West's

2004–2005

ARIZONA

Education Code

As amended through the Second Regular Session
of the Forty-sixth Legislature (2004)

With

Official Classification

Tables

Selected Provisions from:

Title 13. Criminal Code

Title 34. Public Buildings and Improvements

Title 38. Public Officers and Employees

Combined Index

THOMSON
WEST™

Mat #40212771

ISBN 0–314–11372–X

PREFACE

This pamphlet contains the complete text of the Education Code, as enacted by Laws 1981, Chapter 1, § 2, effective January 23, 1981, and as subsequently amended by laws enacted through the Second Regular Session of the Forty-sixth Legislature (2004), set out under the classification and arrangement of the Arizona Revised Statutes, as approved by the Director of the Arizona Legislative Council under the authority of A.R.S. §§ 41–1304.01 to 41–1304.03.

Provisions selected from Title 13, Criminal Code, Title 34, Public Buildings and Improvements, and provisions from Title 38, Public Officers and Employees, relating to Public Meetings and Proceedings, Social Security, the State Retirement System, the Long–Term Disability Program, tax deferred annuity and deferred compensation programs, computer access by minors in public schools or libraries, conflicts of interest, and disclosure of information by public employees are included in this pamphlet. These provisions are also completely up to date through the Second Regular Session of the Forty-sixth Legislature (2004).

Footnotes, notes relating to repealed sections of the Arizona Revised Statutes or to Session Law provisions not classified as a specified section of the Statutes, and italic notes revealing the source of chapters and articles of the Statutes or giving special notice of pertinent facts are included in this pamphlet.

For other laws, annotations to the judicial construction and application of the Arizona laws, including this Code, detailed historical notes explaining legislative changes in the laws, cross references, references to law review commentaries, and many other informative features and aids to research, the user should consult West's Arizona Revised Statutes—Annotated.

For copies of laws enacted at subsequent sessions of the Legislature, see the Arizona Legislative Service or Westlaw AZ–LEGIS.

Disposition and derivation tables are included herein to give a convenient means of finding particular provisions of the new Education Code and corresponding sections of the former Code.

THE PUBLISHER

October, 2004

PREFACE

Internet Access

Contact the West Editorial Department directly with your questions and suggestions by e-mail at west.editor@thomson.com.

Visit West's home page at http://west.thomson.com.

RELATED PRODUCTS FROM WEST

ARIZONA PRACTICE SERIES

Arizona Law of Evidence 4th
Robert Bartells, Joseph M. Livermore, Ann Holt Hameroff

Arizona Civil Trial Practice
Daniel J. McAuliffe and Shirley J. Wahl

Arizona Practice Civil Rules Handbook
Daniel J. McAuliffe

Arizona Marriage Dissolution Practice
Charles M. Smith and Irwin Cantor

Arizona Community Property Law 3rd
Thomas A. Jacobs

Arizona Juvenile Law and Practice
Thomas A. Jacobs

Arizona Corporate Practice
Terence W. Thompson, John L. Hay, James P. O'Sullivan, Robert A. Royal and Thomas J. McDonald

Arizona Trial Handbook
Ben Cooper and Kevin M. Judiscak

ARIZONA LEGAL FORMS

Arizona Civil Procedure Forms
Daniel J. McAuliffe

Arizona Debtor–Creditor Forms 2nd
Lisa C. Thompson

Arizona Domestic Relations Forms
Catherine Creighton

Arizona Commercial Transactions Forms
David L. Abney

Arizona Criminal Procedure Forms
Crane McClennen

Arizona Business Organizations—Corporation Forms
Thomas H. Curzon

Arizona Business Organizations—2d Limited Liability Companies and Partnership Forms
Gary A. Gotto and Laurie B. Fields

RELATED PRODUCTS

West's Arizona Revised Statutes—Annotated
West's Arizona Revised Statutes—Compact Edition
West's Arizona Legislative Service
West's Arizona Civil Practice Law Pamphlet
West's Arizona Criminal and Motor Vehicle Law Pamphlet
West's Arizona Criminal Law and Rules Pamphlet
West's Arizona Education Code Pamphlet
West's Arizona Family Law and Rules Pamphlet
West's Arizona Probate Law and Rules Pamphlet
West's Arizona Rules of Court—State
West's Arizona Rules of Court—Federal
West's Arizona Reports
West's Arizona Digest
West's Arizona Law Finder

West CD–ROM Libraries™

Westlaw
WIN®
WESTCheck® and WESTMATE®

To order any of these Arizona practice tools, call your West Representative or **1–800–328–9352**.

NEED RESEARCH HELP?

You can get quality research results with free help—call the West Reference Attorneys when you have questions concerning Westlaw or West Publications at 1–800–733–2889.

INTERNET ACCESS

Contact the West Editorial Department directly with your questions and suggestions by email at west.editor@thomson.com. Visit West's home page at http://west.thomson.com

*

TABLE OF CONTENTS

TITLE 15
EDUCATION

Section Analysis, see beginning of each Chapter.

TABLE OF CONTENTS

WESTLAW ELECTRONIC RESEARCH GUIDE

Westlaw, Computer Assisted Legal Research

Westlaw is part of the research system provided by West. With Westlaw, you find the same quality and integrity that you have come to expect from West books. For the most current and comprehensive legal research, combine the strengths of West books and Westlaw.

Westlaw Adds to Your Library

Whether you wish to expand or update your research, Westlaw can help. For instance, Westlaw is the most current source for case law, including slip opinions and unreported decisions. In addition to case law, the online availability of statutes, statutory indexes, legislation, court rules and orders, administrative materials, looseleaf publications, texts, periodicals, news and business information makes Westlaw an important asset to any library. Check the online Westlaw Directory or the print *Westlaw Database Directory* for a list of available databases and services. Following is a brief description of some of the capabilities that Westlaw offers.

Natural Language Searching

You can now search most Westlaw databases using WIN®, the revolutionary Natural Language search method. As an alternative to formulating a query using terms and connectors, WIN allows you to simply enter a description of your research issue in plain English:

> What is the government's obligation to warn military personnel of the danger of past exposure to radiation?

Westlaw then retrieves the set of documents that have the highest statistical likelihood of matching your description.

Retrieving a Specific Document

When you know the citation to a case or statute that is not in your library, use the Find service to retrieve the document on Westlaw. Access Find and type a citation like the following:

863 P3d 263

AZ ST s 13–1204

Updating Your Research

You can use Westlaw to update your research in many ways:

- Retrieve cases citing a particular statute.
- Update a state statute by accessing the Update service from the displayed statute using the jump marker, or by accessing the KeyCite servic

- Retrieve newly enacted legislation by searching in the appropriate legislative service database.
- Retrieve cases not yet reported by searching in case law databases.
- Read the latest U.S. Supreme Court opinions within an hour of their release.
- Update West digests by searching with topic and key numbers.

KeyCite

Cases and other legal materials listed in KeyCite Scope can be researched through West's KeyCite service on Westlaw. Use KeyCite to check citations for form, parallel references, prior and later history, and comprehensive citator information, including citations to other decisions and secondary materials.

Additional Information

For more detailed information or assistance, contact your Westlaw Account Representative or call 1–800–REF–ATTY (1–800–733–2889).

TABLE OF CONTENTS

TITLE 15
EDUCATION

Section Analysis, see beginning of each Chapter.

TABLE OF CONTENTS

TABLE OF CONTENTS

TABLE OF CONTENTS

TITLE 13
CRIMINAL CODE

TITLE 34
PUBLIC BUILDINGS AND IMPROVEMENTS

TABLE OF CONTENTS

TITLE 38

PUBLIC OFFICERS AND EMPLOYEES

COMBINED INDEX

*

DISPOSITION TABLE

Showing where the subject matter of the sections of former Title 15 was covered by new sections effective January 23, 1981:

Former Sections	New Sections
15–101	15–202
15–101.01	15–201
15–102	15–203
	15–213
15–103	15–531
15–111	15–231
15–112	15–237
15–113	15–237
15–121	15–251
15–121.01	15–251
15–122	15–252
	15–253
15–123	15–255
15–124	None
15–141	None
15–141	15–301
15–142[1]	None
15–142[2]	15–302
	15–308
15–143[1]	None
15–143[2]	15–303
15–144[1]	None
15–144[2]	15–304
15–145	15–305
15–146	15–306
15–147	15–307
15–148	15–309
15–151[3]	15–141
15–151[4]	None
15–152	15–141
15–153	15–141
15–154	15–141
15–201	15–521
15–202	15–705
15–203	15–535
15–204	15–843
15–205	38–501
	38–502
	38–503
	38–504
15–206	15–505
15–207	15–508
15–208	15–509
	15–521
	15–550
15–209[5]	15–543
15–209[6]	15–323
	15–421
15–210	15–507
15–231	15–504
15–232	15–504
15–233	15–532
15–234	15–534
15–235	15–533
15–236	15–203
15–251	15–501
15–252	15–536
15–253	15–539
15–254	15–540
15–255	15–549
15–256	15–540
15–257	15–544
15–258	15–545
15–259	15–536
15–260	15–546
15–261	16–547
15–262	15–541
15–263	15–542
15–264	15–543
15–265	15–538

[1] Laws 1955, 3rd S.S., Ch. 3 version.

[2] Laws 1980, 2nd S.S., Ch. 9 version.

[3] Laws 1978, Ch. 7, § 2 version.

[4] Laws 1974, Ch. 163, § 1 version.

[5] Laws 1912, Ch. 77, § 93 version.

[6] Laws 1978, Ch. 213, § 7 version.

DISPOSITION TABLE

Former Sections	New Sections
15–268	15–537
15–301	15–801
15–302	15–803
	15–821
	15–823
15–302.01	15–821
15–303	15–822
15–304	15–825
15–305	15–841
15–306	None
15–307	15–827
15–321	15–802
15–322	None
15–323	15–802
15–324	15–804
15–325	15–805
15–326	None
15–327	15–826
15–328	15–851
15–329	15–852
15–341	15–803
15–342	15–803
15–343	15–803
15–401	15–441
15–402	15–442
15–403	15–460
15–403.01	None
15–403.02	15–908
	15–950
15–403.03	15–1033
15–404	15–458
15–405	15–458
15–406	15–461
15–407	15–462
15–408	15–443
15–409	15–459
15–410	15–459
15–411	15–430
15–412	15–322
15–413	15–469
15–421	15–453
15–421.01	15–455
15–421.02	15–456
15–421.03	15–429
15–421.04	15–975
15–421.05	15–457
15–421.06	15–491
	15–997
15–431	15–421
	15–425
15–432	15–321
15–433	15–324
15–434	15–325
15–435	15–326
15–436	15–381
15–436.01	15–381
15–437	15–341
15–438	15–343
15–439	15–327
15–440	15–341
15–441	15–323
	15–341
	15–381
15–441.01	15–384
15–441.02	15–382
15–442	15–341
	15–342
	15–721
	15–1102
	15–1103
	15–1104
15–442.01	15–721
15–443	15–502
15–443.01	15–344
15–444	15–503
15–444.02	15–548
15–445	15–962
15–445.01[7]	None
15–445.01[8]	15–961
15–446	15–842
15–447	15–329
15–448	15–703
15–449	15–824
15–450	15–362
15–451	15–1105
15–452	15–363
15–453	15–383
15–454	15–385
15–461	15–1141

[7] Laws 1974, 1st S.S., Ch. 3, § 10 version.

[8] Laws 1980, 2nd S.S., Ch. 9, § 21 version.

DISPOSITION TABLE

Former Sections	New Sections
15–462	15–1142
15–463	15–1143
15–471	15–424
15–472	15–421
15–472.01	15–423
15–473	15–401
15–473.01	15–402
15–474	15–422
15–475	15–403
15–476	15–404
15–477	15–405
15–478	15–426
15–479	15–406
15–491	15–448
15–492	None
15–495	15–448
15–496	None
15–497	15–1032
15–498	15–448
15–501	15–444
	15–447
15–502	15–445
15–503	15–446
15–504	15–467
15–505	15–993
15–521	15–449
15–522	15–449
15–523	15–450
15–524	15–451
15–525	15–468
15–531	15–452
15–541	15–421
15–542	15–427
15–543	15–428
15–544	15–321
	15–322
	15–324
15–545	15–341
	15–721
	15–722
	15–724
15–545.01	15–722
15–546	15–701
15–547[9]	15–824

Former Sections	New Sections
15–547[10]	15–702
15–547.01	15–824
15–548	None
15–551	15–463
15–561	15–454
15–601	15–1402
15–602	15–1441
	15–1444
15–603	15–1462
	15–1463
	15–1464
	15–1465
15–611	16–1402
15–612	15–1403
15–613	15–1403
	15–1404
	15–1405
15–614	15–1404
	15–1405
15–615	15–1462
	15–1463
	15–1464
	15–1465
15–621	15–1441
15–622	15–1442
15–623	15–1443
15–624	15–1444
15–631	15–1445
15–632	15–1466
	15–1468
15–633	15–1467
15–651	15–101
	15–1401
15–652	None
15–653	None
15–656	15–1421
15–657	15–1422
15–658	15–1423
15–659	15–1424
15–660	15–1425
15–661	None
15–662	None
15–663	15–1426
15–664	15–1427
15–666	15–1402

[9] Laws 1925, Ch. 28, § 1 version.

[10] Laws 1976, Ch. 37, § 1 version.

DISPOSITION TABLE

Former Sections	New Sections
15-667	15-1403
15-668	15-1404
15-669	15-1405
15-676	15-1421
	15-1441
15-676.01	15-1441
15-677	15-1442
15-678	15-1443
15-679	15-1444
15-686	15-1463
	15-1464
	15-1465
15-687	15-1445
15-688	15-1461
15-689	15-1462
15-690	15-1466
15-690.01	15-1468
15-691	15-1467
15-692	None
15-693	15-1469
15-696	15-1481
15-696.01	15-1482
15-696.02	15-1483
15-696.03	15-1484
15-696.04	15-1485
15-696.05	15-1486
15-696.06	15-1487
15-696.07	15-1488
15-696.08	15-1489
15-696.09	15-1490
15-696.10	15-1491
15-701	15-1601
15-702	15-1602
15-702.01	15-1604
15-702.02	15-1605
15-703	15-1603
15-704	15-1606
15-705	15-1631
15-721	15-1621
15-722	15-1622
15-723	15-1623
15-724	15-1625
15-725	15-1624
	15-1626
15-725.01	15-1627
15-725.02	15-1628
15-726	15-1626
15-727	15-1629
15-728	15-1632
15-729	None
15-730	15-1630
15-741	15-1661
15-742	15-1662
15-743	15-1663
15-744	15-1664
15-745	15-1665
15-746	15-1666
15-747	15-1667
15-748	15-1668
15-749	15-1669
15-761	15-1742
15-761.01	15-1743
15-762	15-1741
15-763	15-1744
15-764	15-1745
15-765	15-1746
15-768	15-1721
15-768.01	15-1722
15-768.02	15-1723
15-768.03	15-1724
15-768.04	15-1725
15-768.05	15-1726
15-771	15-1701
15-772	15-1702
15-773	15-1703
15-774	15-1704
15-775	15-1705
15-776	15-1706
15-777	15-1707
15-778	15-1708
15-779	15-1709
15-780	15-1710
15-781	15-1711
15-782	15-1681
15-782.01	15-1682
15-782.02	15-1683
15-782.03	15-1684
15-782.04	15-1685
15-782.05	15-1686
15-782.06	15-1687
15-782.07	15-1688
15-782.08	15-1689
15-782.09	15-1690

DISPOSITION TABLE

Former Sections	New Sections
15–782.10	15–1691
15–782.11	15–1692
15–782.12	15–1693
15–782.13	15–1694
15–782.14	15–1695
15–791	15–1801
15–792	15–1802
15–792.01	15–1803
15–793	15–1804
15–794	15–1805
15–795	15–1806
15–798	15–1807
15–801	15–1301
15–802	15–1302
15–803	15–1303
15–804	15–1304
15–805	None
15–811	15–1321
15–812	15–1322
15–813	15–1323
15–814	15–1324
15–815	15–1325
15–816	15–1326
15–817	15–1327
15–818	15–1328
15–819	15–1329
15–831	15–1341
15–832	15–1342
15–833	15–1343
15–833.01	15–1344
15–834	15–1345
15–835	15–1346
15–836	15–1347
15–837	15–1348
15–838	15–1349
15–839	15–1350
15–851	15–1361
15–901	15–1651
15–902	15–1652
15–903	15–1653
15–911	15–464
Former	New
Sections	Sections
15–912	15–465
15–913	15–465
15–914	15–466
15–915	15–909
15–916	15–974
15–921	15–361
15–931	32–3001
15–932	32–3002
15–932.01	32–3003
15–933	32–3004
15–934	32–3005
15–935	32–3006
15–936	32–3007
15–937	32–3008
15–938	32–3009
15–939	32–3010
15–940	32–3011
15–941	32–3012
15–942	32–3013
15–943	32–3014
15–944	32–3015
15–945	32–3016
15–946	32–3017
15–1001	15–231
15–1002	15–231
15–1003	15–708
15–1004	15–708
15–1005	15–709
15–1006	15–769
15–1010	15–763
15–1011	15–761
15–1012	15–235
	15–762
15–1013	15–766
15–1014	15–767
15–1015	15–764
	15–765
15–1015.01	15–203
15–1015.02	15–768
15–1016	15–204
15–1017	15–769
15–1017.01	15–236
15–1018[11]	15–763
	15–764
	15–765
15–1018[12]	None

[11] Laws 1967, Ch. 127, § 1 version.

[12] Laws 1972, Ch. 161, § 4 version.

DISPOSITION TABLE

Former Sections	New Sections
15–1018[13]	15–236
15–1019[14]	15–769
15–1019[15]	15–1181
	15–1201
15–1020[16]	None
15–1020[17]	15–1182
15–1020.01	15–1183
15–1020.02	15–1184
15–1020.03	15–1185
15–1020.04	15–1186
15–1020.05	15–1185
15–1020.06	15–1184
15–1020.10	15–1201
15–1020.11	15–1202
15–1020.12	15–1203
15–1020.13	15–1204
15–1020.14	15–1205
15–1020.15	15–1205
15–1020.16	15–1204
15–1021	15–710
15–1022	15–203
15–1023	15–712
15–1024	15–704
15–1025	15–711
15–1026	15–522
15–1027	15–522
15–1031	15–254
	15–506
15–1032	15–254
15–1041	15–232
15–1042	15–233
15–1043	15–234
15–1051	15–782
15–1051.01	15–781
15–1052	15–783
15–1053	15–784
15–1054	15–785
15–1055	15–786
15–1056	15–788
15–1061	15–1171
15–1062	15–1172
15–1063	15–1173
15–1064	15–1174
15–1065	15–1175
15–1071	15–713
15–1072	15–713
15–1073	15–714
15–1074	15–713
15–1081	15–761
15–1082	15–764
	15–765
15–1083	15–769
15–1091	15–784
15–1092	15–787
15–1093	15–789
15–1094	15–786
15–1095	15–790
15–1097	15–706
15–1098	15–707
15–1099	None
15–1101	15–723
15–1102	15–725
15–1103	15–725
15–1104	15–725
15–1105	15–725
15–1106	15–727
15–1107	15–727
15–1108	15–728
15–1109	15–726
15–1121	15–101
	15–1151
15–1122	15–1153
15–1123	15–1152
15–1124	15–1154
15–1125	15–1155
15–1126	15–1156
15–1127	15–1157
15–1128	15–1158
15–1131[18]	15–741
	15–742
	15–743

[13] Laws 1975 Ch. 140, § 3 version.

[14] Laws 1967, 3rd S.S., Ch. 19, § 4 version.

[15] Laws 1979, Ch. 195, § 26 version.

[16] Laws 1961, Ch. 40, § 1 version.

[17] Laws 1976, Ch. 185, § 4 version.

[18] Laws 1974, Ch. 38, § 1 version.

DISPOSITION TABLE

Former Sections	New Sections
15–1131[19]	15–741
15–1132[20]	15–741
15–1132[19]	15–742
15–1133[20]	15–741
15–1133[19]	15–743
15–1134[21]	15–743
15–1134[19]	15–744
15–1135[20]	None
15–1135[19]	15–741
15–1137	15–853
15–1137.01	15–854
15–1137.02	15–855
15–1139	15–1901
15–1141	15–206
15–1142	15–207
15–1143	15–208
15–1144	15–209
15–1145	15–210
15–1151	15–211
15–1152	15–212
15–1161	15–205
15–1165	15–365
15–1166	15–365
15–1167	15–365
15–1171	15–364
15–1172	15–364
15–1175	15–1141
15–1176	15–1142
15–1177	15–1143
15–1181	41–1971
15–1182	41–1972
15–1183	41–1973
15–1184	41–1974
15–1185	41–1975
15–1186	41–1976
15–1191	15–131
15–1192	15–132
15–1193	15–133
15–1194	15–134
15–1195	15–135
15–1198	15–121
15–1199[22]	15–791
15–1199[23]	15–1901
15–1199.01	15–792
15–1199.02	None
15–1201	15–903
15–1201.01	15–949
15–1201.02[24]	None
15–1201.02[25]	None
15–1201.02[26]	15–1003
15–1201.03	15–729
15–1201.04	15–271
	15–904
15–1201.05	15–272
15–1201.06	15–1106
15–1202	15–905
15–1202.01	15–481
15–1202.02[27]	None
15–1202.02[28]	15–101
	15–901
15–1202.03[29]	None
15–1202.03[30]	15–941
15–1202.04	15–942
15–1202.05	15–943
15–1202.06[29]	15–961
	15–962
15–1202.06[30]	15–944
15–1202.07[31]	None

[19] Laws 1980, 2nd S.S., Ch. 9, § 48 version.
[20] Laws 1969, Ch. 59, § 2 version.
[21] Laws 1973, Ch. 98, § 2 version.
[22] Laws 1971, Ch. 184, § 7 version.
[23] Laws 1980, Ch. 161, § 1 version.
[24] Laws 1967, 3rd S.S., Ch. 19, § 8 version.
[25] Laws 1979, Ch. 167, § 1 version.
[26] Laws 1980, 2nd S.S., Ch. 9, § 57 version.
[27] Laws 1977, Ch. 152, § 5 version.
[28] Laws 1980, Ch. 167, § 5 version.
[29] Laws 1974, 1st S.S., Ch. 3, § 23 version.
[30] Laws 1980, 2nd S.S., Ch. 9, § 62 version.
[31] Laws 1974, 1st S.S., Ch. 3, § 24 version (not effective).

DISPOSITION TABLE

Former Sections	New Sections
15-1202.07[30]	15-945
15-1202.08	15-946
15-1202.09	15-947
15-1202.10	15-971
15-1202.11	15-972
15-1202.12	15-948
15-1203[32]	None
15-1203[33]	None
15-1203.01	None
15-1204	15-906
15-1205	15-328
15-1210.01	15-922
15-1210.02	15-923
15-1210.03	15-921
15-1211	15-973
15-1211.01	None
15-1212	15-901
	15-902
	15-973
15-1213	15-769
15-1214	15-976
15-1221	15-901
15-1222	15-973
15-1223	None
15-1224	None
15-1225	None
15-1228	15-971
15-1228.01	15-971
15-1228.02	15-973
15-1231	15-996
15-1232	15-998
15-1233	15-991
15-1234	15-902
15-1235	None
15-1236	15-992
15-1236.01	15-994
15-1237	15-995
15-1238	15-1000
15-1239	None
15-1240	None
15-1241	None
15-1242	None
15-1243	None
15-1244	None

[32] Laws 1961, Ch. 15, § 2 version.

[33] Laws 1977, Ch. 152, § 6 version.

Former Sections	New Sections
15-1245	15-907
15-1246	15-1001
15-1247	15-1002
15-1248	15-1101
15-1249	15-999
15-1261	None
15-1262	None
15-1263	None
15-1271	15-1121
15-1272	15-1122
15-1273	15-1123
15-1274	15-1124
15-1281	15-1125
15-1282	15-1126
15-1301	15-1021
15-1302	15-491
15-1302.01	15-491
15-1303	15-492
15-1304	15-493
15-1305	None
15-1321	15-1023
15-1322	15-1024
15-1323	15-1025
15-1324	15-1024
15-1325	15-1026
15-1326	15-1027
15-1327	15-1022
15-1328	15-1028
15-1329	15-1029
15-1330	15-1030
15-1331	15-1031
15-1401	15-621
15-1402	15-622
15-1403	15-623
15-1404	15-624
15-1405	15-625
15-1406	15-626
15-1407	15-627
15-1408	15-628
15-1409	15-629
15-1410	15-630
15-1411	15-631
15-1412	15-632
15-1413	15-633
15-1414	15-634

DISPOSITION TABLE

Former Sections	New Sections
15–1415	15–635
15–1416	15–636
15–1417	15–637
15–1418	15–638
15–1419	15–639
15–1420	15–640
15–1421	15–641
15–1422	15–642
15–1423	15–643
15–1424	15–644
15–1425	15–645
15–1426	15–645
15–1427	None
15–1428	None
15–1429	None
15–1430	None
15–1431	None
15–1432	None
15–1433	None
15–1434	None
15–1435	None
15–1436	None
15–1437	None
15–1438	15–646
15–1439	15–647
15–1440	15–648
15–1441	15–649
15–1442	15–650
15–1443	15–651
15–1444	15–652
15–1445	15–653
15–1446	15–654
15–1461	15–601
15–1462	15–602
15–1463	15–603
15–1464	15–604
15–1465	15–604
15–1466	15–605
15–1467	15–606
15–1468	15–607
15–1469	15–608
15–1470	15–609
15–1471	15–610
15–1501	15–151
15–1601	15–101
	15–901
15–1602	None
15–1603	15–971
15–1604	15–974
15–1621	15–101
	15–901
15–1622	None
15–1623	15–922
15–1624	15–921
15–1625	15–945
	15–946
15–1626	15–923
15–1627	None
15–1628	None
15–1629	None
15–1661	None
15–1662	None
15–1663	None
15–1664	None
15–1665	None
15–1701	15–1201
15–1702	15–1202
15–1703	15–1203
15–1704	15–1204
15–1705	15–1205
15–1706	15–1205
15–1707	15–1204

*

DERIVATION TABLE

Showing where the subject matter of sections of the Education Code, as added by Laws 1981, Ch. 1, § 2, effective January 23, 1981, was covered by former sections:

Former Sections	New Sections
15–101	15–651
	15–1121
	15–1202.02[1]
	15–1601
	15–1621
15–121	15–1198
15–131	15–1191
15–132	15–1192
15–133	15–1193
15–134	15–1194
15–135	15–1195
15–141	15–151[2]
	15–152
	15–153
	15–154
15–151	15–1501
15–201	15–101.01
15–202	15–101
15–203	15–102
	15–236
	15–1015.01
	15–1022
15–204	15–1016
15–205	15–1161
15–206	15–1141
15–207	15–1142
15–208	15–1143
15–209	15–1144
15–210	15–1145
15–211	15–1151
15–212	15–1152
15–213	15–102
15–231	15–111
	15–1001
	15–1002
15–232	15–1041
15–233	15–1042
15–234	15–1043
15–235	15–1012
15–236	15–1017.01
	15–1018[3]
15–237	15–112
	15–113
15–251	15–121
	15–121.01
15–252	15–122
15–253	15–122
15–254	15–1031
	15–1032
15–255	15–123
15–271	15–1201.04
15–272	15–1201.05
15–301	15–141
15–302	15–142
15–303	15–143
15–304	15–144
15–305	15–145
15–306	15–146
15–307	15–147
15–308	15–142
15–309	15–148
15–321	15–432
	15–544
15–322	15–412
	15–544
15–323	15–209[4]
	15–441
15–324	15–433
	15–544
15–325	15–434
15–326	15–435
15–327	15–439
15–328	15–1205
15–329	15–447

[1] Laws 1980, Ch. 167, § 5 version.

[2] Laws 1978, Ch. 7, § 2 version.

[3] Laws 1975, Ch. 140, § 3 version.

[4] Laws 1978, Ch. 213, § 7 version.

DERIVATION TABLE

Former Sections	New Sections
15–341	15–437
	15–440
	15–441
	15–442
	15–545
15–342	15–442
15–343	15–438
15–344	15–443.01
15–361	15–921
15–362	15–450
15–363	15–452
15–364	15–1171
	15–1172
15–365	15–1165
	15–1166
	15–1167
15–381	15–436
	15–436.01
	15–441
15–382	15–441.02
15–383	15–453
15–384	15–441.01
15–385	15–454
15–401	15–473
15–402	15–473.01
15–403	15–475
15–404	15–476
15–405	15–477
15–405	15–477
15–406	15–479
15–421[5]	15–209
	15–431
	15–472
	15–541
15–422	15–474
15–423	15–472.01
15–424	15–471
15–425	15–431
15–426	15–478
15–427	15–542
15–428	15–543
15–429	15–421.03
15–430	15–411
15–441	15–401
15–442	15–402

Former Sections	New Sections
15–443	15–408
15–444	15–501
15–445	15–502
15–446	15–503
15–447	15–501
15–448	15–491
	15–495
	15–498
15–449	15–521
	15–522
15–450	15–523
15–451	15–524
15–452	15–531
15–453	15–421
15–454	15–561
15–455	15–421.01
15–456	15–421.02
15–457	15–421.05
15–458	15–404
	15–405
15–459	15–409
	15–410
15–460	15–403
15–461	15–406
15–462	15–407
15–463	15–551
15–464	15–911
15–465	15–912
	15–913
15–466	15–914
15–467	15–504
15–468	15–525
15–469	15–413
15–481	15–1202.01
15–491	15–421.06
	15–1302
	15–1302.01
15–492	15–1303
15–493	15–1304
15–501	15–205
	15–251
15–502	15–205
	15–443
15–503	15–205
	15–444
15–504	15–205

[5] Laws 1978, Ch. 213, § 7 version.

DERIVATION TABLE

Former Sections	New Sections
	15–231
	15–232
15–505	15–206
15–506	15–1031
15–507	15–210
15–508	15–207
15–509	15–208
15–521	15–201
	15–208
15–522	15–1026
	15–1027
15–531	15–103
15–532	15–233
15–533	15–235
15–534	15–234
15–535	15–203
15–536	15–252
	15–259
15–537	15–268
15–538	15–265
15–539	15–253
15–540	15–254
	15–256
15–541	15–262
15–542	15–263
15–543	15–209[6]
	15–264
15–544	15–257
15–545	15–258
15–546	15–260
15–547	15–261
15–548	15–444.02
15–549	15–255
15–550	15–208
15–601	15–1461
15–602	15–1462
15–603	15–1463
15–604	15–1464
	15–1465
15–605	15–1466
15–606	15–1467
15–607	15–1468
15–608	15–1469
15–609	15–1470

Former Sections	New Sections
15–610	15–1471
15–621	15–1401
15–622	15–1402
15–623	15–1403
15–624	15–1404
15–625	15–1405
15–626	15–1406
15–627	15–1407
15–628	15–1408
15–629	15–1409
15–630	15–1410
15–631	15–1411
15–632	15–1412
15–633	15–1413
15–634	15–1414
15–635	15–1415
15–636	15–1416
15–637	15–1417
15–638	15–1418
15–639	15–1419
15–640	15–1420
15–641	15–1421
15–642	15–1422
15–643	15–1423
15–644	15–1424
15–645	15–1425
	15–1426
15–646	15–1438
15–647	15–1439
15–648	15–1440
15–649	15–1441
15–650	15–1442
15–651	15–1443
15–652	15–1444
15–653	15–1445
15–654	15–1446
15–701	15–546
15–702	15–547[7]
15–703	15–448
15–704	15–1024
15–705	15–202
15–706	15–1097
15–707	15–1098
15–708	15–1003
	15–1004

[6] Laws 1912, Ch. 77, § 93 version.

[7] Laws 1976, Ch. 37, § 1 version.

DERIVATION TABLE

Former Sections	New Sections
15–709	15–1005
15–710	15–1021
15–711	15–1025
15–712	15–1023
15–713	15–1071
	15–1072
	15–1074
15–714	15–1073
15–721	15–442
	15–442.01
	15–545
15–722	15–545
	15–545.01
15–723	15–1101
15–724	15–545
15–725	15–1102
	15–1103
	15–1104
	15–1105
15–726	15–1109
15–727	15–1106
	15–1107
15–728	15–1108
15–729	15–1201.03
15–741	15–1131[8]
	15–1131[9]
	15–1132[10]
	15–1133[10]
	15–1135[9]
	15–742
	15–1131[11]
	15–1132[12]
15–743	15–1131[11]
	15–1133[12]
	15–1134[13]
15–744	15–1134[12]
15–761	15–1011
	15–1081

Former Sections	New Sections
15–762	15–1012
15–763	15–1010
	15–1018
15–764	15–1015
	15–1018[14]
	15–1082
15–765	15–1015
	15–1018[14]
	15–1082
15–766	15–1013
15–767	15–1014
15–768	15–1015.02
15–769	15–1006
	15–1017
	15–1019[15]
	15–1083
	15–1213
15–781	15–1051.01
15–782	15–1051
15–783	15–1052
15–784	15–1053
	15–1091
15–785	15–1054
15–786	15–1055
	15–1094
15–787	15–1092
15–788	15–1056
15–789	15–1093
15–790	15–1095
15–801	15–301
15–802	15–321
	15–323
15–803	15–302
	15–341
	15–342
	15–343
15–804	15–324
15–805	15–325
15–821	15–302

[8] Laws 1974, Ch. 38, § 1 version.

[9] Laws 1980, 2nd S.S., Ch. 9, § 48 version.

[10] Laws 1969, Ch. 59, § 2 version.

[11] Laws 1974, Ch. 38, § 1 version.

[12] Laws 1980, 2nd S.S., Ch. 9, § 48 version.

[13] Laws 1973, Ch. 98, § 2 version.

[14] Laws 1967, Ch. 127, § 1 version.

[15] Laws 1967, 3rd S.S., Ch. 19, § 4 version.

DERIVATION TABLE

Former Sections	New Sections
	15–302.01
15–822	15–303
15–823	15–302
15–824	15–449
	15–547[16]
	15–547.01
15–825	15–304
15–826	15–327
15–827	15–307
15–841	15–305
15–842	15–446
15–843	15–204
15–851	15–328
15–852	15–329
15–853	15–1137
15–854	15–1137.01
15–855	15–1137.02
15–901	15–1202.02[17]
	15–1212
	15–1221
	15–1601
	15–1621
15–902	15–1212
	15–1234
15–903	15–1201
15–904	15–1201.04
15–905	15–1202
15–906	15–1204
15–907	15–1245
15–908	15–403.02
15–909	15–915
15–921	15–1210.03
	15–1624
15–922	15–1210.01
	15–1623
15–923	15–1210.02
	15–1626
15–941	15–1202.03[18]
15–942	15–1202.04
15–943	15–1202.05
15–944	15–1202.06[19]
15–945	15–1202.07[20]
	15–1625
15–946	15–1202.08
	15–1625
15–947	15–1202.09
15–948	15–1202.12
15–949	15–1201.01
15–950	15–403.02
15–961	15–445.01[21]
15–962	15–445
	15–1202.06[22]
15–971	15–1202.10
	15–1228
	15–1228.01
	15–1603
15–972	15–1202.11
15–973	15–1211
	15–1212
	15–1222
	15–1228.02
15–974	15–916
	15–1604
15–975	15–421.04
15–976	15–1214
15–991	15–1233
15–992	15–1236
15–993	15–505
15–994	15–1236.01
15–995	15–1237
15–996	15–1231
15–997	15–421.06
15–998	15–1232
15–999	15–1249
15–1000	15–1238
15–1001	15–1246
15–1002	15–1247
15–1003	15–1201.02[23]

[16] Laws 1925, Ch. 28, § 1 version.

[17] Laws 1980, Ch. 167, § 5 version.

[18] Laws 1980, 2nd S.S., Ch. 9, § 62 version.

[19] Laws 1980, 2nd S.S., Ch. 9, § 62 version.

[20] Laws 1980, 2nd S.S., Ch. 9, § 62 version.

[21] Laws 1980, 2nd S.S., Ch. 9, § 21 version.

[22] Laws 1974, 1st S.S., Ch. 3, § 23 version.

[23] Laws 1980 2nd S.S., Ch. 9, § 57 version.

DERIVATION TABLE

Former Sections	New Sections
15–1021	15–1301
15–1022	15–1327
15–1023	15–1321
15–1024	15–1322
	15–1324
15–1025	15–1323
15–1026	15–1325
15–1027	15–1326
15–1028	15–1328
15–1029	15–1329
15–1030	15–1330
15–1031	15–1331
15–1032	15–497
15–1033	15–403.03
15–1101	15–1248
15–1102	15–442
15–1103	15–442
15–1104	15–442
15–1105	15–451
15–1106	15–1201.06
15–1121	15–1271
15–1122	15–1272
15–1123	15–1273
15–1124	15–1274
15–1125	15–1281
15–1126	15–1282
15–1141	15–461
	15–1175
15–1142	15–462
	15–1176
15–1143	15–463
	15–1177
15–1151	15–1121
15–1152	15–1123
15–1153	15–1122
15–1154	15–1124
15–1155	15–1125
15–1156	15–1126
15–1157	15–1127
15–1158	15–1128
15–1171	15–1061
15–1172	15–1062
15–1173	15–1063

Former Sections	New Sections
15–1174	15–1064
15–1175	15–1065
15–1181	15–1019[24]
15–1182	15–1020[25]
15–1183	15–1020.01
15–1184	15–1020.02
	15–1020.06
15–1185	15–1020.03
	15–1020.05
15–1186	15–1020.04
15–1201	15–1019[26]
	15–1020.10
	15–1701
15–1202	15–1020.11
	15–1702
15–1203	15–1020.12
	15–1703
15–1204	15–1020.13
	15–1020.16
	15–1704
	15–1707
15–1205	15–1020.14
	15–1020.15
	15–1705
	15–1706
15–1301	15–801
15–1302	15–802
15–1303	15–803
15–1304	15–804
15–1321	15–811
15–1322	15–812
15–1323	15–813
15–1324	15–814
15–1325	15–815
15–1326	15–816
15–1327	15–817
15–1328	15–818
15–1329	15–819
15–1341	15–831
15–1342	15–832
15–1343	15–833
15–1344	15–833.01
15–1345	15–834
15–1346	15–835

[24] Laws 1979, Ch. 195, § 26 version.

[25] Laws 1976, Ch. 185, § 4 version.

[26] Laws 1979, Ch. 195, § 26 version.

DERIVATION TABLE

Former Sections	New Sections
15–1347	15–836
15–1348	15–837
15–1349	15–838
15–1350	15–839
15–1361	15–851
15–1401	15–651
15–1402	15–601
	15–611
	15–666
15–1403	15–612
	15–613
	15–667
15–1404	15–613
	15–614
	15–668
15–1405	15–613
	15–614
	15–669
15–1421	15–656
	15–676
15–1422	15–657
15–1423	15–658
15–1424	15–659
15–1425	15–660
15–1426	15–663
15–1427	15–664
15–1441	15–602
	15–621
	15–676
	15–676.01
15–1442	15–622
	15–677
15–1443	15–623
	15–678
15–1444	15–602
	15–624
	15–679
15–1445	15–631
	15–687
15–1461	15–688
15–1462	15–603
	15–615
	15–689
15–1463	15–603
	15–615
	15–686

Former Sections	New Sections
15–1464	15–603
	15–615
	15–686
15–1465	15–603
	15–615
	15–686
15–1466	15–632
	15–690
15–1467	15–633
	15–691
15–1468	15–632
	15–690.01
15–1469	15–693
15–1481	15–696
15–1482	15–696.01
15–1483	15–696.02
15–1484	15–696.03
15–1485	15–696.04
15–1486	15–696.05
15–1487	15–696.06
15–1488	15–696.07
15–1489	15–696.08
15–1490	15–696.09
15–1491	15–696.10
15–1601	15–701
15–1602	15–702
15–1603	15–703
15–1604	15–702.01
15–1605	15–702.02
15–1606	15–704
15–1621	15–721
15–1622	15–722
15–1623	15–723
15–1624	15–725
15–1625	15–724
15–1626	15–725
	15–726
15–1627	15–725.01
15–1628	15–725.02
15–1629	15–727
15–1630	15–730
15–1631	15–705
15–1632	15–728
15–1651	15–901
15–1652	15–902
15–1653	15–903
15–1661	15–741

DERIVATION TABLE

Former Sections	New Sections
15–1662	15–742
15–1663	15–743
15–1664	15–744
15–1665	15–745
15–1666	15–746
15–1667	15–747
15–1668	15–748
15–1669	15–749
15–1681	15–782
15–1682	15–782.01
15–1683	15–782.02
15–1684	15–782.03
15–1685	15–782.04
15–1686	15–782.05
15–1687	15–782.06
15–1688	15–782.07
15–1689	15–782.08
15–1690	15–782.09
15–1691	15–782.10
15–1692	15–782.11
15–1693	15–782.12
15–1694	15–782.13
15–1695	15–782.14
15–1701	15–771
15–1702	15–772
15–1703	15–773
15–1704	15–774
15–1705	15–775
15–1706	15–776
15–1707	15–777
15–1708	15–778
15–1709	15–779
15–1710	15–780
15–1711	15–781
15–1721	15–768
15–1722	15–768.01
15–1723	15–768.02
15–1724	15–768.03
15–1725	15–768.04
15–1726	15–768.05
15–1741	15–762
15–1742	15–761
15–1743	15–761.01
15–1744	15–763
15–1745	15–764
15–1746	15–765
15–1801	15–791
15–1802	15–792
15–1803	15–792.01
15–1804	15–793
15–1805	15–794
15–1806	15–795
15–1807	15–798
15–1901	15–1139
	15–1199[27]

[27] Laws 1980, Ch. 161, § 1 version.

CITE THIS PAMPHLET

Thus: A.R.S. § ____

*

TITLE 15

EDUCATION

Title 15, consisting of Chapters 1 to 14, was added by Laws 1981, Ch. 1, § 2, effective January 23, 1981.

Chapter 15 was added by renumbering Article 2 of Chapter 1, § 15–121, as Article 1, § 15–1901, of Chapter 15.

Former Title 15, consisting of Chapters 1, 1.1, 2 to 4, 4.1, 5, 6, 6.1, 7, 7.1, and 8 to 17, was, except for Chapter 9, Article 4, repealed by Laws 1981, Ch. 1, § 1, effective January 23, 1981.

Former Chapter 9, Article 4, §§ 15–931 to 15–946, was transferred for placement in Title 32, Chapter 30 as Article 1, consisting of §§ 32–3001 to 32–3017, by Laws 1981, Ch. 1, § 3, effective January 23, 1981.

Historical and Statutory Notes

Laws 1981, Ch. 1, §§ 28 and 29 provide:

"**Sec. 28. Legislative intent**

"The legislature intends by this act to provide for a substantial and orderly relocation of existing provisions of the law relating to education within title 15, Arizona Revised Statutes. This act is not intended to change the meaning or substance of existing provisions of law but is enacted solely for the purpose of facilitating access to existing statutes by placing them in an orderly sequence."

"**Sec. 29. Saving clause**

"This act does not affect any legal acts taken or proceedings initiated pursuant to title 15 except chapter 9, article 4 [Section 15–961 et seq.] of such title in the Arizona Revised Statutes prior to its repeal by this act or any legal acts or proceedings taken pursuant to title 15, chapter 9, article 4, Arizona Revised Statutes, prior to its transfer to title 32, chapter 30, article 1, [Section 32–3001 et seq.] Arizona Revised Statutes. All legal acts taken or proceedings initiated pursuant to title 15, Arizona Revised Statutes, prior to its repeal or transfer shall remain valid and shall have the same effect as if such acts were taken or proceedings initiated pursuant to the appropriate section of the law as reorganized in the new title 15 of this act or as renumbered in the new title 32, chapter 30, article 1, Arizona Revised Statutes."

CHAPTER 1

GENERAL PROVISIONS

ARTICLE 1. GENERAL PROVISIONS

ARTICLE 2. EMPLOYEE ANNUITY AND DEFERRED COMPENSATION PLANS

ARTICLE 3. TEACHER EXCHANGE

ARTICLE 4. EDUCATIONAL RECORDS

ARTICLE 5. SAFETY REQUIREMENTS

ARTICLE 6. STATE PROHIBITIONS

ARTICLE 7. COMPREHENSIVE SCHOOL HEALTH POLICY COUNCIL [REPEALED]

ARTICLE 8. CHARTER SCHOOLS

Chapter 1, consisting of Article 1, § 15–101, Article 2, § 15–121 (Article 3, § 15–131 prior to renumbering), Article 3, §§ 15–131 to 15–135 (Article 4, §§ 15–141 to 15–145 prior to renumbering), Article 4, § 15–141 (Article 5, § 15–151 prior to renumbering), and Article 5, § 15–151 (Article 6, § 15–161 prior to renumbering), was added by Laws 1981, Ch. 1, § 2, effective January 23, 1981.

Another Article 2, consisting of § 15–121 as added by Laws 1981, Ch. 1, § 2, effective January 23, 1981, was renumbered as Chapter 15, Article 1, § 15–1901.

Executive Order:

Executive Order No. 91–9, dated April 23, 1991 established the Governor's Task Force on Educational Reform.

ARTICLE 1. GENERAL PROVISIONS

§ 15–101. Definitions

In this title, unless the context otherwise requires:

1. "Accommodation school" means either:

(a) A school which is operated through the county board of supervisors and the county school superintendent and which the county school superintendent administers to serve a military reservation or territory which is not included within the boundaries of a school district.

(b) A school that provides educational services to homeless children or alternative education programs as provided in § 15-308, subsection B.

2. "Assessed valuation" means the valuation derived by applying the applicable percentage as provided in title 42, chapter 15, article 1 [1] to the full cash value or limited property value, whichever is applicable, of the property.

3. "Charter school" means a public school established by contract with a district governing board, the state board of education or the state board for charter schools pursuant to article 8 of this chapter [2] to provide learning that will improve pupil achievement.

4. "Child with a disability" means a child with a disability as defined in § 15-761.

5. "Class A bonds" means general obligation bonds approved by a vote of the qualified electors of a school district at an election held on or before December 31, 1998.

6. "Class B bonds" means general obligation bonds approved by a vote of the qualified electors of a school district at an election held from and after December 31, 1998.

7. "Competency" means a demonstrated ability in a skill at a specified performance level.

8. "Course" means organized subject matter in which instruction is offered within a given period of time and for which credit toward promotion, graduation or certification is usually given. A course consists of knowledge selected from a subject for instructional purposes in the schools.

9. "Course of study" means a list of required and optional subjects to be taught in the schools.

10. "Fiscal year" means the year beginning July 1 and ending June 30.

11. "Governing board" means a body organized for the government and management of the schools within a school district or a county school superintendent in the conduct of an accommodation school.

12. "Lease" means an agreement for conveyance and possession of real or personal property.

13. "Limited property value" means the value determined pursuant to title 42, chapter 13, article 7.[3] Limited property value shall be used as the basis for assessing, fixing, determining and levying primary property taxes.

14. "Parent" means the natural or adoptive parent of a child or a person who has custody of a child.

15. "Person who has custody" means a parent or legal guardian of a child, a person to whom custody of the child has been given by order of a court or a person who stands in loco parentis to the child.

16. "P.L. 81-874" means P.L. 81-874 or its successors.

17. "Primary property taxes" means all ad valorem taxes except for secondary property taxes.

18. "Private school" means a nonpublic institution where instruction is imparted.

19. "School" means any public institution established for the purposes of offering instruction to pupils in programs for preschool children with disabilities, kindergarten programs or any combination of grades one through twelve.

20. "School district" means a political subdivision of this state with geographic boundaries organized for the purpose of the administration, support and maintenance of the public schools or an accommodation school.

21. "Secondary property taxes" means ad valorem taxes used to pay the principal of and the interest and redemption charges on any bonded indebtedness or other lawful long-term obligation issued or incurred for a specific purpose by a school district or a community college district and amounts levied pursuant to an election to exceed a budget, expenditure or tax limitation.

22. "Subject" means a division or field of organized knowledge, such as English or mathematics, or a selection from an organized body of knowledge for a course or teaching unit, such as the English novel or elementary algebra.

Added by Laws 1981, Ch. 1, § 2, eff. Jan. 23, 1981. Amended by Laws 1982, Ch. 197, § 1; Laws 1983, Ch. 182, § 1; Laws 1983, Ch. 325, § 1; Laws 1984, Ch. 349, § 1; Laws 1990, Ch. 348, § 1, eff. June 26, 1990; Laws 1992, Ch. 172, § 2; Laws 1994, Ch. 315, § 5; Laws 1994, 9th S.S., Ch. 2, § 1; Laws 1995, Ch. 268, § 2; Laws 1996, Ch. 316, § 1, eff. May 1, 1996; Laws 1997, Ch. 231, § 1; Laws 1998, Ch. 1, § 44, eff. Jan. 1, 1999; Laws 1998, 5th S.S., Ch. 1, § 4, eff. July 9, 1998; Laws 1999, Ch. 299, § 2; Laws 2000, Ch. 236, § 1, eff. April 12, 2000.

[1] Section 42-15001 et seq.

[2] Section 15-181 et seq.

[3] Section 42-133001 et seq.

Historical and Statutory Notes

Source:

Laws 1947, Ch. 98, § 1.
Code 1939, Supp.1952, § 54-1801.
A.R.S. former §§ 15-651, 15-1121, 15-1202.02, 15-1601, 15-1621.
Laws 1960, Ch. 119, § 1.
Laws 1971, Ch. 146, § 1.
Laws 1974, 1st S.S., Ch. 3, §§ 23, 38.
Laws 1975, Ch. 88, § 1.
Laws 1976, Ch. 166, § 1.
Laws 1977, Ch. 152, § 9.
Laws 1978, 1st S.S., Ch. 1, § 1.
Laws 1980, 2nd S.S., Ch. 9, §§ 27, 62.
Laws 1980, Ch. 167, § 5.

Laws 1983, Ch. 267, § 5, effective April 25, 1983, provided for an exemption from revenue control limits for compliance with court ordered desegregation for the 1983-1984 and 1984-1985 fiscal years.

Laws 1991, Ch. 222, § 1 provided for the establishment of a joint legislative committee to study consolidation of school districts. The provision was repealed Nov. 10, 1992 under § 2 of the act.

Laws 1994, 9th S.S., Ch. 2, § 21, provides:

"**Sec. 21. District and department of education reports**

"**A.** For fiscal years 1995-1996 through 2000-2001, by September 1 each school district shall submit on behalf of its schools to the department of education the following information on a form prescribed by the department:

"1. The number of nonresident pupils who:

"(a) Applied for admission to the school for enrollment in the current fiscal year.

"(b) Were accepted for admission to the school for enrollment in the current fiscal year.

"(c) Actually enrolled in the school for the current fiscal year.

"2. The number of pupils who were transported by the school or school district and who met the economic eligibility requirements established under the national school lunch and child nutrition acts (42 United States Code §§ 1751 through 1785) for free or reduced price lunches.

"3. The ethnicity of pupils transferring in and out of the school or school district.

"4. The reasons given by the parents or guardians for the transfer of their children in and out of a school or school district.

"5. The number of resident pupils who transferred to a different school within the same district.

"6. Any other information prescribed by the department for data collection and reporting.

"**B.** By December 1 of each year the department of education shall submit a report to the legislature that summarizes the information received pursuant to subsection A."

Laws 1994, 9th S.S., Ch. 2, § 24, as amended by Laws 1995, Ch. 4, § 1, eff. March 9, 1995, provides:

"**Sec. 24. Capital needs assessment of school districts; definition**

"**A.** The joint committee on capital review, by July 1, 1995, shall conduct a statewide school district facilities inventory and needs assessment and issue a report to the president of the senate, the speaker of the house of representatives and the joint legislative budget committee containing recommendations regarding the facilities needs of school districts. The joint committee on capital review shall issue a request for proposal and contract with a professional firm specializing in facilities assessment. The joint committee on capital review shall:

"1. Develop statewide standards for public school facilities.

"2. Ensure that the contracted firm selects appropriate personnel from school districts and other facilities and construction professionals designated by the joint committee on capital review to conduct the needs assessment.

"3. Ensure that data collected during the conduct of the inventory and needs assessment include at least the following:

"(a) The district's building asset value per pupil.

"(b) Age, condition and capacity utilization of existing buildings in the district.

"(c) The balance contained in the district's capital outlay reserve fund and in the district's school plant fund.

"(d) The unused amount of the district's bonding capacity.

"(e) Maintenance and operations expenditures in excess of the district's revenue control limit.

"(f) The district's cash balance.

"(g) Recent successful subdivision, unification or consolidation attempts by the school district.

"(h) Student enrollment growth in the district.

"(i) The proportion and dollar amount of the district's capital outlay revenue limit that has been transferred to the maintenance and operation section of the budget.

"(j) Facility needs relative to the standards developed in paragraph 1 of this subsection.

"4. Review the data collected pursuant to paragraph 3 of this subsection and work with the contracted firm to make recommendations for funding school district facilities needs.

"**B.** The joint committee on capital review shall conduct the inventory and needs assessment for those school districts for which the secondary assessed valuation per pupil for the district is less than the median secondary assessed valuation per pupil for all districts of the same district group in this state. The inventory and needs assessment shall also be conducted for a representative sample of not more than thirty-seven per cent of schools in districts for which the secondary assessed valuation per pupil for the district is more than the median secondary assessed valuation per pupil for all districts of the same district group in this state. For the purpose of this subsection, "district group" means:

"1. If the school district is a unified school district, a group consisting of all unified schools.

"2. If the school district is a high school district or a common school district, a group that includes all high school and common school districts."

Laws 1996, Ch. 316, § 5, provides:

"**Sec. 5. Applicability**

"Sections 15-101, 15-973 and 15-974, Arizona Revised Statutes, as amended by this act, apply to fiscal year 1995-1996 and thereafter."

Laws 1998, 5th S.S., Ch. 1, § 1, provides:

"**Section 1. Designation of act**

"This act shall be known and may be cited as 'The Students FIRST Act of 1998.' "

Laws 1998, 5th S.S., Ch. 1, § 2, provides:

"**Sec. 2. Repeal**

"Laws 1998, third special session, chapter 1, Laws 1998, chapter 164, Laws 1998, chapter 219 and Laws 1998, chapter 286, § 1 are repealed."

Reviser's Notes:

1983 Note. Prior to the 1984 amendment, this section contained the amendments made by Laws 1983, Ch. 182, § 1 and Ch. 325, § 1 which were blended together pursuant to authority of § 41-1304.03. Additionally, pursuant to authority of § 41-1304.02, paragraph 5, as added by Laws 1983, Ch. 182, was renumbered as paragraph 8 and paragraphs 10 and 14, as added by Laws 1983, Ch. 325, were renumbered respectively as paragraphs 11 and 15.

1995 Note. Pursuant to authority of § 41-1304.02, in Laws 1995, Ch. 4, § 1, amending Laws 1994, 9th S.S., Ch. 2, § 24, subsection A, first sentence "district" was inserted after the first "school" to correct a manifest clerical error.

1998 Note. Prior to the 1999 amendment, this section contained the amendments made by Laws 1998, Second Regular Session, Ch. 1, sec. 44 and Laws 1998, Fifth Special Session, Ch. 1, sec. 4 that were blended together pursuant to authority of § 41–1304.03.

§ 15–102. Parental involvement in the school; definition

A. The governing board, in consultation with parents, teachers and administrators, shall develop and adopt a policy to promote the involvement of parents and guardians of children enrolled in the schools within the school district, including:

1. A plan for parent participation in the schools which is designed to improve parent and teacher cooperation in such areas as homework, attendance and discipline.

2. Procedures by which parents may learn about the course of study for their children and review learning materials.

3. Procedures by which parents who object to any learning material or activity on the basis that it is harmful may withdraw their children from the activity or from the class or program in which the material is used. Objection to a learning material or activity on the basis that it is harmful includes objection to a material or activity because it questions beliefs or practices in sex, morality or religion.

B. The policy adopted by the governing board pursuant to this section may also include the following components:

1. A plan by which parents will be made aware of the district's parental involvement policy and the provisions of this section, including:

(a) Rights under the family educational rights and privacy act of 1974 relating to access to children's official records.

(b) The parent's right to inspect the school district policies and curriculum.

2. Efforts to encourage the development of parenting skills.

3. The communication to parents of techniques designed to assist the child's learning experience in the home.

4. Efforts to encourage access to community and support services for children and families.

5. The promotion of communication between the school and parents concerning school programs and the academic progress of the parents' children.

6. Identifying opportunities for parents to participate in and support classroom instruction at the school.

7. Efforts to, with appropriate training, support parents as shared decision makers and to encourage membership on school councils.

8. The recognition of the diversity of parents and the development of guidelines that promote widespread parental participation and involvement in the school at various levels.

9. The development of preparation programs and specialized courses for certificated employees and administrators that promote parental involvement.

10. The development of strategies and programmatic structures at schools to encourage and enable parents to participate actively in their children's education.

C. For the purposes of this section, "parent" means the parent or person who has custody of the child.

Added by Laws 1987, Ch. 320, § 1. Amended by Laws 1995, Ch. 268, § 3.

Historical and Statutory Notes

Laws 1987, Ch. 320, § 3 provides:

"**Sec. 3. Parental involvement policy; adoption by school district governing boards**

"Notwithstanding § 15-102, Arizona Revised Statutes, as added by this act, school district governing boards are not required to adopt a policy on parental involvement in the schools until January 1, 1988."

ARTICLE 2. EMPLOYEE ANNUITY AND DEFERRED COMPENSATION PLANS

Laws 1982, Ch. 133, § 2 substituted "Employee Annuity and Deferred Compensation Plans" for "Employee Annuities" as the heading for this article.

§ 15-121. Permitting school employees to participate in federal annuity program and deferred compensation plans; prohibition against use of public monies; exception

A. Employees of school districts, accommodation school employees, employees of the community college districts, employees of the universities and all other certificated and noncertificated employees of the schools of this state, including those located at state institutions, may participate in the federal tax sheltered annuity plan as provided in 26 United States Code § 403, [1] if the governing body approves.

B. Upon election by an employee to participate in the federal annuity plan, the governing board of a school district, the county school superintendent, the community college district governing board, the Arizona board of regents or other governing body or employer of the employee shall invest an amount to be reduced from the regular annual salary of the employee, as the employee may authorize, in annuities as provided in 26 United States Code § 403.

C. An employee may also participate in a deferred compensation plan approved by the governing body and may authorize the necessary deductions from his regular salary.

D. The amount to be invested shall be determined by the employee not less than fifteen days prior to his first payday in the school year, or at any time during the school year at the option of the governing body. The employing body or county school superintendent shall assume no responsibility other than to make the requested payments during the actual time of the employment of the employee. The employer shall transfer to the fund manager the employee contributions within ten working days after each and every payroll date. Contributions transferred after that date shall include a penalty of six per cent a year for each day the contributions are late. The penalty shall be paid by the employer. If the employee changes his employment to another school or school district, he may authorize his new employer to continue the payments if the governing body approves.

E. State, county, district or other public monies shall not be used in the purchase of any annuity or payment of any deferred compensation authorized by this article, except for monies authorized to be paid and used for severance pay, sick leave payouts or vacation payouts.

Added as § 15-131 by Laws 1981, Ch. 1, § 2, eff. Jan. 23, 1981. Renumbered as § 15-121. Amended by Laws 1982, Ch. 133, § 1; Laws 1983, Ch. 114, § 1, eff. April 13, 1983; Laws 2003, Ch. 264, § 1.

[1] 26 U.S.C.A. § 403.

Historical and Statutory Notes

Source:

Laws 1963, Ch. 19, § 1.
A.R.S. former § 15-1198.
Laws 1969, Ch. 19, § 1.
Laws 1980, Ch. 225, § 2.
Laws 1980, Ch. 237, § 1.

Laws 2003, Ch. 264, § 17, provides:

"**Sec. 17. State treasurer; new school facilities transfer**

"Notwithstanding § 15-2002, subsection A, paragraph 10, Arizona Revised Statutes, as amended by this act, or any other law, the state treasurer shall disregard any instructions of the school facilities board relating to the new school facilities fund transfers for fiscal year 2003-2004."

Laws 2003, Ch. 264, § 18, provides:

"**Sec. 18. State treasurer; deficiencies correction transfer**

"Notwithstanding § 15-2002, subsection A, paragraph 10, Arizona Revised Statutes, as amended by this act, or any other law, the state treasurer shall disregard any instructions of the school facilities board relating to the deficiencies correction fund transfers for fiscal year 2003-2004."

Laws 2003, Ch. 264, § 20, provides:

"**Sec. 20. State board of education; charter school sponsorship**

"Notwithstanding title 15, chapter 1, article 8, Arizona Revised Statutes, the state board of education shall not sponsor any additional charter schools for fiscal year 2003-2004 and the state board of education and the state board for charter schools shall enter into an intergovernmental agreement for fiscal year 2003-2004 that requires the state board for charter schools to provide the same type of oversight that year for charter schools that are sponsored by the state board of education as the state board for charter schools provides for charter schools sponsored by the state board for charter schools."

Laws 2003, Ch. 264, § 25, provides:

"**Sec. 25. Securing principal and interest; refunding bonds**

"**A.** In connection with issuing state school trust revenue bonds authorized by this act and to secure the principal and interest on the bonds, the school facilities board by resolution may:

"1. Segregate the state school trust revenue bond debt service fund into one or more accounts and subaccounts and provide that bonds issued under this act may be secured by a lien on all or part of the monies paid into the state school trust revenue bond debt service fund or into any account or subaccount in the fund.

"2. Provide that the bonds issued under this act are secured by a first lien on the monies paid into the state school trust revenue bond debt service fund as provided in this act and pledge and assign to or in trust for the benefit of the holder or holders of the bonds all or part of the monies in the state school trust revenue bond debt service fund, in any account or subaccount in the state school trust revenue bond debt service fund or in the state school trust revenue bond proceeds fund as is necessary to secure and pay the principal, the interest and any premium on the bonds as they come due.

"3. Establish priorities among bondholders based on criteria adopted by the board.

"4. Set aside, regulate and dispose of reserves and sinking accounts.

"5. Prescribe the procedure, if any, by which the terms of any contract with bondholders may be amended or abrogated, the amount of bonds the holders of which must consent to and the manner in which the consent may be given.

"6. Provide for payment of bond related expenses from the proceeds of the sale of the bonds or other revenues authorized by this act and available to the board.

"7. Provide for the services of trustees, cotrustees, agents and consultants and other specialized services with respect to the bonds.

"8. Take any other action that in any way may affect the security and protection of the bonds or interest on the bonds.

"9. Refund any bonds issued by the board by issuing new bonds, if these bonds are secured from the same source of revenues as the bonds authorized by this act.

"10. Issue bonds partly to refund outstanding bonds and partly for any other purpose consistent with this act.

"**B.** If bonds are issued pursuant to this act, the executive director of the school facilities board shall provide to the state treasurer and the state land department a schedule of the amount needed to pay each fiscal year's debt service on outstanding state school trust revenue bonds including sinking fund deposits pursuant to the terms of the bonds, and the state treasurer and the state land department shall follow the schedule in making transfers to the state school trust revenue bond debt service fund pursuant to this act.

"**C.** Bonds issued to refund any bonds issued by the board as provided by subsection A, paragraphs 9 and 10 of this section are not subject to the limit on principal amount prescribed by § 22, subsection A of this act but are subject to the limitation on total annual debt service prescribed by § 22, subsection D of this act."

Laws 2003, Ch. 264, § 26, provides:

"**Sec. 26. Lien of pledge**

"**A.** Any pledge made under this act in connection with state school trust revenue bonds is valid and binding from the time when the pledge is made.

"**B.** The monies pledged and received by the school facilities board to be placed in the state school trust revenue bond debt service fund are immediately subject to the lien of the pledge without any future physical delivery or further act. Any lien of any pledge is valid and binding against all parties that have claims of any kind against the board, regardless of whether the parties have notice of the lien. The official resolution or trust indenture or any instrument by which this pledge is created, when adopted by the school facilities board, is notice to all concerned of the creation of the pledge, and those instruments need not be recorded in any other place to perfect the pledge."

Laws 2003, Ch. 264, § 27, provides:

"**Sec. 27. Bond purchase; cancellation**

"The school facilities board may purchase bonds for cancellation out of any monies available for the purchase, at a price of not more than either of the following:

"1. If the bonds are redeemable at the time of the purchase, the applicable redemption price plus accrued interest to the next interest payment date on the bonds.

"2. If the bonds are not redeemable at the time of the purchase, the applicable redemption price on the first date after the purchase on which the bonds become subject to redemption plus accrued interest to that date."

Laws 2003, Ch. 264, § 28, provides:

"**Sec. 28. Payment of revenue bonds**

"**A.** The state school trust revenue bonds shall be paid solely from monies from the state school trust revenue bond debt service fund established pursuant to this act.

"**B.** The state treasurer or the paying agent for the revenue bonds shall cancel all revenue bonds when paid."

Laws 2003, Ch. 264, § 30, provides:

"**Sec. 30. Audit**

"**A.** The school facilities board shall cause an annual audit to be made of the state school trust revenue bond proceeds fund established pursuant to this act and the state school trust revenue bond debt service fund established pursuant to this act, including all accounts and subaccounts in the funds. A certified public accountant shall conduct the audit within ninety days after the end of each fiscal year.

"**B.** The school facilities board shall immediately file a certified copy of the audit with the auditor general. The auditor general may make any further audits and examinations that are necessary and may take appropriate action relating to the audit or examination pursuant to title 41, chapter 7, article 10.1, Arizona Revised Statutes. If the auditor general takes no official action within thirty days after the audit is filed, the audit is considered to be sufficient.

"**C.** The school facilities board shall pay negotiated and approved fees and costs of the certified public accountant and auditor general under this section from the state school trust revenue bond debt service fund established pursuant to this act."

Laws 2003, Ch. 264, § 31, provides:

"**Sec. 31. Characteristics of bonds; negotiable; exemption from taxation; obligation; legal investments**

"**A.** State school trust revenue bonds issued under this act are fully negotiable within the meaning and for all purposes of the uniform commercial code, subject only to any provisions for registration, regardless of whether the bonds actually constitute negotiable instruments under the uniform commercial code.

"**B.** The bonds, their transfer and the income from the bonds are at all times free from taxation in this state.

"**C.** Bonds issued under this act:

"1. Are obligations of the school facilities board. The members of the board and persons executing the bonds are not personally liable for payment of the bonds.

"2. Are payable only according to their terms.

"3. Are not general, special or other obligations of this state.

"4. Do not constitute a debt of this state.

"5. Are not enforceable against this state nor is the payment of the bonds enforceable out of any monies other than the revenue pledged and assigned to, or in trust for the benefit of, the holder or holders of the bonds.

"6. Are securities in which public officers and bodies of this state and of municipalities and political subdivisions of this state, all companies, associations and other persons carrying on an insurance business, all financial institutions, investment companies and other persons carrying on a banking business, all fiduciaries and all other persons who are authorized to invest in government obligations may properly and legally invest.

"7. Are securities that may be deposited with public officers or bodies of this state and municipalities and political subdivisions of this state for purposes that require the deposit of government bonds or obligations."

Laws 2003, Ch. 264, § 32, provides:

"**Sec. 32. Effect of changing circumstances on bonds; agreement of state**

"**A.** State school trust revenue bonds issued under this act remain valid and binding obligations of the school facilities board notwithstanding that before the delivery of the bonds any of the persons whose signatures appear on the bonds cease to be members of the school facilities board.

"**B.** An amendment of any provision of this act does not diminish or impair the validity of bonds issued under this act or the remedies and rights of bondholders.

"**C.** This state pledges to and agrees with the holders of the bonds authorized by this act that this state will not limit, alter or impair the rights and remedies of the bondholders, until all bonds issued under this act, together with interest on the bonds, interest on any unpaid installments of principal or interest and all costs and expenses in connection with any action or proceedings by or on behalf of the bondholders, are fully met and discharged. The school facilities board, as agent for this state, may include this pledge and undertaking in its resolutions and indentures authorizing and securing the bonds."

Laws 2003, Ch. 264, § 33, provides:

"**Sec. 33. Validity of bonds; certification by attorney general**

"**A.** This act constitutes full authority for authorizing and issuing state school trust revenue bonds without reference to any other law of this state. No other law with regard to authorizing or issuing obligations or that in any way impedes or restricts performing the acts authorized by this act may be construed to apply to any proceedings taken or acts done pursuant to this act.

"**B.** The validity of bonds issued under this act does not depend on and is not affected by the legality of any proceeding relating to any action by the school facilities board in granting or lending monies or the acquisition, construction or improvement of any facility paid with monies provided by the school facilities board.

"**C.** The school facilities board may submit to the attorney general revenue bonds to be issued under this act after all proceedings for authorizing the bonds have been completed. Within fifteen days after submission, the attorney general shall examine the bonds and pass on the validity of the bonds and the regularity of the proceedings. If the bonds and proceedings comply with the Constitution of Arizona and this act, and if the bonds when delivered and paid for will constitute binding and legal obligations of the board, the attorney general shall certify in substance that the bonds are issued according to the constitution and laws of this state. The certificate shall also state that the bonds are also validly secured by the obligation to transfer monies from designated sources of revenue, including income on the permanent state school fund as provided by this act, to cover any insufficiencies.

"**D.** The bonds shall recite that they are regularly issued pursuant to this act. That recital, together with the certification by the attorney general under subsection C of this section, constitutes prima facie evidence of the legality and validity of the bonds. From and after the sale and delivery of the bonds, they are incontestable by the school facilities board or this state."

Laws 2003, Ch. 264, § 34, provides:

"**Sec. 34. State treasurer and state board of investment to comply with agreements**

"Notwithstanding any other law, the state treasurer and the state board of investment shall comply with all agreements made by the school facilities board with or for the benefit of the owners of its state school trust revenue bonds regarding the investment of the assets of the permanent state school fund."

Laws 2003, Ch. 264, § 35, provides:

"**Sec. 35. Project bids; joint committee on capital review approval**

"**A.** Before the issuance of any state school trust revenue bonds pursuant to this act, the school facilities board shall:

"1. Receive bids for the cost of all deficiencies correction projects that will be financed with the revenue bond proceeds.

"2. Submit a list of the projects, the project bids and the estimated annual principal and interest payments related to the bond agreement to the joint committee on capital review for approval.

"**B.** The school facilities board shall report to the joint committee on capital review the cost of the remaining projects in the Tucson Unified School District, the Mesa Unified School District and the Glendale Union High School District after receiving bids for projects in those districts."

Laws 2003, Ch. 264, § 36, provides:

"**Sec. 36. Reduction in school district state aid apportionment; fiscal year 2003-2004**

"**A.** Notwithstanding § 15-973, subsection B, paragraph 10, Arizona Revised Statutes, the state board of education shall defer until July 1, 2004 $191,000,000 of the basic state aid and additional state aid payment that otherwise would be apportioned to school districts under that law on June 15, 2004.

"**B.** The funding deferral required by this section does not apply to charter schools."

Reviser's Notes:

1981 Note. The above article and section which comprises it were added by Laws 1981, Ch. 1, § 2 as article 3 and § 15-131 and were renumbered as article 2 and § 15-121 pursuant to authority of § 41-1304.02.

ARTICLE 3. TEACHER EXCHANGE

§ 15-131. Exchange teacher agreements

A. The governing board of any school district in this state or the Arizona board of regents may enter into agreements with any foreign country, state, territory or possession of the United States or other school district within the state for the exchange and employment of teachers or professors having required certificates in this state and teachers or professors in the public schools, universities or colleges of any foreign country, state, territory or possession of the United States or other school district within the state having certification or qualifications equivalent to that of the exchange teacher or professor of this state.

B. In all cases of the exchange of any foreign teacher or professor such exchange shall be contracted for and effected exclusively through the teacher exchange program as authorized by federal statutes enacted by the congress of the United States.

Added as § 15-141 by Laws 1981, Ch. 1, § 2, eff. Jan. 23, 1981. Renumbered as § 15-131.

Historical and Statutory Notes

Source:

Laws 1956, Ch. 76, § 1.
A.R.S. former § 15-1191.

Reviser's Notes:

1981 Note. The above article and sections which comprise it were added by Laws 1981, Ch. 1, § 2 as article 4 and §§ 15-141 through 15-145 and were renumbered as article 3 and §§ 15-131 through 15-135 pursuant to authority of § 41-1304.02.

§ 15-132. Certification of exchange teachers and professors

The state board of education shall issue temporary certificates to exchange teachers and professors of foreign countries and other states whose training and background comply with the rules promulgated by the board for certification and are equivalent to those of the local teacher with whom the exchange is made.

Added as § 15-142 by Laws 1981, Ch. 1, § 2, eff. Jan. 23, 1981. Renumbered as § 15-132.

Historical and Statutory Notes

Source:

Laws 1956, Ch. 76, § 1.
A.R.S. former § 15-1192.

Reviser's Notes:

1981 Note. The above article and sections which comprise it were added by Laws 1981, Ch. 1, § 2 as article 4 and §§ 15-141 through 15-145 and were renumbered as article 3 and §§ 15-131 through 15-135 pursuant to authority of § 41-1304.02.

§ 15-133. Terms of employment

No exchange teacher or professor may be employed in this state unless he has been issued proper certification and may not be employed for more than one school year, except that, by consent of the governing board or the Arizona board of regents and the two exchange teachers concerned, the period may be extended to two years.

Added as § 15-143 by Laws 1981, Ch. 1, § 2, eff. Jan. 23, 1981. Renumbered as § 15-133.

Historical and Statutory Notes

Source:

Laws 1956, Ch. 76, § 1.
A.R.S. former § 15-1193.

Reviser's Notes:

1981 Note. The above article and sections which comprise it were added by Laws 1981, Ch. 1, § 2 as article 4 and §§ 15-141 through 15-145 and were renumbered as article 3 and §§ 15-131 through 15-135 pursuant to authority of § 41-1304.02.

§ 15-134. Payment of salaries of exchange teachers

During the exchange teaching provided for in this article, the salaries of the exchange teachers or professors may be paid by either the school districts or universities or colleges by which they are regularly employed, or by the school districts or universities or colleges in which the exchange teaching service is rendered. The school district or university or college shall pay the salary of only one of the two exchange teachers and in an amount not to exceed the annual salary of its regularly employed teachers or professors.

Added as § 15-144 by Laws 1981, Ch. 1, § 2, eff. Jan. 23, 1981. Renumbered as § 15-134.

Historical and Statutory Notes

Source:

Laws 1956, Ch. 76, § 1.
A.R.S. former § 15-1194.
Laws 1963, Ch. 23, § 1.

Reviser's Notes:

1981 Note. The above article and sections which comprise it were added by Laws 1981, Ch. 1, § 2 as article 4 and §§ 15-141 through 15-145 and were renumbered as article 3 and §§ 15-131 through 15-135 pursuant to authority of § 41-1304.02.

§ 15-135. Deductions for retirement; preservation of rights

A. All regular deductions for retirement as required by law shall be made from the salary of the local teacher or professor participating in exchange teaching pursuant to this article.

B. No such teacher or professor shall lose any right of certification, retirement, salary status or other benefit provided by law or by the rules of the governing board of the school district or the Arizona board of regents due to exchange teaching under this article.

Added as § 15-145 by Laws 1981, Ch. 1, § 2, eff. Jan. 23, 1981. Renumbered as § 15-135. Amended by Laws 1986, Ch. 399, § 1.

Historical and Statutory Notes

Source:

Laws 1956, Ch. 76, § 1.
A.R.S. former § 15-1195.

Reviser's Notes:

1981 Note. The above article and sections which comprise it were added by Laws 1981, Ch. 1, § 2 as article 4 and §§ 15-141 through 15-145 and were renumbered as article 3 and §§ 15-131 through 15-135 pursuant to authority of § 41-1304.02.

ARTICLE 4. EDUCATIONAL RECORDS

§ 15-141. Educational records; injunction; special action

A. The right to inspect and review educational records and the release of or access to these records, other information or instructional materials is governed by federal law in the family educational and privacy rights act of 1974 (20 United States Code §§ 1232g, 1232h and 1232i),[1] and federal regulations issued pursuant to such act.

B. In addition to the enforcement procedures provided in the family educational and privacy rights act of 1974, the superior court may grant injunctive or special action relief if any educational agency or institution or an officer or employee of an agency or institution fails to comply with the act regardless of whether the agency or institution is the recipient of any federal funds subject to termination pursuant to the act or whether administrative remedies through any federal agency have been exhausted.

C. Notwithstanding any financial debt owed by the pupil, the governing board of a school district shall release to the department of juvenile corrections all educational records relating to a pupil who is awarded to the department of juvenile corrections within ten working days after the date the request is received.

D. A juvenile court may require a school district to provide the court with the educational records of a juvenile who is accused of committing a delinquent or incorrigible act before the juvenile is adjudicated. The educational records shall include the juvenile's cumulative file and discipline file and, if applicable, records that are compiled pursuant to the individuals with disabilities education act (P.L. 91-230; 84 Stat. 175; 20 United States Code § 1400) and the rehabilitation act of 1973 (P.L. 93-112; 87 Stat. 394; 29 United States Code § 794). The presiding judge of the juvenile court shall adopt procedures for the transmission of the educational records from the school district to the juvenile court. The disclosure of the educational records shall comply with the family educational and privacy rights act of 1974 (20 United States Code § 1232g) and shall ensure the ability of the juvenile court to effectively serve, before adjudication, the juvenile whose records are released. Nothing in this subsection shall be considered to prevent the juvenile court from adjudicating a juvenile prior to receiving educational records pursuant to this subsection.

E. A school district may release pupil attendance, disciplinary and other educational records to a law enforcement agency and county attorney pursuant to an intergovernmental agreement among the school district, law enforcement agency, county attorney and other state, local or tribal government agencies to create a local or tribal governmental juvenile justice network for the purpose of:

1. Providing appropriate programs and services to intervene with juveniles currently involved in the juvenile justice system.

2. Providing appropriate programs and services designed to deter at-risk juveniles from dropping out of school or other delinquent behavior.

3. Increasing the safety and security of the community and its children by reducing juvenile crime.

F. Educational records provided pursuant to an intergovernmental agreement entered into pursuant to subsection E shall be used solely for the purposes of the agreement and shall not be disclosed to any other party, except as provided by law.

Added as § 15–151 by Laws 1981, Ch. 1, § 2, eff. Jan. 23, 1981. Renumbered as § 15–141. Amended by Laws 1989, Ch. 266, § 8, eff. July 1, 1991; Laws 1991, Ch. 210, § 10; Laws 1995, Ch. 178, § 14; Laws 1999, Ch. 245, § 2; Laws 2002, Ch. 340, § 1.

[1] 20 U.S.C.A. §§ 1232g, 1232h and 1232i.

Historical and Statutory Notes

Source:

Laws 1974, Ch. 163, § 1.
A.R.S. former §§ 15–151, 15–152, 15–153, 15–154.

The 1989 amendment, in subsec. A, substituted "of 1974, as amended" for ", title", inserted parentheses, and inserted a reference to § 1232i; and added subsec. C.

The 1991 amendment by Ch. 210, rewrote subsec. C, which had read:

"**C.** Notwithstanding any financial debt owed by the pupil, the governing board of a school district shall release to the state department of juvenile corrections all educational records relating to a pupil who is awarded to the state department of juvenile corrections within ten working days after the date the request is received."

The 1995 amendment by Ch. 178, in subsec. C, substituted "department of juvenile corrections" for "department of youth treatment and rehabilitation" and "the facility" for "such facility" twice; and made other nonsubstantive changes.

The 1999 amendment by Ch. 245, in subsec. A, substituted "family educational and privacy rights act of 1974" for "family educational rights and privacy act of 1974, as amended"; in subsec. B, substituted "the family educational and privacy rights act of 1974, the superior court" for "such act, the superior court of this state", "an officer or employee of an agency" for "officer or employee of such agency", "the act" for "such act" twice, and "the agency" for "such agency"; and added subsec. D.

The 2002 amendment by Ch. 340 added subsecs. E and F.

Reviser's Notes:

1981 Note. The above article and section which comprises it were added by Laws 1981, Ch. 1, § 2 as article 5 and § 15–151 and were renumbered as article 4 and § 15–141 pursuant to authority of § 41–1304.02.

§ 15–142. Access to directory information relating to pupils and to school property

A. If the governing board of a school district permits the release of directory information relating to pupils or permits access to school buildings, school grounds or other school property to persons who inform pupils of educational or occupational opportunities, the governing board shall provide access to directory information relating to pupils and to school property on the same basis for official recruiting representatives of the militia of this state and the armed services of the united states for the purpose of informing pupils of educational and occupational opportunities available in the militia and the armed services.

B. Notwithstanding subsection A of this section, pupil transcripts shall not be released to representatives of postsecondary institutions, the militia of this state or the armed services of the united states unless the pupil consents in writing to the release of the pupil's transcript. The governing board of the school district shall provide the pupil with a transcript release form that allows the pupil to designate in separate check boxes whether the transcript is to be released to postsecondary institutions, the militia of this state or the armed services of the united states, or to any combination of these entities.

C. This section shall not be construed to authorize school districts to release information that would violate the family educational and privacy rights act of 1974 (20 united states code § 1232g).

Added by Laws 2001, Ch. 130, § 1.

Historical and Statutory Notes

Former § 15-142, added by Laws 1982, Ch. 178, § 1, which related to access to directory information relating to pupils and school property, was repealed by Laws 1996, Ch. 284, § 3.

ARTICLE 5. SAFETY REQUIREMENTS

§ 15-151. Eye protective devices; definition

A. Every student, teacher and visitor in public and private schools, community colleges, colleges and universities shall wear appropriate eye protective ware while participating in or when observing vocational, technical, industrial arts, art or laboratory science activities involving exposure to:

1. Molten metals or other molten materials.
2. Cutting, shaping and grinding of materials.
3. Heat treatment, tempering or kiln firing of any metal or other materials.
4. Welding fabrication processes.
5. Explosive materials.
6. Caustic solutions.
7. Radioactive materials.

B. The governing board of every school district, the governing board of every community college district, the Arizona board of regents and every person maintaining a private or parochial school in this state shall equip schools within their jurisdiction with eye protective ware for use as required in this article.

C. Standards and rules for the enforcement of this article shall be prescribed by the governing board of every school district, the community college district governing board of each community college district and the Arizona board of regents.

D. Schools, community colleges, colleges and universities may receive and expend federal, state and local monies to provide eye protective devices.

E. For purposes of this article, "eye protective wear" means devices meeting the standards of the [1] American national standards institute's standards for occupational and education eye protection, Z87.1-1989.

Added as § 15-161 by Laws 1981, Ch. 1, § 2, eff. Jan. 23, 1981. Renumbered as § 15-151. Amended by Laws 1996, Ch. 284, § 4.

[1] So in original. The phrase "standards of the" should be stricken.

Historical and Statutory Notes

Source:

Laws 1968, Ch. 132, § 1.
A.R.S. former § 15-1501.

Reviser's Notes:

1981 Note. The above article and section which comprises it were added by Laws 1981, Ch. 1, § 2 as article 6 and § 15-161 and were renumbered as article 5 and § 15-151 pursuant to authority of § 41-1304.02.

§ 15-152. Pest management at schools; notice

A. The governing board of each school district, in consultation with teachers, parents, guardians, administrators, members of the public, a certified applicator, and at least one health professional, shall develop and adopt a policy to provide pupils and employees with at least forty-eight hours' notice before pesticides are applied on school property. The policy shall include at least the following:

1. Procedures for providing the notification including:

(a) Procedures for oral notification to pupils and employees during a regular school session.

(b) Procedures for written notification to parents or guardians during a regular school session.

(c) Procedures for the posting of signs to identify pesticide application areas.

2. Procedures for requiring any contracted pest control applicator to provide detailed and sufficient information to the schools for the purpose of completing the posting materials.

3. Procedures providing for continuing instruction for pupils who are absent because of pesticide application on school property.

B. Each school district shall maintain written records of pesticide application notifications. The school district may delegate to the pest control applicator the duty to fill out and post notices required by district policy.

C. For purposes of this section "pesticides" does not include nonrestricted use disinfectants, sanitizers or deodorizers regulated by the federal insecticide, fungicide and rodenticide act but includes other pesticides regulated under the federal insecticide, fungicide and rodenticide act (P.L. 100-532; 102 Stat. 2654; 7 United States Code § 136).

Added by Laws 1993, Ch. 102, § 1. Amended by Laws 1996, Ch. 284, § 5.

Historical and Statutory Notes

Reviser's Notes:

1993 Note. Pursuant to authority of § 41-1304.02, in subsection A the spelling of "hours' " was corrected.

§ 15-153. School safety program oversight committee; membership; duties; staff; compensation; definition

A. The school safety program oversight committee is established consisting of the following members:

1. Two members of the senate who are from different political parties and who are appointed by the president of the senate. These members serve as advisory members. The president of the senate shall select one member to cochair the committee.

2. Two members of the house of representatives who are from different political parties and who are appointed by the speaker of the house of representatives. These members serve as advisory members. The speaker of the house of representatives shall select one member to cochair the committee.

3. The governor, or the governor's designee.

4. The superintendent of public instruction, or the superintendent's designee.

5. A law enforcement officer who is appointed by the speaker of the house of representatives.

6. A juvenile probation officer who is appointed by the chief justice of the supreme court.

7. A public school principal who is appointed by the superintendent of public instruction.

8. A representative from the field of law related education who is appointed by the governor.

B. Members serve at the pleasure of the appointing entity.

C. The committee shall review plans submitted by the applicants for participation in the school safety program and shall select sites that are eligible to receive funding based on school safety needs. The committee shall also review renewal applications from participating sites.

D. The committee shall evaluate the program and report annually to the president of the senate, the speaker of the house of representatives, the governor and the joint legislative audit committee by November 1.

E. For purposes of this section, "advisory member" means a member who advises the committee but who is not eligible to vote and is not a member for the purposes of determining a quorum.

Added by Laws 1997, Ch. 220, § 78.

Termination under Sunset Law

The school safety program oversight committee shall terminate on July 1, 2007, unless continued. See §§ 41-3007.09 and 41-2955.

Sections 15-153, 15-154 and 15-155, are repealed on January 1, 2008, by § 41-3007.09.

Historical and Statutory Notes

Laws 1997, Ch. 220, §§ 102, 104, provide:

"Sec. 102. Terms of board members

"Notwithstanding § 15–153, Arizona Revised Statutes, as added by this act, a person who is serving as a member of the joint legislative committee on school safety on the effective date of this act is eligible to serve on the school safety program oversight committee for the remainder of the person's scheduled term. All subsequent appointments shall be made as prescribed by statute."

"Sec. 104. Purpose

"The purpose of the school safety program oversight committee is to provide a proactive approach to prevent juvenile referrals to the court system of this state and to prevent detention in the state department of juvenile corrections, county jails and the state department of corrections."

§ 15–154. Public school safety program proposal; requirements; purpose; definitions

A. A public school district may apply to participate or may complete an application to continue in the school safety program as provided in this section for any fiscal year by submitting by April 15 a program proposal or an application to continue the program to the school safety program oversight committee. New applicants are restricted to unencumbered monies that have been appropriated in previous fiscal years or monies appropriated to expand the program. The program proposal shall contain:

1. A detailed description of the school safety needs of the public school or school district.

2. A plan for implementing a law related education program or a plan that demonstrates the existence of a law related education program as a school safety prevention strategy.

3. A plan to use trained school resource officers or juvenile probation officers in the schools, or both.

B. The state board of education shall administer the program in cooperation with the courts, law enforcement agencies and law related education providers. Representatives from the state board of education shall use relevant crime statistics and shall visit schools located in school districts that submit program proposals in order to verify the information contained in the program proposals.

C. The department of education, at the direction of the state board of education, shall distribute monies to the school districts whose plans have been approved by the school safety program oversight committee.

D. Any appropriations that are made to the department of education for the school safety program are exempt from the provisions of § 35–190 relating to the lapsing of appropriations. All monies that are not used for an approved school safety plan during the fiscal year for which the monies were appropriated revert to the department of education for distribution to the program in the following fiscal year.

E. Monies received by a school district under the program shall be spent to implement the approved plans.

F. For purposes of this section:

1. "Law related education" means interactive education to equip children and youth with knowledge and skills pertaining to the law, school safety and effective citizenship.

2. "Law related education program" means a program designed to provide children and youth with knowledge, skills and activities pertaining to the law and legal process and to promote law-abiding behavior with the purpose of preventing children and youth from engaging in delinquency or violence and enabling them to become productive citizens.

Added by Laws 1997, Ch. 220, § 78. Amended by Laws 1999, 1st S.S., Ch. 4, § 1.

Termination under Sunset Law

The school safety program oversight committee shall terminate on July 1, 2007, unless continued. See §§ 41–3007.09 and 41–2955.

Sections 15–153, 15–154 and 15–155, are repealed on January 1, 2008, by § 41–3007.09.

§ 15–154.01. Character education matching grant program; program termination

A. Any public or charter school that teaches a character education curriculum pursuant to § 15–719 is eligible for a state matching grant of up to one thousand five hundred dollars annually. The school shall provide matching monies from any lawful source, except that the school shall not use resources obtained from a federal character education grant as matching monies to obtain a second state character education grant.

B. The character education program shall be an age-specific, stand-alone character education curriculum with the following elements:

1. Applicable definitions for character qualities that include at least five of the following attributes:

(a) Attentiveness.

(b) Caring.

(c) Citizenship.

(d) Compassion.

(e) Diligence.

(f) Discernment.

(g) Forgiveness.

(h) Generosity.

(i) Gratefulness.

(j) Initiative.

(k) Orderliness.

(*l*) Respect.

(m) Responsibility.

(n) Sincerity.

(*o*) Trustworthiness.

(p) Virtue.

(q) Wisdom.

2. Activities that provide a forum for practical application and an environment in which character-related behavior is identified, recognized and reinforced such as literature or visual media presentations or discussion of character values as they relate to a specific story.

3. Stories from the lives of our nation's leaders, where character qualities are demonstrated.

4. Mentors or teachers who demonstrate the character qualities defined in the lessons presented.

5. Mentor and teacher training for praising students who demonstrate specific character qualities.

6. A precourse and postcourse survey of parents, teachers and students on their assessment of the program.

C. The department of education shall contract with and distribute state matching grant monies to the Arizona K–12 center at Northern Arizona University. The Arizona K–12 center at Northern Arizona University shall administer the program and distribute the state matching grant monies. Programs must demonstrate proven and effective curriculum and training to receive matching grant funds.

D. The state department of education shall apply for all applicable character education grants from the federal government.

E. The department of education shall work in cooperation with the Arizona K–12 center at Northern Arizona University to evaluate the effectiveness of all character education programs funded by state and federal resources.

F. The program established by this section ends on July 1, 2010 pursuant to § 41–3102.

Added by Laws 2000, 5th S.S., Ch. 1, § 1. Amended by Laws 2001, Ch. 174, § 1.

Historical and Statutory Notes

Laws 2000, 5th S.S. Ch. 1, § 65, provides:

"**Sec. 65. Conforming legislation; blending**

"**A.** The legislative council staff shall prepare proposed legislation conforming the Arizona Revised Statutes to the provisions of this act for consideration in the forty-fifth legislature, first regular session.

"**B.** The executive director of the legislative council is authorized to blend the nonconflicting changes made to the Arizona Revised Statutes during the forty-fourth legislature, second regular session, with the changes made to those same statutes by this act."

Laws 2000, 5th S.S., Ch. 1, §§ 66 and 67, provide:

"**Sec. 66. Delayed implementation**

"This act shall not be implemented until from and after May 31, 2001.

"**Sec. 67. Conditional enactment**

"This act does not become effective unless the qualified electors of this state in the general election that will be held in November, 2000 approve an increase in state transaction privilege tax rates of six-tenths of one per cent in order to fund the provisions of this act."

Proposition 301, approved by the electors at the Nov. 7, 2000 general election, effective Nov. 27, 2000, included a provision increasing the state transaction privilege tax rate six-tenths of one per cent. Therefore, the conditions of the 5th S.S. Ch. 1 were met, and the act became effective.

§ 15–155. School safety program; funding

A. The department of education shall cooperate with the county school superintendent, the county sheriff and the local chief of police to permit a law enforcement agency, with the consent of the school, to assign a peace officer to participate in the safe schools program in each school in the county. The cost of the peace officer is a state charge that is funded by the department of education.

B. In cooperation with the department of education and the county school superintendent and with the consent of the school, the presiding judge of the juvenile court may assign juvenile probation officers to participate in the safe schools program in each school in the county. The cost of juvenile probation officers is a state charge that is funded by the department of education.
Added by Laws 1997, Ch. 220, § 78.

Termination under Sunset Law

The school safety program oversight committee shall terminate on July 1, 2007, unless continued. See §§ 41–3007.09 and 41–2955.

Sections 15–153, 15–154 and 15–155, are repealed on January 1, 2008, by § 41–3007.09.

§ 15–156. Liquid roofing systems; violation; classification; definition

A. A person shall not knowingly apply or allow to be applied a liquid roofing system that the person knows or with the exercise of reasonable care should know contains at least one-tenth of one per cent by weight or volume of any diisocyanate on a building that is owned or operated by a public school while a teacher or student is present in the building.

B. A person shall not knowingly allow any teacher or student to remain in a building that is owned or operated by a public school during, and for at least two hours after, a liquid roofing system has been applied that the person knows or with the exercise of reasonable care should know contains at least one-tenth of one per cent by weight or volume of any diisocyanate.

C. Current material safety data sheets must be supplied to the school prior to the application of liquid roofing systems containing more than one-tenth of one per cent by weight or volume of any diisocyanate on a building owned or operated by a public school. Applicators of liquid roofing systems must follow all applicable occupational safety and health administration regulations. All federal, state, and local regulations governing the use, shipment, and disposal of diisocyanates shall be followed and strictly adhered to.

D. A person who violates this section is guilty of a class 2 misdemeanor.

E. For the purposes of this section, "diisocyanate" means any diisocyanate used in a liquid applied roofing system including methylene bisphenyl diisocyanate, also known as methylene diphenyl diisocyanate or MDI, polymeric methylene bisphenyl diisocyanate, also known as polymeric MDI, or hexamethylene diisocyanate or HDI.
Added by Laws 1998, Ch. 104, § 1.

Historical and Statutory Notes

Reviser's Notes:

1998 Note. Pursuant to authority of § 41-1304.02, in the section heading "Liquid" was substituted for "Spray polyurethane".

ARTICLE 6. STATE PROHIBITIONS

Article 6, consisting of § 15-161, was added by Laws 1983, Ch. 325, § 2, effective July 27, 1983.

§ 15-161. State control over private schools

Nothing in this title shall be construed to provide the state board of education or the governing boards of school districts control or supervision over private schools.

Added by Laws 1983, Ch. 325, § 2.

Historical and Statutory Notes

Former § 15-161 was renumbered as § 15-151.

Reviser's Notes:

1983 Note. Pursuant to authority of § 41-1304.02, in the heading of this section the word "Prohibiting" was deleted.

ARTICLE 7. COMPREHENSIVE SCHOOL HEALTH POLICY COUNCIL [REPEALED]

Article 7, added by Laws 1992, Ch. 305, § 2, relating to the Arizona Comprehensive School Health Policy Council, was repealed on January 1, 2003, by § 41-3002.17.

§§ 15-171, 15-172. Repealed by Laws 1995, Ch. 268, § 4

Historical and Statutory Notes

The repealed sections, added by Laws 1992, Ch. 305, § 2, related to the comprehensive school health policy council and the comprehensive school health fund.

ARTICLE 8. CHARTER SCHOOLS

Article 8, Charter Schools, consisting of §§ 15-181 to 15-189, was added by Laws 1994, 9th S.S., Ch. 2, § 2, effective September 16, 1994.

Another Article 8, Family Literacy Pilot Program, was renumbered as Article 9. See Article 9, §§ 15-191 and 15-191.01.

Historical and Statutory Notes

Laws 2004, Ch. 278, § 8, provides:

"**Sec. 8. State board of education; charter school sponsorship**

"Notwithstanding title 15, chapter 1, article 8, Arizona Revised Statutes, the state board of education shall not sponsor any additional charter schools for fiscal year 2004-2005 and the state board of education and the state board for charter schools shall enter into an intergovernmental agreement for fiscal year 2004-2005 that requires the state board for charter schools to provide the same type of oversight that year for charter schools that are sponsored by the state board of education as the state board for charter schools provides for charter schools sponsored by the state board for charter schools."

Laws 2004, Ch. 278, § 21, provides:

"**Sec. 21. Retroactivity**

"**A.** Except as provided in subsection B of this section, this act applies retroactively to from and after June 30, 2004.

"**B.** Laws 2002, chapter 330, § 49, as amended by this act, applies retroactively to from and after June 29, 2004."

§ 15-181. Charter schools; purpose; scope

A. Charter schools may be established pursuant to this article to provide a learning environment that will improve pupil achievement. Charter schools provide additional academic choices for parents and pupils. Charter schools may consist of new schools or all or any portion of an existing school. Charter schools are public schools that serve as alternatives to traditional public schools and charter schools are not subject to the requirements of article XI, § 1, Constitution of Arizona, or chapter 16 of this title.

B. Charter schools shall comply with all provisions of this article in order to receive state funding as prescribed in § 15-185.

Added by Laws 1994, 9th S.S., Ch. 2, § 2. Amended by Laws 1998, 5th S.S., Ch. 1, § 5, eff. July 9, 1998.

Historical and Statutory Notes

The purported amendment of this section by Laws 1998, 3rd S.S., Ch. 1, failed to became effective because Ch. 1 was repealed in its entirety by Laws 1998, 5th S.S., Ch. 1, § 2, effective July 1, 1998.

Laws 1998, 5th S.S., Ch. 1, § 2, provides:

"**Sec. 2. Repeal**

"Laws 1998, third special session, chapter 1, Laws 1998, chapter 164, Laws 1998, chapter 219 and Laws 1998, chapter 286, § 1 are repealed."

Another § 15-181 was renumbered as § 15-191.

§ 15-182. State board for charter schools; membership; terms; compensation; duties

A. The state board for charter schools is established consisting of the following members:

1. The superintendent of public instruction or the superintendent's designee.

2. Six members of the general public, at least two of whom shall reside in a school district where at least sixty per cent of the children who attend school in the district meet the eligibility requirements established under the national school lunch and child nutrition acts (42 United States Code §§ 1751 through 1785) for free lunches, and at least one of whom shall reside on an Indian reservation, who are appointed by the governor pursuant to § 38-211.

3. Two members of the business community who are appointed by the governor pursuant to § 38-211.

4. A teacher who provides classroom instruction at a charter school and who is appointed by the governor pursuant to § 38-211.

5. An operator of a charter school who is appointed by the governor pursuant to § 38-211.

6. Three members of the legislature who shall serve as advisory members and who are appointed jointly by the president of the senate and the speaker of the house of representatives.

B. The superintendent of public instruction shall serve a term on the state board for charter schools that runs concurrently with the superintendent's term of office. The members appointed pursuant to subsection A, paragraph 6 of this section shall serve two year terms on the state board for charter schools that begin and end on the third Monday in January and that run concurrently with their respective terms of office. Members appointed pursuant to subsection A, paragraphs 2, 3, 4 and 5 of this section shall serve staggered four year terms that begin and end on the third Monday in January.

C. The state board for charter schools shall annually elect a president and such other officers as it deems necessary from among its membership.

D. Members of the state board for charter schools are not eligible to receive compensation but are eligible for reimbursement of expenses pursuant to title 38, chapter 4, article 2.[1]

E. The state board for charter schools shall:

1. Exercise general supervision over charter schools sponsored by the board and recommend legislation pertaining to charter schools to the legislature.

2. Grant charter status to qualifying applicants for charter schools pursuant to § 15-183.

3. Adopt and use an official seal in the authentication of its acts.

4. Keep a record of its proceedings.

5. Adopt rules for its own government.

6. Determine the policy of the board and the work undertaken by it.

7. Delegate to the superintendent of public instruction the execution of board policies.

8. Prepare a budget for expenditures necessary for the proper maintenance of the board and the accomplishment of its purpose.

F. The state board for charter schools may:

1. Contract.

2. Sue and be sued.

Added by Laws 1994, 9th S.S., Ch. 2, § 2. Amended by Laws 1996, Ch. 356, § 1; Laws 1997, Ch. 231, § 2; Laws 2004, Ch. 257, § 1.

[1] Section 38-621 et seq.

Termination Under Sunset Law

The state board for charter schools shall terminate on July 1, 2014, unless continued. See §§ 41-3014.15 and 41-2955.

Section 15-182, relating to the state board for charter schools, is repealed on January 1, 2015, by § 41-3014.15.

Historical and Statutory Notes

Laws 1994, 9th S.S., Ch. 2, §§ 19 and 22, provide:

"**Sec. 19. Purpose**

"The purpose of the state board for charter schools is to:

"1. Grant charter status to qualifying applicants for charter schools that are sponsored by the state board for charter schools.

"2. Exercise general supervision over charter schools sponsored by the state board for charter schools.

"3. Recommend proposed legislation pertaining to charter schools to the legislature."

"**Sec. 22. State board for charter schools; initial terms**

"**A.** Notwithstanding § 15-182, Arizona Revised Statutes, as added by this act, the initial appointments of the members of the state board for charter schools shall be made on October 1, 1994 and the initial terms of the members of the state board for charter schools are:

"1. For members appointed pursuant to § 15-182, subsection A, paragraph 2, Arizona Revised Statutes, one term ending on the third Monday in January, 1997 and one term ending on the third Monday in January, 1999.

"2. For members appointed pursuant to § 15-182, subsection A, paragraph 3, Arizona Revised Statutes, one term ending on the third Monday in January, 1997, one term ending on the third Monday in January, 1998 and one term ending on the third Monday in January, 1999.

"3. For members appointed pursuant to § 15-182, subsection A, paragraph 4, Arizona Revised Statutes, one term ending on the third Monday in January, 1997, and one term ending on the third Monday in January, 1999.

"**B.** All subsequent appointments shall be made as prescribed by statute."

Laws 1996, Ch. 356, § 7, provides:

"**Sec. 7. Retention of members**

"Notwithstanding § 15-182, Arizona Revised Statutes, as amended by this act, members of the state board of education who are members of the state board for charter schools on the effective date of this act shall continue to serve until the expiration of the term to which the member was appointed or their resignation, whichever occurs first."

Laws 2004, Ch. 257, §§ 4 and 5, provide:

"**Sec. 4. Purpose**

"Pursuant to § 41-2955, subsection B, Arizona Revised Statutes, the legislature continues the state board for charter schools, the purpose of which is to:

"1. Grant charter status to qualifying applications for charter schools that are sponsored by the state board for charter schools.

"2. Exercise general supervision over charter schools sponsored by the state board for charter schools.

"3. Recommend proposed legislation pertaining to charter schools to the legislature.

"**Sec. 5. State board for charter schools; appointment of resident of Indian reservation**

"On the next expiration that occurs after the effective date of § 1 of this act of the term of office of a member of the general public appointed to the state board for charter schools pursuant to § 15-182, subsection A, paragraph 2, Arizona Revised Statutes, as amended by this act, the governor shall appoint a person who resides on an Indian reservation to the state board for charter schools."

Another § 15-182 was renumbered as § 15-191.01.

§ 15-183. Charter schools; application; requirements; immunity; exemptions; renewal of application; reprisal

A. An applicant seeking to establish a charter school shall submit a written application to a proposed sponsor as prescribed in subsection C of this section. The application shall include a detailed business plan for the charter school and may include a mission statement for the charter school, a description of the charter school's organizational structure and the governing body, a financial plan for the first three years of operation of the charter school, a description of the charter school's hiring policy, the name of the charter school's applicant or applicants and requested sponsor, a description of the charter school's facility and the location of the school, a description of the grades being served and an outline of criteria designed to measure the effectiveness of the school.

B. The sponsor of a charter school may contract with a public body, private person or private organization for the purpose of establishing a charter school pursuant to this article.

C. The sponsor of a charter school may be either a school district governing board, the state board of education or the state board for charter schools, subject to the following requirements:

1. For charter schools that submit an application for sponsorship to a school district governing board:

(a) An applicant for a charter school may submit its application to a school district governing board, which shall either accept or reject sponsorship of the charter school within ninety days. An applicant may submit a revised application for reconsideration by the governing board. If the governing board rejects the application, the governing board shall notify the applicant in writing of the reasons for the rejection. The applicant may request, and the governing board may provide, technical assistance to improve the application.

(b) In the first year that a school district is determined to be out of compliance with the uniform system of financial records, within fifteen days of the determination of noncompliance, the school district shall notify by certified mail each charter school sponsored by the school district that the school district is out of compliance with the uniform system of financial records. The notification shall include a statement that if the school district is determined to be out of compliance for a second consecutive year, the charter school will be required to transfer sponsorship to another entity pursuant to subdivision (c) of this paragraph.

(c) In the second consecutive year that a school district is determined to be out of compliance with the uniform system of financial records, within fifteen days of the determination of noncompliance, the school district shall notify by certified mail each charter school sponsored by the school district that the school district is out of compliance with the uniform system of financial records. A charter school that receives a notification of school district noncompliance pursuant to this subdivision shall file a written sponsorship transfer application within forty-five days with the state board of education, the state board for charter schools or the school district governing board if the charter school is located within the geographic boundaries of that school district. A charter school that receives a notification of school district noncompliance may request an extension of time to file a sponsorship transfer application and the state board of education, the state board for charter schools or a school district governing board may grant an extension of not more than an additional thirty days if good cause exists for the extension. The state board of education and the state board for charter schools shall approve a sponsorship transfer application pursuant to this paragraph.

(d) Beginning July 1, 2000, a school district governing board shall not grant a charter to a charter school that is located outside the geographic boundaries of that school district.

(e) A school district that has been determined to be out of compliance with the uniform system of financial records during either of the previous two fiscal years shall not sponsor a new or transferring charter school.

2. The applicant may submit the application to the state board of education or the state board for charter schools. The state board of education or the state board for charter schools may approve the application if the application meets the requirements of this article and may approve the charter if the proposed sponsor determines, within its sole discretion, that the applicant is sufficiently qualified to operate a charter school. The state board of education or the state

board for charter schools may approve any charter schools transferring charters. The state board of education and the state board for charter schools shall approve any charter schools transferring charters from a school district that is determined to be out of compliance with the uniform system of financial records pursuant to this section, but may require the charter school to sign a new charter that is equivalent to the charter awarded by the former sponsor. If the state board of education or the state board for charter schools rejects the preliminary application, the state board of education or the state board for charter schools shall notify the applicant in writing of the reasons for the rejection and of suggestions for improving the application. An applicant may submit a revised application for reconsideration by the state board of education or the state board for charter schools. The applicant may request, and the state board of education or the state board for charter schools may provide, technical assistance to improve the application.

3. Each applicant seeking to establish a charter school shall submit a full set of fingerprints to the approving agency for the purpose of obtaining a state and federal criminal records check pursuant to § 41-1750 and Public Law 92-544. If an applicant will have direct contact with students, the applicant shall possess a valid fingerprint clearance card that is issued pursuant to title 41, chapter 12, article 3.1. [1] The department of public safety may exchange this fingerprint data with the federal bureau of investigation. The criminal records check shall be completed before the issuance of a charter.

4. All persons engaged in instructional work directly as a classroom, laboratory or other teacher or indirectly as a supervisory teacher, speech therapist or principal shall have a valid fingerprint clearance card that is issued pursuant to title 41, chapter 12, article 3.1. A charter school shall not employ a teacher whose certificate has been revoked for a violation of § 15-507 or 15-550 or for any offense that placed a pupil in danger. All other personnel shall be fingerprint checked pursuant to § 15-512. Before employment, the charter school shall make documented, good faith efforts to contact previous employers of a person to obtain information and recommendations that may be relevant to a person's fitness for employment as prescribed in § 15-512, subsection F. The charter school shall notify the department of public safety if the charter school or sponsor receives credible evidence that a person who possesses a valid fingerprint clearance card is arrested for or is charged with an offense listed in § 41-1758.03, subsection B.

5. If a charter school operator is not already subject to a public meeting or hearing by the municipality in which the charter school is located, the operator of a charter school shall conduct a public meeting at least thirty days before the charter school operator opens a site or sites for the charter school. The charter school operator shall post notices of the public meeting in at least three different locations that are within three hundred feet of the proposed charter school site.

D. A board that is authorized to sponsor charter schools pursuant to this article has no legal authority over or responsibility for a charter school sponsored by a different board. This subsection does not apply to the state board of education's duty to exercise general supervision over the public school system pursuant to § 15-203, subsection A, paragraph 1.

E. The charter of a charter school shall ensure the following:

1. Compliance with federal, state and local rules, regulations and statutes relating to health, safety, civil rights and insurance. The department of education shall publish a list of relevant rules, regulations and statutes to notify charter schools of their responsibilities under this paragraph.

2. That it is nonsectarian in its programs, admission policies and employment practices and all other operations.

3. That it provides a comprehensive program of instruction for at least a kindergarten program or any grade between grades one and twelve, except that a school may offer this curriculum with an emphasis on a specific learning philosophy or style or certain subject areas such as mathematics, science, fine arts, performance arts or foreign language.

4. That it designs a method to measure pupil progress, toward the pupil outcomes adopted by the state board of education pursuant to § 15–741.01 including participation in the Arizona instrument to measure standards test and the nationally standardized norm-referenced achievement test as designated by the state board and the completion and distribution of an annual report card as prescribed in chapter 7, article 3 of this title. [2]

5. That, except as provided in this article and in its charter, it is exempt from all statutes and rules relating to schools, governing boards and school districts.

6. That, except as provided in this article, it is subject to the same financial and electronic data submission requirements as a school district including the uniform system of financial records as prescribed in chapter 2, article 4 of this title, [3] procurement rules as prescribed in § 15–213 and audit requirements. The auditor general shall conduct a comprehensive review and revision of the uniform system of financial records to ensure that the provisions of the uniform system of financial records that relate to charter schools are in accordance with commonly accepted accounting principles used by private business. A school's charter may include exceptions to the requirements of this paragraph that are necessary as determined by the district governing board, the state board of education or the state board for charter schools. The department of education or the office of the auditor general may conduct financial, program or compliance audits.

7. Compliance with all federal and state laws relating to the education of children with disabilities in the same manner as a school district.

8. That it provides for a governing body for the charter school that is responsible for the policy decisions of the charter school.

9. That it provides a minimum of one hundred seventy-five instructional days before June 30 of each fiscal year unless it is operating on an alternative calendar approved by its sponsor. The superintendent of public instruction shall adjust the apportionment schedule accordingly to accommodate a charter school utilizing an alternative calendar.

F. The charter of a charter school shall include a description of the charter school's personnel policies, personnel qualifications and method of school governance and the specific role and duties of the sponsor of the charter school. A charter school shall keep on file the resumes of all current and former employees who provide instruction to pupils at the charter school. Resumes shall include an individual's educational and teaching background and experience in a particular academic content subject area. A charter school shall inform parents and guardians of the availability of the resume information and shall make the resume information available for inspection on request of parents and guardians of pupils enrolled at the charter school. Nothing in this subsection shall be construed to require any charter school to release personally identifiable information in relation to any teacher or employee including the teacher's or employee's address, salary, social security number or telephone number.

G. The charter of a charter school may be amended at the request of the governing body of the charter school and on the approval of the sponsor.

H. Charter schools may contract, sue and be sued.

I. An approved plan to establish a charter school is effective for fifteen years from the first day of operation. At the conclusion of the first fourteen years of operation, the charter school may apply for renewal. In addition to any other requirements, the application for renewal shall include a detailed business plan for the charter school. The sponsor may deny the request for renewal if, in its judgment, the charter school has failed to complete the obligations of the contract or has failed to comply with this article. A sponsor shall give written notice of its intent not to renew the charter school's request for renewal to the charter school at least twelve months before the expiration of the approved plan to allow the charter school an opportunity to apply to another sponsor to transfer the operation of the charter school. If the operation of the charter school is transferred to another sponsor, the fifteen year period of the current charter shall be maintained. A sponsor shall review a charter at five year intervals and may revoke a charter at any time if the charter school breaches one or more provisions of its charter. At least ninety days before the effective date of the proposed revocation the sponsor shall give written notice to the operator of the charter school of its intent to revoke the charter. Notice of the sponsor's intent to revoke the charter shall be delivered personally to the operator of the charter school or sent by certified mail, return receipt requested, to the address of the charter school. The notice shall incorporate a statement of reasons for the proposed revocation of the charter. The sponsor shall allow the charter school at least ninety days to correct the problems associated with the reasons for the proposed revocation of the charter. The final determination of whether to revoke the charter shall be made at a public hearing called for such purpose.

J. After renewal of the charter at the end of the fifteen year period described in subsection I of this section, the charter may be renewed for successive periods of fifteen years if the charter school and its sponsor deem that the school is in compliance with its own charter and the provisions of this article.

K. A charter school that is sponsored by the state board of education or the state board for charter schools may not be located on the property of a school district unless the district governing board grants this authority.

L. A governing board or a school district employee who has control over personnel actions shall not take unlawful reprisal against another employee of the school district because the employee is directly or indirectly involved in an application to establish a charter school. A governing board or a school district employee shall not take unlawful reprisal against an educational program of the school or the school district because an application to establish a charter school proposes the conversion of all or a portion of the educational program to a charter school. As used in this subsection, "unlawful reprisal" means an action that is taken by a governing board or a school district employee as a direct result of a lawful application to establish a charter school and that is adverse to another employee or an education program and:

1. With respect to a school district employee, results in one or more of the following:

(a) Disciplinary or corrective action.

(b) Detail, transfer or reassignment.

(c) Suspension, demotion or dismissal.

(d) An unfavorable performance evaluation.

(e) A reduction in pay, benefits or awards.

(f) Elimination of the employee's position without a reduction in force by reason of lack of monies or work.

(g) Other significant changes in duties or responsibilities that are inconsistent with the employee's salary or employment classification.

2. With respect to an educational program, results in one or more of the following:

(a) Suspension or termination of the program.

(b) Transfer or reassignment of the program to a less favorable department.

(c) Relocation of the program to a less favorable site within the school or school district.

(d) Significant reduction or termination of funding for the program.

M. Charter schools shall secure insurance for liability and property loss. The governing body of a charter school that is sponsored by the state board of education or the state board for charter schools may enter into an intergovernmental agreement or otherwise contract to participate in an insurance program offered by a risk retention pool established pursuant to § 11–952.01 or 41–621.01 or the charter school may secure its own insurance coverage. The pool may charge the requesting charter school reasonable fees for any services it performs in connection with the insurance program.

N. Charter schools do not have the authority to acquire property by eminent domain.

O. A sponsor, including members, officers and employees of the sponsor, is immune from personal liability for all acts done and actions taken in good faith within the scope of its authority.

P. Charter school sponsors and this state are not liable for the debts or financial obligations of a charter school or persons who operate charter schools.

Q. The sponsor of a charter school shall establish procedures to conduct administrative hearings upon determination by the sponsor that grounds exist to revoke a charter. Procedures for administrative hearings shall be similar to procedures prescribed for adjudicative proceedings in title 41, chapter 6, article 10.[4] Except as provided in § 41–1092.08, subsection H, final decisions of the state board of education and the state board for charter schools from hearings conducted pursuant to this subsection are subject to judicial review pursuant to title 12, chapter 7, article 6.[5]

R. The sponsoring entity of a charter school shall have oversight and administrative responsibility for the charter schools that it sponsors.

S. Charter schools may pledge, assign or encumber their assets to be used as collateral for loans or extensions of credit.

T. All property accumulated by a charter school shall remain the property of the charter school.

U. Charter schools may not locate a school on property that is less than one-fourth mile from agricultural land regulated pursuant to § 3–365, except that the owner of the agricultural land may agree to comply with the buffer zone requirements of § 3–365. If the owner agrees in writing to comply with the buffer zone requirements and records the agreement in the office of the county recorder as a restrictive covenant running with the title to the land, the charter school may locate a school within the affected buffer zone. The agreement may include any stipulations regarding the charter school, including conditions for future expansion of the school and changes in the operational status of the school that will result in a breach of the agreement.

V. A transfer of a charter to another sponsor, a transfer of a charter school site to another sponsor or a transfer of a charter school site to a different charter shall be completed before the beginning of the fiscal year that the transfer is scheduled to become effective. An entity that sponsors charter schools may accept a transferring school after the beginning of the fiscal year if the transfer is approved by the superintendent of public instruction. The superintendent of public instruction shall have the discretion to consider each transfer during the fiscal year on a case by case basis. If a charter school is sponsored by a school district that is determined to be out of compliance with this title, the uniform system of financial records or any other state or federal law, the charter school may transfer to another sponsoring entity at any time during the fiscal year.

Added by Laws 1994, 9th S.S., Ch. 2, § 2. Amended by Laws 1995, Ch. 273, § 1; Laws 1996, Ch. 284, § 6; Laws 1996, Ch. 356, § 2; Laws 1997, Ch. 221, § 63; Laws 1997, Ch. 231, § 3; Laws 1998, Ch. 71, § 1; Laws 1998, Ch. 183, § 1; Laws 2000, Ch. 90, § 2; Laws 2000, Ch. 113, § 38; Laws 2000, Ch. 342, § 1; Laws 2002, 5th S.S, Ch. 4, § 2, eff. Aug. 5, 2002; Laws 2003, Ch. 214, § 2, eff. Oct. 1, 2003.

[1] Section 41–1788 et seq.
[2] Section 15–741 et seq.
[3] Section 15–271 et seq.
[4] Section 41–1092 et seq.
[5] Section 12–901 et seq.

Retroactive Application

This section, as amended by Laws 2000, Ch. 90, applies retroactively to July 1, 2000.

Historical and Statutory Notes

Laws 1996, Ch. 356, § 5, provides:

"**Sec. 5. Duration of existing charters**

"Notwithstanding § 15-183, Arizona Revised Statutes, as amended by this act, the charter of a charter school that possesses a charter on the effective date of this act shall be extended for an additional fifteen years from the effective date of this act."

Laws 1999, 1st S.S., Ch. 4, § 15, provides:

"**Sec. 15. Charter school financial and compliance audits; financial statement audits; oversight responsibility**

"**A.** Notwithstanding § 15-271, subsection D, Arizona Revised Statutes, or any other law, the state board of education and the state board for charter schools, rather than the auditor general, are responsible for notifying a charter school under the board's jurisdiction if the school has failed to establish and maintain the uniform system of financial records.

"**B.** Notwithstanding § 15-271, subsection E, Arizona Revised Statutes, or any other law, the state board of education and the state board for charter schools, rather than the auditor general, are responsible for reporting to the department of education any charter school under the board's jurisdiction that either fails to establish and maintain the uniform system of financial records that is prescribed by the auditor general or fails to correct deficiencies in the system within ninety days after receiving notice of the deficiencies.

"**C.** Notwithstanding § 15-914, subsection D, Arizona Revised Statutes, or any other law, an independent certified public accountant who conducts an audit pursuant to § 15-914, subsections A, B and C, Arizona Revised Statutes, shall submit a uniform system of financial records compliance questionnaire to the state board that sponsors the audited charter school, rather than to the auditor general.

"**D.** Notwithstanding § 15-914, subsection E, Arizona Revised Statutes, or any other law, contracts for all financial and compliance audits and financial statement audits for charter schools that are sponsored by the state board of education or the state board for charter schools, and the completed audits for those schools, shall be approved by the state board that sponsors the charter school affected rather than by the auditor general.

"**E.** The requirements in subsections A and B of this section do not pertain to exceptions to requirements of the uniform system of financial records that the state board of education or the state board for charter schools include in the charter of a charter school pursuant to § 15-183, subsection E, paragraph 6, Arizona Revised Statutes."

Laws 2000, Ch. 90, §§ 6, 7 and 8, provide:

"**Sec. 6. Procedures for charter schools sponsored by school districts that are out of compliance before July 1, 2000**

"Notwithstanding § 15-183, Arizona Revised Statutes, as amended by this act, if a school district is determined to have been out of compliance with the uniform system of financial records in the fiscal year that ends on June 30, 2000, both of the following shall occur:

"1. The school district shall immediately notify each of the charter schools sponsored by the school district that the school district is out of compliance with the uniform system of financial records. The notification shall include a statement that if the school district is determined to be out of compliance for a second consecutive year, the charter school will be required to transfer sponsorship to another entity pursuant to section 15-183, subsection C, paragraph 1, subdivision (c), Arizona Revised Statutes.

"2. The fiscal year that begins on July 1, 2000 shall be considered the second year of potential noncompliance for purposes of § 15-183, subsection C, paragraph 1, subdivision (c), Arizona Revised Statutes. The department of education shall determine whether to require any charter schools that were sponsored by a school district that is determined to be out of compliance for a second consecutive year to file a sponsorship transfer application with the state board of education, the state board for charter schools or school district governing board if the charter school is located within the boundaries of that school district.

"**Sec. 7. Procedures for district sponsored charter schools located outside district boundaries before July 1, 2000**

"Except as provided in § 15-183, Arizona Revised Statutes, as amended by this act, the charter of a charter school that was sponsored by a school district before July 1, 2000 and that is located outside the boundaries of the school district remains valid.

"Sec. 8. **Retroactivity**

Section 15-183, Arizona Revised Statutes, as amended by this act, applies retroactively to from and after June 30, 2000."

"1. The school district shall immediately notify each of the charter schools sponsored by the school district that the school district is out of compliance with the uniform system of financial records. The notification shall include a statement that if the school district is determined to be out of compliance for a second consecutive year, the charter school will be required to transfer sponsorship to another entity pursuant to § 15-183, subsection C, paragraph 1, subdivision (c), Arizona Revised Statutes.

"2. The fiscal year that begins on July 1, 2000 shall be considered the second year of potential noncompliance for purposes of § 15-183, subsection C, paragraph 1, subdivision (c), Arizona Revised Statutes. The department of education shall determine whether to require any charter schools that were sponsored by a school district that is determined to be out of compliance for a second consecutive year to file a sponsorship transfer application with the state board of education, the state board for charter schools or school district governing board if the charter school is located within the boundaries of that school district.

Laws 2002, 5th S.S., Ch. 4, § 5, provides:

"**Sec. 5. Applicability**

"Notwithstanding § 15-183, subsection C, paragraph 4, Arizona Revised Statutes, as amended by this act, a charter school may employ a person who does not have a valid class one or class two fingerprint clearance card to engage in instructional work directly as a classroom, laboratory or other teacher or indirectly as a supervisory teacher, speech therapist or principal if:

"1. The person is employed by the charter school on the effective date of this act, the person applies for a class one or class two fingerprint clearance card on or before October 1, 2002 and the person's application has not been denied.

"2. The person begins employment with the charter school after October 1, 2002 and before May 1, 2003, the person applies for a class one or class two fingerprint clearance card on or before the seventh day following the date the person was hired and the person's application has not been denied.

"3. The person is employed by the charter school, has timely applied for a class one or class two fingerprint clearance card as provided in this section, and is awaiting the outcome of a good cause exception determination pursuant to § 41-619.55, Arizona Revised Statutes."

Laws 2002, 5th S.S., Ch. 4, § 7, provides:

"**Sec. 7. Department of public safety; report of information to department of education**

"The department of public safety shall report to the department of education information about class one and class two fingerprint clearance cards that are required to be obtained by charter school teachers under § 15-183, Arizona Revised Statutes."

Laws 2003, Ch. 264, § 20, provides:

"**Sec. 20. State board of education; charter school sponsorship**

"Notwithstanding title 15, chapter 1, article 8, Arizona Revised Statutes, the state board of education shall not sponsor any additional charter schools for fiscal year 2003-2004 and the state board of education and the state board for charter schools shall enter into an intergovernmental agreement for fiscal year 2003-2004 that requires the state board for charter schools to provide the same type of oversight that year for charter schools that are sponsored by the state board of education as the state board for charter schools provides for charter schools sponsored by the state board for charter schools."

Reviser's Notes:

1996 Note. Prior to the 1997 amendments, this section contained the amendments made by Laws 1996, Ch. 284, sec. 6 and Ch. 356, sec. 2 that were blended together pursuant to authority of § 41-1304.03. Pursuant to authority of § 41-1304.02, in subsection I, seventh sentence the words "At least ninety days before the effective date of the proposed revocation" were transposed to the beginning of the sentence.

1997 Note. Prior to the 1998 amendments, this section contained the amendments made by Laws 1997, Ch. 221, § 63 and Ch. 231, § 3 that were blended together pursuant to authority of § 41-1304.03.

1998 Note. Prior to the 2000 amendments, this section contained the amendments made by Laws 1998, Ch. 71, sec. 1 and Ch. 183, sec. 1 that were blended together pursuant to authority of § 41-1304.03. Pursuant to authority of § 41-1304.02, in subsection V, last sentence the spelling of "breach" was corrected.

2000 Note. Prior to the 2002 amendment, this section contained the amendments made by Laws 2000, Ch. 90, sec. 2, Ch. 113, sec. 38 and Ch. 342, sec. 1 that were blended together pursuant to authority of § 41-1304.03.

§ 15-184. Charter schools; admission requirements

A. A charter school shall enroll all eligible pupils who submit a timely application, unless the number of applications exceeds the capacity of a program, class, grade level or building. A charter school shall give enrollment preference to pupils returning to the charter school in the second or any subsequent year of its operation and to siblings of pupils already enrolled in the charter school. A charter school that is sponsored by a school district governing board shall give enrollment preference to eligible pupils who reside within the boundaries of the school district where the charter school is physically located. If capacity is insufficient to enroll all pupils who submit a timely application, the charter school shall select pupils through an equitable selection process such as a lottery except that preference shall be given to siblings of a pupil selected through an equitable selection process such as a lottery.

B. Except as provided in subsection C, a charter school shall not limit admission based on ethnicity, national origin, gender, income level, disabling condition, proficiency in the English language or athletic ability.

C. A charter school may limit admission to pupils within a given age group or grade level.

D. A charter school shall admit pupils who reside in the attendance area of a school or who reside in a school district that is under a court order of desegregation or that is a party to an agreement with the United States department of education office for civil rights directed toward remediating alleged or proven racial discrimination unless notice is received from the resident school that the admission would violate the court order or agreement. If a charter school admits a pupil after notice is received that the admission would constitute such a violation, the charter school is not allowed to include in its student count the pupils wrongfully admitted.

E. A charter school may refuse to admit any pupil who has been expelled from another educational institution or who is in the process of being expelled from another educational institution.

Added by Laws 1994, 9th S.S., Ch. 2, § 2. Amended by Laws 1996, Ch. 284, § 7; Laws 1999, Ch. 114, § 1.

§ 15-185. Charter schools; financing; definitions

A. Financial provisions for a charter school that is sponsored by a school district governing board are as follows:

1. The charter school shall be included in the district's budget and financial assistance calculations pursuant to paragraph 3 of this subsection and chapter 9 of this title, [1] except for chapter 9, article 4 of this title. The charter of the charter school shall include a description of the methods of funding the charter school by the school district. The school district shall send a copy of the charter and application, including a description of how the school district plans to fund the school, to the state board of education before the start of the first fiscal year of operation of the charter school. The charter or application shall include an estimate of the student count for the charter school for its first fiscal year of operation. This estimate shall be computed pursuant to the requirements of paragraph 3 of this subsection.

2. A school district is not financially responsible for any charter school that is sponsored by the state board of education or the state board for charter schools.

3. A school district that sponsors a charter school may:

(a) Increase its student count as provided in subsection B, paragraph 2 of this section during the first year of the charter school's operation to include those charter school pupils who were not previously enrolled in the school district. A charter school sponsored by a school district governing board is eligible for the assistance prescribed in subsection B, paragraph 4 of this section. The soft capital allocation as provided in § 15-962 for the school district sponsoring the charter school shall be increased by the amount of the additional assistance. The school district shall include the full amount of the additional assistance in the funding provided to the charter school.

(b) Compute separate weighted student counts pursuant to § 15-943, paragraph 2, subdivision (a) for its noncharter school versus charter school pupils in order to maintain eligibility for small school district support level weights authorized in § 15-943, paragraph 1 for its noncharter school pupils only. The portion of a district's student count that is attributable to charter school pupils is not eligible for small school district support level weights.

4. If a school district uses the provisions of paragraph 3 of this subsection, the school district is not eligible to include those pupils in its student count for the purposes of computing an increase in its revenue control limit and district support level as provided in § 15-948.

5. A school district that sponsors a charter school is not eligible to include the charter school pupils in its student count for the purpose of computing an increase in its capital outlay revenue limit as provided in § 15-961, subsection C, except that if the charter school was previously a school in the district, the district may include in its student count any charter school pupils who were enrolled in the school district in the prior year.

6. A school district that sponsors a charter school is not eligible to include the charter school pupils in its student count for the purpose of computing the revenue control limit which is used to determine the maximum budget increase as provided in chapter 4, article 4 of this title [2] unless the charter school is located within the boundaries of the school district.

7. If a school district converts one or more of its district public schools to a charter school and receives assistance as prescribed in subsection B, paragraph 4 of this section, and subsequently converts the charter school back to a district public school, the school district shall repay the state the total additional assistance received for the charter school for all years that the charter school was in operation. The repayment shall be in one lump sum and shall be reduced from the school district's current year equalization assistance. The school district's general budget limit shall be reduced by the same lump sum amount in the current year.

B. Financial provisions for a charter school that is sponsored by the state board of education or the state board for charter schools are as follows:

1. The charter school shall calculate a base support level as prescribed in § 15-943, except that §§ 15-941 and 15-942 do not apply to these charter schools.

2. Notwithstanding paragraph 1 of this subsection, the student count shall be determined initially using an estimated student count based on actual registration of pupils before the beginning of the school year. After the first one hundred days or two hundred days in session, as applicable, the charter school shall revise the student count to be equal to the actual average daily membership, as defined in § 15–901, or the adjusted average daily membership, as prescribed in § 15–902, of the charter school. Before the one hundredth day or two hundredth day in session, as applicable, the state board of education or the state board for charter schools may require a charter school to report periodically regarding pupil enrollment and attendance and the department of education may revise its computation of equalization assistance based on the report. A charter school shall revise its student count, base support level and additional assistance before May 15. A charter school that overestimated its student count shall revise its budget before May 15. A charter school that underestimated its student count may revise its budget before May 15.

3. A charter school may utilize § 15–855 for the purposes of this section. The charter school and the department of education shall prescribe procedures for determining average daily attendance and average daily membership.

4. Equalization assistance for the charter school shall be determined by adding the amount of the base support level and additional assistance. The amount of the additional assistance is one thousand three hundred three dollars ninety-seven cents per student count in kindergarten programs and grades one through eight and one thousand five hundred nineteen dollars seventy-five cents per student count in grades nine through twelve.

5. The state board of education shall apportion state aid from the appropriations made for such purposes to the state treasurer for disbursement to the charter schools in each county in an amount as determined by this paragraph. The apportionments shall be made in twelve equal installments of the total amount to be apportioned during the fiscal year on the fifteenth day of each month of the fiscal year.

6. Notwithstanding paragraph 5 of this subsection, if sufficient appropriated monies are available after the first forty days in session of the current year, a charter school may request additional state monies to fund the increased state aid due to anticipated student growth through the first one hundred days or two hundred days in session, as applicable, of the current year as provided in § 15–948. In no event shall a charter school have received more than three-fourths of its total apportionment before April 15 of the fiscal year. Early payments pursuant to this subsection must be approved by the state treasurer, the director of the department of administration and the superintendent of public instruction.

7. The charter school shall not charge tuition, levy taxes or issue bonds.

8. Not later than noon on the day preceding each apportionment date established by paragraph 5 of this subsection, the superintendent of public instruction shall furnish to the state treasurer an abstract of the apportionment and shall certify the apportionment to the department of administration, which shall draw its warrant in favor of the charter schools for the amount apportioned.

C. If a pupil is enrolled in both a charter school and a public school that is not a charter school, the sum of the daily membership, which includes enrollment as prescribed in § 15–901, subsection A, paragraph 2, subdivisions (a) and (b) and daily attendance as prescribed in § 15–901, subsection A, paragraph 6, for that pupil in the school district and the charter school shall not exceed 1.0. If a pupil is enrolled in both a charter school and a public school that is not a charter school, the department of education shall direct the average daily membership to the school with the most recent enrollment date. Upon validation of actual enrollment in both a charter school and a public school that is not a charter school and if the sum of the daily membership or daily attendance for that pupil is greater than 1.0, the sum shall be reduced to 1.0 and shall be apportioned between the public school and the charter school based on the percentage of total time that the pupil is enrolled or in attendance in the public school and the charter school. The uniform system of financial records shall include guidelines for the apportionment of the pupil enrollment and attendance as provided in this section.

D. Charter schools are allowed to accept grants and gifts to supplement their state funding, but it is not the intent of the charter school law to require taxpayers to pay twice to educate the same pupils. The base support level for a charter school or for a school district sponsoring a charter school shall be reduced by an amount equal to the total amount of monies received by a charter school from a federal or state agency if the federal or state monies are intended for the basic maintenance and operations of the school. The superintendent of public instruction shall estimate the amount of the reduction for the budget year and shall revise the reduction to reflect the actual amount before May 15 of the current year. If the reduction results in a negative amount, the negative amount shall be used in computing all budget limits and equalization assistance, except that:

1. Equalization assistance shall not be less than zero.

2. For a charter school sponsored by the state board of education or the state board for charter schools, the total of the base support level, the capital outlay revenue limit, the soft capital allocation and the additional assistance shall not be less than zero.

3. For a charter school sponsored by a school district, the base support level for the school district shall not be reduced by more than the amount that the charter school increased the district's base support level, capital outlay revenue limit and soft capital allocation.

E. If a charter school was a district public school in the prior year and is now being operated for or by the same school district and sponsored by the state board of education, the state board for charter schools or a school district governing board, the reduction in subsection D of this section applies. The reduction to the base support level of the charter school or the sponsoring district of the charter school shall equal the sum of the base support level and the additional assistance received in the current year for those pupils who were enrolled in the traditional public school in the prior year and are now enrolled in the charter school in the current year.

F. Equalization assistance for charter schools shall be provided as a single amount based on average daily membership without categorical distinctions between maintenance and operations or capital.

G. At the request of a charter school, the county school superintendent of the county where the charter school is located may provide the same educational services to the charter school as prescribed in § 15–308, subsection A. The county school superintendent may charge a fee to recover costs for providing educational services to charter schools.

H. If the sponsor of the charter school determines at a public meeting that the charter school is not in compliance with federal law, with the laws of this state or with its charter, the sponsor of a charter school may submit a request to the department of education to withhold up to ten per cent of the monthly apportionment of state aid that would otherwise be due the charter school. The department of education shall adjust the charter school's apportionment accordingly. The sponsor shall provide written notice to the charter school at least seventy-two hours before the meeting and shall allow the charter school to respond to the allegations of noncompliance at the meeting before the sponsor makes a final determination to notify the department of education of noncompliance. The charter school shall submit a corrective action plan to the sponsor on a date specified by the sponsor at the meeting. The corrective action plan shall be designed to correct deficiencies at the charter school and to ensure that the charter school promptly returns to compliance. When the sponsor determines that the charter school is in compliance, the department of education shall restore the full amount of state aid payments to the charter school.

I. A charter school may receive and spend monies distributed by the department of education pursuant to § 42–5029, subsection E and § 37–521, subsection B.

J. For the purposes of this section:

1. "Monies intended for the basic maintenance and operations of the school" means monies intended to provide support for the educational program of the school, except that it does not include supplemental assistance for a specific purpose or P.L. 81–874 monies. The auditor general shall determine which federal or state monies meet the definition in this paragraph.

2. "Operated for or by the same school district" means the charter school is either governed by the same district governing board or operated by the district in the same manner as other traditional schools in the district or is operated by an independent party that has a contract with the school district. The auditor general and the department of education shall determine which charter schools meet the definition in this subsection.

Added by Laws 1994, 9th S.S., Ch. 2, § 2. Amended by Laws 1995, Ch. 273, § 2; Laws 1996, Ch. 284, § 8; Laws 1997, 1st S.S., Ch. 4, § 1; Laws 1997, Ch. 231, § 4; Laws 1998, Ch. 167, § 1; Laws 1998, Ch. 168, § 1; Laws 1998, 5th S.S., Ch. 1, § 6, eff. July 9, 1998; Laws 1999, Ch. 96, § 3; Laws 1999, Ch. 299, § 3; Laws 1999, 1st S.S., Ch. 4, § 2; Laws 2000, Ch. 90, § 3; Laws 2000, 5th S.S., Ch. 1, § 2; Laws 2003, Ch. 166, § 1; Laws 2003, Ch. 264, § 2; Laws 2004, Ch. 120, § 1; Laws 2004, Ch. 278, § 1.

[1] Section 15–901 et seq.

[2] Section 15–481 et seq.

Historical and Statutory Notes

Laws 1996, 5th S.S., Ch. 4, § 2, provides:

"**Sec. 2. Charter schools; transportation state aid; 1996-1997 fiscal year**

"Notwithstanding §§ 15-185, 15-186 and 15-816.01, Arizona Revised Statutes, the transportation support level for the 1996-1997 fiscal year for each charter school that is sponsored by the state board of education or the state board for charter schools shall be $174 multiplied by the school's student count."

Laws 1996, Ch. 284, §§ 82 and 83, provide:

"**Sec. 82. Charter school finance provisions**

"Notwithstanding § 15-185, subsection D, Arizona Revised Statutes, as amended by this act, for fiscal year 1996-1997 and fiscal year 1997-1998 for a charter school that was granted a charter prior to July 1, 1996 and receives federal monies from a federal agency for the basic maintenance and operations of the school, the amount of the reduction prescribed by § 15-185, subsection D, Arizona Revised Statutes, shall be zero.

"**Sec. 83. Termination of charters**

"If a charter school is affected by the provisions of § 15-185, subsection D, Arizona Revised Statutes, as amended by this act, the charter may be terminated after June 30, 1996, at the request of either the charter school or the sponsor."

Laws 1997, Ch. 231, §§ 34 and 39, provide:

"**Sec. 34. Charter school sponsors; budget capacity reduction; exemption**

"Notwithstanding Laws 1997, first special session, chapter 4, § 16, a school district that sponsored a charter school in fiscal year 1995-1996 but that no longer sponsors that charter school in fiscal year 1996-1997 may expend any portion of its cash balance reserves in fiscal year 1996-1997 up to the amount of the school district's budget capacity in fiscal year 1996-1997 prior to enactment of Laws 1997, first special session, chapter 4, § 16."

"**Sec. 39. State sponsored charter school apportionment schedule; exception**

"Notwithstanding § 15-185, subsection B, paragraph 6, Arizona Revised Statutes, as amended by this act, for fiscal year 1997-1998 all charter schools sponsored by either the state board of education or the state board for charter schools shall use the apportionment method established in § 15-185, subsection B, paragraph 6, subdivision (a), as amended by this act."

Laws 1997, 1st S.S., Ch. 4, §§ 14 to 16 and 18, provide:

"**Sec. 14. Charter schools; transportation state aid; 1997-1998 fiscal year**

"Notwithstanding § 15-185, as amended by this act, and §§ 15-186 and 15-816.01, Arizona Revised Statutes, the transportation support level for the 1997-1998 fiscal year for each charter school that is sponsored by the state board of education or the state board for charter schools is one hundred seventy-four dollars multiplied by the school's student count.

"**Sec. 15. Charter schools; federal receipts zero reductions**

"**A.** Notwithstanding § 15-185, subsection D, Arizona Revised Statutes, as amended by this act, or any other provision of law, for fiscal year 1996-1997 and fiscal year 1997-1998 for a charter school that was granted a charter and that was in operation before July 1, 1996 and that receives federal monies from a federal agency for the basic maintenance and operations of the school, the amount of the reduction prescribed by § 15-185, subsection D, Arizona Revised Statutes, as amended by this act, is zero.

"**B.** Notwithstanding § 15-185, subsection D, Arizona Revised Statutes, as amended by this act, or any other provision of law, for fiscal year 1996-1997 for a charter school that was granted a charter prior to July 1, 1996 but that was not in operation before July 1, 1996 and that receives federal monies from a federal agency for the basic maintenance and operations of the school, the amount of the reduction prescribed by § 15-185, subsection D, Arizona Revised Statutes, is zero.

"**C.** Notwithstanding Laws 1996, chapter 284, § 82, the provisions of § 15-185, subsection D, Arizona Revised Statutes, as amended by this act, shall apply, starting in fiscal year 1997-1998, to a charter school that was granted a charter prior to July 1, 1996 but that was not in operation prior to July 1, 1996 and receives federal monies from a federal agency for the basic maintenance and operations of the school.

"**Sec. 16. District sponsored charter schools; student counts**

"**A.** Notwithstanding § 15-902 and § 15-185, subsection A, Arizona Revised Statutes, as amended by this act, or any other law, changes in a school district's student count that are attributable to a district sponsored charter school switching sponsors or ceasing to operate do not entitle a school district to make an adjustment for rapid decline in student count pursuant to § 15-942, Arizona Revised Statutes.

"**B.** Notwithstanding § 15-902 and § 15-185, subsection A, Arizona Revised Statutes, as amended by this act, or any other law, any school district that sponsored a charter school in fiscal year 1995-1996 but that no longer sponsors that charter school in fiscal year 1996-1997 shall subtract from its average daily membership for fiscal year 1995-1996 that portion of the average daily membership that was attributable to the charter school that it sponsored in fiscal year 1995-1996. This adjustment shall result in such a school district receiving the amount of basic state aid funding for fiscal year 1996-1997 that it would have been entitled to if it had not sponsored in fiscal year 1995-1996 the charter school that it no longer sponsors in fiscal year 1996-1997. This provision of law is effective for fiscal year 1996-1997. Any school district affected by this provision for fiscal year 1996-1997 shall adjust its fiscal year 1996-1997 budget before May 15, 1997 in order to reflect the requirements of this law."

"**Sec. 18. Retroactivity**

"Section 16 of this act is effective retroactively to from and after March 31, 1997."

The purported amendment of this section by Laws 1998, Ch. 164 failed to become effective because Chapter 164 was repealed in its entirety by Laws 1998, 5th S.S., Ch. 1, § 2, effective July 1, 1998.

The purported amendment of this section by Laws 1998, 3rd S.S., Ch. 1, failed to became effective because Ch. 1 was repealed in its entirety by Laws 1998, 5th S.S., Ch. 1, § 2, effective July 1, 1998.

Laws 1998, 4th S.S., Ch. 8, § 12, provides:

"**Sec. 12. Charter schools; transportation state aid; 1998-1999 fiscal year**

"Notwithstanding §§ 15-185 and 15-816.01, Arizona Revised Statutes, the transportation support level for the 1998-1999 fiscal year for each charter school that is sponsored by the state board of education or the state board for charter schools is one hundred seventy-four dollars multiplied by the school's student count."

Laws 1998, 5th S.S., Ch. 1, § 2, provides:

"**Sec. 2. Repeal**

"Laws 1998, third special session, chapter 1, Laws 1998, chapter 164, Laws 1998, chapter 219 and Laws 1998, chapter 286, § 1 are repealed."

Laws 1999, Ch. 96, § 7, provides:

"**Sec. 7. Retroactivity**

"This act applies retroactively to from and after June 30, 1999."

Laws 2000, 5th S.S. Ch. 1, § 65, provides:

"**Sec. 65. Conforming legislation; blending**

"**A.** The legislative council staff shall prepare proposed legislation conforming the Arizona Revised Statutes to the provisions of this act for consideration in the forty-fifth legislature, first regular session.

"**B.** The executive director of the legislative council is authorized to blend the nonconflicting changes made to the Arizona Revised Statutes during the forty-fourth legislature, second regular session, with the changes made to those same statutes by this act."

Laws 2004, Ch. 278, § 15, provides:

"**Sec. 15. Fund transfer; allocation**

"The sum of $600,000 is transferred from the certificates of participation fund to the department of education for allocation in fiscal year 2004-2005 to a school district that included at least one hundred fifty pupils from unorganized territories in its average daily membership count for fiscal year 2002-2003. A school district that receives funding pursuant to this section may use the funding only to purchase pupil transportation vehicles and may increase its capital outlay revenue limit for fiscal year 2004-2005 by the amount of funding received pursuant to this section."

Laws 2004, Ch. 278, § 21, provides:

"**Sec. 21. Retroactivity**

"**A.** Except as provided in subsection B of this section, this act applies retroactively to from and after June 30, 2004.

"**B.** Laws 2002, chapter 330, § 49, as amended by this act, applies retroactively to from and after June 29, 2004."

Reviser's Notes:

1996 Note. In the chapter version in subsection B, paragraph 10 "The" is shown as existing, or downstyle, language, but it is new language. Pursuant to authority of § 41-1304.02, to correct a manifest clerical error, in the chapter version "The" is shown as new, or upstyle, language.

1997 Note. Prior to the 1998 amendments, this section contained the amendments made by Laws 1997, First Special Session, Ch. 4, sec. 1 and Laws 1997, First Regular Session, Ch. 231, sec. 4 that were blended together pursuant to authority of § 41-1304.03.

1998 Note. Prior to the 1999 amendments, this section contained the amendments made by Laws 1998, Second Regular Session, Ch. 167, sec. 1 and Ch. 168, sec. 1 and Laws 1998, Fifth Special Session, Ch. 1. sec. 6 that were blended together pursuant to authority of § 41-1304.03.

1999 Note. Prior to the 2000 blend, this section contained the amendments made by Laws 1999, First Regular Session, Ch. 96, sec. 3 and Ch. 299, sec. 3 and First Special Session, Ch. 4, sec. 2 that were blended together pursuant to authority of § 41-1304.03. Pursuant to authority of § 41-1304.02, in subsection B the paragraph designation "4." was substituted for "4," to correct a manifest clerical error.

2000 Note. Prior to the 2003 amendments, this section contained the amendments made by Laws 2000, Ch. 90, sec. 3 and 5th S.S., Ch. 1, sec. 2 that were blended together pursuant to authority of § 41-1304.03.

2003 Note. Prior to the 2004 amendment, this section contained the amendments made by Laws 2003, Ch. 166, sec. 1 and Ch. 264, sec. 2 that were blended together pursuant to authority of § 41-1304.03.

2004 Note. This section contains the amendments made by Laws 2004, Ch. 120, sec. 1 and Ch. 278, sec. 1 that were blended together as shown pursuant to authority of § 41-1304.03.

§ 15-185.01. Repealed by Laws 1998, 5th S.S., Ch. 1, § 7, eff. July 1, 1999

Historical and Statutory Notes

The repealed section, added by Laws 1997, 1st S.S., Ch. 4, § 2, provided additional capital assistance for charter schools.

A purported repeal of this section by Laws 1998, 3rd S.S., Ch. 1, failed to became effective because Ch. 1 was repealed in its entirety by Laws 1998, 5th S.S., Ch. 1, § 2, effective July 1, 1998.

§ 15-186. Repealed by Laws 1998, 4th S.S., Ch. 8, § 1

Historical and Statutory Notes

The repealed section, added by Laws 1994, 9th S.S., Ch. 2, § 2, amended by Laws 1995, Ch. 1, § 1, related to charter school transportation provisions.

Laws 1996, Ch. 356, § 6, provides:

"**Sec. 6. Charter school transportation; fiscal year 1995-1996**

"**A.** Notwithstanding § 15-186, Arizona Revised Statutes, as amended by Laws 1995, chapter 1, § 1, and § 15-945, Arizona Revised Statutes, as amended by Laws 1995, chapter 191, § 14, for fiscal year 1995-1996, the transportation support level for a charter school that is sponsored by the state board of education or the state board for charter schools shall be calculated as if 'eligible students' had been defined as in subsection B of this section and by dividing third party passenger vehicle miles traveled after December 22, 1995 by seven.

"**B.** In this section, 'eligible students' means:

"1. For students with disabilities whose individualized education plan specifies that transportation is necessary for fulfillment of the plan and students who meet the economic eligibility requirements established under the national school lunch and child nutrition acts (42 United States Code §§ 1751 through 1785) for free or reduced price lunches, those whose place of actual residence is more than one mile from the school facility of attendance if attending common school or whose place of actual residence is more than one and one-half miles from the school facility of attendance if attending high school. Transportation for these students is limited to no more than twenty miles each way to and from the school of attendance.

"2. For other students, those whose place of actual residence is more than one mile from the school facility of attendance if attending common school or whose place of actual residence is more than one and one-half miles from the school facility of attendance if attending high school."

Laws 1996, 5th S.S., Ch. 4, § 2, provides:

"**Sec. 2. Charter schools; transportation state aid; 1996-1997 fiscal year**

"Notwithstanding §§ 15-185, 15-186 and 15-816.01, Arizona Revised Statutes, the transportation support level for the 1996-1997 fiscal year for each charter school that is sponsored by the state board of education or the state board for charter schools shall be $174 multiplied by the school's student count."

§ 15-187. Charter schools; teachers; employment benefits

A. A teacher who is employed by or teaching at a charter school and who was previously employed as a teacher at a school district shall not lose any right of certification, retirement or salary status or any other benefit provided by law, by the rules of the governing board of the school district or by the rules of the board of directors of the charter school due to teaching at a charter school on the teacher's return to the school district.

B. A teacher who is employed by or teaching at a charter school and who submits an employment application to the school district where the teacher was employed immediately before employment by or at a charter school shall be given employment preference by the school district if both of the following conditions are met:

1. The teacher submits an employment application to the school district no later than three years after ceasing employment with the school district.

2. A suitable position is available at the school district.

C. A charter school that is sponsored by a school district governing board, the state board of education or the state board for charter schools is eligible to participate in the Arizona state retirement system pursuant to title 38, chapter 5, article 2.[1] The charter school is a political subdivision of this state for purposes of title 38, chapter 5, article 2.

Added by Laws 1994, 9th S.S., Ch. 2, § 2. Amended by Laws 1995, Ch. 273, § 3.

[1] Section 38–711 et seq.

Historical and Statutory Notes

The 1995 amendment by Ch. 273 added subsec. C.

§ 15–187.01. Optional inclusion of charter school employees in state health and accident coverage; payment of premiums; advance notice; minimum period of participation; definition

A. If a governing body of a charter school determines that state health and accident insurance coverage is necessary or desirable and in the best interest of the charter school, it may provide for inclusion of the charter school's employees and spouses and dependents of the charter school's employees in state health and accident insurance coverage pursuant to § 38–651.

B. If the charter school elects to participate in the state health and accident insurance coverage, it shall be the only health and accident insurance coverage offered to charter school employees.

C. A charter school governing body that elects to include its employees in the state health and accident insurance coverage shall notify the department of administration of its intention to do so by January 15 of the calendar year prior to the school year starting after June 30 in which the charter school's employees would be eligible to receive state health and accident insurance coverage.

D. A charter school governing body that elects to include its employees in the state health and accident insurance coverage shall participate in state health and accident insurance coverage for at least two years.

E. Charter schools that opt to participate in the state health and accident insurance coverage shall agree to accept the benefit level, plan design, insurance providers, premium level and other terms and conditions determined by the department of administration and shall accept such other contractual arrangements made by the department of administration with health and accident insurance providers.

F. Charter schools shall reimburse the department of administration for administrative and operational costs associated with charter schools participating in the state health and accident insurance coverage determined pursuant to § 38–651, subsection K.

G. As used in this section, "state health and accident insurance coverage" means the health and accident coverage procured by the department of administration under § 38–651.
Added by Laws 1998, Ch. 212, § 1.

§ 15–188. Charter schools stimulus fund

A. The charter schools stimulus fund is established for the purpose of providing financial support to charter school applicants and charter schools for start-up costs and costs associated with renovating or remodeling existing buildings and structures. The fund consists of monies appropriated by the legislature and grants, gifts, devises and donations from any public or private source. The department of education shall administer the fund.

B. The state board of education shall adopt rules to implement the provisions of this section, including application and notification requirements. If sufficient monies are appropriated for this purpose, monies from the charter schools stimulus fund shall be distributed to qualifying charter school applicants and charter schools in the following manner:

1. Each qualifying charter school applicant or charter school shall be awarded an initial grant of up to one hundred thousand dollars during or before the first year of the charter school's operation. If an applicant for a charter school receives an initial grant pursuant to this paragraph and fails to begin operating a charter school within the next eighteen months, the applicant shall reimburse the department of education for the amount of the initial grant plus interest calculated at a rate of ten per cent a year.

2. Applicants for charter schools and charter schools that received initial grants pursuant to paragraph 1 may apply to the department of education for an additional grant of up to one hundred thousand dollars. If an applicant for a charter school receives an additional grant pursuant to this paragraph and fails to begin operating a charter school within the next eighteen months, the applicant shall reimburse the department of education for the amount of the additional grant plus interest calculated at a rate of ten per cent a year. A reimbursement required by this paragraph is in addition to any reimbursement required by paragraph 1.

C. Monies in the charter schools stimulus fund are exempt from the provisions of § 35–190 relating to lapsing of appropriations.
Added by Laws 1994, 9th S.S., Ch. 2, § 2. Amended by Laws 2000, Ch. 193, § 105.

§ 15–189. Charter schools; vacant buildings; list

The department of education, in conjunction with the department of administration, shall annually publish a list of vacant and unused buildings and vacant and unused portions of buildings that are owned by this state or by school districts in this state and that may be suitable for the operation of a charter school. The department of education shall make the list available to applicants for charter schools and to existing charter schools. The list shall include the address of each building, a short description of the building and the name of the owner of the building. Nothing in this section requires the owner of a building on the list to sell or lease the building or a portion of the building to a

charter school or to any other school or to any other prospective buyer or tenant.
Added by Laws 1994, 9th S.S., Ch. 2, § 2.

§ 15-189.01. Charter schools; zoning; development fees

A. Charter schools shall be classified as public schools for the purposes of the assessment of zoning fees, site plan fees and development fees. Municipalities and counties shall adopt procedures to ensure that hearings and administrative reviews involving charter schools are scheduled and conducted on an expedited basis and that charter schools receive a final determination from the municipality or county within thirty days of the beginning of processes requiring only an administrative review and within ninety days of the beginning of processes requiring a public hearing and allowing an appeal to a board of adjustment, city or town council or board of supervisors.

B. No political subdivision of this state may enact or interpret any law, rule or ordinance in a manner that conflicts with subsection A.
Added by Laws 1996, Ch. 356, § 3.

§ 15-189.02. Charter schools; public bidding requirements

A. A charter school's procurement is exempt from public bidding requirements if the aggregate dollar amount of the procurement does not exceed the maximum amount of the exemption authorized by title 41, chapter 23 [1] or pursuant to rules adopted by the director of the department of administration.

B. Notwithstanding subsection A, the state board for charter schools may authorize an exemption from public bidding requirements that exceeds the maximum exemption prescribed in subsection A of this section for any charter school sponsored by the state board for charter schools.
Added by Laws 1996, Ch. 356, § 3.

[1] Section 41-2501 et seq.

§ 15-189.03. Academic credits; transfer

If a pupil who was previously enrolled in a charter school enrolls in a public school in this state, the public school shall accept credits earned by the pupil in courses or instructional programs at the charter school in a uniform and consistent manner and according to the same criteria that are used to accept academic credits from other public schools.
Added by Laws 1999, Ch. 9, § 1.

ARTICLE 9. FAMILY LITERACY PROGRAM

Article 9, Family Literacy Pilot Program, consisting of §§ 15-191 and 15-191.01, was added by Laws 1994, 9th S.S., Ch. 1, § 7, effective September 16, 1994, as Article 8, §§ 15-181, 15-182, and was renumbered by the reviser.

The heading of Article 9 was changed from "Family Literacy Pilot Program" to "Family Literacy Program" by Laws 1998, Ch. 295, § 5, eff. June 1, 1998.

Historical and Statutory Notes

Laws 1999, Ch. 211, § 1, par. 7, provides:

"**Section 1. Purpose**"

"7. Laws 1998, chapter 295, § 5 amended the article heading of title 15, chapter 1, article 9, Arizona Revised Statutes, but incorrectly identified the article as article 8. This act amends Laws 1998, chapter 295, § 5 to correct the article number."

Reviser's Notes:

1994 Note. The above article and the sections that comprise it were added by Laws 1994, Ninth Special Session, Ch. 1, sec. 7 as title 15, chapter 1, article 8 and §§ 15–181 and 15–182 and were renumbered as article 9 and §§ 15–191 and 15–191.01, respectively, pursuant to authority of § 41–1304.02.

§ 15–191. Definitions

In this article, unless the context otherwise requires:

1. "Eligible parent" means a parent who meets the following requirements:

(a) Has a three year old or four year old child.

(b) Lacks sufficient mastery of basic educational or basic English language skills needed to function effectively in society or lacks a high school diploma or its equivalent.

(c) Is a citizen or a legal resident of the United States or is otherwise lawfully present in the United States.

2. "Family literacy program" means a program that is established pursuant to this article and that is designed to promote the acquisition of learning and reading skills by parents and their preschool children in a shared instructional setting.

Added as § 15–181 by Laws 1994, 9th S.S., Ch. 1, § 7. Renumbered as § 15–191. Amended by Laws 1998, Ch. 295, § 6, eff. June 1, 1998.

Historical and Statutory Notes

Laws 1994, 9th S.S., Ch. 1, §§ 1 and 9, provide:

"**Section 1. Intent**

"**A.** The intent of this act is to establish the healthy families pilot program, the family literacy pilot program and the health start pilot program to create a coordinated effort between state agencies and private organizations to encourage increased prenatal care, reduce and eliminate early childhood diseases, reduce the incidence of low birth weight in infants, reduce child abuse and neglect and reduce family illiteracy. These statewide pilot programs seek to link at-risk children and families with beneficial services to accomplish the objectives of this act.

"**B.** The healthy families pilot program is intended to reduce child abuse and neglect, promote child wellness, identify school readiness programs, strengthen family relations, promote family unity, reduce the dependency on drugs and alcohol and encourage the development of a strong, supportive environment for at-risk families in order to promote healthy families. The pilot program is intended to achieve its objectives through the use of trained professionals.

"**C.** The health start pilot program is intended to serve children and pregnant women in order to increase prenatal care, reduce the incidence of low birth weight in infants, reduce the incidence of childhood diseases, increase immunizations, provide preventative care information and assist families to identify school readiness programs so that children may receive a healthy start in life. The pilot program is intended to achieve its objectives through the use of lay workers.

"**D.** The family literacy pilot program is intended to serve the parents of preschool children by improving their basic academic skills in order to increase family literacy. The pilot program is intended to achieve its objectives through organizational partnerships involving public schools, private preschools and adult education programs.

"**E.** It is the intent of this act that the provisions of this act related to preventing child abuse, increasing prenatal care for needy mothers, and enhanced literacy programs and other social services programs may serve as the state commitment that may be used to match any federal monies that may be provided to a city or county under a federal empowerment zone or enterprise community."

"**Sec. 9. Program evaluation**

"**A.** The auditor general shall conduct an annual programmatic evaluation of the health start pilot program established in § 36–697, Arizona Revised Statutes, as added by this act, the healthy families pilot program established in § 8–701, Arizona Revised Statutes, as added by this act, and the family literacy pilot program established in § 15–191.01, Arizona Revised Statutes, as added by this act. The auditor general shall provide annual programmatic evaluations to the speaker of the house of representatives, the president of the senate, the governor and the joint committee on children and families on or before December 31, 1995 and December 31, 1996 and a final evaluation on or before December 31, 1997.

"**B.** The annual programmatic evaluations shall examine the effectiveness of the programs, the organizational structure and efficiency of the programs, the level and scope of services included within the programs, the type and level of criteria used to establish eligibility within the programs and the number and demographic characteristics of the persons who receive services by the programs.

"**C.** The annual programmatic evaluations shall include:

"1. Information on the number and characteristics of the program participants.

"2. Information on contractors and program service providers.

"3. Information on program revenues and expenditures.

"4. Information on the number and characteristics of enrollment and disenrollment.

"5. Information on the average cost for each participant in the programs.

"6. Information concerning progress of program participants in achieving goals and objectives.

"7. Recommendations regarding program administration.

"8. Recommendations regarding informational materials distributed through the programs.

"9. Recommendations pertaining to program expansion.

"10. Recommendations regarding the method used in preparing the Arizona children and families resource directory.

"**D.** In preparing the annual programmatic evaluations, the auditor general shall not rely solely on information concerning program participants and program performance prepared by contractors and program services providers but shall independently develop information for the annual programmatic evaluations. The evaluations shall include information and statistics for each pilot program and for each site in the program.

"**E.** The final evaluation shall include the information required in the annual programmatic evaluations and the following:

"1. Statistical information measuring the effectiveness of the programs in accomplishing the goals and objectives established in this act in § 8–701, subsection C, § 15–191.01, subsection A, and § 36–697, subsection B, Arizona Revised Statutes, as added by this act.

"2. The attitudes and concerns of program participants.

"**F.** The final evaluation shall also:

"1. Evaluate the educational process for parents on developmental assessments so that early identification of any learning disabilities, physical handicaps or behavioral health needs are determined.

"2. Measure the effects on program participants of promoting family unity and strengthening family relations.

"3. Review the impact on program participants of the counseling and coping support services received.

"4. Evaluate the method for selecting eligible program participants.

"5. Evaluate the overall effectiveness of the program based on performance based outcome measurements including a reduced dependency on welfare, increased employment and increased self-sufficiency.

"6. Estimate the long-term savings for providing early intervention services established in the health start and healthy families pilot programs.

"**G.** Notwithstanding any law to the contrary, the auditor general has access to all relevant information and records held by the department of health services and the department of economic security in order to conduct the evaluation required by this section. The auditor general shall keep this information confidential."

Laws 1994, 9th S.S., Ch. 1, § 10, as amended by Laws 1995, Ch. 272, § 2, and Laws 1996, Ch. 247, § 1, providing for a joint committee on community program evaluation, was repealed by Laws 1996, Ch. 247, § 5, eff. July 1, 1998.

Laws 1994, 9th S.S., Ch. 1, § 12, which provided for delayed repeal of this section effective July 1, 1998, was itself repealed by Laws 1998, Ch. 295, § 9, eff. June 1, 1998.

Laws 1996, Ch. 247, § 2, providing for a health start program coordination study, was repealed by § 5 of that act effective July 1, 1998.

Reviser's Notes:

1994 Note. The above article and the sections that comprise it were added by Laws 1994, Ninth Special Session, Ch. 1, sec. 7 as title 15, chapter 1, article 8 and §§ 15–181 and 15–182 and were renumbered as article 9 and §§ 15–191 and 15–191.01, respectively, pursuant to authority of § 41–1304.02.

1994 Note. Pursuant to authority of § 41–1304.02, in [Laws 1994, 9th S.S., Ch. 1, § 10] subsection D, first sentence the reference to; "article 9" was substituted for the reference to "article 8" to conform to the reviser's renumbering of that article.

1996 Note. Pursuant to authority of § 41–1304.02, in Laws 1996, Ch. 247, § 1, subsection C, paragraph 4, subdivision (b) a period was inserted at the end of the sentence to correct a manifest clerical error.

§ 15–191.01. Family literacy program; procedures; curriculum; eligibility plan

A. The family literacy program is established in the state board of education through the division of adult education to increase the basic academic and literacy skills of eligible parents and their preschool children in accordance with this article. The state board of education shall establish family literacy projects as part of the overall program at locations where there is a high incidence of economic and educational disadvantage as determined by the state board of education in consultation with the department of economic security and, as appropriate, other state agencies.

B. The state board of education shall adopt procedures necessary to implement the family literacy program.

C. The state board of education shall establish guidelines for requiring program participants to engage in community service activities in exchange for benefits received from the program. Participants shall be allowed to choose from a variety of community and faith-based service providers that are under contract with the department to provide community service opportunities or program services. Participants shall be allowed and encouraged to engage in community services within their own communities. Participants shall be allowed to fulfill the requirements of this subdivision [1] by providing community services to the program from which they received services.

D. [2]Submit an annual report by December 31 to the governor, the speaker of the house of representatives and the president of the senate regarding the community service activities of program participants pursuant to subsection C, including information on the number of participants, the types of community service performed and the number of hours spent in community service activities.

E. Local education agencies and adult education programs funded by the department of education are eligible for grants if the state board of education determines that a high percentage of adults in the county, the local school district or the targeted local school service area have not graduated from high school. Selection criteria for grant awards shall include at a minimum the educational needs of the adult population, the incidence of unemployment in the county, district or local targeted school service area, the degree to which community collaboration and partnership demonstrate the ability to bring additional resources to the program and the readiness and likelihood of the proposing organizations to establish a successful family literacy project.

F. Each project team shall include representatives from each of the following:

1. One or more local school districts or the county school superintendent's office.

2. An adult education provider funded by the division of adult education.

3. A private or public early childhood education provider.

4. Any other social service, governmental or private agency that may provide assistance for the planning and operation of the project.

G. In addition to the grants prescribed in subsection H, the state board of education shall authorize two grants to existing literacy programs in this state that can offer training and serve as models and training resources for the establishment and expansion of other programs throughout this state. Existing literacy programs shall submit a grant application to the state board of education in the same manner as prescribed in subsection I[3].

H. The state board of education shall authorize additional grants through the division of adult education in areas of educational and economic need.

I. Selected projects shall use either:

1. A nationally recognized family literacy model such as models developed by the national center for family literacy or its successor.

2. A model that, in the determination of the project team and the state board of education, is superior to a nationally recognized family literacy model.

J. Eligible parents shall be instructed in adult basic education and general educational development. Preschool children shall receive instruction in developmentally appropriate early childhood programs. Other planned, structured activities involving parents and children in learning activities may be established as a part of the curriculum.

K. Each grant application shall include a plan to address at least the following:

1. Identification and recruitment of eligible parents and children.

2. Screening and preparation of parents and children for participation in the program.

3. Food services for program participants.

4. Instructional programs that promote academic and literacy skills and that equip parents to provide needed support for the educational growth and success of their children.

5. A determination that at least ten but no more than twenty parents with children will enroll and be eligible for the program.

6. Provision of child care through either private or public providers.

7. A transportation plan for participants.

8. An organizational partnership involving at a minimum a common school, a private preschool provider and an adult education program funded by the department of education.

Added as § 15-182 by Laws 1994, 9th S.S., Ch. 1, § 7. Renumbered as § 15-191.01. Amended by Laws 1998, Ch. 295, § 7, eff. June 1, 1998.

[1] So in original. Should read "subsection".

[2] So in original. Should read "The state board of education shall".
[3] So in original. Should read "K".

Repeal

This section is repealed by Laws 1998, Ch. 295, § 10, as amended by Laws 2003, Ch. 264, § 46, effective January 2, 2014.

Historical and Statutory Notes

Laws 1994, 9th S.S., Ch. 1, § 9, provides:

"**Sec. 9. Program evaluation**

"**A.** The auditor general shall conduct an annual programmatic evaluation of the health start pilot program established in § 36–697, Arizona Revised Statutes, as added by this act, the healthy families pilot program established in § 8–701, Arizona Revised Statutes, as added by this act, and the family literacy pilot program established in § 15–191.01, Arizona Revised Statutes, as added by this act. The auditor general shall provide annual programmatic evaluations to the speaker of the house of representatives, the president of the senate, the governor and the joint committee on children and families on or before December 31, 1995 and December 31, 1996 and a final evaluation on or before December 31, 1997.

"**B.** The annual programmatic evaluations shall examine the effectiveness of the programs, the organizational structure and efficiency of the programs, the level and scope of services included within the programs, the type and level of criteria used to establish eligibility within the programs and the number and demographic characteristics of the persons who receive services by the programs.

"**C.** The annual programmatic evaluations shall include:

"1. Information on the number and characteristics of the program participants.

"2. Information on contractors and program service providers.

"3. Information on program revenues and expenditures.

"4. Information on the number and characteristics of enrollment and disenrollment.

"5. Information on the average cost for each participant in the programs.

"6. Information concerning progress of program participants in achieving goals and objectives.

"7. Recommendations regarding program administration.

"8. Recommendations regarding informational materials distributed through the programs.

"9. Recommendations pertaining to program expansion.

"10. Recommendations regarding the method used in preparing the Arizona children and families resource directory.

"**D.** In preparing the annual programmatic evaluations, the auditor general shall not rely solely on information concerning program participants and program performance prepared by contractors and program services providers but shall independently develop information for the annual programmatic evaluations. The evaluations shall include information and statistics for each pilot program and for each site in the program.

"**E.** The final evaluation shall include the information required in the annual programmatic evaluations and the following:

"1. Statistical information measuring the effectiveness of the programs in accomplishing the goals and objectives established in this act in § 8–701, subsection C, § 15–191.01, subsection A, and § 36–697, subsection B, Arizona Revised Statutes, as added by this act.

"2. The attitudes and concerns of program participants.

"**F.** The final evaluation shall also:

"1. Evaluate the educational process for parents on developmental assessments so that early identification of any learning disabilities, physical handicaps or behavioral health needs are determined.

"2. Measure the effects on program participants of promoting family unity and strengthening family relations.

"3. Review the impact on program participants of the counseling and coping support services received.

"4. Evaluate the method for selecting eligible program participants.

"5. Evaluate the overall effectiveness of the program based on performance based outcome measurements including a reduced dependency on welfare, increased employment and increased self-sufficiency.

"6. Estimate the long-term savings for providing early intervention services established in the health start and healthy families pilot programs.

"**G.** Notwithstanding any law to the contrary, the auditor general has access to all relevant information and records held by the department of health services and the department of economic security in order to conduct the evaluation required by this section. The auditor general shall keep this information confidential."

Laws 1994, 9th S.S., Ch. 1, § 12, which provided for delayed repeal of this section effective July 1, 1998, was itself repealed by Laws 1998, Ch. 295, § 9, eff. June 1, 1998.

Laws 1997, 1st S.S., Ch. 4, § 9, amended by 1997, Ch. 231, § 33, provides:

"**Sec. 9. State block grant for early childhood education**

"**A.** Funding for the state block grant for early childhood programs in fiscal year 1997–1998 shall be allocated based on the number of K-3 students at each charter school or school district who were eligible for free lunches during fiscal year 1996–1997 under the national school lunch and child nutrition acts (42 United States Code §§ 1751 through 1785). Any charter school or school district that did not determine for fiscal year 1996–1997 if its K-3 students were eligible for free lunches under the national school lunch and child nutrition acts shall receive funding for the state block grant for early childhood education based on the number of K-3 students that would have been eligible according to the statewide K-3 eligibility average for all school districts and charter schools collectively for fiscal year 1996–1997.

"**B.** School districts or charter schools that devote part or all of their fiscal year 1997–1998 state block grant for early childhood funding to preschool programs shall comply with all of the following:

"1. Restrict the preschool program only to children who have reached four years of age by September 1, 1997 and who are eligible for free or reduced price lunches under the national school lunch and child nutrition acts (42 United States Code §§ 1751 through 1785).

"2. Allow the parents or guardians of all children selected for the program to request to have their children receive preschool services from a federally funded or private child care provider of the parent or guardian's own choosing. A school district or charter school shall allow at least fifty per cent of children selected from the program to receive services from a federally funded or private child care provider, unless the parents or guardians of fewer than fifty per cent of the children selected for the program request to have their children receive services from a federally funded or private child care provider, in which case the school district or charter school shall allow all children whose parents or guardians request that their children be served by a federally funded or private child care provider to receive services from a federally funded or private child care provider.

"3. Allow participating students to receive preschool services only from a public, federally funded or private child care provider licensed by the department of health services.

"4. Limit the use of contracts with federally funded and private child care providers primarily to matters pertaining to numbers of children to be served, hours of service to be provided per child, payment rates and other financial aspects of the program.

"5. Pay participating federally funded and private child care providers in a timely manner.

"**C.** It is the intent of the legislature that before July 1, 1999 all public, federally funded and private child care providers that receive funding through this program become accredited by a state board of education approved organization that provides accreditation for preschool programs."

Laws 1998, Ch. 295, § 10, as amended by Laws 2003, Ch. 264, § 46, provides:

"**Sec. 10. Delayed repeal**

"Section 15-191.01, Arizona Revised Statutes, is repealed from and after January 1, 2014."

Reviser's Notes:

1994 Note. The above article and the sections that comprise it were added by Laws 1994, Ninth Special Session, Ch. 1, sec. 7 as title 15, chapter 1, article 8 and §§ 15-181 and 15-182 and were renumbered as article 9 and §§ 15-191 and 15-191.01, respectively, pursuant to authority of § 41-1304.02.

1994 Note. Pursuant to authority of § 41-1304.02, in [Laws 1994, 9th S.S., Ch. 1, § 9] subsection A, first sentence, and subsection E, paragraph 1 the reference to "§ 15-191.01" was substituted for the reference to "§ 15-182" to conform to the reviser's renumbering of that section.

CHAPTER 2

STATE GOVERNANCE OF SCHOOLS

ARTICLE 1. STATE BOARD OF EDUCATION

Section

ARTICLE 2. DEPARTMENT OF EDUCATION

ARTICLE 3. SUPERINTENDENT OF PUBLIC INSTRUCTION

ARTICLE 4. UNIFORM SYSTEM OF FINANCIAL RECORDS

Chapter 2, consisting of Article 1, §§ 15–201 to 15–213, Article 2, §§ 15–231 to 15–237, Article 3, §§ 15–251 to 15–255, and Article 4, §§ 15–271 and 15–272, was added by Laws 1981, Ch. 1, § 2, effective January 23, 1981.

ARTICLE 1. STATE BOARD OF EDUCATION

§ 15–201. State board of education; members; appointment; terms

Text of section pending conditional amendment

A. The state board of education shall be composed of the superintendent of public instruction, the president of a state university or a state college, three lay members, a member of the state board of directors for community colleges, a superintendent of a high school district, a classroom teacher and a county school superintendent. A member who is a president of a state university or a state college shall not succeed himself.

B. The governor shall appoint each member, other than the superintendent of public instruction, pursuant to § 38–211 for a term of four years beginning on the third Monday in January.

Added by Laws 1981, Ch. 1, § 2, eff. Jan. 23, 1981. Amended by Laws 1981, Ch. 314, § 1.

For text of conditional amendment, see § 15–201, post

Historical and Statutory Notes

Source:

Laws 1965, Ch. 3, § 1.
A.R.S. former § 15–101.01.
Laws 1972, Ch. 163, § 11.

This section was conditionally amended by Laws 1982, Ch. 332, § 2, but the condition failed to occur. See, note, post.

Proposition 104, based on Laws 1982, S.C.R. No. 1003 proposing an amendment of Const. Art. 11, § 3 to change the composition of the state board of education and providing for incumbents' continuance in office and the filling of any vacancies on the board, was rejected by the electors at the November 2, 1982 general election as proclaimed by the governor on November 30, 1982.

§ 15–201. State board of education; members; appointment; terms

Text of conditional amendment

A. The state board of education shall be composed of the superintendent of public instruction, the president of a state university or a state college, three lay members, a president or chancellor of a community college district, a superintendent of a high school district, a classroom teacher and a county school superintendent. A member who is a president of a state university or a state college shall not succeed himself.

B. The governor shall appoint each member, other than the superintendent of public instruction, pursuant to § 38-211 for a term of four years beginning on the third Monday in January.

Added by Laws 1981, Ch. 1, § 2, eff. Jan. 23, 1981. Amended by Laws 1981, Ch. 314, § 1; Laws 2004, Ch. 336, § 2.

For text of section pending conditional amendment, see § 15-201, ante

Historical and Statutory Notes

Laws 2004, Ch. 336, § 34, provides:

"**Sec. 34. Retention of members**

"Notwithstanding §§ 15-201, 15-1851, 15-1863, 15-1872 and 41-617, Arizona Revised Statutes, as amended by this act, the persons serving as the representatives of the state board of directors for community colleges on the state board of education, the commission for postsecondary education, the Arizona student program investing resources for education selection committee, the family college savings program oversight committee and the Arizona drug and gang policy council on the effective date of this act may continue to serve until the expiration of their normal terms."

Laws 2004, Ch. 336, § 35, provides:

"**Sec. 35. Conditional enactment**

"Section 15-201, Arizona Revised Statutes, as amended by this act, does not become effective unless a corresponding change to article XI, § 3, Constitution of Arizona, is approved by a vote of the people at the next general election."

§ 15-202. Meetings; majority required for validation; travel expenses; immunity

A. The state board of education shall hold four regular meetings annually at times it directs. Special meetings may be held on the call of the presiding officer.

B. Concurrence of a majority of all members of the board is necessary for validation of an act of the board.

C. Members shall be allowed travel expenses and reimbursement for subsistence, as provided by title 38, chapter 4, article 2,[1] to be paid upon claims approved by the superintendent of public instruction, as other claims against the state are paid, from the appropriation for the board authorized in the general appropriation bill.

D. Members of the board are immune from personal liability with respect to all acts done and actions taken in good faith within the scope of their authority during duly constituted regular and special meetings with approval of a majority of the board.

Added by Laws 1981, Ch. 1, § 2, eff. Jan. 23, 1981.

[1] Section 38-621 et seq.

Historical and Statutory Notes

Source:
Laws 1912, Ch. 77, § 3.
Civ. Code 1913, § 2696.
Laws 1921, Ch. 134, § 1.
Laws 1922, Ch. 35, § 119.
Rev. Code 1928, § 988.
Code 1939, § 54-101.
A.R.S. former § 15-101.
Laws 1960, Ch. 127, § 1.
Laws 1972, Ch. 109, § 1.

§ 15-203. Powers and duties

A. The state board of education shall:

1. Exercise general supervision over and regulate the conduct of the public school system.

2. Keep a record of its proceedings.

3. Make rules for its own government.

4. Determine the policy and work undertaken by it.

5. Appoint its employees, on the recommendation of the superintendent of public instruction.

6. Prescribe the duties of its employees if not prescribed by statute.

7. Delegate to the superintendent of public instruction the execution of board policies.

8. Recommend to the legislature changes or additions to the statutes pertaining to schools.

9. Prepare, publish and distribute reports concerning the educational welfare of this state.

10. Prepare a budget for expenditures necessary for proper maintenance of the board and accomplishment of its purposes and present the budget to the legislature.

11. Aid in the enforcement of laws relating to schools.

12. Prescribe a minimum course of study in the common schools, minimum competency requirements for the promotion of pupils from the third grade and minimum course of study and competency requirements for the promotion of pupils from the eighth grade. The state board of education shall prepare a fiscal impact statement of any proposed changes to the minimum course of study or competency requirements and, on completion, shall send a copy to the director of the joint legislative budget committee and the executive director of the school facilities board. The state board of education shall not adopt any changes in the minimum course of study or competency requirements in effect on July 1, 1998 that will have a fiscal impact on school capital costs.

13. Prescribe minimum course of study and competency requirements for the graduation of pupils from high school. The state board of education shall prepare a fiscal impact statement of any proposed changes to the minimum course of study or competency requirements and, on completion, shall send a copy to the director of the joint legislative budget committee and the executive director of the school facilities board. The state board of education shall not adopt any changes in the minimum course of study or competency require-

ments in effect on July 1, 1998 that will have a fiscal impact on school capital costs.

14. Supervise and control the certification of persons engaged in instructional work directly as any classroom, laboratory or other teacher or indirectly as a supervisory teacher, speech therapist, principal or superintendent in a school district, including school district preschool programs, or any other educational institution below the community college, college or university level, and prescribe rules for certification, including rules for certification of teachers who have teaching experience and who are trained in other states, which are not unnecessarily restrictive and are substantially similar to the rules prescribed for the certification of teachers trained in this state. Until July 1, 2006, the rules shall require applicants for all certificates for common school instruction to complete a minimum of forty-five classroom hours or three college level credit hours, or the equivalent, of training in research based systematic phonics instruction from a public or private provider. The rules shall not require a teacher to obtain a master's degree or to take any additional graduate courses as a condition of certification or recertification. The rules shall allow a general equivalency diploma to be substituted for a high school diploma in the certification of emergency substitute teachers.

15. Adopt a list of approved tests for determining special education assistance to gifted students as defined in § 15-761 and as provided in § 15-764. The adopted tests shall provide separate scores for quantitative reasoning, verbal reasoning and nonverbal reasoning and shall be capable of providing reliable and valid scores at the highest ranges of the score distribution.

16. Adopt rules governing the methods for the administration of all proficiency examinations.

17. Adopt proficiency examinations for its use. The state board of education shall determine the passing score for the proficiency examination.

18. Include within its budget the cost of contracting for the purchase, distribution and scoring of the examinations as provided in paragraphs 16 and 17 of this subsection.

19. Supervise and control the qualifications of professional nonteaching school personnel and prescribe standards relating to qualifications.

20. Impose such disciplinary action, including the issuance of a letter of censure, suspension, suspension with conditions or revocation of a certificate, upon a finding of immoral or unprofessional conduct.

21. Establish an assessment, data gathering and reporting system for pupil performance as prescribed in chapter 7, article 3 of this title. [1]

22. Adopt a rule to promote braille literacy pursuant to section 15-214.

23. Adopt rules prescribing procedures for the investigation by the department of education of every written complaint alleging that a certificated person has engaged in immoral conduct.

24. For purposes of federal law, serve as the state board for vocational and technological education and meet at least four times each year solely to execute the powers and duties of the state board for vocational and technological education.

25. Develop and maintain a handbook for use in the schools of this state that provides guidance for the teaching of moral, civic and ethical education. The handbook shall promote existing curriculum frameworks and shall encourage school districts to recognize moral, civic and ethical values within instructional and programmatic educational development programs for the general purpose of instilling character and ethical principles in pupils in kindergarten programs and grades one through twelve.

26. Require pupils to recite the following passage from the declaration of independence for pupils in grades four through six at the commencement of the first class of the day in the schools, except that a pupil shall not be required to participate if the pupil or the pupil's parent or guardian objects:

We hold these truths to be self-evident, that all men are created equal, that they are endowed by their creator with certain unalienable rights, that among these are life, liberty and the pursuit of happiness. That to secure these rights, governments are instituted among men, deriving their just powers from the consent of the governed. . . .

27. Adopt rules that provide for teacher certification reciprocity. The rules shall provide for a one year reciprocal teaching certificate with minimum requirements including valid teacher certification from a state with substantially similar criminal history or teacher fingerprinting requirements and proof of the submission of an application for a fingerprint clearance card pursuant to title 41, chapter 12, article 3.1.[2]

28. Adopt rules that will be in effect until December 31, 2006 and that provide for the presentation of an honorary high school diploma to a person who has never obtained a high school diploma and who meets each of the following requirements:

(a) Is at least sixty-five years of age.

(b) Currently resides in this state.

(c) Provides documented evidence from the Arizona department of veterans' services that the person enlisted in the armed forces of the United States before completing high school in a public or private school.

(d) Was honorably discharged from service with the armed forces of the United States.

29. Cooperate with the Arizona–Mexico commission in the governor's office and with researchers at universities in this state to collect data and conduct projects in the United States and Mexico on issues that are within the scope of the duties of the department of education and that relate to quality of life, trade and economic development in this state in a manner that will help the Arizona–Mexico commission to assess and enhance the economic competitiveness of this state and of the Arizona–Mexico region.

30. Adopt rules to define and provide guidance to schools as to the activities that would constitute immoral or unprofessional conduct of certificated persons.

31. Adopt guidelines to encourage pupils in grades nine, ten, eleven and twelve to volunteer for twenty hours of community service before graduation from high school. A school district that complies with the guidelines adopted

pursuant to this paragraph is not liable for damages resulting from a pupil's participation in community service unless the school district is found to have demonstrated wanton or reckless disregard for the safety of the pupil and other participants in community service. For the purposes of this paragraph "community service" may include service learning. The guidelines shall include the following:

(a) A list of the general categories in which community service may be performed.

(b) A description of the methods by which community service will be monitored.

(c) A consideration of risk assessment for community service projects.

(d) Orientation and notification procedures of community service opportunities for pupils entering grade nine including the development of a notification form. The notification form shall be signed by the pupil and the pupil's parent or guardian, except that a pupil shall not be required to participate in community service if the parent or guardian notifies the principal of the pupil's school in writing that the parent or guardian does not wish the pupil to participate in community service.

(e) Procedures for a pupil in grade nine to prepare a written proposal that outlines the type of community service that the pupil would like to perform and the goals that the pupil hopes to achieve as a result of community service. The pupil's written proposal shall be reviewed by a faculty advisor, a guidance counselor or any other school employee who is designated as the community service program coordinator for that school. The pupil may alter the written proposal at any time before performing community service.

(f) Procedures for a faculty advisor, a guidance counselor or any other school employee who is designated as the community service program coordinator to evaluate and certify the completion of community service performed by pupils.

B. The state board of education may:

1. Contract.

2. Sue and be sued.

3. Distribute and score the tests prescribed in chapter 7, article 3 of this title.

4. Provide for an advisory committee to conduct hearings and screenings to determine whether grounds exist to impose disciplinary action against a certificated person, whether grounds exist to reinstate a revoked or surrendered certificate and whether grounds exist to approve or deny an initial application for certification or a request for renewal of a certificate. The board may delegate its responsibility to conduct hearings and screenings to its advisory committee. Hearings shall be conducted pursuant to title 41, chapter 6, article 6.[3]

5. Proceed with the disposal of any complaint requesting disciplinary action or with any disciplinary action against a person holding a certificate as prescribed in subsection A, paragraph 14 of this section after the suspension or expiration of the certificate or surrender of the certificate by the holder.

6. Assess costs and reasonable attorney fees against a person who files a frivolous complaint or who files a complaint in bad faith. Costs assessed pursuant to this paragraph shall not exceed the expenses incurred by the state board in the investigation of the complaint.

Added by Laws 1981, Ch. 1, § 2, eff. Jan. 23, 1981. Amended by Laws 1981, Ch. 105, § 1; Laws 1981, Ch. 314, § 2; Laws 1982, Ch. 169, § 1; Laws 1982, Ch. 332, § 3; Laws 1983, Ch. 154, § 1; Laws 1983, Ch. 325, § 3; Laws 1984, Ch. 277, § 1; Laws 1984, Ch. 379, § 1; Laws 1985, Ch. 166, § 1, eff. April 18, 1985; Laws 1985, Ch. 254, § 1, eff. April 29, 1985; Laws 1985, Ch. 347, § 1, eff. May 14, 1985; Laws 1985, Ch. 350, § 4; Laws 1985, Ch. 345, § 1; Laws 1986, Ch. 250, § 2; Laws 1987, Ch. 220, § 1; Laws 1989, Ch. 237, § 1; Laws 1990, Ch. 136, § 1; Laws 1990, Ch. 340, § 1; Laws 1990, Ch. 402, § 1, eff. July 6, 1990; Laws 1991, Ch. 218, § 1, eff. June 10, 1991; Laws 1991, Ch. 292, § 1, eff. June 28, 1991; Laws 1991, Ch. 298, § 6, eff. Sept. 12, 1991, retroactively effective to July 1, 1991; Laws 1992, Ch. 314, § 1; Laws 1993, Ch. 202, § 1, eff. April 21, 1993; Laws 1994, Ch. 165, § 1; Laws 1995, Ch. 108, § 1; Laws 1995, Ch. 268, § 5; Laws 1996, Ch. 1, § 1; Laws 1996, Ch. 284, § 9; Laws 1997, Ch. 137, § 1; Laws 1997, Ch. 221, § 64; Laws 1998, Ch. 169, § 1; Laws 1998, Ch. 231, § 1; Laws 1998, 5th S.S., Ch. 1, § 8, eff. July 9, 1998; Laws 1999, Ch. 256, § 1; Laws 2000, Ch. 97, § 1; Laws 2000, Ch. 257, § 1; Laws 2000, Ch. 271, § 1, eff. April 17, 2000; Laws 2001, Ch. 56, § 1; Laws 2001, Ch. 141, § 1; Laws 2001, Ch. 231, § 2; Laws 2001, Ch. 241, § 1; Laws 2003, Ch. 160, § 1; Laws 2003, Ch. 214, § 3, eff. Oct. 1, 2003.

[1] Section 15-741 et seq.

[2] Section 41-1758 et seq.

[3] Section 41-1061 et seq.

Historical and Statutory Notes

Source:

Laws 1912, Ch. 77, § 4.
Civ. Code 1913, § 2697.
Laws 1921, Ch. 134, § 1.
Laws 1921, Ch. 140, §§ 1, 2.
Laws 1925, Ch. 69, § 1.
Rev. Code 1928, §§ 989, 1064.
Code 1939, § 54-806.
Laws 1953, Ch. 49, § 1.
Code 1939, Supp.1953, § 54-102.
A.R.S. former §§ 15-102, 15-236, 15-1015.01, 15-1022.
Laws 1960, Ch. 120, § 1.
Laws 1960, Ch. 127, §§ 2, 46.
Laws 1961, Ch. 61, § 1.
Laws 1963, Ch. 91, § 1.
Laws 1966, Ch. 80, § 1.
Laws 1970, Ch. 175, § 1.
Laws 1970, Ch. 190, § 10.
Laws 1972, Ch. 111, § 1.
Laws 1972, Ch. 168, § 1.
Laws 1974, 1st S.S., Ch. 3, § 75.
Laws 1974, Ch. 146, § 1.
Laws 1975, Ch. 33, § 1.
Laws 1976, Ch. 156, § 1.
Laws 1976, Ch. 165, § 4.
Laws 1977, Ch. 155, § 1.
Laws 1978, Ch. 188, § 1.
Laws 1979, Ch. 37, § 1.
Laws 1979, Ch. 90, § 1.
Laws 1979, Ch. 111, § 2.
Laws 1979, Ch. 118, § 2.
Laws 1979, Ch. 185, § 2.
Laws 1980, 2nd S.S., Ch. 9, §§ 6, 9.
Laws 1980, Ch. 170, § 1.

Laws 1982, Ch. 332, § 1 provides:

"**Section 1. Purpose**

"The purpose of this act is to:

"1. Direct the state board for vocational and technical education, which is the state board of education, to perform its duties as provided by law and to work as equal partners with the state board of directors for community colleges in the coordination and articulation of vocational and technical education programs offered under their respective jurisdictions.

"2. Provide direction to the educational institutions of this state relating to their responsibilities for providing vocational and technical education. The primary responsibilities of the educational institutions are as follows:

"(a) School district governing boards have the primary responsibility for providing career exploration and entry level vocational education.

"(b) Community college district governing boards have the primary responsibility for providing technical education and advanced vocational and technical education, including the retraining and upgrading of a student's occupational skills. Community college district governing boards in conjunction with the state board of private technical and business schools have the major responsibility for providing vocational and technical education which focuses on the economic development of this state.

"(c) Universities have the primary responsibility for research related to vocational and technical education and career exploration."

Laws 1984, Ch. 346, §§ 1 to 7 and 10, relating to purpose, legislative intent, state board of education, school district proposals, requirements for school district teacher career ladder plans, and joint select education committee, expired on January 1, 1986.

Laws 1985, Ch. 177, §§ 1 to 5, effective April 18, 1985, providing for a joint legislative committee on career ladders, career ladder plan requirements, career ladder plan programs, and study of such programs, was repealed by Laws 1986, Ch. 364, § 1.

The amendment of this section by Laws 1985, Ch. 254, § 1 was repealed by Laws 1985, Ch. 350, § 5.

Laws 1985, Ch. 350, § 1, paragraph 2 provides:

"**Section 1. Purpose**"

"2. Section 15-203, Arizona Revised Statutes, was amended by Laws 1985, chapter 166, § 1 and chapter 254, § 1. The chapter 254 version failed to set forth in full the text of § 15-203 as amended by Laws 1985, chapter 166, § 1 (an emergency act) as is required by Constitution of Arizona article IV, part 2, § 14. In order to accomplish the intent of the 1985 enactments, in this enactment the chapter 166 version is amended to incorporate the amendments made by the chapter 254 version and the chapter 254 version is repealed."

This section, as amended by Laws 1985, Ch. 345, § 1, was repealed by Laws 1986, Ch. 250, § 1, effective August 13, 1986.

Laws 1987, Ch. 83, § 1, effective April 16, 1987, provided for a study by the state board of education of certification requirements of teachers trained in other states.

Laws 1987, Ch. 201, § 1, effective May 1, 1987, as amended by Laws 1988, Ch. 44, § 3, effective May 9, 1988, directed the state board of education to enter into an intergovernmental agreement with the Arizona board of regents for the conduct of school finance studies.

Laws 1990, Ch. 233, § 17, provides:

"**Sec. 17. Effective date**

"Sections 1 through 11 and § 15 of this act are effective from and after June 30, 1991."

The purported amendment of this section by Laws 1990, Ch. 330, § 2, was repealed prior to taking effect by Laws 1990, Ch. 402, § 9, effective July 6, 1990.

The purported amendment of this section by Laws 1990, Ch. 233, § 1, effective July 1, 1991, was repealed prior to taking effect by Laws 1991, Ch. 218, § 2, effective June 10, 1991.

The purported amendment of this section by Laws 1990, Ch. 233, § 1, effective July 1, 1991, was repealed by Laws 1991, Ch. 298, § 7, effective September 21, 1991, retroactively effective to July 1, 1991.

The 1991 amendment of this section by Ch. 218 explicitly amended the 1990 amendment of this section by Chs. 136, 340 and 402.

The 1991 amendment of this section by Ch. 292 explicitly amended the 1991 amendment of this section by Ch. 218.

The 1991 amendment of this section by Ch. 298 explicitly amended the 1990 amendments of this section by Chs. 136, 340 and 402.

The amendment of this section by Laws 1991, Ch. 298, § 6 was repealed by Laws 1992, Ch. 319, § 7.

Laws 1991, Ch. 298, § 1, par. 3 provides:

"**Section 1. Purpose**"

"3. Section 15-203, Arizona Revised Statutes, was amended by Laws 1990, chapter 136, § 1, chapter 233, § 1, chapter 340, § 1 and chapter 402, § 1. The chapter 233 version could not be blended because of its delayed effective date. In order to blend these versions the 1990 blended version of § 15-203, Arizona Revised Statutes, is amended to incorporate the amendments made by Laws 1990, chapter 233 and the chapter 233 version is repealed."

Laws 1991, Ch. 298, § 47, subsec. B provides:

"**Sec. 47. Retroactivity**"

"**B.** Sections 6, 7, 8 and 9 of this act are effective retroactively to from and after June 30, 1991."

The 1992 amendment of this section by Ch. 314 explicitly amended the 1991 amendment of this section by Ch. 292.

Laws 1992, Ch. 319, § 1, par. 4, provides:

"**Section 1. Purpose**"

"4. Section 15-203, Arizona Revised Statutes, was amended by Laws 1991, chapter 218, § 1 and Laws 1991, chapter 292, § 1. The chapter 218 version had an emergency clause and the chapter 292 version amended the chapter 218 version and also had an emergency clause. However, Laws 1991, chapter 298, § 6 also amended § 15-203, Arizona Revised Statutes, and failed to comply with article IV, part 2, § 14, Constitution of Arizona. Since the substance of the Laws 1991, chapter 298 version was incorporated in the Laws 1991, chapter 218 version of § 15-203, Arizona Revised Statutes, in this act the chapter 298 version is repealed."

Laws 1995, Ch. 108, § 3, provides:

"**Sec. 3. Preliminary notice of inadequacy of classroom performance; review of time frame; report**

"If after reviewing the time frame related to a teacher's opportunity to improve after receiving preliminary notice of inadequacy of classroom performance required pursuant to § 15-203, subsection A, paragraph 34, Arizona Revised Statutes, the state board of education determines that other time frames or deadlines need to be modified in §§ 15-536 through 15-543, Arizona Revised Statutes, the state board of education shall report its findings and recommendations to the legislature by December 15, 1995."

The 1996 amendment of this section by Ch. 284 explicitly amended the amendment of this section by Laws 1996, Ch. 1, § 1.

Laws 1998, Ch. 231, § 4, provides:

"**Sec. 4. Training in research based systematic phonics instruction; exemption for teachers certificated by June 30, 1999**

"A teacher who holds a valid certificate to provide common school instruction on June 30, 1999 is exempt from the research based systematic phonics instruction training requirements of § 15-203, Arizona Revised Statutes, as amended by this act."

Laws 1998, Ch. 231, § 6 as amended by Laws 1999, Ch. 256, § 4, and Laws 2000, Ch. 32, § 21, provides:

"**Sec. 6. Delayed repeal**

"Section 15-718, Arizona Revised Statutes, and §§ 4 and 5 of this act are repealed from and after June 30, 2006."

The purported amendment of this section by Laws 1998, Ch. 164 failed to become effective because Chapter 164 was repealed in its entirety by Laws 1998, 5th S.S., Ch. 1, § 2, effective July 1, 1998.

The purported amendment of this section by Laws 1998, 3rd S.S., Ch. 1, failed to became effective because Ch. 1 was repealed in its entirety by Laws 1998, 5th S.S., Ch. 1, § 2, effective July 1, 1998.

Laws 2000, Ch. 32, § 1, par. 13, provides:

"**Section 1. Purpose**"

"13. Laws 1999, chapter 256, § 4 amended Laws 1998, chapter 231, § 6 to specify what sections of Laws 1998, chapter 231 were subject to a delayed repeal. This act further specifies that the delayed repeal of Laws 1998, chapter 231, § 2 refers to § 15-718, Arizona Revised Statutes."

Laws 2000, Ch. 271, § 2, provides:

"**Sec. 2. Exemption from rule-making requirements**

"Notwithstanding any other law, the state board of education is exempt from the provisions of title 41, chapter 6, Arizona Revised Statutes, with respect to the rules establishing teacher certification reciprocity as provided by this act."

Reviser's Notes:

1981 Note. Prior to the 1982 amendments, this section contained the amendments made by Laws 1981, Ch. 105, § 1 and Ch. 314, § 2 which were blended together pursuant to authority of § 41-1304.03.

1982 Note. Prior to the 1983 amendments, this section contained the amendments made by Laws 1982, Ch. 169, § 1 and Ch. 332, § 3 which were blended together pursuant to authority of § 41-1304.03. Pursuant to authority of § 41-1304.02, in subsection A, paragraph 21, a comma following the word "college" was transposed to follow the words "community college" and "community college," was transposed between the words "the" and "college".

1983 Note. Prior to the 1984 amendments, this section contained the amendments made by Laws 1983, Ch. 154, § 1 and Ch. 325, § 3 which were blended together pursuant to authority of § 41-1304.03.

1984 Note. Prior to the 1985 amendments, this section contained the amendments made by Laws 1984, Ch. 277, § 1 and Ch. 379, § 1 which were blended together pursuant to authority of § 41-1304.03.

1985 Notes. The amendment of this section by Laws 1985, Ch. 345, § 1 failed to set forth in full the text of the section as amended by Laws 1985, Ch. 166, § 1, an emergency act, as required by Constitution of Arizona Art. IV, part 2, § 14.

Prior to the 1986 amendment, this section contained the amendments made by Laws 1985, Ch. 347, § 1 and Ch. 350, § 4 which were blended together pursuant to authority of § 41-1304.03.

1990 Note. Prior to the 1991 amendments this section contained the amendments made by Laws 1990, Ch. 136, § 1 and Ch. 340, § 1 and Ch. 402, § 1 which were blended together pursuant to authority of § 41-1304.03.

1990 Note. The independent and valid amendment of this section by Laws 1990, Ch. 136, § 1, Ch. 233, § 1, Ch. 340, § 1 and Ch. 402, § 1 could not be blended because of the delayed effective date of Ch. 233.

1991 Note. The amendment of this section by Laws 1991, Ch. 298, sec. 6 failed to set forth in full the text of the section as amended by Laws 1991, Ch. 218 and Ch. 292, emergency acts, as required by Constitution of Arizona Art. IV, part 2, sec. 14.

1995 Note. Prior to the 1996 amendment this section contained the amendments made by Laws 1995, Ch. 108, sec. 1 and Ch. 268, sec. 5 that were blended together pursuant to authority of § 41-1304.03.

1997 Note. Prior to the 1998 amendments, this section contained the amendments made by Laws 1997, Ch. 137, sec. 1 and Ch. 221, sec. 64 that were blended together pursuant to authority of § 41-1304.03.

1998 Note. Prior to the 1999 amendment, this section contained the amendments made by Laws 1998, Second Regular Session, Ch. 169, sec. 1 and Ch. 231, sec. 1 and Laws 1998, Fifth Special Session, Ch. 1. sec. 8 that were blended together pursuant to authority of § 41-1304.03.

2000 Note. Prior to the 2001 amendments, this section contained the amendments made by Laws 2000, Ch. 97, sec. 1, Ch. 257, sec. 1 and Ch. 271, sec. 1 that were blended together pursuant to authority of § 41-1304.03. Pursuant to authority of § 41-1304.02, in subsection A, paragraph 27, second sentence the spelling of "one year" was corrected.

2001 Note. Prior to the 2003 amendment, this section contained the amendments made by Laws 2001, Ch. 56, sec. 1, Ch. 141, sec. 1, Ch. 231, sec. 2 and Ch. 241, sec. 1 that were blended together pursuant to authority of section 41-1304.03. Pursuant to authority of § 41-1304.02, in subsection A, paragraph 28, subdivision (c) the spelling of "veterans'" was corrected.

2003 Note. This section contains the amendments made by Laws 2003, Ch. 160, sec. 1 and Ch. 214, sec. 3 that were blended together as shown pursuant to authority of § 41-1304.03.

§ 15-204. Acceptance of gifts and grants; gifts and grants fund; use; unexpended monies

A. The state board of education may accept gifts or grants of monies or real or personal property from public and private organizations, if the purpose of the gift or grant specified by the donor is approved by the board and is within the scope of the board's powers and duties. There is established a fund for the placement of such monies which shall be designated as the gift and grant fund.

B. Any such monies received by the state board shall be placed in the appropriate gift and grant fund and expended for the purpose specified by the donor.

C. If all or part of the monies accepted by the board from a donor are not expended prior to the end of the fiscal year in which the gift or grant was accepted, the balance of the amount donated shall remain in the gift or grant fund until needed for the purpose specified by the donor.

Added by Laws 1981, Ch. 1, § 2, eff. Jan. 23, 1981. Amended by Laws 1988, Ch. 106, § 1.

Historical and Statutory Notes

Source:

Laws 1970, Ch. 169, § 3.
A.R.S. former § 15-1016.
Laws 1971, Ch. 184, § 4.

Reviser's Notes:

1988 Note. Pursuant to authority of § 41-1304.02, in the section heading "gifts and grants fund;" was added after "grants;".

§ 15-205. Education of Indians in state schools; contracts with department of interior

A. The state board of education may enter into contracts with the department of the interior for the welfare and education of Indians in schools of this state, in accordance with the act of congress approved April 16, 1934, as amended by the act of June 4, 1936. The board shall administer the expenditure of federal funds provided under such contracts.

B. No contract as provided for in subsection A shall be binding on the school district affected until it is approved by the district governing board.

Added by Laws 1981, Ch. 1, § 2, eff. Jan. 23, 1981.

Historical and Statutory Notes

Source:

Laws 1937, Ch. 38, § 1.
Code 1939, § 54-103.
A.R.S. former § 15-1161.

§ 15-206. Federal grants for educational purposes; administration

A. The state board of education may accept on behalf of this state from any federal agency monies which have been appropriated by act of Congress for defense in education, reduction of illiteracy, teaching of immigrants, employment and training, educational support services or other educational purpose.

B. The state board of education shall not reserve funds for state use in excess of actual cost not to exceed ten per cent of the grants to this state for provision to school district governing boards under the elementary and secondary education act of 1965, as amended (20 United States Code §§ 2911 through 2952 and 2971 through 2976).[1]

C. The state board of education, following regular educational fiscal procedure for counties, shall be the chief educational authority for administration and supervision of the expenditure of federal appropriations described in subsection A, and the state treasurer shall be trustee thereof.

Added by Laws 1981, Ch. 1, § 2, eff. Jan. 23, 1981. Amended by Laws 1982, Ch. 268, § 1; Laws 1988, Ch. 106, § 2; Laws 1991, Ch. 120, § 1.

[1] 20 U.S.C.A. §§ 2911 through 2952, 2971 through 2976.

Historical and Statutory Notes

Source:

Laws 1942, 1st S.S., Ch. 15, § 1.
Code 1939, Supp.1952, App. 4(A).
A.R.S. former § 11-1141.

Laws 1988, Ch. 44, § 2, effective May 9, 1988, as amended by Laws 1990, Ch. 233, § 14, provides:

"Sec. 2. Use of federal grants for fiscal years 1988-1989, 1989-1990, 1990-1991, 1991-1992 and 1992-1993

"Notwithstanding § 15-206, subsection B, Arizona Revised Statutes, for fiscal years 1988-1989, 1989-1990, 1990-1991, 1991-1992, 1992-1993, 1993-1994 and 1994-1995 the state board of education may reserve for state use one hundred sixty thousand dollars in addition to ten per cent of the grants to this state appropriated under the education consolidation and improvement act of 1981, as amended (20 United States Code §§ 1511 through 1521). The state board of education shall prepare a report on how the monies prescribed in this act are being utilized and present the report to the legislature by December 1, 1990."

Laws 1988, Ch. 44, § 2, as amended by Laws 1990, Ch. 233, § 14 and by Laws 1991, Ch. 120, § 2, provides:

"Sec. 2. Use of federal grants for fiscal years 1988-1989 through 1994-1995

"**A.** Notwithstanding § 15-206, subsection B, Arizona Revised Statutes, the state board of education may reserve monies for state use in addition to ten per cent of the grants to this state appropriated under the elementary and secondary education act of 1965, as amended (20 United States Code §§ 2911 through 2952 and 2971 through 2976) as follows:

"1. For fiscal years 1988-1989 through 1990-1991, one hundred sixty thousand dollars.

"2. For fiscal years 1991-1992 through 1994-1995, two hundred twelve thousand dollars.

"**B.** The state board of education shall prepare a report on how the monies prescribed in this act are being utilized and present the report to the legislature by December 1, 1991."

Reviser's Notes:

1988 Note. Pursuant to authority of § 41-1304.02, in subsection A the words "from any federal agency" following "monies" were transposed to follow the second "state".

§ 15–207. Apportionment and expenditure of federal grants for educational purposes

A. The state board of education shall apportion the monies described in § 15–206 for the aid of the school districts of this state to supplement monies otherwise provided therefor.

B. Monies so apportioned shall be expended by the school districts for the purposes and in the manner set forth in the federal grant. In the absence of federal regulation the state board of education shall determine the purposes and methods of expenditure in accordance with § 15–206. The state board of education may, with the approval of the board of supervisors, authorize expenditure of monies received pursuant to § 15–206 in excess of the annual budgets of school districts.

Added by Laws 1981, Ch. 1, § 2, eff. Jan. 23, 1981.

Source:

Laws 1942, 1st S.S., Ch. 15, § 2.
Code 1939, Supp.1952, App. 4(A).
A.R.S. former § 15–1142.

§ 15–208. Application by school district for apportionment of federal monies; hearing

A. A school district which, by reason of an emergency, finds it necessary to expend monies in excess of its annual budget for any purpose set forth in § 15–206 may apply to the state board of education for an apportionment from federal funds available under § 15–207.

B. The board shall conduct a hearing and an investigation concerning the application. If the hearing and investigation disclose that the district needs additional funds for the proper conduct of its school, the board may, in its discretion, apportion such monies as it deems necessary to the district.

Added by Laws 1981, Ch. 1, § 2, eff. Jan. 23, 1981.

Historical and Statutory Notes

Source:

Laws 1942, 1st S.S., Ch. 15, § 3.
Code 1939, Supp.1952, App. 4(A).
A.R.S. former § 15–1143.

§ 15–209. Disbursement of apportioned federal funds

If monies are apportioned to a school district pursuant to § 15–207, the state board of education shall direct the department of administration division of finance to draw a warrant for the amount apportioned, and the state treasurer shall pay the warrant upon presentation, as provided by law. The school district shall immediately deposit the monies with the county treasurer of the county in which the district is located, and the treasurer shall place it in the appropriate fund to the credit of the district. Thereafter the monies shall be disbursed by the county treasurer only on the voucher of the school district and the warrant of the county school superintendent.

Added by Laws 1981, Ch. 1, § 2, eff. Jan. 23, 1981.

Historical and Statutory Notes

Source:

Laws 1942, 1st S.S., Ch. 15, § 4.

Code 1939, Supp.1952, App. 4(A).
A.R.S. former § 15-1144.
Laws 1970, Ch. 190, § 17.
Laws 1976, Ch. 163, § 8.

§ 15-210. Unlawful expenditure of federal monies

If a school district expends or attempts to expend monies received pursuant to § 15-207 in a manner other than as directed by the state board of education or as provided by the federal grant, the state board of education shall immediately deliver to the county treasurer of the county in which such district is located written notice directing him to refuse to pay further warrants drawn against monies so provided in the fund prescribed in § 15-209. Copies of the notice shall be served upon the governing board of the school district and the county school superintendent. No further expenditures shall be made by the school district from such monies, and no further monies shall be apportioned or paid to the district until it has complied with the federal regulations and directions of the state board of education. Upon compliance to the satisfaction of the state board of education, the state board shall deliver written notice to the county treasurer and the county school superintendent and thereafter the monies may be expended as provided in § 15-206.

Added by Laws 1981, Ch. 1, § 2, eff. Jan. 23, 1981.

Historical and Statutory Notes

Source:

Laws 1942, 1st S.S., Ch. 15, § 5.
Code 1939, Supp.1952, App.4(A).
A.R.S. former § 15-1145.

§ 15-211. Repealed by Laws 1988, Ch. 106, § 3

Historical and Statutory Notes

The repealed section, added by Laws 1981, Ch. 1, § 2, derived from Laws 1962, Ch. 40, § 1 and A.R.S. former § 15-1151, related to the administration of private grants for educational purposes.

§ 15-212. Expenditure of private funds; exemption

A. Prior to expenditure of any monies granted to the state board of education by a private organization, the superintendent of public instruction shall present a plan governing the expenditure of such funds to the state board of education for approval.

B. Upon approval of the plan by the state board of education, the superintendent of public instruction may expend the private grants as provided in the plan.

C. Any funds granted to the state board of education as a private grant shall be exempt from the provisions of § 35-190, relating to lapsing of appropriations.

Added by Laws 1981, Ch. 1, § 2, eff. Jan. 23, 1981.

Historical and Statutory Notes

Source:

Laws 1962, Ch. 40, § 1.
A.R.S. former § 15-1152.
Laws 1976, Ch. 59, § 2.

Laws 1976, Ch. 59, [which amended former § 15-1152] provided in § 1:

"**Section 1. Intent**

"The legislature intends through the enactment of this bill to clarify and conform the amended sections to various other statutory activities of recent years. Most changes relate to the identification of the appropriate state officer, agency or department. Several amendments pertain to an altered procedure for the allotment of state monies. Some amendments merely substitute more suitable terminology for that which has been superseded elsewhere in the statutes."

§ 15–213. Procurement practices of school districts and charter schools; definitions

A. The state board of education shall adopt rules prescribing procurement practices for all school districts in this state as follows:

1. The state board shall submit to the auditor general proposed rules consistent with the procurement practices prescribed in title 41, chapter 23, [1] modifying the provisions for public notice of invitation for bids, requests for proposals and requests for qualifications to allow a governing board to give public notice of the invitation for bids, requests for proposals and requests for qualifications by publication in the official newspaper of the county as defined in § 11–255, modifying the provisions relating to disposal of materials to comply with § 15–342, paragraph 18, providing for governing board delegation of procurement authority and modifying as necessary other provisions which the state board determines are not appropriate for school districts, for procurement of construction, construction services, materials or services when the total procurement exceeds thirty thousand dollars in total cost. The rules shall include provisions specifying that school districts are not required to engage in competitive bidding in order to make the decision to participate in programs pursuant to § 15–382 and that a program authorized by § 15–382 is not required to engage in competitive bidding for the services necessary to administer the program or for purchase of insurance or reinsurance. The rules for procurement of construction projects shall include provisions specifying that surety bonds furnished as bid security and performance and payment bonds shall be executed and furnished as required by title 34, chapter 2 or 6, [2] as applicable.

2. The state board of education shall adopt rules for procurements involving construction not exceeding one hundred fifty thousand dollars which shall be known as the simplified school construction procurement program. At a minimum, the rules for a simplified construction procurement program shall require that:

(a) A list be maintained by each county school superintendent of persons who desire to receive solicitations to bid on construction projects to which additions shall be permitted throughout the year.

(b) The list of persons be available for public inspection.

(c) A performance bond and a payment bond as required by this section be provided for contracts for construction by contractors.

(d) All bids for construction be opened at a public opening and the bids shall remain confidential until the public opening.

(e) All persons desiring to submit bids be treated equitably and the information related to each project be available to all eligible persons.

(f) Competition for construction projects under the simplified school construction procurement program be encouraged to the maximum extent possible. At a minimum, a school district shall submit information on each project to all persons listed with the county school superintendent by any school district within that county.

(g) A provision, covenant, clause or understanding in, collateral to or affecting a construction contract that makes the contract subject to the laws of another state or that requires any litigation, arbitration or other dispute resolution proceeding arising from the contract to be conducted in another state is against this state's public policy and is void and unenforceable.

3. On or before December 31, 2004, the state board of education shall adopt rules for the procurement of goods and information services by school districts and charter schools using electronic, on-line bidding. The rules adopted by the state board shall include the use of reverse auctions and shall be consistent with the procurement practices prescribed in title 41, chapter 23, article 13, [3] modifying as necessary those provisions and the rules adopted pursuant to that article that the state board determines are not appropriate for school districts and charter schools. Until the rules are adopted school districts and charter schools may procure goods and information services pursuant to title 41, chapter 23, article 13 using the rules adopted by the department of administration in implementing that article.

4. The auditor general shall review the proposed rules to determine whether the rules are consistent with the procurement practices prescribed in title 41, chapter 23 and any modifications are required to adapt the procedures for school districts.

5. If the auditor general approves the proposed rules, the auditor general shall notify the state board in writing and the state board shall adopt such rules.

6. If the auditor general objects to the proposed rules, the auditor general shall notify the state board of the objections in writing and the state board, in adopting the rules, shall conform the proposed rules to meet the objections of the auditor general or revise the proposed rules to which an objection has been made and submit the revisions to the auditor general for approval.

B. After the bids submitted in response to an invitation for bids are opened and the award is made or after the proposals or qualifications are submitted in response to a request for proposals or a request for qualifications and the award is made, the governing board shall make available for public inspection all information, all bids, proposals and qualifications submitted and all findings and other information considered in determining whose bid conforms to the invitation for bids and will be the most advantageous with respect to price, conformity to the specifications and other factors or whose proposal or qualifications are to be selected for the award. The invitation for bids, request for proposals or request for qualifications shall include a notice that all information and bids, proposals and qualifications submitted will be made available for public inspection. The rules adopted by the state board shall prohibit the use in connection with procurement of specifications in any way proprietary to one supplier unless the specification includes all of the following:

1. A statement of the reasons why no other specification is practicable.

2. A description of the essential characteristics of the specified product.

3. A statement specifically permitting an acceptable alternative product to be supplied.

C. No project or purchase may be divided or sequenced into separate projects or purchases in order to avoid the limits prescribed by the state board under subsection A of this section.

D. A contract for the procurement of construction or construction services shall include a provision which provides for negotiations between the school district and the contractor for the recovery of damages related to expenses incurred by the contractor for a delay for which the school district is responsible, which is unreasonable under the circumstances and which was not within the contemplation of the parties to the contract. This subsection shall not be construed to void any provision in the contract which requires notice of delays, provides for arbitration or other procedure for settlement or provides for liquidated damages.

E. The auditor general may conduct discretionary reviews, investigations and audits of the financial and operational procurement activities of school districts, nonexempt charter schools and school purchasing cooperatives. The auditor general has final review and approval authority over all school district, nonexempt charter school and school purchasing cooperative audit contracts and any audit reports issued in accordance with this section.

F. In addition to the requirements of §§ 15–914 and 15–914.01, school districts, nonexempt charter schools and school purchasing cooperatives, in connection with any audit conducted by a certified public accountant, shall contract for a systematic review of purchasing practices using methodology consistent with sampling guidelines established by the auditor general. The auditor general shall consider cost when establishing guidelines pursuant to this subsection and to the extent possible shall attempt to minimize the cost of the review. The purpose of the review is to determine whether the school district, nonexempt charter school or school purchasing cooperative is in compliance with the procurement laws and applicable procurement rules of this state. A copy of the review shall be submitted upon completion to the auditor general. The auditor general may conduct discretionary reviews of school districts, nonexempt charter schools and school purchasing cooperatives not required to contract for independent audits.

G. The attorney general or county attorney has jurisdiction to enforce this section. The attorney general or county attorney may seek relief for any violation of this section through an appropriate civil or criminal action in superior court including an action to enjoin a threatened or pending violation of this section and including an action to enforce compliance with any request for documents made by the auditor general pursuant to this section.

H. The department of education shall enact policies and procedures for the acceptance and disposition of complaints from the public regarding school procurement practices and shall forward all school procurement complaints to the attorney general.

I. The state board of education shall adjust the total cost provided for in subsection A, paragraph 1 of this section by the annual percentage change in the GDP price deflator as defined in § 41-563.

J. The state board of education and the auditor general shall adopt rules authorizing school districts to procure construction services by construction-manager-at-risk, design-build, qualified select bidders list and job-order-contracting methods of project delivery. The rules adopted shall require each school district that uses construction-manager-at-risk, design-build, qualified select bidders list or job-order-contracting to procure construction services to submit, on or before January 15 of each year, a report to the secretary of state on the benefits associated with the use of such procurement methods. The report shall include the number of projects completed in the preceding calendar year using that procurement method, the cost and description of each project and an estimate of any cost savings or other benefits realized through the use of that procurement method.

K. The dollar amount of each job order under any job-order-contracting construction services program shall not be more than the dollar amount determined pursuant to § 41-2578, subsection J, paragraph 1.

L. A school district or charter school may evaluate general services administration contracts for materials and services. The governing board or governing body may authorize purchases under a current contract for materials or services without complying with the requirements of the procurement rules adopted by the state board of education if the governing board or governing body determines in writing that all of the following apply:

1. The price for materials or services is equal to or less than the contractor's current federal supply contract price with the general services administration.

2. The contractor has indicated in writing that the contractor is willing to extend the current federal supply contract pricing, terms and conditions to the school district or charter school.

3. The purchase order adequately identifies the federal supply contract on which the order is based.

4. The purchase contract is cost effective and is in the best interests of the school district or charter school.

M. For the purposes of this section:

1. "Nonexempt charter school" means a charter school that is not exempted from procurement laws pursuant to § 15-183, subsection E, paragraph 6.

2. "School purchasing cooperative" means an entity engaged in cooperative purchasing as defined in § 41-2631.

3. "Total cost" means the cost of all materials and services, including the cost of labor performed by employees of the school district, for all construction as provided in subsection A of this section.

Added by Laws 1981, Ch. 1, § 2, eff. Jan. 23, 1981. Amended by Laws 1984, Ch. 80, § 1; Laws 1984, Ch. 251, § 6, eff. Jan. 1, 1985; Laws 1985, Ch. 31, § 2, eff. April 2, 1985; Laws 1986, Ch. 17, § 1; Laws 1987, Ch. 266, § 1; Laws 1987, Ch. 293, § 1, eff. May 13, 1987; Laws 1989, Ch. 273, § 1, eff. June 26, 1989; Laws 1991, Ch. 138, § 1; Laws 1991, Ch. 319, § 1; Laws 1994, Ch. 194, § 1; Laws 1996, Ch. 284, § 10; Laws

1997, Ch. 277, § 1; Laws 1998, Ch. 139, § 2, eff. Oct. 1, 1998; Laws 1999, Ch. 238, § 1; Laws 2000, Ch. 135, § 1, eff. April 4, 2000; Laws 2000, Ch. 233, § 1; Laws 2001, Ch. 227, § 1, eff. April 23, 2001; Laws 2002, Ch. 240, § 2; Laws 2003, Ch. 179, § 1; Laws 2003, Ch. 215, § 1, eff. May 14, 2003, retroactively effective to Aug. 22, 2002; Laws 2004, Ch. 50, § 1.

[1] Section 41–2501 et seq.

[2] Sections 34–201 et seq. and 34–601 et seq.

[3] Section 41–2671 et seq.

Historical and Statutory Notes

Source:

Laws 1912, Ch. 77, § 4.
Civ. Code 1913, § 2697.
Laws 1921, Ch. 134, § 1.
Laws 1925, Ch. 69, § 1.
Rev. Code 1928, § 989.
Laws 1953, Ch. 49, § 1.
Code 1939, Supp.1953, § 54–102.
A.R.S. former § 15–102.
Laws 1960, Ch. 120, § 1.
Laws 1960, Ch. 127, § 2.
Laws 1961, Ch. 61, § 1.
Laws 1963, Ch. 91, § 1.
Laws 1966, Ch. 80, § 1.
Laws 1970, Ch. 175, § 1.
Laws 1970, Ch. 190, § 10.
Laws 1972, Ch. 111, § 1.
Laws 1972, Ch. 168, § 1.
Laws 1974, 1st S.S., Ch. 3, § 75.
Laws 1974, Ch. 146, § 1.
Laws 1975, Ch. 33, § 1.
Laws 1976, Ch. 156, § 1.
Laws 1977, Ch. 155, § 1.
Laws 1978, Ch. 188, § 1.
Laws 1979, Ch. 37, § 1.
Laws 1979, Ch. 90, § 1.
Laws 1979, Ch. 111, § 2.
Laws 1979, Ch. 118, § 2.
Laws 1979, Ch. 185, § 2.
Laws 1980, 2nd S.S., Ch. 9, § 6.
Laws 1980, Ch. 170, § 1.

The amendment of this section by Laws 1984, Ch. 80, § 1, was repealed by Laws 1985, Ch. 31, § 1, effective April 2, 1985.

The 1996 amendment by Ch. 284, in subsec. A, in par. 1, the first sentence, substituted "for procurement of construction, materials or services when the total procurement exceeds twenty thousand dollars in total cost" for "all construction which exceeds fifteen thousand dollars in total cost, for all materials which exceed ten thousand dollars in total cost and for all services which exceed ten thousand dollars in total cost"; and inserted new subsec. A, par. 2, redesignating the existing pars. 2 to 4, as 3 to 5, accordingly.

The 1997 amendment by Ch. 277 substituted "thirty thousand dollars" for "twenty thousand dollars" in the first sentence of subsec. A, par. 1; rewrote the first sentence of subsec. A, par. 2; inserted "school" in the phrase "simplified school construction procurement program" where it occurs; inserted "into separate projects or purchases" in subsec. C; and added subsec. G. The first sentence of subsec. A, par. 2, had read: "The state board of education may adopt rules for a procurement involving construction not exceeding one hundred thousand dollars which shall be known as the simplified construction procurement program."

The 1998 amendment by Ch. 139, rewrote subsec. A, par. 1, which had read:

"1. The state board shall submit to the auditor general proposed rules consistent with the procurement practices prescribed in title 41, chapter 23, modifying the provisions for public notice of invitation for bids to allow a governing board to give public notice of the invitation for bids by publication in the official newspaper of the county as defined in § 11–255, modifying the provisions relating to disposal of materials to comply with § 15–342, paragraph 18, providing for governing board delegation of procurement authority and modifying as necessary other provisions which the state board determines are not appropriate for school districts, for procurement of construction, materials or services when the total procurement exceeds thirty thousand dollars in total cost. The rules shall include provisions specifying that school districts are not required to engage in competitive bidding in order to make the decision to participate in programs pursuant to § 15–382 for the purchase of health and accident insurance and related employee benefits when such programs comply with competitive bidding requirements for the subsequent purchase of reinsurance or for the joint purchase of insurance or reinsurance. The rules for procurement of construction projects shall include provisions specifying that surety bonds furnished as bid security and performance and payment bonds shall be executed and furnished as required by title 34, chapter 2."

Laws 1998, Ch. 139, § 6, provides:

"**Sec. 6. Effective date**

"This act is effective from and after September 30, 1998."

The 1999 amendment by Ch. 238 inserted subsecs. E and F; redesignated former subsec. E as subsec. G; rewrote subsec. G; inserted subsec. H; redesignated former subsecs. F and G as subsecs. I and J, respectively; in subsec. I, deleted "In fiscal year 1998-1999 and each fiscal year thereafter," from the beginning; and rewrote subsec. J. Prior to revision, subsecs. G and J (former subsecs. E and G) had read:

"**E.** The attorney general may seek relief for any violation of this section or rule adopted pursuant to this section through any appropriate civil action including an action to enjoin a threatened or pending violation of this section.

"**G.** For the purposes of this section, "total cost" means the cost of all materials and services, including the cost of labor performed by employees of the school district, for all construction as provided in subsection A of this section."

Laws 1999, Ch. 238, § 3, provides:

"**Sec. 3. Purpose and applicability**

"This act is intended to clarify applicable law and, where necessary, to provide a means for enhanced oversight and public confidence in the action of school districts, nonexempt charter schools, and school purchasing cooperatives and their officers, employees and governing board members. This act restates the body of law currently applicable to procurement related activities of these entities and public officials, which laws currently apply to school procurement. In addition, this act establishes new provisions relating to school procurement to augment existing law as a means of ensuring public confidence in the procurement related activities undertaken on behalf of school districts, nonexempt charter schools and school purchasing cooperatives in this state."

The 2000 amendment by Ch. 135 inserted, in two places in subsec. A, par. 1, "requests for proposals and requests for qualifications"; added, to the end of the third sentence of the same paragraph, "or 6, as applicable"; rewrote the introductory paragraph of subsec. B; substituted, in the first sentence in subsec. F, "school purchasing cooperatives" for "school district purchasing cooperatives"; added subsec. J, relating to rules and reports and subsec. K, providing for procedures pending adoption of rules; redesignated former subsec. J as subsec. L, and substituted, as par. 2 of subsec. L as so redesignated, " 'School purchasing cooperative' means a an entity engaged in cooperative purchasing as defined in § 41-2631" for " 'School purchasing cooperative' means a school purchasing cooperative as defined in section 41-2631, paragraph 1". Prior to amendment by Laws 2000, Ch. 135, the introductory paragraph of subsec. B read:

"**B.** After the bids are opened and the award is made, the governing board shall make available for public inspection all information and bids submitted by bidders, findings and other information considered in determining whose bid conforms to the invitation for bids and will be the most advantageous with respect to price, conformity to the specifications and other factors. The invitation for bids shall include a notice that all information and bids submitted by bidders will be made available for public inspection. The rules adopted by the state board shall prohibit the use in connection with procurement of specifications in any way proprietary to one supplier unless the specification includes all of the following:".

The 2000 amendment by Ch. 233 inserted subsec. A, par. 2(g); deleted "district" in the phrase "nonexempt charter schools and school district purchasing cooperatives" in subsec. F; and rewrote subsec. J, par. 2, which had read:

"2. "School purchasing cooperative" means a school purchasing cooperative as defined in § 41-2631, paragraph 1."

For applicability provision of Laws 2000, Ch. 233, see Historical and Statutory Notes following § 32-1129.

The 2001 amendment by Ch. 227 inserted references to "construction services" in subsec. A, par. 1 and in subsec. D; deleted ", on or before July 1, 1998," before "shall adopt rules" in subsec. A, par. 2; rewrote subsec. J; and inserted new subsec. L, redesignating existing subsec. L as M, accordingly. Subsection J had read:

"**J.** The state board of education and the auditor general shall adopt rules authorizing school districts to procure construction services by construction-manager-at-risk, design-build and job-order-contracting methods of project delivery. The rules adopted shall require each school district that uses construction-manager-at-risk, design-build or job-order-contracting to procure construction services to submit, on or before January 15 of each year, a report to the secretary of state on the benefits associated with the use of such procurement methods. The report shall include the number of projects completed in the preceding calendar year using that procurement method, the cost and description of each project and an estimate of any cost savings or other benefits realized through the use of that procurement method."

The 2002 amendment by Ch. 240, in subsec. A, par. 1, in the second sentence, substituted "the services necessary to administer the program or for" for "other than the joint"; in subsec. D, in the second sentence, substituted "subsection" for "section"; and deleted subsec. K and redesignated former subsecs. L and M as subsecs. K and L, accordingly. Prior to the amendment, former subsec. K read:

"**K.** Until the rules prescribed in subsection J of this section are adopted, school districts may procure construction services by the construction-manager-at-risk, design-build and job-order-contracting methods of project delivery as provided in title 41, chapter 23, except that the rules adopted by the director of the department of administration do not apply. Any procurement commenced pursuant to this subsection may be completed pursuant to this subsection regardless of the adoption of rules by the state board of education and the auditor general."

The 2003 amendment by Ch. 179, inserted subsec. A, par. 3 and redesignated pars. 4 to 6 accordingly.

The 2003 amendment by Ch. 215, in subsec. J, in the first and second sentences, inserted ", qualified select bidders list".

Laws 2003, Ch. 215, § 5, eff. May 14, 2003, provides:

"**Sec. 5. Retroactivity**

"This act is effective retroactively to August 22, 2002."

The 2004 amendment by Ch. 50, inserted new subsec. L and redesignated existing subsec. L as M, accordingly.

Reviser's Notes:

1984 Note. The amendment made by Laws 1984, Ch. 251, § 6 was inconsistent and incompatible with Laws 1984, Ch. 80, § 1 and therefore could not be blended.

1985 Note. In the section heading "report;" was added after "rules;" pursuant to authority of § 41-1304.02.

1987 Note. Prior to the 1989 amendment, this section contained the amendments made by Laws 1987, Ch. 266, § 1, and Ch. 293, § 1 which were blended together pursuant to authority of § 41-1304.03.

1991 Note. Prior to the 1994 amendment, this section contained the amendments made by Laws 1991, Ch. 138, sec. 1 and Ch. 319, sec. 1 that were blended together pursuant to authority of § 41-1304.03.

1997 Note. Pursuant to authority of § 41-1304.02, subsection F was relettered as subsection G and subsection G was relettered as subsection F.

1999 Note. Pursuant to authority of § 41-1304.02, "Procurement practices of school districts; definitions" was substituted for the previous section heading and in subsection F, first sentence "shall" was transposed to follow "accountant,".

2000 Note. Prior to the 2001 amendment, this section contained the amendments made by Laws 2000, Ch. 135, sec. 1 and Ch. 233, sec. 1 that were blended together pursuant to authority of § 41-1304.03.

2003 Note. Prior to the 2004 amendment, this section contained the amendments made by Laws 2003, Ch. 179, sec. 1 and Ch. 215, sec. 1 that were blended together pursuant to authority of § 41-1304.03.

2004 Note. Pursuant to authority of § 41-1304.02, in subsection L, paragraph 4 the spelling of "cost effective" was corrected.

§ 15-213.01. Procurement practices; guaranteed energy cost savings contracts; definitions

A. Notwithstanding § 15-213, subsection A, a school district may contract for the procurement of a guaranteed energy cost savings contract with a qualified provider through a competitive sealed proposal process as provided by the procurement practices adopted by the state board of education. To the extent the qualified provider subcontracts with contractors who will be involved in any construction associated with the guaranteed energy cost savings contract, the qualified provider must follow the provisions of § 41-2533 in selecting these contractors.

B. A school district may enter into a guaranteed energy cost savings contract with a qualified provider if it determines that the amount it would spend on the energy cost savings measures recommended in the proposal would not exceed the amount to be saved in energy and operational costs within ten years after the date installation or implementation is complete, if the recommendations in the proposal are followed.

C. The school district shall use objective criteria in selecting the qualified provider including the cost of the contract, the energy and operational cost savings, the net projected energy savings, the quality of the technical approach, the quality of the project management plan, the financial solvency of the qualified provider and the experience of the qualified provider with projects of similar size and scope. The school district shall set forth each criterion with its respective numerical weighting in the request for proposal.

D. In selecting a contractor to perform any construction work related to performing the guaranteed energy cost savings contract, the qualified provider may develop and use a prequalification process for contractors wishing to bid on this work. These prequalifications may require the contractor to demonstrate that the contractor is adequately bonded to perform the work and that the contractor has not failed to perform on a prior job. The qualified provider may use performance specifications in soliciting bids from contractors.

E. An in-depth feasibility study shall be performed by the selected qualified provider in order to establish the exact scope of the guaranteed energy cost savings contract, the fixed cost savings guarantee amount and the methodology for determining actual savings. This report shall be reviewed and approved by the school district prior to the actual installation of any equipment. The qualified provider shall transmit a copy of the approved in-depth feasibility study to the superintendent of public instruction.

F. The guaranteed energy savings contract shall require that a qualified provider perform an energy audit of the facility or facilities one year after the energy cost savings measures are installed or implemented and every three years thereafter for the length of the contract. The qualified provider shall transmit a copy of the audit to the superintendent of public instruction. The qualified provider shall pay the cost of the audit. In determining whether the projected energy savings calculations have been met, the energy or operational cost savings shall be computed by comparing the energy baseline before installation or implementation of the energy cost savings measures with the energy consumed and operational costs avoided after installation or implementation of the energy cost savings measures. The qualified provider and the school district may agree to make modifications to the energy baseline only for any of the following:

1. Changes in utility rates.

2. Changes in the number of days in the utility billing cycle.

3. Changes in the square footage of the facility.

4. Changes in the operational schedule of the facility.

5. Changes in facility temperature.

6. Significant changes in the weather.

7. Significant changes in the amount of equipment or lighting utilized in the facility.

G. The information to develop the energy baseline shall be derived from actual energy measurements or shall be calculated from energy measurements at the facility where energy cost savings measures are to be installed or implemented. The measurements shall be taken in the year preceding the installation or implementation of energy cost savings measures.

H. When submitting a proposal for the installation of equipment, the qualified provider shall include information on the projected energy savings associated with each proposed energy cost savings measure.

I. A school district, or two or more school districts, may enter into an installment payment contract or lease-purchase agreement with a qualified provider for the purchase and installation or implementation of energy cost savings measures. The guaranteed energy cost savings contract may provide for payments over a period of not more than ten years. The contract shall provide that all payments, except obligations on termination of the contract before its expiration, shall be made over time.

J. The guaranteed energy cost savings contract shall include a written guarantee of the qualified provider that either the energy or operational costs savings, or both, will meet or exceed the costs of the energy cost savings measures within ten years. The qualified provider shall reimburse the school district for any shortfall of guaranteed energy cost savings on an annual basis.

K. The school district may obtain any required financing as part of the original competitive sealed proposal process.

L. A qualified provider that is awarded the contract shall give a sufficient bond to the school district for its faithful performance of the equipment installment.

M. When selecting subcontractors to perform construction work, the qualified provider is required to make public information in the subcontractor's bids only if the qualified provider is awarded the guaranteed energy savings contract by the school district.

N. This section does not apply to the construction of new buildings.

O. For the purposes of this section:

1. "Construction" means the process of building, altering, repairing, improving or demolishing any school district structure or building, or other public improvements of any kind to any school district real property. Construction does not include the routine operation, routine repair or routine maintenance of existing structures, buildings or real property.

2. "Energy baseline" means a calculation of the amount of energy used in an existing facility before the installation or implementation of the energy cost savings measures.

3. "Energy cost savings measure" means a training program or facility alteration designed to reduce energy consumption or operating costs and may include one or more of the following:

(a) Insulating the building structure or systems in the building.

(b) Storm windows or doors, caulking or weather stripping, multi-glazed windows or door systems, additional glazing, reductions in glass area, or other window and door system modifications that reduce energy consumption.

(c) Automated or computerized energy control systems.

(d) Heating, ventilating or air conditioning system modifications or replacements.

(e) Replacing or modifying lighting fixtures to increase the energy efficiency of the lighting system without increasing the overall illumination of a facility unless an increase in illumination is necessary to conform to the applicable state or local building code for the lighting system after the proposed modifications are made.

(f) Indoor air quality improvements to increase air quality that conform to the applicable state or local building code requirements.

(g) Energy recovery systems.

(h) Installing a new or retrofitting an existing day lighting system.

(i) Any life safety measures that provide long-term operating cost reductions and that comply with state and local codes.

(j) Implementing operation programs through education, training and software that reduce the operating costs.

4. "Guaranteed energy cost savings contract" means a contract for implementing one or more energy cost savings measures.

5. "Operational savings" means reductions in actual budget line items currently being expended or savings realized from the implementation or installation of energy cost savings measures.

6. "Qualified provider" means a person or a business experienced in designing, implementing or installing energy cost savings measures.

Added by Laws 1996, Ch. 212, § 1. Amended by Laws 1999, Ch. 62, § 1; Laws 2003, Ch. 92, § 1.

Historical and Statutory Notes

The repeal of this section by Laws 1996, Ch. 212, § 4, which was to become effective August 1, 1999, was itself repealed by Laws 1999, Ch. 62, § 2.

Reviser's Notes:

1996 Note. Pursuant to authority of § 41-1304.02, in subsection G, last sentence the spelling of "preceding" was corrected.

§ 15-214. Braille literacy; definition

A. The state board of education shall adopt rules to promote braille literacy that:

1. Assure that each blind pupil receives an individualized braille literacy assessment and appropriate educational services resulting from the assessment, establish standards of proficiency and instruction, provide materials in a computer accessible format capable of braille reproduction and require that certified teachers of visually impaired pupils meet braille competencies as specified in this section.

2. Assure that, in developing the individualized written education program for each blind pupil, the presumption shall be that proficiency in braille is essential for that pupil to achieve satisfactory educational progress. Braille instruction and use are not required by this section if, in the course of developing the pupil's individualized education program, all members of the team concur that the pupil's visual impairment does not affect reading and writing performance commensurate with ability. Nothing in this section requires the exclusive use of braille if other special education services are appropriate to the pupil's educational needs. The provision of other appropriate services does not preclude braille use or instruction.

3. Assure that instruction in braille is sufficient to enable each blind pupil to communicate effectively and efficiently in all subject areas with the same level of proficiency expected of the pupil's peers of comparable ability and grade level. The pupil's individualized education program shall specify:

(a) The results of a braille assessment.

(b) The methods by which braille will be implemented.

(c) The date on which braille instruction will begin.

(d) The length of the period of instruction and the frequency and duration of each instructional session.

(e) The level of competency in braille to be achieved by the end of the period of instruction and a description of the objective measures to be used to evaluate the pupil's level of competency.

(f) A list of the appropriate braille materials and equipment needed to allow the pupil to achieve the level of competency specified in the individualized education program.

(g) The rationale for not providing braille if braille is not determined to be an appropriate medium.

4. Assure that the department of education shall require all publishers of textbooks to furnish the department with computer diskettes for literary and nonliterary subjects when diskettes become available for nonliterary subjects, in a standard format approved by the department of education from which braille versions of the textbook can be produced.

5. Assure that teachers certified in the education of blind and visually impaired pupils in this state on or after July 1, 1997 shall be required to demonstrate competence in braille. Competence shall be measured by either:

(a) Successful completion of a nationally validated test, when such a test is available.

(b) Successful completion of a braille test developed in the program in visual impairment at the university of Arizona.

B. As used in this section, "blind pupil" means a pupil who meets one or more of the following conditions:

1. Cannot successfully use vision as a primary and efficient channel for learning.

2. Exhibits such a low degree or amount of visual acuity or visual field that vision is not considered as a primary mode of learning.

3. Has a medically indicated prognosis of visual deterioration.

Added by Laws 1997, Ch. 137, § 2.

Historical and Statutory Notes

Laws 1997, Ch. 137, § 5, provides:

"**Sec. 5. Intent**

"**A.** The purposes of this act are to assure that each blind pupil receives an individualized braille literacy assessment and appropriate educational services resulting from the assessment, to establish standards of proficiency and instruction, to provide materials in a computer accessible format capable of braille reproduction and to require that certified teachers of visually impaired students meet braille competencies as specified in this act.

"B. It is the goal of the legislature to encourage persons who are blind or visually impaired to participate fully in the social and economic life of the state and to engage in remunerative employment. The legislature finds that literacy is essential to achievement of this goal. Furthermore, the legislature finds that literacy for most persons who are blind or visually impaired means the ability to read and write braille with proficiency."

Former § 15-214, added by Laws 1990, Ch. 266, § 2, amended by Laws 1992, Ch. 208, § 1; and Laws 1992, Ch. 349, § 1, which related to an environmental special plate fund, was repealed by Laws 1996, Ch. 243, § 14.

ARTICLE 2. DEPARTMENT OF EDUCATION

§ 15-231. Department of education

A. There is created a department of education.

B. The department shall be administered through:

1. The state board of education which shall be the policy determining body of the department.

2. The superintendent of public instruction in whom all executive, administrative and ministerial functions of the department are vested and who is the executive officer of the state board of education.

C. In addition to any divisions established by law, the superintendent of public instruction may establish such divisions as in the judgment of the superintendent of public instruction are necessary for the proper transaction of the business of the department.

D. The department shall be conducted under the control of the superintendent of public instruction.

Added by Laws 1981, Ch. 1, § 2, eff. Jan. 23, 1981. Amended by Laws 1981, Ch. 163, § 2; Laws 1995, Ch. 268, § 6.

Historical and Statutory Notes

Source:

Laws 1947, Ch. 17, § 3.
Code 1939, Supp.1952, § 54-307.
Laws 1962, Ch. 13, § 2.
Laws 1970, Ch. 175, § 2.
Laws 1970, Ch. 190, § 16.
Laws 1972, Ch. 105, § 3.
A.R.S. former §§ 15-111, 15-1001, 15-1002.
Laws 1978, Ch. 188, § 12.

§ 15-231.01. Public school information hot line; program termination

The department of education shall establish a toll-free telephone number for complaints and requests for information relating to public schools and charter schools, including complaints regarding procurement practices pursuant to § 15-213, subsection H. If appropriate, the department of education shall forward the complaints or refer the complainant to the appropriate state, federal and local agencies for appropriate action. The program established by this section ends on July 1, 2009, pursuant to § 41-3102.

Added by Laws 1999, Ch. 238, § 2.

Historical and Statutory Notes

Reviser's Notes:

1999 Note. Pursuant to authority of § 41-1304.02, in the section heading "hot line; program termination" was substituted for "hotline" and in the first sentence the spelling of "toll free" was corrected.

§ 15–231.02. School safety clearinghouse; program termination

A. The department of education shall Establish a central clearinghouse within the department for information concerning school safety. The department shall employ at least one person to carry out the duties of the clearinghouse. The clearinghouse shall:

1. Respond to requests from the public for information about school safety.

2. Serve as the central repository for violence prevention curriculum, programs and strategies relating to school safety.

3. Establish and maintain a school violence prevention web site for school and public use.

B. The program established by this section ends on July 1, 2010 pursuant to § 41–3102.

Added by Laws 2000, Ch. 226, § 2, eff. April 10, 2000.

§ 15–231.03. School safety survey report

On or before September 15, 2007, and every four years thereafter, the department of education shall conduct a random survey of school districts on school safety and submit a written report that summarizes the results to the governor, the president of the senate and the speaker of the house of representatives and submit a copy of this report to the Arizona state library, archives and public records.

Added by Laws 2000, Ch. 226, § 2, eff. April 10, 2000. Amended by Laws 2003, Ch. 104, § 9.

§ 15–232. Division of adult education; duties

There is established a division of adult education within the department of education, under the jurisdiction of the state board for vocational and technological education, which shall:

1. Prescribe a course of study for adult education in school districts.

2. Make available and supervise the program of adult education in other institutions and agencies of this state.

3. Adopt rules for the establishment and conduct of classes for immigrant and adult education, including the teaching of English to foreigners, in school districts.

4. Devise plans for establishment and maintenance of classes for immigrant and adult education, including the teaching of English to foreigners, stimulate and correlate the Americanization work of various agencies, including governmental, and perform such other duties as may be prescribed by the state board of education and the superintendent of public instruction.

5. Prescribe a course of study to provide training for adults to continue their basic education to the degree of passing a general equivalency diploma test or an equivalency test approved by the state board of education.

Added by Laws 1981, Ch. 1, § 2, eff. Jan. 23, 1981. Amended by Laws 1991, Ch. 218, § 3, eff. June 10, 1991.

Historical and Statutory Notes

Source:

Laws 1921, Ch. 140, §§ 1, 2.
Rev. Code 1928, § 1064.
Code 1939, § 54-806.
A.R.S. former § 15-1041.
Laws 1972, Ch. 104, § 2.

§ 15-233. Night schools for teaching English

The governing board of a school district in which there are fifteen or more persons over sixteen years of age who either do not read and write or speak the English language who desire to attend a night school may establish a night school for teaching the English language, American ideals and an understanding of American institutions.

Added by Laws 1981, Ch. 1, § 2, eff. Jan. 23, 1981.

Historical and Statutory Notes

Source:

Laws 1918, Ch. 10, § 1.
Rev. Code 1928, § 1065.
Code 1939, § 54-807.
A.R.S. former § 15-1042.

§ 15-234. Appropriations for adult education; eligibility; definition

A. Any appropriation made to the state board of education or department of education for the purposes of adult education may be expended for costs to the department of activities related to adult education including the costs of operating the division of adult education. In addition, any of the monies may be allocated to an adult education provider as provided in subsections B and C of this section.

B. An adult education provider which offers a course of study for adult education under § 15-232 is eligible for allocation of funds pursuant to subsection C of this section from the state board of education if the district or county offering such course meets all applicable standards established under rules or regulations of the state board.

C. The state board of education may allocate from its available appropriation for adult education any amount it deems appropriate for the use of an eligible adult education provider to compensate for costs of conducting the course of study of adult education based on an application which shall include a budget and other criteria as established by the state board of education. This application must be approved by the state board of education prior to the commencement of classes or courses of study if the applicant wishes to be compensated. Compensation shall be limited to the approved amount in the application.

D. For purposes of this section, "adult education provider" means a school district, community college district, correctional facility or community-based organization, an institution serving educationally disadvantaged adults, or any other institution that receives public funds to provide adult education services.

Added by Laws 1981, Ch. 1, § 2, eff. Jan. 23, 1981. Amended by Laws 1993, Ch. 202, § 2, eff. April 21, 1993; Laws 1995, Ch. 268, § 7; Laws 2002, Ch. 89, § 1.

Historical and Statutory Notes

Source:

Laws 1972, Ch. 104, § 3.
A.R.S. former § 15-1043.

Reviser's Notes:

1993 Note. Pursuant to authority of § 41-1304.02, in the section heading "of districts and counties" was deleted and "; definition" was added.

§ 15-235. Division of special education; director; duties; qualifications; advisory committee; members

A. A division of special education is established to carry out this section, § 15-236 and chapter 7, article 4 of this title [1] subject to the superintendent of public instruction.

B. There shall be at least one director of the division of special education.

C. The director or directors shall carry out this section, § 15-236 and chapter 7, article 4 of this title and the duties prescribed by the state board of education relating to the administration of this section, § 15-236 and chapter 7, article 4 of this title.

D. The division of special education may review special education programs, including placement of pupils, to determine that program, evaluation and placement procedures comply with §§ 15-766 and 15-767 and the rules approved by the state board of education.

E. Only a person who is experienced in special education is eligible for appointment as a director of the division of special education.

F. A special education advisory committee is established that shall advise and consult with the state board of education, the superintendent of public instruction and the director or directors of the division of special education and that shall engage in other activities as are provided in this section. The advisory committee shall be composed pursuant to the requirements of 20 United States Code § 1412(A)(21)(B) and (C). The state board of education shall appoint the members of the advisory committee for staggered three year terms. Vacancies shall be filled for the unexpired term in the same manner as original appointments.

G. The advisory committee shall have a minimum of two meetings a year.

H. The advisory committee annually shall elect its own chairman and vice-chairman. The state board of education shall regularly submit, as part of its budget request, any item or items sufficient to cover expenses of the operation of the advisory committee, and of its members in connection with their attendance at meetings of the advisory committee and other advisory committee activities.

Added by Laws 1981, Ch. 1, § 2, eff. Jan. 23, 1981. Amended by Laws 1981, Ch. 314, § 3; Laws 1995, Ch. 268, § 8; Laws 2000, Ch. 236, § 2, eff. April 12, 2000.

[1] Section 15-761 et seq.

Historical and Statutory Notes

Source:

Laws 1970, Ch. 169, § 3.
A.R.S. former § 15-1012.
Laws 1973, Ch. 181, § 4.

Laws 1975, Ch. 140, § 1.
Laws 1976, Ch. 165, § 2.

§ 15–236. Cost study of special education programs; program and fiscal audits

A. The department of education shall by December 1, 1981 and every two years thereafter complete a cost study of special education programs. Such study shall include, but is not limited to, the cost of providing special education programs to pupils prescribed by § 15–761.

B. The department of education shall conduct program and fiscal audits of selected district special education programs. The audits shall be designed to determine the degree of compliance with existing statutes and regulations and the appropriate placement of students in special education programs. A report of the findings of such audits shall be completed on or before January 3 of each year. If the department of education determines that a child has been inappropriately placed in a special education program of a school district, the district's weighted student count for educational support services for students in group B as provided in § 15–943 shall be recomputed and the district's entitlement to state aid adjusted accordingly.

C. For each fiscal year the department of education shall request a separate line item appropriation for program and fiscal audits of special education programs in the budget estimate submitted pursuant to § 35–113.

Added by Laws 1981, Ch. 1, § 2, eff. Jan. 23, 1981.

Historical and Statutory Notes

Source:

Laws 1975, Ch. 140, § 3.
A.R.S. former § 15–1018.
Laws 1976, Ch. 165, § 5.
Laws 1976, Ch. 185, § 3.
Laws 1977, Ch. 20, § 3.
Laws 1977, Ch. 89, § 7.
Laws 1980, 2nd S.S., Ch. 9, § 41.

§ 15–237. Publications; production revolving fund

A. The department of education may make available to the public at a reasonable cost publications produced by the department. Each separate production of a department publication shall contain a statement as to the number of copies produced, the total production cost and the cost of production per copy. Monies obtained by the sale of publications shall be deposited in the department's production revolving fund for producing further publications.

B. There is established a department of education production revolving fund for use for expenses incurred for producing and distributing publications of the department.

C. The department of education production revolving fund shall be established as a separate account on the books of the department of education.

D. Monies of the department of education production revolving fund shall not revert to the state general fund.

Added by Laws 1981, Ch. 1, § 2, eff. Jan. 23, 1981. Amended by Laws 1996, Ch. 284, § 11.

Historical and Statutory Notes

Source:

Laws 1978, Ch. 188, § 2.
A.R.S. former §§ 15-112, 15-113.

§ 15-238. Statewide student estimate

Before February 15 of each year the department of education shall submit to the economic estimates commission the total estimated statewide number of students determined for the current year using the unit of measurement prescribed in § 15-902, subsection A.

Added by Laws 1996, Ch. 284, § 12.

Historical and Statutory Notes

Former § 15-238, added by Laws 1983, Ch. 182, § 2, relating to an instructional computer software clearinghouse, was repealed by Laws 1995, Ch. 268, § 9.

Reviser's Notes:

1996 Note. Pursuant to authority of § 41-1304.02, the words "for the current year" were transposed to follow "determined".

§ 15-239. School compliance and recognition; accreditation

A. The department of education may:

1. Monitor school districts to ascertain that laws applying to the school districts are implemented as prescribed by law.

2. Adopt a system of recognition for school districts which meet or exceed the requirements of the law which apply to the school districts.

3. Establish standards and procedures for the accreditation of all schools requesting state accreditation.

B. The department of education may adopt guidelines necessary to implement the provisions of this section.

Added by Laws 1989, Ch. 191, § 1.

Historical and Statutory Notes

Reviser's Notes:

1989 Note. Pursuant to authority of § 41-1304.02, in subsection B "section" was substituted for "act".

§ 15-240. Issuance of subpoenas

A. On the request of any person who is investigating, on behalf of the department of education, a complaint alleging that a certificated person has engaged in immoral or unprofessional conduct, the department of education may issue subpoenas compelling the attendance and testimony of witnesses or demanding the production for examination or copying of documents or any physical evidence.

B. The superior court, on application by the department of education or by the person subpoenaed, has jurisdiction to issue an order either:

1. Requiring the person to appear before the department of education or the duly authorized agent to produce evidence relating to the matter under investigation.

2. Revoking, limiting or modifying the subpoena if in the court's opinion the evidence demanded does not relate to conduct that might constitute grounds for disciplinary action, is not relevant to the subject matter of the investigation or does not describe with sufficient particularity the evidence whose production is required.

C. Any failure to obey an order of the court pursuant to subsection B may be punished by the court as contempt.

Added by Laws 1994, Ch. 165, § 2.

§ 15-241. School accountability; schools failing to meet academic standards; failing schools tutoring fund

A. The department of education shall compile an annual achievement profile for each public school.

B. Each school shall submit to the department any data that is required and requested and that is necessary to compile the achievement profile. A school that fails to submit the information that is necessary is not eligible to receive monies from the classroom site fund established by § 15-977.

C. The department shall establish a baseline achievement profile for each school by October 15, 2001. The baseline achievement profile shall be used to determine a standard measurement of acceptable academic progress for each school and a school classification pursuant to subsection G of this section. Any disclosure of educational records compiled by the department of education pursuant to this section shall comply with the family educational and privacy rights act of 1974 (20 United States Code § 1232g).

D. The achievement profile for schools that offer instruction in kindergarten programs and grades one through eight, or any combination of those programs or grades, shall include the following school academic performance indicators:

1. The Arizona measure of academic progress. The department shall compute the extent of academic progress made by the pupils in each school during the course of each year.

2. The Arizona instrument to measure standards test. The department shall compute the percentage of pupils who meet or exceed the standard on the Arizona instrument to measure standards test, as prescribed by the state board of education.

E. The achievement profile for schools that offer instruction in grades nine through twelve, or any combination of those grades, shall include the following school academic performance indicators:

1. The Arizona instrument to measure standards test. The department shall compute the percentage of pupils pursuant to subsection F of this section who meet or exceed the standard on the Arizona instrument to measure standards test, as prescribed by the state board of education.

2. The annual dropout rate.

3. The annual graduation rate.

F. Subject to final adoption by the state board of education, the department shall determine the criteria for each school classification using a research based methodology. The methodology shall include the performance of pupils at all achievement levels, account for pupil mobility, account for the distribution of pupil achievement at each school and include longitudinal indicators of academic performance. For the purposes of this subsection, "research based methodology" means the systematic and objective application of statistical and quantitative research principles to determine a standard measurement of acceptable academic progress for each school.

G. The achievement profile shall be used to determine a school classification that designates each school as one of the following:

1. An excelling school.
2. A highly performing school.
3. A performing school.
4. An underperforming school.
5. A school failing to meet academic standards.

H. The classification for each school and the criteria used to determine classification pursuant to subsection F of this section shall be included on the school report card prescribed in § 15–746.

I. Subject to final adoption by the state board of education, the department of education shall develop a parallel achievement profile for accommodation schools, alternative schools as defined by the state board of education and schools with a student count of fewer than one hundred pupils.

J. If a school is designated as an underperforming school, within ninety days after receiving notice of the designation, the governing board shall develop an improvement plan for the school, submit a copy of the plan to the superintendent of public instruction and supervise the implementation of the plan. The plan shall include necessary components as identified by the state board of education. Within thirty days after submitting the improvement plan to the superintendent of public instruction, the governing board shall hold a special public meeting in each school that has been designated as an underperforming school and shall present the respective improvement plans that have been developed for each school. The school district governing board, within thirty days of receiving notice of the designation, shall provide written notification of the classification to each residence within the attendance area of the school. The notice shall explain the improvement plan process and provide information regarding the public meeting required by this subsection.

K. A school that has not submitted an improvement plan pursuant to subsection J of this section is not eligible to receive monies from the classroom site fund established by § 15–977 for every day that a plan has not been received by the superintendent of public instruction within the time specified in subsection J of this section plus an additional ninety days. The state board of education shall require the superintendent of the school district to testify before the board and explain the reasons that an improvement plan for that school has not been submitted.

L. If a charter school is designated as an underperforming school, within thirty days the school shall notify the parents of the students attending the school of the classification. The notice shall explain the improvement plan process and provide information regarding the public meeting required by this subsection. Within ninety days of receiving the classification, the charter holder shall present an improvement plan to the charter sponsor at a public meeting and submit a copy of the plan to the superintendent of public instruction. The improvement plan shall include necessary components as identified by the state board of education. For every day that an improvement plan is not received by the superintendent of public instruction, the school is not eligible to receive monies from the classroom site fund established by § 15–977 for ninety days plus every day that a plan is not received. The charter holder shall appear before the sponsoring board and explain why the improvement plan has not been submitted.

M. The department of education shall establish an appeals process, to be approved by the state board of education, for a school to appeal data used to determine the achievement profile of the school. The criteria established shall be based on mitigating factors and may include a visit to the school site by the department of education.

N. If a school remains classified as an underperforming school for a third consecutive year, the department of education shall visit the school site to confirm the classification data and to review the implementation of the school's improvement plan. The school shall be classified as failing to meet academic standards unless an alternate classification is made after an appeal pursuant to subsection M of this section.

O. The school district governing board, within thirty days of receiving notice of the school failing to meet academic standards classification, shall provide written notification of the classification to each residence in the attendance area of the school. The notice shall explain the improvement plan process and provide information regarding the public meeting required by subsection R of this section.

P. The superintendent of public instruction, based on need, shall assign a solutions team to an underperforming school or a school failing to meet academic standards comprised of master teachers, fiscal analysts and curriculum assessment experts who are certified by the state board of education as Arizona academic standards technicians. The department of education may hire or contract with administrators, principals and teachers who have demonstrated experience with the characteristics and situations in an underperforming school or a school failing to meet academic standards and may use these personnel as part of the solutions team. The team shall work with staff at the school to assist in curricula alignment and shall instruct teachers on how to increase pupil academic progress, considering the school's achievement profile. The team shall select two master teachers to be employed by the school. The solutions team shall consider the existing improvement plan to assess the need for changes to curriculum, professional development and resource allocation.

Q. The parent or the guardian of the pupil may apply, either to the school district or the department of education, in a manner determined by the department of education for reimbursement from the failing schools tutoring fund established by this section. The school may apply to the state board of education for grants from the funds provided pursuant to § 42–5029, subsection E, paragraph 7 to provide supplemental instruction. Pupils attending a school designated as an underperforming school or a school failing to meet academic standards may select an alternative tutoring program in academic standards from a provider that is certified by the state board of education. To qualify, the provider must guarantee in writing a stated level of academic improvement for the pupil that includes a timeline for improvement that is agreed to by the parent or guardian of the pupil and the provider shall agree to refund to the state the standards assistance grant monies if the guaranteed level of academic improvement is not met.

R. Within sixty days of receiving notification of designation as a school failing to meet academic standards, the school district governing board shall evaluate needed changes to the existing improvement plan for the school, consider recommendations from the solutions team, submit a copy of the plan to the superintendent of public instruction and supervise the implementation of the plan. Within thirty days after submitting the improvement plan to the superintendent of public instruction, the governing board shall hold a public meeting in each school that has been designated as a school failing to meet academic standards and shall present the respective improvement plans that have been developed for each school.

S. A school that has not submitted an improvement plan pursuant to subsection R of this section is not eligible to receive monies from the classroom site fund established by § 15–977 for every day that a plan has not been received by the superintendent of public instruction within the time specified in subsection R of this section plus an additional ninety days. The state board of education shall require the superintendent of the school district to testify before the board and explain the reasons that an improvement plan for that school has not been submitted.

T. If a charter school is designated as a school failing to meet academic standards, the department of education shall immediately notify the charter school's sponsor. The charter school's sponsor shall either take action to restore the charter school to acceptable performance or revoke the charter school's charter. Within thirty days the school shall notify the parents of the students attending the school of the classification and of any pending public meetings to review the issue.

U. A school that has been designated as a school failing to meet academic standards shall be evaluated by the department of education to determine if the school failed to properly implement its school improvement plan, the alignment of the curriculum with academic standards, teacher training, budget prioritization or other proven strategies to improve academic performance. After visiting the school site pursuant to subsection N of this section, the department of education shall submit to the state board of education a recommendation to proceed pursuant to subsections P, Q and R of this section or that the school be subject to a public hearing to determine if the school failed to properly implement its improvement plan and the reasons for the department's recommendation.

V. If the department does recommend a public hearing, the state board of education shall meet and may provide by a majority vote at the public hearing for the continued operation of the school as allowed by this subsection. The state board of education shall determine whether governmental, nonprofit and private organizations may submit applications to the state board to fully or partially manage the school. The state board's determination shall include:

1. If and to what extent the local governing board may participate in the operation of the school including personnel matters.

2. If and to what extent the state board of education shall participate in the operation of the school.

3. Resource allocation pursuant to subsection X of this section.

4. Provisions for the development and submittal of a school improvement plan to be presented in a public meeting at the school.

5. A suggested time frame for the alternative operation of the school.

W. The state board shall periodically review the status of a school that is operated by an organization other than the school district governing board to determine whether the operation of the school should be returned to the school district governing board. Before the state board makes a determination, the state board or its designee shall meet with the school district governing board or its designee to determine the time frame, operational considerations and the appropriate continuation of existing improvements that are necessary to assure a smooth transition of authority from the other organization back to the school district governing board.

X. If an alternative operation plan is provided pursuant to subsection V of this section, the state board of education shall pay for the operation of the school and shall adjust the school district's student count pursuant to § 15-902, soft capital allocation pursuant to § 15-962, capital outlay revenue limit pursuant to § 15-961, base support level pursuant to § 15-943, monies distributed from the classroom site fund established in § 15-977 and transportation support level pursuant to § 15-945 to accurately reflect any reduction in district services that are no longer provided to that school by the district. The state board of education may modify the school district's revenue control limit, the district support level and the general budget limit calculated pursuant to § 15-947 by an amount that corresponds to this reduction in services. The state board of education shall retain the portion of state aid that would otherwise be due the school district for the school and shall distribute that portion of state aid directly to the organization that contracts with the state board of education to operate the school.

Y. If the state board of education determines that a charter school failed to properly implement its improvement plan, the sponsor of the charter school shall revoke the charter school's charter.

Z. If there are more than two schools in a district and more than one-half, or in any case more than five, of the schools in the district are designated as schools failing to meet academic standards for more than two consecutive years, in the next election of members of the governing board the election ballot shall contain the following statement immediately above the listing of governing board candidates:

Within the last five years, (number of schools) schools in the ________ school district have been designated as "schools failing to meet academic standards" by the superintendent of public instruction.

AA. At least twice each year the department of education shall publish in a newspaper of general circulation in each county of this state a list of schools that are designated as schools failing to meet academic standards.

BB. The failing schools tutoring fund is established consisting of monies collected pursuant to § 42–5029, subsection E as designated for this purpose. The department of education shall administer the fund.

Added by Laws 2000, 5th S.S., Ch. 1, § 3. Amended by Laws 2002, Ch. 284, § 1; Laws 2003, Ch. 147, § 1; Laws 2004, Ch. 34, § 1.

Historical and Statutory Notes

Laws 2000, 5th S.S., Ch. 1, §§ 66 and 67, provide:

"**Sec. 66. Delayed implementation**

"This act shall not be implemented until from and after May 31, 2001.

"**Sec. 67. Conditional enactment**

"This act does not become effective unless the qualified electors of this state in the general election that will be held in November, 2000 approve an increase in state transaction privilege tax rates of six-tenths of one per cent in order to fund the provisions of this act."

Proposition 301, approved by the electors at the Nov. 7, 2000 general election, effective Nov. 27, 2000, included a provision increasing the state transaction privilege tax rate six-tenths of one per cent. Therefore, the conditions of the 5th S.S. Ch. 1 were met, and the act became effective.

Laws 2002, Ch. 284, §§ 2 and 3, provide:

"**Sec. 2. Report; purpose**

"The department of education shall submit an annual report to the legislature on the average progress of pupils expressed as a percentage of one year's academic progress and shall provide a copy of this report to the chairpersons of the senate and the house of representatives education committees. The department of education shall also submit an annual report to the legislature on the actual versus the predicted academic performance of schools based on school level, socioeconomic variables such as demographics and income and shall provide a copy of this report to the chairpersons of the senate and the house of representatives education committees. The publication of these reports is subject to the availability of funds and shall not interfere with other state or federal reporting requirements.

"**Sec. 3. Delayed repeal**

"Section 2 of this act, relating to reports on the average progress of pupils and the academic performance of schools, is repealed from and after December 31, 2004."

Reviser's Notes:

2002 Note. Pursuant to authority of § 41–1304.02, in the section heading "; failing schools" was removed.

2003 Note. Pursuant to authority of § 41–1304.02, in the section heading "; fund" was added.

ARTICLE 3. SUPERINTENDENT OF PUBLIC INSTRUCTION

§ 15–251. Powers and duties

The superintendent of public instruction shall:

1. Superintend the schools of this state.

2. Request the auditor general to investigate when necessary the accounts of school monies kept by any state, county or district officer.

3. Subject to supervision by the state board of education, apportion to the several counties the monies to which each county is entitled for the year. Apportionment shall be made as provided in chapter 9 of this title.[1]

4. Direct the work of all employees of the board who shall be employees of the department of education.

5. Execute, under the direction of the state board of education, the policies which have been decided upon by the state board.

6. Direct the performance of executive, administrative or ministerial functions by the department of education or divisions or employees thereof.

Added by Laws 1981, Ch. 1, § 2, eff. Jan. 23, 1981. Amended by Laws 1982, Ch. 332, § 4; Laws 1991, Ch. 218, § 4, eff. June 10, 1991; Laws 1995, Ch. 268, § 10.

[1] Section 15-901 et seq.

Historical and Statutory Notes

Source:

Laws 1912, Ch. 77, § 12.
Civ. Code 1913, § 2705.
Laws 1922, Ch. 35, §§ 39, 41, 42, 154.
Rev. Code 1928, § 990.
Code 1939, § 54-201.
A.R.S. former §§ 15-121, 15-121.01.
Laws 1957, Ch. 94, § 1.
Laws 1960, Ch. 127, § 3.
Laws 1968, Ch. 97, § 1.
Laws 1968, Ch. 177, § 6.
Laws 1969, Ch. 21, § 1.
Laws 1970, Ch. 175, §§ 3, 4.
Laws 1974, 1st S.S., Ch. 3, § 1.
Laws 1980, 2nd S.S., Ch. 9, § 7.

Laws 1989, Ch. 273, § 26, effective June 26, 1989, provides:

"**Sec. 26. Report to the legislature**

"By January 1, 1992 the superintendent of public instruction shall submit a report to the speaker of the house of representatives and the president of the senate on the adequacy of funding for programs for limited English proficient pupils."

§ 15-252. Powers and duties; publications; payment of claims for printing

A. The superintendent of public instruction shall:

1. Print as needed in pamphlet form the laws relating to schools, including model forms of which the superintendent is unable to supply blanks, and supply copies of the pamphlets to school officers and teachers, school libraries and the Arizona state library, archives and public records.

2. Prepare, print and distribute pamphlets on subjects the state board of education directs, including school sanitation, school architecture and an enumeration of the school holidays established by law.

3. Prepare, print and distribute through the county school superintendents blank forms and school registers, with instructions and rules as to their use, to teachers and officers charged with administration of laws pertaining to schools.

4. Print and distribute the courses of study prescribed by the state board of education.

5. Prepare and print blank forms for teachers' certificates.

B. Claims for the printing of laws and reports of the superintendent shall be approved by the superintendent and paid as other claims against the state are paid from appropriations for the state board of education.

Added by Laws 1981, Ch. 1, § 2, eff. Jan. 23, 1981. Amended by Laws 2000, Ch. 88, § 18.

Historical and Statutory Notes

Source:

Laws 1912, Ch. 77, § 12.
Civ. Code 1913, § 2705.
Laws 1922, Ch. 154, §§ 39, 41, 42, 154.
Rev. Code 1928, § 990.
Code 1939, § 54-201.
A.R.S. former § 15-122.
Laws 1960, Ch. 127, § 4.
Laws 1976, Ch. 104, § 14.
Laws 1978, Ch. 170, § 2.

§ 15-253. Legal opinions relating to school matters

A. The superintendent of public instruction shall:

1. Furnish copies of the attorney general opinions, including opinions of the county attorneys which have been submitted to the attorney general for review as provided in subsection B, relating to school matters to all county attorneys, county school superintendents and to other interested persons who request copies.

2. Require each county school superintendent to furnish copies of all attorney general opinions relating to school matters to all school districts in his county.

B. For the purposes set forth in subsection A, the attorney general shall promptly furnish copies of opinions relating to school matters to the superintendent of public instruction. Each county attorney shall promptly transmit a copy of his opinion relating to school matters to the attorney general who shall concur, revise or decline to review the opinion of the county attorney. If the attorney general does not concur, revise or decline to review the county attorney's opinion within sixty days from its receipt, the opinion shall be deemed affirmed. The opinion of the attorney general shall prevail.

Added by Laws 1981, Ch. 1, § 2, eff. Jan. 23, 1981.

Historical and Statutory Notes

Source:

Laws 1912, Ch. 77, § 12.
Civ. Code 1913, § 2705.
Laws 1922, Ch. 154, §§ 39, 41, 42, 154.
Rev. Code 1928, § 990.
Code 1939, § 54–201.
A.R.S. former § 15–122.
Laws 1960, Ch. 127, § 4.
Laws 1976, Ch. 104, § 14.
Laws 1978, Ch. 170, § 2.

§ 15–254. Repealed by Laws 1995, Ch. 268, § 11

Historical and Statutory Notes

The repealed section, added by Laws 1981, Ch. 1, § 2, amended by Laws 1993, Ch. 202, § 3, derived from:

Laws 1912, Ch. 77, §§ 117 to 119.
Civ. Code 1913, §§ 2843 to 2845.
Laws 1922, Ch. 35, § 50.
Rev. Code 1928, §§ 1066, 1067.
Code 1939, §§ 54–808, 54–809.
A.R.S. former §§ 15–1031, 15–1032.
Laws 1975, Ch. 140, § 4.

related to patriotic exercises and observance of legal holidays in schools.

§ 15–255. Annual report; contents; definition

A. The superintendent of public instruction shall make a report to the governor and the legislature on or before January 15 each year. The report shall be in printed form.

B. The report shall contain:

1. A full statement of the condition and amount of all funds and property apportioned for the purpose of education.

2. The total current expenditures per pupil and separate per pupil amounts for classroom supplies, classroom instruction excluding classroom supplies, district and school administration, support services-students, and all other support services and operations. These per pupil amounts shall be calculated for the state by type of district or school. The method of calculating these per pupil amounts shall be as prescribed in the uniform system of financial records.

3. The number and grades of schools in each county.

4. The number of children attending schools.

5. The average number of children who have attended the schools during each of the two years previous to July 1 of the year in which the report is made.

6. The number of children attending private schools.

7. The amount of school monies derived from county taxes.

8. The amount of school monies derived other than by county taxes.

9. The amount of federal monies that was received during the previous year and that was specified for Indian education aid and emergency operational aid.

10. The amounts expended for salaries of teachers and superintendents and for building of schools.

11. A statement of plans for the management of schools.

12. Such other information relating to the educational interests of this state as the superintendent deems expedient.

C. In addition to the printed report required by subsections A and B of this section, the superintendent of public instruction shall make available in electronic form a supplemental report that provides detail regarding current expenditures by function code for each individual school district. For purposes of this subsection, "function code" means the function codes defined in the uniform system of financial records provided for in § 15–272.

D. For the purposes of this section "type of district or school" means accommodation school, unified school district, common school district not within the boundaries of a high school district, common school district within the boundaries of a high school district, high school district, joint technological education district and charter school.

Added by Laws 1981, Ch. 1, § 2, eff. Jan. 23, 1981. Amended by Laws 1992, Ch. 305, § 3; Laws 1996, Ch. 284, § 13; Laws 1997, 1st S.S., Ch. 4, § 3; Laws 1999, 1st S.S., Ch. 4, § 3.

Historical and Statutory Notes

Source:

Laws 1912, Ch. 77, § 12.
Civ. Code 1913, § 2705.
Laws 1922, Ch. 35, §§ 39, 41, 42, 154.
Rev. Code 1928, § 54–201.
Code 1939, § 54–201.
A.R.S. former § 15–123.
Laws 1960, Ch. 127, § 5.
Laws 1977, Ch. 119, § 2.

§ 15–256. Waivers; federal education flexibility partnership act

Consistent with the purposes, intent and eligibility requirements of the education flexibility partnership act (20 United States Code § 5891), the superintendent of public instruction may issue to schools and school districts waivers of state statutory requirements related to programs described in 20 United States Code § 5891(b).

Added by Laws 2000, Ch. 166, § 1.

ARTICLE 4. UNIFORM SYSTEM OF FINANCIAL RECORDS

§ 15-271. Duties of auditor general for uniform financial records system; annual report

A. The auditor general shall determine the accounting systems, accounting methods and accounting procedures for utilization by school districts.

B. The auditor general in conjunction with the department of education shall prescribe a uniform system of financial records for utilization by all school districts each fiscal year.

C. The uniform system of financial records prescribed by the auditor general shall:

1. Provide for adjustment in consideration of existing capabilities available at a reasonable cost to school districts.

2. Allow schools to maintain necessary records at a minimum cost.

3. Prescribe guidelines applicable to procurement practices for use by school districts for amounts less than those prescribed in § 15-213, subsection A.

4. Prescribe methods for the apportionment of revenues, including apportionment of various revenues to maintenance and operations, capital outlay and adjacent ways.

5. Prescribe methods for the apportionment of revenues in excess of the revenue control limit in the same manner as the revenues in paragraph 4.

6. Prescribe guidelines for the apportionment of the pupil enrollment and attendance as provided in § 15-808, subsection F.

7. Provide the department of education, the auditor general, the governor and the legislature with sufficient uniform information to assist in determining equitable distribution of state aid to school districts.

8. Provide information including at a minimum:

(a) The student count and maintenance and operation expenditures with separate subsections for regular education programs, special education programs and operating expenditures for pupil transportation.

(b) Capital outlay expenditures.

(c) Debt service and special projects of all school districts.

D. The auditor general shall inform any school district which fails to establish and maintain the uniform system of financial records and shall detail in writing the deficiencies of the school district system giving the district ninety days to correct the deficiencies.

E. The auditor general shall report to the department of education any school district which either fails to establish and maintain the uniform system of financial records prescribed by the auditor general or fails to correct deficiencies in the system within ninety days after receiving notice of the deficiencies.

F. A school district may but shall not be required to maintain or provide financial records other than those prescribed by the auditor general.

Added by Laws 1981, Ch. 1, § 2, eff. Jan. 23, 1981. Amended by Laws 1981, Ch. 69, § 1; Laws 1984, Ch. 80, § 2; Laws 1985, Ch. 31, § 3, eff. April 2, 1985; Laws 1985, Ch. 166, § 2, eff. April 18, 1985; Laws 1986, Ch. 125, § 1, eff. April 18, 1986; Laws 1993, Ch. 202, § 4, eff. April 21, 1993; Laws 1996, Ch. 284, § 14; Laws 1998, Ch. 224, § 1; Laws 2000, 5th S.S., Ch. 1, § 4.

Historical and Statutory Notes

Source:

Laws 1974, 1st S.S., Ch. 3, § 23.
A.R.S. former § 15-1201.04.
Laws 1980, 2nd S.S., Ch. 9, § 58.

Laws 1999, 1st S.S., Ch. 4, § 15, provides:

"**Sec. 15. Charter school financial and compliance audits; financial statement audits; oversight responsibility**

"**A.** Notwithstanding § 15-271, subsection D, Arizona Revised Statutes, or any other law, the state board of education and the state board for charter schools, rather than the auditor general, are responsible for notifying a charter school under the board's jurisdiction if the school has failed to establish and maintain the uniform system of financial records.

"**B.** Notwithstanding § 15-271, subsection E, Arizona Revised Statutes, or any other law, the state board of education and the state board for charter schools, rather than the auditor general, are responsible for reporting to the department of education any charter school under the board's jurisdiction that either fails to establish and maintain the uniform system of financial records that is prescribed by the auditor general or fails to correct deficiencies in the system within ninety days after receiving notice of the deficiencies.

"**C.** Notwithstanding § 15-914, subsection D, Arizona Revised Statutes, or any other law, an independent certified public accountant who conducts an audit pursuant to § 15-914, subsections A, B and C, Arizona Revised Statutes, shall submit a uniform system of financial records compliance questionnaire to the state board that sponsors the audited charter school, rather than to the auditor general.

"**D.** Notwithstanding § 15-914, subsection E, Arizona Revised Statutes, or any other law, contracts for all financial and compliance audits and financial statement audits for charter schools that are sponsored by the state board of education or the state board for charter schools, and the completed audits for those schools, shall be approved by the state board that sponsors the charter school affected rather than by the auditor general.

"**E.** The requirements in subsections A and B of this section do not pertain to exceptions to requirements of the uniform system of financial records that the state board of education or the state board for charter schools include in the charter of a charter school pursuant to § 15-183, subsection E, paragraph 6, Arizona Revised Statutes."

Proposition 301, approved by the electors at the Nov. 7, 2000 general election, effective Nov. 27, 2000, included a provision increasing the state transaction privilege tax rate six-tenths of one per cent. Therefore, the conditions of the 5th S.S. Ch. 1 were met, and the act became effective.

Reviser's Notes:

1998 Note. Pursuant to authority of § 41-1304.02, in subsection C, paragraph 5 the reference to "§ 15-808" was substituted for the reference to "§ 15-802.02" to conform to the reviser's renumbering of that section.

§ 15-272. Duties of department of education for uniform system of financial records

A. The department of education shall advise and consult with the auditor general in the preparation and implementation of a uniform system of financial records.

B. The state board of education shall upon report from the auditor general determine whether school districts are maintaining the uniform system of financial records. If the state board of education determines that a school district is not in compliance with the uniform system of financial records or has failed to correct a deficiency within ninety days after receiving notice from the auditor general, the state board of education may direct the superintendent of public instruction to withhold any portion of state funds to the school district from the date of the determination until such time as the auditor general reports compliance with the uniform system of financial records. The auditor general and the department of education shall assist the school district to achieve compliance during such period.

Added by Laws 1981, Ch. 1, § 2, eff. Jan. 23, 1981. Amended by Laws 1981, Ch. 314, § 4; Laws 1986, Ch. 232, § 26, eff. Jan. 1, 1987; Laws 1987, Ch. 62, § 1; Laws 1997, Ch. 221, § 65; Laws 2000, Ch. 113, § 39; Laws 2002, Ch. 167, § 1.

Historical and Statutory Notes

Source:

Laws 1974, 1st S.S., Ch. 3, § 23.
A.R.S. former § 15–1201.05.

§ 15–272. Duties of department of education for uniform system of financial records

A. The department of education shall advise and consult with the auditor general in the preparation and implementation of a uniform system of financial records.

B. The state board of education shall upon report from the auditor general determine whether a school district is maintaining the uniform system of financial records. If the state board of education determines that a school district is not in compliance with the uniform system of financial records or has failed to correct a deficiency within ninety days after notification by the auditor general, the state board of education may direct the superintendent of

CHAPTER 3

LOCAL GOVERNANCE OF SCHOOLS

ARTICLE 1. COUNTY SCHOOL SUPERINTENDENT

ARTICLE 2. ORGANIZATIONAL POWERS OF SCHOOL DISTRICT GOVERNING BOARDS

ARTICLE 3. POWERS AND DUTIES OF SCHOOL DISTRICT GOVERNING BOARDS

ARTICLE 3.1. DECENTRALIZATION PROCESS

ARTICLE 4. ESTABLISHMENT OF SPECIAL SERVICES

Chapter 3, consisting of Article 1, §§ 15–301 to 15–309, Article 2, §§ 15–321 to 15–329, Article 3, §§ 15–341 to 15–344, Article 4, §§ 15–361 to 15–365, and Article 5, §§ 15–381 to 15–385, was added by Laws 1981, Ch. 1, § 2, effective January 23, 1981.

ARTICLE 1. COUNTY SCHOOL SUPERINTENDENT

§ 15-301. Office of county school superintendent; qualifications; travel expenses

A. A person is eligible for election as county school superintendent if the person holds a basic or standard certificate to teach in the schools of this state.

B. In addition to the salary allowed by law, the county school superintendent is eligible for reimbursement of travel expenses.

C. The office of county school superintendent is designated as a local education service agency for the purpose of serving as an education service agency that is eligible to receive and spend local, state and federal monies to provide programs and services to school districts and charter schools within that county.

D. The office of county school superintendent shall be under the jurisdiction of the elected county school superintendent.

Added by Laws 1981, Ch. 1, § 2, eff. Jan. 23, 1981. Amended by Laws 2002, Ch. 290, § 1.

Historical and Statutory Notes

Source:

Laws 1912, Ch. 77, §§ 16, 20.
Civ.Code 1913, §§ 2708, 2712.
Laws 1927, Ch. 36, § 1.
Rev.Code 1928, § 992.
Laws 1941, Ch. 79, § 1.
Code 1939, Supp. 1952, § 54-301.
A.R.S. former § 11-511.
A.R.S. former § 15-141.
Laws 1980, 2nd S.S., Ch. 9, § 8.

§ 15-302. Powers and duties

A. The county school superintendent shall:

1. Distribute all laws, reports, circulars, instructions and forms which he may receive for the use of school officers.

2. Record all official acts.

3. Appoint governing board members of school districts to fill all vacancies, but the term of the appointment shall be until the next regular election for governing board members, at which time a successor shall be elected to serve the unexpired portion of the term. The county school superintendent may, if he deems it in the best interest of the community, call a special election to fill the vacancies. If an election is called, the newly elected member shall serve for the remainder of the unexpired portion of the term.

4. Make reports, when directed by the superintendent of public instruction, showing matters relating to schools in his county as may be required on the forms furnished by the superintendent of public instruction.

5. Have such powers and perform such duties as otherwise prescribed by law.

6. On or before October 1 of each year, make a report to the superintendent of public instruction showing the amount of monies received from state school funds, special school district taxes and other sources, the total expenditures for school purposes and the balance on hand to the credit of each school district at the close of the school year.

7. Contract with the board of supervisors for the board of supervisors to conduct all regular school district elections.

8. Be responsible, in cooperation with the governing boards and the board of supervisors, for all special school district elections.

9. Maintain teacher and administrator certification records of effective dates and expiration dates of teachers' and administrators' certificates in compliance with guidelines prescribed in the uniform system of financial records for those school districts for which the county school superintendent is the fiscal agent. The county school superintendent shall not draw a warrant in payment of a teacher's, substitute teacher's or administrator's salary unless the teacher, substitute teacher or administrator is legally certified during the fiscal year in which the term for payment is demanded.

10. Notify a school district three years before the expiration of a revenue control limit override that the school district's budget must be adjusted in the final two years of the override pursuant to § 15–481, subsections P and Q, if the voters do not approve another override.

11. In collaboration with the department of education and other state agencies, provide assistance to school districts and charter schools on the use of student data, staff development, curriculum alignment and technology to improve student performance.

12. Assist schools in meeting yearly adequate progress goals as defined by criteria established by the state board of education and implemented by the department of education.

B. At the request of school districts and charter schools, the county school superintendent may provide discretionary programs in addition to the programs prescribed in subsection A.

C. The county school superintendent may provide the services prescribed in subsections A and B in the county or jointly with two or more counties pursuant to title 11, chapter 7, article 3.

D. Each county school superintendent may establish an advisory committee to the office of the county school superintendent.

Added by Laws 1981, Ch. 1, § 2, eff. Jan. 23, 1981. Amended by Laws 1982, Ch. 94, § 1; Laws 1987, Ch. 36, § 1; Laws 1992, Ch. 305, § 4; Laws 1995, Ch. 268, § 12; Laws 2002, Ch. 125, § 1; Laws 2002, Ch. 290, § 2.

Historical and Statutory Notes

Source:

Laws 1912, Ch. 77, §§ 16, 20.
Civ.Code 1913, §§ 2607, 2708, 2712.
Laws 1927, Ch. 36, § 1.
Rev.Code 1928, §§ 885, 992.
Code 1939, § 17–1101.
Laws 1941, Ch. 79, § 1.
Code 1939, Supp. 1952, § 54–301.
A.R.S. former § 11–512.
Laws 1963, Ch. 6, § 1.
Laws 1967, Ch. 104, § 1.
Laws 1972, Ch. 138, § 1.
Laws 1975, Ch. 103, § 1.
Laws 1976, Ch. 165, § 1.
Laws 1977, Ch. 119, § 1.
A.R.S. former § 15–142.
Laws 1980, 2nd S.S., Ch. 9, § 8.

Laws 2002, Ch. 125, § 2, effective August 22, 2002, retroactively effective to July 1, 2000, provides:

"**Sec. 2. Computation of general budget limit for fiscal years 2000–2001 and 2001–2002**

"Notwithstanding § 15–481, subsections P and Q, Arizona Revised Statutes, a unified school district for which fiscal year 2001–2002 is the seventh year of revenue control limit budget overrides that are entirely funded with revenues from other than a levy of taxes on the taxable property within the school district pursuant to § 15-481, subsections F and J, Arizona Revised Statutes, may calculate its general budget limit pursuant to § 15-947, Arizona Revised Statutes, for fiscal years 2000-2001 and 2001-2002 by using the initial percentage increases in the revenue control limit authorized by the voters of the school district, provided that all of the following conditions are met:

"1. The original overrides that were approved by the voters of the school district were for the maximum percentage that the school district could have sought at the time that the overrides were approved.

"2. The voters of the school district approved each override by a margin of seventy-five per cent or more.

"3. The school district did not request, and the voters did not disapprove a request, to renew either of the budget overrides."

Laws 2002, Ch. 125, § 3, provides:

"**Sec. 3. Retroactivity**

"This act is effective retroactively to from and after June 30, 2000."

Reviser's Notes:

2002 Note. This section contains the amendments made by Laws 2002, Ch. 125, sec. 1 and Ch. 290, sec. 2 that were blended together as shown pursuant to authority of § 41-1304.03.

§ 15-303. Apportionment of funds

The county school superintendent shall apportion the school monies to each school district of the county. He shall give written notification to the county treasurer of the amount apportioned to each school district and to the governing board of the school district of the amount apportioned to the district.
Added by Laws 1981, Ch. 1, § 2, eff. Jan. 23, 1981.

Historical and Statutory Notes

Source:

Laws 1912, Ch. 77, §§ 16, 20.
Civ.Code 1913, §§ 2708, 2712.
Laws 1927, Ch. 36, § 1.
Rev.Code 1928, § 992.
Laws 1941, Ch. 79, § 1.
Code 1939, Supp. 1952, § 54-301.
A.R.S. former § 11-513.
A.R.S. former § 15-143.
Laws 1980, 2nd S.S., Ch. 9, § 8.

§ 15-304. Warrants; limitations; definition

The county school superintendent, on the voucher of the governing board of a school district, shall draw his warrant on the county treasurer for all necessary expenses against the school fund of the district. The warrants shall be drawn in the order in which the vouchers are filed in his office. A warrant shall not be drawn for an expenditure from the maintenance and operation, capital outlay, adjacent ways and federal and state grant funds for a purpose not included in the budget of the school district or for an expenditure in excess of the amount budgeted and not previously expended, except for expenditures authorized by the board of supervisors as provided in § 15-907. The county school superintendent shall not draw a warrant for an expenditure from any school district fund except the maintenance and operation, capital outlay or adjacent ways fund or federal and state grant funds unless sufficient cash is available in the fund according to the records of the county school superintendent. The county school superintendent may only draw a warrant for an expenditure from a federal or state grant fund when sufficient cash is not available in the grant fund if the county treasurer maintains the two accounts as provided in § 15-996, paragraph 1 and if the county school superintendent determines that the expenditures are included in the budget section of the approved grant application. For purposes of this section, "voucher" means a summary cover sheet and either copies of the invoices of the expenditure or a listing of the invoice detail.

Added by Laws 1981, Ch. 1, § 2, eff. Jan. 23, 1981. Amended by Laws 1982, Ch. 199, § 1; Laws 1983, Ch. 241, § 1; Laws 1985, Ch. 166, § 3, eff. April 18, 1985; Laws 1986, Ch. 125, § 2, eff. April 18, 1986; Laws 1992, Ch. 305, § 5; Laws 1995, Ch. 191, § 1, eff. April 19, 1995.

Historical and Statutory Notes

Source:

Laws 1912, Ch. 77, §§ 16, 20.
Civ.Code 1913, §§ 2708, 2712.
Laws 1927, Ch. 36, § 1.
Rev.Code 1928, § 992.
Laws 1941, Ch. 79, § 1.
Code 1939, Supp. 1952, § 54–301.
A.R.S. former § 11–514.
A.R.S. former § 15–144.
Laws 1980, 2nd S.S., Ch. 9, § 8.

Reviser's Notes:

1992 Note. Pursuant to authority of § 41–1304.02, in the section heading "; definition" was added after "limitations".

§ 15–305. Repealed by Laws 1986, Ch. 49, § 1, eff. Aug. 13, 1986

Historical and Statutory Notes

The repealed section, added by Laws 1981, Ch. 1, § 2, derived from Laws 1912, Ch. 77, §§ 16, 20; Civ.Code 1913, §§ 2708, 2712; Laws 1927, Ch. 36, § 1; Rev.Code 1928, § 992; Laws 1941, Ch. 79, § 1; Code 1939, Supp.1952, § 54–301; A.R.S. former § 11–515; A.R.S. former § 15–145; Laws 1980, 2nd S.S., Ch. 9, § 8, related to salary warrants.

§ 15–306. Register of warrants

The county school superintendent shall keep a register of warrants showing the funds upon which the warrants have been drawn, the number of warrants, in whose favor and for what purpose drawn, and also a receipt from the person to whom the warrant was delivered.

Added by Laws 1981, Ch. 1, § 2, eff. Jan. 23, 1981.

Historical and Statutory Notes

Source:

Laws 1912, Ch. 77, §§ 16, 20.
Civ.Code 1913, §§ 2708, 2712.
Laws 1927, Ch. 36, § 1.
Rev.Code 1928, § 992.
Laws 1941, Ch. 79, § 1.
Code 1939, Supp.1952, § 54–301.
A.R.S. former § 11–516.
A.R.S. former § 15–146.
Laws 1980, 2nd S.S., Ch. 9, § 8.

§ 15–307. Repealed by Laws 1987, Ch. 36, § 2

Historical and Statutory Notes

The repealed section, added by Laws 1981, Ch. 1, § 2, derived from Laws 1912, Ch. 77, § 17; Civ.Code 1913, § 2709; Rev.Code 1928, § 993; Code 1939, § 54–302; A.R.S. former § 11–517; A.R.S. former § 15–147; Laws 1980, 2nd S.S., Ch. 9, § 8, related to the county school superintendent's authority to open school and appoint a teacher if the governing board failed to have the school kept.

§ 15–308. Providing educational services of an accommodation school

A. The county school superintendent may provide educational services of an accommodation school to the school districts in the county using the facilities of the accommodation school. The county school superintendent shall administer the program and shall develop a fiscal year budget according to the process specified for school districts.

B. A county may offer educational services to homeless children or alternative education programs as defined in § 15-796 through an accommodation school.

Added by Laws 1981, Ch. 1, § 2, eff. Jan. 23, 1981. Amended by Laws 1992, Ch. 305, § 6; Laws 1997, Ch. 231, § 5.

Historical and Statutory Notes

Source:

Laws 1967, Ch. 104, § 1.
Laws 1972, Ch. 138, § 1.
Laws 1975, Ch. 103, § 1.
Laws 1976, Ch. 165, § 1.
Laws 1977, Ch. 119, § 1.
A.R.S. former § 15-142.
Laws 1980, 2nd S.S., Ch. 9, § 8.

§ 15-309. Repealed by Laws 1987, Ch. 36, § 2

Historical and Statutory Notes

The repealed section, added by Laws 1981, Ch. 1, § 2, derived from Laws 1912, Ch. 77, § 19; Civ.Code 1913, § 2711; Rev.Code 1928, § 995; Code 1939, § 54-304; A.R.S. former § 11-518; A.R.S. former § 15-148; Laws 1980, 2nd S.S., Ch. 9, § 8, related to the county school superintendent's authority to require the governing board of a school district to repair the school buildings or property or to abate a nuisance in or about the premises and the authority to require the board to provide suitable outhouses.

§ 15-310. Repealed by Laws 1993, Ch. 83, § 2

Historical and Statutory Notes

The repealed section, added by Laws 1982, Ch. 221, § 1, amended by Laws 1985, Ch. 337, § 1, related to nationally standardized norm-referenced achievement test results.

ARTICLE 2. ORGANIZATIONAL POWERS OF SCHOOL DISTRICT GOVERNING BOARDS

§ 15-321. Organization; election of officers of the board; meetings; execution of warrants; exemption

A. For the purpose of organization of the governing board, the board shall meet at the most convenient public facility in the school district. If a public facility is not available within the district, the governing board may meet at any available public facility that is convenient to all governing board members, regardless of the county or school district in which the facility is located. The governing board shall meet between January 1 and January 15 next following the election.

B. At the organization meeting the governing board shall elect from among the membership of the board a president.

C. For the purposes of regular meetings of the governing board, the board shall meet at the most convenient public facility in the school district. If a public facility is not available within the district, the governing board may meet at any available public facility that is convenient to all governing board members, regardless of the county or school district in which the facility is located.

D. The board shall prescribe rules for its own government. It shall hold a regular meeting at least once each month during the regular school year and may hold other meetings as often as called. If action has been taken and documents approved at a meeting, they may be signed subsequently by individual board members.

E. Business shall be conducted at regular or special meetings. Notice of a special meeting, and of the hour for a regular meeting if no hour is fixed by a rule of the board, shall be delivered personally or by telephone.

F. A majority of the members of a governing board constitutes a quorum for the transaction of business.

G. An order on a county school superintendent for a salary or other expense shall be signed by a majority of the governing board. An order for salary or other expense may be signed between board meetings if a resolution to that effect has been passed prior to the signing at a regular or special meeting of the governing board and the order is ratified by the board at the next regular or special meeting of the governing board.

H. This section does not apply to county school superintendents in the conduct of an accommodation school.

Added by Laws 1981, Ch. 1, § 2, eff. Jan. 23, 1981. Amended by Laws 1982, Ch. 197, § 2; Laws 1994, Ch. 315, § 6; Laws 1995, Ch. 268, § 13.

Historical and Statutory Notes

Source:

Laws 1912, Ch. 77, §§ 41, 69, 81, 82.
Civ. Code 1913, §§ 2733, 2765, 2777, 2778.
Laws 1921, Ch. 72, § 5.
Laws 1921, Ch. 137, § 1.
Laws 1925, Ch. 11, § 1.
Laws 1925, Ch. 70, §§ 1 to 4.
Laws 1927, Ch. 88, § 1.
Rev. Code 1928, §§ 1011, 1013, 1074.
Laws 1933, Ch. 18, § 1.
Code 1939, §§ 54–418, 54–907.
Laws 1949, Ch. 110, § 1.
Laws 1951, Ch. 140, § 1.
Laws 1952, Ch. 138, § 1.
Code 1939, Supp.1952, § 54–416.
Laws 1954, Ch. 117, § 2.
A.R.S. former §§ 15–432, 15–544.
Laws 1960, Ch. 127, §§ 22, 42.
Laws 1972, Ch. 138, § 21.
Laws 1975, Ch. 131, § 2.
Laws 1978, Ch. 193, § 2.

§ 15–322. Organization of the governing board of a consolidated school district

A. A meeting of the governing board of the consolidated school district shall be called by the county school superintendent within ten days after their election.

B. At the meeting provided by subsection A the members shall organize the board of the consolidated school district.

1. They shall receive from the boards of the school districts which have been consolidated all property, accounts and records of such boards.

2. Property of the several school districts shall become the property of the newly formed school district.

3. Balances or deficits in the funds of the several school districts consolidated shall become the balances or deficits of the new school district.

4. All bonded indebtedness of the school districts consolidated shall become the bonded indebtedness of the new school district.

Added by Laws 1981, Ch. 1, § 2, eff. Jan. 23, 1981.

Historical and Statutory Notes

Source:

Laws 1912, Ch. 77, §§ 31, 81, 82.
Civ. Code 1913, §§ 2723, 2777, 2778.
Rev. Code 1928, §§ 1001, 1074.
Code 1939, §§ 54-406, 54-907.
A.R.S. former §§ 15-412, 15-544.

§ 15-323. Governing board member; voting eligibility; purchases from board member

A. Notwithstanding any other provision of law, a governing board member is eligible to vote on any budgetary, personnel or other question which comes before the board, except:

1. It shall be unlawful for a member to vote on a specific item which concerns the appointment, employment or remuneration of such member or any person related to such member who is a spouse or a dependent as defined in § 43-1001.

2. No member may vote on the employment of a person who is a member of the governing board or who is the spouse of a member of the governing board and whose membership on the board and employment are prohibited by § 15-421, subsection D.

B. The governing board may make purchases from a board member if the transaction does not exceed three hundred dollars, the total purchases from any board member by the board within any twelve month period do not exceed one thousand dollars and the board has by majority vote adopted within the preceding twelve month period a policy authorizing such purchases.

C. Notwithstanding subsection B of this section, the governing board of a school district having a student count of fewer than three thousand may make purchases from a board member in any amount as provided in this subsection and § 15-213. The governing board must approve each purchase from a board member, and the amount of the purchase or contract for purchase shall be included in the minutes of the meeting at which the governing board approves the purchase.

Added by Laws 1981, Ch. 1, § 2, eff. Jan. 23, 1981. Amended by Laws 1986, Ch. 17, § 2; Laws 1987, Ch. 138, § 1.

Historical and Statutory Notes

Source:

Laws 1912, Ch. 77, § 41.
Civ. Code 1913, § 2733.
Laws 1921, Ch. 72, § 5.
Laws 1921, Ch. 137, § 1.
Laws 1925, Ch. 11, § 1.
Laws 1925, Ch. 70, §§ 1 to 4.
Laws 1927, Ch. 88, § 1.
Rev. Code 1928, § 1011.
Laws 1933, Ch. 18, § 1.
Laws 1949, Ch. 110, § 1.
Laws 1951, Ch. 74, § 1.
Laws 1951, Ch. 140, § 1.
Laws 1952, Ch. 138, § 1.
Code 1939, Supp.1952, § 54-416.
Laws 1954, Ch. 117, § 2.
A.R.S. former §§ 15-209, 15-441.
Laws 1956, Ch. 134, § 1.
Laws 1958, Ch. 88, § 2.
Laws 1960, Ch. 127, § 28.
Laws 1977, Ch. 164, § 1.
Laws 1978, Ch. 213, § 7.
Laws 1980, Ch. 170, § 2.

Reviser's Notes:

1987 Note. Pursuant to authority of § 41-1304.02, in the section heading "; employment prohibition" was deleted.

§§ 15–324, 15–325. Repealed by Laws 1995, Ch. 268, § 14

Historical and Statutory Notes

Section 15–324, added by Laws 1981, Ch. 1, § 2, amended by Laws 1981, Ch. 117, § 1, derived from:

Laws 1912, Ch. 77, §§ 68, 69, 81, 82.
Civ. Code 1913, §§ 2764, 2765, 2777, 2778.
Rev. Code 1928, §§ 1028, 1074.
Code 1939, §§ 54–433, 54–907.
A.R.S. former §§ 15–433, 15–544.
Laws 1960, Ch. 127, § 23.

related to duties of governing board clerks.

Section 15–325, added by Laws 1981, Ch. 1, § 2, derived from:

Laws 1912, Ch. 77, §§ 68, 69.
Civ. Code 1913, §§ 2764, 2765.
Rev. Code 1928, § 1028.
Code 1939, § 54–433.
A.R.S. former § 15–434.
Laws 1960, Ch. 127, § 24.
Laws 1974, 1st S.S., Ch. 3, § 5.
Laws 1980, 2nd S.S., Ch. 9, § 17.

related to compensation of governing board clerks.

§ 15–326. Capacity to sue and be sued and to hold and convey property

The governing board of a school district shall in the district name, as specified in § 15–441, subsection B:

1. Sue and be sued.
2. Hold and convey property for the use and benefit of the district.

Added by Laws 1981, Ch. 1, § 2, eff. Jan. 23, 1981.

Historical and Statutory Notes

Source:

Laws 1912, Ch. 77, § 27.
Civ. Code 1913, § 2719.
Rev. Code 1928, § 996.
Code 1939, § 54–401.
A.R.S. former § 15–435.
Laws 1960, Ch. 127, § 25.

§ 15–327. Advisory meetings of school district electors; notice; procedure; effect

A. The governing board may call meetings of the qualified school electors of the school district for consultation concerning any litigation in which the district is engaged or is likely to become engaged, or concerning any other affairs of the district not otherwise provided for.

B. Upon a petition of fifteen per cent or one thousand of the qualified electors of the school district as shown by the last regular school election, the governing board shall call such meeting.

C. Meetings of electors shall be called by posting notices in three public places in the school district, including the door of the school building, for not less than ten days preceding the meeting. The notices shall specify the purpose for which the meeting is called, and no other business shall be transacted at the meeting.

D. A school district meeting shall be called to order and presided over by the president of the governing board or, in his absence, by an elector chosen by the electors present. At the meetings all voting shall be by ballot of the qualified school electors. In all matters the meeting may exercise advisory power only.

Added by Laws 1981, Ch. 1, § 2, eff. Jan. 23, 1981. Amended by Laws 1995, Ch. 268, § 15.

Historical and Statutory Notes

Source:

Laws 1912, Ch. 77, §§ 41 to 43.
Civ. Code 1913, §§ 2733 to 2735.
Laws 1921, Ch. 72, § 5.
Laws 1921, Ch. 137, § 1.
Laws 1925, Ch. 11, § 1.
Laws 1925, Ch. 70, §§ 1 to 4.
Laws 1927, Ch. 88, § 1.
Rev. Code 1928, §§ 1011, 1012.
Laws 1933, Ch. 18, § 1.
Code 1939, § 54-417.
Laws 1949, Ch. 110, § 1.
Laws 1951, Ch. 140, § 1.
Laws 1952, Ch. 138, § 1.
Code 1939, Supp.1952, § 54-416.
Laws 1954, Ch. 117, § 2.
A.R.S. former § 15-439.
Laws 1960, Ch. 127, § 27.
Laws 1972, Ch. 138, § 8.

§ 15-328. Single administrative program

A. Any common school district and any high school district having common governing board membership and coterminous district boundaries may by resolution of each board provide for the operation of such school districts under a single administrative program.

B. Operation of school districts under a single administrative program shall be commenced on July 1 of any year. The county school superintendent and the superintendent of public instruction shall be notified at least forty-five days before the beginning of a fiscal year of intention to operate under a single administrative program.

C. For purposes of this section, "single administrative program" means that a common school district and a high school district as provided in subsection A may combine administrative functions including but not limited to land acquisition, construction of school buildings, employment of all persons engaged in the administration and operation of the common school district and the high school district, and purchase and use of equipment and services, provided such expenditures are properly prorated to the separate accounts of the common school districts and the high school districts. The proration shall also apply for budget purposes.

D. All other provisions of this title shall be complied with by each of the districts, except that for the purpose of school administration a single administrative program may be conducted.

Added by Laws 1981, Ch. 1, § 2, eff. Jan. 23, 1981.

Historical and Statutory Notes

Source:

Laws 1964, Ch. 77, § 1.
A.R.S. former § 15-1205.

§ 15-329. Repealed by Laws 1983, Ch. 174, § 1

Historical and Statutory Notes

The repealed section, added by Laws 1981, Ch. 1, § 2, authorizing the organization of intermediate schools and requiring governing boards which organize intermediate schools to secure and receive all funds necessary for the maintenance of the schools, was derived from:

Laws 1912, Ch. 77, § 41.
Civ. Code, 1913, § 2733.
Laws 1921, Ch. 72, § 5.
Laws 1921, Ch. 137, § 1.
Laws 1925, Ch. 11, § 1.
Laws 1925, Ch. 70, §§ 1 to 4.
Laws 1927, Ch. 88, § 1.
Rev.Code 1928, § 1011.
Laws 1933, Ch. 18, § 1.

Laws 1949, Ch. 110, § 1.
Laws 1951, Ch. 140, § 1.
Laws 1952, Ch. 138, § 1.
Code 1939, Supp.1952, § 54-416.
Laws 1954, Ch. 117, § 2.
A.R.S. former § 15-447.

ARTICLE 3. POWERS AND DUTIES OF SCHOOL DISTRICT GOVERNING BOARDS

§ 15-341. General powers and duties; immunity; delegation

A. The governing board shall:

1. Prescribe and enforce policies and procedures for the governance of the schools, not inconsistent with law or rules prescribed by the state board of education.

2. Maintain the schools established by it for the attendance of each pupil for a period of not less than one hundred seventy-five school days or two hundred school days, as applicable, or its equivalent as approved by the superintendent of public instruction for a school district operating on a year-round operation basis, to offer an educational program on the basis of a four day school week or to offer an alternative kindergarten program on the basis of a three day school week, in each school year, and if the funds of the district are sufficient, for a longer period, and as far as practicable with equal rights and privileges.

3. Exclude from schools all books, publications, papers or audiovisual materials of a sectarian, partisan or denominational character.

4. Manage and control the school property within its district.

5. Acquire school furniture, apparatus, equipment, library books and supplies for the use of the schools.

6. Prescribe the curricula and criteria for the promotion and graduation of pupils as provided in §§ 15-701 and 15-701.01.

7. Furnish, repair and insure, at full insurable value, the school property of the district.

8. Construct school buildings on approval by a vote of the district electors.

9. Make in the name of the district conveyances of property belonging to the district and sold by the board.

10. Purchase school sites when authorized by a vote of the district at an election conducted as nearly as practicable in the same manner as the election provided in § 15-481 and held on a date prescribed in § 15-491, subsection E, but such authorization shall not necessarily specify the site to be purchased and such authorization shall not be necessary to exchange unimproved property as provided in § 15-342, paragraph 23.

11. Construct, improve and furnish buildings used for school purposes when such buildings or premises are leased from the national park service.

12. Purchase school sites or construct, improve and furnish school buildings from the proceeds of the sale of school property only on approval by a vote of the district electors.

13. Hold pupils to strict account for disorderly conduct on school property.

14. Discipline students for disorderly conduct on the way to and from school.

15. Except as provided in § 15–1224, deposit all monies received by the district as gifts, grants and devises with the county treasurer who shall credit the deposits as designated in the uniform system of financial records. If not inconsistent with the terms of the gifts, grants and devises given, any balance remaining after expenditures for the intended purpose of the monies have been made shall be used for reduction of school district taxes for the budget year, except that in the case of accommodation schools the county treasurer shall carry the balance forward for use by the county school superintendent for accommodation schools for the budget year.

16. Provide that, if a parent or legal guardian chooses not to accept a decision of the teacher as provided in § 15–521, paragraph 3, the parent or legal guardian may request in writing that the governing board review the teacher's decision. Nothing in this paragraph shall be construed to release school districts from any liability relating to a child's promotion or retention.

17. Provide for adequate supervision over pupils in instructional and noninstructional activities by certificated or noncertificated personnel.

18. Use school monies received from the state and county school apportionment exclusively for payment of salaries of teachers and other employees and contingent expenses of the district.

19. Make an annual report to the county school superintendent on or before October 1 each year in the manner and form and on the blanks prescribed by the superintendent of public instruction or county school superintendent. The board shall also make reports directly to the county school superintendent or the superintendent of public instruction whenever required.

20. Deposit all monies received by school districts other than student activities monies or monies from auxiliary operations as provided in §§ 15–1125 and 15–1126 with the county treasurer to the credit of the school district except as provided in paragraph 21 of this subsection and §§ 15–1223 and 15–1224, and the board shall expend the monies as provided by law for other school funds.

21. Establish a bank account in which the board may during a month deposit miscellaneous monies received directly by the district. The board shall remit monies deposited in the bank account at least monthly to the county treasurer for deposit as provided in paragraph 20 of this subsection and in accordance with the uniform system of financial records.

22. Employ an attorney admitted to practice in this state whose principal practice is in the area of commercial real estate, or a real estate broker who is licensed by this state and who is employed by a reputable commercial real estate company, to negotiate a lease of five or more years for the school district if the governing board decides to enter into a lease of five or more years as lessor of school buildings or grounds as provided in § 15–342, paragraph 7 or 10. Any lease of five or more years negotiated pursuant to this paragraph shall provide that the lessee is responsible for payment of property taxes pursuant to the requirements of § 42–11104.

23. Prescribe and enforce policies and procedures for disciplinary action against a teacher who engages in conduct which is a violation of the policies of the governing board but which is not cause for dismissal of the teacher or for revocation of the certificate of the teacher. Disciplinary action may include suspension without pay for a period of time not to exceed ten school days. Disciplinary action shall not include suspension with pay or suspension without pay for a period of time longer than ten school days. The procedures shall include notice, hearing and appeal provisions for violations which are cause for disciplinary action. The governing board may designate a person or persons to act on behalf of the board on these matters.

24. Prescribe and enforce policies and procedures for disciplinary action against an administrator who engages in conduct which is a violation of the policies of the governing board regarding duties of administrators but which is not cause for dismissal of the administrator or for revocation of the certificate of the administrator. Disciplinary action may include suspension without pay for a period of time not to exceed ten school days. Disciplinary action shall not include suspension with pay or suspension without pay for a period of time longer than ten school days. The procedures shall include notice, hearing and appeal provisions for violations which are cause for disciplinary action. The governing board may designate a person or persons to act on behalf of the board on these matters. For violations which are cause for dismissal, the provisions of notice, hearing and appeal in chapter 5, article 3 of this title [1] shall apply. The filing of a timely request for a hearing suspends the imposition of a suspension without pay or a dismissal pending completion of the hearing.

25. Notwithstanding § 13-3108, prescribe and enforce policies and procedures that prohibit a person from carrying or possessing a weapon on school grounds unless the person is a peace officer or has obtained specific authorization from the school administrator.

26. Prescribe and enforce policies and procedures relating to the health and safety of all pupils participating in district sponsored practice sessions, games or other interscholastic athletic activities, including the provision of water. A school district and its employees are immune from civil liability for the consequences of the good faith adoption and implementation of policies and procedures pursuant to this paragraph.

27. Prescribe and enforce policies and procedures regarding the smoking of tobacco within school buildings. The policies and procedures shall be adopted in consultation with school district personnel and members of the community and shall state whether smoking is prohibited in school buildings. If smoking in school buildings is not prohibited, the policies and procedures shall clearly state the conditions and circumstances under which smoking is permitted, those areas in a school building which may be designated as smoking areas and those areas in a school building which may not be designated as smoking areas.

28. Establish an assessment, data gathering and reporting system as prescribed in chapter 7, article 3 of this title. [2]

29. Provide special education programs and related services pursuant to § 15-764, subsection A to all children with disabilities as defined in § 15-761.

30. Administer competency tests prescribed by the state board of education for the graduation of pupils from high school.

31. Secure insurance coverage for all construction projects for purposes of general liability, property damage and workers' compensation and secure performance and payment bonds for all construction projects.

32. Keep on file the resumes of all current and former employees who provide instruction to pupils at a school. Resumes shall include an individual's educational and teaching background and experience in a particular academic content subject area. A school district shall inform parents and guardians of the availability of the resume information and shall make the resume information available for inspection on request of parents and guardians of pupils enrolled at a school. Nothing in this paragraph shall be construed to require any school to release personally identifiable information in relation to any teacher or employee including the teacher's or employee's address, salary, social security number or telephone number.

33. Report to local law enforcement agencies any suspected crime against a person or property that is a serious offense as defined in § 13-604 or that involves a deadly weapon or dangerous instrument or serious physical injury and any conduct that poses a threat of death or serious physical injury to employees, students or anyone on the property of the school. A school district and its employees are immune from liability for any good faith actions taken in furtherance of this paragraph. This paragraph does not limit or preclude the reporting by a school district or an employee of a school district of suspected crimes other than those required to be reported by this paragraph. For the purposes of this paragraph, "dangerous instrument", "deadly weapon" and "serious physical injury" have the same meaning prescribed in § 13-105.

34. In conjunction with local law enforcement agencies and local medical facilities, develop an emergency response plan for each school in the school district in accordance with minimum standards developed jointly by the department of education and the division of emergency management within the department of emergency and military affairs.

35. Annually assign at least one school district employee to participate in a multihazard crisis training program developed or selected by the governing board.

36. Provide written notice to the parents or guardians of all students affected in the school district at least thirty days prior to a public meeting to discuss closing a school within the school district. The notice shall include the reasons for the proposed closure and the time and place of the meeting. The governing board shall fix a time for a public meeting on the proposed closure no less than thirty days before voting in a public meeting to close the school. The school district governing board shall give notice of the time and place of the meeting. At the time and place designated in the notice, the school district governing board shall hear reasons for or against closing the school. The school district governing board is exempt from the provisions of this paragraph if it is determined by the governing board that the school shall be closed because it poses a danger to the health or safety of the pupils or employees of the school.

37. Incorporate instruction on native american history into appropriate existing curricula.

B. Notwithstanding subsection A, paragraphs 8, 10 and 12 of this section, the county school superintendent may construct, improve and furnish school buildings or purchase or sell school sites in the conduct of an accommodation school.

C. If any school district acquires real or personal property, whether by purchase, exchange, condemnation, gift or otherwise, the governing board shall pay to the county treasurer any taxes on the property that were unpaid as of the date of acquisition, including penalties and interest. The lien for unpaid delinquent taxes, penalties and interest on property acquired by a school district:

1. Is not abated, extinguished, discharged or merged in the title to the property.

2. Is enforceable in the same manner as other delinquent tax liens.

D. The governing board may not locate a school on property that is less than one-fourth mile from agricultural land regulated pursuant to § 3–365, except that the owner of the agricultural land may agree to comply with the buffer zone requirements of § 3–365. If the owner agrees in writing to comply with the buffer zone requirements and records the agreement in the office of the county recorder as a restrictive covenant running with the title to the land, the school district may locate a school within the affected buffer zone. The agreement may include any stipulations regarding the school, including conditions for future expansion of the school and changes in the operational status of the school that will result in a breach of the agreement.

E. A school district's governing board members and its school council members are immune from civil liability for the consequences of adoption and implementation of policies and procedures pursuant to subsection A of this section and § 15–342. This waiver does not apply if the school district's governing board members or its school council members are guilty of gross negligence or intentional misconduct.

F. A governing board may delegate in writing to a superintendent, principal or head teacher the authority to prescribe procedures that are consistent with the governing board's policies.

G. Notwithstanding any other provision of this title, a school district governing board shall not take any action that would result in an immediate reduction or a reduction within three years of pupil square footage that would cause the school district to fall below the minimum adequate gross square footage requirements prescribed in § 15–2011, subsection C, unless the governing board notifies the school facilities board established by § 15–2001 of the proposed action and receives written approval from the school facilities board to take the action. A reduction includes an increase in administrative space that results in a reduction of pupil square footage or sale of school sites or buildings, or both. A reduction includes a reconfiguration of grades that results in a reduction of pupil square footage of any grade level. This subsection does not apply to temporary reconfiguration of grades to accommodate new school construction if the temporary reconfiguration does not exceed one year. The sale of equipment that results in an immediate reduction or a reduction within three years that falls below the equipment requirements prescribed in § 15-2011, subsection B is subject to commensurate withholding of school district capital outlay revenue limit monies pursuant to the direction of the school facilities board. Except as provided in § 15-342, paragraph 10, proceeds from the sale of school sites, buildings or other equipment shall be deposited in the school plant fund as provided in § 15-1102.

H. Subsections C through G of this section apply to a county board of supervisors and a county school superintendent when operating and administering an accommodation school.

I. Until the state board of education and the auditor general adopt rules pursuant to § 15-213, subsection J, a school district may procure construction services, including services for new school construction pursuant to § 15-2041, by the construction-manager-at-risk, design-build and job-order-contracting methods of project delivery as provided in title 41, chapter 23, except that the rules adopted by the director of the department of administration do not apply to procurements pursuant to this subsection. Any procurement commenced pursuant to this subsection may be completed pursuant to this subsection.

Added by Laws 1981, Ch. 1, § 2, eff. Jan. 23, 1981. Amended by Laws 1981, Ch. 128, § 1; Laws 1981, Ch. 144, § 1; Laws 1981, Ch. 182, § 1; Laws 1982, Ch. 197, § 3; Laws 1982, Ch. 332, § 5; Laws 1983, Ch. 9, § 1, eff. Feb. 25, 1983; Laws 1983, Ch. 281, § 1; Laws 1983, Ch. 325, § 4; Laws 1984, Ch. 115, § 1, eff. April 13, 1984; Laws 1984, Ch. 349, § 2; Laws 1984, Ch. 379, § 2; Laws 1985, Ch. 127, § 1; Laws 1985, Ch. 254, § 2, eff. April 29, 1985; Laws 1986, Ch. 296, § 1; Laws 1986, Ch. 399, § 2; Laws 1987, Ch. 93, § 1; Laws 1988, Ch. 79, § 1, eff. May 16, 1988; Laws 1988, Ch. 106, § 4; Laws 1988, Ch. 312, § 5; Laws 1989, Ch. 196, § 2; Laws 1989, Ch. 273, § 2, eff. June 26, 1989; Laws 1990, Ch. 293, § 1; Laws 1990, Ch. 322, § 2, eff. June 20, 1990; Laws 1990, Ch. 330, § 3; Laws 1990, Ch. 348, § 2, eff. June 26, 1990; Laws 1990, Ch. 366, § 18; Laws 1991, Ch. 173, § 1; Laws 1991, Ch. 218, § 5, eff. June 10, 1991; Laws 1991, Ch. 257, § 2; Laws 1991, Ch. 298, § 8, eff. Sept. 21, 1991, retroactively effective to July 1, 1991; Laws 1992, Ch. 172, § 3; Laws 1994, Ch. 361, § 1; Laws 1995, Ch. 146, § 1; Laws 1995, Ch. 268, § 16; Laws 1996, Ch. 71, § 1; Laws 1996, Ch. 125, § 1; Laws 1996, Ch. 284, § 15; Laws 1997, Ch. 231, § 6; Laws 1997, Ch. 271, § 1, eff. April 29, 1997; Laws 1998, Ch. 1, § 45, eff. Jan. 1, 1999; Laws 1998, Ch. 71, § 2; Laws 1998, Ch. 167, § 2; Laws 1998, 5th S.S., Ch. 1, § 9, eff. July 9, 1998; Laws 1999, Ch. 68, § 1; Laws 1999, Ch. 76, § 3; Laws 1999, Ch. 299, § 4; Laws 2000, Ch. 90, § 4; Laws 2000, Ch. 226, § 3, eff. April 10, 2000; Laws 2000, Ch. 376, § 3; Laws 2001, Ch. 324, § 6; Laws 2002, Ch. 181, § 6; Laws 2002, Ch. 316, § 1; Laws 2002, Ch. 330, § 1; Laws 2002, Ch. 340, § 2; Laws 2003, Ch. 215, § 2, eff. May 14, 2003, retroactively effective to Aug. 22, 2002; Laws 2004, Ch. 339, § 1.

[1] Section 15-531 et seq.

[2] Section 15-741 et seq.

Historical and Statutory Notes

Source:

Laws 1912, Ch. 77, §§ 41, 54, 55, 81, 82.
Civ. Code 1913, §§ 2733, 2750, 2751, 2777, 2778.
Laws 1921, Ch. 72, §§ 1, 5.
Laws 1921, Ch. 137, § 1.
Laws 1925, Ch. 11, § 1.
Laws 1925, Ch. 70, §§ 1 to 4.
Laws 1927, Ch. 88, § 1.
Rev. Code 1928, §§ 1011, 1025, 1026, 1074.
Laws 1933, Ch. 18, § 1.
Laws 1936, 1st S.S., Ch. 4, § 1.
Code 1939, §§ 54-430, 54-431, 54-907.
Laws 1949, Ch. 110, § 1.
Laws 1951, Ch. 74, § 1.
Laws 1951, Ch. 140, § 1.
Laws 1952, Ch. 138, § 1.
Laws 1954, Ch. 117, § 2.
Code 1939, Supp.1952, § 54-416.
Laws 1954, Ch. 147, § 1.

A.R.S. former §§ 15-437, 15-440, 15-441, 15-442, 15-545.
Laws 1956, Ch. 134, § 1.
Laws 1958, Ch. 88, § 2.
Laws 1960, Ch. 120, § 2.
Laws 1960, Ch. 127, §§ 28, 29.
Laws 1961, Ch. 61, § 2.
Laws 1962, Ch. 92, § 1.
Laws 1962, Ch. 112, § 1.
Laws 1966, Ch. 85, § 1.
Laws 1967, Ch. 69, § 1.
Laws 1967, 3rd S.S., Ch. 19, § 1.
Laws 1969, Ch. 16, § 1.
Laws 1970, Ch. 118, § 1.
Laws 1972, Ch. 115, § 5.
Laws 1973, Ch. 62, § 1.
Laws 1974, 1st S.S., Ch. 3, §§ 8, 10.
Laws 1975, Ch. 50, § 2.
Laws 1976, Ch. 68, § 1.
Laws 1976, Ch. 156, § 2.
Laws 1977, Ch. 79, § 1.
Laws 1977, Ch. 157, § 1.
Laws 1978, Ch. 7, § 3.
Laws 1978, Ch. 8, § 1.
Laws 1978, Ch. 87, § 1.
Laws 1978, Ch. 188, §§ 4, 6.
Laws 1979, Ch. 117, § 1.
Laws 1979, Ch. 118, § 4.
Laws 1979, Ch. 195, § 6.
Laws 1979, 1st S.S., Ch. 2, § 2.
Laws 1980, 2nd S.S., Ch. 9, § 18.
Laws 1980, Ch. 105, § 2.
Laws 1980, Ch. 170, § 2.
Laws 1980, Ch. 225, § 1.

Laws 1984, Ch. 1, § 1, effective January 20, 1984, provides:

"**Section 1. Extension of the minutes of instruction; schools in disaster areas**

"**A.** Notwithstanding § 15-341, subsection A, paragraph 2, § 15-769, subsection B, § 15-901, subsection A, paragraph 2, subdivision (a) and § 15-901, subsection A, paragraph 6, Arizona Revised Statutes, for fiscal year 1983-1984 the governing board of a school district which is located in a disaster area as designated by Presidential Proclamation may extend the number of minutes each pupil must be enrolled each day as provided in § 15-901, Arizona Revised Statutes, by not more than one hundred twenty minutes. The extension of the number of minutes each pupil must be enrolled each day shall total when added to the regularly scheduled days in session the equivalent of not less than one hundred seventy-five days of instructional time as determined by the superintendent of public instruction.

"**B.** The superintendent of public instruction shall determine the eligibility of a school district to extend the number of minutes each pupil must be enrolled each day. The superintendent of public instruction shall prescribe appropriate reporting and recording procedures to implement the provisions of this act."

The amendment of this section by Laws 1988, Ch. 106, § 4, was repealed by Laws 1988, Ch. 312, § 6.

Laws 1988, Ch. 312, § 1, par. 3 provides:

"**Section 1. Purpose**"

"3. Section 15-341, Arizona Revised Statutes, was amended by Laws 1988, chapter 79, § 1 and chapter 106, § 4. The chapter 106 version failed to amend the chapter 79 version, which was an emergency enactment, and therefore did not comply with the requirements of article IV, part 2, § 14, Constitution of Arizona. To accomplish the intent of these enactments, in this enactment the chapter 79 version is amended to incorporate the amendments made by chapter 106 and the chapter 106 version is repealed."

The amendments of this section by Laws 1990, Ch. 330, § 3, Ch. 348, § 2 and Ch. 366, § 18, and the purported amendment of this section by Laws 1990, Ch. 233, § 2, effective July 1, 1991, were repealed by Laws 1991, Ch. 173, § 2, Ch. 218, § 6, effective June 10, 1991, Ch. 257, § 3 and Ch. 298, § 9, effective Sept. 21, 1991, retroactively effective to July 1, 1991.

The 1991 amendment of this section by Ch. 173 explicitly amended the 1990 amendments of this section by Chs. 293 and 322.

The 1991 amendment of this section by Ch. 218 explicitly amended the 1990 amendment of this section by Chs. 293 and 322.

The 1991 amendment of this section by Ch. 257 explicitly amended the 1990 amendments of this section by Chs. 293 and 322.

Laws 1991, Ch. 298, § 1, par. 4 provides:

"**Section 1. Purpose**"

"4. Section 15-341, Arizona Revised Statutes, was amended by Laws 1990, chapter 293, § 1 and chapter 322, § 2, and these two chapters were blended. However, because the chapter 322 version had an emergency clause, the other four amendments to § 15-341, Arizona Revised Statutes, in Laws 1990, chapter 233, § 2, chapter 330, § 3, chapter 348, § 2 and chapter 366, § 18 did not comply with the requirements of article IV, part 2, § 14, Constitution of Arizona. To accomplish the intent of these enactments, in this act the blended version of § 15-341, Arizona Revised Statutes, is amended to incorporate the Laws 1990, chapter 233, chapter 330, chapter 348 and chapter 366 versions and those versions are repealed."

The 1991 amendment of this section by Ch. 298 explicitly amended the 1990 amendments of this section by Chs. 293 and 322.

The 1991 amendments of this section by Ch. 257, § 2 and Ch. 298, § 8 were repealed by Laws 1992, Ch. 319, § 8.

The 1992 amendment of this section by Ch. 172 explicitly amended the 1991 amendment of this section by Ch. 173 and Ch. 218.

Laws 1992, Ch. 319, § 1, par. 5, provides:

"**Section 1. Purpose**"

"5. Section 15-341, Arizona Revised Statutes, was amended by Laws 1991, chapter 173, § 1, Laws 1991, chapter 218, § 5, Laws 1991, chapter 257, § 2 and Laws 1991, chapter 298, § 8. The chapter 257 and chapter 298 versions failed to amend the chapter 218 version, which was an emergency enactment, and therefore did not comply with article IV, part 2, § 14, Constitution of Arizona. Since the substance of the Laws 1991, chapter 257 and Laws 1991, chapter 298 versions was incorporated in the blend version of § 15-341, Arizona Revised Statutes, in this act the chapter 257 and chapter 298 versions are repealed."

Laws 1994, Ch. 254, § 10, as amended by Laws 1996, Ch. 284, § 76, provides:

"**Sec. 10. Teacher survey; report**

"**A.** The governing board of each school district shall conduct a uniform survey prescribed by the department of education of the teachers employed by the governing board each quarter of the one hundred seventy-five day school year. The survey shall be conducted in a manner that enables individual ratings by each teacher to remain anonymous. The survey shall be in substantially the following format:

" 'Please rate the performance of the district administration and the governing board as one of the following: excellent, very good, good, fair, poor.

" 'Please provide suggestions for improvement or describe any problems that you believe should be addressed by the district administration or the governing board.'

"**B.** The school district may change the frequency of or refuse to conduct this survey by a majority vote of the governing board of the school district. The governing board shall vote on this issue at its first meeting conducted during the 1996-1997 school year.

"**C.** The school district governing board shall compile the results of each survey completed pursuant to subsection A of this section and make them available for inspection by any person pursuant to § 39-121, Arizona Revised Statutes. The district shall provide a report of the results of each of the quarterly surveys in a format prescribed by the department of education by October 1 of each year to the department of education. The department of education shall compile the results of the district survey and provide a report by December 1 of each year to the chairman of the senate education committee and the chairman of the house of representatives education committee. The report from the department of education shall contain the following:

"1. An executive summary.

"2. The number of teachers surveyed.

"3. The per cent of responses to questions asked."

The purported amendment of this section by Laws 1998, 3rd S.S., Ch. 1, failed to became effective because Ch. 1 was repealed in its entirety by Laws 1998, 5th S.S., Ch. 1, § 2, effective July 1, 1998.

The purported amendment of this section by Laws 1998, Ch. 164 failed to become effective because Chapter 164 was repealed in its entirety by Laws 1998, 5th S.S., Ch. 1, § 2, effective July 1, 1998.

The amendment of this section by Laws 2000, Ch. 376, § 3 was repealed by Laws 2001, Ch. 324, § 7.

The 2001 amendment of this section by Ch. 324 explicitly amended the amendment of this section by Laws 2000, Ch. 90, § 4, and Laws 2000, Ch. 226, § 3.

Laws 2001, Ch. 324, § 1, par. 3, provides:

"**Section 1. Purpose**"

"3. Section 15-341, Arizona Revised Statutes, was amended by Laws 2000, chapter 90, § 4, Laws 2000, chapter 226, § 3 and Laws 2000, chapter 376, § 3. The chapter 376 version could not be blended because it failed to amend the chapter 226 version, which was an emergency enactment, and therefore did not comply with article IV, part 2, § 14, Constitution of Arizona. To accomplish the intent of these enactments, this act amends the 2000 blended version of § 15-341, Arizona Revised Statutes, to incorporate the amendments made by Laws 2000, chapter 376 and the chapter 376 version is repealed."

Laws 2001, Ch. 324, § 60, subsec. A, provides:

"**Sec. 60. Retroactive application**

"**A.** Sections 2, 3, 6 through 9, 13, 22 through 28, 31 through 34, 36, 37, 44, 45 and 48 of this act apply retroactively to July 18, 2000."

Laws 2002, Ch. 330, § 50, provides:

"**Sec. 50. School district administrative costs; data analysis**

"**A.** Before July 1, 2002, the joint legislative budget committee staff shall analyze school district cost data from fiscal year 2000-2001 in order to determine the average per pupil current expenditure for each school district for administrative functions and whether each district exceeded its predicted per pupil cost level for those functions based on data reported by districts of similar type and size.

"**B.** Before December 1, 2002, the auditor general shall report to the legislature regarding factors that help explain differences in administrative costs for school districts that are identified by the joint legislative budget committee as having reported particularly high or low average per pupil current expenditures for administrative functions for fiscal year 2000-2001. This analysis shall include an emphasis on school districts that are identified as having particularly high or low average per pupil administrative costs for fiscal year 2000-2001 but that were not identified as having had particularly high or low average per pupil administrative costs for fiscal year 1998-1999 and vice versa. The analysis shall discuss factors that caused these districts to report particularly high or low average per pupil administrative costs for only one of the two time periods analyzed."

Laws 2002, Ch. 330, § 58, provides:

"**Sec. 58. Transfer of powers; effect**

"**A.** This act does not alter the effect of any actions that were taken or impair the valid obligations of the state board of directors for community colleges in existence before the effective date of this act.

"**B.** Administrative rules and orders that were adopted by the state board of directors for community colleges prior to June 30, 2002 continue in effect through June 30, 2003. Community college district governing boards shall not adopt any rules that conflict with rules adopted by the state board of directors for community colleges.

"**C.** On the effective date of this act, all real and personal property, fixtures and records that are located on a community college campus in this state are transferred from the state board of directors for community colleges to the community college district board of that community college."

Laws 2002, Ch. 330, § 59, provides:

"**Sec. 59. Assignment of interest in real property**

"**A.** The state board of directors for community colleges shall assign all rights, title and interest in real property it has purchased, received, held and taken leases of that is situated in each community college district to such district's governing board. The chair of the state board of directors for community colleges or the chair's designee shall take all necessary steps to effect such assignment prior to July 1, 2002.

"**B.** The state board of directors for community colleges shall assign all rights, title and interest in real property it has purchased, received, held and taken leases of that is situated in an unorganized community college district that is served by a community college district to the duly elected board of the provisional community college district or, if a provisional community college district has not been formed, to the county board of supervisors of the unorganized county. The chair of the state board of directors for community colleges or the chair's designee shall take all necessary steps to effect such assignment before July 1, 2002."

Laws 2002, Ch. 330, § 64, provides:

"**Sec. 64. Conforming legislation**

"The legislative council staff shall prepare proposed legislation conforming the Arizona Revised Statutes to the provisions of this act for consideration in the forty-sixth legislature, first regular session."

Laws 2002, Ch. 330, became law without the Governor's signature as provided in Arizona Constitution, Article 5, § 7.

Laws 2003, Ch. 215, § 5, eff. May 14, 2003, provides:

"**Sec. 5. Retroactivity**

"This act is effective retroactively to August 22, 2002."

Executive Orders:

Receipt of criminal history record information:

Executive Order No. 88-2, dated January 20, 1988, authorized the Criminal Identification Section of the Department of Public Safety to provide, and the Paradise Valley Unified School District No. 69 to receive, criminal history record information for purposes of evaluating fitness of prospective employees in accordance with rules and regulations issued by the Department of Public Safety.

Executive Order No. 89-1, dated February 3, 1989, authorized the Criminal Identification Section of the Department of Public Safety to provide, and the Washington School District to receive, criminal history record information for purposes of evaluating the fitness of prospective employees in accordance with rules and regulations issued by the Department of Public Safety.

Executive Order No. 89-4, dated February 24, 1989, authorized the Criminal Identification Section of the Department of Public Safety to provide, and the Ash Creek Elementary District No. 53 to receive, criminal history record information for purposes of evaluating the fitness of prospective employees in accordance with rules and regulations issued by the Department of Public Safety.

Executive Order No. 89-5, dated February 24, 1989, authorized the Criminal Identification Section of the Department of Public Safety to provide, and the Sierra Vista Public Schools Unified District No. 68 to receive, criminal history record information for purposes of evaluating the fitness of prospective employees in accordance with rules and regulations issued by the Department of Public Safety.

Executive Order No. 89-6, dated March 7, 1989, authorized the Criminal Identification Section of the Department of Public Safety to provide, and the Parker Unified School District No. 27 to receive, criminal history record information for purposes of evaluating the fitness of prospective employees in accordance with rules and regulations issued by the Department of Public Safety.

Executive Order No. 89-9, dated April 19, 1989, authorized the Criminal Identification Section of the Department of Public Safety to provide, and the chief officer or designee of Bisbee Unified School District No. Two to receive, criminal history record information for purposes of evaluating the fitness of prospective employees in accordance with rules and regulations issued by the Department of Public Safety.

Executive Order No. 89-10, dated April 19, 1989, authorized the Criminal Identification Section of the Department of Public Safety to provide, and the chief officer or designee of Cochise County Educational Services to receive, criminal history record information for purposes of evaluating the fitness of prospective employees in accordance with rules and regulations issued by the Department of Public Safety.

Executive Order No. 89-17, dated June 12, 1989, authorized the Criminal Identification Section of the Department of Public Safety to provide, and the chief officer or designate of Fort Huachuca Accommodation Schools to receive, criminal history record information for purposes of evaluating the fitness of prospective employees in accordance with rules and regulations issued by the Department of Public Safety.

Reviser's Notes:

1981 Note. Prior to the 1982 amendments, this section contained the amendments made by Laws 1981, Ch. 128, § 1, Ch. 144, § 1 and Ch. 182, § 1 which were blended together pursuant to authority of § 41-1304.03.

1982 Note. Prior to the 1983 amendments, this section contained the amendments made by Laws 1982, Ch. 197, § 3 and Ch. 332, § 5 which were blended together pursuant to authority of § 41-1304.03.

1983 Note. Prior to the 1984 amendments, this section contained the amendments made by Laws 1983, Ch. 281, § 1 and Ch. 325, § 4 which were blended together pursuant to authority of § 41-1304.03. Additionally, pursuant to authority of § 41-1304.02, the spelling of "disciplinary" in subsection A, paragraph 25 was corrected and in the fifth sentence of subsection A, paragraphs 25 and 26, the comma following "appeal in chapter 5, article 3" was transposed to follow "days" in the same sentence.

1984 Note. Prior to the 1985 amendments, this section contained the amendments made by Laws 1984, Ch. 349, § 2 and Ch. 379, § 2 which were blended together pursuant to authority of § 41-1304.03.

1985 Note. Prior to the 1986 amendments, this section contained the amendments made by Laws 1985, ch. 127, § 1 and ch. 254, § 2 which were blended together pursuant to authority of § 41-1304.03. Pursuant to authority of § 41-1304.02, in subsection A, paragraph 4, "audio visual" was combined as one word as a correction of a manifest clerical error.

1986 Note. Prior to the 1987 amendment, this section contained the amendments made by Laws 1986, chapter 296, § 1 and chapter 399, § 2 which were blended together pursuant to authority of § 41-1304.03.

1988 Note. Pursuant to authority of § 41-1304.02, in subsection A, paragraph 16 the reference to "§ 15-1223" was renumbered to "§ 15-1224" to conform to the reviser's renumbering of that section.

1989 Note. Prior to the 1990 amendments, this section contained the amendments made by Laws 1989, Ch. 196, § 2 and Ch. 273, § 2 which were blended together pursuant to authority of § 41-1304.03.

1990 Note. The independent and valid amendment of this section by Laws 1990, Ch. 233, § 2, Ch. 293, § 1 and Ch. 322, § 2 could not be blended because of the delayed effective date of Ch. 233.

1990 Note. The amendment of this section by Laws 1990, Ch. 330, § 3, Ch. 348, § 2 and Ch. 366, § 18 failed to set forth in full the text of the section as amended by Laws 1990, Ch. 322, an emergency act, as required by Constitution of Arizona Art. IV, part 2, § 14.

1990 Note. Prior to the 1991 amendments, this section contained the amendments made by Laws 1990, ch. 293, § 1 and ch. 322, § 2 which were blended together pursuant to authority of § 41-1304.03.

1991 Note. Prior to the 1992 amendment, this section contained the amendments made by Laws 1991, Ch. 173, sec. 1 and Ch. 218, sec. 5 that were blended together pursuant to authority of § 41-1304.03.

1991 Note. The amendment of this section by Laws 1991, Ch. 257, sec. 2 and Ch. 298, sec. 8 failed to set forth in full the text of the section as amended by Laws 1991, Ch. 218, an emergency act, as required by Constitution of Arizona Art. IV, part 2, sec. 14.

1995 Note. Prior to the 1996 amendments, this section contained the amendments made by Laws 1995, Ch. 146, sec. 1 and Ch. 268, sec. 16 that were blended together pursuant to authority of § 41-1304.03. In the chapter 268 version in subsection A, paragraph 16 after ~~"subsection~~

A" a comma appears contrary to written instructions. Pursuant to authority of § 41-1304.02, the comma is removed to correct a manifest clerical error.

1996 Note. Prior to the 1997 amendment, this section contained the amendments made by Laws 1996, Ch. 71, sec. 1, Ch. 125, sec. 1 and Ch. 284, sec. 15 that were blended together pursuant to authority of § 41-1304.03.

1997 Note. Prior to the 1998 amendments, this section contained the amendments made by Laws 1997, Ch. 231, sec. 6 and Ch. 271, sec. 1 that were blended together pursuant to authority of § 41-1304.03.

1998 Note. Prior to the 1999 amendments, this section contained the amendments made by Laws 1998, Second Regular Session, Ch. 1, sec. 45, Ch. 71, sec. 2 and Ch. 167, sec. 2 and Laws 1998, Fifth Special Session, Ch. 1. sec. 9 that were blended together pursuant to authority of § 41-1304.03. Pursuant to authority of § 41-1304.02, in subsection C, last sentence the spelling of "breach" was corrected.

1998 Note. Prior to the 1999 amendments, this section contained the amendments made by Laws 1998, Second Regular Session, Ch. 71, sec. 2 and Ch. 167, sec. 2 and Laws 1998, Fifth Special Session, Ch. 1. sec. 9 that were blended together pursuant to authority of § 41-1304.03. Pursuant to authority of § 41-1304.02, in subsection C, last sentence the spelling of "breach" was corrected.

1999 Note. Prior to the 2000 amendments, this section contained the amendments made by Laws 1999, Ch. 68, sec. 1, Ch. 76, sec. 3 and Ch. 299, sec. 4 that were blended together pursuant to authority of § 41-1304.03.

2000 Note. Prior to the 2001 amendment, this section contained the amendments made by Laws 2000, Ch. 90, sec. 4 and Ch. 226, sec. 3 that were blended together pursuant to authority of § 41-1304.03. Pursuant to authority of § 41-1304.02, in subsection A, paragraph 33, first sentence the words "to local law enforcement" were transposed to follow "Report".

2000 Note. The amendment of this section by Laws 2000, Ch. 376, sec. 3 failed to set forth in full the text of the section as amended by Laws 2000, Ch. 226, sec. 3, an emergency act, as required by Constitution of Arizona art. IV, pt. 2, sec. 14.

2002 Note. Prior to the 2003 amendment, this section contained the amendments made by Laws 2002, Ch. 181, sec. 6, Ch. 316, sec. 1, Ch. 330, sec. 1 and Ch. 340, sec. 2 that were blended together pursuant to authority of section 41-1304.03. Pursuant to authority of § 41-1304.02, in subsection A, paragraph 33 the last sentence was transposed to follow the second sentence.

§ 15-341.01. One hundred eighty day school year

A. Notwithstanding any other law, school instruction shall be conducted in each public school in this state for school sessions that total at least one hundred eighty days each school year. The superintendent of public instruction shall cause all relevant school funding formulas to be adjusted to reflect instruction on the one hundred eighty days' equivalency. The department of education shall adjust the amount of state aid distributed to school districts pursuant to § 15-971 to correspond to the increased number of school days prescribed by this section.

B. The legislative council shall prepare draft legislation that conforms the statutes and furthers the purposes of this section pursuant to article IV, part 1, § 1, Constitution of Arizona.

Added by Laws 2000, 5th S.S., Ch. 1, § 5.

Historical and Statutory Notes

Laws 2000, 5th S.S., Ch. 1, § 54, provides:

"**Sec. 54. Increased number of school days; phase-in**

"Notwithstanding §§ 15-341, 15-802, 15-854, 15-855, 15-902 and 15-1001, Arizona Revised Statutes, § 15-901, Arizona Revised Statutes, as amended by this act, and § 15-341.01, Arizona Revised Statutes, as added by this act, the number of mandatory school days offered by school districts shall be increased from the current number of one hundred seventy-five days to one hundred eighty days according to the following schedule:

"1. In fiscal year 2001-2002, each school district governing board shall maintain the schools established by it for the attendance of each pupil for a period of not less than one hundred seventy-six school days.

"2. In fiscal year 2002-2003, each school district governing board shall maintain the schools established by it for the attendance of each pupil for a period of not less than one hundred seventy-seven school days.

"3. In fiscal year 2003-2004, each school district governing board shall maintain the schools established by it for the attendance of each pupil for a period of not less than one hundred seventy-eight school days.

"4. In fiscal year 2004-2005, each school district governing board shall maintain the schools established by it for the attendance of each pupil for a period of not less than one hundred seventy-nine school days.

"5. In fiscal year 2005-2006 and each fiscal year thereafter, each school district governing board shall maintain the schools established by it for the attendance of each pupil for a period of not less than one hundred eighty school days as prescribed by statute."

Proposition 301, approved by the electors at the Nov. 7, 2000 general election, effective Nov. 27, 2000, included a provision increasing the state transaction privilege tax rate six-tenths of one per cent. Therefore, the conditions of the 5th S.S. Ch. 1 were met, and the act became effective.

Laws 2003, Ch. 264, § 41, provides:

"**Sec. 41. Calculation of instructional days for fiscal year 2003-2004**"

"Notwithstanding any other law, for fiscal year 2003-2004, the term " one hundred eighty days" in § 15-341.01, Arizona Revised Statutes, means one hundred eighty days of instruction or an equivalent number of minutes of instruction per school year based on a different number of days of instruction approved by the school district governing board."

"Notwithstanding any other law, for fiscal year 2003-2004, the term " one hundred eighty days" in § 15-341.01, Arizona Revised Statutes, means one hundred eighty days of instruction or an equivalent number of minutes of instruction per school year based on a different number of days of instruction approved by the school district governing board."

Laws 2004, Ch. 278, § 9, provides:

"**Sec. 9. Calculation of instructional days for fiscal year 2004-2005**

"Notwithstanding any other law, for fiscal year 2004-2005, the term " one hundred eighty days" in § 15-341.01, Arizona Revised Statutes, means one hundred eighty days of instruction or an equivalent number of minutes of instruction per school year based on a different number of days of instruction approved by the school district governing board."

Laws 2004, Ch. 278, § 21, provides:

"**Sec. 21. Retroactivity**

"**A.** Except as provided in subsection B of this section, this act applies retroactively to from and after June 30, 2004.

"**B.** Laws 2002, chapter 330, § 49, as amended by this act, applies retroactively to from and after June 29, 2004."

Former § 15-341.01 was renumbered as § 15-349.

§ 15-342. Discretionary powers

The governing board may:

1. Expel pupils for misconduct.

2. Exclude from grades one through eight children under six years of age.

3. Make such separation of groups of pupils as it deems advisable.

4. Maintain such special schools during vacation as deemed necessary for the benefit of the pupils of the school district.

5. Permit a superintendent or principal or representatives of the superintendent or principal to travel for a school purpose, as determined by a majority vote of the board. The board may permit members and members-elect of the board to travel within or without the school district for a school purpose and receive reimbursement. Any expenditure for travel and subsistence pursuant to this paragraph shall be as provided in title 38, chapter 4, article 2.[1] The designated post of duty referred to in § 38-621 shall be construed, for school district governing board members, to be the member's actual place of residence, as opposed to the school district office or the school district boundaries. Such expenditures shall be a charge against the budgeted school district funds. The governing board of a school district shall prescribe procedures and amounts for reimbursement of lodging and subsistence expenses. Reimburse-

ment amounts shall not exceed the maximum amounts established pursuant to section 38–624, subsection C.

6. Construct or provide in rural districts housing facilities for teachers and other school employees which the board determines are necessary for the operation of the school.

7. Sell or lease to the state, a county, a city or a tribal government agency, any school property required for a public purpose, provided the sale or lease of the property will not affect the normal operations of a school within the school district.

8. Annually budget and expend funds for membership in an association of school districts within this state.

9. Enter into leases or lease-purchase agreements for school buildings or grounds, or both, as lessor or as lessee, for periods of less than five years subject to voter approval for construction of school buildings as prescribed in § 15–341, subsection A, paragraph 8.

10. Subject to chapter 16 of this title,[2] sell school sites or enter into leases or lease-purchase agreements for school buildings and grounds, as lessor or as lessee, for a period of five years or more, but not to exceed ninety-nine years, if authorized by a vote of the school district electors in an election called by the governing board as provided in § 15–491, except that authorization by the school district electors in an election is not required if one of the following requirements is met:

(a) The market value of the school property is less than fifty thousand dollars.

(b) The buildings and sites are completely funded with monies distributed by the school facilities board.

(c) The transaction involves the sale of improved or unimproved property pursuant to an agreement with the school facilities board in which the school district agrees to sell the improved or unimproved property and transfer the proceeds of the sale to the school facilities board in exchange for monies from the school facilities board for the acquisition of a more suitable school site. For a sale of property acquired by a school district prior to July 9, 1998, a school district shall transfer to the school facilities board that portion of the proceeds that equals the cost of the acquisition of a more suitable school site. If there are any remaining proceeds after the transfer of monies to the school facilities board, a school district shall only use those remaining proceeds for future land purchases approved by the school facilities board, or for capital improvements not funded by the school facilities board for any existing or future facility.

(d) The transaction involves the sale of improved or unimproved property pursuant to a formally adopted plan and the school district uses the proceeds of this sale to purchase other property that will be used for similar purposes as the property that was originally sold, provided that the sale proceeds of the improved or unimproved property are used within two years after the date of the original sale to purchase the replacement property. If the sale proceeds of the improved or unimproved property are not used within two years after the date of the original sale to purchase replacement property, the sale proceeds shall be used towards payment of any outstanding bonded indebtedness. If any sale proceeds remain after paying for outstanding bonded indebtedness, or if the district has no outstanding bonded indebtedness, sale proceeds shall be used to reduce the district's primary tax levy. A school district shall not use the provisions of this subdivision unless all of the following conditions exist:

(i) The school district is the sole owner of the improved or unimproved property that the school district intends to sell.

(ii) The school district did not purchase the improved or unimproved property that the school district intends to sell with monies that were distributed pursuant to chapter 16 of this title.

(iii) The transaction does not violate § 15-341, subsection G.

11. Review the decision of a teacher to promote a pupil to a grade or retain a pupil in a grade in a common school or to pass or fail a pupil in a course in high school. The pupil has the burden of proof to overturn the decision of a teacher to promote, retain, pass or fail the pupil. In order to sustain the burden of proof, the pupil shall demonstrate to the governing board that the pupil has mastered the academic standards adopted by the state board of education pursuant to §§ 15-701 and 15-701.01. If the governing board overturns the decision of a teacher pursuant to this paragraph, the governing board shall adopt a written finding that the pupil has mastered the academic standards. Notwithstanding title 38, chapter 3, article 3.1,[3] the governing board shall review the decision of a teacher to promote a pupil to a grade or retain a pupil in a grade in a common school or to pass or fail a pupil in a course in high school in executive session unless a parent or legal guardian of the pupil or the pupil, if emancipated, disagrees that the review should be conducted in executive session and then the review shall be conducted in an open meeting. If the review is conducted in executive session, the board shall notify the teacher of the date, time and place of the review and shall allow the teacher to be present at the review. If the teacher is not present at the review, the board shall consult with the teacher before making its decision. Any request, including the written request as provided in section 15-341, the written evidence presented at the review and the written record of the review, including the decision of the governing board to accept or reject the teacher's decision, shall be retained by the governing board as part of its permanent records.

12. Provide transportation or site transportation loading and unloading areas for any child or children if deemed for the best interest of the district, whether within or without the district, county or state.

13. Enter into intergovernmental agreements and contracts with school districts or other governing bodies as provided in § 11-952.

14. Include in the curricula which it prescribes for high schools in the school district career and technical education, vocational education and technology education programs and career and technical, vocational and technology program improvement services for the high schools, subject to approval by the state board of education. The governing board may contract for the provision of career and technical, vocational and technology education as provided in § 15-789.

15. Suspend a teacher or administrator from his duties without pay for a period of time of not to exceed ten school days, if the board determines that

suspension is warranted pursuant to § 15–341, subsection A, paragraphs 23 and 24.

16. Dedicate school property within an incorporated city or town to such city or town or within a county to that county for use as a public right-of-way if both of the following apply:

(a) Pursuant to an ordinance adopted by such city, town or county, there will be conferred upon the school district privileges and benefits which may include benefits related to zoning.

(b) The dedication will not affect the normal operation of any school within the district.

17. Enter into option agreements for the purchase of school sites.

18. Donate surplus or outdated learning materials to nonprofit community organizations where the governing board determines that the anticipated cost of selling the learning materials equals or exceeds the estimated market value of the materials.

19. Prescribe policies for the assessment of reasonable fees for students to use district-provided parking facilities. The fees are to be applied by the district solely against costs incurred in operating or securing the parking facilities. Any policy adopted by the governing board pursuant to this paragraph shall include a fee waiver provision in appropriate cases of need or economic hardship.

20. Establish alternative educational programs that are consistent with the laws of this state to educate pupils, including pupils who have been reassigned pursuant to § 15–841, subsection E or F.

21. Require a period of silence to be observed at the commencement of the first class of the day in the schools. If a governing board chooses to require a period of silence to be observed, the teacher in charge of the room in which the first class is held shall announce that a period of silence not to exceed one minute in duration will be observed for meditation, and during that time no activities shall take place and silence shall be maintained.

22. Require students to wear uniforms.

23. Exchange unimproved property or improved property, including school sites, where the governing board determines that the improved property is unnecessary for the continued operation of the school district without requesting authorization by a vote of the school district electors if the governing board determines that the exchange is necessary to protect the health, safety or welfare of pupils or when the governing board determines that the exchange is based on sound business principles for either:

(a) Unimproved or improved property of equal or greater value.

(b) Unimproved property that the owner contracts to improve if the value of the property ultimately received by the school district is of equal or greater value.

24. For common and high school pupils, assess reasonable fees for optional extracurricular activities and programs conducted when the common or high school is not in session, except that no fees shall be charged for pupils' access to or use of computers or related materials. For high school pupils, the

governing board may assess reasonable fees for fine arts and vocational education courses and for optional services, equipment and materials offered to the pupils beyond those required to successfully complete the basic requirements of any other course, except that no fees shall be charged for pupils' access to or use of computers or related materials. Fees assessed pursuant to this paragraph shall be adopted at a public meeting after notice has been given to all parents of pupils enrolled at schools in the district and shall not exceed the actual costs of the activities, programs, services, equipment or materials. The governing board shall authorize principals to waive the assessment of all or part of a fee assessed pursuant to this paragraph if it creates an economic hardship for a pupil. For the purposes of this paragraph, "extracurricular activity" means any optional, noncredit, educational or recreational activity which supplements the education program of the school, whether offered before, during or after regular school hours.

25. Notwithstanding § 15-341, subsection A, paragraphs 8 and 10, construct school buildings and purchase or lease school sites, without a vote of the school district electors, if the buildings and sites are totally funded from one or more of the following:

(a) Monies in the unrestricted capital outlay fund, except that the estimated cost shall not exceed two hundred fifty thousand dollars for a district that utilizes the provisions of § 15-949.

(b) Monies distributed from the school facilities board established by § 15-2001.

(c) Monies specifically donated for the purpose of constructing school buildings.

Nothing in this paragraph shall be construed to eliminate the requirement for an election to raise revenues for a capital outlay override pursuant to § 15-481 or a bond election pursuant to § 15-491.

26. Conduct a background investigation that includes a fingerprint check conducted pursuant to § 41-1750, subsection G for certificated personnel and personnel who are not paid employees of the school district, as a condition of employment. A school district may release the results of a background check to another school district for employment purposes. The school district may charge the costs of fingerprint checks to its fingerprinted employee, except that the school district may not charge the costs of fingerprint checks for personnel who are not paid employees of the school district.

27. Sell advertising space on the exterior of school buses as follows:

(a) Advertisements shall be age appropriate and not contain promotion of any substance that is illegal for minors such as alcohol, tobacco and drugs or gambling. Advertisements shall comply with the state sex education policy of abstinence.

(b) Advertising approved by the governing board may appear only on the sides of the bus in the following areas:

(i) The signs shall be below the seat level rub rail and not extend above the bottom of the side windows.

(ii) The signs shall be at least three inches from any required lettering, lamp, wheel well or reflector behind the service door or stop signal arm.

(iii) The signs shall not extend from the body of the bus so as to allow a handhold or present a danger to pedestrians.

(iv) The signs shall not interfere with the operation of any door or window.

(v) The signs shall not be placed on any emergency doors.

(c) Establish a school bus advertisement fund that is comprised of revenues from the sale of advertising space on school buses. The monies in a school bus advertisement fund are not subject to reversion and shall be used for the following purposes:

(i) To comply with the energy conservation measures prescribed in § 15–349 in school districts that are in area A as defined in section 49–541, and any remaining monies shall be used to purchase alternative fuel support vehicles and any other pupil related costs as determined by the governing board.

(ii) For any pupil related costs as determined by the governing board in school districts not subject to the provisions of item (i) of this subdivision.

28. Assess reasonable damage deposits to pupils in grades seven through twelve for the use of textbooks, musical instruments, band uniforms or other equipment required for academic courses. The governing board shall adopt policies on any damage deposits assessed pursuant to this paragraph at a public meeting called for this purpose after providing notice to all parents of pupils in grades seven through twelve in the school district. Principals of individual schools within the district may waive the damage deposit requirement for any textbook or other item if the payment of the damage deposit would create an economic hardship for the pupil. The school district shall return the full amount of the damage deposit for any textbook or other item if the pupil returns the textbook or other item in reasonably good condition within the time period prescribed by the governing board. For the purposes of this paragraph, '—i'in reasonably good condition" means the textbook or other item is in the same or a similar condition as it was when the pupil received it, plus ordinary wear and tear.

29. Notwithstanding § 15–1105, expend surplus monies in the civic center school fund for maintenance and operations or unrestricted capital outlay, if sufficient monies are available in the fund after meeting the needs of programs established pursuant to § 15–1105.

30. Notwithstanding § 15–1143, expend surplus monies in the community school program fund for maintenance and operations or unrestricted capital outlay, if sufficient monies are available in the fund after meeting the needs of programs established pursuant to section 15–1142.

Added by Laws 1981, Ch. 1, § 2, eff. Jan. 23, 1981. Amended by Laws 1981, Ch. 145, § 1; Laws 1981, Ch. 182, § 2; Laws 1983, Ch. 9, § 2, eff. Feb. 25, 1983; Laws 1983, Ch. 14, § 1; Laws 1983, Ch. 101, § 8; Laws 1983, Ch. 281, § 2; Laws 1983, Ch. 325, § 5; Laws 1984, Ch. 349, § 3; Laws 1985, Ch. 328, § 2; Laws 1985, Ch. 348, § 1, eff. May 14, 1985; Laws 1986, Ch. 166, § 1; Laws 1988, Ch. 177, § 1; Laws 1989, Ch. 273, § 3, eff. June 26, 1989; Laws 1990, Ch. 348, § 3, eff. June 26, 1990; Laws 1991, Ch. 138, § 2; Laws 1992, Ch. 230, § 1; Laws 1993, Ch. 202, § 5, eff. April 21, 1993; Laws 1994, Ch. 315, § 7; Laws 1995, Ch. 71, § 1; Laws 1995, Ch. 146, § 2; Laws 1995, Ch.

268, § 17; Laws 1996, Ch. 71, § 2; Laws 1996, Ch. 125, § 2; Laws 1996, Ch. 284, § 16; Laws 1997, Ch. 80, § 1; Laws 1997, Ch. 231, § 7; Laws 1997, Ch. 271, § 2, eff. April 29, 1997; Laws 1998, Ch. 41, § 1; Laws 1998, 5th S.S., Ch. 1, § 10, eff. July 9, 1998; Laws 1999, Ch. 68, § 2; Laws 1999, Ch. 95, § 1; Laws 1999, Ch. 163, § 1; Laws 1999, Ch. 299, § 5; Laws 2000, 5th S.S., Ch. 1, § 6; Laws 2001, Ch. 11, § 1, eff. Mar. 15, 2001. Amended by Laws 2002, Ch. 89, § 2; Laws 2002, Ch. 316, § 2.

[1] Section 38-621 et seq.

[2] Section 15-2001 et seq.

[3] Section 38-431 et seq.

Historical and Statutory Notes

Source:

Laws 1912, Ch. 77, §§ 41, 54.
Civ. Code 1913, §§ 2733, 2750.
Laws 1921, Ch. 72, § 5.
Laws 1921, Ch. 137, § 1.
Laws 1925, Ch. 11, § 1.
Laws 1925, Ch. 70, §§ 1 to 4.
Laws 1927, Ch. 88, § 1.
Rev. Code 1928, §§ 1011, 1025.
Laws 1933, Ch. 18, § 1.
Code 1939, § 54-430.
Laws 1949, Ch. 110, § 1.
Laws 1951, Ch. 74, § 1.
Laws 1951, Ch. 140, § 1.
Laws 1952, Ch. 138, § 1.
Code 1939, Supp.1952, § 54-416.
Laws 1954, Ch. 117, § 2.
A.R.S. former § 15-442.
Laws 1960, Ch. 120, § 1.
Laws 1960, Ch. 127, § 29.
Laws 1961, Ch. 61, § 2.
Laws 1962, Ch. 92, § 1.
Laws 1962, Ch. 112, § 1.
Laws 1967, Ch. 69, § 1.
Laws 1967, 3rd S.S., Ch. 19, § 1.
Laws 1969, Ch. 16, § 1.
Laws 1970, Ch. 118, § 1.
Laws 1972, Ch. 115, § 5.
Laws 1973, Ch. 62, § 1.
Laws 1974, 1st S.S., Ch. 3, §§ 8, 10.
Laws 1975, Ch. 50, § 2.
Laws 1976, Ch. 68, § 1.
Laws 1976, Ch. 156, § 2.
Laws 1977, Ch. 79, § 1.
Laws 1977, Ch. 157, § 1.
Laws 1978, Ch. 7, § 3.
Laws 1978, Ch. 8, § 1.
Laws 1978, Ch. 87, § 1.
Laws 1978, Ch. 188, § 6.
Laws 1979, Ch. 117, § 1.
Laws 1979, Ch. 195, § 6.
Laws 1979, 1st S.S., Ch. 2, § 2.
Laws 1980, 2nd S.S., Ch. 9, § 18.
Laws 1980, Ch. 105, § 2.
Laws 1980, Ch. 225, § 1.

The amendment of this section by Laws 1983, Ch. 14, § 1, was repealed by Laws 1983, Ch. 101, § 9.

Laws 1983, Ch. 101, § 1, par. 5 provides:

"**Section 1. Purpose**"

"5. Section 15-342, Arizona Revised Statutes, was amended by Laws 1983, chapter 9, § 2 and chapter 14, § 1. The chapter 9 version had an emergency effective date of February 25, 1983. The chapter 14 version which received final passage on March 15, 1983 did not set forth the full text of § 15-342, Arizona Revised Statutes, as amended by Laws 1983, chapter 9, § 2 as is required by Constitution of Arizona, Article IV, part 2, § 14. In order to accomplish the intent of both 1983 amendments, in this enactment the chapter 9 version is amended to incorporate the amendments made by chapter 14 and the chapter 14 version is repealed."

The purported amendment of this section by Laws 1998, Ch. 164 failed to become effective because Chapter 164 was repealed in its entirety by Laws 1998, 5th S.S., Ch. 1, § 2, effective July 1, 1998.

The purported amendment of this section by Laws 1998, 3rd S.S., Ch. 1, failed to became effective because Ch. 1 was repealed in its entirety by Laws 1998, 5th S.S., Ch. 1, § 2, effective July 1, 1998.

Proposition 301, approved by the electors at the Nov. 7, 2000 general election, effective Nov. 27, 2000, included a provision increasing the state transaction privilege tax rate six-tenths of one per cent. Therefore, the conditions of the 5th S.S. Ch. 1 were met, and the act became effective.

Reviser's Notes:

1981 Note. Prior to the 1983 amendments, this section contained the amendments made by Laws 1981, Ch. 14, § 1 and Ch. 182, § 2 which were blended together pursuant to authority of § 41-1304.03.

1983 Note. Prior to the 1984 amendment, this section contained the amendments made by Laws 1983, Ch. 101, § 8, Ch. 281, § 2 and Ch. 325, § 5 which were blended together pursuant to authority of § 41-1304.03. Additionally, pursuant to authority of § 41-1304.02, paragraph 15, as added by Laws 1983, Ch. 281, was renumbered as paragraph 16 [renumbered as par. 15 in 1984].

1985 Note. Prior to the 1986 amendment, this section contained the amendments made by

Laws 1985, Ch. 328, § 2 and Ch. 348, § 1 which were blended together pursuant to authority of § 41–1304.03.

1995 Note. Prior to the 1996 amendments, this section contained the amendments made by Laws 1995, Ch. 71, sec. 1, Ch. 146, sec. 2 and Ch. 268, sec. 17 that were blended together pursuant to authority of § 41–1304.03.

1996 Note. Prior to the 1997 amendments, this section contained the amendments made by Laws 1996, Ch. 71, sec. 2, Ch. 125, sec. 2 and Ch. 284, sec. 16 that were blended together pursuant to authority of § 41–1304.03.

1997 Note. Prior to the 1998 amendment, this section contained the amendments made by Laws 1997, Ch. 80, sec. 1, Ch. 231, sec. 7 and Ch. 271, sec. 2 that were blended together pursuant to authority of § 41–1304.03. Pursuant to authority of § 41–1304.02, in paragraph 27, subdivision (c), item (i) the comma was transposed to follow "49–541".

1998 Note. Prior to the 1999 amendments, this section contained the amendments made by Laws 1998, Second Regular Session, Ch. 41, sec. 1 and Laws 1998, Fifth Special Session, Ch. 1. sec. 10 that were blended together pursuant to authority of § 41–1304.03.

1999 Note. Prior to the effective date of the 2000 amendment by 5th S.S., Ch. 1, this section contained the amendments made by Laws 1999, Ch. 68, sec. 2, Ch. 95, sec. 1, Ch. 163, sec. 1 and Ch. 299, sec. 5 that were blended together pursuant to authority of § 41–1304.03.

2002 Note. This section contains the amendments made by Laws 2002, Ch. 89, sec. 2 and Ch. 316, sec. 2 that were blended together as shown pursuant to authority of § 41–1304.03.

§ 15–343. Employment of professional help

A. The governing board may employ professional personnel deemed necessary for making surveys and recommendations relating to the curricula, physical plant and other requirements of the district.

B. The governing board may employ an attorney to represent the district if the county attorney consents. The purpose for which an attorney is hired shall be set forth in writing by the board.

C. The governing board may employ legal counsel without the consent of the county attorney when, in its discretion, it deems it advisable.

D. Compensation for legal counsel under subsections B and C of this section is payable from district funds.

E. If an attorney is employed without the consent of the county attorney, the county attorney shall not have the duty to represent the district with regard to any matter for which such attorney was employed and shall not be responsible to the district for any exercise of, or failure to exercise, professional judgment by such attorney in his representation of the district.

F. The county attorney is not required to assume the duty to represent the district on a matter for which an attorney was employed without consent.

G. An attorney employed pursuant to subsection B of this section shall represent the school district with powers and duties otherwise performed by the county attorney, pursuant to § 11–532, subsection A, paragraph 10.

H. The provisions of subsections B and C of this section are in addition to, and not in limitation of, any other powers held by the board.

Added by Laws 1981, Ch. 1, § 2, eff. Jan. 23, 1981.

Historical and Statutory Notes

Source:

Laws 1912, Ch. 77, § 41.
Civ. Code 1913, § 2733.
Laws 1921, Ch. 72, § 5.
Laws 1921, Ch. 137, § 1.
Laws 1925, Ch. 11, § 1.
Laws 1925, Ch. 70, §§ 1 to 4.
Laws 1927, Ch. 88, § 1.
Rev. Code 1928, § 1011.
Laws 1933, Ch. 18, § 1.

Laws 1949, Ch. 110, § 1.
Laws 1951, Ch. 140, § 1.
Laws 1952, Ch. 138, § 1.
Code 1939, Supp.1952, § 54-416.
Laws 1954, Ch. 117, § 2.
A.R.S. former § 15-438.
Laws 1972, Ch. 171, § 3.
Laws 1976, Ch. 184, § 3.

§ 15-344. Administration of prescription, patent or proprietary medications by employees; definition

A. Subject to the limitations and requirements set forth in subsection B of this section, the school district governing board shall establish policies and procedures governing the administration of a prescription medication or a patent or proprietary medication to students by employees.

B. For purposes of this section, "administration" of prescription medication or a patent or proprietary medication means the giving of a single dose of medication or the giving of a treatment package in its original container. In the case of a minor student, such administration shall only occur upon the written or oral request or authorization of a parent or legal guardian.

Added by Laws 1981, Ch. 1, § 2, eff. Jan. 23, 1981. Amended by Laws 1981, Ch. 264, § 9, eff. Sept. 1, 1981; Laws 1985, Ch. 242, § 1; Laws 1989, Ch. 126, § 2; Laws 1996, Ch. 284, § 17.

Historical and Statutory Notes

Source:

Laws 1978, Ch. 41, § 1.
A.R.S. former § 15-443.01.
Laws 1979, Ch. 103, § 1.

Reviser's Notes:

1985 Note. The engrossed copy of S.B. 1248, 37th Legislature, first regular session, which was sent to the governor and enacted as Laws 1985, Ch. 242 contained an erroneous first page. Pursuant to authority of § 41-1304.02, the correct first page was substituted. In addition, subsections B, C and D, added by Laws 1985, Ch. 242, sec. 1 were renumbered as § 15-345, subsections A, B and C. The internal reference in § 15-344, subsection A was relettered to conform to the reviser's renumbering of that subsection and "; chemical abuse prevention policies; definition" was deleted from the section heading.

§ 15-345. Chemical abuse prevention policies and procedures

The school district governing board may adopt chemical abuse prevention policies and procedures in consultation with pupils, school district personnel and members of the community, including parents and local law enforcement agencies.

Formerly § 15-344, subsecs. B, C, and D, as amended by Laws 1985, Ch. 242, § 1. Renumbered as § 15-345. Amended by Laws 1987, Ch. 307, § 30; Laws 1995, Ch. 268, § 18.

Historical and Statutory Notes

Laws 1985, Ch. 242, §§ 3 and 4 provide:

"**Sec. 3. Chemical abuse prevention policies and procedures; duties of school district governing boards and state board of education**

"**A.** Notwithstanding § 15-344 [renumbered as § 15-345], subsection B, Arizona Revised Statutes, as amended by this act, school district governing boards are not required to adopt chemical abuse prevention policies and procedures until September 1, 1986.

"**B.** Notwithstanding § 15-344 [renumbered as § 15-345], subsection C, Arizona Revised Statutes, as amended by this act, the state board of education is not required to distribute model chemical abuse prevention policies and procedures and a recommended procedure for policy development until November 1, 1985.

"**Sec. 4. Joint legislative oversight committee on chemical abuse programs; membership; report**

"A joint legislative oversight committee on chemical abuse prevention programs shall be appointed consisting of three members of the house of representatives appointed by the speaker of the house and three members of the senate appointed by the president of the senate. The joint legislative oversight committee on chemical abuse prevention programs shall monitor the development and implementation of chemical abuse prevention programs in public school districts in this state. The committee shall compile a report to be submitted to the speaker of the house and president of the senate on or before December 31, 1987."

Laws 1987, Ch. 307, § 56 provides:

"**Sec. 56. Duties of state board of education**

"The state board of education, with the assistance of the superintendent of public instruction, shall conduct a survey of each school district in this state to determine the current policies and practices regarding the enforcement of rules for disciplinary action against pupils, teachers or administrators who engage in conduct which is in violation of title 13, chapter 34, Arizona Revised Statutes, and shall recommend to the legislature any statutory or administrative changes which may be needed to ensure that uniform and effective disciplinary action is provided for in each school district. The superintendent shall deliver a report on the results of the survey to the governor and the president of the senate and the speaker of the house of representatives by July 1, 1988."

Reviser's Notes:

1985 Note. Laws 1985, Ch. 242, § 1 added new subsections B, C and D to § 15-344. Pursuant to authority of § 41-1304.02 these subsections were numbered as § 15-345, subsections A, B and C, respectively, with the section heading "Chemical abuse prevention policies; procedures; definition".

1987 Note. Pursuant to authority of § 41-1304.02, in the section heading a semicolon after "policies" was deleted and "and" was added and "; definition" was deleted.

§ 15-346. Policies and procedures concerning pupils with chronic health problems; definition

A. The governing board shall adopt policies and procedures concerning pupils with chronic health problems in consultation with parents, teachers and at least one health professional. The policies and procedures shall be designed to provide continuing learning for pupils with chronic health problems while they are absent from school and to provide for the integration of pupils with chronic health problems into the regular education program as much as possible. The policies and procedures shall include provisions for:

1. Homework availability to ensure that pupils with chronic health problems have the opportunity to keep up with assignments and avoid losing credit because of their absence from school.

2. Flexibility in physical education activity requirements so that pupils with chronic health problems may participate in the regular physical education program to the extent that their health permits.

B. For the purpose of this section, "pupils with chronic health problems" means:

1. Pupils who are unable to attend regular classes for intermittent periods of one or more consecutive days because of illness, disease, pregnancy complications, or accident but who are not homebound. The chronic health problem shall be certified by a person licensed under title 32, chapter 7, 13 or 17.[1]

2. Pupils who have an infant with a severe health problem. The severe health problem of the infant shall be certified by a person licensed under title 32, chapter 7, 13 or 17.

Added by Laws 1986, Ch. 84, § 1. Amended by Laws 1989, Ch. 15, § 1; Laws 1996, Ch. 284, § 18; Laws 2001, Ch. 312, § 1.

[1] Section 32-801 et seq., 32-1401 et seq., or 32-1800 et seq.

Historical and Statutory Notes

Reviser's Notes:

1986 Note. Laws 1986, Ch. 383, § 1 added another new § 15-346 which was renumbered as § 15-914, pursuant to authority of § 41-1304.02.

§ 15-347. Extracurricular activities; cultural tradition

A governing board shall consider the cultural traditions of pupils when establishing or enforcing rules related to a pupil's participation in extracurricular school activities. If district rules or rules regulating a district's participation in an extracurricular program prohibit a student from participating because of a pupil's cultural traditions, the governing board may adopt alternative rules which would allow that pupil to participate but take into consideration the health or safety of the pupil or any other person participating in the activities.

Added by Laws 1988, Ch. 293, § 1.

Historical and Statutory Notes

Laws 1988, Ch. 293, § 5 provides:

"**Sec. 5. Report on policies regarding extracurricular activities**

"The department of education shall prepare a report on the policies regarding extracurricular activities adopted by school districts and shall submit the report to the president of the senate and the speaker of the house of representatives by April 1, 1989."

§ 15-348. Interscholastic athletics noncontact sports

A governing board or an interscholastic athletic association may permit common school students to participate in practice sessions of noncontact sports with secondary school students.

Added by Laws 1988, Ch. 293, § 2.

Historical and Statutory Notes

Reviser's Notes:

1988 Note. Pursuant to authority of § 41-1304.02, a hyphen was removed from "noncontact" in the section heading and the text of the section.

§ 15-349. Operation of motor vehicle fleet; options to conventional fuels

A. The governing board of a school district with an average daily membership as defined in § 15-901 of more than three thousand which is located within or which has bus routes running within area A, as defined in § 49-541, shall develop and implement, subject to the availability of a state air quality funding source, a vehicle fleet plan for vehicles with a gross vehicle weight rating of at least seventeen thousand five hundred pounds for the purpose of encouraging the use of fuels listed pursuant to this subsection in school district owned vehicles. The plan shall provide for at least fifty per cent of the fleet with a gross vehicle weight rating of at least seventeen thousand five hundred pounds to operate on any of the following by December 31, 2004, and each year thereafter:

1. Alternative fuels or clean burning fuels as defined in section 1-215.

2. Ultra low sulfur diesel as defined in § 49-558.01 and that is used in an engine with an emission control device.

3. Vehicles powered by an engine that meets or exceeds an emission standard for diesel particulate matter of 0.05 grams per brake horsepower hour.

B. Engine retrofits or conversions meet the requirements of subsection A of this section if they have been approved for use by any one of the following:

1. The United States environmental protection agency voluntary retrofit program.

2. The United States environmental protection agency verification protocol for retrofit catalyst particulate filter and engine modification control technologies for highway and nonroad use diesel engines.

3. The California air resources board diesel emission control strategy verification procedure.

4. Sections 43100 and 43102 of the health and safety code of the state of California.

5. Actual emission testing performed on the vehicle.

C. This section does not preclude a school district from using any local, federal or private funding sources that may be available in order to comply with the requirements of this section.

Added as 15-341.01 by Laws 1993, 6th S.S., Ch. 1, § 5. Renumbered as 15-349. Amended by Laws 1994, Ch. 353, § 4, eff. April 26, 1994; Laws 1996, 7th S.S., Ch. 6, § 7; Laws 1997, Ch. 269, § 4; Laws 1998, Ch. 217, § 6; Laws 1999, Ch. 168, § 3, eff. May 5, 1999; Laws 2000, Ch. 148, § 3; Laws 2000, Ch. 405, § 4, eff. April 28, 2000; Laws 2001, Ch. 70, § 2; Laws 2002, Ch. 296, § 2, eff. July 1, 2003.

Historical and Statutory Notes

Laws 1994, 6th S.S., Ch. 1, § 41, as amended by Laws 1994, Ch. 353, § 32, eff. April 26, 1994, provides:

"**Sec. 41. School district vehicle conversion; plan; report**

"**A.** Each interested school district in area A, as defined in § 49-541, Arizona Revised Statutes, shall submit a document to the department of commerce energy office by June 1, 1994 detailing its plan for converting its nondiesel powered fleet to alternative fuel use in accordance with the schedule in § 15-349, Arizona Revised Statutes. The document shall include a description of the plan, a listing of the number and type of district vehicles, the student count in the district, the district's annual route miles transporting eligible students on buses owned and operated by the school district and the estimated cost of the conversion.

"**B.** The department of commerce energy office, with the assistance of the department of education, shall notify all districts in area A, as defined in § 49-541, Arizona Revised Statutes, of the availability of these funds as soon as practicable. In this notification, the department of commerce energy office, shall provide minimum guidelines with regard to conversion.

"**C.** After receipt of the plans, the department of commerce energy office shall distribute the $2,900,000 appropriated in § 42 of this act to applying school districts in area A, as defined in § 49-541, Arizona Revised Statutes, by December 31, 1994. The Arizona department of commerce energy office shall determine an allowable expenditure for each bus to pay for the incremental cost of the alternative fueled bus over a conventionally powered bus. This distribution shall be based upon the plan submitted to the department of commerce energy office pursuant to this section. In the event that the appropriation is not sufficient to meet the total distribution, the amount allocated to each school district shall be proportionately adjusted based upon each district's route miles for buses operated by the school district and preference will be given to school districts with an average daily membership greater than three thousand students. Any monies remaining after the conversion of these buses shall be expended for conversion of other nondiesel vehicles or reverted to the oil overcharge fund as provided in § 42 of this act. Expenditures made by school districts shall conform to the procedures pursuant to § 15-213, Arizona Revised Statutes.

"**D.** After distribution of the funds as provided in subsection C of this section, the department of commerce energy office shall allocate remaining monies on a pro rata share of average daily membership to applicant districts in area A, as defined in § 49-541, Arizona Revised Statutes. These monies shall also be expended for conversion of other nondiesel vehicles or reverted to the oil overcharge fund as provided in § 42 of this act. Expenditures made by school districts shall conform to the procedures pursuant to § 15-213, Arizona Revised Statutes.

"**E.** The school districts in area A, as defined in § 49-541, Arizona Revised Statutes, shall complete conversion of vehicles to alternative fuels in accordance with the schedule in § 15-349, Arizona Revised Statutes, and submit a report to the department of commerce energy office by January 31 of the year following the conversion schedule in § 15-349, Arizona Revised Statutes, relating to implementation of the conversion. The department of commerce energy office shall submit a summary of the reports to the president of the senate, the speaker of the house of representatives and the director of the joint legislative budget committee by March 31 of the year following the conversion schedule in § 15-349, Arizona Revised Statutes."

Laws 1994, Ch. 353, § 42, eff. April 26, provides:

"**Sec. 42. School district vehicle conversion plan; revisions**

"A school district which submitted a plan within the timeframe pursuant to Laws 1993, sixth special session, forty-first legislature, chapter 1, § 41 may make reasonable revisions to its initial submission by the date prescribed in § 32 of this act."

Laws 1998, Ch. 217, § 42, as amended by Laws 1999, Ch. 168, § 27, effective May 5, 1999, provides:

"**Sec. 42. Area A expansion; compliance dates; air quality programs; Pinal county**

"**A.** Notwithstanding § 41 as added by this act, and section 49-541, paragraph 1, Arizona Revised Statutes, as amended by this act, relating to the geographical definition of area A, all air quality measures and programs added or modified by this act which are not listed in subsection B of this section, shall be effective from and after December 31, 2000 in the portion of area A which includes Pinal county.

"**B.** Cities, counties and school districts that are located in Pinal county and that have been included within the boundaries of area A shall comply with the provisions of § 9-500.04, subsections C through G, § 15-349 and § 49-474.01, subsections C through E, Arizona Revised Statutes, relating to the conversions of fleet vehicles to alternative fuels according to the following schedule:

"1. At least eighteen per cent of the total fleet by December 31, 2000.

"2. At least twenty-five per cent of the total fleet by December 31, 2001.

"3. At least fifty per cent of the total fleet by December 31, 2003.

"4. At least seventy-five per cent of the total fleet by December 31, 2005."

Laws 1998, Ch. 217, § 42, as amended by Laws 1999, Ch. 295, § 51 provides:

"**Sec. 42. Area A expansion; compliance dates; air quality programs; Pinal county**

"**A.** Notwithstanding § 41 as added by this act, and § 49-541, paragraph 1, Arizona Revised Statutes, as amended by this act, relating to the geographical definition of area A, all air quality measures and programs added or modified by this act which are not listed in subsection B of this section, shall be effective from and after December 31, 2000 in the portion of area A which includes Pinal county.

"**B.** Cities, counties and school districts that are located in Pinal county and that have been included within the boundaries of area A shall comply with the provisions of § 9-500.04, subsections C through G, § 15-349 and § 49-474.01, subsections C through E, Arizona Revised Statutes, relating to the conversions of fleet vehicles to alternative fuels according to the following schedule:

"1. At least eighteen per cent of the total fleet by December 31, 2000.

"2. At least twenty-five per cent of the total fleet by December 31, 2001.

"3. At least fifty per cent of the total fleet by December 31, 2003.

"4. At least seventy-five per cent of the total fleet by December 31, 2005."

Laws 2001, Ch. 371, § 18, subsec. B, provides:

"**Sec. 18. Area A expansion; compliance date; air quality programs**

"**B.** Cities, counties and school districts that have been included within the boundaries of area A shall comply with the provisions of § 9-500.04, subsections C through G, § 15-349 and § 49-474.01, subsections C through E, Arizona Revised Statutes, relating to the conversions of fleet vehicles to alternative fuels according to the following schedule:

"1. At least eighteen per cent of the total fleet by December 31, 2003.

"2. At least twenty-five per cent of the total fleet by December 31, 2004.

"3. At least fifty per cent of the total fleet by December 31, 2006.

"4. At least seventy-five per cent of the total fleet by December 31, 2008."

Laws 2002, Ch. 296, §§ 11, 12 and 13, effective July 1, 2003, provide:

"**Sec. 11. Description of funding source; purpose; notification**

"**A.** The funding described in § 15-349, Arizona Revised Statutes, as amended by this act, for the purpose of implementing a vehicle fleet plan for school districts, relating to vehicles with a gross vehicle weight rating of at least seventeen thousand five hundred pounds, may be from any of the following sources:

"1. The Arizona clean air fund, established pursuant to § 41-1516, Arizona Revised Statutes, as administered by the department of commerce.

"2. The clean air fund, established pursuant to title 49, Arizona Revised Statutes, as administered by the department of environmental quality.

"3. The portion of the air quality fund, established by § 49-551, Arizona Revised Statutes, as administered by the department of environmental quality, that receives monies from the fees established pursuant to section 49-543, subsection B, paragraph 2, Arizona Revised Statutes.

"**B.** The joint legislative budget committee shall promptly notify the governor, the president of the senate and the speaker of the house of representatives when any of the funding sources identified in subsection A of this section become operative.

"**Sec. 12. Conditional schedule revision**

"Notwithstanding § 15-349, Arizona Revised Statutes, as amended by this act, if the beginning production date for the standard for diesel fuel of a maximum sulfur limit of fifteen parts per million, as contained in the United States environmental protection agency rule relating to the control of air pollution from new motor vehicles: heavy duty engine and vehicle standards and highway diesel fuel sulfur control requirements; final rule, as published in the federal register, volume 66, number 12, January 28, 2001, pages 5001 through 5050, is revised by adding more than one year to the beginning production date, the schedule for implementing a vehicle fleet plan for school districts shall be as follows:

"1. The plan shall provide for at least sixty per cent of the fleet with a gross vehicle weight rating of at least seventeen thousand five hundred pounds to operate on the fuels listed pursuant to § 15-349, subsection A, Arizona Revised Statutes, as amended by this act, by December 31, 2005.

"2. The plan shall provide for at least seventy-five per cent of the fleet with a gross vehicle weight rating of at least seventeen thousand five hundred pounds to operate on the fuels listed pursuant to § 15-349, subsection A, Arizona Revised Statutes, as amended by this act, by December 31, 2006, and each year thereafter.

"**Sec. 13. Effective date**

"This act is effective from and after June 30, 2003."

Reviser's Notes:

1993 Note. Pursuant to authority of § 41-1304.02, this section. added by Laws 1993, Sixth Special Session, Ch. 1, sec. 5 as § 15-341.01, was renumbered as § 15-349.

1997 Note. Pursuant to authority of § 41-1304.02, in subsection B, third sentence the spelling of "heavy-duty" was corrected.

1998 Note. Pursuant to authority of § 41-1304.02, "~~E.~~F." was substituted for the second subsection E designation to correct a manifest clerical error.

2000 Note. Prior to the 2001 amendment, this section contained the amendments made by Laws 2000, Ch. 148, sec. 3 and Ch. 405, sec. 4 that were blended together pursuant to authority of § 41-1304.03.

§ 15-350. Investigation of immoral or unprofessional conduct; confidentiality

A. On request of the state board of education, any school or school district that has employed a certificated person during the time in which the person is alleged to have engaged in conduct constituting grounds for disciplinary action shall make available the attendance and testimony of witnesses, documents and any physical evidence within the school district's control for examination or copying. All information received and records or reports kept by the state board of education during an investigation of immoral or unprofessional conduct are confidential and are not a public record.

B. Notwithstanding subsection A of this section, the state board of education may provide information, records or reports relating to the investigation of a certificate holder to any school or school district that currently employs the certificate holder. All information, records or reports received by any school or school district pursuant to this subsection shall be used for employment purposes only, are confidential and are not a public record.

C. An investigator who is regularly employed and paid by the state board of education has the authority to access criminal history records and criminal history record information, as defined in § 41-1750, from law enforcement agencies.

Added by Laws 1994, Ch. 165, § 3. Amended by Laws 1998, Ch. 64, § 1; Laws 2000, Ch. 97, § 2; Laws 2001, Ch. 241, § 2.

Historical and Statutory Notes

The 1998 amendment by Ch. 64 added subsec. B.

The 2000 amendment by Ch. 97 changed "department of education" to "state board of education" throughout; changed "as a result of an investigation" to "during an investigation" in the second sentence of subsec. A; and changed "a school district" to "any school district" in two instances in subsec. B.

The 2001 amendment by Ch. 241 substituted "school or school district" for "school district" in subsec. A; rewrote subsec. B; and added subsec. C. Subsec. B had read:

"**B.** Notwithstanding subsection A, the state board of education may provide information, records or reports relating to the investigation of a certificate holder to any school district or other public school that currently employs the certificate holder. All information, records or reports received by any school district or other public school pursuant to this subsection shall be used for employment purposes only, are confidential and are not a public record."

ARTICLE 3.1. DECENTRALIZATION PROCESS

Article 3.1, Decentralization Process, consisting of §§ 15-351 to 15-353, was added by Laws 1994, 9th S.S., Ch. 2, § 3, effective September 16, 1994.

§ 15-351. School councils; duties; membership

A. The purpose of this section is to ensure that individuals who are affected by the outcome of a decision at the school site share in the decision making process.

B. Each school shall establish a school council. A governing board may delegate to a school council the responsibility to develop a curriculum and may delegate any additional powers that are reasonably necessary to accomplish decentralization. The school council shall take into consideration the ethnic composition of the local community and, except as provided in § 15-352, shall consist of the following members:

1. Parents or guardians of pupils enrolled in the school who are not employed by the school district.
2. Teachers.
3. Noncertified employees.
4. Community members.
5. Pupils, if the school is a high school.
6. The principal of the school.

C. Each group specified in subsection B of this section shall select its school council appointees and shall submit the names of its respective representatives to the principal. The initial representatives shall be selected at public meetings held at the school site, and, thereafter, representatives shall be selected by their groups in the manner determined by the school council. Schools shall give notice of the public meeting where the initial representatives of the groups shall be selected, clearly stating its purpose, time and place. The notice shall be posted in at least three different locations at the school site and in the community and shall be given to pupils for delivery to their parents or guardians.

D. The governing board shall determine the initial number of school council members. Thereafter, the school council shall determine the number. The number of teachers and parents or guardians of pupils enrolled at the school shall be equal. Teachers and parents or guardians of pupils enrolled at the school shall constitute a majority of the school council members.

E. The school council shall adopt written guidelines that specify the number of school council members and the methods for the selection of school council members.

F. The principal shall serve as chairman of the school council unless another person is elected by a majority of the school council members.
Added by Laws 1994, 9th S.S., Ch. 2, § 3. Amended by Laws 1996, Ch. 284, § 19; Laws 1997, Ch. 39, § 1; Laws 2003, Ch. 49, § 1.

Historical and Statutory Notes

Laws 1994, 9th S.S., Ch. 2, § 23, provides:

"**Sec. 23. Establishment of school councils; date**

"Each school in this state shall establish a school council pursuant to § 15-351, Arizona Revised Statutes, as added by this act, no later than December 31, 1995."

§ 15-352. Exemptions

A. The governing board is not obligated to reconstitute previously formed school councils pursuant to this section if the existing school councils include representation by more than one teacher and more than one parent or guardian of a pupil enrolled at the school.

B. The governing board may allow an alternative school to establish an alternative school council with members other than those specified in § 15-351 if teachers and parents or guardians of pupils enrolled at the school are represented.

C. A school district that has only one school or a student population of less than six hundred students may decide by a vote of the governing board to not participate in the decentralization process required by this article. If the governing board votes to not participate, the district is not subject to this article.
Added by Laws 1994, 9th S.S., Ch. 2, § 3. Amended by Laws 1997, Ch. 39, § 2.

§ 15-353. Responsibilities of principals

The principal of every school offering instruction in preschool programs, kindergarten programs or any combination of grades one through twelve is responsible for:

1. Providing leadership for the school.

2. Implementing the goals and the strategic plan of the school.

3. Serving as the administrator of the school.

4. Distributing a parental satisfaction survey to the parent of every child enrolled at the school. The parental satisfaction survey shall be distributed at least once each year and shall be distributed as part of the regular parent communication correspondence.

Added by Laws 1994, 9th S.S., Ch. 2, § 3.

§ 15-354. Principals; supplies and materials purchases

A. Notwithstanding any other law, the governing board of a school district may authorize school principals to sign negotiable instruments on behalf of the school district if the negotiable instruments are used for the purchase of supplies and materials that are necessary to conduct the operations of the school.

B. Purchases made pursuant to this section are exempt from title 41, chapter 23 [1] and the rules prescribed pursuant to § 15-213.

C. A school district that purchases supplies and materials pursuant to this section shall maintain a separate account in its maintenance and operation budget for each authorized school in the district for the purchase of supplies and materials. The amount of available monies in each school's supplies and materials account shall not exceed five thousand dollars.

D. Within thirty days of any purchase made pursuant to this section, the principal shall supply the governing board of the school district with a receipt from the seller of the supplies and materials that shows the price paid for each item purchased.

E. The principal and the governing board shall ensure that all purchases made pursuant to this section comply with the uniform system of financial records.

F. A governing board may delegate the purchasing authority granted pursuant to this section to one or more employees.

Added by Laws 1997, Ch. 231, § 8. Amended by Laws 2004, Ch. 340, § 1.

[1] Section 41-2501 et seq.

ARTICLE 4. ESTABLISHMENT OF SPECIAL SERVICES

§ 15-361. Establishment of evening and night schools; admission of students; tuition

The governing board of a school district may establish an evening or night school when in its judgment the school is necessary or convenient. The school shall be open for admission of children between the ages of fourteen and twenty-one years, but this shall not be construed as a requirement for a full course of study therein nor as requiring the admission of a person to a class beyond his educational attainments. The schools shall be open to persons over twenty-one years of age only upon payment of tuition as provided by law.

Added by Laws 1981, Ch. 1, § 2, eff. Jan. 23, 1981.

Historical and Statutory Notes

Source:

Rev. Code 1928, § 1040a.
Laws 1933, Ch. 65, § 4.
Code 1939, § 54–513.
A.R.S. former § 15–921.

§ 15–362. Libraries; powers and duties; authority to contract with a county free library or other public library

A. The governing board of a school district may establish and maintain libraries. Such libraries shall be under control of the board. The board shall be accountable for the care of the libraries, but it may appoint district librarians, or it may put the libraries under direct charge of a teacher or other qualified person. When requested, the board shall report on the libraries to the county school superintendent on forms supplied by the superintendent of public instruction.

B. The governing board shall:

1. Enforce the rules prescribed for government of school libraries.

2. Exclude from school libraries all books, publications and papers of a sectarian, partisan or denominational character.

C. A district library shall be free to all pupils of suitable age who attend the school. Residents of the district may become entitled to library privileges by payment of fees and compliance with regulations prescribed by the board. The governing board may enter into a contract or agreement with the proper authorities of a county free library or other public library possessing facilities for rendering the desired service for the procurement of reference or other library books or the extension services of such library. The amount so expended shall not exceed two per cent of the total school district budget for the school year during which the services are utilized.

Added by Laws 1981, Ch. 1, § 2, eff. Jan. 23, 1981.

Historical and Statutory Notes

Source:

Laws 1912, Ch. 77, §§ 41, 96, 97.
Civ. Code 1913, §§ 2733, 2813, 2814.
Laws 1921, Ch. 72, § 5.
Laws 1921, Ch. 137, § 1.
Laws 1925, Ch. 11, § 1.
Laws 1925, Ch. 70, §§ 1 to 4.
Laws 1927, Ch. 88, § 1.
Rev. Code 1928, §§ 1011, 1058.
Laws 1933, Ch. 18, § 1.
Laws 1935, Ch. 36, § 1.
Code 1939, § 54–1112.
Laws 1949, Ch. 110, § 1.
Laws 1951, Ch. 140, § 1.
Laws 1952, Ch. 138, § 1.
Code 1939, Supp.1952, § 54–416.
Laws 1954, Ch. 117, § 2.
A.R.S. former § 15–450.
Laws 1960, Ch. 127, § 35.
Laws 1978, Ch. 188, § 9.

§ 15–363. School recreation centers; authority to contract with public recreation boards and agencies

A. The governing board may operate school buildings and grounds for the purpose of providing a public play and recreation center. The governing board may organize and conduct in the center community recreation activities which contribute to the physical, mental and moral welfare of youths residing in the vicinity. A school recreation center may be open at times the governing board deems advisable, including evening hours and vacation days, and shall be conducted in accordance with rules prescribed by the governing board.

B. The governing board may cooperate and enter into contracts with other public recreation boards and agencies in carrying out the purposes of this section.

Added by Laws 1981, Ch. 1, § 2, eff. Jan. 23, 1981.

Historical and Statutory Notes

Source:

Laws 1949, Ch. 44, §§ 1, 2.
Code 1939, Supp.1952, §§ 54–435, 54–436.
A.R.S. former § 15–452.
Laws 1960, Ch. 127, § 36.

§ 15–364. Agreements and expenditure of public monies for recreational facilities on school properties; use of proceeds of bond issues

A. The governing board of a school district may enter into agreements with counties, cities, towns or other school district governing boards, providing for the construction, development, cooperative maintenance, operation and use of parks and recreational facilities, including swimming pools, on properties used for school purposes and under the control of such school districts. The governing boards may expend public monies for the construction and development of such parks or recreational facilities in cooperation with cities, towns and counties.

B. Counties, cities and towns may expend public monies and enter into agreements with cities, towns and school district governing boards for the construction, development, cooperative maintenance, operation and use of parks, swimming pools and other recreational facilities on properties used for school purposes, if the governing authorities having charge and control of such properties give their consent and cooperation.

C. Cities, towns and counties with a population of five hundred thousand persons or more according to the most recent United States decennial census may use the proceeds of bond issues for the purposes of this section.

Added by Laws 1981, Ch. 1, § 2, eff. Jan. 23, 1981. Amended by Laws 1995, Ch. 289, § 1.

Historical and Statutory Notes

Source:

Laws 1955, Ch. 134, §§ 1 to 4.
Code 1939, Supp.1955, §§ 54–2001 to 54–2004.
A.R.S. former §§ 15–1171, 15–1172.
Laws 1971, Ch. 93, § 1.
Laws 1978, Ch. 74, § 2.
Laws 1980, 2nd S.S., Ch. 8, § 14.

§ 15–365. Service programs operated through the office of a county school superintendent; reports; definitions

A. The county school superintendent may establish service programs which shall be available to any local school district governing board officially requesting such programs.

B. Both central administrative costs and general service costs shall be shared on a user basis and budgeted and paid as contract costs by the districts using such programs, except as provided in subsections E, F and H of this section.

C. Agreements or contracts entered into pursuant to this section shall not be subject to the provisions of title 11, chapter 7, article 3 [1] relating to intergovernmental agreements and contracts.

D. Each county school superintendent shall submit to the school districts involved and to the board of supervisors no later than May 31 of each year a program progress report and a fiscal report including actual expenditures through March 31 and estimates for the remainder of the fiscal year on each service program in operation in such county.

E. County school superintendents may establish special small district service programs designed to meet the special needs of school districts with a total student count of fewer than six hundred in such areas as administrative assistance and specialized services as follows:

1. For counties with seven or more school districts with a student count of fewer than six hundred, the small district service program may serve a single county or two or more counties.

2. Except as provided in subsection I of this section, for counties with fewer than seven school districts with a student count of fewer than six hundred, the small district service program shall serve two or more counties as determined by the superintendent of public instruction.

F. The costs of the small district service program are payable in part from the small district service program fund. Costs in excess of the amount available in the small district service program fund shall be shared on a user basis and budgeted and paid as contract costs by the district using such programs. The small district service program fund for each program shall consist of a base amount plus a per district amount for each school district in the county or counties served which has a student count of fewer than six hundred. For fiscal year 1989–1990, the base amount is fifty-six thousand four hundred ninety-four dollars and the per district amount is five thousand eighty-four dollars. Beginning with fiscal year 1990–1991, the base amount and per district amount are the amounts for the prior year adjusted by the growth rate prescribed by law, subject to appropriation. The county treasurer shall pay the appropriate amount into the small district service program fund from monies collected from the tax levy for county equalization assistance for education as provided in § 15–994 before the monies are used to provide equalization assistance for education as provided in § 15–971, subsection C, except that for small district service programs which serve two or more counties payment into the fund shall be as provided in subsection H of this section.

G. School districts which provide only financing for pupils who are instructed by another district shall be included in determining the number of districts counted for the small district service program fund.

H. For each small district service program which serves two or more counties, a county of jurisdiction shall be selected by the superintendent of public instruction. Payment shall be made into the small district service program fund in the county of jurisdiction from monies collected from the tax levy for county equalization assistance for education as provided in § 15–994 before the monies are used to provide equalization assistance as provided in § 15–994 by each county participating in the small district service program as follows:

1. The county treasurer of each county which is not the county of jurisdiction shall pay to the county of jurisdiction an amount determined as follows:

(a) Determine the total amount of the small district service program fund as provided in subsection F of this section.

(b) Determine the total number of school districts with a student count of fewer than six hundred in all counties served by the small district service program.

(c) Divide the amount determined in subdivision (a) of this paragraph by the amount determined in subdivision (b) of this paragraph.

(d) Multiply the number of school districts with a student count of fewer than six hundred in each county by the amount determined in subdivision (c) of this paragraph.

(e) The product determined in subdivision (d) of this paragraph is the amount which shall be paid to the county of jurisdiction.

2. The county treasurer of the county of jurisdiction shall deposit the monies received from the other counties as provided in paragraph 1 of this subsection into the small district service program fund and shall also pay into the fund an amount equal to the quotient obtained in paragraph 1, subdivision (c) of this subsection multiplied by the number of school districts with a student count of fewer than six hundred in the county of jurisdiction.

I. If a small district service program is established before fiscal year 1987–1988, the program may continue to operate as a single county program if the county contains fewer than seven, but at least four, school districts with a student count of fewer than six hundred.

J. A school district with a student count of six hundred or more in the current year which participated in a small district service program and which had a student count of fewer than six hundred in the prior year may continue to participate in the program for the current year and one additional year. The amount in the small district service program fund shall be determined as if the district had a student count of fewer than six hundred.

K. In this section, unless the context otherwise requires:

1. "Central administrative costs" means only those costs which are incurred by the county school superintendent in administering any service program which benefits all the school districts in the program and which are shared on a user basis and budgeted and paid as contract costs by districts, except as provided in subsections E, F and H of this section.

2. "General service costs" means those costs which are directly related to each of the service programs, which are shared on a user basis and which are budgeted and paid as contract costs by districts, except as provided in subsections E, F and H of this section.

3. "Service programs" means those programs which can be accomplished more efficiently and economically as multidistrict or multicounty operations.

4. "Student count" means the student count as defined in § 15–901, subsection A, except that it shall not include pupils enrolled in grades nine through

twelve to whom the district does not provide instruction if the district is a common school district which is not within a high school district.

Added by Laws 1981, Ch. 1, § 2, eff. Jan. 23, 1981. Amended by Laws 1985, Ch. 166, § 4, eff. April 18, 1985; Laws 1989, Ch. 206, § 1; Laws 1990, Ch. 226, § 1; Laws 1992, Ch. 172, § 4; Laws 1993, Ch. 189, § 1; Laws 1995, Ch. 191, § 2, eff. April 19, 1995; Laws 1995, Ch. 196, § 4.

[1] Section 11-951 et seq.

Historical and Statutory Notes

Source:

Laws 1976, Ch. 65, § 1.
A.R.S. former §§ 15-1165 to 15-1167.

For applicability provisions of Laws 1995, Ch. 196, see the Historical and Statutory Notes following § 1-254.

The amendment of this section by Laws 1995, Ch. 196, § 4, was repealed by Laws 1996, Ch. 248, § 2.

Laws 1996, Ch. 248, § 1, provides:

"**Section 1. Purpose**

"Sections 15-365, 15-782.01, 15-905, 15-913, 15-914, 15-945, 15-961, 15-962, 15-1184, 15-1424 and 15-1466, Arizona Revised Statutes, were amended by both Laws 1995, chapter 191 and Laws 1995, chapter 196. The two versions of each statute could not be blended because of conflicting language concerning the school district growth rate. The practical effect of both versions of each statute is to change the determination of the school district growth rate from a specified formula to an amount 'prescribed by law, subject to legislative appropriation'. However, the chapter 191 versions of each of these statutes used the phrase 'prescribed by law, subject to legislative appropriation' and the chapter 196 versions of each of these statutes accomplishes the same result by changing an internal reference to another statute that uses the phrase 'prescribed by law, subject to legislative appropriation'. In this act the chapter 196 version of each of these statutes is repealed, except for § 15-1466, Arizona Revised Statutes, in which the two versions contain substantively conflicting language and the chapter 191 version is repealed."

Reviser's Notes:

1995 Note. The amendment made by Laws 1995, Ch. 196, sec. 4 was inconsistent and incompatible with Laws 1995, Ch. 191, sec. 2 and therefore could not be blended.

ARTICLE 5. PROVISIONS FOR INSURANCE COVERAGE

§ 15-381. Liabilities of the governing board; payment of liabilities; immunity

A. The governing board is liable as such, in the name of the school district, for a judgment against the district for salary due a teacher on contract and for all debts contracted under this title. It shall pay judgments or liabilities from the school monies to the credit of the district.

B. The governing board members shall have no personal liability for acts done in reliance upon written opinions of the attorney general or upon written opinions of the county attorney:

1. Which are deemed to be affirmed by the attorney general pursuant to § 15-253.
2. With which the attorney general concurs.
3. Which the attorney general declines to review.
4. As revised by a written opinion of the attorney general.

C. Members of a governing board are immune from personal liability with respect to all acts done and actions taken in good faith within the scope of their authority during duly constituted regular and special meetings.

Added by Laws 1981, Ch. 1, § 2, eff. Jan. 23, 1981. Amended by Laws 1989, Ch. 273, § 4, eff. June 26, 1989.

Historical and Statutory Notes

Source:

Laws 1912, Ch. 77, §§ 41, 57.
Civ. Code 1913, §§ 2733, 2753.
Laws 1921, Ch. 72, § 5.
Laws 1921, Ch. 137, § 1.
Laws 1925, Ch. 70, §§ 1 to 4.
Laws 1927, Ch. 88, § 1.
Rev. Code 1928, §§ 1011, 1027.
Laws 1933, Ch. 18, § 1.
Code 1939, § 54-432.
Laws 1949, Ch. 110, § 1.
Laws 1951, Ch. 74, § 1.
Laws 1951, Ch. 140, § 1.
Laws 1952, Ch. 138, § 1.
Code 1939, Supp.1952, § 54-416.
Laws 1954, Ch. 117, § 2.
A.R.S. former §§ 15-436, 15-436.01, 15-441.
Laws 1956, Ch. 134, § 1.
Laws 1958, Ch. 88, § 2.
Laws 1960, Ch. 127, §§ 26, 28.
Laws 1972, Ch. 109, § 2.
Laws 1974, Ch. 113, § 1.
Laws 1980, Ch. 167, § 1.
Laws 1980, Ch. 170, § 2.

The 1989 amendment by Ch. 273, § 4, deleted former subsec. D and added new subsecs. D to G, which subsections were subsequently renumbered as § 15-387 [see, Reviser's Note, post].

Subsection D, prior to the 1989 amendment, had read:

"The governing board may provide financial protection for its members against damages incurred because of their position as members of the board, through the purchase of surety bonds and public liability and property damage insurance."

Reviser's Notes:

1989 Note. Laws 1989, Ch. 273, § 4 amended this section by adding subsections D, E, F and G. Pursuant to authority of § 41-1304.02, these subsections were relettered as § 15-387, subsections A, B, C and D and in the heading of this section "; purchase of insurance" was deleted.

§ 15-382. Authorization to self-insure; pooling agreements; joint agreements; trustees; liability coverage and pool requirements; remedies; definition

A. The school district governing board may determine that self-insurance is necessary or desirable in the best interest of the district and may provide for a self-insurance program or programs for the district including risk management consultation. Any risk management consultant or insurance administrator employed by a school district governing board must be licensed under title 20, chapter 2, article 3 or 9, [1] and such license shall be verified by the school district governing board prior to employment.

B. The school district governing board may:

1. Enter into intergovernmental agreements or contracts with pools operated pursuant to § 11-952.01 for participation in programs offered by public agency pools. In addition to the joint purchasing of insurance or reinsurance or the pooling of the retention of risks for property, fidelity and liability losses, these programs may include the joint purchasing of health benefits plan, life or disability insurance, prepaid legal insurance or the pooling of the retention of their risks of losses for health, accident, life or disability claims or the provision of the health and medical services enumerated in § 36-2907.

2. Separately contract with a trustee or board of trustees that provides a common self-insurance program or programs with pooled funds and risks to more than one district, a community college district formed pursuant to title 15, chapter 12, article 3 [2] or an association of school districts within this state that is funded by member school districts pursuant to § 15-342, paragraph 8.

3. Enter into cooperative procurement agreements with other districts pursuant to rules adopted pursuant to § 15-213 to participate in programs for either self-insurance or the joint purchase of insurance.

4. Separately establish a self-insurance program solely for its district.

C. If the school district governing board, either alone or in combination with another school district or an association of school districts in this state that is funded by member school districts pursuant to § 15–342, paragraph 8, establishes a self-insurance program, the governing board or an association of school districts shall place all funds into a trust to be used for payment of uninsured losses, claims, defense costs, costs of training designed to reduce losses and claims, the cost of related employee benefits including wellness programs, life, disability and other fully and partially insured group insurance plans, programs that allow for participation in a cafeteria plan that meets the requirements of the United States internal revenue code of 1986, costs of administration and other related expenses. If a member of the governing board or employee of the school district is acting as a trustee, the trust shall be administered by at least five joint trustees, of whom no more than one may be a member of the governing board and no more than one may be an employee of the school district. Funds budgeted for self-insurance programs shall be subject to district budgetary requirements, including but not limited to the requirements that the funds be budgeted within the maintenance and operation section and the budget limitation on increases as prescribed in § 15–905. The funds, upon being placed in the trust, shall not lapse at the close of the fiscal year, except that any cash balance remaining after termination of the program and settlement of all outstanding claims shall be used for reduction of school district taxes for the budget year. The trustees of the trust must be bonded, a stop-loss provision must be incorporated in the trust agreement, and an annual audit must be performed by a certified public accountant and a copy of the report kept on file in the district office for a period of not less than five years.

D. If the self-insurance is for liability losses, excess liability coverage or reinsurance must be obtained as follows:

1. For a single school district, the coverage may include an annual aggregate limit of no more than three million dollars and the maximum retention per occurrence shall be one-half of one per cent of the district's maintenance and operation budget.

2. For a pool, the coverage may include an annual aggregate limit set by the pool and the maximum retention per occurrence shall not exceed one-half of one per cent of the combined maintenance and operation budgets of the districts in the pool.

E. "Self–insurance program" as used in this section means programs established and wholly or partially funded by the school district governing board. Self–insurance programs shall not include a decision by the governing board not to carry insurance upon a particular risk or risks.

Added by Laws 1981, Ch. 1, § 2, eff. Jan. 23, 1981. Amended by Laws 1985, Ch. 206, § 1; Laws 1986, Ch. 391, § 4, eff. May 21, 1986; Laws 1998, Ch. 139, § 3, eff. Oct. 1, 1998; Laws 2001, Ch. 139, § 1; Laws 2002, Ch. 240, § 3; Laws 2004, Ch. 230, § 3.

[1] Sections 20–281 et seq. or 20–485 et seq.

[2] Section 15–1441 et seq.

Historical and Statutory Notes

Source:

Laws 1979, Ch. 185, § 3.
A.R.S. former § 15-441.02.

The 1985 amendment rewrote subsec. B, which had read:

"The school district governing board may enter into governmental agreements or contracts pursuant to title 11, chapter 7, article 3 providing for a self-insurance program or programs by districts."

The 1986 amendment deleted "for employee benefits" following "self-insurance program or programs" in subsec. A; in subsec. B, deleted "do either of the following" from the end of the introductory paragraph, inserted "or the joint purchase of insurance" in par. 1, deleted ", excluding workers' compensation programs," preceding "with pooled funds" in par. 2 and inserted par. 3; deleted the designation of former subsec. D and incorporated its provisions in subsec. C as its concluding sentence; substituted "a certified accountant" for "an external auditor" in the sentence incorporated into subsec. C; inserted a new subsec. D; and in subsec. E, deleted "an employee benefit program or" preceding "programs established" in the first sentence and inserted "governing" in the second sentence.

Laws 1998, Ch. 139, § 6, provides:

"**Sec. 6. Effective date**

"This act is effective from and after September 30, 1998."

The 2002 amendment by Ch. 240, rewrote subsec. B, paragraph 1, which had read:

"1. Enter into intergovernmental agreements or contracts pursuant to § 11-952.01 for participation in programs offered by public agency pools. These programs may include the joint purchasing of health benefits plan insurance or the joint providing of the health and medical services enumerated in § 36-2907."

The 2004 amendment by Ch. 230 inserted "or reinsurance" in subsec. D; and rewrote pars. 1 and 2 of subsec. B, which had read:

[**B.**] "1. Enter into intergovernmental agreements or contracts pursuant to § 11-952.01 for participation in programs offered by public agency pools. these programs may include the joint purchasing of health benefits plan, life or disability insurance or the pooling of the retention of losses for health, accident, life or disability claims or the provision of the health and medical services enumerated in § 36-2907.

"2. Separately contract with a trustee or board of trustees which provides a common self-insurance program or programs with pooled funds and risks to more than one district or an association of school districts within this state that is funded by member school districts pursuant to § 15-342, paragraph 8."

Reviser's Notes:

1985 Note. Pursuant to authority of § 41-1304.02, in subsection B, paragraph 2, "workers'" was substituted for "workers" [deleted by 1986 amendment].

§ 15-383. Insurance on school bus operator; authority of the governing board to purchase

A. The governing board may purchase public liability and property damage insurance covering school bus drivers while driving school buses.

B. The governing board of any school district may require the operator of a school bus used for transportation of pupils attending schools in the district to carry public liability insurance in amounts not to exceed twenty thousand dollars for personal injury to any one person, and one hundred thousand dollars for personal injuries arising out of any one accident, covering any liability to which the operator may be subject on account of personal injuries to a passenger or other person caused or contributed to by an act of the operator while operating a school bus. If the policy of insurance is filed with and approved by the governing board of the school district, the governing board may increase the compensation otherwise payable to the operator by an amount equal to the cost to the operator of the insurance.

Added by Laws 1981, Ch. 1, § 2, eff. Jan. 23, 1981.

Historical and Statutory Notes

Source:

Laws 1941, Ch. 96, § 1.

Code 1939, Supp.1952, § 54-434.
A.R.S. former § 15-453.
Laws 1958, Ch. 88, § 3.

§ 15-384. Authorization for insurance coverage for students

A. The governing board of any school district, or the county school superintendent concerning accommodation schools, may provide or make available health benefits plan coverage for the school district. Such services may be secured only by either of the following methods:

1. Obtaining membership in nonprofit corporations pursuant to § 11-952.01 which shall defray the cost of the health and medical services and benefits.

2. Obtaining group, blanket or individual policies of health benefits plan insurance from insurers authorized to transact such business in this state.

B. The cost of membership in the nonprofit corporation or the health benefits plan insurance premiums may be paid by the school district, or by the county in the case of accommodation schools, or by the student or the student's parent or guardian, provided that no monies from the school district's maintenance and operation budget shall be used to pay for such membership or premiums.

Added by Laws 1981, Ch. 1, § 2, eff. Jan. 23, 1981. Amended by Laws 1998, Ch. 139, § 4, eff. Oct. 1, 1998.

Historical and Statutory Notes

Source:

Laws 1964, Ch. 84, § 1.
A.R.S. former § 15-441.01.
Laws 1998, Ch. 139, § 6, provides:

"**Sec. 6. Effective date**

"This act is effective from and after September 30, 1998."

§ 15-385. Premiums of a bond or insurance for accommodation schools or federally owned buildings on Indian reservation

A. When by the provisions of an agreement entered into between the state, an officer or agency thereof or a school district of this state, and the government of the United States or an agency or officer thereof, for the use of school buildings on Indian reservations, whereby a school district is required to execute a bond in favor of the federal government or an officer or agency thereof, or to procure and pay for insurance for protection of federally owned buildings or equipment being used for school purposes, the bond or insurance may be executed by the governing board of the school district, and the district or governing board may procure and pay for the bond or insurance as is necessary for protection of the buildings or equipment. Premiums paid for a bond or insurance shall be a charge against the funds of the school district.

B. The provisions of this section shall apply also to accommodation schools under the jurisdiction of the county school superintendent and payment of premiums for a bond or insurance may be made by the county school superintendent from the county school reserve fund.

Added by Laws 1981, Ch. 1, § 2, eff. Jan. 23, 1981.

Historical and Statutory Notes

Source:
Laws 1943, Ch. 21, § 1.
Code 1939, Supp.1952, § 54-104.
A.R.S. former § 15-454.

§ 15-386. Insurance refund fund

A. Monies retained for insurance premium payments which are refunded to a school district at the end of a fiscal year by an insurer with which the governing board contracted for that fiscal year may be deposited with the county treasurer who shall credit the deposits to the insurance refund fund of the district.

B. The insurance refund fund of a school district is a continuing fund not subject to reversion. Monies from the insurance refund fund may:

1. Be expended for insurance premium payments.

2. Be placed into a trust to be used for payments of uninsured losses, claims, defense costs and other related expenses as provided in § 15-382.

3. Be used for reduction of taxes in the budget year.

Added by Laws 1985, Ch. 170, § 1, eff. April 18, 1985.

§ 15-387. Procurement of insurance; eligibility of governing board members, former board members and surviving spouse and dependents; deposit of monies

A. Notwithstanding § 15-323, the governing board may procure insurance from any insurer authorized by the director of the department of insurance or may establish a self-insurance program as provided in § 15-382 for the management and administration of a system for direct payment of benefits, losses or claims or any combination of insurance and direct payments, including risk management consultation, to provide:

1. Health, accident, life or disability benefits for employees of the school district and their dependents and for members of the governing board and their dependents as provided in subsection B of this section.

2. Payment of any property or fidelity loss sustained, legal expenses incurred or lawful claim of liability or fortuitous loss made against the school district or its employees, including leased employees, or officers if the employees, leased employees or officers are acting in the scope of their employment or authority.

3. Coverage for all construction projects for purposes of general liability, property damage and workers' compensation.

B. A governing board member is eligible to participate in an insurance plan provided as an employee benefit pursuant to subsection A, paragraph 1 of this section if the member pays the full premium and the participation of the member does not result in an expenditure of school district monies.

C. If the governing board allows its members to participate in the insurance plan, a governing board may also adopt a policy allowing participation in an insurance plan provided as an employee benefit pursuant to subsection A, paragraph 1 of this section for former board members and for surviving spouses and dependents of board members or former board members as follows:

1. The board may allow a former board member to continue to participate if the former board member served at least four consecutive years on the board, was covered under the insurance plan while serving on the board and pays the full premium and the participation does not result in an expenditure of school district monies.

2. The board may allow the surviving spouse and dependent of the board member or former board member to continue to participate in the insurance plan if the surviving spouse or dependent pays the full premium and the participation of the surviving spouse and dependent does not result in an expenditure of school district monies and if:

(a) The deceased board member or former board member met the qualifications for eligibility pursuant to paragraph 1 of this subsection.

(b) The deceased board member or former board member would have met the qualifications for eligibility pursuant to paragraph 1 of this subsection if the deceased board member or former board member had not died in office.

D. Monies that are provided by employees, board members, former board members and surviving spouses and dependents of board members or former board members and that are received pursuant to this section shall be deposited in an account as provided in § 15-1223.

Formerly § 15-381, subsecs. D to G, as amended by Laws 1989, Ch. 273, § 4, eff. June 26, 1989. Renumbered as § 15-387. Amended by Laws 1999, Ch. 299, § 6; Laws 2004, Ch. 230, § 4.

Historical and Statutory Notes

Reviser's Notes:

1989 Note. Laws 1989, Chapter 273 added subsections D, E, F and G to § 15-381. Pursuant to authority of § 41-1304.02, these subsections were relettered as a new § 15-387, subsections A, B, C and D, the reference in subsection A, paragraph 1 to "subsection B" was substituted for the reference to "subsection E" and the references in subsections B and C to "subsection A" were substituted for the reference to "subsection D" to conform to the reviser's relettering and "Procurement of insurance; eligibility of governing board members, former board members and surviving spouse and dependents; deposit of monies" was added as the section heading.

§ 15-388. Optional inclusion of school district employees in state health and accident coverage; payment of premiums; advance notice; minimum period of participation; definition

A. If a governing board of a school district determines that state health and accident insurance coverage is necessary or desirable and in the best interest of the district, it may provide for inclusion of the district's employees and spouses and dependents of school district employees in state health and accident insurance coverage pursuant to § 38-651.

B. If the school district elects to participate in the state health and accident insurance coverage, it shall be the only health and accident insurance coverage offered to school district employees.

C. A school district governing board that elects to include its employees in the state health and accident insurance coverage shall notify the department of administration of its intention to do so by January 15 of the calendar year prior to the school year starting after June 30 in which the school district's employees would be eligible to receive state health and accident insurance coverage.

D. A school district governing board that elects to include its employees in the state health and accident insurance coverage shall participate in state health and accident insurance coverage for at least two years.

E. School districts that opt to participate in the state health and accident insurance coverage shall agree to accept the benefit level, plan design, insurance providers, premium level and other terms and conditions determined by the department of administration and shall accept such other contractual arrangements made by the department of administration with health and accident insurance providers.

F. School districts shall reimburse the department of administration for administrative and operational costs associated with school districts participating in the state health and accident insurance coverage determined pursuant to § 38-651, subsection K.

G. As used in this section, "state health and accident insurance coverage" means the health and accident coverage procured by the department of administration under § 38-651.

Added by Laws 1991, Ch. 319, § 2, eff. Aug. 1, 1993. Amended by Laws 1998, Ch. 212, § 2; Laws 2001, Ch. 127, § 1.

Historical and Statutory Notes

Laws 1991, Ch. 319, § 7, subsec. A, provides:

"**Sec. 7. Delayed effective date**

"**A.** Sections 2 and 3 of this act are effective from and after July 31, 1993."

ARTICLE 6. JOINT TECHNOLOGICAL EDUCATION DISTRICTS

Article 6, consisting of §§ 15-391 to 15-396, was added by Laws 1990, Ch. 248, § 1, effective September 27, 1990, retroactively effective to July 15, 1990.

The article heading was changed from "Joint Vocational and Technical Education Districts" to "Joint Technological Education Districts" by Laws 1991, Ch. 154, § 1, effective May 20, 1991.

Historical and Statutory Notes

Laws 1990, Ch. 248, § 8 as amended by Laws 1991, Ch. 154, § 13, effective May 20, 1991, provides:

"**Sec. 8. Staffing for joint technological education district**

"If an existing vocational and technical school operated by a single public school district becomes a joint technological education school operated in accordance with § 15-393, Arizona Revised Statutes, all staff employed at the existing vocational and technical school on March 15 of the school year prior to the first year of operation of the joint technological school are entitled to employment by the joint district if they would have been employed if the vocational and technical school had continued to be operated by the single school district. Staff employed by the joint technological education district pursuant to this section shall retain employment benefits, including previously established years of employment and sick leave."

Laws 1990, Ch. 399, § 23, provides:

"Sec. 23. Laws 1990, chapter 248 is amended by adding section 10 to read:

"**Sec. 10. Retroactivity**

"This act is effective retroactively to July 15, 1990."

§ 15–391. Definitions

In this article, unless the context otherwise requires:

1. "Joint board" means a joint technological education district governing board.

2. "Joint district" means a joint technological education district.

3. "State board" means the state board of education.

Added by Laws 1990, Ch. 248, § 1, eff. Sept. 27, 1990, retroactively effective to July 15, 1990. Amended by Laws 1991, Ch. 154, § 2, eff. May 20, 1991; Laws 2002, Ch. 89, § 3.

Historical and Statutory Notes

For retroactivity provision of Laws 1990, Ch. 248, amended by Laws 1990, Ch. 399, § 23, see Historical and Statutory Notes preceding § 15–391.

§ 15–392. Formation of district

A. Notwithstanding any other provision of law, districts interested in forming a joint technological education district shall conduct a study to determine the need to establish a joint technological education district in an area consisting of two or more school districts. The districts shall also initiate a plan for the establishment and operation of the joint district, which shall include a proposed budget based on a reasonable estimate of student enrollment in the new joint district. Any school district may assist in the preparation and payment of costs of the study and plan. The districts shall file a copy of the plan with the governing board of each school district included in the plan for the joint district. The districts shall submit the results of the study and the plan, along with evidence of approval by the governing board of each school district included in the selected plan for the joint district, to the state board of education.

B. If the state board of education determines that the plan submitted for the proposed joint district has met the requirements of this section, until December 31, 2001, the question shall be submitted to the qualified electors of each school district at a general election or at any other election held on a date prescribed in § 16–204. After December 31, 2001, the question shall be submitted to the qualified electors of the district seeking to become a part of the joint district at an election held on the first Tuesday after the first Monday in November. The question that is submitted to the qualified electors must describe the tax rate that is associated with joining the joint district and the estimated cost of that tax rate for the owner of a single family home that is valued at one hundred thousand dollars. If the electors in a district approve, then that district is authorized to participate in a joint technological education district. The joint district shall become operational on July 1 following the election held pursuant to this subsection, except as provided in subsection D of this section.

C. The governing boards of the school districts participating in the joint district may pay on a proportional basis the administrative, clerical and other expenses necessary for the establishment and operation of the joint district until monies are otherwise provided.

D. A joint technological education district after receiving voter approval as provided in subsection B of this section shall be governed by a joint board consisting of members elected pursuant to § 15-393, except that the initial composition of the joint board shall consist of one person who is not currently a board member of any school district and who is appointed by the governing board of each district participating in the joint technological education district. The terms of office of the joint board members shall become effective on January 1 following the election held pursuant to subsection B of this section. Upon the effective date of the term of office for joint board members, the joint board may begin necessary operations and activities related to making the district operational pursuant to subsection B of this section. If less than five districts are participating in the joint district, the initial composition of the joint board shall consist of two persons who are not currently board members of any school district and who are appointed by each participating district's governing board. The appointed members shall serve until January 1 following the next general election. At the general election held next following the formation of the joint district and thereafter, joint board members shall be elected as prescribed in § 15-393.

Added by Laws 1990, Ch. 248, § 1, eff. Sept. 27, 1990, retroactively effective to July 15, 1990. Amended by Laws 1991, Ch. 154, § 3, eff. May 20, 1991; Laws 1992, Ch. 305, § 7; Laws 1999, Ch. 152, § 1; Laws 2001, Ch. 251, § 1; Laws 2002, Ch. 89, § 4; Laws 2002, Ch. 330, § 2.

Historical and Statutory Notes

For retroactivity provision of Laws 1990, Ch. 248, amended by Laws 1990, Ch. 399, § 23, see Historical and Statutory Notes preceding § 15-391.

Laws 1992, Ch. 305, §§ 30 and 31, provide:

"**Sec. 30. Joint technological education district; general election of board members**

"Notwithstanding § 15-392, Arizona Revised Statutes, the first general election for members of a joint technological education district governing board for a joint technological education district established prior to the effective date of this act shall be held in 1994.

"**Sec. 31. Retention of members**

"Notwithstanding § 15-392, Arizona Revised Statutes, as amended by this act, all persons serving as members of a joint technological education district governing board shall continue to serve until the general election held pursuant to § 30 of this act, unless a vacancy occurs due to the member's resignation, death or removal. If a vacancy occurs, a member shall be appointed to fill the remainder of the unexpired term pursuant to the provisions of § 15-392, Arizona Revised Statutes, as amended by this act."

Laws 1999, Ch. 152, § 3, provides:

"**Sec. 3. Retroactivity**

"This act applies retroactively to from and after July 1, 1998."

Laws 2001, Ch. 251, became law without the Governor's signature as provided in Arizona Constitution, Article 5, § 7.

Laws 2002, Ch. 330, became law without the Governor's signature as provided in Arizona Constitution, Article 5, § 7.

Laws 2004, Ch. 278, § 21, provides:

"**Sec. 21. Retroactivity**

"**A.** Except as provided in subsection B of this section, this act applies retroactively to from and after June 30, 2004.

"**B.** Laws 2002, chapter 330, § 49, as amended by this act, applies retroactively to from and after June 29, 2004."

Laws 2002, Ch. 330, § 51, as amended by Laws 2004, Ch. 278, § 7; Laws 2004, Ch. 341, § 10, provides:

"**Sec. 51. Temporary prohibition on joining or forming joint technological education districts**

"**A.** Notwithstanding §§ 15-392 and 15-395, Arizona Revised Statutes, school districts shall not be allowed to:

"1. Form any new joint technological education district between November 30, 2002 and June 30, 2005, unless both of the following requirements are met:

"(a) At least two school district governing boards voted to participate as part of the joint technological education district before February 1, 2002.

"(b) The joint technological education district is approved by the voters before November 30, 2002.

"2. Join a joint technological education district between the effective date of this act and June 30, 2005, unless the school district shares a border with a school district that currently belongs to the joint district or, if the school district does not share a border with a school district that currently belongs to the joint district, the governing board of the school district voted to become part of the joint technological education district at a public meeting before March 7, 2002 and the joinder is approved by the voters before November 30, 2002. The election requirements prescribed in §§ 15-392 and 15-395, Arizona Revised Statutes, apply to any joinders entered into pursuant to this paragraph.

"**B.** For fiscal year 2004-2005, basic state aid funding to a new joint technological education district formed pursuant to subsection A, paragraph 1 of this section shall be limited to no more than the amount of basic state aid funding that the district received in fiscal year 2003-2004."

Laws 2004, Ch. 341, § 13, subsec. B, provides:

"**Sec. 13. Conditional enactment**"

"**B.** Section 10 of this act, relating to a temporary prohibition on joining or forming joint technological education districts, is not effective unless senate bill 1405, § 7, forty-sixth legislature, second regular session, as transmitted to the governor, becomes law."

Reviser's Notes:

2002 Note. This section contains the amendments made by Laws 2002, Ch. 89, sec. 4 and Ch. 330, sec. 2 that were blended together as shown pursuant to authority of § 41-1304.03.

§ 15-393. Joint technological education district governing board

A. The management and control of the joint district are vested in the joint technological education district governing board. Unless the governing boards of the school districts participating in the formation of the joint district vote to implement an alternative election system as provided in subsection B of this section, the joint board shall consist of five members elected from five single member districts formed within the joint district. The single member district election system shall be submitted as part of the plan for the joint district pursuant to § 15-392 and shall be established in the plan as follows:

1. The governing boards of the school districts participating in the formation of the joint district shall define the boundaries of the single member districts so that the single member districts are as nearly equal in population as is practicable, except that if the joint district lies in part in each of two or more counties, at least one single member district may be entirely within each of the counties comprising the joint district if this district design is consistent with the obligation to equalize the population among single member districts.

2. The boundaries of each single member district shall follow election precinct boundary lines, as far as practicable, in order to avoid further segmentation of the precincts.

3. A person who is a registered voter of this state and who is a resident of the single member district is eligible for election to the office of joint board member from the single member district. The terms of office of the members of the joint board shall be as prescribed in § 15-427, subsection B.

4. Nominating petitions shall be signed by the number of qualified electors of the single member district as provided in § 16-322.

B. The governing boards of the school districts participating in the formation of the joint district may vote to implement any other alternative election system for the election of joint district board members. If an alternative election system is selected, it shall be submitted as part of the plan for the joint district pursuant to § 15-392, and the implementation of the system shall be as approved by the United States justice department.

C. The joint technological education district shall be subject to the following provisions of this title:

1. Chapter 1, articles 1 through 6. [1]
2. Sections 15-208, 15-210, 15-213 and 15-234.
3. Chapter 3, articles 2, 3 and 5. [2]
4. Section 15-361.
5. Chapter 4, articles 1, 2 and 5. [3]
6. Chapter 5, articles 1, 2 and 3. [4]
7. Sections 15-701.01, 15-722, 15-723, 15-724, 15-727, 15-728, 15-729 and 15-730.
8. Chapter 7, article 5. [5]
9. Chapter 8, articles 1, 3 and 4. [6]
10. Sections 15-828 and 15-829.
11. Chapter 9, articles 1, 6 and 7. [7]
12. Sections 15-941, 15-943.01, 15-948, 15-952, 15-953 and 15-973.
13. Sections 15-1101 and 15-1104.
14. Chapter 10, articles 2, 3, 4 and 8. [8]

D. Notwithstanding subsection C of this section, the following apply to a joint technological education district:

1. A joint district may issue bonds for the purposes specified in § 15-1021 and in chapter 4, article 5 of this title to an amount in the aggregate, including the existing indebtedness, not exceeding one per cent of the taxable property used for secondary tax purposes, as determined pursuant to title 42, chapter 15, article 1, [9] within the joint technological education district as ascertained by the last property tax assessment previous to issuing the bonds.

2. The number of governing board members for a joint district shall be as prescribed in subsection A of this section.

3. If a career and technical education and vocational education course or program provided pursuant to this article is provided in a facility owned and operated by a school district in which a pupil is enrolled, the sum of the daily attendance, as provided in § 15-901, subsection A, paragraph 6, for that pupil in both the school district and joint technological education district shall not exceed 1.250 and the sum of the fractional student enrollment, as provided in § 15-901, subsection A, paragraph 2, subdivision (a), shall not exceed 1.250 for the courses taken in the school district and the facility. The school district and the joint district shall determine the apportionment of the daily attendance and fractional student enrollment for that pupil between the school district and the joint district.

4. The student count for the first year of operation of a joint technological education district as provided in this article shall be determined as follows:

(a) Determine the estimated student count for joint district classes that will operate in the first year of operation. This estimate shall be based on actual registration of pupils as of March 30 scheduled to attend classes that will be operated by the joint district. The student count for the district of residence of the pupils registered at the joint district shall be adjusted. The adjustment shall cause the district of residence to reduce the student count for the pupil to reflect the courses to be taken at the joint district. The district of residence shall review and approve the adjustment of its own student count as provided in this subdivision before the pupils from the school district can be added to the student count of the joint district.

(b) The student count for the new joint district shall be the student count as determined in subdivision (a).

(c) After the first one hundred days or two hundred days in session, as applicable, for the first year of operation, the joint district shall revise the student count to the actual student count for students attending classes in the joint district. A joint district shall revise its student count, the base support level as provided in § 15–943.02, the revenue control limit as provided in § 15–944.01, the capital outlay revenue limit and the soft capital allocation as provided in § 15–962.01 prior to May 15. A joint district that overestimated its student count shall revise its budget prior to May 15. A joint district that underestimated its student count may revise its budget prior to May 15.

(d) After the first one hundred days or two hundred days in session, as applicable, for the first year of operation, the district of residence shall adjust its student count by reducing it to reflect the courses actually taken at the joint district. The district of residence shall revise its student count, the base support level as provided in § 15–943, the revenue control limit as provided in § 15–944, the capital outlay revenue limit as provided in § 15–961 and the soft capital allocation as provided in § 15–962 prior to May 15. A district that underestimated the student count for students attending the joint district shall revise its budget prior to May 15. A district that overestimated the student count for students attending the joint district may revise its budget prior to May 15.

(e) A joint district for the first year of operation shall not be eligible for the provisions of § 15–948.

(f) The procedures for implementing the provisions of this paragraph shall be as prescribed in the uniform system of financial records.

(g) If the district of residence utilizes the provisions of § 15–942 to determine its student count, the district shall reduce its student count as provided in this paragraph by subtracting the appropriate count from the student count determined as provided in § 15–942.

For the purposes of this paragraph, "district of residence" means the district that included the pupil in its average daily membership for the year before the first year of operation of the joint district and that would have included the pupil in its student count for the purposes of computing its base support level for the fiscal year of the first year of operation of the joint district if the pupil had not enrolled in the joint district.

5. A student includes any person enrolled in the joint district without regard to the person's age or high school graduation status, except that a student who is over twenty-two years of age shall not be included in the student count of the joint district for the purposes of chapter 9, articles 3, 4 and 5 of this title.

6. A joint district may operate for more than one hundred seventy-five days per year, with expanded hours of service.

7. A joint district may use the excess utility costs provisions of § 15–910 in the same manner as a school district for fiscal years 1999–2000 and 2000–2001, except that the base year shall be the first full fiscal year of operations.

8. A joint district may use the carryforward provisions of § 15–943. 01 retroactively to July 1, 1993.

E. The joint board shall appoint a superintendent as the executive officer of the joint district.

F. Taxes may be levied for the support of the joint district as prescribed in chapter 9, article 6 of this title. Except for the taxes levied pursuant to § 15–994, such taxes shall be obtained from a levy of taxes on the taxable property used for secondary tax purposes.

G. The schools in the joint district are available to all persons who reside in the joint district subject to the rules for admission prescribed by the joint board.

H. The joint board may collect tuition for adult students and the attendance of pupils who are residents of school districts that are not participating in the joint district pursuant to arrangements made between the governing board of the district and the joint board.

I. The joint board may accept gifts, grants, federal monies, tuition and other allocations of monies to erect, repair and equip buildings and for the cost of operation of the schools of the joint district.

J. One member of the joint board shall be selected chairman. The chairman shall be selected annually on a rotation basis from among the participating school districts. The chairman of the joint board shall be a voting member.

K. A joint board and a community college district may enter into agreements for the provision of administrative, operational and educational services and facilities.

Added by Laws 1990, Ch. 248, § 1, eff. Sept. 27, 1990, retroactively effective to July 15, 1990. Amended by Laws 1991, Ch. 154, § 4, eff. May 20, 1991; Laws 1997, Ch. 300, § 8; Laws 1998, Ch. 1, § 46, eff. Jan. 1, 1999; Laws 1998, Ch. 52, § 4; Laws 1998, Ch. 167, § 3; Laws 1998, 5th S.S., Ch. 1, § 11, eff. July 9, 1998; Laws 1999, Ch. 152, § 2; Laws 1999, Ch. 299, § 7; Laws 2000, Ch. 342, § 2; Laws 2000, Ch. 344, § 1; Laws 2001, Ch. 251, § 2; Laws 2002, Ch. 89, § 5; Laws 2004, Ch. 263, § 1.

[1] Sections 15–101 et seq. through 15–161 et seq.

[2] Sections 15–321 et seq., 15–341 et seq. and 15–381 et seq.

[3] Sections 15–401 et seq., 15–421 et seq. and 15–491 et seq.

[4] Sections 15–501 et seq., 15–521 et seq. and 15–531 et seq.

[5] Section 15–781 et seq.

[6] Sections 15–801 et seq., 15–840 et seq. and 15–851 et seq.

[7] Sections 15–901 et seq., 15–991 et seq. and 15–1021 et seq.

[8] Sections 15–1121 et seq., 15–1141 et seq., 15–1151 et seq., 15–1221 et seq.

[9] Section 42–15001 et seq.

Retroactive Application

This section, as amended by Laws 2000, Ch. 344, applies retroactively to July 1, 1993.

Historical and Statutory Notes

For retroactivity provision of Laws 1990, Ch. 248, amended by Laws 1990, Ch. 399, § 23, see Historical and Statutory Notes preceding § 15-391.

Laws 1991, chapter 154, § 14, as amended by Laws 1992, Ch. 305, § 28, provides:

"**Sec. 14. Joint technological education district; first year student count for fiscal year 1991-1992; student count for fiscal year 1992-1993**

"Notwithstanding § 15-901, Arizona Revised Statutes, and § 15-393, subsection D, paragraph 4, Arizona Revised Statutes, as amended by this act:

"1. For the purposes of calculating a base support level, capital outlay revenue limit and capital levy revenue limit for fiscal year 1991-1992, the total student count for the joint district shall not exceed 834. For fiscal year 1991-1992 the student count of the district of residence of the pupils registered at the joint district shall be reduced by 0.400 for each pupil taking three classes in the joint district and shall be reduced by 1.000 for each pupil taking four or more classes in the joint district. The district of residence shall review and approve the adjustment of its own student count as provided in this subsection before the pupils from the school district can be added to the student count of the joint district.

"2. For the purposes of determining the student count for fiscal year 1992-1993:

"(a) The joint district shall follow the procedures prescribed in § 15-393, subsection D, paragraph 4, Arizona Revised Statutes, as added by this act, as if fiscal year 1992-1993 were the first year of operation of the joint district.

"(b) If the number of pupils enrolled in the joint district from a district of residence exceeds the number of pupils so enrolled from the district in fiscal year 1991-1992, the district of residence shall adjust its student count by the amount prescribed in § 15-393, subsection D, paragraph 4, Arizona Revised Statutes, less the amount its student count was adjusted for fiscal year 1991-1992 due to the enrollment of pupils in the joint district during fiscal year 1991-1992."

The 1998 amendment of this section by Ch. 52, § 4, explicitly amended the amendment of this section by Laws 1998, Ch. 1, § 46.

Laws 1998, Ch. 52, § 74, as amended by Laws 1998, Ch. 113, § 68, provides:

"**Sec. 74. Effective date**

"Sections 9-432, 15-393, 15-991.01, 15-1021, 27-234, 42-5008, 42-5404, 42-11109, 42-12159, 42-13001, 42-14357, 42-15064, 42-16214, 42-17251, 42-17254, 42-17256, 48-574, 48-614, 48-616 and 48-807, Arizona Revised Statutes, as amended by this act, are effective from and after December 31, 1998."

Laws 1998, Ch. 113, § 1, par. 40, provides:

"**Section 1. Purpose.**"

"40. Sections 9-432, 15-393, 15-991.01, 15-1021 and 27-234, Arizona Revised Statutes, were amended by Laws 1998, chapter 1 with a delayed effective date of January 1, 1999. The Laws 1998, chapter 1 versions of these sections were subsequently amended by Laws 1998, chapter 52 with a general effective date. In order to correct a potentially defective enactment, this act amends Laws 1998, chapter 52, § 74 that prescribes an effective date of January 1, 1999 for other sections in the act to include §§ 9-432, 15-393, 15-991.01, 15-1021 and 27-234, Arizona Revised Statutes."

The purported amendment of this section by Laws 1998, 3rd S.S., Ch. 1, failed to became effective because Ch. 1 was repealed in its entirety by Laws 1998, 5th S.S., Ch. 1, § 2, effective July 1, 1998.

Laws 1999, Ch. 152, § 3, provides:

"**Sec. 3. Retroactivity**

"This act applies retroactively to from and after July 1, 1998."

Laws 2000, Ch. 344, § 4, provides:

Sec. 4. Retroactivity

"Section 15-393, Arizona Revised Statutes, as amended by this act, applies retroactively to July 1, 1993."

Laws 2001, Ch. 251, § 6, provides:

"**Sec. 6. Report on joint student enrollment**

"**A.** By September 1, 2001, each superintendent of a joint technological education district operating during the school year 2000-2001 shall submit a report to the joint legislative budget committee staff containing the following information:

"1. The total number of students enrolled during the 2000-2001 school year at the joint technological education district.

"2. The average daily membership for the 2000-2001 school year.

"3. A description of the classes or courses offered by the joint technological education district and the total number of instructional hours provided for each course.

"4. The location where each course is taught.

"5. The number of students enrolled in each course.

"6. Identify which courses, if any, the student received community college credit.

"7. Identify which courses, if any, that a community college may include the instructional hours toward the college's full-time equivalent student count.

"8. The amount of funding, if any, that the joint technological district provides to a community college for courses taught on a community college campus or by a community college instructor.

"9. The number of subjects, if any, that the student took during school year 2000-2001 from a high school program at either a charter school or school district.

"10. The number of nonhigh school enrolled students taking courses through the joint technological district.

"**B.** The joint legislative budget committee staff shall develop the form and instructions for the reporting of this information."

Laws 2001, Ch. 251, became law without the Governor's signature as provided in Arizona Constitution, Article 5, § 7.

Reviser's Notes:

1990 Note. Pursuant to authority of § 41-1304.02, in the section heading "district" was added after "education".

1998 Note. Prior to the 1999 amendments, this section contained the amendments made by Laws 1998, Second Regular Session, Ch. 52, sec. 4 and Ch. 167, sec. 3 and Laws 1998, Fifth Special Session, Ch. 1, sec. 11 that were blended together pursuant to authority of § 41-1304.03.

1998 Note. Prior to the 1999 amendments, this section contained the amendments made by Laws 1998, Second Regular Session, Ch. 167, sec. 3 and Laws 1998, Fifth Special Session, Ch. 1, sec. 11 that were blended together pursuant to authority of § 41-1304.03.

1999 Note. Prior to the 2000 amendments, this section contained the amendments made by Laws 1999, Ch. 152, sec. 2 and Ch. 299, sec. 7 that were blended together pursuant to authority of § 41-1304.03.

2000 Note. Prior to the 2001 amendment, this section contained the amendments made by Laws 2000, Ch. 342, sec. 2 and Ch. 344, sec. 1 that were blended together pursuant to authority of§ 41-1304.03.

§ 15-394. Preservation of years of employment

The years of employment of a certificated teacher who has been employed by a school district for more than the major portion of three consecutive school years shall be preserved if such teacher moves from a school district to a joint technological education district or from a joint technological education district to a school district if the governing board recognizes the previously established years of employment of the teacher, provided such districts are participating in the joint technological education district.

Added by Laws 1990, Ch. 248, § 1, eff. Sept. 27, 1990, retroactively effective to July 15, 1990. Amended by Laws 1991, Ch. 154, § 5, eff. May 20, 1991.

Historical and Statutory Notes

For retroactivity provision of Laws 1990, Ch. 248, amended by Laws 1990, Ch. 399, § 23, see Historical and Statutory Notes preceding § 15-391.

§ 15-395. Enlarging joint district

A. To add school districts to a joint district, the joint board shall first publish a copy of a proposed resolution accepting the school district into the joint district in a newspaper of general circulation in the school district proposing to join the joint district once a week for at least two weeks immediately before the date of the consideration of the adoption of the proposed resolution by the joint board.

B. After adoption by the joint board of the resolution accepting the school district into the joint district, until December 31, 2001, the question shall be

submitted to the qualified electors of the district seeking to become a part of the joint district at a general election or at any other election held on a date prescribed in § 16–204. After December 31, 2001, the question shall be submitted to the qualified electors of the district seeking to become a part of the joint district at an election held on the first Tuesday after the first Monday in November. The question that is submitted to the qualified electors shall describe the tax rate that is associated with joining the joint district and the estimated cost of that tax rate for the owner of a single family home that is valued at one hundred thousand dollars. Authorization is required through an intergovernmental agreement between the joint district and the district seeking to become part of the joint district in order to enlarge the joint district.
Added by Laws 1990, Ch. 248, § 1, eff. Sept. 27, 1990, retroactively effective to July 15, 1990. Amended by Laws 1991, Ch. 154, § 6, eff. May 20, 1991; Laws 2000, Ch. 342, § 3; Laws 2000, Ch. 344, § 2; Laws 2001, Ch. 251, § 3; Laws 2002, Ch. 330, § 3.

Historical and Statutory Notes

For retroactivity provision of Laws 1990, Ch. 248, amended by Laws 1990, Ch. 399, § 23, see Historical and Statutory Notes preceding § 15–391.

Laws 2001, Ch. 251, became law without the Governor's signature as provided in Arizona Constitution, Article 5, § 7.

Laws 2002, Ch. 330, became law without the Governor's signature as provided in Arizona Constitution, Article 5, § 7.

Laws 2004, Ch. 278, § 21, provides:

"**Sec. 21. Retroactivity**

"**A.** Except as provided in subsection B of this section, this act applies retroactively to from and after June 30, 2004.

"**B.** Laws 2002, chapter 330, § 49, as amended by this act, applies retroactively to from and after June 29, 2004."

Laws 2002, Ch. 330, § 51, as amended by Laws 2004, Ch. 278, § 7; Laws 2004, Ch. 341, § 10, provides:

"Sec. 51. Temporary prohibition on joining or forming joint technological education districts

"**A.** Notwithstanding §§ 15–392 and 15–395, Arizona Revised Statutes, school districts shall not be allowed to:

"1. Form any new joint technological education district between November 30, 2002 and June 30, 2005, unless both of the following requirements are met:

"(a) At least two school district governing boards voted to participate as part of the joint technological education district before February 1, 2002.

"(b) The joint technological education district is approved by the voters before November 30, 2002.

"2. Join a joint technological education district between the effective date of this act and June 30, 2005, unless the school district shares a border with a school district that currently belongs to the joint district or, if the school district does not share a border with a school district that currently belongs to the joint district, the governing board of the school district voted to become part of the joint technological education district at a public meeting before March 7, 2002 and the joinder is approved by the voters before November 30, 2002. The election requirements prescribed in §§ 15–392 and 15–395, Arizona Revised Statutes, apply to any joinders entered into pursuant to this paragraph.

"**B.** For fiscal year 2004–2005, basic state aid funding to a new joint technological education district formed pursuant to subsection A, paragraph 1 of this section shall be limited to no more than the amount of basic state aid funding that the district received in fiscal year 2003–2004."

Laws 2004, Ch. 341, § 13, subsec. B, provides:

"**Sec. 13. Conditional enactment**"

"**B.** Section 10 of this act, relating to a temporary prohibition on joining or forming joint technological education districts, is not effective unless senate bill 1405, § 7, forty-sixth legislature, second regular session, as transmitted to the governor, becomes law."

Reviser's Notes:

2000 Note. Prior to the 2001 amendment, this section contained the amendments made by Laws 2000, Ch. 342, sec. 3 and Ch. 344, sec. 2 that were blended together pursuant to authority of § 41–1304.03.

§ 15–395.01. Reducing the size of a joint district

A. To withdraw a school district from a joint district, the governing boards of a majority of the school districts participating in the joint district shall approve by a majority vote the withdrawal of the district. If a majority of the governing boards approve the withdrawal, the joint board shall consider the withdrawal, and to approve the withdrawal the proposed withdrawal must receive the affirmative vote of a majority of the members of the board. If the joint board approves, the question of the withdrawal from the joint district shall be submitted to the qualified electors of the school district seeking to withdraw from the joint district at the next general election.

B. If the withdrawal of a school district is approved as prescribed in subsection A of this section, the qualifying tax rate shall remain in effect for the remainder of the current tax year.

C. The school district withdrawn pursuant to this section shall not be entitled to ownership of any assets held by the joint district.

D. If a joint district from which a school district withdraws pursuant to this section has outstanding bonded indebtedness, the debt shall continue to be levied upon taxable property for all bonds issued prior to the withdrawal of the school district in the same manner as was levied and collected prior to the withdrawal of the school district.

Added by Laws 1991, Ch. 154, § 7, eff. May 20, 1991.

Historical and Statutory Notes

Reviser's Notes:

1991 Note. Pursuant to authority of § 41–1304.02, in subsection A, second sentence the comma following the third "withdrawal" was transposed to follow the second "withdrawal".

§ 15–396. Dissolution of district

A. On approval of a majority of the full membership of the joint board or on the receipt by the joint board of resolutions adopted by the governing boards of the school districts participating in the joint district, the joint board shall adopt and send to the state board a resolution requesting the dissolution of the joint district. The resolution shall state the reasons for the proposed dissolution, set forth a plan for equitable adjustment, division and disposition of the assets and liabilities of the joint district and provide that each participating school district will assume its share of the outstanding indebtedness of the joint district.

B. On approval of the resolution by the state board, the joint district is dissolved in accordance with the provisions of the resolution.

Added by Laws 1990, Ch. 248, § 1, eff. Sept. 27, 1990, retroactively effective to July 15, 1990.

Historical and Statutory Notes

For retroactivity provision of Laws 1990, Ch. 248, amended by Laws 1990, Ch. 399, § 23, see Historical and Statutory Notes preceding § 15–391.

CHAPTER 4

SCHOOL ELECTIONS

ARTICLE 1. GENERAL PROVISIONS

ARTICLE 2. SCHOOL DISTRICT GOVERNING BOARD ELECTIONS

ARTICLE 3. SCHOOL DISTRICT BOUNDARY PROVISIONS AND ELECTIONS

Chapter 4, consisting of Article 1, §§ 15–401 to 15–406, Article 2, §§ 15–421 to 15–430, Article 3, §§ 15–441 to 15–469, Article 4, § 15–481, and Article 5, §§ 15–491 to 15–493, was added by Laws 1981, Ch. 1, § 2, effective January 23, 1981.

ARTICLE 1. GENERAL PROVISIONS

§ 15–401. Qualifications of school electors; school district registers; challenge; tally lists

A. A person who is a qualified elector of this state under § 16–121 in the boundaries of the school district twenty-nine days immediately preceding the election is qualified to vote at an election of the school district in the precinct in which he is registered. For the purposes of this title, the term "qualified school elector", "qualified elector", "school elector" or "elector" shall have the qualifications prescribed in this subsection.

B. All school elections shall be conducted by use of school district precinct registers and in the manner as provided in §§ 16–579, 16–580 and 16–584. A person offering to vote may be challenged, and the election officers shall thereupon have the powers and duties of general election officers.

C. The forms for the tally list shall be furnished by the county board of supervisors, and the tally lists must be completed and returned to the county school superintendent and shall be kept by him for not less than five years.

Added by Laws 1981, Ch. 1, § 2, eff. Jan. 23, 1981. Amended by Laws 1981, Ch. 301, § 1; Laws 1990, Ch. 321, § 3, eff. Nov. 19, 1990; Laws 1993, Ch. 98, § 2, eff. Jan. 1, 1994.

Historical and Statutory Notes

Source:

Laws 1912, Ch. 77, §§ 38, 39.
Civ. Code 1913, §§ 2730, 2731.
Laws 1925, Ch. 12, § 1.
Rev. Code 1928, § 1009.
Code 1939, § 54–414.
Laws 1954, Ch. 107, § 1.
A.R.S. former § 15–473.
Laws 1960, Ch. 127, § 38.
Laws 1972, Ch. 138, § 12.
Laws 1973, Ch. 183, § 3.
Laws 1980, Ch. 210, § 2.

Laws 1990, 5th Sp.Sess., Ch. 1, § 7, subsec. A, provides:

"Laws 1990, chapter 321, §§ 1 through 12, 14 and 15 are effective on the effective date of this act [the 5th Sp.Sess. chapter was effective November 19, 1990]."

§ 15–402. Voting by early ballot

A qualified elector of a school district, who meets the requirements may vote by early ballot.

Added by Laws 1981, Ch. 1, § 2, eff. Jan. 23, 1981. Amended by Laws 1999, Ch. 32, § 1.

Historical and Statutory Notes

Source:

Laws 1972, Ch. 54, § 1.
A.R.S. former § 15–473.01.
Laws 1979, Ch. 209, § 12.

§ 15–403. Special election; notice; bond election procedure; qualifications of voters; closing of registrations; election precincts; polling places

A. The county school superintendent shall cause notices of a special election except a bond election to be posted at least ninety days previous to the date of the election. The notices shall be posted in at least three public places in the school district. One notice shall be posted at the school if there is one. Bond election notices and procedures shall comply with the requirements of title 35, chapter 3, article 3.[1]

B. The notices shall specify the day and the polling places of the special election and the time the polls will be open. A special election may be held only on a date prescribed by § 16-204.

C. If the county school superintendent fails to give notice as provided in subsections A and B of this section, any two qualified electors who reside within the district may give similar notice of the special election at least seventy-five days prior to the special election.

D. A person is not entitled to vote at a special election or an election held at a time and place other than a general election in a school district who has not been a qualified elector in a precinct in the boundaries of the school district for twenty-nine days preceding the election, who is not qualified to register to vote as provided in § 16-101 and who has not registered to vote prior to midnight of the twenty-ninth day preceding the date of the election.

E. The governing board of a school district shall establish school district election precincts that have the same boundaries as the county election precincts as provided in § 16-411 and designate one polling place within each precinct, except that the governing board of a union high school district may divide a county election precinct along the boundaries of common school districts within the boundaries of the union high school district and establish polling places within each common school district. In those cases where a school district boundary bisects a county election precinct, that portion of the election precinct that is within the school district shall be the school district election precinct. The governing board may consolidate school district election precincts if it deems it necessary for each special election and designate one polling place for the election precincts which it consolidates. If school district election precincts are consolidated, a school district precinct register shall be prepared for the consolidated precinct. Upon a specific finding of the board, included in the order or resolution designating polling places pursuant to this subsection, that no suitable polling place is available within a precinct of the school district, a polling place for such precinct may be designated within an adjacent precinct. The adjacent precinct need not be within the school district. Any such polling places shall be listed in a separate section of the order or resolution.

F. All special elections which are called either by the county school superintendent or the governing board of a school district and which are held at a time other than the general election shall be conducted by the use of school district precinct registers.

Added by Laws 1981, Ch. 1, § 2, eff. Jan. 23, 1981. Amended by Laws 1981, Ch. 301, § 2; Laws 1983, Ch. 151, § 1; Laws 1988, Ch. 187, § 1, eff. June 8, 1988; Laws 1990, Ch. 321, § 4, eff. Nov. 19, 1990; Laws 1993, Ch. 98, § 3, eff. Jan. 1, 1994; Laws 1994, Ch. 361, § 2; Laws 1996, Ch. 271, § 11, eff. April 23, 1996.

[1] Section 35-451 et seq.

Historical and Statutory Notes

Source: Laws 1912, Ch. 77, § 35.

Civ. Code 1913, § 2727.
Rev. Code 1928, § 1005.
Code 1939, § 54–410.
A.R.S. former § 15–475.
Laws 1972, Ch. 138, § 14.
Laws 1978, Ch. 188, § 10.
Laws 1980, Ch. 210, § 3.

For effective date provision of Laws 1990, 5th Sp.Sess., Ch. 1, changing the effective dates of sections of Laws 1990, Ch. 321, see Historical and Statutory Notes following § 15–401.

§ 15–404. Election officers; compensation

A. In school district elections held at a time and place other than general elections, at least twenty days before the school district election the county school superintendent or other authority conducting the election shall appoint for each election precinct or combination of precincts not fewer than one inspector and two judges as election officers and may appoint additional clerks and marshals necessary to properly conduct the election.

B. For the purpose of this section, an employee of a school district shall not serve as an election officer for the school district. If those appointed are not present at the opening of the polls, the electors present may select them. In all school district elections each election officer shall receive the same compensation as other election officers of a general election.

Added by Laws 1981, Ch. 1, § 2, eff. Jan. 23, 1981. Amended by Laws 1981, Ch. 301, § 3; Laws 1986, Ch. 155, § 1; Laws 1988, Ch. 187, § 2, eff. June 8, 1988.

Historical and Statutory Notes

Source:

Laws 1912, Ch. 77, § 36.
Civ. Code 1913, § 2728.
Rev. Code 1928, § 1006.
Laws 1947, Ch. 6, § 1.
Laws 1952, Ch. 146, § 2.
Laws 1953, Ch. 107, § 1.
Code 1939, Supp.1953, § 54–411.
A.R.S. former § 15–476.
Laws 1972, Ch. 138, § 15.
Laws 1973, Ch. 183, § 4.
Laws 1978, Ch. 188, § 10.
Laws 1980, Ch. 210, § 3.

§ 15–405. Opening and closing of polls

At all school elections the polls shall be open during the same hours as are applicable to general elections. The inspector and two judges shall determine when the hour for opening and closing the polls has arrived. A voter within the polling place at the closing of the polls shall be allowed to vote.

Added by Laws 1981, Ch. 1, § 2, eff. Jan. 23, 1981.

Historical and Statutory Notes

Source:

Laws 1912, Ch. 77, § 37.
Civ. Code 1913, § 2729.
Laws 1915, Ch. 11, § 1.
Rev. Code 1928, § 1008.
Laws 1953, Ch. 108, § 1.
Code 1939, Supp.1953, § 54–413.
A.R.S. former § 15–477.
Laws 1968, Ch. 96, § 1.
Laws 1972, Ch. 138, § 16.

§ 15–406. Cost of elections

A. The cost of all special elections provided in this title, including the preparation of ballots, shall be charged against the funds of the school district or districts involved.

B. The county school superintendent shall contract with the board of supervisors for holding regular school district elections. The contracted cost of

such school elections shall be a charge against the county school superintendent who shall prorate such costs to the districts.
Added by Laws 1981, Ch. 1, § 2, eff. Jan. 23, 1981.

Historical and Statutory Notes

Source:
Laws 1960, Ch. 127, § 40.
A.R.S. former § 15-479.
Laws 1972, Ch. 138, § 18.

§ 15-407. School district ballot option

The governing body of a school district may choose to use either electromechanical or electronic vote recording and ballot counting equipment, or paper ballots for any special election held pursuant to this chapter.
Added by Laws 1990, Ch. 278, § 1, eff. June 2, 1991.

ARTICLE 2. SCHOOL DISTRICT GOVERNING BOARD ELECTIONS

§ 15-421. Governing board; members; qualifications

A. The governing body of a school district shall be a governing board. There shall be three governing board members, except as otherwise provided by this section and § 15-425, subsection A.

B. The governing body of a high school district shall be a governing board composed of:

1. In a single district, the governing board members of the common school district.

2. In a union high school district, five members.

C. A person who is a registered voter of this state and has been a resident of the school district for one year immediately preceding the day of election is eligible for election to the office of governing board member.

D. No employee of a school district or the spouse of such employee may hold membership on a governing board of a school district by which such employee is employed.

E. A member of one governing board is ineligible to be a candidate for nomination or election to or serve simultaneously as a member of any other governing board, except that a member of a governing board may be a candidate for nomination or election for any other governing board if the member is serving in the last year of a term of office. A member of a governing board shall resign the member's seat on the governing board before becoming a candidate for nomination or election to the governing board of any other school district, unless the member of the governing board is serving in the last year of a term of office.
Added by Laws 1981, Ch. 1, § 2, eff. Jan. 23, 1981. Amended by Laws 2001, Ch. 37, § 1.

Historical and Statutory Notes

Source:
Laws 1912, Ch. 77, §§ 34, 79.
Civ. Code 1913, §§ 2726, 2775.
Laws 1921, Ch. 72, §§ 2, 7.

Laws 1925, Ch. 73, § 1.
Rev. Code 1928, §§ 1004, 1072.
Laws 1933, Ch. 65, § 1.
Code 1939, § 54-905.
Laws 1952, Ch. 146, § 1.
Code 1939, Supp.1952, § 54-409.
Laws 1954, Ch. 117, §§ 1, 3.
Laws 1955, Ch. 49, § 1.
Code 1939, Supp.1955, § 54-409a.
A.R.S. former §§ 15-209, 15-431, 15-541.
Laws 1960, Ch. 127, § 21.
Laws 1972, Ch. 138, § 7.
Laws 1977, Ch. 164, § 1.
Laws 1978, Ch. 213, § 7.

Laws 2001, Ch. 37, § 4, provides:

"**Sec. 4. Applicability**

"This act applies only to those persons who are candidates for an election that is held after the effective date of this act and to persons who take office after the effective date of this act."

§ 15-422. Nominating petitions; ballots

A. Nominating petitions shall be filed with the county school superintendent as prescribed by title 16, chapter 3. Nominating petitions shall be signed by a number of qualified electors of the district as provided in § 16-322. Nominating petitions for persons seeking to fill a vacancy on a governing board shall be designated as provided in § 16-314.

B. The county school superintendent may cause separate ballots to be prepared, or such school district candidates' names may be included as a part of the regular ballot. In any event the names of all persons whose petitions have been filed shall appear on a ballot, without partisan or other designation except the title of the office.

Added by Laws 1981, Ch. 1, § 2, eff. Jan. 23, 1981. Amended by Laws 1983, Ch. 171, § 1; Laws 1991, Ch. 243, § 1; Laws 2000, Ch. 24, § 1, eff. March 20, 2000.

Historical and Statutory Notes

Source:

Laws 1912, Ch. 77, §§ 38, 39.
Civ. Code 1913, §§ 2730, 2731.
Laws 1921, Ch. 72, § 3.
Laws 1925, Ch. 12, § 1.
Laws 1927, Ch. 78, § 1.
Rev. Code 1928, §§ 1007, 1009.
Code 1939, §§ 54-412, 54-414.
Laws 1954, Ch. 107, § 1.
A.R.S. former §§ 15-472, 15-474.
Laws 1960, Ch. 127, §§ 37, 39.
Laws 1972, Ch. 54, § 2.
Laws 1972, Ch. 138, § 13.
Laws 1975, Ch. 131, § 1.

§ 15-423. School district precinct registers; date of preparation; contents; copies

A. By the fifth day preceding the elections for membership on school district governing boards the county recorder shall prepare from the original affidavits of registration at least four printed or typed lists of all uncanceled registrations of each school district in the county, and the lists are the official school district precinct registers.

B. The official school district precinct registers shall contain all information required to be included on precinct registers. The county recorder may combine the precinct register and the official school district precinct register into one common register.

C. The county recorder shall, upon request, provide copies of school district precinct registers in the manner and for the fees prescribed in § 16-168, or § 16-172 for political subdivisions, for copies of precinct registers.

D. By the fifth day preceding a special election or an election held at a time and place other than a general election in a school district, the county recorder shall prepare from the original affidavits of registration at least four printed or typed lists of all uncanceled registrations of each school district election precinct, and the lists are the official school district precinct registers. The official school district precinct registers shall contain all information required to be included on precinct registers. The governing board of the school district shall request of the county recorder and the county recorder shall provide to the school district copies of school district precinct registers in the manner and for the fees prescribed in § 16–172 for copies of precinct registers.

Added by Laws 1981, Ch. 1, § 2, eff. Jan. 23, 1981. Amended by Laws 1981, Ch. 301, § 4.

Historical and Statutory Notes

Source:

Laws 1972, Ch. 138, § 11.
A.R.S. former § 15–472.01.
Laws 1973, Ch. 183, § 2.
Laws 1979, Ch. 209, § 11.
Laws 1980, Ch. 210, § 1.

Reviser's Notes:

1981 Note. Pursuant to authority of § 41–1304.02, in the heading of this section the word "precinct" was added following the word "district".

§ 15–424. Election of governing board members; terms; statement of contributions and expenditures

A. A regular election shall be held for each school district at the time and place, and in the manner, of general elections as provided in title 16.[1]

B. Except as provided in subsection C of this section and §§ 15–429 and 15–430, the term of office for each member shall be four years from January 1 next following his election.

C. At the first general election held for a newly formed district, three members shall be elected. The candidate receiving the highest number of votes shall be elected to a four year term, and the candidates having the second and third highest number of votes shall be elected to two year terms. A district increasing its governing board to five members shall at the next general election elect members in the following manner:

1. If one of the previous three offices is to be filled, the three candidates receiving the highest, the second highest and the third highest number of votes shall be elected to four year terms.

2. If two of the previous three offices are to be filled, the candidates receiving the highest, the second highest and the third highest number of votes shall be elected to four year terms. The candidate receiving the fourth highest number of votes shall be elected to a two year term. Thereafter all such offices shall have four year terms.

D. If only one person files or no person files a nominating petition for an election to fill a district office, the board of supervisors up to seventy-five days before the election, may cancel the election for the position and appoint the person who filed the nominating petition to fill the position. If no person files a nominating petition for an election to fill a district office, the board of supervisors up to seventy-five days before the election, may cancel the election for that office and that office is deemed vacant and shall be filled as provided in § 15–302. A person who is appointed pursuant to this section is fully vested with the powers and duties of the office as if elected to that office.

E. If two or more candidates receive an equal number of votes for the same office, and a higher number than any other candidate for that office, whether upon the tally by the school election board or canvass of returns by the board of supervisors, or upon recount by a court, the officer or board whose duty it is to declare the result shall determine by lot and in the presence of the candidates which candidate shall be declared elected.

F. Position of the names of candidates for each office shall be rotated so that each candidate occupies each position on the ballot an equal number of times, insofar as is possible, for each ballot style. For candidates seeking election to fill a vacancy on the governing board, the ballot shall be designated as provided in § 16–502.

G. This section does not require that a school election at which no member is to be elected be held on a general election day.

H. All candidates for the office of school district governing board member shall file with the county school superintendent a statement of contributions and expenditures as provided in § 16–913.

Added by Laws 1981, Ch. 1, § 2, eff. Jan. 23, 1981. Amended by Laws 1981, Ch. 314, § 5; Laws 1984, Ch. 59, § 1; Laws 1991, Ch. 243, § 2; Laws 2003, Ch. 203, § 1.

[1] Section 16–101 et seq.

Historical and Statutory Notes

Source:

Laws 1912, Ch. 77, § 34.
Civ. Code 1913, § 2726.
Laws 1921, Ch. 72, § 2.
Rev. Code 1928, § 1004.
Laws 1933, Ch. 65, § 1.
Laws 1952, Ch. 146, § 1.
Code 1939, Supp.1952, § 54–409.
Laws 1954, Ch. 117, § 1.
A.R.S. former § 15–471.
Laws 1963, Ch. 7, § 1.
Laws 1972, Ch. 138, § 10.
Laws 1973, Ch. 183, § 1.
Laws 1979, Ch. 209, § 10.

Reviser's Notes:

2003 Note. Pursuant to authority of § 41–1304.02, in subsection D, in the first two sentences "may" was transposed to follow "election,".

§ 15–425. Election to determine whether membership of governing board shall increase to five members; form of ballot; reconsideration procedure if negative vote; appointment or election of new members

A. A qualified elector of a school district may submit to the county school superintendent a petition, signed by not less than ten per cent of the qualified school electors of the district, requesting the county school superintendent to call a special election to determine whether or not the number of members of the governing board for the school district should be increased to five. Upon receipt of the petition, in proper form and with the necessary signatures, the county school superintendent shall thereafter call a special election not later than ninety days prior to the general election to determine the question of whether the membership of the governing board for the school district shall be increased to five.

B. Public notices of a special election called to determine whether there shall be five governing board members shall be posted in not less than three public places in the district at least ten days prior to the election. The election shall be held as prescribed by the county school superintendent and electors shall possess the qualifications as prescribed for the election of governing board members.

C. The ballots shall contain the words: "Five governing board members, yes. Five governing board members, no."

D. If the majority of the electors voting on the question votes in the affirmative, the school district shall elect five governing board members, as provided in § 15-424. If the majority of the electors voting on the question of increasing the number of governing board members votes in the negative, the question shall not again be placed upon the ballot of an election in the district until the lapse of one year from the date of such election.

E. Notwithstanding § 15-424 and subsection D of this section, if the voters approve an increase in the size of the governing board at least one year before the next general election, the county school superintendent may appoint the two new members or call a special election pursuant to § 15-302.

F. The term of the two new members appointed by the county school superintendent or elected through a special election expires January 1 following the next general election. At the first general election following the increase in the size of the governing board, the candidates elected and their terms shall be determined pursuant to § 15-424, subsection C.

Added by Laws 1981, Ch. 1, § 2, eff. Jan. 23, 1981. Amended by Laws 1989, Ch. 35, § 1, eff. April 14, 1989, retroactively effective to Nov. 8, 1988.

Historical and Statutory Notes

Source:

Laws 1912, Ch. 77, § 34.
Civ. Code 1913, § 2726.
Laws 1921, Ch. 72, § 2.
Rev. Code 1928, § 1004.
Laws 1933, Ch. 65, § 1.
Laws 1952, Ch. 146, § 1.
Code 1939, Supp.1952, § 54-409.
Laws 1954, Ch. 117, § 1.
Laws 1955, Ch. 49, § 1.
Code 1939, Supp.1955, § 54-409a.
A.R.S. former § 15-431.
Laws 1960, Ch. 127, § 21.
Laws 1972, Ch. 138, § 7.
Laws 1978, Ch. 193, § 2.

Laws 1989, Ch. 35, § 2, effective April 14, 1989, provides:

"**Sec. 2. Retroactivity**

"This act is effective retroactively to November 8, 1988."

Reviser's Notes:

1989 Note. Pursuant to authority of § 41-1304.02, in the section heading "; appointment or election of new members" was added after "vote".

§ 15-426. Tally and canvass of votes; certificate of election; oath of office

A. The officers of a special election shall, as soon as the polls are closed, tally the votes cast, enclose one list of the persons voting and one copy of the tally sheet in a cover and seal and direct the cover and its contents to the county school superintendent. The inspector shall place in the ballot box one list of the persons voting, one copy of the tally sheets and the ballots. The inspector shall lock the ballot box until the county school superintendent and the chairman of the board of supervisors meet to canvass the returns. Unless otherwise specified in this title, the officers of a regular school election shall proceed in the manner provided in title 16 for the tally of votes.

B. The county school superintendent and the chairman of the board of supervisors shall meet within thirty days, unless otherwise specified in this title, following the date of any school election and canvass the returns in accordance with procedures for the canvass of returns in a general election. The county school superintendent shall declare the results of the election, shall declare elected the person receiving the highest number of votes for each office to be filled, and shall issue to him a certificate of election.

C. When each governing board member elected subscribes to the oath of office attached to the certificate, it shall be forwarded on the same day to the county school superintendent. Members of governing boards may administer the oath of office to each other.

Added by Laws 1981, Ch. 1, § 2, eff. Jan. 23, 1981. Amended by Laws 1995, Ch. 268, § 19.

Historical and Statutory Notes

Source:

Laws 1912, Ch. 77, § 40.
Civ. Code 1913, § 2732.
Laws 1925, Ch. 30, § 1.
Laws 1927, Ch. 86, § 1.
Rev.Code 1928, § 1010.
Code 1939, § 54–415.
Laws 1955, Ch. 90, § 1.
A.R.S. former § 15–478.
Laws 1972, Ch. 138, § 17.
Laws 1979, Ch. 209, § 13.

§ 15–427. Governing board of a union high school district; qualifications; terms

A. The members of the governing board of a union high school district shall be qualified school electors of the district. Members shall be elected from the union high school district at large except as provided in § 15–431.

B. The term of office of the members of the union high school district governing board shall be four years, except:

1. Upon formation of a union high school district, the governing board shall be appointed by the county school superintendent and shall hold office until January 1 following the next general election.

2. At the first general election after formation of the district, members shall be elected in the following manner:

(a) The three candidates receiving the highest, the second highest and the third highest number of votes shall be elected to four year terms.

(b) The two candidates receiving the fourth and fifth highest number of votes shall be elected for two year terms. Thereafter all such offices shall have four year terms.

Added by Laws 1981, Ch. 1, § 2, eff. Jan. 23, 1981. Amended by Laws 1981, Ch. 314, § 6; Laws 1985, Ch. 238, § 1; Laws 1990, Ch. 369, § 1; Laws 1993, Ch. 202, § 6, eff. April 21, 1993; Laws 2001, Ch. 37, § 2.

Historical and Statutory Notes

Source:

Laws 1912, Ch. 77, §§ 79, 80.
Civ. Code 1913, §§ 2775, 2776.
Laws 1921, Ch. 72, §§ 7, 8.
Laws 1925, Ch. 73, § 1.
Laws 1927, Ch. 82, § 1.
Rev. Code 1928, §§ 1072, 1073.
Code 1939, §§ 54–905, 54–906.
Laws 1954, Ch. 117, § 3.
A.R.S. former § 15–542.
Laws 1960, Ch. 127, § 42.
Laws 1972, Ch. 138, § 21.
Laws 1975, Ch. 131, § 2.
Laws 1977, Ch. 47, § 1.

Laws 2001, Ch. 37, § 4, provides:

"Sec. 4. Applicability

"This act applies only to those persons who are candidates for an election that is held after the effective date of this act and to persons who take office after the effective date of this act."

§ 15–428. Election of governing board members of a union high school district

A. Members of the governing board of a union high school district shall be elected at the time and place and in the manner that members of other school districts are elected, as nearly as is practicable, except as provided in § 15–427, subsection B.

B. Election officers shall certify the returns to the county school superintendent who shall meet with the chairman of the board of supervisors within thirty days following the date of the election and canvass the returns and issue certificates of election, as provided in § 15–426.

Added by Laws 1981, Ch. 1, § 2, eff. Jan. 23, 1981. Amended by Laws 1985, Ch. 238, § 2.

Historical and Statutory Notes

Source:

Laws 1912, Ch. 77, § 79.
Civ. Code 1913, § 2775.
Laws 1921, Ch. 72, § 7.
Laws 1925, Ch. 73, § 1.
Rev.Code 1928, § 1072.
Code 1939, § 54–905.
Laws 1954, Ch. 117, § 3.
A.R.S. former § 15–543.
Laws 1972, Ch. 138, § 22.
Laws 1973, Ch. 157, § 15.
Laws 1979, Ch. 118, § 4.

§ 15–429. Election of governing board members of a joint common school district

A. A joint common school district shall be governed by a board of five members, one of whom shall reside in and be elected from each of the counties comprising the district and the remaining number shall reside in the district and be elected at large unless the district has implemented an alternative election system as provided in § 15–431. Within ten days after the creation of the joint common school district, the county school superintendent of the jurisdictional county, after notifying the county school superintendent of any other county whose territory, or a portion thereof, is in the new district, shall call a special election, which shall be held within twenty days after the issuance of such call, to elect a governing board for the joint common school district. The polling places for the election shall be located in each county of the district. The election shall be conducted as provided by law for other school districts, except that the members first elected shall serve until January 1 following the next general election. At the general election held next following the special election, and thereafter, the members shall be elected as prescribed for five member boards in §§ 15–424 and 15–427.

B. The county school superintendent shall call the first meeting of the newly formed governing board within ten days after its election. Each member shall be given five days' written notice in advance of the meeting. The meeting shall be held at a location convenient to all members. Business shall be conducted as provided by law for the conduct of school districts.

Added by Laws 1981, Ch. 1, § 2, eff. Jan. 23, 1981. Amended by Laws 1990, Ch. 369, § 2.

Historical and Statutory Notes

Source:
Laws 1970, Ch. 12, § 1.
A.R.S. former § 15-421.03.
Laws 1972, Ch. 138, § 6.

§ 15-430. Governing board members of newly consolidated district; election of members

A. If school districts are consolidated as provided in § 15-459, the terms of the governing board members of the previously existing school districts do not expire on the effective date of the consolidation and continue until January 1 following the next general election, during which time the members of the governing boards of the previously existing school districts shall serve as the governing board of the new school district.

B. At the next general election held following the consolidation and thereafter, five members shall be elected as prescribed in § 15-427, subsection B. The new board shall take office on January 1 following the general election.

Added by Laws 1981, Ch. 1, § 2, eff. Jan. 23, 1981. Amended by Laws 1983, Ch. 118, § 1; Laws 1985, Ch. 238, § 3; Laws 1986, Ch. 312, § 1; Laws 1989, Ch. 210, § 1; Laws 1994, Ch. 264, § 1.

Historical and Statutory Notes

Source:
Laws 1912, Ch. 77, § 31.
Civ. Code 1913, § 2723.
Rev. Code 1928, § 1001.
Code 1939, § 54-406.
A.R.S. former § 15-411.
Laws 1972, Ch. 138, § 5.
Laws 1974, 1st S.S., Ch. 3, § 64.
Laws 1975, Ch. 103, § 6.

Reviser's Notes:

1994 Note. Pursuant to authority of § 41-1304.02, in the section heading "; terms" was deleted and in subsection B, first sentence "next" was transposed to follow "At the".

§ 15-431. Alternative election procedure of governing board members

A. If, for the prior school year, a school district had an average daily membership of at least one thousand and the total minority enrollment in the district, as reported to the department of education, was at least twenty-five per cent of the total enrollment of the district, the governing board may vote to implement an alternative election system for the election of governing board members. The alternative election system implemented by the board may include a vote by the board to divide the school district into as many single member districts as there are governing board members or a vote by the board to implement any other election method that is consistent with § 2 of the voting rights act of 1965 (42 United States Code § 1973), as amended. A school district that has implemented an alternative election system for the election of governing board members as provided by this subsection may continue to elect governing board members using the alternative election system even if the average daily membership of the school district or percentage of minority pupils enrolled in the district falls below the levels prescribed in this subsection. If the average daily membership of the school district or percentage of minority pupils enrolled in the district falls below the levels prescribed in this subsection, the governing board may vote to elect governing board members using the at large election method as prescribed in § 15-429.

B. If the governing board of a school district has implemented a single member district election system as provided in subsection A of this section, the system shall be implemented as follows:

1. The governing board shall define the boundaries of the single member district so that the single member districts are as nearly equal in population as is practicable, except that if the school district lies in part in each of two or more counties, at least one single member district may be entirely within each of the counties comprising the school district if this district design is consistent with the obligation to equalize the population among single member districts.

2. The boundaries of the single member district shall follow election precinct boundary lines, as far as practicable, in order to avoid further segmentation of the precincts.

3. A number shall be assigned to each of the new single member districts in ascending order according to the percentage of the district's minority population in each single member district.

4. As the terms of the governing board members who were elected at large expire, the members shall be replaced by members who are elected from the single member districts in ascending order of single member district number.

5. A person who is a registered voter of this state and who is a resident of the single member district is eligible for election to the office of school board member from the single member district.

6. Nominating petitions shall be signed by the number of qualified electors of the single member district as provided in § 16-322.

C. If the governing board has voted to implement any other alternative election system for the election of governing board members, as provided in subsection A of this section, the implementation of the system shall be as approved by the United States justice department.

Added by Laws 1990, Ch. 369, § 3.

ARTICLE 3. SCHOOL DISTRICT BOUNDARY PROVISIONS AND ELECTIONS

§ 15-441. School districts; designation

A. The bases of the educational organization of the county and state are the school districts as defined in § 15-101. Existing districts shall be continued, and new districts may be formed as provided in this title.

B. Each school district shall be designated as school district no. ______ (insert the number of the district), of ________ county (insert the name of the county).

Added by Laws 1981, Ch. 1, § 2, eff. Jan. 23, 1981.

Historical and Statutory Notes

Source:

Laws 1912, Ch. 77, § 27.
Civ. Code 1913, § 2719.
Rev. Code 1928, § 996.
Code 1939, § 54-401.
A.R.S. former § 15-401.

§ 15-442. Record of school district boundaries; limitation on change; notice to governing board

A. The county school superintendent shall, on or before December 1 each year, file with the board of supervisors and the county assessor a transcript of the boundaries of each school district within the county. The boundaries shown in the transcript shall become the legal boundaries of the districts as of the following July 1.

B. The boundaries of a school district shall not be changed except as provided in this title and then only after the governing boards of the districts affected have had written notice of the proposed change from the county school superintendent and have had an opportunity to be heard.

Added by Laws 1981, Ch. 1, § 2, eff. Jan. 23, 1981.

Historical and Statutory Notes

Source:
Laws 1912, Ch. 77, § 29.
Civ. Code 1913, § 2721.
Rev. Code 1928, § 998.
Code 1939, § 54–403.
Laws 1954, Ch. 135, § 1.
A.R.S. former § 15–402.
Laws 1971, Ch. 4, § 2.
Laws 1972, Ch. 138, § 2.
Laws 1974, 1st S.S., Ch. 3, § 76.

§ 15–443. Formation of new common school district

A. New common school districts may be formed in unorganized territory on presentation to the county school superintendent of a petition which:

1. Is signed by the parents or guardians of at least ten pupils. Persons who sign the petition shall:

(a) Be residents of the proposed new common school district.

(b) Reside more than four miles from any school district schoolhouse.

2. Set forth the boundaries of the proposed common school district.

B. For any common school district formed after July 1, 1988, the tax rate levied for the district shall be at a rate not less than the rate prescribed in § 15–971, subsection B, paragraph 2. Any monies received from the tax levy in excess of the additional amounts prescribed in § 15–991 shall be deposited in the state general fund.

Added by Laws 1981, Ch. 1, § 2, eff. Jan. 23, 1981. Amended by Laws 1985, Ch. 238, § 4; Laws 1988, Ch. 271, § 1, eff. July 1, 1988.

Historical and Statutory Notes

Source:
Laws 1912, Ch. 77, § 28.
Civ. Code 1913, § 2720.
Rev. Code 1928, § 997.
Code 1939, § 54–402.
A.R.S. former § 15–408.

§ 15–444. Formation of union high school district; petition for establishment; election; notice

A. Two or more adjoining school districts jointly having a student count of not less than two hundred pupils and an assessed valuation of not less than two million dollars may unite and form a union high school district. No union high school district may be formed of territory already embodied in a union high school district unless the remaining territory of the original union high school district is contiguous and has an assessed valuation of not less than five million dollars.

B. If a majority of the governing boards of each of two or more adjoining school districts unites in a petition to the county school superintendent for establishment of a union high school district, or if ten per cent of each of two or more adjoining school districts unite in a petition for establishment of a union high school district, the county school superintendent shall call an election to be held at the next regular election of the governing board, if within ninety days after receipt of the petition, to determine the question, or a special election called for that purpose within sixty days.

C. Public notices of the election, not less than three in each school district comprising the proposed union high school district, shall be posted, one to be upon the door of the schoolhouse in each district, at least ten days before the election.

D. The election shall be conducted as nearly as practicable in the manner prescribed in § 15-459. The ballots shall contain the words "union high school district, yes" and "union high school district, no", and the voter shall signify his desired choice.

E. If a majority of the persons voting within each school district comprising the proposed union high school district votes in favor of establishment of a union high school district, the union high school district shall become effective as provided in § 15-459, subsection G.

F. If a union high school district is established from a unified school district as provided in this section, a common school district is established with boundaries coterminous with the boundaries of the former unified school district.

Added by Laws 1981, Ch. 1, § 2, eff. Jan. 23, 1981. Amended by Laws 1981, Ch. 314, § 7; Laws 1985, Ch. 238, § 5; Laws 1986, Ch. 310, § 1.

Historical and Statutory Notes

Source:

Laws 1912, Ch. 77, §§ 74 to 76.
Civil Code 1913, §§ 2270 to 2272.
Laws 1917, Ch. 5, § 1.
Rev. Code 1928, §§ 1068, 1069.
Laws 1931, Ch. 50, § 1.
Code 1939, §§ 54-901, 54-902.
A.R.S. former §§ 15-445 and 15-502.
Laws 1960, Ch. 127, § 41.
Laws 1972, Ch. 138, § 19.
Laws 1973, Ch. 183, § 5.
Laws 1974, 1st S.S., Ch. 3, § 12.
Laws 1980, 2nd S.S., Ch. 9, § 24.
Laws 1981, Ch. 1, § 2.
Laws 1981, Ch. 301, § 5.

§ 15-444.01. Common school districts within a high school district; proposed expansion or reduction; notification

The governing board of a common school district that is located within a high school district shall notify and obtain permission from the governing board of the high school district before taking any action that results in the expansion or reduction of the common school district's boundaries. The notification and permission required by this section shall take place at least ninety days before the beginning of the fiscal year in which the proposed expansion or reduction is scheduled to take effect.

Added by Laws 1997, Ch. 276, § 1.

§§ 15-445, 15-446. Repealed by Laws 1985, Ch. 238, § 11

Historical and Statutory Notes

Section 15-445, added by Laws 1981, Ch. 1, § 2, amended by Laws 1981, Ch. 301, § 5 and derived from:

Laws 1912, Ch. 77, §§ 75, 76.
Civ.Code 1913, §§ 2771, 2772.
Rev.Code 1928, § 1069.
Code 1939, § 54-902.
A.R.S. former § 15-502.
Laws 1972, Ch. 138, § 19.
Laws 1973, Ch. 183, § 5.

related to petitions for establishment of high schools in common school districts and to elections conducted following such petitions. See, now, § 15-444.

Section 15-446, added by Laws 1981, Ch. 1, § 2 and derived from:

Laws 1912, Ch. 77, § 77.
Civ.Code 1913, § 2773.
Rev.Code 1928, § 1070.
Code 1939, § 54-903.
A.R.S. former § 15-503.

related to elections to determine the location of schools.

§ 15-447. Offer of instruction in high school subjects by common school districts; limitations

The state board of education may grant permission to the governing board of a common school district to offer instruction in high school subjects, grades nine through twelve, except that the state board shall not grant permission if the qualified electors of a common school district have voted against the formation of a high school district within the last five years. If the qualified electors of a common school district vote against the formation of a high school district within one year after the state board has granted permission to the governing board to offer instruction in high school subjects, the governing board shall cease to offer instruction in high school subjects at the end of the current year and shall not offer such instruction until such time as the state board has again granted permission in accordance with this section. Enrollment of pupils in grades nine through twelve shall be deemed to be enrollment in high school. For purposes of computing the base support level, the support level weight for high school districts shall be used. Successful completion of a prescribed course of study in grades nine through twelve entitles a pupil to a certificate of high school graduation.

Added by Laws 1981, Ch. 1, § 2, eff. Jan. 23, 1981. Amended by Laws 1983, Ch. 174, § 2.

Historical and Statutory Notes

Source:

Laws 1912, Ch. 77, § 74.
Civ. Code 1913, § 2770.
Laws 1917, Ch. 5, § 1.
Rev. Code 1928, § 1068.
Laws 1931, Ch. 50, § 1.
Code 1939, § 54-901.
A.R.S. former § 15-501.
Laws 1960, Ch. 127, § 41.
Laws 1974, 1st S.S., Ch. 3, § 12.
Laws 1980, 2nd S.S., Ch. 9, § 24.

§ 15-448. Formation of unified school district; board membership; budget

A. One or more common school districts and a high school district with coterminous or overlapping boundaries may establish a unified school district pursuant to this section. Unification of a common school district and a high school district is not authorized by this section if any of the high school facilities owned by the new unified school district would not be located within its boundaries.

B. Formation of a unified school district shall be by resolutions approved by the governing boards of the unifying school districts and certification of approval by such governing boards to the county school superintendent of the county or counties in which such individual school districts are located. A common school district and high school district that unify pursuant to this section shall not exclude from the same unification a common school district that has overlapping boundaries with the high school district and that wishes to unify. The formation of a unified school district shall become effective on July 1 of the next fiscal year following the certification of the county school superintendent. An election shall not be required to form a unified school district pursuant to this section.

C. The boundaries of the unified school district shall be the boundaries of the former common school district or districts that unify. The boundaries of the common school district or districts that are not unifying remain unchanged. The county school superintendent, immediately upon receipt of the approved resolutions prescribed by subsection B of this section, shall file with the board of supervisors, the county assessor and the superintendent of public instruction a transcript of the boundaries of the unified school district. The boundaries shown in the transcript shall become the legal boundaries of the school districts on July 1 of the next fiscal year.

D. On formation of the unified school district, the governing board consists of the members of the former school district governing boards and the members shall hold office until January 1 following the first general election after formation of the district.

E. Beginning on January 1 following the first general election after formation of the unified school district, the governing board shall have five members. At the first general election after the formation of the district, members shall be elected in the following manner:

1. The three candidates receiving the highest, the second highest and the third highest number of votes shall be elected to four year terms.

2. The two candidates receiving the fourth and fifth highest number of votes shall be elected to two year terms. Thereafter all offices shall have four year terms.

F. The new unified school district may appoint a resident of the remaining common school district to serve as a nonvoting member of the governing board to represent the interests of the high school pupils who reside in the remaining common school district and who attend school in the unified school district.

G. For the first year of operation, the unified school district governing board shall prepare a consolidated budget based on the student counts from the school districts comprising the unified school district, except that for purposes of determining budget amounts and equalization assistance, the student count for the former high school district shall not include the prior year average daily membership attributable to high school pupils from a common school district that was part of the former high school district but is not part of the unified school district. The unified school district shall charge the remaining common school district tuition for these pupils as provided in subsection J of this section and shall not include such pupils for the purpose of making any adjustment for rapid decline in student count pursuant to § 15–942. The unified school district may budget for unification assistance pursuant to § 15–912.01.

H. The governing board of the unified school district shall prepare policies, curricula and budgets for the district. These policies shall require that:

1. The base compensation of each certificated teacher for the first year of operation of the new unified school district shall not be lower than the certificated teacher's base compensation for the prior year in the previously existing school districts.

2. The certificated teacher's years of employment in the previously existing school districts shall be included in determining the teacher's certificated years of employment in the new unified school district.

I. Upon formation of a unified school district any existing override authorization of the former high school district and the former common school district or districts shall continue until expiration based on the revenue control limit of the school district or districts that had override authorization prior to unification. The unified school district may request new override authorization for the budget year as provided in § 15–481 based on the combined revenue control limit of the new district after unification. If the unified school district's request for override authorization is approved, it will replace any existing override for the budget year.

J. The unified school district shall admit high school pupils who reside in a common school district that was located within the boundaries of the former high school district. Tuition shall be paid to the unified school district by the common school district in which such pupils reside. Such tuition amount shall be calculated in accordance with § 15–824, subject to the following modifications:

1. If the former high school district had outstanding bonded indebtedness at the time of unification, the combined tuition for the group of high school pupils who reside in each common school district shall include a debt service amount for the former high school district's outstanding bonded indebtedness that is determined as follows:

(a) Divide the total secondary assessed valuation of the common school district in which the group of pupils reside by the total secondary assessed valuation of the former high school district. For the purposes of this subdivision, "secondary assessed valuation" means secondary assessed valuation for the tax year prior to the year when the unification occurs and includes the values used to determine voluntary contributions collected pursuant to title 9, chapter 4, article 3 [1] and title 48, chapter 1, article 8. [2]

(b) Multiply the quotient obtained in subdivision (a) of this paragraph by the unified school district's annual debt service expenditure.

2. The debt service portion of such tuition payments calculated pursuant to paragraph 1 of this subsection shall be used exclusively for debt service of the outstanding bonded indebtedness of the former high school district. When such indebtedness is fully extinguished, the debt service portion of a pupil's tuition shall be determined in accordance with paragraph 3 of this subsection.

3. If the former high school district had no outstanding bonded indebtedness at the time of unification, the tuition calculation shall include the actual school district expenditures for the portion of any debt service of the unified school district that pertains to any construction or renovation of high school facilities divided by the school district's student count for the high school portion of the school district.

4. The unified school district shall not include in the tuition calculation any debt service that pertains to any construction or renovation of school facilities for preschool through grade eight.

5. Notwithstanding § 15–951, subsection H, the revenue control limit of the common school district shall include the full amount of the debt service portion of the tuition calculated pursuant to this subsection.

K. All assets and liabilities of the unifying school districts shall be transferred and assumed by the new unified school district. Any existing bonded indebtedness of a common school district or a high school district unifying pursuant to this section shall be assumed by the new unified school district and shall be regarded as an indebtedness of the new unified school district for the purpose of determining the debt incurring authority of the district. Taxes for the payment of such bonded indebtedness shall be levied on all taxable property in the new unified school district, but nothing in this subsection shall be construed to relieve from liability to taxation for the payment of all taxable property of the former high school district if necessary to prevent a default in the payment of any bonded indebtedness of the former high school district. The residents of a common school district that does not unify shall not vote in bond or override elections of the unified school district and shall not be assessed taxes as a result of a bond or override election of the unified school district.

L. If the remaining common school district had authorization for an override as provided in § 15–481 or 15–482, the override authorization continues for the remaining common school district or districts in the same manner as before the formation of the unified school district.

M. The bonding authorization and bonding limitations continue for the remaining common school district or districts in the same manner as before the formation of the unified school district.

N. Nothing in this section shall be construed to relieve a school district formed pursuant to § 15–457 or 15–458 of its liability for any outstanding bonded indebtedness.

O. For school districts that become unified after July 1, 2004 and where all of the common schools were eligible for the small school district weight pursuant to § 15–943, paragraph 1, subdivision (a) when computing their base support level and base revenue control limit before unification, the unified school district may continue to use the small school district weight as follows:

1. Annually determine the common school student count and the weighted student count pursuant to § 15–943, paragraph 1, subdivision (a) for each common school district before unification.

2. Calculate the sum of the common school districts' student counts and weighted student counts determined in paragraph 1 of this subsection.

3. Divide the sum of the weighted student counts by the sum of the student counts determined in paragraph 2 of this subsection.

4. The amount determined in paragraph 3 of this subsection shall be the weight for the common schools in the unified school district.

P. A unified school district may calculate its revenue control limit and district support level by using the provisions of subsection O of this section as follows:

1. Determine the number of individual school districts that existed before unification into a single school district.

2. Multiply the amount determined in paragraph 1 of this subsection By six hundred.

3. Multiply the amount determined in paragraph 2 of this subsection By 0.80.

4. If the amount determined in paragraph 3 of this subsection Exceeds the student count of the unified school district, the unified school district is eligible to use the provisions of subsection O of this section.

Q. The provisions of subsections o and p of this section shall remain in effect until the aggregate student count of the common school districts before unification exceeds the aggregate number of students of the common school districts before unification authorized to utilize the provisions of § 15–943, paragraph 1, subdivision (a).

Added by Laws 1981, Ch. 1, § 2, eff. Jan. 23, 1981. Amended by Laws 1996, Ch. 284, § 20; Laws 1999, Ch. 280, § 1; Laws 2000, Ch. 211, § 1; Laws 2004, Ch. 341, § 1.

[1] Section 9–431 et seq.

[2] Section 48–241 et seq.

Historical and Statutory Notes

Source:

Laws 1974, 1st S.S., Ch. 3, § 65.

A.R.S. former §§ 15–491, 15–495, 15–498.

Laws 1986, Ch. 407, § 1, effective May 23, 1986, provides:

"**Section 1. Provisions for certain unified school districts**

"**A.** Notwithstanding any other law to the contrary, for fiscal year 1986–1987, the governing board of a unified school district which offers instruction in the ninth grade and which pays tuition to another school district for at least four hundred pupils in grades ten, eleven, and twelve may increase its revenue control limit and district support level by one hundred thousand dollars.

"**B.** Until December 31, 1989, a unified school district which is eligible to utilize the provisions of subsection A of this section may, by a majority vote of the qualified school electors of the school district, disunite to form a common school district with boundaries coterminous with the boundaries of the unified school district as follows:

"1. If a majority of the governing board of the unified school district unites in a petition to the county school superintendent for disunification to form a common school district, the county school superintendent shall call an election to be held at the next regular election of the governing board, if within ninety days after receipt of the petition, to determine the question, or shall call a special election for that purpose within sixty days.

"2. Not less than five public notices of the election shall be posted, one to be on the door of the schoolhouse in the district, at least ten days before the election.

"3. The election shall be conducted as nearly as practicable in the manner prescribed in § 15–439, [So in original. Should be '§ 15–459.'] Arizona Revised Statutes. The ballots shall contain the words 'common school district, yes' and 'common school district, no' and the voters shall signify their desired choice.

"4. If a majority of the persons voting in the unified school district votes in favor of disunification to form a common school district, the common school district becomes effective as provided in § 15-459, subsection G, Arizona Revised Statutes.

"C. If a unified school district disunites to form a common school district as provided in subsection B of this section, the newly formed common school district may offer instruction in grade nine if the state board of education approves."

Laws 1996, Ch. 284, § 84, provides:

"**Sec. 84. Override provisions upon unification of a high school district and a common school district**

"Notwithstanding § 15-448, Arizona Revised Statutes, as amended by this act, if a high school district and a common school district have adopted resolutions to become a unified district pursuant to § 15-448, Arizona Revised Statutes, the common school district may request an override for the new district to begin in fiscal year 1996-1997 as provided in § 15-482, Arizona Revised Statutes, based on the revenue control limit of the common school district."

§ 15-449. Formation of unified school district by common school district; petition for establishment; election; notice

A. A common school district having a student count of not less than two hundred pupils and an assessed valuation of not less than two million dollars may, by a majority vote of the qualified school electors of the school district, establish a unified school district with boundaries coterminous with the boundaries of the common school district.

B. If a majority of the governing board of the common school district unites in a petition to the county school superintendent for establishment of a unified school district, or if ten per cent of the residents of the common school district unite in a petition for establishment of a unified school district, the county school superintendent shall call an election to be held at the next regular election of the governing board, if within ninety days after receipt of the petition, to determine the question, or shall call a special election for that purpose within sixty days.

C. Not less than five public notices of the election shall be posted, one to be on the door of the schoolhouse in the district, at least ten days before the election.

D. The election shall be conducted as nearly as practicable in the manner prescribed in § 15-459. The ballots shall contain the words "unified school district, yes" and "unified school district, no", and the voter shall signify his desired choice.

E. If a majority of the persons voting in the common school district votes in favor of establishment of a unified school district, the unified school district becomes effective as provided in § 15-459, subsection G.

Added by Laws 1986, Ch. 310, § 2.

Historical and Statutory Notes

Former § 15-449, added by Laws 1981, Ch. 1, § 2, amended by Laws 1981, Ch. 301, § 6, and relating to the establishment of county union high school districts, was derived from:

Laws 1913, 2nd S.S., Ch. 18, §§ 1, 2.
Civ.Code 1913, §§ 2781, 2782.
Rev.Code 1928, §§ 1077, 1078.
Code 1939, §§ 54-910, 54-911.
A.R.S. former §§ 15-521, 15-522.
Laws 1968, Ch. 2, §§ 1, 2.
Laws 1972, Ch. 138, § 20.
Laws 1973, Ch. 183, § 6.

§ 15–450. Formation of a new joint unified school district; petition; report; election; notice; ballots; canvass of votes; appointment of governing board

A. Notwithstanding any other statute, a new joint unified school district may be formed if the formation is approved by the state board of education and if the following requirements are met:

1. The boundaries of the proposed new joint unified school district include an incorporated city that is divided by two counties.

2. The proposed new joint unified school district includes territory within the boundaries of two or more existing school districts.

3. The proposed new joint unified school district would have a student count of not less than six hundred.

4. A high school is not located within the boundaries of the proposed new joint unified school district.

5. The assessed valuation of the proposed school district is at least two million dollars.

6. The governing boards of the districts affected have been given notice of the proposed change and an opportunity to be heard pursuant to § 15–442, subsection B.

B. If it is desired that a new joint unified school district be formed pursuant to the provisions of this section, ten per cent or more of the qualified electors residing within the boundaries of the proposed joint unified school district shall file petitions with the county school superintendents of the counties in which the territory of the proposed district is situated. The petitions shall describe the territory to be included in the proposed joint unified school district and shall request that the formation of the proposed district be submitted to the qualified electors who reside within the proposed district.

C. Each county school superintendent with whom petitions for the formation of a joint unified school district are filed shall examine the petitions within fifteen days of the date of receipt to determine their sufficiency including the adequacy of the signatures from the portion of the proposed district within his county. If the petitions are found sufficient, the county school superintendent shall transmit the petitions to the state board of education.

D. The state board of education shall promptly schedule a review of the issue of the formation of the proposed joint unified school district after receiving the petitions from the county school superintendents pursuant to subsection C of this section. The board shall approve or reject the formation of the proposed joint unified school district within sixty days of the date of receipt of the petitions. The board shall consider:

1. Operational costs of the existing and proposed districts.

2. Travel times and distances.

3. Climatic conditions.

4. Local terrain.

5. The number of pupils.

6. The fairness and appropriateness of any redistribution of taxable wealth from an existing school district to a proposed joint unified school district.

7. Whether the assessed valuation of the proposed joint unified school district is sufficient to support the district in a manner comparable to other districts of similar size.

If the state board after considering all such factors determines that the proposed new district will not cause an undue adverse effect on the operations of any existing school district, jeopardize the operation of the proposed joint common school district or cause a disproportionate amount of taxable wealth to be redistributed, it shall approve the petitions and return them to the respective county school superintendents.

E. On approval from the state board of education, the county school superintendent of each county whose territory or a portion of whose territory will be included in the proposed joint unified school district shall submit the question of the formation of the proposed joint unified school district to the voters at a general election or at a special election to be held for that purpose. If no general election is scheduled to be held within sixty days after the date the county school superintendent receives the approved petitions from the state board of education, he shall promptly call a special election to be held within sixty days after receipt of the approved petitions. Notice of the election shall be given by the county school superintendent to the boards of supervisors. At least ten days before the election, the county school superintendent shall cause notice of the proposed election to be posted in not less than three public places in the proposed district and to be published at least once in a newspaper of general circulation in the proposed district. The notice shall state the following:

1. The question to be voted on and the boundaries of the proposed joint unified school district with sufficient definiteness to make them readily ascertainable.

2. A description of voter qualifications, including requirements that the voters shall be residents of the proposed district.

3. The location of voting places within the proposed district, at least one of which shall be in each county.

F. Within ten days after the election the county school superintendent and the chairman of the board of supervisors of each county shall canvass the vote. If a majority of the votes cast in each county of persons who reside within the proposed district favors formation of the proposed joint unified school district, the boards of supervisors shall jointly declare the election and the joint unified school district shall become operative from and after June 30 next following the election.

G. If the joint unified school district includes territory located in two or more counties, the county of jurisdiction is the county in which the largest number of qualified electors of the joint unified school district resides, except that if all of the existing school buildings are located in one county, that county is the county of jurisdiction. The county school superintendent of the jurisdictional county shall perform all duties for and with respect to the joint unified school district required to be performed by county school superintendents. The board of supervisors of the jurisdictional county shall perform all duties for and with respect to the joint unified school district required to be performed by boards of supervisors, except that school district taxes to be levied on property in the portion of the joint unified school district lying in another county shall be levied by the board of supervisors of the other county or counties and on receipt shall be transferred to the county of jurisdiction.

H. If a new joint unified school district is authorized, the governing boards of the existing school districts shall prepare a projected list of assets for the existing districts prior to the end of the fiscal year in which the election is held. The governing boards of the original school districts and the new joint unified school district shall prepare a final statement of assets for the formerly existing school districts as of the end of the fiscal year in which the election was held and shall have the statement of cash and bonded indebtedness certified by the county treasurers by August 30 of the year in which the new school district becomes operative. The governing boards of the original school districts and the new joint unified school district shall set aside sufficient assets or provide other means to satisfy the liabilities of the former existing districts except for bonded indebtedness and approve the final division of all assets by September 15 of the year in which the new school district becomes operative. If one or more of the governing boards fail to provide for satisfying the liabilities and fail to approve the division of assets by September 15, the county attorney or attorneys shall determine the means to satisfy the liabilities and final division of assets by October 1 of the fiscal year in which the new school district becomes operative.

I. The division of bonded indebtedness of the original school districts shall be in accordance with the provisions of § 15-457, subsection B. In addition, any debt due to lease purchase agreements shall be handled in a similar manner as outlined for bonded indebtedness in § 15-457, subsection B.

J. Sections 15-457, 15-975 and 15-997 apply to joint unified school districts formed under this section.

K. A joint unified school district shall not be formed if any of the resulting school districts would have a student count for the current year of less than six hundred.

L. The governing board of the joint unified school district shall prepare policies, curricula and budgets for the new school district. These policies shall require that:

1. The base salary of each teacher for the first year of operation of the new school district shall not be lower than the teacher's base salary for the prior year in the previously existing school district.

2. The teacher's years of employment in the previously existing school district shall be included in determining the teacher's years of employment in the new joint unified school district.

M. If a new joint unified school district is authorized, the governing board of a district which will have its boundaries reduced by creation of the new joint unified district may hold an override election for the year beginning July 1 after the election that authorized the formation of the new joint unified district. The governing board of a school district which will have its boundaries reduced by creation of the new joint unified district may hold a bond election for bonds applicable to and paid solely by the school district as it will exist after the formation of the new joint unified school district. The electors who reside in an area which property will not be subject to taxation for operation or payment of the bonds of the school district calling the override or bond election after creation of the new joint unified school district are not eligible to vote in such an override or bond election.

Added by Laws 1990, Ch. 329, § 2.

Historical and Statutory Notes

Laws 1990, Ch. 329, § 1, provides:

"**Section 1. Legislative intent**

"The legislature determines that special circumstances exist that make an alternative method for the formation of a joint unified school district necessary if an existing city that is divided by two counties is also divided by two or more school districts. It is the intent of this legislation that the qualified electors of a community that meets this criteria be permitted an opportunity to vote on the formation of such a district in the belief that the best interests of the pupils, as well as the residents, of such a community will be served thereby."

Former § 15-450, added by Laws 1981, Ch. 1, § 2, derived from:

Laws 1913, 2nd S.S., Ch. 18, § 4.
Civ.Code 1913, § 2784.
Rev.Code 1928, § 1079.
Code 1939, § 54-912.
A.R.S. former § 15-523.
Laws 1968, Ch. 2, § 3.

relating to the composition of county union high school districts, was repealed by Laws 1982, Ch. 41, § 1.

§ 15-451. Appointment of governing board for joint unified school districts

A. If the election results in the formation of the joint unified school district, the governing board shall contain the same governing board members of the former school district governing boards. The members shall have authority to adopt a budget and perform such other functions necessary for the school district to become operative at the beginning of the next fiscal year and shall serve until January 1 following the next general election. At the general election held next following the formation and thereafter, members shall be elected as prescribed in § 15-448, subsection E, except that all governing board members of a newly formed unified school district shall be elected to four year terms at the first general election.

B. If any members of the governing boards of the original school districts are residents of the new joint unified school district, those members shall continue to serve on the governing boards of the original school districts until the joint unified school district becomes operative and upon the joint unified school district becoming operative shall be replaced by members who are appointed by the appropriate county school superintendent. The appointed members shall serve until January 1 following the next general election. At the general election next following the formation, new members shall be elected as prescribed in § 15-448, subsection E, except that all governing board members of a newly formed unified school district shall be elected to four year terms at the first general election.

Added by Laws 1990, Ch. 329, § 2. Amended by Laws 1999, Ch. 280, § 2; Laws 2000, Ch. 211, § 2.

Historical and Statutory Notes

Former § 15-451, added by Laws 1981, Ch. 1, § 2, derived from:

Laws 1913, 2nd S.S., Ch. 18, § 5.
Civ.Code 1913, § 2785.
Rev.Code 1928, § 1079.
Code 1939, § 54-912.
A.R.S. former § 15-524.
Laws 1968, Ch. 2, § 4.

relating to government of county union high school districts, was repealed by Laws 1982, Ch. 41, § 1.

§ 15-452. Repealed by Laws 1981, Ch. 133, § 1

Historical and Statutory Notes

The repealed section, added by Laws 1981, Ch. 1, § 2, effective January 23, 1981, related to the formation of county high school districts and was derived from:

Laws 1921, Ch. 155, § 1.
Rev.Code 1928, § 1082.
Laws 1950, 2nd S.S., Ch. 10, § 1.
Code 1939, Supp.1952, § 54-915.
A.R.S. former § 15-531.
Laws 1980, Ch. 167, § 2.

§ 15-453. Authority to form joint common school districts; applicability of laws governing other school districts

A. Joint common school districts may be created lying in part in each of two or more counties in the manner set forth in this article. Except as expressly provided in this title, each such district shall have all powers and duties and shall be operated and maintained and shall follow and be subject to such procedures as may be provided by law for the operation of other school districts.

B. Each joint common school district shall be designated as joint common school district no. ____ (insert the number of the district), of ____ counties (insert the name of each county).

C. The provisions of § 15-460, relating to change of district boundaries, are not applicable to the formation of a joint common school district and a joint high school district pursuant to the provisions of this article.

Added by Laws 1981, Ch. 1, § 2, eff. Jan. 23, 1981.

Historical and Statutory Notes

Source:

Laws 1970, Ch. 12, § 1.
A.R.S. former § 15-421.

§ 15-454. Authority to form joint unified or joint high school districts; applicability of other laws governing other school districts

Joint unified school districts or joint high school districts may be created lying in part in each of two or more counties in the same manner as joint common school districts may be created under this article, except as expressly provided in §§ 15-450 and 15-451. Except as expressly provided in §§ 15-429, 15-450, 15-451, 15-453 and 15-455 through 15-457, § 15-491, subsection B, and §§ 15-975 and 15-997, each joint high school district or joint unified school district shall have all powers and duties, shall be operated and maintained and shall follow and be subject to procedures as may be provided by law for the operation of other school districts.

Added by Laws 1981, Ch. 1, § 2, eff. Jan. 23, 1981. Amended by Laws 1981, Ch. 241, § 1, eff. April 27, 1981; Laws 1990, Ch. 329, § 3.

Historical and Statutory Notes

Source:

Laws 1970, Ch. 12, § 2.
A.R.S. former § 15-561.

§ 15-455. Formation of joint common school district; petition; election; notice; canvass

A. A petition for the creation of a joint common school district shall include the following:

1. A description of the territory comprising the proposed district.

2. A request that the question of the creation of the proposed district be submitted to the qualified electors residing within each of the affected districts.

3. The signatures of not less than ten per cent of the qualified electors residing within the portion of the proposed district within the respective county involved. The county school superintendent of each county whose territory, or a portion thereof, will be included in the proposed district shall receive the petitions containing signatures of residents of his county.

B. Each county school superintendent with whom a petition for the creation of a joint common school district is filed shall, within fifteen days of the date of receipt, examine the petition to determine its sufficiency including the adequacy of the signatures from the portion of the proposed district within his county. If the petition is found sufficient, the county school superintendent shall transmit the petition to the state board of education.

C. If the petitions for the creation of the proposed joint common school district are found sufficient by the county school superintendent of each county whose territory or a portion thereof is to be included in the proposed district, the state board of education shall promptly schedule a review of the issue of the creation of the proposed joint common school district. Such review and the board determination on the issue of the creation of the proposed joint common school district shall be completed within sixty days of the date of receipt of the final petition.

D. The review of the issue of the creation of a proposed joint common school district shall include consideration of the following factors:

1. Operational costs.

2. Travel times and distances.

3. Climatic conditions.

4. Local terrain.

5. Number of pupils.

6. The fairness and appropriateness of any redistribution of taxable wealth from an existing school district to a proposed joint common school district.

If the state board after considering all such factors determines that the proposed new district will not cause an undue adverse effect on the operations of any existing school district or jeopardize the operation of the proposed joint common school district or cause a disproportionate amount of taxable wealth to be redistributed, it shall approve the petitions and return them to the respective county school superintendents.

E. Upon receipt of the approved petitions the county school superintendent of each county whose territory, or a portion thereof, will be included in the proposed joint common school district shall submit the question of the formation of the proposed joint common school district at a general election, or at a special election to be held for that purpose. If no general election will be held within sixty days after the date the county school superintendent receives the approved petition from the state board of education, he shall promptly call a special election to be held within forty-five days after receipt of the approved petition. Notice of such election shall be given by the county school superintendent to the boards of supervisors.

F. The county school superintendent shall cause notice of the proposed election to be posted in not less than three public places in the area within each of the affected districts and to be published one time in a newspaper of general circulation in each county, such posting and publication to be made at least ten days before the election. Such notice shall state the following:

1. The question to be voted on and the boundaries of the proposed joint common school district with sufficient definiteness to make them readily ascertainable.
2. Voter qualifications.
3. The voting places within each of the affected districts.

There shall be at least one voting place in each county. The election shall be called and held, and voters shall possess qualifications as prescribed for the election of governing boards and shall be residents of the territory within each of the affected districts. Ballots shall be prepared and the officers of election appointed by the county school superintendent.

G. On the fifth day after the election the county school superintendent and the chairman of the board of supervisors of each county shall canvass the vote. If a majority of the votes cast in each county of persons who reside within each of the affected districts is in favor of creation of the proposed joint common school district, the boards of supervisors shall jointly declare the election and the joint common school district is established. For the purpose of this subsection a majority of the votes cast in each county of persons who reside within each of the affected districts means a majority vote of the qualified electors voting in each county in each part of an affected existing school district or affected area to be included in the proposed joint common school district and a majority vote of the qualified electors voting in each county in each part, if any, of an affected school district not to be included in the proposed joint common school district.

Added by Laws 1981, Ch. 1, § 2, eff. Jan. 23, 1981.

Historical and Statutory Notes

Source:
Laws 1970, Ch. 12, § 1.
A.R.S. former § 15–421.01.
Laws 1976, Ch. 184, § 2.

§ 15-456. Jurisdiction of county board of supervisors and county school superintendent over joint common school district

A. The county of jurisdiction of the proposed joint common school district is that county in which the greater portion of the qualified electors of the proposed joint common school district resides, unless all of the existing school buildings located on territory which will be within the proposed joint common school district are in one county, in which event that county shall be the county of jurisdiction.

B. The jurisdictional county of the joint common school district shall exercise authority as provided for in this section and §§ 15-429, 15-453 through 15-455, 15-457, 15-491, subsection B, 15-975 and 15-997. The county school superintendent of the jurisdictional county shall perform for and in respect to the joint common school district all duties required to be performed by county school superintendents. The board of supervisors of the same county shall have jurisdiction over and perform all duties for and with respect to the joint common school district as required to be performed by boards of supervisors, except that school district taxes to be levied on property in the portion of the joint common school district lying in another county shall be levied by the board of supervisors of such other county.

Added by Laws 1981, Ch. 1, § 2, eff. Jan. 23, 1981.

Historical and Statutory Notes

Source:

Laws 1970, Ch. 12, § 1.
A.R.S. former § 15-421.02.

§ 15-457. Formation of new joint common school district by subdivision of existing school district; effect on bonded indebtedness; transfer of property

A. Any territory incorporated into a joint common school district which is at the time of the creation of such joint common school district part of an existing school district shall thereafter be considered detached from the existing school district.

B. If any such existing school district has outstanding bonded indebtedness, liability for the payment of principal of and interest on such bonded indebtedness shall be prorated between the existing school district and the new joint common school district in the same proportion as the assessed valuation of taxable property in the existing school district bears to the assessed valuation of taxable property in the detached territory, such valuations to be determined according to the assessment rolls of the county in which the existing school district is located, as such rolls exist at the time of the creation of the new joint common school district. Taxes for the payment of such portion of the principal and interest shall be levied on all taxable property in the new joint common school district, but nothing in this subsection shall be construed to relieve from liability to taxation for the payment thereof all taxable property in the theretofore existing school district if necessary to prevent a default in such payment. Voter approval of the creation of the joint common school district shall constitute an approval of such assumption of indebtedness.

C. All school buildings located in the detached territory, as provided in this subsection, together with all equipment and furnishings, shall become the property of the new joint common school district, and the intangible property of the existing school district shall be prorated between the two districts on the same basis used to determine the amount of bonded indebtedness to be assumed.

D. Any assumed indebtedness shall be regarded as an indebtedness of the new joint common school district for the purpose of determining the debt incurring authority of the new joint common school district and the existing school district.

Added by Laws 1981, Ch. 1, § 2, eff. Jan. 23, 1981.

Historical and Statutory Notes

Source:

Laws 1970, Ch. 12, § 1.
A.R.S. former § 15-421.06.

§ 15-458. Formation of new district or districts by subdivision of existing district; division of assets

A. In a school district containing a student count of more than six hundred, a new school district or districts may be formed by a subdivision of the existing school district.

B. On the request of the governing board or on receipt of petitions bearing the signatures of at least ten per cent of the qualified electors in the area proposed to be a new school district or the signatures of at least fifty of the qualified electors in the area proposed to be a new school district, whichever is more, and at least ten per cent of the qualified electors in the area proposed to continue as the existing school district or at least fifty signatures of the qualified electors in the area proposed to continue as the existing school district, whichever is more, the county school superintendent shall within ten days call an election to determine if the existing school district should be divided and a new school district or districts formed, except that if the existing school district is a union high school district, the county school superintendent shall call the election only on the request of the governing boards of the union high school district and each of the common school districts comprising the union high school district or on receipt of petitions bearing the signatures of at least ten per cent of the qualified electors in each of the common school districts or at least fifty signatures of the qualified electors in each of the common school districts, whichever is more. This subsection does not require the submission of the signatures of more than fifty per cent of the qualified electors of the existing school district to the county school superintendent in order to call an election for the purposes of this section. The petition shall state the proposed boundaries of the school district or districts to be formed together with the student count, specific reasons why it is in the best interest of the current district residents to have a new district or districts formed and the amount of real property valuation within the school district or districts to be formed. No new school district may be formed unless the state board of education determines that the real property valuation per student count is sufficient to support the school district in a manner comparable to other school districts of similar size and that a sufficient number of pupils will exist in each of the new districts to ensure that educational programs and services will be of similar or better quality after the subdivision.

C. The election shall be held concurrently and as provided in § 15-459, except that a majority of the votes cast by the qualified electors in each of the areas proposed as a school district must approve the division of the existing school district and the formation of the new school district.

D. The governing board of the existing school district shall prepare a projected list of assets for the existing district prior to the end of the fiscal year in which the election is held. The governing boards of the original and new school district or districts shall prepare a final statement of assets for the formerly existing school district as of the end of the fiscal year in which the election was held and shall have the statement of cash and bonded indebtedness certified by the county treasurer by August 30 of the year in which the new school district or districts become operative. The governing boards of the original school district and the new school district or districts shall set aside sufficient assets or provide other means to satisfy the liabilities of the former existing district except for bonded indebtedness and approve the final division of all assets by September 15 of the year in which the new school district or districts become operative. If one or more of the governing boards fail to provide for satisfying the liabilities and fail to approve the division of assets by September 15, the county attorney shall determine the means to satisfy the liabilities and final division of assets by October 1 of the fiscal year in which the new school district or districts become operative.

E. The division of the bonded indebtedness of the original school district shall be in accordance with the provisions of § 15-457, subsection B.

F. An original or new school district formed by a subdivision of an existing school district or districts after June 30, 1992 is not eligible to determine its budget using the provisions of § 15-949 or the support level weights prescribed in § 15-943, paragraph 1. These districts are also not eligible to participate in a small district service program as prescribed in § 15-365 or to apply to the state board of education for a capital levy adjustment as prescribed in § 15-963.

G. If two or more common school districts are within the boundaries of a union high school district, two or more unified school districts may be formed by a subdivision of the existing union high school district and by unification with the common school districts as provided in this section, subject to the following provisions:

1. Formation of a unified school district pursuant to this subsection shall be initiated if a majority of the governing board members of each of the districts affected unites in a petition to the county school superintendent for the establishment of a unified school district or if ten per cent of the number of qualified electors who voted in whichever of the last two general elections resulted in the higher number of ballots cast and who reside in each of the areas proposed to be the new unified school districts unite in a petition to the county school superintendent for the establishment of a unified school district.

The petition shall include a statement of the proposed boundaries of the new unified school districts and shall request that the subdivision of the union high school district and formation of the unified districts be submitted to the qualified electors who reside within the proposed districts. The petition shall also include a detailed description of desegregation funding and expenses for the resulting school district as set forth in paragraph 7 of this subsection and may include the new school district name and other information as desirable. On receipt of the petitions, the county school superintendent shall examine the petitions within fifteen days of receipt to determine their sufficiency including the adequacy of the signatures of electors. If the petitions are found sufficient, the county school superintendent shall call an election to be held to determine the question. The county school superintendent shall prepare and the governing board shall distribute a subdivision and unification plan that includes:

(a) The proposed boundary changes.

(b) The impact of the proposed boundary changes, including where pupils will attend school, changes in pupil transportation services, changes in availability of special education services, changes in pupil-teacher ratio and operational costs.

(c) If paragraph 7 of this subsection applies to one or more of the existing school districts, a detailed description of desegregation funding and expenses for the resulting school districts as set forth in paragraph 7 of this subsection.

(d) Any other information the county school superintendent deems appropriate to include.

2. If the governing boards or the petitioners wish the new districts to receive unification assistance as provided in § 15–912.01, they shall notify the department of education and the joint legislative budget committee by August 1 of the fiscal year before the new districts would begin operation and provide the department and the joint legislative budget committee with information required to project the costs of unification assistance to the new districts for the first year of operation. The department shall include sufficient monies to cover these unification costs in its budget request for state aid for the following fiscal year.

3. The election shall be held as provided in § 15–459, except that the ballot shall contain the words "subdivision and unification, yes" and " subdivision and unification, no", and there shall be one of the following two ballot questions, whichever is applicable, stated as follows:

(a) Should (insert the name of the district) union high school district be subdivided with boundaries identical to the boundaries of (insert the name of the districts) common school districts and simultaneously creating (insert the number of the districts) unified school districts with the respective common school districts as specified in the subdivision and unification plan?

(b) Should (insert the name of the district) union high school district be subdivided simultaneously with the subdivision of (insert the name of the districts) common school districts and simultaneously creating (insert the number of the districts) unified school districts with the subdivided common school districts as specified in the subdivision and unification plan?

4. If the formation of the new unified school districts is authorized, the terms of the governing board members of the common and union high school districts do not expire on the effective date of unification but continue until January 1 following the next general election, during which time the members of the governing boards of the previously existing school districts shall serve as the governing board of the new school district in which they reside. At the next general election held after the formation and thereafter, members shall be elected as prescribed in § 15-448, subsection E. The governing boards of the new unified school districts shall prepare policies, curricula and budgets for the new unified school districts. The policies prepared by the governing boards shall include the provisions of § 15-459, subsection M.

5. If the common school district is not subdivided, the new unified school district that includes the boundaries of the previously existing common school district shall assume the bonded indebtedness of that previously existing common school district. If the common school district is subdivided, the provisions of subsection E of this section shall apply.

6. If the common school district is not subdivided, existing bond authorization of the common school districts automatically continues for the original purpose authorized. If the common school district is subdivided, the existing bond authorization of the common school district will expire unless it is divided between the new unified school districts as specified in the subdivision and unification plan.

7. If any of the school districts were authorized to budget for expenses of complying with or continuing to implement activities that were required or permitted by court order of desegregation or administrative agreement with the United States department of education office for civil rights directed towards remediating alleged or proven racial discrimination pursuant to § 15-910, this authorization does not expire on the effective date of the subdivision and unification but only applies to schools included in the court order or administrative agreement.

8. If the union high school district and the common school district or districts with which it is unified all have authorization for an override as provided in § 15-481 that would have continued after the subdivision and unification, the override authorization continues for the new district and expires at the time that the earliest override would have expired.

9. If one or more of the previously existing school districts were participating in a career ladder program pursuant to chapter 9, article 1.1 of this title [1] before subdivision and unification, notwithstanding any other law the state board shall expedite the processing of and may approve an updated application for program reapproval for the new school district that includes the existing school district that was participating in the program.

10. The employee's years of employment in the previously existing school district shall be included in determining the employee's years of employment in the new school district after a subdivision and unification. An employee who was entitled to continuing contract status in the previously existing school district is entitled to continuing employment contract status in the new school district.

11. The base salary and benefits of each employee for the first year of operation of the new school district after a subdivision and unification shall not be lower than the employee's base salary and benefits for the prior year in the previously existing school district.

12. Notwithstanding paragraphs 10 and 11 of this subsection and pursuant to § 15–544, nothing in this section shall be construed to restrict the ability of the governing board to implement a reduction in force or to scale back salaries of certified teachers, administrators or noncertificated employees for reasons of economy or to improve the efficient conduct of schools within the district following a subdivision and unification.

Added by Laws 1981, Ch. 1, § 2, eff. Jan. 23, 1981. Amended by Laws 1984, Ch. 168, § 1, eff. April 18, 1984, retroactively effective to March 1, 1984; Laws 1985, Ch. 238, § 6; Laws 1986, Ch. 310, § 3; Laws 1989, Ch. 210, § 2; Laws 1990, Ch. 278, § 2, eff. June 2, 1991; Laws 1991, Ch. 187, § 1; Laws 1993, Ch. 202, § 7, eff. April 21, 1993; Laws 1994, Ch. 264, § 2; Laws 1999, Ch. 280, § 3; Laws 2000, Ch. 211, § 3.

[1]Section 15–918 et seq.

Historical and Statutory Notes

Source:

Laws 1912, Ch. 77, §§ 28, 32, 33.
Civ. Code 1913, §§ 2720, 2724, 2725.
Rev. Code 1928, §§ 997, 1002.
Code 1939, §§ 54–402, 54–407.
A.R.S. former §§ 15–404, 15–405.
Laws 1959, Ch. 70, § 1.
Laws 1974, 1st S.S., Ch. 3, § 3.
Laws 1974, Ch. 113, § 2.
Laws 1980, 2nd S.S., Ch. 9, § 14.

The 1991 amendment of this section by Ch. 187 explicitly amended the 1990 amendment of this section by Ch. 278.

Laws 1993, Ch. 202, § 16, eff. April 21, 1993, provides:

"**Sec. 16. Support level weights for fiscal years 1991–1992 through 1993–1994**

"If a school district was subject to the provisions of § 15–458, subsection F, Arizona Revised Statutes, but adopted budgets for fiscal years 1991–1992 and 1992–1993 using incorrect budget limits due to utilization of the support level weights prescribed in § 15–943, subsection G, paragraph 1, Arizona Revised Statutes, the district is exempt from the provisions of § 15–905, subsections L and M, Arizona Revised Statutes, and § 15–915, Arizona Revised Statutes, for those fiscal years for the amount of the excess budget capacity caused by the use of the incorrect weights."

Reviser's Notes:

1985 Note. Pursuant to authority of § 41–1304.02, in the section heading "or districts" was inserted following the first "district".

1994 Note. Pursuant to authority of § 41–1304.02, in subsection G, paragraph 2, first sentence the reference to "§ 15–912.01" was substituted for the reference to "§ 15–913" to conform to the reviser's renumbering of that section.

§ 15–459. Consolidation of districts; petition; election; notice; report; ballots; canvass of votes; governing board

A. On the request of the governing boards of two or more school districts in the same county or in adjacent counties or on receipt of petitions bearing the signatures of ten per cent or more of the number of qualified electors who voted in whichever of the last two general elections resulted in the higher number of ballots cast and who reside in each of two or more school districts in the same county or in adjacent counties to consolidate the school districts or parts of the districts, the county school superintendent of each of the counties affected shall within ten days call an election to determine the question on consolidation.

B. Consolidations allowed pursuant to subsection A of this section include:

1. To change the boundaries of a school district to include any part of an adjacent school district.

2. If all the common school districts within the boundaries of an existing union high school district desire to consolidate into one common school district.

3. If two or more adjacent school districts of like character, either common, high or unified school districts, desire to consolidate into one common, high or unified school district.

4. If a common school district that is not a part of a union high school district desires to consolidate with an adjacent unified school district.

5. If two or more common school districts desire to consolidate into one school district and unify the consolidated district with a union high school district to form one unified school district.

C. Notice of the election to determine consolidation of school districts shall be posted in not less than three public places in each of the school districts proposed to be consolidated at least twenty-five days before the election.

D. The county school superintendent shall prepare and the governing board shall distribute a report on the proposed boundary changes in a manner similar to that prescribed in § 15-481, subsection B. The report shall contain the following information:

1. The date of the election.

2. The polling places and times they are open.

3. A consolidation plan to include:

(a) The proposed boundary changes.

(b) The impact of the proposed boundary changes, including where pupils will attend school, changes in pupil transportation services, changes in availability of special education services, changes in pupil-teacher ratio and operational costs.

(c) If the provisions of subsection P of this section apply to one or more of the existing school districts, a detailed description of desegregation funding and expenses for the resulting school district as set forth in subsection P of this section.

(d) Any other information the county school superintendent deems appropriate to include.

E. Ballots shall be prepared by the county school superintendent, shall be delivered to the inspector at least forty-eight hours before the opening of the polls as prescribed in § 16-509 and shall contain: "Consolidation includes the assumption of liability by the resulting school district for all indebtedness of existing school districts or those parts of school districts proposed for consolidation. Do you support consolidation under the specified provisions of the consolidation plan? Yes ( ) No ( )." If the election is to simultaneously consolidate and unify two or more common school districts, the ballot shall contain: "Do you support the consolidation of the (insert names of common school districts) and the subsequent unification of the consolidated districts with the (insert name of union high school district) to form one unified school district under the consolidation and unification plan? Yes ( ) No ( )."

F. The county school superintendent shall hold the election during the fiscal year preceding the fiscal year consolidation is proposed to be effective on a date prescribed by § 16–204. The election shall be held in the manner and electors shall possess qualifications as prescribed for the election of governing board members. The results of the election shall be reported to the county school superintendent.

G. The county school superintendent and the chairman of the board of supervisors shall, on the seventh day after the election, canvass the vote. If a majority of the votes cast in each district favors consolidation, the districts are consolidated and become one district from and after June 30 next following the election. If parts of two or more school districts are proposed to be consolidated, a majority of the voters in the part of a school district or districts not affected by the proposed consolidation and a majority of the voters in the part of the school district or districts proposed for consolidation must approve the consolidation.

H. If a school district provides only financing for pupils who are instructed by another school district in the same county or in an adjacent county, the school district or any part of the school district may be consolidated with the school district providing the instructional program as follows:

1. The governing board of the financing school district approves the consolidation or ten per cent of the qualified electors residing in the school district, or that part of the school district proposed for consolidation, petitions the county school superintendent to call an election to approve the proposed consolidation.

2. The governing board of the school district providing instruction approves the consolidation.

3. At an election called by the county school superintendent of each of the counties affected, a majority of the persons voting in the school district, or that part of the school district providing financing, approves the proposed consolidation and a majority of the persons voting in the district providing instruction approves the proposed consolidation.

I. Elections held as provided in subsection H of this section shall be conducted in the same manner as elections prescribed in subsections C through G of this section and shall be held concurrently as prescribed in § 15–458.

J. If the consolidated district includes territory located in two or more counties, the county of jurisdiction is the county in which the largest number of qualified electors of the consolidated school district resides, except that if all of the existing school buildings are in one county, that county is the county of jurisdiction. The county school superintendent of the jurisdictional county shall perform all duties for and with respect to the consolidated school district as required to be performed by county school superintendents. The board of supervisors of the jurisdictional county shall perform all duties for and with respect to the consolidated school district as required to be performed by boards of supervisors, except that school district taxes to be levied on property in the portion of the consolidated school district lying in another county shall be levied by the board of supervisors of the other county or counties and on receipt shall be transferred to the county of jurisdiction. All school buildings located within the consolidated school district, together with all equipment and furnishings, become the property of the consolidated school district. Any assumed indebtedness is an indebtedness of the consolidated school district for the purpose of determining the debt incurring authority of the consolidated school district.

K. Sections 15-457, 15-975 and 15-997 apply to school districts which are consolidated as provided in subsection H of this section.

L. Consolidation pursuant to this section is not allowed if the resulting school district would have a student count for the current year of more than ten per cent of the total student count of all school districts in this state.

M. The governing board shall prepare policies, curricula and budgets for the new school district. These policies shall require that:

1. The base salary and benefits of each employee for the first year of operation of the new school district shall not be lower than the employee's base salary and benefits for the prior year in the previously existing school district.

2. The employee's years of employment in the previously existing school district shall be included in determining the employee's years of employment in the new school district. An employee who was entitled to continuing employment contract status in the previously existing school district is entitled to continuing employment contract status in the new school district.

3. Notwithstanding paragraphs 1 and 2 of this subsection and pursuant to § 15-544, nothing in this section shall be construed to restrict the ability of the governing board to implement a reduction in force or to scale back salaries of certified teachers, administrators or noncertificated employees for reasons of economy or to improve the efficient conduct of schools within the district following a school district consolidation.

N. If all of the districts to be consolidated have authorization for an override as provided in § 15-481 that would have continued after the consolidation, the override authorization continues for the new district and expires at the time that the earliest override would have expired.

O. If one or more, but not all, of the districts to be consolidated have authorization for an override as provided in § 15-481 that would have continued after the consolidation, the override authorization shall only apply to the schools included under the terms of the prior override authorization. Consolidation of school districts does not consolidate or pool the liability to be taxed for the override and only property that was located within the boundaries of the district that approved the override prior to consolidation are to pay taxes to support the override. This subsection also applies if all of the districts to be consolidated have authorization for overrides, but the authorizations are pursuant to different subsections of § 15-481 or the override amounts are not the same percentage of the revenue control limit.

P. Notwithstanding § 15-457, consolidation of school districts does not consolidate or pool the liability of the former school districts into the resulting school district. Outstanding indebtedness incurred by a school district before consolidation shall be repaid without interruption according to existing debt schedules as determined by the county board of supervisors. If a school district consolidates after July 1, 2004, the new school district may pay tuition to the district of attendance when a pupil is precluded by distance or lack of transportation from attending school in the district of a pupil's residence.

Q. If one or more of the previously existing school districts was authorized to budget for expenses of complying with or continuing to implement activities that were required or permitted by court order of desegregation or administrative agreement with the United States department of education office for civil rights directed toward remediating alleged or proven racial discrimination pursuant to § 15–910, this authorization does not expire on the effective date of consolidation but only applies to schools included in the court order or administrative agreement.

R. If one or more of the previously existing school districts was participating in a career ladder program pursuant to chapter 9, article 1.1 of this title [1] before consolidation, notwithstanding any other law the state board shall expedite the processing of and may approve an updated application for program reapproval that incorporates the geographic boundaries of the resulting school district and the inclusion of the additional staff in the career ladder program.

S. If the formation of a new consolidated and unified school district is authorized, the terms of the governing board members of the common and union high school districts do not expire on the effective date of the unification. The governing board members of the previously existing school districts shall serve as provided in § 15–430, except that the power of the governing board members of the previously existing school districts acting as the governing board of the unified school district is limited to the maintenance and operation of the previously existing school districts and compliance with the consolidation and unification plan.

Added by Laws 1981, Ch. 1, § 2, eff. Jan. 23, 1981. Amended by Laws 1983, Ch. 118, § 2; Laws 1985, Ch. 238, § 7; Laws 1986, Ch. 312, § 2; Laws 1988, Ch. 187, § 3, eff. June 8, 1988; Laws 1989, Ch. 210, § 3; Laws 1993, Ch. 98, § 4, eff. Jan. 1, 1994; Laws 1994, Ch. 264, § 3; Laws 1996, Ch. 271, § 12, eff. April 23, 1996; Laws 1997, Ch. 276, § 2; Laws 1999, Ch. 280, § 4; Laws 2004, Ch. 341, § 2.

[1] Section 15–918 et seq.

Historical and Statutory Notes

Source:

Laws 1912, Ch. 77, § 31.
Civ. Code 1913, § 2723.
Rev. Code 1928, § 1001.
Code 1939, § 54–406.
A.R.S. former §§ 15–409, 15–410.
Laws 1972, Ch. 138, § 4.
Laws 1974, 1st S.S., Ch. 3, § 63.
Laws 1975, Ch. 103, § 5.

Reviser's Notes:

1997 Note. Pursuant to authority of § 41–1304.02, in subsection O, second sentence, the words "without interruption" were transposed to follow "repaid".

§ 15–460. Change of school district boundaries

A. On request of the governing board of a school district or on receipt of a petition bearing the signatures of ten per cent or more of the qualified electors residing in the school district to change the boundaries of the school district in such a manner as to include adjacent unorganized territory, setting forth the boundaries desired and the reasons for such change, the county school superintendent shall submit the question of including the unorganized territory within the existing school district to the qualified electors of the new proposed school district. The election shall be held as provided in § 15–459, except that a majority of the qualified electors voting on the question in the unorganized territory and a majority of the qualified electors voting on the question in the existing school district must approve the change. If approved, the change is effective from and after June 30 next following the election.

B. When ten per cent or more of the qualified electors residing in a school district desire that the boundaries of the school district be diminished, they may present a petition to the county school superintendent setting forth the change of boundaries desired and the reasons for such change. The county school superintendent shall prepare and transmit to the governing board of the school district proposed to be diminished a report providing specific information regarding the future availability of educational programs in the area of the district to be detached and in the area which will constitute the remaining district, availability of pupil transportation services and the financial impact on taxpayers. The governing board shall mail or distribute the report to all households located in the school district. The county school superintendent shall submit the question of diminishing the school district boundaries to the qualified electors of the school district. The election shall be held as provided in § 15–459. A majority of the qualified electors voting on the question in the territory to remain in the existing school district and a majority of the qualified electors voting on the question in the territory to be excluded must approve the change. If approved, the change is effective from and after June 30 next following the election.

C. Notwithstanding subsections A and B of this section and this chapter, the governing boards of two adjacent common, union or unified school districts may authorize minor boundary adjustments to both school districts and the governing boards of a unified school district and adjacent common and union high school districts may authorize minor boundary adjustments to the three school districts if all of the following are true:

1. The school districts authorizing the boundary adjustment have not previously made more than one minor boundary adjustment pursuant to this subsection.

2. A majority of the electors within the geographic boundaries of a portion of a school district, as specified in the petition, presents a petition to the governing boards of the district or districts in which the petitioners currently reside and the district to which the petitioners desire to be annexed. If there are no electors within the geographic boundaries of the territory to be annexed, a majority of the property owners in the territory may submit the petition. The petition shall set forth the boundaries of the portion of the district to be annexed.

3. A majority of the members of the governing boards of each district approves the minor boundary adjustment.

4. The boundary adjustment would result in the transfer of no more than one and one-half per cent of the student count of the district from which the pupils will transfer.

5. The boundary adjustment would not result in the transfer of any school buildings, equipment or furnishings from one school district to another school district.

6. No member of the governing board of the school district to be diminished is a resident of the territory that is being transferred to the adjacent school district.

7. The governing boards of the school districts have agreed on a means to satisfy any liabilities.

D. If a majority of the members of the governing boards of school districts to which petitions were presented pursuant to subsection C of this section approves the petitions, the petitions shall be transmitted with the endorsements of the governing boards to the county school superintendent. The county school superintendent, if no petition opposing annexation signed by a majority of the school electors representing either the resident district or the district to which annexation is proposed is received within fifteen days after the transmittal of the petition requesting annexation, shall make the records of boundaries conform to the petition for annexation and notify the boards of supervisors and the county assessor of the boundary change. The change is effective from and after June 30 next following the notification of the boards of supervisors.

E. Notwithstanding subsection A of this section, if the qualified electors residing in a school district have previously voted to accept unorganized territory into the district's boundaries in two consecutive elections called for this purpose, the school district governing board may annex any election precinct within the unorganized territory that is contiguous to the school district if both of the following conditions exist:

1. At least one hundred fifty pupils who reside in the election precinct are enrolled in one or more school districts in the county.

2. The qualified electors of the precinct have previously voted in favor of the annexation.

Added by Laws 1981, Ch. 1, § 2, eff. Jan. 23, 1981. Amended by Laws 1981, Ch. 314, § 8; Laws 1983, Ch. 118, § 3; Laws 1985, Ch. 238, § 8; Laws 1990, Ch. 244, § 1; Laws 1994, Ch. 264, § 4; Laws 1996, Ch. 126, § 1; Laws 2002, Ch. 75, § 1.

Historical and Statutory Notes

Source:

Laws 1912, Ch. 77, § 30.
Civ. Code 1913, § 2722.
Rev. Code 1928, § 999.
Code 1939, § 54–404.
A.R.S. former § 15–403.
Laws 1956, Ch. 131, § 1.
Laws 1972, Ch. 138, § 3.
Laws 1974, 1st S.S., Ch. 3, § 6.1.
Laws 1975, Ch. 103, § 2.
Laws 1976, Ch. 184, § 1.
Laws 1977, Ch. 173, § 1.
Laws 1980, 2nd S.S., Ch. 9, § 12.

§§ 15-461, 15-462. Repealed by Laws 1985, Ch. 238, § 11

Historical and Statutory Notes

Section 15-461, added by Laws 1981, Ch. 1, § 2, related to annexation of school districts and was derived from:

Laws 1921, Ch. 72, § 1.
Rev.Code 1928, § 1000.
Code 1939, § 54-405.
A.R.S. former § 15-406.

Section 15-462, added by Laws 1981, Ch. 1, § 2, related to annexation of common school districts to high school districts and was derived from:

Laws 1925, Ch. 72, § 1.
Rev.Code 1928, § 1003.
Code 1939, § 54-408.
Laws 1954, Ch. 159, § 1.
A.R.S. former § 15-407.

§ 15-463. Annexation of military reservation to high school district or union high school district; procedure; notice; hearing

A. A high school district, or union high school district, any portion of which is contiguous to a military reservation, may at any time, and as provided in subsection B, annex all or any contiguous part of said military reservation for high school purposes only.

B. When a majority of the governing board of a high school district or a union high school district petitions the board of supervisors of the county in which the school district is located, requesting the annexation of all or a contiguous part of a military reservation, and such petition is accompanied by a petition containing the same request signed by ten or more qualified school electors residing in the school district, the board of supervisors shall within fifteen days give written notice of the proposed annexation to the commanding officer of the military reservation and to the governing board of any other high school districts or union high school districts contiguous to the military reservation, which notice shall fix a time and place not more than fifteen days after the serving of said notice for a hearing on the petitions. If, at the hearing, the commanding officer of the military reservation or other higher military authority, or the authorized agent of either, objects to the annexation, no further action shall be taken. If, however, no such objection is made at the hearing, the board of supervisors, within ten days after the hearing, shall either allow or deny the petitions. If the petitions are allowed, the board of supervisors shall forthwith notify the commanding officer of the military reservation and the county school superintendent and the annexation shall take effect immediately.

C. A high school district which annexes any or all of a contiguous part of a military reservation as provided in this section and a common school district which is coterminous with the portion of the high school district which is not part of the military reservation may operate as a unified school district under a single governing board.

Added by Laws 1981, Ch. 1, § 2, eff. Jan. 23, 1981. Amended by Laws 1981, Ch. 156, § 1, eff. April 17, 1981.

Historical and Statutory Notes

Source:

Laws 1959, Ch. 26, § 1.
A.R.S. former § 15-551.

The 1981 amendment added subsec. C.

Reviser's Notes:

1981 Note. Pursuant to authority of § 41-1304.02, in the heading of this section the words "or union high school district" were added following the word "district".

§ 15-464. Withdrawal of military reservation from school district; petition; hearing

When a common school district or a high school district adjacent to or embracing all or a portion of a military reservation has a larger school population than it had the previous year, as shown by a census enumeration certified by the county school superintendent, and it is not feasible educationally and economically for the school district to provide adequate school facilities for the military reservation, the school district governing board or the authorities of the military reservation may petition the state board of education to withdraw the military reservation from the school district. Within thirty days after receipt of the petition the state board of education shall hold a hearing thereon and within ten days after the hearing shall allow or deny the petition. If allowed, the state board shall direct the county school superintendent to withdraw the military reservation from the school district in which it is in whole or in part included and to report the change of school district boundaries to the board of supervisors.

Added by Laws 1981, Ch. 1, § 2, eff. Jan. 23, 1981.

Historical and Statutory Notes

Source:

Laws 1948, 5th S.S., Ch. 37, § 1.

Code 1939, Supp.1952, § 54-404a.

A.R.S. former § 15-911.

§ 15-465. Accommodation school; establishment on military reservation; expenses; abandonment

A. Upon the withdrawal of a military reservation from any common school district or high school district, as provided in § 15-464, and upon a showing by the military authorities that necessary buildings and facilities for the operation of a school are available, the county school superintendent shall establish an accommodation school on the military reservation.

B. Expenses of conducting the school shall be paid out of the county school reserve fund by the county school superintendent, as the expenses of other accommodation schools are paid.

C. If a military reservation is abandoned in which an accommodation school has been conducted in accordance with the provisions of this section and §§ 15-464 and 15-466, the boundaries of the common school district or the high school district, as they existed prior to withdrawal of the reservation from the school district, shall be deemed automatically reinstated.

Added by Laws 1981, Ch. 1, § 2, eff. Jan. 23, 1981.

Historical and Statutory Notes

Source:

Laws 1948, 5th S.S., Ch. 37, § 2.

Code 1939, Supp.1952, §§ 54-404a, 54-404b.

A.R.S. former §§ 15-912, 15-913.

§ 15-466. Transfer of accommodation schools

A. Facilities, if possible, and pupils of an existing accommodation school operated pursuant to this section and §§ 15-464 and 15-465 may be included in the most accessible adjacent school district as directed by majority vote of the board of supervisors of the county in which such school is located, subject to approval by a majority of members of the governing board of the school district designated to receive such pupils and facilities and a vote of approval at an election called by the county school superintendent of the qualified electors in the area served by the accommodation school.

B. Facilities owned by a governmental entity other than the school district and operated as an accommodation school may be accepted by the school district or operated by the school district pursuant to an agreement with or permit from such other governmental entity.
Added by Laws 1981, Ch. 1, § 2, eff. Jan. 23, 1981.

Historical and Statutory Notes

Source:

Laws 1974, 1st S.S., Ch. 3, § 66.
A.R.S. former § 15-914.

§ 15-467. Change of union high school district to high school district

A. When all the common school districts comprising a union high school district unite, either by annexation or by consolidation, into one common school district, the union high school district shall, as of the first day of the next fiscal year, be deemed to be dissolved, and the terms of office of all governing board members elected to the union high school district shall expire and the union high school district shall thereupon become ipso facto a high school district and be administered as other high school districts are administered.

B. A high school district created as provided by subsection A is liable for all indebtedness, bonded or otherwise, outstanding against the dissolved union high school district, and all property, balances and deficits of the dissolved district become the property, balances and deficits of the high school district.
Added by Laws 1981, Ch. 1, § 2, eff. Jan. 23, 1981.

Historical and Statutory Notes

Source:

Laws 1946, 2nd S.S., Ch. 10, § 1.
Code 1939, Supp.1952, § 54-901a.
A.R.S. former § 15-504.

§ 15-468. Repealed by Laws 1982, Ch. 41, § 1

Historical and Statutory Notes

The repealed section, added by Laws 1981, Ch. 1, § 2, and relating to the discontinuance of county union high school districts, the formation of new high school districts or union high school districts, and the disposition of the county union high school districts' properties, was derived from:

Laws 1913, 2nd S.S., Ch. 18, §§ 6, 7.
Civ. Code 1913, §§ 2786, 2787.
Rev. Code 1928, § 1081.
Code 1939, § 54-914.
A.R.S. former § 15-525.
Laws 1968, Ch. 2, § 5.
Laws 1974, 1st S.S., Ch. 3, § 13.
Laws 1980, 2nd S.S., Ch. 9, § 26.
Laws 1981, Ch. 1, § 2.

§ 15-469. Lapsing of common school district; conditions; procedure; disposition of property of lapsed common school district

A. If in a common school district there has been a student count of less than eight pupils between the ages of six and twenty-one years for three months during the school year, the county school superintendent may at once suspend the common school district and report the suspension and reasons to the board of supervisors at its next meeting.

B. The board of supervisors may declare the common school district lapsed and attach the territory to one or more of the adjoining school districts, dispose of the property of the lapsed common school district and apply the proceeds to the credit of the lapsed common school district. The county school superintendent shall determine all unbonded indebtedness of the lapsed common school district and draw his warrant, on proper vouchers, on the county treasurer in payment of the unbonded indebtedness. Any balance remaining after such payment shall be transferred to the county school fund.

Added by Laws 1981, Ch. 1, § 2, eff. Jan. 23, 1981.

Historical and Statutory Notes

Source:

Laws 1912, Ch. 77, § 107.
Civ. Code 1913, § 2823.
Laws 1921, Ch. 158, § 1.
Rev. Code 1928, § 1096.
Code 1939, § 54-610.
A.R.S. former § 15-413.
Laws 1974, 1st S.S., Ch. 3, § 4.
Laws 1980, 2nd S.S., Ch. 9, § 15.

ARTICLE 4. SCHOOL DISTRICT BUDGET OVERRIDE ELECTIONS

§ 15-481. Override election; budget increases; notice; ballot; effect

A. If the proposed budget of a school district exceeds the aggregate budget limit for the budget year, the governing board shall order an override election to be held not less than ninety days from the date of the order for the purpose of presenting the proposed budget to the qualified electors of the school district who shall by a majority of those voting either affirm or reject the budget. In addition, the governing board shall prepare an alternate budget which does not include an increase in the budget of more than the amount permitted as provided in § 15-905. If the qualified electors approve the proposed budget, the governing board of the school district shall follow the procedures prescribed in § 15-905 for adopting a budget that includes the authorized increase. If the qualified electors disapprove the proposed budget, the governing board shall follow the procedures prescribed in § 15-905 for adopting a budget that does not include the proposed increase or the portion of the proposed increase that exceeds the amount authorized by a previously approved budget increase as prescribed in subsection P of this section.

B. The county school superintendent shall prepare an informational report on the proposed increase in the budget and a sample ballot and, at least thirty-five days prior to the election, shall transmit the report and the ballot to the governing board of the school district. For a school district located in a county with a population of two hundred thousand persons or more, the governing board, upon receipt of the report and the ballot, shall mail or distribute the report and the ballot to the households, in which qualified electors reside, within the school district at least thirty days prior to the election. For a school district located in a county with a population of less than two hundred thousand persons, the governing board, upon receipt of the report and the ballot, shall mail or distribute the report and the ballot to the households within the school district at least thirty days prior to the election. Any distribution of material concerning the proposed increase in the budget shall not be conducted by children enrolled in the school district. The report shall contain the following information:

1. The date of the election.

2. The polling places and times they are open.

3. The proposed total increase in the budget which exceeds the amount permitted pursuant to § 15–905.

4. The total amount of the current year's budget, the total amount of the proposed budget and the total amount of the alternate budget.

5. If the override is for a period of more than one year, a statement indicating the number of years the proposed increase in the budget would be in effect and the percentage of the school district's revenue control limit that the district is requesting for the future years.

6. The proposed total amount of revenues which will fund the increase in the budget and the amount which will be obtained from a levy of taxes upon the taxable property within the school district for the first year for which the budget increase was adopted.

7. The proposed amount of revenues which will fund the increase in the budget and which will be obtained from other than a levy of taxes upon the taxable property within the school district for the first year for which the budget increase was adopted.

8. The dollar amount and the purpose for which the proposed increase in the budget is to be expended for the first year for which the budget increase was adopted.

9. At least two arguments, if submitted, but no more than ten arguments for and two arguments, if submitted, but no more than ten arguments against the proposed increase in the budget. The arguments shall be in a form prescribed by the county school superintendent and each argument shall not exceed two hundred words. Arguments for the proposed increase in the budget shall be provided in writing and signed by the governing board. If submitted, additional arguments in favor of the proposed increase in the budget shall be provided in writing and signed by those in favor. Arguments against the proposed increase in the budget shall be provided in writing and signed by those in opposition. The names of those persons other than the governing board or superintendent submitting written arguments shall not be included in the report without their specific permission, but shall be made available only upon request to the county school superintendent. The county school superintendent shall review all factual statements contained in the written arguments and correct any inaccurate statements of fact. The superintendent shall not review and correct any portion of the written arguments which are identified as statements of the author's opinion. The county school superintendent shall make the written arguments available to the public as provided in title 39, chapter 1, article 2. [1] A deadline for submitting arguments to be included in the informational report shall be set by the county school superintendent.

10. A statement that the alternate budget shall be adopted by the governing board if the proposed budget is not adopted by the qualified electors of the school district.

11. The full cash value, the assessed valuation and the estimated amount of the secondary tax bill if the proposed budget is adopted for each of the following:

(a) An owner-occupied residence whose assessed valuation is the average assessed valuation of property classified as class three, as prescribed by § 42–12003 for the current year in the school district.

(b) An owner-occupied residence whose assessed valuation is one-half of the assessed valuation of the residence in subdivision (a) of this paragraph.

(c) An owner-occupied residence whose assessed valuation is twice the assessed valuation of the residence in subdivision (a) of this paragraph.

(d) A business whose assessed valuation is the average of the assessed valuation of property classified as class one, as prescribed by § 42–12001, paragraphs 12 and 13 for the current year in the school district.

12. If the election is conducted pursuant to subsection L or m of this section, the following information:

(a) An executive summary of the school district's most recent capital improvement plan submitted to the school facilities board.

(b) A complete list of each proposed capital improvement that will be funded with the budget increase and a description of the proposed cost of each improvement, including a separate aggregation of capital improvements for administrative purposes as defined by the school facilities board.

(c) The tax rate associated with each of the proposed capital improvements and the estimated cost of each capital improvement for the owner of a single family home that is valued at eighty thousand dollars.

C. For the purpose of this section, the school district may use its staff, equipment, materials, buildings or other resources only to distribute the informational report at the school district office or at public hearings and to produce such information as required in subsection B of this section, provided that nothing in this subsection shall preclude school districts from holding or participating in any public hearings at which testimony is given by at least one person for the proposed increase and one person against the proposed increase.

D. The elections prescribed in subsection A of this section shall be held on a date prescribed by § 16–204 and shall be conducted as nearly as practicable in the manner prescribed in article 1 of this chapter, [2] §§ 15–422 through 15–424 and § 15–426, relating to special elections, except that:

1. The notices required pursuant to § 15–403 shall be posted not less than twenty-five days before the election.

2. Ballots shall be counted pursuant to title 16, chapter 4, article 10. [3]

E. If the election is to exceed the revenue control limit and if the proposed increase will be fully funded by a levy of taxes upon the taxable property within the school district, the ballot shall contain the words "budget increase, yes" and "budget increase, no", and the voter shall signify his desired choice. The ballot shall also contain the amount of the proposed increase of the proposed budget over the alternate budget, a statement that the amount of the proposed increase will be based on a percentage of the school district's revenue control limit in future years, if applicable, as provided in subsection P of this section and the following statement:

Any budget increase authorized by this election shall be entirely funded by a levy of taxes upon the taxable property within this school district for the year for which adopted and for ____ subsequent years, shall not be realized from monies furnished by the state and shall not be subject to the limitation on taxes specified in article IX, § 18, Constitution of Arizona. Based on an estimate of assessed valuation used for secondary property tax purposes, the proposed increase in the school district's budget over that allowed by law would result in an estimated increase in the school district's tax rate of ______________ dollar per one hundred dollars of assessed valuation used for secondary property tax purposes and is in addition to the school district's tax rate which will be levied to fund the school district's revenue control limit allowed by law.

F. If the election is to exceed the revenue control limit and if the proposed increase will be fully funded by revenues from other than a levy of taxes upon the taxable property within the school district, the ballot shall contain the words "budget increase, yes" and "budget increase, no", and the voter shall signify the voter's desired choice. The ballot shall also contain:

1. The amount of the proposed increase of the proposed budget over the alternate budget.

2. A statement that the amount of the proposed increase will be based on a percentage of the school district's revenue control limit in future years, if applicable, as provided in subsection P of this section.

3. The following statement:

Any budget increase authorized by this election shall be entirely funded by this school district with revenues from other than a levy of taxes on the taxable property within the school district for the year for which adopted and for ____ subsequent years and shall not be realized from monies furnished by the state.

G. Except as provided in subsection H of this section, the maximum budget increase which may be requested and authorized as provided in subsection E or f of this section or the combination of subsections e and f of this section is ten per cent of the revenue control limit as provided in § 15–947, subsection A for the budget year.

H. Special budget override provisions for school districts with a student count of less than one hundred fifty-four in kindergarten programs and grades one through eight or with a student count of less than one hundred seventy-six in grades nine through twelve are as follows:

1. The maximum budget increase that may be requested and authorized as provided in subsections e and f of this section is the greater of the amount prescribed in subsection G of this section or a limit computed as follows:

(a) For common or unified districts with a student count of less than one hundred fifty-four in kindergarten programs and grades one through eight, the limit computed as prescribed in item (i) or (ii) of this subdivision, whichever is appropriate:

(i)

Student Count		Small School Student Count Limit		Support Level Weight for Small Isolated School Districts		Base Level		Phase Down Reduction Factor
____	−	125	×	1.358 + (0.0005 × (500 − Student Count))	×	$	=	$

Phase down Base		Phase Down Reduction Factor		Small Isolated School District Elementary Limit
$150,000	−	$	=	$

(ii)

Student Count		Small School Student Count Limit		Support Level Weight for Small School Districts		Base Level		Phase Down Reduction Factor
____	−	125	×	1.278 + (0.0003 × (500 − Student Count))	×	$	=	$

Phase Down Base		Phase Down Reduction Factor		Small School District Elementary Limit
$150,000	−	$	=	$

(b) For unified or union high school districts with a student count of less than one hundred seventy-six in grades nine through twelve, the limit computed as prescribed in item (i) or (ii) of this subdivision, whichever is appropriate:

(i)

Student Count		Small School Student Count Limit		Support Level Weight for Small Isolated School Districts		Base Level		Phase Down Reduction Factor
____	−	100	×	1.468 + (0.0005 × (500 − Student Count))	×	$	=	$

Phase down Base		Phase Down Reduction Factor		Small Isolated District Secondary Limit
$350,000	−	$	=	$

(ii)

Student Count		Small School Student Count Limit		Support Level Weight for Small School Districts		Base Level		Phase Down Reduction Factor
____	−	100	×	1.398 + (0.0004 × (500 − Student Count))	×	$	=	$

Phase Down Base		Phase Down Reduction Factor		Small School District Secondary Limit

$350,000 − $ __________ = $ __________

(c) If both subdivisions (a) and (b) of this paragraph apply to a unified school district, its limit for the purposes of this paragraph is the combination of its elementary limit and its secondary limit.

(d) If only subdivision (a) or (b) of this paragraph applies to a unified school district, the district's limit for the purposes of this paragraph is the sum of the limit computed as provided in subdivision (a) or (b) of this paragraph plus ten per cent of the revenue control limit attributable to those grade levels that do not meet the eligibility requirements of this subsection. If a school district budgets monies outside the revenue control limit pursuant to § 15-949, subsection E, the district's limit for the purposes of this paragraph is only the ten per cent of the revenue control limit attributable to those grade levels that are not included under § 15-949, subsection E. For the purposes of this subdivision, the revenue control limit is separated into elementary and secondary components based on the weighted student count as provided in § 15-971, subsection B, paragraph 2, subdivision (a).

2. If a school district utilizes the provisions of this subsection To request an override of more than one year, the ballot shall include an estimate of the amount of the proposed increase in the future years in place of the statement that the amount of the proposed increase will be based on a percentage of the school district's revenue control limit in future years, as prescribed in subsections e and f of this section.

3. Notwithstanding subsection P of this section, the maximum period of an override authorized pursuant to this subsection is five years.

4. Subsection P, paragraphs 1 and 2 of this section do not apply to overrides authorized pursuant to this subsection.

I. If the election is to exceed the revenue control limit as provided in § 15-482 and if the proposed increase will be fully funded by a levy of taxes on the taxable property within the school district, the ballot shall contain the words "budget increase, yes" and "budget increase, no", and the voter shall signify the voter's desired choice. The ballot shall also contain the amount of the proposed increase of the budget over the alternate budget, a statement that the amount of the proposed increase will be based on a percentage of the school district's revenue control limit in future years, if applicable, as provided in subsection Q of this section, and the following statement:

Any budget increase authorized by this election shall be entirely funded by a levy of taxes on the taxable property within this school district for the year for which adopted and for _____ subsequent years, shall not be realized from monies furnished by the state and shall not be subject to the limitation on taxes specified in article IX, § 18, Constitution of Arizona. Based on an estimate of assessed valuation used for secondary property tax purposes, the portion of the proposed increase in the school district's budget over that allowed by law which will be funded by a levy of taxes upon the taxable property within this school district would result in an estimated increase in the school district's tax rate of __________ dollar per one hundred dollars of assessed valuation used for secondary property tax purposes and is in addition to the school district's tax rate that will be levied to fund the school district's revenue control limit allowed by law.

J. If the election is to exceed the revenue control limit as provided in § 15-482 and if the proposed increase will be fully funded by revenues other than a levy of taxes on the taxable property within the school district, the ballot shall contain the words "budget increase, yes" and "budget increase, no", and the voter shall signify the voter's desired choice. The ballot shall also contain the amount of the proposed increase of the proposed budget over the alternate budget, a statement that the amount of the proposed increase will be based on a percentage of the school district's revenue control limit in future years, if applicable, as provided in subsection Q of this section and the following statement:

Any budget increase authorized by this election shall be entirely funded by this school district with revenues from other than a levy of taxes on the taxable property within the school district for the year for which adopted and for ____ subsequent years and shall not be realized from monies furnished by the state.

K. The maximum budget increase that may be requested and authorized as provided in subsection I or j of this section, or a combination of both of these subsections, is five per cent of the revenue control limit as provided in § 15-947, subsection A for the budget year. For a unified school district, a common school district not within a high school district or a common school district within a high school district that offers instruction in high school subjects as provided in § 15-447, five per cent of the revenue control limit means five per cent of the revenue control limit attributable to the weighted student count in preschool programs for children with disabilities, kindergarten programs and grades one through eight as provided in § 15-971, subsection B.

L. If the election is to exceed the capital outlay revenue limit and if the proposed increase will be fully funded by a levy of taxes upon the taxable property within the school district, the ballot shall contain the words "budget increase, yes" and "budget increase, no", and the voter shall signify the voter's desired choice. An election held pursuant to this subsection shall be held on the first Tuesday after the first Monday of November. The ballot shall also contain the amount of the proposed increase of the proposed budget over the alternate budget and the following statement:

Any budget increase authorized by this election shall be entirely funded by a levy of taxes upon the taxable property within this school district for the year in which adopted and for ____ subsequent years, shall not be realized from monies furnished by the state and shall not be subject to the limitation on taxes specified in article IX, § 18, Constitution of Arizona. Based on an estimate of assessed valuation used for secondary property tax purposes, the proposed increase in the school district's budget over that allowed by law would result in an estimated increase in the school district's tax rate of ____________ dollar per one hundred dollars of assessed valuation used for secondary property tax purposes and is in addition to the school district's tax rate which will be levied to fund the school district's capital outlay revenue limit allowed by law.

M. If the election is to exceed the capital outlay revenue limit and if the proposed increase will be fully funded by revenues from other than a levy of taxes upon the taxable property within the school district, the ballot shall contain the words "budget increase, yes" and "budget increase, no", and the voter shall signify the voter's desired choice. An election held pursuant to this subsection shall be held on the first Tuesday after the first Monday of November. The ballot shall also contain the amount of the proposed increase of the proposed budget over the alternate budget and the following statement:

Any budget increase authorized by this election shall be entirely funded by this school district with revenues from other than a levy of taxes on the taxable property within the school district for the year in which adopted and for ______ subsequent years and shall not be realized from monies furnished by the state.

N. If the election is to exceed a combination of the revenue control limit as provided in subsection E or f of this section, the revenue control limit as provided in subsection I or j of this section or the capital outlay revenue limit as provided in subsection L or m of this section, the ballot shall be prepared so that the voters may vote on each proposed increase separately and shall contain statements required in the same manner as if each proposed increase were submitted separately.

O. If the election provides for a levy of taxes on the taxable property within the school district, at least thirty days prior to the election, the department of revenue shall provide the school district governing board and the county school superintendent with an estimate of the school district's assessed valuation used for secondary property tax purposes for the ensuing fiscal year. The governing board and the county school superintendent shall use this estimate to translate the amount of the proposed dollar increase in the budget of the school district over that allowed by law into a tax rate figure.

P. If the voters in a school district vote to adopt a budget in excess of the revenue control limit as provided in subsection E or f of this section, any additional increase shall be included in the aggregate budget limit for each of the years authorized. Any additional increase shall be excluded from the determination of equalization assistance. The school district governing board may, however, levy on the assessed valuation used for secondary property tax purposes of the property in the school district the additional increase if adopted under subsection E of this section for the period of one year, two years or five through seven years as authorized. If an additional increase is approved as provided in subsection F of this section, the school district governing board may only use revenues derived from the school district's prior year's maintenance and operation fund ending cash balance to fund the additional increase. If a budget increase was previously authorized and will be in effect for the budget year or budget year and subsequent years, as provided in subsection E or f of this section, the governing board may request a new budget increase as provided in the same subsection Under which the prior budget increase was adopted which shall not exceed the maximum amount permitted under subsection G of this section. If the voters in the school district authorize the new budget increase amount, the existing budget increase no longer is in effect. If the voters in the school district do not authorize the budget increase amount, the existing budget increase remains in effect for the time period for which it was authorized. The maximum additional increase authorized as provided in subsection E or f of this section and the additional increase which is included in the aggregate budget limit is based on a percentage of a school district's revenue control limit in future years, if the budget increase is authorized for more than one year. If the additional increase:

1. Is for two years, the proposed increase in the second year is equal to the initial proposed percentage increase.

2. Is for five years or more, the proposed increase is equal to the initial proposed percentage increase in the following years of the proposed increase, except that in the next to last year it is two-thirds of the initial proposed percentage increase and it is one-third of the initial proposed percentage increase in the last year of the proposed increase.

Q. If the voters in a school district vote to adopt a budget in excess of the revenue control limit as provided in subsection I or j of this section, any additional increase shall be included in the aggregate budget limit for each of the years authorized. Any additional increase shall be excluded from the determination of equalization assistance. The school district governing board, however, may levy on the assessed valuation used for secondary property tax purposes of the property in the school district the additional increase if adopted under subsection I of this section for the period of one year, two years or five through seven years as authorized. If an additional increase is approved as provided in subsection J of this section, the increase may only be budgeted and expended if sufficient monies are available in the maintenance and operation fund of the school district. If a budget increase was previously authorized and will be in effect for the budget year or budget year and subsequent years, as provided in subsection I or j of this section, the governing board may request a new budget increase as provided in the same subsection Under which the prior budget increase was adopted that does not exceed the maximum amount permitted under subsection K of this section. If the voters in the school district authorize the new budget increase amount, the existing budget increase no longer is in effect. If the voters in the school district do not authorize the budget increase amount, the existing budget increase remains in effect for the time period for which it was authorized. The maximum additional increase authorized as provided in subsection I or j of this section and the additional increase that is included in the aggregate budget limit is based on a percentage of a school district's revenue control limit in future years, if the budget increase is authorized for more than one year. If the additional increase:

1. Is for two years, the proposed increase in the second year is equal to the initial proposed percentage increase.

2. Is for five years or more, the proposed increase is equal to the initial proposed percentage increase in the following years of the proposed increase, except that in the next to last year it is two-thirds of the initial proposed percentage increase and it is one-third of the initial proposed percentage increase in the last year of the proposed increase.

R. If the voters in a school district vote to adopt a budget in excess of the capital outlay revenue limit as provided in subsection L of this section, any additional increase shall be included in the aggregate budget limit for each of the years authorized. The additional increase shall be excluded from the determination of equalization assistance. The school district governing board may, however, levy on the assessed valuation used for secondary property tax purposes of the property in the school district the additional increase for the period authorized but not to exceed ten years. For overrides approved by a vote of the qualified electors of the school district at an election held from and after October 31, 1998, the period of the additional increase prescribed in this subsection shall not exceed seven years for any capital override election.

S. If the voters in a school district vote to adopt a budget in excess of the capital outlay revenue limit as provided in subsection M of this section, any additional increase shall be included in the aggregate budget limit for each of the years authorized. The additional increase shall be excluded from the determination of equalization assistance. The school district governing board may only use revenues derived from the school district's prior year's maintenance and operation fund ending cash balance and capital outlay fund ending cash balance to fund the additional increase for the period authorized but not to exceed ten years. For overrides approved by a vote of the qualified electors of the school district at an election held from and after October 31, 1998, the period of the additional increase prescribed in this subsection shall not exceed seven years for any capital override election.

T. In addition to subsections p and s of this section, from the maintenance and operation fund and capital outlay fund ending cash balances, the school district governing board shall first use any available revenues to reduce its primary tax rate to zero and shall use any remaining revenues to fund the additional increase authorized as provided in subsections f and m of this section.

U. If the voters in a school district disapprove the proposed budget, the alternate budget which, except for any budget increase authorized by a prior election, does not include an increase in the budget in excess of the amount provided in § 15–905 shall be adopted by the governing board as provided in § 15–905.

V. The governing board may request that any override election be cancelled if any change in chapter 9 of this title [4] changes the amount of the aggregate budget limit as provided in § 15–905. The request to cancel the override election shall be made to the county school superintendent at least ten days prior to the date of the scheduled override election.

W. For any election conducted pursuant to subsection L or m of this section:

1. The ballot shall include the following statement in addition to any other statement required by this section:

The capital improvements that are proposed to be funded through this override election are to exceed the state standards and are in addition to monies provided by the state.

__________ school district is proposing to increase its budget by $ __________ to fund capital improvements over and above those funded by the state. Under the students first capital funding system, ________ school district is entitled to state monies for building renewal, new construction and renovation of school buildings in accordance with state law.

2. The ballot shall contain the words "budget increase, yes" and " budget increase, no", and the voter shall signify the voter's desired choice.

3. At least eighty-five days before the election, the school district shall submit proposed ballot language to the director of the Arizona legislative council. The director of the Arizona legislative council shall review the proposed ballot language to determine whether the proposed ballot language complies with this section. If the director of the Arizona legislative council determines that the proposed ballot language does not comply with this section, the director, within ten calendar days of the receipt of the proposed ballot language, shall notify the school district of the director's objections and the school district shall resubmit revised ballot language to the director for approval.

X. If the voters approve the budget increase pursuant to subsection L or m of this section, the school district shall not use the override proceeds for any purposes other than the proposed capital improvements listed in the publicity pamphlet, except that up to ten per cent of the override proceeds may be used for general capital expenses, including cost overruns of proposed capital improvements.

Y. Each school district that currently increases its budget pursuant to subsection L or m of this section is required to hold a public meeting each year between September 1 and October 31 at which an update of the progress of capital improvements financed through the override is discussed and at which the public is permitted an opportunity to comment. At a minimum, the update shall include a comparison of the current status and the original projections on the construction of capital improvements, the costs of capital improvements and the costs of capital improvements in progress or completed since the prior meeting and the future capital plans of the school district. The school district shall include in the public meeting a discussion of the school district's use of state capital aid and voter- approved bonding in funding capital improvements, if any.

Z. If a budget in excess of the capital outlay revenue limit was previously adopted by the voters in a school district and will be in effect for the budget year or budget year and subsequent years, as provided in subsection L or m of this section, the governing board may request an additional budget in excess of the capital outlay revenue limit. If the voters in a school district authorize the additional budget in excess of the capital outlay revenue limit, the existing capital outlay revenue limit budget increase remains in effect.

Added by Laws 1981, Ch. 1, § 2, eff. Jan. 23, 1981. Amended by Laws 1981, Ch. 222, § 1; Laws 1981, Ch. 279, § 1, eff. April 27, 1981; Laws 1982, Ch. 198, § 1; Laws 1984, Ch. 22, § 1, eff. March 30, 1984; Laws 1984, Ch. 324, § 1; Laws 1985, Ch. 166, § 5, eff. April 18, 1985; Laws 1986, Ch. 82, § 1; Laws 1988, Ch. 177, § 2; Laws 1988, Ch. 187, § 4, eff. June 8, 1988; Laws 1989, Ch. 273, § 5, eff. June 26, 1989; Laws 1990, Ch. 278, § 3, eff. June 2, 1991; Laws 1992, Ch. 288, § 2, eff. Sept. 30, 1992, retroactively effective to July 1, 1992; Laws 1992, Ch. 305, § 8; Laws 1993, Ch. 98, § 5, eff. Jan. 1, 1994; Laws 1993, Ch. 219, § 1; Laws 1995, Ch. 191, § 3, eff. April 19, 1995; Laws 1996, Ch. 271, § 13, eff. April 23, 1996; Laws 1996, Ch. 284, § 21; Laws 1997, Ch. 4, § 1, eff. July 21, 1997, retroactively effective to July 1, 1997; Laws 1998, 5th S.S., Ch. 1, § 12, eff. July 9, 1998; Laws 1999, Ch. 299, § 8; Laws 1999, Ch. 344, § 2; Laws 2000, Ch. 236, § 3, eff. April 12, 2000; Laws 2001, Ch. 310, § 1; Laws 2002, Ch. 326, § 1; Laws 2004, Ch. 338, § 1.

[1] Section 39-121 et seq.

[2] Section 15-401 et seq.

[3] Section 16-601 et seq.

[4] Section 15-901 et seq.

Historical and Statutory Notes

Source:

Laws 1974, 1st S.S., Ch. 3, § 23.
A.R.S. former § 15-1202.01.
Laws 1976, Ch. 162, § 17.
Laws 1977, Ch. 164, § 12.
Laws 1980, 2nd S.S., Ch. 9, § 60.

The 1984 amendment of this section by Ch. 324 explicitly amended the 1984 amendment of this section by Ch. 22.

Laws 1990, Ch. 278, § 9, provides:

"**Sec. 9. Effective Date**

"This act is effective from and after June 1, 1991."

The purported amendment of this section by Laws 1992, Ch. 50, § 1, was repealed by Laws 1992, Ch. 288, § 3, eff. Sept. 30, 1992, retroactively effective July 1, 1992, prior to taking effect.

Laws 1992, Ch. 288, §§ 1 and 29, provide:

"**Section 1. Legislative intent**

"The legislature recognizes that extreme variations in school district cash balances create an inequity in revenues available to school districts. The legislature desires to better equalize revenues by redistributing a portion of the cash balances through the state's equalization system. The legislature further recognizes that federal impact aid (P.L. 81-874) monies may contribute in part to the cash balances of some school districts, and in order to avoid considering impact aid in the cash balance reversion in possible violation of 20 United States Code § 240 (d)(2), the reversion is based on the proportionate share of the cash balance which is attributed to non-impact aid revenues, so that no impact aid revenues are included in the reversion."

"**Sec. 29. Retroactivity**

"This act is effective retroactively to July 1, 1992."

Laws 1993, Ch. 202, § 29, eff. April 21, 1993, provides:

"**Sec. 29. Maintenance and operations overrides for fiscal year 1992-1993**

"Notwithstanding § 15-481, subsection P, Arizona Revised Statutes, for fiscal year 1992-1993, the additional increase for an override adopted pursuant to § 15-481, subsection F, Arizona Revised Statutes, may be funded in whole or in part from the school district's prior year's capital outlay fund ending cash balance, after any reversion as required pursuant to § 15-991.02, Arizona Revised Statutes. If the monies in the ending cash balance are in the reserve of the capital outlay fund, the amount in the reserve shall be reduced by the amount used to fund the override."

Laws 1994, Ch. 254, § 9, effective April 24, 1994, provides:

"**Sec. 9. Provisions for unified school districts that exceeded the general budget limit in fiscal year 1992-1993 or 1993-1994**

"**A.** Notwithstanding §§ 15-905 and 15-949, Arizona Revised Statutes, a unified school district is not required to reduce its general budget limit due to excess expenditures for pupils in kindergarten programs and grades one through eight for fiscal year 1992-1993 or 1993-1994 if each of the following conditions apply for the fiscal year in which the excess expenditures were made:

"1. The district adopted a budget which included an adjustment for low student count as provided in § 15-949, Arizona Revised Statutes.

"2. The district's student count in grades nine through twelve was one hundred or less and the district's student count in kindergarten programs and grades one through eight was more than one hundred twenty-five.

"**B.** For fiscal year 1994-1995, a unified school district that meets the conditions of subsection A of this section for fiscal year 1993-1994 may adopt a budget including a budget increase as provided in § 15-481, subsection E or H, Arizona Revised Statutes, as if an election had taken place and the voters had approved the override for that year."

Laws 1997, Ch. 4, § 16, as amended by Laws 1997, 1st S.S., Ch. 9, § 1, provides:

"**Sec. 16. Conditional repeal**

"**A.** If there is a final adjudication [see note, post] in the proceedings resulting from the Arizona supreme court's decision in Roosevelt Elementary School District No. 66 v. Bishop, 179 Ariz. 233, 877 P.2d 806 (1994) that this act, in conjunction with Laws 1996, fifth special session, chapter 8 and Laws 1996, seventh special session, chapter 1, does not ensure a constitutional system of education:

"1. This act and Laws 1996, fifth special session, chapter 8, § 14 are void and are repealed as of the date of the final adjudication.

"2. Laws 1996, fifth special session, chapter 8, §§ 1, 13, 15 and 17 and laws 1996, seventh special session, chapter 1, §§ 3, 4 and 5 are void and are repealed six months after the date of the final adjudication.

"**B.** Subsection A of this section does not invalidate any contractual obligations of the state board for school capital facilities that may have been incurred before the repeal prescribed in subsection A, paragraph 2 of this section, including school districts that have been given preliminary approvals by the state board for school capital facilities before the date of final adjudication, not to exceed the balance of the school capital equity fund established by § 15-1053, Arizona Revised Statutes, on the date of the final adjudication. After the date of final adjudication, the state board shall not enter into any contractual obligations not related to a preliminary approval given before the date of the final adjudication or give any new preliminary approvals. Between the date of final adjudication and the repeal prescribed in subsection A, paragraph 2 of this section, nothing in this section shall be construed to prohibit the board from paying its costs of operation as prescribed by law.

"**C.** On the discontinuation of the state board for school capital facilities, the department of education shall assume responsibility for distributing monies and receiving reports and repayment obligations from school districts pursuant to contracts and preliminary approvals entered into between the state board and school districts before the final adjudication referred to in subsection A of this section. Any monies remitted to the department of education pursuant to this subsection shall be transmitted to the state general fund. The department of education shall submit an annual report to the president of the senate, the speaker of the house of representatives and the governor that summarizes the reports and amount of repayments from school districts."

The conditions for the repeals by this section have been met. The Supreme Court in Order No. CV-97-0369-SA, dated October 24, 1997, declared that the legislature's 1997 school funding plan was unconstitutional; the order of July 28, 1994, was still in effect; and, that the order of the trial court dated August 20, 1997 was approved. A written opinion followed, dated December 23, 1997 (Hull v. Albrecht, 190 Ariz. 520, 950 P.2d 1141 (1997)). An informal Attorney General Opinion considers December 23, 1997, the date the written Supreme Court decision was released, as the final date of adjudication. A subsequent amendment to cure the constitutional infirmity by Laws 1998, 3rd S.S., Ch. 1 was also declared unconstitutional by the Supreme Court (Hull v. Albrecht 192 Ariz. 34, 960 P.2d 634 (1998)).

The purported amendment of this section by Laws 1998, Ch. 164 failed to become effective because Chapter 164 was repealed in its entirety by Laws 1998, 5th S.S., Ch. 1, § 2, effective July 1, 1998.

The purported amendment of this section by Laws 1998, 3rd S.S., Ch. 1, failed to became effective because Ch. 1 was repealed in its entirety by Laws 1998, 5th S.S., Ch. 1, § 2, effective July 1, 1998.

Laws 2004, Ch. 278, §§ 17 to 20, provide:

"**Sec. 17. Appropriation; Hayden-Winkelman unified school district; repayment schedule and terms**

"**A.** Notwithstanding § 15-2084, Arizona Revised Statutes, the sum of $3,215,000 is appropriated from the school improvement revenue bond debt service fund for fiscal year 2004-2005 to the department of education for distribution to Hayden-Winkelman unified school district No. 41. The district shall use the monies solely for the purpose of redeeming its outstanding series 1994 callable general obligation bonds.

"**B.** The district shall levy a tax on the secondary assessment roll to repay the amount appropriated by this section in five annual installments of principal and simple interest at the rate of four per cent per year on July 1, 2011, July 1, 2012, July 1, 2013, July 1, 2014 and July 1, 2015, but not more than a total sum of $830,000 each year. The payments shall be credited to the school improvement revenue bond debt service fund established by § 15-2084, Arizona Revised Statutes.

"**C.** Notwithstanding any other law, through July 1, 2015 the district shall not propose or conduct any election to approve:

"1. Any budget override.

"2. Any authorization to issue bonds or incur any other form of district indebtedness.

"**Sec. 18. Joint legislative study committee; Hayden-Winkelman property taxes**

"**A.** The joint legislative study committee on Hayden-Winkelman property taxes is established consisting of the following members:

"1. Three members of the senate who are appointed by the president of the senate, including the chairperson of the senate appropriations committee and the senator whose legislative district includes the Hayden-Winkelman unified school district No. 41.

"2. Three members of the house of representatives who are appointed by the speaker of the house of representatives, including the chairperson of the house of representatives appropriations committee and one member whose legislative district includes the Hayden-Winkelman unified school district No. 41.

"3. One member who represents a statewide tax research organization and who is appointed by the president of the senate.

"4. One member who owns commercial real property in the Hayden-Winkelman unified school district No. 41 and who is appointed by the speaker of the house of representatives.

"5. One member who is appointed by the president of the senate and who represents a taxpayer that owns taxable property in the Hayden–Winkelman unified school district No. 41 and in the town of Hayden that is valued by the department of revenue pursuant to title 42, chapter 14, Arizona Revised Statutes.

"6. One member who is appointed by the speaker of the house of representatives and who resides in and owns residential real property in the Hayden–Winkelman unified school district No. 41.

"7. One member of the governing body of the Hayden–Winkelman unified school district No. 41 who is appointed by the president of the senate.

"8. One member of the governing body of the town of Hayden who is appointed by the speaker of the house of representatives.

"9. One member who has expertise in public finance and investment banking and who is appointed by the governor.

"**B.** Members of the committee serve without compensation or reimbursement of expenses. The committee shall select a chairperson from its membership. The legislature shall provide meeting space and the joint legislative budget committee shall provide staff support for the study committee.

"**C.** The study committee shall analyze the indebtedness, expenditures, property taxes and other revenues of the Hayden–Winkelman unified school district No. 41 and the town of Hayden and consider all possible solutions to provide long-term relief and stability for the residents, property owners and taxpayers of the community. The study committee shall submit a report of its findings and recommendations to the president of the senate, the speaker of the house of representatives and the governor on or before December 31, 2004 and shall provide a copy of this report to the secretary of state and the director of the Arizona state library, archives and public records.

"**Sec. 19. Repeal**

"Section 18 of this act, relating to the joint legislative study committee on Hayden–Winkelman property taxes, is repealed from and after September 30, 2005.

"**Sec. 20. Publication**

"The publishers of the annotated Arizona Revised Statutes shall include the text of § 17 of this act with the annotations under section 15-481, Arizona Revised Statutes, through 2015."

Laws 2004, Ch. 278, § 21, provides:

"**Sec. 21. Retroactivity**

"**A.** Except as provided in subsection B of this section, this act applies retroactively to from and after June 30, 2004.

"**B.** Laws 2002, chapter 330, § 49, as amended by this act, applies retroactively to from and after June 29, 2004."

Reviser's Notes:

1981 Note. Prior to the 1982 amendment, this section contained the amendments made by Laws 1981, Ch. 222, § 1 and Ch. 279, § 1 which were blended together pursuant to authority of § 41-1304.03. Additionally, pursuant to authority of § 41-1304.02, in subsections M [subsequently deleted] and O [now N] the words "used for secondary property tax purposes" following the word "valuation" were transposed to follow the third "district".

1988 Note. Prior to the 1989 amendment, this section contained the amendments made by Laws 1988, Ch. 177, § 2 and Ch. 187, § 4 which were blended together pursuant to authority of § 41-1304.03.

1992 Note. Prior to the 1993 amendments, this section contained the amendments made by Laws 1992, Ch. 288, sec. 2 and Ch. 305, sec. 8 that were blended together pursuant to authority of § 41-1304.03.

1993 Note. Prior to the 1995 amendment, this section contained the amendments made by Laws 1993, Ch. 98, sec. 5 and Ch. 219, sec. 1 that were blended together pursuant to authority of § 41-1304.03.

1995 Note. In the chapter version in subsection A, third sentence the words "in section" were shown as new, or upstyle, language, but they are existing law. Pursuant to the authority of § 41-1304.02, to correct a manifest clerical error in the chapter version these words are shown as existing, or downstyle, language.

1996 Note. Prior to the 1997 amendment, this section contained the amendments made by Laws 1996, Ch. 271, sec. 13 and Ch. 284, sec. 21 that were blended together pursuant to authority of § 41-1304.03.

1997 Note. This section is subject to a conditional repeal pursuant to Laws 1997, Ch. 4, sec. 16.

1999 Note. Prior to the 2000 amendment, this section contained the amendments made by Laws 1999, Ch. 299, sec. 8 and Ch. 344, sec. 2 that were blended together pursuant to authority of § 41-1304.03. Pursuant to authority of § 41-1304.02, in subsection W, paragraph 2 "no" was substituted for "No" and in paragraph 3, first sentence "a" was substituted for "A" to correct electronic database errors.

§ 15-482. Special budget override provisions; special programs to improve academic achievement of pupils in kindergarten programs and grades one through three

A. An additional budget increase may be requested and authorized as provided in § 15-481, subsections I and J of up to five per cent of the revenue control limit as provided in subsection B of this section if the following conditions are met:

1. The school district uses a task force of educators and other persons to develop a special program designed to improve the academic achievement of low achieving pupils in kindergarten programs and grades one through three, with the goal that all pupils capable of doing so will learn the basic skills necessary for fourth grade work by the end of the third grade.

2. The amount of the proposed budget increase as provided in subsection B of this section is for use for the special program and is to supplement, not supplant, programs for pupils in kindergarten programs and grades one through three which were in existence prior to the budget increase, unless in the fiscal year prior to the fiscal year of the proposed budget increase special programs for pupils in kindergarten programs and grades one through three were in existence and were funded with proceeds from the sale or lease of school property, as provided in § 15-1102.

B. The maximum amount of the budget increase requested and authorized shall not exceed the budgeted expenditures of the proposed special program for each fiscal year, not to exceed a total of five per cent of the revenue control limit for each fiscal year. For a unified school district, a common school district not within a high school district or a common school district within a high school district that offers instruction in high school subjects as provided in § 15-447, five per cent of the revenue control limit means five per cent of the revenue control limit attributable to the weighted student count in preschool programs for children with disabilities, kindergarten programs and grades one through eight as provided in § 15-971, subsection B.

C. For each fiscal year in which a budget increase of up to five per cent of the revenue control limit is authorized as provided in subsection A of this section, the governing board shall:

1. Utilize a separate annual special program budget on a form prescribed by the auditor general in conjunction with the department of education. The budget format shall be designed to allow a school district to plan and provide in detail for expenditures to be incurred as a result of the special program.

2. Prepare as a part of the school district annual financial report a detailed report of expenditures incurred as a result of the special program, in a format prescribed by the auditor general in conjunction with the department of education, as provided in § 15-904.

D. The special program may be designed for any or all of the pupils enrolled in kindergarten programs and grades one through three and may involve efforts to remove barriers to academic achievement as well as efforts to improve instruction or increase the amount of instruction. The special program, at a minimum, shall focus on pupils who, because of innate factors, are not succeeding in the school environment as identified by parents, guardians or school personnel. These pupils may include, but are not limited to, those who do not qualify for special education services, who have measured intelligence quotients of between seventy and eighty-five or who exhibit characteristics of attention deficit disorder or learning patterns attributable to prenatal substance exposure.

E. During any fiscal year in which proceeds from the sale or lease of school property are used for the maintenance and operation section of the budget as provided in § 15–1102, a budget increase is in effect as provided in § 15–481, subsection E or F, or a budget increase is in effect as provided in this section, or any combination of these conditions occurs, the total amount of the proceeds and increases which may be expended is equal to fifteen per cent of the revenue control limit for that year as provided in § 15–947, subsection A, provided that the following maximum amount is attributable to any one of the conditions:

1. Fifteen per cent of the revenue control limit if using the proceeds from the sale or lease of school property for the maintenance and operation section of the budget as provided in § 15–1102.

2. Ten per cent of the revenue control limit if using a budget increase as provided in § 15–481, subsection E or F, or both.

3. Five per cent of the revenue control limit if using a budget increase as provided in this section.

Added by Laws 1984, Ch. 364, § 1. Amended by Laws 1985, Ch. 166, § 6, eff. April 18, 1985; Laws 1986, Ch. 349, § 1, eff. May 9, 1986; Laws 1989, Ch. 32, § 1; Laws 1990, Ch. 348, § 4, eff. June 26, 1990; Laws 1991, Ch. 195, § 1; Laws 1992, Ch. 62, § 1; Laws 1992, Ch. 305, § 9; Laws 2000, Ch. 236, § 4, eff. April 12, 2000; Laws 2004, Ch. 315, § 1.

Historical and Statutory Notes

Reviser's Notes:

1984 Note. Pursuant to authority of § 41–1304.02, in subsection A, paragraph 2 "as provided in subsection B of this section" following "program" was transposed to follow "increase".

1992 Note. Prior to the 2000 amendment, this section contained the amendments made by Laws 1992, Ch. 62, sec. 1 and Ch. 305, sec. 9 that were blended together pursuant to authority of § 41–1304.03.

ARTICLE 5. BOND ELECTIONS

§ 15–491. Elections on school property; exceptions

A. The governing board of a school district may, and upon petition of fifteen per cent of the school electors as shown by the poll list at the last preceding annual school election shall, call an election for the following purposes:

1. To locate or change the location of school buildings.

2. To purchase or sell school sites or buildings or sell school sites pursuant to § 15–342 or to build school buildings, but the authorization by vote of the school district shall not necessarily specify the site to be purchased.

3. To decide whether the bonds of the school district shall be issued and sold for the purpose of raising money for purchasing or leasing school lots, for

building or renovating school buildings, for improving school grounds, for purchasing pupil transportation vehicles or for liquidating any indebtedness already incurred for such purposes. Except as provided in § 15-1021, subsection H, the proceeds of class B bonds or impact aid revenue bonds shall not be used for soft capital purposes except for pupil transportation vehicles. A school district shall not issue class B bonds until the school district has obligated in contract the entire proceeds of any class A bonds issued by the school district. The total amount of class A and class B bonds issued by a school district shall not exceed the debt limitations prescribed in article IX, §§ 8 and 8.1, Constitution of Arizona.

4. To lease for five or more years, as lessor or as lessee, school buildings or grounds. Approval by a majority of the school district electors voting authorizes the governing board to negotiate for and enter into a lease. The ballot shall list the school buildings or grounds for which a lease is sought. If the governing board does not enter into a lease of five or more years of the school buildings or grounds listed on the ballot within five years of the date of the election and the board continues to seek such a lease, the governing board shall call a special election to reauthorize the board to negotiate for and to enter into a lease of five or more years.

B. No petition shall be required for the holding of the first election to be held in a joint common school district for any of the purposes specified in subsection A of this section. The notice of election required by § 15-492 shall be published in each of the counties which comprise the joint common school district. The certification of election results required by § 15-493 shall be made to the board of supervisors of the jurisdictional county.

C. When the election is called to determine whether or not bonds of the school district shall be issued and sold for the purposes enumerated in the call for the election, the question shall be submitted to the vote of the qualified electors of the school district as defined in § 15-401 and subject to the provisions of § 15-402.

D. The governing board shall order the election to be held in the manner prescribed in title 35, chapter 3, article 3. [1] If a petition for an election has been filed with the governing board as provided in subsection A of this section, the board shall act upon the petition within sixty days by ordering the election to be held as provided in this subsection. If a school district bond election is scheduled for the same date a school district will hold an override election, the governing body shall deliver a copy of the notice of election and ballot to the county school superintendent who shall include the notice of election and ballot with the information report and ballot prepared for the override election. Mailing of the information required for both the override and bond elections shall constitute compliance with the notice provisions of this section.

E. The elections to be held pursuant to this section shall only be held on dates prescribed by § 16-204, except that elections held pursuant to this section to decide whether class B bonds shall be issued shall only be held on the first Tuesday after the first Monday of November.

F. Subsection A, paragraph 2 of this section does not apply to the sale of school property if the market value of the school property is less than fifty thousand dollars.

G. Bond counsel fees, financial advisory fees, printing costs and paying agent and registrar fees for bonds issued pursuant to an election under this section shall be paid from either the amount authorized by the qualified electors of the school district or current operating funds. Bond election expenses shall be paid from current operating funds only.

H. For any election conducted to decide whether class B bonds will be issued pursuant to this section:

1. except as provided in paragraph 2 of this subsection, the ballot shall include the following statement:

The capital improvements that are proposed to be funded through this bond issuance are to exceed the state standards and are in addition to monies provided by the state.

__________ school district is proposing to issue class B general obligation bonds totaling $__________ to fund capital improvements over and above those funded by the state. Under the students first capital funding system, __________ school district is entitled to state monies for building renewal, new construction and renovation of school buildings in accordance with state law.

2. For a school district that is a joint technological education district, the ballot shall include the following statement:

__________, a joint technological education district, is proposing to issue class b general obligation bonds totaling $__________ to fund capital improvements at the main campus of the joint technological education district.

3. The ballot shall contain the words "bond approval, yes" and "bond approval, no", and the voter shall signify the voter's desired choice.

4. At least eighty-five days before the election, the school district shall submit proposed ballot language to the director of the Arizona legislative council. The director of the Arizona legislative council shall review the proposed ballot language to determine whether the proposed ballot language complies with this section. If the director of the Arizona legislative council determines that the proposed ballot language does not comply with this section, the director, within ten calendar days of the receipt of the proposed ballot language, shall notify the school district of the director's objections and the school district shall resubmit revised ballot language to the director for approval.

5. No later than ten days before a class B bond election conducted pursuant to this section, the school district shall mail to each qualified elector in the school district a publicity pamphlet. The publicity pamphlet shall contain, at a minimum, the following information:

(a) An executive summary of the school district's most recent capital plan submitted to the school facilities board.

(b) A complete list of each proposed capital improvement that will be funded with the proceeds of the bonds and a description of the proposed cost of each improvement, including a separate aggregation of capital improvements for administrative purposes as defined by the school facilities board.

(c) The tax rate associated with each of the proposed capital improvements and the estimated cost of each capital improvement for the owner of a single family home that is valued at one hundred thousand dollars.

I. For any election conducted to decide whether impact aid revenue bonds shall be issued pursuant to this section:

1. The ballot shall include the following statement:

The capital improvements that are proposed to be funded through this bond issuance are to exceed the state standards and are in addition to monies provided by the state.

________ school district is proposing to issue impact aid revenue bonds totaling $________ to fund capital improvements over and above those funded by the state. Under the students first capital funding system, ________ school district is entitled to state monies for building renewal, new construction and renovation of school buildings in accordance with state law.

2. The ballot shall contain the words "bond approval, yes" and "bond approval, no", and the voter shall signify the voter's desired choice.

3. At least eighty-five days before the election, the school district shall submit proposed ballot language to the director of the legislative council. The director of the legislative council shall review the proposed ballot language to determine whether the proposed ballot language complies with this section. If the director of the legislative council determines that the proposed ballot language does not comply with this section, the director, within ten calendar days of the receipt of the proposed ballot language, shall notify the school district of the director's objections and the school district shall resubmit revised ballot language to the director for approval.

4. No later than ten days before an impact aid revenue bond election conducted pursuant to this section, the school district shall mail to each qualified elector in the school district a publicity pamphlet. The publicity pamphlet shall contain, at a minimum, the following information:

(a) An executive summary of the school district's most recent capital plan submitted to the school facilities board.

(b) A complete list of each proposed capital improvement that will be funded with the proceeds of the bonds and a description of the proposed cost of each improvement, including a separate aggregation of capital improvements for administrative purposes as defined by the school facilities board.

(c) A statement that impact aid revenue bonds will be fully funded by aid that the school district receives from the federal government and do not require a levy of taxes in the district.

(d) A statement that if the bonds are approved the first priority for the impact aid will be to pay the debt service for the bonds and that other uses of the monies are prohibited until the debt service obligation is met.

(e) A statement that if the impact aid revenue bonds are approved, the school district shall not issue or sell class B bonds while the district has existing indebtedness from impact aid revenue bonds, except for bonds issued to refund any bonds issued by the board.

J. If the voters approve the issuance of school district class B bonds or impact aid revenue bonds, the school district shall not use the bond proceeds for any purposes other than the proposed capital improvements listed in the publicity pamphlet, except that up to ten per cent of the bond proceeds may be used for general capital expenses, including cost overruns of proposed capital improvements.

K. Each school district that issues bonds under this section is required to hold a public meeting each year between September 1 and October 31, until the bond proceeds are spent, at which an update of the progress of capital improvements financed through bonding is discussed and at which the public is permitted an opportunity to comment. At a minimum, the update shall include a comparison of the current status and the original projections on the construction of capital improvements, the costs of capital improvements and the costs of capital improvements in progress or completed since the prior meeting and the future capital bonding plans of the school district. The school district shall include in the public meeting a discussion of the school district's use of state capital aid and voter-approved capital overrides in funding capital improvements, if any.

Added by Laws 1981, Ch. 1, § 2, eff. Jan. 23, 1981. Amended by Laws 1982, Ch. 171, § 1; Laws 1983, Ch. 9, § 3, eff. Feb. 25, 1983; Laws 1984, Ch. 349, § 4; Laws 1986, Ch. 296, § 2; Laws 1989, Ch. 273, § 6, eff. June 26, 1989, retroactively effective to Jan. 23, 1981; Laws 1990, Ch. 278, § 4, eff. June 2, 1991; Laws 1990, Ch. 348, § 5, eff. June 26, 1990; Laws 1991, Ch. 246, § 1; Laws 1991, Ch. 298, § 10; Laws 1992, Ch. 230, § 2; Laws 1994, Ch. 361, § 3; Laws 1996, Ch. 271, § 14, eff. April 23, 1996; Laws 1996, Ch. 286, § 3; Laws 1997, Ch. 271, § 3, eff. April 29, 1997; Laws 1998, Ch. 1, § 47, eff. Jan. 1, 1999; Laws 1998, 5th S.S., Ch. 1, § 13, eff. July 9, 1998; Laws 1999, Ch. 299, § 9; Laws 2001, Ch. 228, § 1; Laws 2004, Ch. 341, § 3.

[1] Section 35–451 et seq.

Historical and Statutory Notes

Source:

Laws 1912, Ch. 77, § 44.
Civ.Code 1913, § 2736.
Laws 1919, Ch. 21, § 1.
Laws 1921, Ch. 72, § 6.
Laws 1925, Ch. 24, § 1.
Rev.Code 1928, § 1014.
Code 1939, § 54–419.
Laws 1954, Ch. 107, § 2.
A.R.S. former §§ 15–421.06, 15–1302, 15–1302.06.
Laws 1957, Ch. 82, § 1.
Laws 1960, Ch. 127, § 60.
Laws 1963, Ch. 95, § 1.
Laws 1967, 3rd S.S., Ch. 19, § 21.
Laws 1970, Ch. 12, § 1.
Laws 1970, Ch. 165, § 9.
Laws 1971, Ch. 37, § 3.
Laws 1974, Ch. 134, § 31.
Laws 1978, Ch. 188, § 21.
Laws 1980, 2nd S.S., Ch. 9, § 83.

Laws 1989, Ch. 273, § 31, effective June 26, 1989, provides:

"**Sec. 31. Retroactivity**

"The provisions of § 6 of this act with respect to authorizing an election for the purposes of purchasing pupil transporation [So in original] vehicles are effective retroactively to January 23, 1981. The retroactive effect of this act does not validate the use of monies raised through the sale of bonds for purchasing pupil transporation [So in original] vehicles by a school district if purchasing pupil transportation vehicles was not one of the purposes enumerated in the call for the bond election as prescribed in § 15–492, Arizona Revised Statutes."

The amendment of this section by Laws 1990, Ch. 348, § 5, effective June 26, 1990, was repealed by Laws 1991, Ch. 246, § 2, and by Laws 1991, Ch. 298, § 11.

The 1991 amendment of this section by Ch. 246 explicitly amended the 1990 amendment of this section by Ch. 278.

Laws 1991, Ch. 246, § 5 provides:

"**Sec. 5. Applicability**

"This act does not apply to any election held before January 1, 1992."

The 1991 amendment of this section by Ch. 298 explicitly amended the 1990 amendment of this section by Ch. 278.

Laws 1991, Ch. 298, § 1, par. 5 provides:

"**Section 1. Purpose**"

"5. Section 15-491, Arizona Revised Statutes, was amended by Laws 1990, chapter 278, § 4 and Laws 1990, chapter 348, § 5. These two versions could not be blended because of the delayed effective date of the chapter 278 version. In order to blend these two versions the Laws 1990, chapter 278 version of § 15-491, Arizona Revised Statutes, is amended to incorporate the amendments made by Laws 1990, chapter 348 and the chapter 348 version is repealed."

Laws 1997, Ch. 4, § 16, as amended by Laws 1997, 1st S.S., Ch. 9, § 1, provides:

"**Sec. 16. Conditional repeal**

"**A.** If there is a final adjudication [see note, post] in the proceedings resulting from the Arizona supreme court's decision in Roosevelt Elementary School District No. 66 v. Bishop, 179 Ariz. 233, 877 P.2d 806 (1994) that this act, in conjunction with Laws 1996, fifth special session, chapter 8 and Laws 1996, seventh special session, chapter 1, does not ensure a constitutional system of education:

"1. This act and Laws 1996, fifth special session, chapter 8, § 14 are void and are repealed as of the date of the final adjudication.

"2. Laws 1996, fifth special session, chapter 8, §§ 1, 13, 15 and 17 and laws 1996, seventh special session, chapter 1, §§ 3, 4 and 5 are void and are repealed six months after the date of the final adjudication.

"**B.** Subsection A of this section does not invalidate any contractual obligations of the state board for school capital facilities that may have been incurred before the repeal prescribed in subsection A, paragraph 2 of this section, including school districts that have been given preliminary approvals by the state board for school capital facilities before the date of final adjudication, not to exceed the balance of the school capital equity fund established by § 15-1053, Arizona Revised Statutes, on the date of the final adjudication. After the date of final adjudication, the state board shall not enter into any contractual obligations not related to a preliminary approval given before the date of the final adjudication or give any new preliminary approvals. Between the date of final adjudication and the repeal prescribed in subsection A, paragraph 2 of this section, nothing in this section shall be construed to prohibit the board from paying its costs of operation as prescribed by law.

"**C.** On the discontinuation of the state board for school capital facilities, the department of education shall assume responsibility for distributing monies and receiving reports and repayment obligations from school districts pursuant to contracts and preliminary approvals entered into between the state board and school districts before the final adjudication referred to in subsection A of this section. Any monies remitted to the department of education pursuant to this subsection shall be transmitted to the state general fund. The department of education shall submit an annual report to the president of the senate, the speaker of the house of representatives and the governor that summarizes the reports and amount of repayments from school districts."

The conditions for the repeals by this section have been met. The Supreme Court in Order No. CV-97-0369-SA, dated October 24, 1997, declared that the legislature's 1997 school funding plan was unconstitutional; the order of July 28, 1994, was still in effect; and, that the order of the trial court dated August 20, 1997 was approved. A written opinion followed, dated December 23, 1997 (Hull v. Albrecht, 190 Ariz. 520, 950 P.2d 1141 (1997)). An informal Attorney General Opinion considers December 23, 1997, the date the written Supreme Court decision was released, as the final date of adjudication. A subsequent amendment to cure the constitutional infirmity by Laws 1998, 3rd S.S., Ch. 1 was also declared unconstitutional by the Supreme Court (Hull v. Albrecht 192 Ariz. 34, 960 P.2d 634 (1998)).

The purported amendment of this section by Laws 1998, Ch. 164 failed to become effective because Chapter 164 was repealed in its entirety by Laws 1998, 5th S.S., Ch. 1, § 2, effective July 1, 1998.

The purported amendment of this section by Laws 1998, 3rd S.S., Ch. 1, failed to became effective because Ch. 1 was repealed in its entirety by Laws 1998, 5th S.S., Ch. 1, § 2, effective July 1, 1998.

Laws 1999, Ch. 299, § 41, provides:

"**Sec. 41. Use of class A bonds for furniture and apparatus**

"Notwithstanding § 15-491, subsection A, paragraph 3, Arizona Revised Statutes, as amended by this act, the proceeds of class A bonds may be used for supplying school buildings with furniture and apparatus if these expenditures were approved by the qualified electors of the school district."

Laws 2004, Ch. 341, § 12, provides:

"**Sec. 12. Retroactivity**

"Sections 15-491 and 15-1021, Arizona Revised Statutes, as amended by this act, apply retroactively to from and after May 14, 2004."

Reviser's Notes:

1989 Note. Pursuant to authority of § 41-1304.02, in subsection A, paragraph 3 the spelling of "transportation" was corrected.

1991 Note. Prior to the 1992 amendment, this section contained the amendments made by Laws 1991, Ch. 246, sec. 1 and Ch. 298, sec. 10 that were blended together pursuant to authority of § 41-1304.03. In the Laws 1991, Ch. 246 version in subsection A, paragraph 4, fourth sentence the stricken words "long-term" were incorrectly shown as "long-time". Pursuant to authority of § 41-1304.02, the stricken words "long-term" are substituted for "long-time" to correct a manifest clerical error.

1996 Note. Prior to the 1997 amendments, this section contained the amendments made by Laws 1996, Ch. 271, sec. 14 and Ch. 286, sec. 3 that were blended together pursuant to authority of § 41-1304.03.

1997 Note. The independent and valid amendment of this section by Laws 1997, Ch. 4, sec. 2 and Ch. 271, sec. 3 could not be blended because of the conditional repeal in Laws 1997, Ch. 4, sec. 16.

1998 Note. Prior to the 1999 amendment, this section contained the amendments made by Laws 1998, Second Regular Session, Ch. 1, sec. 47 and Laws 1998, Fifth Special Session, Ch. 1. sec. 13 that were blended together pursuant to authority of § 41-1304.03.

§ 15-492. Bond election; pamphlet

Notice and procedures for an election upon the question of bond issues shall be conducted in the manner prescribed in title 35, chapter 3, article 3,[1] and the county school superintendent shall prepare the required informational pamphlet.

Added by Laws 1981, Ch. 1, § 2, eff. Jan. 23, 1981. Amended by Laws 1990, Ch. 278, § 5, eff. June 2, 1991; Laws 1994, Ch. 361, § 4.

[1] Section 15-451 et seq.

Historical and Statutory Notes

Source:

Laws 1912, Ch. 77, §§ 45 to 47.
Civ.Code 1913, §§ 2737 to 2739.
Rev.Code 1928, § 1015.
Code 1939, § 54-420.
A.R.S. former § 15-1303.
Laws 1977, Ch. 164, § 14.

Reviser's Notes:

1990 Note. Pursuant to authority of § 41-1304.02, in subsection A, first sentence the comma following "ballot" was transposed to follow the second "election".

1994 Note. Pursuant to authority of § 41-1304.02, "procedure ballots;" was deleted from the section heading.

§ 15-493. Canvass of votes; certification of result

The official returns shall be delivered to the county board of supervisors or the appropriate county elections officer. Within fourteen days of the election, the county board of supervisors or the county elections officer shall canvass the results of the election and shall file duplicate copies of the certificate of the result of the election with the clerk of the board of supervisors and with the governing board of the school district.

Added by Laws 1990, Ch. 278, § 7, eff. June 2, 1991.

Historical and Statutory Notes

Source:

Laws 1912, Ch. 77, §§ 48, 49.
Civ.Code 1913, §§ 2740, 2741.
Rev.Code 1928, § 1016.
Code 1939, § 54-421.
A.R.S. former § 15-1304.
A.R.S. former § 15-493.
Laws 1981, Ch. 1, § 2.
Laws 1989, Ch. 9, § 1.

CHAPTER 5

SCHOOL EMPLOYEES

ARTICLE 1. GENERAL PROVISIONS

ARTICLE 2. DUTIES OF TEACHERS

ARTICLE 3. CERTIFICATION AND EMPLOYMENT OF TEACHERS

ARTICLE 4. PRINCIPALS' INSTITUTE

Chapter 5, consisting of Article 1, §§ 15–501 to 15–509, Article 2, §§ 15–521 and 15–522, and Article 3, §§ 15–531 to 15–550, was added by Laws 1981, Ch. 1, § 2, effective January 23, 1981.

ARTICLE 1. GENERAL PROVISIONS

§ 15–501. Definitions

In this chapter, unless the context otherwise requires:

1. "Administrator" means any school district administrator except a school principal devoting not less than fifty per cent of his time to classroom teaching.

2. "Certificated teacher" means a person who holds a certificate from the state board of education to work in the schools of this state and who is employed under contract in a school district in a position which requires certification except a psychologist or an administrator devoting less than fifty per cent of his time to classroom teaching.

3. "Full-time" means employed for a full school day, or its equivalent, or for a full class load, or its equivalent, as determined by the governing board.

4. "Governing board" means the governing board of a school district or a county school superintendent in the case of accommodation schools located in such county.

5. "Major portion of a school year" means full-time employment for fifty-one per cent of the school days during which school is in session, except that a certificated teacher is not deemed to have completed the major portion of the third school year of three consecutive years of employment until the end of the third school year.

6. "Superintendent" means the superintendent of schools of a school district.

7. "Suspension without pay" means suspension without pay for a period of time not to exceed ten school days.

Added by Laws 1981, Ch. 1, § 2, eff. Jan. 23, 1981. Amended by Laws 1983, Ch. 281, § 3; Laws 1984, Ch. 52, § 1; Laws 1986, Ch. 399, § 3; Laws 1987, Ch. 202, § 1.

Historical and Statutory Notes

Source:

Laws 1912, Ch. 77, § 110.
Civ.Code 1913, § 2836.
Rev.Code 1928, § 1057.
Code 1939, § 54–1111.
Laws 1949, Ch. 52, § 1.
Code 1939, Supp.1952, § 54–1009.
A.R.S. former §§ 15–205, 15–251.
Laws 1960, Ch. 127, §§ 10, 14.
Laws 1963, Ch. 49, § 1.

Reviser's Notes:

1984 Note. In subsection A, paragraph 4, "Full-time" was substituted for "Full time" pursuant to authority of § 41–1304.02.

§ 15–502. Employment of school district personnel; payment of wages of discharged employee

A. The governing board may at any time employ and fix the salaries and benefits of employees necessary for the succeeding year. The contracts of all certificated employees shall be in writing, and all employees shall be employed subject to the provisions of § 38–481. The governing board may obtain the services of any employee, including teachers, substitute teachers and administrators, by contracting with a private entity that employs personnel required by the school district.

B. A teacher shall not be employed if the teacher has not received a certificate for teaching granted by the proper authorities. If a teacher has filed an application and completed all of the requirements for a certificate but time does not allow a teacher to receive a certificate before the commencement of employment, the conditional certificate shall serve as a certificate for the payment of wages, provided that the teacher files the conditional certificate with the county school superintendent and the certificate is issued within three months of the date of commencing employment. In order to be paid wages beyond the three month period prescribed in this subsection, the teacher shall file the certificate with the county school superintendent. Any contract issued to a teacher who has completed certificate requirements but has not received a certificate shall be specifically contingent upon receipt of such a certificate. The governing board of a school district that is subject to § 15–914.01 shall adhere to the duties described in § 15–302, subsection A, paragraph 9 for purposes of this subsection.

C. No dependent, as defined in § 43–1001, of a governing board member may be employed in the school district in which the person to whom such dependent is so related is a governing board member, except by consent of the board.

D. The governing board may employ certificated teachers under contract as part-time classroom teachers. Notwithstanding any other statute, a certificated teacher who has been employed by the school district for more than the major portion of three consecutive school years does not lose the entitlement to the procedures prescribed in §§ 15-538.01, 15-539 through 15-544 and 15-547 if the teacher is employed under contract on a part-time basis for at least forty per cent time. As used in this subsection, "forty per cent time" means employed for at least forty per cent of the school day required of full-time teachers of the same grade level or for at least forty per cent of the class load assigned to full-time teachers of the same grade level, as determined by the governing board.

E. Notwithstanding §§ 23-351 and 23-353, if an employee is discharged from the service of a school district, the school district shall pay the wages due to the employee within ten calendar days from the date of discharge.

F. Each school district shall establish policies and procedures to provide teachers with personal liability insurance.

Added by Laws 1981, Ch. 1, § 2, eff. Jan. 23, 1981. Amended by Laws 1984, Ch. 52, § 2; Laws 1984, Ch. 194, § 1; Laws 1985, Ch. 345, § 2; Laws 1986, Ch. 399, § 4; Laws 1987, Ch. 313, § 1; Laws 1990, Ch. 123, § 1; Laws 1990, Ch. 363, § 5; Laws 1995, Ch. 268, § 20; Laws 1998, Ch. 63, § 1; Laws 2000, 5th S.S., Ch. 1, § 7; Laws 2001, Ch. 381, § 1; Laws 2002, Ch. 290, § 3.

Historical and Statutory Notes

Source:

Laws 1912, Ch. 77, §§ 41, 110.
Civ.Code 1913, §§ 2733, 2836.
Laws 1921, Ch. 72, § 5.
Laws 1921, Ch. 137, § 1.
Laws 1925, Ch. 11, § 1.
Laws 1925, Ch. 70, § 1-4.
Laws 1927, Ch. 88, § 1.
Rev.Code 1928, §§ 1011, 1057.
Laws 1933, Ch. 18, § 1.
Code 1939, § 54-1111.
Laws 1949, Ch. 110, § 1.
Laws 1951, Ch. 140, § 1.
Laws 1952, Ch. 138, § 1.
Code 1939, Supp.1952, § 54-416.
Laws 1954, Ch. 117, § 2.
A.R.S. former §§ 15-205, 15-443.
Laws 1960, Ch. 127, §§ 10, 30.
Laws 1962, Ch. 137, § 1.
Laws 1972, Ch. 138, § 9.
Laws 1977, Ch. 164, § 7.
Laws 1979, Ch. 145, § 35.
Laws 1979, Ch. 204, § 2.

Laws 1984, Ch. 52, § 2, added subsec. D.

Laws 1984, Ch. 194, § 1, inserted the second and third sentences in subsec. A.

The 1985 amendment inserted new subsecs. C, D and E; and redesignated former subsecs. C and D as subsecs. F and G.

The 1986 amendment rewrote the second sentence of subsec. G, which had read: "Notwithstanding any other statute, a certificated teacher who obtains continuing teacher status in a school district does not lose continuing teacher status if the teacher is employed under contract on a part-time basis for at least forty per cent time."

The 1987 amendment inserted "all of the following occur" at the end of the introductory paragraph of subsec. C; inserted a new subsec. D; and redesignated existing subsecs. D to G as subsecs. E to H.

The purported amendment of this section by Laws 1990, Ch. 123, § 1 was repealed by Laws 1990, Ch. 363, § 6.

The 1990 amendment by Ch. 363 added subsec. I.

The 1990 amendment of this section by Ch. 363 explicitly amended the 1987 amendment of this section by Ch. 313.

Laws 1990, Ch. 363, § 1, par. 4 provides:

"**Section 1. Purpose**"

"4. Section 15-502, Arizona Revised Statutes, was amended by Laws 1990, chapter 123, § 1. However, Laws 1990, chapter 123, § 1 failed to set forth in full the existing text of § 15-502, Arizona Revised Statutes, as last amended by Laws 1987, chapter 313, § 1 as required by the Constitution of Arizona article IV, part 2, § 14. In order to correct a potentially defective enactment, in this enactment § 15–502, Arizona Revised Statutes, as amended by Laws 1987, chapter 313, § 1, the previously valid version of this section, is amended to incorporate the amendments made by Laws 1990, chapter 123, § 1 and the Laws 1990, chapter 123, § 1 version is repealed."

Laws 1993, Ch. 202, §§ 20 to 24, eff. April 21, 1993, providing for a pilot program for school performance incentives, were repealed by Laws 1994, Ch. 221, § 3.

The 1995 amendment by Ch. 268, substantially rewrote the section, deleting the second and third sentences of subsec. A in their entirety, and deleting subsecs. C to F, redesignating then existing subsecs. G to I, as C to E, accordingly.

The 1998 amendment by Ch. 63 rewrote subsec. B, which had read:

"**B.** A teacher shall not be employed if the teacher has not received a certificate for teaching, granted by the proper authorities. If a teacher has filed an application and completed all of the requirements for a certificate but time does not allow a teacher to receive a certificate before the commencement of employment, the certificate shall be deemed to have been received on the date of application if the certificate is issued within three months of the date of commencing employment, and such teacher shall upon receipt of the certificate and filing such certificate with the county school superintendent be paid as though the certificate was in full force and effect during the period when salary entitlement was earned. Any contract issued to a teacher who has completed certificate requirements but has not received a certificate shall be specifically contingent upon receipt of such a certificate."

The 2000 amendment by 5th S.S., Ch. 1, added subsec. F.

Proposition 301, approved by the electors at the Nov. 7, 2000 general election, effective Nov. 27, 2000, included a provision increasing the state transaction privilege tax rate six-tenths of one per cent. Therefore, the conditions of the 5th S.S. Ch. 1 were met, and the act became effective.

The 2001 amendment by Ch. 381 inserted the last sentence of subsec. A, relating to use of private entities to provide personnel services.

Reviser's Notes:

1984 Note. Prior to the 1985 amendment, this section contained the amendments made by Laws 1984, Ch. 52, § 2 and Ch. 194, § 1 which were blended together pursuant to authority of § 41–1304.03.

1987 Note. Pursuant to authority of § 41–1304.02, in the section heading "district certification;" was deleted.

1995 Note. Pursuant to authority of § 41–1304.02, in the section heading "associate teachers; limitation;" was removed.

§ 15–503. Superintendents, principals, head teachers and school psychologists; term of employment; evaluation; contract delivery; nonretention notice

A. The governing board may:

1. Employ a superintendent or principal, or both.

2. Appoint a head teacher.

3. Jointly with another governing board employ a superintendent or a principal, or both.

B. The term of employment of superintendents or principals may be for any period not exceeding three years, except that if the superintendent's or principal's contract with the school district is for multiple years pursuant to this subsection the school district shall not offer to extend or renegotiate the contract until May of the year preceding the final year of the contract. The school district governing board or the governing body of the charter school shall communicate the superintendent's or principal's duties with respect to the classroom site fund established by § 15–977.

C. The governing board shall establish systems for the evaluation of the performance of principals and other school administrators and certificated school psychologists in the school district. In the development and adoption of these performance evaluation systems, the governing board shall avail itself of the advice of its administrators and certificated school psychologists. Each evaluation shall include recommendations as to areas of improvement in the performance of the certificated school psychologist if the performance of the certificated school psychologist warrants improvement. After transmittal of an assessment, a board designee shall confer with the certificated school psychologist to make specific recommendations as to areas of improvement in the certificated school psychologist's performance. The board designee shall provide assistance and opportunities for the certificated school psychologist to improve his performance and shall follow up with the certificated school psychologist after a reasonable period of time for the purpose of ascertaining that the certificated school psychologist is demonstrating adequate performance. The evaluation process for certificated school psychologists shall include appeal procedures for certificated school psychologists who disagree with the evaluation of their performance, if the evaluation is for use as criteria for establishing compensation or dismissal.

D. On or before May 15 the governing board shall offer a contract for the next school year to each certified administrator and certificated school psychologist who is in the last year of his contract unless, on or before April 15, the governing board, a member of the board acting on behalf of the board or the superintendent of the school district gives notice to the administrator or certificated school psychologist of the board's intention not to offer a new contract. If the governing board has called for an override election for the third Tuesday in May as provided in § 15–481, the governing board shall offer a contract for the next school year to each certified administrator or certificated school psychologist who is in the last year of his contract on or before June 15 unless, no later than five days after the override election excluding Saturday, Sunday and legal holidays, the governing board, a member of the board acting on behalf of the board or the superintendent of the school district gives notice to the administrator or the certificated school psychologist of the board's intention not to offer a new contract. The administrator's or the certificated school psychologist's acceptance of the contract shall be indicated within thirty days from the date of the written contract or the offer is revoked. The administrator or certificated school psychologist accepts the contract by signing the contract and returning it to the governing board or by making a written instrument which accepts the terms of the contract and delivering the written instrument to the governing board.

E. Notice of the board's intention not to reemploy the administrator or certificated school psychologist shall be made by delivering the notice personally to the administrator or the certificated school psychologist or by sending the notice by certified mail, postmarked on or before the applicable deadline prescribed in subsection D of this section, and directed to the administrator or the certificated school psychologist at his place of residence as recorded in the school district records.

Added by Laws 1981, Ch. 1, § 2, eff. Jan. 23, 1981. Amended by Laws 1983, Ch. 281, § 4; Laws 1985, Ch. 207, § 1; Laws 1988, Ch. 148, § 1; Laws 1992, Ch. 314, § 2; Laws 1995, Ch. 268, § 21; Laws 2001, Ch. 379, § 1.

Historical and Statutory Notes

Source:

Laws 1912, Ch. 77, §§ 41, 110.
Civ.Code 1913, §§ 2733, 2836.
Laws 1921, Ch. 72, § 5.
Laws 1921, Ch. 137, § 1.
Laws 1925, Ch. 11, § 1.
Laws 1925, Ch. 70, §§ 1-4.
Laws 1927, Ch. 88, § 1.
Rev.Code 1928, §§ 1011, 1057.
Laws 1933, Ch. 18, § 1.
Code 1939, § 54-1111.
Laws 1949, Ch. 110, § 1.
Laws 1951, Ch. 140, § 1.
Laws 1952, Ch. 138, § 1.
Code 1939, Supp.1952, § 54-416.
Laws 1954, Ch. 117, § 2.
A.R.S. former §§ 15-205, 15-444.
Laws 1956, Ch. 134, § 2.
Laws 1960, Ch. 127, §§ 10, 31.
Laws 1974, 1st S.S., Ch. 3, § 6.
Laws 1979, Ch. 118, § 3.
Laws 1980, 2nd S.S., Ch. 9, § 19.

The 1983 amendment added subsec. C.

The 1985 amendment rewrote subsec. A, which had read:

"**A.** The governing board may:

"1. In school districts having a student count of three hundred or more, employ a superintendent or principal, or both.

"2. In a school district having five or more teachers, employ a principal.

"3. In a school district having less than five teachers, appoint a head teacher.

"4. Jointly employ a superintendent or a principal, or both, if the combined student count of the school districts employing the superintendent or principal meets the requirements of paragraphs 1 and 2 of this subsection."

The 1988 amendment added subsecs. D and E; and made nonsubstantive changes.

The 1992 amendment by Ch. 314 rewrote subsec. C; included contracts of "certificated school psychologist[s]" in subsecs. D and E; and deleted "administrative" before "contract" several places in subsec. C. Subsection C had read:

"**C.** The governing board shall establish a system for the evaluation of the performance of principals and other school administrators in the school district. In the development and adoption of this administrator performance evaluation system, the governing board shall avail itself of the advice of its administrators."

The 1995 amendment by Ch. 268 rewrote subsec. A, which had read:

"**A.** The governing board may:

"In a school district having five or more teachers, employ a superintendent or principal, or both.

"2. "In a school district having fewer than five teachers, employ a principal or appoint a head teacher.

"3. Jointly with another governing board employ a superintendent or a principal, or both, if the combined number of teachers of the school districts employing the superintendent or principal, or both, meets the requirements of paragraph 1 of this subsection.".

The 2001 amendment by Ch. 379 rewrote subsec. B, which had read:

"**B.** The term of employment of superintendents or principals may be for any period not exceeding three years."

§ 15-504. Repealed by Laws 1995, Ch. 268, § 22

Historical and Statutory Notes

The repealed section, added by Laws 1981, Ch. 1, § 2, derived from:

Laws 1912, Ch. 77, § 110.
Civ.Code 1913, § 2836.
Rev.Code 1928, §§ 1041a, 1041b, 1057.
Laws 1935, Ch. 67, §§ 1, 2.
Code 1939, §§ 54-1003, 54-1111.
Laws 1943, Ch. 5, § 1.
Laws 1953, Ch. 54, § 1.
Code 1939, Supp.1953, § 54-1002.
A.R.S. former §§ 15-205, 15-231, 15-232.
Laws 1960, Ch. 127, § 10.
Laws 1976, Ch. 162, § 12.
Laws 1977, Ch. 44, § 1.

related to oaths of office for school employees.

§ 15-505. Examination of persons displaying symptoms of pulmonary disease

A school district employee shall not be required to submit to annual or other regular periodic examinations for tuberculosis, except that in instances where such employee displays symptoms of pulmonary disease the governing board may require such employee to submit to such tests or examinations as a licensed physician deems appropriate.

Added by Laws 1981, Ch. 1, § 2, eff. Jan. 23, 1981. Amended by Laws 1986, Ch. 58, § 1; Laws 1986, Ch. 399, § 5; Laws 1990, Ch. 35, § 1.

Historical and Statutory Notes

Source:

Laws 1912, Ch. 37, § 1.
Civ.Code 1913, § 2809.
Rev.Code 1928, § 1045.
Code 1939, § 54-1007.
A.R.S. former § 15-206.
Laws 1960, Ch. 127, § 11.
Laws 1976, Ch. 22, § 1.

The 1986 amendment of this section by Ch. 399 explicitly amended the 1986 amendment of this section by Ch. 58.

§ 15-506. Flag display; recitation of the pledge of allegiance

School authorities shall purchase a United States flag, flagstaff and appurtenances, display the flag upon or near the school building during school hours and at such other times as they direct and set aside a specific time each day for those students who wish to recite the pledge of allegiance to the United States flag.

Added by Laws 1981, Ch. 1, § 2, eff. Jan. 23, 1981.

Historical and Statutory Notes

Source:

Laws 1912, Ch. 77, §§ 117 to 119.
Civ.Code 1913, §§ 2843, 2844.
Rev.Code 1928, § 1066.
Code 1939, § 54-808.
A.R.S. former § 15-1031.
Laws 1975, Ch. 140, § 4.

§ 15-507. Abuse of teacher or school employee in school; classification

A person who knowingly abuses a teacher or other school employee on school grounds or while the teacher or employee is engaged in the performance of his duties is guilty of a class 3 misdemeanor.

Added by Laws 1981, Ch. 1, § 2, eff. Jan. 23, 1981. Amended by Laws 1989, Ch. 124, § 1.

Historical and Statutory Notes

Source:

Pen.Code 1901, § 606.
Pen.Code 1913, § 696.
Rev.Code 1928, § 4870.
Code 1939, § 43-1309.
A.R.S. former § 15-210.
Laws 1978, Ch. 201, § 255.

The 1989 amendment deleted "insults or" preceding "abuses" inserted "or other school employee"; and inserted "or employee".

§ 15-507.01. Renumbered as §15-515

§ 15-508. Dismissal for failure to comply with certain laws

Wilful neglect or failure on the part of a school superintendent, principal, teacher or other officer of a school to observe and carry out the requirements of §§ 15-532 and 15-710 is sufficient cause for dismissal or removal of such person from his position, and the superintendent of public instruction shall make necessary arrangements for carrying out the provisions of this section.

Added by Laws 1981, Ch. 1, § 2, eff. Jan. 23, 1981.

Historical and Statutory Notes

Source:

Laws 1925, Ch. 40, §§ 4, 5.
Rev.Code 1928, § 1063.
Code 1939, § 54-805.
Laws 1943, Ch. 62, § 3.
A.R.S. former § 15-207.
Laws 1960, Ch. 127, § 12.

§ 15-509. Failure to comply with statutes as unprofessional conduct; penalty

A certificated person who fails to comply with § 15-501, 15-507 or 15-508 is guilty of unprofessional conduct and the certificated person's certificate shall be revoked.

Added by Laws 1981, Ch. 1, § 2, eff. Jan. 23, 1981. Amended by Laws 1990, Ch. 35, § 2; Laws 1995, Ch. 268, § 23.

Historical and Statutory Notes

Source:

Laws 1912, Ch. 77, § 95.
Civ.Code 1913, § 2808.
Rev.Code 1928, § 1044.
Code 1939, § 54-1006.
A.R.S. former § 15-208.

The 1990 amendment deleted a reference to § 15-505.

The 1995 amendment by Ch. 268 substituted "certificated person" for "teacher"; deleted "15-504," following "15-501,"; and made a gender related change.

§ 15-510. Authorization of leaves of absence; application; preservation of rights

A. The governing board may authorize leaves of absence for school district personnel when it deems such leaves of absence to be reasonable and for good cause and not detrimental to education within the school district.

B. Leaves of absence shall be limited to a period of not to exceed one year.

C. Leaves of absence shall be granted upon application stating the purpose of the leave of absence, the facts as to its necessity or advisability and other information helpful to the governing board in making a determination as to whether the leave should be granted.

D. Sabbatical leaves of absence may be granted by the governing board to certificated teachers and administrators under this section upon the following additional conditions for the following purposes only:

1. Sabbatical leave of absence may be granted only for the purposes of continuing professional education.

2. Sabbatical leave may not exceed a period of one year and may only be granted to a certificated teacher or an administrator who has been employed by the school district for a period of seven consecutive years immediately prior to the time the sabbatical leave is to commence, and who has not previously been granted a sabbatical leave of absence by the governing board.

3. The governing board may authorize a salary to be paid to the person to whom sabbatical leave is granted of not to exceed one-half of the salary then received by him.

4. The salary shall be paid to such person upon the condition that he shall return not later than one year after commencement of the sabbatical leave for renewal of employment for at least one school year, and unless he returns

within such period, he shall repay to the school district the amount paid to him during the leave period, and, unless such amount is so paid, the governing board shall direct the county attorney to institute suit against such person to collect such amount.

E. If leave is granted, all rights prescribed in §§ 15-538.01, 15-539 through 15-544 and 15-547 for certificated teachers who have been employed by the school district for more than the major portion of three consecutive school years and all rights of retirement, accrued leave with pay, salary increments and other benefits provided by law shall be preserved and available to the employee after the termination of the leave of absence.

Formerly § 15-548. Added by Laws 1981, Ch. 1, § 2, eff. Jan. 23, 1981. Renumbered as § 15-510 and amended by Laws 1986, Ch. 58, § 2. Amended by Laws 1986, Ch. 399, § 6.

Historical and Statutory Notes

Source:
Laws 1956, Ch. 49, § 1.
A.R.S. former § 15-444.02.
Laws 1964, Ch. 96, § 1.

§ 15-511. Use of school district or charter school resources or employees to influence elections; prohibition; civil penalty; definition

A. A person acting on behalf of a school district or a person who aids another person acting on behalf of a school district shall not use school district or charter school personnel, equipment, materials, buildings or other resources for the purpose of influencing the outcomes of elections. Notwithstanding this section, a school district may distribute informational reports on a proposed budget override election as provided in § 15-481, subsections B and C or informational reports on a proposed bond election as provided in § 15-491, subsection D. Nothing in this section precludes a school district from reporting on official actions of the governing board.

B. An employee of a school district or charter school who is acting as an agent of or working in an official capacity for the school district or charter school may not give pupils written materials to influence the outcome of an election or to advocate support for or opposition to pending or proposed legislation.

C. Employees of a school district or charter school may not use the authority of their positions to influence the vote or political activities of any subordinate employee.

D. Nothing contained in this section shall be construed as denying the civil and political liberties of any person as guaranteed by the United States and Arizona Constitutions.

E. By January 1, 2004, the attorney general shall publish and distribute to school districts and charter schools a detailed guideline regarding activities prohibited under this section. The attorney general may distribute these guidelines through a web site or electronically.

F. The attorney general or the county attorney for the county in which an alleged violation of this section occurred may initiate a suit in the superior court in the county in which the school district or charter school is located for the purpose of complying with this section.

G. For each violation of this section, the court may impose a civil penalty not to exceed five hundred dollars plus any amount of misused funds subtracted from the school district budget against a person who knowingly violates or a person who knowingly aids another person in violating this section. The person determined to be out of compliance with this section shall be responsible for the payment of all penalties and misused funds. School district funds or insurance payments shall not be used to pay these penalties or misused funds. All misused funds collected pursuant to this section shall be returned to the school district or charter school whose funds were misused.

H. An attorney acting on behalf of a public school may request a legal opinion of the county attorney or attorney general as to whether a proposed use of school district resources would violate this section.

I. All penalties collected by the court for a suit initiated in superior court by the attorney general shall be paid to the office of the attorney general for the use and reimbursement of costs of prosecution pursuant to this section. All penalties collected by the court for a suit initiated in superior court by a county attorney shall be paid to the county treasurer of the county in which the court is held for the use and reimbursement of costs of prosecution pursuant to this section.

J. For the purposes of this section, "misused funds" means school district monies or resources used pursuant to subsection A of this section.

Added by Laws 1996, Ch. 286, § 5. Amended by Laws 2003, Ch. 259, § 1.

Historical and Statutory Notes

Source:

A.R.S. former § 15–511.
Laws 1987, Ch. 240, § 1.

Laws 1987, Ch. 240, § 3 provides:

"**Sec. 3. State board rules**

"The state board of education shall prescribe rules limiting the use of school resources to influence the outcomes of elections and rules for policies for political activities of employees as required by § 15–511, Arizona Revised Statutes, as added by this act, no later than December 31, 1987 and school district governing boards shall adopt policies as required by § 15–511, subsection B, Arizona Revised Statutes, as added by this act, no later than June 30, 1988."

The 2003 amendment by Ch. 259, rewrote the section, which had read:

"**A.** A school district shall not use its personnel, equipment, materials, buildings or other resources for the purpose of influencing the outcomes of elections. Notwithstanding this section, a school district may distribute informational reports on a proposed budget override election as provided in § 15–481, subsections B and C or informational pamphlets on a proposed bond election as provided in § 15–491, subsection D. Nothing in this section precludes a school district from reporting on official actions of the governing board.

"**B.** An employee of a school district who is acting as an agent of or working in an official capacity for the school district may not give pupils written materials that are designed to influence the outcome of an election or to advocate support for or opposition to pending or proposed legislation.

"**C.** Employees of a school district may not use the authority of their positions to influence the vote or political activities of any subordinate employee.

"**D.** Nothing contained in this section shall be construed as denying the civil and political liberties of any employee as guaranteed by the United States and Arizona Constitutions."

Former § 15–511, added by Laws 1987, Ch. 240, § 1, amended by Laws 1996, Ch. 284, § 22, relating to similar subject matter, was repealed by Laws 1996, Ch. 286, § 4. See now this section.

Reviser's Notes:

2003 Note. Pursuant to authority of § 41–1304.02, in the section heading "; definition" was added and in subsection E, the spelling of "web site" was corrected.

§ 15-512. Noncertificated personnel; fingerprinting personnel; background investigations; affidavit; civil immunity; violation; classification; definition

A. Noncertificated personnel and personnel who are not paid employees of the school district and who are not either the parent or the guardian of a pupil who attends school in the school district but who are required or allowed to provide services directly to pupils without the supervision of a certificated employee and who are initially hired by a school district after January 1, 1990 shall be fingerprinted as a condition of employment except for personnel who are required as a condition of licensing to be fingerprinted if the license is required for employment or for personnel who were previously employed by a school district and who reestablished employment with that district within one year after the date that the employee terminated employment with the district. A school district may release the results of a background check to another school district for employment purposes. The employee's fingerprints and the form prescribed in subsection D of this section shall be submitted to the school district within twenty days after the date an employee begins work. A school district may terminate an employee if the information on the form provided under subsection D of this section is inconsistent with the information received from the fingerprint check. The school district shall develop procedures for fingerprinting employees. For the purposes of this subsection, "supervision" means under the direction of and, except for brief periods of time during a school day or a school activity, within sight of a certificated employee when providing direct services to pupils.

B. Fingerprint checks shall be conducted pursuant to § 41-1750, subsection G.

C. The school district shall assume the costs of fingerprint checks and may charge these costs to its fingerprinted employee, except that the school district may not charge the costs of the fingerprint check to personnel of the school district who are not paid employees. The fees charged for fingerprinting shall be deposited with the county treasurer who shall credit the deposit to the fingerprint fund of the school district. The costs charged to a fingerprinted employee are limited to and the proceeds in the fund may only be applied to the actual costs, including personnel costs, incurred as a result of the fingerprint checks. The fingerprint fund is a continuing fund which is not subject to reversion.

D. Personnel required to be fingerprinted as prescribed in subsection A of this section shall certify on forms that are provided by the school and notarized whether they are awaiting trial on or have ever been convicted of or admitted in open court or pursuant to a plea agreement committing any of the following criminal offenses in this state or similar offenses in another jurisdiction:

1. Sexual abuse of a minor.
2. Incest.
3. First or second degree murder.

4. Kidnapping.

5. Arson.

6. Sexual assault.

7. Sexual exploitation of a minor.

8. Felony offenses involving contributing to the delinquency of a minor.

9. Commercial sexual exploitation of a minor.

10. Felony offenses involving sale, distribution or transportation of, offer to sell, transport, or distribute or conspiracy to sell, transport or distribute marijuana or dangerous or narcotic drugs.

11. Felony offenses involving the possession or use of marijuana, dangerous drugs or narcotic drugs.

12. Misdemeanor offenses involving the possession or use of marijuana or dangerous drugs.

13. Burglary in the first degree.

14. Burglary in the second or third degree.

15. Aggravated or armed robbery.

16. Robbery.

17. A dangerous crime against children as defined in § 13–604.01.

18. Child abuse.

19. Sexual conduct with a minor.

20. Molestation of a child.

21. Manslaughter.

22. Aggravated assault.

23. Assault.

24. Exploitation of minors involving drug offenses.

E. A school district may refuse to hire or may review or terminate personnel who have been convicted of or admitted committing any of the criminal offenses prescribed in subsection D of this section or of a similar offense in another jurisdiction. A school district which is considering terminating an employee pursuant to the provisions of this subsection shall hold a hearing to determine whether a person already employed shall be terminated. In conducting a review, the governing board shall utilize the guidelines, including the list of offenses that are not subject to review, as prescribed by the state board of education pursuant to § 15–534, subsection C. In considering whether to hire or terminate the employment of a person the governing board shall take into account the following factors:

1. The nature of the crime and the potential for crimes against children.

2. Offenses committed as a minor for which proceedings were held under the jurisdiction of a juvenile or an adult court.

3. Offenses that have been expunged by a court of competent jurisdiction, if the person has been pardoned or if the person's sentence has been commuted.

4. The employment record of the person since the commission of the crime if the crime was committed more than ten years before the governing board's consideration of whether to hire or terminate the person.

5. The reliability of the evidence of an admission of a crime unless made under oath in a court of competent jurisdiction.

F. Before employment with the school district, the district shall make documented, good faith efforts to contact previous employers of a person to obtain information and recommendations which may be relevant to a person's fitness for employment. A governing board shall adopt procedures for conducting background investigations required by this subsection, including one or more standard forms for use by school district officials to document their efforts to obtain information from previous employers. A school district may provide information received as a result of a background investigation required by this section to any other school district, to any other public school and to any public entity that agrees pursuant to a contract or intergovernmental agreement to perform background investigations for school districts or other public schools. School districts and other public schools may enter into intergovernmental agreements pursuant to § 11-952 and cooperative purchasing agreements pursuant to rules adopted in accordance with § 15-213 for the purposes of performing or contracting for the performance of background investigations and for sharing the results of background investigations required by this subsection. Information obtained about an employee or applicant for employment by any school district or other public school in the performance of a background investigation may be retained by that school district or the other public school or by any public entity that agrees pursuant to contract to perform background investigations for school districts or other public schools and may be provided to any school district or other public school that is performing a background investigation required by this subsection.

G. A school district may fingerprint any other employee of the district, whether paid or not, or any other applicant for employment with the school district not otherwise required by this section to be fingerprinted on the condition that the school district may not charge the costs of the fingerprint check to the fingerprinted applicant or nonpaid employee.

H. Subsection A of this section does not apply to a person who provides instruction or other education services to a pupil, with the written consent of the parent or guardian of the pupil, under a work release program, advance placement course or other education program that occurs off school property.

I. Public entities that agree pursuant to contract to perform background investigations, public schools, the department of education and previous employers who provide information pursuant to this section are immune from civil liability unless the information provided is false and is acted on by the school district to the harm of the employee and the public entity, the public school, the previous employer or the department of education knows the information is false or acts with reckless disregard of the information's truth or falsity. A school district which relies on information obtained pursuant to this section in making employment decisions is immune from civil liability for use of the information unless the information obtained is false and the school district knows the information is false or acts with reckless disregard of the information's truth or falsity.

J. The superintendent of a school district or chief administrator of a charter school or the person's designee who is responsible for implementing the governing board's policy regarding background investigations required by subsection F of this section and who fails to carry out that responsibility is guilty of unprofessional conduct and shall be subject to disciplinary action by the state board.

K. A school district may hire noncertificated personnel before receiving the results of the fingerprint check but may terminate employment if the information on the form provided in subsection D of this section is inconsistent with the information received from the fingerprint check. In addition to any other conditions or requirements deemed necessary by the superintendent of public instruction to protect the health and safety of pupils, noncertificated personnel who are required or allowed unsupervised contact with pupils may be hired by school districts before the results of a fingerprint check are received if all of the following conditions are met:

1. The school district that is seeking to hire the applicant shall document in the applicant's file the necessity for hiring and placement of the applicant before a fingerprint check could be completed.

2. The school district that is seeking to hire the applicant shall do all of the following:

(a) Ensure that the department of public safety completes a statewide criminal history information check on the applicant. A statewide criminal history information check shall be completed by the department of public safety every one hundred twenty days until the date that the fingerprint check is completed.

(b) Obtain references from the applicant's current employer and two most recent previous employers except for applicants who have been employed for at least five years by the applicant's most recent employer.

(c) Provide general supervision of the applicant until the date that the fingerprint check is completed.

(d) Report to the superintendent of public instruction on June 30 and December 31 the number of applicants hired prior to the completion of a fingerprint check. In addition, the school district shall report the number of applicants for whom fingerprint checks were not received after one hundred twenty days and after one hundred seventy-five days of hire.

L. Notwithstanding any other law, this section does not apply to pupils who attend school in a school district and who are also employed by a school district.

M. A person who makes a false statement, representation or certification in any application for employment with the school district is guilty of a class 3 misdemeanor.

N. For the purpose of this section, "background investigation" means any communication with an employee's or applicant's former employer that concerns the education, training, experience, qualifications and job performance of the employee or applicant and that is used for the purpose of evaluating the employee or applicant for employment. Background investigation does not include the results of any state or federal criminal history records check.

Added by Laws 1989, Ch. 115, § 1. Amended by Laws 1990, Ch. 291, § 1, eff. June 13, 1990; Laws 1992, Ch. 136, § 1; Laws 1992, Ch. 247, § 2; Laws 1993, Ch. 39, § 1; Laws 1995, Ch. 268, § 24; Laws 1996, Ch. 284, § 23; Laws 1997, Ch. 68, § 1; Laws 1997, Ch. 231, § 9; Laws 1998, Ch. 64, § 2; Laws 1998, Ch. 218, § 1, eff. June 1, 1998; Laws 1998, Ch. 270, § 1, eff. August 17, 1999; Laws 1999, Ch. 316, § 1, eff. May 19, 1999; Laws 2000, Ch. 251, § 2.

Historical and Statutory Notes

The 1990 amendment rewrote the section, which had read:

"**A.** Noncertificated personnel initially hired by a school district after January 1, 1990 shall be fingerprinted as a condition of employment except for personnel who are required as a condition of licensing to be fingerprinted if the license is required for employment. The employee's fingerprints and the form prescribed in subsection D of this section shall be submitted to the school district within twenty days after the date an employee begins work. A school district may terminate an employee if the information on the form provided under subsection D of this section is inconsistent with the information received from the fingerprint check. The school district shall develop procedures for fingerprinting employees.

"**B.** Fingerprint checks shall be conducted pursuant to § 41-1750, subsection G.

"**C.** The school district shall assume the costs of fingerprint checks and may charge these costs not to exceed twenty dollars per employee to its fingerprinted employee. The fees charged for fingerprinting shall be deposited with the county treasurer who shall credit the deposit to the fingerprint fund of the school district. The costs charged to a fingerprinted employee are limited to and the proceeds in the fund may only be applied to the actual costs, including personnel, incurred as a result of the fingerprint checks. The fingerprint fund is a continuing fund which is not subject to reversion.

"**D.** Personnel employed by the school district shall certify on forms that are provided by the school and notarized that they are not awaiting trial on and have never been convicted of or admitted committing any of the following criminal offenses in this state or similar offenses in another jurisdiction:

"1. Sexual abuse of a minor.

"2. Incest.

"3. First or second degree murder.

"4. Kidnapping.

"5. Arson.

"6. Sexual assault.

"7. Sexual exploitation of a minor.

"8. Contributing to the delinquency of a minor.

"9. Commercial sexual exploitation of a minor.

"10. Felony offenses involving distribution of marijuana or dangerous or narcotic drugs.

"11. Burglary.

"12. Robbery.

"13. A dangerous crime against children as defined in § 13-604.01.

"14. Child abuse.

"15. Sexual conduct with a minor.

"16. Molestation of a child.

"**E.** Before employment with the school district, the district shall make documented, good faith efforts to contact previous employers of a person to obtain information and recommendations which may be relevant to a person's fitness for employment. A previous employer who provides information pursuant to this subsection is immune from civil liability unless the information provided is false and is acted on to the harm of the employee by the school district and the previous employer knows the information is false or acts with reckless disregard of the information's truth or falsity. A school district which relies on information obtained pursuant to this subsection in making employment decisions is immune from civil liability for use of the information unless the information obtained is false and the school district knows the information is false or acts with reckless disregard of the information's truth or falsity."

The 1992 amendment by Ch. 136 inserted the third sentence of subsec. F relating to a fingerprint check.

The 1992 amendment by Ch. 247 inserted the provision in subsec. A allowing a school district to release results of background checks to other school districts for employment purposes.

The 1993 amendment by Ch. 39, in subsec. D, inserted "in open court or pursuant to a plea agreement" in the introductory paragraph, inserted "Felony offenses involving" in par. 8, rewrote par. 10, inserted new pars. 11 and 12, redesignated existing par. 11 as par. 13. and inserted "in the first degree", inserted a new par. 14, redesignated existing par. 12 as par. 15

and inserted "Aggravated or armed" in that paragraph, inserted a new par. 16, redesignated existing pars. 14 through 18 as pars. 18 through 22, and inserted pars. 23 and 24; and rewrote subsec. E. Paragraph 10 of subsec. D, and subsec. E, had read:

"10. Felony offenses involving distribution of marijuana or dangerous or narcotic drugs."

"**E.** A school district shall not employ and may terminate personnel who have been convicted of any of the criminal offenses prescribed in subsection D of this section or of a similar offense in another jurisdiction. A school district which is considering terminating an employee pursuant to the provisions of this subsection shall hold a hearing to determine whether a person already employed shall be terminated."

The 1995 amendment by Ch. 268, in subsec. F, deleted the former second sentence, which had read, "For certificated personnel, the district shall also contact the department of education to obtain information contained in the person's certification record which may be relevant to the person's fitness for employment.".

The 1996 amendment by Ch. 284, in subsec. F, substituted "shall" for "may" following "A school district", and deleted "if requested to do so by the person who was the subject of the fingerprint check" at the end of the second sentence.

The 1997 amendment by Ch. 68 deleted material relating to civil liability of the department of education and previous employers who provide information from subsec. F and inserted that material as subsec. H; and redesignated former subsec. H as subsec. I.

The 1997 amendment by Ch. 231 modified a statutory reference.

The 1998 amendment by Ch. 64 deleted "personnel who were previously employed by another school district and who were required as a condition of employment to be fingerprinted" following "required for employment" in the first sentence of subsec. A; deleted "voluntary" preceding "manslaughter" in par. 21 of subsec. D.; rewrote subsec. F; inserted references to public entities and public schools in the first sentence of subsec. H; and inserted a new subsec. I, redesignating former subsec. I as subsec. J.

The 1998 amendment by Ch. 218 deleted "voluntary" in the offense "voluntary manslaughter" in subsec. D, par. 21; inserted a new subsec. I; and redesignated former subsec. I as J, accordingly.

The 1998 amendment by Ch. 270 rewrote the section.

The amendment of this section by Laws 1998, Ch. 270, § 2 was repealed by Laws 1999, Ch. 316, § 2, effective May 19, 1999.

The 1999 amendment by Ch. 316 inserted new subsecs. H and M , and redesignated the remaining subsecs. accordingly; and deleted "Until June 30, 1999" from the beginning of newly designated subsec. K, and pars. 1 and 2 of subsec. K.

The 1999 amendment of this section by Ch. 316 explicitly amended the amendments of this section by Laws 1998, Ch. 64, § 2, and by Laws 1998, Ch. 218, § 1.

The 2000 amendment by Ch. 251 substituted, in subsec. K, par. 2, "do all of the following" for "perform all of the following"; substituted, in the first sentence of par. N, "employee's or applicant's" for "employee or applicant's"; and, in the third sentence of subsec. E, made a conforming correction in statutory citation.

Reviser's Notes:

1992 Note. Prior to the 1995 amendment this section contained the amendments made by Laws 1992, Ch. 136, sec. 1 and Ch. 247, sec. 2 that were blended together pursuant to authority of § 41-1304.03.

1993 Note. Pursuant to authority of § 41-1304.02, in subsection E the second and third sentences, including paragraphs 1 through 5, were moved to the end of the subsection following "terminated."

1997 Note. Prior to the 1998 amendments, this section contained the amendments made by Laws 1997, Ch. 68, sec. 1 and Ch. 231, sec. 9 that were blended together pursuant to authority of § 41-1304.03. Pursuant to authority of § 41-1304.02, in the section heading "; civil immunity" was added after "affidavit" and in subsection H, first sentence the words "by the school district" were transposed to follow "on".

1998 Note. The independent and valid amendment of this section by Laws 1998, Ch. 64, sec. 2, Ch. 218, sec. 1 and Ch. 270, sec. 2 could not be blended because of the delayed effective date of Ch. 270.

1998 Note. Prior to the 1999 amendment, this section contained the amendments made by Laws 1998, Ch. 64, sec. 2 and Ch. 218. sec. 1 that were blended together pursuant to authority of § 41-1304.03. Pursuant to authority of § 41-1304.02, in the section heading "; definition" was added after "immunity", the sixth and seventh sentences of subsection F were designated as subsection L, in the second sentence of new subsection L the quotation marks enclosing "Background investigation" were removed to correct a manifest clerical error and in subsection J, paragraph 2, subdivision (a) "Ensure" was substituted "Ensures" to correct a manifest clerical error.

1999 Note. Pursuant to authority of § 41-1304.02, in subsection H the spelling of "work release" was corrected.

§ 15-513. Transportation employees; chemical abuse education; drug tests; costs; termination from employment; appeal; definition

A. Beginning on January 1, 1991, a transportation employee shall submit to drug and alcohol testing if the supervisor of the employee, or the supervisor's designee, has probable cause that the employee's job performance has been impaired by the use of alcohol or a drug in violation of title 13, chapter 34.[1] Probable cause shall be based on observance of the employee by district personnel or personnel of a contracting person or entity which furnishes transportation services to the school district and shall be documented by an affidavit signed by the person who has observed the behavior and the supervisor of the employee or the supervisor's designee.

B. A transportation employee shall submit to drug and alcohol testing after an accident involving a vehicle used to transport pupils or an accident involving equipment used in the performance of the employee's duties if the supervisor of the employee, or the supervisor's designee, has probable cause, based on knowledge of the events and circumstances of the accident, that the employee's involvement in the accident was influenced by the use of alcohol or a drug in violation of title 13, chapter 34. Probable cause shall be documented by an affidavit signed by the supervisor of the employee, or the supervisor's designee.

C. School districts shall develop procedures for drug and alcohol testing of transportation employees as provided in the section.

D. The school district shall assume the costs of the drug and alcohol testing of a transportation employee. If the results of a test are positive, the school district may charge the costs of the test to the tested employee. The costs charged to the employee are limited to the actual costs incurred as a result of testing. If the results of a test are negative, the school district shall not charge the costs of testing to the tested employee.

E. A transportation employee who refuses to submit to drug and alcohol testing or whose test results are positive may be terminated from employment. School districts shall develop a procedure for an employee to appeal the test findings before termination of the employee.

F. An employee who is terminated or otherwise disciplined under this section shall be entitled to all appeal and review rights the employee would have as a district employee or by contract with another person or entity which furnishes transportation services to the school district.

G. For purposes of this section, "transportation employee" means an individual who is employed by the school district, or by another person or entity which furnishes transportation services to the school district, as the driver of a vehicle used to transport pupils, as a person involved in the maintenance and service of vehicles used to transport pupils, as a person involved in the dispatching or supervision of persons employed as drivers of vehicles used to transport pupils or persons involved in the maintenance and service of vehicles used to transport pupils.

Added by Laws 1990, Ch. 324, § 1.

[1] Section 13-3401 et seq.

Historical and Statutory Notes

Reviser's Notes:

1990 Note. Pursuant to authority of § 41–1304.02, subsection F was relettered as subsection G and subsection G was relettered as subsection F.

§ 15–514. Reports of immoral or unprofessional conduct; immunity

A. Any certificated person or governing board member who reasonably suspects or receives a reasonable allegation that a person certificated by the state board of education has engaged in conduct involving minors that would be subject to the reporting requirements of § 13–3620 shall report or cause reports to be made to the department of education in writing as soon as is reasonably practicable but not later than three business days after the person first suspects or receives an allegation of the conduct.

B. The superintendent of a school district or the chief administrator of a charter school who reasonably suspects or receives a reasonable allegation that an act of immoral or unprofessional conduct that would constitute grounds for dismissal or criminal charges by a certificated person has occurred shall report the conduct to the department of education.

C. A person who reports or provides information pursuant to this section regarding the immoral or unprofessional conduct of a certificated person in good faith is not subject to an action for civil damages as a result.

D. A governing board or school or school district employee who has control over personnel decisions shall not take unlawful reprisal against an employee because the employee reports in good faith information as required by this section. For the purposes of this subsection "unlawful reprisal" means an action that is taken by a governing board as a direct result of a lawful report pursuant to this section and, with respect to the employee, results in one or more of the following:

1. Disciplinary action.

2. Transfer or reassignment.

3. Suspension, demotion or dismissal.

4. An unfavorable performance evaluation.

5. Other significant changes in duties or responsibilities that are inconsistent with the employee's salary or employment classification.

E. Failure to report information as required by this section by a certificated person constitutes grounds for disciplinary action by the state board of education.

F. A governing board or school district employee who has control over personnel decisions and who reasonably suspects or receives a reasonable allegation that a person certificated by the state board of education has engaged in conduct involving minors that would be subject to the reporting requirements of § 13–3620 and this article shall not accept the resignation of the certificate holder until these suspicions or allegations have been reported to the state board of education.

Added by Laws 1994, Ch. 165, § 4. Amended by Laws 1997, Ch. 231, § 10; Laws 1998, Ch. 64, § 3; Laws 2001, Ch. 241, § 3.

Historical and Statutory Notes

The 1997 amendment by Ch. 231 substituted "state board of education" for "department of education" in subsec. A.

The 1998 amendment by Ch. 64 rewrote subsec. B, deleted "or unprofessional" preceding "conduct" in subsec. C, and inserted a new subsec. D, redesignating former subsec. D as subsec. E.

The 2001 amendment by Ch. 241 rewrote the section, which had read:

"**A.** Any certificated person or governing board member who has reasonable grounds to believe that a person certificated by the state board of education has engaged in conduct involving minors that would be subject to the reporting requirements of § 13-3620 shall report or cause reports to be made to the department of education in writing within seventy-two hours of the report made pursuant to § 13-3620.

"**B.** The superintendent of a school district or the chief administrator of a charter school who has reasonable grounds to believe that an act of immoral conduct that would constitute grounds for dismissal or criminal charges by a certificated person has occurred shall report the conduct to the department of education.

"**C.** A certificated person or governing board member who reports or provides information regarding the immoral conduct of a certificated person to the department of education in good faith is not subject to an action for civil damages as a result.

"**D.** A governing board or school district employee who has control over personnel decisions shall not take unlawful reprisal against an employee because the employee reports in good faith information as required by this section. For the purposes of this subsection 'unlawful reprisal' means an action that is taken by a governing board as a direct result of a lawful report pursuant to this section and, with respect to the employee, results in one or more of the following:

"1. Disciplinary action.

"2. Transfer or reassignment.

"3. Suspension, demotion or dismissal.

"4. An unfavorable performance evaluation.

"5. Other significant changes in duties or responsibilities that are inconsistent with the employee's salary or employment classification.

"**E.** Failure to report information as required by this section by a certificated person constitutes grounds for disciplinary action by the state board of education.

§ 15-515. Duty to report violations occurring on school premises

All school personnel who observe a violation of § 13-3102, subsection A, paragraph 12 or § 13-3111 on school premises shall immediately report the violation to the school administrator. The administrator shall immediately report the violation to a peace officer. The peace officer shall report this violation to the department of public safety for inclusion in the statewide and federal uniform crime reports prescribed in § 41-1750, subsection A, paragraph 2.

Added as § 15-507.01 by Laws 1994, Ch. 109, § 5. Renumbered as § 15-515.

Historical and Statutory Notes

Reviser's Notes:

1994 Note. Pursuant to authority of § 41-1304.02, this section, added by Laws 1994, Ch. 109, sec. 5. as § 15-507.01, was renumbered as § 15-515.

ARTICLE 2. DUTIES OF TEACHERS

§ 15-521. Duties of teachers

accountability statute

Every teacher shall:

1. Hold pupils to strict account for disorderly conduct.

2. Keep a school register, which the governing board shall carefully preserve as one of the records of the school.

3. Make the decision to promote or retain a pupil in grade in a common school or to pass or fail a pupil in a course in high school. Such decisions may be overturned only as provided in § 15-342, paragraph 11.

4. Comply with all rules and policies of the governing board that relate to the duties prescribed in this section.

Added by Laws 1981, Ch. 1, § 2. Amended by Laws 1981, Ch. 182, § 3; Laws 1981, Ch. 314, § 9; Laws 1983, Ch. 9, § 4, eff. Feb. 25, 1983; Laws 1983, Ch. 281, § 5; Laws 1983, Ch. 325, § 6; Laws 1984, Ch. 349, § 5; Laws 1987, Ch. 220, § 2; Laws 1991, Ch. 257, § 4; Laws 1995, Ch. 268, § 25.

Historical and Statutory Notes

Source:

Laws 1912, Ch. 77, §§ 92, 95.
Civ.Code 1913, §§ 2805, 2808.
Rev.Code 1928, §§ 1041, 1044.
Code 1939, §§ 54-1001, 54-1006.
A.R.S. former §§ 15-201, 15-208.
Laws 1975, Ch. 50, § 1.
Laws 1979, Ch. 204, § 1.
Laws 1980, Ch. 105, § 1.

The 1981 amendment by Ch. 182, § 3 substituted "the governing board shall carefully preserve" for "shall be carefully preserved by the governing board" in subsec. A, par. 6; and rewrote the first sentence of subsec. A, par. 10, which had read:

"Make the decision for promotion or retention of students.";

and substituted "§ 15-342" for "§ 15-341" and "paragraph 11" for "paragraph 17" in the second sentence of subsec. A, par. 10.

The 1981 amendment by Ch. 314, § 9 substituted "§ 15-342" for "§ 15-341" and "paragraph 11" for "paragraph 17" in subsec. A, par. 10.

The 1983 amendment by Ch. 9, § 4 substituted "paragraph 12" for "paragraph 11" in subsec. A, par. 10.

The 1983 amendment by Ch. 281, § 5 substituted "pass or fail a pupil in" for "pass, fail or withdraw a pupil in or from" in the first sentence of par. 10, and added par. 11 in subsec. A; and substituted "is subject to disciplinary action by the governing board pursuant to § 15-341, subsection A, paragraph 25 and by the state board of education pursuant to § 15-203, subsection A, paragraph 28" for "his certificate shall be revoked" in subsec. B.

The 1983 amendment by Ch. 325, § 6 deleted "and" preceding "in the manner" in par. 8, and substituted "pass or fail a pupil in" for "pass, fail or withdraw a pupil in or from" in the first sentence of par. 10 of subsec. A.

The 1984 amendment by Ch. 349substituted "paragraph 11" for "paragraph 12", in subd. 10, of subsec. A, and "paragraph 26" for "paragraph 28" in subsec. B.

The 1987 amendment by Ch. 220 changed a statutory reference in subsec. B.

The 1991 amendment by Ch. 257 deleted "and regulations" following "rules" in pars. 3 and 11 of subsec. A.

The 1995 amendment by Ch. 268 rewrote the section which formerly read:

"**A.** Every teacher shall:

"1. Before assuming charge of a school, except as provided in § 15-502, subsection B, present his or her certificate to the county school superintendent, who shall record it.

"2. Immediately notify the county school superintendent when taking charge of a school or when closing a term of school.

"3. Enforce the course of study, the use of adopted textbooks and the rules prescribed for schools.

"4. Hold pupils to strict account for disorderly conduct.

"5. Exercise supervision over pupils on the playgrounds and during recess if assigned to such duty.

"6. Keep a school register, which the governing board shall carefully preserve as one of the records of the school.

"7. Furnish reports to the county school superintendent as required by the state board of education upon forms furnished by the superintendent of public instruction.

"8. Make an annual report for the entire school year to the county school superintendent at the time, in the manner and on forms prescribed by the state board of education.

"9. Make such other reports as may be required by the superintendent of public instruction, county school superintendent or governing board.

"10. Make the decision to promote or retain a pupil in grade in a common school or to pass or fail a pupil in a course in high school. Such decisions may be overturned only as provided in § 15-342, paragraph 11.

"11. Comply with all rules and policies of the governing board that relate to the duties prescribed in this subsection.

"**B.** A teacher who fails to comply with this section is guilty of unprofessional conduct, and is subject to disciplinary action by the governing board pursuant to § 15-341, subsection A, paragraph 25 and by the state board of education pursuant to § 15-203, subsection A, paragraph 27."

Reviser's Notes:

1981 Note. Prior to the 1983 amendments, this section contained the amendments made by Laws 1981, Ch. 182, § 3 and Ch. 314, § 9 which were blended together pursuant to authority of § 41-1304.03.

1983 Note. Prior to the 1984 amendment, this section contained the amendments made by Laws 1983, Ch. 281, § 5 and Ch. 325, § 6 which were blended together pursuant to authority of § 41-1304.03.

§ 15-522. Repealed by Laws 1995, Ch. 268, § 26

Historical and Statutory Notes

The repealed section, added by Laws 1981, Ch. 1, § 2, derived from Laws 1980, Ch. 210, § 4, and A.R.S. former §§ 15-1026 and 15-1027, related to periods of silence for meditation in schools.

ARTICLE 3. CERTIFICATION AND EMPLOYMENT OF TEACHERS

§ 15-531. Fees

The state board of education may fix and collect fees for:

1. Issuance and evaluation, singly or both, including provisional, basic or standard teaching certificate, administrative, specialized service, nurse, career and technical education, vocational education or substitute, special subject endorsements including guidance-counselor, art, music, physical education, industrial arts, librarian or driver training, one year and multi-year certificates including adult education, emergency or intern certificates, not less than twenty dollars and not more than thirty dollars.

2. Renewal of any certificate, name changes, duplicates or changes of coding to existing files or certificates, not less than ten dollars and not more than twenty dollars.

3. Administration and evaluation of the examination on the Constitutions of the United States and Arizona, not less than six dollars and not more than twelve dollars for regularly scheduled administrations and not less than twelve dollars and not more than twenty dollars for administrations other than regularly scheduled administrations.

4. Administration and evaluation of the reading, grammar and mathematics proficiency examination for applicants for teaching certificates, not less than ten dollars and not more than twenty dollars.

Added by Laws 1981, Ch. 1, § 2, eff. Jan. 23, 1981. Amended by Laws 1981, Ch. 105, § 2; Laws 1989, Ch. 237, § 2, eff. Jan. 1, 1990; Laws 1992, Ch. 314, § 3; Laws 1995, Ch. 268, § 27; Laws 2002, Ch. 89, § 6.

Historical and Statutory Notes

Source: Laws 1912, Ch. 77, § 4.

Civ.Code 1913, § 2697.
Laws 1921, Ch. 134, § 1.
Laws 1925, Ch. 69, § 1.
Rev.Code 1928, § 989.
Laws 1953, Ch. 49, § 1.
Code 1939, Supp.1953, § 54–102.
A.R.S. former § 15–103.
Laws 1966, Ch. 42, § 1.
Laws 1977, Ch. 33, § 1.
Laws 1989, Ch. 237, § 3, provides:

"**Sec. 3. Effective date**

"Section 15–531, Arizona Revised Statutes, as amended by this act, is effective from and after December 31, 1989."

§ 15–531.01. Repealed by Laws 1997, Ch. 231, § 11

Historical and Statutory Notes

The repealed section, added by Laws 1992, Ch. 314, § 4, amended by Laws 1995, Ch. 268, § 28; Laws 1996, Ch. 284, § 24, related to certification of school nurses.

§ 15–532. Examination on state and United States constitutions; exemption; intergovernmental agreement or contract for administration and evaluation

A. A person applying for a certificate authorizing the person to become superintendent, principal or teacher in a school shall, in addition to fingerprinting and other requirements, either complete the required classes or pass a satisfactory examination upon the provisions and principles of the Constitutions of the United States and Arizona.

B. A person who has not met the requirements of this section at the time application is made but who has met all other requirements shall be granted a certificate for not more than three years, except that a person who has not met the requirements of this section but who has met all other requirements and who applies for a certificate authorizing the person to teach an academic course that focuses predominantly on history, government, social studies, citizenship, law or civics shall be granted a certificate for not more than one year. No additional certificate may be granted until all requirements have been fulfilled as provided by the regulations of the state board of education governing certification of teachers.

C. A noncertified person, qualified under the federal and state plans for vocational education, shall be exempt from the provisions of this section for the purpose of acting as an instructor for special adult and evening classes.

D. The state board of education may enter into intergovernmental agreements or contracts pursuant to title 11, chapter 7, article 3 [1] for the administration and evaluation of the examination on the provisions and principles of the Constitutions of the United States and Arizona. Notwithstanding § 15–531, the intergovernmental agreement or contract shall specify the fee for the administration and evaluation of the examination and may provide for the retention of all or part of the monies by the contractor administering and evaluating the examination.

E. A university under the jurisdiction of the Arizona board of regents shall administer the examination required by this section to students who are pursuing a bachelor of arts degree in education or a bachelor of science degree in education at that university.

Added by Laws 1981, Ch. 1, § 2, eff. Jan. 23, 1981. Amended by Laws 1985, Ch. 254, § 3, eff. April 29, 1985; Laws 2003, Ch. 214, § 4, eff. May 14, 2003.

[1] Section 11-951 et seq.

Historical and Statutory Notes

Source:

Laws 1925, Ch. 40, § 3.
Rev.Code 1928, § 1062.
Laws 1943, Ch. 62, § 2.
Laws 1949, Ch. 9, § 1.
Code 1939, Supp.1952, § 54-804.
A.R.S. former § 15-233.
Laws 1960, Ch. 127, § 13.

§ 15-533. Proficiency examination

Carnel vs. Harris

A. To qualify for either a basic or standard teaching certificate, or equivalent certificate later adopted by the state board of education, a person must pass each component of the proficiency examination developed and administered by the state board of education. The proficiency examination shall consist of only a professional knowledge test and a subject knowledge test. A person is not required to take a component of the examination if the person has passed a component on a proficiency examination which has been adopted by a state board of education or equivalent agency in another state and which has been determined to be equivalent to the applicable component on the examination prescribed in this section by the state board of education in this state. The state board of education may grant a basic or standard teaching certificate for not to exceed one year to a teacher who is a nonresident and who has not met the requirement of this section at the time of application.

B. A person is not required to pass the proficiency examination or the equivalent examination more than once, except that a person who passed the examination seven or more years before qualifying to teach in this state is required to repass the examination.

Added by Laws 1984, Ch. 286, § 2. Amended by Laws 1985, Ch. 191, § 1; Laws 1988, Ch. 69, § 1; Laws 1992, Ch. 305, § 10; Laws 2000, Ch. 97, § 3.

Historical and Statutory Notes

Source:

Laws 1980, 2nd S.S., Ch. 9, § 9.
A.R.S. former §§ 15-235, 15-533.
Laws 1981, Ch. 1, § 2.
Laws 1982, Ch. 288, § 1.

Laws 1984, Ch. 286, § 3 provides:

"**Sec. 3. Admittance or attendance in colleges of education; proficiency examination requirement**

"Any person who has been admitted to or is in the college of education of a university under the jurisdiction of the Arizona board of regents and any person who has graduated from a university under the jurisdiction of the Arizona board of regents on or before the effective date of this act is required to pass each component of the reading, grammar and mathematics proficiency examination before qualifying to teach in this state. Nothing in this section shall require any person having received a basic, standard or equivalent teaching certificate prior to October 1, 1980 to pass each component of the reading, grammar and mathematics proficiency examination."

Laws 1985, Ch. 191, § 2 provides:

"**Sec. 2. Entrance into teacher training program in colleges of education; reading, grammar and mathematics proficiency examination requirement**

"Notwithstanding § 15-533, subsection B, Arizona Revised Statutes, a person may be admitted into any teacher training program in a college of education of a university under the jurisdiction of the Arizona board of regents until December 31, 1985 without having passed each component of the reading, grammar and mathematics proficiency examination, except that the person is required to pass each component of the reading, grammar and mathematics proficiency examination to qualify to teach in this state."

Former § 15-533 (for derivation, see Source note, ante), relating to the same subject matter as this section, was repealed by Laws 1984, Ch. 286, § 1.

Reviser's Notes:

1992 Note. Pursuant to authority of § 41-1304.02, in the section heading "; nonresidents" was added after "examination".

§ 15-534. Fingerprinting; review and disciplinary action; violation; classification

A. A person who applies for a certificate as prescribed in § 15-203 shall have a valid fingerprint clearance card that is issued pursuant to title 41, chapter 12, article 3.1.[1] Applicants who possess a certificate pursuant to § 15-203 and who apply for additional certificates or who apply for renewal of any certificate shall meet one of the following requirements:

1. Have a valid fingerprint clearance card issued pursuant to title 41, chapter 12, article 3.1.

2. Provide proof of the submission of an application for a fingerprint clearance card. Applicants who have been denied a fingerprint clearance card shall also provide proof that the applicant qualifies for a good cause exception hearing pursuant to § 41-619.55.

B. A person who is certified pursuant to § 15-203 shall maintain a valid fingerprint clearance card during the valid period of the person's certificate or certificates.

C. The state board of education may review and determine whether to renew or not issue a certificate to an applicant for certification on a finding that the applicant engaged in conduct that is immoral or unprofessional or engaged in conduct that would warrant disciplinary action if the person had been certified at the time that the alleged conduct occurred. The board shall prescribe guidelines for this process.

D. The state board of education may take disciplinary action against or not renew the certificate of a person on a finding that the certificated person engaged in conduct that is immoral or unprofessional or engaged in conduct that would warrant disciplinary action if the person had been certified at the time that the alleged conduct occurred. The board shall prescribe guidelines for this process.

E. The department of education may issue conditional certification before an applicant has obtained a valid fingerprint clearance card. A conditional certificate may be used only for employment in the school district that submits an application to the department of education for conditional certification pursuant to this subsection. The state board of education may revoke conditional certification if the information on the application for a conditional certificate is false or incomplete, the applicant is denied a fingerprint clearance card or the conditional certificate is used for employment in a school district other than the school district that is indicated on the application for conditional certification. In addition to any other conditions or requirements deemed necessary by the superintendent of public instruction to protect the health and safety of pupils, conditional certification shall be issued before the applicant obtains a fingerprint clearance card if all of the following conditions are met:

1. The school district that is seeking to hire the applicant verifies in writing on a form developed by the department of education the necessity for hiring and placement of the applicant before a fingerprint check is completed.

2. The school district that is seeking to hire the applicant performs all of the following:

(a) Ensures that the department of public safety completes a statewide criminal records check on the applicant. A statewide criminal records check shall be completed by the department of public safety every one hundred twenty days until the date that the fingerprint check is completed.

(b) Completes a search of criminal records in all local jurisdictions outside of this state in which the applicant has lived in the previous five years.

(c) Obtains references from the applicant's current employer and two most recent previous employers except for applicants who have been employed for at least five years by the applicant's most recent employer.

(d) Provides general supervision of the applicant until the applicant receives permanent certification from the department of education.

F. Before employment, schools or school districts shall verify the certification and fingerprint status of applicants who apply for school or school district positions that require certification.

G. The state board of education shall notify the department of public safety if the state board of education receives credible evidence that a person who possesses a valid fingerprint clearance card either:

1. Is arrested for or charged with an offense listed in § 41-1758.03, subsection B.

2. Falsified information on the form required by subsection A of this section.

H. A person who makes a false statement, representation or certification in any application for certification is guilty of a class 3 misdemeanor.

Added by Laws 1989, Ch. 115, § 2. Amended by Laws 1990, Ch. 291, § 2, eff. June 13, 1990; Laws 1993, Ch. 39, § 2; Laws 1995, Ch. 268, § 29; Laws 1996, Ch. 284, § 25; Laws 1997, Ch. 231, § 12; Laws 1998, Ch. 218, § 2, eff. June 1, 1998; Laws 1998, Ch. 270, § 3, eff. August 17, 1999; Laws 1999, Ch. 316, § 3, eff. Aug. 17, 1999; Laws 2000, Ch. 208, § 1; Laws 2000, Ch. 251, § 3; Laws 2001, Ch. 241, § 4; Laws 2003, Ch. 214, § 5, eff. Oct. 1, 2003.

[1] Section 41-1758 et seq.

Historical and Statutory Notes

The 1990 amendment deleted "and shall not exceed twenty dollars per fingerprinted applicant" at the end of subsec. E; in subsec. F, substituted "whether they are awaiting trial on or have ever been convicted" for "that they are not awaiting trial on and have never been convicted" and added pars. 17 and 18; and added subsec. G.

The 1993 amendment rewrote subsecs. F and G, which had read:

"**F.** Applicants shall certify on forms that are provided by the department of education and notarized whether they are awaiting trial on or have ever been convicted of or admitted committing any of the following criminal offenses in this state or similar offenses in another jurisdiction:

"1. Sexual abuse of a minor.

"2. Incest.

"3. First or second degree murder.

"4. Kidnapping.

"5. Arson.

"6. Sexual assault.

"7. Sexual exploitation of a minor.

"8. Contributing to the delinquency of a minor.

"9. Commercial sexual exploitation of a minor.

"10. Felony offenses involving distribution of marijuana or dangerous or narcotic drugs.

"11. Burglary.

"12. Robbery.

"13. A dangerous crime against children as defined in § 13–604.01.

"14. Child abuse.

"15. Sexual conduct with a minor.

"16. Molestation of a child.

"17. Voluntary manslaughter.

"18. Aggravated assault.

"**G.** The department of education shall not issue or renew and may revoke certification of a person who has been convicted of any of the criminal offenses prescribed in subsection F of this section or of a similar offense in another jurisdiction. In considering whether to revoke the certification of a person pursuant to the provisions of this subsection, the state board of education shall hold a hearing on the matter in conjunction with the provisions of § 15–203, subsection A, paragraphs 21 and 27."

The 1995 amendment by Ch. 268 added subsec. H, allowing fingerprints to be submitted up to 18 months before the time of application for certification.

The 1996 amendment by Ch. 284, in subsec. F, deleted "and notarized" following "education" in the introductory paragraph.

The 1997 amendment by Ch. 231 deleted "Beginning January 1, 1990" from the beginning of the section; deleted former subsec. B; and redesignated former subsecs. C to H as B to G, accordingly. Prior to its deletion, subsec. B had read:

"**B.** The department of education may issue or renew certification prior to receiving the results of the fingerprint check but may revoke certification if the information on the form provided under subsection F of this section is inconsistent with the information received from the fingerprint check."

The 1998 amendment by Ch. 218 added subsec. H relating to conditional certification.

The 1998 amendment by Ch. 270 rewrote the section.

The amendment of this section by Laws 1998, Ch. 270, § 3 was repealed by Laws 1999, Ch. 316, § 4, effective August 17, 1999.

The 1999 amendment by Ch. 316 rewrote the section, which, as amended by Laws 1998, Ch. 218, had read:

"**A.** A person applying for a certificate as prescribed in § 15–203 shall be fingerprinted as a condition of certification. The employee's fingerprints and the form prescribed in subsection E of this section shall be submitted to the department of education at the time of application for certification. Applicants for renewal of any certificate shall not be required to be fingerprinted as a condition of renewal unless the school district requests the department of education to fingerprint the applicant. A person who already holds a certificate as provided in § 15–203 and who applies for additional certificates shall not be required to be fingerprinted.

"**B.** The department of education shall develop procedures for the fingerprinting of applicants for certification and renewal of any certificate.

"**C.** Fingerprint checks shall be conducted pursuant to § 41–1750, subsection G.

"**D.** The department of education shall assume the costs of fingerprint checks and may charge these costs to the fingerprinted applicant for certification. Any monies collected shall be deposited in the fingerprint revolving fund and shall be used to defray the costs incurred as a result of fingerprint checks. The department shall establish procedures for the expenditure of fund monies and the reimbursement of monies to the fund. The department of education fingerprint revolving fund shall be established as a separate account on the books of the department of education. Monies of the department of education fingerprint revolving fund shall not revert to the state general fund. If a school district requests that an applicant for renewal of any certificate be fingerprinted as provided in subsection A of this section, the department of education may charge these costs to the school district. The costs charged to a fingerprinted applicant are limited to the actual costs, including personnel costs, incurred as a result of the fingerprint checks.

"**E.** Applicants shall certify on forms that are provided by the department of education whether they are awaiting trial on or have ever been convicted of or admitted in open court or pursuant to a plea agreement committing any of the following criminal offenses in this state or similar offenses in another jurisdiction:

"1. Sexual abuse of a minor.

"2. Incest.

"3. First or second degree murder.

"4. Kidnapping.

"5. Arson.

"6. Sexual assault.

"7. Sexual exploitation of a minor.

"8. Felony offenses involving contributing to the delinquency of a minor.

"9. Commercial sexual exploitation of a minor.

"10. Felony offenses involving sale, distribution or transportation of, offer to sell, transport or distribute or conspiracy to sell, transport or distribute marijuana or dangerous or narcotic drugs.

"11. Felony offenses involving the possession or use of marijuana, dangerous drugs or narcotic drugs.

"12. Misdemeanor offenses involving the possession or use of marijuana or dangerous drugs.

"13. Burglary in the first degree.

"14. Burglary in the second or third degree.

"15. Aggravated or armed robbery.

"16. Robbery.

"17. A dangerous crime against children as defined in § 13–604.01.

"18. Child abuse.

"19. Sexual conduct with a minor.

"20. Molestation of a child.

"21. Voluntary manslaughter.

"22. Aggravated assault.

"23. Assault.

"24. Exploitation of minors involving drug offenses.

"**F.** The state board of education may review and may revoke, not issue or not renew the certificate of a person who has been convicted of or admitted in open court or pursuant to a plea agreement committing any of the criminal offenses prescribed in subsection E of this section or a similar offense in another jurisdiction. The board shall prescribe guidelines for the review process including a list of offenses that are not subject to review. In considering whether to revoke, not issue or not renew the certification of a person, the state board shall take into account the following factors:

"1. The nature of the crime and the potential for crimes against children.

"2. Offenses committed as a minor for which proceedings were held under the jurisdiction of a juvenile or adult court.

"3. Offenses that have been expunged by a court of competent jurisdiction, if the person has been pardoned or if the person's sentence has been commuted.

"4. The employment record of the person since the commission of the crime if the crime was committed more than ten years before the state board's review of the person's certification.

"5. The reliability of the evidence of an admission of a crime unless made under oath in a court of competent jurisdiction.

"**G.** Fingerprints may be submitted up to eighteen months before the time of application for certification.

"**H.** Until June 30, 1999, the department of education may issue conditional certification before receiving the results of the fingerprint check. The state board of education may revoke conditional certification if the information on the form provided under subsection E of this section is inconsistent with the information received from the fingerprint check. In addition to any other conditions or requirements deemed necessary by the superintendent of public instruction to protect the health and safety of pupils, conditional certification shall be issued before receiving the results of a fingerprint check if all of the following conditions are met:

"1. Until June 30, 1999, the school district that is seeking to hire the applicant verifies in writing on a form developed by the department of education the necessity for hiring and placement of the applicant before a fingerprint check is completed.

"2. Until June 30, 1999, the school district that is seeking to hire the applicant performs all of the following:

"(a) Ensures that the department of public safety completes a statewide criminal history information check on the applicant. A statewide criminal history information check shall be completed by the department of public safety every one hundred and twenty days until the date that the fingerprint check is completed.

"(b) Completes a search of criminal records in all local jurisdictions outside of this state in which the applicant has lived in the previous five years.

"(c) Obtain references from the applicant's current employer and two most recent previous employers except for applicants who have been employed for at least five years by the applicant's most recent employer.

"(d) Supervise the applicant until the applicant receives permanent certification from the department of education."

The 1999 amendment of this section by Ch. 316 explicitly amended the amendment of this section by Laws 1998, Ch. 218, § 2.

The 2000 amendment by Ch. 208 rewrote subsec. A, which had provided:

"**A.** A person applying for a certificate as prescribed in § 15–203 shall have a valid class one or class two fingerprint clearance card issued pursuant to title 41, chapter 12, article 3.1. Applicants for renewal of any certificate shall not be required to be fingerprinted as a condition of renewal unless the school district requests the department of education to fingerprint the applicant. A person who already holds a certificate as provided in § 15–203 and who applies for additional certificates shall not be required to be fingerprinted."

The 2000 amendment by Ch. 251 substituted, in two instances in subsec. E, par. 2, item (a), "Criminal history record information" for "criminal history information"; inserted subsec. F, requiring notification by the state board of education of arrests of, or falsifications by, certain fingerprint clearance card possessors; redesignated former subsec. F as subsec. G; and made nonsubstantive wording changes throughout.

The 2001 amendment by Ch. 241 rewrote the section, which had read:

"**A.** A person who applies for a certificate as prescribed in § 15-203 shall have a valid class one or class two fingerprint clearance card that is issued pursuant to title 41, chapter 12, article 3.1. Applicants for renewal of any certificate shall meet one of the following requirements:

"1. Have a valid class one or class two fingerprint clearance card issued pursuant to title 41, chapter 12, article 3.1.

"2. Provide proof of the submission of an application for a class one or class two fingerprint clearance card.

"3. Received a class one or class two fingerprint clearance card issued pursuant to title 41, chapter 12, article 3.1, for the purposes of certification by the state board of education.

"A person who already holds a certificate as provided in § 15-203 and who applies for additional certificates shall not be required to be fingerprinted.

"**B.** Applicants shall certify on forms that are provided by the department of education whether they are awaiting trial on or have ever been convicted of any of the following criminal offenses in this state or similar offenses in another state or jurisdiction:

"1. Sexual abuse of a minor.

"2. Incest.

"3. First or second degree murder.

"4. Kidnapping.

"5. Arson.

"6. Sexual assault.

"7. Sexual exploitation of a minor.

"8. Felony offenses involving contributing to the delinquency of a minor.

"9. Commercial sexual exploitation of a minor.

"10. Felony offenses involving sale, distribution or transportation of, offer to sell, transport or distribute or conspiracy to sell, transport or distribute marijuana, dangerous drugs or narcotic drugs.

"11. Felony offenses involving the possession or use of marijuana, dangerous drugs or narcotic drugs.

"12. Burglary.

"13. Aggravated or armed robbery.

"14. Robbery.

"15. A dangerous crime against children as defined in § 13-604.01.

"16. Child abuse.

"17. Sexual conduct with a minor.

"18. Molestation of a child.

"19. Manslaughter.

"20. Assault or aggravated assault.

"21. Exploitation of minors involving drug offenses.

"22. A violation of § 28-1381, 28-1382 or 28-1383.

"23. Offenses involving domestic violence.

"**C.** The state board of education may review, and may revoke, or not renew the certificate of a person who has been convicted of or admitted in open court or pursuant to a plea agreement committing any of the criminal offenses prescribed in subsection B of this section or a similar offense in another jurisdiction. The board shall prescribe guidelines for the review process including a list of offenses that are not subject to review. In considering whether to revoke or not renew the certification of a person, the state board shall take into account the following factors:

"1. The nature of the crime and the potential for crimes against children.

"2. Offenses that were committed as a minor and for which proceedings were held under the jurisdiction of a juvenile or adult court.

"3. Offenses that have been expunged by a court of competent jurisdiction, if the person has been pardoned or if the person's sentence has been commuted.

"4. The employment record of the person since the commission of the crime if the crime was committed more than ten years before the state board's review of the person's certification.

"5. The reliability of the evidence of an admission of a crime unless made under oath in a court of competent jurisdiction.

"**D.** Fingerprints may be submitted up to eighteen months before the time of application for certification.

"**E.** The department of education may issue conditional certification before an applicant has obtained a valid class one or class two fingerprint clearance card. The state board of education may revoke conditional certification if the information on the form provided under subsection B of this section is false or incomplete or the applicant is denied a class one or class two fingerprint clearance card. In addition to any other conditions or requirements deemed necessary by the superintendent of public instruction to protect the health and safety of pupils, conditional certification shall be issued before the applicant obtains a class one or class two fingerprint clearance card if all of the following conditions are met:

"1. The school district that is seeking to hire the applicant verifies in writing on a form developed by the department of education the necessity for hiring and placement of the applicant before a fingerprint check is completed.

"2. The school district that is seeking to hire the applicant performs all of the following:

"(a) Ensures that the department of public safety completes a statewide criminal history record information check on the applicant. A statewide criminal history record information check shall be completed by the department of public safety every one hundred twenty days until the date that the fingerprint check is completed.

"(b) Completes a search of criminal records in all local jurisdictions outside of this state in which the applicant has lived in the previous five years.

"(c) Obtains references from the applicant's current employer and two most recent previous employers except for applicants who have been employed for at least five years by the applicant's most recent employer.

"(d) Provides general supervision of the applicant until the applicant receives permanent certification from the department of education.

"**F.** The state board of education shall notify the department of public safety if the state board of education receives credible evidence that a person who possesses a valid class one or class two fingerprint clearance card either:

"1. Is arrested for or charged with an offense listed in § 41-1758.03, subsection B or F.

"2. Falsified information on the form required by subsection B of this section.

"**G.** A person who makes a false statement, representation or certification in any application for certification is guilty of a class 3 misdemeanor."

The 2003 amendment by Ch. 214, rewrote the section, which had read:

"**A.** A person who applies for a certificate as prescribed in § 15-203 shall have a valid class one or class two fingerprint clearance card that is issued pursuant to title 41, chapter 12, article 3.1. Applicants for renewal of any certificate shall meet one of the following requirements:

"1. Have a valid class one or class two fingerprint clearance card issued pursuant to title 41, chapter 12, article 3.1.

"2. Provide proof of the submission of an application for a class one or class two fingerprint clearance card.

"3. Have a class one or class two fingerprint clearance card issued pursuant to title 41, chapter 12, article 3.1, for the purposes of certification by the state board of education.

"**B.** A person who already holds a certificate as provided in § 15-203 and who applies for additional certificates shall not be required to be fingerprinted.

"**C.** The state board of education may review and determine whether to renew or not issue a certificate to an applicant for certification on a finding that the applicant engaged in conduct that is immoral or unprofessional or engaged in conduct that would warrant disciplinary action if the person had been certified at the time that the alleged conduct occurred. The board shall prescribe guidelines for this process.

"**D.** The state board of education may take disciplinary action against or not renew the certificate of a person on a finding that the certificated person engaged in conduct that is immoral or unprofessional or engaged in conduct that would warrant disciplinary action if the person had been certified at the time that the alleged conduct occurred. The board shall prescribe guidelines for this process.

"**E.** The department of education may issue conditional certification before an applicant has obtained a valid class one or class two fingerprint clearance card. The state board of education may revoke conditional certification if the information on the application for a conditional certificate is false or incomplete or the applicant is denied a class one or class two fingerprint clearance card. In addition to any other conditions or requirements deemed necessary by the superintendent of public instruction to protect the health and safety of pupils, conditional certification shall be issued before the applicant obtains a class one or class two fingerprint clearance card if all of the following conditions are met:

"1. The school district that is seeking to hire the applicant verifies in writing on a form developed by the department of education the necessity for hiring and placement of the applicant before a fingerprint check is completed.

"2. The school district that is seeking to hire the applicant performs all of the following:

"(a) Ensures that the department of public safety completes a statewide criminal history record information check on the applicant. A statewide criminal history record information check shall be completed by the department of public safety every one hundred twenty days until the date that the fingerprint check is completed.

"(b) Completes a search of criminal records in all local jurisdictions outside of this state in which the applicant has lived in the previous five years.

"(c) Obtains references from the applicant's current employer and two most recent previous employers except for applicants who have been employed for at least five years by the applicant's most recent employer.

"(d) Provides general supervision of the applicant until the applicant receives permanent certification from the department of education.

"**F.** The state board of education shall notify the department of public safety if the state board of education receives credible evidence that a person who possesses a valid class one or class two fingerprint clearance card either:

"1. Is arrested for or charged with an offense listed in § 41-1758.03, subsection B or F.

"2. Falsified information on the form required by subsection B of this section.

"**G.** A person who makes a false statement, representation or certification in any application for certification is guilty of a class 3 misdemeanor."

Former § 15-534, added by Laws 1981, Ch. 1, § 2, derived from Laws 1912, Ch. 77, § 94; Civ.Code 1913, § 2807; Rev.Code 1928, § 1043; Code 1939, § 54-1005; A.R.S. former § 15-234 and relating to certification as a prerequisite to warrant for salary was repealed by Laws 1984, Ch. 94, § 2.

Reviser's Notes:

1995 Note. Pursuant to authority of § 41-1304.02, in subsection H "eighteen" was substituted for "18" to correct a manifest clerical error.

1998 Note. The independent and valid amendment of this section by Laws 1998, Ch. 218, sec. 2 and Ch. 270, sec. 3 could not be blended because of the delayed effective date of Ch. 270.

2000 Note. Prior to the 2001 amendment, this section contained the amendments made by Laws 2000, Ch. 208, sec. 1 and Ch. 251, sec. 3 that were blended together pursuant to authority of § 41-1304.03.

2001 Note. Pursuant to authority of § 41-1304.02, in the section heading "review and disciplinary action" was substituted for "affidavit".

§ 15-534.01. Withdrawal of applications for administrative deficiencies; denial of applications for substantive deficiencies; certification timeframes

A. If an application for certification is administratively incomplete, as prescribed in title 41, chapter 6, article 7.1, [1] the department of education or the state board of education shall issue a written notice requesting the applicant to supply missing documents or other information. The department of education shall consider an application for certification withdrawn if, within sixty days after the date of the notice, the applicant does not supply the documentation or information requested or does not provide reasonable documented justification for the delay. On receipt of documented justification, the department of education shall provide an additional thirty days for the requested documentation or information to be provided before considering an application withdrawn.

B. If an application for certification is substantively incomplete, as prescribed in title 41, chapter 6, article 7.1, the department of education or the state board of education may issue a written notice requesting the applicant to supply additional documents or other information. The state board of education shall deny an application for certification if, within sixty days after the date of the notice, the applicant does not supply the documentation or information requested.

C. If the final day of a deadline imposed by this section falls on a Saturday, Sunday or other legal holiday, the next business day is the final day of the deadline.

D. A notice of denial of an application for certification issued by the state board of education pursuant to subsection B of this section shall comply with § 41-1076.

E. A person who has had an application for certification denied by the state board of education pursuant to subsection B of this section may file a written request for a hearing with the state board of education within fifteen days after receiving the notice of denial. The appeal shall be conducted in accordance with title 41, chapter 6, article 6.[2]

Added by Laws 2004, Ch. 198, § 1.

[1] Section 41-1072 et seq.

[2] Section 41-1061 et seq.

§ 15-534.02. Restrictions on applications for certification after the surrender, revocation or denial of certificate

A. A person shall not submit an application for certification with the state board of education for a period of five years if any of the following occurs:

1. The person surrenders a certificate issued by the state board of education.

2. The person's certificate is revoked by the state board of education on grounds of immoral or unprofessional conduct pursuant to rules adopted by the state board of education pursuant to § 15-203.

3. The person's application for certification is denied by the state board of education on grounds of immoral or unprofessional conduct pursuant to rules adopted by the state board of education pursuant to § 15-203. This paragraph does not apply to a person who, after denial of an application for certification, provides additional information that was not previously considered by the state board of education and that addresses the grounds on which the state board of education denied the application for certification.

B. The five year period prescribed in subsection A begins on the date that the state board of education accepts a surrendered certificate, makes a final decision to revoke a certificate or makes a final determination to deny an application for certification.

C. A person who has had a certificate revoked pursuant to § 15-550 is not eligible to apply for certification with the state board of education.

D. The department of education shall not process an application for certification submitted by a person who is prohibited from submitting an application pursuant to subsections a and c of this section.

Added by Laws 2004, Ch. 198, § 1.

§ 15-534.03. Service of documents; change of address notice requirement

A. Every notice or decision issued by the state board of education pertaining to the denial of an application for initial certification or renewal of a certificate or pertaining to disciplinary action against a certificated person shall be served by personal delivery or certified mail, return receipt requested, to the applicant or certificated person's last address of record with the department of education or by any other method that is reasonably calculated to give actual notice to the applicant or the certificated person.

B. Each applicant or certificated person shall inform the department of education of any change of address within thirty days of the change of address.

Added by Laws 2004, Ch. 198, § 1.

Historical and Statutory Notes

Reviser's Notes:

2004 Note. Pursuant to authority of § 41-1304.02, in the section heading "; change of address notice requirement" was added and the section was divided into subsections A and B with subsection A consisting of the first sentence and subsection B consisting of the second sentence.

§ 15-535. Sectarian instruction prohibited

A teacher who uses sectarian or denominational books or teaches any sectarian doctrine or conducts any religious exercises in school is guilty of unprofessional conduct and his certificate shall be revoked.

Added by Laws 1981, Ch. 1, § 2, eff. Jan. 23, 1981.

Historical and Statutory Notes

Source:

Laws 1912, Ch. 77, § 95.
Civ.Code 1913, § 2808.
Rev.Code 1928, § 1044.
Code 1939, § 54-1006.
A.R.S. former § 15-203.

§ 15-536. Offer of contract to certificated teacher who has not been employed more than three consecutive school years; acceptance; notice to teacher of intention not to reemploy

A. Subject to the provisions of §§ 15-539, 15-540, 15-541, 15-544 and 15-549, the governing board shall, between March 15 and May 15, offer a teaching contract for the next ensuing school year to each certificated teacher who has not been employed by the school district for more than the major portion of three consecutive school years and who is under a contract of employment with the school district for the current school year, unless, on or before April 15, the governing board, a member of the board acting on behalf of the board or the superintendent of the school district gives notice to the teacher of the board's intention not to offer a teaching contract, unless such teacher has been dismissed pursuant to § 15-538, 15-539, 15-541 or 15-544. The teacher's acceptance of the contract for the ensuing year must be indicated within thirty days from the date of the written contract or the offer is revoked. The teacher accepts the contract by signing the contract and returning it to the governing board or by making a written instrument which accepts the terms of the contract and delivering it to the governing board. If the written instrument includes terms in addition to the terms of the contract offered by the board, the teacher fails to accept the contract.

B. Notice of the board's intention not to reemploy the teacher shall be by delivering it personally to the teacher or by sending it by registered or certified mail bearing a postmark of on or before April 15, directed to the teacher at his place of residence as recorded in the school district records. The notice shall incorporate a statement of reasons for not reemploying the teacher. If the reasons are charges of inadequacy of classroom performance as defined by the governing board pursuant to § 15-539, subsection D, the board, or its authorized representative, shall, at least ninety days prior to such notice, give the teacher written preliminary notice of his inadequacy, specifying the nature of the inadequacy with such particularity as to furnish the teacher an opportunity to correct his inadequacies and overcome the grounds for such charge. The governing board may delegate to employees of the governing board the general authority to issue preliminary notices of inadequacy of classroom performance to teachers pursuant to this subsection without the need for prior approval of each notice by the governing board. In all cases in which an employee of the governing board issues a preliminary notice of inadequacy of classroom performance without prior approval by the governing board, the employee shall report its issuance to the governing board within five school days. The written notice of intention not to reemploy shall include a copy of any evaluation pertinent to the charges made and filed with the board.

C. Nothing in this section shall be construed so as to provide a certificated teacher who has not been employed by the school district for more than the major portion of three consecutive school years and who has received notice of the board's intention not to offer a teaching contract with the right to a hearing pursuant to the provisions of § 15-539, subsection G.

Added by Laws 1981, Ch. 1, § 2, eff. Jan. 23, 1981. Amended by Laws 1983, Ch. 281, § 6; Laws 1986, Ch. 103, § 1; Laws 1986, Ch. 399, § 7; Laws 1987, Ch. 202, § 2; Laws 1990, Ch. 123, § 2; Laws 2003, Ch. 64, § 1.

Historical and Statutory Notes

Source:

Laws 1949, Ch. 52, §§ 2, 9.
Code 1939, Supp.1952, §§ 54-1010, 54-1017.
A.R.S. former §§ 15-252, 15-259.
Laws 1960, Ch. 127, § 15.
Laws 1974, Ch. 60, § 1.
Laws 1977, Ch. 164, § 2.
Laws 1978, Ch. 168, § 1.

The 1983 amendment by Ch. 281 rewrote subsec. A, which had read:

"**A.** Subject to the provisions of §§ 15-539, 15-540, 15-544 and 15-549, the governing board shall, between March 15 and May 15, offer a teaching contract for the next ensuing school year to each probationary teacher and a contract renewal for each continuing teacher under a contract of employment with the school district for the current school year, unless, on or before April 15, the governing board, a member thereof acting on behalf of the board or the superintendent of the school district gives notice to the probationary teacher of the board's intention not to offer a teaching contract or a contract renewal in the case of a continuing teacher, unless such teacher has been dismissed pursuant to § 15-538, 15-539, 15-541 or 15-544. The probationary or continuing teacher's acceptance of the contract for the ensuing year must be indicated within thirty days after receipt of the contract or contract renewal by signing and returning the contract or contract renewal or by an acceptance in writing which is delivered to the governing board or the offer of contract or contract renewal is revoked.;"

deleted subsec. B, which had read:

"**B.** If dismissal proceedings in reference to a continuing teacher could not have been completed by April 15 through no fault of the governing board or superintendent, or if the incidents relied on in whole or in part occurred after April 15, dismissal proceedings may continue or be initiated.;"

relettered former subsecs. C and D as subsecs. B and C; and inserted "who has received notice of the board's intention not to offer a teaching contract", and substituted "subsection E" for "subsection D" in subsec. C.

The 1986 amendment by Ch. 103, § 1, modified the statutory reference in subsec. C.

The 1986 amendment by Ch. 399, § 1, substituted references to "certificated teacher" or "certificated teacher who has not been employed by the school district for more than the major portion of three consecutive school years" for "probationary teacher".

The 1987 amendment by Ch. 202 inserted the two sentences preceding the last sentence in subsec. B.

The 1990 amendment by Ch. 123 in subsec. C substituted "§ 15-539, subsection G" for "§ 15-539, subsection F".

The 2003 amendment by Ch. 64, in subsec. B, inserted "as defined by the governing board pursuant to § 15-539, subsection D" in the third sentence, and substituted "subsection" for "section" in the fourth sentence.

§ 15-537. Performance of certificated teachers; evaluation system

A. The governing board of a school district shall establish a system for the evaluation of the performance of certificated teachers in the school district.

The objectives of the teacher performance evaluation system are to improve instruction and maintain instructional strengths. The governing board shall involve its certificated teachers in the development and periodic evaluation of the teacher performance evaluation system.

B. The governing board shall prescribe specific procedures for the teacher performance evaluation system which shall include at least the following elements:

1. A reliable evaluation instrument including specific criteria for measuring effective teaching performance in each area of the teacher's classroom responsibility.

2. An assessment of the competencies of teachers as they relate to the specific criteria for measuring teacher performance prescribed in paragraph 1 of this subsection.

3. A specified minimum number and minimum duration of actual classroom observations of the certificated teacher demonstrating teaching skills by the persons evaluating the teacher.

4. Specific and reasonable plans for the improvement of teacher performance as provided in subsection F.

5. Appeal procedures for teachers who disagree with the evaluation of their performance, if the evaluation is for use as criteria for establishing compensation.

C. A regular evaluation of the performance of each certificated teacher as provided in this section shall be performed at least twice each year for a teacher who has not been employed by the school district for more than the major portion of three consecutive school years and at least once each year for a teacher who has been employed by the school district for more than the major portion of three consecutive school years. The governing board may provide for additional teacher performance evaluations as it deems necessary.

D. The governing board shall designate persons who are qualified to evaluate teachers to serve as evaluators for the district's teacher performance evaluation system. The governing board shall ensure that persons evaluating teachers are qualified to evaluate teachers.

E. An evaluation made as provided in this section shall be in writing, and a copy shall be transmitted to the certificated teacher within five days after completion of the evaluation. The certificated teacher may initiate a written reaction or response to the evaluation.

F. Each evaluation shall include recommendations as to areas of improvement in the performance of the certificated teacher if the performance of the teacher warrants improvement. After transmittal of an assessment a board designee shall confer with the teacher to make specific recommendations as to areas of improvement in the teacher's performance. The board designee shall provide assistance and opportunities for the certificated teacher to improve his performance and follow up with the teacher after a reasonable period of time for the purpose of ascertaining that the teacher is demonstrating adequate classroom performance.

G. Copies of the assessment and evaluation report of a certificated teacher retained by the governing board are confidential, do not constitute a public record and shall not be released or shown to any person except:

1. To the certificated teacher who may make any use of it.

2. To authorized district officers and employees for all personnel matters regarding employment and contracts and for any hearing which relates to personnel matters.

3. For introduction in evidence or discovery in any court action between the governing board and the certificated teacher in which either:

(a) The competency of the teacher is at issue.

(b) The assessment and evaluation were an exhibit at a hearing, the result of which is challenged.

Added by Laws 1983, Ch. 281, § 8. Amended by Laws 1984, Ch. 115, § 2, eff. April 13, 1984; Laws 1984, Ch. 297, § 1; Laws 1985, Ch. 268, § 1; Laws 1986, Ch. 399, § 8; Laws 1987, Ch. 303, § 1; Laws 1996, Ch. 284, § 26.

Historical and Statutory Notes

Source:

A.R.S. former § 15-268.
Laws 1974, Ch. 60, § 4.
A.R.S. former § 15-537.
Laws 1981, Ch. 1, § 2.
Laws 1981, Ch. 314, § 10.

The 1984 amendment by Ch. 115, § 2, eff. April 13, 1984, inserted "if the performance of the teacher warrants improvement" in subsec. F.

The 1984 amendment by Ch. 297, § 1 amended this section as amended by Laws 1984, Ch. 115, by substituting "involve" for "avail itself of the advice of", and "periodic evaluation" for "adoption" in subsec. A; inserting subd. 5 in subsec. B; and inserting "who are" preceding "qualified" in subsec. D.

The 1985 amendment by Ch. 268 substituted in subsec. B.3 "A specified minimum number and minimum duration of actual classroom observations" for "Actual classroom observation", and added the third sentence in subsec. D.

Laws 1985, Ch. 268, §§ 2 and 3 related to the distribution by the state board of education of recommended qualifications for persons evaluating teachers, to the duty of the superintendent of public instruction to seek input concerning the appropriate criteria to use in evaluating teaching skills and competencies, and to a study of teacher evaluation practices.

The 1986 amendment by Ch. 399 added the fourth sentence in subsec. A, and substituted in subsecs. C and H references to teachers employed more or less than the major portion of three consecutive years for reference to probationary and continuing teachers, respectively.

The 1987 amendment by Ch. 303 inserted in the second sentence of subsec. H "evidence that teachers were involved in the development of the teacher performance evaluation system".

The 1996 amendment by Ch. 284, in subsec. A, deleted the former fourth sentence, which had read, "The state board of education shall develop and distribute to governing boards recommended standards for an effective teacher performance evaluation system."; in subsec. D, deleted the former third sentence, which had read, "The state board of education shall develop and distribute to school districts recommended qualifications for persons evaluating teachers, including recommended training."; in subsec. E, made a nonsubstantive language change; and deleted former subsec. H, which had read:

"**H.** The governing board shall file with the department of education by July 1 of each year a report for the school year on the school district's teacher performance evaluation system. The report shall include a copy of the evaluation procedure for the teacher performance evaluation system, evidence that teachers were involved in the development of the teacher performance evaluation system, the number of teachers who have not been employed by the school district for more than the major portion of three consecutive school years and the number of teachers who have been employed by the school district for more than the major portion of three consecutive school years, the number of evaluations made for teachers who have not been employed by the school district for more than the major portion of three consecutive school years and for teachers who have been employed by the school district for more than the major portion of three consecutive school years, the number of certificated teachers who responded in writing to the governing board regarding their evaluation and general examples of recommendations as to areas of improvement in the performance of the teachers."

Former § 15–537 (see Source ante), added by Laws 1981, Ch. 1, § 2, amended by Laws 1981, Ch. 314, § 10, and relating to the same subject matter as this section, was repealed by Laws 1983, Ch. 281, § 7.

§ 15–538. Preliminary notice of inadequacy of classroom performance

A. The governing board of any school district shall give any certificated teacher who has not been employed by the school district for more than the major portion of three consecutive school years notice of intention to dismiss or not to reemploy if such intention is based on charges of inadequacy of classroom performance as defined by the governing board pursuant to § 15–539, subsection D. The governing board, or its authorized representative, shall, at least ninety days prior to such notice, give the teacher written preliminary notice of his inadequacy, specifying the nature thereof with such particularity as to furnish the teacher an opportunity to correct his inadequacies and overcome the grounds for such charge. The governing board may delegate to employees of the governing board the general authority to issue preliminary notices of inadequacy of classroom performance to teachers pursuant to this section without the need for prior approval of each notice by the governing board. In all cases in which an employee of the governing board issues a preliminary notice of inadequacy of classroom performance without prior approval by the governing board, the employee shall report its issuance to the governing board within five school days. The written notice of intention to dismiss or not to reemploy shall include a copy of any evaluation pertinent to the charges made and filed with the governing board.

B. If the preliminary notice required in subsection A of this section is issued as a result of an intention to dismiss, such preliminary notice shall be given at least ninety days prior to service of notice of the intention to dismiss. If the preliminary notice is issued as a result of an intention not to reemploy, such preliminary notice shall be given no later than January 15.

Added by Laws 1981, Ch. 1, § 2, eff. Jan. 23, 1981. Amended by Laws 1983, Ch. 281, § 9; Laws 1986, Ch. 399, § 9; Laws 1987, Ch. 202, § 3; Laws 2003, Ch. 64, § 2.

Historical and Statutory Notes

Source:

Laws 1974, Ch. 60, § 3.
A.R.S. former § 15–265.
Laws 1977, Ch. 164, § 6.

The 1983 amendment by Ch. 281, deleted "continuing or" preceding "probationary teacher" in the first sentence of subsec. A.

The 1986 amendment by Ch. 399 substituted in the first sentence of subsec. B "certificated teacher who has not been employed by the school district for more than the major portion of three consecutive school years" for "probationary teacher".

The 1987 amendment by Ch. 202 inserted the two sentences preceding the last sentence of subsec. A.

The 2003 amendment by Ch. 64, inserted "as defined by the governing board pursuant to § 15–539, subsection D" in subsec. A; and inserted "of this section" in subsec. B.

§ 15–538.01. Offer of contract to certificated teacher employed more than three consecutive school years

A. Subject to the provisions of §§ 15–539, 15–540, 15–541, 15–544 and 15–549, the governing board shall, between March 15 and May 15, offer to each certificated teacher who has been employed by the school district for more than the major portion of three consecutive school years and who is under contract of employment with the school district for the current year a contract renewal for the next ensuing school year unless on or before May 15 the governing board, a member of the school board acting on behalf of the board or the superintendent of the school district gives notice to the teacher of the board's intent not to offer a contract and to dismiss the teacher as provided in § 15–539.

B. The teacher's acceptance of the contract must be indicated within thirty days from the date of the written contract or the offer of a contract is revoked. The teacher accepts the contract by signing the contract and returning it to the governing board or by making a written instrument which accepts the terms of the contract and delivering it to the governing board. If the written instrument includes terms in addition to the terms of the contract offered by the board, the teacher fails to accept the contract.

C. If dismissal proceedings in reference to the teacher cannot be completed by May 15 through no fault of the governing board or the superintendent, or if the incidents relied on in whole or in part occurred after May 15, dismissal proceedings may continue or be initiated.

Added by Laws 1983, Ch. 281, § 10. Amended by Laws 1984, Ch. 115, § 3, eff. April 13, 1984; Laws 1986, Ch. 399, § 10.

Historical and Statutory Notes

The 1984 amendment by Ch. 115 rewrote subsec. A, which had read:

"**A.** Subject to the provisions of §§ 15–539, 15–540, 15–541, 15–544 and 15–549, the governing board shall, between March 15 and May 15, offer a continuing teacher a contract for two years unless on or before May 15 the governing board, a member of the board acting on behalf of the board or the superintendent of the school district gives notice to the continuing teacher of the board's intent not to offer a contract and to dismiss the teacher as provided in § 15–539. Except for contracts offered in 1984, the governing board shall offer a continuing teacher a contract for two years as provided in this section at the end of the first year of the teacher's existing two year contract. If agreed upon by the parties, the new two year contract shall replace the second year of the existing two year contract.";

deleted former subsec. B, which read:

"**B.** Each contract offered pursuant to subsection A of this section shall contain provisions authorizing the governing board to terminate the second year of a two year contract and not offer a new two year contract which would replace the second year of the existing two year contract if the board determines that reduction of salaries or personnel are necessary pursuant to the provisions of § 15–544.";

and redesignated subsecs. C and D as subsecs. B and C.

Laws 1984, Ch. 115, § 5, effective April 13, 1984, related to the rescission by school district governing boards of two-year contracts offered to continuing teachers between March 15, 1984 and April 13, 1984.

The 1986 amendment by Ch. 399 substituted references to "certificated teacher who has been employed by the school district for more than the major portion of three consecutive school years" or "teacher" for "continuing teacher".

§ 15–539. Dismissal of certificated teacher; due process; written charges; notice; hearing on request

A. Upon a written statement of charges presented by the superintendent, charging that there exists cause for the suspension without pay for a period of time greater than ten school days or dismissal of a certificated teacher of the district, the governing board shall, except as otherwise provided in this article, give notice to the teacher of its intention to suspend without pay or dismiss the teacher at the expiration of thirty days from the date of the service of the notice.

B. Whenever the superintendent presents a statement of charges wherein the alleged cause for dismissal constitutes immoral or unprofessional conduct, the governing board may adopt a resolution that a complaint be filed with the department of education. Pending disciplinary action by the state board of education, the certificated teacher may be reassigned by the superintendent or placed on administrative leave by the board pursuant to § 15-540.

C. The governing board shall give a certificated teacher who has been employed by the school district for more than the major portion of three consecutive school years notice of intention to dismiss if its intention to dismiss is based on charges of inadequacy of classroom performance as defined by the governing board pursuant to subsection D of this section. The governing board or its authorized representative shall give the teacher a written preliminary notice of inadequacy of classroom performance at least ten instructional days prior to the start of the period of time within which to correct the inadequacy and overcome the grounds for the charge. The governing board may delegate to employees of the governing board the general authority to issue preliminary notices of inadequacy of classroom performance to teachers pursuant to this section without the need for prior approval of each notice by the governing board. In all cases in which an employee of the governing board issues a preliminary notice of inadequacy of classroom performance without prior approval by the governing board, the employee shall report its issuance to the governing board within five school days. The written preliminary notice of inadequacy of classroom performance shall specify the nature of the inadequacy of classroom performance with such particularity as to furnish the teacher an opportunity to correct the teacher's inadequacies and overcome the grounds for the charge. The written preliminary notice of inadequacy of classroom performance shall be based on a valid evaluation according to school district procedure, shall include a copy of any evaluation pertinent to the charges made and shall state the date by which the teacher has to correct the inadequacy and overcome the grounds for the charge. That evaluation shall not be conducted within two instructional days of any school break of one week or more. The written preliminary notice of inadequacy of classroom performance shall allow the teacher not less than eighty-five instructional days within which to correct the inadequacy and overcome the grounds for the charge. If within the time specified in the written preliminary notice of inadequacy of classroom performance the teacher does not demonstrate adequate classroom performance, the governing board shall dismiss the teacher either within thirty days of the service of a subsequent notice of intention to dismiss or by the end of the contract year in which the subsequent notice of intention to dismiss is served unless the teacher has requested a hearing as provided in subsection G of this section. If the teacher demonstrates adequate classroom performance during the period allowed to correct such deficiencies as specified in the written preliminary notice of inadequacy of classroom performance, the governing board may not dismiss the teacher for the reasons specified in the written preliminary notice of inadequacy of classroom performance. If the governing board of a school district has received approval to budget for a career ladder program, the governing board may define inadequacy of classroom performance by establishing a single level of performance which is required of all teachers or by establishing more than one required level of performance. If more than one level is established, the same level of performance for minimum adequacy shall be required of all teachers who have completed the same number of years of teaching in the district.

D. The governing board shall develop a definition of inadequacy of classroom performance that applies to notices issued pursuant to § 15-536, § 15-538 and this section. The governing board shall develop its definition of inadequacy of classroom performance in consultation with its certificated teachers. The consultation may be accomplished by holding a public hearing, forming an advisory committee, providing teachers the opportunity to respond to a proposed definition or obtaining teacher approval of a career ladder program which defines inadequacy of classroom performance.

E. Any written statement of charges alleging unprofessional conduct, conduct in violation of the rules or policies of the governing board or inadequacy of classroom performance shall specify instances of behavior and the acts or omissions constituting the charge so that the certificated teacher will be able to prepare a defense. If applicable, it shall state the statutes, rules or written objectives of the governing board which the certificated teacher is alleged to have violated and set forth the facts relevant to each occasion of alleged unprofessional conduct, conduct in violation of the rules or policies of the governing board or inadequacy of classroom performance.

F. The notice shall be in writing and shall be served upon the certificated teacher personally or by United States registered or certified mail addressed to the teacher's last known address. A copy of the charges, together with a copy of this section and §§ 15-501, 15-538.01, 15-540, 15-541, 15-542 and 15-544 through 15-547 shall be attached to the notice.

G. The certificated teacher who receives notice that there exists cause for dismissal or suspension without pay shall have the right to a hearing if the teacher files a written request with the governing board within thirty days of service of notice. The filing of a timely request shall suspend the imposition of a suspension without pay or a dismissal pending completion of the hearing.
Added by Laws 1981, Ch. 1, § 2, eff. Jan. 23, 1981. Amended by Laws 1983, Ch. 281, § 11; Laws 1984, Ch. 115, § 4, eff. April 13, 1984; Laws 1986, Ch. 103, § 2; Laws 1986, Ch. 399, § 11; Laws 1987, Ch. 202, § 4; Laws 1988, Ch. 148, § 2; Laws 1990, Ch. 123, § 3; Laws 1994, Ch. 165, § 5; Laws 1995, Ch. 108, § 2; Laws 1996, Ch. 165, § 1; Laws 1996, Ch. 284, § 27; Laws 1998, Ch. 169, § 2; Laws 2003, Ch. 64, § 3.

Historical and Statutory Notes

Source:

Laws 1974, Ch. 60, § 3.
A.R.S. former § 15-253.
Laws 1977, Ch. 164, § 3.

The 1983 amendment by Ch. 281 substituted "suspension without pay or dismissal of a probationary or continuing teacher" for "dismissal of a continuing teacher", deleted "continuing" following "give notice to the", and inserted "suspend him without pay or" in subsec. A; inserted a new subsec. B; relettered former subsecs. B to D as subsecs. C to E; inserted "conduct in violation of the rules, regulations or policies of the governing board" in the first and second sentences of subsec. C; substituted "this section and §§ 15-501, 15-538.01, 15-540 through 15-542, 15-544 through 15-547 and 15-549" for "§§ 15-501, 15-536, 15-538 through 15-547 and 15-549" in subsec. C; and inserted "who receives notice that there exists cause for dismissal or suspension without pay" in the first sentence, and substituted "imposition of any disciplinary action" for "dismissal procedure" in the second sentence of subsec. E.

The 1984 amendment by Ch. 115 rewrote subsec. B, which had read:

"**B.** If the governing board gives a continuing teacher notice of intention to dismiss based on charges of inadequacy of classroom performance, the governing board or its authorized representative shall give the continuing teacher a written preliminary notice by May 15. The notice shall specify the nature of the inadequacy of classroom performance with such particularity as to furnish the teacher an opportunity to correct his inadequacies and overcome the grounds for the charge. The written notice of intention to dismiss or not renew a contract shall include a copy of any evaluation pertinent to the charges made and filed with the governing board. If the teacher does not demonstrate adequate classroom performance by February 1, the governing board shall dismiss the teacher at the end of the contract year. If the teacher demonstrates adequate classroom performance by February 1, the governing board shall offer the teacher a two year contract.";

and substituted "a suspension without pay or a dismissal" for "any disciplinary action" in subsec. E.

The 1986 amendments by Chs. 103 and 399 substantially rewrote this section which, as amended in 1984, provided:

"**A.** Upon a written statement of charges formulated by the governing board, charging that there exists cause for the suspension without pay or dismissal of a probationary or continuing teacher of the district, the governing board shall, except as otherwise provided in this article, give notice to the teacher of its intention to suspend him without pay or dismiss him at the expiration of thirty days from the date of the service of the notice.

"**B.** If the governing board intends to dismiss a continuing teacher based on charges of inadequacy of classroom performance, the governing board or its authorized representative shall give the continuing teacher a written preliminary notice by May 15. The written preliminary notice shall specify the nature of the inadequacy of classroom performance with such particularity as to furnish the teacher an opportunity to correct his inadequacies and overcome the grounds for the charge. The written preliminary notice of intention to dismiss shall include a copy of any evaluation pertinent to the charges made and filed with the governing board and state the date by which the teacher has to correct the inadequacy and overcome the grounds for the charge. The written preliminary notice shall allow the teacher one summer vacation period to obtain additional education if the teacher so desires and one full semester of teaching time subsequent to the opportunity for additional education within which to correct the inadequacy and overcome the grounds for the charge. If within the time specified in the written preliminary notice of intention to dismiss the teacher does not demonstrate adequate classroom performance, the governing board shall dismiss the teacher either within thirty days of the service of a subsequent notice of intention to dismiss or by the end of the contract year in which the subsequent notice of intention to dismiss is served unless the teacher has requested a hearing as provided in subsection E of this section. If the teacher demonstrates adequate classroom performance during the period allowed to correct such deficiencies as specified in the written preliminary notice, the governing board may not dismiss the teacher for the reasons specified in the written preliminary notice.

"**C.** Any written statement of charges alleging unprofessional conduct, conduct in violation of the rules, regulations or policies of the governing board or inadequacy of classroom performance shall specify instances of behavior and the acts or omissions constituting the charge so that the teacher will be able to prepare a defense. It shall, if applicable, state the statutes, rules or written objectives of the governing board which the teacher is alleged to have violated and set forth the facts relevant to each occasion of alleged unprofessional conduct, conduct in violation of the rules, regulations or policies of the governing board or inadequacy of classroom performance.

"**D.** The notice shall be in writing and be served upon the teacher personally or by United States registered or certified mail addressed to him at his last known address. A copy of the charges, together with a copy of this section and §§ 15-501, 15-538.01, 15-540 through 15-542, 15-544 through 15-547 and 15-549 shall be attached to the notice.

"**E.** The teacher who receives notice that there exists cause for dismissal or suspension without pay shall have the right to a hearing if he files a written request with the governing board within thirty days of service of notice. The filing of a timely request shall suspend the imposition of a suspension without pay or a dismissal pending completion of the hearing."

The 1987 amendment by Ch. 202 to subsec. B substituted references throughout to "notice of inadequacy of classroom performance" for "notice of intention to dismiss" and inserted provisions constituting the third and fourth sentences.

The 1988 amendment by Ch. 148 substituted "adopted" for "formulated" in subsec. A.

The 1990 amendment by Ch. 123 , in subsec. A, substituted "presented by the superintendent" for "adopted by the governing board"; inserted subsec. B; and redesignated former subsecs. B, C, D, E, and F as C, D, E, F, and G.

The 1994 amendment by Ch. 165 in subsec. B deleted "authorizing" following "resolution", and substituted "department" for "state board" of education, and "15-540" for "13-540"; substituted reference to subsection "G" for "F" in the introductory paragraph of subsec. C; and, in subsec. E deleted "regulations" from the phrase "rules, regulations or policies" in two instances.

The 1995 amendment by Ch. 108 inserted ", unless another time frame has been adopted by the state board of education for qualified schools pursuant to § 15-203, subsection A, paragraph 34" in subsec. C; and made gender related changes throughout.

The 1996 amendment by Ch. 165, in subsec. C, substituted "at least ten instructional days prior to the start of the period of time within which to correct the inadequacy and overcome the grounds for the charge" for "by the preceding May 15" at the end of the second sentence, inserted "be based on a valid evaluation according to school district procedure and shall" following "performance shall" in the sixth sentence, inserted the seventh sentence, prohibiting evaluations within two instructional days of certain school breaks, substituted "one full semester of teaching time, or an equivalent period of instructional days specified by the state board of education pursuant to § 15-203 to accommodate teachers who are employed in year-round school year operation programs or other schools that do not use a traditional school year calendar, within which to correct the inadequacy and overcome the grounds for the charge" for "one summer vacation period to obtain additional education if the teacher so desires and one full semester of teaching time subsequent to the opportunity for additional education within which to correct the inadequacy and overcome the grounds for the charge, unless another time frame has been adopted by the state board of education for qualified schools pursuant to § 15-203, subsection A, paragraph 34" at the end of the eighth sentence, deleted "the following restrictions shall apply:" following "established,", deleted the former paragraph designations, deleted former par. 1, and added former par. 2 to the end of the last sentence. Former par. 1 of subsec. C, had read:

"1. The governing board may require increased levels of performance only during the first six years of teaching in the school district. A single level of performance to demonstrate minimum adequacy shall be required of teachers who have taught for seven or more years in the district."

The 1996 amendment by Ch. 284, in subsec. C, substituted a reference to § 15-203 for a reference to § 15-203, subsec. A, par. 34 in the seventh sentence.

The 1998 amendment by Ch. 169 changed the number of days allowed for written preliminary notice of inadequacy of class room performance from "one full semester of teaching time, or an equivalent period of instructional days specified by the state board of education pursuant to § 15-203 to accommodate teachers who are employed in year round school year operation programs or other schools that do not use a traditional school year calendar," to "not less than eighty-five instructional days" in subsec. B.

The 2003 amendment by Ch. 64, inserted "pursuant to subsection D of this section" in the first sentence of subsec. C; inserted the first sentence of subsec. D; and made other nonsubstantive changes.

Reviser's Notes:

1996 Note. Prior to the 1998 amendment, this section contained the amendments made by Laws 1996, Ch. 165, sec. 1 and Ch. 284, sec. 27 that were blended together pursuant to authority of § 41-1304.03.

§ 15-540. Suspension prior to dismissal of a certificated teacher; written charges; salary

A. Upon a written statement of charges adopted by the governing board charging a certificated teacher of the school district with cause for suspension without pay or dismissal, the governing board may immediately place the teacher on administrative leave of absence and give him notice of the administrative leave of absence.

B. The notice of administrative leave of absence shall be in writing and be served upon the teacher personally or by United States registered mail addressed to the teacher at his last known address.

C. Any teacher who is placed on administrative leave of absence pursuant to this section shall continue to be paid regular salary during the period of administrative leave of absence.

Added by Laws 1981, Ch. 1, § 2, eff. Jan. 23, 1981. Amended by Laws 1983, Ch. 281, § 12; Laws 1986, Ch. 399, § 12; Laws 1988, Ch. 148, § 3.

Historical and Statutory Notes

Source:

Laws 1949, Ch. 52, § 6.
Code 1939, Supp.1952, § 54-1014.
A.R.S. former §§ 15-254, 15-256.
Laws 1974, Ch. 60, § 3.

The 1983 amendment by Ch. 281 rewrote subsec. A, which had read:

"**A.** Upon a written statement of charges formulated by the governing board, charging a teacher of the school district with cause for dismissal, the governing board may immediately suspend the teacher from his duties and give him notice of suspension.";

substituted "administrative leave of absence" for "suspension" in subsec. B and C; and substituted "placed on "administrative leave of absence" for "suspended" and for "suspension" in subsec. C.

The 1986 amendment by Ch. 399 substituted "certificated" for "probationary or continuing" teacher in subsec. A.

The 1988 amendment by Ch. 148 substituted "adopted" for "formulated" in subsec. A.

§ 15-541. Hearing on dismissal

A. The governing board shall decide whether to hold a hearing on the dismissal or suspension without pay for a period of time longer than ten days of a certificated teacher as provided in this article. If the governing board decides not to hold a hearing, the governing board shall designate a hearing officer to hold the hearing, hear the evidence, prepare a record and issue a recommendation to the governing board for action. The governing board may provide by policy or vote at its annual organizational meeting that all hearings conducted pursuant to this section will be conducted before a hearing officer. The hearing officer will be mutually agreed upon by the parties to the hearing. If the parties cannot mutually agree on a hearing officer, a hearing officer will be selected by the governing board from a list provided by the department of education or the American Arbitration Association. The hearing shall be held not less than ten nor more than twenty-five days after the request is filed unless all parties to the hearing mutually agree to a different hearing date, and notice of the time and place of the hearing shall be given to the teacher not less than three days before the date of the hearing. The teacher may request that the hearing be conducted in public or private. At the hearing the teacher may appear in person and by counsel, if desired, and may present any testimony, evidence or statements, either oral or in writing, in the teacher's behalf. The governing board or the hearing officer shall prepare an official record of the hearing, including all testimony recorded manually or by mechanical device, and exhibits. The teacher who is the subject of the hearing may not request that the testimony be transcribed unless the teacher agrees in writing to pay the actual cost of the transcription. Within ten days after a hearing conducted by the governing board, the board shall determine whether there existed good and just cause for the notice of dismissal or suspension and shall render its decision accordingly, either affirming or withdrawing the notice of dismissal or suspension. Within ten days after a hearing conducted by a hearing officer, the hearing officer shall deliver a written recommendation to the governing board that includes findings of fact and conclusions. Parties to the hearing have the right to object to the findings of the hearing officer and present oral and written arguments to the governing board.

B. A hearing held pursuant to this section may not be conducted by any hearing officer having a personal interest which would conflict with his or her objectivity in the hearing. The governing board has an additional ten days to determine whether good and just cause existed for the notice of dismissal or suspension and shall render its decision accordingly, either affirming or withdrawing the notice of suspension or dismissal. Good and just cause does not include religious or political beliefs or affiliations unless they are in violation of the oath of the teacher.

Added by Laws 1983, Ch. 281, § 14. Amended by Laws 1986, Ch. 399, § 13; Laws 1996, Ch. 165, § 2.

Historical and Statutory Notes

Source:

Laws 1974, Ch. 60, § 3.
A.R.S. former §§ 15-262, 15-541.
Laws 1981, Ch. 1, § 2.
Laws 1983, Ch. 98, § 15.

The 1986 by Ch. 399 amendment inserted "certificated" preceding "teacher" in the first sentence and deleted "termination" preceding "or suspension" in the next to last sentence.

The 1996 amendment by Ch. 165, rewrote the section, which formerly read:

"The governing board shall hold a hearing on the dismissal or suspension of a certificated teacher as provided in this article not less than ten nor more than twenty-five days after the request is filed, and notice of the time and place of the hearing shall be given to the teacher not less than three days before the date of the hearing. The teacher may request a public or private hearing before the board. At the hearing the teacher may appear in person and by counsel, if desired, and may present any testimony, evidence or statements, either oral or in writing, in his behalf. The governing board shall prepare an official record of the hearing, including all testimony recorded manually or by mechanical device, and exhibits, but the board shall not be required to transcribe the record unless requested by the teacher, who shall be furnished with a complete transcript upon the payment of the actual cost. Within ten days following the hearing the board shall determine whether there existed good and just cause for the notice of dismissal or suspension and shall render its decision accordingly, either affirming or withdrawing the notice of dismissal or suspension. Good and just cause does not include religious or political beliefs or affiliations unless they are in violation of the oath of the teacher."

Former § 15-541, derived from Laws 1974, Ch. 60, § 3; Laws 1981, Ch. 1, § 2; and Laws 1983, Ch. 98, § 15, and relating to the same subject matter as this section, was repealed by Laws 1983, Ch. 281, § 13.

§ 15-542. Hearing costs; counsel; limitations on evidence; reinstatement

A. The governing board shall pay all expenses of the hearing. The certificated teacher and the governing board shall pay their own attorney and witness fees, except if the governing board does not suspend the teacher without pay or dismiss the teacher, the governing board shall pay all reasonable attorney and witness fees incurred by the teacher.

B. No witness shall be permitted to testify at the hearing except upon oath or affirmation. No testimony shall be given or evidence introduced relating to adequacy of classroom performance which occurred more than four years prior to the date of the service of the notice. Evidence of records regularly kept by the governing board concerning the teacher may be introduced, but no decision relating to the suspension without pay or dismissal of any teacher shall be made based on charges or evidence relating to adequacy of classroom performance occurring more than four years prior to service of the notice. The four-year time limit shall not apply to the introduction of evidence in any area except that relating to adequacy of classroom performance.

C. If a certificated teacher who has been employed by the school district for more than the major portion of three consecutive school years is placed on administrative leave of absence pending the hearing, he shall be reinstated within five days after the governing board renders a decision not to suspend him without pay or dismiss him.

Added by Laws 1981, Ch. 1, § 2, eff. Jan. 23, 1981. Amended by Laws 1983, Ch. 281, § 15; Laws 1986, Ch. 399, § 14.

Historical and Statutory Notes

Source:

Laws 1974, Ch. 60, § 3.
A.R.S. former § 15-263.
Laws 1977, Ch. 164, § 4.

The 1983 amendment by Ch. 281 substituted "if the governing board does not suspend the teacher without pay or dismiss the teacher," for "if the commission recommends that the teacher not be dismissed," in the second sentence of subsec. A; deleted subsecs. B and C, which had read:

"**B.** Members of the commission shall not be compensated but are eligible for reimbursement, from the school district, of expenses as authorized for state employees under title 38, chapter 4, article 2. [Section 38-621 et seq.]

"**C.** The governing board and the teacher have the right to be represented by counsel at any hearing under this section.";

relettered former subsecs. D and E as subsecs. B and C; substituted "suspension without pay or dismissal" for "dismissal or suspension" in the third sentence of subsec. B; and substituted "placed on administrative leave of absence" for "suspended", and substituted "suspend him without pay or dismiss him" for "dismiss" in subsec. C.

The 1986 amendment by Ch. 399 inserted "certificated" preceding "teacher" in the second sentence of subsec. A, in subsec. C substituted references to teachers who have been employed "by the school district for more than the major portion of three consecutive school years" for references to continuing teachers, and substituted "adequacy of classroom performance" for "teacher adequacy" twice in subsec. B

§ 15-543. Appeal from decision of board

A. The decision of the governing board is final unless the certificated teacher files, within thirty days after the date of the decision, an appeal with the superior court in the county within which he was employed.

B. The decision of the governing board may be reviewed by the court in the same manner as the decision made in accordance with the provisions of § 41-785. The proceeding shall be set for hearing at the earliest possible date and shall take precedence over all other cases, except older matters of the same character and matters to which special precedence is otherwise given by law.

Added by Laws 1983, Ch. 281, § 17. Amended by Laws 1986, Ch. 399, § 15.

Historical and Statutory Notes

Source:

Laws 1912, Ch. 77, § 93.
Civ.Code 1913, § 2806.
Rev.Code 1928, § 1042.
Code 1939, § 54-1004.
A.R.S. former §§ 15-209, 15-264, 15-543.
Laws 1974, Ch. 60, § 3.
Laws 1981, Ch. 1, § 2.

The 1986 amendment by Ch. 399 inserted "certificated" preceding "teacher" in subsec. A.

Former § 15-543 (for derivation, see Source note, ante), relating to the same subject matter as this section, was repealed by Laws 1983, Ch. 281, § 16.

§ 15-544. Limitations on reduction of salaries or personnel

A. A governing board may reduce salaries or eliminate certificated teachers in a school district in order to effectuate economies in the operation of the district or to improve the efficient conduct and administration of the schools of the school district, but no reduction in the salary of a certificated teacher who has been employed by the school district for more than the major portion of three consecutive school years shall be made except in accordance with a general salary reduction in the school district by which the teacher is employed, and in such case the reduction shall be applied equitably among all such teachers.

B. Notice of a general salary reduction shall be given each certificated teacher affected not later than May 15 before the fiscal year in which the reduction is to take effect.

C. A certificated teacher dismissed for reasons of economy or to improve the efficient conduct and administration of the schools of the school district shall have a preferred right of reappointment in the order of original employment by the governing board in the event of an increase in the number of certificated teachers or the reestablishment of services within a period of three years.

D. The provisions of this section do not apply to reductions in salary from monies from the classroom site fund pursuant to § 15–977.

Added by Laws 1981, Ch. 1, § 2, eff. Jan. 23, 1981. Amended by Laws 1986, Ch. 399, § 16; Laws 2004, Ch. 243, § 1.

Historical and Statutory Notes

Source:

Laws 1949, Ch. 52, § 7.
Code 1939, Supp.1952, § 54–1015.
A.R.S. former § 15–257.

The 1986 amendment by Ch. 399 rewrote this section which, prior thereto, provided:

"Nothing in this article shall be interpreted to prevent a governing board from reducing salaries or eliminating teachers in a school district in order to effectuate economies in the operation of the district or to improve the efficient conduct and administration of the schools of the school district, but no reduction in the salary of a continuing teacher shall be made except in accordance with a general salary reduction in the school district by which he is employed, and in such case the reduction shall be applied equitably among all such teachers. Notice of a general salary reduction shall be given each teacher affected not later than May 1 of the calendar year in which the reduction is to take effect. A teacher dismissed for reasons of economy or lack of pupils shall have a preferred right of reappointment in the order of original employment by the governing board in the event of an increase in the number of teachers or the reestablishment of services within a period of three years."

The 2004 amendment by Ch. 243 made a nonsubstantive change in subsec. A; added new subsec. D; and rewrote subsec. B, which had read:

"**B.** Notice of a general salary reduction shall be given each certificated teacher affected not later than May 1 of the calendar year in which the reduction is to take effect."

§ 15–545. Resignation restrictions; unprofessional act; penalty

A certificated teacher shall not resign after signing and returning his contract, unless the resignation is first approved by the governing board. A teacher who resigns contrary to this section shall be deemed to commit an unprofessional act and, upon request of the governing board, shall be subject to such disciplinary action, including suspension or revocation of certificate, as the state board of education deems appropriate.

Added by Laws 1981, Ch. 1, § 2, eff. Jan. 23, 1981. Amended by Laws 1986, Ch. 399, § 17.

Historical and Statutory Notes

Source:

Laws 1949, Ch. 52, § 8.
Code 1939, Supp.1952, § 54–1016.
A.R.S. former § 15–258.
Laws 1960, Ch. 127, § 16.

The 1986 amendment by Ch. 399 substituted "certificated" for "probationary or continuing" preceding "teacher" in the first sentence.

§ 15–546. Rights in employment not vested

The provisions of this article may be modified, amended or repealed at any time and no person shall be deemed to have acquired any vested right to continuing employment under or by virtue of any provision of this article.

Added by Laws 1981, Ch. 1, § 2, eff. Jan. 23, 1981.

Historical and Statutory Notes

Source:

Laws 1949, Ch. 52, § 10.
Code 1939, Supp.1952, § 54-1018.
A.R.S. former § 15-260.

§ 15-547. Preservation of years of employment

The years of employment of a certificated teacher who has been employed by a school district for more than the major portion of three consecutive school years shall be preserved if such teacher transfers from a common school district to a high school district or from a high school district to a common school district if the governing board recognizes the previously established years of employment of the transferred teacher, provided such districts have coterminous boundaries and have a common governing board.

Added by Laws 1981, Ch. 1, § 2, eff. Jan. 23, 1981. Amended by Laws 1986, Ch. 399, § 18.

Historical and Statutory Notes

Source:

Laws 1965, Ch. 74, § 3.
A.R.S. former § 15-261.

The 1986 amendment by Ch. 399 substituted references to teachers who have been employed "by the school district for more than the major portion of three consecutive school years" for references to continuing teachers and substituted "years of employment" for "tenure" in two instances.

§ 15-548. Renumbered as § 15-510

§ 15-549. Compulsory leaves of absence for criminal charges; continued salary

A. If any certificated teacher is charged by criminal complaint, information or indictment with any criminal offense which would be deemed cause for dismissal, the governing board may immediately place the teacher on compulsory leave of absence for a period of time extending for not more than ten days after the date of the entry of the judgment in the proceedings.

B. Any teacher placed upon compulsory leave of absence pursuant to this section shall continue to be paid regular salary during the period of compulsory leave of absence.

Added by Laws 1981, Ch. 1, § 2, eff. Jan. 23, 1981.

Historical and Statutory Notes

Source:

Laws 1974, Ch. 60, § 3.
A.R.S. former § 15-255.

§ 15-550. Conviction as unprofessional conduct; penalty

A. A teacher who has been convicted of a dangerous crime against children as defined in § 13-604.01 or has been convicted of a violation of § 13-1404 or 13-1406 in which the victim was a minor or § 13-1405 or an act committed in another state or territory which if committed in this state would have been a dangerous crime against children or a violation of § 13-1404 in which the victim was a minor or a violation of § 13-1405 or 13-1406 is guilty of unprofessional conduct and the teacher's certificate shall be revoked permanently immediately on notification of conviction by the clerk of the court or the magistrate.

B. A teacher who has been convicted of a preparatory offense as prescribed in § 13-1001 of any of the offenses prescribed in subsection A of this section or any crime that requires the teacher to register as a sex offender is guilty of unprofessional conduct and the teacher's certificate shall be permanently revoked on notification of the conviction by a court of competent jurisdiction.

Added by Laws 1981, Ch. 1, § 2, eff. Jan. 23, 1981. Amended by Laws 1986, Ch. 58, § 3; Laws 1988, Ch. 243, § 1; Laws 2001, Ch. 241, § 5.

Historical and Statutory Notes

Source:

Laws 1912, Ch. 77, § 95.
Civ.Code 1913, § 2808.
Rev.Code 1928, § 1044.
Code 1939, § 54-1006.
A.R.S. former § 15-208.

The 1986 amendment by Ch. 58 substituted statutory reference to § 15-510 for § 15-548 in provisions now comprising subsec. A.

The 1988 amendment by Ch. 243 designated subsections; and added the provisions constituting subsec. B.

The 2001 amendment by Ch. 241 rewrote the section, which had read:

"**A.** A teacher who fails to comply with this article, except §§ 15-531 and 15-510, is guilty of unprofessional conduct and his certificate shall be revoked.

"**B.** A teacher who has been convicted of a dangerous crime against children as defined in § 13-604.01 or has been convicted of a violation of § 13-1404 or 13-1406 in which the victim was a minor or § 13-1405 or an act if committed in another state or territory which if committed in this state would have been a dangerous crime against children or a violation of § 13-1404 in which the victim was a minor or a violation of § 13-1405 or 13-1406 is guilty of unprofessional conduct and the teacher's certificate shall be revoked permanently immediately on notification of conviction by the clerk of the court or the magistrate."

Reviser's Notes:

1981 Note. Pursuant to authority of § 41-1304.02, "A." was deleted as a correction of a manifest clerical error.

§ 15-551. Confidentiality of pupil's name; disciplinary hearing; civil penalty

A. The governing board and the state board of education shall keep confidential the name of a pupil involved in a hearing before either board regarding the dismissal or discipline of a school district employee or an action on a certificate. The board shall not disclose the pupil's name without the consent of the pupil's parent or guardian except by order of the superior court. This section does not prevent either board from disclosing the pupil's name to any party to the hearing.

B. The board shall take a pupil's testimony in executive session. The pupil shall be referred to by a fictitious name during any public portions of the hearing. The pupil's name and testimony are not subject to inspection pursuant to title 39, chapter 1, article 2.[1]

C. A person who participates in a hearing described in subsection A shall keep confidential the name of any pupil involved in the hearing. The county attorney may enforce a civil penalty of five hundred dollars against a person who violates this subsection.

D. The state board shall adopt rules for the implementation of this section.

Added by Laws 1988, Ch. 244, § 1.

[1] Section 39-121 et seq.

Historical and Statutory Notes

Reviser's Notes:

1988 Note. Pursuant to authority of § 41-1304.02, "; civil penalty" was added to the section heading.

ARTICLE 4. PRINCIPALS' INSTITUTE

Article 4, consisting of §§ 15-561 to 15-563, was added by Laws 1984, Ch. 348, § 1, effective August 3, 1984.

§ 15-561. Repealed by Laws 1995, Ch. 268, § 30

Historical and Statutory Notes

The repealed section, added by Laws 1984, Ch. 348, § 1, amended by Laws 1994, 9th S.S., Ch. 2, § 4, related to the principals' institute advisory committee.

§ 15-562. Repealed by Laws 1994, 9th S.S., Ch. 2, § 5

Historical and Statutory Notes

The repealed section, added by Laws 1984, Ch. 348, § 1, related to the principals' institute and its programs.

§ 15-563. Repealed by Laws 1995, Ch. 268, § 30

Historical and Statutory Notes

The repealed section, added by Laws 1984, Ch. 348, § 1, related to administration of the principals' institute.

CHAPTER 6

TEACHERS RETIREMENT SYSTEM [REPEALED]

Chapter 6, consisting of Article 1, Membership of Teachers in State Employees Retirement System, §§ 15–601 to 15–610, and Article 2, Teachers Retirement System, §§ 15–621 to 15–654, as added by Laws 1981, Ch. 1, § 2, effective January 23, 1981, was repealed by Laws 1981, Ch. 314, § 11, effective July 25, 1981.

§§ 15–601 to 15–610. Repealed by Laws 1981, Ch. 314, § 11

Historical and Statutory Notes

The repealed sections, added by Laws 1981, Ch. 1, § 2, effective January 23, 1981, and relating to the membership of teachers in state employees retirement system, were derived from:

Laws 1953, Ch. 137, §§ 1, 3 to 8.
Laws 1954, Ch. 109, §§ 1 to 5.
Code 1939, Supp.1953, §§ 54–1746, 54–1748 to 54–1753.
Code 1939, Supp.1954, §§ 15–1748a to 15–1748c.
Laws 1955, Ch. 67, §§ 1, 2.
A.R.S. former §§ 15–1461 to 15–1471.
Laws 1970, Ch. 190, § 22.
Laws 1976, Ch. 36, § 1.
Laws 1976, Ch. 163, § 12.
Laws 1978, Ch. 209, § 2.

See, generally § 38–711 et seq..

Laws 1981, Ch. 314, § 28 provides:

"**Sec. 28. Savings clause**

"Sections 11 and 22 of this act do not affect rights and duties that matured, penalties that were incurred and proceedings that were begun before their effective dates."

§§ 15–621 to 15–654. Repealed by Laws 1981, Ch. 314, § 11

Historical and Statutory Notes

The repealed sections, added by Laws 1981, Ch. 1, § 2, effective January 23, 1981, and relating to the teachers' retirement system, were derived from:

Laws 1943, Ch. 61, §§ 2 to 16, 29 to 35, 37.
Laws 1947, Ch. 58, §§ 1 to 5.
Laws 1947, Ch. 93, § 1.
Laws 1952, Ch. 148, §§ 1 to 8, 10.
Code 1939, Supp.1952, §§ 54–1702 to 54–1716, 54–1729 to 54–1735, 54–1737.
Laws 1957, Ch. 73, §§ 1 to 3.
Laws 1961, Ch. 20, §§ 1 to 3.
Laws 1961, Ch. 85, §§ 1, 2.
Laws 1968, Ch. 146, § 1.
Laws 1970, Ch. 95, §§ 2 to 4.
Laws 1970, Ch. 190, §§ 19 to 21.
Laws 1953, Ch. 137, § 9.
Laws 1955, Ch. 77, §§ 1 to 3.
A.R.S. former §§ 15–1401 to 15–1426, 15–1438 to 15–1446.
Laws 1975, Ch. 34, § 1.
Laws 1976, Ch. 163, §§ 9 to 11.
Laws 1978, Ch. 201, § 263.
Laws 1978, Ch. 209, § 1.

See, generally § 38–711 et seq.

For savings clause of Laws 1981, Ch. 314, see Historical and Statutory Notes following §§ 15–601 to 15–610.

CHAPTER 7

INSTRUCTION

ARTICLE 1. CURRICULUM

ARTICLE 2. COURSES OF STUDY AND TEXTBOOKS

Chapter 7, consisting of Article 1, §§ 15–701 to 15–714, Article 2, §§ 15–721 to 15–729, Article 3, §§ 15–741 to 15–744, Article 4, §§ 15–761 to 15–769, and Article 5, §§ 15–781 to 15–790, was added by Laws 1981, Ch. 1, § 2, effective January 23, 1981.

ARTICLE 1. CURRICULUM

Historical and Statutory Notes

Laws 1987, Ch. 245 § 1, as amended by Laws 1988, Ch. 55, § 1 and Laws 1989, Ch. 16, § 1, provides:

"**Section 1. Joint legislative committee on goals for Arizona's educational excellence**

"**A.** A joint legislative committee on goals for Arizona's educational excellence is established consisting of:

"1. Three members of the senate, including two members of the joint legislative committee to study funding priorities of the public school system and one member of the senate education committee, who are appointed by the president of the senate, one of whom shall cochair the committee.

"2. Three members of the house of representatives, including two members of the joint legislative committee to study funding priorities of the public school system and one member of the house of representatives education committee, who are appointed by the speaker of the house of representatives, one of whom shall cochair the committee.

"3. One representative of the business community who is a member of the joint legislative committee to study funding priorities of the public school system and is appointed by the president of the senate.

"4. One representative of the educational community who is a member of the joint legislative committee to study funding priorities of the public school system and is appointed by the president of the senate.

"5. One school district governing board member who is appointed by the president of the senate.

"6. One member of the state board of education who is appointed by the speaker of the house of representatives.

"7. One parent of a pupil in a kindergarten program or grades one through twelve who is appointed by the speaker of the house of representatives.

"8. One teacher who is appointed by the speaker of the house of representatives.

"9. One superintendent of a school district who is appointed by the speaker of the house of representatives.

"**B.** The committee may use the expertise and services of legislative staff and the staff of the state board of education.

"**C.** Members of the committee are not eligible to receive compensation, but members appointed pursuant to subsection A, paragraphs 3, 4, 5, 6, 7, 8 and 9 are eligible for reimbursement of expenses by the Arizona legislative council pursuant to title 38, chapter 4, article 2, Arizona Revised Statutes.

"**D.** The committee shall:

"1. Recommend a list of specific, attainable goals for Arizona's educational excellence, to include at least the following areas:

"(a) Achievement levels of pupils at the end of grade three, grade eight and grade twelve.

"(b) High school graduation rate.

"(c) Post-school employment and college enrollment rate.

"2. Report these goals to the superintendent of public instruction by September 15, 1987.

"3. Submit recommendations of goals and indicators for determining if the goals have been met by December 31, 1987 to the president of the senate, the speaker of the house of representatives and the state board of education.

"4. Review the list of skills developed by the state department of education for each adopted student achievement goal area and offer recommendations to the state board of education before the board adopts the list. On board adoption, evaluate each list of skills in relation to the adopted statewide student achievement goals.

"5. Establish a process for the consideration of revisions to goals initially adopted by the committee as set forth in subsection H of this section. This process shall be based on a review of data collected on adopted goal areas as reported by the department of education by November 1 of each year.

"6. If appropriate, develop additional goal areas and indicators.

"7. Review the proposal developed by the department of education and the state board of education concerning a comprehensive assessment program to measure statewide progress toward adopted goals. By December 31, 1989, recommend legislative changes to provide for the implementation of the assessment plan beginning in the fall of 1990.

"8. By December 31, 1991, present a final report of the work of the committee to the president of the senate, the speaker of the house of representatives and the state board of education, including final recommendations on possible revisions to the adopted goals and the comprehensive assessment program.

"**E.** The state board of education shall:

"1. Report to the committee by December 1, 1987:

"(a) Any recommended additions or changes to the goals recommended by the committee.

"(b) Recommendations for specific measures which can be used as indicators to determine if each of the goals have been met, for all of the goals recommended by the committee and for all of the additional proposed goals as provided in subdivision (a) of this paragraph.

"2. Oversee the development, implementation and measurement of a list of skills for the student achievement goal areas adopted by the committee. Before final adoption the board shall present these skills to the committee for its review and recommendations.

"3. In conjunction with the department of education, establish a system for the collection and reporting of nontest indicators by school districts to assess progress toward goals. Nontest indicators represent information acquired through sources other than testing. The board shall recommend specific indicators which are to be assessed by school districts, with the initial collection of indicators to begin during fiscal year 1989–1990. Depending on the type of information collected, the board may recommend a system which utilizes population sampling and pilot testing for some indicators. The recommended system shall be incorporated into the proposal for the comprehensive assessment program developed by the department of education and presented by the department to the joint legislative committee before October 1, 1989.

"4. In conjunction with the department of education, the board of regents and the state board of directors for community colleges, develop a system for collection of data to provide information on progress toward the postschool employment and college enrollment goal. The board shall review the information obtained through the provisions of § 15–1822, Arizona Revised Statutes, and recommend as part of the comprehensive assessment program what revisions if any are required to incorporate this information into the proposed system. The board shall consider the use of a state student identification system to allow tracking of students as part of an assessment program.

"5. By November 1, 1991, submit to the committee recommendations regarding possible revisions to the adopted goals and the comprehensive assessment program.

"**F.** The committee may study and make recommendations regarding other issues related to improving, and assessing progress toward, educational excellence.

"**G.** The department of education shall:

"1. Prepare a proposal for a comprehensive assessment program which would provide data to measure statewide progress toward all adopted goal areas. In preparing this proposal, the department shall:

"(a) Conduct public forums to allow interested persons to have an opportunity for information and input.

"(b) Include all major points of concerns presented during the public forums in a report to the joint legislative committee at the time the proposal is presented.

"(c) Address the role of the state and the local school district in reference to the collection of data for statewide policymaking, diagnostic purposes and educational accountability.

"(d) Incorporate findings from the studies mandated by Laws 1988, chapter 216 in reference to the use of norm-referenced achievement tests for diagnostic purposes and the current statewide norm-referenced testing program.

"(e) Address how current district and state assessment programs, including the continuous uniform evaluation system of pupil achievement prescribed in § 15–203, subsection a, paragraph 38, Arizona Revised Statutes, the minimum course of study and competency requirements prescribed in §§ 15–701, 15–701.01 and 15–203, Arizona Revised Statutes, the testing programs prescribed in § 15–741, Arizona Revised Statutes, the state board adopted essential skills and the adopted state goals will be integrated into the proposal for a comprehensive assessment program.

"(f) Address the needs of special pupil populations.

"(g) In conjunction with the state board of education, recommend a system for the collection and reporting of nontest indicators as part of the comprehensive assessment system.

"(h) Include recommendations for legislation in reference to the implementation of a comprehensive assessment program.

"(i) Present the proposal to the joint legislative committee on goals for educational excellence by October 1, 1989.

"2. Continue to develop and pilot test data collection instruments and the collection of data to assess progress toward all adopted goals.

"3. Report to the committee by November 1 of each year the data that has been collected as measurement of progress toward goals. The first report is due by November 1, 1988.

"**H.** The initially adopted statewide goals are:

"1. That appropriate efforts be made to help all of the students in this state master essential skills at the highest levels of thinking, to graduate from high school and to achieve their postsecondary school goals.

"2. That by 1992, eighty per cent, by 1996, eighty-five per cent and by 2000, ninety per cent of graduates in this state master core competencies as detailed in a list of essential skills adopted by the state board of education for each of the following student achievement goals:

"(a) In communication that graduates be able to:

"(i) Read, comprehend, interpret and draw inferences from written material.

"(ii) Organize information and state it clearly and concisely in a written form that is grammatically correct.

"(iii) Effectively communicate thoughts, knowledge and information through speech.

"(iv) Use listening skills to comprehend information from oral communication.

"(b) In mathematics that graduates achieve the mathematics skills and knowledge of computation, problem solving, data analysis and technological literacy.

"(c) In science that graduates achieve the science skills and knowledge of scientific principles, reasoning, technology and history.

"(d) In social and economic studies that graduates achieve skills and knowledge of citizenship, history, geography, economics and government.

"(e) In humanities and arts that graduates achieve skills and knowledge in the visual arts, performing arts, music, foreign language and literature.

"(f) In physical and health education that graduates achieve health and physical education skills and knowledge which will allow them to develop and maintain positive physical health.

"(g) In occupational areas that graduates achieve the occupational skills and knowledge of technology, career decision making, employability and basic academic skill application which will allow for successful participation in the occupation of their choice.

"3. That by 2000, the high school graduation rate in this state be ninety per cent. Interim goals are:

"(a) By 1992, eighty per cent of the students in this state graduate from high school.

"(b) By 1996, eighty-five per cent of the students in this state graduate from high school.

"4. That for post-high school employment and college enrollment:

"(a) The percentage of high school graduates who are unemployed or underemployed decrease.

"(b) All students, including urban, rural and minority students, have an equal opportunity to pursue postsecondary choices."

Laws 1987, Ch. 245, § 2, as amended by Laws 1988, Ch. 55, § 2, provides:

"**Sec. 2. Expiration date**

"This act expires from and after December 31, 1991."

Laws 1988, Ch. 55, § 3, provides:

"**Sec. 3. Continuation of committee**

"**A.** All members appointed pursuant to Laws 1987, chapter 245, § 1, subsection A, paragraphs 3 through 9, who were serving on the committee on December 31, 1987, shall continue to serve on the committee until December 31, 1991. A vacancy shall be filled in the same manner as an original appointment.

"**B.** Legislative members appointed pursuant to Laws 1987, chapter 245, § 1, subsection A, paragraphs 1 and 2, who were serving on the committee on December 31, 1987, shall continue to serve until expiration of their legislative term. Thereafter, the president of the senate and the speaker of the house of representatives for the thirty-ninth and fortieth legislatures, respectively, shall appoint members from their respective houses whose terms shall be concurrent with their term of office or until expiration of the committee, whichever occurs first."

§ 15–701. Common school; promotions; requirements; certificate; supervision of eighth grades by superintendent of high school district; high school admissions; academic credit

A. The state board of education shall:

1. Prescribe a minimum course of study, as defined in § 15–101 and incorporating the academic standards adopted by the state board of education, to be taught in the common schools.

2. Prescribe competency requirements for the promotion of pupils from the eighth grade and competency requirements for the promotion of pupils from the third grade incorporating the academic standards in at least the areas of reading, writing, mathematics, science and social studies.

3. Distribute guidelines for the school districts to follow in prescribing criteria for the promotion of pupils from grade to grade in the common schools. These guidelines shall include recommended procedures for insuring that the cultural background of a pupil is taken into consideration when criteria for promotion are being applied.

B. Pursuant to the guidelines which the state board of education distributes, the governing board of a school district shall:

1. Prescribe curricula that include the academic standards in the required subject areas pursuant to subsection A, paragraph 1 of this section.

2. Prescribe criteria for the promotion of pupils from grade to grade in the common schools in the school district. These criteria shall include accomplishment of the academic standards in at least reading, writing, mathematics, science and social studies, as determined by district assessment. Other criteria may include additional measures of academic achievement and attendance.

C. The governing board may prescribe the course of study and competency requirements for promotion which are in addition to or higher than the course of study and competency requirements which the state board prescribes.

D. A teacher shall determine whether to promote or retain a pupil in grade in a common school as provided in § 15–521, paragraph 3 on the basis of the prescribed criteria. The governing board, if it reviews the decision of a teacher to promote or retain a pupil in grade in a common school as provided in § 15–342, paragraph 11, shall base its decision on the prescribed criteria.

E. A governing board may provide and issue certificates of promotion to pupils whom it promotes from the eighth grade of a common school. Such certificates shall be signed by the principal or superintendent of schools. Where there is no principal or superintendent of schools, the certificates shall be signed by the teacher of an eighth grade. The certificates shall admit the holders to any high school in the state.

F. A governing board may request certificates of promotion from the county school superintendent. If a governing board requests these certificates from the county school superintendent, the county school superintendent shall furnish and sign the certificates.

G. Within any high school district or union high school district, the superintendent of the high school district shall supervise the work of the eighth grade of all schools employing no superintendent or principal.

H. A school district shall not deny a pupil who is between the ages of sixteen and twenty-one years admission to a high school because the pupil does not hold an eighth grade certificate. Governing boards shall establish procedures for determining the admissibility of pupils who are under sixteen years of age and who do not hold eighth grade certificates.

I. The state board of education shall adopt rules to allow common school pupils who can demonstrate competency in a particular academic course or subject to obtain academic credit for the course or subject without enrolling in the course or subject.

Added by Laws 1981, Ch. 1, § 2, eff. Jan. 23, 1981. Amended by Laws 1982, Ch. 143, § 1; Laws 1983, Ch. 325, § 7; Laws 1985, Ch. 166, § 7, eff. April 18, 1985; Laws 1990, Ch. 233, § 3, eff. July 1, 1991; Laws 1992, Ch. 66, § 1; Laws 1994, Ch. 315, § 8; Laws 1995, Ch. 268, § 31; Laws 1998, Ch. 183, § 2; Laws 1999, Ch. 151, § 1.

Historical and Statutory Notes

Source:

Laws 1912, Ch. 77, § 83.
Civ. Code 1913, § 2779.
Laws 1925, Ch. 28, § 1.
Rev. Code 1928, § 1075.
Code 1939, § 54–908.
A.R.S. former § 15–546.
Laws 1960, Ch. 127, § 43.

Reviser's Notes:

1982 Note. Pursuant to authority of § 41–1304.02, in subsection A the spelling of the second "prescribe" was corrected.

§ 15-701.01. High school; graduation; requirements; community college or university courses; transfer from private schools; academic credit

A. The state board of education shall:

1. Prescribe a minimum course of study, as defined in § 15-101 and incorporating the academic standards adopted by the state board of education, for the graduation of pupils from high school.

2. Prescribe competency requirements for the graduation of pupils from high school incorporating the academic standards in at least the areas of reading, writing, mathematics, science and social studies.

3. Develop and adopt competency tests for the graduation of pupils from high school in at least the areas of reading, writing and mathematics and shall establish passing scores for each such test.

B. The governing board of a school district shall:

1. Prescribe curricula that include the academic standards in the required subject areas pursuant to subsection A, paragraph 1 of this section.

2. Prescribe criteria for the graduation of pupils from the high schools in the school district. These criteria shall include accomplishment of the academic standards in at least reading, writing, mathematics, science and social studies, as determined by district assessment. Other criteria may include additional measures of academic achievement and attendance.

C. The governing board may prescribe the course of study and competency requirements for the graduation of pupils from high school which are in addition to or higher than the course of study and competency requirements which the state board prescribes.

D. The governing board may prescribe competency requirements for the passage of pupils in courses which are required for graduation from high school.

E. A teacher shall determine whether to pass or fail a pupil in a course in high school as provided in § 15-521, paragraph 3 on the basis of the competency requirements, if any have been prescribed. The governing board, if it reviews the decision of a teacher to pass or fail a pupil in a course in high school as provided in § 15-342, paragraph 11, shall base its decision on the competency requirements, if any have been prescribed.

F. Graduation requirements established by the governing board may be met by a pupil who passes courses in the required or elective subjects at a community college or university, if the course is at a higher level than the course taught in the high school attended by the pupil or, if the course is not taught in the high school, the level of the course is equal to or higher than the level of a high school course. The governing board shall determine if the subject matter of the community college or university course is appropriate to the specific requirement the pupil intends it to fulfill and if the level of the community college or university course is less than, equal to or higher than a high school course, and the governing board shall award one-half of a carnegie unit for each three semester hours of credit the pupil earns in an appropriate community college or university course. If a pupil is not satisfied with the decision of the governing board regarding the amount of credit granted or the subjects for which credit is granted, the pupil may request that the state board of education review the decision of the governing board, and the state board shall make the final determination of the amount of credit to be given the pupil and for which subjects. The governing board shall not limit the number of credits required for high school graduation which may be met by taking community college or university courses. For the purposes of this subsection:

1. "Community college" means an educational institution that is operated by a community college district as defined in § 15–1401 or a postsecondary educational institution under the jurisdiction of an Indian tribe recognized by the United States department of the interior.

2. "University" means a university under the jurisdiction of the Arizona board of regents.

G. A pupil who transfers from a private school shall be provided with a list that indicates those credits that have been accepted and denied by the school district. A pupil may request to take an examination in each particular course in which credit has been denied. The school district shall accept the credit for each particular course in which the pupil takes an examination and receives a passing score on a test designed and evaluated by a teacher in the school district who teaches the subject matter on which the examination is based. In addition to the above requirements, the governing board of a school district may prescribe requirements for the acceptance of the credits of pupils who transfer from a private school.

H. The state board of education shall adopt rules to allow high school pupils who can demonstrate competency in a particular academic course or subject to obtain academic credit for the course or subject without enrolling in the course or subject.

Added by Laws 1983, Ch. 325, § 8. Amended by Laws 1984, Ch. 311, § 1; Laws 1990, Ch. 233, § 4, eff. July 1, 1991; Laws 1990, Ch. 288, § 1; Laws 1991, Ch. 298, § 12; Laws 1995, Ch. 268, § 32; Laws 1996, Ch. 284, § 28; Laws 1998, Ch. 183, § 3; Laws 1999, Ch. 151, § 2; Laws 2003, Ch. 253, § 3, eff. Sept. 18, 2003, retroactively effective to July 1, 2003.

Historical and Statutory Notes

Laws 1990, Ch. 228, § 1, effective May 14, 1990, provides:

"**Section 1. High school graduation; additional level**

"The state board of education shall examine the possibility of developing additional graduation levels for pupils who have exceeded the competency requirements for graduation as prescribed in § 15–701.01, Arizona Revised Statutes. The state board shall collect information regarding multiple diplomas from those states which provide for more than one high school diploma and submit a report regarding the findings of its examination of additional graduation levels to the legislature by November 30, 1990."

The amendment of this section by Laws 1990, Ch. 288, § 1 was repealed by Laws 1991, Ch. 298, § 13.

The 1991 amendment of this section by Ch. 298 explicitly amended the 1990 amendment of this section by Ch. 233.

Laws 1991, Ch. 298, § 1, par. 6, provides:

"**Section 1. Purpose**"

"6. Section 15–701.01, Arizona Revised Statutes, was amended by Laws 1990, chapter 233, § 4 and Laws 1990, chapter 288, § 1. These two versions could not be blended because of the delayed effective date of the chapter 233 version. In order to blend these two versions the Laws 1990, chapter 233 version of

§ 15-701.01, Arizona Revised Statutes, is amended to incorporate the amendments made by Laws 1990, chapter 288 and the chapter 288 version is repealed."

Reviser's Notes:

1984 Note. Pursuant to authority of § 41-1304.02, "; community college or university courses" was added to the heading of this section.

1995 Note. Pursuant to authority of § 41-1304.02, in subsection E, first sentence the comma after ~~"subsection A"~~ was removed to correct a manifest clerical error.

§ 15-702. High school equivalency diploma

A. Any person who is sixteen years of age or older and who passes a general educational development test shall be awarded an Arizona high school equivalency diploma by the state board of education and the state superintendent of public instruction. The state board of education may establish eligibility requirements for persons wishing to take a general educational development test, except that the minimum age required to take the test may not be older than sixteen nor shall the board require the completion of any high school credits.

B. A person who meets the minimum course of study and competency requirements prescribed by the state board of education for graduation from high school through a combination of high school credits and community college and university credits, which are converted to high school credits in the same manner as provided in § 15-701.01, subsection F by the governing board or the state board of education, shall be awarded an Arizona high school equivalency diploma.

Added by Laws 1981, Ch. 1, § 2, eff. Jan. 23, 1981. Amended by Laws 1984, Ch. 264, § 1; Laws 1984, Ch. 311, § 2; Laws 1990, Ch. 233, § 5, eff. July 1, 1991; Laws 1994, Ch. 315, § 9.

Historical and Statutory Notes

Source:

Laws 1976, Ch. 37, § 1.
A.R.S. former § 15-547.

Reviser's Notes:

1984 Note. Prior to the 1990 amendment, this section contained the amendments made by Laws 1984, Ch. 264, § 1 and Ch. 311, § 2 which were blended together pursuant to authority of § 41-1304.03. Additionally, pursuant to authority of § 41-1304.02, in subsection B the comma following "subsection D" was transposed to follow the second "education".

§ 15-703. Kindergarten programs and special departments; special teachers

A. The governing board may:

1. Establish departments of industrial arts and consumer education and homemaking.

2. Employ special teachers in special subjects.

B. Each common school district or unified school district shall establish a kindergarten program, unless the governing board of such common school district or unified school district files an exemption claim with the department of education. A district is exempt from establishing a kindergarten program if it files with the department of education an exemption claim which states that the establishment of a kindergarten program will interfere with the work of, or maintenance of efficiency in, the grades and that a kindergarten program is not in the best interests of the district.

C. For the purpose of maintaining a kindergarten program a common school district or unified school district governing board may lease such buildings as may be necessary as provided by law.

Added by Laws 1981, Ch. 1, § 2, eff. Jan. 23, 1981. Amended by Laws 1984, Ch. 349, § 6; Laws 1990, Ch. 348, § 6, eff. June 26, 1990.

Historical and Statutory Notes

Source:

Laws 1912, Ch. 77, § 84.
Civ. Code 1913, § 2780.
Rev. Code 1928, § 1076.
Code 1939, § 54-909.
A.R.S. former § 15-448.
Laws 1957, Ch. 27, § 1.
Laws 1971, Ch. 177, § 2.
Laws 1972, Ch. 161, § 2.

§ 15-704. Reading proficiency; definitions

A. Each school district or charter school that provides instruction in kindergarten programs and grades one through three shall select and administer screening, ongoing diagnostic and classroom based instructional reading assessments, including a motivational assessment, as defined by the state board of education, to monitor student progress. Each school shall use the diagnostic information to plan appropriate and effective intervention.

B. Each school district or charter school that provides instruction for pupils in kindergarten programs and grades one through three shall conduct a curriculum evaluation and adopt a scientifically based reading curriculum that includes the essential components of reading instruction. All school districts and charter schools that offer instruction in kindergarten programs and grades one through three shall provide ongoing teacher training based on scientifically based reading research.

C. Each school district or charter school that provides instruction in kindergarten programs and grades one through three shall devote reasonable amounts of time to explicit instruction and independent reading in grades one through three.

D. A pupil in grade three who does not meet or exceed the reading standards measured by the Arizona instrument to measure standards test administered pursuant to § 15-741 shall be provided intensive reading instruction as defined by the state board of education until the pupil meets these standards.

E. The governing board of each school district and the governing body of each charter school shall determine the percentage of pupils at each school in grade three who do not meet the reading standards prescribed by the state board of education and measured by the Arizona instrument to measure standards test administered pursuant to § 15-741. If more than twenty per cent of students in grade three at either the individual school level or at the school district level do not meet the standards, the governing board or governing body shall conduct a review of its reading program that includes curriculum and professional development in light of current, scientifically based reading research.

F. Based on the review required in subsection E of this section, the governing board or governing body and the school principal of each school that does not meet the reading standards, in conjunction with school council members, if applicable, shall develop methods of best practices for teaching reading based on essential components of reading instruction and supported by scientifically based reading research. These methods shall be adopted at a public meeting and shall be implemented the following academic year.

G. Subsections E and F of this section shall be coordinated with efforts to develop and implement an improvement plan if required pursuant to § 15–241.

H. For the purposes of this section:

1. "Essential components of reading instruction" means explicit and systematic instruction in the following:

(a) Phonemic awareness.

(b) Phonics.

(c) Vocabulary development.

(d) Reading fluency.

(e) Reading comprehension.

2. "Reading" means a complex system of deriving meaning from print that requires all of the following:

(a) The skills and knowledge to understand how phonemes or speech sounds are connected to print.

(b) The ability to decode unfamiliar words.

(c) The ability to read fluently.

(d) Sufficient background information and vocabulary to foster reading comprehension.

(e) The development of appropriate active strategies to construct meaning from print.

(f) The development and maintenance of a motivation to read.

3. "Scientifically based reading research" means research that meets all of the following:

(a) Applies rigorous, systematic and objective procedures to obtain valid knowledge relevant to reading development, reading instruction and reading difficulties.

(b) Employs systematic empirical methods that draw on observation or experiment.

(c) Involves rigorous data analyses that are adequate to test the stated hypotheses and justify the general conclusions drawn.

(d) Relies on measurements or observational methods that provide valid data across evaluators and observers and across multiple measurements and observations.

(e) Has been accepted by a peer reviewed journal or approved by a panel of independent experts through a comparably rigorous, objective and scientific review.

(f) Contains all of the elements of the essential components of reading instruction.

Added by Laws 2002, Ch. 295, § 2.

Historical and Statutory Notes

Laws 2002, Ch. 295, § 6, provides:

"**Sec. 6. State board of education; reading standards**

"The state board of education shall adopt reading standards that reflect current scientifically based reading research and that include definitions for 'reading', 'essential components of reading instruction' and 'scientifically based reading research' as those terms are defined in § 15-704, as added by this act."

Former § 15-704, added by Laws 1981, Ch. 1, § 2, derived from Laws 1970, Ch. 165, § 1; A.R.S. former § 15-1024, which related to oral and silent reading in grades one through eight, was repealed by Laws 2002, Ch. 295, § 1.

Reviser's Notes:

2002 Note. Pursuant to authority of § 41-1304.02, in subsection H, paragraph 3, subdivision (e) the spelling of "peer reviewed" was corrected.

§ 15-705. Extracurricular activities; requirements

A. Each governing board after consultation with parents and teachers shall adopt policies and procedures governing requirements for pupils' participation in extracurricular activities for pupils in grade six, if the grade is part of a middle school, and grades seven through twelve. The consultation by the governing board with parents and teachers may be accomplished by holding a public hearing or forming an advisory committee. The requirements shall meet or exceed the minimum requirements prescribed by the state board.

B. The state board of education shall prescribe rules for policies regarding pupils' participation in extracurricular activities including minimum statewide requirements. The minimum statewide requirements:

1. Shall be appropriate to the grade in which the pupil is enrolled.

2. Shall be based on the number of courses passed or failed, on grades received or on a combination of these factors.

3. May incorporate additional factors.

4. Shall take into consideration the minimum course of study and competency requirements prescribed by the state board pursuant to § 15-701.01.

Added by Laws 1986, Ch. 305, § 1. Amended by Laws 1988, Ch. 293, § 3.

Historical and Statutory Notes

Laws 1986, Ch. 305, §§ 2 and 3 provide:

"**Sec. 2. Adoption of policy and procedures**

"Notwithstanding § 15-705, Arizona Revised Statutes, as added by this act, the state board of education shall prescribe rules for policies regarding participation in extracurricular activities no later than January 1, 1987 and each governing board shall adopt policies and procedures governing pupils' participation in extracurricular activities no later than September 1, 1987 and shall submit a copy of the policies and procedures to the department of education no later than September 30, 1987.

"**Sec. 3. Report on policies regarding extracurricular activities**

"The department of education shall prepare a report on the policies regarding extracurricular activities adopted by school districts and shall submit the report to the president of the senate and the speaker of the house of representatives by December 31, 1987."

Laws 1988, Ch. 293, § 4 provides:

"**Sec. 4. Adoption of policy and procedures**

"Notwithstanding § 15-705, Arizona Revised Statutes, as amended by this act, the state board of education shall prescribe rules for policies regarding pupils' participation in extracurricular activities including statewide minimum standards no later than September 1, 1988. Each governing board shall adopt policies and procedures based on the state board rules and procedures no later than January 1, 1989 and shall submit a copy of the policies and procedures to the department of education no later than January 31, 1989."

Former § 15–705 was repealed by Laws 1984, Ch. 169, § 1. For subject matter and derivation of former § 15–705, see Historical and Statutory Notes under § 15–707.

§ 15–706. Instruction in environmental education; definition

A. The department of education shall establish and maintain an environmental education information resource system to assist school districts that choose to develop and implement environmental education programs. The system shall include a current documentation, referral and dissemination program for environmental education materials and information that promotes knowledge of the environment, including various scientific and economic concepts that impact on environmental and natural resource issues of this state and its citizens.

B. If a school district chooses to provide instruction in environmental education, the environmental education program shall:

1. Be based on current scientific information.

2. Include a discussion of economic and social implications.

C. For the purposes of this section "environmental education" means Educational processes, programs and activities which are specifically designed to enhance student acquisition of knowledge of scientific and economic principles, concepts and facts as they relate to environmental topics and issues and which are taught in an unbiased, fair and balanced manner.

Added by Laws 1990, Ch. 266, § 3. Amended by Laws 1994, Ch. 294, § 2; Laws 1995, Ch. 268, § 33; Laws 2000, Ch. 146, § 1.

Historical and Statutory Notes

Laws 1990, Ch. 266, § 1, provides:

"Section 1. Legislative intent

"The legislature recognizes that the education of the people in this state is critical to maintaining the delicate balance among all forms of life and their environments. It is the intent of the legislature that the public schools, community colleges, state universities and state agencies provide a continuing awareness of the essential mission to preserve the earth's capacity to sustain a quality of life in the most healthful, enjoyable and productive environment possible. It is the further intent of the legislature that the public schools, community colleges, state universities and state agencies integrate environmental education throughout the educational system and public education programs so that awareness of students and the general public is thorough, continuous and meaningful."

Laws 1990, Ch. 266, § 12, as amended by Laws 1991, Ch. 232, § 4, effective June 12, 1991, provides:

"Sec. 12. Implementation of environmental education programs

"**A.** Notwithstanding § 15–706, Arizona Revised Statutes, as added by this act:

"1. School districts shall implement environmental education programs in the academic year following the fiscal year in which the environmental education information resource system is established as provided in paragraph 3 of this subsection.

"2. The state board of education is required to develop guidelines for environmental programs by June 30, 1992 and assessments of environmental education programs by September 1, 1993.

"3. The department of education is required to establish and maintain an environmental education information resource system during the fiscal year in which the department of education environmental education fund contains at least one hundred thousand dollars.

"**B.** Notwithstanding § 15–1643, Arizona Revised Statutes, as added by this act, a university under the jurisdiction of the Arizona board of regents is not required to incorporate training in environmental education into its teacher training programs, provide environmental education training programs to certificated teachers or establish an environmental resource center until fiscal year 1991–1992.

"C. The department of education, in consultation with the Arizona board of regents, shall submit a report on the implementation and assessment of environmental education programs and the training of certificated teachers in environmental education to the president of the senate, the speaker of the house of representatives and the governor by November 15, 1993."

Laws 1997, Ch. 233, § 1, par. 25, provides:

"**Section 1. Purpose**"

"25. Laws 1996, chapter 304, § 5 amended Laws 1994, chapter 294, § 12 but failed to include it in the title of the act. In order to comply with article IV, part 2, § 13, Constitution of Arizona, in this act Laws 1994, chapter 294, § 12 is amended to incorporate the amendment made by Laws 1996, chapter 304, § 5 and Laws 1996, chapter 304, § 5 is repealed."

Laws 1997, Ch. 233, § 48, subsec. A, provides:

"**Sec. 48. Retroactive application**

"**A.** Sections 45 and 46 of this act apply retroactively to from and after March 1, 1996."

Former § 15-706 was repealed by Laws 1984, Ch. 169, § 1. For subject matter and derivation of former § 15-706, see Historical and Statutory Notes under § 15-707.

Reviser's Notes:

1990 Note. Pursuant to authority of § 41-1304.02, in subsection D the reference to "§ 15-1646" was substituted for the reference to "§ 15-1643" to conform to the reviser's renumbering of that section.

§ 15-707. High schools; education about organ donation

Each high school in this state that provides a driver education program may educate the students who are enrolled in the program about the option of organ donation.

Added by Laws 2004, Ch. 125, § 1.

Historical and Statutory Notes

Former § 15-707, added by Laws 1998, Ch. 183, § 4, related to curriculum review, and was repealed by Laws 2002, Ch. 295, § 3.

Other former §§ 15-705 to 15-707, added by Laws 1981, Ch. 1, § 2, which related to English language and bilingual instruction and special instruction in English, were repealed by Laws 1984, Ch. 169, § 1. The sections were derived from:

Laws 1912, Ch. 77, § 73.
Civ.Code 1913, § 2769.
Rev.Code 1928, § 1047.
Code 1939, § 54-1101.
A.R.S. former §§ 15-202, 15-1097, 15-1098.
Laws 1969, Ch. 95, §§ 2, 3.
Laws 1972, Ch. 124, § 2.
Laws 1973, Ch. 169, §§ 1, 5, 6.
Laws 1981, Ch. 1, § 2.

§ 15-707.01. Repealed by Laws 2002, Ch. 295, § 3

Historical and Statutory Notes

The repealed section, added by Laws 1998, Ch. 183, § 4, related to intensive reading instruction.

§ 15-708. Remedial education programs; powers of the governing board; definition

A. Beginning July 1, 1980 school districts with an estimated student count of five thousand or less for the 1980-1981 school year may provide remedial education programs to children with learning problems who are presently being served in special education programs as provided in article 4 of this chapter but who will no longer qualify for special education from and after July 20, 1979.

B. Beginning July 1, 1980 school districts with an estimated student count of more than five thousand for the 1980-1981 school year shall provide remedial education programs to children with learning problems who are presently being served in special education programs as provided in article 4 of this chapter [1] but who will no longer qualify for special education from and after July 20, 1979.

C. Nothing in this section or § 15-709 shall be construed to preclude a school district from providing remedial education programs for children not specifically provided for in this section or § 15-709.

D. The governing board may employ teachers who hold a valid Arizona teachers certificate or supportive personnel as deemed necessary for the operation of a remedial education program.

E. In this section and § 15-709, unless the context otherwise requires, "remedial education programs" means curricula to supplement the regular school curricula to assist children with learning problems in achieving the level they are expected to achieve in the regular classroom.

Added by Laws 1981, Ch. 1, § 2, eff. Jan. 23, 1981.

[1] Section 15-761 et seq.

Historical and Statutory Notes

Source:

A.R.S. former §§ 15-1003, 15-1004.
Laws 1979, Ch. 181, § 2.
Laws 1980, 2nd S.S., Ch. 9, § 37.

§ 15-709. Review of students in remedial education programs

A. The educational development of a child in a remedial education program as provided in this section and § 15-708 shall be reviewed each regular reporting period by the teachers or others instructing the child in the remedial education program and the regular classroom teacher to determine if the child has reached the expected level of achievement. If it is determined that the child is maintaining his expected level of achievement, the child shall no longer be eligible for assistance in the remedial education program.

B. Parents shall be notified of the progress of their child in the remedial education program as provided in this section and § 15-708 by the established reporting method of the school district, which may be the report card.

Added by Laws 1981, Ch. 1, § 2, eff. Jan. 23, 1981.

Historical and Statutory Notes

Source:

A.R.S. former § 15-1005.
Laws 1979, Ch. 181, § 2.

§ 15-710. Instruction in state and federal constitutions, American institutions and history of Arizona

All schools shall give instruction in the essentials, sources and history of the Constitutions of the United States and Arizona and instruction in American institutions and ideals and in the history of Arizona, including the history of native americans in Arizona. The instruction shall be given in accordance with the state course of study for at least one year of the common school grades and high school grades respectively.

Added by Laws 1981, Ch. 1, § 2, eff. Jan. 23, 1981. Amended by Laws 1997, Ch. 231, § 13; Laws 2004, Ch. 339, § 2.

Historical and Statutory Notes

Source:

Laws 1925, Ch. 40, §§ 1, 2.
Rev. Code 1928, § 1061.
Laws 1943, Ch. 62, § 1.
Code 1939, Supp. 1952, § 54–803.
A.R.S. former § 15–1021.
Laws 1969, Ch. 44, § 1.

§ 15–711. Sex education curricula; sexual conduct with a minor

All school districts with existing sex education curricula shall include instruction on the laws relating to sexual conduct with a minor for pupils in grades seven, eight, nine, ten, eleven and twelve. Each school district may develop its own course of study to meet the requirements of this section.

Added as § 15–720 by Laws 2001, Ch. 61, § 1. Renumbered as § 15–711.

Historical and Statutory Notes

Former § 15–711, added by Laws 1981, Ch. 1, § 2, derived from Laws 1971, Ch. 86, § 1, and A.R.S. former § 15–1025, which related to free enterprise system instruction in high schools, was repealed by Laws 1995, Ch. 268, § 34.

Reviser's Notes:

2001 Note. Pursuant to authority of § 41–1304.02, this section, added by Laws 2001, Ch. 61, sec. 1 as § 15–720, was renumbered as § 15–711 and "Sex education curricula; sexual conduct with a minor" was substituted for the previous section heading.

§ 15–712. Instruction on alcohol, tobacco, narcotic drugs, marijuana, date rape drugs and other dangerous drugs; chemical abuse prevention programs; definitions

A. Instruction on the nature and harmful effects of alcohol, tobacco, narcotic drugs, marijuana, date rape drugs and other dangerous drugs on the human system and instruction on the laws related to the control of these substances and the nonuse and prevention of use and abuse of alcohol, tobacco, narcotic drugs, marijuana, date rape drugs and other dangerous drugs may be included in the courses of study in common and high schools, with emphasis on grades four through nine. Instruction on the nature and harmful effects of alcohol, tobacco, narcotic drugs, marijuana, date rape drugs and other dangerous drugs on a human fetus may be included in the courses of study in grades six through twelve. The instruction may be integrated into existing health, science, citizenship or similar studies and shall meet the criteria for chemical abuse prevention education programs developed pursuant to subsection C of this section.

B. At the request of a school district, the department of education shall provide technical assistance to school districts that choose to implement programs to prevent chemical abuse.

C. The department of education and the department of health services, in consultation with the committee established pursuant to § 41–617, shall establish an interagency committee to coordinate their assistance to school districts.

D. The state board of education may accept gifts and grants and shall distribute them and monies appropriated for chemical abuse prevention programs to school districts to assist with the costs of programs designed to prevent chemical abuse by pupils in kindergarten programs and grades one through twelve. School districts which have approved chemical abuse prevention policies and procedures as prescribed in § 15-345 are eligible for a maximum of one dollar for each pupil or one thousand dollars, whichever is more. If sufficient monies are not available to meet all requests, the state board shall determine which school districts to fund based on need, availability of other programs or sources of revenue and the likelihood of the school district's proposed program successfully meeting needs identified by the school district. A school district shall include the monies it receives for chemical abuse prevention programs under this section in the special projects section of the budget as provided in § 15-903, subsection F.

E. For the purpose of this section:

1. "Date rape drug" means a drug prescribed in § 13-3401, paragraph 30, subdivisions (f) through (m).

2. "Narcotic drug", "marijuana" and "dangerous drug" have the same meaning prescribed in § 13-3401.

Added by Laws 1981, Ch. 1, § 2, eff. Jan. 23, 1981. Amended by Laws 1981, Ch. 264, § 10, eff. Sept. 1, 1981; Laws 1985, Ch. 242, § 2; Laws 1986, Ch. 47, § 1; Laws 1987, Ch. 307, § 31; Laws 1990, Ch. 128, § 1; Laws 1995, Ch. 268, § 35; Laws 1996, Ch. 284, § 29; Laws 1999, Ch. 299, § 10; Laws 2001, Ch. 334, § 25.

Historical and Statutory Notes

Source:

Laws 1943, Ch. 66, § 1.
Code 1939, Supp. 1952, § 54-811.
A.R.S. former § 15-1023.
Laws 1973, Ch. 76, § 2.
Laws 1979, Ch. 103, § 2.

The purported amendment of this section by Laws 1998, 3rd S.S., Ch. 1, failed to became effective because Ch. 1 was repealed in its entirety by Laws 1998, 5th S.S., Ch. 1, § 2, effective July 1, 1998.

Reviser's Notes:

1981 Note. Pursuant to authority of § 41-1304.02, in the heading of this section the word "and" was deleted and a comma was added following the word "tobacco" and the words "drugs, marijuana" were added following the word "narcotic".

1987 Note. Pursuant to authority of § 41-1304.02, in subsection C, "§ 41-617" was substituted for "§ 41-2751" to conform to the Reviser's renumbering of that section.

§ 15-713. Training in use of bows or firearms; instruction materials; certification of instructors; cooperating agencies

A. The Arizona game and fish department may provide training in the safe handling and use of bows or firearms and safe hunting practices, in conjunction with the common schools and high schools of the state when the schools request the training.

B. The Arizona game and fish department may prescribe courses of study, approve instruction materials, certify instructors for training programs conducted by private organizations or public agencies and issue certificates of completion of the required course of study.

C. To carry out the purposes of the training program authorized by this section and § 15-714, the Arizona game and fish department may cooperate with other agencies and private organizations.

Added by Laws 1981, Ch. 1, § 2, eff. Jan. 23, 1981. Amended by Laws 1996, Ch. 284, § 30.

Historical and Statutory Notes

Source:
Laws 1955, Ch. 121, §§ 1, 2, 4.
Code 1939, Supp.1955, §§ 54–814, 54–815, 54–817.
A.R.S. former §§ 15–1071, 15–1072, 15–1074.
Laws 1975, Ch. 105, § 12.
Laws 1980, Ch. 224, § 2.

§ 15–714. Eligibility for training in use of bows or firearms

A. Training courses may be offered on a voluntary basis to all persons who have reached the age of ten years, but the game and fish commission may require any hunter whose hunting license has been revoked or suspended to show a certificate of completion of such training course as a condition to issuance or renewal of a license.

B. The courses held for students in the common schools and high schools shall be elective only, and attendance in such classes shall not be considered in computing a school district's student count.

Added by Laws 1981, Ch. 1, § 2, eff. Jan. 23, 1981.

Historical and Statutory Notes

Source:
Laws 1955, Ch. 121, §§ 3, 5.
Code 1939, Supp.1955, §§ 54–816, 54–818.
A.R.S. former § 15–1073.
Laws 1974, 1st S.S., Ch. 3, § 17.
Laws 1975, Ch. 105, § 3.

§ 15–715. Special academic assistance to pupils in kindergarten programs and grades one through three

A. Each common and unified school district shall develop a plan to supplement the regular education program by providing special academic assistance to pupils in kindergarten programs and grades one through three. The purpose of the special academic assistance is to assist pupils in developing the minimum skills necessary for fourth grade work by the end of the third grade. Special academic assistance, at a minimum, shall focus on pupils who, because of innate factors, are not succeeding in the school environment as identified by parents, guardians or school personnel. These pupils may include, but are not limited to, those who do not qualify for special education services, who have measured intelligence quotients of between seventy and eighty-five or who exhibit characteristics of attention deficit disorder or learning patterns attributable to prenatal substance exposure. The plan shall include:

1. Procedures for use in identifying pupils in need of special academic assistance.

2. Special services for provision of special academic assistance through the regular program of instruction.

3. Procedures for involving parents in the program.

4. Evaluation procedures for use in assessing the progress of the pupils in the program.

B. Each common and unified school district shall implement its program of special academic assistance to pupils in kindergarten programs and grades one through three by the 1986–1987 school year.

C. The teacher of a pupil enrolled in a special academic assistance program shall review the pupil's academic achievement each regular reporting period. Parents shall be notified of the progress of their child in the special academic assistance program by the established reporting method of the school district.

D. The state board of education shall develop and provide the following to all common and unified school districts:

1. Competency requirements for the promotion of pupils from the third grade as prescribed in § 15-701.

2. Model plans for special academic assistance programs which include all of the items specified in subsection A of this section.

E. The department of education shall provide technical assistance to school districts in developing and implementing their plan. The assistance shall include assistance with all of the items specified in subsection A of this section.

Added by Laws 1985, Ch. 166, § 8, eff. April 18, 1985. Amended by Laws 1988, Ch. 308, § 1; Laws 1990, Ch. 233, § 6, eff. July 1, 1991; Laws 1992, Ch. 62, § 2; Laws 2004, Ch. 340, § 2.

Historical and Statutory Notes

Laws 1985, Ch. 166, §§ 46 and 47, delayed the requirements for special academic assistance provided for in this section for the 1985–1986 fiscal year and required a report to the legislature.

Laws 1990, Ch. 345, § 1, as amended by Laws 1991, Ch. 251, § 5, Laws 1993, Ch. 77, § 27, and Laws 1994, 9th S.S., Ch. 2, § 26, provides:

"**Section 1. At-risk preschool project grants; needs assessment; application; allocation of monies**

"**A.** A five year project of preschool grants to school districts is established for fiscal years 1990–1991 through 1994–1995. The grants shall be disbursed by the state board of education to school districts to be used in individual schools to provide preschool services to at-risk preschool children who have reached the age of four by September 1 of the current year and who reside in the school attendance area or disbursed by the state board of education as provided in § 29 of this act to provide preschool services to at-risk preschool children who have reached the age of four by September 1 of the current year. In providing preschool services to at-risk preschool children, districts shall provide services that, at a minimum, focus on pupils who, because of innate factors, are not succeeding in the school environment as identified by parents, guardians or school personnel. These pupils may include, but are not limited to, those who do not qualify for special education services, who have measured intelligence quotients of between seventy and eighty-five or who exhibit characteristics of attention deficit disorder or learning patterns attributable to prenatal substance exposure. The grants shall be distributed in two phases. Phase one programs shall consist of those programs initially funded during fiscal year 1990–1991 and phase two programs shall consist of those programs initially funded during fiscal year 1991–1992 or later. A school is eligible to apply for a preschool project if it has been identified by the state board of education as having a large percentage of pupils in kindergarten programs and grades one through three who are at risk of not succeeding in the educational system. The department of education shall make a list of qualifying at-risk school attendance areas available to the public. The state board shall select schools to receive grants based on the percentage of at-risk children in their kindergarten programs through grade three population, the quality of the proposed program to serve at-risk preschool pupils and the school's ability to implement the program. The state board shall establish requirements for application, evaluation, reporting and reapplication as follows:

"1. Initial application requirements for both phase one and phase two programs shall include at least:

"(a) An assessment of the needs of the at-risk preschool children who reside in the school attendance area. The needs assessment shall include a consideration of at least the following factors:

"(i) Academic and readiness needs.

"(ii) The most appropriate number of days and hours per week during which the at-risk preschool program should operate.

"(iii) Child care needs including nutrition.

"(b) A proposal detailing a program specifically designed to provide assistance to the at-risk preschool pupils. This proposal shall describe how the findings of the needs assessment were incorporated into the school application and shall include:

"(i) A description of the procedures used to identify the at-risk preschool children.

"(ii) A description of clearly defined goals for meeting the academic and readiness needs identified pursuant to subdivision (a), item (i) of this paragraph.

"(iii) A description of the instructional approach to be used in meeting the identified needs of the at-risk preschool pupils which is developmentally appropriate and consistent with nationally recognized standards of early childhood education.

"(iv) A list of the qualifications and experience of project staff.

"(v) A plan for the provision of in-service training for personnel involved in the preschool project.

"(vi) A description of the service delivery model including the extent to which the project will collaborate with other at-risk preschool programs in the district attendance area.

"(vii) A plan showing how the programs developed under this act will be articulated with existing programs in kindergarten programs and grades one through three.

"(viii) A plan for involving families of at-risk preschool pupils in the program.

"2. In addition to the application requirements in paragraph 1, initial application requirements for phase two programs shall include evidence of collaboration or consultation with district operated programs for preschool children with disabilities, federally funded at-risk programs, child care centers serving government subsidized children or other similar programs serving at-risk young children to ensure efficient delivery of services and to prevent duplication of services. The evidence shall include the establishment of an early childhood coordinating committee. The coordinating committee shall assist the district in the development of the application to the department of education to request funding for this project. Members of the coordinating committee shall include parents, school and special education personnel, and, if available in the community, representatives from federally funded at-risk preschool programs, representatives from child care centers serving government subsidized children and representatives from other similar programs serving at-risk young children. Other members of the coordinating committee may include representatives from health services and community agencies, members of the community who are knowledgeable about appropriate programs for young children and representatives from local child care resource and referral agencies.

"3. School districts participating in both phases of the at-risk preschool project may subcontract with federally funded at-risk programs, child care centers serving government subsidized children or other similar programs serving at-risk young children. If a school district subcontracts with a program or center, the district shall describe the subcontracting arrangement in the initial application established pursuant to paragraphs 1 and 2 and shall require the subcontractor to provide the program information specified in Laws 1990, chapter 345, § 2, subsection A, paragraph 4, subdivisions (a) through (j), as amended by Laws 1991, chapter 251, § 6. The school district shall submit the required information in the initial application to the state board.

"4. Annual reapplication requirements for both phase one and phase two programs shall include at least an annual report for each fiscal year of participation in the project describing the progress of the program as presented in the proposal, the amount of monies expended on the program as detailed on a form developed by the department of education, the number of pupils receiving assistance from the program and other information requested by the department of education. In addition, all school districts that receive funding pursuant to this act shall annually submit data on or before March 15 to the department of education documenting the nature and level of services that were provided to program participants. The data shall be directly related to the services that the district proposed to deliver in its approved application for these monies. The data shall also include documentation and a description of actual parental involvement and community support. The department of education shall prepare a uniform self-reporting format for the transmission of this data and shall monitor and assist grantees accordingly.

"**B.** The department of education shall review the annual reports prescribed in subsection A, paragraph 4. After reviewing the annual reports and making any on-site visitations, the department of education shall notify those districts which are not in compliance with the district's approved proposal and inform those districts of the types of technical assistance available from the department of education and of the date by which compliance must be achieved. By May 30 of each year of the pilot project, the department of education shall make a report to the state board of education of those districts which continue to be in noncompliance with their approved proposal. The state board shall determine whether such districts are eligible for continued funding.

"**C.** The department of education shall present a report to the president of the senate, the speaker of the house of representatives and the governor by November 15 from 1991 through 1993, on the progress of the preschool at-risk project."

Laws 1990, Ch. 345, § 1, as amended by Laws 1991, Ch. 251, § 5, and Laws 1992, Ch. 305, § 22, was repealed by Laws 1994, 9th S.S., Ch. 2, § 27.

Laws 1990, Ch. 345, § 2, as amended by Laws 1991, Ch. 251, § 6; Laws 1992, Ch. 305, § 23, provides:

"**Sec. 2. Early childhood advisory council**

"**A.** The state board of education shall appoint a state early childhood advisory council on early childhood education. Members of the advisory council shall include teachers, parents of eligible children, public school administrators, the superintendent of public instruction, the director of the governor's office for children and representatives of state human service agencies, business and industry, child care providers, early childhood associations, and state and federal at-risk preschool programs. The advisory council shall:

"1. Advise the department of education relating to the at-risk preschool project.

"2. Establish guidelines for comprehensive early childhood programs for at-risk four year old children. The guidelines shall reflect the best practices on comprehensive early childhood programs.

"3. Review applications and reapplications for at-risk preschool project grants and make recommendations to the state board of education for awards.

"4. Consider the following when recommending initial awards to the state board of education for phase two programs of the at-risk preschool project:

"(a) The quality and background of the staff in early childhood programs, including the specific formal training and background in early childhood education or child development of the individual directly supervising the program.

"(b) The ability of the program to provide for or coordinate with child care services in addition to preschool services for families needing full-day child care.

"(c) A staff-to-child ratio of not less than one staff member per ten children with a group size of no more than twenty.

"(d) The degree to which the program involves and works with parents, includes home visits and offers parents instruction on child development and parenting skills.

"(e) The manner in which health, medical, dental and nutrition needs are addressed by the program.

"(f) The degree to which the program involves collaboration with existing services and services for at-risk four year old children.

"(g) The degree to which the program can be monitored and evaluated to determine its ability to meet its goals.

"(h) The degree to which the program integrates the culture and language of minority children.

"(i) The need to provide or desirability of providing transportation or other auxiliary services in order to enable families to participate in the program.

"(j) The need to provide or desirability of providing staff training and development and staff compensation sufficient to assure continuity of services.

"5. Conduct annual site visits to selected preschool projects funded pursuant to this section.

"6. Submit a report containing the findings and recommendations of the evaluation required pursuant to Laws 1990, chapter 345, § 1, subsection C, as amended by § 5 of this act, to the president of the senate, the speaker of the house of representatives and the governor within six months of the completion of the evaluation and no later than November 15, 1993.

"**B.** The department of education shall provide staff assistance to the council."

Laws 1990, Ch. 392, § 1, as amended by Laws 1992, Ch. 62, § 6, provides:

"**Section 1. Full-day kindergarten for at-risk pupils; definition**

"**A.** The department of education shall rank all schools which provide a kindergarten program and which are operated by a school district according to their population of at-risk pupils and shall notify those schools with the greatest population of at-risk pupils that they are eligible to receive monies to administer a full-day kindergarten program for pupils who are at risk of not succeeding in the educational system. The state board of education shall disburse monies appropriated to applying schools that demonstrate the greatest need based on the ranking. Schools that receive approval to provide a full-day kindergarten program as provided in this act shall receive an amount equal to one thousand two hundred dollars per pupil enrolled in a kindergarten program. If additional monies are available after funding all eligible schools, the remaining monies shall be used to increase the per pupil funding amount for each school approved as provided in this subsection.

"**B.** The full-day kindergarten program, at a minimum, shall focus on pupils who, because of innate factors, are not succeeding in the school environment as identified by parents, guardians or school personnel. These pupils may include, but are not limited to, those who do not qualify for special education services, who have measured intelligence quotients of between seventy and eighty-five or who exhibit characteristics of attention deficit disorder or learning patterns attributable to prenatal substance exposure.

"**C.** A school that has received monies for participation in an at-risk pilot program for pupils in kindergarten programs and grades one through three, as provided in Laws 1988, chapter 308, or has a special budget override in effect designed to improve the academic achievement in kindergarten programs and grades one through three, as provided in § 15-482, Arizona Revised Statutes, and is already using at least a portion of these monies for the provision of a full-day kindergarten program, is not eligible to receive additional monies under this act.

"**D.** For purposes of this act, "full-day kindergarten program" means a minimum of two hundred forty minutes of instruction each day not including lunch periods or recess periods as provided to pupils enrolled in a kindergarten program."

Laws 1991, Ch. 251, § 1, as amended by Laws 1992, Ch. 62, § 7, providing for the establishment of a joint legislative committee to study funding and programs for at-risk pupils was repealed by § 12 of Ch. 251, as amended by § 9 of Ch. 62, on January 1, 1993.

Laws 1991, Ch. 251, § 2, establishing a governor's task force on pupil readiness, was repealed by Laws 1992, Ch. 70, § 2, subsec. G, as amended by Laws 1993, Ch. 174, § 4, on February 1, 1993.

Laws 1991, Ch. 251, § 3, as amended by Laws 1992, Ch. 305, § 25; Laws 1993, 2nd S.S., Ch. 8, § 9, is amended to read:

"**Sec. 3. At-risk pilot project extension**

"**A.** The pilot at-risk project for students in kindergarten through third grades as established by Laws 1988, chapter 308, § 3, as amended by Laws 1989, chapter 273, § 21, the pilot at-risk project for students in grades seven through twelve as established by Laws 1988, chapter 308, § 5, as amended by Laws 1989, chapter 273, § 34, and the use of funds as specified in Laws 1990, chapter 399, § 17 shall be extended until such time that sufficient funding for statewide at-risk programs and services is provided by the legislature through a weight in the funding formula for kindergarten and grades one through twelve.

"**B.** The state board of education shall annually review reapproval applications to determine if the program is in compliance with the provisions of the laws establishing these projects. Beginning with the 1993-1994 school year, monies may only be allocated for practices found to be effective with at-risk populations as determined by the evaluation submitted to the legislature. The total amount to be granted to a recipient for a given fiscal year shall be determined based on the application for that year and is not required to equal the amount received in a prior year. Any monies not allocated to programs applying for reapproval may be allocated to new school districts, schools or educational consortia that meet the eligibility requirements prescribed by law."

Laws 1991, Ch. 251, §§ 10 and 11, provide:

"**Sec. 10. At-risk preschool pilot programs fund; exemption from lapsing**

"Monies appropriated or donated to the department of education for the purpose of funding at-risk preschool pilot programs established pursuant to § 5 of this act shall be deposited by the department in the at-risk preschool pilot programs fund. The department of education at-risk preschool pilot programs fund shall be established as a separate fund on the books of the department of education. The department shall account separately in the at-risk preschool pilot programs fund for the monies for phase one and phase two programs as established pursuant to § 5 of this act. Monies of the department of education at-risk preschool pilot programs fund are exempt from the provisions of § 35-190, Arizona Revised Statutes, relating to lapsing of appropriations.

"**Sec. 11. County detention center education program**

"Of the monies appropriated from the state general fund to support the secondary level at-risk pilot project established pursuant to Laws 1988, chapter 308, § 5, the state board of education may allocate monies to support the pilot education program for pupils within a county detention center which had been initiated pursuant to Laws 1989, chapter 273, § 34."

Laws 1992, Ch. 62, § 11, provides:

"**Sec. 11. Needs assessment**

"**A.** The state board of education shall conduct a needs assessment to determine the number of pupils in this state who, because of innate factors, are not succeeding in the school environment as identified by parents, guardians or school personnel. These pupils may include, but are not limited to, those who do not qualify for special education services or who no longer qualify for special education services, who have measured intelligence quotients of between seventy and eighty-five or who exhibit characteristics of attention deficit disorder or learning patterns attributable to prenatal substance exposure.

"**B.** The needs assessment shall be designed to:

"1. Identify the number of innately at-risk pupils who are currently receiving special assistance and the number of innately at-risk pupils who are not receiving special assistance.

"2. Describe existing programs that serve innately at-risk pupils.

"3. Identify the most appropriate programs for serving innately at-risk pupils.

"4. Serve as the basis for a permanent mechanism for identifying innately at-risk pupils.

"C. The state board of education shall report the results of the needs assessment to the governor, the president of the senate, the speaker of the house of representatives and the chairmen of the joint legislative committee to study funding and programs for at-risk pupils no later than December 31, 1992."

Laws 1993, Ch. 77, § 1, par. 17, provides:

"**Section 1. Purpose**"

"17. Laws 1990, chapter 345, § 1, as amended by Laws 1991, chapter 251, § 5, was amended by Laws 1992, chapter 62, § 8. However, Laws 1992, chapter 62 failed to set forth the full text of Laws 1990, chapter 345, § 1, as amended, as required by article IV, part 2, § 14, Constitution of Arizona. In order to correct a potentially defective enactment, this act amends Laws 1990, chapter 345, § 1, as amended by Laws 1991, chapter 251, § 5, to incorporate the amendments made by Laws 1992, chapter 62 and the chapter 62 version is repealed."

Laws 1993, Ch. 77, § 28, as amended by Laws 1994, Ch. 189, § 19, provides:

"**Sec. 28. Repeal**

"Laws 1990, chapter 345, § 1, as amended by Laws 1991, chapter 251, § 5 and Laws 1992, chapter 62, § 8, is repealed."

Laws 1994, Ch. 189, § 1, par. 9, provides:

"**Section 1. Purpose**"

"9. Laws 1993, chapter 77, § 28 repealed a session law that in one instance had been amended by Laws 1991, chapter 251, § 5. Laws 1993, chapter 77 incorrectly identified the section as § 1. To correct this error, this act amends Laws 1993, chapter 77, § 28 to correct this reference."

Laws 1994, Ch. 266, § 4, provides:

Sec. 4. Secondary level at-risk pilot project

Notwithstanding Laws 1991, chapter 251, § 11, beginning with fiscal year 1994-1995, monies appropriated from the state general fund to support the secondary level at-risk pilot project established pursuant to Laws 1988, chapter 308, § 5 shall not be used to support the pilot education program for pupils within a county detention center.

Laws 1994, 9th S.S., Ch. 2, §§ 28 to 30, provide:

"**Sec. 28. At-risk preschool project; qualified private or federally funded providers**

"**A.** Any private day care operator licensed under title 36, chapter 7.1, article 1, Arizona Revised Statutes, or federally funded preschool that provides services in the school attendance area of a school otherwise eligible to receive funding for the at-risk preschool project is eligible to provide direct services under the at-risk preschool program operated under § 26 of this act.

"**B.** The school district shall provide assistance to the private day care operator or federally funded preschool in meeting the application requirements for both phases one and two programs set forth in Laws 1990, chapter 345, § 1, as amended by Laws 1991, chapter 251, § 5, Laws 1993, chapter 77, § 27 and this act. The criteria used to evaluate the qualifications and training of project staff, the service delivery model and other aspects of the proposed program shall apply to private operators, federally funded preschools and public school programs. An application for participation in the at-risk preschool program may include either a private day care provider, a federally funded preschool or a school, or a combination of any of the three. A private day care provider, a federally funded preschool and a school may provide services in a school attendance area.

"**C.** A private day care operator or a federally funded preschool participating in the program shall provide the program information specified in Laws 1990, chapter 345, § 2, subsection A, paragraph 4, subdivisions (a) through (j), as amended by Laws 1991, chapter 251, section 6 and Laws 1992, chapter 305, § 23.

"**D.** The state board of education shall develop a list of public schools, private day care operators and federally funded preschools that have been selected to participate in the at-risk preschool project. The state board shall distribute the list to all school districts in the state for districts to use in connection with the requirements of § 29 of this act.

"**Sec. 29. At-risk preschool project; qualified private providers; reimbursement**

"**A.** The department of education shall develop a procedure by which school districts shall reimburse private day care operators or federally funded preschools participating in the at-risk preschool program operating under Laws 1990, chapter 345, § 1, as amended by Laws 1991, chapter 251, § 5, Laws 1993, chapter 77, § 27 and this act, on behalf of the parent of a preschool child who resides in a school attendance area that contains a private day care operator or federally funded preschool that has been selected by the state board to participate in the at-risk preschool program and who requests placement in a participating private or federally funded program.

"**B.** The department of education shall transfer the amounts necessary to fund the reimbursements required by subsection A of this section to a school district.

"C. The school district shall reimburse a private day care operator or federally funded preschool participating in the at-risk preschool program for services provided in the manner developed pursuant to subsection A of this section.

"**Sec. 30. Program evaluation**

"**A.** The auditor general shall conduct an annual programmatic evaluation of the at-risk preschool project as prescribed in this act. The auditor general shall provide annual programmatic evaluations to the speaker of the house of representatives, the president of the senate and the governor on or before December 31, 1995 and each year thereafter during which the project continues.

"**B.** The annual programmatic evaluations shall examine the effectiveness of the project, the level and scope of services included within the project, the criteria used to select among applicants for participation in the project and the number and demographic characteristics of the children and the families of children participating in the project.

"**C.** The annual programmatic evaluations shall include:

"1. Information on the number and characteristics of the children and the families of the children participating in the project.

"2. Information on the number of public schools, private day care operators and federally funded preschools participating in the project.

"3. Information on the average cost for each participating child.

"4. Information concerning the scholastic performance of previous participants in the project including, but not limited to:

"(a) The performance of past participants on nationally standardized norm-referenced achievement tests.

"(b) The performance of similar students who did not participate in the project.

"(c) The performance of all students in the same grade level at each of the schools at which a program was operated.

"5. A summary of the program information required to be provided under § 26 of this act.

"6. An evaluation of the overall effectiveness of the pilot project based on performance based outcome measures including the subsequent scholastic performance of participants.

"7. Recommendations regarding the effectiveness of the project.

"8. Recommendations regarding the continuation of the project.

"9. Any other information or evaluative material that the auditor general determines to be useful in considering the programmatic and cost-effectiveness of the project.

"**D.** Notwithstanding any law to the contrary, the auditor general has access to all relevant information and records held by the department of education, the department of health services and the department of economic security in order to conduct the evaluation required by this section. The auditor general shall keep this information confidential."

§ 15-716. Instruction on acquired immune deficiency syndrome; department assistance

A. Each common, high and unified school district may provide instruction to kindergarten programs through the twelfth grade on acquired immune deficiency syndrome and the human immunodeficiency virus.

B. Each district is free to develop its own course of study for each grade. At a minimum, instruction shall:

1. Be appropriate to the grade level in which it is offered.
2. Be medically accurate.
3. Promote abstinence.
4. Discourage drug abuse.
5. Dispel myths regarding transmission of the human immunodeficiency virus.

C. No district shall include in its course of study instruction which:

1. Promotes a homosexual life-style.
2. Portrays homosexuality as a positive alternative life-style.

3. Suggests that some methods of sex are safe methods of homosexual sex.

D. At the request of a school district, the department of health services or the department of education shall review instruction materials to determine their medical accuracy.

E. At the request of a school district, the department of education shall provide the following assistance:

1. A suggested course of study.

2. Teacher training.

3. A list of available films and other teaching aids.

F. At the request of a parent, a pupil shall be excused from instruction on the acquired immune deficiency syndrome and the human immunodeficiency virus as provided in subsection A of this section. The school district shall notify all parents of their ability to withdraw their child from the instruction.

Added by Laws 1991, Ch. 269, § 1. Amended by Laws 1995, Ch. 268, § 36.

Historical and Statutory Notes

Reviser's Notes:

1991 Note. Pursuant to authority of § 41–1304.02, in subsection C, paragraphs 1 and 2 the spelling of "life-style" was corrected and in subsection F, first sentence the second "the" was transposed to follow "on".

§ 15–717. American history and heritage

A teacher or administrator in any school in this state may read or post in any school building copies or excerpts of the following materials:

1. The national motto.

2. The national anthem.

3. The pledge of allegiance.

4. The preamble to the constitution of this state.

5. The declaration of independence.

6. The Mayflower compact.

7. Writings, speeches, documents and proclamations of the founding fathers and the presidents of the United States.

8. Published decisions of the United States Supreme Court.

9. Acts of the United States Congress.

Added by Laws 1993, Ch. 125, § 1.

§ 15–718. Repealed by Laws 2002, Ch. 295, § 3

Historical and Statutory Notes

The repealed section, added by Laws 1998, Ch. 231, § 2, amended by Laws 1999, Ch. 256, § 2, related to research based phonics instruction.

§ 15–719. Character education program instruction; fund

A. Each common, high and unified school district and charter school may provide instruction to kindergarten programs through the twelfth grade on character development.

B. Each district may develop its own course of study for each grade. At a minimum, the character education program must include:

1. Instruction in the definition and application of at least six of the following character traits: truthfulness, responsibility, compassion, diligence, sincerity, trustworthiness, respect, attentiveness, obedience, orderliness, forgiveness, virtue, fairness, caring, citizenship and integrity.

2. The use of activities, discussions and visual media and literacy presentations to illustrate and reinforce the application of the character traits.

3. Presentations by teachers or mentors who demonstrate the character traits.

C. At the request of the school district or charter school, the department of education may certify that the school district or charter school has a character development instruction program that meets all of the requirements in subsection B of this section.

D. Parents may elect for their child not to participate in the program.

E. The school district or charter school may accept donations or charge fees for the program if the program is not offered during regular school hours.

F. A character education special plate fund is established consisting of monies received pursuant to § 28-2421. The department of education shall administer the fund. Monies in the fund are continuously appropriated. Monies from the fund shall be annually distributed by the department by July 1.

G. The character education and development division at the department of education shall allocate monies through at least two but no more than four private character education foundations that are incorporated nonprofit corporations in this state and that are qualified under § 501(c)(3) of the United States internal revenue code [1] for federal income tax purposes. The director of the character education and development division at the department of education shall select private character education foundations that provide character education programs that demonstrate proven and effective research based curriculum and training to receive monies from the character education special plate fund.

H. On notice from the department of education, the state treasurer shall invest and divest monies in the fund as provided by § 35-313, and monies earned from investment shall be credited to the fund.

I. Monies in the fund are exempt from the provisions of § 35-190 relating to lapsing of appropriations.

Added by Laws 2000, Ch. 313, § 1. Amended by Laws 2004, Ch. 316, § 1.

[1] Internal Revenue Code sections may be found in Title 26 of U.S.C.A.

Historical and Statutory Notes

Reviser's Notes:

2004 Note. Pursuant to authority of § 41-1304.02, in subsection F the reference to "§ 28-2421" was substituted for the reference to "§ 28-2420" to conform to the reviser's renumbering of that section.

§ 15-720. Noncurriculum related clubs for grades seven and eight; definitions

A. It is unlawful for any public school that offers instruction in grades seven and eight to deny equal access to pupils, to deny a fair opportunity to pupils or to discriminate against pupils who wish to conduct a meeting within a limited open forum on the basis of religious content, political content, philosophical content or other content of speech at these meetings.

B. A public school that offers instruction in grades seven and eight shall be deemed to offer a fair opportunity to pupils who wish to conduct a meeting within a limited open forum pursuant to this section if the school policy on noncurriculum group meetings conforms to all of the following:

1. The meetings are voluntary and initiated by pupils.

2. The meetings are not sponsored by the school, the school district, the federal government, this state, any of this state's political subdivisions or any officer or employee of the school, the school district, the federal government, this state or any of this state's political subdivisions.

3. Employees or officers of the school, the school district, the federal government, this state or any of this state's political subdivisions may be present at religious meetings only as nonparticipants.

4. The meetings do not materially and substantially interfere with the orderly conduct of the educational activities of the school.

5. Persons who are not officials or employees of the school or the school district shall not direct, conduct, control or regularly attend the meetings.

C. This section shall not be construed to authorize this state or any of its political subdivisions to engage in any of the following:

1. Influence the form or the content of any prayer or other religious activity.

2. Require any person to participate in prayer or any other religious activity.

3. Spend public monies on noncurriculum group meetings other than the incidental costs of providing methods to announce the time and location of a noncurriculum group's meeting to seventh and eighth grade pupils and the incidental costs of providing the facilities to conduct the meetings.

4. Compel any officer or employee of the school or the school district to attend a noncurriculum group meeting if the content of the speech at the meeting is contrary to the beliefs of the officer or employee.

5. Allow meetings that are unlawful to take place on school property.

6. Limit the application of this section to groups of a minimum or maximum number of pupils.

7. Violate the constitutional rights of any person.

D. This section shall not be construed to limit the authority of the school, the school district or the officers or employees of the school or the school district to:

1. Maintain order and discipline on the school premises.

2. Protect the safety of pupils and faculty.

3. Allow a school officer or employee or a school district officer or employee to be present at noncurriculum group meetings.

4. Ensure that the attendance of pupils at noncurriculum group meetings is voluntary.

E. As used in this section:

1. "Limited open forum" means an offering or opportunity provided by a school that provides instruction in grades seven and eight for one or more noncurriculum related groups of pupils to meet on the premises of the school during lunch periods, before the commencement of the day's regularly scheduled courses or after the conclusion of the day's regularly scheduled courses.

2. "Noncurriculum" means that the group's activities do not substantially enhance, extend or reinforce the subject matter of an academic course that is currently offered at the school.

3. "Pupil" means a public school student enrolled in the seventh or eighth grade.

Added by Laws 2001, Ch. 263, § 1.

Historical and Statutory Notes

Another § -15-720 added by Laws 2001, Ch. 61, § 1, was renumbered as § 15-711.

Reviser's Notes:

2001 Note. Laws 2001, Ch. 61, sec. 1 added another new § 15-720 that was renumbered as § 15-711, pursuant to authority of § 41-1304.02.

ARTICLE 2. COURSES OF STUDY AND TEXTBOOKS

§ 15-721. Common schools; course of study; textbooks

A. The governing board shall approve for common schools the course of study, the basic textbook for each course and all units recommended for credit under each general subject title prior to implementation of the course.

B. If any course does not include a basic textbook, the governing board shall approve all supplemental books used in the course prior to approval of the course.

C. If any course includes a basic textbook and uses supplemental books, the governing board may approve all supplemental books and teaching aids, including instructional computer software, used in the course prior to approval of the course.

D. If the course includes a basic textbook and uses supplemental books that have not been approved by the governing board at the time of approval of the course, a teacher may use the supplemental books at any time during the school year. Use of the supplemental books shall be brought to the attention of the governing board during the school year in which they are added for ratification.

E. Notwithstanding any other law, the provisions of subsections B and C do not apply to supplemental books used in courses or programs instituted pursuant to article 4 of this chapter.[1]

F. The governing board shall:

1. Enforce the course of study and select all textbooks used in the common schools and purchase the textbooks from the publishers. District school funds may be budgeted and expended by the governing board for teaching aids, including instructional computer software. For courses that do not require that each student have a textbook other than for classroom instruction the school district need only purchase one textbook for each student in the largest group that would be receiving classroom instruction at any one time.

2. Require that all meetings of committees authorized for the purposes of textbook review and selection be open to the public as prescribed in title 38, chapter 3, article 3.1.[2]

3. Make available at the school district office for review by the public, for a period of sixty days prior to formal selection of textbooks, a copy of each textbook being considered for selection.

Added by Laws 1981, Ch. 1, § 2, eff. Jan. 23, 1981. Amended by Laws 1982, Ch. 81, § 1; Laws 1983, Ch. 182, § 3; Laws 1984, Ch. 379, § 3; Laws 1997, Ch. 231, § 14.

[1] Section 15-761 et seq.

[2] Section 38-431 et seq.

Historical and Statutory Notes

Source:

Laws 1912, Ch. 77, §§ 41, 54, 81, 82.
Civ. Code 1913, §§ 2733, 2750, 2777, 2778.
Laws 1921, Ch. 72, § 5.
Laws 1921, Ch. 137, § 1.
Laws 1925, Ch. 11, § 1.
Laws 1925, Ch. 70, §§ 1 to 4.
Laws 1927, Ch. 88, § 1.
Rev. Code 1928, §§ 1011, 1025, 1074.
Laws 1933, Ch. 18, § 1.
Code 1939, §§ 54-430, 54-907.
Laws 1949, Ch. 110, § 1.
Laws 1951, Ch. 74, § 1.
Laws 1951, Ch. 140, § 1.
Laws 1952, Ch. 138, § 1.
Code 1939, Supp.1952, § 54-416.
Laws 1954, Ch. 117, § 2.
A.R.S. former §§ 15-442, 15-442.01, 15-545.
Laws 1960, Ch. 120, § 2.
Laws 1960, Ch. 127, § 2.
Laws 1961, Ch. 61, § 2.
Laws 1962, Ch. 92, § 1.
Laws 1962, Ch. 112, § 1.
Laws 1966, Ch. 85, § 1.
Laws 1967, Ch. 69, § 1.
Laws 1967, 3rd S.S., Ch. 19, § 1.
Laws 1969, Ch. 16, § 1.
Laws 1970, Ch. 118, § 1.
Laws 1972, Ch. 115, § 5.
Laws 1973, Ch. 62, § 1.
Laws 1974, 1st S.S., Ch. 3, §§ 8, 10.
Laws 1975, Ch. 50, § 2.
Laws 1976, Ch. 68, § 1.
Laws 1976, Ch. 156, § 2.
Laws 1977, Ch. 79, § 1.
Laws 1977, Ch. 157, § 1.
Laws 1977, Ch. 164, § 7.
Laws 1978, Ch. 7, § 3.
Laws 1978, Ch. 8, § 1.
Laws 1978, Ch. 87, § 1.
Laws 1978, Ch. 188, § 6.
Laws 1979, Ch. 117, § 1.
Laws 1979, Ch. 118, § 4.
Laws 1979, Ch. 195, § 6.
Laws 1979, Ch. 218, § 2.
Laws 1979, 1st S.S., Ch. 2, § 2.
Laws 1980, 2nd S.S., Ch. 9, § 18.
Laws 1980, Ch. 105, § 2.
Laws 1980, Ch. 225, § 1.

§ 15-722. High schools; course of study; textbooks

A. The governing board shall approve for high schools the course of study, the basic textbook for each course and all units recommended for credit under each general subject title prior to implementation of such course.

B. If any course does not include a basic textbook, the governing board shall approve all supplemental books used in such course prior to usage.

C. If any course includes a basic textbook and uses supplemental books or instructional computer software, the governing board may approve all supplemental books and instructional computer software used in such course prior to usage.

D. If the course includes a basic text and uses supplemental books which have not been approved by the governing board at the time of approval of the course, a teacher may use such supplemental books at any time during the school year. Use of such supplemental books shall be brought to the attention of the governing board during the school year in which they are added for ratification.

E. The governing board shall prescribe up to five textbooks for each course and the teacher, with the consent of the governing board, may use any one of the prescribed textbooks for the purposes of his course.

Added by Laws 1981, Ch. 1, § 2, eff. Jan. 23, 1981. Amended by Laws 1983, Ch. 182, § 4; Laws 1984, Ch. 379, § 4.

Historical and Statutory Notes

Source:

Laws 1912, Ch. 77, §§ 81, 82.
Civ. Code 1913, §§ 2777, 2778.
Rev. Code 1928, § 1074.
Code 1939, § 54–907.
A.R.S. former §§ 15–545, 15–545.01.
Laws 1966, Ch. 85, § 1.
Laws 1979, Ch. 118, § 4.
Laws 1979, Ch. 218, § 3.

§ 15–723. Furnishing of free textbooks, subject matter materials and supplementary books

A. Free textbooks, subject matter materials and supplementary books shall be furnished in common schools and all state welfare institutions maintaining educational facilities, subject to § 15–727.

B. Governing boards shall furnish free required textbooks and related printed subject matter materials in the high schools, subject to § 15–727.

Added by Laws 1981, Ch. 1, § 2, eff. Jan. 23, 1981. Amended by Laws 1983, Ch. 182, § 5; Laws 1984, Ch. 379, § 5.

Historical and Statutory Notes

Source:

Laws 1912, Ch. 72, §§ 1, 2.
Civ. Code 1913, §§ 2825, 2826.
Laws 1922, Ch. 35, § 49.
Rev. Code 1928, § 1048.
Laws 1933, Ch. 20, § 1.
Laws 1949, Ch. 88, § 1.
Code 1939, Supp.1952, § 54–1102.
Laws 1955, Ch. 25, § 1.
A.R.S. former § 15–1101.
Laws 1960, Ch. 120, § 3.
Laws 1976, Ch. 156, § 3.

Laws 1984, Ch. 379, § 18 provides:

"Sec. 18. Furnishing free required textbooks and related printed subject matter materials in the high schools; phase in

"Notwithstanding § 15–723, Arizona Revised Statutes, as amended by § 5 of this act:

"1. Beginning with the 1985–1986 school year, governing boards shall furnish free required textbooks and related printed subject matter materials for high school pupils in grade nine.

"2. Beginning with the 1986–1987 school year, governing boards shall furnish free required textbooks and related printed subject matter materials for high school pupils in grades nine and ten.

"3. Beginning with the 1987–1988 school year, governing boards shall furnish free required textbooks and related printed subject matter materials for high school pupils in grades nine through eleven.

"4. Beginning with the 1988–1989 school year and each year thereafter, governing boards shall furnish free required textbooks and related printed subject matter materials for high school pupils in grades nine through twelve."

§ 15-724. Purchase of high school textbooks, subject matter materials and supplementary books; budget; rental

A. The governing board may include in its proposed school district budget finances required for the purchase of textbooks, subject matter materials and supplementary books for the use of registered high school pupils.

B. The governing board may charge a reasonable rental fee for the use of nonrequired textbooks, nonrelated subject matter materials and supplementary books by registered high school pupils.

Added by Laws 1981, Ch. 1, § 2, eff. Jan. 23, 1981. Amended by Laws 1984, Ch. 379, § 6.

Historical and Statutory Notes

Source:

Laws 1912, Ch. 77, §§ 81, 82.
Civ. Code 1913, §§ 2777, 2778.
Rev. Code 1928, § 1074.
Code 1939, § 54-907.
A.R.S. former § 15-545.
Laws 1966, Ch. 85, § 1.
Laws 1979, Ch. 118, § 4.

Laws 1984, Ch. 379, § 19 provides:

"**Sec. 19. Rental of textbooks, subject matter materials and supplementary books in the high schools; phase in**

"Notwithstanding § 15-724, Arizona Revised Statutes, as amended by § 6 of this act:

"1. For fiscal year 1984-1985, governing boards may charge a reasonable rental fee for the use of all textbooks, subject matter materials and supplementary books by registered high school pupils in grades nine through twelve.

"2. For the 1985-1986 school year, governing boards may charge a reasonable rental fee for the use of all textbooks, subject matter materials and supplementary books by high school pupils in grades ten through twelve.

"3. For the 1986-1987 school year, governing boards may charge a reasonable rental fee for the use of all textbooks, subject matter materials and supplementary books by high school pupils in grades eleven and twelve.

"4. For the 1987-1988 school year, governing boards may charge a reasonable rental fee for the use of all textbooks, subject matter materials and supplementary books by high school pupils in grade twelve.

"5. Beginning with the 1988-1989 school year and each year thereafter, governing boards may charge a reasonable rental fee for the use of non-required textbooks, non-related subject matter materials and supplementary books by all registered high school pupils in grades nine through twelve."

Reviser's Notes:

1984 Note. Pursuant to authority of § 41-1304.02, in subsection B hyphens were removed from "nonrequired" and "nonrelated".

§ 15-725. Repealed by Laws 1996, Ch. 284, § 31

Historical and Statutory Notes

The repealed section, added by Laws 1981, Ch. 1, § 2, amended by Laws 1983, Ch. 182, § 6; Laws 1984, Ch. 61, § 6; and Laws 1984, Ch. 379, § 7, derived from:

Laws 1912, Ch. 72, §§ 3, 4, 7, 9.
Civ. Code 1913, §§ 2827, 2828, 2831, 2833.
Rev. Code 1928, §§ 1049, 1050, 1053, 1054.
Code 1939, §§ 54-1103, 54-1107, 54-1108.
Laws 1941, Ch. 17, § 1.
Code 1939, Supp.1952, § 54-1104.
A.R.S. former §§ 15-1102, 15-1103, 15-1104, 15-1105.
Laws 1960, Ch. 120, § 4.
Laws 1976, Ch. 156, § 4, 5.

related to contracts for purchases of textbooks and instructional computer software.

§ 15-726. Purchase of textbooks and instructional computer software by schools having four or fewer teachers; welfare institutions

A. In all schools having four or fewer teachers, the county school superintendent may have advisory authority to assist the governing board in the selection and ordering of textbooks and instructional computer software pursuant to this title.

B. State welfare institutions maintaining educational facilities and the various accommodation schools shall purchase textbooks and instructional computer software by the same procedures as provided for the common schools.

C. Welfare institutions shall purchase textbooks and instructional computer software with their own institutional funds, and the textbooks and instructional computer software required for the accommodation schools shall be purchased by the county school superintendents from the county school reserve funds of the various counties.

Added by Laws 1981, Ch. 1, § 2, eff. Jan. 23, 1981. Amended by Laws 1983, Ch. 182, § 7.

Historical and Statutory Notes

Source:

Laws 1960, Ch. 120, § 6.
A.R.S. former § 15-1109.

§ 15-727. Care and issue of textbooks, subject matter materials, supplementary books and instructional computer software

All textbooks, subject matter materials, supplementary books and instructional computer software in the possession of the school districts and those textbooks, subject matter materials, supplementary books and instructional computer software purchased by school districts as provided in this title are and remain the property of the school districts. The school districts shall hold pupils using the textbooks, subject matter materials, supplementary books and instructional computer software responsible for damage or loss of the textbooks, subject matter materials, supplementary books and instructional computer software. If a pupil for any reason requires a second copy of a textbook, subject matter materials or a supplementary book, the pupil shall reimburse the school district for the cost of the textbook, subject matter materials or supplementary book.

Added by Laws 1981, Ch. 1, § 2, eff. Jan. 23, 1981. Amended by Laws 1983, Ch. 182, § 8; Laws 1984, Ch. 379, § 8.

Historical and Statutory Notes

Source:

Laws 1912, Ch. 72, §§ 5, 10.
Civ.Code 1913, §§ 2829, 2834.
Rev. Code 1928, §§ 1051, 1055.
Code 1939, § 54-1109.
Laws 1949, Ch. 88, § 2.
Code 1939, Supp.1954, § 54-1105.
A.R.S. former §§ 15-1106, 15-1107.

§ 15-728. Purchase of books by pupils or parent

A pupil or parent may purchase from the governing board such books as necessary for high school pupils at the price the governing board pays for the books.

Added by Laws 1981, Ch. 1, § 2, eff. Jan. 23, 1981.

Historical and Statutory Notes

Source:
Laws 1912, Ch. 72, § 11.
Civ. Code 1913, § 2835.
Rev. Code 1928, § 1056.
Code 1939, § 54-1110.
A.R.S. former § 15-1108.

§ 15-729. Use of monies received for lost or damaged textbooks, subject matter materials, supplementary books or instructional computer software

A school district may hold and use all monies obtained for lost or damaged school textbooks, subject matter materials, supplementary books or instructional computer software to repair or replace textbooks, subject matter materials, supplementary books or instructional computer software which are lost or damaged. A school district shall use these monies in addition to the monies budgeted for purchase of new textbooks, subject matter materials, supplementary books or instructional computer software.

Added by Laws 1981, Ch. 1, § 2, eff. Jan. 23, 1981. Amended by Laws 1983, Ch. 182, § 9; Laws 1984, Ch. 379, § 9.

Historical and Statutory Notes

Source:
Laws 1972, Ch. 22, § 1.
A.R.S. former § 15-1201.03.
Laws 1980, 2nd S.S., Ch. 9, § 57.

§ 15-730. Access to instructional material by parents and guardians

On written request, school personnel designated by the governing board shall permit parents or guardians access to instructional materials currently used by or being considered for use by the school district by making available at least one copy of the instructional material for review by the parents or guardians. Parents or guardians may take printed textbooks, printed supplementary books and printed subject matter materials from the school district premises for a period of not more than forty-eight hours. Parents or guardians may review all other materials, including films, only on the school district premises.

Added by Laws 1987, Ch. 320, § 2.

ARTICLE 2.1. ACCESSIBILITY TO TEXTBOOKS AND INSTRUCTIONAL MATERIALS

Article 2.1, Accessibility to Textbooks and Instructional Materials, consisting of §§ 15-731, 15-732, was added by Laws 2004, Ch. 202, § 1, effective Aug. 25, 2004.

§ 15-731. Definitions

In this article, unless the context otherwise requires:

1. "Accessible electronic file" means, until a national file format is adopted by the United States department of education, a digital file in a mutually agreed on by the publisher and the local educational agency electronic file format that has been prepared using a markup language that maintains the structural integrity of the information and can be processed by conversion software. If a national file format is adopted by the United States department of education, accessible electronic file means an electronic file conforming to the specifica-

tions of the national file format adopted by the United States department of education.

2. "Available authorized entity" means an authorized entity, as defined by 17 United States code § 121, that commonly provides alternative format school materials that are accessible by schools in this state and that has the vendor's authorization to make alternative formats.

3. "Child with a disability" means a pupil who is subject to an individualized education plan pursuant to the individuals with disabilities education act of 1997 (20 United States code §§ 1400 through 1415) or a pupil with a § 504 plan, and whose individualized education plan or § 504 plan requires the use of instructional materials in a specialized format.

4. "Individualized education plan" has the same meaning prescribed in 20 United States code §§ 1401 and 1412 and § 15-761.

5. "Nonprinted instructional materials" means nonprinted textbooks and related core materials, including those that require the availability of electronic equipment in order to be used as a learning resource, that are written and published primarily for use in elementary school and secondary school instruction and that are required by a state educational agency or a local educational agency for use by pupils in the classroom. These materials shall be available to the extent technologically available and may include software programs and internet based materials.

6. "Printed instructional materials" means textbooks and related printed core materials that are written and published primarily for use in elementary school and secondary school instruction and that are required by a state educational agency or a local educational agency for use by pupils in the classroom.

7. "Section 504 plan" means a written statement developed for a pupil with a disability that includes the provision of regular or special education and related aids and services, including assistive technology, that is designed to meet individual educational needs in accordance with 34 Code of Federal Regulations part 104.

8. "Structural integrity" means the structure of all parts of the printed instructional material are kept intact to the extent feasible and as mutually agreed on by the publisher and the local educational agency. If a national file format is adopted by the United States department of education, the national file format's technical specifications for structural integrity are required in the accessible electronic file.

9. "Vendor" means a person or entity that offers printed or nonprinted instructional materials for commercial sale to a school district and other public schools.

Added by Laws 2004, Ch. 202, § 1.

Historical and Statutory Notes

Reviser's Notes:

2004 Note. Pursuant to authority of § 41-1304.02, in paragraph 1, second sentence the quotation marks enclosing "accessible electronic file" were removed to correct a manifest clerical error.

§ 15-732. Powers and duties; state board of education; governing boards

A. The state board of education shall adopt rules on or before August 1, 2005 that require all school districts and other public schools to purchase adopted printed and nonprinted instructional materials for which accessible electronic files are available or, in the case of nonprinted instructional materials delivered on line, that comply with subsection B of this section. The rules shall establish procedures and timelines to ensure that accessible materials are distributed to a child with a disability at the same time that printed and nonprinted instructional materials are distributed to other students. The rules shall require the vendor to submit the accessible electronic files to one or more authorized entities, for conversion by such authorized entities into accessible formats for use by a child with a disability. The rules shall prohibit unauthorized copying, modification and distribution of the accessible electronic files, including distribution of unencrypted or reproducible accessible electronic files to other than authorized entities. This section applies only to newly adopted printed and nonprinted instructional materials adopted after the 2005-2006 school year and with an original copyright date of 2004 or later.

B. On-line nonprinted instructional materials shall be deemed compliant for purposes of subsection A of this section if they meet or exceed standards for internet accessibility, as set forth in § 508 of the rehabilitation act of 1973, as amended by 29 United States code § 794d, and regulations implementing that act as set forth in part 1194 of title 36 of the Code of Federal Regulations.

C. Printed and on-line nonprinted instructional materials are exempt from this article if providing an accessible electronic file would do any of the following:

1. Fundamentally alter the nature of the instructional activity.

2. Result in undue financial and administrative burdens on any state agency, school district or school.

3. Cause such resources not to meet state content standards, adoption criteria or other applicable specifications.

D. The governing board of each school district or the governing body of another public school that solicits bids pursuant to this section shall provide written notification of the requirements of this article and related and subsequent rules to vendors before soliciting bids for printed and nonprinted instructional materials.

E. This section does not permit reproduction, modification or distribution of accessible electronic files or of printed or nonprinted instructional materials without the permission of the copyright holder, and does not require vendors or copyright holders to provide copies or authorize uses of the electronic files or instructional materials without compensation, except as provided by 17 United States code § 121. School districts and other public schools shall certify that no reproduction or modification shall occur without the express authorization of the copyright holder while materials are in the custody of the school district or other public school.

F. Nothing in this section reduces the obligation of the state board of education and the governing board of a school district or the governing body of another public school to provide for the instruction of visually impaired pupils in the use of braille or to provide braille textbooks as prescribed in § 15–214.

G. If a national file format is adopted by the United States department of education, nothing in this section requires publishers to produce accessible electronic files that are inconsistent with or more stringent than the specifications of the nationally adopted file format.

H. Nothing in this section shall be construed to apply to a private school.

Added by Laws 2004, Ch. 202, § 1.

Historical and Statutory Notes

Reviser's Notes:

2004 Note. Pursuant to authority of § 41–1304.02, in subsection A the spelling of "on line" was corrected and in subsections B and C the spelling of "on-line" was corrected.

ARTICLE 3. ASSESSMENT AND ACCOUNTABILITY

Laws 1990, Ch. 233, § 15, effective July 1, 1991, substituted "Assessment and Accountability" for "Achievement Testing" as the heading for this article.

§ 15–741. Assessment of pupils

A. The state board of education shall:

1. Adopt rules for purposes of this article pursuant to title 41, chapter 6.[1]

2. Adopt and implement an Arizona instrument to measure standards test to measure pupil achievement of the state board adopted academic standards in reading, writing and mathematics in at least four grades designated by the board. The board shall determine the manner of implementation. The board may administer assessments of the academic standards in social studies and science. Prior to the administration of the tests to pupils and following the statewide piloting of the tests, the board shall approve, at a public meeting, the Arizona instrument to measure standards test.

3. Adopt and implement a statewide nationally standardized norm-referenced achievement test in reading, language arts and mathematics, except that the superintendent of public instruction may determine additional grade levels for which pupils are tested. The tests shall be consistent with the state standards and shall be administered during the spring of each year between March 15 and May 1.

4. Ensure that the tests prescribed in this section are uniform throughout the state.

5. Ensure that the tests prescribed in this section are able to be scored in an objective manner and that the tests are not intended to advocate any sectarian, partisan or denominational viewpoint.

6. Ensure that the results of the nationally standardized norm-referenced achievement tests established as provided in this article are comparable to

associated grade equivalents, percentiles and stanines derived from a multistate sample.

7. Include within its budget all costs pertaining to the tests prescribed in this article. If sufficient monies are appropriated, the state board may provide norm-referenced achievement test services to school districts which request assistance in testing pupils in grades additional to those required by this section.

8. Use subtests of the statewide nationally standardized norm-referenced achievement test as designated by the state board to assess pupils in reading, language arts and mathematics, at a level appropriate for their grade level.

9. Survey teachers, principals and superintendents on achievement related nontest indicators, including information on graduation rates by ethnicity and dropout rates by ethnicity for each grade level. Before the survey, the state board of education shall approve at a public meeting the nontest indicators on which data will be collected. In conducting the survey and collecting data, the state board of education shall not violate the provisions of the family educational rights and privacy act (P.L. 93-380), as amended,[2] nor disclose personally identifiable information.

10. Establish a fair and consistent method and standard by which norm-referenced test scores from schools in a district may be evaluated taking into consideration demographic data. The board shall establish intervention strategies to assist schools with scores below the acceptable standard. The board shall annually review district and school scores and shall offer assistance to school districts in analyzing data and implementing intervention strategies. The board shall use the adopted norm-referenced test and methods of data evaluation for a period of at least ten years.

11. Participate in other assessments that provide national comparisons as needed.

B. The standardized norm-referenced achievement tests adopted by the state board as provided in subsection A shall be given annually. The tests shall be administered over a one week period between March 15 and May 1. Nontest indicator data and other information shall be collected at the same time as the collection of standardized norm-referenced achievement test data.

C. Local school district governing boards shall:

1. Administer the tests prescribed in subsection A.

2. Survey teachers, principals and superintendents on achievement related nontest indicator data as required by the state board including information related to district graduation and dropout rates. In conducting the survey and collecting data, the governing board shall not violate the provisions of the family educational rights and privacy act (P.L. 93-380), as amended, nor disclose personally identifiable information.

D. A test for penmanship shall not be required pursuant to this article.

Added by Laws 1990, Ch. 233, § 8, eff. July 1, 1991. Amended by Laws 1991, Ch. 252, § 1, eff. June 18, 1991; Laws 1992, Ch. 288, § 4, eff. Sept. 30, 1992, retroactively effective to July 1, 1992; Laws 1992, Ch. 319, § 9, eff. Sept. 30, 1992, retroactively effective to July 1, 1991; Laws 1996, Ch. 284, § 32; Laws 1997, Ch. 231, § 15; Laws 1998, Ch. 183, § 5; Laws 2000, Ch. 398, § 1; Laws 2000, 5th S.S., Ch. 1, § 8; Laws 2001, Ch. 159, § 1.

[1] Section 41-1001 et seq.

[2] 20 U.S.C.A. § 1232.

Historical and Statutory Notes

Source:

Laws 1969, Ch. 59, § 2.
A.R.S. former §§ 15-1131, 15-1132, 15-1133, 15-1135.
Laws 1973, Ch. 98, § 1.
Laws 1974, Ch. 38, § 1.
Laws 1980, 2nd S.S., Ch. 9, § 48.
A.R.S. former § 15-741.
Laws 1981, Ch. 1, § 2.
Laws 1981, Ch. 314, § 12.
Laws 1985, Ch. 346, § 1.
Laws 1988, Ch. 48, § 1.
Laws 1988, Ch. 216, § 1.

Laws 1990, Ch. 3, § 1, effective March 22, 1990 provides:

"**Sec. 1. Alternative testing dates for 1989-1990 school year**

"Notwithstanding § 15-741, subsection C, Arizona Revised Statutes and rules promulgated pursuant to that section, for the 1989-1990 school year the standardized norm-referenced achievement tests may be given between March 26 and April 13."

Laws 1990, Ch. 233, § 16, provides:

"**Sec. 16 Exemption from writing assessment**

"Notwithstanding § 15-741, subsection E, paragraph 1, Arizona Revised Statutes, as amended by Laws 1988, chapter 216, the state board of education shall not implement the uniform achievement test, which is designed to assess the composition skills of a representative sample of pupils in grades four, eight and eleven, in April, 1991."

Laws 1991, Ch. 2, § 1, effective March 22, 1991, provides:

"**Section 1. Alternative testing dates for 1990-1991 school year**

"Notwithstanding § 15-741, subsection C, Arizona Revised Statutes, as amended by Laws 1988, chapter 216, § 1, and rules adopted pursuant to that section, for the 1990-1991 school year the standardized norm-referenced achievement tests may be given between March 25 and April 12."

Laws 1991, Ch. 288, § 19, effective Sept. 21, 1991, retroactively effective to July 1, 1991, provides:

"**Sec. 19. Norm-referenced testing of pupils; 1991-1992 school year**

"**A.** Notwithstanding the provisions of § 15-741, subsection A, paragraph 3, Arizona Revised Statutes, as amended by Laws 1988, chapter 48, § 1 and chapter 216, § 1 and as added by Laws 1990, chapter 233, § 8, for the 1991-1992 school year, the state board of education shall adopt and implement a nationally standardized norm-referenced achievement test to be administered to pupils in grades four, seven and eleven.

"**B.** Notwithstanding the provisions of § 15-741, subsection A, paragraph 8, Arizona Revised Statutes, as added by Laws 1990, chapter 233, § 8, the state board of education shall use subtests of the statewide nationally standardized norm-referenced achievement test as designated by the state board to assess pupils in grades four, seven and eleven in reading, grammar and mathematics at a level appropriate for their grade level.

"**C.** Notwithstanding the provisions of § 15-744, subsection B, Arizona Revised Statutes, for the 1991-1992 school year, the governing board of a school district may exempt pupils who are limited English proficient and who are enrolled in a program as prescribed in § 15-754, Arizona Revised Statutes, from the testing requirement prescribed in subsections A and B of this act if the pupils have been enrolled in a school district in this state for less than three academic years beginning with the second grade. The instructional program for limited English proficient pupils who are exempt from the nationally standardized norm-referenced testing requirement as provided in this section shall include an alternative assessment of achievement to be administered pursuant to standards prescribed by the state board of education.

"**D.** The state board of education may provide norm-referenced achievement test services to school districts which request assistance in testing additional pupils during the 1991-1992 school year if sufficient monies are appropriated."

The 1991 amendment of this section by Ch. 252 explicitly amended the 1990 addition of this section by Ch. 233.

The amendment of this section by Laws 1991, Ch. 252, § 1, was repealed by Laws 1992, Ch. 288, § 5, effective September 30, 1992, retroactively effective to July 1, 1992, and by Laws 1992, Ch. 319, § 10, effective September 30, 1992, retroactively effective to July 1, 1991.

The 1992 amendment of this section by Ch. 288 explicitly amended the 1991 amendment of this section by Ch. 252.

The 1992 amendment of this section by Ch. 319 explicitly amended the 1990 amendment of this section by Ch. 233.

Laws 1992, Ch. 319, § 1, par. 6, and § 57, subsec. B, provide:

"**Section 1. Purpose**"

"6. Section 15-741, Arizona Revised Statutes, was amended by Laws 1991, chapter 252, § 1 with an emergency effective date. However, the amended version of § 15-741, Arizona Revised Statutes, was not effective until July 1, 1991. In order to correct a potentially defective enactment, in this act the Laws 1990, chapter 233, § 8 version of § 15-741, Arizona Revised Statutes, is amended to incorporate the amendments made by Laws 1991, chapter 252 and the chapter 252 version is repealed."

"**Sec. 57. Retroactivity**"

"**B.** Sections 9 through 12 and 15 through 18 of this act are effective retroactively to July 1, 1991."

Laws 1996, 5th S.S., Ch. 4, § 3, provides:

"**Sec. 3. Board of education; norm-referenced testing**

"Notwithstanding §§ 15-741, 15-741.01, 15-743 and 15-745, Arizona Revised Statutes, the state board of education shall adopt and implement for fiscal year 1996-1997 a statewide nationally standardized norm-referenced test that shall be given to all pupils in grades three through twelve."

Laws 1997, 1st S.S., Ch. 4, § 11, provides:

"**Sec. 11. Essential skills tests; funding; requirement**

"Notwithstanding §§ 15-741, 15-741.01, 15-743 and 15-745, Arizona Revised Statutes, or any other law, the state board of education shall not be required to implement essential skills tests that measure pupil achievement in reading, writing, and mathematics in at least four grades if the amount of appropriated monies is not adequate to fund the costs of the testing program."

Laws 1998, 4th S.S., Ch. 8, § 11, provides:

"**Sec. 11. Norm-referenced testing; grade levels to be tested**

"Notwithstanding § 15-741, subsection A, paragraph 3, Arizona Revised Statutes, for fiscal year 1998-1999 the state board of education shall adopt and implement a statewide nationally standardized norm-referenced achievement test for pupils in grades two through eleven in reading, language arts and mathematics."

Laws 1999, 1st S.S., Ch. 4, § 12, provides:

"**Sec. 12. Norm-referenced testing; grade levels to be tested**

"Notwithstanding § 15-741, subsection A, paragraph 3, Arizona Revised Statutes, the state board of education shall adopt and implement a statewide nationally standardized norm-referenced achievement test for pupils in grades two through eleven in reading, language arts and mathematics."

Laws 2000, 5th S.S. Ch. 1, § 65, provides:

"**Sec. 65. Conforming legislation; blending**

"**A.** The legislative council staff shall prepare proposed legislation conforming the Arizona Revised Statutes to the provisions of this act for consideration in the forty-fifth legislature, first regular session.

"**B.** The executive director of the legislative council is authorized to blend the nonconflicting changes made to the Arizona Revised Statutes during the forty-fourth legislature, second regular session, with the changes made to those same statutes by this act."

Former § 15-741, added by Laws 1981, Ch. 1, § 2 (see Source, ante) which was similar and related to testing of pupils, was repealed by Laws 1990, Ch. 233, § 7, eff. July 1, 1991.

Reviser's Notes:

1990 Note. Pursuant to authority of § 14-1304.02, in subsection A, the second paragraph 9 was renumbered as paragraph 10 and paragraph 10 was renumbered as paragraph 11.

1991 Note. Laws 1991, Ch. 252, sec. 1 amended this section with an emergency clause, effective June 18, 1991. [The] version of § 15-741 added by Laws 1990, Ch. 233, sec. 8 [was] effective on July 1, 1991.

1992 Note. Prior to the 1996 amendment, this section contained the amendments made by Laws 1992, Ch. 288, sec. 4 and Ch. 319, sec. 9 that were blended together pursuant to authority of § 41-1304.03.

2000 Note. Prior to the 2001 amendment, this section contained the amendments made by Laws 2000, Ch. 398, sec. 1 and 5th S.S., Ch. 1, sec. 8 that were blended together pursuant to authority of § 41-1304.03.

§ 15-741.01. Goals for excellence

A. Based on the data reported on the report cards as prescribed in this article, the state board shall adopt specific state level objectives for each of the following goal areas:

1. Achievement levels of pupils at the end of grade three, grade eight and grade twelve.

2. Dropout and high school graduation rates.

3. Postsecondary employment and college enrollment rate.

B. Local district governing boards shall establish specific district level objectives and shall prescribe a method for schools in the district to establish school level objectives for the goal areas in subsection A, as prescribed by the state board.

C. The state board shall publish in the appropriate report cards the objectives written by the state, the districts and the schools, and the state board, districts and schools shall review and revise, if needed, their own objectives annually.

Added by Laws 1990, Ch. 233, § 9, eff. July 1, 1991.

Historical and Statutory Notes

Laws 1996, 5th S.S., Ch. 4, § 3, provides:

"**Sec. 3. Board of education; norm-referenced testing**

"Notwithstanding §§ 15-741, 15-741.01, 15-743 and 15-745, Arizona Revised Statutes, the state board of education shall adopt and implement for fiscal year 1996-1997 a statewide nationally standardized norm-referenced test that shall be given to all pupils in grades three through twelve."

§ 15-742. Contract for purchase of tests

A. The state board of education shall enter into contracts with contractors for the purchase of the tests adopted by the state board. Notwithstanding § 41-2546, the state board may enter into contracts for the purchase of nationally standardized norm-referenced tests pursuant to this section for a duration of up to ten years. The contracts may also provide for the distribution of the tests to the school districts and the scoring of the tests.

B. Contractors shall give a cash or corporate surety bond payable to this state and approved by the state board indemnifying the state in the test purchases in an amount not less than five hundred nor more than ten thousand dollars as may be determined by the state board.

The contractor shall faithfully comply with the conditions of the contract and shall furnish to the state the tests as provided in the contract at prices not exceeding the lowest prices then granted to any buyer.

If there is a decrease in the prices given to a person purchasing such tests from the contractor, the state shall have the benefit of the decrease in price.

C. The contractor shall file with the state board a sworn statement stating the lowest prices for which the contractor's series of tests is sold anywhere in the United States.

D. If a contractor violates a condition of the contract, the attorney general, upon request of the state board of education, shall institute an action for damages on the bond of the contractor.

Added by Laws 1981, Ch. 1, § 2, eff. Jan. 23, 1981. Amended by Laws 1999, Ch. 6, § 1.

Historical and Statutory Notes

Source:

Laws 1969, Ch. 59, § 2.
A.R.S. former §§ 15-1131, 15-1132.
Laws 1973, Ch. 98, § 1.
Laws 1974, Ch. 38, § 1.
Laws 1980, 2nd S.S., Ch. 9, § 48.

§ 15-743. Test results; annual report

A. The state board of education shall provide annual reports for every school and district and the state as a whole. The state board shall annually submit these reports to school districts, the legislature and the county school superintendents and shall make them available to the public. The state board shall publish and distribute the reports by September 1 and shall also provide a cumulative summary of the reports every five years. The annual reports and cumulative summary results shall include:

1. Average and range scores on the Arizona instrument to measure standards test.

2. Standardized test scores by subject area according to percentiles and stanines for the school, school district, county, state and nation.

3. Achievement related nontest indicator data collected in the survey of teachers, principals and superintendents as required by § 15-741, including information related to dropout rates by ethnicity for each grade level and graduation rates and postsecondary employment and education by ethnicity. In reporting such data, the state board of education shall not violate the provisions of the family educational rights and privacy act (P.L. 93-380), as amended, [1] nor disclose personally identifiable information.

4. The numbers of pupils who have completed the academic standards at grades three, eight and twelve.

B. Test results on individual pupils shall not be made available to the public by name or individually identifiable reference.

C. The state board shall provide a copy of the results from the tests prescribed in § 15-741, subsection A for each school district to that school district. No results may be released to the public until ten days after the reports are provided to each school district.

D. The state board shall provide each school district participating in the testing program with a copy of each pupil's standardized norm-referenced test scores in reading, language arts and mathematics, and the associated grade equivalents, percentiles and stanines for the school, school district, county, state and nation, a report of pupil progress on an ongoing and annual basis, showing the trends in gain or loss in pupil achievement over time in reading, language arts and mathematics for all years in which pupils are enrolled in the school district for an entire school year and for which this information is available and a report of the pupil progress for pupils not enrolled in a district for an entire school year. The state board shall also provide each school district with each pupil's Arizona instrument to measure standards test scores and the Arizona instrument to measure standards test scores for the school, district, county and state.

E. The school district shall provide a parent or guardian of each pupil participating in the standardized norm-referenced testing part of the program with a copy of the pupil's score in reading, language arts and mathematics, and the percentiles and stanines. The school district shall provide a parent or guardian of each pupil with a copy of the pupil's scores on the Arizona instrument to measure standards test and the associated scores for the school, district, county and state. The school district shall make available to the public through the reports those scores for each school in the district and for the school district, county, state and nation.

F. Each pupil's Arizona instrument to measure standards test results for grade twelve shall be recorded on the pupil's high school transcript. The state board of education shall prescribe the format for recording Arizona instrument to measure standards test results on high school transcripts.

Added by Laws 1981, Ch. 1, § 2, eff. Jan. 23, 1981. Amended by Laws 1981, Ch. 211, § 1; Laws 1982, Ch. 205, § 1; Laws 1985, Ch. 346, § 2, eff. May 14, 1985; Laws 1987, Ch. 24, § 1; Laws 1988, Ch. 44, § 1, eff. May 9, 1988; Laws 1990, Ch. 233, § 10, eff. July 1, 1991; Laws 1991, Ch. 252, § 2, eff. June 18, 1991; Laws 1992, Ch. 319, § 11, eff. Sept. 30, 1992, retroactively effective to July 1, 1991; Laws 1994, 9th S.S., Ch. 2, § 6; Laws 1997, Ch. 231, § 16; Laws 1998, Ch. 183, § 6; Laws 2002, Ch. 215, § 1.

[1] 20 U.S.C.A. § 1232.

Retroactive Application

This section, as amended by Laws 2002, Ch. 215, applies retroactively to June 2, 2002.

Historical and Statutory Notes

Source:

Laws 1969, Ch. 59, § 2.
A.R.S. former §§ 15–1131, 15–1133, 15–1134.
Laws 1973, Ch. 98, §§ 1, 2.
Laws 1974, Ch. 38, § 1.
Laws 1980, 2nd S.S., Ch. 9, § 48.

Laws 1984, Ch. 231, § 1, relating to pupil achievement tests, cumulative data and effective classrooms and schools and school districts, expired November 1, 1984, by terms of § 4 of that act.

The 1991 amendment of this section by Ch. 252 explicitly amended the 1990 amendment of this section by Ch. 233.

The amendment of this section by Laws 1991, Ch. 252, § 2, effective June 18, 1991, was repealed by Laws 1992, Ch. 319, § 12, effective September 30, 1992, retroactively effective to July 1, 1991.

The 1992 amendment of this section by Ch. 319 explicitly amended the 1990 amendment of this section by Ch. 233.

Laws 1992, Ch. 319, § 1, par. 7, provides:

"**Section 1. Purpose**"

"7. Section 15–743, Arizona Revised Statutes, was amended by Laws 1991, chapter 252, § 2 with an emergency effective date. However, the amended version of § 15–743, Arizona Revised Statutes, was not effective until July 1, 1991. In order to correct a potentially defective enactment, in this act the Laws 1990, chapter 233 version of § 15–743, Arizona Revised Statutes is amended to incorporate the amendments made by Laws 1991, chapter 252 and the chapter 252 version is repealed."

Laws 1996, 5th S.S., Ch. 4, § 3, provides:

"**Sec. 3. Board of education; norm-referenced testing**

"Notwithstanding §§ 15–741, 15–741.01, 15–743 and 15–745, Arizona Revised Statutes, the state board of education shall adopt and implement for fiscal year 1996–1997 a statewide nationally standardized norm-referenced test that shall be given to all pupils in grades three through twelve."

Laws 2002, Ch. 215, § 2, provides:

"**Sec. 2. Retroactivity**

"This act applies retroactively to from and after June 1, 2002."

Reviser's Notes:

1981 Note. Pursuant to authority of § 41–1304.02, in subsection G "8." was omitted and the text beginning with the word "In" was not indented as a correction of a manifest clerical error.

1987 Note. Pursuant to authority of § 41–1304.02, in the section heading "; annual report" was added and in subsection H the spelling of "computerized" was corrected as a manifest clerical error.

1991 Note. Laws 1991, Ch. 252, sec. 2 amended this section with an emergency clause, effective June 18, 1991. This version of § 15–743 is as amended by Laws 1990, Ch. 233, sec. 10 and is effective on July 1, 1991.

§ 15–744. Exemptions

A. The governing board of a school district may exempt pupils who are limited English proficient and who are enrolled in an instructional program as prescribed in § 15–754 from the nationally standardized norm-referenced achievement testing requirement prescribed by this article for not to exceed three consecutive school years. The first year of the exemption is the first academic year in which the pupil is enrolled in a school district in this state in grade two or above. The instructional program for limited English proficient pupils who are exempt from the nationally standardized norm-referenced achievement testing requirement as provided in this subsection shall include an alternative assessment of achievement to be administered annually.

B. School districts shall annually report the number of pupils by category and by grade level which were exempt as provided in this section to the department of education. The department shall include this information in its annual report to the legislature pursuant to § 15–743.

C. At the request of a pupil's parent or guardian, the governing board of a school district shall administer any test required by this article to pupils exempted from the testing requirement pursuant to this section. Test results for these pupils shall not be included in the summary results of tests prescribed in § 15–743, but individual results shall be sent to the school and to the parent or guardian.

Added by Laws 1981, Ch. 1, § 2, eff. Jan. 23, 1981. Amended by Laws 1982, Ch. 205, § 3; Laws 1988, Ch. 48, § 2; Laws 1988, Ch. 128, § 1; Laws 1990, Ch. 47, § 1; Laws 1991, Ch. 173, § 3; Laws 1992, Ch. 172, § 5; Laws 1992, Ch. 305, § 11; Laws 1996, Ch. 284, § 33; Laws 2000, Ch. 236, § 5, eff. April 12, 2000.

Historical and Statutory Notes

Source:

A.R.S. former § 15–1134.
Laws 1980, 2nd S.S., Ch. 9, § 48.

Reviser's Notes:

1982 Note. Pursuant to authority of § 41–1304.02, in subsection B "non-English" was substituted for "nonenglish" as a correction of a manifest clerical error.

1988 Note. Prior to the 1990 amendment, this section contained the amendments made by Laws 1988, ch. 48, § 2 and Ch. 128, § 1 which were blended together pursuant to the authority of § 41–1304.03.

1992 Note. Prior to the 1996 amendment, this section contained the amendments made by Laws 1992, Ch. 172, sec. 5 and Ch. 305, sec. 11 that were blended together pursuant to authority of § 41–1304.03.

§ 15–745. Children instructed at home; testing; prohibition

A. Nothing in this article shall be construed to require the testing of children who are instructed in a home school program while they are receiving home school instruction.

B. A child who enrolls in a kindergarten program or grades one through twelve after receiving instruction in a home school program shall be tested pursuant to this article in order to determine the appropriate grade level for the educational placement of the child.

Added by Laws 1995, Ch. 268, § 38.

Historical and Statutory Notes

Source:

A.R.S. former § 15-745.
Laws 1985, Ch. 337, § 2.
A.R.S. former § 15-745.
Laws 1993, Ch. 83, § 3.

Laws 1996, 5th S.S., Ch. 4, § 3, provides:

"**Sec. 3. Board of education; norm-referenced testing**

"Notwithstanding §§ 15-741, 15-741.01, 15-743 and 15-745, Arizona Revised Statutes, the state board of education shall adopt and implement for fiscal year 1996-1997 a statewide nationally standardized norm-referenced test that shall be given to all pupils in grades three through twelve."

Former § 15-745, added by Laws 1993, Ch. 83, § 3 (see Source, ante), relating to similar subject matter, was repealed by Laws 1995, Ch. 268, § 37.

Another former § 15-745, added by Laws 1985, Ch. 337, § 2, relating to similar subject matter, was repealed by Laws 1993, Ch. 83, § 2.

§ 15-746. School report cards

A. Each school shall distribute an annual report card that contains at least the following information:

1. A description of the school's regular, magnet and special instructional programs.

2. A description of the current academic goals of the school.

3. A summary of the results achieved by pupils enrolled at the school during the prior three school years as measured by the Arizona instrument to measure standards test and the nationally standardized norm-referenced achievement test as designated by the state board and as reported in the annual report prescribed by § 15-743, a summary of the pupil progress on an ongoing and annual basis, showing the trends in gain or loss in pupil achievement over time in reading, language arts and mathematics for all years in which pupils are enrolled in the school district for an entire school year and for which this information is available and a summary of the pupil progress for pupils not enrolled in a district for an entire school year.

4. The school's current expenditures per pupil for classroom supplies, classroom instruction excluding classroom supplies, administration, support services-students, and all other support services and operations. The current expenditures per pupil by school shall include allocation of the district-wide expenditures to each school, as provided by the district. The report shall include a comparison of the school to the state amount for a similar type of district as calculated in § 15-255. The method of calculating these per pupil amounts and the allocation of expenditures shall be as prescribed in the uniform system of financial records.

5. The attendance rate of pupils enrolled at the school as reflected in the school's average daily membership as defined in § 15-901.

6. The number of incidents that occurred on the school grounds and that required the intervention of local, state or federal law enforcement.

7. The percentage of pupils who have either graduated to the next grade level or graduated from high school.

8. A description of the social services available at the school site.

9. The school calendar including the length of the school day and hours of operations.

10. The total number of pupils enrolled at the school during the previous school year.

11. The transportation services available.

12. Beginning in the 2000–2001 school year and until July 1, 2006, the reading instruction programs used by the school for kindergarten programs and grades one, two and three, pursuant to section 15–704. The report card shall include a district comparison of test scores among the different programs of reading instruction and shall identify the program of reading instruction used in each classroom.

13. A description of the responsibilities of parents of children enrolled at the school.

14. A description of the responsibilities of the school to the parents of the children enrolled at the school including dates the report cards are delivered to the home.

15. A description of the composition and duties of the school council as prescribed in § 15–351 if such a school council exists.

16. For the most recent year available, the average current expenditure per pupil for administrative functions compared to the predicted average current expenditure per pupil for administrative functions according to an analysis of administrative cost data by the joint legislative budget committee staff.

17. If the school provides instruction to pupils in kindergarten programs and grades one through three, the ratio of pupils to teachers in each classroom where instruction is provided in kindergarten programs and grades one through three.

18. The average class size per grade level for all grade levels, kindergarten programs and grades one through eight. For the purposes of this paragraph, "average class size" means the weighted average of each class.

B. The department of education shall develop a standardized report card format that meets the requirements of subsection A of this section. The department shall modify the standardized report card as necessary on an annual basis. The department shall distribute to each school in this state a copy of the standardized report card that includes the required test scores for each school. Additional copies of the standardized report card shall be available on request.

C. After each school has completed the report card distributed to it by the department of education, the school, in addition to distributing the report card as prescribed in subsection A of this section, shall send a copy of the report card to the department. The department shall prepare an annual report that contains the report card from each school in this state.

D. The school shall distribute report cards to parents of pupils enrolled at the school, no later than the last day of school of each fiscal year, and shall present a summary of the contents of the report cards at an annual public meeting held at the school. The school shall give notice at least two weeks before the public meeting that clearly states the purposes, time and place of the meeting.

Added by Laws 1994, 9th S.S., Ch. 2, § 7. Amended by Laws 1997, Ch. 4, § 3, eff. July 21, 1997, retroactively effective to July 1, 1997; Laws 1997, 1st S.S., Ch. 4, § 4; Laws 1997, Ch. 231, § 17; Laws 1998, Ch. 183, § 7; Laws 1998, Ch. 231, § 3; Laws 1999, Ch. 256, § 3; Laws 1999, 1st S.S., Ch. 4, § 4; Laws 2000, Ch. 76, § 1; Laws 2002, Ch. 295, § 4.

Historical and Statutory Notes

Laws 1997, Ch. 4, § 16, as amended by Laws 1997, 1st S.S., Ch. 9, § 1, provides:

"**Sec. 16. Conditional repeal**

"**A.** If there is a final adjudication [see note, post] in the proceedings resulting from the Arizona supreme court's decision in Roosevelt Elementary School District No. 66 v. Bishop, 179 Ariz. 233, 877 P.2d 806 (1994) that this act, in conjunction with Laws 1996, fifth special session, chapter 8 and Laws 1996, seventh special session, chapter 1, does not ensure a constitutional system of education:

"1. This act and Laws 1996, fifth special session, chapter 8, § 14 are void and are repealed as of the date of the final adjudication.

"2. Laws 1996, fifth special session, chapter 8, §§ 1, 13, 15 and 17 and laws 1996, seventh special session, chapter 1, §§ 3, 4 and 5 are void and are repealed six months after the date of the final adjudication.

"**B.** Subsection A of this section does not invalidate any contractual obligations of the state board for school capital facilities that may have been incurred before the repeal prescribed in subsection A, paragraph 2 of this section, including school districts that have been given preliminary approvals by the state board for school capital facilities before the date of final adjudication, not to exceed the balance of the school capital equity fund established by § 15–1053, Arizona Revised Statutes, on the date of the final adjudication. After the date of final adjudication, the state board shall not enter into any contractual obligations not related to a preliminary approval given before the date of the final adjudication or give any new preliminary approvals. Between the date of final adjudication and the repeal prescribed in subsection A, paragraph 2 of this section, nothing in this section shall be construed to prohibit the board from paying its costs of operation as prescribed by law.

"**C.** On the discontinuation of the state board for school capital facilities, the department of education shall assume responsibility for distributing monies and receiving reports and repayment obligations from school districts pursuant to contracts and preliminary approvals entered into between the state board and school districts before the final adjudication referred to in subsection A of this section. Any monies remitted to the department of education pursuant to this subsection shall be transmitted to the state general fund. The department of education shall submit an annual report to the president of the senate, the speaker of the house of representatives and the governor that summarizes the reports and amount of repayments from school districts."

The conditions for the repeals by this section have been met. The Supreme Court in Order No. CV–97–0369–SA, dated October 24, 1997, declared that the legislature's 1997 school funding plan was unconstitutional; the order of July 28, 1994, was still in effect; and, that the order of the trial court dated August 20, 1997 was approved. A written opinion followed, dated December 23, 1997 (Hull v. Albrecht, 190 Ariz. 520, 950 P.2d 1141 (1997)). An informal Attorney General Opinion considers December 23, 1997, the date the written Supreme Court decision was released, as the final date of adjudication. A subsequent amendment to cure the constitutional infirmity by Laws 1998, 3rd S.S., Ch. 1 was also declared unconstitutional by the Supreme Court (Hull v. Albrecht 192 Ariz. 34, 960 P.2d 634 (1998)).

Laws 1999, 1st S.S., Ch. 4, § 16, provides:

"**Sec. 16. School district administrative costs; data analysis**

"**A.** Before July 1, 2000, the joint legislative budget committee staff shall analyze school district cost data from fiscal year 1998–1999 in order to determine the average per pupil current expenditure for each school district for administrative functions and whether each district exceeded its predicted per pupil cost level for those functions based on data reported by districts of similar type and size.

"**B.** Before December 1, 2000, the auditor general shall report to the legislature regarding factors that help explain differences in administrative costs for school districts that are identified by the joint legislative budget committee as having reported particularly high or low average per pupil current expenditures for administrative functions for fiscal year 1998–1999."

Laws 1999, 1st S.S., Ch. 5, § 23, provides:

"**Sec. 23. Increased base support level; fiscal year 1999–2000**

"**A.** If the fiscal event described in § 18, subsection A, paragraph 3 of this act occurs, then notwithstanding § 15–901, subsection B, paragraph 2, subdivision (a), Arizona Revised Statutes, the base level is $2,578.41. The increase in the base support level is for fiscal year 1999–2000.

"**B.** If the fiscal event described in § 18, subsection A, paragraph 4 of this act occurs, then notwithstanding § 15–901, subsection B, paragraph 2, subdivision (a), Arizona Revised Statutes, the base level is $2,597.09. The increase in the base support level is for fiscal year 1999–2000.

"**C.** It is the intent of the legislature that any monies under this section shall be used to enhance one or more of the following items:

"1. Classroom teacher salaries.

"2. Employing new teachers.

"3. Teacher training and development.

"4. Classroom technology.

"5. Strengthening programs for pupils in kindergarten programs and grades one, two and three.

"6. Additional school days.

"7. Supplemental learning programs to meet state academic standards.

"8. Reading clinics.

"9. Achieving or maintaining school sizes of fewer than four hundred fifty pupils.

"**D.** For fiscal year 1999–2000, school districts and charter schools shall report on the school report card issued pursuant to § 15–746, Arizona Revised Statutes, a summary of any monies received pursuant to this section and a description of how the monies were used to enhance classrooms to augment pupil learning. School districts and charter schools shall provide to any person on request a detailed itemization of the classroom enhancements and associated expenditures.

"**E.** Notwithstanding § 15–905, subsection A, paragraph 2, Arizona Revised Statutes, school district governing boards and charter schools may include in the proposed and adopted budget for fiscal year 1999–2000 and 2000–2001 any items or amounts authorized by this act. If subsequent events prevent any provision of this act from becoming effective, the governing boards and charter schools shall reduce their budgets by the amount that was budgeted pursuant to this act and that did not become effective.

"**F.** The staff of the Arizona legislative council shall prepare legislation for consideration in the forty-fifth legislature, first regular session to make necessary statutory changes to conform to the enactment of fiscal events pursuant to this section."

Laws 1999, 1st S.S., Ch. 5, § 24 was repealed by Laws 2000, Ch. 48, § 5. See also amendment of the note by Laws 2000, Ch. 398, post.

Laws 1999, 1st S.S., Ch. 5, § 24, was purportedly amended by Laws 2000, Ch. 398, § 3.

Laws 1999, 1st S.S., Ch. 5, § 25, provides:

"**Sec. 25. Retroactivity**

"Section 23 of this act applies retroactively to from and after June 30, 1999."

Laws 2000, Ch. 76, §§ 2 and 3 provide:

"**Sec. 2. K–3 classroom size reduction planning committee**

"**A.** The K–3 classroom size reduction planning committee is established consisting of the following members:

"1. Three members of the house of representatives, no more than two of whom are from the same political party, who are appointed by the speaker of the house of representatives.

"2. Three members of the senate, no more than two of whom are from the same political party, who are appointed by the president of the senate.

"3. One faculty member of a college of education of one of the universities under the jurisdiction of the Arizona board of regents who is appointed by the governor.

"4. One member of a statewide association composed of school district governing board members who is appointed by the president of the senate.

"5. One teacher who is a member of a statewide association composed of teachers and who is appointed by the speaker of the house of representatives.

"6. One member of an association composed of parents of public school children who is appointed by the president of the senate.

"7. One member of an association composed of school administrators who is appointed by the speaker of the house of representatives.

"8. One member of the public who is appointed by the speaker of the house of representatives.

"9. One member of a statewide class size advocacy organization who is appointed by the governor.

"**B.** Appointed members serve at the pleasure of the person who made the appointment.

"**C.** Members of the committee are not eligible to receive compensation, but members are eligible for reimbursement of expenses under title 38, chapter 4, article 2, Arizona Revised Statutes.

"**D.** The committee may use the expertise and services of the staffs of the department of education and the legislature.

"E. The committee shall:

"1. Recommend teacher training programs that are designed to maximize pupil achievement in schools undergoing classroom size reduction for kindergarten programs and grades one through three.

"2. Recommend possible legislative changes for schools that have implemented classroom size reduction programs for kindergarten programs and grades one through three that would increase classroom space for pupils in kindergarten programs and grades one through three.

"3. Examine and analyze any other issues that will promote classroom size reduction in kindergarten programs and grades one through three.

"4. Examine the cost of implementing a classroom size reduction program. The cost estimate shall be included in the annual report.

"5. Submit an annual written report to the governor, the president of the senate, the speaker of the house of representatives, the secretary of state and the department of library, archives and public records by September 15 that contains the committee's study results and recommendations during years 2000 and 2001."

"**Sec. 3. Delayed repeal**

"Section 2 of this act, relating to the K–3 classroom size reduction planning committee, is repealed from and after December 31, 2005."

Reviser's Notes:

1994 Note. Pursuant to authority of § 41–1304.02, in subsection B, third sentence the words "to each school in this state" were transposed to follow "distribute".

1997 Note. Prior to the 1998 amendments, this section contained the amendments made by Laws 1997, First Special Session, Ch. 4, sec. 4 and Laws 1997, First Regular Session, Ch. 231, sec. 17 that were blended together pursuant to authority of § 41–1304.03. Pursuant to authority of § 41–1304.02, in subsection A, paragraph 4, first sentence the second "classroom supplies," was transposed to follow "for".

1997 Note. The independent and valid amendment of this section by Laws 1997, 1st Spec. sess., Ch. 4, sec. 4, Laws 1997, Ch. 4, sec. 3 and Laws 1997, Ch. 231, sec. 17 could not be blended because of the conditional repeal in Laws 1997, Ch. 4, sec. 16.

1998 Note. Prior to the 1999 amendment, this section contained the amendments made by Laws 1998, Ch. 183, sec. 7 and Ch. 231, sec. 3 that were blended together pursuant to authority of § 41–1304.03.

1999 Note. Prior to the 2000 amendment, this section contained the amendments made by Laws 1999, First Regular Session, Ch. 256, sec. 3 and First Special Session, Ch. 4, sec. 4 that were blended together as shown above pursuant to authority of § 41–1304.03.

2000 Note. Pursuant to authority of § 41–1304.02, in subsection A, paragraph 18, first sentence "eight" was substituted for "8".

§ 15–747. Nationally standardized test; exemption from public record requirements; public viewing

A. Except as provided in subsection B of this section, any nationally standardized test that is administered to pupils in this state and to pupils in any other states, and any questions, answers or scoring keys from any such test that appear in any bid, proposal, contract, documentation or other materials, are exempt from title 39, chapter 1, article 2 [1] if both of the following apply:

1. The test is copyrighted.

2. The test will be deprived of value if the questions or answers become known to pupils before the administration of the test.

B. The state board of education shall adopt rules that set forth procedures to allow parents of pupils and the general public to view the nationally standardized norm-referenced achievement test prescribed by § 15–741. The rules shall include procedures to prohibit pupils who are required to take the nationally standardized norm-referenced achievement test from viewing that test before the test is administered to those pupils. The rules adopted pursuant to this subsection shall prohibit the duplication or photocopying of the nationally standardized norm-referenced achievement test. The rules shall prohibit any other activities that would violate the copyright protection afforded by federal law to the copyright holders of the tests and to the copyright holders of related testing materials.

Added by Laws 2002, Ch. 64, § 1.

[1] Section 39-121 et seq.

§§ 15-747, 15-748. Repealed by Laws 2001, Ch. 233, § 1

Historical and Statutory Notes

Section 15-747, added as Laws 1998, 4th S.S., Ch. 8, § 14, renumbered as § 15-747, amended by Laws 1999, 1st S.S., Ch. 4, § 5; Laws 2000, Ch. 388, § 1, related to education accountability measures.

Section 15-748, added as Laws 1998, 4th S.S., Ch. 8, § 14, renumbered as § 15-748, related to the technical advisory committee.

ARTICLE 3.1. ENGLISH LANGUAGE EDUCATION FOR CHILDREN IN PUBLIC SCHOOLS

Article 3.1, English Language Education for Children in Public Schools, consisting of §§ 15-751 to 15-755, was added by Proposition 203, an initiative measure, approved election Nov. 7, 2000, eff. Nov. 27, 2000.

Former Article 3.1, Bilingual Programs and English as a Second Language Programs, consisting of §§ 15-751 to 15-756, added as Article 8, §§ 15-799 to 15-799.05, by Laws 1984, Ch. 169, § 2, effective August 3, 1984, was renumbered as this article and these sections, and was repealed by Proposition 203, an initiative measure, approved election Nov. 7, 2000, eff. Nov. 27, 2000.

§ 15-751. Definitions

In this section

1. "Bilingual education/native language instruction" means a language acquisition process for students in which much or all instruction, textbooks, or teaching materials are in the child's native language other than English.

2. "English language classroom" means a classroom in which English is the language of instruction used by the teaching personnel, and in which such teaching personnel possess a good knowledge of the English language. English language classrooms encompass both English language mainstream classrooms and sheltered English immersion classrooms.

3. "English language mainstream classroom" means a classroom in which the students either are native English language speakers or already have acquired reasonable fluency in English.

4. "English learner" or "limited English proficient student" means a child who does not speak English or whose native language is not English, and who is not currently able to perform ordinary classroom work in English.

5. "Sheltered English immersion" or "structured English immersion" means an English language acquisition process for young children in which nearly all classroom instruction is in English but with the curriculum and presentation designed for children who are learning the language. Books and instructional materials are in English and all reading, writing, and subject

matter are taught in English. Although teachers may use a minimal amount of the child's native language when necessary, no subject matter shall be taught in any language other than English, and children in this program learn to read and write solely in English. This educational methodology represents the standard definition of "sheltered English" or "structured English" found in educational literature.

Added by Proposition 203, an initiative measure, approved election Nov. 7, 2000, eff. Nov. 27, 2000.

Historical and Statutory Notes

Source

A.R.S. former § 15-799.
Laws 1984, Ch. 169, § 2.
A.R.S. former § 15-751.

Proposition 203, based on an Initiative Measure, proposing amendment to Title 15, Chapter 7, by repeal and addition of Article 3.1, relating to English language education, was approved by the electors at the November 7, 2000 general election as proclaimed by the governor on November 27, 2000.

Proposition 203, §§ 1, 4 and 5, part of an initiative measure, approved election Nov. 7, 2000, eff. Nov. 27, 2000, provide:

"**Sec. 1. Findings and Declarations**

"The People of Arizona find and declare:

"1. The English language is the national public language of the United States of america and of the state of Arizona. it is spoken by the vast majority of Arizona residents, and is also the leading world language for science, technology, and international business, thereby being the language of economic opportunity; and

"2. Immigrant parents are eager to have their children acquire a good knowledge of English, thereby allowing them to fully participate in the american dream of economic and social advancement; and

"3. The government and the public schools of Arizona have a moral obligation and a constitutional duty to provide all of Arizona's children, regardless of their ethnicity or national origins, with the skills necessary to become productive members of our society. of these skills, literacy in the English language is among the most important.

"4. The public schools of Arizona currently do an inadequate job of educating immigrant children, wasting financial resources on costly experimental language programs whose failure over the past two decades is demonstrated by the current high drop-out rates and low English literacy levels of many immigrant children.

"5. Young immigrant children can easily acquire full fluency in a new language, such as English, if they are heavily exposed to that language in the classroom at an early age.

"6. Therefore it is resolved that: all children in Arizona public schools shall be taught English as rapidly and effectively as possible.

"7. Under circumstances in which portions of this statute are subject to conflicting interpretations, these findings and declarations shall be assumed to contain the governing intent of the statute."

"**Sec. 4. Severability**

"If a provision of this act or its application to any person or circumstances is held invalid, the invalidity does not affect other provisions or applications of the act that can be given effect without the invalid provision or application, and to this end the provisions of this act are severable.

"**Sec. 5. Application**

"The provisions of this act cannot be waived, modified, or set aside by any elected or appointed official or administrator, except as through the amendment process provided for in the Arizona constitution."

Former § 15-751, added as § 15-799 by Laws 1984, Ch. 169, § 2, renumbered as § 15-751, which also related to definitions, was repealed by Proposition 203, an initiative measure, approved election Nov. 7, 2000, eff. Nov. 27, 2000. See now, this section.

§ 15-752. English language education

Subject to the exceptions provided in § 15-753, all children in Arizona public schools shall be taught English by being taught in English and all children shall be placed in English language classrooms. Children who are English learners shall be educated through sheltered English immersion during a temporary transition period not normally intended to exceed one year. Local schools shall be permitted but not required to place in the same classroom English learners of different ages but whose degree of English proficiency is similar. Local schools shall be encouraged to mix together in the same classroom English learners from different native-language groups but with the same degree of English fluency. Once English learners have acquired a good working knowledge of English and are able to do regular school work in English, they shall no longer be classified as English learners and shall be transferred to English language mainstream classrooms. As much as possible, current per capita supplemental funding for English learners shall be maintained. Foreign language classes for children who already know English shall be completely unaffected, as shall special educational programs for physically-or mentally-impaired students.

Added by Proposition 203, an initiative measure, approved election Nov. 7, 2000, eff. Nov. 27, 2000.

Historical and Statutory Notes

Source:

Laws 1912, Ch. 77, § 73.
Civ.Code 1913, § 2769.
Rev.Code 1928, § 1047.
Code 1939, § 54-1101.
A.R.S. Former §§ 15-202, 15-705, 15-707, 15-1098.
Laws 1969, Ch. 95, §§ 2, 3.
Laws 1972, Ch. 124, § 2.
Laws 1973, Ch. 169, §§ 1, 6.
Laws 1981, Ch. 1, § 2.
A.R.S. former § 15-752.
A.R.S. former § 15-799.01.
Laws 1984, Ch. 169, § 2.
A.R.S. former § 15-752.
Laws 1999, Ch. 249, § 1.

Proposition 203, based on an Initiative Measure, proposing amendment to Title 15, Chapter 7, by repeal and addition of Article 3.1, relating to English language education, was approved by the electors at the November 7, 2000 general election as proclaimed by the governor on November 27, 2000.

Former § 15-752, added as § 15-799.01 by Laws 1984, Ch. 169, § 2, renumbered as § 15-752, amended by Laws 1999, Ch. 249, § 1, which related to conducting schools in English language, was repealed by Proposition 203, an initiative measure, approved election Nov. 7, 2000, eff. Nov. 27, 2000. See now, this section.

§ 15-753. Parental waivers

A. The requirements of § 15-752 may be waived with the prior written informed consent, to be provided annually, of the child's parents or legal guardian under the circumstances specified in this section. Such informed consent shall require that said parents or legal guardian personally visit the school to apply for the waiver and that they there be provided a full description of the educational materials to be used in the different educational program choices and all the educational opportunities available to the child. If a parental waiver has been granted, the affected child shall be transferred to classes teaching English and other subjects through bilingual education techniques or other generally recognized educational methodologies permitted by law. Individual schools in which 20 students or more of a given grade level receive a waiver shall be required to offer such a class; in all other cases, such students must be permitted to transfer to a public school in which such a class is offered.

B. The circumstances in which a parental exception waiver may be applied for under this section are as follows:

1. Children who already know English: the child already possesses good English language skills, as measured by oral evaluation or standardized tests of English vocabulary comprehension, reading, and writing, in which the child

scores approximately at or above the state average for his grade level or at or above the 5th grade average, whichever is lower; or

2. Older children: the child is age 10 years or older, and it is the informed belief of the school principal and educational staff that an alternate course of educational study would be better suited to the child's overall educational progress and rapid acquisition of basic English language skills; or

3. Children with special individual needs: the child already has been placed for a period of not less than thirty calendar days during that school year in an English language classroom and it is subsequently the informed belief of the school principal and educational staff that the child has such special and individual physical or psychological needs, above and beyond the child's lack of English proficiency, that an alternate course of educational study would be better suited to the child's overall educational development and rapid acquisition of English. A written description of no less than 250 words documenting these special individual needs for the specific child must be provided and permanently added to the child's official school records, and the waiver application must contain the original authorizing signatures of both the school principal and the local superintendent of schools. Any such decision to issue such an individual waiver is to be made subject to the examination and approval of the local school superintendent, under guidelines established by and subject to the review of the local governing board and ultimately the state board of education. Teachers and local school districts may reject waiver requests without explanation or legal consequence, the existence of such special individual needs shall not compel issuance of a waiver, and the parents shall be fully informed of their right to refuse to agree to a waiver.

Added by Proposition 203, an initiative measure, approved election Nov. 7, 2000, eff. Nov. 27, 2000.

Historical and Statutory Notes

Proposition 203, based on an Initiative Measure, proposing amendment to Title 15, Chapter 7, by repeal and addition of Article 3.1, relating to English language education, was approved by the electors at the November 7, 2000 general election as proclaimed by the governor on November 27, 2000.

Former § 15-753, added as § 15-799.02 by Laws 1984, Ch. 169, § 2, renumbered as § 15-753, amended by Laws 1996, Ch. 284, § 34; Laws 1999, Ch. 249, § 2, which related to census procedures, was repealed by Proposition 203, an initiative measure, approved election Nov. 7, 2000, eff. Nov. 27, 2000.

§ 15-754. Legal standing and parental enforcement

As detailed in §§ 15-752 and 15-753, all Arizona school children have the right to be provided at their local school with an English language public education. The parent or legal guardian of any Arizona school child shall have legal standing to sue for enforcement of the provisions of this statute, and if successful shall be awarded normal and customary attorney's fees and actual and compensatory damages, but not punitive or consequential damages. Any school board member or other elected official or administrator who willfully and repeatedly refuses to implement the terms of this statute may be held personally liable for fees and actual and compensatory damages by the child's parents or legal guardian, and cannot be subsequently indemnified for such assessed damages by any public or private third party. Any individual found so liable shall be immediately removed from office, and shall be barred from holding any position of authority anywhere within the Arizona public school system for an additional period of five years.

Added by Proposition 203, an initiative measure, approved election Nov. 7, 2000, eff. Nov. 27, 2000.

Historical and Statutory Notes

Proposition 203, based on an Initiative Measure, proposing amendment to Title 15, Chapter 7, by repeal and addition of Article 3.1, relating to English language education, was approved by the electors at the November 7, 2000 general election as proclaimed by the governor on November 27, 2000.

Former § 15-754, added as § 15-799.03 by Laws 1984, Ch. 169, § 2, renumbered as § 15-754, derived from Laws 1969, Ch. 95, § 3; A.R.S. former §§ 15-706, 15-707, 15-1097, 15-1098; Laws 1972, Ch. 124, § 2; Laws 1973, Ch. 169, §§ 5, 6; Laws 1981, Ch. 1, § 2, which related to requirements of bilingual education and English as second language programs, was repealed by Proposition 203, an initiative measure, approved election Nov. 7, 2000, eff. Nov. 27, 2000.

§ 15-755. Standardized testing for monitoring education progress

In order to ensure that the educational progress of all Arizona students in academic subjects and in learning English is properly monitored, a standardized, nationally-normed written test of academic subject matter given in English shall be administered at least once each year to all Arizona public schoolchildren in grades 2 and higher. Only students classified as severely learning disabled may be exempted from this test. The particular test to be used shall be selected by the office of the state superintendent of public instruction, and it is intended that the test shall generally remain the same from year to year. The national percentile scores of students shall be confidentially provided to individual parents, and the aggregated percentile scores and distributional data for individual schools and school districts shall be made publicly available on an internet web site; the scores for students classified as "limited-English" shall be separately sub-aggregated and made publicly available there as well. Although administration of this test is required solely for monitoring educational progress, Arizona public officials and administrators may utilize these test scores for other purposes as well if they so choose.

Added by Proposition 203, an initiative measure, approved election Nov. 7, 2000, eff. Nov. 27, 2000.

Historical and Statutory Notes

Proposition 203, based on an Initiative Measure, proposing amendment to Title 15, Chapter 7, by repeal and addition of Article 3.1, relating to English language education, was approved by the electors at the November 7, 2000 general election as proclaimed by the governor on November 27, 2000.

Former § 15-755, added as § 15-799.04 by Laws 1984, Ch. 169, § 2, renumbered as § 15-755, amended by Laws 1989, Ch. 273, § 7, eff. June 26, 1989, which related to reporting procedures regarding bilingual education and English as second language programs, was repealed by Proposition 203, an initiative measure, approved election Nov. 7, 2000, eff. Nov. 27, 2000.

§ 15-756. Programs for English learners; requirements; federal funding

A. The state board of education shall prescribe the manner in which:

1. The primary or home language for all new pupils who enroll in a school district or charter school shall be identified.

2. The English language proficiency of all pupils with a primary or home language other than English shall be assessed through the administration of English language proficiency exams.

3. The process of reassessment of English learners for the purpose of determining English language proficiency shall be conducted.

4. The evaluation of former English learners shall be conducted.

5. Training may be allowed that is not provided by a college or university to substitute for any of the courses required for a structured English immersion endorsement or a bilingual education endorsement if all of the following conditions apply:

(a) The State Board of Education has reviewed the curriculum, textbooks, grading procedures and attendance policies and determined that the training is comparable in amount, scope and quality to a course offered by a college or university for a structured English immersion or bilingual education endorsement.

(b) The training meets the professional teaching standards adopted by the State Board of Education.

(c) The State Board of Education has reviewed the qualifications of the instructor and determined that the instructor has sufficient experience to effectively conduct the training.

B. The department of education shall develop guidelines for the monitoring of school districts and charter schools for the purposes of ensuring compliance with all federal and state laws regarding English learners, including requiring each school district and charter school to annually submit a report to the department of education that includes the following information identified by grade level and by school:

1. The number of pupils who are classified as English learners for the first time.

2. The number of English learners who achieved English proficiency in the past academic year and who exited the English learner program.

3. The total number of pupils classified as English learners.

4. The number of pupils who are enrolled in each type of language acquisition program offered by the school district or charter school.

5. If requested by the department of education, The test data used to determine English proficiency.

C. The superintendent of public instruction shall attempt to obtain the maximum amount of federal funding that is available for bilingual education programs and structured English immersion programs and any other funding from federal programs that apply to the educational needs of English learners.

D. The department of education shall submit an annual report to the governor, the president of the senate and the speaker of the house of representatives that includes an itemized list of all federal monies received by the department for language acquisition programs and the purposes for which these federal monies are designated. The department shall submit a copy of this report to the secretary of state and the director of the Arizona state library, archives and public records.

E. Nothing in subsection A, paragraph 5 of this section shall be construed to prohibit a school district or charter school from developing or participating in a training program that does not meet the conditions prescribed in subsection A, paragraph 5.

Added by Laws 2001, 2nd S.S., Ch. 9, § 1.

Historical and Statutory Notes

Laws 2002, 2nd S.S., Ch. 9, §§ 6 to 8, provide:

"**Sec. 6. Joint Legislative committee on school maintenance and operations funding**

"**A.** A joint legislative committee on school maintenance and operations funding is established consisting of:

"1. Four members of the house of representatives, no more than two of whom shall be members of the same political party. The leader of each of the two major parties of the house of representatives shall appoint two members to serve on the joint legislative committee. Members appointed pursuant to this paragraph shall be selected within thirty days of the effective date of this act. The speaker of the house of representatives shall select one of the members appointed pursuant to this paragraph to co-chair the joint legislative committee.

"2. Four members of the senate, no more than two of whom shall be members of the same political party. The leader of each of the two major parties of the senate shall appoint two members to serve on the joint legislative committee. Members appointed pursuant to this paragraph shall be selected within thirty days of the effective date of this act. The president of the senate shall select one of the members appointed pursuant to this paragraph to co-chair the joint legislative committee.

"**B.** The committee shall:

"1. Evaluate and make specific recommendations on school district and charter school maintenance and operations funding, including specific recommendations concerning group A and group B weights, with emphasis on the group B weight for English learners and the funding formula for rural and small schools.

"2. Evaluate and make specific recommendations on English learner programs, including, but not limited to the following:

"(a) The manner in which structured English immersion programs and bilingual education programs are implemented in this state.

"(b) The additional requirements for school districts and charter schools necessitated by the ballot initiative that enacted the provisions of title 15, chapter 7, article 3.1 and the consent order dated June 30, 2000 in the Flores v. Arizona litigation.

"(c) The identification of which school districts and charter schools have significantly high reclassification rates and test scores for English learners.

"(d) The incremental amount per student that school districts and charter schools spend on each English learner from any and all funding sources.

"(e) Whether additional compensatory instruction monies that are made available should be distributed to parents of English learners or the school district or charter school.

"(f) The current use of federal monies for English learner programs and the future appropriate use of federal monies for English learner programs.

"(g) The extent to which school districts and charter schools are in compliance with state and federal laws relating to English learner programs, including the consent order dated June 30, 2000 in the Flores v. Arizona litigation.

"3. Review a form developed by the state board of education to be used by all school districts and charter schools for use at the beginning of the 2003–2004 school year for parental waivers pursuant to § 15–753, Arizona Revised Statutes.

"4. Review a parent or legal guardian English learner notification and consent form developed by the state board of education to be used by all school districts and charter schools for use at the beginning of the 2002–2003 school year. The form shall be completed annually by either school district or charter school personnel and the classroom teacher within thirty days of the receipt of the language proficiency test results. The form shall be signed and dated by both the primary classroom teacher and the student's parents or legal guardian. The signed and completed form shall be kept on file by the school district or charter school. The form shall not exceed one page in length and shall contain the following information:

"(a) The pupil's name.

"(b) The reasons that the pupil has been placed in a language acquisition program.

"(c) A check box that indicates whether the pupil has been placed in a structured English immersion program or a bilingual education program.

"(d) A list of the criteria that will be used to determine if the pupil has achieved English proficiency.

"5. Recommend to the state board of education:

"(a) Structured English immersion guidelines and methodologies to be used by school districts and charter schools.

"(b) Guidelines for the courses required pursuant to § 15-1626, Arizona Revised Statutes, as amended by this act, pertaining to provisional structured English immersion endorsements.

"(c) Guidelines and requirements for structured English immersion certification of teachers.

"(d) Other sources of in-service teacher training.

"6. Submit a report of its findings, recommendations and proposed legislation to the president of the senate, the speaker of the house of representatives and the governor on or before December 1, 2004. The committee shall provide a copy of the report to the secretary of state and the director of the Arizona state library, archives and public records.

"**C.** The committee may instruct the auditor general to conduct and complete any and all audits that the committee deems necessary. The auditor general shall report to the committee the results of any audits conducted pursuant to this subsection.

"**D.** The committee may utilize the services and staff of the department of education, the auditor general, legislative council and the legislature.

"**Sec. 7. Delayed repeal**

"Section 6 of this act, relating to the joint legislative committee on school maintenance and operations funding, is repealed from and after December 31, 2004.

"**Sec. 8. Cost study of ELL group B weight; report**

"**A.** The legislative council shall select and contract with a private entity to conduct a cost study of the group B weight for English learners. The cost study shall determine the actual cost of complying with all state and federal laws relating to language acquisition programs and the current use of federal monies for English learner programs and the future appropriate use of federal monies for English learner programs. The cost study shall reflect the requirements listed in the consent order dated June 30, 2000 in the Flores v. Arizona litigation."

"**B.** The joint legislative committee on school maintenance and operations funding shall determine the scope and content of the cost study and the school districts and charter schools that will be selected to participate in the cost study. No fewer than fifty per cent of the school districts and charter schools that are selected to participate in the cost study shall be from school districts and charter schools with the highest number of pupils who are classified as English learners.

"**C.** Legislative council shall award the contract to conduct the cost study to the selected private entity by August 1, 2002. The private entity shall complete the cost study and submit its final report to the joint legislative committee, the governor, the president of the senate and the speaker of the house of representatives on or before August 1, 2004 and shall provide a copy of this report to the secretary of state and the director of the Arizona state library, archives and public records.

Laws 2002, 2nd S.S., Ch. 9, § 17, provides:

"**Sec. 17. Intent**

"**A.** It is the intent of the legislature to identify and fund the most effective and cost efficient English language acquisition programs for our public education institutions. The legislature has held extensive hearings and taken hours of testimony on this issue. Those hearings show that there is a significant array of teaching programs and instructional models currently in place for teaching non-English speaking students. Additionally, there is limited data and few reports of results to help identify a menu of teaching programs that would allow those students to master the standard academic curriculum. It is also apparent that one teaching model will not effectively and efficiently satisfy the needs of all educational institutions.

"**B.** With the information currently available, the legislature finds the level of funding in this legislation to be reasonable. The legislature recognizes that further study and evaluation are necessary to determine whether the funding for this program should be adjusted. Therefore, the legislature is establishing a joint legislative committee and providing the necessary funds to evaluate the various teaching programs in place or available, recommend programs for successful English language acquisition programs of non-English speaking students in Arizona schools and determine whether the level of funding associated with such programs should be adjusted. The legislature is requiring the study to be concluded within a strict, yet realistic timeline of two years and the legislature expects legislative review during the third year. During the study interim the legislature has chosen the Nogales unified school district cost study prepared by the Arizona department of education as the basis for the English learner (ELL) group B weight selected. The legislature evaluated several areas of the cost study that indicated the Nogales number might not be representative of average costs across the state. In those areas the legislature added supplemental funding in an effort to better balance the ELL group B weight.

"**C.** It remains the intent of the legislature to identify and fund effective and cost efficient English language acquisition programs for schools in Arizona. It is important to remember that parents of English learners want their children to be proficient in English. The legislature is trying to find the best way to honor that desire."

Former § 15–756, added as § 15–799.05 by Laws 1984, Ch. 169, § 2, renumbered as § 15–756, amended by Laws 1989, Ch. 273, § 8, eff. June 26, 1989; Laws 1999, Ch. 249, § 3, derived from Laws 1969, Ch. 95, § 3; A.R.S. former §§ 15–706, 15–1097; Laws 1973, Ch. 169, § 5; Laws 1981, Ch. 1, § 2, which related to powers and duties of superintendent of public instruction, was repealed by Proposition 203, an initiative measure, approved election Nov. 7, 2000, eff. Nov. 27, 2000.

Proposition 203, based on an Initiative Measure, proposing amendment to Title 15, Chapter 7, by repeal and addition of Article 3.1, relating to English language education, was approved by the electors at the November 7, 2000 general election as proclaimed by the governor on November 27, 2000.

§ 15–756.01. Contracts with private vendors

School districts and charter schools may enter into contracts with private vendors that provide literacy services that are designed to make participating pupils who begin receiving the services in kindergarten successful at reading, writing and speaking English at the third grade level by the end of the third grade.

Added by Laws 2001, 2nd S.S., Ch. 9, § 1.

ARTICLE 4. SPECIAL EDUCATION FOR EXCEPTIONAL CHILDREN

§ 15–761. Definitions

In this article, unless the context otherwise requires:

1. "Autism" means a developmental disability that significantly affects verbal and nonverbal communication and social interaction and that adversely affects educational performance. Characteristics include irregularities and impairments in communication, engagement in repetitive activities and stereotyped movements, resistance to environmental change or change in daily routines and unusual responses to sensory experiences. Autism does not include children with characteristics of emotional disability as defined in this section.

2. "Child with a disability" means a child who is at least three years but less than twenty-two years of age, who has been evaluated pursuant to § 15–766 and found to have at least one of the following disabilities and who, because of the disability, needs special education and related services:

(a) Autism.

(b) Emotional disability.

(c) Hearing impairment.

(d) Other health impairments.

(e) Specific learning disability.

(f) Mild, moderate or severe mental retardation.

(g) Multiple disabilities.

(h) Multiple disabilities with severe sensory impairment.

(i) Orthopedic impairment.

(j) Preschool moderate delay.

(k) Preschool severe delay.

(*l*) Preschool speech/language delay.

(m) Speech/language impairment.

(n) Traumatic brain injury.

(*o*) Visual impairment.

3. "Educational disadvantage" means a condition which has limited a child's opportunity for educational experience resulting in a child achieving less than a normal level of learning development.

4. "Eligibility for special education" means the pupil must have one of the disabilities contained in paragraph 2 of this section and must also require special education services in order to benefit from an educational program.

5. "Emotional disability":

(a) Means a condition whereby a child exhibits one or more of the following characteristics over a long period of time and to a marked degree that adversely affects the child's performance in the educational environment:

(i) An inability to learn which cannot be explained by intellectual, sensory or health factors.

(ii) An inability to build or maintain satisfactory interpersonal relationships with peers and teachers.

(iii) Inappropriate types of behavior or feelings under normal circumstances.

(iv) A general pervasive mood of unhappiness or depression.

(v) A tendency to develop physical symptoms or fears associated with personal or school problems.

(b) Includes children who are schizophrenic but does not include children who are socially maladjusted unless they are also determined to have an emotional disability as determined by evaluation as provided in § 15–766.

6. "Exceptional child" means a gifted child or a child with a disability.

7. "Foster parent" means a person who has been designated by a court of competent jurisdiction to serve as the parent of a child with a disability if that person has an ongoing, long-term parental relationship with the child, is willing to make educational decisions for the child and has no personal interest that would conflict with the interests of the child.

8. "Gifted child" means a child who is of lawful school age, who due to superior intellect or advanced learning ability, or both, is not afforded an opportunity for otherwise attainable progress and development in regular classroom instruction and who needs special instruction or special ancillary services, or both, to achieve at levels commensurate with the child's intellect and ability.

9. "Hearing impairment" means a loss of hearing acuity, as determined by evaluation pursuant to § 15-766, which interferes with the child's performance in the educational environment and requires the provision of special education and related services.

10. "Home school district" means the school district in which the person resides who has legal custody of the child, as provided in § 15-824, subsection B. If the child is a ward of the state and a specific person does not have legal custody of the child, the home school district is the district that the child last attended or, if the child has not previously attended a public school in this state, the school district within which the child currently resides.

11. "Individualized education program" means a written statement, as defined in 20 United States Code §§ 1401 and 1412, for providing special education services to a child with a disability that includes the pupil's present levels of educational performance, the measurable annual goals and short-term objectives or benchmarks for evaluating progress toward those goals and the specific special education and related services to be provided.

12. "Individualized education program team" means a team whose task is to develop an appropriate educational program for the child and that includes:

(a) The parent.

(b) At least one of the child's regular education teachers.

(c) One of the child's special education teachers.

(d) A representative of the public agency that is qualified to provide or supervise the provision of instruction that is designed specifically for children with disabilities who is knowledgeable about general curriculum and the availability of resources.

(e) A person who can interpret the instructional implications of evaluation results.

(f) The child, if appropriate.

(g) At the discretion of the parent or the public agency, other persons with knowledge or special expertise about the child.

13. "Mental retardation" means a significant impairment of general intellectual functioning that exists concurrently with deficits in adaptive behavior and that adversely affects the child's performance in the educational environment.

14. "Mild mental retardation" means performance on standard measures of intellectual and adaptive behavior between two and three standard deviations below the mean for children of the same age.

15. "Moderate mental retardation" means performance on standard measures of intellectual and adaptive behavior between three and four standard deviations below the mean for children of the same age.

16. "Multidisciplinary evaluation team" means a team of persons including individuals described as the individualized education program team and other qualified professionals who shall determine whether a child is eligible for special education.

17. "Multiple disabilities" means learning and developmental problems resulting from multiple disabilities as determined by evaluation pursuant to § 15-766 that cannot be provided for adequately in a program designed to meet the needs of children with less complex disabilities. Multiple disabilities include any of the following conditions that require the provision of special education and related services:

(a) Two or more of the following conditions:

(i) Hearing impairment.

(ii) Orthopedic impairment.

(iii) Moderate mental retardation.

(iv) Visual impairment.

(b) A child with a disability listed in subdivision (a) of this paragraph existing concurrently with a condition of mild mental retardation, emotional disability or specific learning disability.

18. "Multiple disabilities with severe sensory impairment" means multiple disabilities that include at least one of the following:

(a) Severe visual impairment or severe hearing impairment in combination with another severe disability.

(b) Severe visual impairment and severe hearing impairment.

19. "Orthopedic impairment" means one or more severe orthopedic impairments and includes those that are caused by congenital anomaly, disease and other causes, such as amputation or cerebral palsy, and that adversely affect a child's performance in the educational environment.

20. "Other health impairments" means limited strength, vitality or alertness, including a heightened alertness to environmental stimuli, due to chronic or acute health problems which adversely affect a pupil's educational performance.

21. "Out-of-home care" means the placement of a child with a disability outside of the home environment and includes twenty-four hour residential care, group care or foster care on either a full-time or part-time basis.

22. "Parent" means the natural or adoptive parent of a child, the legal guardian of a child, a relative with whom a child resides and who is acting as the parent of that child, a surrogate parent who has been appointed for a child pursuant to § 15-763.01 or a foster parent as defined in this section.

23. "Preschool child" means a child who is at least three years of age but who has not reached the required age for kindergarten, subject to § 15-771, subsection G.

24. "Preschool moderate delay" means performance by a preschool child on a norm-referenced test that measures at least one and one-half, but not more than three, standard deviations below the mean for children of the same chronological age in two or more of the following areas:

(a) Cognitive development.

(b) Physical development.

(c) Communication development.

(d) Social or emotional development.

(e) Adaptive development.

The results of the norm-referenced measure must be corroborated by information from a comprehensive developmental assessment and from parental input, if available, as measured by a judgment based assessment or survey. If there is a discrepancy between the measures, the evaluation team shall determine eligibility based on a preponderance of the information presented.

25. "Preschool severe delay" means performance by a preschool child on a norm-referenced test that measures more than three standard deviations below the mean for children of the same chronological age in one or more of the following areas:

(a) Cognitive development.

(b) Physical development.

(c) Communication development.

(d) Social or emotional development.

(e) Adaptive development.

The results of the norm-referenced measure must be corroborated by information from a comprehensive developmental assessment and from parental input, if available, as measured by a judgment based assessment or survey. If there is a discrepancy between the measures, the evaluation team shall determine eligibility based on a preponderance of the information presented.

26. "Preschool speech/language delay" means performance by a preschool child on a norm-referenced language test that measures at least one and one-half standard deviations below the mean for children of the same chronological age or whose speech, out of context, is unintelligible to a listener who is unfamiliar with the child. Eligibility under this paragraph is appropriate only if a comprehensive developmental assessment or norm-referenced assessment and parental input indicate that the child is not eligible for services under another preschool category. The evaluation team shall determine eligibility based on a preponderance of the information presented.

27. "Prior written notice" means notice, as defined in 20 United States Code §§ 1414 and 1415, that includes a description of the action proposed or refused by the school, an explanation of why the school proposes or refuses to take the action, a description of any options the school considered and the reasons why those options were rejected, a description of each evaluation procedure, test, record or report the school used as a basis for the proposal or refusal, a description of any other factors that were relevant to the school's proposal or refusal, a full explanation of all of the procedural safeguards available to the parent and a listing of sources for parents to contact to obtain assistance in understanding the notice.

28. "Related services" means those supportive services, as defined in 20 United States Code § 1401, that are required to assist a child with a disability who is eligible to receive special education services in order for the child to benefit from special education.

29. "Residential special education placement" means the placement of a child with a disability in a public or private residential program, as provided in § 15–765, subsection G, in order to provide necessary special education and related services as specified in the child's individualized education program.

30. "Severe mental retardation" means performance on standard measures of intellectual and adaptive behavior measures at least four standard deviations below the mean for children of the same age.

31. "Special education" means the adjustment of the environmental factors, modification of the course of study and adaptation of teaching methods, materials and techniques to provide educationally for those children who are gifted or disabled to such an extent that they need specially designed instruction in order to receive educational benefit. Difficulty in writing, speaking or understanding the English language due to an environmental background wherein a language other than English is spoken primarily or exclusively shall not be considered a disability that requires special education.

32. "Special education referral" means a written request for an evaluation to determine whether a pupil is eligible for special education services that, for referrals not initiated by a parent, includes documentation of appropriate efforts to educate the pupil in the regular education program.

33. "Specific learning disability":

(a) Means a specific learning disorder in one or more of the basic psychological processes involved in understanding or in using language, spoken or written, which may manifest itself in an imperfect ability to listen, think, speak, read, write, spell or do mathematical calculations.

(b) Includes such conditions as perceptual disabilities, minimal brain dysfunction, dyslexia and aphasia.

(c) Does not include learning problems which are primarily the result of visual, hearing, motor or emotional disabilities, of mental retardation or of environmental, cultural or economic disadvantage.

34. "Speech/language impairment" means a communication disorder such as stuttering, impaired articulation, severe disorders of syntax, semantics or vocabulary, or functional language skills, or a voice impairment, as determined by evaluation pursuant to § 15–766, to the extent that it calls attention to itself, interferes with communication or causes a child to be maladjusted.

35. "State placing agency" has the same meaning prescribed in § 15–1181.

36. "Surrogate parent" means a person who has been appointed by the court pursuant to § 15–763.01 in order to represent a child in decisions regarding special education.

37. "Traumatic brain injury":

(a) Means an acquired injury to the brain that is caused by an external physical force and that results in total or partial functional disability or psychosocial impairment, or both, that adversely affects educational performance.

(b) Applies to open or closed head injuries resulting in mild, moderate or severe impairments in one or more areas, including cognition, language, memory, attention, reasoning, abstract thinking, judgment, problem solving, sensory, perceptual and motor abilities, psychosocial behavior, physical functions, information processing and speech.

(c) Does not include brain injuries that are congenital or degenerative or brain injuries induced by birth trauma.

38. "Visual impairment" means a loss in visual acuity or a loss of visual field, as determined by evaluation pursuant to § 15-766, that interferes with the child's performance in the educational environment and that requires the provision of special education and related services.

Added by Laws 1981, Ch. 1, § 2, eff. Jan. 23, 1981. Amended by Laws 1984, Ch. 72, § 1; Laws 1986, Ch. 298, § 1, eff. May 6, 1986; Laws 1987, Ch. 363, § 1, eff. May 22, 1987; Laws 1988, Ch. 281, § 1; Laws 1989, Ch. 15, § 2; Laws 1990, Ch. 207, § 1; Laws 1990, Ch. 258, § 1; Laws 1991, Ch. 173, § 4; Laws 1991, Ch. 209, § 1; Laws 1991, Ch. 257, § 5; Laws 1992, Ch. 172, § 6; Laws 1993, Ch. 189, § 2; Laws 1994, Ch. 91, § 1, eff. April 12, 1994; Laws 2000, Ch. 236, § 6, eff. April 12, 2000; Laws 2004, Ch. 256, § 1.

Historical and Statutory Notes

Source:

Laws 1962, Ch. 110, § 1.
A.R.S. former §§ 15-1011, 15-1081.
Laws 1970, Ch. 169, § 3.
Laws 1971, Ch. 184, § 2.
Laws 1973, Ch. 181, § 3.
Laws 1977, Ch. 89, § 2.
Laws 1978, Ch. 188, § 13.
Laws 1979, Ch. 181, § 3.

Laws 1986, Ch. 298, § 4, effective May 6, 1986, provides:

"**Sec. 4. Budget for fiscal year 1986-1987**

"Governing boards of school districts shall budget for fiscal year 1986-1987 using the provisions of § 15-761, Arizona Revised Statutes, as amended by this act."

Laws 1987, Ch. 363, § 27, effective May 22, 1987, provides:

"**Sec. 27. Budgeting for MHSSI pupils beginning with fiscal year 1988-1989**

"Notwithstanding §§ 15-761, 15-901 and 15-943, Arizona Revised Statutes, as amended by this act, school district governing boards may enroll pupils in a multiple handicapped with severe sensory impairment program beginning with fiscal year 1987-1988, but no pupils may be budgeted in that category until the 1988-1989 budget year."

Laws 1988, Ch. 281, § 11 provides:

"**Sec. 11. Budgeting for preschool handicapped pupils beginning with fiscal year 1989-1990**

"Notwithstanding §§ 15-761, 15-901, 15-943, 15-961, 15-962 and 15-971, Arizona Revised Statutes, as amended by this act, school district governing boards may budget for preschool handicapped pupils beginning with fiscal year 1989-1990 as provided in this act."

Laws 2001, Ch. 356, § 1, provides:

"**Section 1.** Pilot program for the integration of special education services; requirements; report

"**A.** On or before January 1, 2002, the department of education shall, in collaboration with the department of economic security, the department of health services, the administrative office of the courts and the department of juvenile corrections, develop a pilot program for the integration of special education services in five school districts in this state, at least one of which is a school district in a county with a population of less than one hundred thousand persons. The pilot program shall be designed to streamline, expedite and coordinate special education services through the integration of those services at the local level.

"**B.** The department of education shall submit a report no later than December 1, 2002, that reports the number of school districts interested in implementing the pilot program, summarizes the results of the pilot program and recommends proposed legislation to the governor, the president of the senate and the speaker of the house of representatives and provide a copy of this report to the secretary of state and the director of the Arizona state library, archives and public records."

Reviser's Notes:

1990 Note. Prior to the 1991 amendments, this section contained the amendments made by Laws 1990, Ch. 207, § 1 and Ch. 258, § 1 which were blended together pursuant to authority of § 41-1304.03.

1991 Note. Prior to the 1992 amendment, this section contained the amendments made by Laws 1991, Ch. 173, sec. 4 and Ch. 209, sec. 1 and Ch. 257, sec. 5 that were blended together pursuant to authority of § 41-1304.03.

1992 Note. Pursuant to authority § 41-1304.02, paragraph 15 was renumbered as paragraph 14 and the remaining paragraphs were renumbered to conform in order to correct a manifest clerical error.

2000 Note. In the chapter version in paragraph 12, in the lead-in language a stricken comma should have appeared after "~~parent~~". Pursuant to authority of section 41-1304.02, the stricken comma is inserted in the chapter version to correct a manifest clerical error.

§ 15-762. Division of special education

The division of special education as provided in chapter 2, article 2 [1] of this title shall carry out the provisions of this article subject to the superintendent of public instruction.

Added by Laws 1981, Ch. 1, § 2, eff. Jan. 23, 1981.

[1] Section 15-231 et seq.

§ 15-763. Plan for providing special education; definition

A. All school districts and charter schools shall develop policies and procedures for providing special education to all children with disabilities within the district or charter school. All children with disabilities shall receive special education programming commensurate with their abilities and needs. Each child shall be ensured access to the general curriculum and an opportunity to meet the state's academic standards. Special education services shall be provided at no cost to the parents of children with disabilities.

B. For the purposes of determining the services to pupils served by private schools under existing federal law, the state shall consider the term to include home schooled pupils.

C. If federal monies are provided to a school district or a charter school for special education services to home schooled or private schooled pupils, The school district or charter school shall provide the services to both the home schooled pupils and the private schooled pupils in the same manner.

D. For the purposes of this section, "special education" has the same meaning prescribed in § 15-1201.

Added by Laws 1981, Ch. 1, § 2, eff. Jan. 23, 1981. Amended by Laws 1981, Ch. 314, § 13; Laws 2000, Ch. 236, § 7, eff. April 12, 2000; Laws 2001, Ch. 364, § 1.

Historical and Statutory Notes

Source:

Laws 1961, Ch. 40, § 1.
A.R.S. former §§ 15-1010, 15-1018.
Laws 1967, Ch. 127, § 1.
Laws 1973, Ch. 181, § 2.
Laws 1977, Ch. 89, § 1.

Reviser's Notes:

2001 Note. Pursuant to authority of § 41-1304.02, in the section heading "; definition" was added.

§ 15-763.01. Surrogate parent; appointment

A. A petition for the appointment of a surrogate parent for a child with a disability shall be made to a court of competent jurisdiction if any of the following conditions have been met:

1. No parent can be identified.

2. A public agency cannot determine the whereabouts of a parent, after having made three documented and reasonable attempts.

3. The child is a ward of the state.

B. In order for a person to be eligible to receive an appointment as a surrogate parent for a child with a disability all of the following must be true:

1. The person shall be determined by the court to possess knowledge and skills that will ensure adequate representation of the child.

2. The person may not be an employee of a state agency if that agency is involved in the education or care of the child.

3. The person may not have any interests that would conflict with the best interests of the child.

4. The person shall have a valid fingerprint clearance card issued pursuant to title 41, chapter 12, article 3.1.[1]

C. A person who is appointed as a surrogate parent for a child with a disability shall not be deemed to be an employee of the state solely as a result of serving as a surrogate parent and receiving compensation for that service.
Added by Laws 1991, Ch. 209, § 2. Amended by Laws 2000, Ch. 236, § 8, eff. April 12, 2000; Laws 2003, Ch. 214, § 6, eff. Oct. 1, 2003.

[1] Section 41-1758 et seq.

§ 15-764. Powers of the school district governing board or county school superintendent

A. The governing board of each school district or the county school superintendent shall:

1. Provide special education and related services for all children with disabilities and make such programs and services available to all eligible children with disabilities who are at least three years but less than twenty-two years of age.

2. Employ supportive special personnel, which may include a director of special education, for the operation of special school programs and services for exceptional children.

3. To the extent appropriate, educate children with disabilities in the regular education classes. Special classes, separate schooling or other removal of children with disabilities from the regular educational environment shall occur only if, and to the extent that, the nature or severity of the disability is such that education in regular classes, even with the use of supplementary aids and services, cannot be accomplished satisfactorily.

4. Provide necessary specialized transportation in connection with any educational program, class or service as required by the pupil's individualized education program.

5. Establish policy with regard to allowable pupil-teacher ratios and pupil-staff ratios within the school district or county for provision of special education services.

B. The special education programs and services established pursuant to this section and § 15-765 shall be conducted only in a school facility which houses regular education classes or in other facilities approved by the division of special education.

C. The governing board of each school district shall provide special education to gifted pupils identified as provided in § 15-770. Special education for gifted pupils shall only include expanding academic course offerings and supplemental services as may be required to provide an educational program which is commensurate with the academic abilities and potential of the gifted pupil.

D. The governing board may modify the course of study and adapt teaching methods, materials and techniques to provide educationally for those pupils who are gifted and possess superior intellect or advanced learning ability, or both, but may have an educational disadvantage resulting from a disability or a difficulty in writing, speaking or understanding the English language due to an environmental background wherein a language other than English is primarily or exclusively spoken. Programs and services provided for gifted pupils as provided in this subsection may not be separate from programs provided for other gifted pupils and may not be provided in facilities separate from the facilities used for other gifted pupils. Identification of gifted pupils as provided in this subsection shall be based on tests or subtests that are demonstrated to be effective with special populations including those with a disability or difficulty with the English language.

E. The governing body of each school district, county or agency involved in intergovernmental agreements may, in cooperation with another school district or districts, establish special education programs for exceptional children. When two or more governing bodies determine to carry out by joint agreement the duties in regard to the special education programs for exceptional children, the governing bodies shall, in accordance with state law and the rules of the division of special education, establish a written agreement for the provision of services. In such agreements, one governing body of each school district, an agency involved in intergovernmental agreements or the county shall administer the program in accordance with the contract agreement between the school districts. Tuition students may be included in the agreement. The agreement may also include lease-purchase of facilities for the special education programs for exceptional children.

F. The county school superintendent may, upon approval of the division of special education, establish special education programs in the county accommodation schools under the jurisdiction of the superintendent or may cooperate with other school districts by agreement to provide such services for such special programs in accordance with the rules of the division of special education. At the beginning of each school year the county school superintendent shall present an estimate of the current year's accommodation school exceptional programs tuition cost to each school district that has signed an agreement to use the services of the accommodation school. The tuition shall be the estimated per capita cost based on the number of pupils that each school district has estimated will enroll in the program, and the school district shall pay the tuition quarterly in advance on July 1, October 1, January 1 and April 1. Increases in enrollment during the school year over the school district's estimate of July 1 shall cause the tuition charges to be adjusted accordingly. In the event of overpayment by the school district of residence, the necessary adjustment shall be made at the close of the school year.

Added by Laws 1981, Ch. 1, § 2, eff. Jan. 23, 1981. Amended by Laws 1982, Ch. 169, § 2; Laws 1983, Ch. 325, § 9; Laws 1984, Ch. 282, § 1; Laws 1984, Ch. 379, § 10; Laws 1986, Ch. 250, § 3; Laws 1989, Ch. 273, § 9, eff. June 26, 1989; Laws 1991, Ch. 173, § 5; Laws 1991, Ch. 257, § 6; Laws 1992, Ch. 172, § 7; Laws 2000, Ch. 236, § 9, eff. April 12, 2000.

Historical and Statutory Notes

Source:

Laws 1961, Ch. 40, § 1.
A.R.S. former §§ 15-1015, 15-1018, 15-1082.
Laws 1962, Ch. 110, § 1.
Laws 1967, Ch. 127, § 1.
Laws 1970, Ch. 169, § 3.
Laws 1971, Ch. 184, § 3.
Laws 1973, Ch. 181, § 5.
Laws 1974, 1st S.S., Ch. 3, § 15.
Laws 1976, Ch. 165, § 3.
Laws 1976, Ch. 185, § 2.
Laws 1977, Ch. 20, § 2.
Laws 1977, Ch. 89, § 5.
Laws 1978, Ch. 170, § 1.
Laws 1978, Ch. 198, § 7.
Laws 1979, Ch. 195, § 7.
Laws 1979, Ch. 210, § 1.
Laws 1980, 2nd S.S., Ch. 9, § 39.

Reviser's Notes:

1984 Note. Prior to the 1986 amendment, this section contained the amendments made by Laws 1984, Ch. 282, § 1, and Ch. 379, § 10 which were blended together pursuant to authority of § 41-1304.03.

1991 Note. Prior to the 1992 amendment, this section contained the amendments made by Laws 1991, Ch. 173, sec. 5 and Ch. 257, sec. 6 that were blended together pursuant to authority of § 41-1304.03.

§ 15-765. Special education in rehabilitation, corrective or other state and county supported institutions, facilities or homes

A. For the purposes of this section and § 15-764, children with disabilities who are being provided with special education in rehabilitation, corrective or other state and county supported institutions or facilities are the responsibility of that institution or facility, including children with disabilities who are not enrolled in a residential program and who are being furnished with daily transportation. Special education programs at the institution or facility shall conform to the conditions and standards prescribed by the director of the division of special education.

B. Notwithstanding the provisions of subsection A of this section, the department of economic security or the department of health services may request on behalf of a school-age child with a disability residing in a residential facility or foster home operated or supported by the department of economic security or the department of health services that the school district in which the facility or home is located enroll the school-age child in the district, subject to § 15-825. The school district shall, upon the request by the department of economic security or the department of health services, enroll the child and provide any necessary special education and related services, subject to § 15-766. A school district in which a child with a disability is enrolled shall coordinate the development of an individualized education program with the development of an individual program or treatment plan. The provision of special education and related services to a child with a disability may be subject to the provisions of subsection D of this section.

C. Before any placement is made in facilities described in this section, the school district of residence shall insure that a full continuum of alternative placements is available to meet the needs of children with disabilities and that the proposed placement is the least restrictive environment in which appropriate education services can be provided to the child.

D. A school district or county school superintendent may contract with, and make payments to, other public or private schools, institutions and agencies approved by the division of special education, within or without the school district or county, for the education of and provision of services to children with disabilities if the provisions of § 15–766 and the conditions and standards prescribed by the division of special education have been met and if unable to provide satisfactory education and services through its own facilities and personnel in accordance with the rules prescribed by the state board of education. No school district may contract or make payments under the authority of this section or § 15–764 or any other provisions of law for the residential or educational costs of placement of children with disabilities in an approved private special education school, institution or agency unless the children are evaluated and placed by a school district. The following special provisions apply in order to qualify for the group B ED-P weight:

1. If the child is placed in a private special education program, the chief administrative official of the school district or county or other person designated by the school district or county as responsible for special education shall verify that the pupil is diagnosed with an emotional disability as defined in § 15–761, that no appropriate program exists within the school district or county, as applicable, and that no program can feasibly be instituted by the school district or county, as applicable.

2. If the child is placed in a special program that provides intensive services within a school district, the chief administrative official of the school district or county or other person as designated by the school district or county as responsible for special education shall verify that the pupil placed in such a program is diagnosed with an emotional disability as defined in § 15–761 and that appropriate services cannot be provided in traditional resource and self-contained special education classes.

E. When a state placing agency initially places a pupil in a private residential facility, the home school district must conduct an evaluation pursuant to § 15–766 or review the educational placement of a pupil who has previously been determined eligible for special education services. The school district shall notify the appropriate state placing agency when a child requires an evaluation for possible receipt of services provided by that agency or a residential special education placement. The school district and the state agency shall jointly evaluate the child, including consideration of relevant information from additional sources, including probation or parole officers, caseworkers, guardians ad litem and court appointed special advocates.

F. If the child is not eligible for special education or does not require residential special education placement, §§ 15–1182 and 15–1183 apply.

G. If the individualized education program team determines that a residential special education placement is the least restrictive environment in which an appropriate educational program can be provided, the home school district shall submit the following documentation to the department of education:

1. A residential special education voucher application signed by designated representatives of the state placing agency, as defined in § 15-1181, and the home school district, respectively.

2. The educational reasons for recommending the residential special education placement, including an evaluation or addendum to the evaluation that describes the instructional and behavioral interventions that were previously attempted and the educational reasons for recommending the residential special education placement, including documentation that the nature or severity of the disability is such that education in a less restrictive environment is not appropriate.

3. Exit criteria as required in subsection K of this section.

4. That prior written notice for a change in the child's placement was provided.

H. If a residential special education placement is required by the child's individualized education program, the educational component of the residential facility shall be one that is approved by the department of education for the specific special education services required.

I. The residential component of the facility in which the residential special education placement is made shall be licensed by the department of economic security or the department of health services, whichever is appropriate.

J. Following and in accordance with the consensus decision of the individualized education program team as prescribed in § 15-766, a residential special education placement shall be made by the school district and the appropriate state agency. The individualized education program team shall determine whether a residential special education placement is necessary. The state placing agency shall consider the recommendations of the individualized education program team in selecting the specific residential facility. The department of education shall enter into interagency services agreements with the department of economic security or the department of health services to establish a mechanism for resolving disputes if the school district and the department of economic security or the department of health services cannot mutually agree on the specific residential placement to be made. Dispute resolution procedures may not be used to deny or delay residential special education placement.

K. The individualized education program for any child who requires residential special education placement must include exit criteria that indicate when the educational placement of the child shall be reviewed to determine whether the child can be moved to a less restrictive placement.

L. All noneducational and nonmedical costs incurred by the placement of a child with a disability in a private or public school program and concurrent out-of-home care program shall be paid by the department of economic security for those children eligible to receive services through the division of developmental disabilities or the administration for children, youth and families of the department of economic security and by the department of health services for those children eligible to receive services through the division of behavioral health in the department of health services or children's rehabilitation services. Nothing in this section is intended to prevent or limit the department of health services and the department of economic security from joint case management of any child who qualifies for services from both agencies or from sharing the noneducational costs of providing those services. The educational costs incurred by the placement of a child with a disability in an out-of-home care facility shall be paid as follows:

1. Through a residential special education placement voucher as provided in § 15–1184 if the child is determined to require a residential special education placement as defined in § 15–761.

2. Through an initial or continuing residential education voucher if a child is placed in a private residential facility by a state placing agency, as defined in § 15–1181, for care, treatment and safety reasons and the child needs educational services while in that placement.

3. Through a certificate of educational convenience if the child is attending a public school not within the child's school district of residence as provided in § 15–825.

4. By the home school district, pursuant to a contract with a public or private school as provided in subsection D of this section, if the home school district is unable to provide satisfactory education and services through its own facilities and personnel.

M. The department of economic security or the department of health services, whichever is appropriate, shall determine if the child placed for purposes of special education in a private or public school and concurrent out-of-home care is covered by an insurance policy which provides for inpatient or outpatient child or adolescent psychiatric treatment. The appropriate state agency may only pay charges for treatment costs that are not covered by an insurance policy. Notwithstanding any other law, the appropriate state agency may pay for placement costs of the child before the verification of applicable insurance coverage. On the depletion of insurance benefits, the appropriate state agency shall resume payment for all noneducational and nonmedical costs incurred in the treatment of the child. The appropriate state agency may request the child's family to contribute a voluntary amount toward the noneducational and nonmedical costs incurred as a result of residential placement of the child. The amount which the appropriate state agency requests the child's family to contribute shall be based on guidelines in the rules of the appropriate state agency governing the determination of contributions by parents and estates. Nothing in this subsection shall be construed to require parents to incur any costs for required special education and related services or shall be construed to result in a reduction in lifetime insurance benefits available for a child with a disability.

N. If appropriate services are offered by the school district and the parent or the child chooses for the child to attend a private facility, either for day care or for twenty-four hour care, neither the school district nor the respective agency is obligated to assume the cost of the private facility. If residential twenty-four hour care is necessitated by factors such as the child's home condition and is not related to the special educational needs of the child, the agency responsible for the care of the child is not required to pay any additional costs of room and board and nonmedical expenses pursuant to this section.

Added by Laws 1981, Ch. 1, § 2, eff. Jan. 23, 1981. Amended by Laws 1981, Ch. 147, § 1; Laws 1983, Ch. 252, § 1; Laws 1985, Ch. 166, § 9, eff. April 18, 1985; Laws 1988, Ch. 127, § 1; Laws 1990, Ch. 164, § 1; Laws 1991, Ch. 173, § 6; Laws 1992, Ch. 172, § 8; Laws 1994, Ch. 91, § 2, eff. April 12, 1994.

Historical and Statutory Notes

Source:

Laws 1961, Ch. 40, § 1.
A.R.S. former §§ 15-1015, 15-1018, 15-1082.
Laws 1962, Ch. 110, § 1.
Laws 1967, Ch. 127, § 1.
Laws 1970, Ch. 169, § 3.
Laws 1971, Ch. 184, § 3.
Laws 1973, Ch. 181, § 1.
Laws 1974, 1st S.S., Ch. 3, § 15.
Laws 1976, Ch. 165, § 3.
Laws 1976, Ch. 185, § 2.
Laws 1977, Ch. 20, § 2.
Laws 1977, Ch. 89, § 5.
Laws 1978, Ch. 170, § 1.
Laws 1978, Ch. 198, § 7.
Laws 1979, Ch. 195, § 7.
Laws 1979, Ch. 210, § 1.
Laws 1980, 2nd S.S., Ch. 9, § 39.

Laws 1990, Ch. 164, §§ 7 to 9 provide:

"**Sec. 7. Private institution; definition**

"Notwithstanding § 15-1181, Arizona Revised Statutes, as amended by this act, for fiscal years 1990-1991 through 1993-1994, 'private institution' means a child welfare agency which is licensed by the department of economic security or department of health services and for which one of the following also applies:

"1. For special education placements, the agency has been approved by the division of special education pursuant to § 15-765, subsection C, Arizona Revised Statutes, for the purpose of providing special education.

"2. For other than special education placements, the agency has been accredited or has applied for accreditation by the North Central Association of Colleges and Secondary Schools as a special function school.

"**Sec. 8. Transition to voucher funding**

"**A.** School districts which have included in their fiscal year 1990-1991 student count, pupils placed by the department of health services in residential programs and for whom tuition has been paid as provided in § 15-765, subsection E, must reduce their revenue control limit and district support level, capital outlay revenue limit and capital levy revenue limit for fiscal year 1990-1991 by the amounts attributable to these pupils for the days for which tuition was paid and notify the department of education by July 31, 1990 of the amounts. The department of education shall prescribe the method for determining the amount of the reductions. The department of education shall decrease that school district's apportionment of equalization assistance for the fiscal year 1990-1991 by the corresponding amount.

"**B.** It is the intent of the legislature that monies appropriated from the state general fund to the state board of education and the superintendent of public instruction for basic state aid for fiscal year 1990-1991, in an amount equal to the equalization assistance reduction in subsection A shall be used by the state board of education for the permanent voucher fund pursuant to this act.

"**Sec. 9. Reporting requirements**

"By October 1, 1991, the department of education will provide a fiscal impact report regarding this act to the president of the senate and the speaker of the house of representatives."

Reviser's Notes:

1981 Note. Pursuant to authority of § 41-1304.02, in the heading of this section the words "or facilities" were added following the word "institutions".

1988 Note. Pursuant to authority of § 41-1304.02, in subsection C the spelling of the first "education", "exceptional" and the first "prescribed" was corrected and in subsection D the spelling of "multidisciplinary" and "mutually" was corrected.

1994 Note. Pursuant to authority of § 41-1304.02, in subsection E, last sentence "caseworkers" was combined as one word.

§ 15-766. Evaluation of child for placement in special education program

A. A special education referral shall be made under the direction of the chief administrative official of the school district or county, or such person officially designated as responsible for special education, after consultation with the parent or guardian.

B. Before a child who is suspected of having a disability is placed in a special education program, an evaluation shall be made of the capabilities and limitations of the child. A reevaluation shall be conducted at least every three years to determine if the disability remains and to determine continued placement in a special education program. The evaluation and reevaluations shall be made by a multidisciplinary evaluation team under the direction of the chief administrative official of the school district or county or such person officially designated as responsible for special education. The team shall review existing evaluation data and shall collect additional data, if necessary, to determine the eligibility of the pupil for special education and to develop an appropriate individual education program. The school district or county may conduct joint evaluations, directly or indirectly with the department of economic security, the department of health services, the department of juvenile corrections and the juvenile courts, or the school district may contract with any state agency or department for all or a portion of the components of the evaluations required by this section. The determination of eligibility for special education services is solely the responsibility of the multidisciplinary evaluation team. The evaluation pursuant to this section shall contain in writing, but is not limited to:

1. A review of current evaluations, including types of tests and the results of those tests.

2. Information provided by the parents, including medical and developmental information and history.

3. educational history, including the reason for the referral, current classroom based assessments and observations by teachers and related service providers.

4. Documentation of whether the child's educational problems are related to or resulting primarily from reasons of educational disadvantage.

5. A determination of whether the child has a category of disability as defined in § 15–761.

6. The child's present levels of academic performance and current educational needs.

7. A determination of whether the child needs special education and related services.

8. A determination of whether any additions or modifications are needed to allow the child to progress in the general curriculum.

C. The results of the evaluation shall be submitted in writing and with recommendations to the chief administrative official of the school district or county or to such person designated by the chief administrative official as responsible for special education.

D. Any of the evaluation components that are enumerated in subsection B of this section, that are less than three years old and that are appropriate to consider under the specific circumstances may be shared by and among state agencies for the purpose of expediting completion of the evaluation and placement process.

E. The chief administrative official of the school district or county or the person officially designated as responsible for special education shall place the child, based upon the consensus recommendation of the individualized education program team and subject to due process pursuant to 20 United States Code § 1415, except that a child shall not be placed in a special education program without the approval of the child's parent or guardian, or retained in such a program without actual notice to the parent or guardian. Placement may be made or changed pursuant to a hearing officer's decision under 20 United States Code § 1415 or an order from a court of competent jurisdiction. The state board of education shall adopt rules to provide a parent or guardian the opportunity to appeal the selection of a specific hearing officer. The state board of education shall adopt rules prescribing minimum standards for hearing officers and prescribing training requirements for hearing officers.

Added by Laws 1981, Ch. 1, § 2, eff. Jan. 23, 1981. Amended by Laws 1986, Ch. 298, § 2, eff. May 6, 1986; Laws 1988, Ch. 127, § 2; Laws 1991, Ch. 257, § 7; Laws 1992, Ch. 172, § 9; Laws 1992, Ch. 273, § 4; Laws 1995, Ch. 178, § 15; Laws 1996, Ch. 284, § 35; Laws 2000, Ch. 236, § 10, eff. April 12, 2000.

Historical and Statutory Notes

Source:

Laws 1970, Ch. 169, § 3.
A.R.S. former § 15-1013.
Laws 1977, Ch. 89, § 3.
Laws 1978, Ch. 198, § 6.

Reviser's Notes:

1988 Note. Pursuant to the authority of § 41-1304.02, in subsection D, paragraph 4 the spelling of "qualified" was corrected and in subsection E the spelling of "multidisciplinary" was corrected.

1992 Note. Prior to the 1995 amendment this section contained the amendments made by Laws 1992, Ch. 172, sec. 9 and Ch. 273, sec. 4 that were blended together pursuant to authority of § 41-1304.03.

§ 15-767. Review of special education placement; report of educational progress

The parents of each child who is placed in a special education program shall receive reports of the child's progress in the general curriculum and the child's progress in meeting the goals stated in the child's individualized education program at least as often as progress reports are given to parents of children who are not placed in special education programs. The reports of the child's progress shall address whether the child's progress is sufficient to enable the child to achieve the goals stated in the child's individualized education program by the end of the school year.

Added by Laws 2000, Ch. 236, § 12, eff. April 12, 2000.

Historical and Statutory Notes

Source:

Laws 1970, Ch. 169, § 3
A.R.S. former § 15-1014.
Laws 1977, Ch. 89, § 4.
A.R.S. former § 15-767.
Laws 1981, Ch. 1, § 2.
Laws 1981, Ch. 31, § 1.
Laws 1991, Ch. 257, § 8.

Former § 15-767, added by Laws 1981, Ch. 1, § 2, and amended by Laws 1981, Ch. 31, § 1, and Laws 1991, Ch. 257, § 8 (see, also, Source, ante), relating to similar subject matter, was repealed by Laws 2000, Ch. 236, § 11, effective April 12, 2000.

§ 15–768. Repealed by Laws 2000, Ch. 236, § 13, eff. April 12, 2000

Historical and Statutory Notes

The repealed section, relating to reports to the department of education and the department of economic security, was added by Laws 1981, Ch. 1, § 2 and was derived from Laws 1978, Ch. 198, § 8 and A.R.S. former § 15–1015.02. Prior to repeal, § 15–768 was amended by:

Laws 1986, Ch. 298, § 3,

Laws 1987, Ch. 363, § 2,

Laws 1989, Ch. 15, § 3,

Laws 1990, Ch. 207, § 2,

Laws 1990, Ch. 258, § 2,

Laws 1991, Ch. 173, § 7,

Laws 1991, Ch. 209, § 3,

Laws 1991, Ch. 257, § 9, and

Laws 1992, Ch. 172, § 10.

Laws 1992, Ch. 319, § 1, par. 8, provides:

"**Section 1. Purpose**

"8. Section 15–768, Arizona Revised Statutes, was amended by Laws 1991, chapter 173, § 7, Laws 1991, chapter 209, § 3 and Laws 1991, chapter 257, § 9. The chapter 173 version could not be blended because it was inconsistent in part with the blended version. Since the substance of the Laws 1991, chapter 173 version was incorporated in the blend version of § 15–768, Arizona Revised Statutes, in this act the chapter 173 version is repealed."

§ 15–769. Appropriation and apportionment; approval of program

A. Except as provided in this section and § 15–770, all pupils who are children with a disability as defined in § 15–761 shall be included in the entitlement to state aid computed as provided in chapter 9, article 5 of this title [1] and apportionment made as provided in § 15–973.

B. A district may budget using the group B weight for a homebound child with a disability if the educational program meets the minimum standards established by the state board of education. For purposes of computing the base support level, a school district shall not classify a pupil in more than one category of disability.

C. The appropriations and apportionment as provided in chapter 9, article 5 of this title shall not be granted to the governing board of a school district or county school superintendent unless the school district or county complies with the provisions of this article and the conditions and standards prescribed by the superintendent of public instruction pursuant to rules of the state board of education for pupil identification and placement pursuant to §§ 15–766 and 15–767.

D. If a pupil with a group B disability does not receive special education instructional services but receives at least one ancillary service, the pupil shall be considered a special education pupil for the group B funding. If the category of disability has both a resource and self-contained weight, the pupil shall be classified as in a resource program. In this subsection, "ancillary service" means one of the following:

1. Physical therapy.
2. Occupational therapy.
3. Orientation and mobility training.
4. Sign language interpretation services.
5. A full-time aide needed for an individual pupil to benefit from the pupil's educational program as specified in the pupil's individualized education program.

Added by Laws 1981, Ch. 1, § 2, eff. Jan. 23, 1981. Amended by Laws 1982, Ch. 169, § 3; Laws 1984, Ch. 282, § 2; Laws 1985, Ch. 127, § 2; Laws 1989, Ch. 15, § 4; Laws 1990, Ch. 207, § 3; Laws 1992, Ch. 172, § 11.

[1] Section 15–971 et seq.

Historical and Statutory Notes

Source:

Laws 1960, Ch. 55, § 1.
A.R.S. former §§ 15-1006, 15-1017, 15-1019, 15-1083, 15-1213.
Laws 1961, Ch. 40, § 1.
Laws 1962, Ch. 110, § 1.
Laws 1966, Ch. 82, § 2.
Laws 1967, 3rd S.S., Ch. 19, §§ 4, 5.
Laws 1970, Ch. 169, § 3.
Laws 1971, Ch. 184, § 5.
Laws 1972, Ch. 161, § 3.
Laws 1973, Ch. 181, § 6.
Laws 1974, 1st S.S., Ch. 3, § 16.
Laws 1975, Ch. 140, § 2.
Laws 1977, Ch. 89, § 6.
Laws 1978, Ch. 40, § 1.
Laws 1979, Ch. 181, § 2.
Laws 1979, Ch. 195, § 25.
Laws 1980, 2nd S.S., Ch. 9, § 40.

§ 15-770. Gifted pupils; scope and sequence; annual financial report

A. The governing board of each school district shall develop a scope and sequence for the identification process of and curriculum modifications for gifted pupils to ensure that gifted pupils receive special education commensurate with their academic abilities and potentials. The scope and the sequence shall:

1. Provide for routine screening for gifted pupils using one or more tests adopted by the state board as prescribed in § 15-203, subsection A, paragraph 15 and § 15-764. School districts may identify any number of pupils as gifted but shall identify as gifted at least those pupils who score at or above the ninety-seventh percentile, based upon national norms, on a test adopted by the state board.

2. Include an explanation of how special education for the gifted differs from regular education in such areas as:

(a) Content, including broad based interdisciplinary curriculum.

(b) Process, including higher level thinking skills.

(c) Product, including variety and complexity.

(d) Learning environment, including flexibility.

B. The governing board shall submit the scope and the sequence to the department of education for approval on or before July 1 if any changes were made during the previous fiscal year. All school districts shall provide to gifted pupils special education commensurate with their academic abilities and potentials.

C. If the governing board fails to submit the scope and sequence for gifted pupils as prescribed in subsection B of this section or if the scope and sequence submitted by the governing board fails to receive full approval by the superintendent of public instruction, the school district is not eligible to receive state aid for the group A weight for three per cent of the student count and shall compute the weighted student count for pupils in group A as provided in § 15-943 by adjustment of the student count accordingly. By December 1 of each year, the department of education shall notify those school districts which appear to be in noncompliance and note the specific areas of deficiencies which must be corrected by April 1 of the following year to be eligible to use the actual student count rather than an adjusted student count. By April 15, the department shall notify those districts which must use an adjusted student count for the next fiscal year's state aid as provided in chapter 9 of this title.[1]

D. The annual financial report of a school district as prescribed in § 15-904 shall include the amount of monies expended on programs for gifted pupils and the number of pupils enrolled in programs or receiving services by grade level.

Added by Laws 1982, Ch. 169, § 4. Amended by Laws 1986, Ch. 250, § 4; Laws 1987, Ch. 85, § 1; Laws 1989, Ch. 273, § 10, eff. June 26, 1989; Laws 1995, Ch. 268, § 39; Laws 1996, Ch. 284, § 36.

[1] Section 15-901 et seq.

Historical and Statutory Notes

Laws 1986, Ch. 250, § 5 provides:

"**Sec. 5. Submission of revised scope and sequence to the department of education**

"Notwithstanding § 15-770, Arizona Revised Statutes, as amended by this act, the governing board of a school district is not required to revise and submit its scope and sequence for the identification and education of gifted pupils to the department of education for approval until July 1, 1987."

Reviser's Notes:

1982 Note. Pursuant to § 41-1304.02, "; definition" was added to the heading of this section [subsequently deleted].

§ 15-771. Preschool programs for children with disabilities; definition

A. Each school district shall make available an educational program for preschool children with disabilities who reside in the school district and who are not already receiving services that have been provided through the department of education. The state board of education shall prescribe rules for use by school districts in the provision of educational programs for preschool children with disabilities. School districts are required to make available educational programs for and, for the purposes of calculating average daily attendance and average daily membership, may count only those preschool children who meet the definition of one of the following conditions:

1. Hearing impairment.
2. Visual impairment.
3. Preschool moderate delay.
4. Preschool severe delay.
5. Preschool speech/language delay.

The school district may make available an educational program for speech or language impaired preschool children whose performance on a standardized language test measures one and one-half standard deviations, or less, below the mean for children of their chronological age. The superintendent of public instruction shall prescribe guidelines for the eligibility of speech or language impaired children, except that eligibility under this subsection is appropriate only when a comprehensive developmental assessment or norm-referenced assessment and parental input indicate that the child is not eligible for services under another preschool category.

B. The state board of education shall annually distribute to school districts at least ten per cent of the monies it receives under 20 United States Code § 1411(c)(2) for preschool programs for children with disabilities. The state board shall prescribe rules for the distribution of the monies to school districts.

C. The governing board of a school district may submit a proposal to the state board of education as prescribed by the state board to receive monies for preschool programs for children with disabilities as provided in this section. A school district which receives monies as provided in this section shall include the monies in the special projects section of the budget as provided in § 15–903, subsection F.

D. All school districts shall cooperate, if appropriate, with community organizations that provide services to preschool children with disabilities in the provision of the district's preschool program for children with disabilities.

E. A school district may not admit a child to a preschool program for children with disabilities unless the child is evaluated and recommended for placement as provided in §§ 15–766 and 15–767.

F. For the purpose of allocating monies pursuant to 20 United States Code § 1419(g)(1)(B)(i), "jurisdiction" includes high school pupils whose parents reside within the boundaries of a common school district. The common school district shall ensure such high school pupils are not counted by any other school district.

G. For purposes of this section, "preschool child" means a child who is at least three years of age but who has not reached the age required for kindergarten. A preschool child is three years of age as of the date of the child's third birthday. The governing board of a school district may admit otherwise eligible children who are within ninety days of their third birthday, if it is determined to be in the best interest of the individual child. Children who are admitted to programs for preschool children prior to their third birthday are entitled to the same provision of services as if they were three years of age.

Added by Laws 1986, Ch. 388, § 1, eff. Aug. 13, 1986, retroactively effective to July 1, 1986. Amended by Laws 1987, Ch. 363, § 3, eff. May 22, 1987; Laws 1988, Ch. 281, § 2; Laws 1989, Ch. 15, § 5; Laws 1989, Ch. 273, § 11, eff. June 26, 1989; Laws 1990, Ch. 207, § 4; Laws 1990, Ch. 258, § 3; Laws 1991, Ch. 173, § 8; Laws 1991, Ch. 209, § 4; Laws 1991, Ch. 244, § 1, eff. June 17, 1991; Laws 1991, Ch. 257, § 10; Laws 1992, Ch. 172, § 12; Laws 1999, Ch. 299, § 11; Laws 2000, Ch. 236, § 14, eff. April 12, 2000.

Historical and Statutory Notes

Laws 1986, Ch. 388, § 3 provides:

"This act is effective retroactively to July 1, 1986."

Laws 1990, Ch. 258, § 9, provides:

"**Sec. 9. Educational programs for handicapped preschool children for fiscal year 1990–1991**

"Notwithstanding § 15–771, Arizona Revised Statutes, as amended by this act, for fiscal year 1990–1991 a school district is required to make available an educational program for handicapped preschool children only for those handicapped children who are not already receiving services that have been provided through the department of education or the department of economic security and who are at least four years of age but who have not reached the age required for kindergarten. A handicapped child is deemed four years of age if the child has reached the age of four before September 1 of the current school year."

Amendment of this section by Laws 1990, Ch. 207, § 4 was repealed by Laws 1991, Ch. 173, § 9, Ch. 209, § 5, Ch. 244, § 2, effective June 17, 1991, and Ch. 257, § 11.

The 1991 amendment of this section by Ch. 173 explicitly amended the 1990 amendment of this section by Ch. 258.

The 1991 amendment of this section by Ch. 209 explicitly amended the 1990 amendment of this section by Ch. 258.

The 1991 amendment of this section by Ch. 244 explicitly amended the 1990 amendment of this section by Ch. 258.

The 1991 amendment of this section by Ch. 257 explicitly amended the 1991 amendment of this section by Ch. 173.

The purported amendment of this section by Laws 1998, 3rd S.S., Ch. 1, failed to became effective because Ch. 1 was repealed in its entirety by Laws 1998, 5th S.S., Ch. 1, § 2, effective July 1, 1998.

Reviser's Notes:

1986 Note. Pursuant to authority of § 41-1304.02, in subsection A "§ 15-761, paragraphs 1, 6, 9, 10, 14, 15 and 16" was substituted for "§ 15-761, paragraph 4, subdivisions (a), (b), (e), (f), (h), (i) and (j)" to conform to the amendment of § 15-761 by Laws 1986, Ch. 298, § 1.

1989 Note. Prior to the 1990 amendments, this section contained the amendments made by Laws 1989, Ch. 15, § 5 and Ch. 273, § 11 which were blended together pursuant to authority of § 41-1304.03.

1990 Note. The amendment made by Laws 1990, Ch. 258, § 3 was inconsistent and incompatible with Laws 1990, Ch. 207, § 4 and therefore could not be blended.

1991 Note. Prior to the 1992 amendment, this section contained the amendments made by Laws 1991, Ch. 173, sec. 8, Ch. 209, sec. 4, Ch. 244, sec. 1 and Ch. 257, sec. 10 that were blended together pursuant to authority of § 41-1304.03. In the Laws 1991, Ch. 257 version in subsection D "preschool" was incorrectly shown as "PRESCHOOL". Pursuant to authority of § 41-1304.02, in order to correct a manifest clerical error "preschool" is substituted in the blend version.

§ 15-772. Additional assistance for gifted programs

A. School districts which comply with § 15-770 and which submit evidence that all district teachers who have primary responsibility for teaching gifted pupils have obtained or are working toward obtaining the appropriate certification endorsement as required by the state board may apply to the department of education for additional funding for gifted programs equal to fifty-five dollars per pupil for three per cent of the district's student count, or one thousand dollars, whichever is more. As an alternate to the individual district application process, a governing board may request that a county school superintendent apply on its behalf as part of an educational consortia. The consortia may include school districts in more than one county. If additional monies are available after funding all eligible school districts or educational consortia, the additional monies shall be used to increase the per pupil amount for each district or educational consortia funded. If sufficient monies are not available to meet all requests, the state board shall determine the allocation of monies based on the comprehensiveness across grade levels, appropriateness to the population being served, utility and demonstrated effectiveness of the scope and sequence and the likelihood of the school district's or educational consortia's proposed program successfully meeting the needs of the gifted pupils. A school district shall include the monies it receives for gifted programs and services under this section in the special projects section of the budget.

B. School districts which receive additional assistance as provided in this section shall conduct evaluation studies of their programs for the gifted and submit information to the department of education regarding the results of their studies. The department shall develop evaluation guidelines, reporting forms, procedures and time lines.

Added by Laws 1989, Ch. 273, § 12, eff. June 26, 1989.

Historical and Statutory Notes

Reviser's Notes:

1989 Note. Pursuant to authority of § 41-1304.02, in subsection A, first sentence the word "to" following "programs" was transposed to follow "equal".

§ 15-773. Transfer of parental rights at age of majority

A. When a pupil with a disability reaches eighteen years of age, all rights previously accorded to the pupil's parent under part B of the individuals with disabilities education act (20 United States Code §§ 1400 through 1420) and all rights previously accorded to the pupil's parent under the laws of this state are transferred to the pupil, unless the pupil has been declared legally incompetent.

B. A pupil with a disability who is at least eighteen years of age but under twenty-two years of age and who has not been declared legally incompetent, and who manifests the capacity to give and gives informed consent, may execute a delegation of right to make educational decisions pursuant to this section for the purpose of appointing the pupil's parent or agent to represent the educational interests of the pupil. A student shall have the right to terminate the agreement at any time and resume the right to make decisions regarding their education.

C. The delegation of right to make educational decisions shall meet all of the following requirements:

1. Contain language indicating the pupil is eighteen years of age or older but under twenty-two years of age.

2. Contain language that the pupil intends to delegate the pupil's educational rights under state and federal law to a specified individual who is at least eighteen years of age.

3. Contain language that the pupil has not been declared legally incompetent.

4. Contain language that the pupil is entitled to be present during the development of any individualized education plan and that any issues or concerns raised by the pupil will be addressed.

5. Not exceed one year in duration, but may be renewed with the written or other formal authorization of the pupil and the person who accepts the delegation each year until the pupil reaches twenty-two years of age.

6. Contain language permitting the pupil to terminate at any time.

7. Be signed by the pupil or contain some other manifestation of assent that the pupil has agreed to the terms of the delegation.

8. Be signed or assented to by the person who accepts the delegation.

9. Be notarized.

D. A notarized instrument that is signed or assented to by the pupil and the person who accepts the delegation and that is in substantially the following form shall be presumed to satisfy the requirements of subsection C:

Delegation of Right to Make Educational Decisions

I, __________, am eighteen years of age but under twenty-two years of age and a pupil who has the right to make educational decisions for myself under state and federal law. I have not been declared legally incompetent, and As of the date of the execution of this document, I delegate my right to give consent and to make decisions concerning educational matters to

__________, who will be considered my "Parent" for the purposes of 20 United States Code § 1401 and will exercise all the rights and responsibilities concerning my education that are conferred on a parent pursuant to state and federal law. I understand and give my consent that __________ will make all decisions relating to my education on my behalf. I understand that I am entitled to be present during the development of any individualized education plan and that any issues or concerns I may have will be addressed. This delegation will be in effect for one year from today's date and may be renewed only by my written or formal authorization. I understand that I have the right to terminate this agreement at any time and resume the right to make decisions regarding my education.

E. The delegation of right to make educational decisions pursuant to this section may be given in writing, by audio or video means or in any other alternative format that is necessitated by the pupil's disability.

Added by Laws 2001, Ch. 47, § 1.

Historical and Statutory Notes

Another § 15–773 added by Laws 2001, Ch. 233, § 2, was renumbered as § 15–774.

Reviser's Notes:

2001 Note. Laws 2001, Ch. 233, sec. 2 added another new § 15–773 that was renumbered as § 15–774, pursuant to authority of § 41–1304.02.

§ 15–774. Extraordinary special education needs fund; grant application; criteria

A. The extraordinary special education needs fund is established consisting of legislative appropriations, gifts, grants and donations. Monies in the fund are subject to legislative appropriation and are exempt from the provisions of § 35–190 relating to lapsing of appropriations. The state board of education shall administer the fund.

B. A school district may apply to the state board of education for an extraordinary special education needs grant from the fund. The state board of education shall prescribe the format of the applications. The applications shall include the following:

1. Demonstration of extraordinary needs, including a description and documentation of pupil services required and evidence that the district is not able to absorb the costs of these services.

2. Evidence that monies from the fund will not supplant federal, local or other state efforts.

3. Evidence that before making an application for monies from the fund the school district has made sufficient efforts to seek but has not received funding to cover the extraordinary costs applied for pursuant to paragraph 1 of this subsection from all other sources, including federal and other state sources of funding.

C. Extraordinary special education needs grants shall be used in the current year. All unspent grant monies shall be returned to the department of education at the end of the fiscal year for deposit in the extraordinary special education needs fund.

Added as § 15-773 by Laws 2001, Ch. 233, § 2. Renumbered as § 15-774.

Historical and Statutory Notes

Laws 2001, Ch. 233, § 7, provides:

"**Sec. 7. Reduction of kindergarten and first grade average daily membership counts; early kindergarten and early first grade programs; definitions**

"**A.** Notwithstanding any other law, the department of education may reduce the average daily membership count of a school district or charter school for the 2000-2001 school year in order to eliminate pupils enrolled in early kindergarten or early first grade programs during the 1999-2000 or 2000-2001 school years, but may not reduce the average daily membership count of a school district or charter school in order to eliminate pupils enrolled in early kindergarten or early first grade programs during school years prior to the 1999-2000 school year.

"**B.** For the purposes of this section:

"1. "Early first grade program" means a first grade program that was designed to prepare children for first grade and was not designed, based on state standards and district curriculum, to prepare children to advance to the second grade after completing the program.

"2. "Early kindergarten program" means a kindergarten program that was designed to prepare children for kindergarten and was not designed, based on state standards and district curriculum, to prepare children to advance to the first grade after completing the program."

Reviser's Notes:

2001 Note. Pursuant to authority of § 41-1304.02, this section, added by Laws 2001, Ch. 233, sec. 2 as § 15-773, was renumbered as § 15-774 and in the section heading "grant" was added after "fund;".

ARTICLE 5. CAREER AND TECHNICAL EDUCATION AND VOCATIONAL EDUCATION

The heading of Article 5 was changed from "VOCATIONAL EDUCATION" to "CAREER AND TECHNICAL EDUCATION AND VOCATIONAL EDUCATION" by Laws 2002, Ch. 89, eff. August 22, 2002.

Historical and Statutory Notes

Laws 1992, Ch. 305, § 1, provides:

"**Sec. 1. Legislative intent**

"It is the intent of the legislature of [probably should read "legislature that"] the state board of vocational and technological education encourage the development of model programs that will expand opportunities for vocational education in high demand, high wage jobs. In cooperation with the Arizona board of regents, the state board of vocational and technological education shall specify high demand, high wage jobs to be included in the list of programs eligible for state aid through the funding formula."

Laws 1992, Ch. 305, § 26, provides:

"**Sec. 26. State board for vocational and technological education; report**

"The state board for vocational and technological education shall provide an annual report to the president of the senate and the speaker of the house of representatives by December 31 beginning in 1994 and ending in 1999. The report shall contain the information required by section 15-781.01, subsection E, paragraph 18, Arizona Revised Statutes, the number of teachers or support personnel provided preservice and in-service training and any other evaluative information that the board deems relevant."

§ 15-781. Definitions

In this article, unless the context otherwise requires:

1. "Career and technical education and vocational education" means vocational and technical preparation programs for pupils in grades nine through twelve.

2. "Occupation" means the principal employment, paid or unpaid, of a person.

3. "Program improvement services" means those activities, services and functions carried out to develop, support and improve the quality of career and technical education and vocational education programs, including teacher education, curriculum, guidance and administration.

4. "Program standards" means models designed to serve as a guide in the establishment, maintenance and evaluation of quality career and technical, vocational, and technical education programs.

5. "Training provider" means an agency, council or organization providing career and technical education and vocational education or employment training, or both.

6. "Unpaid employment" means work in recognized occupations for which there is no direct financial compensation.

7. "Vocational and technical preparation" means an organized set of specialized courses which is directly related to the preparation of persons for occupations that normally do not require a baccalaureate or advanced degree for paid or unpaid employment or advancement and which is designed in total to provide a pupil with sufficient skills for entry into an occupation.

Added by Laws 1982, Ch. 332, § 7. Amended by Laws 2002, Ch. 89, § 8.

Historical and Statutory Notes

Source:

Laws 1979, Ch. 118, § 6..
A.R.S. former §§ 15-781, 15-1051.01.
Laws 1980, 2nd S.S., Ch. 9, § 44.
Laws 1981, Ch. 1, § 2.

Former § 15-781, added by Laws 1981, Ch. 1, § 2, and relating to the same subject matter as this section, was repealed by Laws 1982, Ch. 332, § 6.

§ 15-781.01. Repealed by Laws 1991, Ch. 8, § 10 (§ 41-2999.04), eff. Jan. 1, 2000

Historical and Statutory Notes

The repealed section, added by Laws 1990, Ch. 402, § 2, amended by Laws 1991, Ch. 218, § 7; Laws 1993, Ch. 202, § 8; Laws 1995, Ch. 268, § 40; Laws 1997, Ch. 231, § 18, related to the state board for vocational and technological education.

The purported enactment of this section by Laws 1990, Ch. 330, § 4, was repealed prior to taking effect by Laws 1990, Ch. 402, § 9, effective July 6, 1990.

Laws 1990, Ch. 402, § 8, which provided for delayed repeal of § 15-781.01, effective January 1, 2000, was itself repealed by Laws 1991, Ch. 8, § 1, subsec. I.

Former § 15-781.01 was renumbered as § 15-790.

§ 15-781.02. Meetings; majority required for validation; travel expenses; immunity

A. The state board of education shall hold four regular meetings annually at times it directs under the provisions of § 15-784 for the purposes of providing career and technical education and vocational education. Special meetings may be held on the call of the presiding officer.

B. Concurrence of a majority of all members of the board is necessary for validation of an act of the board.

C. Members shall be allowed travel expenses and reimbursement for subsistence, as provided by title 38, chapter 4, article 2,[1] to be paid on claims approved by the superintendent of public instruction, as other claims against the state are paid, from the appropriation for the board authorized in the general appropriations act.

D. Members of the board are immune from personal liability with respect to all acts done and actions taken in good faith within the scope of their authority during duly constituted regular and special meetings with approval of a majority of the board.

E. The superintendent of public instruction is the executive officer of the board.

Added by Laws 1991, Ch. 218, § 8, eff. June 10, 1991. Amended by Laws 2002, Ch. 89, § 9.

[1] Section 38-621 et seq.

Historical and Statutory Notes

The 2002 amendment by Ch. 89 rewrote subsec. A; and substituted "general appropriation act" for "general appropriation bill" at the end of subsec. C. Former subsec. A had read:

"**A.** The state board for vocational and technological education shall hold four regular meetings annually at times it directs. Special meetings may be held on the call of the presiding officer."

§ 15-782. Career and technical education and vocational education

A. A school having satisfactory facilities and equipment and which is fit to provide career and technical education and vocational education, such as agriculture, business and office education, health occupations, home economics, industrial education, marketing and distribution and public and personal services, shall, upon application made by the governing board to the state board of education, be designated to maintain a department consisting of such career and technical education and vocational education programs and program improvement services for pupils in grades seven through twelve.

B. Instruction in the department shall be of a practical character.

C. The governing board shall employ trained instructors with qualifications fixed by the state board of education, shall provide suitable classrooms and laboratory facilities for such instruction according to rules established by the state board of education and may provide a tract of land, together with buildings, machinery, tools, equipment and appliances, suitable for field work in agriculture.

Added by Laws 1981, Ch. 1, § 2, eff. Jan. 23, 1981. Amended by Laws 1990, Ch. 330, § 5; Laws 2002, Ch. 89, § 10.

Historical and Statutory Notes

Source:

Laws 1912, Ch. 45, §§ 1 to 3.
Civ.Code 1913, §§ 2791 to 2793.
Rev.Code 1928, §§ 1083, 1084.
Code 1939, §§ 54-916, 54-917.
A.R.S. former § 15-1051.
Laws 1979, Ch. 118, § 5.

§ 15–782.01. Repealed by Laws 1998, 4th S.S., Ch. 8, § 1

Historical and Statutory Notes

The repealed section, added by Laws 1985, Ch. 347, § 2, amended by Laws 1989, Ch. 72, § 1; Laws 1990, Ch. 330, § 6; Laws 1991, Ch. 218, § 9; Laws 1992, Ch. 172, § 13; Laws 1992, Ch. 305, § 12; Laws 1993, Ch. 189, § 3; Laws 1995, Ch. 191, § 4; Laws 1995, Ch. 196, § 5; Laws 1995, Ch. 268, § 41; and Laws 1997, Ch. 231, § 19, related to high cost vocational and technological education programs.

Laws 1997, 1st S.S., Ch. 4, § 10, provides:

"**Sec. 10. State block grant for vocational education; purpose and allocation plan for fiscal year 1997–1998; suspension of group B vocational education weight for fiscal year 1997–1998**

"**A.** Notwithstanding § 15–782.01, Arizona Revised Statutes, monies appropriated by the fiscal year 1997–1998 general appropriation act for the state block grant for vocational education program for fiscal year 1997–1998 shall be allocated ninety-five per cent based on vocational education student counts and five per cent based on placement data for vocational education program completers. Vocational education student counts for fiscal year 1997–1998 shall consist of the number of eleventh and twelfth grade students enrolled in an approved vocational education program in fiscal year 1996–1997, with the counts being adjusted to reflect the relative demand for employees in labor market sectors addressed by each vocational education program area represented in the student count data. Vocational education placement data for fiscal year 1997–1998 shall consist of the number of students from fiscal year 1994–1995 who completed a level III course in an approved vocational education program, graduated from high school and were working in a job requiring the occupational skills taught in the approved program when the fiscal year 1994–1995 program completer follow-up survey was conducted. It is the intent of the legislature that starting in fiscal year 1998–1999 at least twenty per cent of the state block grant for vocational education be allocated based on placement data for vocational education program completers.

"**B.** Notwithstanding § 15–943, paragraph 2, subdivision (b), Arizona Revised Statutes, the support level weight for the vocational education funding category for fiscal year 1997–1998 is zero."

§ 15–782.02. Career and technical education and vocational education programs; expanded hours; tuition

Text of section effective until July 1, 2006

A. School districts with career and technical education and vocational education programs may offer vocational educational services without regard to students' age or high school graduation status. Persons over twenty-two years of age shall not attend vocational programs in high school buildings during regular school hours, except that a person over twenty-two years of age may attend vocational programs on a campus that is not a comprehensive high school campus during regular school hours in a county with a population that exceeds one million persons pursuant to § 15–393, subsection D, paragraph 5 if the vocational program has additional student capacity after the enrollment of persons twenty-two years of age or younger, except that a student who is over twenty-two years of age shall not be included in the student count of the joint district for the purposes of chapter 9, articles 3, 4 and 5 of this title. The governing board of the joint technological education district shall adopt policies that prescribe the circumstances under which students who are twenty-two years of age or younger and persons who are over twenty-two years of age and who are attending vocational programs are allowed in the same classroom at the same time. The policies shall be designed to maximize the safety of students who are twenty-two years of age or younger and who attend programs during regular school hours, including requiring the presence of security personnel on campus. Vocational programs offered by a joint technological education district to persons over twenty-two years of age shall be limited to a high school curriculum unless the programs are offered in conjunction with a community college district. The department of education shall distribute twenty-six dollars for every day that a full-time student attends an extended year or summer school program in a joint technological education district and thirteen dollars for every day that a part-time student attends an extended year or summer school program in a joint technological education district, subject to appropriation except that the department of education shall not distribute monies pursuant to this section for any student who has either graduated from high school or obtained a general education diploma or who has reached twenty-two years of age, whichever occurs first.

B. School districts with career and technical education and vocational education programs may operate those programs for more than one hundred seventy-five days per year, with expanded hours of service.

C. Career and technical education and vocational education programs run by school districts may charge tuition to offset expenses associated with serving adult students.

Added by Laws 1997, Ch. 300, § 9. Amended by Laws 1998, Ch. 166, § 1; Laws 1999, 1st S.S., Ch. 4, § 6; Laws 2002, Ch. 89, § 11; Laws 2004, Ch. 263, § 2.

For text of section effective July 1, 2006, see § 15–782.02, post

§ 15–782.02. Career and technical education and vocational education programs; expanded hours; tuition

Text of section effective July 1, 2006

A. School districts with career and technical education and vocational education programs may offer vocational educational services without regard to students' age or high school graduation status. Persons over twenty-two years of age shall not attend vocational programs in high school buildings during regular school hours. The department of education shall distribute twenty-six dollars for every day that a full-time student attends an extended year or summer school program in a joint technological education district and thirteen dollars for every day that a part-time student attends an extended year or summer school program in a joint technological education district, subject to appropriation except that the department of education shall not distribute monies pursuant to this section for any student who has either graduated from high school or obtained a general education diploma or who has reached twenty-two years of age, whichever occurs first.

B. School districts with career and technical education and vocational education programs may operate those programs for more than one hundred seventy-five days per year, with expanded hours of service.

C. Career and technical education and vocational education programs run by school districts may charge tuition to offset expenses associated with serving adult students.

Added by Laws 1997, Ch. 300, § 9. Amended by Laws 1998, Ch. 166, § 1; Laws 1999, 1st S.S., Ch. 4, § 6; Laws 2002, Ch. 89, § 11; Laws 2004, Ch. 263, § 3, eff. July 1, 2006.

For text of section effective until July 1, 2006, see § 15–782.02, ante

Historical and Statutory Notes

Laws 2004, Ch. 263, § 4, provides:

"Sec. 4. Effective date

"Section 15-782.02, Arizona Revised Statutes, as amended by § 3 of this act, is effective from and after June 30, 2006."

Reviser's Notes:

1997 Note. Pursuant to authority of § 41-1304.02, in the section heading "and tuition" was added after "hours".

§ 15-783. Evaluation of career and technical education and vocational education programs

The governing board of a school district shall provide for a self-evaluation of its career and technical education and vocational education programs annually. The assessment shall be conducted in cooperation with and with assistance from business, industry or labor representatives. The evaluation shall be conducted in the manner prescribed by the state board of education and the results shall be submitted to the department of education as prescribed by the state board.

Added by Laws 1982, Ch. 332, § 11. Amended by Laws 1990, Ch. 330, § 7; Laws 1991, Ch. 218, § 10, eff. June 10, 1991; Laws 2002, Ch. 89, § 12.

Historical and Statutory Notes

Source:

Laws 1912, Ch. 45, § 3.
Civ.Code 1913, § 2793.
Rev.Code 1928, § 1084.
Code 1939, § 54-917.
A.R.S. former §§ 15-783, 15-1052.
Laws 1981, Ch. 1, § 2.

Laws 1982, Ch. 332, § 21 provides:

"Sec. 21. Evaluation of vocational and technical education programs

"Notwithstanding new §§ 15-783 and 15-1447, Arizona Revised Statutes, as added by §§ 11 and 18 of this act, if a vocational and technical education program was evaluated during fiscal year 1980-1981 or 1981-1982 the program does not have to be evaluated for another five years."

Former § 15-783 (for derivation, see Source note, ante), added by Laws 1981, Ch. 1, § 2, and relating to nonresident tuition for vocational training, was repealed by Laws 1982, Ch. 332, § 10.

§ 15-784. Vocational education; acceptance of congressional acts; appropriation; distribution of federal monies

A. The state assents to the provisions and accepts the benefits of the vocational education act of 1917, as amended, and the Carl D. Perkins vocational education act of 1984, as amended by the Carl D. Perkins vocational and applied technological education act amendments of 1990, as amended by the Carl D. Perkins vocational and applied technology act of 1998.

B. The state board of education is the state board of vocational education for the purposes of the acts. The state treasurer is designated custodian for vocational education for the purposes of the acts. The state treasurer shall receive and provide for the custody and disbursement of all monies paid to the state for the purposes of vocational education.

C. There is appropriated from the general fund of the state sufficient monies to meet the requirements of the acts of Congress.

D. The state board of education may distribute the monies it receives as provided in subsection A to any eligible recipient of the monies under the federal law.

E. The state board of education shall distribute to the community college districts in this state at least fifteen per cent of the monies received as provided in subsection A. Provisional community college districts are not eligible to receive monies pursuant to this section.

Added by Laws 1981, Ch. 1, § 2, eff. Jan. 23, 1981. Amended by Laws 1982, Ch. 332, § 9; Laws 1983, Ch. 154, § 2; Laws 1984, Ch. 277, § 2; Laws 1985, Ch. 347, § 3, eff. May 14, 1985; Laws 1990, Ch. 402, § 3, eff. July 6, 1990; Laws 1991, Ch. 218, § 11, eff. June 10, 1991; Laws 2002, Ch. 89, § 13; Laws 2002, Ch. 330, § 4.

Historical and Statutory Notes

Source:

Laws 1917, Ch. 44, §§ 1 to 4.
Rev. Code 1928, § 1059.
Code 1939, § 54–801.
A.R.S. former §§ 15–1053, 15–1091.
Laws 1964, Ch. 112, § 1.
Laws 1970, Ch. 204, § 36.
Laws 1972, Ch. 142, § 17.
Laws 1979, Ch. 118, § 7.

The purported amendment of this section by Laws 1990, Ch. 330, § 8, was repealed prior to taking effect by Laws 1990, Ch. 402, § 9, effective July 6, 1990.

Laws 2002, Ch. 330, § 62, provides:

"**Sec. 62. Vocational education; community colleges; transition**

"The state board of education shall minimize administrative costs associated with vocational education and ensure that the individual community college districts of this state receive from this state the maximum possible amount of federal monies available to this state under the vocational education act of 1917, as amended, and the Carl D. Perkins vocational education act of 1984, as amended by the Carl D. Perkins vocational and applied technological education act amendments of 1990."

Laws 2002, Ch. 330, became law without the Governor's signature as provided in Arizona Constitution, Article 5, § 7.

Reviser's Notes:

2002 Note. This section contains the amendments made by Laws 2002, Ch. 89, sec. 13 and Ch. 330, sec. 4 that were blended together as shown pursuant to authority of § 41–1304.03. Pursuant to authority of § 41–1304.02, in the section heading "acts" was substituted for "act" and "; intergovernmental agreements" was removed.

§ 15–785. Career and technical education and vocational education schools; expenses; allocations from federal funds

Any school district may organize schools or classes in accordance with the provisions of the federal law accepted by § 15–784 and the rules and regulations of the state board of education. The school district shall be eligible for allocations from federal funds and from the appropriation for the state board of an amount which is not more than seventy-five per cent of all the expenditures for vocational education in such schools or classes. The state board shall make allocations upon signed statements of assurances and reports from the school districts covering the details of such expenditures.

Added by Laws 1981, Ch. 1, § 2, eff. Jan. 23, 1981. Amended by Laws 2002, Ch. 89, § 14.

Historical and Statutory Notes

Source:

Laws 1919, Ch. 134, §§ 1 to 3.
Laws 1922, Ch. 35, §§ 46, 47.
Rev.Code 1928, § 1060.
Code 1939, § 54–802.
A.R.S. former § 15–1054.

§ 15–786. Acceptance of gifts or grants; fund; unexpended monies

A. The state board of education may accept gifts or grants of monies or property from public or private sources. The state board shall place the monies in a separate account designated as the career and technical education and vocational education fund.

B. If all or part of the monies accepted by the state board as provided in subsection A are not expended prior to the end of the fiscal year in which the gift or grant was accepted, the remaining balance of the amount remains in the career and technical education and vocational education fund until needed and does not revert to the state general fund at the close of the fiscal year.
Added by Laws 1982, Ch. 332, § 11. Amended by Laws 2002, Ch. 89, § 15.

Historical and Statutory Notes

Source:

Laws 1959, Ch. 8, § 1.
A.R.S. former §§ 15-786, 15-1055, 15-1094.
Laws 1964, Ch. 112, § 1.
Laws 1981, Ch. 1, § 2.

Former § 15-786 (for derivation, see Source note, ante), relating to the same subject matter as this section, was repealed by Laws 1982, Ch. 332, § 10.

Reviser's Notes:

1982 Note. Pursuant to authority of § 41-1304.02, "use" was deleted from and "fund" was added to the heading of this section.

§ 15-787. Eligibility; allocation; plan

A. A school district or a district formed for the purposes of this article as prescribed by the terms of this article may be eligible for allocation of funds from the state board of education provided the district offering career and technical education and vocational education meets minimum standards and requirements approved by the state board of vocational education.

B. The state board of education may allocate from its available appropriation any amount it deems appropriate for the use of a school district or a district formed for the purposes of this article, and such allocation may be for administrative costs, equipment or capital outlay.

C. The state board of education shall develop a state plan for career and technical education and vocational education which provides for the distribution of career and technical education and vocational education funds to school districts or districts formed for the purposes of this article meeting the minimum requirements provided for in the state plan for career and technical education and vocational education.
Added by Laws 1981, Ch. 1, § 2, eff. Jan. 23, 1981. Amended by Laws 1981, Ch. 314, § 14; Laws 2002, Ch. 89, § 16.

Historical and Statutory Notes

Source:

Laws 1964, Ch. 112, § 1.
A.R.S. former § 15-1092.
Laws 1974, 1st S.S., Ch. 3, § 18.

§ 15-788. Exemption from certain requirements; exception

A. Any building, structure, addition or alteration constructed by vocational education students shall be exempt from § 34-201 and title 41, chapter 23 [1] and may be constructed without advertising for bids. This exemption shall not be construed to permit teaching or nonteaching school personnel to do any construction, building or alteration to a building while under the jurisdiction of a school program without complying with § 34-201 and title 41, chapter 23.

B. All purchases of supplies, materials and equipment for such construction by career and technical education and vocational education students shall follow bidding procedures as established by the state board of education pursuant to § 15-213.

Added by Laws 1981, Ch. 1, § 2, eff. Jan. 23, 1981. Amended by Laws 1984, Ch. 251, § 7, eff. Jan. 1, 1985; Laws 2002, Ch. 89, § 17.

[1] Section 41-2501 et seq.

Historical and Statutory Notes

Source:

Laws 1979, Ch. 90, § 2.

A.R.S. former § 15-1056.

Laws 1980, 2nd S.S., Ch. 9, § 45.

§ 15-789. Contracting and cooperative arrangements for career and technical education and vocational education; advisory committee

A. The governing board of a school district may contract with any public body or with any private person for the purpose of providing career and technical education and vocational education. For the purposes of this subsection, school districts are exempt from § 15-213.

B. School districts or community college districts may independently or jointly make application for career and technical education and vocational education monies.

C. School districts and community college districts may provide for joint cooperation among themselves and with each other and with any educational institution eligible to receive career and technical education and vocational education monies as provided in § 15-784 for the purposes of providing career and technical education and vocational education and for the use of each other's facilities and personnel.

D. School districts, among themselves or with community college districts, may jointly purchase, sell, lease or lease-purchase land, buildings or other real or personal property for the purposes of providing career and technical education and vocational education, including establishing a jointly owned and operated vocational and technical center, if:

1. The districts enter into an intergovernmental agreement pursuant to § 11-952.

2. The state board of education and, if a community college district is a party to the agreement, the governing board of the community college district approve the intergovernmental agreement.

E. If one or more school districts, among themselves or with a community college district, enter into an intergovernmental agreement to establish a jointly owned and operated vocational and technical center, the governing boards of the districts shall establish a joint advisory committee for the vocational and technical center consisting of:

1. At least one member of each school district governing board or a designated district staff representative appointed by the respective school district governing board.

2. If a community college is a party to the agreement, members of the community college district board or designated district staff representatives

appointed by the community college district board equal in number to the total number of persons appointed pursuant to paragraph 1 of this subsection.

3. Members engaged in commerce or industry in this state equal in number to the total number of persons appointed pursuant to paragraph 1 of this subsection, jointly appointed by the district governing boards.

F. A school district and a community college district may jointly accept gifts or grants of monies, land or other real or personal property for the purpose of providing career and technical education and vocational education and may administer or dispose of the property in accordance with the purpose of the gift or grant.

Added by Laws 1982, Ch. 332, § 11. Amended by Laws 1984, Ch. 277, § 3; Laws 1986, Ch. 142, § 1; Laws 1988, Ch. 288, § 1, eff. July 8, 1988; Laws 1990, Ch. 348, § 7, eff. June 26, 1990; Laws 2002, Ch. 89, § 18; Laws 2003, Ch. 253, § 4, eff. Sept. 18, 2003, retroactively effective to July 1, 2003.

Historical and Statutory Notes

Source:

Laws 1964, Ch. 112, § 1.
A.R.S. former §§ 15–789, 15–1093.
Laws 1979, Ch. 118, § 10.
Laws 1981, Ch. 1, § 2.

Former § 15–789 (for derivation, see Source note, ante), relating to the same subject matter as this section, was repealed by Laws 1982, Ch. 332, § 10.

§ 15–790. Primary responsibility of school districts, community college districts and universities

A. School district governing boards have the primary responsibility for providing career exploration and entry level career and technical education and vocational education.

B. Community college district governing boards have the primary responsibility for providing postsecondary technological education and advanced career and technical education and vocational education, including the retraining and upgrading of a student's occupational skills. Community college district governing boards in conjunction with the state board for private postsecondary education have the major responsibility for providing career and technical education and vocational education which focuses on the economic development of this state.

C. Universities have the primary responsibility for research related to career and technical education and vocational education.

Added as § 15–781.01 by Laws 1982, Ch. 332, § 8. Renumbered as § 15–790. Amended by Laws 1989, Ch. 72, § 2; Laws 1991, Ch. 274, § 1, eff. June 21, 1991; Laws 2002, Ch. 89, § 19.

Historical and Statutory Notes

Former § 15–790, added by Laws 1981, Ch. 1, § 2, and relating to the applicability of this article, was repealed by Laws 1982, Ch. 332, § 10. The source of the former section was:

Laws 1964, Ch. 112, § 1.
A.R.S. former § 15–1095.

Reviser's Notes:

1982 Note. Pursuant to authority of § 41–1304.02, this section, added by Laws 1982, Ch. 332, § 8 as § 15–781.01, was renumbered as § 15–790.

§ 15-790.01. Repealed by Laws 1995, Ch. 268, § 42

Historical and Statutory Notes

The repealed section, added by Laws 1992, Ch. 305, § 13, amended by Laws 1993, Ch. 166, § 1, related to the vocational and technological education restructuring fund.

ARTICLE 6. CAREER EDUCATION PROGRAMS [REPEALED]

Article 6, Career Education Programs, consisting of §§ 15-791 and 15-792, was added by Laws 1981, Ch. 308, § 2, effective July 25, 1981, and was repealed by Laws 1997, Ch. 231, § 20, eff. July 21, 1997.

§§ 15-791, 15-792. Repealed by Laws 1997, Ch. 231, § 20

Historical and Statutory Notes

The repealed sections, derived from A.R.S. §§ 15-1199, 15-1199.01; Laws 1971, Ch. 184, § 7, added by Laws 1981, Ch. 308, § 2, amended by Laws 1982, Ch. 332, §§ 12, 13; Laws 1983, Ch. 101, § 10; Laws 1993, Ch. 202, § 9; Laws 1996, Ch. 284, § 37, related to career exploration programs.

ARTICLE 7. ALTERNATIVE EDUCATION PROGRAMS

Article 7, consisting of §§ 15-796 to 15-798, was added by Laws 1982, Ch. 307, § 1, effective July 24, 1982.

§ 15-796. Alternative education programs; contract with public body or private persons; definition

A. The governing board of a school district may contract with any public body or private person for the purpose of providing alternative education programs.

B. On the approval of the parent or guardian of a pupil or of a pupil who is an emancipated person, the superintendent of a school district may recommend to the governing board the placement of the pupil in an alternative education program as provided in this article.

C. For the purposes of this section, "alternative education" means the modification of the school course of study and adoption of teaching methods, materials and techniques to provide educationally for those pupils in grades six through twelve who are unable to profit from the regular school course of study and environment.

Added by Laws 1982, Ch. 307, § 1. Amended by Laws 1986, Ch. 336, § 1.

Historical and Statutory Notes

Reviser's Notes:

1982 Note. Pursuant to authority of § 41-1304.02, "private schools" was deleted from and "public body or private person" [changed to "persons" in the 1986 amendment] was added to the heading of this section.

§ 15-797. Financial provisions for pupils in alternative education programs

A. School districts may count pupils for daily attendance as provided in § 15-901 who are not actually and physically in attendance in a recognized common or high school but who are enrolled in and actually and physically in attendance in an alternative education program which is provided by any public body or private person and which meets the standards that the state board of education and the governing board prescribe for the course of study given in the common and high schools.

B. The governing board of a school district shall prescribe procedures for verifying the attendance of pupils enrolled in an alternative education program which is provided by any public body or private person.

C. The governing board may make payments for the cost of the education of pupils as provided in this article not to exceed the cost per student count as provided in § 15-824, subsection G.

D. School districts operating alternative schools pursuant to this section and charter schools operating on approved alternative calendars pursuant to § 15-183 may count pupils as having attended full time in any week for which the pupil was enrolled in and physically attended at least twenty hours of instruction during that week.

E. School districts operating alternative schools pursuant to this section and charter schools operating on approved alternative calendars pursuant to § 15-183 shall comply with the annual hours of instruction requirement pursuant to § 15-901.

Added by Laws 1982, Ch. 307, § 1. Amended by Laws 1986, Ch. 336, § 2; Laws 1990, Ch. 367, § 2; Laws 1999, Ch. 243, § 1; Laws 2002, Ch. 189, § 1.

§ 15-798. Governing board responsibility

Notwithstanding the provisions of this article, governing boards retain the responsibility for the education of the pupils under their jurisdiction.

Added by Laws 1982, Ch. 307, § 1.

ARTICLE 8. BILINGUAL PROGRAMS AND ENGLISH AS A SECOND LANGUAGE PROGRAMS [RENUMBERED]

Article 8, consisting of §§ 15-799 to 15-799.05, as added by Laws 1984, Ch. 169, § 2, effective August 3, 1984, was renumbered as Article 3.1, §§ 15-751 to 15-756.

§§ 15-799 to 15-799.05. Renumbered as §§ 15-751 to 15-756

CHAPTER 8

SCHOOL ATTENDANCE

ARTICLE 1. SCHOOL YEAR AND ATTENDANCE REQUIREMENTS

Section

ARTICLE 1.1. OPEN SCHOOL ENROLLMENT

ARTICLE 2. ADMISSION REQUIREMENTS

ARTICLE 3. SUSPENSION AND EXPULSION OF PUPILS

Chapter 8, consisting of Article 1, §§ 15–801 to 15–805, Article 2, §§ 15–821 to 15–827, Article 3, §§ 15–841 to 15–843, and Article 4, §§ 15–851 to 15–855, was added by Laws 1981, Ch. 1, § 2, effective January 23, 1981.

ARTICLE 1. SCHOOL YEAR AND ATTENDANCE REQUIREMENTS

§ 15–801. School year; school month; holidays

A. Except as may be otherwise authorized by the superintendent of public instruction to accommodate a year-round school operation, an educational program offered on the basis of a four day school week or an alternative kindergarten program offered on the basis of a three day school week, the school year shall begin July 1 and end June 30 and a school month is twenty school days, or four weeks of five days each.

B. When July 4, Veterans' Day, December 25 or Thanksgiving Day occurs within the school week, the schools shall be closed and the compensation of the teachers shall not be diminished on that account. Governing boards of school districts may declare a recess during the Christmas holiday season of not to exceed two school weeks and teachers shall receive compensation during the recess.

Added by Laws 1981, Ch. 1, § 2, eff. Jan. 23, 1981. Amended by Laws 1985, Ch. 127, § 3; Laws 1987, Ch. 93, § 2; Laws 1990, Ch. 322, § 3, eff. June 20, 1990.

Historical and Statutory Notes

Source:

Laws 1912, Ch. 77, §§ 70, 71.
Civ. Code 1913, §§ 2766, 2767.
Rev. Code 1928, § 1029.
Laws 1933, Ch. 6, § 1.
Code 1939, § 54-501.
A.R.S. former § 15-301.
Laws 1969, Ch. 146, § 2.
Laws 1972, Ch. 115, § 2.
Laws 1980, 2nd S.S., Ch. 9, § 10.

Laws 1995, Ch. 236, § 4, eff. April 19, 1995, provides:

"**Sec. 4. Rules**

"The department of economic security and the department of revenue shall adopt emergency rules to administer the provisions of this act.

§ 15-802. School instruction; exceptions; violations; classification; definitions

A. Every child between the ages of six and sixteen years shall attend a school and shall be provided instruction in at least the subjects of reading, grammar, mathematics, social studies and science. The person who has custody of the child shall choose a public, private, charter or home school as defined in this section to provide instruction.

B. The parent or person who has custody shall do the following:

1. If the child will attend a public, private or charter school, enroll the child in and ensure that the child attends a public, private or charter school for the full time school is in session. If a child attends a school which is operated on a year-round basis the child shall regularly attend during school sessions that total not less than one hundred seventy-five school days or two hundred school days, as applicable, or the equivalent as approved by the superintendent of public instruction.

2. If the child will attend a private school or home school, file an affidavit of intent with the county school superintendent stating that the child is attending a regularly organized private school or is being provided with instruction in a home school. The affidavit of intent shall include:

(a) The child's name.

(b) The child's date of birth.

(c) The current address of the school the child is attending.

(d) The names, telephone numbers and addresses of the persons who currently have custody of the child.

3. If the child will attend home school, the child has not reached eight years of age by September 1 of the school year and the person who has custody of the child does not desire to begin home instruction until the child has reached eight years of age, file an affidavit of intent pursuant to paragraph 2 of this subsection stating that the person who has custody of the child does not desire to begin home school instruction.

C. An affidavit of intent shall be filed within thirty days from the time the child begins to attend a private school or home school and is not required thereafter unless the private school or the home school instruction is terminated and then resumed. The person who has custody of the child shall notify the county school superintendent within thirty days of the termination that the child is no longer being instructed at a private school or a home school. If the private school or home school instruction is resumed, the person who has custody of the child shall file another affidavit of intent with the county school superintendent within thirty days.

D. A person is excused from the duties prescribed by subsection A or B of this section if any of the following are shown to the satisfaction of the school principal or the school principal's designee:

1. The child is in such physical or mental condition that instruction is inexpedient or impracticable.

2. The child has completed the high school course of study necessary for completion of grade ten as prescribed by the state board of education.

3. The child has presented reasons for nonattendance at a public school which are satisfactory to the school principal or the school principal's designee. For purposes of this paragraph, the principal's designee may be the school district governing board.

4. The child is over fourteen years of age and is, with the consent of the person who has custody of him, employed at some lawful wage earning occupation.

5. The child is enrolled in a work training, career education, career and technical education, vocational education or manual training program which meets the educational standards established and approved by the department of education.

6. The child was either:

(a) Suspended and not directed to participate in an alternative education program.

(b) Expelled from a public school as provided in article 3 of this chapter. [1]

7. The child is enrolled in an education program provided by a state educational or other institution.

E. Unless otherwise exempted in this section or § 15–803, a parent of a child between six and sixteen years of age or a person who has custody of a child, who does not provide instruction in a home school and who fails to enroll or fails to ensure that the child attends a public, private or charter school pursuant to this section is guilty of a class 3 misdemeanor. A parent who fails to comply with the duty to file an affidavit of intent to provide instruction in a home school is guilty of a petty offense.

F. For the purposes of this section:

1. "Home school" means a school conducted primarily by the parent, guardian or other person who has custody of the child or instruction provided in the child's home.

2. "Private school" means a nonpublic institution, other than the child's home, where academic instruction is provided for at least the same number of days and hours each year as a public school.

Added by Laws 1993, Ch. 83, § 4. Amended by Laws 1994, Ch. 315, § 10; Laws 1995, Ch. 268, § 43; Laws 1996, Ch. 284, § 38; Laws 1996, Ch. 313, § 4; Laws 1998, Ch. 141, § 1; Laws 1998, Ch. 167, § 4; Laws 2002, Ch. 89, § 20.

[1] Section 15-840 et seq.

Historical and Statutory Notes

Source:

Laws 1912, Ch. 77, §§ 89, 90.
Civ. Code 1913, §§ 2802, 2803.
Laws 1921, Ch. 143, § 1.
Rev. Code 1928, §§ 1033, 1034.
Laws 1929, Ch. 93, § 21.
Code 1939, §§ 54-505, 54-506, 54-1521.
A.R.S. former §§ 15-321, 15-323, 15-836, 15-837, 15-1347, 15-1348.
Laws 1960, Ch. 127, § 44.
Laws 1972, Ch. 40, §§ 1, 3.
Laws 1972, Ch. 115, § 3.
Laws 1978, Ch. 201, §§ 256, 259, 260.
A.R.S. former § 15-802.
Laws 1981, Ch. 1, § 2.
Laws 1982, Ch. 221, § 2.
Laws 1983, Ch. 325, § 10.
Laws 1984, Ch. 6, § 8.
Laws 1984, Ch. 379, § 11.
Laws 1985, Ch. 337, § 3.
Laws 1987, Ch. 363, § 4.
Laws 1988, Ch. 216, § 2.
Laws 1990, Ch. 233, § 11.
Laws 1990, Ch. 322, § 4.
Laws 1991, Ch. 228, § 1.
Laws 1991, Ch. 298, § 14.

The 1994 amendment reworded subsec. B and rewrote subsec. E which, prior thereto provided:

"**E.** A person who has custody of a child in a home school program and who violates any provision of this section or who fails to comply with the duty to secure testing or evaluation of the child required in § 15-745 is guilty of a petty offense."

The 1995 amendment by Ch. 268, in subsec. B, inserted "who has custody" in the introductory paragraph, deleted the former second sentence in par. 2, which had read, "If the child is home schooled, the child shall take a nationally standardized norm-referenced achievement test or complete an academic evaluation.", and deleted former par. 2, subd. (e); and in subsec. E, deleted "or secure testing or evaluation of the child required in § 15-745" following "provide instruction in a home school". Subsection B, paragraph 2, subdivision (e) had read:

"(e) If the child is instructed at home, a statement that the child will either take a nationally standardized norm-referenced achievement test or complete an academic evaluation at least every three years as required in § 15-745, subsection G."

The 1996 amendment by Ch. 284, in subsec. D, substituted a reference to high school course of study for a reference to high school courses in par. 2.

The 1996 amendment by Ch. 313, in subsec. E, deleted the former third sentence, which had read, "A violation of this section shall be charged, heard and disposed of pursuant to § 8-232.".

Laws 1997, Ch. 231, § 31, provides:

"**Sec. 31. School attendance; exception**

"**A.** Notwithstanding § 15-802, Arizona Revised Statutes, for the school year beginning July 1, 1996 and ending June 30, 1997, a county school superintendent may submit to the superintendent of public instruction a request to reduce the number of days in a school session from one hundred seventy-five to one hundred and seventy-one days.

"**B.** The superintendent of public instruction may authorize the reduction in the number of days in a school session to one hundred seventy-one days. Such authorization shall be given on a case to case basis. The superintendent of public instruction shall only authorize a reduction in the number of days in a school session if the school was closed due to inclement weather or a state of emergency."

The 1998 amendment by Ch. 141 inserted references to charter schools throughout; inserted "shall attend a school and" in subsec. A; added subsec. B, par. 3, relating to children who will attend home school who have not reached eight years of age by September 1; and rewrote subsec. D which had read:.

"**D.** A person is excused from the duties prescribed by subsection A or B of this section if it is shown to the satisfaction of the county school superintendent that:

"1. The child is in such physical or mental condition that instruction is inexpedient or impracticable.

"2. The child has completed the high school course of study necessary for completion of grade ten as prescribed by the state board of education.

"3. The child has presented reasons for nonattendance at a public school which are satisfactory to a board consisting of the president of the local governing board, the teacher of the child and the probation officer of the superior court in the county.

"4. The child is over fourteen years of age and is, with the consent of the person who has custody of him, employed at some lawful wage earning occupation.

"5. The child is enrolled in a work training, career education, vocational or manual training program which meets the educational standards established and approved by the department of education.

"6. The child was suspended or expelled from a public school as provided in article 3 of this chapter.

"7. The child is enrolled in an education program provided by a state educational or other institution.

"8. The child has not reached eight years of age by September 1 of the school year and the county school superintendent is notified in writing by the person who has custody of the child that that person does not desire to have the child attend school."

The 1998 amendment by Ch. 167 inserted "or two hundred school days, as applicable" in the second sentence of par. 1 of subsec. B.

The 2002 amendment by Ch. 89 modified an internal reference in subsec. B, par. 3; and substituted "career and technical education, vocational education or manual training program" for "vocational or manual training program", in subsec. D, par. 5.

Former § 15–802, added by Laws 1981, Ch. 1, § 2 (see Source, ante), relating to similar subject matter, was repealed by Laws 1993, Ch. 83, § 2. See, now, this section.

Reviser's Notes:

1993 Note. Pursuant to authority of § 41–1304.02, in the section heading "definition" was deleted and "; classification; definitions" was added after "violations".

1996 Note. Prior to the 1998 amendments, this section contained the amendments made by Laws 1996, Ch. 284, sec. 38 and Ch. 313, sec. 4 that were blended together pursuant to authority of § 41–1304.03.

1998 Note. Prior to the 2002 amendment, this section contained the amendments made by Laws 1998, Ch. 141, sec. 1 and Ch. 167. sec. 4 that were blended together pursuant to authority of § 41–1304.03.

§ 15–802.01. Children instructed at home; eligibility to participate in interscholastic activities

A. Notwithstanding any other law, a child who resides within the attendance area of a public school and who is instructed at home shall be allowed to try out for interscholastic activities on behalf of the public school in the same manner as a pupil who is enrolled in that public school. registration, age eligibility requirements, fees, insurance, transportation, physical condition, qualifications, responsibilities, event schedules, standards of behavior and performance policies for home schooled students shall be consistent with those policies established for students enrolled in that public school. The individual providing the primary instruction of a child who is instructed at home shall submit written verification that provides:

1. Whether the student is receiving a passing grade in each course or subject being taught.

2. Whether the student is maintaining satisfactory progress towards advancement or promotion.

B. A child who is instructed at home and who was previously enrolled in a school shall be ineligible to participate in interscholastic activities for the remainder of the school year during which the child was enrolled in a school.

C. A school district shall not contract with any private entity that supervises interscholastic activities if the private entity prohibits the participation of children instructed at home in interscholastic activities at public, private or charter schools.

Added by Laws 1995, Ch. 268, § 44. Amended by Laws 1997, Ch. 35, § 1; Laws 1999, Ch. 69, § 1.

§ 15–802.02. Renumbered as § 15–808

§ 15–803. School attendance; exemptions; definitions

A. It is unlawful for any child between six and sixteen years of age to fail to attend school during the hours school is in session, unless either:

1. The child is excused pursuant to § 15–802, subsection D or § 15–901, subsection A, paragraph 6, subdivision (c).

2. The child is accompanied by a parent or a person authorized by a parent.

3. The child is provided with instruction in a home school.

B. A child who is habitually truant or who has excessive absences may be adjudicated an incorrigible child as defined in § 8–201. Absences may be considered excessive when the number of absent days exceeds ten per cent of the number of required attendance days prescribed in § 15–802, subsection B, paragraph 1.

C. As used in this section:

1. "Habitually truant" means a truant child who is truant for at least five school days within a school year.

2. "Truant" means an unexcused absence for at least one class period during the day.

3. "Truant child" means a child who is between six and sixteen years of age and who is not in attendance at a public or private school during the hours that school is in session, unless excused as provided by this section.

Added by Laws 1994, Ch. 315, § 11. Amended by Laws 1998, Ch. 141, § 2; Laws 2000, Ch. 277, § 1.

Historical and Statutory Notes

Former § 15–803, repealed by Laws 1990, Ch. 208, § 1, effective January 1, 1992, which related to immunization for school attendance, was added by Laws 1981, Ch. 1, § 2, amended by Laws 1981, Ch. 283, § 1, and was derived from:

Laws 1912, Ch. 77, §§ 72, 85.
Civ. Code 1913, §§ 2768, 2798.
Laws 1925, Ch. 71, § 1.
Rev. Code 1928, § 1030.
Laws 1933, Ch. 65, § 2.
Code 1939, § 54–502.
A.R.S. former §§ 15–302, 15–341, 15–342, 15–343.
Laws 1958, Ch. 21, § 1.
Laws 1960, Ch. 127, § 17.
Laws 1961, Ch. 14, § 1.
Laws 1976, Ch. 127, § 1.
Laws 1978, Ch. 93, § 1.
Laws 1978, Ch. 178, § 1.
Laws 1979, Ch. 3, § 2.
Laws 1979, Ch. 83, §§ 1 to 3.
Laws 1980, Ch. 195, § 1.

Reviser's Notes:

2000 Note. In the chapter version in subsection A, paragraph 2 after the period "~~or~~" should have appeared instead of "~~Or~~". Pursuant to authority of § 41–1304.02, "~~or~~" is substituted in the chapter version to correct a manifest clerical error.

§ 15–804. Attendance officer; appointment; salary

A. The governing board of a school district may appoint an attendance officer for the school district. The salary of the attendance officer shall be fixed by the governing board and paid from the funds of the school district.

B. If in the opinion of the governing boards of two or more school districts one officer will adequately serve such districts, such officer may be appointed

by the districts jointly. His salary may be apportioned as the governing boards provide and shall be paid from the funds of the school districts.
Added by Laws 1981, Ch. 1, § 2, eff. Jan. 23, 1981.

Historical and Statutory Notes

Source:
Laws 1921, Ch. 143, § 1.
Rev. Code 1928, § 1035.
Laws 1933, Ch. 65, § 3.
Code 1939, § 54-507.
A.R.S. former § 15-324.

§ 15-805. Attendance officer; powers and duties

A. The attendance officer may enforce the law relating to:

1. School attendance of children between the ages of six and sixteen years.

2. The provisions of § 15-802, subsection E, and § 15-803.

3. Employment of children between the ages of six and sixteen years.

B. The attendance officer may:

1. Issue a citation to an adult or child who is alleged to be in violation of laws specified in subsection A of this section to appear before a court of competent jurisdiction and shall advise the person to whom the citation is issued that failure to appear at the time and place specified in the citation may result in the issuance of a warrant for the person's arrest. A citation that is issued to a child under eighteen years of age shall require the child's parent or person having custody to appear with the child at the time and place specified in the citation. The attendance officer shall notify the child's parent or person having custody that the citation was issued and that the parent or person having custody is required to appear in court with the child and shall give proof of the notice to the court.

2. Issue a citation on an Arizona traffic ticket and complaint form for any violation of laws specified in subsection A of this section.

3. Report a violation of a law specified in subsection A of this section to the local law enforcement agency and request an investigation of the violation. The law enforcement agency shall, when sufficient cause exists, refer the matter for prosecution.

4. Enter all places where children may be employed to investigate and enforce the law.

Added by Laws 1981, Ch. 1, § 2, eff. Jan. 23, 1981. Amended by Laws 1985, Ch. 337, § 4; Laws 1991, Ch. 228, § 3; Laws 1994, Ch. 315, § 12.

Historical and Statutory Notes

Source:
Laws 1912, Ch. 77, § 91.
Civ. Code 1913, § 2804.
Laws 1921, Ch. 143, § 3.
Rev. Code 1928, § 1036.
Code 1939, § 54-508.
A.R.S. former § 15-325.

§ 15-806. Excuse from school attendance for religious purposes

The governing board of each school district shall adopt a policy governing the excuse of pupils for religious purposes. The policy may permit a pupil to be excused from school attendance for religious purposes, including participation in religious exercises or religious instruction. If the policy permits a pupil to be excused for religious purposes, the policy shall stipulate the conditions under which the excuse will be granted. These conditions shall include at least the following:

1. The person who has custody of the pupil has given written consent.

2. Any religious instruction or exercise takes place at a suitable place away from school property designated by the church or religious denomination or group.

Added by Laws 1986, Ch. 381, § 1. Amended by Laws 1996, Ch. 284, § 39.

Historical and Statutory Notes

Laws 1986, Ch. 381, § 2 provides:

"**Sec. 2. Policies governing excuse from school attendance for religious purposes**

"Notwithstanding § 15-806, Arizona Revised Statutes, as added by this act, the state board of education shall prescribe guidelines for policies governing the excuse of pupils for religious purposes by December 31, 1986 and school district governing boards shall adopt a policy governing the excuse of pupils for religious purposes by June 30, 1987."

§ 15-807. Absence from school; notification of parent or person having custody of pupil; immunity

A. If a pupil in a kindergarten program or grades one through eight is absent from school without excuse as provided in this article or without notice to the school in which the pupil is enrolled of authorization of the absence by the parent or other person who has custody of the pupil, the school in which the pupil is enrolled, within two hours after the first class in which the pupil is absent, shall make a reasonable effort to promptly telephone and notify the parent or other person who has custody of the pupil of the pupil's absence from school.

B. On or before the enrollment of a pupil in a kindergarten program or grades one through eight, the school district shall notify parents or other persons who have custody of a pupil of their responsibility to authorize any absence of the pupil from school and to notify the school in which the pupil is enrolled in advance or at the time of any absence and that the school district requires that at least one telephone number, if available, be given for purposes of this section. The school district shall require that the telephone number, if available, be given at the time of enrollment of the pupil in school and that the school of enrollment be promptly notified of any change in the telephone number.

C. A school district, governing board members of a school district and employees or agents of a school district are not liable for failure to notify the parent or other person who has custody of a pupil of the pupil's absence from school as provided in this section.

Added by Laws 1987, Ch. 273, § 1.

§ 15-808. Technology assisted project-based instruction program; report

A. A technology assisted project-based instruction program shall be instituted on a pilot basis to meet the needs of pupils in the information age. until June 30, 2003, the state board of education shall select up to four existing traditional public schools, at least one of which shall serve pupils in kindergarten programs and grades one through twelve, and beginning July 1, 2003, the state board of education shall select seven existing traditional public schools and the state board for charter schools shall select seven charter schools to participate in the program based on the following criteria:

1. The depth and breadth of curriculum choices.

2. The variety of educational methodologies employed by the school and the means of addressing the unique needs and learning styles of targeted pupil populations including computer assisted learning systems, virtual classrooms, virtual laboratories, electronic field trips, electronic mail, virtual tutoring, online help desk, group chat sessions and noncomputer based activities performed under the direction of a certificated teacher.

3. The availability of an intranet or private network to safeguard pupils against predatory and pornographic elements of the internet.

4. The availability of filtered research access to the internet.

5. The availability of private individual electronic mail between pupils, teachers, administrators and parents in order to protect the confidentiality of pupil records and information.

6. The availability of broadcast quality television production and editing facilities on campus.

7. The availability of faculty members who are experienced in broadcast television production.

8. The availability of faculty members who are experienced with computer networks, the internet and computer animation.

9. The extent to which the school intends to develop partnerships with universities, community colleges and private businesses.

10. The services offered to developmentally disabled populations.

11. The grade levels that will be served by the program.

B. Beginning July 1, 2003, notwithstanding subsection A of this section, any school that was approved to participate before January 1, 2003 is not required to reapply for participation in the program. A pupil is not eligible to participate in the program unless the pupil was previously enrolled in and attended a public school in the previous school year, except that a kindergarten pupil may participate in the program if the pupil has a sibling who is currently enrolled in and attending the program. Pupils who participate in the program are subject to the testing requirements prescribed in chapter 7, article 3 of this title. [1] Upon enrollment, the school shall notify the parents or guardians of the pupil of the state testing requirements. If a pupil fails to comply with the testing requirements and the school administers the tests pursuant to this subsection To less than ninety-five per cent of the pupils in the program, the pupil shall not be allowed to participate in the program.

C. Each school selected by the state board of education to participate in the technology assisted project-based instruction program shall submit an annual report to the state board of education and the joint legislative budget committee. Beginning July 1, 2003, each school selected by the state board for charter schools to participate in the technology assisted project-based instruction program shall submit an annual report to the state board for charter schools and the joint legislative budget committee. The reports shall be submitted by August 1 and shall include the following information:

1. A description of the educational services that are offered under the program and that specifically relate to the depth and breadth of the curriculum choices offered by the school.

2. A description of the effects of media and technology on the delivery of specific educational services to specific pupil populations.

3. A measurement of academic achievement of pupils in the programs, including academic advancement as measured by the increase in grade level equivalent scores each academic year on the nationally standardized norm-referenced achievement test prescribed in § 15-741 and a summary of essential skills test scores, scores on the nationally standardized norm-referenced achievement test, individual pupil portfolios and other assessment tools used by the school. The superintendent of public instruction shall evaluate current nationally standardized norm-referenced achievement tests offered to pupils in kindergarten and grade one. The evaluation shall include the impact on the pupils, the costs associated with each test and the academic value associated with each test. The superintendent of public instruction may recommend at least one nationally standardized norm-referenced achievement test for schools participating in the program pursuant to this section to be offered to pupils. Each participating school may offer this test to its pupils and if the test is offered, each participating school shall be responsible for the costs of administering the standardized norm-referenced achievement test to pupils in kindergarten programs and grade one. Each participating school shall analyze the results of the standardized norm-referenced achievement tests administered to pupils in kindergarten programs and grade one.

4. Academic advancement as measured in grade level equivalents each academic year based on a standardized norm-referenced achievement test.

5. The results of a survey of pupil satisfaction with the program, including:

(a) Pupils' attitudes about delivery modalities employed by the school.

(b) Changes in pupils' attitudes toward learning in general.

(c) Changes in pupils' attitudes about their own ability to learn and about their own academic progress.

(d) Pupils' attitudes about the school they attend.

6. The results of a survey of parental satisfaction with the program, including:

(a) Parents' and their children's attitudes about the delivery modalities employed by the school.

(b) Changes in their children's attitudes about learning in general.

(c) Changes in their children's attitudes about their ability to learn and about their academic progress.

(d) Parents' and their children's attitudes about the school that the child attends.

7. A description of the availability and equitable distribution of educational services provided under the program including specific descriptions of the effectiveness of technology tools and modalities used to address the needs of any underserved populations targeted by the school.

8. A description of the operational and administrative efficiency of the program.

9. A description of the cost-effectiveness of the program.

D. The state board of education and joint legislative budget committee shall collaboratively compile and evaluate the information submitted in the annual reports by schools participating in the pilot program, pursuant to subsection C of this section. The state board of education and the joint legislative budget committee shall report their findings to the governor, the speaker of the house of representatives and the president of the senate by November 15 of each year.

E. Each school selected for the technology assisted project-based instruction program shall ensure that a daily log is maintained for each pupil who participates in the program. The daily log shall describe the amount of time spent by each pupil participating in the program pursuant to this section on academic tasks. The daily log shall be used by the school district or charter school to qualify the pupils who participate in the program in the school's average daily attendance calculations pursuant to § 15-901.

F. If a pupil is enrolled in a school district or charter school and also participates in the technology assisted project-based instruction program, the sum of the average daily membership, which includes enrollment as prescribed in § 15-901, subsection A, paragraph 2, subdivisions (a) and (b) and daily attendance as prescribed in § 15-901, subsection A, paragraph 6, for that pupil in the school district or charter school and in the technology assisted project-based instruction program shall not exceed 1. 0. If the pupil is enrolled in a school district or a charter school and also participates in the technology assisted project-based instruction program and the sum of the daily membership or daily attendance for that pupil is greater than 1.0, the sum shall be reduced to 1.0 and shall be apportioned between the school district or charter school and the technology assisted project-based instruction program based on the percentage of total time that the pupil is enrolled or in attendance in the school district or charter school and the technology assisted project-based instruction program. The uniform system of financial records shall include guidelines for the apportionment of the pupil enrollment and attendance as provided in this subsection.

Added as § 15-802.02 by Laws 1998, Ch. 224, § 2. Renumbered as § 15-808. Amended by Laws 2003, Ch. 241, § 1, eff. May 20, 2003.

[1] Section 15-741 et seq.

Historical and Statutory Notes

Laws 1998, Ch. 224, §§ 3 and 4, provide:

"**Sec. 3. Intent**

"The technology assisted project-based instruction program instituted by § 15-802.02, Arizona Revised Statutes, as added by this act, is intended to improve pupil achievement and extend academic options beyond the four walls of the traditional classroom.

"**Sec. 4. Review and approval of technology assisted project-based instruction programs**

"**A.** Before selecting public schools to participate in the technology assisted project-based instruction program, the state board of education and the joint legislative budget committee shall review the proposed curriculum of each potential pilot school and shall evaluate the projected costs of operating a technology assisted project-based instruction program.

"**B.** After conducting the review required by subsection A, the state board of education shall select four public schools to participate in the technology assisted project-based program."

Reviser's Notes:

1998 Note. Pursuant to authority of § 41-1304.02, this section, added by Laws 1998, Ch. 224, sec. 2 as § 15-802.02, was renumbered as section 15-808.

1998 Note. Pursuant to authority of § 41-1304.02, the reference to "§ 15-808" was substituted for the reference to "section 15-802.02" to conform to the reviser's renumbering of that section.

§ 15-809. AIMS intervention and dropout prevention program; program termination; definitions

A. The department of education shall establish an AIMS intervention and dropout prevention program. The department of education shall develop application procedures, selection criteria and minimum performance standards for service providers that wish to participate in the program. Service providers that receive monies to participate in the program shall demonstrate that their dropout prevention program is offered in the public schools in this state and meets all of the following requirements:

1. Serves at-risk pupils in grade nine, ten, eleven or twelve.

2. Serves pupils who both:

(a) Are most likely to drop out of high school without graduating.

(b) Have documented academic, personal or vocational barriers to success in high school and the workplace.

3. Consists of all of the following for each participating pupil:

(a) At least nine consecutive months of academic support, including tutoring and remediation, to ensure that participating pupils meet the academic standards adopted by the state board of education.

(b) Comprehensive instruction on Arizona workplace skills adopted by the state board of education.

(c) Instruction on leadership and civic duty.

4. Requires pupils who participate in the program to earn credits toward graduation from high school. Pupils who participate in the program shall perform volunteer activities or community service or shall be engaged in employment during summer vacation periods. Each pupil who participates in the program shall continue to participate in the program for twelve months after graduation from high school during which the service provider shall provide follow-up assistance that is designed to assist the pupil's transition to postsecondary education, vocational or job training, military service or employment. A participating school district may develop a dual credit course program in order to meet the requirements of this paragraph.

B. The service providers selected to participate in the AIMS intervention and dropout prevention program shall annually report at least the following information to the department of education:

1. The percentage of pupils who participate in the program and who graduate from high school or obtain a general equivalency degree on or within twelve months after the scheduled graduation date for the pupil's classmates.

2. The percentage of pupils who participate in the program, who graduate from high school or obtain a general equivalency degree and who begin participation in postsecondary education, employment, vocational or job training or military service within twelve months after the scheduled graduation date for the pupil's classmates.

3. The percentage of pupils who participate in the program and who are either enrolled full time at a postsecondary education institution, employed full time, enrolled in a full-time vocational or job training program or on active duty in the armed forces of the united states, or any combination of these activities that in totality amounts to full-time activity, within twelve months after the scheduled graduation date for the pupil's classmates.

4. The percentage of pupils who participate in the program and who pass each aims component.

C. The department of education shall contract with a private entity to conduct an annual performance audit of the AIMS intervention and dropout prevention program.

D. Beginning in 2001, the department of education shall submit an annual report concerning the AIMS intervention and dropout prevention program to the governor, the president of the senate and the speaker of the house of representatives by December 15 that includes an evaluation of the effectiveness of the program. The department of education shall provide a copy of the report to the secretary of state and the director of the department of library, archives and public records.

E. The program established by this section ends on July 1, 2010, pursuant to § 41–3102.

F. For purposes of this section:

1. "AIMS" means the arizona instrument to measure standards test prescribed in § 15–741.

2. "Service providers" means all of the following:

(a) Public agencies, including schools and school districts, that have demonstrated documented success in delivering dropout prevention services as prescribed in this section.

(b) Private entities that are certified by the department of education and that have demonstrated documented success in delivering dropout prevention services as prescribed in this section.

Added by Laws 2000, Ch. 377, § 1.

ARTICLE 1.1. OPEN SCHOOL ENROLLMENT

Article 1.1, consisting of §§ 15–816 to 15–816.07, was added by Laws 1994, 9th S.S., Ch. 2, § 8, effective September 16, 1994.

The heading of Article 1.1 was changed from "Open School Enrollment and Parental Choice" to "Open School Enrollment" by Laws 1995, Ch. 1, § 3, effective Feb. 20, 1995.

§ 15-816. Definitions

In this article, unless the context otherwise requires:

1. "Nonresident pupil" means a pupil who resides in this state and who is enrolled in or is seeking enrollment in a school district other than the school district in which the pupil resides.

2. "Open enrollment" means a policy adopted and implemented by a school district governing board to allow resident transfer pupils to enroll in any school within the school district, to allow resident pupils to enroll in any school located within other school districts in this state and to allow nonresident pupils to enroll in any school within the district pursuant to § 15-816.01.

3. "Resident school" means a school within the designated attendance area in which a pupil resides.

4. "Resident transfer pupil" means a resident pupil who is enrolled in or seeking enrollment in a school that is within the school district but outside the attendance area of the pupil's residence.

Added by Laws 1994, 9th S.S., Ch. 2, § 8. Amended by Laws 1995, Ch. 1, § 2, eff. Feb. 20, 1995.

Historical and Statutory Notes

Laws 1994, 9th S.S., Ch. 2, § 34, as amended by Laws 1995, Ch. 1, § 9, provides:

"Sec. 34. Open enrollment; pupil transportation; fiscal year 1995-1996

"For fiscal year 1995-1996, the governing board of a school district may increase its transportation support level, as provided in § 15-945, Arizona Revised Statutes, and its transportation revenue control limit, as provided in § 15-946, Arizona Revised Statutes, to account for the additional route miles and bus tokens attributable to the pupils for whom transportation is provided pursuant to title 15, chapter 8, article 1.1, Arizona Revised Statutes, as prescribed by the uniform system of financial records."

§ 15-816.01. Enrollment policies

A. School district governing boards shall establish policies and shall implement an open enrollment policy without charging tuition. Tuition may be charged to nonresident pupils only when the tuition is authorized under § 15-764, subsection E, § 15-797, subsection C, § 15-823, subsection A, § 15-824, subsection A or § 15-825. These policies shall include admission criteria, application procedures and transportation provisions. A copy of the district policies for open enrollment shall be filed with the department of education.

B. The governing board of the district educating the pupil may provide transportation limited to no more than twenty miles each way to and from the school of attendance or to and from a pickup point on a regular transportation route or for the total miles traveled each day to an adjacent district for eligible nonresident pupils who meet the economic eligibility requirements established under the national school lunch and child nutrition acts (42 United States Code §§ 1751 through 1785) for free or reduced price lunches.

C. The governing board of the district educating the pupil shall provide transportation limited to no more than twenty miles each way to and from the school of attendance or to and from a pickup point on a regular transportation route or for the total miles traveled each day to an adjacent district for nonresident pupils with disabilities whose individualized education program specifies that transportation is necessary for fulfillment of the program.

Added by Laws 1995, Ch. 1, § 5, eff. Feb. 20, 1995. Amended by Laws 1995, Ch. 268, § 45; Laws 2000, Ch. 236, § 15, eff. April 12, 2000.

Historical and Statutory Notes

Source:

A.R.S. former § 15–816.01.
Laws 1994, 9th S.S., Ch. 2, § 8.

The 1995 amendment of this section by Ch. 268 explicitly amended the addition of this section by Ch. 1, § 5.

Laws 1996, 5th S.S., Ch. 4, § 2, provides:

"**Sec. 2. Charter schools; transportation state aid; 1996–1997 fiscal year**

"Notwithstanding §§ 15–185, 15–186 and 15–816.01, Arizona Revised Statutes, the transportation support level for the 1996–1997 fiscal year for each charter school that is sponsored by the state board of education or the state board for charter schools shall be $174 multiplied by the school's student count."

Laws 1998, 4th S.S., Ch. 8, § 12, provides:

"**Sec. 12. Charter schools; transportation state aid; 1998–1999 fiscal year**

"Notwithstanding §§ 15–185 and 15–816.01, Arizona Revised Statutes, the transportation support level for the 1998–1999 fiscal year for each charter school that is sponsored by the state board of education or the state board for charter schools is one hundred seventy-four dollars multiplied by the school's student count."

Former § 15–816.01, added by Laws 1994, 9th S.S., Ch. 2, § 8, relating to similar subject matter, was repealed by Laws 1995, Ch. 1, § 4, effective February 20, 1995.

§ 15–816.02. Desegregation provisions

A school shall admit pupils who reside in the attendance area of a school that is under a court order of desegregation or that is a party to an agreement with the United States department of education office for civil rights directed toward remediating alleged or proven racial discrimination unless notice is received from the resident school that the admission would violate the court order or agreement. If a school admits a pupil after notice is received that the admission would constitute such a violation, the school's district is not allowed to include in its student count the pupils wrongfully admitted. A school shall not be required to admit nonresident or resident transfer pupils if the admission would violate the provisions of the court order or agreement.

Added as § 15–816.04 by Laws 1994, 9th S.S., Ch. 2, § 8. Renumbered as § 15–816.02 and amended by Laws 1995, Ch. 1, § 6, eff. Feb. 20, 1995.

Historical and Statutory Notes

Former § 15–816.02, added by Laws 1994, 9th S.S., Ch. 2, § 8, relating to admission criteria, was repealed by Laws 1995, Ch. 1, § 4, effective February 20, 1995.

§ 15–816.03. Repealed by Laws 1995, Ch. 1, § 4, eff. Feb. 20, 1995

Historical and Statutory Notes

The repealed section, added by Laws 1994, 9th S.S., Ch. 2, § 8, related to children with disabilities.

§ 15-816.04. Renumbered as § 15-816.02

§§ 15-816.05, 15-816.06. Repealed by Laws 1995, Ch. 1, § 7, eff. Feb. 20, 1995

Historical and Statutory Notes

The repealed sections, added by Laws 1994, 9th S.S., Ch. 2, § 8, related to application procedures and transportation provisions, respectively.

§ 15-816.07. District and school immunity

A school district and its employees are immune from civil liability for decisions that concern the acceptance or rejection of a nonresident pupil for enrollment and that are based on a good faith application of the requirements of this article and the standards adopted pursuant to this article.

Added by Laws 1994, 9th S.S., Ch. 2, § 8.

ARTICLE 2. ADMISSION REQUIREMENTS

§ 15-821. Admission of children; required age

A. Unless otherwise provided by article 1.1 of this chapter or by any other law, all schools shall admit children between the ages of six and twenty-one years who reside in the school district and who meet the requirements for enrollment in one of the grades or programs offered in the school.

B. If a preschool program for children with disabilities is maintained, a child is eligible for admission as prescribed in § 15-771.

C. If a kindergarten program is maintained, a child is eligible for admission to kindergarten if the child is five years of age. A child is deemed five years of age if the child reaches the age of five before September 1 of the current school year. A child is eligible for admission to first grade if the child is six years of age. A child is deemed six years of age if the child reaches the age of six before September 1 of the current school year. The governing board may admit children who have not reached the required age as prescribed by this subsection if it is determined to be in the best interest of the children. For children entering the first grade, such determination shall be based upon one or more consultations with the parent, parents, guardian or guardians, the children, the teacher and the school principal. Such children must reach the required age of five for kindergarten and six for first grade by January 1 of the current school year.

D. Notwithstanding any other law, a child who resides with a family member other than the child's parent and is residing with the family member while awaiting the outcome of a legal guardianship or custody proceeding is deemed to reside in the school district where that family member resides if the family member provides written documentary proof of one of the following:

1. The family member is attempting to obtain legal guardianship of the child in an unresolved and uncontested guardianship proceeding commenced in superior court. The family member shall provide documentation to the school district within thirty days of enrollment that the family member is attempting to

obtain legal guardianship of the child. Upon obtaining legal guardianship, the family member shall provide documentation to the school district.

2. The family member is attempting to obtain custody of the child in an unresolved and uncontested child custody proceeding commenced in superior court. The family member shall provide documentation to the school district within thirty days of enrollment that the family member is attempting to obtain custody of the child. Upon obtaining custody, the family member shall provide documentation to the school district.

Added by Laws 1981, Ch. 1, § 2, eff. Jan. 23, 1981. Amended by Laws 1981, Ch. 314, § 15; Laws 1988, Ch. 281, § 3; Laws 1994, Ch. 315, § 13; Laws 1994, 9th S.S., Ch. 2, § 9, eff. July 1, 1995; Laws 1995, Ch. 268, § 46; Laws 1999, Ch. 46, § 1.

Historical and Statutory Notes

Source:

Laws 1912, Ch. 77, §§ 72, 85.
Civ. Code 1913, §§ 2768, 2798.
Laws 1925, Ch. 71, § 1.
Rev. Code 1928, § 1030.
Laws 1933, Ch. 65, § 2.
A.R.S. former §§ 15-302, 15-302.01.
Laws 1958, Ch. 21, § 1.
Laws 1960, Ch. 127, §§ 17, 18.
Laws 1961, Ch. 14, § 1.
Laws 1978, Ch. 93, § 1.
Laws 1979, Ch. 3, § 2.
Laws 1980, Ch. 195, § 1.

Laws 1994, 9th S.S., Ch. 2, § 35, as amended by Laws 1995, Ch. 1, § 10, effective February 20, 1995, provides:

"**Sec. 35. Delayed effective dates**

"Sections 15-821 and 15-973, Arizona Revised Statutes, as amended by this act, are effective from and after June 30, 1995."

The 1995 amendment of this section by Ch. 268 explicitly amended the amendment of this section by 9th S.S., Ch. 2, § 9.

§ 15-822. Repealed by Laws 1994, Ch. 315, § 14

Historical and Statutory Notes

The repealed section, which related to admission of beginners, was added by Laws 1981, Ch. 1, § 2, and was derived from:

Laws 1912, Ch. 77, §§ 72, 85.
Civ. Code 1913, §§ 2768, 2798.
Laws 1925, Ch. 71, § 1.
Rev. Code 1928, § 1030.
Laws 1933, Ch. 65, § 2.
Code 1939, § 54-502.
A.R.S. former § 15-303.

§ 15-823. Admission; residents of other school districts; nonresidents of this state; tuition

A. Except as provided in subsections B, C, D and E of this section, children of nonresidents of this state may be admitted upon payment of a reasonable tuition fixed by the governing board.

B. The governing board shall admit children of nonresident teaching and research faculty of community college districts and state universities and children of nonresident graduate or undergraduate students of community college districts and state universities whose parent's presence at the district or university is of international, national, state or local benefit without payment of tuition.

C. The governing board shall admit children who are residents of the United States but are nonresidents of this state without payment of tuition if evidence indicates that the child's physical, mental, moral or emotional health is best served by placement with a grandparent, brother, sister, stepbrother, stepsister, aunt or uncle who is a resident within the school district, unless the governing board determines that the placement is solely for the purpose of obtaining an education in this state without payment of tuition.

D. The governing board may admit nonresident foreign students who are in exchange programs without payment of tuition or as it may otherwise prescribe.

E. The governing board may admit children who are residents of the United States without payment of tuition if evidence indicates that because the parents are homeless or the child is abandoned, as defined in § 8-201, the child's physical, mental, moral or emotional health is best served by placement with a person who does not have legal custody of the child and who is a resident within the school district, unless the governing board determines that the placement is solely for the purpose of obtaining an education in this state without payment of tuition.

F. Children admitted under this section shall be counted or not counted as resident pupils as prescribed in § 15-824, subsection D.

Added by Laws 1981, Ch. 1, § 2, eff. Jan. 23, 1981. Amended by Laws 1990, Ch. 367, § 3; Laws 1994, 9th S.S., Ch. 2, § 10, eff. Feb. 20, 1995; Laws 1995, Ch. 191, § 5, eff. April 19, 1995; Laws 1996, Ch. 284, § 40; Laws 1998, Ch. 276, § 39.

Historical and Statutory Notes

Source:

Laws 1912, Ch. 77, §§ 72, 85.
Civ. Code 1913, §§ 2768, 2798.
Laws 1925, Ch. 71, § 1.
Rev. Code 1928, § 1030.
Laws 1933, Ch. 65, § 2.
Code 1939, § 54-502.
A.R.S. former § 15-302.
Laws 1958, Ch. 21, § 1.
Laws 1960, Ch. 127, § 17.
Laws 1961, Ch. 14, § 1.
Laws 1978, Ch. 93, § 1.
Laws 1978, Ch. 178, § 1.
Laws 1979, Ch. 3, § 2.
Laws 1980, Ch. 195, § 1.

Laws 1995, Ch. 1, § 11, effective February 20, 1995, provides:

"**Sec. 11. Effective date**

"Sections 15-823, 15-824 and 15-825, Arizona Revised Statutes, as amended by Laws 1994, ninth special session, chapter 2, §§ 10, 11 and 12, are effective on the effective date of this act."

Laws 1995, Ch. 191, § 25, effective April 19, 1995, provides:

"**Sec. 25. Department of education; tuition payments for fiscal year 1994-1995**

"Notwithstanding § 15-823, Arizona Revised Statutes, as amended by § 5 of this act, § 15-824, Arizona Revised Statutes, as amended by § 6 of this act, and § 15-825, Arizona Revised Statutes, as amended by Laws 1994, ninth special session, chapter 2, § 12, for fiscal year 1994-1995, the department of education shall make tuition payments in the amount to which each school district was entitled as of July 15, 1994."

§ 15-824. Admission of pupils of other school districts; homeless children; tuition charges; definitions

A. The governing board of a school district shall admit pupils from another school district or area as follows:

1. Upon the presentation of a certificate of educational convenience issued by the county school superintendent pursuant to § 15-825.

2. For three hundred fifty or fewer pupils, to a high school without the presentation of such certificate, if the pupil is a resident of a common school district within this state which is not within a high school district and which does not offer instruction in the pupil's grade. The three hundred fifty or fewer pupil limitation prescribed in this paragraph does not apply to a small isolated

school district as defined in § 15-901. Tuition shall be charged as prescribed in subsection E of this section for each pupil admitted pursuant to this paragraph, each pupil from a school district that provides only financing for pupils who are instructed by another school district and each pupil from a unified district that does not offer instruction in the pupil's grade. The school membership of such pupils is deemed, for the purpose of determining student count and for apportionment of state aid, to be enrollment in the school district of the pupil's residence.

B. The residence of the person having legal custody of the pupil is considered the residence of the pupil, except as provided in subsection C of this section and in § 15-825, subsection B.

C. The current residence of a homeless pupil who does not reside with the person having legal custody of the pupil is considered to be the residence of the homeless pupil if the person having legal custody of the pupil is a resident of the United States. For the purposes of this subsection, "homeless pupil" means a pupil who has a primary residence that is:

1. A supervised publicly or privately operated shelter designed to provide temporary living accommodations.

2. An institution that provides a temporary residence for individuals intended to be institutionalized.

3. A public or private place not designed for, or ordinarily used as, a regular sleeping accommodation for human beings.

D. The school enrollment of a pupil who is a resident of this state or who is admitted to a school district under § 15-823, subsection B, C or E is deemed, for the purpose of determining student count and for apportionment of state aid, to be enrollment in the school district of actual attendance, except as provided in § 15-825, subsection A, paragraph 1 and subsection A, paragraph 2 of this section and except for pupils for whom the superintendent of public instruction is charged tuition pursuant to § 15-825, subsections B and D and § 15-976 or for whom another school district is charged tuition as provided in subsections E and G of this section.

E. If tuition is required to be charged for pupils attending school in a school district other than that of their residence, the tuition shall be determined and paid in the following manner:

1. The number of high school pupils for which tuition may be charged to a common school district which is not within a high school district is equal to the average daily membership in the district of attendance from the common school district for the prior fiscal year, except that for the first year in which a common school district not within a high school district stops teaching high school subjects, the district of attendance may charge tuition for the number of pupils which is equal to the average daily membership for high school pupils in the common school district for the prior fiscal year. This number may be adjusted if the common school district increases its revenue control limit and district support level or recomputes its revenue control limit as provided in § 15-948.

2. The tuition for pupils attending school in a school district other than that of their residence, except pupils provided for by § 15–825, subsections B and D and any pupils included in the definition of child with a disability in § 15–761, shall not exceed the cost per student count of the school district attended, as determined for the current school year. Tuition for pupils included in the definition of child with a disability in § 15–761 shall not exceed the actual cost of the school attended for each pupil as determined for the current year. The school district of attendance shall not include in the cost per student count a charge for transportation if no transportation is provided, and the charge for transportation shall not exceed the actual costs of providing transportation for the pupils served, as prescribed in the uniform system of financial records. The school district of attendance shall provide the school district of residence with the final tuition charge for the current year and with an estimate of the budget year's tuition charge by May 1 of the current year. The school district of residence shall pay at least one-fourth of the total amount of the estimated tuition by September 30, December 31 and March 31, and it shall pay the remaining amount it owes after adjustments are made by June 30.

3. Tuition of pupils as provided in § 15–825, subsection D shall not exceed the excess costs for group B children with disabilities in the cost study prescribed in § 15–236 minus the amount generated by the equalization base as determined in § 15–971, subsection A for these pupils. A school district may submit to the superintendent of public instruction a record of actual excess costs to educate a group B child with a disability if the costs are higher than the calculated excess costs or if a pupil has been placed in a private school for special education services. The superintendent shall determine if the additional costs will be paid, and if the costs are paid, whether the additional costs will be paid by the state or the resident district.

4. The amount received representing contributions to capital outlay as provided in subsection G, paragraph 1, subdivision (b) of this section shall be applied to the capital outlay fund or the debt service fund of the school district.

5. The amount received representing contributions to debt service as provided in subsection G, paragraph 1, subdivisions (c) and (d) of this section shall be applied to the debt service fund of the school district if there is one. Otherwise such amount shall be credited to the capital outlay fund of the school district.

F. A school district may submit to the superintendent of public instruction a record of actual costs paid by the school district to educate a pupil who qualifies for a certificate of educational convenience under § 15–825, subsection B. If the actual costs for that pupil exceed the costs per student count computed pursuant to subsection G of this section, the superintendent of public instruction shall reimburse the school district for these additional costs subject to legislative appropriation.

G. For the purposes of this section:

1. "Costs per student count" means the sum of the following for the common or high school portion of the school district attended, whichever is applicable to the pupil involved, as prescribed in the uniform system of financial records:

(a) The actual school district expenditures for the regular education program subsection of the maintenance and operation section of the budget divided by the school district's student count for the common or high school portion of the school district, whichever is applicable.

(b) The actual school district expenditures for the capital outlay section of the budget as provided in §§ 15-903 and 15-905 excluding expenditures for transportation equipment and buildings if no transportation is provided and expenditures for the acquisition of building sites, divided by the school district's student count for the common or high school portion of the school district, whichever is applicable.

(c) The actual school district expenditures for debt service divided by the school district's student count for the common or high school portion of the school district, whichever is applicable.

(d) The result obtained in subdivision (c) of this paragraph shall not exceed:

(i) Seven hundred fifty dollars if the pupil's school district of residence pays tuition for seven hundred fifty or fewer pupils to other school districts or one hundred fifty dollars if the state pays tuition for seven hundred fifty or fewer pupils to a school district pursuant to § 15-825, subsection D or § 15-976.

(ii) Eight hundred dollars if the pupil's school district of residence pays tuition for one thousand or fewer, but more than seven hundred fifty, pupils to other school districts or two hundred dollars if the state pays tuition for one thousand or fewer, but more than seven hundred fifty, pupils to a school district pursuant to § 15-825, subsection D or § 15-976.

(iii) The actual cost per student count if either the pupil's school district of residence or the state pays tuition for more than one thousand pupils to other school districts.

2. "Legal custody" means:

(a) Custody exercised by the natural or adoptive parents with whom a pupil resides.

(b) Custody granted by order of a court of competent jurisdiction to a person or persons with whom a pupil resides unless the primary purpose for which custody was requested was to circumvent the payment of tuition as provided in this section.

Added by Laws 1981, Ch. 1, § 2, eff. Jan. 23, 1981. Amended by Laws 1981, Ch. 181, § 1; Laws 1982, Ch. 183, § 1; Laws 1985, Ch. 156, § 1; Laws 1985, Ch. 166, § 10, eff. April 18, 1985; Laws 1986, Ch. 100, § 1; Laws 1986, Ch. 125, § 3, eff. April 18, 1986; Laws 1986, Ch. 387, § 1; Laws 1990, Ch. 75, § 1; Laws 1990, Ch. 367, § 4; Laws 1991, Ch. 288, § 1, eff. Sept. 21, 1991, retroactively effective to July 1, 1991; Laws 1991, Ch. 292, § 2, eff. June 28, 1991; Laws 1992, Ch. 172, § 14; Laws 1993, Ch. 189, § 4; Laws 1994, 9th S.S., Ch. 2, § 11, eff. Feb. 20, 1995; Laws 1995, Ch. 191, § 6, eff. April 19, 1995; Laws 1995, Ch. 234, § 1; Laws 1996, Ch. 115, § 1; Laws 1996, Ch. 358, § 1; Laws 1999, Ch. 243, § 2; Laws 2002, Ch. 286, § 1, eff. Aug. 22, 2002, retroactively effective to March 2, 2002.

Historical and Statutory Notes

Source:

Laws 1912, Ch. 77, §§ 41, 83.

Civ. Code 1913, §§ 2733, 2779.

Laws 1921, Ch. 72, § 5.

Laws 1921, Ch. 137, § 1.
Laws 1925, Ch. 28, § 1.
Laws 1925, Ch. 70, §§ 1 to 4.
Laws 1927, Ch. 88, § 1.
Rev. Code 1928, §§ 1011, 1075.
Laws 1933, Ch. 18, § 1.
Code 1939, § 54–908.
Laws 1949, Ch. 110, § 1.
Laws 1951, Ch. 140, § 1.
Laws 1952, Ch. 138, § 1.
Code 1939, Supp.1952, § 54–416.
Laws 1954, Ch. 117, § 2.
A.R.S. former §§ 15–449, 15–547, 15–547.01.
Laws 1960, Ch. 127, §§ 19, 34.
Laws 1961, Ch. 14, § 2.
Laws 1964, Ch. 134, § 2.
Laws 1971, Ch. 165, § 3.
Laws 1974, 1st S.S., Ch. 3, § 11.
Laws 1979, Ch. 184, § 1.
Laws 1980, 2nd S.S., Ch. 9, § 22.
Laws 1980, Ch. 195, § 2.

Laws 1985, Ch. 166, § 43, effective April 18, 1985, provides:

"**Sec. 43. Provisions for the fiscal year 1984–1985**

"Notwithstanding §§ 15–824, 15–901, 15–921, 15–922, 15–943, 15–945, 15–947, 15–961, 15–962, 15–971 and 15–974, Arizona Revised Statutes, as amended by this act, for the fiscal year 1984–1985 § 15–824, as amended by Laws 1982, chapter 183, § 1, § 15–901, as amended by Laws 1984, chapter 219, § 1, chapter 235, § 1 and chapter 314, § 1, § 15–921, as added by Laws 1981, chapter 1, § 2, § 15–922, as amended by Laws 1984, chapter 235, § 2, § 15–943, as amended by Laws 1981, chapter 308, § 4, § 15–945, as amended by Laws 1984, chapter 314, § 3, § 15–947, as amended by Laws 1984, chapter 327, § 1, chapter 340, § 3 and chapter 349, § 8, § 15–961, as amended by Laws 1984, chapter 349, § 9 and chapter 379, § 14, § 15–962, as amended by Laws 1984, chapter 349, § 10, § 15–971, as amended by Laws 1984, chapter 379, § 15 and § 15–974, as amended by Laws 1984, chapter 327, § 2 and chapter 340, § 5, apply."

Laws 1990, Ch. 75, § 2 provides:

"**Sec. 2. Report to the legislature**

"The department of education shall submit a report to the president of the senate and the speaker of the house of representatives by December 1, 1991 on the effectiveness of the method used to determine the amount of tuition that is charged for handicapped pupils for whom a certificate of educational convenience has been issued, as provided in § 15–824, Arizona Revised Statutes, as amended by this act. The report shall include comparative cost information on the three methods prescribed by § 15–824, subsection D, paragraph 4, subdivisions (a) through (c), Arizona Revised Statutes, and analysis of the impact on the state in selected cases."

Laws 1990, Ch. 367, § 1, provides:

"**Section 1. Legislative intent**

"It is the intent of the legislature through this act to provide access to public education for homeless children."

Laws 1991, Ch. 288, § 25, provides:

"**Sec. 25. Retroactivity**

"This act is effective retroactively to July 1, 1991."

Laws 1994, 9th S.S., Ch. 2, § 20, provides:

"**Sec. 20. Phasing out tuition payments**

"**A.** For fiscal year 1994–1995, payment of tuition for pupils who receive a certificate of educational convenience pursuant to § 15–825, Arizona Revised Statutes, as amended by Laws 1993, chapter 189, § 5, shall be as prescribed in § 15–824, Arizona Revised Statutes, as amended by Laws 1993, chapter 189, § 4, and § 15–825, Arizona Revised Statutes, as amended by Laws 1993, chapter 189, § 5, except that the school of enrollment of a pupil is deemed for the purpose of determining student count to be enrollment in the school district of attendance. Tuition shall not be collected by the district of attendance within the state for fiscal year 1995–1996 and thereafter except as provided in § 15–825, subsection D, Arizona Revised Statutes, as amended by this act.

"**B.** Notwithstanding subsection A of this section, for pupils who receive a certificate of educational convenience to attend a school out of this state, the school enrollment of the pupil is deemed for the purpose of determining student count to be enrollment in the school district of residence.

"**C.** For fiscal year 1994–1995, school districts may continue to admit pupils who do not reside in the school district but who reside in this state on such terms as the school district prescribes and may charge tuition for pupils. If a school district is charging tuition pursuant to this subsection, except for tuition paid by parents or guardians or for pupils enrolled as prescribed in § 15–824, subsection A, paragraph 2, Arizona Revised Statutes, as amended by Laws 1993, chapter 189, § 4, the tuition shall be determined pursuant to § 15–824, subsection E, Arizona Revised Statutes, as amended by Laws 1993, chapter 189, § 4. If a school district is charging tuition to another school district, except for pupils enrolled as provided in § 15–824, subsection A, paragraph 2, Arizona Revised Statutes, as amended by Laws 1993, chapter 189, § 4, the school enrollment for these pupils is deemed in the school district of attendance for the purpose of determining student count for the last year in which the tuition is charged.

"**D.** For the purposes of computing an increase due to growth in student count as provided in § 15–948, Arizona Revised Statutes, pupils who are enrolled under the provisions established in subsections A and C of this section shall not be included during a year in which tuition is paid."

Laws 1995, Ch. 1, § 11, effective February 20, 1995, provides:

"**Sec. 11. Effective date**

"Sections 15-823, 15-824 and 15-825, Arizona Revised Statutes, as amended by Laws 1994, ninth special session, chapter 2, §§ 10, 11 and 12, are effective on the effective date of this act."

The 1995 amendments of this section by Ch. 191 and by Ch. 234 explicitly amended the amendment of this section by Laws 1994, 9th S.S., Ch. 2, § 11.

Laws 1995, Ch. 234, § 4, provides:

"**Sec. 4. Tuition charged to the superintendent of public instruction for fiscal years 1995-1996 and 1996-1997**

"Notwithstanding § 15-824, subsection F, Arizona Revised Statutes, as amended by this act, for fiscal years 1995-1996 and 1996-1997, if tuition is charged to the superintendent of public instruction as provided in § 15-824, subsection E, paragraph 3, Arizona Revised Statutes, as amended by this act or § 5 of this act, the computation of actual excess costs shall not include amounts per student count for bond issues in excess of the following:

"(a) One hundred fifty dollars if the superintendent of public instruction is charged tuition for seven hundred fifty or fewer pupils by the school district of attendance.

"(b) Two hundred dollars if the superintendent of public instruction is charged tuition for one thousand or fewer, but more than seven hundred fifty pupils by the school district of attendance.

"(c) The actual cost per student count if the pupil's school district of residence pays tuition for more than one thousand pupils to other school districts."

Laws 1996, Ch. 115, § 2, provides:

"**Sec. 2. Tuition for high school pupils who are residents of common school districts not within high school districts; fiscal years 1996-1997 and 1997-1998**

"**A.** Notwithstanding § 15-824, subsection F, paragraph 4, subdivisions (a) and (b), Arizona Revised Statutes, as amended by this act:

"1. For fiscal year 1996-1997, the result obtained in § 15-824, subsection F, paragraph 3, Arizona Revised Statutes, as amended by this act, shall not exceed:

"(a) Six hundred twenty-five dollars if the pupil's school district of residence pays tuition to other school districts for seven hundred fifty or fewer pupils.

"(b) Six hundred seventy-five dollars if the pupil's school district of residence pays tuition to other school districts for more than seven hundred fifty pupils but less than one thousand and one pupils.

"2. For fiscal year 1997-1998, the result obtained in § 15-824, subsection F, paragraph 3, Arizona Revised Statutes, as amended by this act, shall not exceed:

"(a) Six hundred seventy-five dollars if the pupil's school district of residence pays tuition to other school districts for seven hundred fifty or fewer pupils.

"(b) Seven hundred twenty-five dollars if the pupil's school district of residence pays tuition to other school districts for more than seven hundred fifty pupils but less than one thousand and one pupils.

"**B.** This section does not apply to pupils for whom the state pays tuition to a school district."

Laws 1996, Ch. 358, § 6, provides:

"**Sec. 6. Retroactivity**

"Sections 1, 2, 3 and 4 of this act apply retroactively to July 1, 1995."

Laws 2002, Ch. 286, § 3, provides:

"**Sec. 3. Retroactivity**

"This act is effective retroactively to from and after March 1, 2002."

Reviser's Notes:

1985 Note. Prior to the 1986 amendments, this section contained the amendments made by Laws 1985, Ch. 156, § 1 and Ch. 166, § 10 which were blended together pursuant to authority of § 41-1304.03.

1990 Note. Prior to the 1991 amendments, this section contained the amendments made by Laws 1990, Ch. 75, § 1 and Ch. 367, § 4 which were blended together pursuant to authority of § 41-1304.03.

1991 Note. Prior to the 1992 amendment, this section contained the amendments made by Laws 1991, Ch. 288, sec. 1 and Ch. 292, sec. 2 that were blended together pursuant to authority of § 41-1304.03.

1994 Note. Pursuant to authority of § 41-1304.02, in the section heading "definition" was substituted for "definitions".

1995 Note. Prior to the 1996 amendments, this section contained the amendments made by Laws 1995, Ch. 191, sec. 6 and Ch. 234, sec. 1 that were blended together pursuant to authority of § 41-1304.03.

1996 Note. Prior to the 1999 amendment, this section contained the amendments made by Laws 1996, Ch. 115, sec. 1 and Ch. 358, sec. 1

that were blended together pursuant to authority of § 41-1304.03.

§ 15-825. Certificate of educational convenience; issuance; effect on enrollment records

A. A pupil who is precluded by distance or lack of adequate transportation facilities from attending a school in the school district or county of the pupil's residence or who resides in unorganized territory may apply to the county school superintendent for a certificate of educational convenience. If it appears to the county school superintendent that it is not feasible for the pupil to attend a school in the school district or county of residence, the county school superintendent shall issue a certificate authorizing the pupil to attend a school in an adjoining school district or county, whether within or without this state. If a certificate of educational convenience is issued as provided in this subsection, the school enrollment of a pupil is as follows:

1. The school enrollment of a pupil who is precluded from attending a school in this state and who must attend school in another state, when certified to the county school superintendent by the official in charge of the school attended, is deemed for the purpose of determining student count to be enrollment in the school of the county or school district of the student's residence.

2. The school enrollment of a pupil from unorganized territory or from another school district is deemed for the purpose of determining student count to be enrollment in the school district of actual attendance.

B. The county school superintendent of any county in which a pupil is placed as described in this subsection shall issue a certificate of educational convenience for the pupil to attend school in the school district or adjoining school district to that in which the pupil is placed by an agency of this state or a state or federal court of competent jurisdiction in one of the following:

1. A state rehabilitation or corrective institution.

2. A foster home or child care agency or institution which is licensed and supervised by the department of economic security or the department of health services.

3. A residential facility operated or supported by the department of economic security or the department of health services.

4. Under the supervision of the department of juvenile corrections in a residence pursuant to the interstate compact on juveniles. Notwithstanding § 41-1959, the placing agency, department or institution shall provide the school district of attendance with the necessary information to enable the district to obtain a certificate of educational convenience pursuant to this subsection.

C. A pupil attending school under a certificate of educational convenience issued pursuant to subsection B of this section is deemed for the purpose of determining student count to be enrolled in the school district of attendance. The county school superintendent of any county shall not issue a certificate of educational convenience as provided in subsection B of this section if the pupil is placed in the same district of his parents' or legal guardians' residence or if the pupil is placed without a court order and his parents or legal guardians are not residents of this state.

D. If a certificate of educational convenience is issued as provided in subsection B of this section, or for a pupil whose parent or guardian is employed and domiciled by a state institution as prescribed by § 15-976, tuition may be charged as follows:

1. For group B children with disabilities:

(a) Who are from unorganized territory, whose parent or guardian is employed by a state institution as prescribed by § 15-976 or who have been issued a certificate of educational convenience pursuant to subsection B of this section, the superintendent of public instruction shall reimburse the district of attendance for the excess costs as provided in § 15-824, subsection E, paragraph 3.

(b) Who are from another school district, the school district of residence shall reimburse the district of attendance for the excess costs as provided in § 15-824, subsection E, paragraph 3.

2. For pupils who are precluded from attending a school in this state and who must attend a school in another state:

(a) If the pupil resides in a school district in this state, the district of residence shall pay the amount charged by the district of attendance.

(b) If the pupil resides in unorganized territory, the superintendent of public instruction shall pay the amount charged by the district of attendance.

E. The county school superintendent who issues a certificate of educational convenience shall notify the superintendent of public instruction of the issuance of the certificate. The superintendent of public instruction shall draw a warrant in favor of the school district of actual attendance for the amount charged, whether for common or high school attendance, as provided in § 15-824.

F. The total amount of state monies that may be spent in any fiscal year by the superintendent of public instruction for certificates of educational convenience shall not exceed the amount appropriated or authorized by § 35-173 for that purpose. This section shall not be construed to impose a duty on an officer, agent or employee of this state to discharge a responsibility or to create any right in a person or group if the discharge or right would require an expenditure of state monies in excess of the expenditure authorized by legislative appropriation for that specific purpose.

Added by Laws 1981, Ch. 1, eff. Jan. 23, 1981. Amended by Laws 1981, Ch. 181, § 2; Laws 1982, Ch. 183, § 2; Laws 1991, Ch. 288, § 2, eff. Sept. 21, 1991, retroactively effective to July 1, 1991; Laws 1992, Ch. 172, § 15; Laws 1993, Ch. 189, § 5; Laws 1994, 9th S.S., Ch. 2, § 12, eff. Feb. 20, 1995; Laws 1995, Ch. 178, § 16; Laws 1995, Ch. 196, § 6; Laws 1996, Ch. 358, § 2; Laws 2000, Ch. 193, § 106.

Historical and Statutory Notes

Source:

Laws 1949, Ch. 12, § 2.
Laws 1952, Ch. 138, § 2.
Code 1939, Supp.1952, § 54-616.
A.R.S. former § 15-304.
Laws 1958, Ch. 21, § 2.
Laws 1960, Ch. 127, § 20.
Laws 1964, Ch. 134, § 1.

Laws 1971, Ch. 165, § 2.
Laws 1974, 1st S.S., Ch. 3, § 2.
Laws 1978, Ch. 198, § 5.
Laws 1980, 2nd S.S., Ch. 9, § 11.

Laws 1994, 9th S.S., Ch. 2, § 20, provides:

"**Sec. 20. Phasing out tuition payments**

"**A.** For fiscal year 1994–1995, payment of tuition for pupils who receive a certificate of educational convenience pursuant to § 15–825, Arizona Revised Statutes, as amended by Laws 1993, chapter 189, § 5, shall be as prescribed in § 15–824, Arizona Revised Statutes, as amended by Laws 1993, chapter 189, § 4, and § 15–825, Arizona Revised Statutes, as amended by Laws 1993, chapter 189, § 5, except that the school of enrollment of a pupil is deemed for the purpose of determining student count to be enrollment in the school district of attendance. Tuition shall not be collected by the district of attendance within the state for fiscal year 1995–1996 and thereafter except as provided in § 15–825, subsection D, Arizona Revised Statutes, as amended by this act.

"**B.** Notwithstanding subsection A of this section, for pupils who receive a certificate of educational convenience to attend a school out of this state, the school enrollment of the pupil is deemed for the purpose of determining student count to be enrollment in the school district of residence.

"**C.** For fiscal year 1994–1995, school districts may continue to admit pupils who do not reside in the school district but who reside in this state on such terms as the school district prescribes and may charge tuition for pupils. If a school district is charging tuition pursuant to this subsection, except for tuition paid by parents or guardians or for pupils enrolled as prescribed in § 15–824, subsection A, paragraph 2, Arizona Revised Statutes, as amended by Laws 1993, chapter 189, § 4, the tuition shall be determined pursuant to § 15–824, subsection E, Arizona Revised Statutes, as amended by Laws 1993, chapter 189, § 4. If a school district is charging tuition to another school district, except for pupils enrolled as provided in § 15–824, subsection A, paragraph 2, Arizona Revised Statutes, as amended by Laws 1993, chapter 189, § 4, the school enrollment for these pupils is deemed in the school district of attendance for the purpose of determining student count for the last year in which the tuition is charged.

"**D.** For the purposes of computing an increase due to growth in student count as provided in § 15–948, Arizona Revised Statutes, pupils who are enrolled under the provisions established in subsections A and C of this section shall not be included during a year in which tuition is paid."

Laws 1995, Ch. 1, § 11, effective February 20, 1995, provides:

"**Sec. 11. Effective date**

"Sections 15–823, 15–824 and 15–825, Arizona Revised Statutes, as amended by Laws 1994, ninth special session, chapter 2, §§ 10, 11 and 12, are effective on the effective date of this act."

Laws 1996, Ch. 358, § 6, provides:

"**Sec. 6. Retroactivity**

"Sections 1, 2, 3 and 4 of this act apply retroactively to July 1, 1995."

Reviser's Notes:

1995 Note. Prior to the 1996 amendment, this section contained the amendments made by Laws 1995, Ch. 178, sec. 16 and Ch. 196, sec. 6 that were blended together pursuant to authority of § 41–1304.03.

§ 15–825.01. Certificates of educational convenience; pupils attending out-of-state schools

A. A school district is eligible to receive payment from state school monies for excess tuition if the following conditions are met:

1. The county school superintendent issues a certificate of educational convenience pursuant to § 15–825, subsection A, for one or more pupils who reside in the district to attend a school in an adjacent state which is proximate to the school district when the pupils are precluded by distance or lack of adequate transportation facilities from attending a school in the school district or county of the pupils' residence.

2. The superintendent of public instruction determines that the development of an interstate compact with another state or an intergovernmental agreement between the sending and receiving school districts, which provides for tuition-free attendance in the receiving district, is impracticable or not in the best interests of this state.

3. The total amount of tuition charged by the receiving district is greater than the equalization base amount as determined by § 15-971, subsection A, for all of the pupils for whom tuition is being paid pursuant to paragraph 1 of this subsection.

B. The excess tuition payment shall be calculated as follows:

1. Determine the amount of tuition being charged by the receiving district for pupils attending the district pursuant to subsection A, paragraph 1 of this section.

2. Determine the lesser of the amount determined in paragraph 1 of this subsection or the guaranteed tuition level. The guaranteed tuition level for the receiving district shall be determined for the tuitioned pupils by the department of education based upon the receiving state's school finance formula or the actual costs of educating pupils in the receiving district, whichever is appropriate.

3. Subtract the equalization base amount as provided in subsection A, paragraph 3 of this section, from the amount determined in paragraph 2 of this subsection.

C. The excess tuition payment is exempt from the revenue control limit as provided in § 15-947.

Added by Laws 1993, Ch. 202, § 10, eff. April 21, 1993.

§ 15-826. Education of children to whom school inaccessible

The county school superintendent, with the consent of the board of supervisors, may allow on his warrant an amount not to exceed ten dollars per school month per pupil toward the education of children of compulsory school age living at such a distance or inaccessible place that compulsory attendance is impracticable. The monies may be used by the county school superintendent as he deems best for the interest of the pupil and shall be paid from the reserve fund of the county.

Added by Laws 1981, Ch. 1, § 2, eff. Jan. 23, 1981.

Historical and Statutory Notes

Source:

Laws 1919, Ch. 89, § 1.
Rev. Code 1928, § 1038.
Code 1939, § 54-510.
A.R.S. former § 15-327.

§ 15-827. Presentation of withdrawal form

A. A pupil who enters a school shall present to the principal of the school a properly executed withdrawal form if such pupil previously attended another school in this state.

B. The withdrawal form prescribed by subsection A shall be prepared and distributed by the office of the superintendent of public instruction. The withdrawal form shall in addition to any other data required by the superintendent of public instruction contain space for the reason for withdrawal and the signature of an official of the school from which the pupil has withdrawn.

Added by Laws 1981, Ch. 1, § 2, eff. Jan. 23, 1981.

Historical and Statutory Notes

Source:

Laws 1963, Ch. 38, § 1.
A.R.S. former § 15–307.

§ 15–828. Birth certificate; school records; exception

A. On enrollment of a pupil for the first time in a particular school district or private school offering instruction to pupils in any kindergarten programs or grades one through twelve, that school or school district shall notify the person enrolling the pupil in writing that within thirty days the person must provide one of the following:

1. A certified copy of the pupil's birth certificate.

2. Other reliable proof of the pupil's identity and age, including the pupil's baptismal certificate, an application for a social security number or original school registration records and an affidavit explaining the inability to provide a copy of the birth certificate.

3. A letter from the authorized representative of an agency having custody of the pupil pursuant to title 8, chapter 2 [1] certifying that the pupil has been placed in the custody of the agency as prescribed by law.

B. If a child is instructed at home pursuant to § 15–802, the person who has custody of the child shall, within thirty days after the home instruction begins, provide to the county school superintendent of the county in which the child resides one of the following:

1. A certified copy of the child's birth certificate.

2. Other reliable proof of the child's identity and age, including the child's baptismal certificate, an application for a social security number or original school registration records and an affidavit explaining the inability to provide a copy of the birth certificate.

3. A letter from the authorized representative of an agency having custody of the pupil pursuant to title 8, chapter 2 certifying that the pupil has been placed in the custody of the agency as prescribed by law.

C. On presentation of a document pursuant to this section, a photocopy of the document shall be placed in the pupil's file and the document that is presented shall be returned.

D. On the failure of a person enrolling a pupil or instructing a child at home to comply with subsection A or B of this section, the school, school district or county school superintendent shall notify that person in writing that, unless the person complies within ten days, the case shall be referred to the local law enforcement agency for investigation. If compliance is not obtained within the ten day period, the school, school district or county school superintendent shall refer the case to the local law enforcement agency.

E. The school, school district or county school superintendent shall immediately report to the local law enforcement agency any affidavit received pursuant to this section which appears inaccurate or suspicious in form or content.

F. Within five school days after enrolling a transfer pupil from a private school or another school district, a school shall request directly from the pupil's previous school a certified copy of the pupil's record. The requesting school shall exercise due diligence in obtaining the copy of the record requested. Notwithstanding any financial debt owed by the pupil, any school requested to forward a copy of a transferring pupil's record to the new school shall comply and forward the record within ten school days after receipt of the request unless the record has been flagged pursuant to § 15–829. If the record has been flagged, the requested school shall not forward the copy and shall notify the local law enforcement agency of the request. School districts shall include in the educational records required by this subsection data collected pursuant to §§ 15–741 and 15–766, as prescribed by the state board of education.

G. Any disclosure of educational records by the school district or charter school shall comply with the family educational rights and privacy act of 1974 (20 United States code § 1232g).

H. The provisions of this section do not apply to homeless pupils as defined in § 15–824, subsection C.

Added by Laws 1987, Ch. 254, § 1. Amended by Laws 1989, Ch. 273, § 13, eff. June 26, 1989; Laws 1990, Ch. 157, § 1; Laws 1990, Ch. 233, § 12; Laws 1990, Ch. 367, § 5; Laws 1991, Ch. 298, § 16; Laws 2000, Ch. 236, § 16, eff. April 12, 2000.

[1] Section 8–201 et seq.

Historical and Statutory Notes

The amendment of this section by Laws 1990, Ch. 233, § 12, was repealed by Laws 1991, Ch. 298, § 17.

Laws 1991, Ch. 298, § 1, par. 8, provides:

"**Section 1. Purpose**"

"8. Section 15–828, Arizona Revised Statutes, was amended by Laws 1990, chapter 157, § 1, Laws 1990, chapter 233, § 12 and Laws 1990, chapter 367, § 5. The chapter 233 version could not be blended because it was incompatible in part with the blended version. Since the substance of the chapter 233 version was not inconsistent, it was incorporated into the 1990 blended version of § 15–828, Arizona Revised Statutes, and the chapter 233 version is repealed."

The 1991 amendment of this section by Ch. 298 explicitly amended the 1990 amendments of this section by Chs. 157 and 367.

Reviser's Notes:

1990 Note. Prior to the 1991 amendment, this section contained the amendments made by Laws 1990, Ch. 157, § 1 and Ch. 367, § 5 which were blended together pursuant to authority of § 41–1304.03. Pursuant to authority of § 41–1304.02, in the section heading "; exception" was added.

1990 Note. The amendment made by Laws 1990, Ch. 233, § 12 was inconsistent and incompatible with Laws 1990, Ch. 157 and Laws 1990, Ch. 367 and therefore could not be blended.

2000 Note. Pursuant to authority of § 41–1304.02, in subsection G "rights" was transposed to follow "educational".

§ 15–829. Missing child; notification of school; flagging records; definitions

A. When a child is reported missing by a parent or guardian, the law enforcement agency receiving the report shall notify as soon as is appropriate the school the child was attending, if any, or the county school superintendent if the child was being instructed at home. The notification shall include all of the following:

1. The missing child's name.
2. The missing child's date of birth.

3. The missing child's county and state of birth.

4. The missing child's social security number, if any.

5. The physical description of the missing child.

B. When a school is notified pursuant to subsection A that a child is missing, the school shall flag the records of the child. If a copy of or information regarding the records is requested the school shall immediately report the request concerning the flagged records to a local law enforcement agency.

C. The law enforcement agency receiving the report shall notify the school or county school superintendent if the missing child is recovered and the school or county school superintendent shall remove the flag on the records.

D. For purposes of this section:

1. "Flag" means to mark or identify as pertaining to a missing child, or an indication identifying an item as pertaining to a missing child.

2. "Missing child" means a person who is under the age of eighteen years, whose temporary or permanent residence is in this state or is believed to be in this state, whose location has not been determined and who has been reported as missing to a law enforcement agency.

Added by Laws 1987, Ch. 254, § 1.

ARTICLE 3. SUSPENSION AND EXPULSION OF PUPILS

Historical and Statutory Notes

Reviser's Notes:

1981 Note. Pursuant to authority of § 41–1304.02, in the heading of this article the word "pupils" was substituted for the word "students".

§ 15–840. Definitions

In this article, unless the context otherwise requires:

1. "Expulsion" means the permanent withdrawal of the privilege of attending a school unless the governing board reinstates the privilege of attending the school.

2. "Suspension" means the temporary withdrawal of the privilege of attending a school for a specified period of time.

Added by Laws 1985, Ch. 195, § 1.

§ 15–841. Responsibilities of pupils; expulsion; alternative education programs; community service; placement review committee

A. Pupils shall comply with the rules, pursue the required course of study and submit to the authority of the teachers, the administrators and the governing board. A teacher may send a pupil to the principal's office in order to maintain effective discipline in the classroom. If a pupil is sent to the principal's office pursuant to this subsection, the principal shall employ appropriate discipline management techniques that are consistent with rules adopted by the school district governing board. A teacher may remove a pupil from the classroom if either of the following conditions exists:

1. The teacher has documented that the pupil has repeatedly interfered with the teacher's ability to communicate effectively with the other pupils in the classroom or with the ability of the other pupils to learn.

2. The teacher has determined that the pupil's behavior is so unruly, disruptive or abusive that it seriously interferes with the teacher's ability to communicate effectively with the other pupils in the classroom or with the ability of the other pupils to learn.

B. A pupil may be expelled for continued open defiance of authority, continued disruptive or disorderly behavior, violent behavior that includes use or display of a dangerous instrument or a deadly weapon as defined in § 13–105, use or possession of a gun, or excessive absenteeism. A pupil may be expelled for excessive absenteeism only if the pupil has reached the age or completed the grade after which school attendance is not required as prescribed in § 15–802. A school district may expel pupils for actions other than those listed in this subsection as the school district deems appropriate.

C. A school district may refuse to admit any pupil who has been expelled from another educational institution or who is in the process of being expelled from another educational institution.

D. A school district may annually or upon the request of any pupil or the parent or guardian review the reasons for expulsion and consider readmission.

E. As an alternative to suspension or expulsion, the school district may reassign any pupil to an alternative education program if the pupil does not meet the requirements for participation in the alternative to suspension program prescribed in subsection H of this section and if good cause exists for expulsion or for a long-term suspension.

F. A school district may also reassign a pupil to an alternative educational program if the pupil refuses to comply with rules, refuses to pursue the required course of study or refuses to submit to the authority of teachers, administrators or the governing board.

G. A school district or charter school shall expel from school for a period of not less than one year a pupil who is determined to have brought a firearm to a school within the jurisdiction of the school district or the charter school, except that the school district or charter school may modify this expulsion requirement for a pupil on a case by case basis. This subsection shall be construed consistently with the requirements of the individuals with disabilities education act (20 United States Code §§ 1400 through 1420). For the purposes of this subsection:

1. "Expel" may include removing a pupil from a regular school setting and providing educational services in an alternative setting.

2. "Firearm" means a firearm as defined in 18 United States Code § 921.

H. A school district or charter school shall expel from school for at least one year a pupil who is determined to have threatened an educational institution as defined in § 13–2911, except that the school district or charter school may modify this expulsion requirement for a pupil on a case by case basis if the pupil participates in mediation, community service, restitution or other programs in which the pupil takes responsibility for the results of the threat. This subsection shall be construed consistently with the requirements of the individuals with disabilities education act (20 United States Code §§ 1400 through 1420). A school district may reassign a pupil who is subject to expulsion pursuant to this subsection to an alternative education program pursuant to subsection E of this section if the pupil participates in mediation, community service, restitution or other programs in which the pupil takes responsibility for the threat. a school district or charter school may require the pupil's parent or guardian to participate in mediation, community service, restitution or other programs in which the parent or guardian takes responsibility with the pupil for the threat. For the purposes of this subsection, "threatened an educational institution" means to interfere with or disrupt an educational institution by doing any of the following:

1. For the purpose of causing, or in reckless disregard of causing, interference with or disruption of an educational institution, threatening to cause physical injury to any employee of an educational institution or any person attending an educational institution.

2. For the purpose of causing, or in reckless disregard of causing, interference with or disruption of an educational institution, threatening to cause damage to any educational institution, the property of any educational institution, the property of any employee of an educational institution or the property of any person attending an educational institution.

3. Going on or remaining on the property of any educational institution for the purpose of interfering with or disrupting the lawful use of the property or in any manner as to deny or interfere with the lawful use of the property by others.

4. Refusing to obey a lawful order to leave the property of an educational institution.

I. By January 1, 2001, Each school district shall establish an alternative to suspension program in consultation with local law enforcement officials or school resource officers. The school district governing board shall adopt policies to determine the requirements for participation in the alternative to suspension program. Pupils who would otherwise be subject to suspension pursuant to this article and who meet the school district's requirements for participation in the alternative to suspension program shall be transferred to a location on school premises that is isolated from other pupils or transferred to a location that is not on school premises. The alternative to suspension program shall be discipline intensive and require academic work, and may require community service, groundskeeping and litter control, parent supervision, and evaluation or other appropriate activities. The community service, groundskeeping and litter control, and other appropriate activities may be performed on school grounds or at any other designated area.

J. Each school shall establish a placement review committee to determine the placement of a pupil if a teacher refuses to readmit the pupil to the teacher's class and to make recommendations to the governing board regarding the readmission of expelled pupils. The process for determining the placement of a pupil in a new class or replacement in the existing class shall not exceed three business days from the date the pupil was first removed from the existing class. The principal shall not return a pupil to the classroom from which the pupil was removed without the teacher's consent unless the committee determines that the return of the pupil to that classroom is the best or only practicable alternative. The committee shall be composed of two teachers who are employed at the school and who are selected by the faculty members of the school and one administrator who is employed by the school and who is selected by the principal. The faculty members of the school shall select a third teacher to serve as an alternate member of the committee. If the teacher who refuses to readmit the pupil is a member of the committee, that teacher shall be excused from participating in the determination of the pupil's readmission and the alternate teacher member shall replace that teacher on the committee until the conclusion of all matters relating to that pupil's readmission.

Added by Laws 1981, Ch. 1, § 2, eff. Jan. 23, 1981. Amended by Laws 1984, Ch. 393, § 1; Laws 1994, Ch. 315, § 15; Laws 1995, Ch. 268, § 47; Laws 1995, Ch. 280, § 1; Laws 1997, Ch. 82, § 1; Laws 2000, Ch. 82, § 1; Laws 2000, Ch. 226, § 4, eff. April 10, 2000.

Historical and Statutory Notes

Source:

Laws 1912, Ch. 77, §§ 86, 87.
Civ. Code 1913, §§ 2799, 2800.
Laws 1921, Ch. 145, § 1.
Rev. Code 1928, § 1031.
Code 1939, § 54-503.
A.R.S. former § 15-305.

The 1984 amendment deleted "or" preceding "habitual", deleted "and" preceding "vulgarity", inserted "or excessive absenteeism" in the first sentence, and added the second sentence in subsec. B.

The 1994 amendment rewrote this section which, prior to amendment, provided:

"**A.** Pupils shall comply with the regulations, pursue the required course of study and submit to the authority of the teachers and the governing board.

"**B.** Continued open defiance of authority, habitual profanity, vulgarity or excessive absenteeism constitute good causes for expulsion. A pupil may be expelled for excessive absenteeism only if the pupil has reached the age or completed the grade after which school attendance is not required as prescribed in § 15-802."

The 1995 amendment by Ch. 268 added a subsec. G, relating to programs allowing pupils to perform community service as an alternative to suspension.

The 1995 amendment by Ch. 280, in subsec. B, deleted "only" following "A pupil may", and added the last sentence providing that the school district may expel pupils for actions other than those listed in the subsection; and added a subsec. G, relating to expulsion of a student who brings a firearm to school.

The 1997 amendment by Ch. 82 rewrote subsec. A, and added subsec. I. Subsec. A had read, "Pupils shall comply with the rules, pursue the required course of study and submit to the authority of the teachers, the administrators and the governing board."

The 2000 amendment by Ch. 82 inserted, in subsec. E, "the pupil does not meet the requirements for participation in the alternative to suspension program prescribed in subsection H of this section and if" preceding "good cause exists"; substituted "pupil " for "student" in two instances in subsec. G; and rewrote subsec. H, which formerly read:

"**H.** School districts may develop a program that will allow pupils to perform community service as am alternative to suspension. The community service may be performed on school grounds or at any other designated area."

The 2000 amendment by Ch. 226, in addition to some minor, nonsubstantive changes, inserted a new subsec. H, redesignating subsequent subsections accordingly.

Reviser's Notes:

1994 Note. Pursuant to authority of § 41-1304.02, in the section heading "certain" was deleted.

1995 Note. Prior to the 1997 amendment, this section contained the amendments made by Laws 1995, Ch. 268, sec. 47 and Ch. 280, sec. 1 that were blended together pursuant to authority of § 41-1304.03. Pursuant to authority of § 41-1304.02, in the section heading "; definitions" was removed.

1997 Note. Pursuant to authority of § 41-1304.02, in the section heading "; placement review committee" was added after "service".

2000 Note. This section contains the amendments made by Laws 2000, Ch. 82, sec. 1 and Ch. 226, sec. 4 that were blended together as shown above pursuant to authority of § 41-1304.03. Pursuant to authority of § 41-1304.02, "Responsibilities of pupils; expulsion; alternative education programs; community service; placement review committee" was substituted for the previous section heading.

§ 15-842. Damage to school property; suspension or expulsion of pupil; liability of parent

A. A pupil who cuts, defaces or otherwise injures any school property may be suspended or expelled.

B. Upon complaint of the governing board, the parents or guardians of minors who have injured school property shall be liable for all damages caused by their children or wards.

Added by Laws 1981, Ch. 1, § 2, eff. Jan. 23, 1981.

Historical and Statutory Notes

Source:

Laws 1912, Ch. 77, § 88.
Civ. Code 1913, § 2801.
Rev. Code 1928, § 1032.
Code 1939, § 54-504.
A.R.S. former § 15-446.
Laws 1960, Ch. 127, § 33.

§ 15-843. Pupil disciplinary proceedings

A. An action concerning discipline, suspension or expulsion of a pupil is not subject to the provisions of title 38, chapter 3, article 3.1, [1] except that the governing board of a school district shall post regular notice and shall take minutes of any hearing held by the governing board concerning the discipline, suspension or expulsion of a pupil.

B. The governing board of any school district shall, in consultation with the teachers and parents of the school district, prescribe rules for the discipline, suspension and expulsion of pupils. The rules shall be consistent with the constitutional rights of pupils and shall include at least the following:

1. Penalties for excessive pupil absenteeism pursuant to § 15-803 including failure in a subject, failure to pass a grade, suspension or expulsion.

2. Procedures for the use of corporal punishment if allowed by the governing board.

3. Procedures for the reasonable use of physical force by certificated or classified personnel in self-defense, defense of others and defense of property.

4. Procedures for dealing with pupils who have committed or are believed to have committed a crime.

5. A notice and hearing procedure for cases concerning the suspension of a pupil for more than ten days.

6. Procedures and conditions for readmission of a pupil who has been expelled or suspended for more than ten days.

7. Procedures for appeal to the governing board of the suspension of a pupil for more than ten days, if the decision to suspend the pupil was not made by the governing board.

8. Procedures for appeal of the recommendation of the hearing officer or officers designated by the board as provided in subsection F at the time the board considers the recommendation.

C. Penalties adopted under subsection B, paragraph 1 for excessive absenteeism shall not be applied to pupils who have completed the course requirements and whose absence from school is due solely to illness, disease or accident as certified by a person licensed under title 32, chapter 7, 13 or 17.[2]

D. The governing board shall:

1. Support and assist teachers in the implementation and enforcement of the rules prescribed in subsection B.

2. Develop procedures allowing teachers and principals to recommend the suspension or expulsion of pupils.

3. Develop procedures allowing teachers and principals to temporarily remove disruptive pupils from a class.

4. Delegate to the principal the authority to remove a disruptive pupil from the classroom.

E. If a pupil withdraws from school after receiving notice of possible action concerning discipline, expulsion or suspension, the governing board may continue with the action after the withdrawal and may record the results of such action in the pupil's permanent file.

F. In all action concerning the expulsion of a pupil, the governing board of a school district shall:

1. Be notified of the intended action.

2. Decide, in executive session, whether to hold a hearing or to designate one or more hearing officers to hold a hearing to hear the evidence, prepare a record and bring a recommendation to the board for action and whether the hearing shall be held in executive session.

3. Give written notice, at least five working days prior to the hearing by the governing board or the hearing officer or officers designated by the governing board, to all pupils subject to expulsion and their parents or guardians of the date, time and place of the hearing. If the governing board decides that the hearing is to be held in executive session, the written notice shall include a statement of the right of the parents or legal guardians or an emancipated pupil subject to expulsion to indicate their objection to the governing board's decision to have the hearing held in executive session. Objections shall be made in writing to the governing board.

G. If a parent, legal guardian or emancipated pupil subject to expulsion disagrees that the hearing should be held in executive session, then it shall be held in an open meeting unless:

1. If only one pupil is subject to expulsion and disagreement exists between that pupil's parents or legal guardians, the governing board, after consultations with the pupil's parents or legal guardians or the emancipated pupil, shall decide in executive session whether the hearing will be in executive session.

2. If more than one pupil is subject to expulsion and disagreement exists between the parents or guardians of different pupils, then separate hearings shall be held subject to the provisions of this section.

H. Nothing in this section shall be construed to prevent the pupil who is subject to expulsion or suspension, and the pupil's parents or legal guardians and legal counsel, from attending any executive session pertaining to the proposed disciplinary action, from having access to the minutes and testimony of the executive session or from recording the session at the parent's or legal guardian's expense.

I. In schools employing a superintendent or a principal, the authority to suspend a pupil from school is vested in the superintendent, principal or other school officials granted this power by the governing board of the school district.

J. In schools that do not have a superintendent or principal, a teacher may suspend a pupil from school.

K. In all cases of suspension, it shall be for good cause and shall be reported within five days to the governing board by the superintendent or the person imposing the suspension.

L. A teacher who fails to comply with this section is guilty of unprofessional conduct and the teacher's certificate may be revoked.

M. The principal of each school shall insure that a copy of all rules pertaining to discipline, suspension and expulsion of pupils is distributed to the parents of each pupil at the time the pupil is enrolled in school.

N. The principal of each school shall insure that all rules pertaining to the discipline, suspension and expulsion of pupils are communicated to students at the beginning of each school year, and to transfer students at the time of their enrollment in the school.

Added by Laws 1981, Ch. 1, § 2, eff. Jan. 1, 1981. Amended by Laws 1983, Ch. 146, § 1; Laws 1984, Ch. 393, § 2; Laws 1985, Ch. 195, § 2; Laws 1986, Ch. 84, § 2; Laws 1994, 9th S.S., Ch. 2, § 13; Laws 1996, Ch. 284, § 41; Laws 1997, Ch. 231, § 21; Laws 2000, Ch. 277, § 2.

[1] Section 38-431 et seq.

[2] Section 32-801 et seq., 32-1401 et seq., or 32-1801 et seq.

Historical and Statutory Notes

Source:

Laws 1912, Ch. 77, § 92.
Civ. Code 1913, § 2805.
Rev. Code 1928, § 1041.
Code 1939, § 54-1001.
A.R.S. former § 15-204.
Laws 1960, Ch. 127, § 9.
Laws 1971, Ch. 14, § 1.
Laws 1978, Ch. 193, § 1.
Laws 1979, Ch. 181, § 1.

The 1983 amendment inserted a new subsec. B; relettered former subsecs. B to H as subsecs. C to I; substituted "expulsion or suspension for more than ten days" for "discipline, suspension or expulsion" in the first sentence of subsec. C, inserted a new par. 1, and renumbered former pars. 1 and 2 as pars. 2 and 3 of subsec. C; and added subsecs. J and K.

The 1984 amendment, in subsec. A, deleted "or pupils" following "pupil"; in subsec. B, inserted "in consultation with the teachers and parents of the school district", and "the rules shall include at least the following:" in the introduction, and inserted pars. 1 through 4; inserted subsecs. C and D, relettered subsequent subsections; and in subsec. E, deleted "or pupils" following "pupil"; in subsec. F, deleted "parents," following "parent," substituted "disagrees" for "disagree"; in subsec. G, deleted "or pupils" following "pupil", substituted "is" for "are", and "his" for "their".

The 1985 amendment added pars. 5 to 7 to subsec. A, rewrote subsec. E, substituted in subsec. F, "expulsion" for "the proposed action", substituted "expulsion or suspension" for "the action" in subsec. G, and substituted in subsec. J, "the superintendent or the person imposing the suspension" for "the person imposing it". Prior to amendment subsec. E provided:

"**E.** In all action concerning the suspension for more than ten days or expulsion of a pupil, the governing board of a school district shall:

"1. Be notified of the intended action.

"2. Decide, in executive session, whether a hearing is necessary.

"3. Give written notice, at least five working days prior to the hearing, to all pupils subject to the proposed action and their parents or legal guardians of the board's decision to hold the hearing in executive session, the date, time and place of the hearing and the right of the parents or legal guardians or an emancipated pupil subject to the proposed action to indicate their objection to the board's decision to have an executive session. Such objections shall be made in writing to the governing board."

The 1986 amendment inserted a new subsec. C, and redesignated other subsections accordingly.

The 1994 amendment by 9th S.S., Ch. 2, in subsec. D, inserted "and principals" in pars. 2 and 3, and added par. 4.

The 1996 amendment by Ch. 284, in subsec. B, deleted the former second sentence of par. 2, which had read, "These procedures shall be consistent with guidelines prescribed by the state board of education."; in subsec. F, substituted a reference to guardians for a reference to legal guardians in the first sentence of par. 3; and in subsec. H, made a nonsubstantive language and punctuation change.

The 1997 amendment by Ch. 231 inserted "by certificated or classified personnel" in subsec. B, par. 3; and inserted "or guardians" in par. 2 of subsec. G.

The 2000 amendment by Ch. 277, in subsec. A, inserted 'not' preceding 'subject' and substituted 'an action' for 'no action'; in subsec. B, inserted 'shall be consistent with the constitutional rights of pupils' in the second sentence; in subsec. B, par 1, inserted 'pursuant to § 15-803' after 'absenteeism'; added subsec. B, par 6, relating to readmission and renumbering the remainder; and in subsec. L, substituted 'may' for 'shall' and 'the teacher's' for 'his.'

Reviser's Notes:

1981 Note. Pursuant to authority of § 41-1304.02, in the heading of this section the word "pupil" was substituted for the word "student".

1983 Note. Pursuant to authority of § 41-1304.02, in subsection C "suspension for more than ten days" and "or" were transposed to precede "expulsion".

§ 15-844. Suspension and expulsion proceedings for children with disabilities

Notwithstanding §§ 15-841 and 15-842, the suspension or expulsion of children with disabilities, as defined in § 15-761, shall be in accordance with the individuals with disabilities education act (20 United States Code §§ 1410 through 1485) [1] and federal regulations issued pursuant to the individuals with disabilities education act.

Added by Laws 1991, Ch. 190, § 1. Amended by Laws 1992, Ch. 172, § 16; Laws 1999, Ch. 67, § 1.

[1] 20 U.S.C.A. §§ 1410 through 1485.

Historical and Statutory Notes

The 1992 amendment by Ch. 172 rewrote the section, which had read:

"Notwithstanding §§ 15-841, 15-842 and 15-843, the suspension or expulsion of handicapped children, as defined in § 15-761, shall be in accordance with rules prescribed by the state board of education which shall be in conformity with the individuals with disabilities education act, (20 United States Code §§ 1410 through 1485)."

The 1999 amendment by Ch. 67 rewrote the section, which had read:

"Notwithstanding §§ 15-841, and 15-843, the suspension or expulsion of children with disabilities, as defined in § 15-761, shall be in accordance with rules which are prescribed by the state board of education and which shall incorporate the change of placement requirements of the individuals with disabilities education act (20 United States Code §§ 1410 through 1485) and applicable case law regarding suspension and expulsion of children with disabilities."

Reviser's Notes:

1991 Note. Pursuant to authority of § 41-1304.02, in the section heading "; definitions" was deleted.

ARTICLE 4. PART–TIME SCHOOLS AND YEAR–ROUND SCHOOL YEAR OPERATION

Laws 1990, Ch. 322, § 17, effective June 20, 1990, substituted "Part-time Schools and Year-round School Year Operation" for "Part-time Schools and Extended School Year Operation" as the heading for this article.

§§ 15–851, 15–852. Repealed by Laws 1993, Ch. 202, § 11, eff. April 21, 1993

Historical and Statutory Notes

Section 15–851, added by Laws 1981, Ch. 1, § 2, which related to part-time schools for employed children and school hours counted as employment, was derived from:

Section 15–852, added by Laws 1981, Ch. 1, § 2, which related to rules and regulations governing the establishment of part-time schools and reimbursement of the school district for expenses, was derived from:

§ 15–853. Repealed by Laws 1996, Ch. 284, § 42

Historical and Statutory Notes

The repealed section, added by Laws 1981, Ch. 1, § 2, amended by Laws 1990, Ch. 322, § 5; Laws 1995, Ch. 191, § 7, derived from A.R.S. former § 15–1137; Laws 1972, Ch. 115, § 4; Laws 1980, 2nd S.S., Ch. 9, § 50, related to the powers and duties of the state board of education in year-round school year operation.

§ 15–854. Year-round school year operation; powers and duties of superintendent of public instruction

A. The superintendent of public instruction shall:

1. Prepare and distribute all necessary forms for application by any school district for state authorization for a school district year-round school year operation program.

2. Prepare and distribute all necessary budget or reporting forms which may be required for the purpose of this section and § 15–855.

3. Cooperate with and provide continued supervision of all year-round school year operation programs to determine compliance with the provisions of this section and § 15–855.

B. The superintendent of public instruction may:

1. Authorize a school district with program approval for year-round school year operation to employ a fiscal year other than one beginning on July 1 and ending on June 30, and to appropriately adjust the respective budget dates.

2. Authorize and assist in arrangements for any necessary adjustments of employment contracts, the dates and respective percentages of apportionments of state aid and the student count to be based on each pupil's attendance during the respective one hundred seventy-five days or two hundred days, as applicable, of school operation, or the equivalent as approved by the superintendent of public instruction, in which the pupil is enrolled.

Added by Laws 1981, Ch. 1, § 2, eff. Jan. 23, 1981. Amended by Laws 1990, Ch. 322, § 6, eff. June 20, 1990; Laws 1996, Ch. 284, § 43; Laws 1998, Ch. 167, § 5; Laws 2000, Ch. 97, § 4.

Historical and Statutory Notes

Source:
Laws 1972, Ch. 115, § 4.
A.R.S. former § 15–1137.01.
Laws 1980, 2nd S.S., Ch. 9, § 51.

§ 15–855. School or school district operation on a year-round school year basis; separate budget

A. Any school district which is qualified may operate on a four quarter, three semester or other year-round school year operation basis in cooperation with and under the supervision of the superintendent of public instruction.

B. Any school district which operates some but not all of its schools on a year-round school year operation basis shall remove such schools from the school district budget, proportionately reduce the school district budget amounts and employ a separate budget for each of its schools with a year-round school year operation.

C. The superintendent of public instruction shall supervise the conversion of any school district budget as required by subsection B of this section to insure application of all budget requirements.

D. For school districts which maintain an approved year-round school year operation, entitlement to state aid shall be based on the one hundred seventy-five days' equivalency or two hundred days' equivalency, as applicable, of instructional time as approved by the superintendent of public instruction during which each student is enrolled.

Added by Laws 1981, Ch. 1, § 2, eff. Jan. 23, 1981. Amended by Laws 1990, Ch. 322, § 7, eff. June 20, 1990; Laws 1990, Ch. 399, § 1, eff. July 5, 1990; Laws 1991, Ch. 298, § 18; Laws 1998, Ch. 167, § 6; Laws 2000, Ch. 97, § 5.

Historical and Statutory Notes

Source:
Laws 1972, Ch. 115, § 4.
A.R.S. former § 15–1137.02.
Laws 1976, Ch. 162, § 19.
Laws 1980, 2nd S.S., Ch. 9, § 52.

Laws 1991, Ch. 298, § 1, par. 9, provides:

"**Section 1. Purpose**"

"9. Section 15–855, Arizona Revised Statutes, was amended by Laws 1990, chapter 322, § 7 and Laws 1990, chapter 399, § 1. The chapter 399 version failed to amend the chapter 322 version, which was an emergency enactment, and therefore did not comply with the requirements of article IV, part 2, § 14, Constitution of Arizona. To accomplish the intent of these enactments, in this act the Laws 1990, chapter 322 version of § 15–855, Arizona Revised Statutes, is amended to incorporate the amendments made by Laws 1990, chapter 399 and the chapter 399 version is repealed."

The amendment of this section by Laws 1990, Ch. 399, § 1, eff. July 5, 1990, was repealed by Laws 1991, Ch. 298, § 19.

The 1991 amendment of this section by Ch. 298 explicitly amended the 1990 amendment of this section by Ch. 322.

Reviser's Notes:

1990 Note. The amendment of this section by Laws 1990, Ch. 399, § 1 failed to set forth in full the text of the section as amended by Laws 1990, Ch. 322, § 7, an emergency act, as required by Constitution of Arizona Art. IV, part 2, § 14.

ARTICLE 5. FOUR DAY SCHOOL WEEK AND ALTERNATIVE KINDERGARTEN PROGRAMS

Article 5, consisting of § 15–861, was added by Laws 1985, Ch. 127, § 4, effective August 7, 1985.

Laws 1987, Ch. 93, § 3 substituted "Four Day School Week and Alternative Kindergarten Programs" for "Four Day School Week Programs" as the heading for this article.

§ 15-861. Four day school week and alternative kindergarten programs

A. A governing board, after at least two public hearings in the school district, may offer an educational program on the basis of a four day school week or an alternative kindergarten program on the basis of a three day school week, or both.

B. The instructional time in an educational program offered on the basis of a four day school week or in an alternative kindergarten program offered on the basis of a three day school week must be equal to the instructional time in an educational program or kindergarten program, as applicable, offered on the basis of a five day school week. Notwithstanding § 15-901, subsection A, paragraph 6, for school districts which offer an educational program on the basis of a four day school week in common schools or an alternative kindergarten program on the basis of a three day school week, or both, as provided in this section, the minimum number of minutes required for daily attendance shall be increased so that the number of minutes per day multiplied by the total number of school days per school year is at least equal to the number of minutes prescribed for that program or grade in § 15-901, subsection A, paragraph 6, multiplied by one hundred seventy-five.

Added by Laws 1985, Ch. 127, § 4. Amended by Laws 1987, Ch. 93, § 4; Laws 1988, Ch. 281, § 4; Laws 1996, Ch. 284, § 44.

ARTICLE 6. SCHOOL IMMUNIZATION

Article 6, School Immunization, consisting of §§ 15-871 to 15-874, was added by Laws 1990, Ch. 208, § 2, effective January 1, 1992.

Another Article 6, consisting of § 15-871, added by Laws 1990, Ch. 322, § 8, effective June 20, 1990, was transferred and renumbered as Article 7, consisting of § 15-881.

Historical and Statutory Notes

Laws 1990, Ch. 208, § 6, provides:

"**Sec. 6. Effective date**

"This act is effective from and after December 31, 1991."

Reviser's Notes:

1990 Note. Laws 1990, Ch. 322, § 8 added another new title 15, chapter 8, article 6 and § 15-871 that were renumbered as title 15, chapter 8, article 7 and § 15-881 pursuant to authority of § 41-1304.02.

§ 15-871. Definitions

In this article, unless the context otherwise requires:

1. "Documentary proof" means written evidence that a pupil has been immunized or has laboratory evidence of immunity which conforms with the standards promulgated pursuant to § 15-872.

2. "Dose" means the number in a series of immunizations which may be prescribed pursuant to § 36-672.

3. "Health agency" means a local health department or similar governmental agency established pursuant to the laws of another state or country and its officers and employees.

4. "Homeless pupil" means a pupil who has a primary residence that is:

(a) A supervised publicly or privately operated shelter designed to provide temporary living accommodations.

(b) An institution that provides a temporary residence for individuals intended to be institutionalized.

(c) A public or private place not designed for, or ordinarily used as a regular sleeping accommodation for, human beings.

5. "Immunization" means the process of inoculation with a specific antigen to promote antibody formation in the body.

6. "Immunized" means the required initial immunization and boosters or reimmunization prescribed pursuant to § 36–672.

7. "Laboratory evidence of immunity" means written evidence of serologic confirmation of the presence of specific antibodies against an immunization-preventable disease which is signed by a physician or an authorized representative of a health agency.

8. "Local health department" means a local health department established pursuant to title 36, chapter 1, article 4.[1]

9. "Physician" means a person licensed pursuant to title 32, chapter 13, 17 or 29 [2] or a person licensed to practice allopathic or osteopathic medicine under the laws of another state or country.

10. "Pupil" means a person who is eligible to receive instruction at a school and includes pre-kindergarten age children receiving either services for children with disabilities or day care on a school campus otherwise exempt from day care rules pursuant to § 36–884.

11. "School" means a public, private or parochial school that offers instruction at any level or grade through twelfth grade, except for day care facilities regulated pursuant to title 36, chapter 7.1.[3]

12. "School administrator" means the principal or person having general daily control and supervision of the school or that person's designee.

13. "Suspension" or "suspended" means:

(a) For a pupil attending a public school, the temporary withdrawal of the privilege of attending school pursuant to § 15–843.

(b) For a pupil attending a private or parochial school, the temporary withdrawal of the privilege of attending school pursuant to the policies and procedures of the private or parochial school.

Added by Laws 1990, Ch. 208, § 2, eff. Jan. 1, 1992. Amended by Laws 2000, Ch. 11, § 1; Laws 2000, Ch. 236, § 17, eff. April 12, 2000.

[1] Sections 36–161 et seq., 36–181 et seq.

[2] Sections 32–1401 et seq., 32–1800 et seq., and 32–2901 et seq.

[3] Section 36–881 et seq.

Historical and Statutory Notes

Another § 15–871 was renumbered as § 15–881.

For applicable retroactive application provision of Laws 2000, Ch. 11, see note preceding § 48–5901.

Reviser's Notes:

2000 Note. This section contains the amendments made by Laws 2000, Ch. 11, sec. 1 and Ch. 236, sec. 17 that were blended together as shown above pursuant to authority of § 41-1304.03.

§ 15-872. Proof of immunization; noncompliance; notice to parents; civil immunity

A. The director of the department of health services, in consultation with the superintendent of public instruction, shall develop by rule standards for documentary proof.

B. A pupil shall not be allowed to attend school without submitting documentary proof to the school administrator unless the pupil is exempted from immunization pursuant to § 15-873.

C. Each public school shall make full disclosure of the requirements and exemptions as prescribed in §§ 15-872 and 15-873.

D. On enrollment, the school administrator shall suspend that pupil if the administrator does not have documentary proof and the pupil is not exempted from immunization pursuant to § 15-873.

E. Notwithstanding subsections B and D of this section, a pupil may be admitted to or allowed to attend a school if the pupil has received at least one dose of each of the required immunizations prescribed pursuant to § 36-672 and has established a schedule for the completion of required immunizations. The parent, guardian or person in loco parentis of a pupil shall present to the school administrator documentary proof of the immunizations received and a schedule prepared by the pupil's physician or a health agency for completion of additional required immunizations.

F. The school administrator shall review the school immunization record for each pupil admitted or allowed to continue attendance pursuant to subsection E of this section at least twice each school year until the pupil receives all of the required immunizations and shall suspend a pupil as prescribed in subsection G of this section who fails to comply with the immunization schedule. Immunizations received by a pupil shall be entered in the pupil's school immunization record.

G. Unless proof of an exemption from immunization pursuant to § 15-873 is provided, a pupil who is admitted or allowed to continue to attend and who fails to comply with the immunization schedule within the time intervals specified by the schedule shall be suspended from school attendance until documentary proof of the administration of another dose of each appropriate immunizing agent is provided to the school administrator.

H. The provisions of subsections B, D and E of this section do not apply to homeless pupils until the fifth calendar day after enrollment.

I. A school and its employees are immune from civil liability for decisions concerning the admission, readmission and suspension of a pupil which are based on a good faith implementation of the requirements of this article.
Added by Laws 1990, Ch. 208, § 2, eff. Jan. 1, 1992.

Historical and Statutory Notes

Laws 1990, Ch. 208, § 5, effective January 1, 1992, provides:

"**Sec. 5. Applicability**

"Notwithstanding § 15-872, Arizona Revised Statutes, as added by this act, pupils enrolled in any school in this state before the effective date of this act are not required to submit additional documentary proof if the parent, guardian or person in loco parentis of the pupil has previously submitted a statement to the school administrator in that school district in accordance with the laws in effect at the time of admission stating that the pupil has received the required immunizations. A pupil is not exempted from being required to receive additional doses of an immunizing agent or additional immunizations if the department of health services determines that additional doses or immunizations are necessary."

§ 15-873. Exemptions; nonattendance during outbreak

A. Documentary proof is not required for a pupil to be admitted to school if one of the following occurs:

1. The parent or guardian of the pupil submits a signed statement to the school administrator stating that the parent or guardian has received information about immunizations provided by the department of health services, understands the risks and benefits of immunizations and the potential risks of nonimmunization and that due to personal beliefs, the parent or guardian does not consent to the immunization of the pupil.

2. The school administrator receives written certification which is signed by the parent or guardian and by a physician, which states that one or more of the required immunizations may be detrimental to the pupil's health and which indicates the specific nature and probable duration of the medical condition or circumstance which precludes immunization.

B. An exemption pursuant to subsection A, paragraph 2 is only valid during the duration of the circumstance or condition which precludes immunization.

C. Pupils who lack documentary proof of immunization shall not attend school during outbreak periods of communicable immunization-preventable diseases as determined by the department of health services or local health department. The department of health services or local health department shall transmit notice of this determination to the school administrator responsible for the exclusion of the pupils.

Added by Laws 1990, Ch. 208, § 2, eff. Jan. 1, 1992.

§ 15-874. Records; reporting requirements

A. Each pupil's immunizations shall be recorded on the school immunization record. The school immunization record shall be a standardized form developed by the department of health services in conjunction with the department of education and provided by the department of health services and shall be a part of the mandatory permanent student record. The records are open to inspection by the department of health services and the local health department.

B. Each immunization record shall contain at least the following information:

1. The pupil's name and birth date.

2. The date of the pupil's admission to the school.

3. The type of immunizing agents administered to the pupil.

4. The date each dose of immunizing agent is administered to the pupil.

5. The established schedule for completion of immunizations if the pupil is admitted to or allowed to continue to attend a school pursuant to § 15-872, subsection E.

6. Laboratory evidence of immunity if this evidence is presented as part of a pupil's documentary proof.

7. If an exemption from immunization as provided in § 15-873 is submitted to the school administrator, the date the exemption is submitted and the reason for the exemption.

8. Additional information prescribed by the director of the department of health services by rule.

C. A school shall transfer an immunization record with the mandatory permanent student record and provide at no charge, on request, a copy of the immunization record to the parent or guardian of the pupil.

D. By November 30 of each school year, each school district and private school shall complete and file a report with the local health department and the department of health services, using forms provided by the department of health services. The report shall state the number of pupils attending who have completed required immunizations or who have submitted laboratory evidence of immunity, the number of pupils attending with uncompleted required immunizations and the number of pupils attending with an exemption from immunization pursuant to § 15-873.

Added by Laws 1990, Ch. 208, § 2, eff. Jan. 1, 1992.

ARTICLE 7. EXTENDED SCHOOL YEAR FOR HANDICAPPED PUPILS

Article 7, Extended School Year for Handicapped Pupils, consisting of § 15-881 (added as Article 6, consisting of § 15-871, by Laws 1990, Ch. 322, § 8, effective June 20, 1990) was transferred for placement here and renumbered.

§ 15-881. Extended school year programs for pupils with disabilities; eligibility and program structure; definition

A. Each school district shall make an extended school year program available to all pupils with disabilities for whom such a program is necessary in order to either:

1. Prevent irreparable harm to the pupil's ability to maintain identified skills or behavior.

2. Accommodate critical learning periods for pupils who are unlikely to receive another opportunity to learn or generalize targeted skills or behavior.

B. The state board of education shall prescribe rules for use by school districts in determining the eligibility of pupils with disabilities for an extended school year program. The rules adopted by the state board pursuant to this subsection shall include the following criteria for determining the eligibility of pupils with disabilities in an extended school year program:

1. Regression-recoupment factors.
2. Critical learning stages.
3. Least restrictive environment considerations.
4. Teacher and parent interviews and recommendations.
5. Data-based observations of the pupil.
6. Considerations of the pupil's previous history.
7. Parental skills and abilities.
8. Factors that are inappropriate considerations for eligibility.
9. Any other considerations deemed necessary and appropriate by the state board of education.

C. Rules that are adopted pursuant to subsection B of this section shall clarify that attendance in the program is not compulsory, that the program is not required for all pupils with disabilities and that eligibility for participation in the program is not based on need or desire for any of the following:

1. A day care or respite care service for pupils with disabilities.
2. A program to maximize the academic potential of pupils with disabilities.
3. A summer recreation program for pupils with disabilities.

D. For purposes of this section "extended school year" means additional special education and related services for pupils with disabilities to supplement the normal school year which are provided as part of a free and appropriate public education as defined in P.L.

Added as § 15–871 by Laws 1990, Ch. 322, § 8, eff. June 20, 1990. Renumbered as § 15–881. Amended by Laws 1996, Ch. 284, § 45; Laws 2000, Ch. 236, § 18, eff. April 12, 2000.

Historical and Statutory Notes

Laws 1990, Ch. 322, § 1, effective June 20, 1990, provides:

"**Section 1. Legislative intent**

"It is the intent of the legislature to ensure that all handicapped pupils receive a free and appropriate public education as required by Public Law 94–142 and that the additional monies provided by this act be used for the purpose of providing an extended school year program for handicapped pupils who are deemed eligible to participate in such a program."

Reviser's Notes:

1990 Note. The above article and section that comprises it were added by Laws 1990, Ch. 322, § 8 as title 15, chapter 8, article 6 and § 15–871 and were renumbered as title 15, chapter 8, article 7 and § 15–881 pursuant to authority of § 41–1304.02. In addition, in the section heading "; definition" was added after "structure" and in subsection C, paragraph 1 the hyphen was deleted between the words "day" and "care".

CHAPTER 9

SCHOOL DISTRICT BUDGETING AND FINANCIAL ASSISTANCE

ARTICLE 1. GENERAL PROVISIONS FOR SCHOOL DISTRICT BUDGETS

ARTICLE 1.1. CAREER LADDER AND OTHER PERFORMANCE INCENTIVE PROGRAMS

Section

ARTICLE 5. STATE AND LOCAL ASSISTANCE TO SCHOOL DISTRICTS AND ACCOMMODATION SCHOOLS

ARTICLE 6. COUNTY FINANCE RESPONSIBILITIES FOR SCHOOL DISTRICTS

ARTICLE 7. BOND ISSUES AND BONDED INDEBTEDNESS

Chapter 9, School District Budgeting and Financial Assistance, consisting of Article 1, §§ 15–901 to 15–909, Article 2, §§ 15–921 to 15–923, Article 3, §§ 15–941 to 15–950, Article 4, §§ 15–961 and 15–962, Article 5, §§ 15–971 to 15–976, Article 6, §§ 15–991 to 15–1003, and Article 7, §§ 15–1021 to 15–1033, was added by Laws 1981, Ch. 1, § 2, effective January 23, 1981.

ARTICLE 1. GENERAL PROVISIONS FOR SCHOOL DISTRICT BUDGETS

§ 15–901. Definitions

A. In this title, unless the context otherwise requires:

1. "Average daily attendance" or "ADA" means actual average daily attendance through the first one hundred days or two hundred days in session, as applicable.

2. "Average daily membership" means the total enrollment of fractional students and full-time students, minus withdrawals, of each school day through the first one hundred days or two hundred days in session, as applicable, for the current year. Withdrawals include students formally withdrawn from schools and students absent for ten consecutive school days, except for excused absences as identified by the department of education. For computation

purposes, the effective date of withdrawal shall be retroactive to the last day of actual attendance of the student.

(a) "Fractional student" means:

(i) For common schools, until fiscal year 2001–2002, a preschool child who is enrolled in a program for preschool children with disabilities of at least three hundred sixty minutes each week or a kindergarten student at least five years of age prior to January 1 of the school year and enrolled in a school kindergarten program that meets at least three hundred forty-six instructional hours during the minimum number of days required in a school year as provided in § 15–341. In fiscal year 2001–2002, the kindergarten program shall meet at least three hundred forty-eight hours. In fiscal year 2002–2003, the kindergarten program shall meet at least three hundred fifty hours. In fiscal year 2003–2004, the kindergarten program shall meet at least three hundred fifty-two hours. In fiscal year 2004–2005, the kindergarten program shall meet at least three hundred fifty-four hours. In fiscal year 2005–2006 and each fiscal year thereafter, the kindergarten program shall meet at least three hundred fifty-six hours. Lunch periods and recess periods may not be included as part of the instructional hours unless the child's individualized education program requires instruction during those periods and the specific reasons for such instruction are fully documented. In computing the average daily membership, preschool children with disabilities and kindergarten students shall be counted as one-half of a full-time student. For common schools, a part-time student is a student enrolled for less than the total time for a full-time student as defined in this section. A part-time common school student shall be counted as one-fourth, one-half or three-fourths of a full-time student if the student is enrolled in an instructional program that is at least one-fourth, one-half or three-fourths of the time a full-time student is enrolled as defined in subdivision (b) of this paragraph.

(ii) For high schools, a part-time student who is enrolled in less than four subjects that count toward graduation as defined by the state board of education in a recognized high school and who is taught in less than twenty instructional hours per week prorated for any week with fewer than five school days. A part-time high school student shall be counted as one-fourth, one-half or three-fourths of a full-time student if the student is enrolled in an instructional program that is at least one-fourth, one-half or three-fourths of a full-time instructional program as defined in subdivision (c) of this paragraph.

(b) "Full–time student" means:

(i) For common schools, a student who is at least six years of age prior to January 1 of a school year, who has not graduated from the highest grade taught in the school district and who is regularly enrolled in a course of study required by the state board of education. Until fiscal year 2001–2002, first, second and third grade students, ungraded students at least six, but under nine, years of age by September 1 or ungraded group B children with disabilities who are at least five, but under six, years of age by September 1 must be enrolled in an instructional program that meets for a total of at least six hundred ninety-two hours during the minimum number of days required in a school year as provided in § 15–341. In fiscal year 2001–2002, the program shall meet at least six hundred ninety-six hours. In fiscal year 2002–2003, the program shall meet at least seven hundred hours. In fiscal year 2003–2004, the program shall meet at least seven hundred four hours. In fiscal year 2004–2005, the program shall meet at least seven hundred eight hours. In fiscal year 2005–2006 and in each fiscal year thereafter, the program shall meet at least seven hundred twelve hours. Until fiscal year 2001–2002, fourth, fifth and sixth grade students or ungraded students at least nine, but under twelve, years of age by September 1 must be enrolled in an instructional program that meets for a total of at least eight hundred sixty-five hours during the minimum number of school days required in a school year as provided in § 15-341. In fiscal year 2001–2002, the program shall meet at least eight hundred seventy hours. In fiscal year 2002–2003, the program shall meet at least eight hundred seventy-five hours. In fiscal year 2003–2004, the program shall meet at least eight hundred eighty hours. In fiscal year 2004–2005, the program shall meet at least eight hundred eighty-five hours. In fiscal year 2005–2006 and each fiscal year thereafter, the program shall meet at least eight hundred ninety hours. Until fiscal year 2001–2002, seventh and eighth grade students or ungraded students at least twelve, but under fourteen, years of age by September 1 must be enrolled in an instructional program that meets for a total of at least one thousand thirty-eight hours during the minimum number of days required in a school year as provided in § 15-341. In fiscal year 2001–2002, the program shall meet at least one thousand forty-four hours. In fiscal year 2002–2003, the program shall meet at least one thousand fifty hours. In fiscal year 2003–2004, the program shall meet at least one thousand fifty-six hours. In fiscal year 2004–2005, the program shall meet at least one thousand sixty-two hours. In fiscal year 2005–2006 and each fiscal year thereafter, the program shall meet at least one thousand sixty-eight hours. Lunch periods and recess periods may not be included as part of the instructional hours unless the student is a child with a disability and the child's individualized education program requires instruction during those periods and the specific reasons for such instruction are fully documented.

(ii) For high schools, a student not graduated from the highest grade taught in the school district, or an ungraded student at least fourteen years of age by September 1, and enrolled in at least a full-time instructional program of subjects that count toward graduation as defined by the state board of education in a recognized high school. A full-time student shall not be counted more than once for computation of average daily membership.

(iii) For homebound or hospitalized, a student receiving at least four hours of instruction per week.

(c) "Full-time instructional program" means:

(i) Through fiscal year 2000–2001, at least four subjects, each of which, if taught each school day for the minimum number of days required in a school year, would meet a minimum of one hundred twenty hours a year, or the equivalent, or one or more subjects taught in amounts of time totaling at least twenty hours per week prorated for any week with fewer than five school days.

(ii) For fiscal year 2001–2002, an instructional program that meets at least a total of seven hundred four hours during the minimum number of days required and includes at least four subjects each of which, if taught each school day for the minimum number of days required in a school year, would meet a minimum of one hundred twenty-two hours a year, or the equivalent, or one or more subjects taught in amounts of time totaling at least twenty hours per week prorated for any week with fewer than five school days.

(iii) For fiscal year 2002–2003, an instructional program that meets at least a total of seven hundred eight hours during the minimum number of days required and includes at least four subjects each of which, if taught each school day for the minimum number of days required in a school year, would meet a minimum of one hundred twenty-two hours a year, or the equivalent, or one or more subjects taught in amounts of time totaling at least twenty hours per week prorated for any week with fewer than five school days.

(iv) For fiscal year 2003–2004, an instructional program that meets at least a total of seven hundred twelve hours during the minimum number of days required and includes at least four subjects each of which, if taught each school day for the minimum number of days required in a school year, would meet a minimum of one hundred twenty-three hours a year, or the equivalent, or one or more subjects taught in amounts of time totaling at least twenty hours per week prorated for any week with fewer than five school days.

(v) For fiscal year 2004–2005, an instructional program that meets at least a total of seven hundred sixteen hours during the minimum number of days required and includes at least four subjects each of which, if taught each school day for the minimum number of days required in a school year, would meet a minimum of one hundred twenty-three hours a year, or the equivalent, or one or more subjects taught in amounts of time totaling at least twenty hours per week prorated for any week with fewer than five school days.

(vi) For fiscal year 2005–2006 and each fiscal year thereafter, an instructional program that meets at least a total of seven hundred twenty hours during the minimum number of days required and includes at least four subjects each of which, if taught each school day for the minimum number of days required in a school year, would meet a minimum of one hundred twenty-three hours a year, or the equivalent, or one or more subjects taught in amounts of time totaling at least twenty hours per week prorated for any week with fewer than five school days.

3. "Budget year" means the fiscal year for which the school district is budgeting and which immediately follows the current year.

4. "Common school district" means a political subdivision of this state offering instruction to students in programs for preschool children with disabilities and kindergarten programs and grades one through eight.

5. "Current year" means the fiscal year in which a school district is operating.

6. "Daily attendance" means:

(a) For common schools, days in which a pupil:

(i) Of a kindergarten program or ungraded, but not group B children with disabilities, and at least five, but under six, years of age by September 1 attends at least three-quarters of the instructional time scheduled for the day. If the total instruction time scheduled for the year is at least three hundred forty-six hours but is less than six hundred ninety-two hours such attendance shall be counted as one-half day of attendance. If the instructional time scheduled for the year is at least six hundred ninety-two hours, "daily attendance" means days in which a pupil attends at least one-half of the instructional time scheduled for the day. Such attendance shall be counted as one-half day of attendance.

(ii) Of the first, second or third grades, ungraded and at least six, but under nine, years of age by September 1 or ungraded group B children with disabilities and at least five, but under six, years of age by September 1 attends more than three-quarters of the instructional time scheduled for the day.

(iii) Of the fourth, fifth or sixth grades or ungraded and at least nine, but under twelve, years of age by September 1 attends more than three-quarters of the instructional time scheduled for the day, except as provided in § 15-797.

(iv) Of the seventh or eighth grades or ungraded and at least twelve, but under fourteen, years of age by September 1 attends more than three-quarters of the instructional time scheduled for the day, except as provided in § 15-797.

(b) For common schools, the attendance of a pupil at three-quarters or less of the instructional time scheduled for the day shall be counted as follows, except as provided in § 15-797 and except that attendance for a fractional student shall not exceed the pupil's fractional membership:

(i) If attendance for all pupils in the school is based on quarter days, the attendance of a pupil shall be counted as one-fourth of a day's attendance for each one-fourth of full-time instructional time attended.

(ii) If attendance for all pupils in the school is based on half days, the attendance of at least three-quarters of the instructional time scheduled for the day shall be counted as a full day's attendance and attendance at a minimum of one-half but less than three-quarters of the instructional time scheduled for the day equals one-half day of attendance.

(c) For common schools, the attendance of a preschool child with disabilities shall be counted as one-fourth day's attendance for each thirty-six minutes of attendance not including lunch periods and recess periods, except as provided in paragraph 2, subdivision (a), item (i) of this subsection for children with disabilities up to a maximum of three hundred sixty minutes each week.

(d) For high schools or ungraded schools in which the pupil is at least fourteen years of age by September 1, the attendance of a pupil shall not be counted as a full day unless the pupil is actually and physically in attendance and enrolled in and carrying four subjects, each of which, if taught each school day for the minimum number of days required in a school year, would meet a minimum of one hundred twenty hours a year, or the equivalent, that count toward graduation in a recognized high school except as provided in § 15-797 and subdivision (e) of this paragraph. Attendance of a pupil carrying less than the load prescribed shall be prorated.

(e) For high schools or ungraded schools in which the pupil is at least fourteen years of age by September 1, the attendance of a pupil may be counted as one-fourth of a day's attendance for each sixty minutes of instructional time in a subject that counts toward graduation, except that attendance for a pupil shall not exceed the pupil's full or fractional membership.

(f) For homebound or hospitalized, a full day of attendance may be counted for each day during a week in which the student receives at least four hours of instruction.

(g) For school districts which maintain school for an approved year-round school year operation, attendance shall be based on a computation, as prescribed by the superintendent of public instruction, of the one hundred eighty days' equivalency or two hundred days' equivalency, as applicable, of instructional time as approved by the superintendent of public instruction during which each pupil is enrolled.

7. "Daily route mileage" means the sum of:

(a) The total number of miles driven daily by all buses of a school district while transporting eligible students from their residence to the school of attendance and from the school of attendance to their residence on scheduled routes approved by the superintendent of public instruction.

(b) The total number of miles driven daily on routes approved by the superintendent of public instruction for which a private party, a political subdivision or a common or a contract carrier is reimbursed for bringing an eligible student from the place of his residence to a school transportation pickup point or to the school of attendance and from the school transportation scheduled return point or from the school of attendance to his residence. Daily route mileage includes the total number of miles necessary to drive to transport eligible students from and to their residence as provided in this paragraph.

8. "District support level" means the base support level plus the transportation support level.

9. "Eligible students" means:

(a) Students who are transported by or for a school district and who qualify as full-time students or fractional students, except students for whom transportation is paid by another school district or a county school superintendent, and:

(i) For common school students, whose place of actual residence within the school district is more than one mile from the school facility of attendance or students who are admitted pursuant to § 15-816.01 and who meet the economic eligibility requirements established under the national school lunch and child nutrition acts (42 United States Code §§ 1751 through 1785) for free or reduced price lunches and whose actual place of residence outside the school district boundaries is more than one mile from the school facility of attendance.

(ii) For high school students, whose place of actual residence within the school district is more than one and one-half miles from the school facility of attendance or students who are admitted pursuant to § 15-816.01 and who meet the economic eligibility requirements established under the national school lunch and child nutrition acts (42 United States Code §§ 1751 through 1785) for free or reduced price lunches and whose actual place of residence outside the school district boundaries is more than one and one-half miles from the school facility of attendance.

(b) Kindergarten students, for purposes of computing the number of eligible students under subdivision (a), item (i) of this paragraph, shall be counted as full-time students, notwithstanding any other provision of law.

(c) Children with disabilities, as defined by § 15–761, who are transported by or for the school district or who are admitted pursuant to chapter 8, article 1.1 of this title[1] and who qualify as full-time students or fractional students regardless of location or residence within the school district or children with disabilities whose transportation is required by the pupil's individualized education program.

(d) Students whose residence is outside the school district and who are transported within the school district on the same basis as students who reside in the school district.

10. "Enrolled" or "enrollment" means when a pupil is currently registered in the school district.

11. "GDP price deflator" means the average of the four implicit price deflators for the gross domestic product reported by the United States department of commerce for the four quarters of the calendar year.

12. "High school district" means a political subdivision of this state offering instruction to students for grades nine through twelve or that portion of the budget of a common school district which is allocated to teaching high school subjects with permission of the state board of education.

13. "Revenue control limit" means the base revenue control limit plus the transportation revenue control limit.

14. "Student count" means average daily membership as prescribed in this subsection for the fiscal year prior to the current year, except that for the purpose of budget preparation student count means average daily membership as prescribed in this subsection for the current year.

15. "Submit electronically" means submitted in a format and in a manner prescribed by the department of education.

16. "Total bus mileage" means the total number of miles driven by all buses of a school district during the school year.

17. "Total students transported" means all eligible students transported from their place of residence to a school transportation pickup point or to the school of attendance and from the school of attendance or from the school transportation scheduled return point to their place of residence.

18. "Unified school district" means a political subdivision of the state offering instruction to students in programs for preschool children with disabilities and kindergarten programs and grades one through twelve.

B. In this title, unless the context otherwise requires:

1. "Base" means the revenue level per student count specified by the legislature.

2. "Base level" means:

(a) For fiscal year 2003–2004, two thousand eight hundred twenty-two dollars seventy-four cents.

(b) For fiscal year 2004–2005, two thousand eight hundred ninety-three dollars eighteen cents.

3. "Base revenue control limit" means the base revenue control limit computed as provided in § 15–944.

4. "Base support level" means the base support level as provided in § 15–943.

5. "Certified teacher" means a person who is certified as a teacher pursuant to the rules adopted by the state board of education, who renders direct and personal services to school children in the form of instruction related to the school district's educational course of study and who is paid from the maintenance and operation section of the budget.

6. "ED, MIMR, SLD, SLI and OHI" means programs for children with emotional disabilities, mild mental retardation, a specific learning disability, a speech/language impairment and other health impairments.

7. "ED–P" means programs for children with emotional disabilities who are enrolled in private special education programs as prescribed in § 15–765, subsection D, paragraph 1 or in an intensive school district program as provided in § 15–765, subsection D, paragraph 2.

8. "ELL" means English learners who do not speak English or whose native language is not English, who are not currently able to perform ordinary classroom work in English and who are enrolled in an English language education program pursuant to §§ 15–751, 15–752 and 15–753.

9. "Full–time equivalent certified teacher" or "FTE certified teacher" means for a certified teacher the following:

(a) If employed full time as defined in § 15–501, 1.00.

(b) If employed less than full time, multiply 1.00 by the percentage of a full school day, or its equivalent, or a full class load, or its equivalent, for which the teacher is employed as determined by the governing board.

10. "Group A" means educational programs for career exploration, a specific learning disability, an emotional disability, mild mental retardation, remedial education, a speech/language impairment, homebound, bilingual, preschool moderate delay, preschool speech/language delay, other health impairments and gifted pupils.

11. "Group B" means educational improvements for pupils in kindergarten programs and grades one through three, educational programs for autism, a hearing impairment, moderate mental retardation, multiple disabilities, multiple disabilities with severe sensory impairment, orthopedic impairments, preschool severe delay, severe mental retardation and emotional disabilities for school age pupils enrolled in private special education programs or in school district programs for children with severe disabilities or visual impairment and English learners enrolled in a program to promote English language proficiency pursuant to § 15–752.

12. "HI" means programs for pupils with hearing impairment.

13. "Homebound" or "hospitalized" means a pupil who is capable of profiting from academic instruction but is unable to attend school due to

illness, disease, accident or other health conditions, who has been examined by a competent medical doctor and who is certified by that doctor as being unable to attend regular classes for a period of not less than three school months or a pupil who is capable of profiting from academic instruction but is unable to attend school regularly due to chronic or acute health problems, who has been examined by a competent medical doctor and who is certified by that doctor as being unable to attend regular classes for intermittent periods of time totaling three school months during a school year. The medical certification shall state the general medical condition, such as illness, disease or chronic health condition, that is the reason that the pupil is unable to attend school. Homebound or hospitalized includes a student who is unable to attend school for a period of less than three months due to a pregnancy if a competent medical doctor, after an examination, certifies that the student is unable to attend regular classes due to risk to the pregnancy or to the student's health.

14. "K–3" means kindergarten programs and grades one through three.

15. "MD–R, A–R and SMR–R" means resource programs for pupils with multiple disabilities, autism and severe mental retardation.

16. "MD–SC, A–SC and SMR–SC" means self-contained programs for pupils with multiple disabilities, autism and severe mental retardation.

17. "MDSSI" means a program for pupils with multiple disabilities with severe sensory impairment.

18. "MOMR" means programs for pupils with moderate mental retardation.

19. "OI–R" means a resource program for pupils with orthopedic impairments.

20. "OI–SC" means a self-contained program for pupils with orthopedic impairments.

21. "PSD" means preschool programs for children with disabilities as provided in § 15–771.

22. "P–SD" means programs for children who meet the definition of preschool severe delay as provided in § 15–771.

23. "Qualifying tax rate" means the qualifying tax rate specified in § 15–971 applied to the assessed valuation used for primary property taxes.

24. "Small isolated school district" means a school district which meets all of the following:

(a) Has a student count of fewer than six hundred in kindergarten programs and grades one through eight or grades nine through twelve.

(b) Contains no school which is fewer than thirty miles by the most reasonable route from another school, or, if road conditions and terrain make the driving slow or hazardous, fifteen miles from another school which teaches one or more of the same grades and is operated by another school district in this state.

(c) Is designated as a small isolated school district by the superintendent of public instruction.

25. "Small school district" means a school district which meets all of the following:

(a) Has a student count of fewer than six hundred in kindergarten programs and grades one through eight or grades nine through twelve.

(b) Contains at least one school which is fewer than thirty miles by the most reasonable route from another school which teaches one or more of the same grades and is operated by another school district in this state.

(c) Is designated as a small school district by the superintendent of public instruction.

26. "Transportation revenue control limit" means the transportation revenue control limit computed as prescribed in § 15–946.

27. "Transportation support level" means the support level for pupil transportation operating expenses as provided in § 15–945.

28. "VI" means programs for pupils with visual impairments.

29. "Voc. Ed." means career and technical education and vocational education programs, as defined in § 15–781.

Added by Laws 1981, Ch. 1, § 2, eff. Jan. 23, 1981. Amended by Laws 1981, Ch. 93, § 1; Laws 1981, Ch. 308, § 3; Laws 1982, Ch. 307, § 2; Laws 1982, Ch. 332, § 14; Laws 1983, Ch. 9, § 5, eff. Feb. 25, 1983; Laws 1984, Ch. 219, § 1; Laws 1984, Ch. 235, § 1; Laws 1984, Ch. 314, § 1, eff. April 30, 1984; Laws 1985, Ch. 166, § 11, eff. April 18, 1985; Laws 1985, Ch. 347, § 4, eff. May 14, 1985; Laws 1986, Ch. 336, § 3; Laws 1987, Ch. 333, § 1, eff. May 21, 1987; Laws 1987, Ch. 363, § 5, eff. May 22, 1987; Laws 1988, Ch. 281, § 5; Laws 1988, Ch. 288, § 2, eff. July 8, 1988; Laws 1989, Ch. 15, § 6; Laws 1989, Ch. 72, § 3; Laws 1989, Ch. 273, § 14, eff. June 26, 1989; Laws 1990, Ch. 258, § 4; Laws 1990, Ch. 322, § 9, eff. June 20, 1990; Laws 1991, Ch. 257, § 12; Laws 1991, Ch. 292, § 3, eff. June 28, 1991; Laws 1992, Ch. 172, § 17; Laws 1992, Ch. 305, § 14; Laws 1993, Ch. 189, § 6; Laws 1994, Ch. 315, § 16; Laws 1994, 9th S.S., Ch. 2, § 14; Laws 1995, Ch. 1, § 8, eff. Feb. 20, 1995; Laws 1995, Ch. 191, § 8; Laws 1995, Ch. 196, § 7; Laws 1996, Ch. 284, § 46; Laws 1997, 1st S.S., Ch. 4, § 5; Laws 1998, Ch. 167, § 7; Laws 1998, 4th S.S., Ch. 8, § 2; Laws 1999, 1st S.S., Ch. 4, § 7; Laws 2000, Ch. 236, § 19, eff. April 12, 2000; Laws 2000, Ch. 342, § 4; Laws 2000, 5th S.S., Ch. 1, § 10; Laws 2001, Ch. 233, § 3; Laws 2001, Ch. 312, § 2; Laws 2001, 2nd S.S., Ch. 9, § 2; Laws 2002, Ch. 89, § 21; Laws 2002, Ch. 189, § 2; Laws 2003, Ch. 264, § 3; Laws 2004, Ch. 278, § 2.

[1] Section 15–816 et seq.

Historical and Statutory Notes

Source:

Laws 1912, Ch. 77, § 99.
Civ. Code 1913, § 2816.
Laws 1921, Ch. 158, § 1.
Laws 1922, Ch. 35, § 131.
Rev. Code 1928, § 1089.
Laws 1933, Ch. 65, § 8.
Laws 1941, Ch. 79, § 3.
Laws 1947, Ch. 85, § 2.
Laws 1949, Ch. 12, § 1.
Code 1939, Supp.1952, § 54–602.
Laws 1955, Ch. 108, § 2.
A.R.S. former §§ 15–1202.02, 15–1212, 15–1221, 15–1601, 15–1621.
Laws 1959, Ch. 90, §§ 2, 3.
Laws 1967, Ch. 127, § 50.
Laws 1961, Ch. 12, § 2.
Laws 1965, 3rd S.S., Ch. 1, § 5.
Laws 1967, 3rd S.S., Ch. 19, §§ 11, 12.
Laws 1968, Ch. 166, § 1.
Laws 1970, Ch. 11, § 1.
Laws 1970, Ch. 165, § 4.
Laws 1971, Ch. 177, §§ 5, 6.
Laws 1972, Ch. 115, § 6.
Laws 1973, Ch. 157, § 17.
Laws 1974, 1st S.S., Ch. 3, §§ 26, 38.
Laws 1975, Ch. 88, § 1.
Laws 1976, Ch. 66, § 1.
Laws 1976, Ch. 166, § 1.
Laws 1976, Ch. 184, § 4.
Laws 1977, Ch. 20, § 4.
Laws 1977, Ch. 152, § 9.

Laws 1978, Ch. 188, § 19.
Laws 1978, 1st S.S. Ch. 1, § 1.
Laws 1979, Ch. 184, § 2.
Laws 1980, 2nd S.S., Ch. 9, §§ 62, 65.
Laws 1980, Ch. 167, §§ 5, 6.

Laws 1987, Ch. 333, §§ 2 to 4, relating to a dropout prevention program for fiscal years 1987 to 1990, were repealed by Laws 1990, Ch. 399, § 15, effective July 1, 1990.

The 1989 amendment of this section by Ch. 72 explicitly amended the 1988 amendment of this section by Ch. 281.

The 1989 amendment of this section by Ch. 273 explicitly amended the 1989 amendment of this section by Ch. 15. See Reviser's Note, post.

This section as amended by Laws 1988, Ch. 288, § 2 was repealed by Laws 1989, Ch. 15, § 7 and by Ch. 72, § 4.

Laws 1990, Ch. 258, § 4 specifically amended § 15-901, as amended by Laws 1989, Ch. 15, § 6 and Ch. 72, § 3.

The 1990 amendment of this section by Ch. 322 explicitly amended the 1989 amendment of this section by Chs. 15 and 72.

Amendment of this section by Laws 1989, Ch. 273, § 14 was repealed by Laws 1990, Ch. 258, § 5 and Laws 1990, Ch. 322, § 10.

Laws 1990, Ch. 357, §§ 1 to 4, relating to school restructuring incentives, was repealed by § 7 of that act effective July 1, 1994.

Laws 1990, Ch. 399, § 16, as amended by Laws 1991, Ch. 252, § 3, eff. June 18, 1991; Laws 1992, Ch. 62, § 10; Laws 2000, Ch. 398, § 2, provides:

"**Sec. 16. Dropout prevention program for fiscal years 1991-1992 and 1992-1993**

"**A.** For fiscal years 1991-1992 and 1992-1993, a school district which participated in the dropout prevention program as originally established by Laws 1987, chapter 333 and continued by Laws 1990, chapter 399 during fiscal year 1990-1991 is eligible to continue to participate in the dropout prevention program for the 1991-1992 and 1992-1993 fiscal years at a level budgeted during fiscal year 1990-1991 if it is granted approval by the state board of education for that fiscal year after demonstrating that it meets the following requirements:

"1. The governing board continues a comprehensive dropout prevention program for grades four through twelve as stipulated in its dropout prevention plan as submitted to and approved by the state board of education and that, at a minimum, focuses on pupils who, because of innate factors, are not succeeding in the school environment as identified by parents, guardians or school personnel. These pupils may include, but are not limited to, those who do not qualify for special education services, who have measured intelligence quotients of between seventy and eighty-five or who exhibit characteristics of attention deficit disorder or learning patterns attributable to prenatal substance exposure.

"2. The governing board submits to the state board of education a detailed proposed budget for dropout prevention program expenditures for fiscal year 1991-1992 or 1992-1993, whichever is appropriate, an expenditure report on the dropout prevention program for the prior fiscal year and documentation of how participation in the dropout prevention program has improved the performance and retention of pupils for the two previous school years. Examples of documentation of improvements may include, but are not limited to, a decrease in the dropout rate of the school district, reduced course failures, increased graduation rates, improved performance on the annual norm-referenced achievement examination and decreased absence rates. Budget information and other documentation as required by this paragraph shall be submitted to the state board on forms that are developed and made available to the governing board by the department of education.

"3. Those school districts which are not unified but are eligible to participate in the dropout prevention program as provided in this subsection shall continue articulation with their feeder districts as part of the dropout prevention program.

"4. The governing board shall submit a resolution to continue participation in the program, any plan modifications and other documentation as required by paragraph 2 of this subsection to the department of education by August 1, 1991 and 1992. The department of education shall submit the documentation as required by paragraph 2 of this subsection and a summary of this information to the legislature by September 1, 1991 and 1992 in order to assist the legislature in making long term funding decisions regarding dropout prevention and at-risk programs.

"**B.** If the state board of education determines that the governing board has submitted insufficient documentation, pursuant to subsection A, paragraph 2 of this section, the state board may either prohibit the district from continuation of the dropout prevention program or approve participation at a funding level that is lower than was authorized for fiscal year 1990-1991. The school district governing board shall revise its maintenance and operation budget to fully reflect any reduction.

"**C.** The department of education and the auditor general shall include in the maintenance and operation section of the budget, as provided in § 15-903, Arizona Revised Statutes, a separate line for dropout prevention program expenditures as provided in this act. The additional maintenance and operation budget capacity provided in this act shall only be used for expenditures for the dropout prevention program as provided in this act.

"**D.** The primary property tax rate set to fund a dropout prevention program as provided in this section shall not be included in the computation of additional state aid for education as provided in § 15-972, Arizona Revised Statutes.

"**E.** Monies raised or allocated for dropout prevention programs shall not be used to fund school-based health clinics.

"**F.** No more than five per cent of monies raised or allocated for dropout prevention programs shall be used for administrator salaries."

Laws 1991, Ch. 154, § 14, effective May 20, 1991, as amended by Laws 1992, Ch. 305, § 28, provides:

"**Sec. 14. Joint technological education district; first year student count for fiscal year 1991-1992; student count for fiscal year 1992-1993**

"Notwithstanding § 15-901, Arizona Revised Statutes, and § 15-393, subsection D, paragraph 4, Arizona Revised Statutes, as amended by this act:

"1. For the purposes of calculating a base support level, capital outlay revenue limit and capital levy revenue limit for fiscal year 1991-1992, the total student count for the joint district shall not exceed 834. For fiscal year 1991-1992 the student count of the district of residence of the pupils registered at the joint district shall be reduced by 0.400 for each pupil taking three classes in the joint district and shall be reduced by 1.000 for each pupil taking four or more classes in the joint district. The district of residence shall review and approve the adjustment of its own student count as provided in this subsection before the pupils from the school district can be added to the student count of the joint district.

"2. For the purposes of determining the student count for fiscal year 1992-1993:

"(a) The joint district shall follow the procedures prescribed in § 15-393, subsection D, paragraph 4, Arizona Revised Statutes, as added by this act, as if fiscal year 1992-1993 were the first year of operation of the joint district.

"(b) If the number of pupils enrolled in the joint district from a district of residence exceeds the number of pupils so enrolled from the district in fiscal year 1991-1992, the district of residence shall adjust its student count by the amount prescribed in § 15-393, subsection D, paragraph 4, Arizona Revised Statutes, less the amount its student count was adjusted for fiscal year 1991-1992 due to the enrollment of pupils in the joint district during fiscal year 1991-1992."

Laws 1992, Ch. 288, § 22, eff. Sept. 30, 1992, retroactively effective to July 1, 1992, provides:

"**Sec. 22. Fiscal year 1992-1993 school district growth rate**

"**A.** Notwithstanding § 15-901, subsection B, paragraph 4, subdivision (f), Arizona Revised Statutes, or any other provision of law, the school district growth rate for the fiscal year 1992-1993 is zero per cent, except that the base level prescribed in § 15-901, subsection B, paragraph 4, Arizona Revised Statutes, and the state support level for each approved route mile, as provided in § 15-945, subsection A, paragraph 5, Arizona Revised Statutes, shall be increased by one-half of one per cent, except as provided in subsection F of this section.

"**B.** The governing board of a school district may adopt a budget which reflects the amounts as provided by subsection A of this section.

"**C.** On or before July 24, 1992 the superintendent of public instruction shall compute an estimate of the amount of the increase in budget capacity produced by the one-half of one per cent growth rate as provided in subsection A of this section and notify the county school superintendent.

"**D.** Prior to estimating the amount of school monies required by each school district as prescribed in § 15-991, Arizona Revised Statutes, the county school superintendent shall consult with the school districts regarding their intent to utilize the provisions of this section in order to make an accurate estimate of the additional amounts needed for each school district from the primary property tax. The county school superintendent shall, on a date prescribed by and on forms prescribed by the department of education, transmit to the department of education the estimates used in setting the tax rates.

"**E.** The modified ending cash balance, as defined in subsection H of this section, of each school district shall be reduced by the amount prescribed in subsection C of this section, except that a school district that is not eligible for equalization assistance shall not have its modified ending cash balance reduced by the amount prescribed in subsection C of this section. If the reduction amount exceeds the modified ending cash balance, the reduction shall equal the modified ending cash balance. The amount of the reduction shall be prorated as prescribed in § 15-991.02, subsection D, Arizona Revised Statutes, as added by this act, to the maintenance and operation, capital outlay and adjacent ways funds and is not available to reduce the primary tax rate as prescribed in § 15-906, Arizona Revised Statutes, as amended by this act. After receiving notice from the department of education of the final increase in budget capacity and the final reduction amounts as prescribed in subsection F of this section, the county treasurer, on or before March 1, 1993, shall deposit the final reduction amounts into a separate account within the county aid for equalization assistance for education fund of the county and distribute the money as prescribed in § 15-971, subsection C, Arizona Revised Statutes, as amended by this act. For the purposes of computing state aid for equalization assistance, the final reduction amounts as prescribed in this subsection shall be added to the total amount of county aid as prescribed by § 15-971, subsection D, paragraph 6, Arizona Revised Statutes, as amended by this act. On or before April 1, 1993, the county treasurer shall report to the department of education the amount deposited in the county aid for equalization assistance for education fund as prescribed by this subsection by each school district.

"**F.** The superintendent of public instruction shall compute the increase in the amount of state aid for equalization assistance as of January 15, 1993 resulting from the provisions of subsection A of this section. If the increase is more than two million five hundred thousand dollars, the superintendent of public instruction shall proportionally reduce the percentage increase as provided in subsection A of this section for both the base level and support level for each approved route mile, so that the cost of the increase in state aid for equalization assistance comes as near as practicable to, but does not exceed, two million five hundred thousand dollars. On or before February 1, 1993, the superintendent of public instruction shall recompute the amount of increase in budget capacity based upon the provisions of this subsection and compute the final reduction amount, as prescribed in subsection E of this section, from the modified ending cash balance and notify the governing boards of school districts and the county treasurers of the recomputed amounts.

"**G.** If a school district governing board had included in its budget the additional monies provided by subsection A of this section and if the base level and support level for each approved route mile are reduced as provided in subsection F of this section, the school district governing board shall reduce its expenditures based on the resulting revised budget limits. The governing board may adopt a revised budget by May 15, 1993 to reflect the new amounts.

"**H.** For purposes of this section "modified ending cash balance" means any cash balances at the close of fiscal year 1991-1992 remaining in the maintenance and operation, capital outlay and adjacent ways funds after the payment of encumbrances as provided in § 15-906, Arizona Revised Statutes, as amended by this act, except monies accumulated in the reserve of the capital outlay fund and reverted monies as provided in § 15-991.02, Arizona Revised Statutes, as added by this act."

Laws 1992, Ch. 305, § 32, provides:

"**Sec. 32. Extension of dropout prevention programs**

"The dropout prevention program provisions of Laws 1990, chapter 399, § 16, as amended by Laws 1991, chapter 252, § 3 shall be extended until such time that adequate funds are appropriated to fully fund dropout prevention efforts statewide as determined by the legislature."

Laws 1993, 2nd S.S., Ch. 8, § 6, provides:

"**Sec. 6. Fiscal year 1993-1994 school district growth rate**

"Notwithstanding § 15-901, subsection B, paragraph 2, subdivision (f), Arizona Revised Statutes, as amended by Laws 1992, chapter 305, § 14, or any other law, the school district growth rate for fiscal year 1993-1994 is zero per cent."

The 1993 amendment of this section by Ch. 189 explicitly amended the 1992 amendment of this section by Ch. 305.

Amendment of this section by Laws 1992, Ch. 172, § 17, was repealed by Laws 1993, Ch. 189, § 7.

Laws 1994, 8th S.S., Ch. 3, § 5, provides:

"**Sec. 5. Fiscal year 1994-1995 school district growth rate; use of monies**

"**A.** Notwithstanding § 15-901, subsection B, paragraph 2, subdivision (f), Arizona Revised Statutes, or any other law, the school district growth rate for fiscal year 1994-1995 is 2.0 per cent.

"**B.** For fiscal year 1994-1995 the amounts attributable to the school district growth rate prescribed in subsection A of this section as used in determining a district's base support level and capital outlay revenue limit, shall be transferred into the classroom improvement fund. The amount to be transferred into the classroom improvement fund shall be determined by a school district governing board as follows:

"1. Compute the total of a district's base support level as determined in § 15-943, § 15-943.02 or § 15-951, Arizona Revised Statutes, and capital outlay revenue limit as determined in § 15-951, 15-961 or 15-962.01, Arizona Revised Statutes, for fiscal year 1994-1995 using the growth rate prescribed in subsection A of this section.

"2. Compute the total of a district's base support level as determined in § 15-943, § 15-943.02 or § 15-951, Arizona Revised Statutes, and capital outlay revenue limit as determined in § 15-951, 15-961 or 15-962.01, Arizona Revised Statutes, for fiscal year 1994-1995 using a growth rate of zero per cent.

"3. Subtract the amount determined in paragraph 2 of this subsection from the amount determined in paragraph 1 of this subsection.

"4. The amount of monies determined in paragraph 3 of this subsection shall be transferred into the classroom improvement fund.

"**C.** The monies in the classroom improvement fund are intended to be used in the classroom for such items as textbooks and related printed subject matter materials, instructional aids, library books, computers and computer software. The monies in the fund may also be used for school improvements, such as reduction in class size, and increased program offerings.

"**D.** Monies in the classroom improvement fund may be expended for maintenance and operation and capital outlay, but shall not be used to supplant existing monies or for salary increases or benefit increases of currently employed personnel whose duties have not changed.

"**E.** Expenditures from the classroom improvement fund shall not exceed the amount of monies determined in subsection B, paragraph 3 of this section. If the expenditures exceed this amount, or if any unauthorized expenditures are made, the provisions of § 15–905, subsections L and M, Arizona Revised Statutes, shall apply.

"**F.** The financial and compliance audit as provided in § 5–914, Arizona Revised Statutes, shall include the classroom improvement fund.

"**G.** The computation required in subsection B of this section does not apply to increases in a district's revenue control limit and district support level as provided in § 15–948, Arizona Revised Statutes.

"**H.** The district's general budget limit, as prescribed in § 15–947 or 15–947.01, Arizona Revised Statutes, as determined by using the growth rate prescribed in subsection A of this section shall be reduced by the amount of monies determined in subsection B, paragraph 3 of this section.

"**I.** Notwithstanding § 15–905, subsection F, Arizona Revised Statutes, a district shall not budget in the capital outlay section of the fiscal year 1994–1995 budget an amount of monies less than the capital base amount. When determining the amount budgeted in the capital outlay section of the fiscal year 1994–1995 budget, the amount shall not include amounts attributable to capital outlay overrides, capital outlay desegregation and monies budgeted from the capital reserve. The capital base amount shall be determined as follows:

"1. Determine the district's budgeted expenditures for the capital outlay section of the fiscal year 1993–1994 budget, excluding amounts attributable to capital outlay overrides, capital outlay desegregation and monies budgeted from the capital reserve.

"2. Divide the amount determined in paragraph 1 of this subsection by the student count used in determining the fiscal year 1993–1994 budget.

"3. Multiply the quotient determined in paragraph 2 of this subsection by the student count used by the district in determining the fiscal year 1994–1995 budget.

"4. The product determined in paragraph 3 of this subsection is the capital base amount.

"**J.** A district may seek an exemption from the provision contained in subsection I of this section, by applying to the state board of education. The state board may grant such an exemption to the district if the provisions contained in subsection I of this section would create a hardship and if such an exemption would not violate other provisions of this section.

"**K.** The department of education shall develop forms for the computation and budget preparation required in subsections B and I of this section and provide them to school district governing boards.

"**L.** The provisions of subsections B through K of this section do not apply to small school districts as provided in § 15–949, Arizona Revised Statutes.

"**M.** Any cash balance remaining in the classroom improvement fund on June 30, 1995 shall be used for reduction of school district taxes for fiscal year 1995–1996, unless the monies are placed in the reserve of the capital outlay fund."

Laws 1995, 1st S.S., Ch. 4, § 2, provides:

"**Sec. 2. Fiscal year 1995–1996 base level and school district growth rate**

"**A.** For fiscal year 1995–1996, the base level for fiscal year 1994–1995, as prescribed in § 15–901, subsection B, paragraph 2, Arizona Revised Statutes, shall be increased by thirty dollars.

"**B.** Notwithstanding § 15–901, subsection B, paragraph 2, subdivision (f), Arizona Revised Statutes, or any other law, the school district growth rate for fiscal year 1995–1996 is 0.0 per cent."

The amendment of this section by Laws 1995, Ch. 191, § 8, was repealed by Laws 1996, Ch. 248, § 4, and by Laws 1996, Ch. 284, § 47.

The 1995 amendment of this section by Ch. 196 explicitly amended the amendment of this section by Laws 1995, Ch. 1, § 8.

The 1996 amendment of this section by Ch. 284 explicitly amended the amendment of this section by Laws 1995, Ch. 196, § 7.

Laws 1997, 1st S.S., Ch. 4, § 17, provides:

"**Sec. 17. Legislative purpose; base level funding**

The purpose of the increase in the funding in § 15-901, subsection B, paragraph 2, Arizona Revised Statutes, as amended by section 5 of this act, is to provide direct assistance to the classroom, including classroom supplies, classroom support services, hiring of additional teachers, and increasing teacher salaries."

The purported amendment of this section by Laws 1998, Ch. 164 failed to become effective because Chapter 164 was repealed in its entirety by Laws 1998, 5th S.S., Ch. 1, § 2, effective July 1, 1998.

The purported amendment of this section by Laws 1998, 3rd S.S., Ch. 1, failed to became effective because Ch. 1 was repealed in its entirety by Laws 1998, 5th S.S., Ch. 1, § 2, effective July 1, 1998.

The amendment by Laws 1998, 4th S.S., Ch. 8, § 2, specifically amended the amendment of this section by Laws 1997, 1st S.S., Ch. 4, § 5.

Laws 1999, 1st S.S., Ch. 5, § 23, provides:

"Sec. 23. Increased base support level; fiscal year 1999-2000

"**A.** If the fiscal event described in § 18, subsection A, paragraph 3 of this act occurs, then notwithstanding § 15-901, subsection B, paragraph 2, subdivision (a), Arizona Revised Statutes, the base level is $2,578.41. The increase in the base support level is for fiscal year 1999-2000.

"**B.** If the fiscal event described in § 18, subsection A, paragraph 4 of this act occurs, then notwithstanding § 15-901, subsection B, paragraph 2, subdivision (a), Arizona Revised Statutes, the base level is $2,597.09. The increase in the base support level is for fiscal year 1999-2000.

"**C.** It is the intent of the legislature that any monies under this section shall be used to enhance one or more of the following items:

"1. Classroom teacher salaries.

"2. Employing new teachers.

"3. Teacher training and development.

"4. Classroom technology.

"5. Strengthening programs for pupils in kindergarten programs and grades one, two and three.

"6. Additional school days.

"7. Supplemental learning programs to meet state academic standards.

"8. Reading clinics.

"9. Achieving or maintaining school sizes of fewer than four hundred fifty pupils.

"**D.** For fiscal year 1999-2000, school districts and charter schools shall report on the school report card issued pursuant to § 15-746, Arizona Revised Statutes, a summary of any monies received pursuant to this section and a description of how the monies were used to enhance classrooms to augment pupil learning. School districts and charter schools shall provide to any person on request a detailed itemization of the classroom enhancements and associated expenditures.

"**E.** Notwithstanding § 15-905, subsection A, paragraph 2, Arizona Revised Statutes, school district governing boards and charter schools may include in the proposed and adopted budget for fiscal year 1999-2000 and 2000-2001 any items or amounts authorized by this act. If subsequent events prevent any provision of this act from becoming effective, the governing boards and charter schools shall reduce their budgets by the amount that was budgeted pursuant to this act and that did not become effective.

"**F.** The staff of the Arizona legislative council shall prepare legislation for consideration in the forty-fifth legislature, first regular session to make necessary statutory changes to conform to the enactment of fiscal events pursuant to this section."

Laws 1999, 1st S.S., Ch. 5, § 24 was repealed by Laws 2000, Ch. 48, § 5. See also amendment of the note by Laws 2000, Ch. 398, post.

Laws 1999, 1st S.S., Ch. 5, § 24, was purportedly amended by Laws 2000, Ch. 398, § 3.

Laws 1999, 1st S.S., Ch. 5, § 25, provides:

"Sec. 25. Retroactivity

"Section 23 of this act applies retroactively to from and after June 30, 1999."

Laws 2000, Ch. 48, § 9, as conditionally amended by Laws 2000, 5th S.S., Ch. 1, § 56, provides [condition met by approval of electors of Proposition 301, proclaimed by the Governor, Nov. 27, 2000]:

"Sec. 9. Increased base support level; fiscal year 2000-2001

"**A.** Notwithstanding § 15-901, subsection B, paragraph 2, subdivision (a), Arizona Revised Statutes, if the fiscal event described in § 8, subsection B of this act occurs, the base support level for fiscal year 2000-2001 is $2,621.62.

"**B.** It is the intent of the legislature that these monies be used for the same purposes described in § 8, subsection A of this act.

"**C.** For fiscal year 2000-2001, school districts and charter schools shall report on the school report card issued pursuant to § 15-746, Arizona Revised Statutes, a summary of any monies received pursuant to this section and a description of how the monies were used.

"**D.** Notwithstanding § 15-905, subsection A, paragraph 2, Arizona Revised Statutes, school district governing boards and charter schools may include in the proposed and adopted budget for fiscal year 2000-2001 any items or amounts authorized by this act. If subsequent events prevent any provision of this act from becoming effective, the governing boards and charter schools shall reduce their budgets by any amount that was budgeted pursuant to this act and that did not become effective.

"**E.** The staff of the legislative council shall prepare legislation for consideration in the forty-fifth legislature, first regular session to make necessary statutory changes to conform to the enactment of fiscal events pursuant to this section."

The amendment of this section by Laws 2000, Ch. 342, § 4 was conditionally repealed by Laws 2000, 5th S.S., Ch. 1, § 9.

Laws 2000, 5th S.S., Ch. 1, § 9, provides:

"**Sec. 9. Repeal**

"Section 15-901, Arizona Revised Statutes, as amended by Laws 2000, chapter 342, § 4, is repealed."

The 2000 amendment of this section by 5th S.S., Ch. 1, explicitly amended the amendment of this section by Laws 2000, Ch. 236 § 19.

Laws 2000, 5th S.S., Ch. 1, § 54, provides:

"**Sec. 54. Increased number of school days; phase-in**

"Notwithstanding §§ 15-341, 15-802, 15-854, 15-855, 15-902 and 15-1001, Arizona Revised Statutes, § 15-901, Arizona Revised Statutes, as amended by this act, and § 15-341.01, Arizona Revised Statutes, as added by this act, the number of mandatory school days offered by school districts shall be increased from the current number of one hundred seventy-five days to one hundred eighty days according to the following schedule:

"1. In fiscal year 2001-2002, each school district governing board shall maintain the schools established by it for the attendance of each pupil for a period of not less than one hundred seventy-six school days.

"2. In fiscal year 2002-2003, each school district governing board shall maintain the schools established by it for the attendance of each pupil for a period of not less than one hundred seventy-seven school days.

"3. In fiscal year 2003-2004, each school district governing board shall maintain the schools established by it for the attendance of each pupil for a period of not less than one hundred seventy-eight school days.

"4. In fiscal year 2004-2005, each school district governing board shall maintain the schools established by it for the attendance of each pupil for a period of not less than one hundred seventy-nine school days.

"5. In fiscal year 2005-2006 and each fiscal year thereafter, each school district governing board shall maintain the schools established by it for the attendance of each pupil for a period of not less than one hundred eighty school days as prescribed by statute."

Proposition 301, approved by the electors at the Nov. 7, 2000 general election, effective Nov. 27, 2000, included a provision increasing the state transaction privilege tax rate six-tenths of one per cent. Therefore, the conditions of the 5th S.S. Ch. 1 were met, and the act became effective.

Laws 2001, Ch. 299, § 1, providing for a school breakfast program and a report, was repealed by section 2 of the act, on January 1, 2004.

The 2002 amendment of this section by Ch. 89 explicitly amended the amendment of this section by Laws 2001, 2nd S.S., Ch. 9, § 2.

Laws 2004, Ch. 278, § 16, provides:

"**Sec. 16. Desegregation budget; limit**

"Notwithstanding § 15-910, Arizona Revised Statutes, the maximum amount that a school district may budget for desegregation activities for fiscal year 2004-2005 shall be computed as follows:

"1. Determine the amount that the district budgeted for desegregation activities for fiscal year 2003-2004 pursuant to Laws 2002, chapter 68, § 3.

"2. Compute the percentage increase in average daily membership for the district, as defined in § 15-901, Arizona Revised Statutes, for the 2003-2004 school year above the 2002-2003 school year. If average daily membership for the district decreased for the 2003-2004 school year below the 2002-2003 school year, assume a per cent increase of zero.

"3. Multiply the amount determined in paragraph 1 of this section by the percentage determined in paragraph 2 of this section.

"4. Multiply the amount determined in paragraph 1 of this section by two per cent for assumed inflation.

"5. Add the amounts determined in paragraphs 1, 3 and 4 of this section."

Laws 2004, Ch. 278, § 21, provides:

"**Sec. 21. Retroactivity**

"**A.** Except as provided in subsection B of this section, this act applies retroactively to from and after June 30, 2004.

"**B.** Laws 2002, chapter 330, § 49, as amended by this act, applies retroactively to from and after June 29, 2004."

Reviser's Notes:

1981 Note. Prior to the 1982 amendments, this section contained the amendments made by Laws 1981, Ch. 93, § 1 and Ch. 308, § 3 which were blended together pursuant to authority of § 41-1304.03.

1982 Note. Prior to the 1983 amendment, this section contained the amendments made by Laws 1982, Ch. 307, § 2 and Ch. 332, § 14 which were blended together pursuant to authority of § 41-1304.03.

1984 Note. Prior to the 1985 amendments, this section contained the amendments made by Laws 1984, Ch. 219, § 1, Ch. 235, § 1 and Ch. 314, § 1 which were blended together pursuant to authority of § 41-1304.03.

1987 Note. Prior to the 1988 amendments this section contained the amendments made by Laws 1987, Ch. 333, § 1 and Ch. 363, § 5 which were blended together pursuant to authority of § 41-1304.03.

1988 Note. The amendment made by Laws 1988, Ch. 288, § 2 was inconsistent and incompatible with Laws 1988, Ch. 281, § 5 and therefore could not be blended.

1989 Notes. Prior to the 1990 amendments, this section contained the amendments made by Laws 1989, Ch. 15, § 6 and Ch. 72, § 3 which were blended together pursuant to authority of § 41-1304.03.

Laws 1989, chapter 273, § 14 amended this section with an emergency clause, effective June 26, 1989, by amending this section as amended by Laws 1989, chapter 15, § 6, which was effective on September 15, 1989.

1990 Note. Prior to the 1991 amendments, this section contained the amendments made by Laws 1990, Ch. 258, § 4 and Ch. 322, § 9 which were blended together pursuant to authority of § 41-1304.03. Pursuant to authority of § 41-1304.02, in subsection A, paragraph 9, subdivision (c) in the Laws 1990, Ch. 258 version after the first "district" "and" was inserted to correct a manifest clerical error and in subsection B, paragraph 9 was renumbered as paragraph 21 and the following paragraphs were renumbered accordingly.

1991 Note. Prior to the 1992 amendments, this section contained the amendments made by Laws 1991, Ch. 257, sec. 12 and Ch. 292, sec. 3 that were blended together pursuant to authority of § 41-1304.03. In the Laws 1991, Ch. 292 version in subsection B, paragraph 21 the first "and" was incorrectly shown as "AND". Pursuant to authority of § 41-1304.02, in order to correct a manifest clerical error "and" is substituted in the blend version.

1992 Note. The amendment made by Laws 1992 Ch. 305, sec. 14 was inconsistent and incompatible with Laws 1992, Ch. 172, sec. 17 and therefore could not be blended.

1993 Note. In the chapter version, in paragraph 7 the quotation mark following "ED-P" was missing but it is existing law. Pursuant to authority of § 41-1304.02, the quotation mark is inserted as a correction of a manifest clerical error.

1995 Note. In the chapter version in subsection B, paragraph 2, subdivision (b) was stricken, but after "~~per cent~~" the stricken language contained "~~by any~~" and these words are not existing law. Pursuant to authority of § 41-1304.02, in the chapter version the words "~~by any~~" are removed. The amendment of this section by Laws 1995, Ch. 191, sec. 8 failed to set forth in full the text of the section as amended by Laws 1995, Ch. 1, sec. 8, an emergency act, as required by Constitution of Arizona art. IV, pt. 2, sec. 14.

1998 Note. Prior to the 1999 amendment, this section contained the amendments made by Laws 1998, Second Regular Session, Ch. 167, sec. 7 and Laws 1998, Fourth Special Session, Ch. 8. sec. 2 that were blended together pursuant to authority of § 41-1304.03.

2000 Note. The amendment of this section by Laws 2000, Ch. 342, sec. 4 failed to set forth in full the text of the section as amended by Laws 2000, Ch. 236, sec. 19, an emergency act, as required by Constitution of Arizona art. IV, pt. 2, sec. 14.

2001 Note. Prior to the 2001 2nd Special Session amendment, this section contained the amendments made by Laws 2001, Ch. 233, sec. 3 and Ch. 312, sec. 2 that were blended together to authority of § 41-1304.03.

2002 Note. Prior to the 2003 amendment, this section contained the amendments made by Laws 2002, Ch. 89, sec. 21 and Ch. 189, sec. 2 that were blended together pursuant to authority of § 41-1304.03.

§ 15-901.01. Inflation adjustments

If approved by the qualified electors voting at a statewide general election, for fiscal years 2001-2002 through 2005-2006, the legislature shall increase the base level or other components of the revenue control limit by two per cent. For fiscal year 2006-2007 and each fiscal year thereafter, the legislature shall increase the base level or other components of the revenue control limit by a minimum growth rate of either two per cent or the change in the GDP price deflator, as defined in § 41-563, from the second preceding calendar year to the calendar year immediately preceding the budget year, whichever is less, except that the base level shall never be reduced below the base level established for fiscal year 2001-2002.

Added by Laws 2000, 5th S.S., Ch. 1, § 11, approved election Nov. 7, 2000, eff. Nov. 27, 2000.

Historical and Statutory Notes

Laws 2000, 5th S.S., Ch. 1, § 64, provides:

"**Sec. 64. Election to authorize additional state transaction privilege and use tax increments**

"**A.** The secretary of state shall place on the ballot of the 2000 state general election the issue of:

"1. An incremental increase in the rate of state transaction privilege tax, as provided by § 42-5010, subsection G, Arizona Revised Statutes, as amended by this act, an incremental increase in the state use tax, as provided by § 42-5155, subsection D, Arizona Revised Statutes, as amended by this act and the distribution of those monies as provided by § 42-5029, Arizona Revised Statutes, as amended by this act.

"2. Inflation adjustments in the state aid to education base level and other components of the revenue control limit pursuant to § 15-901.01, Arizona Revised Statutes, as added by this act.

"3. A termination of the exemption from the revenue control limit for excess utility costs as provided by § 15-910, subsection A, Arizona Revised Statutes, as amended by this act.

"4. A limitation on the school district qualifying tax rates and the county equalization assistance for education rate as provided by section 41-1276, subsection H, Arizona Revised Statutes, as amended by this act.

"5. A state income tax credit in mitigation of increased transaction privilege and use taxes, as provided by § 43-1072.01, Arizona Revised Statutes, as added by this act.

"**B.** As provided by § 19-124, Arizona Revised Statutes, the legislative council shall prepare an analysis of the proposition, and the secretary of state shall include the analysis with any submitted arguments that advocate or oppose the proposition in the general election publicity pamphlet.

"**C.** In addition to any other ballot requirements prescribed by law, the secretary of state shall print on the official general election ballot:

"1. The official title and number of the measure to be voted on.

"2. A descriptive title, not exceeding fifty words, containing a summary of the issue, prepared by the secretary of state and approved by the attorney general.

"3. The phrases:

"A 'yes' vote has the effect of approving an increase in the state transaction privilege (sales) tax and the state use tax of six-tenths of one per cent to raise revenues in support of education, a state income tax credit in mitigation of those tax increases, inflation adjustments in state aid for education, a termination of an exemption from education funding revenue control limits for excess utility costs and a limitation on the school district qualifying tax rates and the county equalization assistance for education rate.

"A 'no' vote has the effect of rejecting the proposed increase in state taxes and the other proposed tax mitigations and education budgetary controls."

Conditionally added § 15-901.01, was placed in Proposition 301, and was approved by the electors at the November 7, 2000 general election as proclaimed by the Governor on November 27, 2000.

§ 15-901.02. Full-day kindergarten instruction; study committee; full-day kindergarten fund

A. A school or charter school that is provided and accepts monies pursuant to this section for full-day kindergarten shall offer full-day kindergarten instruction to all pupils who meet the enrollment requirements for kindergarten programs. Parents of pupils who meet the enrollment requirements for voluntary kindergarten programs in a school or charter school that is required to provide full-day kindergarten instruction shall choose either half-day kindergarten instruction or full-day kindergarten instruction.

B. The legislature shall develop a plan, including capital monies, considering recommendations of the joint legislative study committee on full-day kindergarten established in subsection D of this section, to provide statewide full-day kindergarten instruction by fiscal year 2009–2010. Schools and charter schools that are provided full-day kindergarten funding pursuant to this subsection and subsection C of this section shall continuously be provided full-day kindergarten funding throughout the statewide implementation of the full-day kindergarten plan adopted by the legislature.

C. Funding for full-day kindergarten shall be provided for fiscal year 2004–2005 to schools or charter schools with a student count in which at least ninety per cent of the pupils meet the economic eligibility requirements established under the national school lunch and child nutrition acts (42 United States code §§ 1751 through 1785). The school district or charter school shall receive monies for full-day kindergarten pursuant to this section for each pupil who attends kindergarten instruction.

D. The joint legislative study committee on full-day kindergarten is established and shall consist of three members of the house of representatives appointed by the speaker of the house of representatives, no more than two shall be from the same political party, three members of the senate appointed by the president of the senate, no more than two shall be from the same political party and three members appointed by the governor who represent school districts or charter schools that offer kindergarten programs. The joint legislative study committee shall forward preliminary recommendations by December 1, 2004 to the speaker of the house of representatives, the president of the senate and the governor for full-day kindergarten implementation. The joint legislative study committee shall consider funding for each year of implementation, capital accommodations and program implementation issues such as professional development and diagnostic assessment.

E. The full-day kindergarten fund is established consisting of monies appropriated to the department of education for this purpose. The department of education shall administer the fund. If there are insufficient monies available in the fund to provide full funding pursuant to this section, the department of education shall prorate the amount per pupil distributed to each school district and charter school that is eligible to receive monies from the fund. The amount budgeted by the school district or charter school pursuant to this section shall not be included in the allowable budget balance carryforward calculated pursuant to § 15–943.01. The full-day kindergarten fund terminates on July 1, 2009, and any unencumbered monies remaining in the fund on that date shall be transferred to the state general fund.

F. Monies in the full-day kindergarten fund are continuously appropriated and are exempt from the provisions of § 35–190 relating to lapsing of appropriations, and the allocation to each charter school and school district for a fiscal year shall equal the per pupil amount established in this section for the fiscal year multiplied by the weighted student count for the school district or charter school for the fiscal year pursuant to § 15–943, paragraph 2, subdivision (a). For the purposes of this subsection, the weighted student count for a school district that serves as the district of attendance for nonresident pupils shall be increased to include nonresident pupils who attend school in the school district.

G. Monies distributed from the full-day kindergarten fund shall be spent only for full-day kindergarten instruction.

H. School districts and charter schools that receive monies from the full-day kindergarten fund shall submit a report to the superintendent of public instruction on a per school basis that provides an accounting of the expenditures of monies distributed from the fund during the school year, a description of any professional development required under this section, class size and any district class size policies, data collected from state or district assessments of kindergarten pupils in both full-day and half-day programs, the number of pupils, the number of pupils not served and the reasons those pupils were not served and other information determined by the department of education and the office of the auditor general. The department of education in conjunction with the auditor general shall prescribe the format and due date of the report required under this subsection.

I. School districts and charter schools that receive monies from the full-day kindergarten fund shall receive these monies monthly in an amount not to exceed one-twelfth of the monies estimated pursuant to subsection C of this section, except that if there are insufficient monies in the fund that month to make payments, the distribution for that month shall be prorated for each school district or charter school. The department of education may make an additional payment in the current month for any prior month or months in which school districts or charter schools received a prorated payment if there are sufficient monies in the fund that month for the additional payments. The state is not required to make payments to a school district or charter school full-day kindergarten fund if the monies in the state full-day kindergarten fund are insufficient to meet the estimated allocations to school districts and charter schools pursuant to subsection C of this section.

J. The Arizona state schools for the deaf and the blind shall receive monies from the full-day kindergarten fund in the same manner as school districts and charter schools. The Arizona state schools for the deaf and the blind are subject to this section in the same manner as school districts and charter schools.

K. Each school district and charter school shall establish a local level full-day kindergarten fund to receive allocations from the state level full-day kindergarten fund. The local level full-day kindergarten fund shall be a budgetary controlled account. Interest charges for any registered warrants for the local level full-day kindergarten fund shall be a charge against the local level full-day kindergarten fund. Interest earned on monies in the local level full-day kindergarten fund shall be added to the local level full-day kindergarten fund. This state shall not be required to make payments to a school district or charter school local level full-day kindergarten fund that are in addition to monies appropriated to the state level full-day kindergarten fund.

L. If the state board of education, the department of education, the auditor general or the attorney general determines that a school district is substantially and deliberately not in compliance with this title, and if the school district has failed to correct the deficiency within ninety days after receiving notice from the department of education, the state board of education may direct the superintendent of public instruction, pursuant to state board of education rules, to withhold the monies the school district would otherwise be entitled to receive from the full-day kindergarten fund from the date of the determination of noncompliance until the department of education determines that the school district is in compliance with this title.

M. If the sponsor of the charter school determines at a public meeting that the charter school is not in compliance with federal law, with the laws of this state or with its charter, the sponsor of a charter school shall notify the department of education to withhold the monies that the charter school would otherwise be entitled to receive from the full-day kindergarten fund. The sponsor shall provide written notice to the charter school at least seventy-two hours before the meeting and shall allow the charter school to respond to the allegations of noncompliance at the meeting before the sponsor makes a final determination to notify the department of education of noncompliance. When the sponsor determines that the charter school is in compliance, the department of education shall restore the amount of monies that the charter school is entitled to receive from the full-day kindergarten fund.

N. Schools are not required to offer full-day kindergarten instruction to qualifying students if there is insufficient classroom space. Schools shall not accept monies from the full-day kindergarten fund if space limitations result in class sizes that exceed the average class size of the district or charter school.

O. All schools that accept monies from the full-day kindergarten fund shall provide professional development that is directly related to the delivery of kindergarten standards in a full-day program. Any school that has not yet undergone professional development for implementation of the delivery of a research-based reading curriculum as prescribed in § 15–704 may not receive money from the full-day kindergarten fund until this training has been received by the kindergarten instructors on staff.

P. For any school district that funds voluntary full-day kindergarten instruction with monies from a desegregation levy or a special budget override pursuant to § 15–482 and that qualifies for monies from the full-day kindergarten fund and if the desegregation monies or special budget override monies are used solely to provide full-day kindergarten instruction, the governing board shall hold a public meeting to determine the reallocation of those monies to other programs or whether those monies shall be used to reduce the school district's primary or secondary property tax levy, or both.

Added by Laws 2004, Ch. 278, § 3.

Historical and Statutory Notes

Laws 2004, Ch. 278, § 21, provides:

"**Sec. 21. Retroactivity**

"**A.** Except as provided in subsection B of this section, this act applies retroactively to from and after June 30, 2004.

"**B.** Laws 2002, chapter 330, § 49, as amended by this act, applies retroactively to from and after June 29, 2004."

Reviser's Notes:

2004 Note. Pursuant to authority of § 41–1304.02, in the section heading "study committee;" was added after "instruction;" and in subsection C a period was substituted for the comma after "1785)" to correct a manifest clerical error.

§ 15–902. Determination of student count

A. For a common or a unified school district in which the average daily membership through the first one hundred days or two hundred days in session, as applicable, of the current year has exceeded the average daily attendance through the first one hundred days or two hundred days in session, as applicable, of the current year by more than six per cent, the student count shall be determined by an adjusted average daily membership computed by multiplying the actual average daily attendance by one hundred six per cent.

B. For a high school district in which the average daily membership through the first one hundred days in session of the current year exceeds the average daily attendance through the first one hundred days in session of the current year by more than eight and one-half per cent, the student count shall be determined by an adjusted average daily membership computed by multiplying the actual average daily attendance by one hundred eight and one-half per cent. If the high school district which utilized adjusted average daily membership pursuant to this subsection does not qualify for equalization assistance as provided by § 15–971, the computation of additional state aid for education as provided in § 15–972 for that district shall not include in the primary property tax rate the amount of primary property taxes necessary to fund an amount computed as follows:

1. Determine the revenue control limit, capital outlay revenue limit and soft capital allocation using the adjusted average daily membership.

2. Add the amounts determined in paragraph 1 of this subsection.

3. Determine the revenue control limit, capital outlay revenue limit and soft capital allocation using a student count computed by multiplying the actual average daily attendance by one hundred six per cent.

4. Add the amounts determined in paragraph 3 of this subsection.

5. Subtract the sum determined under paragraph 4 of this subsection from the sum determined under paragraph 2 of this subsection.

C. A school district required to utilize adjusted average daily membership as provided in this section may apply to the department of education for a further adjustment if student absences result from any of the following reasons:

1. Widespread illness for any period of three consecutive days or more.

2. Adverse weather conditions for any period of three consecutive days or more.

3. Concerted refusal by students to attend classes for any period of three consecutive days of more.

4. Threats of violence against school property, school personnel or students for any period of one day or more.

D. All student absence figures shall be submitted by the school district on a school by school basis to the department of education pursuant to subsection C of this section and shall be certified by the governing board of the school district. The department of education shall review the materials and documents submitted and may, if it determines that the absences resulted from the reasons prescribed by this section, further adjust the average daily membership figures of the school district.

E. A school district required to use adjusted average daily membership as provided in this section may apply to the department of education for a further adjustment due to absences of pupils with chronic health problems as defined in § 15–346 if the school district is providing services to the pupils during their absence from school.

F. A pupil is enrolled if the pupil is currently registered in the school district. In addition, the uniform system of financial records shall contain procedures to ensure that enrollment is determined by all school districts on a uniform basis.

G. Any determination of average daily attendance and average daily membership shall be based on the records of the superintendent of public instruction.

H. For school districts which maintain an approved year-round school year operation program, an educational program offered on the basis of a four day school week or an alternative kindergarten program offered on the basis of a three day school week, student count shall be based on a computation as prescribed by the superintendent of public instruction on the one hundred seventy-five days' equivalency or two hundred days' equivalency, as applicable, of instructional time as approved by the superintendent of public instruction during which each pupil is enrolled.

I. School districts shall be required to record electronically membership and attendance on a school by school basis for each day school is in session. Records shall be certified and forwarded to the department of education electronically within twelve days after the first forty days in session and within twelve days after the first one hundred days in session.

J. Absences shall be made part of the attendance record and shall be forwarded electronically by the school district on a school by school basis with other records to the department of education.

K. If a new school district is formed by the subdivision of an existing school district as provided in § 15–458, the new school district shall determine its student count, the approved daily route mileage and the number of eligible students transported on the basis of where pupils reside within the boundaries of the new school district when computing assistance as provided in this chapter. The school district shall determine its student count, the approved daily route mileage and the number of eligible students transported on the basis of where pupils reside within the diminished boundaries of the school district when computing a school district budget limit and assistance as provided in this chapter. The combined student count in the new districts may not exceed the student count of the school district which would have existed if the subdivision had not occurred.

Added by Laws 1981, Ch. 1, § 2, eff. Jan. 23, 1981. Amended by Laws 1983, Ch. 229, § 1, eff. April 22, 1983; Laws 1985, Ch. 127, § 5; Laws 1986, Ch. 84, § 3; Laws 1987, Ch. 93, § 5; Laws 1990, Ch. 322, § 11, eff. June 20, 1990; Laws 1991, Ch. 314, § 1; Laws 1993, Ch. 202, § 12, eff. April 21, 1993; Laws 1998, Ch. 167, § 8; Laws 1998, 5th S.S., Ch. 1, § 14, eff. July 9, 1998; Laws 1999, Ch. 299, § 12; Laws 2000, Ch. 342, § 5; Laws 2001, Ch. 329, § 1.

Historical and Statutory Notes

Source:

Laws 1912, Ch. 77, § 99.
Civ. Code 1913, § 2816.
Laws 1919, Ch. 32, § 1.
Laws 1921, Ch. 158, § 1.
Laws 1922, Ch. 35, § 131.

Rev. Code 1928, §§ 1089, 1098.
Laws 1933, Ch. 65, § 8.
Code 1939, § 54-612.
Laws 1941, Ch. 79, § 3.
Laws 1947, Ch. 85, § 2.
Laws 1949, Ch. 12, § 1.
Code 1939, Supp.1952, § 54-602.
Laws 1955, Ch. 108, § 2.
A.R.S. former §§ 15-1212, 15-1234.
Laws 1959, Ch. 90, § 2.
Laws 1960, Ch. 127, § 50.
Laws 1961, Ch. 12, § 2.
Laws 1967, 3rd S.S., Ch. 19, § 11.
Laws 1968, Ch. 166, § 1.
Laws 1970, Ch. 11, § 1.
Laws 1971, Ch. 177, § 5.
Laws 1972, Ch. 115, § 6.
Laws 1973, Ch. 157, § 17.
Laws 1974, 1st S.S., Ch. 3, § 26.
Laws 1976, Ch. 66, § 1.
Laws 1976, Ch. 184, § 4.
Laws 1977, Ch. 20, § 4.
Laws 1978, Ch. 188, § 19.
Laws 1979, Ch. 184, § 2.
Laws 1980, 2nd S.S., Ch. 9, § 65.
Laws 1980, Ch. 167, § 6.

Laws 1990, Ch. 329, § 5, provides:

"**Sec. 5. Student revenue loss phase-down**

"**A.** Notwithstanding § 15-902, subsection I, Arizona Revised Statutes, a school district which loses at least five hundred students from its student count as a result of the formation of a joint unified school district pursuant to § 15-450, Arizona Revised Statutes, and does not receive tuition for those students for the budget year, may increase its revenue control limit for the budget year by an amount as follows:

"1. For the first year of the loss, six hundred fifty thousand dollars.

"2. For the second year following the loss, six hundred thousand dollars.

"3. For the third year following the loss, five hundred thousand dollars.

"4. For the fourth year following the loss, three hundred thousand dollars.

"5. For the fifth year following the loss, one hundred thousand dollars.

"**B.** Notwithstanding § 15-902, subsection I, Arizona Revised Statutes, a union high school district which loses at least seventy students from its student count as a result of the formation of a joint unified school district pursuant to § 15-450, Arizona Revised Statutes, and does not receive tuition for those students for the budget year, may increase its revenue control limit for the budget year by an amount as follows:

"1. For the first year of the loss, one hundred thousand dollars.

"2. If during the second year following the initial loss of students the union high school district loses an additional seventy students as a result of the formation of a joint unified school district pursuant to § 15-450, Arizona Revised Statutes, and does not receive tuition for those students for the budget year, two hundred thousand dollars.

"3. If during the third year following the initial loss of students the union high school district loses an additional seventy students beyond the second year's additional loss as a result of the formation of a joint unified school district pursuant to § 15-450, and does not receive tuition for those students for the budget year, three hundred twenty-five thousand dollars.

"4. If the union high school district was eligible for the three hundred twenty-five thousand dollars as provided in paragraph 3 of this subsection, for the fourth year following the initial loss of students, two hundred thousand dollars.

"5. If the union high school district was eligible for the two hundred thousand dollars as provided in paragraph 4 of this subsection, for the fifth year following the initial loss of students, one hundred thousand dollars."

Laws 1991, Ch. 314, § 2, provides:

"**Sec. 2. Budget revisions for fiscal year 1991-1992**

"If a school district governing board has adopted a budget for fiscal year 1991-1992 based on forms and instructions provided by the auditor general and the department of education for that fiscal year and if, as a result of the enactment or nonenactment of proposed legislation during the fortieth legislature, first regular session, the budget is based on incorrect limits, does not include items authorized by law or does not otherwise conform with law, the governing board may revise its budget to conform with the law at a public hearing before October 31, 1991. If the governing board does not revise the budget before October 31, 1991 and if the budget includes any items not authorized by law or if the budget exceeds any limits, the governing board shall adjust or revise the budget as provided in § 15-905, subsection E, Arizona Revised Statutes."

The purported amendment of this section by Laws 1998, Ch. 164 failed to become effective because Chapter 164 was repealed in its entirety by Laws 1998, 5th S.S., Ch. 1, § 2, effective July 1, 1998.

The purported amendment of this section by Laws 1998, 3rd S.S., Ch. 1, failed to became effective because Ch. 1 was repealed in its entirety by Laws 1998, 5th S.S., Ch. 1, § 2, effective July 1, 1998.

Laws 1998, 5th S.S., Ch. 1, § 54, provides:

"**Sec. 54. Electronic reporting; implementation**

"Notwithstanding § 15–902, 15–903, 15–904 and 15–905, Arizona Revised Statutes, as amended by this act, schools and school districts shall not be required to submit electronic data to the department of education until fiscal year 2000–2001."

Reviser's Notes:

1998 Note. Prior to the 1999 amendment, this section contained the amendments made by Laws 1998, Second Regular Session, Ch. 167, sec. 8 and Laws 1998, Fifth Special Session, Ch. 1. sec. 14 that were blended together pursuant to authority of § 41–1304.03.

1998 Note. Pursuant to authority of § 41–1304.02 [in Laws 1998, 5th S.S., Ch. 1, § 54], a period was inserted at the end of the sentence to correct a manifest clerical error.

§ 15–902.01. Student revenue loss phase-down

A. Notwithstanding § 15–902, subsection I a school district which loses at least five hundred students from its student count as a result of the formation of a joint unified school district pursuant to § 15–450 and does not receive tuition for those students for the budget year, may increase its base support level for the budget year by an amount as follows:

1. For the first year of the loss, six hundred fifty thousand dollars.
2. For the second year following the loss, six hundred thousand dollars.
3. For the third year following the loss, five hundred thousand dollars.
4. For the fourth year following the loss, three hundred thousand dollars.
5. For the fifth year following the loss, one hundred thousand dollars.

B. In addition to any adjustment for tuition loss received pursuant to § 15–954 a union high school district which loses at least fifty students from its tuition count as a result of the formation of a joint unified school district pursuant to § 15–450 and does not receive tuition for those students for the budget year, may increase its base support level for the budget year by an amount as follows:

1. For the first year of the loss, one hundred thousand dollars.
2. If during the second year following the initial loss of students the union high school district loses an additional fifty students as a result of the formation of a joint unified school district pursuant to § 15–450 and does not receive tuition for those students for the budget year, two hundred thousand dollars.
3. If during the third year following the initial loss of students the union high school district loses an additional fifty students beyond the second year's additional loss as a result of the formation of a joint unified school district pursuant to § 15–450 and does not receive tuition for those students for the budget year, three hundred twenty-five thousand dollars.
4. If the union high school district was eligible for the three hundred twenty-five thousand dollars as provided in paragraph 3 of this subsection, for the fourth year following the initial loss of students, two hundred thousand dollars.
5. If the union high school district was eligible for the two hundred thousand dollars as provided in paragraph 4 of this subsection, for the fifth year following the initial loss of students, one hundred thousand dollars.

Added by Laws 1995, Ch. 191, § 22.

Historical and Statutory Notes

Reviser's Notes:

1995 Note. Pursuant to authority of § 41-1304.02, this section, enacted as § 22 of Laws 1995, Ch. 191, was added to Arizona Revised Statutes as § 15-902.01. In addition, ", Arizona Revised Statutes," was deleted in six places as a conforming change and in subsection B, paragraph 3 "additional" was substituted for "addition" to correct a manifest clerical error.

§ 15-902.02. Optional two hundred day average daily membership calculation

A school district governing board shall calculate its average daily membership on the two hundredth day of instruction if the school district elects to provide two hundred days of instruction. A school district that elects to provide two hundred days of instruction may calculate its budget based on an estimated average daily membership and may increase its base level by five per cent. A school district shall adjust its budget for the budget year based on any discrepancies between the estimated average daily membership for the previous year and the actual average daily membership on the two hundredth day of instruction for the previous year. A school district that elects to provide two hundred days of instruction shall ensure that the last day of instruction in any school year occurs before June 30.

Added by Laws 1998, Ch. 167, § 9. Amended by Laws 1999, 1st S.S., Ch. 4, § 8.

Historical and Statutory Notes

Reviser's Notes:

1998 Note. Pursuant to authority of § 41-1304.02, in the section heading the spelling of "two hundred" was corrected and the subsection designation "A." was removed to correct manifest clerical errors.

§ 15-903. Budget format; prohibited expenditures

A. The superintendent of public instruction in conjunction with the auditor general shall prepare and prescribe a budget format to be utilized by all school districts on a school by school basis.

B. The budget format shall be designed to allow all school districts to plan and provide in detail for the use of available funds on a school by school basis, except that the budget format shall not be required to provide details on a school by school basis in fiscal years 2004-2005 and 2005-2006. The budget format shall contain distinct sections for, but need not be limited to, maintenance and operation, debt service, special projects, capital outlay, adjacent ways and classroom site fund. The maintenance and operation section shall include, but need not be limited to, separate subsections for regular education programs, special education programs and operational expenditures for pupil transportation. Each subsection shall clearly distinguish classroom instruction expenditures. The sections for individual schools shall only contain aggregate summaries by major function for the maintenance and operation, unrestricted capital outlay and soft capital allocation funds. A school district shall prepare budgets for each individual school in the district and shall make these individual school budgets available to the public on request. The special education program subsection shall include, but is not limited to, programs for each disability classification as defined in § 15-761 and programs for gifted, vocational and technological education, remedial education and bilingual students.

The total expenditures for each of these programs shall be included on the budget form. The pupil transportation subsection shall include all operational expenditures relating to the transportation of pupils, including all operational expenditures within a contract if the school district contracts for pupil transportation.

C. The capital outlay section of the budget shall include separate subsections for unrestricted capital outlay and soft capital allocation. The soft capital allocation subsection shall include budgeted expenditures as prescribed in § 15–962. The unrestricted capital outlay subsection shall include budgeted expenditures for acquisitions by purchase, lease-purchase or lease of capital items as defined in the uniform system of financial records. These sections and subsections shall include:

1. Land, buildings and improvements to land and buildings, including labor and related employee benefits costs and material costs if work is performed by school district employees.

2. Furniture, furnishings, athletic equipment and other equipment, including computer software.

3. Pupil and nonpupil transportation vehicles and equipment, including all capital expenditures within a contract if the school district contracts for pupil transportation.

4. Textbooks and related printed subject matter materials adopted by the governing board.

5. Instructional aids.

6. Library books.

7. Payment of principal and interest on bonds.

8. School district administration emergency needs that are directly related to pupils.

D. The budget format shall contain distinct subsections for the following:

1. Special programs to improve academic achievement of pupils in kindergarten programs and grades one through three as provided in § 15–482.

2. School plant funds.

3. Capital outlay budget increases as provided in § 15–481.

4. Property taxation including the following:

(a) The primary tax rates for the school district for the current year and the budget year.

(b) The secondary tax rates for maintenance and operation, K–3 and capital overrides for the school district for the current year and the budget year.

(c) The secondary tax rates for class A bonds for the school district for the current year and the budget year.

(d) The secondary tax rates for class B bonds for the school district for the current year and the budget year.

5. A description of any corrections or adjustments made to the budget pursuant to § 15–915.

E. The budget format shall also contain:

1. A statement identifying proposed pupil-teacher ratios and pupil-staff ratios relating to the provision of special education services for the budget year.

2. A statement identifying the number of full-time equivalent certified employees.

3. If a governing board uses § 15-942 relating to the adjustment for rapid decline in student count, a statement identifying the actual per cent decline in student count and a statement identifying the additional allowable expenditures attributable to using the rapid decline provisions as provided in § 15-942.

F. The special projects section shall include budgeted expenditures for state special projects, including special adult projects, career education, deficiencies correction fund projects, building renewal fund projects and new school facilities fund projects, such federal special projects as ESEA title programs, vocational education and title IV Indian education, and other special projects.

G. A school district shall not make expenditures for campaign literature associated with school district or charter school officials. If the superintendent of public instruction determines that a school district has violated this subsection, the superintendent of public instruction may withhold any portion of the school district's apportionment of state aid.

H. The budget format shall include an electronic format that shall be submitted for each proposed, adopted and revised budget.

Added by Laws 1981, Ch. 1, § 2, eff. Jan. 23, 1981. Amended by Laws 1982, Ch. 179, § 1; Laws 1984, Ch. 314, § 2, eff. April 30, 1984; Laws 1984, Ch. 364, § 2; Laws 1985, Ch. 166, § 12, eff. April 18, 1985; Laws 1986, Ch. 125, § 4, eff. April 18, 1986; Laws 1987, Ch. 164, § 1; Laws 1990, Ch. 348, § 8, eff. June 26, 1990; Laws 1992, Ch. 172, § 18; Laws 1996, 5th S.S., Ch. 8, § 2; Laws 1997, 1st S.S., Ch. 4, § 6; Laws 1998, 5th S.S., Ch. 1, § 15, eff. July 9, 1998; Laws 1999, Ch. 299, § 13; Laws 2000, Ch. 342, § 9; Laws 2000, 5th S.S., Ch. 1, § 12; Laws 2002, Ch. 333, § 1, eff. June 4, 2002; Laws 2004, Ch. 340, § 3.

Historical and Statutory Notes

Source:

Laws 1955, 3rd S.S., Ch. 3, § 1.
A.R.S. former § 15-1201.
Laws 1974, 1st S.S., Ch. 3, § 21.
Laws 1976, Ch. 165, § 6.
Laws 1977, Ch. 89, § 9.
Laws 1977, Ch. 152, § 3.
Laws 1978, Ch. 62, § 8.
Laws 1978, Ch. 188, § 15.
Laws 1980, 2nd S.S., Ch. 9, § 54.
Laws 1980, Ch. 167, § 4.

Laws 1980, 2nd S.S., Ch. 9, § 1, provides:

"**Section 1. Purpose**

"The legislature intends by this act to increase the authority and responsibility of local school boards in determining how revenues will be utilized. Beginning in the 1980-81 fiscal year disparities in operational revenues among districts will be reduced on an annual basis until complete equalization is reached in the 1985-86 fiscal year. Each year a revenue control limit for operational expenses will be established for each district taking into account general maintenance and operation costs, special education, vocational education, teacher experience, operational expenditures for pupil transportation and the size of the school district. Also included, but under a separate fund and excluded from the five year equalization provisions of the school finance plan, is capital outlay. Capital outlay revenue limits will be established. Local leeway will be allowed through budget override provisions. It should also be noted that federal categorical programs are not included as part of the proposed school finance plan.

"With the exception of capital outlay the proposed funding concept is a block grant system which will provide revenues to school districts for operating expenses. Under this single fund concept each school district will be responsible for allocating funds to educational programs within the school district. This is in contrast to the existing system where revenues for specific programs are allocated to schools by the state. Accordingly, the responsibility and authority for establishing program priorities as well as for seeking more efficient and effective means of educating students will rest with the locally elected school board.

"In addition, the legislature recognizes that the early years of a pupil's education are crucial to his future and that mastery of the basic skills of reading, penmanship, grammar and mathematics is essential to the future educational and personal success of an individual. The first priority of the public schools of this state shall be to assure that all Arizonans, to the extent that their individual physical, mental and emotional capacities permit, shall achieve mastery of the basic skills.

"The legislature recognizes the need for increased accountability for the expenditures of state and local funds for education in this state, therefore, the legislature intends to provide such accountability by implementing provisions for pupil and teacher proficiency examinations."

Laws 1987, Ch. 9, § 1, effective March 16, 1987, provided for budgeting for excess insurance costs for fiscal year 1987–1988.

Laws 1988, Ch. 288, § 10, effective July 8, 1988, provided for budgeting for excess insurance costs for fiscal year 1988–1989, and for a limitation on expenditures.

Laws 1989, Ch. 26, § 1, eff. April 13, 1989, prescribes methods of budgeting for excess liability insurance costs exempt from the revenue control limit.

Laws 1990, Ch. 65, § 1, as amended by Laws 1991, Ch. 69, § 1, provides:

"**Section 1. Excess insurance costs for fiscal years 1990–1991 and 1991–1992; limitation on expenditures**

"**A.** The governing board of a school district may budget for excess insurance costs which are specifically exempt from the revenue control limit for the school district for fiscal years 1990–1991 and 1991–1992. The department of education and the auditor general shall include in the maintenance and operation section of the budget format, as provided in § 15–903, Arizona Revised Statutes, a separate line for all property and casualty insurance expenditures and a special excess insurance cost category. The special excess insurance cost category shall contain budgeted expenditures for excess insurance costs, determined as follows:

"1. Determine the actual charges for all property and casualty insurance for fiscal year 1984–1985.

"2. Increase or decrease the amount in paragraph 1 of this subsection by the total percentage increase or decrease in the revenue control limit and the capital outlay revenue limit as provided in § 15–947, Arizona Revised Statutes, for fiscal year 1990–1991 or 1991–1992, whichever is appropriate, over the revenue control limit and the capital outlay revenue limit for fiscal year 1985–1986 excluding monies available from a career ladder program or a teacher compensation program as provided in § 15–952, Arizona Revised Statutes.

"3. Multiply the amount in paragraph 2 of this subsection by 2.50. The product is the amount budgeted in the insurance cost expenditure line.

"4. Expenditures for insurance costs in excess of the amount budgeted in the insurance cost expenditure line may be budgeted in the excess insurance cost category.

"**B.** The governing board may expend from the excess insurance cost category only after it has expended for property and casualty insurance purposes the full amount budgeted in the insurance cost expenditure line of the budget. Notwithstanding § 15–905, subsection N, Arizona Revised Statutes, the governing board of a school district shall not prepay property and casualty insurance premiums in a fiscal year if the governing board has budgeted for excess insurance costs for that fiscal year. The maximum amount that may be expended from the excess insurance cost category in a year in which payment is made to a self-insurance trust fund for property and casualty losses is determined as follows:

"1. Determine the actual charges for all property and casualty insurance for the fiscal year before the first fiscal year in which payments are made into a self-insurance trust fund for property and casualty losses.

"2. Increase the amount determined in paragraph 1 of this subsection by the percentage increase in the revenue control limit and capital outlay revenue limit between the year utilized in paragraph 1 of this subsection and the current year.

"3. Subtract the amount budgeted in the property and casualty insurance expenditure line for the current year from the amount determined in paragraph 2 of this subsection.

"4. The difference in paragraph 3 of this subsection is the maximum amount that may be expended from the excess insurance cost category.

"**C.** The governing board, after notice is given and a public meeting is held as provided in § 15–905, subsection D, Arizona Revised Statutes, may revise at any time before May 15, 1991 the amount budgeted in the excess insurance cost category for fiscal year 1990–1991 and before May 15, 1992 the amount budgeted in the excess insurance cost category for fiscal year 1991–1992.

"**D.** If the revised excess insurance cost category results in an expenditure of monies in excess of school district revenues for fiscal year 1990–1991 or 1991–1992 the county school superintendent shall include within the revenue estimate for the following fiscal year monies necessary to meet the liabilities incurred by the school district in fiscal year 1990–1991 or 1991–1992, whichever is appropriate, in excess of revenues received for that year.

"**E.** The department of education shall describe the method for determining actual charges for all property and casualty insurance."

Laws 1992, Ch. 52, § 1, eff. April 27, 1992, provides:

"**Section 1. Excess insurance costs for fiscal year 1992–1993; limitation on expenditures**

"**A.** The governing board of a school district may budget for excess insurance costs that are specifically exempt from the revenue control limit for fiscal year 1992–1993. The department of education and the auditor general shall include in the maintenance and operation section of the budget format, as provided in § 15–903, Arizona Revised Statutes, a separate line for all property and casualty insurance expenditures and a special excess insurance cost category. The special excess cost category shall contain budgeted expenditures for excess insurance costs, determined as follows:

"1. Determine the actual charges for all property and casualty insurance for fiscal year 1984–1985.

"2. Increase or decrease the amount in paragraph 1 of this subsection by the total percentage increase or decrease in the revenue control limit and the capital outlay revenue limit as provided in § 15–947, Arizona Revised Statutes, for fiscal year 1992–1993 over the revenue control limit and the capital outlay revenue limit for fiscal year 1985–1986 excluding monies available from a career ladder program or a teacher compensation program as provided in § 15–952, Arizona Revised Statutes.

"3. Multiply the amount in paragraph 2 of this subsection by a factor of 2.50. The product is the amount budgeted in the insurance cost expenditure line.

"4. Expenditures for insurance costs in excess of the amount budgeted in the insurance cost expenditure line may be budgeted in the excess cost category.

"**B.** The governing board may expend from the excess insurance cost category only after it has expended for property and casualty insurance purposes the full amount budgeted in the insurance cost expenditure line of the budget. Notwithstanding § 15–905, subsection N, Arizona Revised Statutes, the governing board of a school district shall not prepay property and casualty insurance premiums in a fiscal year if the governing board has budgeted for excess insurance costs for that fiscal year. The maximum amount that may be expended from the excess insurance cost category in a year in which payment is made to a self-insurance trust fund for property and casualty losses is determined as follows:

"1. Determine the actual charges for all property and casualty insurance for the fiscal year before the first fiscal year in which payments are made into a self-insurance trust fund for property and casualty losses.

"2. Increase the amount determined in paragraph 1 of this subsection by the percentage increase in the revenue control limit and the capital outlay revenue limit between the year utilized in paragraph 1 of this subsection and the current year.

"3. Subtract the amount budgeted in the property and casualty insurance expenditure line for the current year from the amount determined in paragraph 2 of this subsection.

"4. The difference in paragraph 3 of this subsection is the maximum amount that may be expended from the excess insurance cost category.

"**C.** The governing board, after notice is given and a public meeting is held as provided in § 15–905, subsection D, Arizona Revised Statutes, may revise at any time before May 15, 1993 the amount budgeted in the excess insurance cost category for fiscal year 1992–1993.

"**D.** If the excess insurance cost category results in an expenditure of monies in excess of school district revenues for fiscal year 1992–1993 the county school superintendent shall include within the revenue estimate for fiscal year 1993–1994 monies necessary to meet the liabilities incurred by the school district in fiscal year 1992–1993 in excess of revenues received for that year.

"**E.** The department of education shall describe the method for determining actual charges for all property and casualty insurance."

Laws 1993, Ch. 202, § 27, eff. April 21, 1993, provides:

"**Sec. 27. Excess insurance costs for fiscal year 1993–1994; limitation on expenditures**

"**A.** The governing board of a school district may budget for excess insurance costs that are specifically exempt from the revenue control limit for fiscal year 1993–1994. The department of education and the auditor general shall include in the maintenance and operation section of the budget format, as provided in § 15–903, Arizona Revised Statutes, a separate line for all property and casualty insurance expenditures and a special excess insurance cost category. The special excess cost category shall contain budgeted expenditures for excess insurance costs, determined as follows:

"1. Determine the actual charges for all property and casualty insurance for fiscal year 1984-1985.

"2. Increase or decrease the amount in paragraph 1 of this subsection by the total percentage increase or decrease in the revenue control limit and the capital outlay revenue limit as provided in § 15-947, Arizona Revised Statutes, for fiscal year 1993-1994 over the revenue control limit and the capital outlay revenue limit for fiscal year 1985-1986 excluding monies available from a career ladder program or a teacher compensation program as provided in § 15-952, Arizona Revised Statutes.

"3. Multiply the amount in paragraph 2 of this subsection by a factor of 2.50. The product is the amount budgeted in the insurance cost expenditure line.

"4. Expenditures for insurance costs in excess of the amount budgeted in the insurance cost expenditure line may be budgeted in the excess cost category.

"**B.** The governing board may expend from the excess insurance cost category only after it has expended for property and casualty insurance purposes the full amount budgeted in the insurance cost expenditure line of the budget. Notwithstanding § 15-905, subsection N, Arizona Revised Statutes, the governing board of a school district shall not prepay property and casualty insurance premiums in a fiscal year if the governing board has budgeted for excess insurance costs for that fiscal year. The maximum amount that may be expended from the excess insurance cost category in a year in which payment is made to a self-insurance trust fund for property and casualty losses is determined as follows:

"1. Determine the actual charges for all property and casualty insurance for the fiscal year before the first fiscal year in which payments are made into a self-insurance trust fund for property and casualty losses.

"2. Increase the amount determined in paragraph 1 of this subsection by the percentage increase in the revenue control limit and the capital outlay revenue limit between the year utilized in paragraph 1 of this subsection and the current year.

"3. Subtract the amount budgeted in the property and casualty insurance expenditure line for the current year from the amount determined in paragraph 2 of this subsection.

"4. The difference in paragraph 3 of this subsection is the maximum amount that may be expended from the excess insurance cost category.

"**C.** The governing board, after notice is given and a public meeting is held as provided in § 15-905, subsection D, Arizona Revised Statutes, may revise at any time before May 15, 1994 the amount budgeted in the excess insurance cost category for fiscal year 1993-1994.

"**D.** If the excess insurance cost category results in an expenditure of monies in excess of school district revenues for fiscal year 1993-1994 the county school superintendent shall include within the revenue estimate for fiscal year 1994-1995 monies necessary to meet the liabilities incurred by the school district in fiscal year 1993-1994 in excess of revenues received for that year.

"**E.** The department of education shall describe the method for determining actual charges for all property and casualty insurance."

Laws 1994, Ch. 254, § 7, effective April 24, 1994, provides:

"**Sec. 7. Excess insurance costs for fiscal year 1994-1995; limitation on expenditures**

"**A.** The governing board of a school district may budget for excess insurance costs that are specifically exempt from the revenue control limit for fiscal year 1994-1995. The department of education and the auditor general shall include in the maintenance and operation section of the budget format, as provided in § 15-903, Arizona Revised Statutes, a separate line for all property and casualty insurance expenditures and a special excess insurance cost category. The special excess cost category shall contain budgeted expenditures for excess insurance costs, determined as follows:

"1. Determine the actual charges for all property and casualty insurance for fiscal year 1984-1985.

"2. Increase or decrease the amount in paragraph 1 of this subsection by the total percentage increase or decrease in the revenue control limit and the capital outlay revenue limit as provided in § 15-947, Arizona Revised Statutes, for fiscal year 1994-1995 over the revenue control limit and the capital outlay revenue limit for fiscal year 1985-1986 excluding monies available from a career ladder program or a teacher compensation program as provided in § 15-952, Arizona Revised Statutes.

"3. Multiply the amount in paragraph 2 of this subsection by a factor of 2.50. The product is the amount budgeted in the insurance cost expenditure line.

"4. Expenditures for insurance costs in excess of the amount budgeted in the insurance cost expenditure line may be budgeted in the excess cost category.

"**B.** The governing board may expend from the excess insurance cost category only after it has expended for property and casualty insurance purposes the full amount budgeted in the insurance cost expenditure line of the budget.

Notwithstanding § 15-905, subsection N, Arizona Revised Statutes, the governing board of a school district shall not prepay property and casualty insurance premiums in a fiscal year if the governing board has budgeted for excess insurance costs for that fiscal year. The maximum amount that may be expended from the excess insurance cost category in a year in which payment is made to a self-insurance trust fund for property and casualty losses is determined as follows:

"1. Determine the actual charges for all property and casualty insurance for the fiscal year before the first fiscal year in which payments are made into a self-insurance trust fund for property and casualty losses.

"2. Increase the amount determined in paragraph 1 of this subsection by the percentage increase in the revenue control limit and the capital outlay revenue limit between the year utilized in paragraph 1 of this subsection and the current year.

"3. Subtract the amount budgeted in the property and casualty insurance expenditure line for the current year from the amount determined in paragraph 2 of this subsection.

"4. The difference in paragraph 3 of this subsection is the maximum amount that may be expended from the excess insurance cost category.

"**C.** The governing board, after notice is given and a public meeting is held as provided in § 15-905, subsection D, Arizona Revised Statutes, may revise at any time before May 15, 1994 the amount budgeted in the excess insurance cost category for fiscal year 1994-1995.

"**D.** If the excess insurance cost category results in an expenditure of monies in excess of school district revenues for fiscal year 1994-1995 the county school superintendent shall include within the revenue estimate for fiscal year 1995-1996 monies necessary to meet the liabilities incurred by the school district in fiscal year 1994-1995 in excess of revenues received for that year.

"**E.** The department of education shall describe the method for determining actual charges for all property and casualty insurance."

Laws 1995, Ch., § 191, § 24, eff. April 19, 1995, provides:

"**Sec. 24. Excess insurance costs for fiscal years 1995-1996 through 1999-2000; limitation on expenditures**

"**A.** The governing board of a school district may budget for excess insurance costs that are specifically exempt from the revenue control limit for fiscal years 1995-1996 through 1999-2000. The department of education and the auditor general shall include in the maintenance and operation section of the budget format, as provided in § 15-903, Arizona Revised Statutes, a separate line for all property and casualty insurance expenditures and a special excess insurance cost category. The special excess cost category shall contain budgeted expenditures for excess insurance costs, determined as follows:

"1. For fiscal year 1995-1996, an amount equal to eighty-five per cent of the amount expended for excess insurance costs for fiscal year 1994-1995 under the provisions of Laws 1994, chapter 254, § 7.

"2. For fiscal year 1996-1997, an amount equal to sixty-eight per cent of the amount expended for excess insurance costs for fiscal year 1994-1995 under the provisions of Laws 1994, chapter 254, § 7.

"3. For fiscal year 1997-1998, an amount equal to fifty-one per cent of the amount expended for excess insurance costs for fiscal year 1994-1995 under the provisions of Laws 1994, chapter 254, § 7.

"4. For fiscal year 1998-1999, an amount equal to thirty-four per cent of the amount expended for excess insurance costs for fiscal year 1994-1995 under the provisions of Laws 1994, chapter 254, § 7.

"5. For fiscal year 1999-2000, an amount equal to seventeen per cent of the amount expended for excess insurance costs for fiscal year 1994-1995 under the provisions of Laws 1994, chapter 254, § 7."

The purported amendment of this section by Laws 1998, Ch. 164 failed to become effective because Chapter 164 was repealed in its entirety by Laws 1998, 5th S.S., Ch. 1, § 2, effective July 1, 1998.

Laws 2000, 5th S.S. Ch. 1, § 65, provides:

"**Sec. 65. Conforming legislation; blending**

"**A.** The legislative council staff shall prepare proposed legislation conforming the Arizona Revised Statutes to the provisions of this act for consideration in the forty-fifth legislature, first regular session.

"**B.** The executive director of the legislative council is authorized to blend the nonconflicting changes made to the Arizona Revised Statutes during the forty-fourth legislature, second regular session, with the changes made to those same statutes by this act."

Laws 2002, Ch. 333, §§ 3 and 4, eff. June 4, 2002, provides:

"**Sec. 3. Extension of state aid or budget limit errors for certain school districts**

"Notwithstanding § 15-915, subsection A, paragraph 1, Arizona Revised Statutes, the superintendent of public instruction may allow a common school district that is not within a high school district and that had an average daily membership for kindergarten and grades one through eight of fewer than eighty-five pupils in fiscal year 1999-2000 to complete the correction of state aid errors or budget limit errors made in fiscal year 1999-2000 no later than four years after the determination by the superintendent of public instruction of the miscalculation."

"**Sec. 4. Budget revisions**

"A school district in fiscal year 2001-2002 may reallocate the revenue control limit and capital outlay revenue limit between the maintenance and operations and the unrestricted portions of the budget for the 2001-2002 school year using the provisions of the general budget limit that were available at the time of the original budget adoption."

Laws 2004, Ch. 340, § 6, provides:

"**Sec. 6. Excess utilities; funding plan; review**

"Through June 30, 2009, each school district that budgets for excess utilities shall conduct the following at the same public meeting where the school district budget is proposed and adopted:

"1. A review that includes the current year budget, the current year estimated expenditures and the proposed budget for the direct operational costs of each of the following that are contained within the revenue control limit and of the excess utilities budget outside the revenue control limit:

"(a) Heating.

"(b) Cooling.

"(c) Water.

"(d) Electricity.

"(e) Telephone communications.

"(f) Sanitation fees.

"2. A review of specific financial goals to enable the school district to pay for utility costs by June 30, 2009 as required by the voters of this state in a referendum designated as Proposition 301 at the 2000 general election.

"3. A review of the district's plan to ensure that the school district is making progress toward the achievement of the financial goals prescribed in paragraph 2."

Laws 2004, Ch. 340, § 7, provides:

"**Sec. 7. Retroactivity**

"Sections 15-903 and 15-904, Arizona Revised Statutes, as amended by this act, apply retroactively to from and after June 30, 2004."

Reviser's Notes:

1984 Note. Prior to the 1985 amendment, this section contained the amendments made by Laws 1984, Ch. 314, § 2, and Ch. 364, § 2 which were blended together pursuant to authority of § 41-1304.03.

2000 Note. Prior to the 2002 amendment, this section contained the amendments made by Laws 2000, Ch. 342, sec. 6 and 5th S.S., Ch. 1, sec. 12 that were blended together pursuant to authority of § 41-1304.03.

2002 Note. Pursuant to authority of § 41-1304.02, in the section heading "; prohibited expenditures" was added.

§ 15-904. School district annual financial report; publication; summary; exemption

A. The governing board of each school district shall publish an annual financial report on a school by school basis for the prior fiscal year by November 15, except that the annual financial report shall not be required to include information on a school by school basis in fiscal years 2004-2005 and 2005-2006. The auditor general in conjunction with the department of education shall prescribe the format of the financial report to be used by school districts. The financial report shall contain budgeted and actual expenditures for the preceding fiscal year and shall be prepared and distributed by October 15 by the school district with a copy to the county school superintendent. A copy of the annual financial report shall be submitted electronically by the school district to the superintendent of public instruction by October 15. The annual financial report shall be approved by the county school superintendent in an electronic procedure as prescribed by the department of education. School districts that are subject to § 15-914.01 are not required to send a copy to the county school superintendent.

B. In addition to the information required in subsection A of this section, the annual financial report shall contain detailed information on the school district budgeted and actual expenditures from the bond building fund, the soft capital allocation fund, the deficiencies correction fund, the building renewal fund and the new school facilities fund, including but not limited to information on classified salaries, employee benefits, interest and fiscal charges, capital lease agreements, land and improvements, buildings and improvements, furniture and equipment, technology and vehicles and transportation equipment for pupils. The information shall specify whether the expenditures are for school district renovation or for new construction, the cost per square foot, and land acquisition costs, as appropriate. The reporting by individual schools shall be limited to annual expenditures aggregated by major function for the maintenance and operation, unrestricted capital outlay and soft capital allocation funds.

C. Except as provided in subsection D of this section, the governing board shall publish, by November 15, the annual financial report for the school district on a school by school basis in a newspaper of general circulation within the school district or in the official newspaper of the county as defined in § 11-255 or the governing board may mail the annual financial report to each household in the school district, except that the annual financial report shall not be required to include information on a school by school basis in fiscal years 2004-2005 and 2005-2006. If the governing board chooses to publish the report in a newspaper, the size of the newspaper print shall be at least eight-point type. The cost of publication or mailing shall be a charge against the school district. The publisher's affidavit of publication shall be filed by the governing board of the school district with the superintendent of public instruction within thirty days after publication.

D. The governing board may publish or mail a summary of the annual financial report in the same manner as provided in subsection C of this section. The auditor general in conjunction with the department of education shall prescribe the form of the summary of the annual financial report for use by the governing boards.

E. The superintendent of public instruction shall compile the financial reports of the school districts on a school by school basis and shall report to the governor and the legislature on or before January 15 of each year as provided in § 15-255, except that the financial reports shall not be required to include information on a school by school basis in fiscal years 2004-2005 and 2005-2006.

Added by Laws 1981, Ch. 1, § 2, eff. Jan. 23, 1981. Amended by Laws 1981, Ch. 314, § 16; Laws 1982, Ch. 197, § 4; Laws 1982, Ch. 273, § 1, eff. April 27, 1982; Laws 1983, Ch. 224, § 6; Laws 1987, Ch. 36, § 3; Laws 1987, Ch. 343, § 1, eff. May 22, 1987; Laws 1992, Ch. 305, § 15; Laws 1995, Ch. 268, § 48; Laws 1996, Ch. 62, § 1; Laws 1996, 7th S.S., Ch. 1, § 1; Laws 1998, Ch. 63, § 2; Laws 1998, 5th S.S., Ch. 1, § 16, eff. July 9, 1998; Laws 1999, Ch. 299, § 14; Laws 2000, Ch. 342, § 7; Laws 2002, Ch. 333, § 2, eff. June 4, 2002; Laws 2004, Ch. 340, § 4.

Historical and Statutory Notes

Source:

Laws 1974, 1st S.S., Ch. 3, § 23.
A.R.S. former § 15-1201.04.
Laws 1980, 2nd S.S., Ch. 9, § 58.

The purported amendment of this section by Laws 1998, 3rd S.S., Ch. 1, failed to became effective because Ch. 1 was repealed in its entirety by Laws 1998, 5th S.S., Ch. 1, § 2, effective July 1, 1998.

Laws 2004, Ch. 340, § 6, provides:

"**Sec. 6. Excess utilities; funding plan; review**

"Through June 30, 2009, each school district that budgets for excess utilities shall conduct the following at the same public meeting where the school district budget is proposed and adopted:

"1. A review that includes the current year budget, the current year estimated expenditures and the proposed budget for the direct operational costs of each of the following that are contained within the revenue control limit and of the excess utilities budget outside the revenue control limit:

"(a) Heating.

"(b) Cooling.

"(c) Water.

"(d) Electricity.

"(e) Telephone communications.

"(f) Sanitation fees.

"2. A review of specific financial goals to enable the school district to pay for utility costs by June 30, 2009 as required by the voters of this state in a referendum designated as Proposition 301 at the 2000 general election.

"3. A review of the district's plan to ensure that the school district is making progress toward the achievement of the financial goals prescribed in paragraph 2."

Laws 2004, Ch. 340, § 7, provides:

"**Sec. 7. Retroactivity**

"Sections 15-903 and 15-904, Arizona Revised Statutes, as amended by this act, apply retroactively to from and after June 30, 2004."

Reviser's Notes:

1982 Note: Prior to the 1983 amendment, this section contained the amendments made by Laws 1982, Ch. 197, § 4 and Ch. 273, § 1 which were blended together pursuant to authority of § 41-1304.03. In addition, pursuant to authority of § 41-1304.02 "; summary" was added to the section heading and the last sentence in this section was lettered as new subsection E.

1987 Note. Prior to the 1996 amendment, this section contained the amendments made by Laws 1987, Ch. 36, § 3 and Ch. 343, § 1 which were blended together pursuant to authority of § 41-1304.03. Pursuant to authority of § 41-1304.02, "School district annual financial report; publication; summary; exemption" was substituted for the previous section heading.

1996 Note. The amendment of this section by Laws 1996, 7th Spec. Sess., Ch. 1, sec. 1 failed to set forth in full the text of the section as last amended by Laws 1996, Ch. 62, sec. 1 as required by Constitution of Arizona art. IV, pt. 2, sec. 14.

1998 Note. Prior to the 1999 amendment, this section contained the amendments made by Laws 1998, Second Regular Session, Ch. 63, sec. 2 and Laws 1998, Fifth Special Session, Ch. 1. sec. 16 that were blended together pursuant to authority of § 41-1304.03.

§ 15-905. School district budgets; notice; adoption; aggregate budget limit; summary; adjustments; definition

A. Not later than July 5 of each year or no later than the publication of notice of the public hearing and board meeting as required by this section, the governing board of each school district shall prepare and furnish to the superintendent of public instruction and the county school superintendent, unless waived by the county school superintendent, a proposed budget in electronic format for the budget year, which shall contain the information and be in the form as provided by the department of education. The proposed budget shall include the following:

1. The total amount of revenues from all sources that was necessary to meet the school district's budget for the current year.

2. The total amount of revenues by source that will be necessary to meet the proposed budget of the school district, excluding property taxes. The governing board shall prepare the proposed budget and a summary of the proposed budget. Both documents shall be kept on file at the school district office and shall be made available to the public upon request. The auditor general in conjunction with the department of education shall prescribe the form of the summary of the proposed budget for use by governing boards. School district

governing boards may include in the proposed budget any items or amounts which are authorized by legislation filed with the secretary of state and which will become effective during the budget year. If subsequent events prevent the legislation from becoming effective, school district governing boards must reduce their budgets by the amounts budgeted pursuant to the legislation which did not become effective.

B. The governing board of each school district shall prepare a notice fixing a time not later than July 15 and designating a public place within each school district at which a public hearing and board meeting shall be held. The governing board shall present the proposed budget for consideration of the residents and the taxpayers of the school district at such hearing and meeting.

C. The governing board of each school district shall publish or mail, prior to the hearing and meeting, a copy of the proposed budget or the summary of the proposed budget and, in addition, a notice of the public hearing and board meeting no later than ten days prior to the meeting. The proposed budget and the summary of the proposed budget shall contain the percentage of increase or decrease in each budget category of the proposed budget as compared to each category of the budget for the current year. Notification shall be either by publication in a newspaper of general circulation within the school district in which the size of the newspaper print shall be at least eight-point type or by mailing the information to each household in the school district. The cost of publication or mailing shall be a charge against the school district. The publisher's affidavit of publication shall be filed by the governing board with the superintendent of public instruction within thirty days after publication. If the budget or proposed budget and notice are mailed, the board shall file an affidavit of mailing with the superintendent of public instruction within thirty days after the mailing. If a truth in taxation notice and hearing is required under § 15-905.01, the governing board may combine the notice and hearing under this section with the truth in taxation notice and hearing.

D. At the time and place fixed in the notice, the governing board shall hold the public hearing and present the proposed budget to the persons attending the hearing. Upon request of any person, the governing board shall explain the budget, and any resident or taxpayer of the school district may protest the inclusion of any item. A governing board member who has a substantial interest, as defined in § 38-502, in a specific item in the school district budget shall refrain from voting on the specific item. A governing board member may without creating a conflict of interest participate in adoption of a final budget even though the member may have substantial interest in specific items included in the budget.

E. Immediately following the public hearing the president shall call to order the governing board meeting for the purpose of adopting the budget. The governing board shall adopt the budget which shall not exceed the general budget limit, the unrestricted capital budget limit or the soft capital allocation limit, making such deductions as it sees fit but making no additions to the proposed budget total for maintenance and operations or capital outlay, and shall enter the budget as adopted in its minutes. Not later than July 18, the budget as finally adopted shall be filed by the governing board with the county school superintendent who shall immediately transmit a copy to the board of supervisors. Not later than July 18, the budget as finally adopted shall be submitted electronically to the superintendent of public instruction. On or before October 30, the superintendent of public instruction shall review the budget and notify the governing board if the budget is in excess of the general budget limit, the unrestricted capital budget limit or the soft capital allocation limit. If the governing board receives notification that the budget is in excess of the general budget limit, the unrestricted capital budget limit or the soft capital allocation limit by fewer than one thousand dollars, the governing board shall adjust the budget and expenditures so as not to exceed the general budget limit, the unrestricted capital budget limit or the soft capital allocation limit for the current year. If the governing board receives notification that the budget is in excess of the general budget limit, the unrestricted capital budget limit or the soft capital allocation limit by one thousand dollars or more, it shall on or before December 15, after it gives notice and holds a public meeting in a similar manner as provided in subsections C and D of this section, adopt a revised budget for the current year which shall not exceed the general budget limit, the unrestricted capital budget limit or the soft capital allocation limit. On or before December 18, the governing board shall file the revised budget which it adopts with the county school superintendent who shall immediately transmit a copy to the board of supervisors. Not later than December 18, the budget as revised shall be submitted electronically to the superintendent of public instruction. School districts that are subject to section 15–914.01 are not required to send a copy of revised budgets to the county school superintendent. Procedures for adjusting expenditures or revising the budget shall be as prescribed in the uniform system of financial records.

F. The governing board of each school district may budget for expenditures within the school district budget as follows:

1. Amounts within the general budget limit, as provided in section 15–947, subsection C, may only be budgeted in the following sections of the budget:

(a) The maintenance and operation section.

(b) The capital outlay section.

2. Amounts within the unrestricted capital budget limit, as provided in § 15–947, subsection D, may only be budgeted in the unrestricted capital outlay subsection of the budget. Monies received pursuant to the unrestricted capital budget limit shall be placed in the unrestricted capital outlay fund. The monies in the fund are not subject to reversion.

3. The soft capital allocation limit, as provided in § 15–947, subsection E, may only be budgeted in the soft capital allocation subsection of the budget.

G. The governing board may authorize the expenditure of monies budgeted within the maintenance and operation section of the budget for any subsection within the section in excess of amounts specified in the adopted budget only by action taken at a public meeting of the governing board and if the expenditures for all subsections of the section do not exceed the amount budgeted as provided in this section. Until June 30, 1999, the governing board may authorize the expenditure of monies to exceed the budgeted expenditures of the capital outlay section of the budget only by action taken at a public meeting of the governing board and if monies are available in the reserve.

H. The aggregate budget limit is the sum of the following:

1. The general budget limit as determined in § 15-947 for the budget year.

2. The unrestricted capital budget limit as determined in section 15-947 for the budget year.

3. The soft capital allocation limit for the budget year as determined in § 15-947.

4. Federal assistance, excluding P.L. 81-874 monies.

I. School districts which overestimated tuition revenues as provided in § 15-947, subsection C, paragraph 2 shall adjust the general budget limit and expenditures based upon tuition revenues for attendance of nonresident pupils during the current fiscal year. School districts which underestimated tuition revenues may adjust their budgets prior to May 15 based upon tuition revenues for attendance of nonresident pupils during the current fiscal year. School districts which overestimated revenues as provided in § 15-947, subsection C, paragraph 2, subdivision (a), items (iii), (iv) and (v) and subdivision (d) shall adjust the general budget limit and expenditures based on actual revenues during the current fiscal year. School districts which underestimated such revenues may adjust their budgets before May 15 based on actual revenues during the current fiscal year. Procedures for completing adjustments shall be as prescribed in the uniform system of financial records. Not later than May 18, the budget as adjusted shall be submitted electronically to the superintendent of public instruction.

J. A common school district not within a high school district whose estimated tuition charge for high school pupils exceeds the actual tuition charge for high school pupils shall adjust the general budget limit and expenditures based on the actual tuition charge. Not later than May 18, the budget as adjusted shall be submitted electronically to the superintendent of public instruction. A common school district not within a high school district whose estimated tuition charge for high school pupils is less than the actual tuition charge for high school pupils may adjust its budget before May 15 based on the actual tuition charge. Procedures for completing adjustments shall be as prescribed in the uniform system of financial records. If the adjusted general budget limit requires an adjustment of state aid and if the adjustment to state aid is not made in the current year, the superintendent of public instruction shall adjust by August 15 of the succeeding fiscal year the apportionment of state aid to the school district to correct any overpayment or underpayment of state aid received during the current year.

K. The governing board may include P.L. 81-874 assistance allocated for children with disabilities, children with specific learning disabilities and children residing on Indian lands which is in addition to basic assistance when determining the general budget limit as prescribed in § 15-947, subsection C. The governing board may adjust before May 15 the budget for the current year based on any adjustments which result in increases over the amount estimated by the superintendent of public instruction for P.L. 81-874 assistance for such pupils for the fiscal year preceding the current year. The governing board shall adjust before May 15 the budget for the current year based on any adjustments which result in decreases in the amount estimated by the superintendent of public instruction for P.L. 81–874 assistance for such pupils for the fiscal year preceding the current year. Not later than May 18, the budget as adjusted shall be submitted electronically to the superintendent of public instruction. Procedures for complying with the provisions of this subsection shall be as prescribed in the uniform system of financial records.

L. The state board of education shall hold a hearing if expenditures by any school district exceed the general budget limit prescribed in § 15–947, subsection C, the unrestricted capital budget limit, the soft capital allocation limit prescribed in § 15–947, subsection E, the school plant fund limits prescribed in § 15–1102, subsection B, the maintenance and operation section of the budget or the capital outlay section of the budget. If the expenditures of any school district exceed these limits or sections of the budget without authorization as provided in § 15–907, the state board of education shall reduce the state aid for equalization assistance for education for the school district computed as provided in § 15–971 during the fiscal year subsequent to the fiscal year in which the excess expenditures were made by an amount equal to the excess expenditures, except that in case of hardship to the school district, the superintendent of public instruction may approve reductions partly in the first subsequent year and partly in the second subsequent year.

M. The governing board of a school district shall reduce the general budget limit, the unrestricted capital budget limit or the soft capital allocation limit, for the year subsequent to the year in which the expenditures were in excess of the applicable limit or section of the budget by the amount determined in subsection L of this section, except that in case of hardship to the school district, the superintendent of public instruction may approve reductions partly in the first subsequent year and partly in the second subsequent year. The reduction in the limit is applicable to each school district which has exceeded the general budget limit, the unrestricted capital budget limit, the soft capital allocation limit or a section of the budget even if the reduction exceeds the state aid for equalization assistance for education for the school district.

N. Except as provided in § 15–916, no expenditure shall be made by any school district for a purpose not included in the budget or in excess of the aggregate budget limit prescribed in this section, except that if no budget has been adopted, from July 1 to July 15 the governing board may make expenditures if the total of the expenditures does not exceed ten per cent of the prior year's aggregate budget limit. Any expenditures made from July 1 to July 15 and prior to the adoption of the budget shall be included in the total expenditures for the current year. No expenditure shall be made and no debt, obligation or liability shall be incurred or created in any year for any purpose itemized in the budget in excess of the amount specified for the item irrespective of whether the school district at any time has received or has on hand funds in excess of those required to meet the expenditures, debts, obligations and liabilities provided for under the budget except expenditures from cash controlled funds as defined by the uniform system of financial records and except as provided in § 15–907 and subsection G of this section. This subsection does not prohibit any school district from prepaying insurance premiums or magazine subscriptions, or from prepaying any item which is normally prepaid in order to procure the service or to receive a discounted price for the service, as prescribed by the uniform system of financial records.

O. The governing board of a school district which is classified as a heavily impacted school district having twenty per cent or more pupils pursuant to 20 United States Code § 238(d)1(A) may determine its eligibility to increase the amount that may be included in determining the general budget limit as provided in subsection K of this section and may increase the amount as follows:

1. For fiscal year 1988–1989:

(a) Multiply one thousand ninety-four dollars by the number of children with disabilities or children with specific learning disabilities, excluding children who also reside on Indian lands, reported to the division of impact aid, United States department of education in the district's application for fiscal year 1987–1988.

(b) Multiply five hundred forty-seven dollars by the number of children residing on Indian lands, excluding children who have disabilities or also have specific learning disabilities, reported to the division of impact aid, United States department of education in the district's application for fiscal year 1987–1988.

(c) Multiply one thousand nine hundred fourteen dollars by the number of children residing on Indian lands who have disabilities or also have specific learning disabilities reported to the division of impact aid, United States department of education in the district's application for fiscal year 1987–1988.

(d) Add the amounts determined in subdivisions (a) through (c).

(e) If the amount of P.L. 81–874 assistance as provided in subsection K of this section is less than the sum determined in subdivision (d) of this paragraph, the district is eligible to use the provisions of this subsection.

2. For budget years after 1988–1989, use the provisions of paragraph 1 of this subsection, but increase each dollar amount by the growth rate for that year as prescribed by law, subject to appropriation and use the number of children reported in the appropriate category for the current fiscal year.

3. If the district is eligible to use the provisions of this subsection, subtract the amount of P.L. 81–874 assistance determined in subsection K of this section from the sum determined in paragraph 1, subdivision (d) of this subsection. The difference is the increase in the amount that may be included in determining the general budget limit as provided in subsection K of this section, if including this amount does not increase the district's primary tax rate for the budget year. If the amount of P.L. 81–874 assistance determined in subsection K of this section is adjusted for the current year, the increase determined in this paragraph shall be recomputed using the adjusted amount and the recomputed increase shall be reported to the department of education by May 15 on a form prescribed by the department of education.

4. If a district uses the provisions of this subsection, the district is not required to adjust its budget for the current year based on adjustments in the estimated amount of P.L. 81–874 assistance as provided in subsection K of this section.

P. A school district, except for an accommodation school, which applies for P.L. 81-874 assistance during the current year may budget an amount for P.L. 81-874 administrative costs for the budget year. The amount budgeted for P.L. 81-874 administrative costs is exempt from the revenue control limit and may not exceed an amount determined for the budgeted year as follows:

1. Determine the minimum cost. The minimum cost for fiscal year 1990-1991 is two thousand three hundred forty-three dollars. For fiscal year 1991-1992 and thereafter, the minimum cost is the minimum cost for the prior year increased by the growth rate as prescribed by law, subject to appropriation.

2. Determine the hourly rate. The hourly rate for fiscal year 1990-1991 is nine dollars thirty-eight cents. For fiscal year 1991-1992 and thereafter, the hourly rate is the hourly rate for the prior year increased by the growth rate as prescribed by law, subject to appropriation.

3. Determine the P.L. 81-874 revenues available by subtracting the amount of P.L. 81-874 assistance used to increase the general budget limit as provided in subsections K and O of this section for the current fiscal year from the total amount of P.L. 81-874 revenues received in the current fiscal year.

4. Determine the total number of administrative hours as follows:

(a) Determine the sum of the following:

(i) 1.00 hours for each high impact pupil who is not disabled or does not have specific learning disabilities.

(ii) 1.25 hours for each high impact pupil who is disabled or has specific learning disabilities.

(iii) 0.25 hours for each low impact pupil who is not disabled or does not have specific learning disabilities.

(iv) 0.31 hours for each low impact pupil who is disabled or has specific learning disabilities.

(b) For the purposes of this paragraph:

(i) "High impact pupil" means a pupil who resides on Indian lands or a pupil who resides on federal property or in low rent housing and whose parent is employed on federal property or low rent housing property or is on active duty in uniformed service, as provided in P.L. 81-874, § 3(a) and as reported in the application for P.L. 81-874 assistance in the current year.

(ii) "Low impact pupil" means a pupil who resides on nonfederal property and has a parent who is employed on federal property or low rent housing property or is on active duty in a uniformed service or a pupil who resides on federal property or in low rent housing and who does not have a parent who is employed on federal property or low rent housing property or is on active duty in uniformed service, as provided in P.L. 81-874, § 3(b) and as reported in the application for P.L. 81-874 assistance in the current year.

5. Multiply the total number of administrative hours determined in paragraph 4 of this subsection by the hourly rate determined in paragraph 2 of this subsection.

6. Determine the greater of the minimum cost determined in paragraph 1 of this subsection or the product determined in paragraph 5 of this subsection.

7. Add to the amount determined in paragraph 6 of this subsection the amount, if any, to be expended by the school district in the budget year through an intergovernmental agreement with other school districts or the department of education to provide P.L. 81-874 technical assistance to participating districts.

8. Determine the lesser of the amount determined in paragraph 7 of this subsection or the revenues available as determined in paragraph 3 of this subsection.

9. The amount determined in paragraph 8 of this subsection is the maximum amount which may be budgeted for P.L. 81-874 administrative costs for the budget year as provided in this subsection.

10. If the governing board underestimated the amount that may be budgeted for P.L. 81-874 administrative costs for the current year, the board may adjust the general budget limit and the budget before May 15. If the governing board overestimated the amount that may be budgeted for P.L. 81-874 administrative costs for the current year, the board shall adjust the general budget limit and the budget before May 15.

Q. If a school district governing board has adopted a budget for a fiscal year based on forms and instructions provided by the auditor general and the department of education for that fiscal year and if, as a result of the enactment or nonenactment of proposed legislation after May 1 of the previous fiscal year, the budget is based on incorrect limits, does not include items authorized by law or does not otherwise conform with law, the governing board may revise its budget at a public hearing on or before September 15 to conform with the law. Not later than September 18, the budget as adjusted shall be submitted electronically to the superintendent of public instruction. If the governing board does not revise the budget on or before September 15 and if the budget includes any items not authorized by law or if the budget exceeds any limits, the governing board shall adjust or revise the budget as provided in subsection E of this section.

R. For the purposes of this section, "P.L. 81-874 assistance" means, for the current year, an amount equal to the final determination of P. L. 81-874 assistance for the fiscal year preceding the current year as confirmed by the division of impact aid, United States department of education or, if a final determination has not been made, the amount estimated by the superintendent of public instruction as confirmed by the division of impact aid, United States department of education and, for the budget year, an amount equal to the determination of P.L. 81-874 assistance for the fiscal year preceding the budget year as estimated by the superintendent of public instruction.

Added by Laws 1981, Ch. 1, § 2, eff. Jan. 23, 1981. Amended by Laws 1981, Ch. 175, § 1; Laws 1982, Ch. 142, § 1, eff. April 16, 1982; Laws 1982, Ch. 198, § 2; Laws 1982, Ch. 273, § 2, eff. April 27, 1982; Laws 1983, Ch. 101, § 12; Laws 1984, Ch. 233, § 1; Laws 1984, Ch. 340, § 1, eff. Aug. 3, 1984, retroactively effective to May 1, 1984; Laws 1984, Ch. 379, § 12; Laws 1985, Ch. 166, § 13, eff. April 18, 1985; Laws 1985, Ch. 273, § 1, eff. May 1, 1985; Laws 1986, Ch. 125, § 5, eff. April 18, 1986; Laws 1987, Ch. 338, § 1; Laws 1988, Ch. 221, § 1, eff. June 14, 1988, retroactively effective to July 1, 1987; Laws 1989, Ch. 273, § 15, eff. June 26, 1989; Laws 1990, Ch. 143, § 1, eff. April 26, 1990; Laws 1990, Ch. 348, § 9, eff. June 26, 1990; Laws 1990, Ch. 399, § 2, eff. July 5, 1990; Laws 1991, Ch. 244, § 3, eff. June 17, 1991; Laws 1991, Ch. 292, § 4, eff. June

28, 1991; Laws 1992, Ch. 288, § 6, eff. Sept. 30, 1992, retroactively effective to July 1, 1992; Laws 1992, Ch. 329, § 1; Laws 1993, Ch. 189, § 8; Laws 1994, Ch. 369, § 1; Laws 1995, Ch. 191, § 9, eff. April 19, 1995; Laws 1995, Ch. 196, § 8; Laws 1996, 5th S.S., Ch. 8, § 3; Laws 1996, Ch. 62, § 2; Laws 1996, Ch. 284, § 48; Laws 1997, Ch. 274, § 1; Laws 1998, Ch. 63, § 3; Laws 1998, 5th S.S., Ch. 1, § 17, eff. July 9, 1998; Laws 1999, Ch. 299, § 15; Laws 2000, Ch. 236, § 20, eff. April 12, 2000; Laws 2000, Ch. 342, § 8; Laws 2001, Ch. 324, § 8.

Historical and Statutory Notes

Source:

Laws 1974, 1st S.S., Ch. 3, § 23.
A.R.S. former § 15–1202.
Laws 1975, Ch. 157, § 2.
Laws 1977, Ch. 152, § 4.
Laws 1977, Ch. 164, § 11.
Laws 1978, Ch. 62, § 10.
Laws 1978, Ch. 170, § 3.
Laws 1979, Ch. 183, § 1.
Laws 1980, 2nd S.S., Ch. 9, § 59.

The amendment of this section by Laws 1982, Ch. 273, § 2, was repealed by Laws 1983, Ch. 101, § 13.

Laws 1983, Ch. 101, § 1, par. 7 provides:

"**Section 1. Purpose**"

"7. Section 15–905, Arizona Revised Statutes, was amended by Laws 1982, chapter 142, § 1, chapter 198, § 2 and chapter 273, § 2. Chapter 142, an emergency measure, became effective April 16, 1982. Chapter 198, effective on the general effective date, was sent to the governor for his signature on April 16. The chapter 142 and chapter 198 versions were blended together pursuant to authority of § 41–1304.02, Arizona Revised Statutes. The text of the section amended by chapter 273, an emergency measure, become [so in original; probably should read "became"] effective April 27 and failed to reflect the text of the section as amended by chapter 142 and therefore did not set forth in full the text of the section being amended as required by Constitution of Arizona Article IV, part 2, § 14. In order to effect the intent of chapter 273, in this enactment the blended version of § 15–905, Arizona Revised Statutes, is amended to incorporate the amendment intended to be made by chapter 273 and the chapter 273 version is repealed."

Laws 1984, Ch. 340, § 8 provides:

"**Sec. 8. Retroactivity**

"This act is effective retroactively to May 1, 1984."

Laws 1988, Ch. 221, § 8 provides:

"**Sec. 8. Retroactivity**

"Sections 1, 3 and 5 of this act are effective retroactively to July 1, 1987."

Laws 1989, Ch. 26, § 1, eff. April 13, 1989, prescribes methods of budgeting for excess liability insurance costs exempt from the revenue control limit.

Laws 1990, Ch. 193, § 1, provides:

"**Budget overrides; miscalculation; expenditure; definition**

"**A.** Notwithstanding § 15–905, subsections E and L and § 15–915, Arizona Revised Statutes, a school district which calculated its budget limits in fiscal years 1988–1989 and 1989–1990 without complying with statutory requirements may expend the amount miscalculated without penalty or reduction in state aid if all of the following apply:

"1. The failure to comply with statutory requirements was the result of not obtaining voter approval to expend monies deposited in a school plant fund in excess of ten per cent of the revenue control limit as provided in § 15–1102, subsection F, Arizona Revised Statutes.

"2. The amount of the miscalculation did not exceed five per cent of the revenue control limit.

"**B.** "Miscalculation", as used in this act, means the difference between the calculation of the school district's budget limit which failed to conform with statutory requirements and the calculation of the school district's budget limits which would have complied with statutory requirements."

The 1990 amendment of this section by Ch. 348 explicitly amended the 1990 amendment of this section by Ch. 143.

Laws 1990, Ch. 399, § 19, provides:

"**Sec. 19. Budget revisions for fiscal year 1990–1991**

"If a school district governing board has adopted a budget for fiscal year 1990–1991 based on forms and instructions provided by the auditor general and the department of education, and if, as a result of the enactment or nonenactment of proposed legislation during the thirty-ninth legislature, second regular session or third special session, the budget does not include items authorized by law or does not conform with law, the governing board may revise its budget at a public hearing before October 31, 1990, unless a later budget revision date is authorized by law, to include omitted items or otherwise modify the budget to conform with law. If the governing board does not revise the budget before October 31, 1990 and if the budget includes any items not authorized by law, the governing board shall adjust or revise the budget as provided in § 15-905, subsection E, Arizona Revised Statutes."

The 1990 amendment of this section by Ch. 399 explicitly amended the 1990 amendment of this section by Ch. 143.

The amendment of this section by Laws 1990, Ch. 399, § 2, was repealed by Laws 1991, Ch. 244, § 4, effective June 17, 1991, and Ch. 292, § 5, effective June 28, 1991.

The 1991 amendment of this section by Ch. 244 explicitly amended the 1990 amendment of this section by Ch. 207.

The 1991 amendment of this section by Ch. 292 explicitly amended the 1990 amendment of this section by Ch. 348.

Laws 1991, Ch. 244, § 13, effective June 17, 1991, provides:

"**Sec. 13. Budget revisions for fiscal year 1991-1992**

"If a school district governing board has adopted a budget for fiscal year 1991-1992 based on forms and instructions provided by the auditor general and the department of education for that fiscal year and if, as a result of the enactment or nonenactment of proposed legislation during the fortieth legislature, first regular session, the budget is based on incorrect limits, does not include items authorized by law, or does not otherwise conform with law, the governing board may revise its budget to conform with the law at a public hearing before October 31, 1991. If the governing board does not revise the budget before October 31, 1991 and if the budget includes any items not authorized by law or if the budget exceeds any limits, the governing board shall adjust or revise the budget as provided in § 15-905, subsection E, Arizona Revised Statutes."

Amendment of this section by Laws 1991, Ch. 292, § 4, was repealed by Laws 1992, Ch. 288, § 7.

The 1992 amendments of this section by Chs. 288 and 329 explicitly amended the 1991 amendment of this section by Ch. 244.

The purported amendment of this section by Laws 1992, Ch. 50, § 2 and Laws 1992 Ch. 172, § 19, and the purported repeal of Laws 1991, Ch. 292, § 4, by Laws 1992, Ch. 50, § 3 and Laws 1992, Ch. 172, § 20, were repealed by Laws 1992, Ch. 288, § 7, eff. Sept. 30, 1992, retroactively effective to July 1, 1992, prior to taking effect.

Laws 1993, Ch. 202, § 16, eff. April 21, 1993, provides:

"Sec. 16. **Support level weights for fiscal years 1991-1992 through 1993-1994**

"If a school district was subject to the provisions of § 15-458, subsection F, Arizona Revised Statutes, but adopted budgets for fiscal years 1991-1992 and 1992-1993 using incorrect budget limits due to utilization of the support level weights prescribed in § 15-943, subsection G, paragraph 1, Arizona Revised Statutes, the district is exempt from the provisions of § 15-905, subsections L and M, Arizona Revised Statutes, and § 15-915, Arizona Revised Statutes, for those fiscal years for the amount of the excess budget capacity caused by the use of the incorrect weights."

Laws 1994, Ch. 254, § 7, effective April 24, 1994, provides:

"**Sec. 7. Excess insurance costs for fiscal year 1994-1995; limitation on expenditures**

"**A.** The governing board of a school district may budget for excess insurance costs that are specifically exempt from the revenue control limit for fiscal year 1994-1995. The department of education and the auditor general shall include in the maintenance and operation section of the budget format, as provided in § 15-903, Arizona Revised Statutes, a separate line for all property and casualty insurance expenditures and a special excess insurance cost category. The special excess cost category shall contain budgeted expenditures for excess insurance costs, determined as follows:

"1. Determine the actual charges for all property and casualty insurance for fiscal year 1984-1985.

"2. Increase or decrease the amount in paragraph 1 of this subsection by the total percentage increase or decrease in the revenue control limit and the capital outlay revenue limit as provided in § 15-947, Arizona Revised Statutes, for fiscal year 1994-1995 over the revenue control limit and the capital outlay revenue limit for fiscal year 1985-1986 excluding monies available from a career ladder program or a teacher compensation program as provided in § 15-952, Arizona Revised Statutes.

"3. Multiply the amount in paragraph 2 of this subsection by a factor of 2.50. The product is the amount budgeted in the insurance cost expenditure line.

"4. Expenditures for insurance costs in excess of the amount budgeted in the insurance cost expenditure line may be budgeted in the excess cost category.

"**B.** The governing board may expend from the excess insurance cost category only after it has expended for property and casualty insurance purposes the full amount budgeted in the insurance cost expenditure line of the budget. Notwithstanding § 15-905, subsection N, Arizona Revised Statutes, the governing board of a school district shall not prepay property and casualty insurance premiums in a fiscal year if the governing board has budgeted for excess insurance costs for that fiscal year. The maximum amount that may be expended from the excess insurance cost category in a year in which payment is made to a self-insurance trust fund for property and casualty losses is determined as follows:

"1. Determine the actual charges for all property and casualty insurance for the fiscal year before the first fiscal year in which payments are made into a self-insurance trust fund for property and casualty losses.

"2. Increase the amount determined in paragraph 1 of this subsection by the percentage increase in the revenue control limit and the capital outlay revenue limit between the year utilized in paragraph 1 of this subsection and the current year.

"3. Subtract the amount budgeted in the property and casualty insurance expenditure line for the current year from the amount determined in paragraph 2 of this subsection.

"4. The difference in paragraph 3 of this subsection is the maximum amount that may be expended from the excess insurance cost category.

"**C.** The governing board, after notice is given and a public meeting is held as provided in § 15-905, subsection D, Arizona Revised Statutes, may revise at any time before May 15, 1994 the amount budgeted in the excess insurance cost category for fiscal year 1994-1995.

"**D.** If the excess insurance cost category results in an expenditure of monies in excess of school district revenues for fiscal year 1994-1995 the county school superintendent shall include within the revenue estimate for fiscal year 1995-1996 monies necessary to meet the liabilities incurred by the school district in fiscal year 1994-1995 in excess of revenues received for that year.

"**E.** The department of education shall describe the method for determining actual charges for all property and casualty insurance."

Laws 1994, Ch. 254, § 8, effective April 24, 1994, as amended by Laws 1995, Ch. 191, § 23, effective April 19, 1995, provides:

"Sec. 8. Budget and expenditure provisions for certain elementary and union high school districts for fiscal year 1992-1993

"**A.** If a union high school district with a student count of less than two thousand was eligible to budget for excess utilities pursuant to § 15-910, Arizona Revised Statutes, for fiscal year 1992-1993 but did not so budget, for the purposes of § 15-905, subsections L and M, Arizona Revised Statutes, the district's general budget limit and the maintenance and operations section of the budget for that year are deemed to have been increased by the amount by which the district was authorized to budget for excess utilities.

"**B.** Notwithstanding § 15-905, subsection M, Arizona Revised Statutes, if a common school district or union high school district with a student count of less than two thousand is required to reduce its general budget limit due to excess expenditures in fiscal year 1992-1993, the district may make part of the reduction in the third subsequent year."

Laws 1994, Ch. 254, § 9, effective April 24, 1994, provides:

"**Sec. 9. Provisions for unified school districts that exceeded the general budget limit in fiscal year 1992-1993 or 1993-1994**

"**A.** Notwithstanding §§ 15-905 and 15-949, Arizona Revised Statutes, a unified school district is not required to reduce its general budget limit due to excess expenditures for pupils in kindergarten programs and grades one through eight for fiscal year 1992-1993 or 1993-1994 if each of the following conditions apply for the fiscal year in which the excess expenditures were made:

"1. The district adopted a budget which included an adjustment for low student count as provided in § 15-949, Arizona Revised Statutes.

"2. The district's student count in grades nine through twelve was one hundred or less and the district's student count in kindergarten programs and grades one through eight was more than one hundred twenty-five.

"**B.** For fiscal year 1994-1995, a unified school district that meets the conditions of subsection A of this section for fiscal year 1993-1994 may adopt a budget including a budget increase as provided in § 15-481, subsection E or H, Arizona Revised Statutes, as if an election had taken place and the voters had approved the override for that year."

For applicability provisions of Laws 1995, Ch. 196, see the Historical and Statutory Notes following § 1-254.

The amendment of this section by Laws 1995, Ch. 196, § 8, was repealed by Laws 1996, Ch. 62, § 3.

The amendment of this section by Laws 1995, Ch. 196, § 8, was repealed by Laws 1996, Ch. 248, § 5.

The amendment of this section by Laws 1995, Ch. 196, § 8 was repealed by Laws 1996, Ch. 284, § 49.

The amendment of this section by Laws 1995, Ch. 196, § 8, was repealed by Laws 1996, 5th S.S., Ch. 8, § 4.

Laws 1996, 5th S.S., Ch. 8, § 20, as amended by Laws 1996, Ch. 284, § 77; Laws 1997, Ch. 271, § 6, provides:

"**Sec. 20. Adjustment for the capital outlay transfer limit**

"**A.** Notwithstanding § 15–905, subsection R, paragraph 4, Arizona Revised Statutes, as amended by this act, use zero for the amount determined in § 15–905, subsection R, paragraph 4, subdivision (e) for fiscal year 1996–1997.

"**B.** For fiscal year 1996–1997, the amount determined pursuant to § 15–905, subsection R, paragraph 1, Arizona Revised Statutes, as amended by this act, shall not exceed the actual amount of capital outlay revenue limit monies budgeted for maintenance and operation in fiscal year 1995–1996 as of March 15, 1996.

"**C.** Notwithstanding subsection B of this section and notwithstanding the actual amount of capital outlay revenue limit monies budgeted for maintenance and operation in fiscal year 1995–1996 as of March 15, 1996, for a school district that had a successful election as provided in § 15–481, Arizona Revised Statutes, in 1990 and did not conduct an election as provided in § 15–481, Arizona Revised Statutes, in 1995 or 1996:

"1. For budget years 1996–1997 and 1997–1998, the amount determined pursuant to § 15–905, subsection R, paragraph 1, Arizona Revised Statutes, as amended by this act, shall be fifty-two per cent of the total capital outlay revenue limit.

"2. Beginning with fiscal year 1998–1999, a school district that utilized the provisions of this subsection is subject to the provisions of § 15–905, subsection R, paragraph 1, Arizona Revised Statutes, using the base established for fiscal year 1997–1998."

The 1996 amendment of this section by Ch. 62 explicitly amended the 1995 amendment of this section by Ch. 191.

The 1996 amendment of this section by Ch. 284 explicitly amended the amendment of this section by Laws 1996, 5th S.S., Ch. 8, § 3.

The purported amendment of this section by Laws 1998, Ch. 164 failed to become effective because Chapter 164 was repealed in its entirety by Laws 1998, 5th S.S., Ch. 1, § 2, effective July 1, 1998.

The purported amendment of this section by Laws 1998, 3rd S.S., Ch. 1, failed to became effective because Ch. 1 was repealed in its entirety by Laws 1998, 5th S.S., Ch. 1, § 2, effective July 1, 1998.

Laws 1998, 4th S.S., Ch. 8, § 13, provides:

"**Sec. 13. Capital outlay transfer limit adjustment; fiscal year 1998–1999**

"Notwithstanding § 15–905, subsection R, paragraph 5, Arizona Revised Statutes, for fiscal year 1998–1999 the amount determined in § 15–905, subsection R, paragraph 5, Arizona Revised Statutes, shall be zero."

Laws 1998, 5th S.S., Ch. 1, § 59, provides:

"**Sec. 59. Capital outlay revenue limit provisions for fiscal year 1998–1999**

"Notwithstanding §§ 15–905, subsection R, 15–947, subsection D, paragraph 4 and 15–947.01, subsection C, Arizona Revised Statutes, as amended by this act, for fiscal year 1998–1999, the capital outlay revenue limit for the budget year is included in the general budget limit and not included in the capital budget limit and a school district is not subject to the provisions of § 15–905, subsection R, Arizona Revised Statutes."

Laws 1999, 1st S.S., Ch. 5, § 23, provides:

"**Sec. 23. Increased base support level; fiscal year 1999–2000**

"**A.** If the fiscal event described in § 18, subsection A, paragraph 3 of this act occurs, then notwithstanding § 15–901, subsection B, paragraph 2, subdivision (a), Arizona Revised Statutes, the base level is $2,578.41. The increase in the base support level is for fiscal year 1999–2000.

"**B.** If the fiscal event described in § 18, subsection A, paragraph 4 of this act occurs, then notwithstanding § 15–901, subsection B, paragraph 2, subdivision (a), Arizona Revised Statutes, the base level is $2,597.09. The increase in the base support level is for fiscal year 1999–2000.

"**C.** It is the intent of the legislature that any monies under this section shall be used to enhance one or more of the following items:

"1. Classroom teacher salaries.

"2. Employing new teachers.

"3. Teacher training and development.

"4. Classroom technology.

"5. Strengthening programs for pupils in kindergarten programs and grades one, two and three.

"6. Additional school days.

"7. Supplemental learning programs to meet state academic standards.

"8. Reading clinics.

"9. Achieving or maintaining school sizes of fewer than four hundred fifty pupils.

"**D.** For fiscal year 1999–2000, school districts and charter schools shall report on the school report card issued pursuant to § 15–746, Arizona Revised Statutes, a summary of any monies received pursuant to this section and a description of how the monies were used to enhance classrooms to augment pupil learning. School districts and charter schools shall provide to any person on request a detailed itemization of the classroom enhancements and associated expenditures.

"**E.** Notwithstanding § 15-905, subsection A, paragraph 2, Arizona Revised Statutes, school district governing boards and charter schools may include in the proposed and adopted budget for fiscal year 1999-2000 and 2000-2001 any items or amounts authorized by this act. If subsequent events prevent any provision of this act from becoming effective, the governing boards and charter schools shall reduce their budgets by the amount that was budgeted pursuant to this act and that did not become effective.

"**F.** The staff of the Arizona legislative council shall prepare legislation for consideration in the forty-fifth legislature, first regular session to make necessary statutory changes to conform to the enactment of fiscal events pursuant to this section."

Laws 1999, 1st S.S., Ch. 5, § 24 was repealed by Laws 2000, Ch. 48, § 5. See also amendment of the note by Laws 2000, Ch. 398, post.

Laws 1999, 1st S.S., Ch. 5, § 24, was purportedly amended by Laws 2000, Ch. 398, § 3.

Laws 1999, 1st S.S., Ch. 5, § 25, provides:

"**Sec. 25. Retroactivity**

"Section 23 of this act applies retroactively to from and after June 30, 1999."

Laws 1999, Ch. 248, § 1, provides:

"**Section 1. School district budget adjustments; extension of time**

"Notwithstanding § 15-905, subsection Q, Arizona Revised Statutes, if a school district governing board has adopted a budget for a fiscal year based on forms and instructions provided by the auditor general and the department of education for that fiscal year and if, as a result of the enactment of Laws 1998, fifth special session, chapter 1, the budget is based on incorrect limits, does not include items authorized by law or does not otherwise conform with law, the governing board may revise its budget at a public hearing at any time before September 15, 1999 to conform with the law."

Laws 2000, Ch. 48, § 9, eff. March 26, 2000, provides:

"**Sec. 9. Increased base support level; fiscal year 2000-2001**

"**A.** Notwithstanding § 15-901, subsection B, paragraph 2, subdivision (a), Arizona Revised Statutes, if the fiscal event described in § 8, subsection B of this act occurs, the base support level for fiscal year 2000-2001 is $2,621.62."

"**B.** It is the intent of the legislature that these monies be used for the same purposes described in § 8, subsection A of this act."

"**C.** For fiscal year 2000-2001, school districts and charter schools shall report on the school report card issued pursuant to § 15-746, Arizona Revised Statutes, a summary of any monies received pursuant to this section and a description of how the monies were used to enhance classrooms to augment pupil learning. School districts and charter schools shall provide to any person on request a detailed itemization of the classroom enhancements and associated expenditures."

"**D.** Notwithstanding § 15-905, subsection A, paragraph 2, Arizona Revised Statutes, school district governing boards and charter schools may include in the proposed and adopted budget for fiscal year 2000-2001 any items or amounts authorized by this act. If subsequent events prevent any provision of this act from becoming effective, the governing boards and charter schools shall reduce their budgets by any amount that was budgeted pursuant to this act and that did not become effective."

"**E.** The staff of the legislative council shall prepare legislation for consideration in the forty-fifth legislature, first regular session to make necessary statutory changes to conform to the enactment of fiscal events pursuant to this section."

Laws 2000, Ch. 48, § 9, as conditionally amended by Laws 2000, 5th S.S., Ch. 1, § 56, provides:

"**Sec. 9. Increased base support level; fiscal year 2000-2001**

"**A.** Notwithstanding § 15-901, subsection B, paragraph 2, subdivision (a), Arizona Revised Statutes, if the fiscal event described in § 8, subsection B of this act occurs, the base support level for fiscal year 2000-2001 is $2,621.62.

"**B.** It is the intent of the legislature that these monies be used for the same purposes described in § 8, subsection A of this act.

"**C.** For fiscal year 2000-2001, school districts and charter schools shall report on the school report card issued pursuant to § 15-746, Arizona Revised Statutes, a summary of any monies received pursuant to this section and a description of how the monies were used.

"**D.** Notwithstanding § 15-905, subsection A, paragraph 2, Arizona Revised Statutes, school district governing boards and charter schools may include in the proposed and adopted budget for fiscal year 2000-2001 any items or amounts authorized by this act. If subsequent events prevent any provision of this act from becoming effective, the governing boards and charter schools shall reduce their budgets by any amount that was budgeted pursuant to this act and that did not become effective.

"**E.** The staff of the legislative council shall prepare legislation for consideration in the forty-fifth legislature, first regular session to make necessary statutory changes to conform to the enactment of fiscal events pursuant to this section."

The amendment of this section by Laws 2000, Ch. 342, § 8 was repealed by Laws 2001, Ch. 324, § 9.

The 2001 amendment of this section by Ch. 324 explicitly amended the amendment of this section by Laws 2000, Ch. 236, § 20.

Laws 2001, Ch. 324, § 1, par. 4, provides:

"**Section 1. Purpose**"

"4. Section 15-905, Arizona Revised Statutes, was amended by Laws 2000, chapter 236, § 20 and Laws 2000, chapter 342, § 8. The chapter 342 version failed to amend the chapter 236 version, which was an emergency enactment, and therefore did not comply with article IV, part 2, section 14, Constitution of Arizona. To accomplish the intent of these enactments, this act amends the Laws 2000, chapter 236 version of § 15-905, Arizona Revised Statutes, to incorporate the amendments made by Laws 2000, chapter 342 and the chapter 342 version is repealed."

Laws 2001, Ch. 324, § 60, subsec. A, provides:

"**Sec. 60. Retroactive application**

"**A.** Sections 2, 3, 6 through 9, 13, 22 through 28, 31 through 34, 36, 37, 44, 45 and 48 of this act apply retroactively to July 18, 2000."

Laws 2003, Ch. 144, § 1, provides:

"**Sec. 1. Errors in school district budget calculation; correction**

"**A.** Notwithstanding §§ 15-905 and 15-915, Arizona Revised Statutes, school districts that miscalculated their budgets during fiscal year 2001-2002 shall be required to correct these errors over a five-year period beginning in fiscal year 2002-2003 and ending in fiscal year 2006-2007 if each of the following conditions exists:

"1. The school district provides evidence to the superintendent of public instruction that the school district's budget for the current year is properly calculated and will not result in any overexpenditures.

"2. The total amount of the correction that would otherwise be required under § 15-915, Arizona Revised Statutes, is more than six hundred thousand dollars but less than seven hundred thousand dollars.

"**B.** In addition to the monies required to be repaid pursuant to subsection A of this section, accrued interest is required to be paid at a rate determined by the superintendent of public instruction."

Reviser's Notes:

1982 Note. Prior to the 1983 amendment, this section contained the amendments made by Laws 1982, Ch. 142, § 1 and Ch. 198, § 2 which were blended together pursuant to authority of § 41-1304.03. Additionally, pursuant to authority of § 41-1304.02, subsection K, as added by Laws 1982, Ch. 142, was relettered as subsection M and the reference to subsection K in subsection J, as amended by Laws 1982, chapter 142 and relettered as subsection L by Laws 1982, Ch. 198, was relettered as subsection M to conform.

The amendment of this section by Laws 1982, Ch. 273, § 2 failed to set forth in full the text of the section as amended by Laws 1982, Ch. 142, § 1, an emergency act, as required by Constitution of Arizona Article IV, Part 2, § 14. Additionally, pursuant to authority of § 41-1304.02, "summary;" was added to the section heading and in the second sentence of subsection A "a summary of" was transposed to follow "and".

1984 Note. Prior to the 1985 amendments, this section contained the amendments made by Laws 1984, Ch. 233, § 1, Ch. 340, § 1 and Ch. 379, § 12 which were blended together pursuant to authority of § 41-1304.03.

1989 Note. Laws 1989, Ch. 273 deleted the requirements in this section for special board meetings, but the title of this chapter did not describe these changes.

1990 Note. The amendment of this section by Laws 1990, Ch. 399, § 2 failed to set forth in full the text of the section as amended by Laws 1990, Ch. 348, an emergency act, as required by Constitution of Arizona Art. IV, part 2, § 14.

1991 Note. The amendment of this section by Laws 1991, Ch. 292, sec. 4 failed to set forth in full the text of the section as amended by Laws 1991, Ch. 244, an emergency act, as required by Constitution of Arizona Art. IV, part 2, sec. 14.

1992 Note. Prior to the 1993 amendment, this section contained the amendments made by Laws 1992, Ch. 288, sec. 6 and Ch. 329, sec. 1 that were blended together pursuant to authority of § 41-1304.03.

1995 Note. Pursuant to authority of § 41-1304.02, in Laws 1995, Ch. 191, § 23, subsection A "the" was inserted before "purposes" to correct a manifest clerical error.

1995 Note. The amendment made by Laws 1995, Ch. 196, sec. 8 was inconsistent and incompatible with Laws 1995, Ch. 191, sec. 9 and therefore could not be blended.

1996 Note. Prior to the 1997 amendment, this section contained the amendments made by Laws 1996, Ch. 62, sec. 2 and Ch. 284, sec. 48 that were blended together pursuant to authority of § 41-1304.03. Pursuant to authority of § 41-1304.02, in subsection K, first sentence, "(C)" was substituted for "(c)" to correct a manifest clerical error. In the Laws 1996, Ch. 284 version in subsection K, first sentence, after "(d)," the word "paragraph" appears, but this word was stricken in the Laws 1996, 5th Spec. Sess., Ch. 8 amendment of this section. Pursuant to authority of § 41-1304.02, to correct a manifest clerical error "paragraph" is omitted from the blend version.

1998 Note. Prior to the 1999 amendment, this section contained the amendments made by Laws 1998, Second Regular Session, Ch. 63, sec. 3 and Laws 1998, Fifth Special Session, Ch. 1. sec. 17 that were blended together pursuant to authority of § 41-1304.03.

2000 Note. The amendment of this section by Laws 2000, Ch. 342, sec. 8 failed to set forth in full the text of the section as amended by Laws 2000, Ch. 236, sec. 20, an emergency act, as required by Constitution of Arizona art. IV, pt. 2, sec. 14.

§ 15-905.01. Truth in taxation; calculation; notice and hearing; vote on tax increase

A. Each school district shall determine its truth in taxation base limit for expenditures as follows:

1. Determine the amounts budgeted in fiscal year 1999-2000 for expenditures in the following categories:

(a) Desegregation pursuant to § 15-910.

(b) Dropout prevention programs.

(c) Excess utilities pursuant to § 15-910.

(d) Career and technical education and vocational education center operations pursuant to § 15-910.01.

(e) Small school adjustments pursuant to § 15-949.

2. The sum of the expenditures in paragraph 1 of this subsection for fiscal year 1999-2000 shall become the truth in taxation base limit.

3. For any year after fiscal year 1999-2000, a school district whose aggregate budgeted expenditures for the expenditures prescribed in paragraph 1 of this subsection exceed the truth in taxation base limit shall publish a truth in taxation hearing notice that meets the requirements of subsection B of this section. If the amount exceeding the previous truth in taxation base limit is approved by the school district governing board following the hearing prescribed in subsection B of this section, the excess amount plus the previous truth in taxation base limit becomes the school district's new truth in taxation base limit.

4. If a school district no longer qualifies for one or more of the expenditures prescribed in paragraph 1 of this subsection, the amount budgeted for the most recent fiscal year in which the school district was eligible for that expenditure shall be deducted from the school district's truth in taxation base limit.

B. For any fiscal year in which a school district governing board budgets an amount that is higher than the truth in taxation base limit calculated pursuant to subsection A of this section, any fiscal year in which a school district levies any amount for adjacent ways pursuant to § 15-995 or any fiscal year in which the school district levies any amount for liabilities in excess of the school district budget pursuant to § 15-907:

1. The school district shall publish a notice that meets the following requirements:

(a) The notice shall be published once in a newspaper of general circulation in the school district. The publication shall be at least ten but not more than twenty days before the date of the hearing.

(b) The notice shall be published in a location other than the classified or legal advertising section of the newspaper in which it is published.

(c) The notice shall be at least one-fourth page in size and shall be surrounded by a solid black border at least one-eighth inch in width.

(d) The notice shall be in the following form, excluding the parenthetical explanations, and with the "truth in taxation hearing—notice of tax increase" headline in at least eighteen point type:

Truth in Taxation Hearing
Notice of Tax Increase

In compliance with § 15-905.01, Arizona Revised Statutes, ________ school district is notifying its property taxpayers of ________ school district's intention to raise its primary property taxes over the current level to pay for increased expenditures in those areas where the governing board has the authority to increase property taxes for the fiscal year beginning July 1, ____. The ________ school district is proposing an increase in its primary property tax levy of $________ (amount of levy increase to pay for truth in taxation base increase, the amount of the total levy for the adjacent ways fund and amounts for liabilities in excess of the school district budget pursuant to § 15-907).

The amount proposed above will cause ________ school district's primary property taxes on a $100,000 home to increase from $________ (the amount used to pay for the current year's truth in taxation base limit [the amount divided by the current net assessed value available February 10 pursuant to § 42-17052] applied to $100,000) to $________ (the amount used to pay for the budget year's proposed truth in taxation base limit and adjacent ways levy, including adjacent ways and liabilities in excess of the school district budget [the amount divided by the current net assessed value available February 10 pursuant to § 42-17052] applied to $100,000).

These amounts proposed are above the qualifying tax levies as prescribed by state law, if applicable. The increase is also exclusive of any changes that may occur from property tax levies for voter approved bonded indebtedness or budget and tax overrides.

All interested citizens are invited to attend the public hearing on the proposed tax increase scheduled to be held ________ (date and time) at ________ (location).

2. In lieu of publishing the truth in taxation notice, the governing board may mail the truth in taxation notice prescribed by paragraph 1, subdivision (d) of this subsection to all registered voters in the district at least ten but not more than twenty days before the date of the hearing.

3. In addition to publishing the truth in taxation notice under paragraph 1 of this subsection or mailing the notice under paragraph 2 of this subsection,

the governing board shall issue a press release containing the truth in taxation notice to all newspapers of general circulation in the school district.

4. The governing board shall consider a motion to levy the increased property taxes by roll call vote.

5. Within three days after the hearing, the governing board shall mail a copy of the truth in taxation notice, a statement of its publication or mailing and the result of the governing board's vote under paragraph 4 of this subsection to the property tax oversight commission established by § 42-17002.

6. The governing board shall hold the truth in taxation hearing on or before the adoption of the school district budget under § 15-905.

7. Expenditures for adjacent ways and liabilities in excess of the school district budget do not become part of the school district's truth in taxation base limit.

C. The department of education shall maintain a listing of each school district's truth in taxation base limit and shall verify the accuracy of the school district's computations. A school district governing board shall notify the department of education of any change in the district's truth in taxation base limit.

D. The department of education shall develop a budget form for school districts to show the primary tax rate associated for each of the expenditure categories mentioned in subsection A, paragraph 1 of this section and for expenditures for adjacent ways pursuant to § 15-995 or any other expenditure in excess of the school district budget pursuant to § 15-907. A school district shall make this information available to the general public at truth in taxation hearings and shall submit the information to the department of education. Added by Laws 1997, Ch. 274, § 2. Amended by Laws 1998, Ch. 1, § 48, eff. Jan. 1, 1999; Laws 1999, Ch. 108, § 1; Laws 2000, Ch. 390, § 1, eff. July 18, 2000, retroactively effective to May 1, 2000; Laws 2002, Ch. 89, § 22; Laws 2003, Ch. 197, § 1, eff. May 12, 2003.

Historical and Statutory Notes

Laws 2000, Ch. 390, § 26, provides:

"**Sec. 26. Refund of erroneously assessed special district taxes**

"**A.** A person who owned property on May 1, 1998 that was erroneously assessed city improvement district taxes or irrigation and drainage district taxes in tax year 1996, 1997 or 1998 and that was thereafter sold before the county assessor mailed a notice of error may apply to the county treasurer for a refund of the erroneously paid taxes. The person shall submit the application on or before October 31, 2000, and the county treasurer shall pay any valid claim, without interest, on or before December 31, 2000. A failure to file a claim on or before October 31, 2000 constitutes a waiver of the claim for refund under this section.

"**B.** The burden is on the property owner to establish the facts that qualify the owner for the refund under this section.

"**C.** Each affected district and the county shall enter into an intergovernmental agreement, pursuant to title 11, chapter 7, article 3, Arizona Revised Statutes, for recovery of the amounts paid by the county treasurer pursuant to this section, either by direct payment by the district to the county or by withholding the amounts from future property tax distributions to the district."

Laws 2000, Ch. 390, § 29, provides:

"**Sec. 29. Retroactive effective date**

"Section 15-905.01, Arizona Revised Statutes, as amended by § 1 of this act, is effective retroactively to from and after April 30, 2000."

Reviser's Notes:

1998 Note. Pursuant to authority of § 41-1304.02, in subsection A, paragraph 1, subdivision (d) the main words of the notice heading were capitalized to correct an electronic data base error.

1999 Note. Pursuant to authority of § 41-1304.02, in the section heading "; calculation" was transposed to follow "taxation" and in subsection A, paragraph 1, subdivision (b) the spelling of "Dropout" was corrected.

§ 15-906. Procedure for payment of levy fund liabilities payable on June 30; lapsing of levy funds with balance for reduction of taxes

A. Annually on or before June 30, each school district shall prepare for all levy funds a list of liabilities for goods received or services rendered on or before June 30 which will not be paid by June 30 of the current fiscal year.

B. Each school district having levy fund liabilities payable on June 30 shall file an advice of encumbrance with the county school superintendent on or before July 18, in the manner and upon a form to be prescribed in the uniform system of financial records. The county school superintendent shall encumber amounts that are included in year to date expenditures not to exceed the budget and that are available to pay the liabilities pursuant to § 15-304. Any cash balances remaining in the maintenance and operation, the unrestricted capital outlay, the soft capital allocation and the adjacent ways funds after encumbrances on June 30 of the current year except reverted monies as provided in § 15-991.02 that will be budgeted in the unrestricted capital outlay fund in the following fiscal year pursuant to § 15-947, subsection D, paragraphs 4 and 5 [1] and that will be budgeted in the soft capital allocation fund in the following fiscal year pursuant to § 15-947, subsection E, paragraphs 2 and 3 shall be used for reduction of school district taxes for the budget year.

C. The county school superintendent may draw warrants against the obligated in contract amounts pursuant to subsection B of this section for a period of sixty days immediately following the close of the fiscal year.

D. After expiration of the period of sixty days immediately following the close of each fiscal year, the remaining obligated in contract balance shall lapse and no further payments from the maintenance and operation, unrestricted capital outlay, soft capital allocation and adjacent ways funds shall be made on any claim for expenditures of the prior fiscal year.

E. School districts that are subject to § 15-914.01 shall adhere to the duties described in § 15-304 for the purposes of this section.

Added by Laws 1981, Ch. 1, § 2, eff. Jan. 23, 1981. Amended by Laws 1981, Ch. 186, § 1, eff. April 22, 1981; Laws 1982, Ch. 198, § 3; Laws 1984, Ch. 379, § 13; Laws 1985, Ch. 166, § 14, eff. April 18, 1985; Laws 1986, Ch. 125, § 6, eff. April 18, 1986; Laws 1992, Ch. 288, § 8, eff. Sept. 30, 1992, retroactively effective to July 1, 1992; Laws 1998, Ch. 63, § 4; Laws 1998, 5th S.S., Ch. 1, § 18, eff. July 9, 1998; Laws 1999, Ch. 299, § 16.

[1] So in original. "[P]aragraphs 4 and 5" should read "paragraph 3".

Historical and Statutory Notes

Source:

Laws 1962, Ch. 39, § 1.
A.R.S. former § 15-1204.
Laws 1973, Ch. 54, § 1.
Laws 1974, 1st S.S., Ch. 3, § 25.
Laws 1977, Ch. 156, § 1.

The purported amendment of this section by Laws 1998, Ch. 164 failed to become effective because Chapter 164 was repealed in its entirety by Laws 1998, 5th S.S., Ch. 1, § 2, effective July 1, 1998.

The purported amendment of this section by Laws 1998, 3rd S.S., Ch. 1, failed to became effective because Ch. 1 was repealed in its entirety by Laws 1998, 5th S.S., Ch. 1, § 2, effective July 1, 1998.

Reviser's Notes:

1998 Note. Prior to the 1999 amendment, this section contained the amendments made by Laws 1998, Second Regular Session, Ch. 63, sec. 4 and Laws 1998, Fifth Special Session, Ch. 1. sec. 18 that were blended together pursuant to authority of § 41-1304.03. In the chapter version in subsection C, before "amounts" and in subsection D, before "balance" "~~encumbered~~ OBLIGATED IN CONTRACT" should have appeared instead of "obligated in contract". Pursuant to authority of § 41-1304.02, to correct a manifest clerical error in the chapter 1 version "~~encumbered~~" is inserted and "obligated in contract" is shown as new, or upstyle, language.

§ 15-907. Incurring liabilities in excess of school district budget; petition; approval; procedure for expenditures

A. In the event of excessive and unexpected legal expenses or for an emergency for which the school district did not receive funding from the school facilities board pursuant to § 15-2022 because there were insufficient monies in the emergency deficiencies correction fund, the governing board of the school district may petition the county school superintendent, or in the case of an accommodation school, the county school superintendent may petition the county board of supervisors, requesting authority to incur liabilities in excess of the school district budget, in an amount the governing board deems necessary. The governing board of the school district shall follow the procedures for the truth in taxation notice and hearing prescribed in § 15-905.01, subsection B.

B. The county school superintendent shall forward the petition together with the superintendent's recommendation and a copy of the budget of the school district to the board of supervisors.

C. The board of supervisors shall hold a hearing on the petition within twenty days after receipt and shall determine whether the petition shall be allowed, allowed after revision or denied.

D. If the petition is allowed in whole or in part, the governing board shall be authorized to incur liabilities in accordance with the petition, and a copy of the order of the board of supervisors authorizing the incurring of such liabilities shall be filed with the county school superintendent. The county school superintendent, upon presentation of proper vouchers, shall draw warrants against the additional allowance. Any liability so incurred shall be in addition to the aggregate budget estimate of the school district for the succeeding year.

E. The portion of the primary tax rate to fund these liabilities in excess of the school district budget as provided in this section shall not be included in the computation of additional state aid for education prescribed in § 15-972.

Added by Laws 1981, Ch. 1, § 2, eff. Jan. 23, 1981. Amended by Laws 1981, Ch. 97, § 1; Laws 1982, Ch. 180, § 1; Laws 1982, Ch. 197, § 5; Laws 1986, Ch. 80, § 1, eff. April 11, 1986; Laws 1995, Ch. 268, § 49; Laws 1997, Ch. 274, § 3; Laws 1999, Ch. 108, § 2; Laws 2001, Ch. 297, § 1.

Historical and Statutory Notes

Source:

Laws 1912, Ch. 77, § 105.
Civ.Code 1913, § 2821.
Laws 1921, Ch. 158, § 1.
Rev.Code 1928, § 1094.
Laws 1933, Ch. 65, § 12.
Laws 1941, Ch. 79, § 8.
Laws 1947, Ch. 85, § 6.
Code 1939, Supp.1952, § 54-808.
Laws 1955, Ch. 108, § 5.

A.R.S. former § 15-1245.
Laws 1960, Ch. 127, § 57.
Laws 1974, 1st S.S., Ch. 3, § 36.
Laws 1980, 2nd S.S., Ch. 9, § 72.

Reviser's Notes:

1982 Note. Prior to the 1986 amendment, this section contained the amendments made by Laws 1982, Ch. 180, § 1 and Ch. 197, § 5 which were blended together pursuant to authority of § 41-1304.03.

§ 15-908. Revenue control limit for school district after consolidation

A resulting school district after consolidation of a school district and unorganized territory or areas within another school district as provided in § 15-459, subsection H or § 15-460, subsection A shall compute its allowable revenue control limit for the first budget year as follows:

1. Divide the allowable revenue control limit for the budget year of the school district prior to consolidation by the student count for the school district for the budget year.

2. Multiply the quotient obtained in paragraph 1 of this section by the student count of the resulting school district for the budget year. The product is the revenue control limit of the resulting school district in the first budget year.

3. The student count used for unorganized territory is the student count of pupils who resided in the unorganized territory prior to consolidation.

Added by Laws 1981, Ch. 1, § 2, eff. Jan. 23, 1981. Amended by Laws 1985, Ch. 238, § 9.

Historical and Statutory Notes

Source:

Laws 1974, 1st S.S., Ch. 3, § 62.
A.R.S. former § 15-403.02.
Laws 1975, Ch. 103, § 3.
Laws 1980, 2nd S.S., Ch. 9, § 13.

§ 15-909. Financial provisions for accommodation schools; definition

A. An accommodation school shall compute a revenue control limit, a capital outlay revenue limit and a soft capital allocation limit for each fiscal year of operation.

B. For the purpose of computing a revenue control limit, a capital outlay revenue limit and a soft capital allocation limit, "accommodation school" means:

1. A common school district within a high school district if the school does not offer instruction in grade nine, ten, eleven or twelve or has not received permission to offer instruction in high school subjects as provided in § 15-447.

2. A unified school district if the school offers instruction in grade nine, ten, eleven or twelve and has received permission to offer instruction in high school subjects as provided in § 15-447.

C. State aid shall be apportioned as provided in § 15-973 to each county accommodation school.

Added by Laws 1981, Ch. 1, § 2, eff. Jan. 23, 1981. Amended by Laws 1988, Ch. 288, § 3, eff. July 8, 1988; Laws 1989, Ch. 273, § 16, eff. June 26, 1989; Laws 1998, 5th S.S., Ch. 1, § 19, eff. July 9, 1998; Laws 1999, Ch. 299, § 17.

Historical and Statutory Notes

Source:

A.R.S. former § 15-915.
Laws 1980, 2nd S.S., Ch. 9, § 36.

The purported amendment of this section by Laws 1998, Ch. 164 failed to become effective because Chapter 164 was repealed in its entirety by Laws 1998, 5th S.S., Ch. 1, § 2, effective July 1, 1998.

The purported amendment of this section by Laws 1998, 3rd S.S., Ch. 1, failed to became effective because Ch. 1 was repealed in its entirety by Laws 1998, 5th S.S., Ch. 1, § 2, effective July 1, 1998.

§ 15-910. School district budgets; excess utility costs; desegregation costs; tuition costs for bond issues; costs for registering warrants; report

A. The governing board may budget for the district's excess utility costs which are specifically exempt from the district's revenue control limit. If approved by the qualified electors voting at a statewide general election, the exemption from the revenue control limit under this subsection expires at the end of the 2008-2009 budget year. The uniform system of financial records shall specify expenditure items allowable as excess utility costs, which are limited to direct operational costs of heating, cooling, water and electricity, telephone communications and sanitation fees. The department of education and the auditor general shall include in the maintenance and operation section of the budget format, as provided in § 15-903, a separate line for utility expenditures and a special excess utility cost category. The special excess utility cost category shall contain budgeted expenditures for excess utility costs, determined as follows:

1. Determine the lesser of the total budgeted or total actual utility expenditures for fiscal year 1984-1985.

2. Multiply the amount in paragraph 1 of this subsection by the total percentage increase or decrease in the revenue control limit and the capital outlay revenue limit for the budget year over the revenue control limit and the capital outlay revenue limit for fiscal year 1984-1985 excluding monies available from a career ladder program or a teacher compensation program provided for in § 15-952.

3. The sum of the amounts in paragraphs 1 and 2 of this subsection is the amount budgeted in the utility expenditure line.

4. Additional expenditures for utilities are budgeted in the excess utility cost category.

B. The governing board shall apply the same percentage increase or decrease allowed in the revenue control limit and the capital outlay revenue limit as provided in § 15-905, subsection E or § 15-948 to the utility expenditure line of the budget.

C. The governing board may expend from the excess utility cost category only after it has expended for utility purposes the full amount budgeted in the utility expenditure line of the budget.

D. The governing board may, after notice is given and a public meeting is held as provided in § 15-905, subsection D, revise at any time before May 15 the amount budgeted in the excess utility cost category for the current year.

Not later than May 18, the budget as revised shall be submitted electronically to the superintendent of public instruction.

E. If the revised excess utility cost category results in an expenditure of monies in excess of school district revenues for the current year, the county school superintendent shall include within the revenue estimate for the budget year monies necessary to meet the liabilities incurred by the school district in the current year in excess of revenues received for the current year.

F. If a school district receives a refund of utility expenditures or a rebate on energy saving devices or services, the refund or rebate shall be applied against utility expenditures for the current year as a reduction of the expenditures, except that the reduction of expenditures shall not exceed the amount of actual utility expenditures.

G. The governing board may budget for expenses of complying with or continuing to implement activities which were required or permitted by a court order of desegregation or administrative agreement with the United States department of education office for civil rights directed toward remediating alleged or proven racial discrimination which are specifically exempt in whole or in part from the revenue control limit and the capital outlay revenue limit. This exemption applies only to expenses incurred for activities which are begun before the termination of the court order or administrative agreement.

H. If a governing board chooses to budget monies outside of the revenue control limit as provided in subsection G of this section, the governing board may do one of the following:

1. Use monies from the maintenance and operation fund equal to any excess desegregation or compliance expenses beyond the revenue control limit before June 30 of the current year.

2. Notify the county school superintendent to include the cost of the excess expenses in the county school superintendent's estimate of the additional amount needed for the school district from the primary property tax as provided in § 15–991.

3. Employ the provisions of both paragraphs 1 and 2 of this subsection provided that the total amount transferred and included in the amount needed from property taxes does not exceed the total amount budgeted as prescribed in subsection J, paragraph 1 of this section.

I. Through fiscal year 2003–2004, the maximum amount which a governing board may budget outside of the capital outlay revenue limit as provided in subsection G of this section is twelve per cent of the maintenance and operation desegregation budget as provided in subsection J of this section or the amount that it budgeted pursuant to this subsection for fiscal year 2001–2002, whichever is less. If a governing board chooses to budget monies outside of the capital outlay revenue limit as provided in subsection G of this section, the governing board may notify the county school superintendent to include the cost of the excess expenses in the county school superintendent's estimate of the additional amount needed for the school district from the primary property tax as provided in § 15–991.

J. A governing board using subsections G, H and I of this section:

1. Shall prepare and employ a separate maintenance and operation desegregation budget and capital outlay desegregation budget on a form prescribed by the superintendent of public instruction in conjunction with the auditor general. The budget format shall be designed to allow a school district to plan and provide in detail for expenditures to be incurred solely as a result of compliance with or continuing to implement activities which were required or permitted by a court order of desegregation or administrative agreement with the United States department of education office for civil rights directed toward remediating alleged or proven racial discrimination.

2. Shall prepare as a part of the annual financial report a detailed report of expenditures incurred solely as a result of compliance with or continuing to implement activities which were required or permitted by a court order of desegregation or administrative agreement with the United States department of education office for civil rights directed toward remediating alleged or proven racial discrimination, in a format prescribed by the auditor general in conjunction with the department of education as provided by § 15-904.

3. On or before September 30, 2003 and At least once every two years thereafter, shall collect and report data regarding activities related to a court order of desegregation or an administrative agreement with the united states department of education office for civil rights to the department of education in a format prescribed by the department of education. The department shall compile and submit copies of the reports to the governor, the president of the senate, the speaker of the house of representatives, and the chairpersons of the education committees of the senate and the House of Representatives. The reports shall include:

(a) A copy of the annual financial report related to desegregation activities as prescribed in this article.

(b) The cost per pupil of desegregation activities, listed separately for each school district and for each program.

(c) A summary of the results of all desegregation activities, including a demonstration of demographic and academic achievement trends. All demographic and achievement data shall be listed separately for each activity and this data shall be compared to the data for the rest of the school district.

(d) A chronological summary of all relevant court filings, pleadings and correspondence to which the school district is a party in any desegregation proceeding. If the school district has an agreement with the united states department of education office for civil rights, any changes to the agreement, any correspondence between the school district and the office of civil rights and a chronological summary of these events shall be submitted with the other information required by this subdivision.

(e) The actions currently being taken by school districts under court orders of desegregation to achieve unitary status, including an estimate of any costs that may be incurred in order to achieve unitary status.

(f) Any other information that the department of education deems necessary in order to carry out the purposes of this paragraph.

K. The governing board may budget for the bond issues portion of the cost of tuition charged the district as provided in § 15-824 for the pupils attending school in another school district, except that if the district is a common school district not within a high school district, the district may only include that part of tuition which is excluded from the revenue control limit and district support level as provided in § 15-951. The bond issues portion of the cost of tuition charged is specifically exempt from the revenue control limit of the school district of residence, and the primary property tax rate set to fund this amount shall not be included in the computation of additional state aid for education as provided in § 15-972, except as provided in § 15-972, subsection E. The department of education and the auditor general shall include in the maintenance and operation section of the budget format, as provided in § 15-903, a separate category for the bond issues portion of the cost of tuition.

L. The governing board may budget for interest expenses it incurred for registering warrants drawn against a fund of the school district or net interest expense on tax anticipation notes as prescribed in § 35-465.05, subsection C for the fiscal year preceding the current year if the county treasurer pooled all school district monies for investment as provided in § 15-996 for the fiscal year preceding the current year and, in those school districts that receive state aid, the school districts applied for an apportionment of state aid before the date set for the apportionment as provided in § 15-973 for the fiscal year preceding the current year. The governing board may budget an amount for interest expenses for registering warrants or issuing tax anticipation notes equal to or less than the amount of the warrant interest expense or net interest expense on tax anticipation notes as prescribed in § 35-465.05, subsection C for the fiscal year preceding the current year as provided in this subsection which is specifically exempt from the revenue control limit. For the purposes of this subsection, "state aid" means state aid as determined in §§ 15-971 and 15-972.

Added by Laws 1983, Ch. 267, § 1, eff. April 25, 1983. Amended by Laws 1984, Ch. 340, § 2, eff. Aug. 3, 1984, retroactively effective to May 1, 1984; Laws 1985, Ch. 166, § 15, eff. April 18, 1985; Laws 1986, Ch. 125, § 7, eff. April 18, 1986; Laws 1986, Ch. 392, § 1, eff. May 21, 1986; Laws 1987, Ch. 188, § 1; Laws 1987, Ch. 296, § 1, eff. May 13, 1987; Laws 1988, Ch. 288, § 4, eff. July 8, 1988; Laws 1990, Ch. 83, § 1; Laws 1991, Ch. 242, § 1, eff. June 17, 1991; Laws 1992, Ch. 117, § 1; Laws 1992, Ch. 243, § 1, eff. Sept. 30, 1992, retroactively effective to July 1, 1990; Laws 1994, Ch. 254, § 1, eff. April 24, 1994; Laws 1995, Ch. 234, § 2; Laws 1998, 5th S.S., Ch. 1, § 20, eff. July 9, 1998; Laws 1999, Ch. 99, § 1, eff. Aug. 6, 1999, retroactively effective to July 1, 1996; Laws 1999, Ch. 299, § 18; Laws 2000, Ch. 342, § 9; Laws 2000, 5th S.S., Ch. 1, § 13, approved election Nov. 7, 2000, eff. Nov. 27, 2000; Laws 2002, Ch. 68, § 1.

Historical and Statutory Notes

Laws 1988, Ch. 288, § 11, eff. July 8, 1988 provides:

"**Sec. 11. Budget revisions for fiscal year 1988-1989**

"If the governing board of a school district adopts a budget for fiscal year 1988-1989 in which the amounts budgeted in the utility expenditure line and in the excess utility cost category were determined using a method which differs from that prescribed in § 15-910, subsection A, paragraph 1, Arizona Revised Statutes, as amended by this act, and if use of the prescribed method would decrease the amount budgeted in the utility expenditure line and increase the amount budgeted in the excess utility cost category, the governing board may revise its budget at a public hearing before September 15, 1988 to adjust the amounts budgeted in the utility expenditure line and in the excess utility cost category as provided in § 15-190 [So in original], subsection A, paragraph 1, Arizona Revised Statutes, as amended by this act."

Laws 1990, Ch. 399, §§ 20, 21, provide:

"**Sec. 20. Desegregation study**

"**A.** The auditor general, in conjunction with the superintendent of public instruction, shall conduct a study of school district desegregation programs and expenditures of those school districts which have budgeted for desegregation expenditures pursuant to § 15-910, subsection H, Arizona Revised Statutes.

"**B.** In order to conduct the study as provided in subsection A of this section, the governing boards of school districts which have budgeted expenditures pursuant to § 15-910, subsection H, Arizona Revised Statutes, shall provide, by the date specified by the auditor general, all of the following:

"1. A copy of the original court order or administrative agreement with the United States department of education office for civil rights under which the school district is currently budgeting for desegregation expenditures pursuant to § 15-910, subsection H, Arizona Revised Statutes, and a summary of the court order or administrative agreement in a format as prescribed by the auditor general in conjunction with the superintendent of public instruction.

"2. A detailed report of items that were budgeted for the previous three years for desegregation expenses pursuant to § 15-910, subsection H, Arizona Revised Statutes, in a format as prescribed by the auditor general in conjunction with the superintendent of public instruction.

"3. A detailed report of actual expenditures for the previous three years for desegregation costs pursuant to § 15-910, subsection H, Arizona Revised Statutes, in a format as prescribed by the auditor general in conjunction with the superintendent of public instruction.

"4. A copy of any reports that have been submitted to either the court of jurisdiction or the United States department of education office for civil rights relating to the progress of any programs that have been implemented to remediate alleged or proven racial discrimination.

"5. Any other information deemed appropriate by the auditor general and the superintendent of public instruction.

"**C.** The auditor general in conjunction with the superintendent of public instruction, as a component of conducting the study as prescribed in subsection A of this section, shall at least:

"1. Determine whether the items that were budgeted pursuant to § 15-910, subsection H, Arizona Revised Statutes, correlated directly with such actual expenditures.

"2. Determine whether the expenditures budgeted pursuant to § 15-910, subsection H, Arizona Revised Statutes, were related directly to the stipulations of the court order or administrative agreement and whether such expenditures were used to supplement and not supplant any other sources of monies for operational or capital purposes.

"3. Compare the expenditures budgeted pursuant to § 15-910, subsection H, Arizona Revised Statutes, to the expenditures of other school districts of similar size and character that have not budgeted expenditures pursuant to § 15-910, subsection H, Arizona Revised Statutes.

"4. Determine the process by which desegregation plans and administrative agreements with the United States department of education office for civil rights directed toward remediating alleged or proven racial or national origin discrimination are developed and approved.

"5. Gather information for comparison purposes from other states in which there are school districts under a court order of desegregation or which are a party to an agreement with the United States department of education office for civil rights directed toward remediating alleged or proven racial discrimination. The auditor general shall include information regarding the degree to which the state's government is involved in the implementation of the court order or agreement.

"6. In conjunction with the attorney general's office and related to the research conducted pursuant to paragraph 5 of this section, review relevant court cases from Arizona and from jurisdictions outside Arizona relating to desegregation.

"7. Examine options for providing funding for desegregation programs.

"8. Examine the impact of expenditures budgeted pursuant to § 15-910, subsection H, Arizona Revised Statutes, on the equalization of school district expenditures.

"**D.** The auditor general, in conjunction with the superintendent of public instruction, as a component of conducting the study as prescribed in subsection A of this section shall establish an advisory committee consisting of not more than nine members, all of whom shall have expertise in the area of desegregation policies and expenditures and at least one of whom shall be an attorney experienced in desegregation law and at least one of whom shall represent a school district currently implementing a court order or administrative agreement. The committee shall provide technical assistance as necessary to conduct the study, shall review and comment on the final report that is to be submitted to the legislature as provided in subsection E of this section and shall assist in the formulation of recommendations to the legislature for possible legislative action as prescribed in subsection E of this section.

"**E.** The auditor general, in conjunction with the superintendent of public instruction, shall submit a report to the joint legislative committee to study funding priorities of the public school system by November 15, 1990 on the findings of the study and recommendations for possible legislative action. The joint legislative committee to study funding priorities of the public school system shall review the report and shall submit a report on its findings and recommendations for possible legislative action to the president of the senate, the speaker of the house of representatives and members of the senate and house of representatives education committees by December 1, 1990.

"**Sec. 21. Desegregation expenditures; fiscal year 1990–1991 and fiscal year 1991–1992**

"**A.** If a school district budgeted for desegregation expenditures pursuant to § 15–910, subsection H, Arizona Revised Statutes, for fiscal year 1989–1990 and if for fiscal year 1990–1991 the district budgets an amount for desegregation expenditures that exceeds the amount budgeted for fiscal year 1989–1990 by more than 4.1 per cent, the district shall submit a report to the auditor general and the superintendent of public instruction detailing the expenditures and demonstrating the reasons that the additional amounts are necessary in order to comply with the court order or agreement. The report submitted by the district shall document at least the amount of the expenditures, the reason for the expenditures and the number of pupils the district anticipates will benefit from the expenditures. The auditor general, in conjunction with the superintendent of public instruction, shall review all reports submitted and, by November 15, 1990, shall submit as a component of the study prescribed in § 20 of this act an analysis of the reports submitted by the school districts and shall make the reports available to the joint legislative committee to study funding priorities of the public school system.

"**B.** If a school district did not budget for desegregation expenditures pursuant to § 15–910, subsection H, Arizona Revised Statutes, for fiscal year 1989–1990, but budgets an amount for desegregation expenditures for fiscal year 1990–1991, the district shall submit a report to the auditor general and the superintendent of public instruction detailing the expenditures, including at least the amount of the expenditures, the reason for the expenditures and the number of pupils the district anticipates will benefit from the expenditures if that portion of the expenditures required to remedy alleged or proven discrimination against pupils who are limited English proficient on the basis of inadequacy of the educational program provided to those pupils exceeds the unfunded cost for limited English proficient instruction, determined as follows:

"1. Determine the amount that will be received by the district for the budget year for pupils who are limited English proficient, pursuant to § 15–943, paragraph 2, Arizona Revised Statutes.

"2. Determine the state average total cost of educating a pupil who is limited English proficient as determined by the cost study conducted pursuant to Laws 1987, chapter 201, § 1.

"3. Increase the amount determined in paragraph 2 by the growth rate prescribed in § 15–901, subsection B, paragraph 2, subdivision (f), Arizona Revised Statutes, for each year following the cost study.

"4. Multiply the amount determined in paragraph 3 by the limited English proficient student count for the district for the budget year.

"5. Subtract the amount determined in paragraph 1 from the amount determined in paragraph 4.

"The auditor general, in conjunction with the superintendent of public instruction, shall review all reports submitted and, by November 15, 1990, shall submit as a component of the study prescribed in § 20 of this act an analysis of the reports submitted by the school districts and shall make the reports available to the joint legislative committee to study funding priorities of the public school system."

Laws 1992, chapter 243, § 4, as amended by Laws 1992, Ch. 305, § 34, provides:

"**Sec. 4. Retroactivity**

"Sections 15–910, 15–947 and 35–465.05, Arizona Revised Statutes, as amended by this act, are effective retroactively to July 1, 1990."

Laws 1994, Ch. 254, § 2, provides:

"**Sec. 2. Energy saving devices and services for fiscal year 1994–1995; limitations; definitions**

"**A.** Subject to the provisions of subsection E of this section, for fiscal years 1993–1994 through 1998–1999 the governing board of a school district may budget for the cost of purchasing energy saving devices, the amount of which is specifically exempt from the capital outlay revenue limit, provided that the energy saving device results in a documented reduction in utility expenditures in the current year or a rebate in the current year, or both, in an amount equal to at least the cost of the energy saving device or the portion of the cost that is budgeted as provided in this subsection.

"**B.** If a governing board budgets for an energy saving device pursuant to subsection A of this section, for fiscal years 1993–1994 through 1998–1999 the governing board may include the operational costs of energy saving devices as excess utility costs as provided in § 15–910, Arizona Revised Statutes. The uniform system of financial records shall specify expenditure items allowable as operational costs of energy saving devices.

"**C.** For fiscal years 1993–1994 through 1998–1999 the governing board of a school district may include the costs of purchasing energy saving services as excess utility costs as provided in § 15–910, Arizona Revised Statutes, provided that the energy saving service results in a documented reduction in utility expenditures in the current year or a rebate in the current year, or both, in an amount equal to at least the cost of the energy saving service or the portion of the cost that is budgeted as provided in this subsection.

"**D.** If a governing board budgets for an energy saving device or service pursuant to subsection A, B or C of this section, prior to the budget decision, justification for the purchase of the energy saving device or the energy saving services shall be presented to the governing board and shall include a written evaluation of the total cost of the device or service, including the proposed capital, operation and maintenance costs compared to the savings anticipated.

"**E.** Notwithstanding § 41–2632, Arizona Revised Statutes, a school district may not budget for the cost of energy saving devices or services that are specifically exempt from the revenue control limit or the capital outlay revenue limit pursuant to subsection A, B or C of this section if either of the following conditions apply:

"1. The contract was approved after June 30, 1995.

"2. The contract was approved between the effective date of this act and June 30, 1995 and any of the following apply:

"(a) The costs will be incurred in connection with the construction of new buildings.

"(b) The costs will be incurred in connection with construction projects for which bonds have been approved by the qualified electors of the school district.

"(c) The contract for the portion of the project that comprises the cost of energy saving devices was not awarded pursuant to a competitive, sealed bidding process pursuant to § 15–213, Arizona Revised Statutes, and did not include performance guarantees as part of the bidding process.

"**F.** As used in this section:

"1. 'Energy saving device' means any instrument, mechanism, appliance or any other apparatus which assists in reducing the costs of heating, cooling, water and electricity.

"2. 'Energy saving service' means a service which assists in reducing the use of heating, cooling, water or electricity including training, materials and monitoring services which apply proven management methods to control of energy and utility use."

Laws 1994, Ch. 254, § 8, as amended by Laws 1995, Ch. 191, § 23, effective April 19, 1995, provides:

"**Sec. 8. Budget and expenditure provisions for certain elementary and union high school districts for fiscal year 1992–1993**

"**A.** If a union high school district with a student count of less than two thousand was eligible to budget for excess utilities pursuant to § 15–910, Arizona Revised Statutes, for fiscal year 1992–1993 but did not so budget, for the purposes of § 15–905, subsections L and M, Arizona Revised Statutes, the district's general budget limit and the maintenance and operations section of the budget for that year are deemed to have been increased by the amount by which the district was authorized to budget for excess utilities.

"**B.** Notwithstanding § 15–905, subsection M, Arizona Revised Statutes, if a common school district or union high school district with a student count of less than two thousand is required to reduce its general budget limit due to excess expenditures in fiscal year 1992–1993, the district may make part of the reduction in the third subsequent year."

The purported amendment of this section by Laws 1998, 3rd S.S., Ch. 1, failed to became effective because Ch. 1 was repealed in its entirety by Laws 1998, 5th S.S., Ch. 1, § 2, effective July 1, 1998.

Laws 1999, Ch. 99, § 3, provides:

"**Sec. 3. Retroactivity**

"Section 1 of this act is effective retroactively to from and after June 30, 1996."

Laws 2000, 5th S.S., Ch. 1, § 64, provides:

"**Sec. 64. Election to authorize additional state transaction privilege and use tax increments**

"**A.** The secretary of state shall place on the ballot of the 2000 state general election the issue of:

"1. An incremental increase in the rate of state transaction privilege tax, as provided by § 42–5010, subsection G, Arizona Revised Statutes, as amended by this act, an incremental increase in the state use tax, as provided by § 42–5155, subsection D, Arizona Revised Statutes, as amended by this act and the distribution of those monies as provided by § 42–5029, Arizona Revised Statutes, as amended by this act.

"2. Inflation adjustments in the state aid to education base level and other components of the revenue control limit pursuant to § 15–901.01, Arizona Revised Statutes, as added by this act.

"3. A termination of the exemption from the revenue control limit for excess utility costs as provided by § 15-910, subsection A, Arizona Revised Statutes, as amended by this act.

"4. A limitation on the school district qualifying tax rates and the county equalization assistance for education rate as provided by section 41-1276, subsection H, Arizona Revised Statutes, as amended by this act.

"5. A state income tax credit in mitigation of increased transaction privilege and use taxes, as provided by § 43-1072.01, Arizona Revised Statutes, as added by this act.

"**B.** As provided by § 19-124, Arizona Revised Statutes, the legislative council shall prepare an analysis of the proposition, and the secretary of state shall include the analysis with any submitted arguments that advocate or oppose the proposition in the general election publicity pamphlet.

"**C.** In addition to any other ballot requirements prescribed by law, the secretary of state shall print on the official general election ballot:

"1. The official title and number of the measure to be voted on.

"2. A descriptive title, not exceeding fifty words, containing a summary of the issue, prepared by the secretary of state and approved by the attorney general.

"3. The phrases:

"A 'yes' vote has the effect of approving an increase in the state transaction privilege (sales) tax and the state use tax of six-tenths of one per cent to raise revenues in support of education, a state income tax credit in mitigation of those tax increases, inflation adjustments in state aid for education, a termination of an exemption from education funding revenue control limits for excess utility costs and a limitation on the school district qualifying tax rates and the county equalization assistance for education rate.

"A 'no' vote has the effect of rejecting the proposed increase in state taxes and the other proposed tax mitigations and education budgetary controls."

Conditionally amended § 15-910, was placed in Proposition 301, and was approved by the electors at the November 7, 2000 general election as proclaimed by the Governor on November 27, 2000.

Laws 2002, Ch. 68, § 3, provides:

"**Sec. 3. Desegregation budget; limit; sunset review; recommendations**

"Notwithstanding § 15-910, Arizona Revised Statutes, through fiscal year 2003-2004, a school district shall not budget more on desegregation activities in any single fiscal year than the school district budgeted for these purposes in fiscal year 2001-2002. By December 1, 2003, the committees of reference for the education committees of the senate and the house of representatives shall conduct a sunset review of the funding mechanisms for desegregation activities. The committees of reference shall make recommendations for proposed legislation for consideration during the forty-sixth legislature, second regular session."

Laws 2002, Ch. 330, § 56, provides:

"**Sec. 56. School district excess utility costs; temporary cap**

"Notwithstanding § 15-910, Arizona Revised Statutes, the maximum amount that a school district may budget in the excess utility cost category for fiscal years 2002-2003 and 2003-2004 is the amount that it budgeted in the excess utility cost category for fiscal year 2001-2002."

Laws 2003, 1st. S.S., Ch. 3, § 1, as amended by Laws 2003, Ch. 264, § 16, provides:

"**Section 1. School district excess utility costs; temporary limitation**

"Notwithstanding Laws 2002, chapter 330, § 56, the maximum amount that a school district may budget in the excess utility cost category for fiscal year 2003-2004 is the amount that it expended from the excess utility cost category for fiscal year 2001-2002."

Laws 2003, 1st S.S., Ch. 3, became law without the Governor's signature as provided in Arizona Constitution, Article 5, § 7.

Laws 2004, Ch. 278, § 16, provides:

"**Sec. 16. Desegregation budget; limit**

"Notwithstanding § 15-910, Arizona Revised Statutes, the maximum amount that a school district may budget for desegregation activities for fiscal year 2004-2005 shall be computed as follows:

"1. Determine the amount that the district budgeted for desegregation activities for fiscal year 2003-2004 pursuant to Laws 2002, chapter 68, § 3.

"2. Compute the percentage increase in average daily membership for the district, as defined in § 15-901, Arizona Revised Statutes, for the 2003-2004 school year above the 2002-2003 school year. If average daily membership for the district decreased for the 2003-2004 school year below the 2002-2003 school year, assume a per cent increase of zero.

"3. Multiply the amount determined in paragraph 1 of this section by the percentage determined in paragraph 2 of this section.

"4. Multiply the amount determined in paragraph 1 of this section by two per cent for assumed inflation.

"5. Add the amounts determined in paragraphs 1, 3 and 4 of this section."

Laws 2004, Ch. 278, § 21, provides:

"**Sec. 21. Retroactivity**

"**A.** Except as provided in subsection B of this section, this act applies retroactively to from and after June 30, 2004.

"**B.** Laws 2002, chapter 330, § 49, as amended by this act, applies retroactively to from and after June 29, 2004."

Reviser's Notes:

1983 Note. Laws 1983, Ch. 89, § 1 added another new § 15-910 which was renumbered as § 15-911 pursuant to authority of § 41-1304.02.

1987 Note. Prior to the 1988 amendment, this section contained the amendments made by Laws 1987, Ch. 188, § 1 and Ch. 296, § 1 which were blended together pursuant to authority of § 41-1304.03.

1992 Note. Prior to the 1994 amendment, this section contained the amendments made by Laws 1992, Ch. 117, sec. 1 and Ch. 243, sec. 1 that were blended together pursuant to authority of § 41-1304.03. Pursuant to authority of § 41-1304.02, in the section heading "; definitions" was added after "warrants".

1994 Note. Pursuant to authority of § 41-1304.02, in the section heading "; definitions" was deleted.

1995 Note. Pursuant to authority of § 41-1304.02, in Laws 1995, Ch. 191, § 23, subsection A "the" was inserted before "purposes" to correct a manifest clerical error.

1999 Note. Prior to the 2000 amendment, this section contained the amendments made by Laws 1999, Ch. 99, sec. 1 and Ch. 299, sec. 18 that were blended together pursuant to authority of § 41-1304.03.

2000 Note. Prior to the 2002 amendment, this section contained the amendments made by Laws 2000, Ch. 342, sec. 9 and 5th S.S., Ch. 1, sec. 13 that were blended together pursuant to authority of § 41-1304.03.

§ 15-910.01. School district budgets; career and technical education and vocational education center expenses

A. The governing board of a school district which has entered into an intergovernmental agreement to establish a jointly owned and operated career and technical education and vocational education center as provided in § 15-789 may budget for vocational maintenance and operation expenses which are specifically exempt in whole or part from the revenue control limit for a period of not to exceed three years beginning the first year that the career and technical education and vocational education center is operating and serving students. The governing board shall notify the state board of education before adopting a budget as provided in this section for the first year of operation of the career and technical education and vocational education center to demonstrate that the center is ready to begin operations.

B. For each year that a school district is authorized to budget for a joint career and technical education and vocational education center as provided in this section, the district shall determine the budget amount as follows:

1. Estimate the average daily membership or adjusted average daily membership for the budget year of students to be enrolled in courses held at the joint career and technical education and vocational education center pursuant to §§ 15-901 and 15-902.

2. Multiply 0.142 by the base level and multiply this product by the average daily membership or adjusted average daily membership as determined in paragraph 1 of this subsection.

C. Before May 15, school districts which overestimate the average daily membership as provided in subsection B, paragraph 1 of this section shall adjust the general budget limit and expenditures based on the actual average daily membership during the current fiscal year. School districts which underestimate the average daily membership may adjust their budgets before May 15 based on the actual average daily membership during the current fiscal year. Procedures for completing adjustments shall be prescribed in the uniform system of financial records. Not later than May 18, the budget as revised shall be submitted electronically to the superintendent of public instruction.

D. A governing board which budgets for career and technical education and vocational education center expenses pursuant to this section shall:

1. Prepare and employ a separate maintenance and operation budget for the career and technical education and vocational education center on a form prescribed by the superintendent of public instruction in conjunction with the auditor general. The budget format shall be designed to allow a school district to plan and provide in detail for expenditures to be incurred solely for the maintenance and operation of the career and technical education and vocational education center.

2. Prepare as a part of the annual financial report a detailed report of expenditures incurred solely for the maintenance and operation of the career and technical education and vocational education center.

E. The part of the primary tax rate set to fund the vocational maintenance and operations expenses as provided in this section shall not be included in the computation of additional state aid for education as prescribed in § 15-972.

Added by Laws 1988, Ch. 288, § 5, eff. July 8, 1988. Amended by Laws 2000, Ch. 342, § 10; Laws 2002, Ch. 89, § 23.

§ 15-910.02. Energy conservation measures; report; definition

A. A school district governing board may adopt measures to reduce excess utility costs and include expenditures for employee training, the use of energy services consultants or other contractual arrangements with energy specialists who advise the district and its employees on energy savings, conservation measures or efforts to improve energy efficiency. Expenditures pursuant to this subsection shall not include capital expenditures.

B. Notwithstanding § 15-910, subsection A, excess utility costs include the costs of implementing measures to reduce energy costs pursuant to subsection A of this section.

C. A school district that adopts measures pursuant to subsection A of this section may include in its budget an energy reduction adjustment based on a reduction of excess utility costs in the fiscal years following the fiscal year of implementation using an estimate of one-half of the energy cost savings. After the audit prescribed in subsection H of this section, a school district which underestimated the energy cost savings may adjust its energy reduction adjustment before May 15 based on the actual energy cost savings. A school district which overestimated the energy cost savings shall decrease its energy reduction adjustment before May 15 of the current fiscal year based on the actual energy cost savings. Not later than May 18, the budget as revised shall be submitted electronically to the superintendent of public instruction.

D. Energy cost savings shall be calculated as follows:

1. Determine the excess utility costs for the base year. The base year shall be the fiscal year prior to implementation and the base expenditures shall only include buildings for which utility services have been provided and billed for the previous twelve consecutive months prior to June 30 of the base year. The

base expenditures shall be decreased proportionately to account for building closings or nonuse for the school district's purposes.

2. Determine the excess utility costs for the fiscal year prior to the current fiscal year for buildings included in the base expenditures.

3. To determine the energy cost savings, subtract paragraph 2 of this subsection from paragraph 1 of this subsection.

E. The unexpended revenue resulting from one-half of the energy cost savings determined in subsection D of this section shall be used for reduction of school district taxes as provided in § 15–906.

F. For any fiscal year that the excess utility costs exceed the excess utility costs for the base year, a school district shall not budget an energy reduction adjustment.

G. For the fiscal year following the year of implementation the excess utility levy must be decreased by no less than the amount of the expenditures associated with the implementation of energy cost reduction measures pursuant to subsection A of this section. Except for the fiscal year of implementation, a school district participating in this program shall not levy for excess utility costs an amount that is more than the fiscal year of implementation minus the amount of the expenditures associated with the implementation of energy cost reduction measures. The implementation year is the year immediately following the base year and is the only year school districts participating in the program may increase the excess utility levy for the costs of implementing energy cost reduction measures.

H. The actual energy cost savings shall be certified by the governing board and verified by an independent audit pursuant to §§ 15–914 or 15–914.01 before the budget may be revised pursuant to this section. The audit shall consider changes in utility rates or energy costs not related to energy conservation and efficiency measures taken before making a final determination of actual energy cost savings. Information required to perform this audit shall be applied uniformly to all school districts in this state pursuant to administrative policies and recommendations of the department of commerce energy office.

I. The superintendent of public instruction shall submit a report on the school districts' energy cost savings as a result of participating in this program to the speaker of the house of representatives and the president of the senate on January 15, 2001 and January 15, 2003 and shall submit a final comprehensive report on January 15, 2005.

J. The governing board shall consider measures for energy conservation and efficiency at the public hearing for which specific notice has been given at the hearing for the adoption and revision of the annual budget pursuant to § 15–905.

K. For purposes of this section "energy cost savings" means an actual reduction in excess utility costs pursuant to § 15–910 and this section.

Added by Laws 1998, Ch. 271, § 1. Amended by Laws 2000, Ch. 342, § 11.

Repeal

This section is repealed by Laws 1998, Ch. 271, § 3, effective July 1, 2005.

Historical and Statutory Notes

Laws 1998, Ch. 271, § 3, provides:

"**Sec. 3. Delayed repeal**

"Section 15–910.02, Arizona Revised Statutes, as added by this act, is repealed from and after June 30, 2005."

Laws 2001, Ch. 32, § 1, provides:

"**School district participation in energy conservation measures; eligibility**

"School districts are ineligible to adjust the budget limit for energy conservation measures pursuant to § 15–947, Arizona Revised Statutes, if the school district did not participate in energy conservation measures pursuant to § 15–910.02, Arizona Revised Statutes, during school year 2000–2001."

Reviser's Notes:

1998 Note. Pursuant to authority of § 41–1304.02, in the section heading "definition" was substituted for "definitions", in subsection D, paragraph 1, last sentence the spelling of "nonuse" was corrected and in subsection K the words "§ 15–910 and this section" were substituted for "§§ 15–910 and 15–910.02".

§ 15–911. Aggregate expenditure limitation; aggregate expenditures of local revenues; adjustments

A. The legislature shall on or before June 1 of each year transmit to the state board of education the aggregate expenditure limitation for all school districts for the following fiscal year which the economic estimates commission determines as provided in § 41–563, subsection C.

B. On or before November 1 of each year the state board of education shall determine and report to the president of the senate, the speaker of the house of representatives and the chairman of the joint legislative budget committee the aggregate expenditures of local revenues as defined in article IX, § 21, subsection (4), Constitution of Arizona, for all school districts for the current year.

C. If the aggregate expenditures of local revenues which the state board determines as provided in subsection B of this section are in excess of the expenditure limitation determined as provided in § 41–563, subsection C:

1. On or before November 1 the state board shall notify each school district that may be affected by subsections D and E of this section and inform it of the amount by which it may have to reduce its expenditures of local revenues.

2. On or before March 1 the legislature, on approval of two-thirds of the membership of each house of the legislature, may authorize the expenditures of local revenues in excess of the expenditure limitation for the current fiscal year.

D. The state board of education shall:

1. Determine the amount of the expenditures of local revenues in excess of the expenditure limitation.

2. Determine the amount of expenditures of local revenues for each school district and the total amount for all of the school districts.

3. Divide the amount determined in paragraph 1 of this subsection by the total amount determined in paragraph 2 of this subsection.

4. Multiply the quotient determined in paragraph 3 of this subsection by the amount determined in paragraph 2 of this subsection for each school district.

E. If the legislature fails to authorize the expenditures of local revenues in excess of the expenditure limitation as provided in subsection C, paragraph 2 of this section, on or before March 5 the state board of education shall inform each school district of the amount it is to reduce its expenditures of local revenues, and each school district shall reduce its expenditures of local revenues by the amount determined in subsection D, paragraph 4 of this section. The governing board of each school district shall on or before April 1, after it gives notice and holds a public meeting in a similar manner as provided in § 15–905, subsections C and D, adopt a revised budget for the current year which shall not exceed the previously adopted budget for the current year less the amount which the state board of education specifies for reduction in expenditures of local revenues. Not later than April 4, the budget as revised shall be submitted electronically to the superintendent of public instruction.

Added as § 15–910 by Laws 1983, Ch. 89, § 1, eff. July 2, 1985. Renumbered as § 15–911. Amended by Laws 2000, Ch. 342, § 12.

Historical and Statutory Notes

Laws 1983, Ch. 89, § 2 provides:

"**Sec. 2. Effective date**

"The provisions of this act shall become effective from and after July 1, 1985."

Reviser's Notes:

1983 Note. This section, added by Laws 1983, Ch. 89, § 1 as § 15–910, was renumbered as § 15–911 pursuant to authority of § 41–1304.02.

§ 15–912. Consolidation assistance

A. A resulting school district after merger of school districts may budget for consolidation assistance as provided in subsection B of this section if the school districts which merge include any of the following:

1. A common school district and at least one other common school district or at least one unified school district.

2. A high school district and at least one other high school district or at least one unified school district.

3. A unified school district and at least one other unified school district or at least one high school district or at least one common school district.

B. The eligible school district may increase the revenue control limit and the district support level for the first three years of operation by an amount determined as follows:

1. In the first year for which a budget is computed, ten per cent of the revenue control limit.

2. In the second year for which a budget is computed, seven per cent of the revenue control limit.

3. In the third year for which a budget is computed, four per cent of the revenue control limit.

C. A school district which budgets for consolidation assistance pursuant to this section may not budget for unification assistance pursuant to § 15–912.01 during the three year period for which the consolidation assistance is in effect plus an additional two years immediately thereafter.

Added by Laws 1985, Ch. 166, § 16, eff. April 18, 1985. Amended by Laws 1989, Ch. 210, § 4; Laws 1994, Ch. 264, § 5.

Historical and Statutory Notes

Reviser's Notes:

1994 Note. Pursuant to authority of § 41–1304.02, in subsection C the reference to "§ 15–912.01" was substituted for the reference to "§ 15–913" to conform to the reviser's renumbering of that section.

§ 15–912.01. Unification assistance

A. New unified school districts formed after a subdivision and unification as provided in § 15–458, subsection G or § 15–459, subsection B, paragraph 5 or new unified school districts formed from a common school district and a high school district pursuant to § 15–448, may budget for unification assistance as provided in subsection B of this section.

B. The eligible school district may increase the revenue control limit and the district support level for the first three years of operation by an amount determined as follows:

1. In the first year for which a budget is computed, ten per cent of the revenue control limit.

2. In the second year for which a budget is computed, seven per cent of the revenue control limit.

3. In the third year for which a budget is computed, four per cent of the revenue control limit.

C. A school district which budgets for unification assistance pursuant to this section may not budget for consolidation assistance pursuant to § 15–912 during the three year period for which the unification assistance is in effect plus an additional two years immediately thereafter.

Added as § 15–913 by Laws 1994, Ch. 264, § 6. Renumbered as § 15–912.01. Amended by Laws 1997, Ch. 276, § 3; Laws 1999, Ch. 280, § 5; Laws 2000, Ch. 211, § 4.

Historical and Statutory Notes

Reviser's Notes:

1994 Note. Pursuant to authority of § 41–1304.02, this section, added by Laws 1994, Ch. 264, sec. 6 as § 15–913, was renumbered as § 15–912.01.

§ 15–913. Education program; juvenile detention centers

A. Each county that operates a juvenile detention center shall offer an education program to serve all school-age children in its juvenile detention center. The county school superintendent and the presiding juvenile court judge in each county shall agree on the method of delivery of the juvenile detention center education program.

B. The state board of education shall prescribe standards and achievement testing requirements for county juvenile detention center education programs that shall attempt to ensure that the programs are compatible with public school education goals and requirements. The county school superintendent shall attempt to coordinate the program with each pupil's school district of residence to assist the pupil's transition back to the school district at the appropriate time.

C. A county may operate its juvenile detention center education program through an existing accommodation school.

D. If a county chooses not to operate its juvenile detention center education program through an existing accommodation school, the county school superintendent may establish a detention center education fund to provide financial support to the program. The detention center education fund for each program shall consist of a base amount plus a variable amount. For fiscal year 1994–1995 the base amount is twenty thousand dollars and the variable amount shall be determined pursuant to subsection E of this section. Beginning with fiscal year 1995–1996 the base amount is the amount for the prior year adjusted by the growth rate prescribed by law, subject to appropriation. The county treasurer shall deposit the appropriate amount into the detention center education fund from monies that are collected from the tax levy for county equalization assistance for education pursuant to § 15–994 after the monies are used pursuant to § 15–365, subsection F and before the monies are used to provide equalization assistance for education pursuant to § 15–971, subsection C, except that if a county detention center education program serves more than one county, payment into the fund shall be pursuant to subsection F of this section.

E. The variable amount shall be determined as follows:

1. Determine the number of days in the prior fiscal year that each child who had been in the detention center for more than forty-eight hours received an instructional program of at least two hundred forty minutes. No school district may count a child as being in attendance in that school district on a day that the child is counted for the purposes of this paragraph.

2. Multiply the number of days determined under paragraph 1 of this subsection by the following amount:

(a) For fiscal year 1994–1995, fifteen dollars.

(b) For fiscal year 1995–1996 and thereafter, the amount for the prior year adjusted by the growth rate prescribed by law, subject to appropriation.

3. For each child with a disability as defined in § 15–761 who had been in the detention center for more than forty-eight hours:

(a) Determine the amount prescribed in § 15–1204, subsection E, paragraph 1 or 2 and add one hundred dollars for capital outlay costs.

(b) Divide the sum determined under subdivision (a) of this paragraph by one hundred seventy-five.

(c) Subtract the amount prescribed in paragraph 2, subdivision (a) or (b) of this subsection from the quotient determined in subdivision (b) of this paragraph.

(d) Determine the number of days in the prior fiscal year that the child received an instructional program of at least two hundred forty minutes.

(e) Multiply the amount determined in subdivision (d) of this paragraph by the difference determined in subdivision (c) of this paragraph.

4. Add the amounts determined in paragraph 3 of this subsection for all children with disabilities.

5. Add the sum determined in paragraph 4 of this subsection to the product determined in paragraph 2 of this subsection. This sum is the variable amount.

F. If a county detention center education program serves more than one county, the county school superintendents and the presiding juvenile court judges of the counties being served shall agree on a county of jurisdiction. The county treasurer shall pay the appropriate amount into the detention center education fund of the county of jurisdiction from monies collected pursuant to subsection D of this section as follows:

1. The total base amount shall be prorated among the counties based on the total number of days as determined under subsection E, paragraph 1 of this section that children from each county were served.

2. The variable amount shall be calculated separately for each county.

3. The county treasurer of each county that is not the county of jurisdiction shall pay its variable amount and its portion of the base amount to the county of jurisdiction.

4. The county treasurer of the county of jurisdiction shall deposit the monies received from the other counties pursuant to paragraph 3 of this subsection into the detention center education fund and shall pay into the fund its variable amount and its portion of the base amount.

G. If a county operated a juvenile detention center education program through an accommodation school in the year before it begins to operate its juvenile detention center education program as provided in subsection D of this section, for the first year of operation as provided in subsection D of this section, the student count of the accommodation school shall be reduced by the student count attributable to the detention center program. The provisions of § 15-942 shall not apply to this reduction in student count.

Added by Laws 1994, Ch. 266, § 1. Amended by Laws 1995, Ch. 191, § 10, eff. April 19, 1995; Laws 1995, Ch. 196, § 9.

Historical and Statutory Notes

Laws 1994, Ch. 266, § 3, provides:

"**Sec. 3. Funding for new or expanded juvenile detention center programs for fiscal year 1994-1995**

"Notwithstanding § 15-913, subsection E, Arizona Revised Statutes, as added by this act, for fiscal year 1994-1995, if a juvenile detention center education program is newly established or if the number of days determined as provided in § 15-913, subsection E, paragraph 1, Arizona Revised Statutes, as added by this act, for fiscal year 1994-1995 is expected to exceed the number of such days for fiscal year 1993-1994 by at least ten per cent, the superintendent of public instruction may authorize payment into the county detention center education fund based on an estimate of the number of days determined as provided in § 15-913, subsection E, paragraph 1 and paragraph 3, subdivision (d), Arizona Revised Statutes, as added by this act. The estimate shall be adjusted before the end of the fiscal year to reflect the actual number of days through June 15 and an estimate of the number of days from June 16 through June 30. Any variation between the final estimate and the actual number of days for the fiscal year shall be added to or subtracted from the number of days used to determine payment into the fund for fiscal year 1995-1996."

For applicability provisions of Laws 1995, Ch. 196, see the Historical and Statutory Notes following § 1-254.

The amendment of this section by Laws 1995, Ch. 196, § 9, was repealed by Laws 1996, Ch. 248, § 6.

Another § 15-913 was renumbered as § 15-912.01.

Former § 15-913, added by Laws 1986, Ch. 364, § 2, which related to career ladder programs, was repealed by Laws 1990, Ch. 319, § 1. See, now, § 15-918 et seq.

Reviser's Notes:

1994 Note. Laws 1994, Ch. 264, sec. 6 added another new § 15-913 that was renumbered as § 15-912.01, pursuant to authority of § 41-1304.02.

1995 Note. The amendment made by Laws 1995, Ch. 196, sec. 9 was inconsistent and incompatible with Laws 1995, Ch. 191, sec. 10 and therefore could not be blended.

§ 15–913.01. Education program; county jails

A. Each county that operates a county jail shall offer an education program to serve all prisoners who are under eighteen years of age and prisoners with disabilities who are age twenty-one or younger and who are confined in the county jail. The county school superintendent and the sheriff in each county shall agree on the method of delivery of the education program.

B. The county school superintendent shall develop policies and procedures for the transfer of educational records of any prisoner confined in a county jail who has been transferred from a juvenile detention center or from any other public agency which has provided educational services to that prisoner.

C. A county may operate its county jail education program through an accommodation school that provides alternative education services pursuant to § 15–308, except that each pupil enrolled in the accommodation school county jail education program shall be funded at an amount equal to seventy-two per cent of the amount for that pupil if that pupil was enrolled in another accommodation school program.

D. If a county chooses not to operate its county jail education program through an accommodation school, the county school superintendent may establish a county jail education fund to provide financial support to the program. The county jail education fund for each program shall consist of a base amount plus a variable amount. For fiscal year 1999–2000 the base amount is fourteen thousand four hundred dollars and the variable amount shall be determined pursuant to subsection E of this section. The county treasurer shall deposit the appropriate amount into the county jail education fund from monies that are collected from the tax levy for county equalization assistance for education pursuant to § 15–994 after the monies are used pursuant to § 15–365, subsection F and before the monies are used to provide equalization assistance for education pursuant to § 15–971, subsection C, except that if a county jail education program serves more than one county, payment into the fund shall be pursuant to subsection F of this section.

E. The variable amount shall be determined as follows:

1. Determine the number of days in the prior fiscal year that each pupil who is a prisoner and had been in the county jail for more than forty-eight hours received an instructional program of at least two hundred forty minutes. No school district may count a pupil as being in attendance in that school district on a day that the pupil is counted as a prisoner for the purposes of this paragraph.

2. Multiply the number of days determined under paragraph 1 of this subsection by the following amount:

(a) For fiscal year 1999–2000, ten dollars and eighty cents.

(b) For fiscal year 2000–2001 and each year thereafter, the amount for the prior year adjusted by any growth rate prescribed by law, subject to legislative appropriation.

3. For each pupil who is a child with a disability as defined in § 15–761, who is a prisoner and who had been in the county jail for more than forty-eight hours:

(a) Determine the amount prescribed in § 15–1204, subsection E, paragraph 1 or 2, multiply the amount by .72 and add seventy-two dollars for capital outlay costs.

(b) Divide the sum determined under subdivision (a) of this paragraph by one hundred seventy-five.

(c) Subtract the amount prescribed in paragraph 2 of this subsection from the quotient determined in subdivision (b) of this paragraph.

(d) Determine the number of days in the prior fiscal year that the pupil received an instructional program of at least two hundred forty minutes.

(e) Multiply the amount determined in subdivision (d) of this paragraph by the difference determined in subdivision (c) of this paragraph.

4. Add the amounts determined in paragraph 3 of this subsection for all pupils with disabilities who are prisoners.

5. Add the sum determined in paragraph 4 of this subsection to the product determined in paragraph 2 of this subsection. This sum is the variable amount.

F. If a county jail education program serves more than one county, the county school superintendents and the sheriffs of the counties being served shall agree on a county of jurisdiction. The county treasurer shall pay the appropriate amount into the county jail education fund of the county of jurisdiction from monies collected pursuant to subsection D of this section as follows:

1. The total base amount shall be prorated among the counties based on the total number of days as determined under subsection E, paragraph 1 of this section that pupils who are prisoners from each county were served.

2. The variable amount shall be calculated separately for each county.

3. The county treasurer of each county that is not the county of jurisdiction shall pay its variable amount and its portion of the base amount to the county of jurisdiction.

4. The county treasurer of the county of jurisdiction shall deposit the monies received from the other counties pursuant to paragraph 3 of this subsection into the county jail education fund and shall pay into the fund its variable amount and its portion of the base amount.

G. If a county operated a county jail education program through an accommodation school in the year before it begins to operate its county jail education program as provided in subsection D of this section, for the first year of operation as provided in subsection D of this section, the student count of the accommodation school shall be reduced by the average daily membership attributable to the accommodation school's county jail program in its last fiscal year of operation. The provisions of § 15–942 shall not apply to this reduction in student count.

Added by Laws 1995, Ch. 158, § 1. Amended by Laws 1999, Ch. 242, § 1.

Historical and Statutory Notes

Laws 1995, Ch. 158, § 6, provides:

"**Sec. 6. Funding for expanded county jail education programs for fiscal year 1995-1996**

"**A.** Notwithstanding § 15-913.01, subsection E, Arizona Revised Statutes, for fiscal year 1995-1996, if the number of days determined pursuant to § 15-913.01, subsection E, paragraph 1, Arizona Revised Statutes, is expected to exceed the number of days for fiscal year 1994-1995 by at least ten per cent, the superintendent of public instruction may authorize payment into the county jail education fund based on an estimate of the number of days determined pursuant to § 15-913.01, subsection E, paragraph 1 and paragraph 3, subdivision (d), Arizona Revised Statutes. The estimate shall be adjusted before the end of the fiscal year to reflect the actual number of days through June 15 and an estimate of the number of days from June 16 through June 30. Any variation between the final estimate and the actual number of days for the fiscal year shall be added to or subtracted from the number of days used to determine payment into the fund for fiscal year 1996-1997.

"**B.** Notwithstanding § 15-948, Arizona Revised Statutes, for fiscal year 1995-1996, if a county operates its county jail education program through an existing accommodation school, the accommodation school may adjust its revenue control limit and district support level by an amount determined as follows:

"1. Determine the average daily membership or adjusted average daily membership, whichever is applicable, of pupils who are served in the county jail education program through the first one hundred days in session.

"2. Multiply the amount that is determined pursuant to paragraph 1 of this subsection by one-half of the base level for the accommodation school.

"**C.** If the accommodation school uses subsection B of this section and § 15-948, subsection A, Arizona Revised Statutes, the amount that is determined pursuant to subsection B, paragraph 2 of this section shall be subtracted from the amount that is determined pursuant to § 15-948, subsection A, paragraph 2, Arizona Revised Statutes."

§ 15-914. Financial and compliance audits

A. The governing board of a school district which is required to comply with the single audit act amendments of 1996 (P. L. 104-156; 110 Stat. 1396; 31 United States code §§ 7501 through 7507) shall contract for at least annual financial and compliance audits of financial transactions and accounts subject to the single audit act amendments of 1996 and kept by or for the school district. beginning with fiscal year 2003-2004, the governing board of a school district that is not required to comply with the single audit act and that has adopted an expenditure budget of two million dollars or more for the maintenance and operation fund pursuant to § 15-905 shall contract for an annual financial statement audit. Beginning with fiscal year 2004-2005, the governing board of a school district that is not required to comply with the single audit act and that has adopted an expenditure budget of less than two million dollars but more than seven hundred thousand dollars for the maintenance and operation fund pursuant to § 15-905 shall contract for a biennial financial statement audit. An independent certified public accountant shall conduct the audit in accordance with generally accepted governmental auditing standards.

B. The governing board of a charter school that is required to comply with the single audit act amendments of 1996 shall contract for an annual financial and compliance audit of financial transactions and accounts subject to the single audit act amendments of 1996 and kept by or for the charter school.

C. A charter school that is not subject to the single audit act amendments of 1996 shall contract for at least an annual financial statement audit conducted in accordance with generally accepted governmental auditing standards. An independent certified public accountant shall conduct the audit.

D. For all audits referred to in subsections A, B and C of this section the independent certified public accountant shall submit a uniform system of financial records compliance questionnaire to the auditor general with the applicable audit reports.

E. Contracts for all financial and compliance audits and financial statement audits and the completed audits shall be approved by the auditor general as provided in § 41-1279.21. Contracts for all financial and compliance audits and financial statement audits shall comply with the rules for competitive sealed proposals as prescribed by the state board of education in § 15-213.

F. If the school district or charter school will incur costs of financial and compliance audits for the budget year, the governing board of a school district or the governing body of the charter school may increase its base support level for the budget year by an amount equal to the amount expended for the district's or charter school's financial and compliance audits in the year before the current year, increased by the growth rate as prescribed by law, subject to appropriation. In determining the amount expended for the district's or charter school's financial and compliance audits, the school district or charter school shall include only the portion of the audit which must be paid from monies other than federal monies. The department of education and the auditor general shall prescribe a method for determining the increase in the base support level and shall include in the maintenance and operation section of the budget format, as provided in § 15-903, a separate line for financial and compliance audits expenditures.

G. Beginning in fiscal year 2003-2004, every audit contract shall include a systematic review of average daily membership, as defined in § 15-901, using methodology that is consistent with guidelines established by the auditor general. The auditor general shall consider cost when establishing guidelines pursuant to this subsection and, to the extent possible, shall attempt to minimize the cost of the review. The purpose of the review is to determine whether the average daily membership reported by the charter school or school district is in compliance with the laws of this state and the uniform systems of financial records for charter schools and school districts.

Added as § 15-346 by Laws 1986, Ch. 383, § 1, eff. May 21, 1986. Renumbered as § 15-914. Amended by Laws 1990, Ch. 399, § 3, eff. July 5, 1990; Laws 1992, Ch. 172, § 21; Laws 1992, Ch. 305, § 16; Laws 1993, Ch. 189, § 9; Laws 1995, Ch. 191, § 11, eff. April 19, 1995; Laws 1995, Ch. 196, § 10; Laws 1997, Ch. 231, § 22; Laws 2003, Ch. 94, § 1.

Historical and Statutory Notes

For applicability provisions of Laws 1995, Ch. 196, see the Historical and Statutory Notes following § 1-254.

The amendment of this section by Laws 1995, Ch. 196, § 10, was repealed by Laws 1996, Ch. 248, § 7.

For purpose of Laws 1996, Ch. 248, see Historical and Statutory Notes following § 15-365.

Laws 1999, 1st S.S., Ch. 4, § 15, provides:

"**Sec. 15. Charter school financial and compliance audits; financial statement audits; oversight responsibility**

"**A.** Notwithstanding § 15-271, subsection D, Arizona Revised Statutes, or any other law, the state board of education and the state board for charter schools, rather than the auditor general, are responsible for notifying a charter school under the board's jurisdiction if the school has failed to establish and maintain the uniform system of financial records.

"**B.** Notwithstanding § 15-271, subsection E, Arizona Revised Statutes, or any other law, the state board of education and the state board for charter schools, rather than the auditor general, are responsible for reporting to the department of education any charter school under the board's jurisdiction that either fails to establish and maintain the uniform system of financial records that is prescribed by the auditor general or fails to correct deficiencies in the system within ninety days after receiving notice of the deficiencies.

"**C.** Notwithstanding § 15–914, subsection D, Arizona Revised Statutes, or any other law, an independent certified public accountant who conducts an audit pursuant to § 15–914, subsections A, B and C, Arizona Revised Statutes, shall submit a uniform system of financial records compliance questionnaire to the state board that sponsors the audited charter school, rather than to the auditor general.

"**D.** Notwithstanding § 15–914, subsection E, Arizona Revised Statutes, or any other law, contracts for all financial and compliance audits and financial statement audits for charter schools that are sponsored by the state board of education or the state board for charter schools, and the completed audits for those schools, shall be approved by the state board that sponsors the charter school affected rather than by the auditor general.

"**E.** The requirements in subsections A and B of this section do not pertain to exceptions to requirements of the uniform system of financial records that the state board of education or the state board for charter schools include in the charter of a charter school pursuant to § 15–183, subsection E, paragraph 6, Arizona Revised Statutes."

Laws 2003, Ch. 94, became law without the Governor's signature as provided in Arizona Constitution, Article 5, § 7.

Reviser's Notes:

1986 Note. Pursuant to authority of § 41–1304.02, this section, added by Laws 1986, Ch. 383, § 1 as § 15–346, was renumbered as § 15–914. In subsection A, "subject to the single audit act of 1984 (P.L. 98–502)" was transposed to follow "accounts".

1992 Note. Prior to the 1993 amendment, this section contained the amendments made by Laws 1992, Ch. 172, sec. 21 and Ch. 305, sec. 16 that were blended together pursuant to authority of § 41–1304.03.

1995 Note. The amendment made by Laws 1995, Ch. 196, sec. 10 was inconsistent and incompatible with Laws 1995, Ch. 191, sec. 11 and therefore could not be blended.

§ 15–914.01. Accounting responsibility; definition

A. School districts with a student count of at least four thousand may apply to the state board of education to assume accounting responsibility.

B. A school district applying to the state board of education to assume accounting responsibility shall develop and file with the department of education an accounting responsibility plan and document in the plan:

1. Administrative and internal accounting controls designed to achieve compliance with the uniform system of financial records and the objectives of this section including:

(a) Procedures for approving, preparing and signing vouchers and warrants.

(b) Procedures to ensure verification of administrators' and teachers' certification records with the department of education for all classroom and administrative personnel required to hold a certificate by the state board of education pursuant to § 15–203 before issuing warrants for their services.

(c) Procedures to account for all revenues, including allocation of certain revenues to funds.

(d) Procedures for reconciling the accounting records monthly to the county treasurer.

2. A compilation of resources required to implement accounting responsibility, including, at a minimum, personnel, training and equipment, and comprehensive analysis of the budgetary implications of accounting responsibility for the school district and the county treasurer.

C. Prior to January 1 of the fiscal year preceding the fiscal year of implementation and Before submitting an application to assume accounting responsibility a school district shall apply for evaluation by the auditor general. On completion of the evaluation the auditor general may recommend approval or denial of accounting responsibility to the state board of education. The evaluation by the auditor general shall be performed contingent on staff availability and may be billed to the school district at cost. Evaluation at a minimum shall include the following:

1. The most recent financial statements audited by an independent certified public accountant.

2. The most recent report on internal control, report on compliance and uniform system of financial records compliance questionnaire prepared by an independent certified public accountant or procedural review completed by the auditor general.

3. The working papers of the independent certified public accountant responsible for auditing the school district, if deemed appropriate by the auditor general.

4. A procedural review if deemed appropriate by the auditor general.

D. School districts that are approved by the state board of education to assume accounting responsibility shall contract with an independent certified public accountant for an annual financial and compliance audit. The auditor general may reevaluate the school district annually based on the audit to determine compliance with the uniform system of financial records.

E. To assume accounting responsibility a school district shall notify the county treasurer and the county school superintendent of its intention before March 1 of the fiscal year preceding the fiscal year of implementation. On notification, the county treasurer shall establish acceptable standards for interface by school districts with the county treasurer, including specifications for computer hardware and software compatibility and procedures to ensure the capacity of each school district for reconciliation of accounts with those of the county treasurer.

F. Any school district that fails to maintain accounting standards as provided by the uniform system of financial records and is found to be in noncompliance with the uniform system of financial records by the state board of education as provided in § 15–272 is not eligible to participate in the program provided by this section.

G. Any school district that has assumed accounting responsibility pursuant to this section that fails to maintain accounting standards as provided by the uniform system of financial records and is found to be in noncompliance with the uniform system of financial records by the state board of education as provided in § 15–272 is no longer eligible to participate in the program provided by this section.

H. For the purposes of this section, "accounting responsibility" means authority for a school district to operate with full independence from the county school superintendent with respect to revenues and expenditures, including allocating revenues, monitoring vouchers, authorizing and issuing warrants and maintaining and verifying staff records for certification and payroll purposes.

Added by Laws 1995, Ch. 107, § 1, eff. July 13, 1995, retroactively effective to July 1, 1994.

Historical and Statutory Notes

Laws 1995, Ch. 107, §§ 2 and 3, provide:

"**Sec. 2. Requirements for fiscal year 1994–1995**

"School districts approved to assume accounting responsibility for 1994–1995 are not required to submit a plan pursuant to § 15–914.01, subsection B, Arizona Revised Statutes, as added by this act, or to be evaluated by the auditor general pursuant to § 15–914.01, subsection C, Arizona Revised Statutes, as added by this act.

"**Sec. 3. Retroactivity**

"This act is effective retroactively to from and after June 30, 1994."

§ 15–914.02. School district audit

A school district that is subject to audit pursuant to § 41–1279.03 shall comply with the reporting, follow-up and hearing participation requirements of that section.

Added by Laws 2003, Ch. 264, § 4.

§ 15–915. Correction of state aid or budget limit errors; definition

A. If the superintendent of public instruction determines that the calculation of state aid for a school district or charter school or the calculation of the school district's or charter school's budget limits within the previous three years did not conform with statutory requirements, the superintendent shall require correction of the errors as follows:

1. Corrections may be made in the current year or in the budget year, except that in case of hardship to the school district, the superintendent may approve corrections partly in one year and partly in the year after that year.

2. Errors in the calculation of state aid shall be corrected by increasing or decreasing the state aid to the school district or charter school in the year or years in which the correction is made.

3. Errors in the calculation of the school district's or charter school's budget limits shall be corrected at a public hearing by requiring the governing board to reduce or by allowing it to increase its budget by the amount of the correction to be made that year. Overbudgeting errors corrected as provided in this paragraph are exempt from the provisions of § 15–905, subsections L and M. Not later than three days after the hearing and correction, the budget as revised shall be submitted electronically to the superintendent of public instruction.

B. Subject to the review by the joint legislative budget committee, the superintendent of public instruction shall adjust state aid for a school district in the current year if the governing board of a school district requests the recalculation of state aid for a prior year due to a change in assessed valuation that occurred as the result of a judgment in accordance with § 42–16213.

C. For purposes of this section, "state aid":

1. For school districts means state aid as determined in § 15-971 and additional state aid as determined in § 15-972.

2. For charter schools means state aid as determined in § 15-185.

Added by Laws 1988, Ch. 221, § 2, eff. June 14, 1988. Amended by Laws 1996, Ch. 316, § 2, eff. May 1, 1996; Laws 1998, Ch. 1, § 49, eff. Jan. 1, 1999; Laws 2000, Ch. 342, § 13.

Historical and Statutory Notes

Laws 1993, Ch. 202, §§ 16 and 26, eff. April 21, 1993, provide:

"**Sec. 16. Support level weights for fiscal years 1991-1992 through 1993-1994**

"If a school district was subject to the provisions of § 15-458, subsection F, Arizona Revised Statutes, but adopted budgets for fiscal years 1991-1992 and 1992-1993 using incorrect budget limits due to utilization of the support level weights prescribed in § 15-943, subsection G, paragraph 1, Arizona Revised Statutes, the district is exempt from the provisions of § 15-905, subsections L and M, Arizona Revised Statutes, and § 15-915, Arizona Revised Statutes, for those fiscal years for the amount of the excess budget capacity caused by the use of the incorrect weights."

"**Sec. 26. Errors in capital levy budget limit calculation in fiscal year 1990-1991**

"Notwithstanding § 15-915, Arizona Revised Statutes, if a school district incorrectly calculated the capital levy budget limit for fiscal year 1990-1991 by increasing the capital levy budget limit to include tax revenues for a prior fiscal year, the superintendent of public instruction may approve the correction to be made over the next consecutive four years."

Laws 1997, Ch. 252, § 1, provides:

"**Section 1. Errors in school district budget calculation; correction**

"**A.** Notwithstanding §§ 15-905, subsections L and M, and 15-915, Arizona Revised Statutes, school districts that miscalculated their budgets shall be required to correct these errors over a ten-year period beginning in fiscal year 1997-1998 and ending in fiscal year 2006-2007 as prescribed in subsection B of this section if each of the following conditions exists:

"1. The school district's combined tax rate exceeds the statewide average combined tax rate for school districts by more than one hundred per cent.

"2. The area within the boundaries of the school district is more than five hundred square miles but less than seven hundred square miles.

"3. The school district miscalculated its budget in each of the previous five fiscal years.

"4. The school district provides evidence to the superintendent of public instruction that the school district's budget for the current year is properly calculated and will not result in any overexpenditures.

"5. The total amount of the correction that would otherwise be required under § 15-915, Arizona Revised Statutes, is more than nine hundred thousand dollars but less than one million one hundred thousand dollars.

"**B.** The annual amount of the correction for a school district meeting the requirements of subsection A of this section shall be equal to ten per cent of the total required correction amount."

Laws 2002, Ch. 333, § 5, eff. June 4, 2002, provides:

"**Sec. 5. Exemption from state aid correction; early kindergarten and early first grade programs**

"Notwithstanding the provisions of Laws 2002, third special session, chapter 1, § 17, the superintendent of public instruction shall not reduce state aid in fiscal year 2001-2002 to a school district if the total student population did not exceed two thousand five hundred fifty students in fiscal years 1998-1999, 1999-2000 and 2000-2001 and that experienced a rapid decline in student population over the same fiscal years, pursuant to § 15-942, Arizona Revised Statutes, in part due to the elimination of the early kindergarten or early first grade programs."

For provisions of Laws 1990, Ch. 193, relating to budget overrides and expenditure of amount miscalculated, see Historical and Statutory Notes following § 15-905.

Laws 2003, Ch. 144, § 1, provides:

"**Section 1. Errors in school district budget calculation; correction**

"**A.** Notwithstanding §§ 15-905 and 15-915, Arizona Revised Statutes, school districts that miscalculated their budgets during fiscal year 2001-2002 shall be required to correct these errors over a five-year period beginning in fiscal year 2002-2003 and ending in fiscal year 2006-2007 if each of the following conditions exists:

"1. The school district provides evidence to the superintendent of public instruction that the school district's budget for the current year is properly calculated and will not result in any overexpenditures.

"2. The total amount of the correction that would otherwise be required under § 15-915,

Arizona Revised Statutes, is more than six hundred thousand dollars but less than seven hundred thousand dollars.

"**B.** In addition to the monies required to be repaid pursuant to subsection A of this section, accrued interest is required to be paid at a rate determined by the superintendent of public instruction."

Laws 2003, Ch. 264, § 43, provides:

"**Sec. 43. Errors in school district budget calculation; correction**

"**A.** Notwithstanding §§ 15-905 and 15-915, Arizona Revised Statutes, school districts that miscalculated their maintenance and operations budget during fiscal year 2001-2002 shall be required to correct these errors over a five-year period beginning in fiscal year 2002-2003 and ending in fiscal year 2006-2007 if each of the following conditions exists:

"1. The school district provides evidence to the superintendent of public instruction that the school district's budget for the current year is properly calculated and will not result in any overexpenditures.

"2. The total amount of the correction that would otherwise be required under § 15-915, Arizona Revised Statutes, is more than one million seven hundred thousand dollars but less than one million nine hundred thousand dollars.

"**B.** In addition to the monies required to be repaid pursuant to subsection A of this section, accrued interest is required to be paid at a rate determined by the superintendent of public instruction."

Reviser's Notes:

1988 Note. Pursuant to authority of § 41-1304.02, in subsection A, paragraph 3, first sentence the words "at a public hearing" following the second "budget" were transposed to follow "corrected".

§ 15-916. Expenditure of state grant monies not included in budget

If the governing board of a school district receives a grant from this state for a specific program and did not include the grant in the district's budget, the governing board may, with the approval of the county school superintendent, authorize the expenditure of the grant monies in excess of the budget by action taken at a public meeting of the governing board. Within thirty days of the action, the governing board shall notify the department of education of the amount of the expenditures authorized. The amount which the district may expend in excess of the budget is equal to the amount of the grant monies which were not included in the budget for that fiscal year.

Added by Laws 1988, Ch. 221, § 2, eff. June 14, 1988.

§ 15-917. Repealed by Laws 1995, Ch. 191, § 12, eff. April 19, 1995

Historical and Statutory Notes

The repealed section, added by Laws 1990, Ch. 310, § 1, amended by Laws 1991, Ch. 292, § 6; Laws 1992, Ch. 288, § 9, related to retirement adjustment.

Section 15-917 was also amended by Laws 1995, Ch. 32, § 6, eff. March 30, 1995, to read:

"**§ 15-917. State aid to schools; retirement adjustment**

"**A.** If the employer retirement contribution rate prescribed in § 38-737is less than 5.09 per cent for the current year, school district expenditures for employer contributions to the Arizona state retirement system and state aid shall be reduced for the current year as follows:

"1. The governing board of each school district shall report to the state board of education by October 1 the estimated employer contribution savings for the current year based on a rate reduction from 5.09 per cent to the rate established for the current year.

"2. Before May 1, the governing board shall calculate the actual amount of employer contribution savings.

"3. The county school superintendent may adjust the actual amount of the employer contribution savings to correct for errors and omissions, and, if an adjustment is made, the adjusted actual amount shall be used as the final amount of employer contribution savings.

"4. Before May 15, the governing board shall decrease its revenue control limit and its district support level by the final amount of employer contribution savings as prescribed in paragraph 3 of this subsection.

"5. The governing board shall adjust expenditures for the current fiscal year based on the reduction in the revenue control limit.

"6. Equalization assistance and apportionment of state aid for that fiscal year as prescribed in article 5 of this chapter shall be determined based on the revenue control limit and the district support level as determined in paragraph 4 of this subsection.

"7. If a school district does not qualify for equalization assistance after the reduction of the revenue control limit and district support level as provided in paragraph 4 of this subsection, the additional state aid to which the district is entitled for the fiscal year as provided in § 15-972 shall be reduced by an amount equal to the actual amount of employer contribution savings less the amount, if any, of equalization assistance to which the district was entitled before the reduction of the revenue control limit and the district support level as provided in paragraph 4 of this subsection.

"8. The state board of education may begin reducing the apportionment of state aid with the October 15 apportionment, as provided in § 15-973, based on the estimate provided in paragraph 1 of this subsection.

"**B.** Procedures for computing the employer contribution savings shall be as prescribed by the auditor general in the uniform system of financial records and shall include the following requirements:

"1. The salary base upon which the savings are computed shall not include salaries paid from funds other than maintenance and operation or capital outlay or from separate subsections of the maintenance and operation or capital outlay sections of the budget which are exempt from the revenue control limit or capital outlay revenue limit and which are limited to specific programs or purposes.

"2. The salary base upon which the savings are computed shall be adjusted to subtract salaries paid from maintenance and operation budget increases authorized pursuant to § 15-481 and § 15-905, subsections K and O as follows:

"(a) Determine the total amount included in the general budget limit for maintenance and operation overrides as provided in § 15-947, subsection C, paragraph 4 and for P.L. 81-874 assistance as provided in § 15-947, subsection C, paragraph 3, subdivision (e), less the amount budgeted in a separate subsection of the maintenance and operation section of the budget for P.L. 81-874 assistance for handicapped children and children with specific learning disabilities.

"(b) Determine the total maintenance and operation section of the budget as prescribed in § 15-903, subsection B, less the amounts budgeted in separate subsections as provided in paragraph 1 of this subsection.

"(c) Divide the difference determined in subdivision (a) of this paragraph by the difference determined in subdivision (b) of this paragraph.

"(d) Reduce the salary base by the percentage determined in subdivision (c) of this paragraph.

"3. A school district of residence which pays tuition to another school district shall include in its employer contribution savings an amount corresponding to the savings attributable to the salaries included in the tuition. The school district of attendance shall adjust its calculation of actual tuition costs based on the retirement rate reduction as prescribed in this section and notify the district of residence and the department of education of the amount by May 1."

ARTICLE 1.1. CAREER LADDER AND OTHER PERFORMANCE INCENTIVE PROGRAMS

Article 1.1, consisting of §§ 15-918 to 15-918.04, was added by Laws 1990, Ch. 319, § 2, effective September 27, 1990.

The heading of Article 1.1 was changed from "Career Ladder Programs" to "Career Ladder And Other Performance Incentive Programs" by Laws 1994, Ch. 221, § 2.

§ 15-918. Career ladder programs; definitions

A. A school district governing board may apply to the state board of education for approval to budget for a career ladder program under the provisions established in this article. The application may be for one or more schools in the district or for the entire district. Applications for initial program approval or reapproval shall be submitted annually by November 15 to the state career ladder advisory committee which is established pursuant to § 15-918.01 and which shall review the applications and forward recommendations to the state board. The board shall provide notice to the applicants of approval or disapproval by February 15.

B. Based on the requirements established in this article and the recommendations of the state career ladder advisory committee, the state board shall prescribe specific procedures for application and requirements as needed for approval to budget for a career ladder program.

C. If a governing board receives approval to budget for a career ladder program, it may calculate its budget using an increase in the base level authorized by the state board. Dependent on the district's implementation stage pursuant to § 15–918.03 and other criteria as prescribed in § 15–918.02, the state board may authorize an increase of up to five and one-half per cent of the base level.

D. The total amount of state monies that may be expended in any fiscal year for the state board of education for career ladder programs shall not exceed the amount appropriated or authorized by § 35–173 for that purpose. This section shall not be construed to impose a duty on an officer, agent or employee of this state to discharge a responsibility or to create any right in a person or group if the discharge or right would require an expenditure of state monies in excess of the expenditure authorized by legislative appropriation for that specific purpose.

E. For the purposes of this article:

1. "Career ladder program" means a program which:

(a) Establishes a multilevel system of teaching positions.

(b) Provides opportunities to teachers for continued professional advancement.

(c) Requires at least improved or advanced teaching skill for advancement to a higher level and other components such as additional higher level instructional responsibilities and demonstration of pupil academic progress.

(d) Uses a performance based compensation system.

2. "Governing board" means any of the following:

(a) A school district governing board.

(b) The governing body of a school if it has been delegated authority over a career ladder program by a school district governing board.

Added by Laws 1990, Ch. 319, § 2. Amended by Laws 1992, Ch. 158, § 1, eff. Sept. 30, 1992, retroactively effective to June 30, 1991; Laws 1994, Ch. 360, § 1; Laws 1995, Ch. 184, § 1, eff. April 19, 1995; Laws 1995, Ch. 196, § 11.

Historical and Statutory Notes

Source:

A.R.S. former § 15–913.
Laws 1986, Ch. 364, § 2.

Laws 1988, Ch. 124, §§ 7 and 8 provide:

"Sec. 7. Salary reduction authorization for career ladder school districts

"Notwithstanding § 15–544, Arizona Revised Statutes, if the governing board of a school district has received approval to budget for a career ladder program as provided by Laws 1986, chapter 364, as amended by this act, or § 15–913, Arizona Revised Statutes, the governing board may reduce the salary of a teacher who has been placed on the career ladder as follows, except that if the teacher was employed by the district before receiving career ladder compensation, the teacher's salary may not be reduced lower than it was for the year before the teacher first received career ladder compensation:

"1. If the district does not receive reapproval to continue to budget for a career ladder program, if legislation authorizing the career ladder program is repealed or if funding percentages are reduced, the salary of a teacher on the career ladder may be reduced in one of the following ways:

"(a) If the district has an alternative salary system established by the board for teachers not on the career ladder, the teacher's salary may be reduced to the salary for which the teacher qualifies using the alternative salary system.

"(b) If the governing board adopts a new salary system to replace the career ladder salary system, the teacher's salary may be reduced to the salary for which the teacher qualifies using the new salary system.

"2. If the governing board adjusts its career ladder salary system by lowering the salary for one or more levels or steps within a level, the teacher's salary may be reduced to the salary for which the teacher qualifies using the new salary system.

"3. If the district's approved career ladder program so specifies, reductions may be made under the following circumstances:

"(a) If the teacher fails to maintain the level of performance required to earn a given salary on the career ladder, the teacher's salary may be reduced to the salary which the board has established for the level of performance actually demonstrated by the teacher.

"(b) If the teacher voluntarily or involuntarily transfers from the career ladder salary system to an alternative salary system established by the board for teachers not on the career ladder, the teacher's salary may be reduced to the salary for which the teacher qualifies using the alternative salary system.

"(c) If a portion of a teacher's compensation was based on the performance of specific responsibilities which are no longer being performed, the teacher's salary may be reduced by the amount of compensation awarded for those responsibilities in the prior fiscal year.

"(d) If a teacher chooses to move to a lower level on the career ladder, the teacher's salary may be reduced to reflect the lower level of placement on the career ladder.

"Sec. 8. Peer review immunity

"Employees of school districts are immune from personal liability with respect to all acts done and actions taken in good faith and without malice while performing assigned duties pursuant to a formal peer review program adopted by the governing board as part of a career ladder program."

Laws 1990, chapter 319, § 14, as amended by Laws 1994, Ch. 360, § 6, provides:

"Sec. 14. Provisions for reapproval of school districts which participated in the pilot career ladder program

"**A.** Notwithstanding title 15, chapter 9, article 1.1, Arizona Revised Statutes, as added by this act, in determining whether to reapprove school districts which had received approval to budget for a career ladder program pursuant to Laws 1986, chapter 364, as amended by Laws 1988, chapter 124, to increase their base level by five per cent, the state board shall utilize the career ladder program requirements as prescribed in Laws 1986, chapter 364, as amended by Laws 1988, chapter 124, except that those districts which had been required to base their program on a career development evaluation model may make modifications to these requirements as necessary.

"**B.** When the state board determines that such districts have met the following conditions the board may authorize the district to budget for a career ladder program using an increase of the base level of five and one-half per cent, rather than an increase of five per cent:

"1. Multiple announced and unannounced classroom observations must be utilized as part of the teacher evaluation system.

"2. Multiple persons must be involved in determining a teacher's career ladder program.

"3. Teachers are required to master increasingly higher level teaching criteria for placement at the higher levels of the career ladder.

"4. Teachers are required to complete increasingly higher level instructional responsibilities for placement at the highest career ladder levels.

"5. Teachers are required to master increasingly higher levels of pupil academic progress for placement at the higher levels of the career ladder.

"6. Districts must demonstrate that district level pupil academic progress has been made since the implementation of their career ladder program.

"7. Periodic district evaluation and review are occurring.

"8. The program participation rate is at least fifty per cent. The participation rate shall be computed as prescribed by the state board of education pursuant to § 15–918.03, paragraph 4, Arizona Revised Statutes, as amended by this act.

"**C.** Notwithstanding § 15–918, subsection A, Arizona Revised Statutes, as added by this act, applications for reapproval to budget for a career ladder program for fiscal year 1991–1992 shall be submitted to the state career ladder advisory committee by January 1, 1991.

The state board shall provide notice to the applicants of approval or disapproval by February 28, 1991.

"**D.** Notwithstanding subsection A of this section, § 15–918.04, subsection A, paragraph 5, Arizona Revised Statutes, as amended by this act, applies to school districts that received approval to budget for a career ladder program pursuant to Laws 1986, chapter 364, as amended by Laws 1988, chapter 124."

Laws 1990, Ch. 319, § 16, as amended by Laws 1992, Ch. 246, § 3, provides:

"**Sec. 16. State board of education; authorization to approve additional districts for career ladder programs**

"**A.** Notwithstanding title 15, chapter 9, article 1.1, Arizona Revised Statutes, as added by this act, fiscal year 1992–1993 is the first period for which the state board is authorized to approve additional districts to budget for a career ladder program for the first time, and the maximum number of new districts which may be approved is seven. In fiscal year 1993–1994, the state board is authorized to approve additional districts to budget for a career ladder program for the first time, except that:

"1. The state board may approve no more than twenty districts for a given year.

"2. If the total number of districts approved is more than five, the total average daily membership of districts approved for a given year may not exceed ten per cent of the state's average daily membership.

"**B.** Beginning in fiscal year 1994–1995, the state board is authorized to approve additional districts to budget for a career ladder program for the first time until all interested and qualified districts are included, except that the state board may approve additional districts only to the extent that the legislature appropriates, in advance, sufficient monies to cover the costs of the development phase for such districts.

"**C.** School districts may develop consortia for purposes of participating in the career ladder program, which may include but not be limited to cooperative activities such as program development, student assessment and evaluation. If a group of districts applies as a consortium, it shall be considered as one district for the purposes of the career ladder program.

"**D.** Notwithstanding subsection A of this section, if it is determined that successful career ladder model components are not available by April 15, 1991, the state career ladder advisory committee shall recommend to the state board of education not to approve additional districts to budget for a career ladder program for the first time until such time that the committee has determined that successful model components are available. The state board of education shall not approve additional districts to budget for a career ladder program for the first time until such time that the state career ladder advisory committee has determined that successful model components are available. At the time such components are developed, the state board shall establish a new time schedule for approving the seven additional districts to budget for a career ladder program.

"**E.** By November 15, 1991, the state board of education shall present recommendations to the legislature regarding the expansion of the program and any other revisions to title 15, chapter 9, article 1.1, Arizona Revised Statutes, as added by this act.

"**F.** By September 1, 1992, the state career ladder advisory committee shall consider the need for modifications in the type and specificity of career ladder program requirements, including the possibility of waivers for districts demonstrating outstanding student academic progress, and report its recommendations to the state board of education. If the state board determines that there is a need for revisions to title 15, chapter 9, article 1.1, Arizona Revised Statutes, the state board shall submit its recommendations to the legislature by November 15, 1992".

Laws 1992, Ch. 158, § 3, provides:

"**Sec. 3. Retroactivity**

"Section 1 of this act is retroactive to June 30, 1991."

For applicability provisions of Laws 1995, Ch. 196, see the Historical and Statutory Notes following § 1–254.

Reviser's Notes:

1994 Note. Pursuant to authority of § 41–1304.02, in the section heading "definitions" was substituted for "definition".

1995 Note. This section contains the amendments made by Laws 1995, Ch. 184, sec. 1 and Ch. 196, sec. 11 that were blended together as shown above pursuant to authority of § 41–1304.03.

§ 15–918.01. State career ladder advisory committee

A. The state board of education shall establish a state career ladder advisory committee which shall:

1. Provide recommendations to the state board on matters related to the implementation, operation and monitoring of career ladder programs in this state's school districts.

2. Develop criteria for the additional incentive components allowed pursuant to § 15-918.02, subsection B subject to the approval of the state board of education.

3. Oversee and administer the optional performance incentive programs in this state's school districts pursuant to this article.

B. The advisory committee shall consist of no more than fifteen members and shall be composed of representatives from the educational, business and general community. No more than one-third of the members of the advisory committee may represent districts which have been authorized to budget for a career ladder program.

C. The state board of education shall appoint the members of the advisory committee for staggered three year terms. Vacancies shall be filled for an unexpired term in the same manner as original appointments. The advisory committee shall annually elect a chair and vice-chair.

D. Members of the committee are not eligible to receive compensation, but if monies are available, members are eligible to receive reimbursement of expenses pursuant to title 38, chapter 4, article 2.[1]

Added by Laws 1990, Ch. 319, § 2. Amended by Laws 1997, Ch. 173, § 1; Laws 1999, Ch. 262, § 3.

[1] Section 38-621.

Historical and Statutory Notes

Laws 1990, Ch. 319, § 15, provides:

"**Sec. 15. State career ladder advisory committee; initial composition and responsibilities**

"**A.** Notwithstanding 15-918.01, Arizona Revised Statutes, as added by this act, for fiscal years 1990-1991 through 1993-1994, the state career ladder advisory committee shall consist of fifteen members, of which eleven shall be representatives of the following groups as they had been established pursuant to Laws 1986, chapter 364, as amended by Laws 1988, chapter 124:

"1. Six persons who had served on the joint legislative committee on career ladders.

"2. Four members of school districts which had been authorized to budget for a career ladder program.

"3. One member of the evaluation team which conducted the study of the career ladder programs.

"**B.** Beginning with fiscal year 1993-1994, the terms of one-third of the original members shall expire. Beginning with fiscal year 1994-1995, the terms of another one-third of the original members shall expire, and beginning with fiscal year 1995-1996, the terms of the final one-third of the original members shall expire. As the terms of the original members expire, new members representing the educational, business and community in general shall be appointed.

"**C.** The advisory committee in conjunction with the department of education shall complete the following:

"1. Utilizing the requirements submitted to the state board of education by the joint legislative committee on career ladders on December 1, 1990, develop specific application requirements for those districts currently budgeting for a career ladder program, including information necessary to request up to a five year waiver.

"2. By April 15, 1991, develop model components reflective of those components found to be successful during the pilot career ladder program, and specific application requirements for those districts applying to budget for a career ladder program under the provisions of this act.

"3. Develop other specific program requirements as necessary to implement the provisions of this act."

Laws 1999, Ch. 262, § 1, provides:

"**Section 1. Purpose**

"It is the intent of the legislature that study committees, boards and commissions make efficient use of citizens' and legislators' varying expertise and that the legislature be disciplined in the establishment of these committees, boards and commissions to ensure that the scope, membership and duration are appropriate for the issue. The legislature intends that all committees, boards and commissions engage in thoughtful, focused deliberations and that their actions, including recommendations, result from sufficient public input. In many cases, committee, board and commission discussions and actions are best conducted by parents, professionals, agency officials and other public citizens and do not require the formal participation of members of the legislature. In other cases, an informal working group is best able to develop compromise recommendations to a challenging public policy issue. In all cases, the recommendations of these committees, boards and commissions have the opportunity to be enacted or modified by the legislature, making legislative participation on the committees, boards and commissions unnecessary."

Reviser's Notes:

1997 Note. Pursuant to authority of § 41-1304.02, in subsection A, paragraph 2 the words "allowed pursuant to § 15-918.02, subsection B" were transposed to follow "components".

§ 15-918.02. Career ladder program; requirements; optional component

A. To receive approval to budget for a career ladder program as provided in this article, a school district's career ladder program or the district's plan for the implementation of its program must contain at least the following components:

1. A structure which provides teachers with opportunities for professional career advancement based primarily on improved or advanced teaching skills, evidence of pupil academic progress and higher level instructional responsibilities. Advancement shall not be based on years of teaching experience or the number of educational credits earned.

2. Provisions requiring all teachers new to the district to be evaluated for the career ladder program.

3. Provisions for ensuring that the placement of teachers on the career ladder shall be based on more than one measure of teacher performance incorporating the areas of instructional performance and pupil academic progress and requirements for higher level instructional responsibilities. The following specific requirements shall exist:

(a) The evaluation of teacher performance shall be based on an evaluation system as provided in § 15-537 and shall include at least the following:

(i) A minimum of one evaluation that consists of both announced and unannounced observations of teacher performance.

(ii) Procedures for ongoing review and refinement of the evaluation instruments and procedures, including a process for establishing inter-rater reliability among all evaluators.

(iii) Increasingly higher levels of instructional criteria against which teachers are evaluated for placement on higher career ladder levels.

(iv) Provisions for formative evaluations and other opportunities for improvement of teacher performance.

(b) The evaluation of a teacher's pupil academic progress shall include at least the following:

(i) Specific criteria and requirements for the demonstration of pupil academic progress for placement at each level of the career ladder. Teachers shall be required to demonstrate increasingly higher levels of pupil academic progress for placement at the higher levels of the career ladder.

(ii) The use of various methods of assessment which have been established by the district for the evaluation of pupil progress. A variety of evaluation procedures may be used depending on the grade levels and the academic disciplines involved. The system must evaluate the teacher in terms of pupil progress as opposed to absolute performance which does not take into account entering ability.

(iii) Specific district procedures for the review and refinement of pupil academic progress criteria, assessments and procedures. Means for measuring pupil progress and the methodology for incorporating this information into the teacher's placement on the ladder must be consistent for all teachers.

(c) The requirement that teachers must perform higher level instructional responsibilities as part of placement at the highest career ladder levels. In addition to these higher level instructional responsibilities required for placement, districts may utilize monies budgeted for the career ladder program to support additional higher level instructional responsibilities for teachers placed on the career ladder.

4. Provisions for the placement of teachers on the career ladder include at least the following:

(a) Specific criteria for placement at each level and step on the ladder.

(b) More than one person who is responsible for determining the placement of the teacher on the ladder.

(c) An appeal process which includes both teachers and administrators to review situations in which teachers disagree with their placement.

(d) Procedures for ensuring the fair and objective placement of teachers on the career ladder including the establishment of inter-rater reliability among persons responsible for determining placement.

5. The program shall utilize a compensation system which is based on a completely restructured salary schedule in which a salary range is established for each career ladder level and a salary is set for each step within a level. The salary range established for a teacher is determined by that teacher's performance and subsequent career ladder placement and not by that teacher's salary at the time of placement. The compensation system must be based on equal pay for equal performance and shall not be the traditional schedule based on experience and education with additional stipends for career ladder placement. If participation in the career ladder program is optional for teachers already teaching in the district when the program is implemented, the traditional salary schedule may be retained for those teachers who choose not to participate in the program.

6. The program shall include provisions for the administration of the career ladder program which include the establishment of at least the following:

(a) A steering committee composed of teachers, administrators, board members and parents to assist in the development and refinement of the district's career ladder program.

(b) Procedures to allow for regular communication of information related to the district's career ladder program, including formalized procedures for teacher, administrator and community input.

(c) Provisions for adequate program management in which the district recognizes the additional responsibilities associated with the management of the program and assigns this task to a person or group of people.

(d) Provisions to provide additional support to building level administrators in recognition of the additional responsibilities associated with the evaluation of teachers for the career ladder program.

7. The program shall include provisions for the periodic review and evaluation of the district's career ladder program and procedures for refining program components based on the evaluation results.

8. The program shall include provisions for providing appropriate amounts and types of staff development for teachers and administrators on the requirements of the career ladder program and assistance in improving performance.

B. In addition to the requirements of subsection A of this section, the program may include additional incentive components in which awards are based upon group, team, school, or district performance, except that awards shall not be based upon extra pay for extra work. Monies budgeted for the career ladder program may be used to support these additional incentive components. These components may provide performance rewards to a single school regardless of whether the components are provided to other schools in the district or to employees regardless of whether they are participating in the main career ladder program as prescribed in subsection A of this section. Examples of incentive components that may be included pursuant to this subsection are as follows:

1. A system for basing rewards on improved performance of a school on the measures included in the school's report card as provided in section 15-743, subsection A, or other objective measures.

2. A system which is based on principles of effective organizations, teamwork, parental and pupil involvement and support of teachers, that utilizes measures of quality including parental satisfaction or rating of educational quality, teacher job satisfaction or rating of support and pupil satisfaction with the quality of education being received.

C. Each district that includes an additional incentive component as provided in subsection B of this section shall develop an assessment plan for the measures of performance by November 1 of each year. Monies used for the planning and development of the additional incentive components shall not exceed five per cent of the monies that are allocated for the additional incentive components.

Added by Laws 1990, Ch. 319, § 2. Amended by Laws 1992, Ch. 246, § 1; Laws 1994, Ch. 360, § 2; Laws 1996, Ch. 284, § 50; Laws 1997, Ch. 173, § 2.

§ 15-918.03. Career ladder programs; implementation phases

The state board of education shall utilize the following implementation phases and requirements when approving districts to budget for a career ladder program:

1. The application phase is the first phase of the career ladder implementation process. During this phase, districts shall assess their readiness to imple-

ment a career ladder program and shall develop the general outline of their program based on model components adopted by the advisory committee but are not authorized to increase their budgets. To receive approval for advancement to the second phase, districts must submit, at a minimum, evidence that the plan was developed in consultation with teachers, administrators and school board members, the district's readiness to implement the plan and a time line indicating when various components, such as the refinement of the district's teacher evaluation instrument and procedures, an appropriate staff development program and the development of pupil assessments, will occur.

2. The development phase is the second implementation phase undertaken by districts following their completion of the application phase. During this phase, districts shall develop the specifics of their career ladder programs and are allowed to budget for a career ladder program as provided in § 15-918.04. To receive approval for advancement to the third phase, districts must submit, at a minimum, evidence that teacher and pupil academic progress evaluation instruments and procedures have been refined and pilot tested, appropriate levels of staff development have been provided and any specific areas of weaknesses associated with the district's readiness to implement a career ladder program have been adequately rectified.

3. The evaluation phase is the third implementation phase undertaken by districts following their completion of the development phase. During this phase, districts shall evaluate teachers, shall provide teacher career ladder placement contracts for the following year and are allowed to budget for a career ladder program as provided in § 15-918.04. To receive approval for advancement to the fourth phase, districts must submit, at a minimum, evidence that teachers have been fairly evaluated and placed and that the district is evaluating its program.

4. The placement phase is the fourth implementation phase undertaken by districts following their completion of the evaluation phase. During this phase, a district shall continue to evaluate teachers and is allowed to budget for a career ladder program as provided in § 15-918.04. To receive approval for advancement to the fifth phase, a district must submit, at a minimum, evidence that the program participation rate is at least fifty per cent, except that if a school district is devoting at least thirty per cent of its career ladder funding to additional incentive components pursuant to § 15-918.02, subsection B, the school district may report its program participation rate to be one hundred per cent, that district level pupil academic progress has occurred and, if not already included, that provisions to require all teachers new to the district to be evaluated for the career ladder program have been included. The state board of education shall prescribe a method of computing the program participation rate that treats all career ladder programs equitably by taking into account variations in program definitions.

5. The effective career ladder phase is the fifth and final implementation phase undertaken by districts following their completion of the placement phase. During this phase, districts shall fully implement their career ladder programs and are allowed to budget for a career ladder program as provided in § 15-918.04. During this phase, the state board may grant districts up to a five year waiver of any program requirements prescribed in § 15-918, subsection

B, or § 15–918.02. Waivers may be granted to districts that meet all of the following conditions:

(a) The district has submitted a request for the waiver that explains how the proposed waiver will improve its program and how this program improvement will enhance pupil achievement.

(b) The district has integrated its career ladder program with other reforms or programs that are designed to improve pupil achievement.

(c) The district is actively evaluating and reviewing its career ladder program and making adjustments as necessary, including analysis of the impact of the program on pupil achievement.

(d) The career ladder program is strongly supported by teachers, administrators and the governing board.

Added by Laws 1990, Ch. 319, § 2. Amended by Laws 1992, Ch. 246, § 2; Laws 1994, Ch. 360, § 3; Laws 1997, Ch. 173, § 3.

§ 15–918.04. Career ladder programs

A. To budget for a career ladder program as approved by the state board, a school district that is implementing the program in all schools in the district may calculate its budget using an increase in the base level as follows:

1. For the fiscal year or years a district is implementing the program at the development phase, 0.5 per cent, except that a district shall:

(a) Be allowed to budget at least the amount in column 2 of this subdivision that corresponds to the student count classification in column 1 of this subdivision:

Column 1 Student count	Column 2 Minimum amount
1–199	$5,000
200–599	$10,000
600–999	$15,000
1,000–1,399	$20,000
1,400 or more	$25,000

(b) Not budget more than one hundred fifty thousand dollars.

2. For the fiscal year or years a district is implementing the program at the evaluation phase, 1.0 per cent, except that a district shall:

(a) Be allowed to budget the amount in column 2 of this subdivision that corresponds to the student count classification in column 1 of this subdivision:

Column 1 Student count	Column 2 Minimum amount
1–199	$10,000
200–599	$20,000
600–999	$30,000
1,000–1,399	$40,000
1,400 or more	$50,000

(b) Not budget more than three hundred thousand dollars.

3. For the fiscal year or years a district is implementing the program at the placement phase, not greater than 2.5 per cent. After the successful completion of at least one year in the placement phase, the board may approve a funding level of not greater than 4.0 per cent.

4. For the fiscal years a district is implementing the program at the effective career ladder phase, not greater than 5.5 per cent.

5. In addition to the amount authorized in paragraphs 3 and 4, a school district for which the formula produces an amount of less than three hundred thousand dollars may increase its base support level by an amount computed as follows:

(a) Determine ten per cent of the funding increase.

(b) Subtract the amount determined in subdivision (a) of this paragraph from the amount in column 2 of this subdivision that corresponds to the student count classification in column 1 of this subdivision:

Column 1 Student count	Column 2 Small district adjustment
1–599	$10,000
600–1,399	$20,000
1,400 or more	$30,000

B. If a career ladder program has been approved for fewer than all of the schools in a school district, the percentage increase in the base level prescribed in subsection A of this section shall be reduced proportionately, based on the ratio of the student count in the career ladder schools to the student count of the school district as a whole. The minimum and maximum dollar amounts apply to the school or schools in one school district as if they were a school district.

C. Notwithstanding any other law, a school district that has implemented a career ladder program may budget any budget balance in the maintenance and operation section of the budget that is directly attributable to a budgeted increase in the base level as prescribed in this section from the current fiscal year for use in career ladder programs in the budget year. The amount budgeted pursuant to this subsection shall not be included in the allowable budget balance carry forward calculated pursuant to § 15–943.01. The amount budgeted pursuant to this subsection is specifically exempt from the revenue control limit. For purposes of this subsection, "budget balance" means the difference between actual career ladder expenditures and the budgeted increase in the base level as prescribed in this section.

Added by Laws 1990, Ch. 319, § 2. Amended by Laws 1993, 2nd S.S., Ch. 8, § 1; Laws 1994, Ch. 360, § 4; Laws 1995, Ch. 184, § 2, eff. April 19, 1995.

Historical and Statutory Notes

Reviser's Notes:

1994 Note. In the chapter version, the beginning of this section reading:

"15–918.04. Career ladder programs

A. To budget for a career ladder program as approved by the state board, a school district THAT IS IMPLEMENTING THE PROGRAM IN ALL SCHOOLS . . ." is missing and subsection A, paragraph 5, subdivision (a) and part of subdivision (b) reading "(b) Subtract the amount determined in subdivision (a) from THE AMOUNT IN COLUMN 2 OF THIS SUBDIVI-

SION THAT" are repeated contrary to amendment instructions. Pursuant to authority of § 41-1304.02, the missing language is inserted and the repeated language is removed to correct manifest clerical errors.

§ 15-918.05. Career ladder programs; determination of equalization assistance payments from county and state monies

A school district that has chosen to calculate its budget using an increase in the base level, as prescribed in § 15-918.04, shall notify the state board of its decision and shall have its equalization assistance for education as computed in § 15-971 computed as follows:

1. For a high school district or a common school district within a high school district that does not offer instruction in high school subjects as provided in § 15-447, the qualifying tax rate as provided in § 15-971, subsection B, paragraph 1 shall be increased by two cents for each percentage increase in the base level as provided in § 15-918.04.

2. For a unified school district, a common school district not within a high school district or a common school district within a high school district that offers instruction in high school subjects as provided in § 15-447, the qualifying tax rate as provided in § 15-971, subsection B, paragraph 2 shall be increased by four cents for each percentage increase in the base level as provided in § 15-918.04.

Added by Laws 1993, 2nd S.S., Ch. 8, § 2. Amended by Laws 1994, 8th S.S., Ch. 3, § 1; Laws 1994, Ch. 360, § 5.

Historical and Statutory Notes

Reviser's Notes:

1994 Note. This section contains the amendments made by Laws 1994, Eighth Special Session, Ch. 3, sec. 1 and Laws 1994, Second Regular Session, Ch. 360, sec. 5 that were blended together as shown above pursuant to authority of § 41-1304.03.

§ 15-919. Optional performance incentive program; definition

A. A school district governing board may apply to the superintendent of public instruction for approval to budget for an optional performance incentive program under the provisions established in this article. Applications for initial program approval or reapproval shall be submitted annually by March 15 to the superintendent of public instruction. The superintendent of public instruction shall review the applications and make recommendations to the state board by May 15. Applications for new programs may be requested only if advanced appropriations have been made to cover the cost of the first year of implementation for new districts for that year. The state board shall provide notice to the applicants of approval or disapproval by July 1, based on the recommendations of the superintendent of public instruction.

B. Notwithstanding subsection A of this section, if the superintendent of public instruction submits recommendations to the state board after May 15, a school district, before October 1, may calculate its budget using the increase in the base level that the school district anticipates will be authorized by the state board. If a school district calculates its budget pursuant to this subsection, the school district shall signify in writing that the increase is pending approval by the state board. If state board approval is not received by October 1, the school district shall recalculate its budget without the increase in the base level that was anticipated pursuant to this subsection. Not later than May 18, the budget as revised shall be submitted electronically to the superintendent of public instruction.

C. Based on the requirements established in this article and the superintendent's recommendations, the superintendent of public instruction shall prescribe specific procedures for application and requirements as needed for approval to budget for an optional performance incentive program.

D. If a governing board receives approval to budget for an optional performance incentive program, it may calculate its budget using an increase in the base level recommended by the superintendent of public instruction and authorized by the state board. Dependent on the guidelines developed by the superintendent of public instruction pursuant to § 15-919.03 and other criteria as prescribed in § 15-919.02, the state board may authorize an increase of up to five and one-half per cent of the base level.

E. For the purposes of this article, "optional performance incentive program" means a program that:

1. Is an alternative to the career ladder program established in this article.

2. Is based on principles of effective organizations, teamwork, parental and pupil involvement and support of teachers.

3. Uses measures of quality including parental satisfaction or rating of educational quality, teacher job satisfaction or rating of support and pupil satisfaction with the quality of education being received.

4. Uses a performance based compensation system.

Added by Laws 1994, Ch. 221, § 1. Amended by Laws 1997, Ch. 200, § 1; Laws 1999, Ch. 262, § 4; Laws 2000, Ch. 342, § 14.

§ 15-919.01. Repealed by Laws 1999, Ch. 262, § 5, eff. Jan. 1, 2000

Historical and Statutory Notes

The repealed section, added by Laws 1994, Ch. 221, § 1, amended by Laws 1997, Ch. 200, § 2, related to the state performance incentive program oversight committee.

§ 15-919.02. Optional performance incentives program; requirements

To receive approval to budget for an optional performance incentives program, a school district's optional performance incentives program or the district's plan for the implementation of its program shall meet at least the following requirements:

1. The program shall be based on principles of effective organizations, teamwork, parental and pupil involvement and support of teachers.

2. The program shall contain documented evidence of support by school district employees.

Added by Laws 1994, Ch. 221, § 1.

§ 15-919.03. Optional performance incentives programs; implementation phases

The superintendent of public instruction may develop and utilize up to five implementation phases when approving districts to budget for an optional performance incentives program. Movement upwards through the implementation phases shall reflect increased performance by the district based on various measures of quality.

Added by Laws 1994, Ch. 221, § 1. Amended by Laws 1999, Ch. 262, § 6; Laws 2000, Ch. 342, § 15.

§ 15-919.04. Optional performance incentives program; funding; limitation

A. The superintendent of public instruction may authorize a district participating in the optional performance incentives program to calculate its budget using an increase in the base level of up to five and one-half per cent.

B. If implementation phases are used, the superintendent of public instruction shall increase a district's funding level based on the district's achievement of successively higher implementation phases.

C. Notwithstanding subsection B of this section, the state performance incentive oversight committee may authorize a district that is a career ladder district to budget for an increase in its base level that is equal to the base level increase that the district was authorized to budget for pursuant to § 15-918.04 at the time of original application to the optional performance incentives program. A school district shall not budget for both the career ladder program and the optional performance incentives program at the same time.

D. Notwithstanding any other law, a school district that has implemented an optional performance incentive program may budget any budget balance in the maintenance and operation section of the budget that is directly attributable to a budgeted increase in the base level as prescribed in this section from the current fiscal year for use in optional performance incentive programs in the budget year. The amount budgeted pursuant to this subsection shall not be included in the allowable budget balance carryforward calculated pursuant to § 15-943.01. The amount budgeted pursuant to this subsection is specifically exempt from the revenue control limit. For purposes of this subsection, "budget balance" means the difference between actual optional performance incentive program expenditures and the budgeted increase in the base level as prescribed in this section.

Added by Laws 1994, Ch. 221, § 1. Amended by Laws 1996, Ch. 284, § 51; Laws 1999, Ch. 262, § 7; Laws 2000, Ch. 342, § 16.

§ 15-919.05. Optional performance incentive programs; determination of equalization assistance payments from county and state monies

A. A school district that has chosen to calculate its budget using an increase in the base level shall notify the state board of its decision and shall have its equalization assistance for education as prescribed in § 15-971 computed as follows:

1. For a high school district or a common school district within a high school district that does not offer instruction in high school subjects as provided in § 15-447, the qualifying tax rate as provided in § 15-971, subsec-

tion B, paragraph 1 shall be increased by two cents for each percentage increase in the base level as provided in § 15-919.04.

2. For a unified school district, a common school district not within a high school district or a common school district within a high school district that offers instruction in high school subjects as provided in § 15-447, the qualifying tax rate as provided in § 15-971, subsection B, paragraph 2 shall be increased by four cents for each percentage increase in the base level as provided in § 15-919.04.

B. Except as provided in § 15-972, subsection E, the primary property tax rate set to fund the amount specified pursuant to subsection A of this section shall not be included in the computation of additional state aid for education as provided in § 15-972.

Added by Laws 1994, Ch. 221, § 1. Amended by Laws 1997, Ch. 120, § 1.

§ 15-919.06. Optional performance incentive programs; unexpended and unencumbered monies; portion nonlapsing

A. A school district that is authorized by the state board to budget for an optional performance incentive program and that by the end of the current fiscal year has additional authorized budget capacity for that fiscal year unexpended and unencumbered shall notify the department of education by July 15 of the following fiscal year of this unexpended and unencumbered amount. The department of education shall decrease that school district's apportionment of state aid for the following fiscal year by an amount equal to twenty per cent of the total unexpended and unencumbered capacity.

B. Notwithstanding § 15-943.01, the maximum amount that may be budgeted as the budget balance carry forward by the governing board of a school district that has received approval to participate in an optional performance incentive program is the maximum amount prescribed in § 15-943.01 further increased by eighty per cent of any unexpended optional performance incentive program monies reported to the department of education pursuant to subsection A of this section.

C. The governing board of a school district that budgets as part of the budget balance carry forward optional performance incentive program monies pursuant to subsection B of this section shall account separately in its budget for the optional performance incentive program monies carried forward and shall use these monies only for the purposes of the optional performance incentive program authorized pursuant to this article.

Added by Laws 1994, Ch. 221, § 1.

§ 15-920. Performance pay; budget balance carryforward; definitions

A. Notwithstanding any other law, a school district that uses a performance pay component in its salary schedule may budget any budget balance in the maintenance and operation section of the budget that is attributable to performance pay and that is not earned in the current fiscal year for use in the budget year. The carryforward shall be used in the following year's performance pay component of the salary schedule. The amount budgeted pursuant to this subsection shall not be included in the allowable budget balance carryforward calculated pursuant to § 15-943.01. The amount budgeted pursuant to this subsection is specifically exempt from the revenue control limit.

B. For purposes of this section:

1. "Budget balance" means the difference between actual and budgeted expenditures for the performance pay component of the salary schedule.

2. "Performance pay component" means any portion of a school district's salary schedule, other than a career ladder program or an optional performance incentives program established pursuant to this article, that is based on factors directly related to a teacher's classroom performance.

Added by Laws 1997, Ch. 114, § 1.

Historical and Statutory Notes

Reviser's Notes:

1997 Note. Pursuant to authority of § 41-1304.02, in the section heading and in subsection A, in two places the spelling of "carryforward" was corrected.

ARTICLE 2. PUPIL TRANSPORTATION

§ 15-921. Duties of superintendent of public instruction

A. The superintendent of public instruction shall supervise the provision of pupil transportation services.

B. The superintendent of public instruction shall evaluate the transportation program and routes for the purpose of evaluating accurate transportation support levels for the budget year.

C. For each fiscal year the superintendent of public instruction shall, on or before May 15, inform each school district of the daily route mileage which shall be used in the determination of the school district's transportation support level for the budget year.

D. The superintendent of public instruction shall be responsible for assembling the information provided by the school district and for determining the accuracy of such information.

Added by Laws 1981, Ch. 1, § 2, eff. Jan. 23, 1981. Amended by Laws 1985, Ch. 166, § 17, eff. April 18, 1985; Laws 1998, 4th S.S., Ch. 8, § 3.

Historical and Statutory Notes

Source:

Laws 1974, 1st S.S., Ch. 3, § 38.
A.R.S. former §§ 15-1210.03, 15-1624.
Laws 1976, Ch. 166, § 3.
Laws 1978, 1st S.S., Ch. 1, § 3.
Laws 1980, 2nd S.S., Ch. 9, § 64.

§ 15-922. Duties of the school district; definition

A. Each school district shall within twelve days after the first one hundred days or two hundred days in session, as applicable, certify to the superintendent of public instruction, in an electronic format as prescribed by the department of education, the following:

1. The daily route mileage of the school district in the current year. The route mileage shall not include more than twenty miles each way to and from the school of attendance or to and from a pickup point on a regular transporta-

tion route to transport eligible students who reside in nonadjacent school districts.

2. The route mileage of the school district in the current year transporting eligible students for an extended school year program in accordance with § 15-881.

3. The number of eligible students transported during the current year.

B. Each school district shall on or before July 15 of the current year certify to the superintendent of public instruction the following:

1. For each bus operated by the school district, the following:

(a) The odometer reading as of the end of the current year.

(b) An inventory of each school bus owned by the school district including:

(i) Manufacturer of the bus.

(ii) Date of purchase.

(iii) Purchase price.

(iv) Capacity for passengers.

(v) Type of fuel used.

2. The total bus mileage during the current year.

3. The road conditions upon which eligible students are transported reported in a format specified by the superintendent of public instruction.

4. The total bus mileage for the current year for academic and career and technical education and vocational education and athletic trips reported in a format specified by the superintendent of public instruction.

C. A school district shall meet the requirements of this section to receive state aid. The superintendent of public instruction may withhold a school district's apportionment of state aid if it is determined by the superintendent of public instruction that the school district is not complying with the requirements of this section.

D. For the purposes of this article and § 15-901, "school bus" or "bus" means a bus as defined in § 28-101, except that the passenger capacity standards prescribed in that section do not apply.

Added by Laws 1981, Ch. 1, § 2, eff. Jan. 23, 1981. Amended by Laws 1981, Ch. 142, § 1; Laws 1984, Ch. 235, § 2; Laws 1985, Ch. 166, § 18, eff. April 18, 1985; Laws 1987, Ch. 294, § 1; Laws 1989, Ch. 220, § 2, eff. Jan. 1, 1990; Laws 1990, Ch. 322, § 12, eff. June 20, 1990; Laws 1994, 9th S.S., Ch. 2, § 15; Laws 1998, Ch. 167, § 10; Laws 2000, Ch. 342, § 17; Laws 2002, Ch. 89, § 24.

Historical and Statutory Notes

Source:

Laws 1974, 1st S.S., Ch. 3, § 38.
A.R.S. former §§ 15-1210.01, 15-1623.
Laws 1976, Ch. 166, § 2.
Laws 1978, 1st S.S., Ch. 1, § 2.
Laws 1980, 2nd S.S., Ch. 9, § 64.

Laws 1980, 2nd S.S., Ch. 9, § 94, subsec. B, as amended by Laws 1982, Ch. 26, § 1, Laws 1983, Ch. 9, § 11, effective February 25, 1983, Laws 1984, Ch. 56, § 1, Laws 1985, Ch. 267, § 1 and Laws 1986, Ch. 27, § 1, provides:

"**B.** The legislative council shall contract with a competent private individual or organization for a detailed transportation cost study to be completed and submitted to the legislature on or before January 1, 1982. The detailed transportation cost study shall be similar to the 'general fund cost study, Arizona school districts', which was submitted to the legislature on July 11, 1979, and shall, among other areas, specifically include the area of energy costs. The legislature shall review the transportation cost study and determine if any changes are required in the current statutory language concerning transportation."

Laws 1989, Ch. 220, § 64 provides:

"This act is effective from and after December 31, 1989."

An amendment of this section by Laws 1996, Ch. 284 failed to become operative. See note, post.

Laws 1996, Ch. 284, § 81, provides:

"Sec. 81. Conditional enactment

"Sections 52, 55, 56 and 80 do not become effective unless H.B. 2308, relating to charter school transportation, is enacted into law [H.B. 2308 failed to become law]."

Reviser's Notes:

1990 Note. Pursuant to authority of § 41-1304.02, in subsection A, paragraph 2 the reference to "§ 15-881" was substituted for the reference to "§ 15-871" to conform to the reviser's renumbering of that section.

§ 15-923. Contracts for transportation

A. As an alternative to maintaining and operating a transportation program or in conjunction with a transportation program, a school district may, if it is found to be economically advantageous, contract for transportation. Contracts may be with another political subdivision, a common or contract carrier or a private party.

B. In addition to other powers and duties prescribed by title 11, chapter 2, article 4, [1] any board of supervisors may at the request of any or all of the governing boards of the school districts within the county provide necessary student transportation. If the board of supervisors and the governing board or boards of such school districts mutually agree that such an arrangement is economically advantageous, the governing board of the school district is authorized to sell or lease its bus or buses to the board of supervisors for such purposes. Agreement between the parties shall be by written contract.

C. In no event shall an eligible student who is transported part by contract and part by school district transportation facilities be counted as more than one eligible student.

D. Each school district shall submit electronically to the department of education the routes contracted, the contractor contract information, the number of eligible students transported by each contractor and any additional information requested by the department of education.

Added by Laws 1981, Ch. 1, § 2, eff. Jan. 23, 1981. Amended by Laws 1985, Ch. 166, § 19, eff. April 18, 1985; Laws 2000, Ch. 342, § 18.

[1] Section 11-251 et seq.

Historical and Statutory Notes

Source:

Laws 1974, 1st S.S., Ch. 3, § 38.
A.R.S. former §§ 15-1210.02, 15-1626.
Laws 1976, Ch. 166, § 5.
Laws 1978, 1st S.S., Ch. 1, § 5.
Laws 1980, 2nd S.S., Ch. 9, § 64.

ARTICLE 3. SCHOOL DISTRICT REVENUE LIMITATION FOR MAINTENANCE AND OPERATION

WESTLAW Electronic Research

See WESTLAW Electronic Research Guide following the Preface.

§ 15-941. Teacher experience index; computation; definition

A. The teacher experience index for each school district shall be computed as follows:

1. For the school district:

Number of years of experience		Number of FTE certified teachers		Number of FTE years of experience of certified teachers
1	×	_____	=	_____
2	×	_____	=	_____
3	×	_____	=	_____
4	×	_____	=	_____
5	×	_____	=	_____
6	×	_____	=	_____
7	×	_____	=	_____
8	×	_____	=	_____
9	×	_____	=	_____
10	×	_____	=	_____
11	×	_____	=	_____
12	×	_____	=	_____
13	×	_____	=	_____
14	×	_____	=	_____
15 (or more)	×	_____	=	_____
	Total	A		B

2. Divide total B by total A to determine the average number of FTE years of experience of FTE certified teachers in the school district.

3. For the state:

Number of years of experience		Number of FTE certified teachers		Number of FTE years of experience of certified teachers
1	×	_____	=	_____
2	×	_____	=	_____
3	×	_____	=	_____
4	×	_____	=	_____
5	×	_____	=	_____
6	×	_____	=	_____
7	×	_____	=	_____
8	×	_____	=	_____
9	×	_____	=	_____
10	×	_____	=	_____
11	×	_____	=	_____
12	×	_____	=	_____
13	×	_____	=	_____
14	×	_____	=	_____
15 (or more)	×	_____	=	_____
	Total	C		D

4. Divide total D by total C to determine the average number of FTE years of experience of FTE certified teachers in the state.

5. Subtract the quotient obtained in paragraph 4 of this subsection from the quotient obtained in paragraph 2 of this subsection and multiply the remainder by 0.0225.

6. Add 1.00 to the product obtained in paragraph 5 of this subsection.

B. Librarians, guidance counselors, curriculum coordinators and other personnel who do not conduct regularly scheduled classes shall not be included as certified teachers and shall be coded separately from certified teachers in the uniform system of financial records.

C. Each school district shall on or before October 15 submit to the superintendent of public instruction in electronic format the data prescribed in subsection A, paragraphs 1 and 2 for the current year. The superintendent of public instruction shall use the data to compute the teacher experience index of each school district for the budget year.

D. The superintendent of public instruction shall on or before March 15 notify each school district of its teacher experience index for the budget year. The teacher experience index for the budget year shall not be recalculated after March 15 unless the superintendent of public instruction determines that the school district has submitted data resulting in an overstatement of the teacher experience index for the budget year.

E. For the purposes of this section, "number of years of experience" means the number of years of classroom instruction conducted by a certified teacher in the school district in which the certified teacher is currently employed including the number of years of experience of the certified teacher granted by the school district for the certified teacher on the district's salary schedule for experience outside of the school district.

Added by Laws 1981, Ch. 1, § 2, eff. Jan. 23, 1981. Amended by Laws 1984, Ch. 178, § 1; Laws 1988, Ch. 288, § 6, eff. July 8, 1988; Laws 1990, Ch. 399, § 4, eff. July 5, 1990; Laws 2000, Ch. 342, § 19.

Historical and Statutory Notes

Source:

Laws 1980, 2nd S.S., Ch. 9, § 62.
A.R.S. former § 15–1202.03.

Laws 1988, Ch. 310, § 1, eff. July 7, 1988, provides:

"**Section 1. Additional teacher experience index expenditures**

"**A.** For fiscal years 1988–1989 and 1989–1990 the governing board of a school district which has a teacher experience index of greater than 1.0, pursuant to § 15–941, subsection D, Arizona Revised Statutes, may budget an amount for additional teacher experience expenditures which is specifically exempt in whole or in part from the revenue control limit. The maximum amount which may be so budgeted is determined as follows:

"1. Determine the teacher experience index for the district for the budget year.

"2. Subtract 1.0 from the number determined in paragraph 1 of this subsection.

"3. Multiply the difference determined in paragraph 2 of this subsection by 0.25.

"4. Multiply the product determined in paragraph 3 of this subsection by the district's base level for the budget year and multiply this product by the district's weighted student count for the budget year pursuant to § 15–944, subsection A, paragraph 2, subdivision (c), Arizona Revised Statutes.

"5. The product determined in paragraph 4 of this subsection is the maximum amount which may be budgeted for the additional teacher experience expenditures.

"**B.** If the governing board of a school district is entitled to use the provisions of subsection A of this section and adopted a budget for fiscal year 1988–1989 without including an amount for additional teacher experience expenditures as provided in subsection A of this section, the governing board may revise its budget to include this amount before September 15, 1988.

"**C.** The part of the primary tax rate set to fund the additional teacher experience expenditures as provided in this section shall not be included in the computation of additional state aid for education as prescribed in § 15–972, Arizona Revised Statutes."

Laws 1990, Ch. 399, § 14, provides:

"**Sec. 14. Additional teacher experience expenditures**

"**A.** For fiscal years 1990–1991, 1991–1992 and 1992–1993, the governing board of a school district which has a teacher experience index of greater than 1.0, pursuant to § 15–941, subsection D, Arizona Revised Statutes, may budget an amount for additional teacher experience expenditures which is specifically exempt in whole or in part from the revenue control limit. The maximum amount which may be so budgeted is determined as follows:

"1. Determine the teacher experience index for the district for the budget year.

"2. Subtract 1.0 from the number determined in paragraph 1.

"3. Multiply the difference determined in paragraph 2 by one of the following:

"(a) For fiscal year 1990–1991, 0.11.

"(b) For fiscal year 1991–1992, 0.067.

"(c) For fiscal year 1992–1993, 0.022.

"4. Multiply the product determined in paragraph 3 by the district's base level for the budget year and multiply this product by the district's weighted student count for the budget year pursuant to § 15–944, subsection A, paragraph 2, subdivision (c), Arizona Revised Statutes.

"5. The product determined in paragraph 4 is the maximum amount which may be budgeted for the additional teacher experience expenditures.

"**B.** If the governing board of a school district is entitled to use the provisions of subsection A of this section and has adopted a budget for fiscal year 1990–1991 without including an amount for additional teacher experience expenditures as provided in subsection A of this section, the governing board may revise its budget to include this amount before September 15, 1990.

"**C.** The part of the primary tax rate set to fund the additional teacher experience expenditures as provided in this section shall not be included in the computation of additional state aid for education as prescribed in § 15–972, Arizona Revised Statutes."

§ 15–941.01. Repealed by Laws 1996, Ch. 284, § 53

Historical and Statutory Notes

The repealed section, added by Laws 1995, Ch. 191, § 13, related to base levels for budget years.

§ 15–942. Adjustment for rapid decline in student count

A. If the student count in grades kindergarten through eight or grades nine through twelve for the budget year is less than the student count in grades kindergarten through eight or grades nine through twelve for the current year or the adjusted student count in grades kindergarten through eight or grades nine through twelve for the current year determined as provided in this section by:

1. At least five per cent but less than nine per cent, a school district may use the student count in grades kindergarten through eight or grades nine through twelve for the current year or the adjusted student count in grades kindergarten through eight or grades nine through twelve for the current year determined as provided in this section multiplied by 0.95 in computing the budget for the budget year and entitlement to state aid.

2. At least nine per cent but less than thirteen per cent, a school district may use the student count in grades kindergarten through eight or grades nine through twelve for the current year or the adjusted student count in grades kindergarten through eight or grades nine through twelve for the current year determined as provided in this section multiplied by 0.93 in computing the budget for the budget year and entitlement to state aid.

3. At least thirteen per cent but less than twenty per cent, a school district may use the student count in grades kindergarten through eight or grades nine through twelve for the current year or the adjusted student count in grades kindergarten through eight or grades nine through twelve for the current year determined as provided in this section multiplied by 0.90 in computing the budget for the budget year and entitlement to state aid.

4. At least twenty per cent but less than thirty per cent, a school district may use the student count in grades kindergarten through eight or grades nine through twelve for the current year or the adjusted student count in grades kindergarten through eight or grades nine through twelve for the current year determined as provided in this section multiplied by 0.87 in computing the budget for the budget year and entitlement to state aid.

5. Thirty per cent or more, a school district may use the student count in grades kindergarten through eight or grades nine through twelve for the current year or the adjusted student count in grades kindergarten through eight or grades nine through twelve for the current year determined as provided in this section multiplied by 0.85 in computing the budget for the budget year and entitlement to state aid.

B. The governing board of a school district utilizing the adjusted student count as provided in this section shall include notification of the actual per cent decline in student count and the additional allowable revenues by computing the base revenue control limit by utilization of the adjustment for rapid decline in student count in the proposed budget presented at the public meeting as provided in § 15–905.

C. When determining its student count or adjusted student count for the current year, the governing board of a school district utilizing the adjusted student count as provided in this section shall not include:

1. Pupils who are residents of the attendance area of another school district as a result of a school district consolidation, subdivision or other boundary change.

2. Pupils whose district of attendance has not changed but who are being included in the student count of a different school district for the budget year as a result of a change in an agreement regarding which district will include the pupils in its student count.

3. Pupils whose attendance has changed to a charter school sponsored by, operated by or operated for a school district, as provided in § 15–185, subsection E.

D. The provisions of this section shall not apply to any reduction in student count resulting from enrollment in a joint technological education district formed pursuant to chapter 3, article 6 of this title. [1]

E. This section does not apply to any reduction in student count resulting from a district sponsored charter school switching sponsors or ceasing to operate.

F. This section does not apply to any reduction in student count resulting from the elimination of early kindergarten or early first grade programs.

Added by Laws 1981, Ch. 1, § 2, eff. Jan. 23, 1981. Amended by Laws 1982, Ch. 273, § 3, eff. April 27, 1982; Laws 1990, Ch. 248, § 3, eff. Sept. 27, 1990, retroactively effective to July 15, 1990; Laws 1990, Ch. 329, § 4; Laws 1991, Ch. 154, § 8, eff. May 20, 1991; Laws 1993, 2nd S.S., Ch. 8, § 3; Laws 1998, 4th S.S., Ch. 8, § 4; Laws 1999, 1st S.S., Ch. 4, § 9; Laws 2002, 3rd S.S., Ch. 1, § 2, eff. Mar. 21, 2002.

[1] Section 15-391 et seq.

Historical and Statutory Notes

Source:

Laws 1980, 2nd S.S., Ch. 9, § 62.
A.R.S. former § 15-1202.04.

Laws 1992, Ch. 288, § 23, eff. Sept. 30, 1992, retroactively effective to July 1, 1992, provides:

"**Sec. 23. Fiscal year 1992-1993 adjustment for rapid decline in student count**

"Notwithstanding § 15-942, Arizona Revised Statutes, for fiscal year 1992-1993, the adjustment for rapid decline in student count in kindergarten programs through grade eight or grades nine through twelve shall be determined as follows:

"1. Determine the adjusted student count for fiscal year 1992-1993 as prescribed by § 15-942, Arizona Revised Statutes.

"2. From the amount determined in paragraph 1 of this section, subtract the student count for fiscal year 1992-1993 as prescribed by §§ 15-901 and 15-902, Arizona Revised Statutes.

"3. Multiply the difference determined in paragraph 2 of this section by 0.64.

"4. Add the product determined in paragraph 3 of this section to the student count determined in paragraph 2 of this section. The sum is the adjusted student count for fiscal year 1992-1993 for the purposes of § 15-942, Arizona Revised Statutes."

Laws 2001, 3rd S.S., Ch. 1, § 17, effective March 21, 2002, provides:

"**Sec. 17. Correction of state aid for fiscal years 1999-2000 and 2000-2001; early kindergarten and early first grade programs**

"Pursuant to § 15-915, Arizona Revised Statutes, and § 15-942, Arizona Revised Statutes, as amended by this act, the superintendent of public instruction shall reduce state aide to school districts and charter schools during fiscal years 2001-2002 and 2002-2003 in order to recapture rapid decline funding that they received during fiscal years 1998-1999, 1999-2000 and 2000-2001 due to elimination of early kindergarten or early first grade programs."

Laws 2002, Ch. 333, § 5, eff. June 4, 2002, provides:

"**Sec. 5. Exemption from state aid correction; early kindergarten and early first grade programs**

"Notwithstanding the provisions of Laws 2002, third special session, chapter 1, § 17, the superintendent of public instruction shall not reduce state aid in fiscal year 2001-2002 to a school district if the total student population did not exceed two thousand five hundred fifty students in fiscal years 1998-1999, 1999-2000 and 2000-2001 and that experienced a rapid decline in student population over the same fiscal years, pursuant to § 15-942, Arizona Revised Statutes, in part due to the elimination of the early kindergarten or early first grade programs."

A provision of Laws 2003, Ch. 264, was line item vetoed by the Governor. See Governor's veto message dated June 17, 2003. The vetoed provision read:

"Notwithstanding § 15-942, Arizona Revised Statutes, for fiscal year 2003-2004, the department of education shall reduce by fifty per cent the amount of rapid decline funding that a school district would otherwise be eligible to receive pursuant to § 15-942, subsections A through F, Arizona Revised Statutes."

Laws 2004, Ch. 278, § 10, provides:

"**Sec. 10. Adjustment for rapid decline in student count for fiscal year 2004-2005**

"Notwithstanding § 15-942, Arizona Revised Statutes, for fiscal year 2004-2005, the department of education shall reduce by fifty per cent the amount of rapid decline funding that a school district would otherwise be eligible to receive pursuant to § 15-942, subsections A through F, Arizona Revised Statutes."

Laws 2004, Ch. 278, § 21, provides:

"**Sec. 21. Retroactivity**

"**A.** Except as provided in subsection B of this section, this act applies retroactively to from and after June 30, 2004.

"**B.** Laws 2002, chapter 330, § 49, as amended by this act, applies retroactively to from and after June 29, 2004."

Reviser's Notes:

1990 Note. Prior to the 1991 amendment, this section contained the amendments made by

Laws 1990, Ch. 248, § 3 and Ch. 329, § 4 which were blended together pursuant to authority of § 41-1304.03.

§ 15-943. Base support level

The base support level for each school district shall be computed as follows:

1. The following support level weights shall be used in paragraph 2, subdivision (a) for the following school districts:

(a) For school districts whose student count in kindergarten programs and grades one through eight is classified in column 1 of this subdivision, the support level weight for kindergarten programs and grades one through eight is the corresponding support level weight prescribed in column 2 or 3 of this subdivision, whichever is appropriate:

Column 1 Student Count	Column 2 Support Level Weight For Small Isolated School Districts	Column 3 Support Level Weight For Small School Districts
1–99	1.559	1.399
100–499	1.358 + [0.0005 x (500 - student count)]	1.278 + [0.0003 x (500 - student count)]
500–599	1.158 + [0.002 x (600 - student count)]	1.158 + [0.0012 x (600 - student count)]

(b) For school districts whose student count in grades nine through twelve is classified in column 1 of this subdivision, the support level weight for grades nine through twelve is the corresponding support level weight prescribed in column 2 or 3 of this subdivision, whichever is appropriate:

Column 1 Student Count	Column 2 Support Level Weight For Small Isolated School Districts	Column 3 Support Level Weight For Small School Districts
1–99	1.669	1.559
100–499	1.468 + [0.0005 x (500 - student count)]	1.398 + [0.0004 x (500 - student count)]
500–599	1.268 + [0.002 x (600 - student count)]	1.268 + [0.0013 x (600 - student count)]

2. Subject to paragraph 1, determine the weighted student count as follows:

(a)

Grade	Base		Group A		Support Level Weight		Student Count		Weighted Student Count
PSD	1.000	+	0.450	=	1.450	x	________	=	________
K–8	1.000	+	0.158	=	1.158	x	________	=	________
9–12	1.163	+	0.105	=	1.268	x	________	=	________
							Subtotal	A	________

(b)

Funding Category	Support Level Weight		Student Count		Weighted Student Count
HI	4.771	x	________	=	________
K–3	0.060	x	________	=	________
ELl	0.115	x	________	=	________
MD–R, A–R and SMR–R	6.024	x	________	=	________
MD–SC, A–SC and SMR–SC	5.833	x	________	=	________

MD-SSI	6.531	x	______	=	______
OI-R	3.158	x	______	=	______
OI-SC	5.576	x	______	=	______
P-SD	3.595	x	______	=	______
ED, MIMR, SLD, SLI and OHI	0.003	x	______	=	______
ED-P	4.647	x	______	=	______
MOMR	4.421	x	______	=	______
VI	4.806	x	______	=	______
			Subtotal	B	

(c) Total of subtotals A and B: ______

3. Multiply the total determined in paragraph 2 by the base level.

4. Multiply the teacher experience index of the district or 1.00, whichever is greater, by the product obtained in paragraph 3.

Added by Laws 1981, Ch. 1, § 2, eff. Jan. 23, 1981. Amended by Laws 1981, Ch. 308, § 4; Laws 1985, Ch. 166, § 20, eff. April 18, 1985; Laws 1985, Ch. 347, § 5, eff. May 14, 1985; Laws 1987, Ch. 363, § 6, eff. May 22, 1987; Laws 1988, Ch. 281, § 6; Laws 1989, Ch. 273, § 17, eff. June 26, 1989; Laws 1990, Ch. 258, § 6; Laws 1990, Ch. 322, § 13, eff. June 20, 1990; Laws 1991, Ch. 288, § 3, eff. Sept. 21, 1991, retroactively effective to July 1, 1991; Laws 1992, Ch. 172, § 22; Laws 1993, Ch. 189, § 10; Laws 1996, 5th S.S., Ch. 8, § 5; Laws 1997, 1st S.S., Ch. 4, § 7; Laws 1998, 4th S.S., Ch. 8, § 5; Laws 1999, 1st S.S., Ch. 4, § 10; Laws 2001, Ch. 233, § 4; Laws 2001, 2nd S.S., Ch. 9, § 3, eff. July 1, 2002.

Historical and Statutory Notes

Source:

Laws 1980, 2nd S.S., Ch. 9, § 62.
A.R.S. former § 15-1202.05.

Laws 1990, Ch. 399, § 13, provides:

"Sec. 13. Teacher experience index expenditures; computation of the base support level for fiscal year 1990-1991

"For the purpose of computing the base support level for fiscal year 1990-1991, the teacher experience index shall be calculated using the method prescribed by § 15-941, Arizona Revised Statutes, as amended by this act."

Laws 1993, Ch. 202, § 16, eff. April 21, 1993, provides:

"Sec. 16. **Support level weights for fiscal years 1991-1992 through 1993-1994**

"If a school district was subject to the provisions of § 15-458, subsection F, Arizona Revised Statutes, but adopted budgets for fiscal years 1991-1992 and 1992-1993 using incorrect budget limits due to utilization of the support level weights prescribed in § 15-943, subsection G, paragraph 1, Arizona Revised Statutes, the district is exempt from the provisions of § 15-905, subsections L and M, Arizona Revised Statutes, and § 15-915, Arizona Revised Statutes, for those fiscal years for the amount of the excess budget capacity caused by the use of the incorrect weights."

Laws 1995, Ch. 158, § 8, provides:

"Sec. 8. Equalization assistance for adult correctional education

"Notwithstanding § 15-1372, Arizona Revised Statutes:

"1. For fiscal year 1996-1997, the student count is one hundred sixty-four and the weighted student count is 271.051 for the correctional education programs provided by § 15-1372, subsection B, Arizona Revised Statutes, as amended by this act.

"2. For fiscal year 1996-1997, the number of correctional education students that may be counted as ED-P as provided in § 15-943, Arizona Revised Statutes, is equal to twenty-five per cent of the student count or the actual number of pupils determined to be ED-P, whichever is more."

Laws 1999, 1st S.S., Ch. 4, § 13, provides:

"Sec. 13. K-3 group B weight for fiscal year 1999-2000

"Notwithstanding § 15-943, paragraph 2, subdivision (b), Arizona Revised Statutes, as amended by this act, the K-3 group B weight for fiscal year 1999-2000 shall be 0.050 rather than 0.060."

Laws 2001, 2nd. S.S., Ch. 9, § 9, provides:

"Sec. 9. Effective date

"Section 15-943, Arizona Revised Statutes, as amended by this act, is effective from and after June 30, 2002."

Reviser's Notes:

1990 Note. Prior to the 1991 amendment, this section contained the amendments made by Laws 1990, Ch. 258, § 6 and Ch. 322, § 13 which were blended together pursuant to authority of § 41–1304.03.

§ 15–943.01. Maintenance and operation budget balance; definition

A. The governing board of a school district may budget any budget balance in the maintenance and operation section of the budget, as provided in § 15–903, from the current fiscal year for use in the maintenance and operation section of the budget in the budget year. The amount which may be budgeted as the budget balance carryforward in any one fiscal year shall not exceed four per cent of the school district's revenue control limit, as provided in § 15–947, subsection A, for the current year and shall not include any budget balance attributable to any reduction in the district's general budget limit including reductions for items which are exempt from the revenue control limit and for which expenditures are limited to a designated purpose such as excess insurance costs or excess utility costs or for the bond issues portion of the cost of tuition. A school district may include in the budget balance carryforward in any fiscal year up to fifty per cent of the unspent proceeds of an override election conducted pursuant to § 15–482. The amount budgeted as the budget balance carryforward is specifically exempt from the revenue control limit.

B. If the actual amount of the allowable budget balance carryforward is less than the amount budgeted for the budget balance carryforward, the governing board shall adjust the general budget limit and expenditures before May 15 based on the actual allowable budget balance carryforward. If the actual amount of the allowable budget balance carryforward is more than the amount budgeted for the budget balance carryforward, the governing board may adjust its budget before May 15 based on the actual amount of the allowable fund balance carryforward. Not later than May 18, the budget as revised shall be submitted electronically to the superintendent of public instruction.

C. If the governing board is eligible to budget for a budget balance carryforward as provided in subsection A of this section, the governing board may transfer an amount from the district's ending cash balance of the maintenance and operations fund to the school opening fund. The maximum amount that may be transferred is the lesser of the district's ending cash balance in the maintenance and operations fund or the amount the district is eligible to budget as a budget balance carryforward. The school opening fund is a cash controlled fund as provided in § 15–905, subsection N, and may only be expended for the additional maintenance and operations expenses incurred in the first year of operation of a new school within the school district. The monies in the school opening fund are not subject to reversion, except that at the end of five years of no activity in the fund, any remaining monies shall be reverted to the maintenance and operations fund. Any monies so reverted may be considered additional budget balance for that fiscal year.

D. If a governing board transfers monies as provided in subsection C of this section, the amount so transferred in a fiscal year shall be subtracted from the amount the district would otherwise be eligible to budget for that fiscal year as provided in subsection A of this section. The difference, if any, is the maximum amount that may be budgeted for that fiscal year as a budget balance carryforward.

E. For the purposes of this section, "budget balance" means the difference between actual and budgeted expenditures.

Added by Laws 1990, Ch. 399, § 5, eff. July 5, 1990. Amended by Laws 1991, Ch. 207, § 1, eff. June 10, 1991; Laws 1994, Ch. 369, § 2; Laws 1996, Ch. 284, § 54; Laws 2000, Ch. 342, § 20; Laws 2004, Ch. 315, § 2.

Historical and Statutory Notes

Laws 1990, Ch. 357, is amended by Laws 1991, Ch. 244, § 12, effective June 17, 1991, by adding § 8, to read:

"**Sec. 8. Restructuring monies; nonlapsing**

"Notwithstanding § 15–943.01, Arizona Revised Statutes, the maximum amount that may be budgeted as the budget balance carry forward by the governing board of a school district that contains a school or schools that have received approval to participate in a school restructuring incentives program is the maximum amount prescribed in § 15–943.01, Arizona Revised Statutes, further increased by any unexpended school restructuring incentives program fund monies, as certified by the principal of the participating school."

Laws 1992, Ch. 288, § 27, eff. Sept. 30, 1992, retroactively effective to July 1, 1992 provides:

"Sec. 27. **Maintenance and operation budget balance; definition; fiscal year 1992–1993**

"Notwithstanding § 15–943.01, subsection A, Arizona Revised Statutes, for fiscal year 1992–1993 the amount which may be budgeted as the budget balance carry forward shall not exceed three per cent of the school district's revenue control limit, as provided in § 15–947, subsection A, Arizona Revised Statutes, for fiscal year 1991–1992."

Reviser's Notes:

1994 Note. Pursuant to authority of § 41–1304.02, in subsection C, third sentence the spelling of "cash controlled" was corrected.

§ 15–943.02. Base support level for joint vocational and technical education districts

A. The base level for each joint vocational and technical education district shall be computed as follows:

Grade/ Category	Support Level Weight		Student Count		Weighted Student Count
9–12	1.339	X	______	=	______

B. Multiply the total determined in subsection A by the base level.

C. Multiply the teacher experience index of the district or 1.00, whichever is greater, by the product obtained in subsection B.

Added as § 15–941.01 by Laws 1990, Ch. 248, § 2, eff. Sept. 27, 1990, retroactively effective to July 15, 1990. Renumbered as § 15–943.02. Amended by Laws 2002, Ch. 89, § 25.

Historical and Statutory Notes

Reviser's Notes:

1990 Note. Pursuant to authority of § 41–1304.02, this section, added by Laws 1990, Ch. 248, § 2 as § 15–941.01, was renumbered as § 15–943.02 and in the section heading "and technical" was added after "vocational".

§ 15–943.03. Budget balance exemption

Charter schools are exempt from the budget balance carry forward limitation prescribed in § 15–943.01, subsection A.

Added by Laws 1996, Ch. 356, § 4.

§ 15–943.04. English learner classroom personnel bonus fund; payment of English language classroom personnel bonuses

The English learner classroom personnel bonus fund is established consisting of monies appropriated for this purpose. The department of education shall administer the fund. Monies in the fund are continuously appropriated. applications from school districts and charter schools for monies from the fund shall be submitted by February 28 of each year. The department of education shall distribute monies in the fund to school districts and charter schools in equal amounts not to exceed two hundred fifty dollars for every English learner, as defined in § 15–751, who was instructed in an English learner program in the past academic year, who achieved English proficiency and who exited the English learner program. School districts and charter schools shall use the monies distributed pursuant to this section to pay bonuses directly to classroom personnel, excluding principals and administrators, who are involved in English learner programs. A school district or charter school shall not receive more than one distribution from the English learner classroom personnel bonus fund for the same pupil.

Added by Laws 2001, 2nd S.S., Ch. 9, § 4. Amended by Laws 2004, Ch. 341, § 4.

§ 15–944. Base revenue control limit

A. The base revenue control limit for each school district for fiscal year 1980–1981 is computed as follows:

1. Add the amounts in the fiscal year 1979–1980 budget effective May 15, 1980 for general operating and special education.

2. Subtract the following budgeted revenues from the sum obtained in paragraph 1 of this subsection:

(a) Tuition paid for attendance of nonresident pupils.

(b) State assistance as provided in § 15–976.

(c) Special education revenues as provided in § 15–825, subsection D and § 15–1204.

(d) Proceeds from the sale or lease of school property as provided in § 15–1102.

3. Add the increase in the base support level from fiscal year 1979–1980 to fiscal year 1980–1981 to the difference obtained in paragraph 2 of this subsection.

B. The equalization factor for each school district is computed as follows:

1. Divide the sum obtained in subsection A, paragraph 3 of this section by the base support level for fiscal year 1980–1981.

2. Subtract 1.0 from the quotient obtained in paragraph 1 of this subsection to obtain the equalization factor.

C. The revenue variation factor for each fiscal year is as follows:

1. For fiscal year 1981–1982, 0.80.

2. For fiscal year 1982–1983, 0.60.

3. For fiscal year 1983–1984, 0.40.

4. For fiscal year 1984–1985, 0.20.

D. The base revenue control limit for each school district during the five years in which the equalization plan is in operation is computed as follows:

1. Multiply the equalization factor by the revenue variation factor for the applicable year. Beginning with fiscal year 1983–1984 if the resulting product is less than negative 0.08, use negative 0.08 for computation purposes as provided in paragraph 2 of this subsection.

2. Multiply the product obtained in paragraph 1 of this subsection by the base support level for the applicable year.

3. Add the base support level for the applicable year to the product obtained in paragraph 2 of this subsection.

E. For fiscal year 1985–1986 and each fiscal year thereafter, the base revenue control limit equals the base support level for the same fiscal year.

Added by Laws 1981, Ch. 1, § 2, eff. Jan. 23, 1981. Amended by Laws 1981, Ch. 181, § 3; Laws 1982, Ch. 291, § 1, eff. May 3, 1982; Laws 1983, Ch. 220, § 1; Laws 1984, Ch. 349, § 7; Laws 1990, Ch. 322, § 14, eff. June 20, 1990; Laws 1990, Ch. 348, § 10, eff. June 26, 1990; Laws 1990, Ch. 399, § 6, eff. July 5, 1990; Laws 1991, Ch. 244, § 5, eff. June 17, 1991.

Historical and Statutory Notes

Source:

Laws 1980, 2nd S.S., Ch. 9, § 62.
A.R.S. former § 15-1202.06.

The amendment of this section by Laws 1990, Ch. 399, § 6 was repealed by Laws 1991, Ch. 244, § 6, effective June 17, 1991.

The 1991 amendment of this section by Ch. 244 explicitly amended the 1990 amendment of this section by Chs. 322 and 348.

Reviser's Notes:

1990 Note. Prior to the 1991 amendment, this section contained the amendments made by Laws 1990, ch. 322, § 14 and Ch. 348, § 10 which were blended together pursuant to authority of § 41-1304.03.

1990 Note. The amendment of this section by Laws 1990, Ch. 399, § 6 failed to set forth in full the text of the section as amended by Laws 1990, Ch. 322 and Ch. 348, emergency acts, as required by Constitution of Arizona Art. IV, part 2, § 14.

§ 15-944.01. Additional expenditures exempt in whole or in part from revenue control limit

Beginning January 1, 1990, no school district is permitted to budget for items that are exempt either in whole or in part from the revenue control limit and that are funded by revenues generated by a levy of taxes on the taxable property in the school district, except that a school district may budget for those items that are exempt either in whole or in part from the revenue control limit as authorized by law before January 1, 1990.

Added by Laws 1990, Ch. 399, § 7, eff. July 5, 1990.

§ 15-945. Transportation support level

A. The support level for to and from school for each school district for the current year shall be computed as follows:

1. Determine the approved daily route mileage of the school district for the fiscal year prior to the current year.

2. Multiply the figure obtained in paragraph 1 of this subsection by one hundred seventy-five.

3. Determine the number of eligible students transported in the fiscal year prior to the current year.

4. Divide the amount determined in paragraph 1 of this subsection by the amount determined in paragraph 3 of this subsection to determine the approved daily route mileage per eligible student transported.

5. Determine the classification in column 1 of this paragraph for the quotient determined in paragraph 4 of this subsection. Multiply the product obtained in paragraph 2 of this subsection by the corresponding state support level for each route mile as provided in column 2 of this paragraph.

Column 1 Approved Daily Route Mileage per Eligible Student Transported	Column 2 State Support Level per Route Mile for Fiscal Year 2004–2005
0.5 or less	$2.11
More than 0.5 through 1.0	$1.71
More than 1.0	$2.11

6. Add the amount spent during the prior fiscal year for bus tokens and bus passes for students who qualify as eligible students as defined in § 15–901.

B. The support level for academic education, career and technical education, vocational education and athletic trips for each school district for the current year is computed as follows:

1. Determine the classification in column 1 of paragraph 2 of this subsection for the quotient determined in subsection A, paragraph 4 of this section.

2. Multiply the product obtained in subsection A, paragraph 5 of this section by the corresponding state support level for academic education, career and technical education, vocational education and athletic trips as provided in column 2, 3 or 4 of this paragraph, whichever is appropriate for the type of district.

Column 1 Approved Daily Route Mileage per Eligible Student Transported	Column 2 District Type 02 or 03	Column 3 District Type 04	Column 4 District Type 05
0.5 or less	0.15	0.10	0.25
More than 0.5 through 1.0	0.15	0.10	0.25
More than 1.0	0.18	0.12	0.30

For the purposes of this paragraph, "district type 02" means a unified school district or an accommodation school that offers instruction in grades nine through twelve, "district type 03" means a common school district not within a high school district, "district type 04" means a common school district within a high school district or an accommodation school that does not offer instruction in grades nine through twelve and "district type 05" means a high school district.

C. The support level for extended school year programs for pupils with disabilities is computed as follows:

1. Determine the sum of the following:

(a) The total number of miles driven by all buses of a school district while transporting eligible pupils with disabilities on scheduled routes from their residence to the school of attendance and from the school of attendance to their residence on routes for an extended school year program in accordance with § 15-881.

(b) The total number of miles driven on routes approved by the superintendent of public instruction for which a private party, a political subdivision or a common or a contract carrier is reimbursed for bringing an eligible pupil with a disability from the place of the pupil's residence to a school transportation pickup point or to the school facility of attendance and from the school transportation scheduled return point or from the school facility to the pupil's residence for an extended school year program in accordance with § 15-881.

2. Multiply the sum determined in paragraph 1 of this subsection by the state support level for the district determined as provided in subsection A, paragraph 5 of this section.

D. The transportation support level for each school district for the current year is the sum of the support level for to and from school as determined in subsection A of this section and the support level for academic education, career and technical education, vocational education and athletic trips as determined in subsection B of this section and the support level for extended school year programs for pupils with disabilities as determined in subsection C of this section.

E. The state support level for each approved route mile, as provided in subsection A, paragraph 5 of this section, shall be adjusted by the growth rate prescribed by law, subject to appropriation.

Added by Laws 1981, Ch. 1, § 2, eff. Jan. 23, 1981. Amended by Laws 1984, Ch. 314, § 3, eff. April 30, 1984; Laws 1985, Ch. 166, § 21, eff. April 18, 1985; Laws 1990, Ch. 322, § 15, eff. June 20, 1990; Laws 1992, Ch. 172, § 23; Laws 1993, Ch. 28, § 1, eff. April 2, 1993; Laws 1993, Ch. 189, § 11; Laws 1994, 9th S.S., Ch. 2, § 16; Laws 1995, Ch. 191, § 14, eff. April 19, 1995; Laws 1995, Ch. 196, § 12; Laws 1998, 4th S.S., Ch. 8, § 6; Laws 1999, Ch. 168, § 4, eff. May 5, 1999; Laws 2000, Ch. 236, § 21, eff. April 12, 2000; Laws 2000, 7th S.S., Ch. 1, § 2, eff. Dec. 14, 2000; Laws 2002, Ch. 89, § 26; Laws 2003, Ch. 264, § 5; Laws 2004, Ch. 278, § 4.

Historical and Statutory Notes

Source:

Laws 1974, 1st S.S., Ch. 3, § 38.
A.R.S. former §§ 15-1202.07, 15-1625.
Laws 1976, Ch. 166, § 4.
Laws 1978, 1st S.S., Ch. 1, § 4.
Laws 1980, 2nd S.S., Ch. 9, § 62.

Laws 1993, Ch. 28, §§ 2 and 3, eff. April 2, 1993, provide:

"**Sec. 2. Provisions for accommodation schools serving military bases that close**

"If a county school superintendent operates both an accommodation school that serves a military reservation and an accommodation school that serves territory that is not located within the boundaries of a school district, and the enrollment of the military reservation accommodation school declines as a result of the closure of the military base that the accommodation school serves, the county school superintendent may, prior to July 1, 1995, incorporate the military reservation accommodation school into the accommodation school that serves unorganized territory and may combine the student count of the two schools if the resulting accommodation school continues to serve pupils from the military reservation for at least part of the next school year, subject to the following provisions:

"1. The resulting accommodation school becomes effective on July 1 following the decision to incorporate the military reservation accommodation school into the accommodation school that serves unorganized territory."

"2. The resulting accommodation school shall not be eligible for consolidation assistance as provided in § 15–912, Arizona Revised Statutes.

"3. Beginning in the first school year in which the resulting accommodation school no longer enrolls any pupils from the military reservation, the resulting accommodation school shall not be eligible to compute an adjustment for rapid decline in student count as provided in § 15–942 for pupils formerly enrolled from the military reservation.

"**Sec. 3. Budget and state aid adjustments**

"If an accommodation school utilized the provisions of § 15–945, subsection B, paragraph 2, Arizona Revised Statutes, prior to the effective date of this act, the school is not subject to the provisions of § 15–905, subsections L and M, Arizona Revised Statutes, and § 15–915, Arizona Revised Statutes, for any amounts related to the computation of the support level for academic and vocational and technological education and athletic trips."

The 1993 amendment of this section by Ch. 189 explicitly amended the 1993 amendment of this section by Ch. 28.

For applicability provisions of Laws 1995, Ch. 196, see the Historical and Statutory Notes following § 1–254.

The amendment of this section by Laws 1995, Ch. 196, § 12, was repealed by Laws 1996, Ch. 248, § 8.

An amendment of this section by Laws 1996, Ch. 284, § 55, and repeal of the Laws 1995, Ch. 196, § 8, amendment by Laws 1996, Ch. 284, § 56 failed to become law, see note post.

Laws 1996, Ch. 284, § 81, provides:

"**Sec. 81. Conditional enactment**

"Sections 52, 55, 56 and 80 do not become effective unless H.B. 2308, relating to charter school transportation, is enacted into law [H.B. 2308 failed to become law]."

Laws 1997, 1st S.S., Ch. 4, § 8, provides:

"**Sec. 8. School districts; transportation state aid; 1997–1998 fiscal year**

"Notwithstanding § 15–945, subsection A, Arizona Revised Statutes, or any other law, the transportation support level for the to and from school component of the transportation support level for each school district for fiscal year 1997–1998 shall be computed using the approved daily route mileage and number of eligible students transported for the school district in fiscal year 1996–1997."

Laws 1997, Ch. 231, § 36, provides:

"**Sec. 36. Appropriation; transportation stimulus funding; 1997–1998 fiscal year**

"**A.** Notwithstanding § 15–945, Arizona Revised Statutes, a unified school district that wants to expand transportation services for eligible students as defined in § 15–901, subsection A, paragraph 9, subdivision (a), Arizona Revised Statutes, shall compute an estimated transportation support level and transportation revenue control limit for fiscal year 1997–1998 as prescribed in § 15–945, Arizona Revised Statutes, based on estimated eligible students and daily route mileage, if both of the following conditions exist:

"1. In fiscal year 1996–1997, the school district only provided pupil transportation services for eligible students as defined in § 15–901, subsection A, paragraph 9, subdivision (c), Arizona Revised Statutes.

"2. The school district's number of eligible students transported for fiscal year 1996–1997 is less than four per cent of its student count for fiscal year 1996–1997.

"**B.** After the first one hundred days in session, a school district that used the provisions of subsection A of this section shall revise its transportation support level and transportation revenue control limit to be equal to the actual transportation support level and transportation revenue control limit for fiscal year 1997–1998. A school district that overestimated its transportation support level and transportation revenue control limit shall revise its budget before May 15. A school district that underestimated its transportation support level and transportation revenue control limit may revise its budget before May 15.

"**C.** Notwithstanding subsection A of this section, the transportation support level for fiscal year 1997–1998 shall not exceed the transportation support level for fiscal year 1996–1997 by more than $300,000.

"**D.** The sum of $300,000 is appropriated from the state general fund to the department of education in fiscal year 1997–1998 for the increase in basic state aid as provided by this section."

The amendment of this section by Laws 2000, Ch. 405, § 5, which was to become effective July 1, 2001, was repealed prior to taking effect by Laws 2000, 7th S.S., Ch. 1, § 1, eff. Dec. 14, 2000.

Laws 2000, 7th S.S., Ch. 1, § 40, provides:

"**Sec. 40. Severability**

"If a provision of this act or its application to any person or circumstance is held invalid, the invalidity does not affect other provisions or applications of the act that can be given effect without the invalid provision or application, and to this end the provisions of this act are severable."

Laws 2004, Ch. 278, § 21, provides:

"**Sec. 21. Retroactivity**

"**A.** Except as provided in subsection B of this section, this act applies retroactively to from and after June 30, 2004.

"**B.** Laws 2002, chapter 330, § 49, as amended by this act, applies retroactively to from and after June 29, 2004."

Reviser's Notes:

1990 Note. Pursuant to authority of § 41-1304.02, in subsection C, paragraph 1, subdivisions (a) and (b) the reference to "§ 15-881" was substituted for the reference to "§ 15-871" to conform to the reviser's renumbering of that section.

1995 Note. The amendment made by Laws 1995, Ch. 196, sec. 12 was inconsistent and incompatible with Laws 1995, Ch. 191, sec. 14 and therefore could not be blended.

2000 Note. The amendment of this section by Laws 2000, Ch. 405, sec. 5 failed to set forth in full the text of the section as amended by Laws 2000, Ch. 236, sec. 21, an emergency act, as required by Constitution of Arizona art. IV, pt. 2, sec. 14.

§ 15-946. Transportation revenue control limit

A. The transportation revenue control limit for each school district for the fiscal years 1985-1986, 1986-1987 and 1987-1988 is computed as follows:

1. Determine the adopted operational expenditure budget for pupil transportation for the fiscal year 1984-1985 effective January 1, 1985.

2. Determine the transportation revenue control limit for the school district for the fiscal year 1984-1985 as provided in this section before April 18, 1985.

3. If the school district's transportation revenue control limit for the fiscal year 1984-1985 as provided in paragraph 2 of this subsection is equal to or greater than the amount determined in paragraph 1 of this subsection, the transportation revenue control limit for the fiscal year 1985-1986 is the change in the transportation support level from the fiscal year 1984-1985 to the fiscal year 1985-1986 plus the transportation revenue control limit for the fiscal year 1984-1985 as provided in paragraph 2 of this subsection. For the fiscal years 1986-1987 and 1987-1988 the transportation revenue control limit is the transportation revenue control limit for the current year plus the change in the transportation support level for the current year to the budget year.

4. If the school district's transportation revenue control limit for the fiscal year 1984-1985 as provided in paragraph 2 of this subsection is less than the amount determined in paragraph 1 of this subsection, the transportation revenue control limit for the fiscal year 1985-1986 is the sum of the following:

(a) The transportation revenue control limit for the school district for the fiscal year 1984-1985 as provided in paragraph 2 of this subsection.

(b) The change in the transportation support level from the fiscal year 1984-1985 to the fiscal year 1985-1986.

(c) One-third of the amount obtained by subtracting the transportation revenue control limit for fiscal year 1984-1985 as provided in paragraph 2 of this subsection from the amount determined in paragraph 1 of this subsection.

5. If the transportation revenue control limit of the school district for the fiscal year 1984-1985 as provided in paragraph 2 of this subsection is less than the amount determined in paragraph 1 of this subsection, the transportation revenue control limit for the fiscal years 1986-1987 and 1987-1988 is the sum of the following:

(a) The transportation revenue control limit for the current year.

(b) The change in the transportation support level from the current year to the budget year.

(c) One-third of the amount obtained by subtracting the transportation revenue control limit for the fiscal year 1984-1985 as provided in paragraph 2 of this subsection from the amount determined in paragraph 1 of this subsection.

B. The transportation revenue control limit for each school district for the fiscal year 1988-1989 and each year thereafter shall be the transportation revenue control limit for the current year plus the increase in the transportation support level from the current year to the budget year. for a school district that sponsors a charter school, its transportation revenue control limit for the budget year shall be calculated as follows:

1. Calculate separately, as prescribed by the department of education, the total transportation support level for the current year for all charter schools under the district's sponsorship in the current year.

2. Calculate separately, as prescribed by the department of education, the total transportation support level for the budget year for all charter schools under the district's sponsorship in the budget year.

3. Subtract the amount determined in paragraph 2 of this subsection from the amount determined in paragraph 1 of this subsection. If the result is zero or less, use zero in paragraph 4 of this subsection.

4. Subtract the amount determined in paragraph 3 of this subsection from the district's transportation revenue control limit for the current year. This is the adjusted transportation revenue control limit for the current year.

5. The transportation revenue control limit for the budget year is the adjusted transportation revenue control limit for the current year determined in paragraph 4 of this subsection plus the increase in the transportation support level from the current year to the budget year.

Added by Laws 1981, Ch. 1, § 2, eff. Jan. 23, 1981. Amended by Laws 1985, Ch. 166, § 22, eff. April 18, 1985; Laws 1986, Ch. 323, § 1; Laws 2000, Ch. 90, § 5.

Historical and Statutory Notes

Source:

Laws 1974, 1st S.S., Ch. 3, § 38.
A.R.S. former §§ 15-1202.08, 15-1625.
Laws 1976, Ch. 166, § 4.
Laws 1978, 1st S.S., Ch. 1, § 4.
Laws 1980, 2nd S.S., Ch. 9, § 62.

§ 15-947. Revenue control limit; district support level; general budget limit; unrestricted total capital budget limit; soft capital allocation limit

A. The revenue control limit for a school district is equal to the sum of the base revenue control limit determined in § 15-944 and the transportation revenue control limit determined in § 15-946.

B. The district support level for a school district is equal to the sum of the base support level determined in § 15-943 and the transportation support level determined in § 15-945.

C. The general budget limit for each school district, for each fiscal year, is the sum of the following:

1. The maintenance and operations portion of the revenue control limit for the budget year.

2. The maintenance and operation portion of the following amounts:

(a) Amounts that are fully funded by revenues other than a levy of taxes upon the taxable property within the school district, as listed below:

(i) Amounts budgeted as the budget balance carryforward as provided in § 15-943.01.

(ii) Tuition revenues for attendance of nonresident pupils.

(iii) State assistance as provided in § 15-976.

(iv) Special education revenues as provided in § 15-825, subsection D and § 15-1204.

(v) P.L. 81-874 assistance determined for children with disabilities, children with specific learning disabilities and children residing on Indian lands as provided in § 15-905, subsections K and O.

(vi) P.L. 81-874 administrative costs as provided in § 15-905, subsection P.

(vii) State assistance for excess tuition as provided in § 15-825.01.

(viii) Amounts received from the state board of education pursuant to § 15-973.01.

(b) Amounts approved pursuant to an override election as provided in § 15-481 for the applicable fiscal year.

(c) Expenditures for excess utility costs as provided in § 15-910.

(d) Amounts authorized by the county school superintendent pursuant to § 15-974, subsection C.

(e) Expenditures for complying with a court order of desegregation as provided in § 15-910.

(f) Expenditures for the bond issues portion of the cost of tuition as provided in § 15-910.

(g) Interest on registered warrants or tax anticipation notes as provided in § 15-910.

(h) Amounts budgeted for a jointly owned and operated career and technical education and vocational education center as provided in § 15-910.01.

(i) Amount of energy reduction adjustment pursuant to section 15-910.02.

3. The maintenance and operations portion of the capital outlay revenue limit for the budget year.

4. Any other budget item that is budgeted in the maintenance and operation section of the budget and that is specifically exempt from the revenue control limit or the capital outlay revenue limit.

D. The unrestricted capital budget limit, for each school district for each fiscal year, is the sum of the following:

1. The federal impact adjustment as determined in § 15-964 for the budget year.

2. Any other budget item that is budgeted in the capital outlay section of the budget and that is specifically exempt from the capital outlay revenue limit.

3. The capital portion of the amounts contained in subsection C, paragraph 2 of this section.

4. The unexpended budget balance in the unrestricted capital outlay fund from the previous fiscal year.

5. The net interest earned in the unrestricted capital outlay fund the previous fiscal year.

E. The soft capital allocation limit for each school district for each fiscal year is the sum of the following:

1. The soft capital allocation for the budget year.

2. The unexpended budget balance in the soft capital allocation fund from the previous fiscal year.

3. The net interest earned in the soft capital allocation fund the previous fiscal year.

Added by Laws 1981, Ch. 1, § 2, eff. Jan. 23, 1981. Amended by Laws 1981, Ch. 181, § 4; Laws 1982, Ch. 198, § 4; Laws 1982, Ch. 290, § 1, eff. May 3, 1982; Laws 1982, Ch. 291, § 2, eff. May 3, 1982; Laws 1983, Ch. 267, § 2, eff. April 25, 1983; Laws 1984, Ch. 327, § 1; Laws 1984, Ch. 340, § 3, eff. Aug. 3, 1984, retroactively effective to May 1, 1984; Laws 1984, Ch. 349, § 8; Laws 1985, Ch. 166, § 23, eff. April 18, 1985; Laws 1986, Ch. 125, § 8, eff. April 18, 1986; Laws 1986, Ch. 392, § 2, eff. May 21, 1986; Laws 1987, Ch. 188, § 2; Laws 1988, Ch. 221, § 3, eff. June 14, 1988, retroactively effective to July 1, 1987; Laws 1988, Ch. 288, § 7, eff. July 8, 1988; Laws 1990, Ch. 143, § 2, eff. April 26, 1990; Laws 1990, Ch. 322, § 16, eff. June 20, 1990; Laws 1990, Ch. 348, § 11, eff. June 26, 1990; Laws 1990, Ch. 399, § 8, eff. July 5, 1990; Laws 1991, Ch. 244, § 7, eff. June 17, 1991; Laws 1991, Ch. 292, § 7, eff. June 28, 1991; Laws 1992, Ch. 243, § 2, eff. Sept. 30, 1992, retroactively effective to July 1, 1990; Laws 1993, Ch. 202, § 13, eff. April 21, 1993; Laws 1996, 5th S.S., Ch. 8, § 6; Laws 1998, Ch. 271, § 2; Laws 1998, 5th S.S., Ch. 1, § 21, eff. July 9, 1998; Laws 1999, Ch. 299, § 19; Laws 2000, Ch. 236, § 22, eff. April 12, 2000; Laws 2000, 5th S.S., Ch. 1, § 14; Laws 2002, Ch. 89, § 27; Laws 2002, Ch. 301, § 1, eff. May 23, 2002.

Historical and Statutory Notes

Source:

Laws 1980, 2nd S.S., Ch. 9, § 62.
A.R.S. former § 15-1202.09.

Laws 1986, Ch. 249, §§ 1 and 2, effective April 30, 1986, prescribe methods of budgeting for excess liability insurance costs exempt from the revenue control limit.

The 1988 amendment of this section by Ch. 288 explicitly amended the 1988 amendment of this section by Ch. 221.

Laws 1989, Ch. 26, § 1, eff. April 13, 1989, prescribes methods of budgeting for excess liability insurance costs exempt from the revenue control limit.

The 1990 amendment of this section by Chs. 399 and 322 explicitly amended the 1990 amendment of this section by Ch. 143.

The amendment of this section by Laws 1990, Ch. 399, § 8, was repealed by Laws 1991, Ch. 244, § 8, effective June 17, 1991, and Ch. 292, § 8, effective June 28, 1991.

The 1991 amendment of this section by Ch. 244 explicitly amended the 1990 amendments of this section by Chs. 322 and 348.

The 1991 amendment of this section by Ch. 292 explicitly amended the 1990 amendment of this section by Chs. 322 and 348.

The 1991 amendment of this section by Laws 1991, Ch. 292, § 7, effective June 28, 1991, was repealed by Laws 1992, Ch. 319, § 14.

The 1992 amendment of this section by Ch. 243 explicitly amended the 1992 amendment of this section by Ch. 244.

Laws 1992, chapter 243, § 4, as amended by Laws 1992, Ch. 305, § 34, provides:

"**Sec. 4. Retroactivity**

"Sections 15–910, 15–947 and 35–465.05, Arizona Revised Statutes, as amended by this act, are effective retroactively to July 1, 1990."

Laws 1992, Ch. 319, § 1, par. 9, provides:

"**Section 1. Purpose**"

"9. Section 15–947, Arizona Revised Statutes, was amended by Laws 1991, chapter 244, § 7 and Laws 1991, chapter 292, § 7. The chapter 292 version failed to amend the chapter 244 version, which was an emergency enactment, and therefore did not comply with article IV, part 2, § 4, Constitution of Arizona. Since the substance of the Laws 1991, chapter 292 version was incorporated in the Laws 1991, chapter 244 version of § 15–947, Arizona Revised Statutes, in this act the chapter 292 version is repealed."

Laws 1993, Ch. 202, § 25, eff. April 21, 1993, provides:

"**Sec. 25. Tuition payments received in fiscal year 1991–1992**

"Notwithstanding § 15–947, Arizona Revised Statutes, and the uniform system of financial records, if a school district received in fiscal year 1991–1992 a payment of tuition for one or more prior years as a result of litigation, the tuition so received shall be considered as tuition received in fiscal year 1990–1991 for the purposes of computing the school district's budget and expenditure limits for fiscal year 1990–1991."

The purported amendment of this section by Laws 1998, Ch. 164 failed to become effective because Chapter 164 was repealed in its entirety by Laws 1998, 5th S.S., Ch. 1, § 2, effective July 1, 1998.

A purported amendment of this section by Laws 1998, Ch. 286, was repealed by Laws 1998, 5th S.S., Ch. 1, § 2. See note, post.

The purported amendment of this section by Laws 1998, 3rd S.S., Ch. 1, failed to became effective because Ch. 1 was repealed in its entirety by Laws 1998, 5th S.S., Ch. 1, § 2, effective July 1, 1998.

Laws 1998, 5th S.S., Ch. 1, § 2, provides:

"**Sec. 2. Repeal**

"Laws 1998, third special session, chapter 1, Laws 1998, chapter 164, Laws 1998, chapter 219 and Laws 1998, chapter 286, § 1 are repealed."

Laws 1998, 5th S.S., Ch. 1, § 57, provides:

"**Sec. 57. Existing monies in the reserve of the capital outlay fund**

"Notwithstanding § 15–947, subsection D, Arizona Revised Statutes, as amended by this act, for fiscal year 2000 school districts may budget any monies accumulated in the reserve of the capital outlay fund as of June 30, 1999 as if the monies were the ending unexpended budget balance in the unrestricted capital outlay fund."

The 2000 amendment of this section by 5th S.S., Ch. 1 explicitly amended the amendment of this section by Laws 2000, Ch. 236, § 22. Proposition 301, approved by the electors at the Nov. 7, 2000 general election, effective Nov. 27, 2000, included a provision increasing the state transaction privilege tax rate six-tenths of one per cent. Therefore, the conditions of the 5th S.S. Ch. 1 were met, and the act became effective.

Laws 2002, Ch. 125, § 2, effective August 22, 2002, retroactively effective to July 1, 2000, provides:

"**Sec. 2. Computation of general budget limit for fiscal years 2000–2001 and 2001–2002**

"Notwithstanding § 15–481, subsections P and Q, Arizona Revised Statutes, a unified school district for which fiscal year 2001–2002 is the seventh year of revenue control limit budget overrides that are entirely funded with revenues from other than a levy of taxes on the taxable property within the school district pursuant to § 15–481, subsections F and J, Arizona Revised Statutes, may calculate its general budget limit pursuant to § 15–947, Arizona Revised Statutes, for fiscal years 2000–2001 and 2001–2002 by using the initial percentage increases in the revenue control limit authorized by the voters of the school district, provided that all of the following conditions are met:

"1. The original overrides that were approved by the voters of the school district were for the maximum percentage that the school district could have sought at the time that the overrides were approved.

"2. The voters of the school district approved each override by a margin of seventy-five per cent or more.

"3. The school district did not request, and the voters did not disapprove a request, to renew either of the budget overrides."

Reviser's Notes:

1982 Note. Prior to the 1983 amendment, this section contains the amendments made by Laws 1982, Ch. 198, § 4, Ch. 290, § 1 and Ch. 291, § 2 which were blended together pursuant to authority of § 41–1304.03.

1984 Note. Prior to the 1985 amendment, this section contained the amendments made by Laws 1984, Ch. 327, § 1, Ch. 340, § 3 and Ch. 349, § 8 which were blended together pursuant to authority of § 41–1304.03.

1990 Note. The amendment of this section by Laws 1990, Ch. 399, § 8 failed to set forth in full the text of the section as amended by Laws 1990, Ch. 322 and Ch. 348, emergency acts, as required by Constitution of Arizona Art. IV, part 2, § 14.

1990 Note. Prior to the 1991 amendments, this section contained the amendments made by Laws 1990, Ch. 322, § 16 and Ch. 348, § 11 which were blended together pursuant to authority of § 41-1304.03.

1991 Note. The amendment of this section by Laws 1991, Ch. 292, sec. 7 failed to set forth in full the text of the section as amended by Laws 1991, Ch. 244, an emergency act, as required by Constitution of Arizona Art. IV, part 2, sec. 14.

1998 Note. Prior to the 1999 amendment, this section contained the amendments made by Laws 1998, Second Regular Session, Ch. 271, sec. 2 and Laws 1998, Fifth Special Session, Ch. 1. sec. 21 that were blended together pursuant to authority of § 41-1304.03.

2002 Note. This section contains the amendments made by Laws 2002, Ch. 89, sec. 27 and Ch. 301, sec. 1 that were blended together as shown pursuant to authority of § 41-1304.03.

§ 15-947.01. Revenue control limit; general budget limit; total capital budget limit for joint technological education districts

A. The revenue control limit and district support level for a joint technological education district are equal to the base support level determined in § 15-943.02.

B. The general budget limit for each joint technological education district, for each fiscal year, is the sum of the following:

1. The revenue control limit for the budget year.
2. The capital outlay revenue limit for the budget year.
3. Tuition revenues for attendance of nonresident pupils.
4. P.L. 81-874 assistance determined for children with disabilities, children with specific learning disabilities and children residing on Indian lands as provided in § 15-905, subsections K and O.
5. Expenditures for excess utility costs as provided in § 15-910.

C. The unrestricted capital budget limit for each joint technological education district for the budget year is as provided in § 15-947, subsection D.

D. The soft capital allocation limit for each joint technological education district for the budget year is as provided in § 15-947, subsection E.

Added by Laws 1990, Ch. 248, § 4, eff. Sept. 27, 1990, retroactively effective to July 15, 1990. Amended by Laws 1991, Ch. 154, § 9, eff. May 20, 1991; Laws 1996, 5th S.S., Ch. 8, § 7; Laws 1998, 5th S.S., Ch. 1, § 22, eff. July 9, 1998; Laws 1999, Ch. 299, § 20; Laws 2000, Ch. 236, § 23, eff. April 12, 2000; Laws 2001, Ch. 251, § 4.

Historical and Statutory Notes

The purported amendment of this section by Laws 1998, Ch. 164 failed to become effective because Chapter 164 was repealed in its entirety by Laws 1998, 5th S.S., Ch. 1, § 2, effective July 1, 1998.

The purported amendment of this section by Laws 1998, 3rd S.S., Ch. 1, failed to became effective because Ch. 1 was repealed in its entirety by Laws 1998, 5th S.S., Ch. 1, § 2, effective July 1, 1998.

Laws 2001, Ch. 251, became law without the Governor's signature as provided in Arizona Constitution, Article 5, § 7.

Reviser's Notes:

1990 Note. Pursuant to authority of § 41-1304.02, in the section heading "and technical" was added after "vocational" and in subsection A the reference to "§ 15-943.02" was substituted for the reference to "§ 15-941.01" to conform to the reviser's renumbering of that section.

§ 15-948. Adjustment for growth in student count

A. Any school district may, after the first one hundred days or two hundred days in session, as applicable, of the current year, determine if it is eligible to increase its revenue control limit and district support level for the current year due to growth in the student population as follows:

1. Determine the student count used for calculating the base support level for the current year.

2. Determine the average daily membership or adjusted average daily membership, whichever is applicable, through the first one hundred days or two hundred days in session, as applicable, of the current year.

3. Subtract the amount determined in paragraph 1 of this subsection from the amount determined in paragraph 2 of this subsection.

4. If the amount determined in paragraph 2 of this subsection is greater than the amount determined in paragraph 1 of this subsection, the governing board of the school district may compute an increase to its revenue control limit and district support level for the current year.

B. A school district may, after the first one hundred days or two hundred days in session, as applicable, of the current year, determine if it is eligible to compute an increase to its revenue control limit for the current year due to growth in the number of pupils in the group B categories of moderate or severe mental retardation, visual impairment, hearing impairment, multiple disabilities, multiple disabilities with severe sensory impairment, orthopedic impairment, preschool severe delay and emotionally disabled pupils enrolled in private special education programs or in school district programs for pupils with severe disabilities as follows:

1. Determine the weighted student count for all group B children with disabilities used for calculating the base support level for the current year.

2. Determine the weighted average daily membership for all group B children with disabilities through the first one hundred days or two hundred days in session, as applicable, of the current year.

3. Subtract the amount determined in paragraph 1 of this subsection from the amount determined in paragraph 2 of this subsection.

4. If the amount determined in paragraph 2 of this subsection is greater than the amount determined in paragraph 1 of this subsection, the governing board of the school district may compute an increase to its revenue control limit and district support level for the current year by using the amount determined in paragraph 3 of this subsection for the weighted student count and the base level for the district for the current year.

C. If a school district meets the criteria specified in subsection A or B of this section, or both, the governing board of the school district may, after notice is given and a public hearing held as provided in § 15-905, subsection D, at any time prior to May 15 revise its budget to include the increase in its revenue control limit and district support level for the current year utilizing the procedure prescribed in subsection A or B of this section, or both. Not later than May 18, the budget as revised shall be submitted electronically to the superintendent of public instruction.

D. If the revised budget is adopted by the governing board at the public hearing and submitted electronically as provided in subsection C of this section, the school district shall receive state aid based upon the adjusted revenue control limit or the adjusted district support level in the manner specified in § 15–971, except that in no event shall the school district receive less state aid than it would have received if it had not used this section.

E. If the adjusted revenue control limit results in an expenditure of funds in excess of school district revenues for the current year, the county school superintendent shall include within the revenue estimate for the budget year funds necessary to meet the liabilities incurred by the school district in the current year in excess of revenues received for the current year.

Added by Laws 1981, Ch. 1, § 2, eff. Jan. 23, 1981. Amended by Laws 1981, Ch. 218, § 1, eff. April 27, 1981; Laws 1982, Ch. 140, § 1; Laws 1983, Ch. 229, § 2, eff. April 22, 1983; Laws 1985, Ch. 166, § 24, eff. April 18, 1985; Laws 1985, Ch. 289, § 1; Laws 1986, Ch. 387, § 2; Laws 1987, Ch. 363, § 7, eff. May 22, 1987; Laws 1988, Ch. 288, § 8, eff. July 8, 1988; Laws 1990, Ch. 258, § 7; Laws 1992, Ch. 172, § 24; Laws 1992, Ch. 305, § 17; Laws 1996, 5th S.S., Ch. 8, § 8; Laws 1998, Ch. 167, § 11; Laws 2000, Ch. 342, § 21.

Historical and Statutory Notes

Source:

Laws 1980, 2nd S.S., Ch. 9, § 62.
A.R.S. former § 15–1202.12.

Laws 1991, Ch. 288, § 16, effective Sept. 21, 1991, retroactively effective to July 1, 1991, provides:

"**Sec. 16. Fiscal year 1991–1992 school district growth in student count; formula**

"Notwithstanding § 15–948, subsections A and B, Arizona Revised Statutes, for fiscal year 1991–1992, the adjustment for growth in student count shall be determined as follows:

"1. Determine the total increase in the revenue control limit and district support level for fiscal year 1991–1992 as prescribed by § 15–948, subsections A and B, Arizona Revised Statutes.

"2. Multiply the amount determined in paragraph 1 of this section by 0.64."

Laws 1992, Ch. 288, § 24, eff. Sept. 30, 1992, retroactively effective to July 1, 1992, provides:

"**Sec. 24. Fiscal year 1992–1993 school district growth in student count; formula**

"Notwithstanding § 15–948, subsections A and B, Arizona Revised Statutes, for fiscal year 1992–1993, the adjustment for growth in student count shall be determined as follows:

"1. Determine the total increase in the revenue control limit and district support level for fiscal year 1992–1993 as prescribed by § 15–948, subsections A and B, Arizona Revised Statutes.

"2. Multiply the amount determined in paragraph 1 of this section by 0.64."

Laws 1993, 2nd S.S., Ch. 8, § 7, provides:

"**Sec. 7. Fiscal year 1993–1994 school district growth in student count; formula**

"Notwithstanding § 15–948, subsections A and B, Arizona Revised Statutes, for fiscal year 1993–1994, the adjustment for growth in student count shall be determined as follows:

"1. Determine the total increase in the revenue control limit and district support level for fiscal year 1993–1994 as prescribed by § 15–948, subsections A and B, Arizona Revised Statutes.

"2. Multiply the amount determined in paragraph 1 of this section by 0.75."

Laws 1996, 5th S.S., Ch. 8, § 16, provides:

"**Sec. 16. Adjustment for growth in student count during fiscal year 1996–1997**

"**A.** Notwithstanding § 15–948, subsection A, Arizona Revised Statutes, as amended by this act, during fiscal year 1996–1997, a school district may, after the first one hundred days in session of fiscal year 1996–1997, determine if it is eligible to increase its revenue control limit and district support level for the current year due to growth in the student population as follows:

"1. Determine the student count used for calculating the base support level for fiscal year 1996–1997.

"2. Determine the average daily membership or adjusted average daily membership, whichever is applicable, through the first one hundred days in session of fiscal year 1996–1997.

"3. Multiply the student count determined in paragraph 1 of this subsection by 1.02.

"4. Subtract the amount determined in paragraph 3 of this subsection from the amount determined in paragraph 2 of this subsection.

"5. If the amount determined in paragraph 2 of this subsection is greater than the amount determined in paragraph 3 of this subsection, the governing board of the school district may compute an increase to its revenue control limit and district support level for fiscal year 1996–1997 by using the amount determined in paragraph 4 of this subsection for the student count and the base level for the district.

"**B.** Notwithstanding § 15-948, subsection B, Arizona Revised Statutes, as amended by this act, during fiscal year 1996–1997, a school district may, after the first one hundred days in session of fiscal year 1996–1997, determine if it is eligible to compute an increase to its revenue control limit and district support level for fiscal year 1996–1997 due to growth in the number of pupils in the group B categories of moderate or severe mental retardation, visual impairment, hearing impairment, multiple disabilities, multiple disabilities with severe sensory impairment, orthopedic impairment, preschool severe delay and emotionally disabled pupils enrolled in private special education programs or in school district programs for pupils with severe disabilities as follows:

"1. Determine the weighted student count for all group B children with disabilities used for calculating the base support level for fiscal year 1996–1997.

"2. Determine the weighted student average daily membership for all group B children with disabilities through the first one hundred days in session of fiscal year 1996–1997.

"3. Multiply the student count determined in paragraph 1 of this subsection by 1.02.

"4. Subtract the amount determined in paragraph 3 of this subsection from the amount determined in paragraph 2 of this subsection.

"5. If the amount determined in paragraph 2 of this subsection is greater than the amount determined in paragraph 3 of this subsection, the governing board of the school district may compute an increase to its revenue control limit for fiscal year 1996–1997 by using the amount determined in paragraph 4 of this subsection for the weighted student count and the base level for the district."

Reviser's Notes:

1992 Note. Prior to the 1996 amendment, this section contained the amendments made by Laws 1992, Ch. 172, sec. 24 and Ch. 305, sec. 17 that were blended together pursuant to authority of § 41-1304.03.

§ 15-949. Small school districts; exemption from general budget limit; budget revision

A. The governing board of a common school district with a student count in kindergarten programs and grades one through eight of one hundred twenty-five or less, the governing board of a high school district with a student count of one hundred or less or the governing board of a unified school district or the county school superintendent for an accommodation school with a student count of one hundred twenty-five or less in kindergarten programs and grades one through eight or with a student count of one hundred or less in grades nine through twelve shall compute a revenue control limit and a general budget limit, but the governing board or the county school superintendent may:

1. Adopt a budget in excess of the general budget limit without the necessity of an election under § 15-481, provided that for a unified school district or for an accommodation school the excess amount of expenditures shall be attributable to the student count in kindergarten programs and grades one through eight or to the student count in grades nine through twelve as provided in this subsection.

2. Revise its budget to include the costs for additional pupils who were not anticipated when the budget was adopted, if it receives permission as follows:

(a) If a governing board:

(i) The governing board shall send a petition to the county school superintendent requesting authority to revise its budget. The petition shall include a copy of the proposed budget.

(ii) The county school superintendent shall recommend the action to be taken on the petition and forward the recommendation and the petition to the board of supervisors.

(iii) The board of supervisors shall hold a hearing on the petition within twenty days after receipt of the petition and shall determine whether to allow the petition, allow the petition after revision or deny the petition.

(b) If a county school superintendent, the county school superintendent shall send the revised budget to the board of supervisors, and the board of supervisors shall hold a hearing on the recommendation within twenty days after receipt of the recommendation and shall determine whether to allow the revised budget, allow the revised budget after further revision or deny the revision.

B. If the board of supervisors revises or denies the petition or recommendation presented pursuant to subsection A, paragraph 2, subdivision (a), item (iii) or subdivision (b) of this section the reasons for revision or denial shall be stated in writing.

C. School districts that in any year after fiscal year 1984–1985 but before fiscal year 1999–2000 have operated under the provisions of the small school adjustment as provided for in subsection A of this section and that have subsequently exceeded the student count limits expressed in subsection A of this section may continue in successive years to adopt a budget greater than the general budget limit without the necessity of an election under § 15–481, except that the amount greater than the general budget limit shall not exceed fifty thousand dollars. The amount that is adopted without the use of an election under § 15–481 and that is greater than the general budget limit is specifically exempt from the revenue control limit.

D. Notwithstanding subsection C of this section, school districts that exceeded the student count limits prescribed in subsection A of this section may adopt, in the first year that these limits are exceeded, a budget that exceeds the general budget limit without an election conducted pursuant to § 15–481 or pursuant to subsection E of this section, except that the amount that exceeds the general budget limit shall not exceed the amount authorized pursuant to subsection C of this section plus the limit prescribed in subsection E of this section. The amount that is adopted without an election and that exceeds the general budget limit is exempt from the revenue control limit.

E. School districts that in any year after fiscal year 1998–1999 have operated under the provisions of the small school adjustment as provided in subsection A of this section and that have subsequently exceeded the student count limits prescribed in subsection A of this section may continue in successive years to adopt a budget greater than the general budget limit subject to an election, except that the amount that is greater than the general budget limit shall not exceed the amount that is prescribed in this subsection. The amount that is adopted pursuant to this subsection is specifically exempt from the revenue control limit and shall be funded by a levy on secondary property taxes in the school district. The maximum amount that may be adopted pursuant to this subsection is computed as follows:

1. For a unified school district, separate the revenue control limit into elementary and secondary components based on the weighted student count as provided in § 15–971, subsection B, paragraph 2, subdivision (a). Use the elementary component of the revenue control limit for the purposes of para-

graph 2 of this subsection and the secondary component of the revenue control limit for the purposes of paragraph 3 of this subsection.

2. For a common or unified district that used the provisions of subsection A of this section based on its elementary student count, the amount is determined as follows:

(a) Subtract one hundred twenty-five from the elementary student count.

(b) Multiply the difference in subdivision (a) of this paragraph by 0.45 per cent.

(c) Subtract the product determined in subdivision (b) of this paragraph from thirty-five per cent. If the result is zero or less than zero, the district is not eligible to use the provisions of this paragraph.

(d) Multiply the difference determined in subdivision (c) of this paragraph by the elementary revenue control limit.

3. For a high school or unified district that used the provisions of subsection A of this section based on its secondary student count, the amount is determined as follows:

(a) Subtract one hundred from the secondary student count.

(b) Multiply the difference in subdivision (a) of this paragraph by 0.65 per cent.

(c) Subtract the product determined in subdivision (b) of this paragraph from sixty-five per cent. If the result is zero or less than zero, the district is not eligible to use the provisions of this paragraph.

(d) Multiply the difference determined in subdivision (c) of this paragraph by the secondary revenue control limit.

4. For a unified school district that used the provisions of subsection A of this section for both its elementary and secondary pupils, combine the amounts determined in paragraphs 2 and 3 of this subsection.

F. For the purposes of subsection E of this section:

1. "Elementary" means kindergarten programs and grades one through eight.

2. "Secondary" means grades nine through twelve.

G. The part of the primary tax rate set to fund the small school district adjustment as provided in subsections D and e of this section shall not be included in the computation of additional state aid for education as prescribed in § 15–972.

H. The election required pursuant to subsection E of this section shall conform to the procedural requirements for calling the election, preparing the informational report and preparing the ballot as prescribed in § 15–481, subsections A, B, C and D. The maximum number of years that a budget override approved pursuant to subsection E of this section may be in effect is five years.

I. If the proposed budget override will be fully funded by a levy of taxes on the taxable property within the school district, the ballot shall contain the words "budget override, yes" and "budget override, no", and the voter shall signify the voter's desired choice. The ballot shall also contain the amount of the proposed budget override compared to the amount the school district budgeted in the preceding year and the amount the school district would be allowed to budget for if the measure is not approved by the voters. The statement shall also include the estimated amount of the override for each year the override is sought. The ballot shall also include the following statement:

School district to levy property taxes in excess of the property tax levy allowed by law to fund the school district's revenue control limit. The property tax levy for the year for which adopted and for ____ subsequent years will be annually adjusted based on a formula that authorizes the __________ school district to exceed the revenue control limit by up to thirty-five per cent for kindergarten programs and grades one through eight or up to sixty-five per cent for grades nine through twelve. The levy shall not be realized from monies furnished by the state and shall not be subject to the limitation on taxes specified in article IX, § 18, Constitution of Arizona. Based on an estimate of assessed valuation used for secondary property tax purposes, the proposed override in the ______________ school district's budget over that allowed by the revenue control limit would result in an estimated increase in the school district's tax rate of ________________ dollars per one hundred dollars of assessed valuation for the secondary property tax purposes.

J. If the proposed budget override will be fully funded by revenues from other than a levy of taxes on the taxable property within the school district, the ballot shall contain the words "budget override, yes" and "budget override, no", and the voter shall signify the voter's desired choice. The ballot shall also contain the amount of the proposed budget override compared to the amount the school district budgeted in the preceding year and the amount the school district would be allowed to budget for if the measure is not approved by the voters. The statement shall also include the estimated amount of the override for each year the override is sought. The ballot shall also include the following statement:

K. For the purposes of subsections h and i of this section, levy of taxes on the taxable property does not include a levy of the government property lease or park property lease excise taxes assessed pursuant to title 42, chapter 6, article 5.[1]

Added by Laws 1981, Ch. 1, § 2, eff. Jan. 23, 1981. Amended by Laws 1982, Ch. 198, § 5; Laws 1985, Ch. 166, § 25, eff. April 18, 1985, retroactively effective to Jan. 1, 1985; Laws 1990, Ch. 348, § 12, eff. June 26, 1990; Laws 1991, Ch. 292, § 9, eff. June 28, 1991; Laws 1993, Ch. 219, § 2; Laws 1996, Ch. 284, § 57; Laws 2001, Ch. 310, § 2; Laws 2004, Ch. 338, § 2; Laws 2004, Ch. 341, § 5.

[1] Section 42–6201 et seq.

Historical and Statutory Notes

Source:

Laws 1960, Ch. 127, § 48.
A.R.S. former § 15–1201.01.
Laws 1965, 3rd S.S., Ch. 1, § 1.
Laws 1967, 3rd S.S., Ch. 19, § 7.
Laws 1971, Ch. 177, § 4.
Laws 1974, 1st S.S., Ch. 3, § 22.
Laws 1975, Ch. 106, § 3.
Laws 1975, Ch. 157, § 1.
Laws 1978, Ch. 152, § 1.
Laws 1978, Ch. 188, § 16.
Laws 1980, 2nd S.S., Ch. 9, § 55.

Laws 1985, Ch. 166, § 48, effective April 18, 1985, provides:

"**Sec. 48. Retroactivity**

"Section 15-949, Arizona Revised Statutes, as amended by this act, is effective retroactively to January 1, 1985."

Laws 1994, Ch. 254, § 9, effective April 24, 1994, provides:

"**Sec. 9. Provisions for unified school districts that exceeded the general budget limit in fiscal year 1992-1993 or 1993-1994**

"**A.** Notwithstanding §§ 15-905 and 15-949, Arizona Revised Statutes, a unified school district is not required to reduce its general budget limit due to excess expenditures for pupils in kindergarten programs and grades one through eight for fiscal year 1992-1993 or 1993-1994 if each of the following conditions apply for the fiscal year in which the excess expenditures were made:

"1. The district adopted a budget which included an adjustment for low student count as provided in § 15-949, Arizona Revised Statutes.

"2. The district's student count in grades nine through twelve was one hundred or less and the district's student count in kindergarten programs and grades one through eight was more than one hundred twenty-five.

"**B.** For fiscal year 1994-1995, a unified school district that meets the conditions of subsection A of this section for fiscal year 1993-1994 may adopt a budget including a budget increase as provided in § 15-481, subsection E or H, Arizona Revised Statutes, as if an election had taken place and the voters had approved the override for that year."

Reviser's Notes:

2001 Note. Pursuant to authority of § 41-1304.02, subsection G, paragraphs 1 and 2 were relettered as subsections H and I, respectively.

2004 Note. This section contains the amendments made by Laws 2004, Ch. 338, sec. 2 and Ch. 341, sec. 5 that were blended together as shown pursuant to authority of § 41-1304.03.

§ 15-950. Revenue control limits for new school districts

A resulting common, high or unified school district after consolidation of school districts as provided in § 15-459, subsection B, paragraph 2 or 3 or subsection H shall in the first budget year determine its allowable revenue control limit as follows:

1. Determine the allowable revenue control limit for the budget year for each of the school districts to be consolidated as it would have been in the absence of the consolidation.

2. Add the revenue control limits determined in paragraph 1 of this section. The sum is the revenue control limit of the resulting school district in the first year for which a budget is computed.

Added by Laws 1981, Ch. 1, § 2, eff. Jan. 23, 1981. Amended by Laws 1983, Ch. 118, § 4; Laws 1985, Ch. 238, § 10.

Historical and Statutory Notes

Source:

Laws 1974, 1st S.S., Ch. 3, § 62.
A.R.S. former § 15-403.02.
Laws 1975, Ch. 103, § 3.
Laws 1980, 2nd S.S., Ch. 9, § 13.

§ 15-951. Revenue control limit, capital outlay revenue limit, soft capital allocation, district support level and student count for a common school district not within a high school district

A. Notwithstanding § 15-947, the revenue control limit for a common school district not within a high school district is the sum of the following:

1. The base revenue control limit computed as prescribed in § 15-944 but excluding pupils admitted to another school district as provided in § 15-824, subsection A, paragraph 2.

2. The tuition payable for high school pupils who attend school in another school district as provided in § 15-824, subsection A, paragraph 2, including any transportation charge, except as provided in subsection H of this section.

3. The transportation revenue control limit for all pupils who reside in the district except those high school pupils transported by another district.

B. Notwithstanding subsection A of this section, for the purposes of §§ 15-481, 15-482 and 15-1102, the revenue control limit for a common school district not within a high school district is the sum of the following:

1. The base revenue control limit for pupils computed as prescribed in § 15-944 but excluding pupils admitted to another school district as provided in § 15-824, subsection A, paragraph 2.

2. The transportation revenue control limit for all pupils who reside in the district except those high school pupils transported by another district.

C. Notwithstanding § 15-961, the capital outlay revenue limit for a common school district not within a high school district is the capital outlay revenue limit computed as prescribed in § 15-961 but excluding pupils who are admitted to another school district as provided in § 15-824, subsection A, paragraph 2.

D. Notwithstanding § 15-962, the soft capital allocation for a common school district not within a high school district is the soft capital allocation computed as prescribed in § 15-962 but excluding pupils who are both admitted to another school district as provided in § 15-824, subsection A, paragraph 2 and not transported by the common school district.

E. Notwithstanding § 15-947, the district support level for a common school district not within a high school district is the sum of the following:

1. The base support level computed as prescribed in § 15-943 but excluding pupils who are admitted to another school district as provided in § 15-824, subsection A, paragraph 2.

2. The tuition payable for high school pupils who are admitted to another school district as provided in § 15-824, subsection A, paragraph 2, including any transportation charge, except as provided in subsection H of this section.

3. The transportation support level for all pupils who reside in the school district except those high school pupils transported by another school district.

F. For the purpose of determining eligibility to adjust the student count as provided in § 15-942, the student count for a common school district not within a high school district is the student count for pupils in the school district less the student count for pupils enrolled in another school district as provided in § 15-824, subsection A, paragraph 2.

G. For the purpose of determining eligibility to increase the revenue control limit and district support level or recompute the revenue control limit as provided in § 15-948, the student count for a common school district not within a high school district is the student count for pupils in kindergarten programs and grades one through twelve, including pupils enrolled in another school district as provided in § 15-824, subsection A, paragraph 2.

H. The tuition amount in subsections A and E of this section shall not include amounts per student count for bond issues as prescribed by § 15-824, subsection G, paragraph 1, subdivision (c) in excess of the following:

1. One hundred fifty dollars if the pupil's school district of residence pays tuition for seven hundred fifty or fewer pupils to other school districts.

2. Two hundred dollars if the pupil's school district of residence pays tuition for one thousand or fewer, but more than seven hundred fifty pupils to other school districts.

3. The actual cost per student count if the pupil's school district of residence pays tuition for more than one thousand pupils to other school districts.
Added by Laws 1985, Ch. 166, § 26, eff. April 18, 1985. Amended by Laws 1986, Ch. 387, § 3; Laws 1995, Ch. 234, § 3; Laws 1996, Ch. 358, § 3; Laws 1998, 5th S.S., Ch. 1, § 23, eff. July 9, 1998; Laws 1999, Ch. 243, § 3; Laws 1999, Ch. 299, § 21.

Retroactive Application

This section, as amended by Laws 1996, Ch. 358, applies retroactively to July 1, 1995.

Historical and Statutory Notes

Laws 1996, Ch. 358, § 6, provides:

"**Sec. 6. Retroactivity**

"Sections 1, 2, 3 and 4 of this act apply retroactively to July 1, 1995."

The purported amendment of this section by Laws 1998, 3rd S.S., Ch. 1, failed to become effective because Ch. 1 was repealed in its entirety by Laws 1998, 5th S.S., Ch. 1, § 2, effective July 1, 1998.

Reviser's Notes:

1995 Note. Pursuant to authority of § 41-1304.02, in subsection H, subdivisions (a), (b) and (c) were renumbered as paragraphs 1, 2 and 3, respectively.

1999 Note. This section contains the amendments made by Laws 1999, Ch. 243, sec. 3 and Ch. 299, sec. 21 that were blended together as shown above pursuant to authority of § 41-1304.03.

§ 15-952. Additional monies for teacher compensation; definitions

A. The governing board of a school district may calculate its revenue control limit and district support level for the budget year using the base level prescribed in § 15-901, subsection B, paragraph 2 increased by 1.25 per cent if granted approval by the state board of education according to the following procedure:

1. If the governing board did not receive approval to increase the school district's base level as provided in this section for the current year:

(a) The governing board shall submit evidence to the state board by May 1 that the school district has met the following requirements:

(i) The school district's teacher performance evaluation system meets the standards recommended by the state board as prescribed in § 15-537.

(ii) The persons evaluating teachers for retention decisions meet the minimum qualifications for evaluators recommended by the state board as prescribed in § 15-537.

(b) The state board shall notify the governing board by June 1 whether it has met the requirements and has preliminary approval to increase the school district's base level for the budget year.

(c) If the governing board receives preliminary approval to increase the school district's base level as prescribed in subdivision (b) of this paragraph for the budget year and wishes to receive final approval, the governing board shall prepare and submit to the state board by June 15 two proposed budgets as follows:

(i) One proposed budget showing the amount budgeted for teacher compensation if final approval to increase the school district's base level is not granted.

(ii) One proposed budget showing the amount budgeted for teacher compensation if final approval to increase the school district's base level is granted.

(d) If the school district's proposed budgets demonstrate that the governing board has budgeted the additional monies for additional teacher compensation as provided in this section, the state board shall give final approval to the governing board to increase the school district's base level as provided in this section and shall notify the governing board of the approval by July 1.

2. If the governing board received approval to increase the school district's base level as provided in this section for the current year but not for the year before the current year:

(a) The governing board shall submit evidence to the state board by February 1 that the school district:

(i) Continues to meet the requirements prescribed in paragraph 1, subdivision (a) of this subsection.

(ii) Adopted the budget for the current year which it submitted to the state board as provided in paragraph 1, subdivision (c), item (ii) of this subsection.

(b) The state board shall notify the governing board by March 1 whether its application to increase the base level is approved for the budget year.

3. If the governing board received approval to increase the school district's base level as provided in this section for the current year and for the year before the current year:

(a) The governing board shall submit evidence to the state board by February 1 that the school district continues to meet the requirements prescribed in paragraph 1, subdivision (a) of this subsection.

(b) The state board shall notify the governing board by March 1 whether its application to increase the base level is approved for the budget year.

B. The state board shall prescribe the methods for demonstrating that the requirements in subsection A of this section have been met.

C. For any fiscal year in which a governing board receives approval to increase the school district's base level as provided in this section, the governing board may only expend the additional monies for additional teacher compensation.

D. In this section:

1. "Additional monies" means the amount of the increase in the base support level produced by increasing the base level as provided in subsection A of this section.

2. "Teacher compensation" means salaries and employee fringe benefits and other nonsalary benefits for certificated teachers.

Added by Laws 1986, Ch. 399, § 19, eff. Jan. 1, 1987. Amended by Laws 1992, Ch. 172, § 25; Laws 1993, Ch. 189, § 12.

Historical and Statutory Notes

Laws 1986, Ch. 399, § 21 provides:

"**Sec. 21. Conditional enactment; delayed effective date**

"Section 19 of this act does not become effective unless article IX, § 21, Constitution of Arizona, relating to public debt, revenue, and taxation, is amended by vote of the people at the next general election, or at the next special election called for such purpose, to increase the aggregate expenditure limitation for school districts, as provided by article XXI, Constitution of Arizona. If the proposed amendment is approved, § 19 of this act is effective from and after December 31, 1986 and additional monies for additional teacher compensation may be expended beginning with fiscal year 1987-1988 as provided in § 19 of this act." [Approved; see note, post.]

Proposition 101, based on Laws 1985, S.C.R. No. 1003 proposing that Const. Art. 9, § 21 be amended to provide annual increases in the aggregate expenditure limitation for school districts, was approved by the electors in the November 4, 1986 general election as proclaimed by the governor on December 16, 1986.

Laws 1989, Ch. 26, § 1, eff. April 13, 1989, prescribes methods of budgeting for excess liability insurance costs exempt from the revenue control limit.

§ 15-953. Increases in the base level

If a school district receives approval to calculate its budget using an increase in the base level as provided in § 15-918 or 15-952 or any other law for a given fiscal year, that increase in the base level applies only to the fiscal year for which approval was given. In order to calculate its budget using an increase in the base level for any subsequent fiscal year the school district must receive specific approval to do so as prescribed by law.

Added by Laws 1987, Ch. 235, § 1, eff. May 7, 1987. Amended by Laws 1990, Ch. 319, § 3.

§ 15-954. Adjustment for tuition loss

A. The district may increase its base support level for tuition loss as prescribed in subsection B of this section if all of the following apply:

1. A school district receives tuition for high school pupils from a school district which is inside or outside of this state and which does not offer instruction in one or more high school grade levels.

2. The school district which had received the tuition loses the tuition because the other school district begins to offer instruction in one or more high school grade levels not previously offered.

3. The number of pupils for whom the district loses the tuition is equal to at least five per cent of the average daily membership of pupils educated by the district in grades nine through twelve for the year prior to the year in which the other school district begins to offer the instruction.

B. The maximum amount by which a district may increase its base support level for tuition loss is determined as follows:

1. Determine the amount of tuition lost between the year before the other school district begins to offer instruction, which is the base year, and the year after the base year.

2. For the year after the base year, the maximum amount is seventy-five per cent of the amount determined in paragraph 1.

3. For the second year after the base year, the maximum amount is fifty per cent of the amount determined in paragraph 1.

4. For the third year after the base year, the maximum amount is twenty-five per cent of the amount determined in paragraph 1.

C. If the resident school district is a joint unified district and phases in the instruction over more than one year:

1. The computation prescribed by subsection A, paragraph 3 of this section shall be made separately for each phase by dividing the number of pupils in the phase by the average daily membership of pupils in grades nine through twelve who are educated by the district of attendance in the year prior to the year in which the resident district begins to offer instruction for this phase.

2. The base year and the maximum amounts determined pursuant to subsection B of this section shall be computed separately for each phase.

3. The total increase in the base support level for a given fiscal year shall be the sum of the computations for each phase calculated pursuant to paragraph 2 of this subsection.

D. If the school district does not qualify for equalization assistance as provided in § 15–971, the part of the primary property tax rate set to fund the tuition loss as provided in this section shall not be included in the computation of additional state aid revenues as prescribed in § 15–972.

Added by Laws 1990, Ch. 399, § 9, eff. July 5, 1990. Amended by Laws 1991, Ch. 292, § 10, eff. June 28, 1991; Laws 1998, Ch. 108, § 1.

Historical and Statutory Notes

Laws 1998, Ch. 108, § 2, provides:

"**Sec. 2. Retroactivity**

"Section 15–954, Arizona Revised Statutes, as amended by this act, applies retroactively to from and after June 30, 1995."

Reviser's Notes:

1990 Note. Pursuant to authority of § 41–1304.02, in subsection A the words "the district may increase its base support level for tuition loss as prescribed in subsection B of this section" were transposed to follow "A." and the comma following the third "instruction" was transposed to follow "offered".

1991 Note. Pursuant to authority of § 41–1304.02, in subsection A a stricken period was removed as the correction of an electronic data base error.

ARTICLE 4. PROVISIONS FOR CAPITAL OUTLAY AND CAPITAL LEVY

WESTLAW Electronic Research

See WESTLAW Electronic Research Guide following the Preface.

Historical and Statutory Notes

Reviser's Notes:

1981 Note. Pursuant to authority of § 41–1304.02, in the article heading to article 4, as added by Laws 1981, Ch. 1, § 2, a duplicate "and" was deleted as a correction of a manifest clerical error.

§ 15–961. Capital outlay revenue limit; growth rate

A. A capital outlay revenue limit per student count is established for fiscal year 1984–1985 as follows:

1. For kindergarten programs and grades one through eight multiply one hundred fifty-five dollars by the weight which corresponds to the student count for kindergarten programs and grades one through eight for the school district

as provided in § 15–943, paragraph 1, subdivision (a), column 3. For a school district with a student count of six hundred or more in kindergarten programs and grades one through eight multiply one hundred fifty-five dollars by 1.158.

2. For grades nine through twelve multiply one hundred sixty-eight dollars by the weight which corresponds to the student count for grades nine through twelve for the school district as provided in § 15–943, paragraph 1, subdivision (b), column 3. For a school district with a student count of six hundred or more in grades nine through twelve multiply one hundred sixty-eight dollars by 1.268.

3. For programs for preschool children with disabilities multiply one hundred fifty-five dollars by 1.158.

B. For fiscal year 1985–1986 and each year thereafter the capital outlay revenue limit prescribed in subsection A of this section shall be adjusted by the growth rate prescribed by law, subject to appropriation.

C. For fiscal year 1985–1986 and each year thereafter the capital outlay revenue limit for a school district shall be computed as follows:

1. Select the applicable capital outlay revenue limit or limits per student count for the school district.

2. Multiply the amount or amounts selected in paragraph 1 of this subsection by the appropriate student count of the school district. The student count of the school district shall not include any pupils in a charter school sponsored by the district pursuant to § 15–185, subsection A, paragraph 3.

3. If a school district's student count used for the budget year is greater than one hundred five per cent of the student count used for the current year's budget, increase the adjusted capital outlay revenue limit determined in paragraph 2 of this subsection by the actual percentage increase in the school district's student count.

D. For fiscal year 1985–1986 and each year thereafter, an amount for the purchase of required textbooks and related printed subject matter materials shall be used to increase the capital outlay revenue limit for a school district as determined in subsection C, paragraph 2 or 3 of this section, whichever is applicable. For fiscal year 1985–1986, the funding level is fifty-seven dollars fifty cents. For fiscal year 1986–1987 and each year thereafter, the funding level is the funding level of the previous year adjusted by the growth rate prescribed by law, subject to appropriation. The amount to be added to the amount in subsection C, paragraph 2 or 3 of this section, whichever is applicable, to determine the capital outlay revenue limit for a school district is computed as follows:

1. For fiscal year 1985–1986, multiply the student count in grade nine by the funding level for the applicable year as prescribed in this subsection.

2. For fiscal year 1986–1987, multiply the student count in grades nine and ten by the funding level for the applicable year as prescribed in this subsection.

3. For fiscal year 1987–1988, multiply the student count in grades nine through eleven by the funding level for the applicable year as prescribed in this subsection.

4. For fiscal year 1988–1989 and each year thereafter, multiply the student count in grades nine through twelve by the funding level for the applicable year as prescribed in this subsection.

Added by Laws 1981, Ch. 1, § 2, eff. Jan. 23, 1981. Amended by Laws 1981, Ch. 217, §§ 1, 2, eff. April 27, 1981; Laws 1982, Ch. 179, § 2; Laws 1982, Ch. 198, § 6; Laws 1982, Ch. 290, § 2, eff. May 3, 1982; Laws 1983, Ch. 9, § 6; Laws 1983, Ch. 182, § 10; Laws 1984, Ch. 349, § 9; Laws 1984, Ch. 379, § 14; Laws 1985, Ch. 166, § 27, eff. April 18, 1985; Laws 1988, Ch. 281, § 7; Laws 1992, Ch. 172, § 26; Laws 1993, Ch. 189, § 13; Laws 1995, Ch. 191, § 15, eff. April 19, 1995; Laws 1995, Ch. 196, § 13; Laws 1998, 5th S.S., Ch. 1, § 24, eff. July 9, 1998; Laws 1999, Ch. 299, § 22.

Historical and Statutory Notes

Source:

Laws 1974, 1st S.S., Ch. 3, § 23.
A.R.S. former §§ 15–445.01, 15–1202.06.
Laws 1980, 2nd S.S., Ch. 9, §§ 21, 62.

This section, as amended by Laws 1982, Ch. 179, § 2 and Laws 1982, Ch. 198, § 6, was repealed by Laws 1983, Ch. 9, § 7, eff. Feb. 25, 1983.

For applicability provisions of Laws 1995, Ch. 196, see the Historical and Statutory Notes following § 1–254.

The amendment of this section by Laws 1995, Ch. 196, § 13, was repealed by Laws 1996, Ch. 248, § 9.

The purported amendment of this section by Laws 1998, 3rd S.S., Ch. 1, failed to became effective because Ch. 1 was repealed in its entirety by Laws 1998, 5th S.S., Ch. 1, § 2, effective July 1, 1998.

Reviser's Notes:

1981 Note. Pursuant to authority of § 41–1304.02, in the heading of this section the word "; exemption" was added following the word "expended".

1981 Note. Subsection I was added by Laws 1981, Ch. 217, § 2 as § 15–961.01 and was renumbered as § 15–961, subsection I [deleted in the 1985 amendment] pursuant to authority of § 41–1304.02.

1982 Note. The amendments made by Laws 1982, Ch. 179, § 2, Laws 1982, Ch. 198, § 6 and Laws 1982, Ch. 290, § 2 were inconsistent and incompatible and therefore could not be blended.

1984 Note. Prior to the 1985 amendment, this section contained the amendments made by Laws 1984, Ch. 349, § 9 and Ch. 379, § 14 which were blended together pursuant to authority of § 41–1304.03.

1995 Note. The amendment made by Laws 1995, Ch. 196, sec. 13 was inconsistent and incompatible with Laws 1995, Ch. 191, sec. 15 and therefore could not be blended.

§ 15–961.01. Renumbered as § 15–961, in part

§ 15–962. Soft capital allocation

A. A soft capital allocation per student count is established for fiscal year 1999–2000, as follows:

1. For kindergarten programs and grades one through eight, multiply one hundred ninety-four dollars thirty cents by the weight which corresponds to the student count for kindergarten programs and grades one through eight for the school district as provided in § 15–943, paragraph 1, subdivision (a), column 3.

2. For grades nine through twelve, multiply one hundred ninety-four dollars thirty cents by the weight which corresponds to the student count as provided in § 15–943, paragraph 1, subdivision (a), column 3.

3. For a school district with a student count of six hundred or more in kindergarten programs and grades one through eight or grades nine through twelve, multiply one hundred ninety-four dollars thirty cents by 1.158.

4. For programs for preschool children with disabilities, multiply one hundred ninety-four dollars thirty cents by 1.158.

B. Beginning with fiscal year 1999–2000, the soft capital allocation prescribed in subsection A of this section shall be adjusted by the growth rate prescribed by law, subject to appropriation.

C. Beginning in fiscal year 1999–2000, the soft capital allocation for a school district is computed as follows:

1. Select the applicable soft capital allocation per student count for the school district as provided in subsection A of this section.

2. Multiply the amount selected in paragraph 1 of this subsection by the appropriate student count of the school district. The student count of the school district shall not include any pupils in a charter school sponsored by the school district pursuant to § 15–185, subsection A, paragraph 3.

D. A school district shall receive its soft capital allocation in the amount determined in this section from monies appropriated for this purpose to the department of education. Soft capital allocation monies shall only be used for short-term capital items that are required to meet academic adequacy standards such as technology, textbooks, library resources, instructional aids, pupil transportation vehicles, furniture and equipment. School districts shall not use any portion of soft capital allocation monies for maintenance and operation expenses. School districts may use soft capital allocation monies to meet administrative soft capital purposes after complying with the adequacy standards prescribed in § 15–2011.

E. School districts shall establish a district soft capital allocation fund and shall use the monies only for the purposes prescribed in subsection D of this section. The ending unexpended budget balance in the school district's soft capital allocation fund may be used in following fiscal years for short-term capital items. School districts shall provide to the superintendent of public instruction an itemized accounting on forms provided by the department of education that details the expenditures of soft capital allocation monies at each school in the district. The superintendent of public instruction shall forward a copy of the report to the school facilities board established by § 15–2001.

F. A school district governing board may petition the state board of education for authority to budget and accumulate for school construction, building renovation or soft capital purposes a portion of the prior year's ending cash balance, not to exceed the amount of P.L. 81–874 monies which the school district was entitled to receive in the prior year, as computed by the superintendent of public instruction, if:

1. The governing board filed with the United States department of education division of impact aid an approved application for federal assistance for construction under P.L. 81–815 for the current or budget year and has been advised by the division of impact aid that no federal monies are available to fund its application.

2. The school district has a computed assessed valuation per pupil which is below the median amount computed by the superintendent of public instruction for all school districts.

3. The governing board has used any available revenues to reduce its primary tax rate to zero for any year in which it petitions to budget and

accumulate monies received under P.L. 81-874 for school construction purposes.

The state board of education may grant approval to a school district governing board to annually budget in the unrestricted capital outlay section of the budget a portion of the cash balance, not to exceed the amount of P.L. 81-874 monies which the school district was entitled to receive in the prior year as computed by the superintendent of public instruction.

G. The state board of education shall not include in the aggregate expenditures of local revenues as determined in § 15-911 the amount of revenues collected pursuant to the soft capital allocation limit. The amount of revenues collected for the soft capital allocation limit is the capital levy as authorized by law.

Added by Laws 1981, Ch. 1, § 2, eff. Jan. 23, 1981. Amended by Laws 1981, Ch. 29, § 1; Laws 1981, Ch. 128, § 2; Laws 1983, Ch. 39, § 1, eff. April 6, 1983; Laws 1984, Ch. 349, § 10; Laws 1985, Ch. 166, § 28, eff. April 18, 1985; Laws 1985, Ch. 285, § 1; Laws 1986, Ch. 125, § 9, eff. April 18, 1986; Laws 1986, Ch. 296, § 3; Laws 1988, Ch. 80, § 1; Laws 1988, Ch. 281, § 8; Laws 1989, Ch. 24, § 1; Laws 1990, Ch. 143, § 3, eff. April 26, 1990; Laws 1990, Ch. 348, § 13, eff. June 26, 1990; Laws 1991, Ch. 292, § 11, eff. June 28, 1991, retroactively effective to March 1, 1989; Laws 1992, Ch. 288, § 10, eff. Sept. 30, 1992, retroactively effective to July 1, 1992; Laws 1993, Ch. 189, § 14; Laws 1994, Ch. 361, § 5; Laws 1995, Ch. 191, § 16, eff. April 19, 1995; Laws 1995, Ch. 196, § 14; Laws 1996, Ch. 62, § 4; Laws 1998, 5th S.S., Ch. 1, § 25, eff. July 9, 1998; Laws 1999, Ch. 299, § 23.

Historical and Statutory Notes

Source:

Laws 1912, Ch. 77, § 41.
Civ.Code 1913, § 2733.
Laws 1921, Ch. 72, § 5.
Laws 1921, Ch. 137, § 1.
Laws 1925, Ch. 11, § 1.
Laws 1925, Ch. 70, §§ 1 to 4.
Laws 1927, Ch. 88, § 1.
Rev.Code 1928, § 1011.
Laws 1933, Ch. 18, § 1.
Laws 1949, Ch. 110, § 1.
Laws 1951, Ch. 140, § 1.
Laws 1952, Ch. 138, § 1.
Code 1939, Supp.1952, § 54-416.
Laws 1954, Ch. 117, § 2.
A.R.S. former §§ 15-445, 15-1202.06.
Laws 1958, Ch. 29, § 1.
Laws 1960, Ch. 127, § 32.
Laws 1967, 3rd S.S., Ch. 19, § 2.
Laws 1970, Ch. 165, § 8.
Laws 1974, 1st S.S., Ch. 3, § 9.
Laws 1974, 1st S.S., Ch. 3, § 23.
Laws 1975, Ch. 94, § 1.
Laws 1975, Ch. 125, § 1.
Laws 1977, Ch. 129, § 1.
Laws 1978, Ch. 74, § 1.
Laws 1978, Ch. 188, § 7.
Laws 1980, 2nd S.S., Ch. 9, § 20.

Laws 1986, Ch. 125, § 13, effective April 18, 1986, provides:

"**Sec. 13. Plan for the use of the reserve of the capital outlay fund**

"The plan for the use of the reserve of the capital outlay fund required in § 15-962, Arizona Revised Statutes, as amended by this act, is the major capital items plan required in § 15-962, Arizona Revised Statutes, as amended by Laws 1985, chapter 285, § 1, and the capital levy plan required in § 15-962, Arizona Revised Statutes, as amended by Laws 1984, chapter 349, § 10."

The 1990 amendment of this section by Ch. 348 explicitly amended the 1990 amendment of this section by Ch. 143.

Laws 1991, Ch. 292, § 29, effective June 28, 1991, provides:

"**Sec. 29. Retroactivity**

"Section 15-962, Arizona Revised Statutes, as amended by this act, is effective retroactively to March 1, 1989."

The purported amendment of this section by Laws 1992, Ch. 172, § 27, was repealed by Laws 1992, Ch. 288, § 11, eff. Sept. 30, 1992, retroactively effective to July 1, 1992, prior to taking effect.

Laws 1993, 2nd S.S., Ch. 8, § 8, provides:

"Sec. 8. **Fiscal year 1993-1994 capital levy revenue limit**

"**A.** Notwithstanding § 15-962, Arizona Revised Statutes, the capital levy revenue limit per student count for fiscal year 1993-1994 is the amount prescribed by § 15-962, Arizona Revised Statutes, reduced by fifteen dollars.

"**B.** If by January 1, 1993 the governing board of a school district has entered into a lease-purchase agreement or otherwise contractually obligated the expenditure of anticipated capital levy revenue limit monies for fiscal year 1993-1994, and if the amount so obligated in fiscal year 1993-1994 is in excess of the total of the district's capital levy revenue limit and capital outlay revenue limit for fiscal year 1993-1994, the governing board may budget for the excess amount for fiscal year 1993-1994. The excess amount shall not exceed the difference between the capital levy revenue limit computed pursuant to § 15-962, Arizona Revised Statutes, and the capital levy revenue limit computed pursuant to subsection A of this section. The excess amount shall be specifically exempt from the capital levy revenue limit as prescribed in § 15-947, Arizona Revised Statutes."

Laws 1993, Ch. 202, § 17, eff. April 21, 1993, provides:

"**Sec. 17. Capital outlay reserve for fiscal year 1993-1994**

"For the purpose of computing the maximum amounts that may be placed or accumulated in the reserve of the capital outlay fund as provided in § 15-962, subsection D, Arizona Revised Statutes, the capital outlay revenue limit for fiscal year 1993-1994 shall be considered to be the amount prescribed by § 15-962, Arizona Revised Statutes, before the subtraction of fifteen dollars as prescribed by Laws 1993, second special session, chapter 8, § 8."

For applicability provisions of Laws 1995, Ch. 196, see the Historical and Statutory Notes following § 1-254.

The amendment of this section by Laws 1995, Ch. 196, § 14, was repealed by Laws 1996, Ch. 62, § 5.

The amendment of this section by Laws 1995, Ch. 196, § 14, was repealed by Laws 1996, Ch. 248, § 10.

The 1996 amendment of this section by Ch. 62 explicitly amended the 1995 amendment of this section by Ch. 191.

The purported amendment of this section by Laws 1998, Ch. 164 failed to become effective because Chapter 164 was repealed in its entirety by Laws 1998, 5th S.S., Ch. 1, § 2, effective July 1, 1998.

The purported amendment of this section by Laws 1998, 3rd S.S., Ch. 1, failed to became effective because Ch. 1 was repealed in its entirety by Laws 1998, 5th S.S., Ch. 1, § 2, effective July 1, 1998.

Laws 1998, 5th S.S., Ch. 1, § 56, provides:

"**Sec. 56. Provisions for fiscal year 1998-1999**

"**A.** For fiscal year 1998-1999, the capital levy revenue limit per student count for fiscal year 1998-1999 is increased by $42.82 before the weights are applied pursuant to § 15-962, subsection A, Arizona Revised Statutes, as amended by Laws 1996, chapter 62, § 4. School districts may revise their budgets within sixty days of the effective date of this act to include the increase, but may only expend the additional monies for items included in § 15-962, subsection F, Arizona Revised Statutes, as amended by this act.

"**B.** For fiscal year 1998-1999, the charter school capital allocation pursuant to § 15-185.01, Arizona Revised Statutes, is increased by three hundred fifty dollars.

"**C.** For fiscal year 1998-1999, all restrictions on general obligation bonding as provided in this act apply to joint technological education districts."

Reviser's Notes:

1981 Note. Prior to the 1983 amendment, this section contained the amendments made by Laws 1981, Ch. 29, § 1 and Ch. 128, § 2 which were blended together pursuant to authority of § 41-1304.03.

1988 Note. Prior to the 1989 amendment, this section contained the amendments made by Laws 1988, Ch. 80, sec. 1 and Ch. 281, sec. 8 which were blended together pursuant to authority of § 41-1304.03.

1995 Note. The amendment made by Laws 1995, Ch. 196, sec. 14 was inconsistent and incompatible with Laws 1995, Ch. 191, sec. 16 and therefore could not be blended.

1999 Note. Pursuant to authority of § 41-1304.02, in the section heading "Capital levy revenue limit;" was removed.

§ 15-962.01. Capital outlay revenue limit and soft capital allocation for joint technological education districts; district soft capital allocation fund

A. The capital outlay revenue limit for a joint technological education district shall be the amount for students in grades nine through twelve for districts with a student count of six hundred or more as prescribed in § 15-961.

B. The soft capital allocation for a joint technological education district shall be the amount for students in grades nine through twelve for districts with a student count of six hundred or more as prescribed in § 15-962.

C. Joint technological education districts shall establish a district soft capital allocation fund and shall use the monies only for the purposes prescribed in § 15–962, subsection D. The ending unexpended budget balance in the district's soft capital allocation fund may be used in following fiscal years for short-term capital items. Districts shall provide to the superintendent of public instruction an itemized accounting on forms provided by the department of education that details the expenditures of soft capital allocation monies at each school in the joint technological education district. The superintendent of public instruction shall forward a copy of the report to the school facilities board established by § 15–2001.

Added by Laws 1990, Ch. 248, § 5, eff. Sept. 27, 1990, retroactively effective to July 15, 1990. Amended by Laws 1991, Ch. 154, § 10, eff. May 20, 1991; Laws 1998, 5th S.S., Ch. 1, § 26, eff. July 9, 1998; Laws 1999, Ch. 299, § 24.

Historical and Statutory Notes

The purported amendment of this section by Laws 1998, Ch. 164 failed to become effective because Chapter 164 was repealed in its entirety by Laws 1998, 5th S.S., Ch. 1, § 2, effective July 1, 1998.

The purported amendment of this section by Laws 1998, 3rd S.S., Ch. 1, failed to became effective because Ch. 1 was repealed in its entirety by Laws 1998, 5th S.S., Ch. 1, § 2, effective July 1, 1998.

Reviser's Notes:

1990 Note. Pursuant to authority of § 41–1304.02, in the section heading "and technical" was added after "vocational".

1998 Note. Pursuant to authority of § 41–1304.02, in the section heading "; district soft capital allocation fund" was added after "districts".

§ 15–963. Capital transportation adjustment for small school districts

A. A school district may apply to the state board of education for a capital transportation adjustment for the purchase of a transportation vehicle if the district meets all of the following requirements:

1. Has a student count of fewer than six hundred in kindergarten programs and grades one through twelve.

2. Transports as eligible students at least one-third of the total student count of the school district.

3. Has an approved daily route mileage per eligible student transported of more than 1.0, computed as prescribed in § 15–945, subsection A, paragraph 4.

B. If a school district receives a capital transportation adjustment as provided in this section, the soft capital allocation limit for that district shall be equal to the capital levy revenue limit or the soft capital allocation limit determined as prescribed in § 15–962 plus any additional amount approved by the state board of education.

C. The state board of education may grant a capital transportation adjustment to a school district which meets the qualifications prescribed in subsection A of this section, except that the total amount of all additional amounts approved as capital transportation adjustments for all school districts for a fiscal year shall not exceed twenty per cent of the total amount which a county may budget for that fiscal year in all small district service program funds as provided in § 15–365, subsection F.

Added by Laws 1985, Ch. 166, § 29, eff. April 18, 1985. Amended by Laws 1989, Ch. 206, § 2; Laws 1990, Ch. 348, § 14, eff. June 26, 1990; Laws 1998, 5th S.S., Ch. 1, § 27, eff. July 9, 1998; Laws 1999, Ch. 299, § 25.

Historical and Statutory Notes

The purported amendment of this section by Laws 1998, 3rd S.S., Ch. 1, failed to became effective because Ch. 1 was repealed in its entirety by Laws 1998, 5th S.S., Ch. 1, § 2, effective July 1, 1998.

Reviser's Notes:

1999 Note. Pursuant to authority of § 41-1304.02, in the section heading "Capital levy adjustment and" was removed.

§ 15-964. Federal impact adjustment

A. The governing board of a school district may compute a federal impact adjustment to the unrestricted capital budget limit. The maximum amount of the federal impact adjustment is the sum of the following:

1. Twenty-five per cent of the monies received from forest reserve funds by the school district in the prior fiscal year as provided in § 41-736.

2. For a school district that is not an accommodation school, the lesser of:

(a) Twenty-five per cent of the P.L. 81-874 revenues received in the prior fiscal year.

(b) The total amount of P.L. 81-874 revenues received in the prior fiscal year minus the sum of the following:

(i) The amount of P.L. 81-874 assistance used to increase the general budget limit as provided in § 15-905, subsections K and O for the prior fiscal year.

(ii) The amount budgeted for P.L. 81-874 administrative costs as provided in § 15-905, subsection P for the current year.

(iii) The amount budgeted for principal and interest on impact aid revenue bonds pursuant to § 15-2104 for the current year.

B. The federal impact adjustment shall only be budgeted and expended for new construction, major renovation of buildings or soft capital.

C. The governing board may not compute a federal impact adjustment for any year in which it budgets as provided in § 15-962, subsection F.

D. If the governing board underestimated the amount of the federal impact adjustment for the current year, the board may adjust the unrestricted capital budget limit and the budget before May 15. If the board overestimated the amount of the federal impact adjustment for the current year, the board shall adjust the unrestricted capital budget limit and the budget before May 15. Not later than May 18, the budget as revised shall be submitted electronically to the superintendent of public instruction.

Added by Laws 1990, Ch. 143, § 4, eff. April 26, 1990. Amended by Laws 1991, Ch. 292, § 12, eff. June 28, 1991; Laws 1996, 5th S.S., Ch. 8, § 9; Laws 1998, 5th S.S., Ch. 1, § 28, eff. July 9, 1998; Laws 1999, Ch. 299, § 26; Laws 2000, Ch. 342, § 22; Laws 2001, Ch. 228, § 2.

Historical and Statutory Notes

The purported amendment of this section by Laws 1998, Ch. 164 failed to become effective because Chapter 164 was repealed in its entirety by Laws 1998, 5th S.S., Ch. 1, § 2, effective July 1, 1998.

The purported amendment of this section by Laws 1998, 3rd S.S., Ch. 1, failed to became effective because Ch. 1 was repealed in its entirety by Laws 1998, 5th S.S., Ch. 1, § 2, effective July 1, 1998.

Reviser's Notes:

1999 Note. Pursuant to authority of § 41-1304.02, in the section heading "Federal impact capital levy adjustment;" was removed.

§ 15-965. Schools; impact aid; teacher housing

Notwithstanding any other law, a school district that receives federal impact aid may use those monies for maintenance and renovation of teacher housing and may transfer those monies into the teacherage account.

Added as Laws 2004, Ch. 209, § 1. Redesignated as § 15-965.

Historical and Statutory Notes

Reviser's Notes:

2004 Note. Pursuant to authority of § 41-1304.02, this section, enacted as § 1 of Laws 2004, Ch. 209, was added to Arizona Revised Statutes as § 15-965.

ARTICLE 5. STATE AND LOCAL ASSISTANCE TO SCHOOL DISTRICTS AND ACCOMMODATION SCHOOLS

§ 15-971. Determination of equalization assistance payments from county and state funds for school districts

A. Equalization assistance for education is computed by determining the total of the following:

1. The lesser of a school district's revenue control limit or district support level as determined in § 15-947 or 15-951.

2. The capital outlay revenue limit of a school district as determined in § 15-951 or 15-961.

3. The soft capital allocation of a school district as determined in § 15-951 or 15-962.

B. From the total of the amounts determined in subsection A of this section subtract:

1. The amount that would be produced by levying the applicable qualifying tax rate determined pursuant to § 41-1276 for a high school district or a common school district within a high school district which does not offer instruction in high school subjects as provided in § 15-447.

2. The amount that would be produced by levying the applicable qualifying tax rate determined pursuant to § 41-1276 for a unified school district, a common school district not within a high school district or a common school district within a high school district which offers instruction in high school subjects as provided in § 15-447. The qualifying tax rate shall be applied in the following manner:

(a) For the purposes of the amount determined in subsection A, paragraph 1 of this section:

(i) Determine separately the percentage that the weighted student count in preschool programs for children with disabilities, kindergarten programs and grades one through eight and the weighted student count in grades nine through twelve is to the weighted student count determined in subtotal A as provided in § 15–943, paragraph 2, subdivision (a).

(ii) Apply the percentages determined in item (i) of this subdivision to the amount determined in subsection A, paragraph 1 of this section.

(b) For the purposes of the amounts determined in subsection A, paragraphs 2 and 3 of this section determine separately the amount of the capital outlay revenue limit and the amount of the soft capital allocation attributable to the student count in preschool programs for children with disabilities, kindergarten programs and grades one through eight and grades nine through twelve.

(c) From the amounts determined in subdivisions (a) and (b) of this paragraph subtract the levy which would be produced by the current qualifying tax rate for a high school district or a common school district within a high school district that does not offer instruction in high school subjects as provided in § 15–447. If the qualifying tax rate generates a levy which is in excess of the total determined in subsection A of this section, the school district shall not be eligible for equalization assistance. In this subsection "assessed valuation" includes the values used to determine voluntary contributions collected pursuant to title 9, chapter 4, article 3 [1] and title 48, chapter 1, article 8. [2]

3. The amount that would be produced by levying a qualifying tax rate in a joint vocational and technological education district, which shall be five cents per one hundred dollars assessed valuation unless the legislature sets a lower rate by law.

4. The amount of government property lease excise tax monies that were distributed to the district pursuant to § 42–6205 during the preceding fiscal year.

C. County aid for equalization assistance for education shall be computed as follows:

1. Determine the total equalization assistance for all school districts in the county as provided in subsections A and B of this section.

2. Determine the total amount of county aid collected for all school districts in the county as provided in § 15–994.

3. Divide the amount determined in paragraph 2 of this subsection by the amount determined in paragraph 1 of this subsection.

4. Multiply the amount determined in subsections A and B of this section by the quotient determined in paragraph 3 of this subsection for each school district.

5. The amount determined in paragraph 4 of this subsection shall be the county aid for equalization assistance for education for a school district.

D. State aid for equalization assistance for education for a school district shall be computed as follows:

1. Determine the equalization assistance for education for a school district as provided in subsections A and B of this section.

2. For each county, determine the levy that would be produced by the tax rate for equalization assistance for education prescribed in § 15–994, subsection A.

3. For each county, determine the total amount to be paid from monies collected from the tax levy for equalization assistance for education into the small district service program fund as prescribed by § 15-365 and into the detention center education fund as prescribed by § 15-913.

4. Subtract the amount determined in paragraph 3 of this subsection from the amount determined in paragraph 2 of this subsection.

5. Prorate the amount determined in paragraph 4 of this subsection to each school district in the county as prescribed by subsection C of this section.

6. Subtract the amount determined in paragraph 5 of this subsection from the amount determined in paragraph 1 of this subsection.

E. Equalization assistance for education shall be paid from appropriations for that purpose to the school districts as provided in § 15-973.

F. A school district shall report expenditures on approved career and technical education and vocational education programs in the annual financial report according to uniform guidelines prescribed by the uniform system of financial records and in order to facilitate compliance with §§ 15-255 and 15-904.

G. The additional weight for state aid purposes given to special education as provided in § 15-943 shall be given to school districts only if special education programs comply with the provisions of chapter 7, article 4 of this title [3] and the conditions and standards prescribed by the superintendent of public instruction pursuant to rules of the state board of education for pupil identification and placement pursuant to §§ 15-766 and 15-767.

H. In addition to general fund appropriations, all amounts received pursuant to § 37-521, subsection B, paragraph 3 and § 42-5029, subsection E, paragraph 5 and from any other source for the purposes of this section are appropriated for state aid to schools as provided in this section.

I. The total amount of state monies that may be spent in any fiscal year for state equalization assistance shall not exceed the amount appropriated or authorized by § 35-173 for that purpose. This section shall not be construed to impose a duty on an officer, agent or employee of this state to discharge a responsibility or to create any right in a person or group if the discharge or right would require an expenditure of state monies in excess of the expenditure authorized by legislative appropriation for that specific purpose.

Added by Laws 1981, Ch. 1, § 2, eff. Jan. 23, 1981. Amended by Laws 1981, Ch. 291, § 1; Laws 1982, Ch. 164, § 1; Laws 1982, Ch. 198, § 7; Laws 1982, Ch. 332, § 15; Laws 1983, Ch. 62, § 1; Laws 1983, Ch. 325, § 11; Laws 1984, Ch. 379, § 15; Laws 1985, Ch. 166, § 30, eff. April 18, 1985; Laws 1985, Ch. 254, § 4, eff. April 29, 1985; Laws 1985, Ch. 347, § 6, eff. May 14, 1985; Laws 1985, Ch. 350, § 6; Laws 1988, Ch. 221, § 4, eff. June 14, 1988; Laws 1988, Ch. 271, § 2, eff. July 1, 1988; Laws 1988, Ch. 281, § 9; Laws 1990, Ch. 248, § 6, eff. Sept. 27, 1990, retroactively effective to July 15, 1990; Laws 1990, Ch. 330, § 9; Laws 1991, Ch. 154, § 11, eff. May 20, 1991; Laws 1991, Ch. 212, § 5; Laws 1991, Ch. 218, § 12, eff. June 10, 1991; Laws 1991, Ch. 288, § 4, eff. Sept. 21, 1991, retroactively effective to July 1, 1991; Laws 1992, Ch. 288, § 12, eff. Sept. 30, 1992, retroactively effective to July 1, 1992; Laws 1992, Ch. 319, § 15, eff. Sept. 30, 1992, retroactively effective to July 1, 1991; Laws 1994, Ch. 266, § 2; Laws 1995, Ch. 196, § 15; Laws 1995, Ch. 268, § 50; Laws 1996, Ch. 349, § 2; Laws 1996, 7th S.S., Ch. 2, § 1; Laws 1997, Ch. 231, § 23; Laws 1998, Ch. 1, § 50, eff. Jan. 1,

1999; Laws 1998, Ch. 153, § 1, eff. Jan. 1, 1999; Laws 1998, 5th S.S., Ch. 1, § 29, eff. July 9, 1998; Laws 1999, Ch. 299, § 27; Laws 2000, Ch. 187, § 2; Laws 2000, Ch. 236, § 24, eff. April 12, 2000; Laws 2000, 5th S.S., Ch. 1, § 15; Laws 2002, Ch. 89, § 28.

[1] Section 9–431 et seq.

[2] Section 48–241 et seq.

[3] Section 15–761 et seq.

Retroactive Application

This section, as amended by Laws 1996, 7th Special Session, Ch. 2, applies retroactively to tax years beginning January 1, 1996.

Historical and Statutory Notes

Source:

Laws 1967, 3rd S.S., Ch. 19, § 17.
A.R.S. former §§ 15–1202.10, 15–1228, 15–1228.01, 15–1603.
Laws 1970, Ch. 165, § 7.
Laws 1974, 1st S.S., Ch. 3, § 38.
Laws 1976, Ch. 66, § 4.
Laws 1980, 2nd S.S., Ch. 9, § 62.

Laws 1985, Ch. 350, § 1, paragraph 3 provides:

"3. Section 15–971, Arizona Revised Statutes, was amended by Laws 1985, chapter 166, § 30 and chapter 254, § 4. The chapter 254 version failed to set forth in full the text of § 15–971 as amended by Laws 1985, chapter 166, § 30 (an emergency act) as is required by Constitution of Arizona article IV, part 2, § 14. In order to accomplish the intent of the 1985 enactments, in this enactment the chapter 166 version is amended to incorporate the amendments made by the chapter 254 version and the chapter 254 version is repealed."

This section, as amended by Laws 1985, Ch. 254, § 4, was repealed by Laws 1985, Ch. 350, § 7.

The 1988 amendment of this section by Ch. 281 explicitly amended the 1988 amendment of this section by Ch. 221.

Laws 1988, Ch. 271, § 36, eff. July 1, 1988, provides:

"**Sec. 36. Additional state aid to education**

"**A.** Notwithstanding § 15–971, Arizona Revised Statutes, and in addition to the provisions of § 15–972, Arizona Revised Statutes, there may be additional state aid for education for the benefit of school districts in which voluntary contributions, pursuant to title 48, chapter 1, article 8, Arizona Revised Statutes, are made which additional state aid shall be computed as provided in subsection B of this section.

"**B.** The clerk of the board of supervisors shall compute each year an amount for additional state aid for education under this section as follows:

"1. Determine the tax rate for primary property taxes for each school district which would be levied without inclusion of voluntary contributions pursuant to title 48, chapter 1, article 8, Arizona Revised Statutes.

"2. Determine the tax rate for primary property taxes for each school district which would be levied with inclusion of voluntary contributions collected pursuant to title 48, chapter 1, article 8, Arizona Revised Statutes.

"3. Subtract the rate determined pursuant to paragraph 1 of this subsection from the rate determined pursuant to paragraph 2 of this subsection.

"4. The maximum tax rate increase for class five property in the district determined in § 42–227, Arizona Revised Statutes, shall be fifty cents per one hundred dollars of assessed valuation in 1988. Each year after 1988 the maximum tax rate increase is the prior year's maximum tax rate increase plus fifty cents per one hundred dollars of assessed valuation.

"5. Subtract the maximum tax rate increase determined pursuant to paragraph 4 of this subsection from the result determined pursuant to paragraph 3 of this subsection. If the result is less than zero, the result shall be zero.

"6. Multiply the result determined in paragraph 5 of this subsection as a rate per one hundred dollars assessed valuation by the assessed valuation used for primary property taxes of the class five property in the district, as determined in § 42–227, Arizona Revised Statutes.

"**C.** The board of supervisors shall reduce the property tax rate or rates that would be levied under §§ 15–971 and 15–972, Arizona Revised Statutes, as amended by this act, by the school district or districts on the assessed valuation used for primary property taxes of the class five property in the school district or districts, as determined in § 42–227, Arizona Revised Statutes, by the rate determined in subsection B, paragraph 5 of this section.

"**D.** The clerk of the board of supervisors shall report to the department of revenue not later than September 5 of each year the amount, by school district, of additional state aid for education and the data used for computing the amount as provided in this section.

"E. The department of revenue shall report to the state board of education not later than October 12 of each year the amount by school district of additional state aid for education as provided in this section. The additional state aid for education provided in this section shall be apportioned as provided in § 15-973, Arizona Revised Statutes, except that payments for additional state aid for education for unsecured property shall be paid on the fifteenth day of the month based on claims submitted by the department of revenue. The department of revenue shall submit claims for unsecured property before the first day of each month for which payments are requested."

Laws 1990, Ch. 248, § 9, provides:

"**Sec. 9. Determination of qualifying tax rate**

"Notwithstanding § 15-971, Arizona Revised Statutes, as amended by this act, for fiscal year 1991-1992, the qualifying tax rate in a vocational and technical education district shall be three cents per one hundred dollars assessed valuation."

Laws 1990, Ch. 319, § 17, as amended by Laws 1992, Ch. 158, § 2, provides:

"**Sec. 17. Department of education; technical assistance**

"A. Notwithstanding § 15-971, Arizona Revised Statutes, for fiscal years 1990-1991 and 1991-1992, districts which have been authorized to budget for a career ladder program pursuant to Laws 1986, chapter 364, as amended by Laws 1988, chapter 124, shall have their apportionment of state aid decreased by an amount equal to 0.000375 multiplied by their base support level.

"B. Of the monies appropriated from the state general fund to the state board of education and the superintendent of public instruction for basic state aid for fiscal year 1990-1991 and 1991-1992, an amount equal to the decrease prescribed in subsection A of this section shall be used by the department of education to hire personnel and for other costs associated with providing technical assistance to the state board of education, the state career ladder advisory committee and school districts for matters relating to the implementation, operation and monitoring of career ladder programs.

"C. For fiscal year 1992-1993 and thereafter, the department of education shall regularly submit, as part of its budget request, any item or items sufficient to cover expenses of providing career ladder program technical assistance to the state board, the career ladder advisory committee and school districts.

"D. For fiscal year 1992-1993 and each year thereafter, school districts which have career ladder programs shall have their apportionment of state aid decreased by the amount provided in subsection A of this section to be used for the purposes provided in subsection B of this section if monies sufficient to cover expenses of providing career ladder program technical assistance to the state board, the state career ladder advisory committee and school districts are not specifically appropriated for that fiscal year to the state board of education and superintendent of public instruction, except that:

"1. The state board of education may reduce the amount multiplied by the base support level as provided in subsection A of this section.

"2. A school district's apportionment of state aid shall not be decreased unless the district's funding level is at least a two and one half per cent increase in the base level."

For conditional enactment provision of Laws 1991, Ch. 212, and occurrence of the condition, see Historical and Statutory Notes preceding § 9-431.

The 1991 amendment of this section by Ch. 218 explicitly amended the 1991 amendment of this section by Ch. 154.

Amendment of this section by Laws 1991, Ch. 212, § 5, was repealed by Laws 1992, Ch. 288, § 13, eff. Sept. 30, 1992, retroactively effective to July 1, 1992, and by Laws 1992, Ch. 319, § 16, eff. Sept. 30, 1992, retroactively effective to July 1, 1991.

The 1991 amendment of this section by Ch. 288 explicitly amended the 1991 amendment of this section by Ch. 218.

The 1992 amendment of this section by Ch. 288 explicitly amended the 1991 amendment of this section by Ch. 288.

The 1992 amendment of this section by Ch. 319 explicitly amended the 1991 amendment of this section by Ch. 288.

Laws 1992, Ch. 319, § 1, par. 10, provides:

"**Section 1. Purpose**"

"10. Section 15-971, Arizona Revised Statutes, was amended by Laws 1991, chapter 154, § 11 and Laws 1991, chapter 212, § 5. The chapter 212 version failed to amend the chapter 154 version, which was an emergency enactment, and therefore did not comply with article IV, part 2, § 14, Constitution of Arizona. Two subsequent amendments to the section by Laws 1991, chapter 218, § 12 and Laws 1991, chapter 288, § 4 amended § 15-971, Arizona Revised Statutes, in the manner required by the constitution. To accomplish the intent of these enactments, in this act the Laws 1991, chapter 288 version of § 15-971, Arizona Revised Statutes, is amended to incorporate the amendments made by Laws 1991, chapter 212 and the chapter 212 version is repealed."

Laws 1995, Ch. 234, § 5, provides:

"**Sec. 5. Tuition for pupils residing in unorganized territory**

"Notwithstanding any other law, for fiscal years 1995-1996 and 1996-1997, tuition for pupils who are residents of this state and who reside in unorganized territory shall be paid from state school monies. The amount of tuition shall not include the portion of the total equalization base as determined in § 15-971, subsection A, Arizona Revised Statutes, for such pupils. The enrollment of such pupils in a school district shall be included in determining the apportionment of the state aid for that school district."

For applicability provisions of Laws 1995, Ch. 196, see the Historical and Statutory Notes following § 1-254.

Laws 1996, 7th S.S., Ch. 2, § 16, subsec. A, provides:

"**Sec. 16. Retroactivity**

"**A.** Sections 1, 2, 3, 5 through 8, 10, 12 and 15 apply retroactively to tax years beginning from and after December 31, 1995."

Laws 1997, Ch. 231, § 35, provides:

"**Sec. 35. Charter school enrollment calculation**

"**A.** For a common school district within a high school district which chartered and operated a high school in fiscal year 1996-1997, enrollment of pupils in grades nine through twelve shall be deemed to be enrollment in high school. For purposes of computing the base support level, the support level weight for high schools shall be used.

"**B.** Equalization assistance shall be calculated as prescribed in § 15-971, Arizona Revised Statutes, as amended by this act, for a common school district within a high school district which offers instruction in high school subjects as provided in § 15-447, Arizona Revised Statutes. The common school district within a high school district which chartered and operated a high school in 1996-1997 may use cash reserves up to the amount of the school district's budget capacity to fund the operation of the charter school for 1996-1997."

The 1998 amendment of this section by Ch. 153, § 1, explicitly amended the amendment of this section by Laws 1998, Ch. 1, § 50.

Laws 1998, Ch. 153, § 5, provides:

"**Sec. 5. Effective date**

"This act is effective from and after December 31, 1998."

The purported amendment of this section by Laws 1998, Ch. 164 failed to become effective because Chapter 164 was repealed in its entirety by Laws 1998, 5th S.S., Ch. 1, § 2, effective July 1, 1998.

The purported amendment of this section by Laws 1998, 3rd S.S., Ch. 1, failed to became effective because Ch. 1 was repealed in its entirety by Laws 1998, 5th S.S., Ch. 1, § 2, effective July 1, 1998.

The 2000 amendment of this section by 5th S.S., Ch. 1 explicitly amended the amendment of this section by Laws 2000, Ch. 236, § 24.

Laws 2000, 5th S.S. Ch. 1, § 65, provides:

"**Sec. 65. Conforming legislation; blending**

"**A.** The legislative council staff shall prepare proposed legislation conforming the Arizona Revised Statutes to the provisions of this act for consideration in the forty-fifth legislature, first regular session.

"**B.** The executive director of the legislative council is authorized to blend the nonconflicting changes made to the Arizona Revised Statutes during the forty-fourth legislature, second regular session, with the changes made to those same statutes by this act."

Reviser's Notes:

1982 Note. Prior to the 1983 amendments, this section contained the amendments made by Laws 1982, Ch. 164, § 1, Ch. 198, § 7 and Ch. 332, § 15 which were blended together pursuant to authority of § 41-1304.03.

1983 Note. Prior to the 1984 amendment, this section contained the amendments made by Laws 1983, Ch. 62, § 1 and Ch. 325, § 11 which were blended together pursuant to authority of § 41-1304.03.

1985 Note. Prior to the 1988 amendments, this section contained the amendments made by Laws 1985, Ch. 347, § 6 and Ch. 350, § 6 which were blended together pursuant to authority of § 41-1304.03.

1988 Note. Prior to the 1990 amendment, this section contained the amendments made by Laws 1988, Ch. 271, sec. 2 and Ch. 281, sec. 9 which were blended together pursuant to authority of § 41-1304.03.

1990 Note. Prior to the 1991 amendments, this section contained the amendments made by Laws 1990, Ch. 248, § 6 and Ch. 330, § 9 which were blended together pursuant to authority of § 41-1304.03.

1991 Note. The amendment of this section by Laws 1991, Ch. 212, sec. 5 failed to set forth in full the text of the section as amended by Laws 1991, Ch. 154, an emergency act, as required by Constitution of Arizona Art. IV, part 2, sec. 14.

1992 Note. Prior to the 1994 amendment, this section contained the amendments made by Laws 1992, Ch. 288, sec. 12 and Ch. 319, sec. 15 that were blended together pursuant to authority of § 41-1304.03.

1995 Note. Prior to the 1996 amendments, this section contained the amendments made by

Laws 1995, Ch. 196, sec. 15 and Ch. 268, sec. 50 that were blended together pursuant to authority of § 41–1304.03.

1998 Note. Prior to the 1999 amendment, this section contained the amendments made by Laws 1998, Second Regular Session, Ch. 153, sec. 1 and Laws 1998, Fifth Special Session, Ch. 1. sec. 29 that were blended together pursuant to authority of § 41–1304.03.

2000 Note. Prior to the 2002 amendment, this section contained the amendments made by Laws 2000, Ch. 187, sec. 2 and Laws 2000, 5th S.S., Ch. 1, sec. 15, that were blended together pursuant to authority of § 41–1304.03.

§ 15–972. State limitation on homeowner property taxes; additional state aid to school districts; definition

A. Notwithstanding § 15–971, there shall be additional state aid for education computed for school districts as provided in subsection B of this section.

B. The clerk of the board of supervisors shall compute such additional state aid for education as follows:

1. For a high school district or for a common school district within a high school district which does not offer instruction in high school subjects as provided in § 15–447:

(a) Determine the tax rate for primary property taxes for the school district which would be levied in lieu of the provisions of this section.

(b) Determine thirty-five per cent of the tax rate determined in subdivision (a) of this paragraph.

(c) Select the lesser of the amount determined in subdivision (b) of this paragraph or the current qualifying tax rate for the district.

(d) Multiply the rate selected in subdivision (c) of this paragraph as a rate per one hundred dollars assessed valuation by the assessed valuation used for primary property taxes of the residential property in the school district.

2. For a unified school district, for a common school district not within a high school district or for a common school district which offers instruction in high school subjects as provided in § 15–447:

(a) Determine the tax rate for primary property taxes for the school district which would be levied in lieu of the provisions of this section.

(b) Determine thirty-five per cent of the tax rate determined in subdivision (a) of this paragraph.

(c) Select the lesser of the amount determined in subdivision (b) of this paragraph or the current qualifying tax rate for the district.

(d) Multiply the rate selected in subdivision (c) of this paragraph as a rate per one hundred dollars assessed valuation by the assessed valuation used for primary property taxes of the residential property in the district.

C. The clerk of the board of supervisors shall report to the department of revenue not later than the Friday following the third Monday in August of each year the amount by school district of additional state aid for education and the data used for computing the amount as provided in subsection B of this section. The department of revenue shall verify all of the amounts and report to the county board of supervisors not later than August 30 of each year the property tax rate or rates which shall be used for property tax reduction as provided in subsection E of this section.

D. The board of supervisors shall reduce the property tax rate or rates that would be levied in lieu of the provisions of this section by the school district or districts on the assessed valuation used for primary property taxes of the residential property in the school district or districts by the rate or rates selected in subsection B, paragraph 1, subdivision (c) and paragraph 2, subdivision (c) of this section. The reduction in property taxes on a parcel of property resulting from the reduction in the property tax rate pursuant to this subsection shall not exceed five hundred dollars except as provided in subsection I of this section. The excess of the reduction in property taxes for a parcel of property resulting from the reduction in the property tax rate pursuant to this subsection over five hundred dollars shall be deducted from the amount of additional state aid for education.

E. Prior to the levying of taxes for school purposes the board of supervisors shall determine whether the total primary property taxes to be levied for all taxing jurisdictions on each parcel of residential property, in lieu of the provisions of this subsection, violate article IX, section 18, Constitution of Arizona. For those properties that qualify for property tax exemptions pursuant to article IX, §§ 2, 2.1 and 2.2, Constitution of Arizona, eligibility for the credit is determined on the basis of the limited property value that corresponds to the taxable assessed value after reduction for the applicable exemption. If the board of supervisors determines that such a situation exists, the board shall apply a credit against the primary property taxes due from each such parcel in the amount in excess of article IX, § 18, Constitution of Arizona. Such excess amounts shall also be additional state aid for education for the school district or districts in which such parcel of property is located.

F. The clerk of the board of supervisors shall report to the department of revenue not later than September 5 of each year the amount by school district of additional state aid for education and the data used for computing the amount as provided in subsection B of this section. The department of revenue shall verify all of the amounts and report to the board of supervisors not later than September 10 of each year the property tax rate which shall be used for property tax reduction as provided in subsection E of this section.

G. The clerk of the board of supervisors shall report to the department of revenue not later than September 30 of each year in writing the following:

1. The data processing specifications used in the calculations provided for in subsections B and E of this section.

2. At a minimum, copies of two actual tax bills for residential property for each distinct tax area.

H. The department of revenue shall report to the state board of education not later than October 12 of each year the amount by school district of additional state aid for education as provided in this section. The additional state aid for education provided in this section shall be apportioned as provided in § 15-973, except that payments for additional state aid for education for unsecured property shall be paid on the fifteenth day of the month based on claims submitted by the department of revenue. The department of revenue shall submit claims for unsecured property before the first day of each month for which payments are requested.

I. If a parcel of property is owned by a cooperative apartment corporation or is owned by the tenants of a cooperative apartment corporation as tenants in common, the reduction in the property taxes prescribed in subsection D of this section shall not exceed five hundred dollars for each owner occupied housing unit on the property. The assessed value used for determining the reduction in taxes for the property is equal to the total assessed value of the property times the ratio of the number of owner occupied housing units to the total number of housing units on the property. As used in this subsection, "cooperative apartment corporation" means a corporation:

1. Having only one class of outstanding stock.

2. All of the stockholders of which are entitled, solely by reason of their ownership of stock in the corporation, to occupy for dwelling purposes apartments in a building owned or leased by such corporation and who are not entitled, either conditionally or unconditionally, except upon a complete or partial liquidation of the corporation, to receive any distribution not out of earnings and profits of the corporation.

3. Eighty per cent or more of the gross income of which is derived from tenant-stockholders. For purposes of this paragraph, "gross income" means gross income as defined by the United States internal revenue code, as defined in § 43–105.

J. The total amount of state monies that may be spent in any fiscal year for state aid for education in this section shall not exceed the amount appropriated or authorized by § 35–173 for that purpose. This section shall not be construed to impose a duty on an officer, agent or employee of this state to discharge a responsibility or to create any right in a person or group if the discharge or right would require an expenditure of state monies in excess of the expenditure authorized by legislative appropriation for that specific purpose.

K. For purposes of this section, "residential property" means residential property as defined in article IX, § 18, subsection (1), Constitution of Arizona, except that it does not mean leased or rented property that is listed as class four pursuant to § 42–12004.

Added by Laws 1981, Ch. 1, § 2, eff. Jan. 23, 1981. Amended by Laws 1981, Ch. 291, § 2; Laws 1981, Ch. 317, § 5; Laws 1982, Ch. 164, § 2; Laws 1983, Ch. 62, § 2; Laws 1985, Ch. 166, § 31, eff. April 18, 1985; Laws 1987, Ch. 188, § 3; Laws 1988, Ch. 271, § 3, eff. July 1, 1988; Laws 1989, Ch. 111, § 1; Laws 1990, 3rd S.S., Ch. 3, § 3; Laws 1991, Ch. 182, § 3, eff. June 3, 1991; Laws 1994, Ch. 41, § 3; Laws 1995, Ch. 196, § 16; Laws 1997, Ch. 14, § 1; Laws, 1998, Ch. 1, § 52, eff. Jan. 1, 1999; Laws 1998, Ch. 153, § 2, eff. Jan. 1, 1999; Laws 1999, Ch. 344, § 3.

Historical and Statutory Notes

Source:

Laws 1980, 2nd S.S., Ch. 9, § 62.
A.R.S. former § 15–1202.11.

Laws 1988, Ch. 271, § 44, provides:

"**Sec. 44. Retroactivity**

"Sections 3, 4, 25 through 35, 38 and 39 of this act apply retroactively to taxable years beginning from and after December 31, 1987."

Laws 1989, Ch. 111, § 2 provides:

"**Sec. 2. Retroactivity**

"This act applies retroactively to taxable years beginning from and after December 31, 1987."

Laws 1990, 3rd S.S., Ch. 3, § 62, subsec. B, provides:

"**Sec. 62. Effective dates**

"**B.** Sections 1, 3, 4, 8, 15, 16, 19 through 35, 37 through 46, 49 through 52, 58 and 59 of this act apply retroactively to taxable years beginning from and after December 31, 1989."

Laws 1991, Ch. 182, effective June 3, 1991, § 1, provides:

"**Section 1. Intent**

"The purpose of this act, relating to §§ 2 through 5, are curative in nature and are intended to clarify statutory intent and ratify historical administrative interpretation, and does not provide for any substantive change in the law."

Laws 1991, Ch. 182, § 8, effective June 3, 1991, as amended by Laws 1991, Ch. 303, § 7, effective June 28, 1991, provides:

"**Sec. 8. Retroactivity**

"Sections 1 through 5 of this act apply retroactively to tax years beginning from and after December 31, 1985."

For applicability provisions of Laws 1995, Ch. 196, see the Historical and Statutory Notes following § 1-254.

The 1998 amendment of this section by Ch. 153, § 2, explicitly amended the amendment of this section by Laws 1998, Ch. 1, § 51.

Laws 1998, Ch. 153, § 5, provides:

"**Sec. 5. Effective date**

"This act is effective from and after December 31, 1998."

Reviser's Notes:

1981 Note. Prior to the 1982 amendment, this section contained the amendments made by Laws 1981, Ch. 291, § 2 and Ch. 317, § 5 which were blended together pursuant to authority of § 41-1304.03.

§ 15-973. Apportionment of funds; expenditure limitation

A. The state board of education shall apportion state aid from appropriations made for such purpose to the several counties on the basis of state aid entitlement for the school districts in each county. No allowance shall be made for nonresident alien children nor for wards of the United States for whom tuition is paid, but attendance of a student in a school of a county adjoining the county of his residence outside the state under a certificate of educational convenience as provided by § 15-825 shall be deemed to be enrollment in the school of the county or school district of his residence.

B. Apportionments shall be made as follows:

1. On July 15, one-twelfth of the total amount to be apportioned during the fiscal year.

2. On September 15, one-twelfth of the total amount to be apportioned during the fiscal year.

3. On October 15, one-twelfth of the total amount to be apportioned during the fiscal year.

4. On December 15, one-twelfth of the total amount to be apportioned during the fiscal year.

5. On January 15, one-twelfth of the total amount to be apportioned during the fiscal year.

6. On February 15, one-twelfth of the total amount to be apportioned during the fiscal year.

7. On March 15, one-twelfth of the total amount to be apportioned during the fiscal year.

8. On April 15, one-sixth of the total amount to be apportioned during the fiscal year.

9. On May 15, one-sixth of the total amount to be apportioned during the fiscal year.

10. On June 15, one-twelfth of the total amount to be apportioned during the fiscal year, except that if the total amount of monies available to make the payment is less than the amount of the payment, a portion of the June 15 payment may be delayed no later than June 30 to allow for the receipt of income from the permanent state common school fund.

The superintendent of public instruction shall furnish to the county treasurer and the county school superintendent an abstract of the apportionment and shall certify the apportionment to the department of administration, which shall draw its warrant in favor of the county treasurer of each county for the amount apportioned. Upon receipt of the warrant the county treasurer shall notify the county school superintendent of the amount, together with any other monies standing to the credit of such school district in the county school fund.

C. Notwithstanding the provisions of subsection B of this section, if sufficient appropriated funds are available and on a showing by a school district that additional state monies are necessary for current expenses, an apportionment or part of an apportionment of state aid may be paid to the school district prior to the date set for such apportionment by subsection B of this section. After the first forty days in session of the current year a school district may request additional state monies to fund the increased state aid due to anticipated student growth through the first one hundred days or two hundred days in session, as applicable, of the current year as provided in § 15–948. In no event shall a school district have received more than three-fourths of its total apportionment before April 15 of the fiscal year. Early payments pursuant to this subsection must be approved by the state treasurer, the director of the department of administration and the superintendent of public instruction. If the computation of state aid for an accommodation school is based on P.L. 81–874 monies to be received in the current year pursuant to § 15–974, subsection A, paragraph 2, the maximum early payment to an accommodation school shall be determined using an estimate of the P.L. 81–874 monies to be received during the fiscal year.

D. Until June 30, 1999, at such time and as provided by federal law or regulation, state aid shall be reduced as follows:

1. The superintendent of public instruction shall compute the amount of monies which each school district is eligible to receive under P.L. 81–874, less P.L. 81–874 monies for children with disabilities, children with specific learning disabilities and children residing on Indian lands which are in addition to the basic assistance as provided in 20 United States Code § 238(d)2(C) and (D), and for which monies have been appropriated.

2. The superintendent of public instruction shall deduct from state aid for each school district which is eligible to receive monies under P.L. 81–874 and for which monies are appropriated as provided in paragraph 1 of this subsection the lesser of:

(a) The maximum allowed by law or regulation.

(b) The amount computed as follows:

(i) For fiscal year 1982–1983, twenty-five per cent of the amount computed in paragraph 1 of this subsection.

(ii) For fiscal year 1983–1984, fifty per cent of the amount computed in paragraph 1 of this subsection.

(iii) For fiscal year 1984–1985, seventy-five per cent of the amount computed in paragraph 1 of this subsection.

(iv) Beginning with fiscal year 1985–1986, ninety-five per cent of the amount computed in paragraph 1 of this subsection.

3. The reduction in state aid shall be made from equalization assistance as prescribed in § 15–971 or from additional state aid as prescribed in § 15–972 during the fiscal year following the fiscal year in which the monies are received. The superintendent of public instruction shall make additional adjustments in state aid for allowable deductions which were not made in any previous fiscal year which is not more than five years earlier than the year in which the adjustments are made. The superintendent of public instruction shall give the school district prior notice of the intention to make the additional adjustments and may distribute the adjustments over more than one year after considering the effects of the adjustments on the school district.

E. The superintendent of public instruction shall not make application to the federal government to utilize P.L. 81–874 monies in determining the apportionment prescribed in this section.

F. If a school district which is eligible to receive monies pursuant to this article is unable to meet a scheduled payment on any lawfully incurred long-term obligation for debt service as provided in § 15–1022, the county treasurer shall use any amount distributed pursuant to this section to make the payment. The county treasurer shall keep a record of all the instances in which a payment is made pursuant to this subsection. Any monies subsequently collected by the district to make the scheduled payment shall be used to replace the amount diverted pursuant to this subsection. When determining the total amount to be funded by a levy of secondary taxes upon property within the school district for the following fiscal year, the county board of supervisors shall add to the amounts budgeted to be expended during the following fiscal year an amount equal to the total of all payments pursuant to this subsection during the current fiscal year which were not repaid during the current year.

G. The total amount of state monies that may be spent in any fiscal year by the state board of education for apportionment of state aid for education shall not exceed the amount appropriated or authorized by § 35–173 for that purpose. This section shall not be construed to impose a duty on an officer, agent or employee of this state to discharge a responsibility or to create any right in a person or group if the discharge or right would require an expenditure of state monies in excess of the expenditure authorized by legislative appropriation for that specific purpose.

Added by Laws 1981, Ch. 1, § 2, eff. Jan. 23, 1981. Amended by Laws 1982, Ch. 291, § 3, eff. May 3, 1982; Laws 1983, Ch. 98, § 16; Laws 1983, Ch. 220, § 2; Laws 1984, Ch. 340, § 4, eff. Aug. 3, 1984, retroactively effective to May 1, 1984; Laws 1985, Ch. 285, § 2; Laws 1988, Ch. 221, § 5, eff. June 14, 1988, retroactively effective to July 1, 1987; Laws 1989, Ch. 183, § 1; Laws 1990, Ch. 143, § 5, eff. April 26, 1990; Laws 1990, Ch. 399, § 10, eff. July 5, 1990; Laws 1991, Ch. 244, § 9, eff. June 17, 1991; Laws 1991, Ch. 288, § 5, eff. Sept. 21, 1991, retroactively effective to July 1, 1991; Laws 1992, Ch. 319, § 17, eff. Sept. 30, 1992, retroactively effective to July 1, 1991; Laws

1994, 9th S.S., Ch. 2, § 17, eff. July 1, 1995; Laws 1995, Ch. 196, § 17; Laws 1996, Ch. 316, § 3, eff. May 1, 1996; Laws 1996, 5th S.S., Ch. 8, § 10; Laws 1997, Ch. 231, § 24; Laws 1998, Ch. 167, § 12; Laws 1998, 5th S.S., Ch. 1, § 30, eff. July 9, 1998; Laws 1999, Ch. 299, § 28.

Historical and Statutory Notes

Source:

Laws 1912, Ch. 77, §§ 98, 99.
Civ.Code 1913, §§ 2815, 2816.
Laws 1915, 1st S.S., Ch. 3, § 51.
Laws 1917, Ch. 90, § 47.
Laws 1919, Ch. 30, § 1.
Laws 1921, Ch. 158, § 1.
Laws 1922, Ch. 35, §§ 130, 131.
Rev.Code 1928, §§ 1088, 1089.
Laws 1933, Ch. 65, §§ 7, 8.
Laws 1935, Ch. 106, § 1.
Laws 1941, Ch. 79, § 3.
Laws 1947, Ch. 85, §§ 1, 2.
Laws 1949, Ch. 12, § 1.
Code 1939, Supp.1952, §§ 54-601, 54-601a, 54-602.
Laws 1955, Ch. 108, §§ 1, 2.
A.R.S. former §§ 15-1211, 15-1212, 15-1222, 15-1228.02.
Laws 1959, Ch. 90, §§ 1 to 3.
Laws 1960, Ch. 127, §§ 50, 51.
Laws 1961, Ch. 12, §§ 1, 2.
Laws 1965, 3rd S.S., Ch. 1, §§ 3, 6.
Laws 1967, 3rd S.S., Ch. 19, §§ 10, 11, 13, 17.
Laws 1968, Ch. 166, § 1.
Laws 1970, Ch. 11, § 1.
Laws 1971, Ch. 177, § 5.
Laws 1972, Ch. 115, § 6.
Laws 1973, Ch. 157, § 17.
Laws 1974, 1st S.S., Ch. 3, § 26.
Laws 1976, Ch. 66, § 1.
Laws 1976, Ch. 184, § 4.
Laws 1977, Ch. 20, § 4.
Laws 1978, Ch. 188, § 19.
Laws 1979, Ch. 184, § 2.
Laws 1980, 2nd S.S., Ch. 9, § 65.
Laws 1980, Ch. 167, § 6.

Laws 1988, Ch. 296, § 1 provides:

"**Section 1. Reduction in state aid apportionment for fiscal year 1988-1989; reimbursement**

"**A.** Notwithstanding any provision of law to the contrary, the state board of education shall reduce, on a pro rata basis, the June 15, 1989, apportionment of basic state aid and additional state aid required pursuant to § 15-973, subsection B, Arizona Revised Statutes, by a total of eighty million dollars.

"**B.** Notwithstanding any provision of law to the contrary, for fiscal year 1989-1990, if the governing board of a school district incurred interest expenses for registering warrants in fiscal year 1988-1989 due to the reduction provided by subsection A of this section, the governing board may budget for fiscal year 1989-1990 an amount for interest expenses equal to the amount of reimbursement to be received for such expenses from the state board of education and the superintendent of public instruction in fiscal year 1989-1990. Amounts received for such reimbursement are specifically exempt from the revenue control limit in fiscal year 1989-1990."

Laws 1989, Ch. 273, § 30 effective June 30, 1989, provides:

"**Sec. 30. Reduction in state aid apportionment for fiscal year 1989-1990; reimbursement**

"**A.** Notwithstanding any other law, the state board of education shall reduce, on a pro rata basis, the June 15, 1990 apportionment of basic state aid and additional state aid required pursuant to § 15-973, subsection B, Arizona Revised Statutes, by a total of one hundred million dollars. If the June 15, 1990 apportionment is estimated to be less than one hundred million dollars, the remaining portion of the reduction shall be taken from the May 15, 1990 apportionment of basic state aid and additional state aid.

"**B.** Notwithstanding any other law, if the governing board of a school district incurred interest expenses for registering warrants in fiscal year 1989-1990 due to the reduction prescribed in subsection A of this section, the governing board may budget for fiscal year 1990-1991 an amount for interest expenses equal to the amount of reimbursement to be received for these expenses from the state board of education and the superintendent of public instruction in fiscal year 1990-1991. Amounts received for the reimbursement are specifically exempt from the revenue control limit in fiscal year 1990-1991."

The 1990 amendment of this section by Ch. 399 explicitly amended the 1990 amendment of this section by Ch. 143.

Laws 1991, 1st S.S., Ch. 1, § 7, provides:

"**Sec. 7. Reduction in state aid apportionment for fiscal year 1990-1991; reimbursement**

"**A.** Notwithstanding any other law, the state board of education shall reduce, on a pro rata basis, the June 15, 1991 apportionment of basic state aid and additional state aid pursuant to § 15-973, subsection B, Arizona Revised Statutes, by a total of one hundred forty-two million five hundred thousand dollars. If the June 15, 1991 apportionment is estimated to be less than one hundred forty-two million five hundred thousand dollars, the remaining portion of the reduction shall be taken from the May 15, 1991 apportionment of basic state aid and additional state aid.

"**B.** Notwithstanding any other law, if the governing board of a school district incurred interest expenses for registering warrants in fiscal year 1990-1991 due to the reduction prescribed in subsection A of this section, the governing board may budget for fiscal year 1991-1992 an amount for interest expenses equal to the amount of reimbursement to be received for these expenses from the state board of education and the superintendent of public instruction in fiscal year 1991-1992. Amounts received for the reimbursement are specifically exempt from the revenue control limit in fiscal year 1991-1992."

Laws 1991, Ch. 288, § 18, effective Sept. 21, 1991, retroactively effective to July 1, 1991, provides:

"**Sec. 18. Reduction in state aid apportionment for fiscal year 1991-1992; reimbursement**

"**A.** Notwithstanding any other law, the state board of education shall reduce, on a pro rata basis, the May and June 1992 apportionments of basic state aid and additional state aid pursuant to § 15-973, subsection B, Arizona Revised Statutes, by a total of one hundred forty-two million five hundred thousand dollars.

"**B.** Notwithstanding any other law, if the governing board of a school district incurred interest expenses for registering warrants in fiscal year 1991-1992 due to the reduction prescribed in subsection A of this section, the governing board may budget for fiscal year 1992-1993 an amount for interest expenses equal to the amount of reimbursement to be received for these expenses from the state board of education and the superintendent of public instruction in fiscal year 1992-1993. Amounts received for the reimbursement are specifically exempt from the revenue control limit in fiscal year 1992-1993."

Laws 1992, Ch. 288, § 25, eff. Sept. 30, 1992, retroactively effective to July 1, 1992, provides:

"**Sec. 25. Reduction in state aid apportionment for fiscal year 1992-1993; reimbursement**

"**A.** Notwithstanding any other law, the state board of education shall reduce, on a pro rata basis, the May and June 1993 apportionments of basic state aid and additional state aid pursuant to § 15-973, subsection B, Arizona Revised Statutes, by a total of one hundred forty-two million five hundred thousand dollars.

"**B.** Notwithstanding any other law, if the governing board of a school district incurred interest expenses for registering warrants in fiscal year 1992-1993 due to the reduction prescribed in subsection A of this section, the governing board may budget for fiscal year 1993-1994 an amount for interest expenses equal to the amount of reimbursement to be received for these expenses from the state board of education and the superintendent of public instruction in fiscal year 1993-1994. Amounts received for the reimbursement are specifically exempt from the revenue control limit in fiscal year 1993-1994.

Laws 1992, Ch. 288, § 26, eff. Sept. 30, 1992, retroactively effective to July 1, 1992, as amended by Laws 1994, 9th S.S., Ch. 2, § 32, provides:

"**Sec. 26. Suspension of state aid reductions for fiscal years 1992-1993 and 1995-1996; condition**

"**A.** Notwithstanding the provisions of § 15-973, subsection D, Arizona Revised Statutes, for fiscal years 1992-1993 through 1995-1996 the superintendent of public instruction shall not reduce state aid as prescribed in § 15-973, subsection D, paragraph 2, Arizona Revised Statutes.

"**B.** Notwithstanding the provisions of § 15-973, subsection E, Arizona Revised Statutes, the superintendent of public instruction shall withdraw the fiscal year 1992-1993 application to the federal government for certification to make reductions and shall not make such application for fiscal years 1993-1994 through 1995-1996.

"**C.** The provisions of subsections A and B of this section do not become effective until federal legislation is enacted that provides that Arizona is deemed to have met the requirements of 20 United States Code § 240 (d)(2) for the purposes of receiving certification to take impact aid into consideration in determining state aid for fiscal years 1988-1989 through 1991-1992."

The 1992 amendment of this section by Ch. 319 explicitly amended the 1991 amendment of this section by Ch. 244.

The amendment of this section by Laws 1991, Ch. 288, § 5, effective September 21, 1991, retroactively effective to July 1, 1991, was repealed by Laws 1992, Ch. 319, § 18, effective September 30, 1992, retroactively effective to July 1, 1991.

Laws 1992, Ch. 319, § 1, par. 11, provides:

"**Section 1. Purpose**"

"11. Section 15-973, Arizona Revised Statutes, was amended by Laws 1991, chapter 244, § 9 and Laws 1991, chapter 288, § 5. The chapter 288 version failed to amend the chapter 244 version, which was an emergency enactment, and therefore did not comply with article IV, part 2, § 14, Constitution of Arizona. To accomplish the intent of these enactments, in this act the Laws 1991, chapter 244 version of § 15-973, Arizona Revised Statutes, is amended to incorporate the amendments made by Laws 1991, chapter 288 and the chapter 288 version is repealed."

Laws 1993, 2nd S.S., Ch. 8, § 10, provides:

"**Sec. 10. Reduction in state aid apportionment for fiscal year 1993-1994; reimbursement**

"**A.** Notwithstanding any other law, the state board of education shall reduce, on a pro rata basis, the May and June, 1994 apportionments of basic state aid and additional state aid pursuant to § 15-973, subsection B, Arizona Revised Statutes, by a total of $142,500,000.

"**B.** Notwithstanding any other law, if the governing board of a school district incurs interest expenses for registering warrants in fiscal year 1993-1994 due to the reduction prescribed in subsection A of this section, the governing board may budget for fiscal year 1994-1995 an amount for interest expenses equal to the amount of reimbursement to be received for these expenses from the state board of education and the superintendent of public instruction in fiscal year 1994-1995. Amounts received for the reimbursement are specifically exempt from the revenue control limit in fiscal year 1994-1995."

Laws 1994, 9th S.S., Ch. 2, § 35, as amended by Laws 1995, Ch. 1, § 10, effective February 20, 1995, provides:

"**Sec. 35. Delayed effective dates**

"Sections 15-821 and 15-973, Arizona Revised Statutes, as amended by this act, are effective from and after June 30, 1995."

For applicability provisions of Laws 1995, Ch. 196, see the Historical and Statutory Notes following § 1-254.

Laws 1996, Ch. 316, § 5, provides:

"**Sec. 5. Applicability**

"Sections 15-101, 15-973 and 15-974, Arizona Revised Statutes, as amended by this act, apply to fiscal year 1995-1996 and thereafter."

The purported amendment of this section by Laws 1998, 3rd S.S., Ch. 1, failed to became effective because Ch. 1 was repealed in its entirety by Laws 1998, 5th S.S., Ch. 1, § 2, effective July 1, 1998.

Laws 2003, Ch. 264, § 36, provides:

"**Sec. 36. Reduction in school district state aid apportionment; fiscal year 2003-2004**

"**A.** Notwithstanding § 15-973, subsection B, paragraph 10, Arizona Revised Statutes, the state board of education shall defer until July 1, 2004 $191,000,000 of the basic state aid and additional state aid payment that otherwise would be apportioned to school districts under that law on June 15, 2004.

"**B.** The funding deferral required by this section does not apply to charter schools."

Laws 2004, Ch. 278, § 11, provides:

"**Sec. 11. Reduction in school district state aid apportionment; fiscal year 2004-2005**

"**A.** Notwithstanding § 15-973, subsection B, paragraph 10, Arizona Revised Statutes, the state board of education shall defer until July 1, 2005 $191,000,000 of the basic state aid and additional state aid payment that otherwise would be apportioned to school districts under that law on June 15, 2005.

"**B.** The funding deferral required by this section does not apply to charter schools."

Laws 2004, Ch. 278, § 21, provides:

"**Sec. 21. Retroactivity**

"**A.** Except as provided in subsection B of this section, this act applies retroactively to from and after June 30, 2004.

"**B.** Laws 2002, chapter 330, § 49, as amended by this act, applies retroactively to from and after June 29, 2004."

Reviser's Notes:

1983 Note. Prior to the 1984 amendment, this section contained the amendments made by Laws 1983, Ch. 98, § 16 and Ch. 220, § 2 which were blended together pursuant to authority of § 41-1304.03. Additionally, pursuant to authority of § 41-1304.02, in subsection D, paragraph 7, "(B)" was substituted for "(b)" in two places as the correction of a manifest clerical error [subsequently amended].

1991 Note. The amendment of this section by Laws 1991, Ch. 288, sec. 5 failed to set forth in full the text of the section as amended by Laws 1991, Ch. 244, an emergency act, as required by Constitution of Arizona Art. IV, part 2, sec. 14.

1996 Note. Prior to the 1997 amendment, this section contained the amendments made by Laws 1996, 5th Spec. Sess., Ch. 8, sec. 10 and 2nd Reg. Sess., Ch. 316, sec. 3 that were blended together pursuant to authority of § 41-1304.03.

1998 Note. Prior to the 1999 amendment, this section contained the amendments made by Laws 1998, Second Regular Session, Ch. 167, sec. 12 and Laws 1998, Fifth Special Session, Ch. 1. sec. 30 that were blended together pursuant to authority of § 41-1304.03.

§ 15-973.01. Assistance for education fund

A. The assistance for education fund is established consisting of monies received pursuant to § 43-617.

B. The state board of education shall administer the fund. On notice from the state board, the state treasurer shall invest and divest monies in the fund as provided by § 35–313 and monies earned from investments shall be credited to the fund. Monies in the fund:

1. Are continuously appropriated to the state board of education.

2. Are exempt from the provisions of § 35–190, relating to lapsing of appropriations.

C. The state board of education shall distribute monies in the fund to school districts at the same time, in the same manner and in the same proportions as state aid from appropriations made pursuant to § 15–973.

D. Monies in the fund shall not be used to reduce the general fund requirement for state aid.

Added by Laws 1998, Ch. 286, § 2.

§ 15–974. Equalization assistance for education for accommodation schools; definition

A. Equalization assistance for education for accommodation schools shall be computed as follows:

1. Determine the total of the lesser of an accommodation school's revenue control limit or district support level as determined in § 15–947, an accommodation school's capital outlay revenue limit as determined in § 15–961 and an accommodation school's soft capital allocation as determined in § 15–962.

2. From the amount determined in paragraph 1 of this subsection subtract the monies received from P.L. 81–874 for the prior fiscal year if the amount to be received in the current fiscal year is equal to or greater than the amount received in the prior fiscal year. If the amount to be received during the current fiscal year is less than the amount received in the prior fiscal year, the subtraction shall be determined as follows:

(a) Subtract the amount to be received in the current fiscal year, adjusting the final payment to reflect actual receipts during the fiscal year.

(b) If additional P.L. 81–874 monies are received after the computation of the last payment of state aid but before the end of the fiscal year, the amount received late shall be subtracted from the equalization assistance for the following fiscal year, except that the total amount reduced pursuant to subdivision (a) of this paragraph and this subdivision shall not exceed the amount of P.L. 81–874 monies received in the prior year.

3. Equalization assistance for an accommodation school shall be the amount determined in paragraph 2 of this subsection.

B. Equalization assistance for education for accommodation schools shall be paid from appropriations for that purpose to the school districts as provided in § 15–973.

C. When an accommodation school has a positive total cash balance at the end of a fiscal year in its maintenance and operation fund, the county school superintendent of the county in which the accommodation school is located may authorize an addition to the accommodation school's revenue control limit as provided in § 15–947, subsection A for the following fiscal year. The county school superintendent may not authorize an addition that exceeds the lesser of the ending cash balance less the amount budgeted for the budget balance carryforward as provided in § 15–943.01 or ten per cent of the revenue control limit of the accommodation school. If an accommodation school has a cash balance in excess of the amount needed to fund the budget balance carryforward, the addition authorized pursuant to this subsection and the items listed in § 15–947, subsection C, paragraph 2, subdivisions (c) and (f) for the following fiscal year, the remaining cash balance shall be used to reduce the amount of state aid for equalization assistance for education for the accommodation school as provided in § 15–971, subsection D for the following year.

D. The provisions of subsection C of this section shall not apply to an accommodation school with a student count of one hundred twenty-five or less in kindergarten programs and grades one through eight or to an accommodation school which offers instruction in grades nine, ten, eleven or twelve and which has a student count of one hundred or less in grades nine through twelve.

E. For the purpose of this section, "monies received from P.L. 81–874" means total P.L. 81–874 monies less P.L. 81–874 monies for children with disabilities, children with specific learning disabilities and children residing on Indian lands which are in addition to the basic assistance as provided in 20 United States Code § 238, subsection (d), paragraph 2, clauses (C) and (D).

Added by Laws 1981, Ch. 1, § 2, eff. Jan. 23, 1981. Amended by Laws 1982, Ch. 198, § 8; Laws 1984, Ch. 327, § 2; Laws 1984, Ch. 340, § 5, eff. Aug. 3, 1984, retroactively effective to May 1, 1984; Laws 1985, Ch. 166, § 32, eff. April 18, 1985; Laws 1988, Ch. 288, § 9, eff. July 8, 1988; Laws 1989, Ch. 273, § 18, eff. June 26, 1989; Laws 1990, Ch. 348, § 15, eff. June 26, 1990; Laws 1996, Ch. 316, § 4, eff. May 1, 1996; Laws 1997, Ch. 231, § 25; Laws 1998, 5th S.S., Ch. 1, § 31, eff. July 9, 1998; Laws 1999, Ch. 299, § 29; Laws 2000, Ch. 236, § 25, eff. April 12, 2000; Laws 2002, Ch. 301, § 2, eff. May 23, 2002.

Retroactive Application

This section, as amended by Laws 2002, Ch. 301, applies retroactively to July 1, 2001.

Historical and Statutory Notes

Source:

Laws 1974, 1st S.S., Ch. 3, § 38.
A.R.S. former §§ 15–916, 15–1604.
Laws 1980, 2nd S.S., Ch. 9, § 36.

Laws 1996, Ch. 316, § 5, provides:

"**Sec. 5. Applicability**

"Sections 15–101, 15–973 and 15–974, Arizona Revised Statutes, as amended by this act, apply to fiscal year 1995–1996 and thereafter."

The purported amendment of this section by Laws 1998, Ch. 164 failed to become effective because Chapter 164 was repealed in its entirety by Laws 1998, 5th S.S., Ch. 1, § 2, effective July 1, 1998.

The purported amendment of this section by Laws 1998, 3rd S.S., Ch. 1, failed to became effective because Ch. 1 was repealed in its entirety by Laws 1998, 5th S.S., Ch. 1, § 2, effective July 1, 1998.

Laws 2002, Ch. 301, § 7, provides:

"**Sec. 7. Retroactivity**

"Sections 2 through 6 of this act apply retroactively to from and after June 30, 2001."

Reviser's Notes:

1984 Note. Prior to the 1985 amendment, this section contained the amendments made by Laws 1984, Ch. 327, § 2 and Ch. 340, § 5 which were blended together pursuant to authority of § 41–1304.03. Additionally, pursuant to authority of § 41–1304.02, in the section heading "; definition" was added and subsections B and C were transposed and relettered accordingly.

1989 Note. Pursuant to authority of § 41-1304.02, in subsection A, paragraph 1 the comma following "15-947" was added as a correction of a manifest clerical error.

§ 15-975. Method of determining funds payable to a joint common school district

In determining the amount of state, county and federal monies or school aid payable to a joint common school district, the portion of the territory of the joint common school district within each county shall be regarded as a separate school district lying within such county. Records of student count shall be kept as to make readily ascertainable the attendance of pupils residing in the portion of the school district in each county. The forms and reports required by law to be filed shall be appropriately filed. Student enrollment and attendance information required by this subsection shall be submitted electronically to the superintendent of public instruction in a format provided. For purposes of applying to a joint common school district the provisions of § 15-101, "assessed valuation" means the net valuation of the part of the school district in the county, and the part of the school district in each county shall be regarded as a school district employing five or more contract classroom teachers.
Added by Laws 1981, Ch. 1, § 2, eff. Jan. 23, 1981. Amended by Laws 1982, Ch. 197, § 6; Laws 2000, Ch. 342, § 23.

Historical and Statutory Notes

Source:

Laws 1970, Ch. 12, § 1.
A.R.S. former § 15-421.04.
Laws 1976, Ch. 162, § 13.
Laws 1980, 2nd S.S., Ch. 9, § 16.

§ 15-976. Assistance for school districts for children whose parents are employed by certain state institutions; expenditure limitation

A. The superintendent of public instruction shall assist school districts in educating children whose parents or legal guardians are employed by and domiciled at the following state institutions and stations: the state hospital, the Arizona state schools for the deaf and the blind, mental retardation centers, port of entry inspection stations and institutions and facilities maintained by the state department of corrections. The school enrollment is deemed for the purpose of determining student count to be enrollment in the school district of actual attendance. The assistance shall be by payment of tuition as follows:

1. For group B children with disabilities, as provided in § 15-825, subsection D.

2. For children other than group B children with disabilities, the costs per student count as prescribed in § 15-824, subsection G minus the amount generated by the equalization base as determined in § 15-971, subsection A for those pupils, except that in no case shall the tuition for any pupil exceed an amount equal to seven thousand dollars minus the amount generated by the equalization base as determined in § 15-971, subsection A.

B. Claims for such payments shall be made by the school districts through the county school superintendent to the superintendent of public instruction.

C. The total amount of state monies that may be spent in any fiscal year by the superintendent of public instruction pursuant to subsection A of this section shall not exceed the amount appropriated or authorized by § 35-173 for that purpose. This section shall not be construed to impose a duty on an officer, agent or employee of this state to discharge a responsibility or to create any right in a person or group if the discharge or right would require an expenditure of state monies in excess of the expenditure authorized by legislative appropriation for that specific purpose.

Added by Laws 1981, Ch. 1, § 2, eff. Jan. 23, 1981. Amended by Laws 1991, Ch. 288, § 6, eff. Sept. 21, 1991, retroactively effective to July 1, 1991; Laws 1995, Ch. 196, § 18; Laws 1996, Ch. 358, § 4; Laws 1999, Ch. 243, § 4.

Historical and Statutory Notes

Source:

Laws 1961, Ch. 111, § 1.
A.R.S. former § 15-1214.
Laws 1962, Ch. 19, § 1.
Laws 1968, Ch. 89, § 11.
Laws 1972, Ch. 97, § 1.
Laws 1973, Ch. 157, § 19.
Laws 1974, 1st S.S., Ch. 3, § 27.
Laws 1980, 2nd S.S., Ch. 9, § 66.

Laws 1991, Ch. 288, § 17, effective Sept. 21, 1991, retroactively effective to July 1, 1991, provides:

"**Sec. 17. Student count limitation; 1991-1992 determination**

"For the purposes of computing a base support level, capital outlay revenue limit and capital levy revenue limit, a district shall not include in its student count for fiscal year 1991-1992 pupils for whom the district received payment in fiscal year 1990-1991 pursuant to § 15-976, Arizona Revised Statutes, prior to amendment by this act. The provisions of § 15-942, Arizona Revised Statutes, do not apply to the reduction in student count prescribed by this section."

For applicability provisions of Laws 1995, Ch. 196, see the Historical and Statutory Notes following § 1-254.

Laws 1996, Ch. 358, § 6, provides:

"**Sec. 6. Retroactivity**

"Sections 1, 2, 3 and 4 of this act apply retroactively to July 1, 1995."

§ 15-977. Classroom site fund; definitions

A. The classroom site fund is established consisting of monies transferred to the fund pursuant to § 37-521, subsection B and § 42-5029, subsection E, paragraph 10. The department of education shall administer the fund. School districts and charter schools may not supplant existing school site funding with revenues from the fund. All monies distributed from the fund are intended for use at the school site. Each school district or charter school shall allocate forty per cent of the monies for teacher compensation increases based on performance and employment related expenses, twenty per cent of the monies for teacher base salary increases and employment related expenses and forty per cent of the monies for maintenance and operation purposes as prescribed in subsection C of this section. Teacher compensation increases based on performance or teacher base salary increases distributed pursuant to this subsection shall supplement, and not supplant, teacher compensation monies from any other sources. The school district or charter school shall notify each school principal of the amount available to the school by April 15. The district or charter school shall request from the school's principal each school's priority for the allocation of the funds available to the school for each program listed under subsection C of this section. The amount budgeted by the school district or charter school pursuant to this section shall not be included in the allowable budget balance carryforward calculated pursuant to § 15-943.01.

B. Monies in the fund are continuously appropriated, are exempt from the provisions of § 35-190 relating to lapsing of appropriations and shall be distributed as follows:

1. By March 30 of each year the staff of the joint legislative budget committee shall determine a per pupil amount from the fund for the budget year using the estimated statewide weighted count for the current year pursuant to § 15–943, paragraph 2, subdivision (a) and based on estimated available resources in the classroom site fund for the budget year.

2. The allocation to each charter school and school district for a fiscal year shall equal the per pupil amount established in paragraph 1 of this subsection for the fiscal year multiplied by the weighted student count for the school district or charter school for the fiscal year pursuant to § 15–943, paragraph 2, subdivision (a). For the purposes of this paragraph, the weighted student count for a school district that serves as the district of attendance for nonresident pupils shall be increased to include nonresident pupils who attend school in the school district.

C. Monies distributed from the classroom site fund shall be spent for the following maintenance and operation purposes:

1. Class size reduction.
2. Teacher compensation increases.
3. AIMS intervention programs.
4. Teacher development.
5. Dropout prevention programs.
6. Teacher liability insurance premiums.

D. The district governing board or charter school shall allocate the classroom site fund monies to include, wherever possible, the priorities identified by the principals of the schools while assuring that the funds maximize classroom opportunities and conform to the authorized expenditures identified in subsection A of this section.

E. School districts and charter schools that receive monies from the classroom site fund shall submit a report by November 15 of each year to the superintendent of public instruction on a per school basis that provides an accounting of the expenditures of monies distributed from the fund during the previous fiscal year and a summary of the results of district and school programs funded with monies distributed from the fund. The department of education in conjunction with the auditor general shall prescribe the format of the report under this subsection.

F. School districts and charter schools that receive monies from the classroom site fund shall receive these monies monthly in an amount not to exceed one-twelfth of the monies estimated pursuant to subsection B of this section, except that if there are insufficient monies in the fund that month to make payments, the distribution for that month shall be prorated for each school district or charter school. The department of education may make an additional payment in the current month for any prior month or months in which school districts or charter schools received a prorated payment if there are sufficient monies in the fund that month for the additional payments. The state is not required to make payments to a school district or charter school classroom site fund if the state classroom site fund revenue collections are insufficient to meet the estimated allocations to school districts and charter schools pursuant to subsection B of this section.

G. The state education system for committed youth shall receive monies from the classroom site fund in the same manner as school districts and charter schools. The Arizona state schools for the deaf and the blind shall receive monies from the classroom site fund in an amount that corresponds to the weighted student count for the current year pursuant to § 15–943, paragraph 2, subdivision (b) for each pupil enrolled in the Arizona state schools for the deaf and the blind. Except as otherwise provided in this subsection, the Arizona state schools for the deaf and the blind and the state education system for committed youth are subject to this section in the same manner as school districts and charter schools.

H. Each school district and charter school, including school districts that unify pursuant to § 15–448 or consolidate pursuant to § 15–459, shall establish a local level classroom site fund to receive allocations from the state level classroom site fund. The local level classroom site fund shall be a budgetary controlled account. Interest charges for any registered warrants for the local level classroom site fund shall be a charge against the local level classroom site fund. Interest earned on monies in the local level classroom site fund shall be added to the local level classroom site fund as provided in § 15–978. In no event shall this state be required to make payments to a school district or charter school local level classroom site fund that are in addition to monies transferred to the state level classroom site fund pursuant to § 37–521, subsection B and § 42–5029, subsection E, paragraph 10.

I. Monies distributed from the classroom site fund for class size reduction, AIMS intervention and dropout prevention programs shall only be used for instructional purposes in the instruction function as defined in the uniform system of financial records except that monies shall not be used for school sponsored athletics.

J. For the purposes of this section:

1. "AIMS intervention" means summer programs, after school programs, before school programs or tutoring programs that are specifically designed to ensure that pupils meet the Arizona academic standards as measured by the Arizona instrument to measure standards test prescribed by § 15–741.

2. "Class size reduction" means any maintenance and operations expenditure that is designed to reduce the ratio of pupils to classroom teachers, including the use of persons who serve as aides to classroom teachers.

Added by Laws 2000, 5th S.S., Ch. 1, § 16. Amended by Laws 2001, Ch. 379, § 2; Laws 2001, 2nd S.S., Ch. 6, § 1, eff. Dec. 19, 2001; Laws 2002, Ch. 301, § 3, eff. May 23, 2002; Laws 2003, Ch. 138, § 1; Laws 2004, Ch. 341, § 6.

Retroactive Application

This section, as amended by Laws 2002, Ch. 301, applies retroactively to July 1, 2001.

Historical and Statutory Notes

Laws 1993, Ch. 202, § 18, eff. April 21, 1993, provides:

"**Sec. 18. Repayment of housing facilities funds**

"The governing board of a school district which has received a loan pursuant to Laws 1986, chapter 403, or Laws 1990, third special session, chapter 1, prior to the repeal of § 15-977, Arizona Revised Statutes, shall continue to repay the loan received pursuant to this section."

Laws 2000, 5th S.S., Ch. 1, §§ 66 and 67, provide:

"**Sec. 66. Delayed implementation**

"This act shall not be implemented until from and after May 31, 2001.

"**Sec. 67. Conditional enactment**

"This act does not become effective unless the qualified electors of this state in the general election that will be held in November, 2000 approve an increase in state transaction privilege tax rates of six-tenths of one per cent in order to fund the provisions of this act." [See note, post.]

Proposition 301, approved by the electors at the Nov. 7, 2000 general election, effective Nov. 27, 2000, included a provision increasing the state transaction privilege tax rate six-tenths of one per cent. Therefore, the conditions of the 5th S.S. Ch. 1 were met, and the act became effective.

Laws 2001, 2nd S.S., Ch. 6, § 13, provides:

"**Sec. 13. Retroactivity**

"Section 15-977, Arizona Revised Statutes, as amended by this act, applies retroactively to May 31, 2001."

Laws 2002, Ch. 301, § 7, provides:

"**Sec. 7. Retroactivity**

"Sections 2 through 6 of this act apply retroactively to from and after June 30, 2001."

Former § 15-977, added by Laws 1986, Ch. 403, § 1, relating to housing facilities funds, was repealed by Laws 1986, Ch. 403, § 4, eff. Jan. 1, 1992.

§ 15-978. Classroom site fund budget limit; school district

The classroom site fund budget limit for each school district is the sum of the following:

1. The allocation that is computed for the school district pursuant to § 15-977, subsection B, paragraph 2.

2. The unexpended budget balance from the classroom site fund for the prior fiscal year.

3. The net interest earned on monies in the classroom site fund during the prior fiscal year.

Added by Laws 2002, Ch. 301, § 4, eff. May 23, 2002.

Retroactive Application

This section, as added by Laws 2002, Ch. 301, applies retroactively to July 1, 2001.

Historical and Statutory Notes

Laws 2002, Ch. 301, § 7, provides:

"**Sec. 7. Retroactivity**

"Sections 2 through 6 of this act apply retroactively to from and after June 30, 2001."

Another § 15-978 was renumbered as § 15-979.

§ 15-979. Instructional improvement fund

A. The instructional improvement fund is established consisting of monies deposited pursuant to §§ 5-601.02(H)(3)(a)(i) and 5-601.02(H)(3)(b)(i), and interest earned on those monies. The department of education shall administer the fund. The fund is not subject to appropriation, and expenditures from the fund are not subject to outside approval notwithstanding any statutory provision to the contrary.

B. Monies received pursuant to § 5-601.02 shall be deposited directly with the instructional improvement fund. On notice from the department of education, the state treasurer shall invest and divest monies in the fund as provided by § 35-313, and monies earned from investment shall be credited to the fund. No monies in the instructional improvement fund shall revert to or be deposited in any other fund, including the state general fund. Monies in the instructional improvement fund are exempt from the provisions of § 35-190 relating to the lapsing of appropriations. Monies provided from the instructional improvement fund shall supplement, not supplant, existing state and local monies.

C. The department of education shall pay the monies in the fund to school districts and charter schools. The department of education shall determine the amount of monies from the fund to be paid to each school district and charter school as follows:

1. Determine the student count for each school district and charter school as provided in § 15-943.

2. Determine the student count for all school districts and charter schools as provided in § 15-943.

3. Divide the amount determined in paragraph 1 of this subsection by the total amount determined in paragraph 2 of this subsection.

4. Multiply the quotient determined in paragraph 3 of this subsection by the total amount of instructional improvement fund monies available to be distributed to school districts and charter schools under this section.

D. Each school district and charter school may utilize up to fifty percent of the amount of monies determined pursuant to subsection C for teacher compensation increases and class size reduction as provided in § 15-977.

E. Monies that are not utilized as provided in subsection D shall be utilized for the following maintenance and operation purposes:

1. Dropout prevention programs.

2. Instructional improvement programs including programs to develop minimum reading skills for students by the end of third grade.

F. School districts and charter schools that receive monies from the instructional improvement fund shall submit a report by November 15 of each year to the department of education that provides an accounting of the expenditure of monies distributed from the fund during the previous fiscal year. The department of education in conjunction with the auditor general shall prescribe the format of the report under this subsection.

Added as § 15-978 by Initiative Measure, Proposition 202, approved election Nov. 5, 2002, eff. Nov. 25, 2002. Renumbered as § 15-979 by Laws 2003, Ch. 176, § 2.

Historical and Statutory Notes

Proposition 202, based on an initiative measure, proposing amendments to Arizona Revised Statutes by addition of §§ 5-601.02, 15-978, 17-299, 36-2903.07, 41-1505.12, by amendment of §§ 13-3301, 41-2306 (as amended by Laws 2000, Ch. 375, § 3), and by repeal of §§ 5-601.01 and 41-2306 (as amended by Laws 2000, Ch. 372, § 3) relating to tribal-state compacts, was approved by the electors at the November 5, 2002 general election as proclaimed by the governor on November 25, 2002.

Laws 2003, Ch. 176, § 1, par. 1, provides:

"**Section 1. Purpose**

"Pursuant to § 41-1304.01, paragraph 2, Arizona Revised Statutes, the purpose of this act is to renumber statutes added by ballot propositions in the 2002 general election that were also added by the legislature in 2002 and to combine legislative amendments to statutes enacted in 2001 and 2002 with amendments to the same statutes enacted by ballot propositions in the 2002 general election as follows:

"1. Section 15-978, Arizona Revised Statutes, was added by Laws 2002, chapter 301, § 4 and by 2002 Proposition 202, § 6. The version added by Laws 2002, chapter 301 relates the classroom site fund budget limit and the version added by 2002 Proposition 202 relates to the instructional improvement fund. In order to resolve these conflicting multiple enactments, this act renumbers § 15-978, Arizona Revised Statutes, as added by 2002 Proposition 202, § 6, as § 15-979."

§ 15-980. Uncollected property tax; supplemental state aid

A. If a county treasurer certifies to a school district after January 1 that, in the treasurer's reasonable belief, more than twenty per cent of the primary property tax revenues that the school district is entitled by law to receive pursuant to § 42-18052 will not be remitted to the district due to property tax delinquencies, the district is eligible for supplemental state aid pursuant to this section.

B. On receiving a certificate pursuant to subsection A of this section, the school district may apply to the department of education for supplemental state aid. The application shall include the county treasurer's certified estimate of the total amount of uncollected primary property taxes for the school district for the tax year payable in the current fiscal year.

C. Within forty-five days after receiving a complete and correct application, the state board of education shall pay to the school district from amounts appropriated for state aid the amount determined in subsection B of this section. The department of education shall notify the county treasurer and the county school superintendent of the amount and the date of the payment of the supplemental state aid. Supplemental state aid paid under this section shall be excluded from the calculation made pursuant to § 15-973, subsection C.

D. The superintendent of a school district that receives supplemental state aid shall report to the department of education between May 5 and May 25 the actual amount of primary property taxes that were not collected and remitted to the district during the current fiscal year, based on information from the county treasurer. If the amount of supplemental state aid paid pursuant to subsection C of this section exceeds the actual amount of the uncollected primary property taxes that the district is entitled to receive, the state board of education shall deduct the difference between the amount of supplemental state aid paid and the amount of the uncollected primary property taxes from the June 15 and, if necessary, subsequent apportionments of state aid pursuant to § 15-973, subsection B.

E. Beginning on June 1 after the payment of supplemental state aid, the county school superintendent shall report quarterly to the department of education the amount of any payments of delinquent primary property taxes received by the district during the previous quarter with respect to a tax year for which the supplemental state aid was paid and not previously deducted from state aid pursuant to subsection D of this section. The department shall deduct the amount reported from the next apportionment of state aid to the district pursuant to § 15-973, subsection B until the supplemental state aid is repaid. If the district does not receive any apportionment pursuant to § 15-973, subsection B, the department shall direct the school district superintendent to pay that amount to the state treasurer for deposit in the state general fund.

Added by Laws 2004, Ch. 278, § 5. Amended by Laws 2004, Ch. 341, § 7.

Historical and Statutory Notes

Laws 2004, Ch. 278, § 21, provides:

"**Sec. 21. Retroactivity**

"**A.** Except as provided in subsection B of this section, this act applies retroactively to from and after June 30, 2004.

"**B.** Laws 2002, chapter 330, § 49, as amended by this act, applies retroactively to from and after June 29, 2004."

Laws 2004, Ch. 341, § 13, subsec. A, provides:

"**Sec. 13. Conditional enactment**

"**A.** Section 15-980, Arizona Revised Statutes, as amended by this act, is not effective unless § 15-980, Arizona Revised Statutes, as added by senate bill 1405, § 5, forty-sixth legislature, second regular session, and as transmitted to the governor becomes law." [S.B. 1405 was approved by Governor and became Laws 2004, Ch. 278.]

ARTICLE 6. COUNTY FINANCE RESPONSIBILITIES FOR SCHOOL DISTRICTS

§ 15-991. Annual estimate by county school superintendent of monies for ensuing year

A. The county school superintendent, not later than August 1 each year, shall file in writing with the governing board of each school district in the county and the board of supervisors the superintendent's estimate of the amount of school monies required by each school district for the ensuing year, based on the budgets adopted by the governing boards of the school districts. The estimate shall contain:

1. A statement of the student count of each school district.

2. The total amount to be received for the year by each school district from the county school fund and the special county school reserve fund.

3. The ending cash balance from the previous year for each school district.

4. The anticipated interest earnings for each school district.

5. Revenues equal to the amount included in the adopted budget for the maintenance and operation section of the budget permitted by § 15-947, subsection C, paragraph 2, subdivision (a), items (ii), (iii), (iv), (v) and (vi) and subdivision (d). The county school superintendent shall estimate the additional amounts needed for each school district from the primary property tax and the secondary property tax and shall certify such amounts to the board of supervisors in writing at the time of filing the estimate. When estimating the additional amount needed from the primary property tax for a school district that is not eligible for any equalization assistance as provided in § 15-971, the county school superintendent shall include the school district governing board's estimate of the increase in the revenue control limit as prescribed by § 15-948 for the applicable year, except that the percentage increase in average daily membership used to compute the estimated increase in the revenue control

limit may not exceed the average of the percentage increase in average daily membership in the three years before the year for which the estimate is made.

B. The county school superintendent shall recompute equalization assistance for education for each school district as provided in § 15–971, subsection A using the property values provided by the county assessor as provided in § 42–17052. The county school superintendent shall certify in writing the amount of equalization assistance for education and the amount needed for each school district from the primary property tax to the board of supervisors on or before the third day prior to the day the board of supervisors is required to levy school district taxes as provided in § 15–992.

C. The county school superintendent shall compute the additional amount to be levied as provided in § 15–992, subsection B, using the property values provided in § 42–17052. The county school superintendent shall certify in writing the additional amount to be levied to the county board of supervisors on or before the third day prior to the day the board of supervisors is required to levy school district taxes as provided in § 15–992.

D. On or before September 1, the governing board of a school district shall file with the county school superintendent an estimate of the amount of P.L. 81–874 monies which it is eligible to receive during the current year. On or before June 1, the governing board shall file with the county school superintendent and the superintendent of public instruction a statement of the actual amount of P.L. 81–874 monies it received during the current year. This subsection does not apply to accommodation schools.

E. The department may collect any other similar or related information from school districts that the department may determine is necessary to carry out the purposes of this section.

Added by Laws 1981, Ch. 1, § 2, eff. Jan. 23, 1981. Amended by Laws 1983, Ch. 214, § 1; Laws 1984, Ch. 233, § 2; Laws 1985, Ch. 166, § 33, eff. April 18, 1985; Laws 1985, Ch. 273, § 2, eff. May 1, 1985; Laws 1990, Ch. 348, § 16, eff. June 26, 1990; Laws 1990, Ch. 399, § 11, eff. July 5, 1990; Laws 1991, Ch. 244, § 10, eff. June 17, 1991; Laws 1992, Ch. 288, § 14, eff. Sept. 30, 1992, retroactively effective to July 1, 1992; Laws 1996, 5th S.S., Ch. 8, § 11; Laws 1998, Ch. 1, § 52, eff. Jan. 1, 1999; Laws 1998, Ch. 63, § 5; Laws 1999, Ch. 211, § 15; Laws 2000, Ch. 342, § 24; Laws 2003, Ch. 141, § 1; Laws 2004, Ch. 340, § 5.

Historical and Statutory Notes

Source:

Laws 1912, Ch. 77, § 101.
Civ.Code 1913, § 2818.
Laws 1917, Ch. 45, § 1.
Laws 1921, Ch. 158, § 1.
Rev.Code 1928, § 1091.
Laws 1933, Ch. 65, § 11.
Laws 1941, Ch. 79, § 6.
Laws 1947, Ch. 85, § 4.
Code 1939, Supp.1952, § 54–605.
Laws 1955, Ch. 108, § 4.
A.R.S. former § 15–1233.
Laws 1974, 1st S.S., Ch. 3, § 28.
Laws 1977, Ch. 152, § 7.
Laws 1980, 2nd S.S., Ch. 9, § 67.
Laws 1980, Ch. 167, § 7.

The amendment of this section by Laws 1990, Ch. 399, § 11 was repealed by Laws 1991, Ch. 244, § 11, effective June 17, 1991.

The 1991 amendment of this section by Ch. 244, explicitly amended the 1990 amendment of this section by Ch. 348.

The 1998 amendment of this section by Ch. 63 explicitly amended the amendment of this section by Laws 1998, Ch. 1, § 52.

The amendment of this section by Laws 1998, Ch. 63, § 5 was repealed by Laws 1999, Ch. 211, § 16.

The 1999 amendment of this section by Ch. 211 explicitly amended the amendment of this section by Laws 1998, Ch. 1, § 52.

Laws 1999, Ch. 211, § 1, par. 8, provides:

"**Section 1. Purpose**"

"8. Section 15-991, Arizona Revised Statutes, was amended by Laws 1998, chapter 1, § 52 and Laws 1998, chapter 63, § 5. Chapter 63 amended the chapter 1 version. However, the chapter 1 version was not effective until January 1, 1999 and the chapter 63 version had an effective date of August 21, 1998. In order to correct a potentially defective enactment, this act amends the Laws 1998, chapter 1 version of section 15-991, Arizona Revised Statutes, to incorporate the amendments made by Laws 1998, chapter 63 and the chapter 63 version is repealed."

Reviser's Notes:

1990 Note. The amendment of this section by Laws 1990, Ch. 399, § 11 failed to set forth in full the text of the section as amended by Laws 1990, Ch. 348, an emergency act, as required by Constitution of Arizona Art. IV, part 2, § 14.

1998 Note. Laws 1998, Ch. 63, sec. 5 amended this section with an effective date of August 21, 1998. This section, as amended by Laws 1998, Ch. 1, sec. 52, is effective on January 1, 1999.

§ 15-991.01. Tax levy for property not located in a school district

A. The board of supervisors of each county, at the time of levying other taxes, shall annually levy a tax on property not located in a school district. The tax levy shall be at a rate equal to one-half the qualifying tax rate prescribed in § 15-971, subsection B, paragraph 2, per one hundred dollars of assessed valuation used for primary property taxes. The tax shall be levied and collected in the same manner as general county taxes on the property. The tax levy provided for in this section is not subject to title 42, chapter 17, articles 2 and 3.[1] The monies received pursuant to this section shall be transmitted by the county treasurer to the state treasurer to be deposited in the state general fund to aid in school financial assistance.

B. The reduction in taxes prescribed in § 15-972 applies to taxes levied pursuant to this section on residential property, except that the state shall not make the payments prescribed in § 15-972, subsection H for this reduction in taxes.

Added by Laws 1989, Ch. 312, § 2. Amended by Laws 1991, Ch. 182, § 4, eff. June 3, 1991; Laws 1998, Ch. 1, § 53, eff. Jan. 1, 1999; Laws 1998, Ch. 52, § 5, eff. Jan. 1, 1999.

[1] Sections 42-17051 et seq., 42-17101 et seq.

Historical and Statutory Notes

Laws 1989, Ch. 312, § 25, subsec. B provides:

"**Sec. 25. Retroactivity**

"**B.** Sections 1, 2, 3, 18 and 19 of this act apply retroactively to from and after June 30, 1989."

Laws 1989, Ch. 312, § 26, provides:

"**Sec. 26. Conditional enactment**"

"This act does not become effective unless Senate Bill 1129 [Laws 1989, Ch. 310], relating to retirement, and Senate Bill 1140 [Laws 1989, Ch. 311], relating to general appropriations, thirty-ninth legislature, first regular session, are enacted into law."

For retroactive application provisions of Laws 1991, Ch. 182, as amended by Laws 1991, Ch. 303, see Historical and Statutory Notes following § 15-972.

The 1998 amendment of this section by Ch. 52, § 5, explicitly amended the amendment of this section by Laws 1998, Ch. 1, § 53.

Laws 1998, Ch. 52, § 74, as amended by Laws 1998, Ch. 113, § 68, provides:

"**Sec. 74. Effective date**

"Sections 9-432, 15-393, 15-991.01, 15-1021, 27-234, 42-5008, 42-5404, 42-11109, 42-12159, 42-13001, 42-14357, 42-15064, 42-16214, 42-17251, 42-17254, 42-17256, 48-574, 48-614, 48-616 and 48-807, Arizona Revised Statutes, as amended by this act, are effective from and after December 31, 1998."

Laws 1998, Ch. 113, § 1, par. 40, provides:

"**Section 1. Purpose**"

"40. Sections 9-432, 15-393, 15-991.01, 15-1021 and 27-234, Arizona Revised Statutes, were amended by Laws 1998, chapter 1 with a delayed effective date of January 1, 1999. The Laws 1998, chapter 1 versions of these sections were subsequently amended by Laws 1998, chapter 52 with a general effective date. In order to correct a potentially defective enactment, this act amends Laws 1998, chapter 52, § 74 that prescribes an effective date of January 1, 1999 for other sections in the act to include §§ 9-432, 15-393, 15-991.01, 15-1021 and 27-234, Arizona Revised Statutes."

Former § 15-991.01, added by Laws 1988, Ch. 271, § 4, and relating to similar subject matter, was repealed by Laws 1989, Ch. 312, § 1.

§ 15-991.02. Repealed by Laws 1998, 5th S.S., Ch. 1, § 32, eff. July 9, 1998

Historical and Statutory Notes

The purported repeal of this section by Laws 1998, 3rd S.S., Ch. 1, failed to became effective because Ch. 1 was repealed in its entirety by Laws 1998, 5th S.S., Ch. 1, § 2, effective July 1, 1998.

The repealed section, added by Laws 1992, Ch. 288, § 15, related to the equalization assistance account.

§ 15-992. School district tax levy; additional tax in districts ineligible for equalization assistance; definition

A. The board of supervisors of each county shall annually, at the time of levying other taxes, levy school district taxes on the property in any school district in which additional amounts are required, which shall be at rates sufficient to provide the additional amounts. No delinquency factor for estimated uncollected taxes may be included in the computation of the primary tax rate for school district taxes. No local property taxes may be levied for any deficit in the classroom site fund. The taxes shall be added to and collected in the same manner as other county taxes on the property within the school district. The amount of the school district taxes levied upon the property in a particular school district shall be paid into the school fund of such school district.

B. At the same time of levying taxes as provided in subsection A of this section, the county board of supervisors shall annually levy an additional tax in each school district that is not eligible for equalization assistance as provided in § 15-971 in an amount determined as follows:

1. Determine the levy that would be produced by fifty per cent of the applicable qualifying tax rate, prescribed in § 15-971, subsection B, per one hundred dollars assessed valuation.

2. Subtract the amount determined in § 15-971, subsection A from the levy determined in paragraph 1 of this subsection. This difference is the additional amount levied or collected as voluntary contributions pursuant to title 48, chapter 1, article 8,[1] except that if the difference is zero or is a negative number, there shall be no levy.

C. Monies collected pursuant to subsection B of this section shall be transmitted to the state treasurer for deposit in the state general fund to aid in school financial assistance.

D. The additional tax prescribed in subsection B of this section is considered to be primary property tax for purposes of § 15-972, subsection B, except that this state is not required to make the payments prescribed in § 15-972, subsection H for these reductions in taxes.

E. For the purposes of this section, "assessed valuation" includes the values used to determine voluntary contributions collected pursuant to title 9, chapter 4, article 3[2] and title 48, chapter 1, article 8.

Added by Laws 1981, Ch. 1, § 2, eff. Jan. 23, 1981. Amended by Laws 1989, Ch. 312, § 3; Laws 1990, 3rd S.S., Ch. 3, § 4; Laws 1996, 7th S.S., Ch. 2, § 2; Laws 1997, Ch. 274, § 4; Laws 2002, Ch. 301, § 5, eff. May 23, 2002.

[1] Section 48–241 et seq.
[2] Section 9–431 et seq.

Retroactive Application

This section, as amended by Laws 2002, Ch. 301, applies retroactively to July 1, 2001.

This section, as amended by Laws 1996, 7th Special Session, Ch. 2, applies retroactively to tax years beginning January 1, 1996.

Historical and Statutory Notes

Source:

Laws 1912, Ch. 77, § 101.
Civ.Code 1913, § 2818.
Laws 1917, Ch. 45, § 1.
Laws 1921, Ch. 158, § 1.
Rev.Code 1928, § 1091.
Laws 1933, Ch. 65, § 11.
Laws 1941, Ch. 79, § 6.
Laws 1947, Ch. 85, § 4.
Code 1939, Supp.1952, § 54–605.
Laws 1955, Ch. 108, § 4.
A.R.S. former § 15–1236.
Laws 1980, 2nd S.S., Ch. 9, § 68.
Laws 1980, Ch. 167, § 8.

This section, as amended by Laws 1990, 3rd S.S., Ch. 3, applies retroactively to taxable years beginning January 1, 1990.

Laws 1996, 7th S.S., Ch. 2, § 16, subsec. A, provides:

"**Sec. 16. Retroactivity**

"**A.** Sections 1, 2, 3, 5 through 8, 10, 12 and 15 apply retroactively to tax years beginning from and after December 31, 1995."

Laws 2002, Ch. 301, § 7, provides:

"**Sec. 7. Retroactivity**

"Sections 2 through 6 of this act apply retroactively to from and after June 30, 2001."

§ 15–993. Tax levy for high schools

In the school district or union high school district which determines to establish a high school, an annual tax shall be levied, the amount of which shall be estimated by the governing board of the school district and certified to the county school superintendent on or before July 1. The board of supervisors, after deducting the amount allowed from state and county funds, shall levy a tax rate upon the property of the high school district or union high school district which will produce the remaining amount so estimated.

Added by Laws 1981, Ch. 1, § 2, eff. Jan. 23, 1981.

Historical and Statutory Notes

Source:

Laws 1912, Ch. 77, § 78.
Civ.Code 1913, § 2774.
Rev.Code 1928, § 1071.
Laws 1933, Ch. 65, § 6.
Code 1939, § 54–904.
A.R.S. former § 15–505.
Laws 1980, 2nd S.S., Ch. 9, § 24.

§ 15–994. Tax levy; county equalization assistance for education

A. The board of supervisors of each county shall annually, at the time of levying other taxes, levy a county equalization assistance for education tax on the property within the county. The tax levy for county equalization assistance for education shall be at a rate determined pursuant to § 41–1276. The tax levy provided for in this section shall not be subject to title 42, chapter 17, articles 2 and 3.[1] Except as provided in § 15-365, the county treasurer shall apportion all monies collected from the county equalization assistance for education tax levy to the school districts within the county in accordance with § 15-971, subsection C at the same time as other tax levy monies are apportioned as provided in § 42-18001.

B. At the same time the county assessor is required to transmit values to the county school superintendent as provided in § 42-17052, the assessor of each county shall provide in electronic format to the superintendent of public instruction the assessed valuation used for determining the primary property tax rate and the secondary property tax rate for each school district in the county. On or before January 15 the county assessor of each county shall provide in electronic format to the superintendent of public instruction the actual assessed valuation used for determining the primary property tax rate and the secondary property tax rate for each school district in the county including any revisions made due to changes in the valuation of unsecured personal property after the tax rates were determined.

Added by Laws 1981, Ch. 1, § 2, eff. Jan. 23, 1981. Amended by Laws 1981, Ch. 291, § 3; Laws 1983, Ch. 214, § 2; Laws 1985, Ch. 166, § 34, eff. April 18, 1985; Laws 1988, Ch. 221, § 6, eff. June 14, 1988; Laws 1990, Ch. 399, § 12, eff. July 5, 1990; Laws 1991, Ch. 288, § 7, eff. Sept. 21, 1991, retroactively effective to July 1, 1991; Laws 1998, Ch. 1, § 54, eff. Jan. 1, 1999; Laws 1998, Ch. 153, § 3, eff. Jan. 1, 1999; Laws 2000, Ch. 187, § 3; Laws 2000, Ch. 342, § 25; Laws 2001, Ch. 115, § 2.

[1] Sections 42-17051 et seq., 42-17101 et seq.

Historical and Statutory Notes

Source:

Laws 1980, 2nd S.S., Ch. 9, § 69.
A.R.S. Former § 15-1236.01.
Laws 1980, Ch. 167, § 9.

The 1998 amendment of this section by Ch. 153, § 3, explicitly amended the amendment of this section by Laws 1998, Ch. 1, § 54.

Laws 1998, Ch. 153, § 5, provides:

"**Sec. 5. Effective date**

"This act is effective from and after December 31, 1998."

Laws 2001, Ch. 115, § 36, subsec. A, provides:

"**Sec. 36. Retroactivity**

"**A.** Section 15-994, Arizona Revised Statutes, as amended by this act, applies retroactively to July 18, 2000."

Reviser's Notes:

1988 Note. Pursuant to authority of § 41-1304.02, in the first sentence of subsection C the spelling of the second "assessor" was corrected.

2000 Note. Prior the 2001 amendment, this section contained the amendments made by Laws 2000, Ch. 187, sec. 3 and Ch. 342, sec. 25 that were blended together pursuant to authority of § 41-1304.03.

§ 15-995. Special district assessment for adjacent ways by school district

A. The governing board of a school district may contract for constructing, maintaining or otherwise improving any public way adjacent to any parcel of land owned by the school district or leased for school purposes by the school district, or an intersection of any public way adjoining a quarter block in which the parcel of land is situated, and for the construction of sidewalks, sewers, utility lines, roadways and other related improvements in or along such streets and intersections, and to pay for such improvements by the levy of a special assessment upon the taxable property in the school district. A school district shall not use any portion of the monies generated from the special assessment for any construction, maintenance or other improvements to the school district's property except improvements necessary to assure the safe ingress to and egress from public school property directly adjacent to the public way for buses and fire equipment. The assessment shall be made a part of the itemized statement regularly filed with the county school superintendent and showing the amount of monies needed for the expenses of schools within the school district for the ensuing year.

B. If any property owned by a school district or leased by a school district for school purposes from any city or county, the state or the United States is included within the assessment district to be assessed to pay the costs and expenses of any public improvements initiated by a city, as to make the assessments thereon payable by the city in which the improvement is initiated, the governing board may contract with the municipality or its improvement district to reimburse it for the amount of the assessment against the property and to pay the amount so contracted for by the levy of a special assessment as provided by subsection A of this section.

C. The governing board of the school district shall follow the truth in taxation notice and hearing requirements prescribed in § 15-905.01, subsection B.

D. The portion of the primary tax rate to fund adjacent ways as provided in this section shall not be included in the computation of additional state aid for education as prescribed in § 15-972.

Added by Laws 1981, Ch. 1, § 2, eff. Jan. 23, 1981. Amended by Laws 1989, Ch. 125, § 1; Laws 1997, Ch. 231, § 26; Laws 1997, Ch. 271, § 4, eff. April 29, 1997; Laws 1997, Ch. 274, § 5; Laws 1999, Ch. 108, § 3.

Historical and Statutory Notes

Source:

Civ.Code 1913, § 2864.
Laws 1915, Ch. 27, § 1.
Laws 1922, Ch. 40, § 1.
Rev.Code 1928, § 1099.
Code 1939, § 54-613.
A.R.S. former § 15-1237.
Laws 1960, Ch. 127, § 54.

Reviser's Notes:

1997 Note. Prior to the 1999 amendment, this section contained the amendments made by Laws 1997, Ch. 231, § 26, Ch. 271, § 4 and Ch. 274, § 5 that were blended together pursuant to authority of § 41-1304.03.

§ 15-996. Duties of county treasurer relating to school district's monies

The county treasurer shall:

1. Receive and hold all school district monies and keep a separate account for each school district and for the special county school reserve fund. The county treasurer may maintain separate accounts for each fund of a school district or the county treasurer may maintain only two accounts for each school district's monies in addition to the funds provided for in §§ 15-1024, 15-1025, 15-2021, 15-2031 and 15-2041. If only two accounts are maintained, the first account shall consist of maintenance and operation, unrestricted capital outlay, soft capital allocation and adjacent ways monies and the classroom site fund prescribed in § 15-977 and the second account shall consist of federal and state grant monies and all other monies.

2. Pool school district monies for investment except as provided in §§ 15-1024 and 15-1025. Interest earned on the monies pooled for investment shall

be apportioned at least quarterly to the appropriate school district based on an average monthly balance as prescribed in the uniform system of accounting for county treasurers as provided in § 41–1279.21.

3. Notwithstanding § 11–605, register warrants only as follows:

(a) If separate accounts are maintained for each fund, warrants may only be registered on the maintenance and operation, unrestricted capital outlay, soft capital allocation and adjacent ways accounts and the classroom site fund prescribed in § 15–977 and only if the total cash balance of all three accounts is insufficient to pay the warrants.

(b) If the county treasurer maintains only two accounts as provided in paragraph 1 of this section:

(i) The county treasurer may register warrants only on the first account and only if the balance of that account is insufficient to pay the warrants.

(ii) The county treasurer may honor warrants for any federal or state grant fund with a negative balance as long as the total balance in the second account is positive. If the second account total balance is negative the warrant for a federal or state grant fund shall be charged to the maintenance and operation fund. Any interest charged to the federal or state grant fund as a result of a negative balance that is in excess of interest earned on the fund shall be transferred to the maintenance and operation fund at the end of the fiscal year or the end of the grant year. If a federal or state grant fund has a negative balance at the end of the fiscal year or grant year, sufficient expenditures shall be transferred to the maintenance and operation fund to eliminate the negative balance.

4. Notify the county school superintendent by the fifteenth day of each calendar month of the month end balances of each school district account.

5. Pay warrants issued by the county school superintendent and duly endorsed by the person entitled to receive the monies.

6. On each property tax bill and each property tax statement prepared, separately state and identify by name each school district's primary property tax rate, the secondary property tax rate that is associated with overrides, the secondary property tax rate that is associated with class A bonds and the secondary property tax rate that is associated with class B bonds. For purposes of this paragraph, "class A bonds" and "class B bonds" have the same meanings prescribed in § 15–101.

Added by Laws 1983, Ch. 241, § 3. Amended by Laws 1987, Ch. 345, § 1; Laws 1995, Ch. 191, § 17, eff. April 19, 1995; Laws 1998, 5th S.S., Ch. 1, § 33, eff. July 9, 1998; Laws 1999, Ch. 299, § 30; Laws 2002, Ch. 301, § 6, eff. May 23, 2002.

Retroactive Application

This section, as amended by Laws 2002, Ch. 301, applies retroactively to July 1, 2001.

Historical and Statutory Notes

Source:

Laws 1912, Ch. 77, § 103.
Civ.Code 1913, § 2819.
Laws 1921, Ch. 158, § 1.
Rev.Code 1928, § 1092.

Laws 1941, Ch. 79, § 7.
Code 1939, Supp.1952, § 54-606.
A.R.S. former §§ 15-996, 15-1231.
Laws 1981, Ch. 1, § 2.
Laws 1981, Ch. 97, § 2.
Laws 1982, Ch. 199, § 2.

The purported amendment of this section by Laws 1998, Ch. 164 failed to become effective because Chapter 164 was repealed in its entirety by Laws 1998, 5th S.S., Ch. 1, § 2, effective July 1, 1998.

The purported amendment of this section by Laws 1998, 3rd S.S., Ch. 1, failed to became effective because Ch. 1 was repealed in its entirety by Laws 1998, 5th S.S., Ch. 1, § 2, effective July 1, 1998.

Laws 2002, Ch. 301, § 7, provides:

"**Sec. 7. Retroactivity**

"Sections 2 through 6 of this act apply retroactively to from and after June 30, 2001."

Former § 15-996, added by Laws 1981, Ch. 1, § 2 (see Source, ante), relating to the same subject matter as this section, was repealed by Laws 1983, Ch. 241, § 2.

Reviser's Notes:

1987 Note. Pursuant to authority of § 41-1304.02, in the section heading "monies" was substituted for "funds".

§ 15-997. Authority of county officers as to funds, taxes and boundaries of joint common school district

A. The county treasurer of the jurisdictional county shall have custody of the funds of a joint common school district and shall perform all duties imposed by law for the control and accounting of other school funds. Warrants drawn against the funds of a joint common school district shall be drawn by the county school superintendent of the jurisdictional county. Any estimates or other information required by the boards of supervisors of the counties in the joint common school district as a basis for action by such boards shall be supplied by the county school superintendent of the jurisdictional county. The board of supervisors of each county shall perform all duties required by law with respect to county appropriation of funds and levy of taxes for joint common school districts in the same manner as though the portion of the joint common school district in its county were a separate school district, except that all such tax proceeds and monies shall be paid over to the treasurer of the jurisdictional county.

B. The statement of school district boundaries required to be filed annually by the county school superintendent shall be filed in each county.

C. All amounts required to be raised by the school district through the levy of ad valorem taxes shall be raised through the levy of taxes at the same rate on all taxable property in the school district regardless of location as to county. The county school superintendent of the jurisdictional county shall file with the board of supervisors of each county a statement and estimate upon which taxes are to be based which shall include the assessed valuation of all taxable property in the school district and the tax rate necessary to be levied.

D. The board of supervisors of the jurisdictional county shall hold a budget hearing as required by law and shall have control over the investment of the debt service funds of the joint common school district.

Added by Laws 1981, Ch. 1, § 2, eff. Jan. 23, 1981.

Historical and Statutory Notes

Source:

Laws 1970, Ch. 12, § 1.
A.R.S. former § 15-421.06.

§ 15-998. Liability of treasurer for failure to keep separate account or give notice; enforcement

If the county treasurer fails to keep a separate account for each school district and for the special county school reserve fund or give the notice required by § 15-996, he is liable to the county in the amount of five hundred dollars, and the county attorney shall, upon direction of the board of supervisors, bring an action in the name of the county against the treasurer for the recovery of the five hundred dollars. Monies collected are payable into the county school fund.

Added by Laws 1981, Ch. 1, § 2, eff. Jan. 23, 1981. Amended by Laws 1981, Ch. 97, § 3; Laws 1982, Ch. 199, § 3.

Historical and Statutory Notes

Source:

Laws 1912, Ch. 77, § 104.
Civ.Code 1913, § 2820.
Rev.Code 1928, § 1093.
Code 1939, § 54-607.
A.R.S. former § 15-1232.

§ 15-999. Preference of payment of warrants; use of balance of school fund remaining at close of fiscal year

A. All warrants registered after January 1, 1936 and drawn on the county treasurer against the school fund of the school district by the county school superintendent or finance officer of a school district that has assumed accounting responsibility pursuant to § 15-914.01 on the order of the governing board shall be entitled to preference of payment out of the school fund according to priority of registration.

B. Unless otherwise provided in this chapter and chapter 10 of this title,[1] if a balance remains in the school fund of a school district at the close of a fiscal year, such balance shall be used for reduction of school district taxes for the budget year.

C. A warrant that is drawn on the school fund of the school district by the county school superintendent or finance officer of a school district that has assumed accounting responsibility pursuant to § 15-914.01 and that is not presented for payment within one year after the date of issuance is void. All warrants not presented within one year shall have no further force or effect, and any monies held at the expiration of such time in any fund or account for the payment of the warrants shall be transferred or reverted to the fund upon which the warrants were drawn.

Added by Laws 1981, Ch. 1, § 2, eff. Jan. 23, 1981. Amended by Laws 1997, Ch. 147, § 3; Laws 1998, Ch. 233, § 5; Laws 2001, Ch. 28, § 1.

[1] Sections 15-901 et seq., 15-1101 et seq.

Historical and Statutory Notes

Source:

Laws 1912, Ch. 77, § 55.
Civ.Code 1913, § 2751.
Rev.Code 1928, § 1026.
Laws 1936, 1st S.S., Ch. 4, § 1.
Code 1939, § 54-431.
Laws 1954, Ch. 147, § 1.
A.R.S. former § 15-1249.
Laws 1960, Ch. 85, § 1.
Laws 1980, 2nd S.S., Ch. 9, § 76.

§ 15-1000. County school fund

The county school fund of each county shall consist of all revenues accruing to the credit of each county from:

1. That portion of the payments made under § 36-1419 which represents payment in lieu of the county levy for school purposes.

2. Taylor Grazing Act monies as provided in § 37-723.

3. All receipts from the lease of public lands as provided in § 37-724.

4. All balances remaining in the county school fund and in the special county school reserve fund at the end of the fiscal year and all balances of lapsed school districts remaining after the payments authorized under § 15-469.

5. All dividends, proceeds from sales, refunds, credits arising from cancelled warrants and any other sums or amounts that are attributable to the county school fund.

6. All other federal lieu taxes which are not specifically allocated by law.

7. Any gratuity or devise designated for specific school purposes.

Added by Laws 1981, Ch. 1, § 2, eff. Jan. 23, 1981.

Historical and Statutory Notes

Source:
Laws 1954, Ch. 149, § 1.
Code 1939, Supp.1954, § 54-608a.
Laws 1955, Ch. 128, § 1.
A.R.S. former § 15-1238.
Laws 1960, Ch. 127, § 55.
Laws 1974, 1st S.S., Ch. 3, § 31.
Laws 1980, 2nd S.S., Ch. 9, § 70.

§ 15-1001. Special county school reserve fund

A. The board of supervisors of each county shall annually budget for the special county school reserve fund an amount to meet the requirements of that fund. Warrants drawn on the special county school reserve fund shall be approved prior to payment by the board of supervisors, as other county warrants are approved, or this responsibility may be delegated by the board of supervisors to the county school superintendent. The budgeted amounts for the special county school reserve fund shall be itemized and estimated to meet the following needs:

1. For transportation of school children to and from one-room and two-room rural schools that are determined by the county school superintendent to be in need of such aid.

2. For transportation to and from unorganized territory to school districts of children who are eligible to receive state aid.

3. For transportation to and from the nearest high school of pupils residing in common school districts which are contiguous or not contiguous to and which are not within a high school district if it is determined by the county school superintendent that such common school districts are in need of such aid to supplement the monies received as provided in subsection B of this section.

4. For one-room and two-room school districts, an amount which when added to the state aid for a school district will provide not more than five thousand dollars for a one-room school and not more than nine thousand dollars for a two-room school, provided that such schools are maintained for a minimum of one hundred seventy-five days or two hundred days, as applicable, per year.

5. For necessary expenses for the establishment and conduct of accommodation schools pursuant to § 15-308.

6. For expenditures necessary to establish and maintain, for the first year of operation, a county special education program for children with disabilities as provided in chapter 7, article 4 of this title.[1]

B. The county school superintendent shall determine the eligibility for transportation aid for the transportation of children from unorganized territory to school districts within that county in the manner provided in this chapter for other school districts and shall certify the eligibility to the department of education.

C. The county school superintendent shall determine the amount of transportation aid for transportation of children from unorganized territory to school districts within that county based upon the provisions of § 15-945, subsection A, paragraphs 1 and 2, except that such transportation aid shall not exceed the actual cost of providing such transportation. The county school superintendent shall certify the amount to the department of education which shall apportion the monies no later than the second Monday in September, December, March and June.

Added by Laws 1981, Ch. 1, § 2, eff. Jan. 23, 1981. Amended by Laws 1981, Ch. 142, § 2; Laws 1985, Ch. 166, § 35, eff. April 18, 1985; Laws 1997, Ch. 231, § 27; Laws 1998, Ch. 167, § 13; Laws 2000, Ch. 236, § 26, eff. April 12, 2000.

[1] Section 15-761 et seq.

Historical and Statutory Notes

Source:
Rev.Code 1928, § 1090a.
Laws 1933, Ch. 65, § 10.
Laws 1941, Ch. 79, § 5.
Laws 1947, Ch. 85, § 3.
Code 1939, Supp.1952, § 54-604.
Laws 1955, Ch. 108, § 3.
A.R.S former § 15-1246.
Laws 1960, Ch. 127, § 58.
Laws 1967, 3rd S.S., Ch. 19, § 20.
Laws 1970, Ch. 169, § 4.
Laws 1974, 1st S.S., Ch. 3, § 37.
Laws 1980, 2nd S.S., Ch. 9, § 73.

§ 15-1002. Administration of county school reserve fund; uses

A. The special county school reserve fund may be used only for:

1. Transportation of children to and from one-room and two-room rural schools that are determined by the county school superintendent to be in need of such aid.

2. Transportation from unorganized territory to school districts of children who are eligible to receive state aid for such children.

3. Transportation to and from the nearest high school of pupils residing in common school districts which are contiguous or not contiguous to and which

are not within a high school district, if it is determined by the county school superintendent that such common school districts are in need of such aid.

4. Costs of maintaining one-room and two-room rural schools in any school district in excess of the amount available for such schools from the county school fund and their school district levy, but not to exceed the additional amount required and estimated for such purpose by the county school superintendent in fixing the amount of the special county school reserve fund under the provisions of § 15-1001.

5. Necessary expenses in excess of the per capita apportionment from the county school fund for the establishment and conduct of schools in unorganized territory.

6. Expenditures necessary to establish and maintain, for the first year of operation, a county special education program for children with disabilities as provided in chapter 7, article 4 of this title.[1]

7. Expenditures for service programs pursuant to § 15-365.

B. The county school superintendent shall apportion the special county school reserve fund. If at the end of any school year any part of the reserve fund remains unexpended, such amount shall be shown in the estimate of the county school superintendent for the succeeding year as a balance of county school funds on hand, except as prescribed by the terms of subsection C of this section.

C. If an accommodation school accepting federal funds becomes a school district, the board of supervisors may order the county school superintendent to transfer the cash balance credited to the accommodation school as of July 1 of the fiscal year in which the transfer occurred to the newly organized school district. In addition, all property both real and personal, title of which is vested in the accommodation school, shall become the property of the newly formed school district.

Added by Laws 1981, Ch. 1, § 2, eff. Jan. 23, 1981. Amended by Laws 2000, Ch. 236, § 27, eff. April 12, 2000.

[1] Section 15-761 et seq.

Historical and Statutory Notes

Source:

Laws 1912, Ch. 77, § 105.
Civ.Code 1913, § 2821.
Laws 1921, Ch. 158, § 1.
Rev.Code 1928, § 1094.
Laws 1933, Ch. 65, § 12.
Laws 1941, Ch. 79, § 8.
Laws 1947, Ch. 85, § 6.
Code 1939, Supp.1954, § 54-608.
Laws 1955, Ch. 108, § 5.
A.R.S. former § 15-1247.
Laws 1960, Ch. 127, § 59.
Laws 1967, Ch. 29, § 1.
Laws 1970, Ch. 169, § 5.
Laws 1976, Ch. 65, § 3.
Laws 1980, 2nd S.S., Ch. 9, § 74.

§ 15-1003. Repealed by Laws 1984, Ch. 314, § 4, eff. April 30, 1984

Historical and Statutory Notes

The repealed section, added by Laws 1981, Ch. 1, § 2, derived from Laws 1980, 2nd S.S., Ch. 9, § 57, and A.R.S. former § 15-1201.02, and amended by Laws 1981, Ch. 159, § 1 and Laws 1983, Ch. 98, § 17, related to the payment of contributions under a federal agreement and to contributions to the state retirement plan.

Laws 1984, Ch. 314, § 8, effective April 30, 1984, provides:

"**Sec. 8. Transition of payment of employer contributions for certificated employees; appropriation; lapsing**

"**A.** Notwithstanding § 4 of this act, the employer contributions required under title 38, chapter 5, article 1, [§ 38-701 et seq.] Arizona Revised Statutes, for certificated employees of school districts and employer contributions to the state retirement plan on behalf of certificated employees of school districts which are based on salaries earned in fiscal year 1983–1984 shall be paid by the department of administration. The employer contributions for certificated employees of school districts which are based on salaries earned in fiscal year 1984–1985 and thereafter shall be paid by the school districts.

"**B.** The sum of two million five hundred thousand dollars is appropriated from the state general fund for fiscal year 1984–1985 to the department of administration for the purposes provided in subsection A of this section.

"**C.** The balance of the appropriation made in subsection B of this section lapses when the purpose for which it is made is accomplished."

ARTICLE 7. BOND ISSUES AND BONDED INDEBTEDNESS

§ 15-1021. Limitation on bonded indebtedness; limitation on authorization and issuance of bonds

A. Until December 31, 1999, a school district may issue class A bonds for the purposes specified in this section and chapter 4, article 5 of this title [1] to an amount in the aggregate, including the existing indebtedness, not exceeding fifteen per cent of the taxable property used for secondary property tax purposes, as determined pursuant to title 42, chapter 15, article 1, [2] within a school district as ascertained by the last property tax assessment previous to issuing the bonds.

B. From and after December 31, 1998, a school district may issue class B bonds for the purposes specified in this section and chapter 4, article 5 of this title to an amount in the aggregate, including the existing class B indebtedness, not exceeding five per cent of the taxable property used for secondary property tax purposes, as determined pursuant to title 42, chapter 15, article 1, within a school district as ascertained by the last assessment of state and county taxes previous to issuing the bonds, or one thousand five hundred dollars per student count as determined pursuant to § 15-902, whichever amount is greater. A school district shall not issue class B bonds until the proceeds of any class A bonds issued by the school district have been obligated in contract. The total amount of class A and class B bonds issued by a school district shall not exceed the debt limitations prescribed in article IX, § 8, Constitution of Arizona.

C. Until December 31, 1999, a unified school district, as defined under article IX, § 8.1, Constitution of Arizona, may issue class A bonds for the purposes specified in this section and chapter 4, article 5 of this title to an amount in the aggregate, including the existing indebtedness, not exceeding thirty per cent of the taxable property used for secondary property tax purposes, as determined pursuant to title 42, chapter 15, article 1, within a unified school district as ascertained by the last property tax assessment previous to issuing the bonds.

D. From and after December 31, 1998, a unified school district, as defined under article IX, § 8.1, Constitution of Arizona, may issue class B bonds for the purposes specified in this section and chapter 4, article 5 of this title to an amount in the aggregate, including the existing class B indebtedness, not exceeding ten per cent of the taxable property used for secondary tax purposes, as determined pursuant to title 42, chapter 15, article 1, within a school district as ascertained by the last assessment of state and county taxes previous to issuing the bonds, or one thousand five hundred dollars per student count as determined pursuant to § 15-902, whichever amount is greater. A unified school district shall not issue class B bonds until the proceeds of any class A bonds issued by the unified school district have been obligated in contract. The total amount of class A and class B bonds issued by a unified school district shall not exceed the debt limitations prescribed in article IX, § 8.1, Constitution of Arizona.

E. No bonds authorized to be issued by an election held after July 1, 1980 may be issued more than six years after the date of the election, except that class A bonds shall not be issued after December 31, 1999.

F. Class A bond proceeds shall not be expended for items whose useful life is less than the average life of the bonds issued, except that bond proceeds shall not be expended for items whose useful life is less than five years.

G. Except as provided in subsection H of this section, class B bond proceeds shall not be expended for soft capital items, computer hardware, or other items whose useful life is less than the average useful life of the bonds issued, except that bond proceeds shall not be expended for items whose useful life is less than five years. For the purposes of this subsection, "computer hardware" means an electronic device with an integrated circuit that performs logic, arithmetic or memory functions by the manipulations of electronic or magnetic impulses and includes all input, output, processing, storage, software or communication facilities that are connected or related to such a device in a system or network.

H. Class b bond proceeds for a new facility at the main campus of a joint technological education district may be expended for soft capital items, computer hardware, furniture or other equipment, except that no bonds may be issued for these purposes for a duration of more than five years. The total amount of bonds that a joint technological education district may issue pursuant to this subsection shall not exceed thirty per cent of the cost of the new school facility, including monies received for the new school facility pursuant to this section.

I. Notwithstanding subsections F and G of this section, bond proceeds may be expended for purchasing pupil transportation vehicles.

J. A school district shall not authorize, issue or sell bonds pursuant to this section if the school district has any existing indebtedness from impact aid revenue bonds pursuant to chapter 16, article 8 of this title, [3] except for bonds issued to refund any bonds issued by the governing board.

Added by Laws 1981, Ch. 1, § 2, eff. Jan. 23, 1981. Amended by Laws 1996, 5th S.S., Ch. 8, § 12; Laws 1997, Ch. 4, § 4, eff. July 21, 1997, retroactively effective to July 1, 1997; Laws 1998, Ch. 1, § 55, eff. Jan. 1, 1999; Laws 1998, Ch. 52, § 6, eff. Jan. 1, 1999; Laws 1998, 5th S.S., Ch. 1, § 34, eff. July 9, 1998; Laws 1999, Ch. 5, § 2; Laws 1999, Ch. 299, § 31; Laws 2001, Ch. 228, § 3; Laws 2002, Ch. 188, § 1; Laws 2004, Ch. 341, § 8.

[1] Section 15-491 et seq.

[2] Section 42-15001 et seq.

[3] Section 15-2101 et seq.

Historical and Statutory Notes

Source:

Laws 1912, Ch. 77, §§ 48, 49.
Civ.Code 1913, §§ 2740, 2741.
Rev.Code 1928, § 1016.
Code 1939, § 54-421.
A.R.S. former § 15-1301.
Laws 1980, 2nd S.S., Ch. 9, § 82.

Laws 1980, 2nd S.S., Ch. 9, [which amended former § 15-1301] § 99, subsec. A, provides:

"**Sec. 99. Conditional enactment**

"**A.** The provisions contained in § 82 of this act shall not become effective unless the Constitution of Arizona is amended by vote of the people at the next special election called for such purpose to ratify the provisions of article IX, §§ 8 and 8.1 of the Constitution of Arizona as prescribed by Senate Concurrent Resolution 1001, thirty-fourth legislature, second special session."

The proposed amendment by Laws 1980, 2nd S.S., S.C.R. No. 1001 was adopted by the electors at the June 3, 1980 special election.

Laws 1997, Ch. 4, § 16, as amended by Laws 1997, 1st S.S., Ch. 9, § 1, provides:

"**Sec. 16. Conditional repeal**

"**A.** If there is a final adjudication [see note, post] in the proceedings resulting from the Arizona supreme court's decision in Roosevelt Elementary School District No. 66 v. Bishop, 179 Ariz. 233, 877 P.2d 806 (1994) that this act, in conjunction with Laws 1996, fifth special session, chapter 8 and Laws 1996, seventh special session, chapter 1, does not ensure a constitutional system of education:

"1. This act and Laws 1996, fifth special session, chapter 8, § 14 are void and are repealed as of the date of the final adjudication.

"2. Laws 1996, fifth special session, chapter 8, §§ 1, 13, 15 and 17 and laws 1996, seventh special session, chapter 1, §§ 3, 4 and 5 are void and are repealed six months after the date of the final adjudication.

"**B.** Subsection A of this section does not invalidate any contractual obligations of the state board for school capital facilities that may have been incurred before the repeal prescribed in subsection A, paragraph 2 of this section, including school districts that have been given preliminary approvals by the state board for school capital facilities before the date of final adjudication, not to exceed the balance of the school capital equity fund established by § 15-1053, Arizona Revised Statutes, on the date of the final adjudication. After the date of final adjudication, the state board shall not enter into any contractual obligations not related to a preliminary approval given before the date of the final adjudication or give any new preliminary approvals. Between the date of final adjudication and the repeal prescribed in subsection A, paragraph 2 of this section, nothing in this section shall be construed to prohibit the board from paying its costs of operation as prescribed by law.

"**C.** On the discontinuation of the state board for school capital facilities, the department of education shall assume responsibility for distributing monies and receiving reports and repayment obligations from school districts pursuant to contracts and preliminary approvals entered into between the state board and school districts before the final adjudication referred to in subsection A of this section. Any monies remitted to the department of education pursuant to this subsection shall be transmitted to the state general fund. The department of education shall submit an annual report to the president of the senate, the speaker of the house of representatives and the governor that summarizes the reports and amount of repayments from school districts."

The conditions for the repeals by this section have been met. The Supreme Court in Order No. CV-97-0369-SA, dated October 24, 1997, declared that the legislature's 1997 school funding plan was unconstitutional; the order of July 28, 1994, was still in effect; and, that the order of the trial court dated August 20, 1997 was approved. A written opinion followed, dated December 23, 1997 (Hull v. Albrecht, 190 Ariz. 520, 950 P.2d 1141 (1997)). An informal Attorney General Opinion considers December 23, 1997, the date the written Supreme Court decision was released, as the final date of adjudication. A subsequent amendment to cure the constitutional infirmity by Laws 1998, 3rd S.S., Ch. 1 was also declared unconstitutional by the Supreme Court (Hull v. Albrecht 192 Ariz. 34, 960 P.2d 634 (1998)).

The 1998 amendment of this section by Ch. 52, § 6, explicitly amended the amendment of this section by Laws 1998, Ch. 1, § 55.

Laws 1998, Ch. 52, § 74, as amended by Laws 1998, Ch. 113, § 68, provides:

"**Sec. 74. Effective date**

"Sections 9-432, 15-393, 15-991.01, 15-1021, 27-234, 42-5008, 42-5404, 42-11109, 42-12159, 42-13001, 42-14357, 42-15064, 42-16214, 42-17251, 42-17254, 42-17256, 48-574, 48-614, 48-616 and 48-807, Arizona Revised Statutes, as amended by this act, are effective from and after December 31, 1998."

Laws 1998, Ch. 113, § 1, par. 40, provides:

"**Section 1. Purpose**"

"40. Sections 9-432, 15-393, 15-991.01, 15-1021 and 27-234, Arizona Revised Statutes, were amended by Laws 1998, chapter 1 with a delayed effective date of January 1, 1999. The Laws 1998, chapter 1 versions of these sections were subsequently amended by Laws 1998, chapter 52 with a general effective date. In order to correct a potentially defective enactment, this act amends Laws 1998, chapter 52, § 74 that prescribes an effective date of January 1, 1999 for other sections in the act to include §§ 9-432, 15-393, 15-991.01, 15-1021 and 27-234, Arizona Revised Statutes."

The purported amendment of this section by Laws 1998, Ch. 164 failed to become effective because Chapter 164 was repealed in its entirety by Laws 1998, 5th S.S., Ch. 1, § 2, effective July 1, 1998.

The purported amendment of this section by Laws 1998, 3rd S.S., Ch. 1, failed to became effective because Ch. 1 was repealed in its entirety by Laws 1998, 5th S.S., Ch. 1, § 2, effective July 1, 1998.

Laws 1999, Ch. 287, §§ 1 and 2, provide:

"**School districts; debt restrictions; bonded indebtedness**

"**A.** Notwithstanding § 15-1021, Arizona Revised Statutes, a debt restricted school district may continue to issue class A bonds until December 31, 2002, although no class A bonds shall be issued pursuant to this act more than six years after the date of the election. The total amount of class A bonds issued by a debt restricted school district pursuant to this section shall not exceed ten million dollars and shall be issued for the purposes specified in title 15, chapter 4, article 5, Arizona Revised Statutes, and § 15-1021, Arizona Revised Statutes. For the purposes of this section, "debt restricted school district" means a school district that received voter approval to issue class A bonds at an election held prior to December 31, 1998 but which cannot issue and sell the full amount of such authorization before December 31, 1999 because of article IX, §§ 8 and 8.1, Constitution of Arizona and debt limitations set forth in § 15-1021, Arizona Revised Statutes, or the limitation prescribed in Laws 1996, chapter 332, § 9.

"**B.** Nothing in this section shall be construed to exempt a school district from the debt limitations prescribed in article IX, §§ 8 and 8.1, Constitution of Arizona.

"**Sec. 2. Intent**

"This act is intended to aid the transition of local funding of school construction to a state funded system by permitting needy districts that have received voter authorization to issue bonds an opportunity to issue some or all of their voted authorization that otherwise could not be completed by December 31, 1999 due to debt restrictions. If this act is a special law, no general law can be made applicable that will accomplish the purposes of this act."

Laws 2004, Ch. 341, § 12, provides:

"**Sec. 12. Retroactivity**

"Sections 15-491 and 15-1021, Arizona Revised Statutes, as amended by this act, apply retroactively to from and after May 14, 2004."

Reviser's Notes:

1997 Note. This section is subject to a conditional repeal pursuant to Laws 1997, Ch. 4, § 16.

1998 Note. Prior to the 1999 amendments, this section contained the amendments made by Laws 1998, Second Regular Session, Ch. 52, sec. 6 and Laws 1998, Fifth Special Session, Ch. 1. sec. 34 that were blended together pursuant to authority of § 41-1304.03.

1999 Note. Prior to the 2001 amendment, this section contained the amendments made by Laws 1999, Ch. 5, sec. 2 and Ch. 299, sec. 31 that were blended together pursuant to authority of § 41-1304.03.

§ 15-1022. Tax levy for bonds; administration and disposition of tax; cancellation of paid bonds

A. The board of supervisors, at the time of making the levy of taxes for county purposes, shall levy a tax for the year upon the taxable property in a school district or former school district canceled by election, which has outstanding school bonds for the interest and redemption of the bonds. The tax shall not be less than sufficient to pay the interest of the bonds for the year and the portion of the principal of the bonds becoming due during the year and in any event shall be enough to raise, annually, for the first half of the term of the bonds a sufficient amount to pay the interest thereon, and during the remainder of the term enough to pay the annual interest and to pay, annually, a portion of the principal of the bonds equal to an amount produced by taking the whole amount of bonds outstanding and dividing it by the number of years the bonds then have to run.

B. All monies, when collected, shall be paid into the county treasury to the credit of the debt service fund of the school district and shall be used only for payment of principal and interest on the bonds. The county treasurer shall keep the debt service fund separate from all other funds in the county treasury. The principal and interest on the bonds shall be paid by the county treasurer from the fund provided therefor.

C. The county treasurer or the treasurer's designated agent shall cancel all bonds and coupons when paid.

Added by Laws 1981, Ch. 1, § 2, eff. Jan. 23, 1981. Amended by Laws 1983, Ch. 183, § 12; Laws 1996, Ch. 111, § 19; Laws 1997, Ch. 276, § 4.

Historical and Statutory Notes

Source:

Laws 1912, Ch. 77, § 51.
Civ.Code 1913, § 2747.
Rev.Code 1928, § 1022.
Code 1939, § 54-427.
A.R.S. former § 15-1327.

§ 15-1023. Issuance of bonds

A. Upon receipt of the certificate of the appropriate election officer as provided in § 15-493 that a majority of votes cast at the bond election favors issuing the bonds, the school district governing board shall issue the bonds of the school district in the number and amount provided in the proceedings, payable from the debt service fund of the school district, naming the fund, and the monies shall be raised by taxation upon the taxable property in the school district for redemption of the bonds and payment of interest thereon.

B. The governing board of the school district by an order entered upon its minutes shall prescribe the form of the bonds and the interest coupons attached thereto and fix the time when the whole or any part of the principal of the bonds is payable, which shall not be more than twenty years from the date thereof.

Added by Laws 1981, Ch. 1, § 2, eff. Jan. 23, 1981. Amended by Laws 1983, Ch. 183, § 13; Laws 1990, Ch. 278, § 8, eff. June 2, 1991; Laws 1996, Ch. 267, § 1.

Historical and Statutory Notes

Source:

Laws 1912, Ch. 77, §§ 48, 49.
Civ.Code 1913, §§ 2740, 2741.
Rev.Code 1928, § 1016.
Code 1939, § 54-421.
A.R.S. former § 15-1321.

§ 15-1023.01. Municipal property corporation financing prohibited; definition

A. Except as provided in subsection C, a school district shall not directly or indirectly pledge its full faith and credit nor incur any direct or indirect obligation of any kind against or pay school district revenues to a municipal property corporation or a special district under title 48 as a means of financing the acquisition or construction of school capital facilities.

B. This section does not apply to any valid obligation initially incurred by a school district on or before December 31, 1998.

C. A school district may pledge school district revenues to a municipal property corporation or a special district under title 48 for the purpose of constructing teacher housing facilities or for any project financed with a loan from the United States department of agriculture.

D. For purposes of this section, "municipal property corporation" means a corporation organized by or at the direction of a city, town or school district to construct and own a capital facility that the school district pledges to lease or lease-purchase and finance with school district revenues.

Added by Laws 1998, 5th S.S., Ch. 1, § 35, eff. July 9, 1998. Amended by Laws 2001, Ch. 11, § 2, eff. Mar. 15, 2001.

Historical and Statutory Notes

The purported addition of this section by Laws 1998, 3rd S.S., Ch. 1, failed to became effective because Ch. 1 was repealed in its entirety by Laws 1998, 5th S.S., Ch. 1, § 2, effective July 1, 1998.

§ 15–1024. Interest on bonds; sale; disposition of proceeds; definition

A. The bonds shall bear interest, payable semiannually at the rate or rates set by the accepted bid, which shall not exceed the maximum rate of interest set forth in the resolution calling the election. The bonds may be made payable at such place within the United States as the governing board of the school district directs and shall be sold in the manner prescribed by the governing board of the school district for not less than par.

B. The proceeds of the sale of the bonds shall be deposited in the county treasury to the credit of the bond building fund of the school district. Such deposits may be drawn out for the purposes authorized by this article as other school monies are drawn. If a balance remains in the bond building fund after the acquisition or construction of facilities is completed for which the bonds were issued and upon written request of the governing board:

1. If the school district has outstanding bonded indebtedness, the balance remaining in the bond building fund shall be transferred to the debt service fund of the district.

2. If the district has no outstanding bonded indebtedness, the balance remaining in the bond building fund shall be transferred to the general fund of the district.

C. When bonds are sold and the proceeds are not required to be used for a period of ten days or more, such proceeds may be invested as provided by § 15–1025, subsection B. All monies earned as interest or otherwise derived from the investment of the proceeds of the sale of the bonds shall be credited to the debt service fund, except that the monies shall be credited to the bond building fund if the voters authorized such use of the monies in a separate question at the bond election. The separate question shall inform the voters that the monies will be credited to the debt service fund, and may therefore reduce the amount of the secondary property tax, if the measure authorizing the monies to be credited to the bond building fund does not pass.

D. The amount of net premium associated with a bond issue may not exceed the greater of:

1. Two per cent of the par value of the bond issue.

2. One hundred thousand dollars.

E. Any net premium not used to pay the costs of the bond issue shall be deposited in a debt service fund and used to pay interest on the bonds.

F. For purposes of this section "net premium" means the difference between the par amount of the bond issue and the bond issue price determined pursuant to United States treasury regulations.

Added by Laws 1981, Ch. 1, § 2, eff. Jan. 23, 1981. Amended by Laws 1983, Ch. 183, § 14; Laws 1985, Ch. 244, § 1; Laws 1996, Ch. 267, § 2; Laws 1996, Ch. 332, § 1, eff. July 20, 1996, retroactively effective to April 1, 1996.

Historical and Statutory Notes

Source:

Laws 1913, 2nd S.S., Ch. 6, § 1.
Civ.Code 1913, §§ 2742, 2743, 2746.
Laws 1927, Ch. 76, § 1.
Rev.Code 1928, §§ 1017, 1018, 1021.
Code 1939, § 54-422.
Laws 1953, Ch. 68, §§ 1, 2.
Code 1939, Supp.1953, §§ 54-423, 54-426.
A.R.S former §§ 15-1322, 15-1324.
Laws 1956, Ch. 119, § 25.
Laws 1970, Ch. 89, § 12.
Laws 1978, Ch. 74, § 4.

Laws 1996, Ch. 332, §§ 9 and 10, provide:

"**Sec. 9. Prohibition on use of premium related capacity**

"Bonds shall not be issued if the bonds would be valid within constitutional debt limits only by virtue of unused debt capacity available on March 31, 1996 as a result of the issuance of refunding bonds with a par amount less than the par amount of the bonds refunded. Debt capacity resulting from the repayment of bonds, increase in value of taxable property or changes in law may be utilized.

"**Sec. 10. Retroactive effective dates**

"Sections 15-1024, 35-457, 35-471 and 35-473.01, Arizona Revised Statutes, as amended by this act, and § 9 of this act are effective retroactively from and after March 31, 1996."

The purported amendment of this section by Laws 1998, 3rd S.S., Ch. 1, failed to became effective because Ch. 1 was repealed in its entirety by Laws 1998, 5th S.S., Ch. 1, § 2, effective July 1, 1998.

Reviser's Notes:

1996 Note. This section contains the amendments made by Laws 1996, Ch. 267, sec. 2 and Ch. 332, sec. 1 that were blended together as shown above pursuant to authority of § 41-1304.03.

§ 15-1025. Investment and reinvestment of debt service fund

A. The governing board of a school district may invest and reinvest all monies belonging or credited to the school district as a debt service fund. Consent may be requested prior to the beginning of any fiscal year for the adoption of a resolution of continuing effect. The investment shall be made for the best interests of the school district.

B. The funds may be invested and reinvested in any of the following:

1. Bonds or other evidences of indebtedness of the United States of America or any of its agencies or instrumentalities when such obligations are guaranteed as to principal and interest by the United States of America or by any agency or instrumentality thereof.

2. Bonds or other evidences of indebtedness of this state, or of any of the counties or incorporated cities, towns or school districts of this state.

3. Bonds, notes or evidences of indebtedness of any county, municipality or municipal district utility within this state, which are payable from revenues or earnings specifically pledged for the payment of the principal and interest on such obligations, and for the payment of which a lawful debt service fund or reserve fund has been established and is being maintained, but only if no default in payment of principal or interest on the obligations to be purchased has occurred within five years of the date of investment therein or, if such obligations were issued less than five years prior to the date of investment, no default in payment of principal or interest has occurred on the obligations to be

purchased, nor on any other obligations of the issuer within five years of such investment.

4. Bonds, notes or evidences of indebtedness issued by any municipal improvement district in this state to finance local improvements authorized by law, if the principal and interest of such obligations are payable from assessments on real property within such local improvement district. No such investment shall be made if the face value of all such obligations and similar obligations outstanding exceeds fifty per cent of the market value of the real property and improvements upon which such bonds or the assessments for the payment of principal and interest thereon are liens inferior only to the liens for general ad valorem property taxes. Such investment shall be made only if no default in payment of principal or interest on the obligations to be purchased has occurred within five years of the date of investment therein or, if such obligations were issued less than five years prior to the date of investment, no default in payment of principal or interest has occurred on the obligations to be purchased, nor on any other obligation of the issuer within five years of such investment.

5. Interest bearing savings accounts or certificates of deposit insured in banks or savings and loan associations doing business in Arizona by the federal deposit insurance corporation, but only if they are secured by the depository to the same extent and in the same manner as required by the general depository law of this state. Security shall not be required for that portion of any deposit that is insured under any law of the United States.

6. Bonds, debentures or other obligations issued by the federal land banks, the federal intermediate credit banks or the banks for cooperatives.

C. The purchase of the securities shall be made by the county treasurer or the treasurer's designated agent upon authority of a resolution of the governing board. The county treasurer shall be the custodian of all securities so purchased. The securities may be sold upon an order of the governing board.

D. All monies earned as interest or otherwise derived by virtue of the provisions of this section shall be credited to the debt service fund.

Added by Laws 1981, Ch. 1, § 2, eff. Jan. 23, 1981. Amended by Laws 1996, Ch. 111, § 20; Laws 1996, Ch. 267, § 3; Laws 1998, Ch. 233, § 6.

Historical and Statutory Notes

Source:

Civ.Code 1913, § 2743.
Laws 1927, Ch. 76, § 1.
Rev.Code 1928, § 1018.
Laws 1953, Ch. 68, § 1.
Code 1939, Supp.1953, § 54-423.
A.R.S. former § 15-1323.
Laws 1956, Ch. 119, § 24.
Laws 1959, Ch. 67, § 1.
Laws 1971, Ch. 113, § 2.
Laws 1975, Ch. 37, § 4.
Laws 1978, Ch. 74, § 3.

Reviser's Notes:

1996 Note. Prior to the 1998 amendment, this section contained the amendments made by Laws 1996, Ch. 111, sec. 20 and Ch. 267, sec. 3 that were blended together pursuant to authority of § 41-1304.03.

§ 15-1026. Repealed by Laws 1996, Ch. 111, § 21

Historical and Statutory Notes

The repealed section, added by Laws 1981, Ch. 1, § 2, related to interest on, and securities for, investments or deposits, and was derived from:

Civ.Code 1913, § 2744.
Rev.Code 1928, § 1019.
Code 1939, § 54-424.
A.R.S. former § 15-1325.

§ 15-1027. Administration of school district debt service funds by county treasurer

The county treasurer shall keep an account of all school district debt service funds, showing the school district to which each fund belongs. On or before the fifteenth day of each month the treasurer shall credit the amount of monies collected during the preceding month to which the school district is entitled. The treasurer shall receive and credit any and all interest or income earned by the debt service fund.

Added by Laws 1981, Ch. 1, § 2, eff. Jan. 23, 1981. Amended by Laws 1996, Ch. 111, § 22; Laws 1998, Ch. 233, § 7.

Historical and Statutory Notes

Source:

Civ.Code 1913, § 2745.
Rev.Code 1928, § 1020.
Code 1939, § 54-425.
A.R.S. former § 15-1326.

§ 15-1028. Disposition of surplus tax monies

A. If a bond issue and interest thereon have been fully paid and a balance remains in the debt service fund from taxes collected for payment of the bonds and interest, the balance may be applied on the payment of other outstanding bonded indebtedness of the school district payable from the levy of taxes on property within the school district in which the excess tax monies were collected, or if there is no outstanding bonded indebtedness, the balance remaining in or accruing to the debt service fund shall, upon written request of the governing board of the school district, be transferred to the general fund of the school district.

B. When a school bond issue and interest thereon have been fully paid and a tax levy has thereafter been made upon and taxes collected from property the situs of which is in a school district other than the original school district for which the levy was made, such taxes shall belong to the school district from which they were collected, and the county treasurer shall credit such taxes to the general school fund of the school district. The taxes may be expended by the governing board of the school district as other monies in its general school fund are expended.

Added by Laws 1981, Ch. 1, § 2, eff. Jan. 23, 1981. Amended by Laws 1983, Ch. 183, § 15.

Historical and Statutory Notes

Source:

Laws 1941, Ch. 21, § 1.
Code 1939, Supp.1952, § 54-427a.
A.R.S. former § 15-1328.

§ 15–1029. Rights of bondholder; additional state tax

A. If the board of supervisors fails to make the levy necessary to pay school district bonds or interest coupons at maturity and such bonds or coupons are presented to the county treasurer and payment is refused, the owner may file the bond, together with all unpaid coupons, with the department of administration, taking his receipt therefor. Such bonds and coupons shall be registered with the department of administration.

B. The department of revenue shall add to the tax to be levied by the school district which issued the bonds a sufficient rate to obtain the amount of principal or interest past due prior to the next levy. The tax shall be levied and collected as a part of the school district tax but shall be paid into the state treasury, shall be passed to the special credit of the school district bond tax and shall, as payments mature, be paid by warrants to the holder of registered obligations as shown by the register in the department of administration until such obligations are fully satisfied and discharged. Any balance then remaining shall be remitted to the general account and credit of the school district.

Added by Laws 1981, Ch. 1, § 2, eff. Jan. 23, 1981. Amended by Laws 1996, Ch. 267, § 4; Laws 1996, 7th S.S., Ch. 2, § 3.

Retroactive Application

This section, as amended by Laws 1996, 7th Special Session, Ch. 2, applies retroactively to tax years beginning January 1, 1996.

Historical and Statutory Notes

Source:

Laws 1912, Ch. 77, § 52.
Civ.Code 1913, § 2748.
Rev.Code 1928, § 1023.
Code 1939, § 54–428.
A.R.S. former § 15–1329.
Laws 1970, Ch. 190, § 18.
Laws 1974, Ch. 164, § 3.

Laws 1996, 7th S.S., Ch. 2, § 16, subsec. A, provides:

"**Sec. 16. Retroactivity**

"**A.** Sections 1, 2, 3, 5 through 8, 10, 12 and 15 apply retroactively to tax years beginning from and after December 31, 1995."

§ 15–1030. Cancellation of unsold bonds; notice; hearing

A. If a bond issue remains unsold for six months after being offered for sale, the governing board of the school district or any school district comprised wholly or partly of territory which at the time of holding the bond election was within the school district may cancel the unsold bonds.

B. The school district governing board shall fix a time for a hearing on the proposed cancellation of the unsold bonds. The school district governing board shall give notice of the time and place of the hearing which shall set forth in general terms the object of the hearing. The notice shall be published for ten days prior to the day of hearing in some newspaper published in the school district. If no newspaper is published in the school district, the notice shall be published in a newspaper published at the county seat of the county in which the school district or some part thereof is located.

C. At the time and place designated in the notice the school district governing board shall hear reasons for or against granting the proposed cancellation of the unsold bonds, and if the board deems it for the best interests of the school district that the unsold bonds be canceled it shall enter an order canceling the unsold bonds, and thereupon the bonds and the vote by which they were authorized to be issued shall be void.

Added by Laws 1981, Ch. 1, § 2, eff. Jan. 23, 1981. Amended by Laws 1996, Ch. 267, § 5.

Historical and Statutory Notes

Source:

Laws 1912, Ch. 77, § 53.
Civ.Code 1913, § 2749.
Rev.Code 1928, § 1024.
Code 1939, § 54-429.
A.R.S. former § 15-1330.

The purported amendment of this section by Laws 1998, 3rd S.S., Ch. 1, failed to became effective because Ch. 1 was repealed in its entirety by Laws 1998, 5th S.S., Ch. 1, § 2, effective July 1, 1998.

§ 15-1031. Power to use outstanding bond authorizations of common school districts or high school districts

A. All outstanding authorizations permitting the issuance of bonds, as provided in this section and §§ 15-1022 through 15-1030, or the incurring of debt by a common school district or a high school district at the time either such district becomes part of a unified school district, shall remain in full force and effect. The unified school district shall be vested with all powers to act for and on behalf of such common school district or high school district to issue the bonds for the purposes for which such authorizations were granted. The school district governing board may submit the bonds for approval by the attorney general.

B. The bonds shall be issued pursuant to this section, chapter 4, article 5 of this title and §§ 15-1021 through 15-1030 except that the effect of the bonds issued pursuant to this section shall be the same as if the questions pertaining to the issuance of the bonds had been submitted to and approved by the electors of the unified school district after its formation.

C. The provisions of this section shall not be construed as authorizing indebtedness in excess of the percentage limitation as prescribed for a unified school district in article IX, § 8.1, Constitution of Arizona.

Added by Laws 1981, Ch. 1, § 2, eff. Jan. 23, 1981. Amended by Laws 1996, Ch. 267, § 6.

Historical and Statutory Notes

Source:

Laws 1976, Ch. 11, § 1.
A.R.S. former § 15-1331.

The purported amendment of this section by Laws 1998, Ch. 164 failed to become effective because Chapter 164 was repealed in its entirety by Laws 1998, 5th S.S., Ch. 1, § 2, effective July 1, 1998.

The purported amendment of this section by Laws 1998, 3rd S.S., Ch. 1, failed to became effective because Ch. 1 was repealed in its entirety by Laws 1998, 5th S.S., Ch. 1, § 2, effective July 1, 1998.

§ 15-1032. Capital facilities; bonded indebtedness liability for unified school districts

A. All school buildings of established school districts which are located within any unified school district shall, together with all equipment and furnishings, become the property of the unified school district.

B. If any established common school district or high school district has a bonded indebtedness liability, the liability or so much of it as is attributable to facilities located within the boundaries of any unified school district shall become an assumed indebtedness liability of the unified school district. The unified school district governing board shall levy a tax against the property of the unified school district for the payment of the principal and interest, but nothing in this section shall be construed to relieve the taxable property in the theretofore existing school districts from liability to taxation for the payment thereof if necessary to prevent a default in such payment. The unified school district shall assume the indebtedness liabilities of the existing school districts which shall be regarded as an indebtedness of the unified school district for the purpose of determining the debt incurring capacity of the unified school district.

Added by Laws 1981, Ch. 1, § 2, eff. Jan. 23, 1981.

Historical and Statutory Notes

Source:

Laws 1974, 1st S.S., Ch. 3, § 65.
A.R.S. former § 15–497.

§ 15–1033. Certification of school district bonds by attorney general

A. Any school district may submit to the attorney general bonds to be issued under this article after the school district has authorized their issuance. Within fifteen days after submission by the school district, the attorney general shall examine the bonds and pass on the validity of the bonds and the regularity of the proceedings authorizing their issuance.

B. If the bonds and proceedings submitted to the attorney general by a school district conform to the laws of this state, and if the bonds when delivered and paid for will constitute binding and legal obligations of the school district according to the terms of the bonds, the attorney general shall certify in substance that the bonds are issued in accordance with the constitution and laws of this state.

Added by Laws 1996, 7th S.S., Ch. 1, § 2.

Historical and Statutory Notes

Former § 15–1033, added by Laws 1981, Ch. 1, § 2, amended by Laws 1983, Ch. 118, § 5, derived from Laws 1974, 1st S.S., Ch. 3, § 62; A.R.S. former § 15–403.03; Laws 1975, Ch. 103, § 4, relating to assumption of indebtedness, was repealed by Laws 1985, Ch. 238, § 11.

ARTICLE 8. STUDENT ACCOUNTABILITY INFORMATION SYSTEM

Article 8, Student Accountability Information System, consisting of §§ 15–1041 to 15–1043, was added by Laws 2000, 5th S.S., Ch. 1, § 17.

Former Article 8, State Board for School Capital Facilities, consisting of §§ 15–1051 to 15–1054, was added by Laws 1996, 5th S.S., Ch. 8, § 13, effective, June 24, 1996, and was repealed by Laws 1997, Ch. 4, § 16, as amended by Laws 1997, 1st S.S., Ch. 9, § 1, six months after the final adjudication of Roosevelt Elementary School District No. 66 v. Bishop, 179 Ariz. 233, 877 P.2d 806 (1994).

§ 15-1041. Student accountability information system

The student accountability information system is established to enable school districts and charter schools to transmit student level data and school finance data electronically through the internet to the department of education for the purposes of complying with the statutory obligations of the department of education and the state board of education.

Added by Laws 2000, 5th S.S., Ch. 1, § 17.

Historical and Statutory Notes

Laws 2000, 5th S.S., Ch. 1, §§ 66 and 67, provide:

"**Sec. 66. Delayed implementation**

"This act shall not be implemented until from and after May 31, 2001.

"**Sec. 67. Conditional enactment**

"This act does not become effective unless the qualified electors of this state in the general election that will be held in November, 2000 approve an increase in state transaction privilege tax rates of six-tenths of one per cent in order to fund the provisions of this act." [See note, post.]

Proposition 301, approved by the electors at the Nov. 7, 2000 general election, effective Nov. 27, 2000, included a provision increasing the state transaction privilege tax rate six-tenths of one per cent. Therefore, the conditions of the 5th S.S. Ch. 1 were met, and the act became effective.

§ 15-1042. Time line; student level data; definition

A. The department of education shall notify school districts and charter schools of electronic data submission procedures and shall distribute a list of the specific student level data elements that school districts and charter schools are required to submit. The department of education shall not make any changes to the student level data elements to be collected except for the following:

1. Student attendance data for a joint technological education district, including entry date and exit date, for classes that count towards the student's graduation requirements as provided for in § 15-701.01.

2. Student attendance data for a community college, unless the college is owned, operated or chartered by an Indian tribe, including entry date and exit date, for classes that count towards the student's graduation requirements as provided for in § 15-701.01.

B. By July 1, 2001, each school district and charter school shall submit electronic data on a school by school basis, including student level data, to the department of education in order for the school district or charter school to receive monies for the cost of educating students pursuant to this title.

C. The department of education shall grant a school district or charter school an extension to the deadline for the submission of student level data or may provide for an alternative method for the submission of student level data if the school district or charter school proves that good cause exists for the extension, and the school district or charter school shall continue to receive monies for the cost of educating students pursuant to this title. A school district or charter school requesting an extension shall notify the department of education no later than June 1, 2001. The request by a school district or charter school for an extension of the deadline for the submission of student level data shall include a justification for the extension and the status of current efforts towards complying with the submission of student level data.

D. A pupil or the parent or guardian of a pupil shall not be required to submit data that does not relate to the provision of educational services or assistance to the pupil.

E. Each student level data element shall include a statutory reference to the law that necessitates its collection.

F. Student level data items submitted to the department of education by school districts pursuant to this section shall not be used to adjust funding levels or calculate the average daily membership for the purpose of funding school districts at any time other than the fortieth, one hundredth and two hundredth day of the school year.

G. A school district or charter school is not required to submit student level data to the department of education more often than once every twenty school days.

H. Notwithstanding subsection K of this section, the student level data shall include reasons for the withdrawal if reasons are provided by the withdrawing pupil or the pupil's parent or guardian. For the purposes of this subsection, the department of education shall include in the specific student level data elements that school districts and charter schools are required to submit data relating to students who withdraw from school because the student is pregnant or because the student is the biological parent of a child.

I. The department of education shall adopt guidelines to remove outdated student level data collected by school districts and charter schools from the student accountability information system beginning in the 2004–2005 school year.

J. All student level data collected pursuant to this section is confidential and is not a public record. The data collected may be used for aggregate research and reporting.

K. For the purposes of this section, "student level data" means all data elements that are compiled and submitted for each student in this state and that are necessary for the completion of the statutory requirements of the department of education and the state board of education relating to the calculation of funding for public education, the determination of student academic progress as measured by student testing programs in this state, state and federal reporting requirements and other duties prescribed to the department of education or the state board of education by law. Student level data does not include data elements related to student behavior, discipline, criminal history, medical history, religious affiliation, personal physical descriptors or family information not authorized by the parent or guardian of the pupil.

Added by Laws 2000, 5th S.S., Ch. 1, § 17. Amended by Laws 2001, Ch. 372, § 1, eff. July 2, 2002; Laws 2002, Ch. 275, § 1; Laws 2003, Ch. 130, § 1.

Retroactive Application

This section, as added by Laws 2000, 5th S.S., Ch. 1, § 17, amended by Laws 2002, Ch. 275, § 1, applies retroactively to April 1, 2002.

Historical and Statutory Notes

Laws 2002, Ch. 275, § 3, provides:

"**Sec. 3. Retroactivity**

"Section 15-1042, Arizona Revised Statutes, as added by Laws 2000, fifth special session, chapter 1, § 17 and as amended by this act, applies retroactively to from and after March 31, 2002."

Proposition 301, approved by the electors at the Nov. 7, 2000 general election, effective Nov. 27, 2000, included a provision increasing the state transaction privilege tax rate six-tenths of one per cent. Therefore, the conditions of the 5th S.S. Ch. 1 were met, and the act became effective.

The 2002 amendment of this section by Ch. 275, explicitly amended the addition of this section by Laws 2000, 5th S.S., Ch. 1, § 17.

The amendment of this section by Laws 2001, Ch. 372, § 1, was repealed by Laws 2002, Ch. 275, § 2.

§ 15-1043. Student level data; confidentiality

Any disclosure of educational records compiled by the department of education pursuant to this article shall comply with the family educational and privacy rights act (20 United States Code § 1232g). Student level data is the property of the school district or charter school and may not be updated unless the change is authorized by the school district or charter school.

Added by Laws 2000, 5th S.S., Ch. 1, § 17.

Historical and Statutory Notes

Proposition 301, approved by the electors at the Nov. 7, 2000 general election, effective Nov. 27, 2000, included a provision increasing the state transaction privilege tax rate six-tenths of one per cent. Therefore, the conditions of the 5th S.S. Ch. 1 were met, and the act became effective.

§§ 15-1051 to 15-1054. Repealed by Laws 1997, Ch. 4, § 16, as amended by Laws 1997, 1st S.S., Ch. 9, § 1

Historical and Statutory Notes

The repealed sections, added by Laws 1996, 5th S.S., Ch. 8, § 13, amended by Laws 1996, Ch. 284, § 58; Laws 1996, 7th S.S., Ch. 1, §§ 3 to 5; Laws 1997, Ch. 4, §§ 5 to 7, eff. July 21, 1997, retroactively effective to July 1, 1997; Laws 1997, Ch. 266, §§ 1, 2, eff. July 1, 1997; Laws 1997, Ch. 271, § 5, related to the state board for school capital facilities and the school capital equity fund. See now, generally, § 15-2001 et seq.

Laws 1997, Ch. 4, §§ 13 and 14, provide:

"**Sec. 13. Existing provisions; school districts and the state board for school capital facilities**

"**A.** The provisions of § 15-1054, Arizona Revised Statutes, as added by Laws 1996, fifth special session, chapter 8, § 13 as amended by Laws 1996, seventh special session, chapter 1, § 5 shall continue to apply to the state board for school capital facilities in processing applications from school districts that have applied for assistance from the school capital equity fund prior to the effective date of this act.

"**B.** The provisions of § 15-1054, Arizona Revised Statutes, as amended by § 6 of this act, shall apply to the state board for school capital facilities and to school districts that apply for assistance from the school capital equity fund after the effective date of this act.

"**Sec. 14. Existing capital outlay revenue limit overrides**

"**A.** Notwithstanding the provisions of § 15-1054, subsection F, Arizona Revised Statutes, as added by this act, the state board for school capital facilities may provide a state grant to a school district if all of the following apply:

"1. The school district has a bonding capacity per pupil equal to or greater than the amounts prescribed in § 15-1054, subsection A, Arizona Revised Statutes.

"2. The school district governing board has made application to the state board for school capital facilities for monies from the school capital equity fund for a capital project for which the district has insufficient bonding capacity.

"3. The voters in the school district vote between January 1, 1997 and June 30, 1997 to adopt a budget in excess of the capital outlay revenue limit as provided in § 15-481, subsections L and M, Arizona Revised Statutes, to fund the entire cost of the capital project.

"4. The state board for school capital facilities approves the project.

"**B.** The amount of the state grant is computed as follows:

"1. Determine the total cost of the approved capital project.

"2. From the amount determined in paragraph 1 of this subsection subtract any available bonding capacity.

"3. Determine the growth weighted student count as provided in § 15-1054, subsection G, paragraph 1, Arizona Revised Statutes, as added by this act.

"4. Divide the amount determined in paragraph 2 of this subsection by the amount determined in paragraph 3 of this subsection.

"5. Divide the amount determined in paragraph 4 of this subsection by one hundred dollars.

"6. Multiply the amount determined in paragraph 5 of this subsection by the applicable tax rate provided in § 15-1054, subsection G, paragraph 4, Arizona Revised Statutes, as added by this act.

"7. Multiply the applicable tax rate determined in paragraph 6 of this subsection by the secondary assessed valuation of the school district for the fiscal year in which the capital project was approved by the state board for school capital facilities.

"8. Multiply the result determined in paragraph 7 of this subsection by five.

"9. Subtract the amount determined in paragraph 8 of this subsection from the amount determined in paragraph 2 of this subsection. If the amount is positive, the result is the amount of the state grant. If the amount is negative, there is no state grant.

"**C.** A school district which receives a state grant under the provisions of this section may apply the amount of the state grant to any of the following:

"1. The approved capital project, by the reduction in the amount needed each year from the capital outlay revenue limit override or by the reduction in the number of years which the capital outlay revenue limit override needs to be in effect.

"2. An additional capital project, provided that it has been approved by the state board for school capital facilities.

"3. Assist in funding an additional capital project, for which a request has been made to, and approval granted by, the state board for school capital facilities, through its use in fully or partially offsetting the computed tax rate amount provided in § 15-1054, subsection G, paragraph 4, Arizona Revised Statutes, as added by this act."

Laws 1997, Ch. 4, § 16, as amended by Laws 1997, 1st S.S., Ch. 9, § 1, provides:

"**Sec. 16. Conditional repeal**

"**A.** If there is a final adjudication [see note, post] in the proceedings resulting from the Arizona supreme court's decision in Roosevelt Elementary School District No. 66 v. Bishop, 179 Ariz. 233, 877 P.2d 806 (1994) that this act, in conjunction with Laws 1996, fifth special session, chapter 8 and Laws 1996, seventh special session, chapter 1, does not ensure a constitutional system of education:

"1. This act and Laws 1996, fifth special session, chapter 8, § 14 are void and are repealed as of the date of the final adjudication.

"2. Laws 1996, fifth special session, chapter 8, §§ 1, 13, 15 and 17 and laws 1996, seventh special session, chapter 1, §§ 3, 4 and 5 are void and are repealed six months after the date of the final adjudication.

"**B.** Subsection A of this section does not invalidate any contractual obligations of the state board for school capital facilities that may have been incurred before the repeal prescribed in subsection A, paragraph 2 of this section, including school districts that have been given preliminary approvals by the state board for school capital facilities before the date of final adjudication, not to exceed the balance of the school capital equity fund established by § 15-1053, Arizona Revised Statutes, on the date of the final adjudication. After the date of final adjudication, the state board shall not enter into any contractual obligations not related to a preliminary approval given before the date of the final adjudication or give any new preliminary approvals. Between the date of final adjudication and the repeal prescribed in subsection A, paragraph 2 of this section, nothing in this section shall be construed to prohibit the board from paying its costs of operation as prescribed by law.

"**C.** On the discontinuation of the state board for school capital facilities, the department of education shall assume responsibility for distributing monies and receiving reports and repayment obligations from school districts pursuant to contracts and preliminary approvals entered into between the state board and school districts before the final adjudication referred to in subsection A of this section. Any monies remitted to the department of education pursuant to this subsection shall be transmitted to the state general fund. The department of education shall submit an annual report to the president of the senate, the speaker of the house of representatives and the governor that summarizes the reports and amount of repayments from school districts."

The conditions for the repeals by this section have been met. The Supreme Court in Order No. CV-97-0369-SA, dated October 24, 1997, declared that the legislature's 1997 school funding plan was unconstitutional; the order of July 28, 1994, was still in effect; and, that the order of the trial court dated August 20, 1997 was approved. A written opinion followed, dated December 23, 1997 (Hull v. Albrecht, 190 Ariz. 520, 950 P.2d 1141 (1997)). An informal Attorney General Opinion considers December 23, 1997, the date the written Supreme Court decision was released, as the final date of adjudication. A subsequent amendment to cure the constitutional infirmity by Laws 1998, 3rd S.S., Ch. 1 was also declared unconstitutional by the Supreme Court (Hull v. Albrecht 192 Ariz. 34, 960 P.2d 634 (1998)).

Laws 1997, 1st S.S., Ch. 4, § 12, provides:

"**Sec. 12. School capital equity fund monies; use**

"Notwithstanding § 15-1054, Arizona Revised Statutes, and subject to legislative appropriation, no more than two per cent of the monies in the school capital equity fund deposited pursuant to § 37-521, Arizona Revised Statutes, may be used by the state board for school capital facilities for fiscal years 1997-1998 and 1998-1999 for administrative costs and technical assistance to school districts. This limit does not apply to monies appropriated by Laws 1997, chapter 4."

Laws 1998, 5th S.S., Ch. 1, §§ 49 and 50, provide:

"**Sec. 49. Termination of state board for school capital facilities**

"Notwithstanding any unfulfilled condition prescribed by Laws 1997, chapter 4, § 16, as amended by Laws 1997, first special session, chapter 9, § 1, the state board for school capital facilities is terminated for all purposes.

"**Sec. 50. Assistance to build classroom monies; reversion to state general fund**

"Notwithstanding any unfulfilled condition prescribed by Laws 1997, chapter 4, § 16, as amended by Laws 1997, first special session, chapter 9, § 1, all unexpended monies remaining in the assistance to build classrooms fund revert to the state general fund."

ARTICLE 9. ASSISTANCE TO BUILD CLASSROOMS [REPEALED]

Article 9, Assistance to Build Classrooms, consisting of §§ 15-1061 and 15-1062, was added by Laws 1997, Ch. 4, § 8, effective July 21, 1997, retroactively effective to July 1, 1997, and was repealed by Laws 1997, Ch. 4, § 16, as amended by Laws 1997, 1st S.S., Ch. 9, § 1, effective October 24, 1997.

§§ 15-1061, 15-1062. Repealed by Laws 1997, Ch. 4, § 16, as amended by Laws 1997, 1st S.S., Ch. 9, § 1, eff. Oct. 24, 1997

Historical and Statutory Notes

Laws 1997, Ch. 4, § 16, as amended by Laws 1997, 1st S.S., Ch. 9, § 1, provides:

"**Sec. 16. Conditional repeal**

"**A.** If there is a final adjudication [see note, post] in the proceedings resulting from the Arizona supreme court's decision in Roosevelt Elementary School District No. 66 v. Bishop, 179 Ariz. 233, 877 P.2d 806 (1994) that this act, in conjunction with Laws 1996, fifth special session, chapter 8 and Laws 1996, seventh special session, chapter 1, does not ensure a constitutional system of education:

"1. This act and Laws 1996, fifth special session, chapter 8, § 14 are void and are repealed as of the date of the final adjudication.

"2. Laws 1996, fifth special session, chapter 8, §§ 1, 13, 15 and 17 and laws 1996, seventh special session, chapter 1, §§ 3, 4 and 5 are void and are repealed six months after the date of the final adjudication.

"**B.** Subsection A of this section does not invalidate any contractual obligations of the state board for school capital facilities that may have been incurred before the repeal prescribed in subsection A, paragraph 2 of this section, including school districts that have been given preliminary approvals by the state board for school capital facilities before the date of final adjudication, not to exceed the balance of the school capital equity fund established by § 15-1053, Arizona Revised Statutes, on the date of the final adjudication. After the date of final adjudication, the state board shall not enter into any contractual obligations not related to a preliminary approval given before the date of the final adjudication or give any new preliminary approvals. Between the date of final adjudication and the repeal prescribed in subsection A, paragraph 2 of this section, nothing in this section shall be construed to prohibit the board from paying its costs of operation as prescribed by law.

"C. On the discontinuation of the state board for school capital facilities, the department of education shall assume responsibility for distributing monies and receiving reports and repayment obligations from school districts pursuant to contracts and preliminary approvals entered into between the state board and school districts before the final adjudication referred to in subsection A of this section. Any monies remitted to the department of education pursuant to this subsection shall be transmitted to the state general fund. The department of education shall submit an annual report to the president of the senate, the speaker of the house of representatives and the governor that summarizes the reports and amount of repayments from school districts."

The conditions for the repeals by this section have been met. The Supreme Court in Order No. CV-97-0369-SA, dated October 24, 1997, declared that the legislature's 1997 school funding plan was unconstitutional; the order of July 28, 1994, was still in effect; and, that the order of the trial court dated August 20, 1997 was approved. A written opinion followed, dated December 23, 1997 (Hull v. Albrecht, 190 Ariz. 520, 950 P.2d 1141 (1997)). An informal Attorney General Opinion considers December 23, 1997, the date the written Supreme Court decision was released, as the final date of adjudication. A subsequent amendment to cure the constitutional infirmity by Laws 1998, 3rd S.S., Ch. 1 was also declared unconstitutional by the Supreme Court (Hull v. Albrecht 192 Ariz. 34, 960 P.2d 634 (1998)).

ARTICLE 10. SCHOOL DISTRICT REVENUE BONDS [REPEALED]

Article 10, School District Revenue Bonds, consisting of §§ 15-1071 to 15-1086, was added by Laws 1997, Ch. 4, § 8, effective July 21, 1997, retroactively effective to July 1, 1997 and was repealed by Laws 1997, Ch. 4, § 16, as amended by Laws 1997, 1st S.S., Ch. 9, § 1, effective October 24, 1997.

§§ 15-1071 to 15-1086. Repealed by Laws 1997, Ch. 4, § 16, as amended by Laws 1997, 1st S.S., Ch. 9, § 1, eff. Oct. 24, 1997

Historical and Statutory Notes

Laws 1997, Ch. 4, § 16, as amended by Laws 1997, 1st S.S., Ch. 9, § 1, provides:

"**Sec. 16. Conditional repeal**

"**A.** If there is a final adjudication [see note, post] in the proceedings resulting from the Arizona supreme court's decision in Roosevelt Elementary School District No. 66 v. Bishop, 179 Ariz. 233, 877 P.2d 806 (1994) that this act, in conjunction with Laws 1996, fifth special session, chapter 8 and Laws 1996, seventh special session, chapter 1, does not ensure a constitutional system of education:

"1. This act and Laws 1996, fifth special session, chapter 8, § 14 are void and are repealed as of the date of the final adjudication.

"2. Laws 1996, fifth special session, chapter 8, §§ 1, 13, 15 and 17 and laws 1996, seventh special session, chapter 1, §§ 3, 4 and 5 are void and are repealed six months after the date of the final adjudication.

"**B.** Subsection A of this section does not invalidate any contractual obligations of the state board for school capital facilities that may have been incurred before the repeal prescribed in subsection A, paragraph 2 of this section, including school districts that have been given preliminary approvals by the state board for school capital facilities before the date of final adjudication, not to exceed the balance of the school capital equity fund established by § 15-1053, Arizona Revised Statutes, on the date of the final adjudication. After the date of final adjudication, the state board shall not enter into any contractual obligations not related to a preliminary approval given before the date of the final adjudication or give any new preliminary approvals. Between the date of final adjudication and the repeal prescribed in subsection A, paragraph 2 of this section, nothing in this section shall be construed to prohibit the board from paying its costs of operation as prescribed by law.

"**C.** On the discontinuation of the state board for school capital facilities, the department of education shall assume responsibility for distributing monies and receiving reports and repayment obligations from school districts pursuant to contracts and preliminary approvals entered into between the state board and school districts before the final adjudication referred to in subsection A of this section. Any monies remitted to the department of education pursuant to this subsection shall be transmitted to the state general fund. The department of education shall submit an annual report to the president of the senate, the speaker of the house of representatives and the governor that summarizes the reports and amount of repayments from school districts."

The conditions for the repeals by this section have been met. The Supreme Court in Order No. CV-97-0369-SA, dated October 24, 1997, declared that the legislature's 1997 school funding plan was unconstitutional; the order of July 28, 1994, was still in effect; and, that the order of the trial court dated August 20, 1997 was approved. A written opinion followed, dated December 23, 1997 (Hull v. Albrecht, 190 Ariz. 520, 950 P.2d 1141 (1997)). An informal Attorney General Opinion considers December 23, 1997, the date the written Supreme Court decision was released, as the final date of adjudication. A subsequent amendment to cure the constitutional infirmity by Laws 1998, 3rd S.S., Ch. 1 was also declared unconstitutional by the Supreme Court (Hull v. Albrecht 192 Ariz. 34, 960 P.2d 634 (1998)).

CHAPTER 10

SCHOOL DISTRICT FUNDS AND RELATED OPERATIONS

ARTICLE 1. REVOLVING FUNDS; SCHOOL PLANT, INSURANCE PROCEEDS, UNEMPLOYMENT COMPENSATION, CIVIC CENTER SCHOOL AND PERMANENT TEACHERAGE FUNDS

Section

15–1101. Revolving funds; purpose and manner of procuring.
15–1102. Disposition of proceeds from sale or lease of school property; school plant monies; payment of bonded indebtedness; definition.
15–1103. Insurance proceeds fund; disposition of proceeds.
15–1104. Unemployment compensation fund.
15–1105. Lease of school property; civic center school fund; reversion to school plant fund; definitions.
15–1106. Permanent teacherage fund; uses; definition.
15–1107. Litigation recovery fund; disposition of proceeds.
15–1108. District services fund.

ARTICLE 2. STUDENT ACTIVITIES AND AUXILIARY OPERATIONS FUNDS

15–1121. Student activities monies defined.
15–1122. Student activities treasurer; assistant student activities treasurer; administration of student activities monies.
15–1123. Record of revenues and expenditures.
15–1124. Student activities revolving fund for expenses.
15–1125. Auxiliary operations fund defined.
15–1126. Accounting; deposit; disposition of monies.

ARTICLE 3. COMMUNITY SCHOOL PROGRAM FUND

15–1141. Definitions.
15–1142. Powers of the governing board.
15–1143. Community school program fund.

ARTICLE 4. SCHOOL LUNCH PROGRAM FUND

15–1151. Definition of school meal programs.
15–1152. School meal programs; nonschool meal programs; powers of state board of education.
15–1153. Federal funds; acceptance; disbursement.
15–1154. Operation of school meal programs by governing boards; school meal program fund; revolving fund.
15–1155. Records, reports, regulations, audits and inspections by state board of education.
15–1156. Repealed.
15–1157. Inclusion of expenses in budget of superintendent of public instruction.
15–1158. Agreements for meals for persons sixty years of age or older.

ARTICLE 5. ARIZONA YOUTH FARM LOAN FUND

15–1171. Trust assets of Arizona rural rehabilitation corporation; transfer to state board of education.
15–1172. Arizona youth farm loan fund.
15–1173. Use of funds.
15–1174. Powers and duties.
15–1175. Liability.

ARTICLE 6. EDUCATION VOUCHER FUND FOR PRIVATE PLACEMENT

15–1181. Definitions.

Chapter 10, School District Funds and Related Operations, consisting of Article 1, §§ 15–1101 to 15–1106, Article 2, §§ 15–1121 to 15–1126, Article 3, §§ 15–1141 to 15–1143, Article 4, §§ 15–1151 to 15–1158,

Article 5, §§ 15-1171 to 15-1175, Article 6, §§ 15-1181 to 15-1186, and Article 7, §§ 15-1201 to 15-1205, was added by Laws 1981, Ch. 1, § 2, effective January 23, 1981.

ARTICLE 1. REVOLVING FUNDS; SCHOOL PLANT, INSURANCE PROCEEDS, UNEMPLOYMENT COMPENSATION, CIVIC CENTER SCHOOL AND PERMANENT TEACHERAGE FUNDS

§ 15-1101. Revolving funds; purpose and manner of procuring

A. If the activities of a school district require immediate cash outlays for items including postage, freight, express, fuel taxes, parcel post, travel or other minor disbursements but not including salaries or wages, which are proper as ultimate claims for payment from school district school funds, the governing board, or the superintendent or chief administrative officer with the approval of the governing board, may apply to the county school superintendent to establish and maintain a revolving fund. The allowable amount of the fund shall be fifty cents per student count, except that for a common school district or high school district, at the request of the governing board, or the superintendent or chief administrative officer with the approval of the governing board, the fund may be increased to an amount of five thousand dollars, but in no event shall the amount of the fund be more than ten thousand dollars, and for a unified school district, at the request of the governing board, or the superintendent or chief administrative officer with the approval of the governing board, the fund may be increased to an amount of ten thousand dollars, but in no event shall the amount of the fund be more than twenty thousand dollars. The application shall state the purposes for which the fund is required and the amount deemed necessary and shall designate the particular official of the school district who shall be the custodian of and be charged with the handling and accounting for the fund.

B. The county school superintendent may allow such application, draw a warrant to the order of the designated custodian and charge the amount against the school district fund, but no revolving fund shall be established unless the designated custodian is bonded for an amount equal to twice the amount of the fund. The cost of the bond shall be a proper charge against the school district.

C. The designated custodian shall periodically submit a voucher with supporting papers covering disbursements from the revolving fund to the county school superintendent who shall issue a warrant for the voucher to reimburse the fund. If the school district is dissolved, consolidated, unified or subdivided, or if the governing board, or the superintendent or chief administrative officer with the approval of the governing board, decides to terminate the revolving fund, the designated employee shall return the original amount of the revolving fund to the county treasurer by the date that the dissolution, consolidation, unification or subdivision of the district becomes effective or within thirty days after the date that the governing board decides to terminate the revolving fund, whichever is appropriate.

Added by Laws 1981, Ch. 1, § 2, eff. Jan. 23, 1981. Amended by Laws 1989, Ch. 23, § 1; Laws 1991, Ch. 292, § 13, eff. June 28, 1991; Laws 1996, Ch. 284, § 59.

Historical and Statutory Notes

Source:

Laws 1955, Ch. 64, § 1.
Code 1939, Supp.1955, § 54-621.
A.R.S. former § 15-1248.
Laws 1956, Ch. 53, § 1.
Laws 1961, Ch. 71, § 1.
Laws 1965, Ch. 41, § 1.
Laws 1974, Ch. 119, § 1.

§ 15-1102. Disposition of proceeds from sale or lease of school property; school plant monies; payment of bonded indebtedness; definition

A. The governing board, or the superintendent or chief administrative officer with the approval of the governing board, may expend the proceeds from the sale or lease of school property for the payment of any outstanding bonded indebtedness of the school district or for the reduction of school district taxes.

B. A common school district or high school district which has an outstanding bonded indebtedness of seven per cent of the current year's assessed valuation or less or a unified school district which has an outstanding bonded indebtedness of fourteen per cent of the current year's assessed valuation or less may expend the proceeds from the sale or lease of school property for maintenance and operation or capital outlay, subject to the following limitations:

1. During the period that proceeds from the sale or lease of school property are used for capital outlay, the school district shall not call an override election to exceed the capital outlay revenue limit, except that during the last year of that period the school district may authorize an override election to exceed the capital outlay revenue limit beginning with the following year.

2. The total sum of the proceeds from the sale of school property before July 1, 1998 or the lease of school property for more than one year expended for maintenance and operation shall not exceed fifteen per cent of the revenue control limit as provided in § 15-947, subsection A in any year of which ten per cent may be used without voter approval and an additional five per cent may be used if the additional amount is approved by a majority of the qualified electors voting in an election called for such purposes. The election shall be conducted and notice and ballots shall be prepared as provided in § 15-481. Proceeds from the sale of school property from and after June 30, 1998 shall not be expended for maintenance and operation.

3. In any fiscal year in which a district utilizes budget increases as authorized in § 15-481, subsection E or F or § 15-482 or utilizes the proceeds from the sale of school property before July 1, 1998 or the lease of school property for more than one year for maintenance and operation or any combination of these provisions, the total amount of these increases which may be expended is equal to fifteen per cent of the revenue control limit for that year as provided in § 15-947, subsection A, provided that the following maximum amount is attributable to the use of any one provision:

(a) Fifteen per cent of the revenue control limit when using the proceeds from the sale before July 1, 1998 or lease of school property for maintenance and operation as provided in this section.

(b) Ten per cent of the revenue control limit when using a budget increase as provided in § 15–481, subsection E or F, or both.

(c) Five per cent of the revenue control limit when using a budget increase as provided in § 15–482.

C. A common school district or high school district which has an outstanding bonded indebtedness of greater than seven per cent of the current year's assessed valuation or a unified school district which has an outstanding bonded indebtedness of greater than fourteen per cent of the current year's assessed valuation may expend the proceeds from the lease or sale of school property as follows:

1. For maintenance and operation the expenditure may not exceed the lesser of the limit in subsection B, paragraph 2 or 3 of this section or the amount of the proceeds from the lease of school property multiplied by .25.

2. For capital outlay, the expenditure of the proceeds:

(a) From the sale of school property may not exceed the amount of the proceeds multiplied by .62.

(b) From the lease of school property is not limited.

D. The governing board, or the superintendent or chief administrative officer with the approval of the governing board, shall promptly deposit monies received for and derived from the sale or lease of school property with the county treasurer who shall establish three school plant funds, one fund for monies received from the sale before July 1, 1998 or lease of school property for more than one year, one fund for monies received from the sale of school property from and after June 30, 1998 and one fund for monies received from the lease of school property for one year or less. The county treasurer shall credit the deposits to the respective school plant fund of the respective school district. Monies placed to the credit of the school plant funds may be expended as provided in this section. The school plant funds are continuing funds not subject to reversion.

E. Notwithstanding subsection C of this section, the governing board, or the superintendent or chief administrative officer with the approval of the governing board, may expend the proceeds from the sale before July 1, 1998 or lease of school property for the additional maintenance and operations expenses incurred as the result of operating on a year-round school year operation basis pursuant to § 15–855. The amount that the governing board, superintendent or chief administrative officer may expend for a year-round school year operation, as provided in this subsection, is limited to the actual maintenance and operations costs incurred as the result of the year-round school year operation as documented in the school district's budget as provided in § 15–855. A governing board, superintendent or chief administrative officer that utilizes the provisions of this subsection is subject to all other limitations prescribed in this section regarding the expenditure of proceeds from the sale before July 1, 1998 or lease of school property.

F. Notwithstanding subsections B and D of this section, if the school district electors approve the sale of school property and the use of the proceeds for the purchase of school sites or the construction, improvement or furnishing of school facilities, the proceeds from the sale shall be put in a separate fund for use for the approved purpose as prescribed by the uniform system of financial records. This fund is a continuing fund not subject to reversion, except that after ten years any unexpended monies shall be put in the school plant fund for use as prescribed in this section.

G. Proceeds from sales by condemnation or sales under threat of condemnation may be deposited with the county treasurer for deposit in the condemnation fund or the school plant fund of the school district. The condemnation fund is a continuing fund not subject to reversion, except that after ten years any unspent monies shall be placed in the school plant fund to be used as prescribed in this section. The governing board, or the superintendent or chief administrative officer with the approval of the governing board, may apply the proceeds in the condemnation fund to:

1. The payment of any outstanding bonded indebtedness of the school district which is payable from the levy of taxes upon property within the school district.

2. Construct, acquire, improve, repair or furnish school facilities or sites after notice and a hearing.

H. Proceeds from a right-of-way settlement shall be deposited with the county treasurer for deposit in the condemnation fund of the school district. The governing board, or the superintendent or chief administrative officer with the approval of the governing board, shall apply such proceeds in the condemnation fund to construct, acquire, improve, repair or furnish school facilities or sites after notice and a hearing.

I. For purposes of this section, "capital outlay" means unrestricted capital outlay as prescribed in § 15–903, subsection C.

Added by Laws 1981, Ch. 1, § 2, eff. Jan. 23, 1981. Amended by Laws 1981, Ch. 318, § 1, eff. May 4, 1981; Laws 1982, Ch. 197, § 7; Laws 1983, Ch. 9, § 8, eff. Feb. 25, 1983; Laws 1983, Ch. 241, § 4; Laws 1983, Ch. 267, § 3, eff. April 25, 1983; Laws 1984, Ch. 349, § 11; Laws 1985, Ch. 166, § 36, eff. April 18, 1985; Laws 1986, Ch. 125, § 10, eff. April 18, 1986; Laws 1986, Ch. 349, § 2, eff. May 9, 1986; Laws 1989, Ch. 13, § 1; Laws 1990, Ch. 348, § 17, eff. June 26, 1990; Laws 1992, Ch. 50, § 4; Laws 1992, Ch. 329, § 2; Laws 1996, Ch. 284, § 60; Laws 1997, Ch. 231, § 28; Laws 1998, 5th S.S., Ch. 1, § 36, eff. July 9, 1998; Laws 2000, Ch. 254, § 1.

Historical and Statutory Notes

Source:

Laws 1912, Ch. 77, §§ 41, 54.
Civ.Code 1913, §§ 2733, 2750.
Laws 1921, Ch. 72, § 5.
Laws 1921, Ch. 137, § 1.
Laws 1925, Ch. 11, § 1.
Laws 1925, Ch. 70, §§ 1 to 4.
Laws 1927, Ch. 88, § 1.
Rev.Code 1928, §§ 1011, 1025.
Laws 1933, Ch. 18, § 1.
Laws 1949, Ch. 110, § 1.
Code 1939, § 54–430.
Laws 1951, Ch. 74, § 1.
Laws 1951, Ch. 140, § 1.
Laws 1952, Ch. 138, § 1.
Code 1939, Supp.1952, § 54–416.
Laws 1954, Ch. 117, § 2.
A.R.S. former § 15–442.
Laws 1960, Ch. 120, § 2.
Laws 1960, Ch. 127, § 29.
Laws 1961, Ch. 61, § 2.
Laws 1962, Ch. 92, § 1.
Laws 1962, Ch. 112, § 1.
Laws 1967, Ch. 69, § 1.
Laws 1967, 3rd S.S., Ch. 19, § 1.
Laws 1969, Ch. 16, § 1.
Laws 1970, Ch. 118, § 1.
Laws 1972, Ch. 115, § 5.
Laws 1973, Ch. 62, § 1.
Laws 1974, 1st S.S., Ch. 3, §§ 8, 10.
Laws 1975, Ch. 50, § 2.
Laws 1976, Ch. 68, § 1.

Laws 1976, Ch. 156, § 2.
Laws 1977, Ch. 79, § 1.
Laws 1977, Ch. 157, § 1.
Laws 1978, Ch. 7, § 3.
Laws 1978, Ch. 8, § 1.
Laws 1978, Ch. 87, § 1.
Laws 1978, Ch. 188, § 6.
Laws 1979, Ch. 117, § 1.
Laws 1979, Ch. 195, § 6.
Laws 1979, 1st S.S., Ch. 2, § 2.
Laws 1980, 2nd S.S., Ch. 9, § 18.
Laws 1980, Ch. 105, § 2.
Laws 1980, Ch. 225, § 1.

Laws 1981, Ch. 318, § 2 provides:

"**Sec. 2. Retroactivity**

"Section 15–1102, Arizona Revised Statutes, as amended by § 1 of this act applies retroactively to any school district that held an election to sell a school building or sold a school building from and after June 30, 1980."

The purported amendment of this section by Laws 1998, 3rd S.S., Ch. 1, failed to became effective because Ch. 1 was repealed in its entirety by Laws 1998, 5th S.S., Ch. 1, § 2, effective July 1, 1998.

Reviser's Notes:

1983 Note. Prior to the 1984 amendment, this section contained the amendments made by Laws 1983, Ch. 241, § 4 and Ch. 267, § 3 which were blended together pursuant to authority of § 41–1304.03.

1990 Note. In the chapter version, at the end of subsection A the existing period was not shown as stricken. Pursuant to authority of § 41–1304.02, the period was deleted as a correction of a manifest clerical error.

1992 Note. Prior to the 1996 amendment, this section contained the amendments made by Laws 1992, Ch. 50, sec. 4 and Ch. 329, sec. 2 that were blended together pursuant to authority of § 41–1304.03. Pursuant to authority of § 41–1304.02, in the section heading the comma after "sale" was deleted and "or" was added.

1997 Note. Pursuant to authority of § 41–1304.02, in the section heading "monies" was substituted for "funds" and "; school building start-up monies" was added after "indebtedness".

1998 Note. Pursuant to authority of § 41–1304.02, in the section heading "school building start-up monies;" was removed.

§ 15–1103. Insurance proceeds fund; disposition of proceeds

A. Monies received for and derived from insurance losses shall be deposited with the county treasurer who shall credit the deposits to the insurance proceeds fund of the respective school district. The insurance proceeds fund of a school district is a continuing fund not subject to reversion.

B. The governing board, or the superintendent or chief administrative officer with the approval of the governing board, may apply the proceeds from insurance recoveries to the payment of any outstanding bonded indebtedness of the school district which is payable from the levy of taxes upon property within the school district.

C. The governing board, or the superintendent or chief administrative officer with the approval of the governing board, may apply the proceeds of insurance recoveries to construct, acquire, improve, repair or furnish school buildings after notice and a hearing.

Added by Laws 1981, Ch. 1, § 2, eff. Jan. 23, 1981. Amended by Laws 1983, Ch. 241, § 5; Laws 1985, Ch. 166, § 37, eff. April 18, 1985; Laws 1996, Ch. 284, § 61; Laws 1998, 5th S.S., Ch. 1, § 37, eff. July 9, 1998.

Historical and Statutory Notes

Source:

Laws 1912, Ch. 77, §§ 41, 54.
Civ.Code 1913, §§ 2733, 2750.
Laws 1921, Ch. 72, § 5.
Laws 1921, Ch. 137, § 1.
Laws 1925, Ch. 11, § 1.
Laws 1925, Ch. 70, §§ 1 to 4.
Laws 1927, Ch. 88, § 1.
Rev.Code 1928, §§ 1011, 1025.
Laws 1933, Ch. 18, § 1.
Laws 1949, Ch. 110, § 1.
Code 1939, § 54–430.
Laws 1951, Ch. 74, § 1.
Laws 1951, Ch. 140, § 1.
Laws 1952, Ch. 138, § 1.
Code 1939, Supp.1952, § 54–416.
Laws 1954, Ch. 117, § 2.
A.R.S. former § 15–442.

Laws 1960, Ch. 120, § 2.
Laws 1960, Ch. 127, § 29.
Laws 1961, Ch. 61, § 2.
Laws 1962, Ch. 92, § 1.
Laws 1962, Ch. 112, § 1.
Laws 1967, Ch. 69, § 1.
Laws 1967, 3rd S.S., Ch. 19, § 1.
Laws 1969, Ch. 16, § 1.
Laws 1970, Ch. 118, § 1.
Laws 1972, Ch. 115, § 5.
Laws 1973, Ch. 62, § 1.
Laws 1974, 1st S.S., Ch. 3, §§ 8, 10.
Laws 1975, Ch. 50, § 2.
Laws 1976, Ch. 68, § 1.
Laws 1976, Ch. 156, § 2.
Laws 1977, Ch. 79, § 1.
Laws 1977, Ch. 157, § 1.
Laws 1978, Ch. 7, § 3.
Laws 1978, Ch. 8, § 1.
Laws 1978, Ch. 87, § 1.
Laws 1978, Ch. 188, § 6.
Laws 1979, Ch. 117, § 1.
Laws 1979, Ch. 195, § 6.
Laws 1979, 1st S.S., Ch. 2, § 2.
Laws 1980, 2nd S.S., Ch. 9, § 18.
Laws 1980, Ch. 105, § 2.
Laws 1980, Ch. 225 § 1.

The purported amendment of this section by Laws 1998, 3rd S.S., Ch. 1, failed to became effective because Ch. 1 was repealed in its entirety by Laws 1998, 5th S.S., Ch. 1, § 2, effective July 1, 1998.

§ 15-1104. Unemployment compensation fund

Unemployment compensation monies shall be deposited with the county treasurer who shall credit the deposits to the unemployment compensation fund of the respective school district. The unemployment compensation fund of a school district is a continuing fund not subject to reversion, except that any monies in the fund determined by the governing board, or the superintendent or chief administrative officer with the approval of the governing board, to be in excess of insurance needs shall be used for reduction of school district taxes for the budget year.

Added by Laws 1981, Ch. 1, § 2, eff. Jan. 23, 1981. Amended by Laws 1983, Ch. 241, § 6; Laws 1996, Ch. 284, § 62.

Historical and Statutory Notes

Source:

Laws 1912, Ch. 77, §§ 41, 54.
Civ.Code 1913, §§ 2733, 2750.
Laws 1921, Ch. 72, § 5.
Laws 1921, Ch. 137, § 1.
Laws 1925, Ch. 11, § 1.
Laws 1925, Ch. 70, §§ 1 to 4.
Laws 1927, Ch. 88, § 1.
Rev.Code 1928, §§ 1011, 1025.
Laws 1933, Ch. 18, § 1.
Laws 1949, Ch. 110, § 1.
Code 1939, § 54-430.
Laws 1951, Ch. 74, § 1.
Laws 1951, Ch. 140, § 1.
Laws 1952, Ch. 138, § 1.
Code 1939, Supp.1952, § 54-416.
Laws 1954, Ch. 117, § 2.
A.R.S. former § 15-442.
Laws 1960, Ch. 120, § 2.
Laws 1960, Ch. 127, § 29.
Laws 1961, Ch. 61, § 2.
Laws 1962, Ch. 92, § 1.
Laws 1962, Ch. 112, § 1.
Laws 1967, Ch. 69, § 1.
Laws 1967, 3rd S.S., Ch. 19, § 1.
Laws 1969, Ch. 16, § 1.
Laws 1970, Ch. 118, § 1.
Laws 1972, Ch. 115, § 5.
Laws 1973, Ch. 62, § 1.
Laws 1974, 1st S.S., Ch. 3, §§ 8, 10.
Laws 1975, Ch. 50, § 2.
Laws 1976, Ch. 68, § 1.
Laws 1976, Ch. 156, § 2.
Laws 1977, Ch. 79, § 1.
Laws 1977, Ch. 157, § 1.
Laws 1978, Ch. 7, § 3.
Laws 1978, Ch. 8, § 1.
Laws 1978, Ch. 87, § 1.
Laws 1978, Ch. 188, § 6.
Laws 1979, Ch. 117, § 1.
Laws 1979, Ch. 195, § 6.
Laws 1979, 1st S.S., Ch. 2, § 2.
Laws 1980, 2nd S.S., Ch. 9, § 18.
Laws 1980, Ch. 105, § 2.
Laws 1980, Ch. 225, § 1.

§ 15-1105. Lease of school property; civic center school fund; reversion to school plant fund; definitions

A. The governing board, or the superintendent or chief administrative officer with the approval of the governing board, may lease school property, including school buildings, grounds, buses and equipment to any person, group or organization for any lawful purpose, including recreational, educational, political, economic, artistic, moral, scientific, social, religious or other civic or governmental purpose in the interest of the community, including extended day resource programs. The governing board, superintendent or chief administrative officer shall charge a reasonable use fee for the lease of the school property, which fee may include goods contributed or services rendered by the person, group or organization to the school district.

B. The governing board, or the superintendent or chief administrative officer with the approval of the governing board, may permit the uncompensated use of school buildings, grounds, buses, equipment and other school property by any school related group, including student political organizations or by any organization whose membership is open to the public and whose activities promote the educational function of the school district as determined in good faith by the school district's governing board, or the superintendent or chief administrative officer with the approval of the governing board, including extended day resource programs, except as provided in § 15-511.

C. A person, group or organization that is otherwise eligible to lease school property shall not be denied use of or charged differentiated fees for school property on the basis of the person, group or organization's beliefs, expression of beliefs or exercise of the rights of association that are protected under the laws of this state, the Constitution of Arizona, the laws of the United States or the United States Constitution.

D. The governing board shall annually approve a fee schedule for the lease of school property. The fee schedule shall include a designation of the persons, groups or organizations that shall have uncompensated use of the school property, and a procedure for determining the value of goods and services being provided as compensation for the use of school property. The governing board, superintendent or chief administrative officer shall require proof of liability insurance for such use or lease of school property.

E. Except as provided in § 15-1102, monies received for and derived from the use or lease of school property under this section shall be promptly deposited with the county treasurer who shall credit the deposits to the civic center school fund of the respective school district. Monies placed to the credit of a civic center school fund may be expended for civic center school purposes by warrants drawn upon order of the school district governing board, or the superintendent or chief administrative officer with the approval of the governing board. The civic center school fund of a school district or multiple school district civic center school program is a continuing fund not subject to reversion, except upon termination of a civic center school program. Upon termination of a civic center school program any remaining funds shall revert to the school plant fund of the school district or districts.

F. For the purposes of this section:

1. "Educational function" means uses that are directly related to the educational mission of the school district as adopted by the school district governing board and includes parent-teacher organizations, youth organizations and school employee organizations.

2. "Extended day resource programs" means activities offered on school property before or after school or at times when school is not customarily in session for children who are of the age required for kindergarten programs and grades one through eight. The program may be offered for children who are of the age required for a kindergarten program or for one grade or for any combination of kindergarten programs and grades. Activities may include physical conditioning, tutoring, supervised homework or arts activities.

3. "Reasonable use fee" means an amount that is at least equal to the school district's cost for utilities, services, supplies or personnel that the school provides to the lessee pursuant to the terms of the lease.

Added by Laws 1981, Ch. 1, § 2, eff. Jan. 23, 1981. Amended by Laws 1983, Ch. 241, § 7; Laws 1984, Ch. 349, § 12; Laws 1985, Ch. 251, § 1, eff. April 29, 1985; Laws 1987, Ch. 240, § 2; Laws 1996, Ch. 284, § 63; Laws 2003, Ch. 254, § 1.

Historical and Statutory Notes

Source:

Laws 1912, Ch. 77, § 41.
Civ.Code 1913, § 2733.
Laws 1921, Ch. 72, § 5.
Laws 1921, Ch. 137, § 1.
Laws 1925, Ch. 11, § 1.
Laws 1925, Ch. 70, §§ 1 to 4.
Laws 1927, Ch. 88, § 1.
Rev.Code 1928, § 1011.
Laws 1933, Ch. 18, § 1.
Laws 1949, Ch. 110, § 1.
Laws 1951, Ch. 140, § 1.
Laws 1952, Ch. 138, § 1.
Code 1939, Supp.1952, § 54-416.
Laws 1954, Ch. 117, § 2.
A.R.S. former § 15-451.
Laws 1973, Ch. 173, § 3.
Laws 1977, Ch. 79, § 2.
Laws 1978, Ch. 7, § 4.
Laws 1979, Ch. 68, § 1.
Laws 1979, Ch. 117, § 2.
Laws 1979, 1st S.S., Ch. 2, § 3.
Laws 1980, 2nd S.S., Ch. 9, § 23.

§ 15-1106. Permanent teacherage fund; uses; definition

A. A school district governing board, or the superintendent or chief administrative officer with the approval of the governing board, may establish a permanent teacherage fund. Such fund shall be comprised of proceeds obtained from the lease of teacherages within the school district. Monies in such fund may be used for any of the following purposes:

1. Maintenance and operation of teacherages.

2. Debt service related to teacherages.

3. Purchase of houses, including mobile or modular housing, to be used exclusively as teacherages for school districts located on Indian and federal lands.

4. Reduction of the local tax levy if accumulation in such fund warrants such use.

B. Monies in a permanent teacherage fund are not subject to reversion.

C. For the purposes of this section, "teacherage" means any housing facilities for teachers and other school employees provided by a school district pursuant to § 15-342, paragraph 6.

Added by Laws 1981, Ch. 1, § 2, eff. Jan. 23, 1981. Amended by Laws 1983, Ch. 14, § 2; Laws 1984, Ch. 349, § 13; Laws 1996, Ch. 284, § 64.

Historical and Statutory Notes

Source:
Laws 1978, Ch. 152, § 2.
A.R.S. former § 15-1201.06.
Laws 1980, Ch. 195, § 4.

§ 15-1107. Litigation recovery fund; disposition of proceeds

A. Monies received for and derived from settlement of legal controversies or from recovery of costs, attorney fees or damages by a school district in litigation by or against the school district shall be deposited with the county treasurer who shall credit the deposits to the litigation recovery fund of the school district. The litigation recovery fund is a continuing fund which is not subject to reversion.

B. If a school district receives monies as provided in subsection A for the purpose of replacing or repairing school buildings or other school property, the governing board, or the superintendent or chief administrative officer with the approval of the governing board, may only apply the proceeds to:

1. Pay any outstanding bonded indebtedness of the school district which is payable from the levy of taxes on property within the school district.

2. Construct, acquire, improve, repair or furnish school buildings after notice and a hearing.

3. Replace or repair the school property other than school buildings.

C. Except as provided in subsection B, the governing board, or the superintendent or chief administrative officer with the approval of the governing board, may apply the proceeds of litigation recoveries to procure legal services or for the costs of litigation.

Added by Laws 1986, Ch. 80, § 2, eff. April 11, 1986. Amended by Laws 1996, Ch. 284, § 65; Laws 1998, 5th S.S., Ch. 1, § 38, eff. July 9, 1998.

Historical and Statutory Notes

The purported amendment of this section by Laws 1998, 3rd S.S., Ch. 1, failed to become effective because Ch. 1 was repealed in its entirety by Laws 1998, 5th S.S., Ch. 1, § 2, effective July 1, 1998.

§ 15-1108. District services fund

A. A school district governing board may establish district services programs to provide goods or services, excluding services provided pursuant to § 15-213, to district schools or departments or other school districts and may charge users on a cost reimbursement basis. Revenues from the operation of a district services program shall be transmitted to the county treasurer for deposit in a district services fund. The governing board may employ personnel, purchase supplies and equipment and incur other necessary expenses related to the operation of a district services program. Examples of district services programs include printing and duplicating, data processing and motor pool services.

B. A district services fund shall be accounted for as prescribed in the uniform system of financial records pursuant to chapter 2, article 4 [1] of this title. A school district governing board may advance monies from the maintenance and operation fund into the district services fund to cover start-up costs.

Monies in the district services fund are not subject to reversion at the end of the fiscal year. The governing board may direct the county treasurer to establish a separate fund pursuant to this section for each district services program.

C. A school or department may choose not to purchase services from a district services program if the school or department determines that it is more advantageous for the school or department to procure the services from another source.

D. The provisions of this section shall not be utilized to replace services provided to a school district by a private enterprise as defined in § 41-2751.

Added by Laws 1996, Ch. 124, § 1.

[1] Section 15-271 et seq.

ARTICLE 2. STUDENT ACTIVITIES AND AUXILIARY OPERATIONS FUNDS

§ 15-1121. Student activities monies defined

All monies raised with the approval of the governing board of a school district by the efforts of students in pursuance of or in connection with all activities of student organizations, clubs, school plays or other student entertainment other than funds specified in §§ 15-1125 and 15-1126 are student activities monies.

Added by Laws 1981, Ch. 1, § 2, eff. Jan. 23, 1981. Amended by Laws 1981, Ch. 144, § 2.

Historical and Statutory Notes

Source:

Laws 1951, Ch. 116, § 1.
Code 1939, Supp.1952, § 54-617.
A.R.S. former § 15-1271.
Laws 1980, 2nd S.S., Ch. 9, § 77.

§ 15-1122. Student activities treasurer; assistant student activities treasurer; administration of student activities monies

A. The governing board of any school district having student activities monies shall establish a student activities fund and appoint a student activities treasurer. The student activities treasurer shall deposit the student activities monies in a bank account designated the student activities account. In school districts which have multiple schools the governing board may designate an assistant student activities treasurer for each school. Each assistant student activities treasurer shall deposit student activities monies in the school district's student activities bank account or in student activities bank accounts established separately for each school. Disbursements from the student activities accounts shall be by check, signed by two persons, one of whom shall be either the student activities treasurer or an assistant student activities treasurer and one of whom shall be any other person authorized to sign by the governing board. The governing board may appoint more than one person to act as cosigner with the student activities treasurer or assistant student activities treasurer. Any disbursement shall be authorized by or on behalf of the student members of the particular club or organization as provided in the uniform system of financial records. The student activities treasurer and assistant student activities treasurers shall give bonds in an amount determined by the governing board, and the cost of bond premiums shall be a charge against the school district.

B. Accounts showing the balances due the respective student organizations as provided in § 15-1121 shall be kept by the student activities treasurer and assistant student activities treasurers and shall be open to inspection by officers of the student bodies concerned.

Added by Laws 1981, Ch. 1, § 2, eff. Jan. 23, 1981. Amended by Laws 1983, Ch. 224, § 7.

Historical and Statutory Notes

Source:
Laws 1951, Ch. 116, § 2.
Code 1939, Supp.1952, § 54-618.
A.R.S. former § 15-1272.
Laws 1968, Ch. 177, § 7.
Laws 1980, 2nd S.S., Ch. 9, § 78.

§ 15-1123. Record of revenues and expenditures

A. The student activities treasurer or assistant student activities treasurer shall maintain an accurate detailed record of all revenues and expenditures of the student activities fund. The record shall be made in such form as the governing board of the school district prescribes. Copies of the record shall be presented to the governing board of the school district not less than once during each calendar month.

B. Student activities fund monies may be invested and reinvested by the governing board of a school district. All monies earned by investment shall be credited to the student activities fund of the school district.

Added by Laws 1981, Ch. 1, § 2, eff. Jan. 23, 1981.

Historical and Statutory Notes

Source:
Laws 1951, Ch. 116, § 3.
Code 1939, Supp.1952, § 54-619.
A.R.S. former § 15-1273.
Laws 1980, 2nd S.S., Ch. 9, § 79.

§ 15-1124. Student activities revolving fund for expenses

The governing board of a school district may, by resolution entered upon its minutes, establish a revolving fund for the purpose of meeting necessary current expenses connected with student activities as defined by this article. The amount of the revolving fund shall be determined by the governing board which establishes the fund and provision for its establishment shall be included in the budget. The amount of monies provided in the revolving fund shall, at the end of each fiscal school year, be returned to the credit of the school district and the fund reestablished as provided in this section.

Added by Laws 1981, Ch. 1, § 2, eff. Jan. 23, 1981.

Historical and Statutory Notes

Source:
Laws 1951, Ch. 116, § 4.
Code 1939, Supp.1952, § 54-620.
A.R.S. former § 15-1274.
Laws 1980, 2nd S.S., Ch. 9, § 80.

§ 15-1125. Auxiliary operations fund defined

The auxiliary operations fund shall consist of all monies raised with the approval of the school district governing board in pursuance of and in connection with all activities of school bookstores and athletic activities.

Added by Laws 1981, Ch. 1, § 2, eff. Jan. 23, 1981.

Historical and Statutory Notes

Source:

Laws 1980, 2nd S.S., Ch. 9, § 81.
A.R.S. former § 15-1281.

§ 15-1126. Accounting; deposit; disposition of monies

A. Auxiliary operations fund monies shall be accounted for in accordance with the requirements of the uniform system of financial records.

B. Auxiliary operations fund monies shall be deposited after authorization by the governing board in a bank account designated as the auxiliary operations fund. Disbursements from the fund shall be authorized by the governing board. Disbursements shall be made by check signed by two employees of the school district designated by the governing board. Persons authorized by the governing board to sign checks shall give a bond in an amount determined by the governing board, and the cost of bond premiums may be a charge against the fund.

C. Auxiliary operations fund monies may be invested and reinvested by the governing board of a school district. All monies earned by investment shall be credited to the auxiliary operations fund of the school district.

D. The governing board may establish an imprest petty cash fund at each school within the school district for activities which require immediate cash outlays for postage, freight, express, parcel post, travel or other minor disbursements, but not including salaries or wages, which are proper as ultimate expenditures from the school district auxiliary operations fund. Imprest petty cash funds established by the governing board shall be funded from the school district auxiliary operations fund in an amount to be determined by the governing board.

E. The governing board may establish a revolving fund bank account for each school within the school district for necessary current expenditures in connection with school bookstore and athletic activities. The revolving funds shall be funded from the auxiliary operations fund in an amount to be determined by the governing board. The school shall return the monies in the revolving fund bank account at the end of each fiscal year to the credit of the school district auxiliary operations fund.

Added by Laws 1981, Ch. 1, § 2, eff. Jan. 23, 1981. Amended by Laws 1982, Ch. 308, § 1; Laws 1990, Ch. 348, § 18, eff. June 26, 1990.

Historical and Statutory Notes

Source:

Laws 1980, 2nd S.S., Ch. 9, § 81.
A.R.S. former § 15-1282.

ARTICLE 3. COMMUNITY SCHOOL PROGRAM FUND

§ 15–1141. Definitions

In this article, unless the context otherwise requires:

1. "Community school" means any school engaged in a community school program.

2. "Community school monies" means monies received as fees, tuitions, grants or donations from any person or agency for a community school program.

3. "Community school program" means the involvement of people in the development of an educationally oriented community. The community school serves the purposes of academic and skill development for all citizens, furnishes supervised recreational and avocational instruction, supplies remedial and supplemental education, furnishes meeting places for community groups and provides facilities for the dissemination of a variety of community related services, including extended day resource programs as defined in § 15–1105.

Added by Laws 1981, Ch. 1, § 2, eff. Jan. 23, 1981. Amended by Laws 1985, Ch. 251, § 2, eff. April 29, 1985.

Historical and Statutory Notes

Source:

Laws 1976, Ch. 79, § 2.
A.R.S. former §§ 15–461, 15–1175.

Laws 1976, Ch. 79, § 1 provides:

"**Section 1. Purpose**

"The purpose of the community school program is to relate the resources of the schools to the self-defined educational needs of the community. Thus the school, as the prime educational institution of the community, commits itself to seeking increased community participation."

§ 15–1142. Powers of the governing board

The governing board of any school district may:

1. Establish and operate a community school program in any school in its school district.

2. Budget and expend from the maintenance and operation section of the budget, as defined in § 15–903, to employ a qualified director necessary for each school or combination of schools engaged in community school programs.

3. Expend community school monies for operation of a community school program.

4. Establish tuition and fee charges for community school programs.

Added by Laws 1981, Ch. 1, § 2, eff. Jan. 23, 1981.

Historical and Statutory Notes

Source:

Laws 1976, Ch. 79, § 2.
A.R.S. former §§ 15–462, 15–1176.

§ 15–1143. Community school program fund

Monies deposited in a community school fund of a school district may be used for community school programs only and are not subject to reversion, except upon termination of a community school program. Upon termination of a community school program any remaining funds shall revert to the operating budget of the school district.

Added by Laws 1981, Ch. 1, § 2, eff. Jan. 23, 1981. Amended by Laws 1983, Ch. 241, § 8.

Historical and Statutory Notes

Source:

Laws 1976, Ch. 79, § 2.
A.R.S. former §§ 15–463, 15–1177.
Laws 1979, Ch. 68, § 3.

ARTICLE 4. SCHOOL LUNCH PROGRAM FUND

§ 15–1151. Definition of school meal programs

In this article, unless the context otherwise requires, "school meal programs" means programs under which meals are served by a public or private school on a nonprofit basis to children in attendance, including a program under which federal assistance is received.

Added by Laws 1981, Ch. 1, § 2, eff. Jan. 23, 1981. Amended by Laws 1991, Ch. 292, § 14, eff. June 28, 1991.

Historical and Statutory Notes

Source:

Laws 1947, Ch. 98, § 1.
Code 1939, Supp.1952, § 54–1801.
A.R.S. former § 15–1121.

Reviser's Notes:

1991 Note. Pursuant to authority of § 41–1304.02, in the section heading "of school meal programs" was added.

§ 15–1152. School meal programs; nonschool meal programs; powers of state board of education

The state board of education may enter into agreements with an agency of the federal government, a governing board or another agency or person, direct the disbursement of federal and state monies in accordance with provisions of federal and state law, direct the distribution of commodities as provided by federal and state law, prescribe regulations, employ personnel, give technical advice and assistance to governing boards in connection with establishment and operation of school meal programs, assist in training personnel engaged in operation of school meal programs and take other action it deems necessary to provide for the establishment and maintenance of school meal programs. The state board of education and the governing boards may also accept gifts for use in connection with a school meal program. Agreements entered into pursuant to this section are exempt from the provisions of § 11–952, subsections D and F. The form to be used in the agreements shall be approved annually by the attorney general prior to its use in such agreements. The department of education shall file with the secretary of state by January 1 one blank copy of the agreement form and a list of the agencies with which the department entered agreements during the preceding year.

Added by Laws 1981, Ch. 1, § 2, eff. Jan. 23, 1981. Amended by Laws 1984, Ch. 138, § 1; Laws 1988, Ch. 195, § 2; Laws 1991, Ch. 292, § 15, eff. June 28, 1991; Laws 1997, Ch. 196, § 2.

Historical and Statutory Notes

Source:

Laws 1947, Ch. 98, § 3.
Code 1939, Supp.1952, § 54-1803.
A.R.S. former § 15-1123.
Laws 1979, Ch. 182, § 1.

§ 15-1153. Federal funds; acceptance; disbursement

A. The state board of education may accept and direct the disbursement of funds appropriated by act of Congress and apportioned to the state for use in connection with school meal programs. The state board shall deposit, pursuant to §§ 35-146 and 35-147, such funds in the school meal program fund. Disbursements from the fund shall be made in accordance with the provisions of § 35-185.

B. Notwithstanding any provision of title 35, chapter 1 [1] limiting the drawing of warrants after the expiration of the fiscal year in which an obligation is incurred, the state board of education may accept and direct the allocation of federal funds apportioned to the state for use in connection with school meal programs, which are received and the allocation effected not later than six months after expiration of the fiscal year for which the allocation is made.
Added by Laws 1981, Ch. 1, § 2, eff. Jan. 23, 1981. Amended by Laws 1991, Ch. 292, § 16, eff. June 28, 1991; Laws 2000, Ch. 193, § 107.

[1] Section 35-101 et seq.

Historical and Statutory Notes

Source:

Laws 1947, Ch. 98, § 2.
Laws 1951, Ch. 119, § 1.
Code 1939, Supp.1952, § 54-1802.
A.R.S. former § 15-1122.

§ 15-1154. Operation of school meal programs by governing boards; school meal program fund; revolving fund

A. A governing board may operate school meal programs, and for that purpose may employ personnel, purchase equipment and food and incur other necessary expenses, making payment therefor through the use of gifts or donations, proceeds of sales of school meals, contributions made available by the federal government or monies obtained by school district levy, but no monies acquired by the levy of state, county or school district taxes shall be expended for food.

B. Any monies received in the operation of a school district school meal program shall be deposited with the county treasurer who shall credit the deposits to the school meal program fund of the respective school district. Monies deposited to the credit of a school meal program fund may be withdrawn by voucher as approved by the governing board for operation of the school district school meal program, except that a revolving fund of five hundred dollars may be established in the manner and for the purposes prescribed in subsection C of this section. The school meal program fund of a school district is a continuing fund not subject to reversion.

C. The governing board of any school district with the consent of the county school superintendent may establish for the operation of school meal programs a revolving fund of five hundred dollars which may be used for payment of freight on commodities, purchase of food required in emergencies, employment of temporary personnel for employment which does not exceed eight hours for any person or other minor disbursements. The revolving fund monies shall be deposited in a federal reserve bank in a designated account and shall be withdrawn by check signed by two bonded employees appointed by the governing board of the school district.

D. Upon approval of a revolving fund as prescribed by subsection C of this section, the county school superintendent shall draw a warrant to the order of the designated employees and charge the amount thereof against the school district school meal program fund, but no revolving fund shall be established unless the designated employees are bonded for an amount equal to twice the amount of the fund. The cost of the bond shall be a proper charge against the school district school meal program fund.

E. The designated employees shall periodically submit a voucher with supporting papers covering disbursements from the school meal revolving fund prescribed by subsection C of this section to the county school superintendent who shall issue a warrant for the voucher to reimburse the fund. If the school district is dissolved, consolidated, unified or subdivided, or if the governing board decides to terminate the revolving fund, the designated employees shall return the original amount of the revolving fund to the county treasurer by the date that the dissolution, consolidation, unification or subdivision becomes effective or within thirty days after the date that the governing board decides to terminate the revolving fund, whichever is appropriate, for deposit in the school meal program fund of the respective school district.

Added by Laws 1981, Ch. 1, § 2, eff. Jan. 23, 1981. Amended by Laws 1983, Ch. 241, § 9; Laws 1991, Ch. 292, § 17, eff. June 28, 1991.

Historical and Statutory Notes

Source:

Laws 1947, Ch. 98, § 4.
Code 1939, Supp.1952, § 54-1804.
A.R.S. former § 15-1124.
Laws 1960, Ch. 127, § 47.
Laws 1962, Ch. 114, § 1.
Laws 1979, Ch. 68, § 2.

Laws 1989, Ch. 17, § 1, as amended by Laws 1991, Ch. 292, § 23, relating to use of maintenance and operation monies for food purchases, was repealed by Laws 1989, Ch. 17, § 2, effective July 1, 1993.

§ 15-1155. Records, reports, regulations, audits and inspections by state board of education

The state board of education shall prescribe regulations for keeping accounts and records and making reports, under the supervision of governing boards. The accounts and records shall be available at all times for inspection and audit by authorized officials and shall be preserved for a period, not exceeding five years, as prescribed by the state board. The state board shall conduct or cause to be conducted audits, inspections and administrative reviews of accounts, records and operations as are necessary to determine whether the school meal programs are being administered according to the provisions of this article and the regulations made by the state board.

Added by Laws 1981, Ch. 1, § 2, eff. Jan. 23, 1981. Amended by Laws 1991, Ch. 292, § 18, eff. June 28, 1991.

Historical and Statutory Notes

Source:
Laws 1947, Ch. 98, § 5.
Code 1939, Supp.1952, § 54-1805.
A.R.S. former § 15-1125.

§ 15-1156. Repealed by Laws 1996, Ch. 284, § 66

Historical and Statutory Notes

The repealed section, added by Laws 1981, Ch. 1, § 2, amended by Laws 1991, Ch. 292, § 19, derived from Laws 1947, Ch. 98, § 5; Code 1939, Supp.1952, § 54-1805; A.R.S. former § 15-1125, related to studies to evaluate school meal programs.

§ 15-1157. Inclusion of expenses in budget of superintendent of public instruction

There shall be included in the budget of the superintendent of public instruction, for presentation to the legislature, such amounts as required by the state board of education for and limited to the administration of this article, including the establishment, maintenance, operation and expansion of school meal programs.

Added by Laws 1981, Ch. 1, § 2, eff. Jan. 23, 1981. Amended by Laws 1991, Ch. 292, § 20, eff. June 28, 1991.

Historical and Statutory Notes

Source:
Laws 1947, Ch. 98, § 7.
Code 1939, Supp.1952, § 54-1807.
A.R.S. former § 15-1127.

§ 15-1158. Agreements for meals for persons sixty years of age or older

A. The governing board of any school district may enter into an agreement with any individual, firm, partnership, corporation, association or public agency whereby the school district agrees to prepare meals for persons sixty years of age or older and their spouses, or any group of such persons, by utilizing the systems and procedures already developed for use in the school meal programs of such school district.

B. An agreement entered into by a governing board of a school district, pursuant to the provisions of this section, shall not:

1. Involve the expenditure by the school district of any federal or state school meal monies or other school monies or the use of any school meal commodities or school district personnel, equipment or facilities unless the agreement includes a provision requiring full reimbursement for such expenditure.

2. Provide for payment to the school district of any amount in excess of the estimated cost of food, personnel, equipment, facilities and other necessary expenditures involved in the performance of the agreement.

3. Permit any program of meals for persons sixty years of age or older and their spouses to interfere in any way with the use of school meal facilities for school purposes.

C. The department of education may cooperate with any individual, firm, partnership, corporation, association or public agency in the planning of programs whereby school districts may prepare meals for persons sixty years of age or older and their spouses, or any group of such persons, by utilizing the systems and procedures already developed for use in the operation of school meal programs.

D. The department of education shall adopt regulations containing guidelines for governing boards of school districts entering into such agreements.
Added by Laws 1981, Ch. 1, § 2, eff. Jan. 23, 1981. Amended by Laws 1991, Ch. 292, § 21, eff. June 28, 1991.

Historical and Statutory Notes

Source:

Laws 1977, Ch. 164, § 10.
A.R.S. former § 15-1128.

ARTICLE 5. ARIZONA YOUTH FARM LOAN FUND

§ 15-1171. Trust assets of Arizona rural rehabilitation corporation; transfer to state board of education

The state board of education is designated as the state agency empowered to make application to the secretary of agriculture of the United States, or any other proper federal official, pursuant and subject to the provisions of act of May 3, 1950 (P.L. 81-499; 40 U.S.C. Sec. 440 et seq.) [1] for the trust assets, either funds or property, held by the United States as trustee on behalf of the Arizona rural rehabilitation corporation.
Added by Laws 1981, Ch. 1, § 2, eff. Jan. 23, 1981. Amended by Laws 2002, Ch. 89, § 29.

[1] 40 U.S.C.A. § 440 et seq. (omitted).

Historical and Statutory Notes

Source:

Laws 1960, Ch. 48, § 1.
A.R.S. former § 15-1061.

§ 15-1172. Arizona youth farm loan fund

Notwithstanding any other law, funds and the proceeds of the trust assets shall be received by the state board of education and shall be deposited, pursuant to §§ 35-146 and 35-147, in a special fund to be known as the Arizona youth farm loan fund that is maintained as a revolving fund and that is appropriated for continuing expenditure or obligation as provided by this article.
Added by Laws 1981, Ch. 1, § 2, eff. Jan. 23, 1981. Amended by Laws 2000, Ch. 193, § 108; Laws 2002, Ch. 89, § 30.

Historical and Statutory Notes

Source:

Laws 1960, Ch. 48, § 1.
A.R.S. former § 15-1062.

§ 15-1173. Use of funds

A. Except as provided in subsection C of this section, monies in the Arizona youth farm loan fund may be used only for such of the rural rehabilitation purposes as are permissible under the Arizona rural rehabilitation corporation's charter as it appeared during the calendar year 1960 and as may from time to time be agreed upon by the state board of education and the secretary of agriculture of the United States or his delegate, including but not limited to furnishing financial assistance to deserving young persons under twenty-five years of age who are students or former students of vocational agriculture or young farmers in organized vocational agriculture classes in becoming satisfactorily established in farming through guaranteed loans, if they cannot obtain needed financing elsewhere on reasonable rates and terms.

B. Administrative expenses of carrying out the provisions of this article, including but not limited to salaries, capital outlay, professional services, travel and current expenditures, shall be paid from annual appropriations made by the legislature to the state board of education, and no part of the trust funds as provided by subsection A of this section may be used for any purpose not expressly listed in subsection A or C of this section.

C. On notice from the state board of vocational education, the state treasurer shall invest and divest monies in the fund as provided by § 35-313, and monies earned from investment shall be credited to the fund.

Added by Laws 1981, Ch. 1, § 2, eff. Jan. 23, 1981. Amended by Laws 1990, Ch. 144, § 7; Laws 2000, Ch. 193, § 109; Laws 2002, Ch. 89, § 31.

Historical and Statutory Notes

Source:

Laws 1960, Ch. 48, § 1.
A.R.S. former § 15-1063.
Laws 1979, Ch. 218, § 4.

§ 15-1174. Powers and duties

The state board of education on behalf of the state of Arizona is authorized and empowered to:

1. Collect, compromise, adjust or cancel claims and obligations arising out of or administered under this article or under any mortgage, lease, contract or other agreement entered into or administered pursuant to this article and, if in its judgment necessary and advisable, pursue the same to final collection in any court having jurisdiction.

2. Bid for and purchase at any execution, foreclosure or other sale, or otherwise to acquire, property upon which the state board has a lien by reason of a judgment or execution, or which is pledged, mortgaged or conveyed or which otherwise secures any loan or other indebtedness owing to or acquired by the state board under this article.

3. Accept title to any property so purchased or acquired, to operate or lease such property for such period as may be deemed necessary to protect the investment therein and to sell or otherwise dispose of such property in a manner consistent with the provisions of this article.

Added by Laws 1981, Ch. 1, § 2, eff. Jan. 23, 1981. Amended by Laws 1984, Ch. 349, § 14; Laws 1990, Ch. 348, § 19, eff. June 26, 1990; Laws 2002, Ch. 89, § 32.

Historical and Statutory Notes

Source:

Laws 1960, Ch. 48, § 1.
A.R.S. former § 15-1064.

§ 15-1175. Liability

The United States, and the secretary of agriculture thereof, shall be held free from liability by virtue of the transfer of the assets to the state board of education pursuant to this article.

Amended by Laws 1981, Ch. 1, § 2, eff. Jan. 23, 1981; Laws 2002, Ch. 89, § 33.

Historical and Statutory Notes

Source:

Laws 1960, Ch. 48, § 1.
A.R.S. former § 15-1065.

ARTICLE 6. EDUCATION VOUCHER FUND FOR PRIVATE PLACEMENT

The article heading was changed from "Special Education Voucher Fund for Private Placement" to "Education Voucher Fund for Private Placement" by Laws 1990, Ch. 164, § 6.

§ 15-1181. Definitions

In this article, unless the context otherwise requires:

1. "Child" means a person who is at least three years of age by September 1 of the current year but who is under twenty-two years of age.

2. "Foster parent" means a person who may serve as the parent of a child with disabilities if that person has an ongoing, long-term parental relationship with the child, is willing to make educational decisions for the child and has no personal interest that would conflict with the interests of the child.

3. "Fund" means the special education fund.

4. "Home school district" has the same meaning prescribed in § 15-761.

5. "Individualized education program" has the same meaning prescribed in § 15-761.

6. "Parent" means the natural or adoptive parent of a child, the legal guardian of a child, a relative with whom a child resides and who is acting as the parent of that child or a surrogate parent who has been appointed for a child pursuant to § 15-763.01. Parent does not mean this state if the child is a ward of the state.

7. "Place" or "placement" means placement of a child in a private residential facility for residential special education placement as defined in § 15-761 or by a state placing agency for care, safety or treatment reasons.

8. "Private residential facility" means a private facility that is licensed by the department of economic security or department of health services and to which one of the following also applies:

(a) For special education placements, the facility has been approved by the division of special education pursuant to § 15-765 for the purpose of providing special education and related services.

(b) For other than special education placements, the facility has been accredited by the north central association of colleges and secondary schools, except that private facilities applying for initial approval as a private school are not required to receive accreditation until three years after the date of initial approval as long as continual progress toward accreditation is maintained.

9. "Related services" means related services as defined in § 15-761.

10. "Residential special education placement" has the same meaning prescribed in § 15-761.

11. "Special education" has the same meaning prescribed in § 15-761.

12. "State placing agency" means the department of juvenile corrections, the department of economic security, the department of health services or the administrative office of the court.

Added by Laws 1994, Ch. 91, § 4, eff. April 12, 1994. Amended by Laws 1995, Ch. 178, § 17; Laws 1998, Ch. 242, § 2, eff. July 1, 1999; Laws 2000, Ch. 236, § 28, eff. April 12, 2000.

Historical and Statutory Notes

Source:

Laws 1976, Ch. 185, § 4.
A.R.S. former § 15-1019.
Laws 1979, Ch. 195, § 26.

Former § 15-1181, which also provided definitions, was added by Laws 1981, Ch. 1, § 2, amended by Laws 1981, Ch. 314, § 17; Laws 1990, Ch. 164, § 2; Laws 1991, Ch. 173, § 10; Laws 1991, Ch. 210, § 11; Laws 1991, Ch. 257, § 13; Laws 1992, Ch. 172, § 28, and was repealed by Laws 1994, Ch. 91, § 3, effective April 12, 1994. See, now, this section.

§ 15-1182. Special education fund; administration

A. There is established a special education fund which shall consist of legislative appropriations made to the fund for purposes of this section and § 15-1202.

B. The fund shall be administered by the superintendent of public instruction for the purposes provided in this article and article 7 of this chapter.

C. Each fiscal year the state board of education shall include in its budget request for assistance to schools a separate line item for the fund.

D. The fund shall provide monies for the education of a child who has been placed in a residential facility by a state placing agency or who requires a residential special education placement as defined in § 15-761.

E. If a child has been placed in a residential facility by a state placing agency, the fund shall provide monies for the following types of vouchers:

1. Initial residential education vouchers to fund the educational costs for any child, whether or not eligible for special education. This paragraph applies to a child who has been placed in a residential facility and who has either not received a comprehensive education evaluation as provided in § 15-766, who has previously received such an evaluation and was determined to be ineligible for special education services or who is eligible for special education and for whom necessary procedures for changing the child's educational placement must be completed. This voucher expires on the expiration of sixty calendar days or completion of the educational evaluation or review of special education placement, whichever occurs first.

2. Continuing residential education vouchers that fund the educational costs for any child, whether or not eligible for special education, who requires placement in a residential facility after the expiration of the initial education voucher and who is not eligible for a residential special education voucher.

F. When a school district makes a residential special education placement, the fund shall provide monies to fund the residential special education placement.

G. Monies in the fund are exempt from the provisions of § 35–190 relating to lapsing of appropriations. Any monies left unexpended may be distributed to school districts by the department of education for the following purposes:

1. To provide educational counseling, training and support services to a child with a disability in order to maintain the child's educational placement in the least restrictive environment.

2. To provide educational transition assistance to children who return to their home after placement in a residential facility.

3. To train personnel for and develop and implement model programs for use by school districts to serve children with emotional disabilities.

H. The total amount of state monies that may be spent in any fiscal year by the superintendent of public instruction for the purposes of this article shall not exceed the amount appropriated or authorized by § 35–173 for that purpose. This article shall not be construed to impose a duty on an officer, agent or employee of this state to discharge a responsibility or to create any right in a person or group if the discharge or right would require an expenditure of state monies in excess of the expenditure authorized by legislative appropriation for that specific purpose.

Added by Laws 1981, Ch. 1, § 2, eff. Jan. 23, 1981. Amended by Laws 1990, Ch. 164, § 3; Laws 1994, Ch. 91, § 5, eff. April 12, 1994; Laws 1995, Ch. 196, § 19; Laws 1998, Ch. 242, § 3, eff. July 1, 1999.

Historical and Statutory Notes

Source:
Laws 1976, Ch. 185, § 4.
A.R.S. former § 15–1020.

For applicability provisions of Laws 1995, Ch. 196, see the Historical and Statutory Notes following § 1–254.

§ 15–1183. Placement; voucher application requirements

A. A voucher may not be issued pursuant to this article and a residential special education placement may not be made in a private residential placement facility unless the requirements of § 15–765, subsection G have been met.

B. If a state placing agency places a child in a private residential facility for care, safety or treatment reasons, the state placing agency is responsible for requesting an initial residential education voucher and notifying the home school district of the placement. The home school district is responsible for completing screening or other identification procedures for determining if the child is a child with a disability as defined in § 15–761 and for reviewing the placement of a child with a disability to determine whether a residential special education placement is necessary. Responsibility for monitoring the educational services during the time a child is placed in the residential facility and for planning for transition from the private residential facility to a public school remains with the home school district.

C. An initial residential education voucher may be extended for good cause, as determined by the director of the division of special education, on application by the home school district. If an extension is denied or a home district fails to complete the requirements for a continuing residential education voucher, the home school district is responsible for payment of educational costs until the requirements of subsection B of this section have been met.

D. In order to receive a continuing residential education voucher, an evaluation pursuant to § 15–766 must be conducted and the following must occur:

1. The home school district shall provide prior written notice to the parent indicating that the child is or is not eligible for special education and shall submit to the department of education a copy of the prior written notice, the evaluation from which the eligibility decision is made and, if the child is eligible for special education but does not require residential special education placement, a copy of the individualized education program indicating the special education to be provided while the child is placed in the residential facility. If the child requires a residential special education placement, § 15–765, subsection G applies.

2. On receipt from the home school district of the documentation specified in paragraph 1, the department of education shall convert the initial residential education voucher to a continuing residential education voucher that is valid for no longer than the remainder of the school year during which it is issued.

Added by Laws 1994, Ch. 91, § 7, eff. April 12, 1994.

Historical and Statutory Notes

Source:

A.R.S. former § 15–1020.01.
Laws 1976, Ch. 185, § 4.
A.R.S. former § 15–1183.
Laws 1981, Ch. 1, § 1.
Laws 1982, Ch. 28, § 1.
Laws 1992, Ch. 172, § 29.

Former § 15–1183, which related to similar subject matter, was added by Laws 1981, Ch. 1, § 1, amended by Laws 1982, Ch. 28, § 1; Laws 1992, Ch. 172, § 29, and was repealed by Laws 1994, Ch. 91, § 6, effective April 12, 1994. See, now, this section.

§ 15–1184. Vouchers; requirements; budgets; prohibited uses

A. The director of the division of special education shall develop requirements for the approval of vouchers, as provided in this section, including the following:

1. For a special education residential placement voucher, documentation that the requirements of § 15–765 have been met.

2. For an initial residential education voucher, documentation that the requirements of § 15–1183, subsection B have been met.

3. For a continuing residential education voucher, documentation that the requirements of § 15–1183, subsection C have been met.

B. The home school district shall consider recommendations from the state placing agency when determining whether the child should be placed solely in the private residential facility or should be placed for part of the school day in a school operated by a school district as provided in § 15-1185.

C. The private residential facility must demonstrate that previously received voucher monies were spent appropriately.

D. If approved, the appropriate voucher shall be issued in an amount not exceeding the sum of the following and shall be paid directly to the private residential facility in a manner prescribed by the superintendent of public instruction:

1. For group A and for placements not requiring special education services, the base level multiplied by two.

2. For group B, the sum of the support level weight as provided in § 15-943, paragraph 2, subdivision (a) for kindergarten programs through grade eight or for grades nine through twelve, whichever is appropriate, and the support level weight for the category, multiplied by the base level.

3. For both group A and group B, two hundred forty dollars for capital outlay costs or related services and fifty dollars for transportation or related services costs. Beginning with fiscal year 1991-1992, the amounts provided in this paragraph for capital outlay and transportation are increased by the growth rate prescribed by law, subject to appropriation.

E. When an initial residential education voucher expires the funding for the initial residential education voucher shall be paid directly to the private facility from the date of initial placement until the date on which the voucher expires pursuant to § 15-1183.

F. For the purpose of this article, the chief official of each state placing agency and the superintendent of public instruction shall jointly prescribe a uniform budgeting format to be submitted by each private institution and to be used in determining instructional costs and residential costs of persons placed.

G. Any residential special education placement or residential education voucher issued pursuant to this article shall not be used in any private residential facility that discriminates on the basis of race, religion, creed, color, national origin or disability.

H. Voucher monies shall only be spent to provide education and related services to children placed as provided in this article. The state board of education may withhold funding from an institution for noncompliance with any applicable statute or any applicable rule adopted by the state board.

I. The individualized education program for any child requiring a residential special education placement must include exit criteria that indicate when the educational placement of the child shall be reviewed in order to determine whether the child can be moved to a less restrictive placement.

Added by Laws 1994, Ch. 91, § 7, eff. April 12, 1994. Amended by Laws 1995, Ch. 191, § 18, eff. April 19, 1995; Laws 1995, Ch. 196, § 20.

Historical and Statutory Notes

Source:

Laws 1976, Ch. 185, § 4.
A.R.S. former §§ 15-1020.02, 15-1020.06.
Laws 1977, Ch. 89, § 8.
Laws 1978, Ch. 62, § 6.
Laws 1980, 2nd S.S., Ch. 9, § 42.

The amendment of this section by Laws 1995, Ch. 196, § 20, was repealed by Laws 1996, Ch. 248, § 11.

For applicability provisions of Laws 1995, Ch. 196, see the Historical and Statutory Notes following § 1–254.

For purpose of Laws 1996, Ch. 248, see Historical and Statutory Notes following § 15–365.

Former § 15–1184, which related to similar subject matter, was added by Laws 1981, Ch. 1, § 2, amended by Laws 1982, Ch. 28, § 2; Laws 1986, Ch. 337, § 1; Laws 1988, Ch. 281, § 10; Laws 1990, Ch. 164, § 4; Laws 1992, Ch. 172, § 30; Laws 1993, Ch. 189, § 15 and was repealed by Laws 1994, Ch. 91. § 3, effective April 12, 1994. See, now, this section.

Reviser's Notes:

1995 Note. The amendment made by Laws 1995, Ch. 196, sec. 20 was inconsistent and incompatible with Laws 1995, Ch. 191, sec. 18 and therefore could not be blended.

§ 15–1185. School district responsibility; integration into a school

A. For a child who is placed in a private residential facility pursuant to this article, the home school district is responsible for reviewing the child's educational progress and planning for integrating the child into a public school when it is educationally appropriate.

B. The private residential facility and the state placing agency shall work with the home school district for purposes of integrating the child into a public school when it is educationally appropriate.

C. If a child who has been placed in a private residential facility for care, safety or treatment reasons attends a public school in other than the home school district on either a part-time or full-time basis, the residential education voucher terminates and the following apply:

1. The school district of attendance must apply for a certificate of educational convenience as provided in § 15–825, subsection B.

2. If the child attends school in the residential facility on a part-time basis, the school district of attendance must apply for a certificate of educational convenience and either provide direct services in the residential facility or contract with the residential facility for that portion of educational services that the private residential facility is to provide.

D. If a child who requires residential special education placement is placed outside of the home school district and is able to attend a nonresidential school on a part-time basis, the residential special education placement voucher terminates. The school district of attendance shall apply for a certificate of educational convenience and pay a prorated tuition amount to the private residential facility.

Added by Laws 1994, Ch. 91, § 7, eff. April 12, 1994.

Historical and Statutory Notes

Former § 15–1185, which related to applications for vouchers, was added by Laws 1981, Ch. 1,§ 2, was amended by Laws 1981, Ch. 108, § 1; Laws 1990, Ch. 164, § 5; Laws 1992, Ch. 172, § 31, and was repealed by Laws 1994, Ch. 91, § 3, effective April 12, 1994. The repealed section was derived from:

Laws 1976, Ch. 185, § 4.
A.R.S. former §§ 15–1020.03, 15–1020.05.
Laws 1980, Ch. 195, § 3.

§ 15-1186. Repealed by Laws 1994, Ch. 91, § 6, eff. April 12, 1994

Historical and Statutory Notes

The repealed section, which related to integration of students in private institutions into public schools, was added by Laws 1981, Ch. 1, § 2, was amended by Laws 1986, Ch. 337, § 2; Laws 1992, Ch. 172, § 32, and was derived from A.R.S. former § 15-1020.04 and Laws 1976, Ch. 185, § 4. See, now, § 15-1185.

ARTICLE 7. SPECIAL EDUCATION VOUCHER FUND FOR STATE INSTITUTIONAL PLACEMENT

§ 15-1201. Definitions

In this article, unless the context otherwise requires:

1. "Fund" means the special education fund established by § 15-1182.

2. "Institution" means the Arizona state schools for the deaf and the blind, the Arizona training program facilities as provided in § 36-551 and the Arizona state hospital.

3. "Place" or "placement" means placement of a person in an institution, as defined in this section, for special education only or for special education and residential and custodial care.

4. "Special education" means the adjustment of the environmental factors, modification of the course of study and adaptation of teaching methods, materials and techniques to provide educationally for those children who are at least three but not more than twenty-one years of age and who are gifted or disabled to such an extent that they do not profit from the regular course of study or need special education services in order to profit. Difficulty in writing, speaking or understanding the English language due to an environmental background in which a language other than English is spoken primarily or exclusively shall not be considered a sufficient handicap to require special education.

Added by Laws 1981, Ch. 1, § 2, eff. Jan. 23, 1981. Amended by Laws 1992, Ch. 172, § 33; Laws 1998, Ch. 242, § 4, eff. July 1, 1999; Laws 2001, Ch. 364, § 2.

Historical and Statutory Notes

Source:

A.R.S. former §§ 15-1020.10, 15-1701.
Laws 1977, Ch. 89, § 10.
Laws 1980, 2nd S.S., Ch. 9, § 43.

§ 15-1202. Special education fund account; administration; expenditure limitation

A. There is established a separate account within the fund which shall consist of legislative appropriations to the account for special education institutional vouchers.

B. The account shall be administered by the superintendent of public instruction for the purposes provided in this article.

C. Each fiscal year the state board of education shall include in its budget request for assistance to schools a separate line item for the account.

D. The total amount of state monies that may be spent in any fiscal year by the superintendent of public instruction for the purposes of this article shall not exceed the amount appropriated or authorized by § 35-173 for that purpose. This article shall not be construed to impose a duty on an officer, agent or employee of this state to discharge a responsibility or to create any right in a person or group if the discharge or right would require an expenditure of state monies in excess of the expenditure authorized by legislative appropriation for that specific purpose.

Added by Laws 1981, Ch. 1, § 2, eff. Jan. 23, 1981. Amended by Laws 1995, Ch. 196, § 21; Laws 1998, Ch. 242, § 5, eff. July 1, 1999.

Historical and Statutory Notes

Source:

Laws 1977, Ch. 89, § 10.
A.R.S. former §§ 15-1020.11, 15-1702.
Laws 1980, 2nd S.S., Ch. 9, § 43.

For applicability provisions of Laws 1995, Ch. 196, see the Historical and Statutory Notes following § 1-254.

§ 15-1203. Placement; requirements

A. No child may be placed for the purpose of special education in an institution unless the institution has applied for and had issued a voucher pursuant to this article. Initial approval for placement shall be given when evaluation information, a copy of the individualized education program and placement documentation are provided to the special education section of the department of education. These documents shall be maintained by the school district or charter school and the receiving institution.

B. A school district may make an interim placement of an eligible child in an institution pursuant to an interim individualized education program. For purposes of this subsection, "interim placement" means placement of a child in an institution for a period of time not to exceed sixty days for the purpose of completing an educational evaluation as required by § 15-766 and making a specific placement.

C. No child who is a resident of an institution may be placed in a school special education program unless the school has applied for and had issued a special education institutional voucher pursuant to this article.

Added by Laws 1981, Ch. 1, § 2, eff. Jan. 23, 1981. Amended by Laws 1992, Ch. 172, § 34; Laws 2000, Ch. 236, § 29, eff. April 12, 2000.

Historical and Statutory Notes

Source:

Laws 1977, Ch. 89, § 10.
A.R.S. former §§ 15-1020.12, 15-1703.
Laws 1980, 2nd S.S., Ch. 9, § 43.

§ 15-1204. Voucher; application; approval; requirements; budgets; prohibited uses; advances

A. When an institution decides to place a person in an institutional special education program, the institution, upon application to and approval by the division of special education, shall have a permanent special education institutional voucher issued pursuant to this article to pay the special education instructional costs of the person at the institution.

B. When an institution decides to place a person who resides in the institution in a school special education program, the school, upon application to and approval by the division of special education, shall have a permanent special education institutional voucher issued pursuant to this article to pay the special education instructional costs of the person in the school.

C. No person residing in an institution and attending a school may have a certificate of educational convenience issued pursuant to § 15-825, subsection A.

D. The director of the division of special education shall develop requirements for the approval of vouchers, pursuant to this section, including the requirement that the person be educationally evaluated.

E. If approved, the voucher, in an amount not exceeding the sum of the following, shall be paid directly to the institution or deposited with the county treasurer to the credit of the school, with notice to the county school superintendent:

1. For group A, the base level multiplied by two.

2. For group B, the sum of the base for kindergarten through eight and the support level weight for the category, multiplied by the base level.

3. For both group A and group B, one hundred dollars for capital outlay costs and fifty dollars for transportation costs.

F. The budget format developed cooperatively between the department of economic security and the department of education pursuant to § 8-503 shall be used by the institutions to determine and segregate residential costs from educational instructional costs.

G. If sufficient appropriated monies are available and upon a showing by an institution that additional state monies are necessary for current expenses, an advance apportionment of state aid may be paid to an institution. In no event shall an institution have received more than three-fourths of its total apportionment under this section before April 15 of the fiscal year. Early payments pursuant to this subsection must be approved by the state treasurer, the director of the department of administration and the superintendent of public instruction.

H. Notwithstanding subsection G of this section, when making the April payment to an institution, the department of education may include an additional amount based on an estimate of monies payable to the institution in May. Before the department of education apportions monies to the institution in June, it shall adjust the June payment to account for any discrepancies between the monies actually paid in April and May and the amount which should have been paid. If an overpayment in May exceeds the total amount payable in June, the institution shall refund to the department of education an amount equal to the overpayment within sixty days of notification of the overpayment. If the overpayment is not refunded within sixty days by the institution, the superintendent of public instruction shall reduce the state aid entitlement to the institution for the succeeding fiscal year to recover any overpayment of state aid received during the current fiscal year.

I. Any special education institutional voucher issued pursuant to this article shall not be used in any school or institution that discriminates on the basis of race, religion, creed, color or national origin.

J. The state board of education may withhold state aid from an institution for noncompliance with any applicable statute or any applicable rule adopted by the state board.

Added by Laws 1981, Ch. 1, § 2, eff. Jan. 23, 1981. Amended by Laws 1984, Ch. 193, § 1; Laws 1987, Ch. 363, § 8, eff. May 22, 1987.

Historical and Statutory Notes

Source:

Laws 1977, Ch. 89, § 10.
A.R.S. former §§ 15–1020.13, 15–1020.16, 15–1704, 15–1707, 15–1708.
Laws 1980, 2nd S.S., Ch., 9, § 43.

§ 15–1205. Voucher; evaluation; placement; definition

A. An application for a voucher pursuant to this article shall not be approved unless the child has been educationally evaluated and recommended for placement in accordance, as nearly as practicable, with the conditions and standards prescribed by the superintendent of public instruction pursuant to rules of the state board of education.

B. In determining the recommendation for placement the chief official of the institution shall consult at a minimum with the following:

1. The parent, as defined in § 15–761 of the child recommended for placement.

2. The person performing the educational evaluation pursuant to this section.

3. A special educator who is certified in an area related to the child's disability.

C. The placing agency may sign a voucher application for submission to the department of education.

D. Nothing in this article shall be construed to prevent a child who has not been educationally evaluated from being placed in an institution if such placement is for the purpose of residential and custodial care only and not for educational reasons. The institutional voucher shall not be paid for such placements.

E. For the purposes of this section, "educationally evaluated" means an evaluation pursuant to § 15–766.

Added by Laws 1981, Ch. 1, § 2, eff. Jan. 23, 1981. Amended by Laws 1992, Ch. 172, § 35.

Historical and Statutory Notes

Source:

Laws 1977, Ch. 89, § 10.
A.R.S. former §§ 15–1020.14, 15–1020.15, 15–1705, 15–1706.
Laws 1980, 2nd S.S., Ch. 9, § 43.
Laws 1980, Ch. 195, § 5.

ARTICLE 7.1. DEPARTMENT OF EDUCATION ENVIRONMENTAL EDUCATION FUND [REPEALED]

Article 7.1, Department of Education Environmental Education Fund, consisting of § 15–1211, was added by Laws 1990, Ch. 266, § 4, effective September 27, 1990, and was repealed by Laws 1997, Ch. 58, § 2, effective July 21, 1997.

§ 15-1211. Repealed by Laws 1997, Ch. 58, § 2

Historical and Statutory Notes

The repealed section, added by Laws 1990, Ch. 266, § 4, related to the department of education environmental education fund.

ARTICLE 8. GOVERNING BOARD BANK ACCOUNTS

Article 8, Governing Board Bank Accounts, consisting of §§ 15-1221 and 15-1222, was added by Laws 1982, Ch. 80, § 1, effective July 24, 1982.

§ 15-1221. Bank account; federal savings bonds; withholdings; vendor electronic payments

A. The governing board may establish a bank account for the purpose of depositing the monies it withholds for each employee for payments under federal savings bond plans until the employee accumulates sufficient monies for the purchase of bonds under the plan. The governing board may make disbursements from the bank account only by check payable to the financial institution in which the monies are deposited for the purchase of bonds by the employee from the financial institution. The bank account may be interest-bearing, and the governing board shall transfer any interest at the end of the fiscal year to the county treasurer for credit to the maintenance and operation fund of the school district.

B. The governing board may establish a bank account for the purpose of making electronic payments to vendors. The account may be a revolving account, funded by the school district by a warrant requested from the county school superintendent and drawn on the county treasurer for an amount equal to the vendor's payment amount. The account may be an interest bearing account. The account shall be a clearing account maintaining a zero balance and shall not accumulate funds except for any account interest balances. The district governing board shall transfer any interest at the end of the fiscal year to the county treasurer for credit to the maintenance and operation fund of the school district.

C. The governing board of a school service program established pursuant to § 15-365 may establish a bank account for the purpose of making electronic payments to vendors. The account may be a revolving account, funded by the school service program by a warrant requested from the county school superintendent and drawn on the county treasurer for an amount equal to the vendor's payment amount. The account may be an interest bearing account. The account shall be a clearing account maintaining a zero balance and shall not accumulate funds except for any account interest balances.

D. The auditor general in conjunction with the department of education shall prescribe the procedures for accounting for the monies withheld pursuant to this section in the uniform system of financial records.

Added by Laws 1982, Ch. 80, § 1. Amended by Laws 1996, Ch. 284, § 67; Laws 1999, Ch. 99, § 2.

Historical and Statutory Notes

Reviser's Notes:

1999 Note. Pursuant to authority of § 41-1304.02, in subsection B, third sentence and subsection C, third sentence the spelling of "interest bearing" was corrected and in subsection C, second sentence the spelling of "vendor's" was corrected.

§ 15-1222. Bank account; employee income tax; withholdings

A. The governing board of a school district may establish a bank account for the purpose of depositing the monies it withholds for each employee for application toward the employee's state income tax liability until the governing board must pay the monies to the department of revenue as provided in § 43-401. The governing board may make disbursements from the bank account only by check payable to the department of revenue. The bank account may be interest-bearing, and the governing board shall transfer any interest at the end of the fiscal year to the county treasurer for credit to the maintenance and operation fund of the school district.

B. The auditor general in conjunction with the state board of education shall prescribe the procedures for accounting for the monies withheld pursuant to this section in the uniform system of financial records.

Added by Laws 1982, Ch. 80, § 1.

Historical and Statutory Notes

Reviser's Notes:

1982 Note. Pursuant to authority of § 41-1304.02, in the section heading a semicolon was inserted between "tax" and "withholdings".

§ 15-1223. Bank accounts; employee insurance; interest; accounting procedures

A. The governing board of a school district may establish bank accounts in which to deposit the monies it withholds for employee insurance programs, the monies contributed by the district for employee insurance programs and the monies received from former employees, board members, former board members and surviving spouses and dependents of board members or former board members for the insurance programs. The governing board may disburse monies from the bank accounts only by check payable to the insurance carriers or to make refunds of insurance to individuals.

B. The bank accounts may be interest-bearing, and the governing board shall transfer any interest at the end of the fiscal year to the county treasurer for credit to the maintenance and operation fund of the school district.

C. The auditor general in conjunction with the department of education shall prescribe the procedures for accounting for monies pursuant to this section in the uniform system of financial records.

Added by Laws 1988, Ch. 79, § 2, eff. May 16, 1988. Amended by Laws 1989, Ch. 273, § 19, eff. June 26, 1989; Laws 1996, Ch. 284, § 68; Laws 1998, Ch. 139, § 5, eff. Oct. 1, 1998.

Historical and Statutory Notes

Laws 1998, Ch. 139, § 6, provides:

"**Sec. 6. Effective date**

"This act is effective from and after September 30, 1998."

Reviser's Notes:

1988 Note. Laws 1988, Ch. 106, § 5 added another new § 15-1223 which was renumbered as § 15-1224, pursuant to authority of § 41-1304.02.

§ 15-1224. Grants to teachers for instruction

A. The governing board shall deposit in a separate bank account grants or gifts which are less than one thousand five hundred dollars and designated for use by a teacher for instructional purposes if the governing board does not deposit the grant or gift as prescribed in § 15-341, subsection A, paragraph 15.

B. A separate record shall be maintained for each grant or gift deposited in the bank account.

C. Disbursements from the bank account shall be by check signed by two employees of the school district appointed by the governing board and shall be authorized by the teacher designated to use the grant or gift as provided in the uniform system of financial records.

D. If any of the monies are not spent before the end of the fiscal year in which the gift or grant was accepted, the balance of the monies shall remain in the bank account until needed for instructional purposes as designated by the teacher, or determined by the grantor.

Added as § 15-1223 by Laws 1988, Ch. 106, § 5. Renumbered as § 15-1224. Amended by Laws 1991, Ch. 257, § 14; Laws 1995, Ch. 268, § 51.

Historical and Statutory Notes

Reviser's Notes:

1988 Note. Pursuant to authority of § 41-1304.02, this section, added by Laws 1988, Ch. 106, § 5 as § 15-1223, was renumbered as § 15-1224.

ARTICLE 9. CAREER AND TECHNICAL EDUCATION AND VOCATIONAL EDUCATION PROJECTS FUND

Article 9, Vocation and Technical Education Projects Fund, consisting of § 15-1231, was added by Laws 1985, Ch. 347, § 7, effective May 14, 1985.

The heading of Article 9 was changed from "VOCATIONAL AND TECHNICAL EDUCATION PROJECTS FUND" to "CAREER AND TECHNICAL EDUCATION AND VOCATIONAL EDUCATION PROJECTS FUND", by Laws 2002, Ch. 89, § 34, eff. August 22, 2002.

§ 15-1231. Career and technical education and vocational education projects fund

A. The governing board of a school district may establish a permanent career and technical education and vocational education projects fund in an amount not to exceed one hundred thousand dollars. The fund shall consist of proceeds from the sale of items produced by career and technical education and vocational education programs. Monies in the fund may be used for any of the following purposes:

1. Purchase of materials for use by career and technical education and vocational education pupils in an instructional program that produces a product that may be sold by the school district.

2. Purchase of equipment, not to exceed five thousand dollars in any one fiscal year, for use by career and technical education and vocational education pupils in an instructional program which produces a product that may be sold by the school district.

3. Expenses directly related to the planning and design of career and technical education and vocational education program products.

B. Monies in the career and technical education and vocational education projects fund may not be used to pay salaries, wages or employee fringe benefits.

C. The career and technical education and vocational education projects fund of a school district is a continuing fund, and monies in the career and technical education and vocational education projects fund are not subject to reversion, except that all monies in the fund in excess of one hundred thousand dollars at the end of the fiscal year shall revert to the school plant fund.
Added by Laws 1985, Ch. 347, § 7, eff. May 14, 1985. Amended by Laws 1996, Ch. 284, § 69; Laws 2002, Ch. 89, § 35.

ARTICLE 10. ACADEMIC CONTESTS FUND

Article 10, consisting of § 15–1241, was added by Laws 1988, Ch. 308, § 2.

§ 15–1241. Academic contests fund; state board of education powers and duties; distribution of monies

A. The state board of education shall establish an academic contests fund consisting of monies appropriated by the legislature or received by the state board as provided in subsection D of this section.

B. The state board of education shall prescribe rules for the distribution of fund monies to school districts for the purpose of sending pupils from the school district who are state level winners of academic contests and their chaperons to the national levels of these contests so that the pupils may represent this state.

C. The criteria on which the state board shall base its rules for the distribution of fund monies shall include at least the following:

1. The contests must be academic in nature and motivate pupils to be creative and to demonstrate excellence.

2. Contests must be sponsored by a recognized national organization.

3. Contests must be open to all pupils, regardless of race, creed, gender or national origin, except that a contest may separate pupils by age or grade level.

4. The opportunity to compete at the national level must be the result of successfully competing at the local or state level, or both, of that contest.

D. The state board of education may accept gifts or grants of monies for deposit in the academic contests fund as provided in this section.

E. A school district which receives monies as provided in this section shall include the monies in the special projects section of the budget as provided in § 15-903, subsection F.

Added by Laws 1988, Ch. 308, § 2. Amended by Laws 1999, Ch. 299, § 32.

Historical and Statutory Notes

The purported amendment of this section by Laws 1998, 3rd S.S., Ch. 1, failed to became effective because Ch. 1 was repealed in its entirety by Laws 1998, 5th S.S., Ch. 1, § 2, effective July 1, 1998.

ARTICLE 11. STATE BLOCK GRANT FOR EARLY CHILDHOOD EDUCATION PROGRAM

Article 11, State Block Grant for Early Childhood Education Program, consisting of § 15-1251, was added by Laws 1998, 4th S.S., Ch. 8, § 7, effective August 13, 1998.

§ 15-1251. State block grant for early childhood education; evaluation

A. The state block grant for early childhood education program is established in the state board of education. The purpose of the program is to promote improved pupil achievement by providing flexible supplemental funding for early childhood programs, including preschool programs for economically disadvantaged children, and programs that serve all public school pupils statewide who are in kindergarten programs and grades one, two and three.

B. Funding for the program for each fiscal year shall be allocated based on the number of pupils in kindergarten programs and grades one, two and three in each charter school or school district who were eligible for free lunches during the prior fiscal year under the national school lunch and child nutrition acts (42 United States Code §§ 1751 through 1785). Any charter school or school district that did not determine for the prior fiscal year if its pupils in kindergarten programs and grades one, two and three were eligible for free lunches under the national school lunch and child nutrition acts shall receive funding for the program in the current fiscal year based on the number of its pupils in kindergarten programs and grades one, two and three who would have been eligible for free lunches in the prior fiscal year according to the statewide kindergarten programs and grades one, two and three eligibility average for all school districts and charter schools collectively for the prior fiscal year. Notwithstanding this section, a school district or charter school with an average daily membership of more than six hundred pupils in kindergarten programs and grades one, two and three in the prior fiscal year shall have participated in the national school lunch and child nutrition acts free lunches program in the prior fiscal year to be eligible for program funding in the current fiscal year.

C. A school district or charter school that devotes part or all of its program funding to preschool programs shall comply with all of the following requirements:

1. Restrict the preschool program only to preschool children eligible for free or reduced price lunches under the national school lunch and child nutrition acts.

2. Allow participating pupils to receive preschool services only from a public, federally funded or private child care provider, each of which shall be licensed by the department of health services and each of which, beginning in fiscal year 1999–2000, also shall be accredited by a state board of education approved organization that provides accreditation for preschool programs.

3. Provide all federally funded or private child care providers located within the school district or within ten miles of the charter school with information necessary for them to participate in the program, including names and addresses of children selected for participation and of their parents or guardians.

4. Provide all parents or guardians of children selected for the program with a list of licensed federally funded or private child care providers located within the school district or within ten miles of the charter school and explain to parents or guardians that they may choose to have their child receive services under the program from any provider on the list if that provider agrees to participate.

5. Allow at least fifty per cent of pupils selected for the program to receive preschool services from a federally funded or private child care provider of their parent's or guardian's own choosing.

6. Allow any eligible child care provider located within the school district or within ten miles of the charter school to participate in the program if it is willing to provide services at a unit cost similar to that paid to other providers in the area under the program.

7. Limit the use of contracts with federally funded and private child care providers to financial agreements pertaining to numbers of children to be served, hours of service to be provided per child, payment rates and other financial aspects of the program.

8. Limit to five per cent the amount of block grant monies that may be used locally for program administration.

9. Pay participating federally funded and private child care providers in a timely manner.

D. The legislative council shall conduct a programmatic evaluation of the state block grant for early childhood education program every three years. For this evaluation, the staff of legislative council shall develop outcome measures to indicate the effectiveness of the early childhood education program. The department of education shall assist the staff of legislative council in collecting any information necessary to complete the evaluation.

Added by Laws 1998, 4th S.S., Ch. 8, § 7. Amended by Laws 2001, Ch. 323, § 1.

Historical and Statutory Notes

Laws 1999, 1st S.S., Ch. 4, § 14, as amended by Laws 2000, Ch. 9, § 1, provides:

"**Sec. 14. Early childhood block grant; deadline for accreditation of preschool programs**

A. Notwithstanding § 15-1251, subsection C, paragraph 2, Arizona Revised Statutes, all sites receiving funding under the early childhood block grant program during fiscal year 1999-2000 shall be accredited by July 1, 1999, except that they may operate on a provisional basis if they provide evidence that shows that they are in the process of becoming accredited. These sites shall attain accreditation no later than July 1, 2000 to be eligible for program funding.

B. Notwithstanding the July 1, 2000 accreditation deadline in subsection A, the agency administering the block grant may extend the accreditation deadline for any site that demonstrates that it is reasonably working toward becoming accredited.

C. Sites that did not participate in the program in the prior funding year are eligible to participate in the program if they have applied for and are working toward accreditation or are accredited. Sites that are not accredited shall become accredited within eighteen months after originally receiving monies.

Laws 2001, Ch. 299, § 1, which provided for a school breakfast program and a report, was repealed by section 2 of the act, on January 1, 2004.

CHAPTER 11

ARIZONA STATE SCHOOL FOR THE DEAF AND THE BLIND

ARTICLE 1. GENERAL PROVISIONS

ARTICLE 2. ADMINISTRATION AND EMPLOYMENT OF PERSONNEL

ARTICLE 3. INSTRUCTION AND STUDENTS

ARTICLE 4. BRANCH SCHOOLS [REPEALED]

For more information on using WESTLAW to supplement your research, see the WESTLAW Electronic Research Guide, which follows the Preface.

Chapter 11, Arizona State School for the Deaf and Blind, consisting of Article 1, §§ 15–1301 to 15–1304, Article 2, §§ 15–1321 to 15–1329, Article 3, §§ 15–1341 to 15–1350, and Article 4, § 15–1361, was added by Laws 1981, Ch. 1, § 2, effective January 23, 1981.

Termination Under Sunset Law

The board of directors of the school for the deaf and the blind shall terminate on July 1, 2013, unless continued. See §§ 41–3013.03 and 41–2955.

Title 15, Chapter 11, relating to the Arizona state school for the deaf and the blind, is repealed on January 1, 2014 by §41–3013.03.

Historical and Statutory Notes

Laws 1986, Ch. 18, § 1, effective April 4, 1986, providing for establishment of a joint legislative committee to study the Arizona state school for the deaf and the blind, expired Nov. 2, 1986 by provisions of § 2 of that act.

Laws 1988, Ch. 237, § 1 provides:

"**Section 1. Purpose**

"The purpose of the Arizona state school for the deaf and the blind is to promote and maintain an educational opportunity of adequate scope and quality for sensory impaired children in this state which will lead to an adult life of independence and self-sufficiency, a meaningful personal, family and community life, and a useful productive occupational life."

Laws 1988, Ch. 237, § 21, which provided for delayed repeal of Title 15, Ch. 11, effective January 1, 1994, was itself repealed by Laws 1991, Ch. 8, § 1, subsec. F.

Laws 1990, Ch. 340, § 3, provides:

"**Sec. 3. Loan forgiveness program for teachers of the deaf and the blind**

"**A.** The Arizona board of regents shall require that the university of Arizona establish and administer a program to provide loans to persons in teacher training programs in the areas of the deaf and the blind within the college of education at the university of Arizona, if funds are appropriated for this purpose.

"**B.** The Arizona board of regents shall adopt rules regarding repayment of the loans. The rules shall include a provision for discharging loan indebtedness if a recipient completes a period of teaching in a state or local school district program for the deaf and the blind which is equal to the amount of time the recipient was supported by a loan pursuant to subsection A."

Laws 1991, Ch. 80, § 31, provides:

"**Sec. 31. Validation of prior acts**

"Every transaction involving the disposal of land of the grant of the United States for the use and benefit of the state school for the deaf and blind that was executed after January 23, 1981 and before the effective date of this act without compliance with § 15–1304, Arizona Revised Statutes, is confirmed, ratified, validated and declared legally effective."

ARTICLE 1. GENERAL PROVISIONS

§ 15–1301. Definitions

In this chapter, unless the context otherwise requires:

1. "Employee classifications" means one of the following:

(a) Management and supervisory staff on a twelve month schedule.

(b) Teachers, credentialed and noncredentialed specialists, on an academic schedule.

(c) Clerical, accounting, maintenance workers and others on a twelve month schedule.

(d) Food service and bus drivers on an academic schedule.

2. "Hearing impairment" means hearing impairment as defined in § 15-761.

3. " Schools" means the Arizona state schools for the deaf and the blind and includes programs and services offered for the deaf and the blind by the schools in conjunction with other educational institutions.

4. "Sensory impairment" means the following conditions, as defined in § 15-761:

(a) Visual impairment.

(b) Hearing impairment.

(c) Both a visual and hearing impairment.

(d) Multiple disabilities, if at least one of the disabilities is a visual or a hearing impairment.

5. "Visual impairment" means visual impairment as defined in § 15-761.

Added by Laws 1981, Ch. 1, § 2, eff. Jan. 23, 1981. Amended by Laws 1987, Ch. 363, § 9, eff. May 22, 1987; Laws 1992, Ch. 172, § 36; Laws 1993, Ch. 204, § 1, eff. April 21, 1993.

Historical and Statutory Notes

Source:

Laws 1955, 3rd S.S., Ch. 3, § 1.
A.R.S. former § 15-801.

§ 15-1302. Arizona state schools for the deaf and the blind; provision of services

A. There shall be Arizona state schools for the deaf and the blind which provide schools and regional programs in appropriate locations in this state.

B. The schools shall be for the education of sensory impaired persons, so that the persons educated there may become self-sustaining and useful citizens.

C. The schools shall be fully recognized as institutions for educational purposes.

D. The schools shall be optional resources to school districts, state institutions and other approved educational programs. Resource services shall include, but are not limited to, the following:

1. Assessments.
2. Special curriculum.
3. Equipment and materials.
4. Supplemental related services.
5. Special short-term programs.
6. Program planning and staff development.
7. Information services for parents, families and the public.

8. Research and development to promote improved educational programs and services.

E. The services prescribed in subsection D shall not duplicate existing services and shall include a variety of methodology as may be requested by the school districts, state institutions and other approved educational programs, including but not limited to oral, auditory, total communication and cued speech.

Added by Laws 1981, Ch. 1, § 2, eff. Jan. 23, 1981. Amended by Laws 1987, Ch. 363, § 10, eff. May 22, 1987; Laws 1990, Ch. 283, § 1, eff. June 12, 1990; Laws 1993, Ch. 204, § 2, eff. April 21, 1993; Laws 1995, Ch. 42, § 1.

Historical and Statutory Notes

Source:

Laws 1929, Ch. 93, §§ 1, 3.
Code 1939, §§ 54-1501, 54-1503.
A.R.S. former § 15-802.

Laws 1987, Ch. 363, § 19, effective May 22, 1987, as amended by Laws 1990, Ch. 283, § 2, effective June 12, 1990, provides:

"**Sec. 19. Pilot program of regional service cooperatives**

"**A.** A pilot program of three regional service cooperatives for sensory impaired pupils is established for fiscal years 1987-1988 through 1993-1994. The cooperatives shall be organized in fiscal year 1987-1988 and services shall be provided in beginning in fiscal year 1988-1989. The cooperatives shall be operated by the Arizona state school for the deaf and the blind through intergovernmental agreements with participating school districts.

"**B.** The state board of education shall determine the geographical area to be served by each cooperative by September 1, 1987, based on the recommendations of the sensory impairment advisory committee as provided in § 20 if this act. Governing boards of school districts within the boundaries established by the state board for a cooperative may elect to participate in the cooperative through an intergovernmental agreement as provided in subsection A of this section.

"**C.** The location of cooperative facilities shall be determined by the Arizona state school for the deaf and the blind in consultation with the participating school districts. The facilities shall be located on or near a public school campus to facilitate part-time attendance of cooperative pupils at the public school when appropriate.

"**D.** Each cooperative shall provide the following services to its participating school districts:

"1. Educational programs and related services shall be provided to all sensory impaired pupils as defined in § 15-1301, Arizona Revised Statutes, as amended by this act, if the school district of residence is participating in the cooperative and cannot provide an appropriate program and if placement at the cooperative is determined to be the most appropriate placement as provided in subsection I of this section. The cooperative may provide a temporary program pending development of a permanent program in the school district of residence.

"2. Supplemental services shall be provided to assist school districts in providing educational and related services to sensory impaired pupils and other areas of need related to sensory impaired pupils. The supplemental services shall include at least the following:

"(a) Evaluations, including audiological, psychological and vision assessment.

"(b) Specialized related services, including orientation and mobility training.

"(c) Specialized curriculum materials and equipment.

"(d) Program and staff development assistance.

"(e) Assistance with screening, identification and registration of sensory impaired pupils.

"**E.** The costs of the services provided in subsection D of this section shall be paid by the participating schools through the intergovernmental agreements as follows:

"1. The costs of educational and related services shall be paid by the school district of residence through a tuition agreement that reflects the cost of the services provided or, beginning with fiscal year 1991-1992 and continuing through fiscal year 1993-1994, by a special education voucher as provided for in title 15, chapter 10, article 7, Arizona Revised Statutes.

"2. The costs of the supplemental services shall be paid by all participating school districts through a basic membership agreement.

"**F.** The Arizona state school for the deaf and the blind shall establish an advisory committee for each cooperative to provide advice on the administration of the cooperative. The advisory committee shall include parents, representatives from participating school districts and representatives from local private organizations which provide services to the sensory impaired.

"G. The cooperative may provide educational programs and related services to pupils from school districts which are not participating in the cooperative on a space available basis. If enrollments must be limited, preference shall be given to pupils from school districts outside of the three established regional service areas. Before a pupil may be placed in a program operated by a cooperative as provided in this subsection, the pupil must be evaluated according to the procedure prescribed in subsection I of this section. The school district of residence shall pay tuition to the cooperative to cover the full unit cost of the educational and related services for a pupil placed in a cooperative as provided in this subsection.

"H. Pupils from school districts which lie outside of the three established regional service areas are eligible for preference in placement at special purpose schools operated by the Arizona state school for the deaf and the blind when placement openings are limited. In order to receive such preference, the appropriate placement must be determined according to subsection I of this section, except that the placement and reevaluation team is not required to include a cooperative representative.

"I. The identification, registration, placement and reevaluation of sensory impaired pupils whose school district of residence is participating in a cooperative shall be as follows:

"1. All sensory impaired children shall be registered with the school district at age five or on moving into the school district.

"2. The school district is responsible for arranging for the evaluation of the sensory impaired pupil.

"3. The appropriate educational placement for the pupil shall be determined by a placement and reevaluation team based on the development of an individualized education program as required by law. The placement and reevaluation team shall consist of at least the following persons:

"(a) The parent or legal guardian of the pupil.

"(b) An administrator of the school district.

"(c) An evaluator.

"(d) A teacher.

"(e) A representative from the cooperative.

"(f) A representative from a special purpose school if referral for placement at a special purpose school is being considered.

"4. The placement and reevaluation team shall consult with other agency experts, experts from private organizations and parent advocates as needed.

"5. Annual reviews of placement as required by law shall be performed by the provider of the educational services.

"6. Reevaluation, required every third year by law, shall be performed by the placement and reevaluation team. Pupils from participating school districts who were not placed in accordance with the procedure prescribed in this subsection shall be reevaluated by a placement and reevaluation team as prescribed in this subsection at the time of their three year reevaluation, except that pupils who are enrolled at a special purpose school at the time of their reevaluation shall be reevaluated by the multidisciplinary team which performs their annual placement review, to which a school district administrator and a cooperative representative shall be added as members. Pupils whose school district of residence is not participating in a cooperative and who are enrolled at a special school at the time of their three year reevaluation shall be reevaluated by the multidisciplinary team which performs their annual placement review, to which a school district administrator or the administrator's designee shall be added.

"For the purposes of this subsection, "special purpose school" means a special purpose school operated by the Arizona state school for the deaf and the blind or a private institution.

"J. For fiscal year 1988–1989, the state board of education shall distribute one hundred thousand dollars from monies received under 20 United States Code § 1411(c)(2) to the cooperatives for the purchase of equipment.

"K. The state board of education, in consultation with the board of directors of the Arizona state school for the deaf and the blind, shall submit a report to the legislature on the pilot program annually by December 1."

Laws 1987, Ch. 363, § 20, effective May 22, 1987, relating to the tuition fund to facilitate appropriate placement of sensory impaired pupils, was repealed by Laws 1990, Ch. 348, § 28, effective June 26, 1990.

Laws 1987, Ch. 363, § 21, as amended by Laws 1988, Ch. 237, § 11 and Laws 1990, Ch. 348, § 29, effective June 26, 1990, provides:

"**Sec. 21. State board of education sensory impairment advisory committee**

"A. The state board of education shall establish a sensory impairment advisory committee consisting of at least the following members:

"1. Three parents of children who are sensory impaired, including one parent of a hearing handicapped child, one parent of a visually handicapped child and one parent of a multiple handicapped child with a severe sensory impairment.

"2. Two sensory impaired adults, including one who has a hearing impairment and one who has a visual impairment.

"3. One representative from a nonpublic organization which provides services to hearing impaired children.

"4. One representative from a nonpublic organization which provides services to visually impaired children.

"5. One representative of the Arizona state school for the deaf and the blind, recommended by the board of directors of the Arizona state school for the deaf and the blind.

"6. One representative from a school district who is experienced in the area of special education for sensory impaired children.

"7. One representative from the department of education who is knowledgeable in the area of special education for sensory impaired children.

"8. Two representatives from the department of economic security, including one representative from the division of developmental disabilities and one representative from the rehabilitation services administration.

"9. One representative from the department of health services who is knowledgeable in the area of screening and evaluation of sensory impaired children.

"**B.** Members of the committee are not eligible to receive compensation, but members appointed pursuant to subsection A, paragraphs 1, 2, 3, 4 and 6 are eligible for reimbursement of expenses by the state board of education pursuant to title 38, chapter 4, article 2, Arizona Revised Statutes.

"**C.** The committee shall:

"1. Review the current rules governing special education programs for sensory impaired pupils and make recommendations to the state board of education regarding modifications necessary to ensure consistency of standards among programs statewide. The recommendations shall include statewide standards for educational and related services, screening, identification and evaluation processes, including qualifications for evaluators, and placement and reevaluation processes. In developing its recommendations, the committee shall consult with relevant experts from public and private agencies and consider the need to:

"(a) Promote greater equity among programs provided by school districts, state supported institutions and private institutions.

"(b) Facilitate mainstreaming by making programs comparable among the various placement options.

"(c) Ensure that continuity of services is available for each pupil within a program.

"(d) Develop a standard which would mandate the establishment of special education programs for the sensory impaired in school districts of a certain size or having a certain population of pupils with sensory impairments, including the minimum services which would be required on establishment.

"2. Review and make recommendations to the legislature regarding the following:

"(a) Establishment of a supplemental or developmental summer program or programs for sensory impaired pupils which emphasize adaptive skills of daily living and socialization that are not generally a part of the regular school course of study. In developing recommendations, the committee shall consider tuition charges as a means of providing funding for a program.

"(b) A classification system for pupils who have both mental and sensory impairments which will ensure placement in the most appropriate program. The recommendations shall identify which classifications, if any, should be excluded from placement at a special purpose school operated by the Arizona state school for the deaf and the blind.

"(c) A framework of a cooperative agreement or agreements between the department of economic security, the department of education and the Arizona state school for the deaf and the blind or a school district which would provide residential placement for sensory impaired pupils who reside in remote areas and are currently limited to special education services at a special purpose school operated by the Arizona state school for the deaf and the blind due to unavailability of other residential placement options. The recommendations shall include the following:

"(i) Development of a process for administering the residential placement program and definition of the specific roles of each agency involved in the program.

"(ii) Establishment of standards to be applied to homes in which pupils are placed.

"(iii) Identification of a funding source or sources to pay the costs of residential placement.

"(d) Admission criteria for placement at a special purpose school operated by the Arizona state school for the deaf and the blind, which includes consideration of the following:

"(i) How appropriateness of residential placement should be determined.

"(ii) Whether any limits should be placed on residential admissions because of the high cost of residential care.

"(iii) Whether statutory provisions regarding admissions to a special purpose school operated by the Arizona state school for the deaf and the blind require modification.

"(iv) The specific responsibility of the school district, the department of education, the Arizona state school for the deaf and the blind and the parent or guardian.

"(v) In developing any recommendations related to admissions, the potential impact of regional service cooperatives both under the pilot program as provided in § 18 of this act and under statewide development of the regional service cooperative concept.

"3. Review and make recommendations to the Arizona board of regents regarding expansion and funding of programs for teachers of the sensory impaired.

"**D.** The committee shall present a report to the joint legislative committee to study the Arizona school for the deaf and the blind on the items specified in subsection C by October 1 of each year beginning in 1988 until 1990.

"**E.** The committee shall serve as the advisory committee for the pilot program of regional service cooperatives, established pursuant to § 18 of this act, by:

"1. Recommending the location of the three regional service cooperatives, giving emphasis to geographic areas that have the greatest overall need for services.

"2. Developing criteria for placement in a regional service cooperative program.

"3. Advising the Arizona state school for the deaf and the blind in the planning, implementation and operation of the regional service cooperatives.

"4. Developing criteria for evaluating the pilot program and contracting with an independent evaluator to evaluate the program. In developing criteria and selecting an evaluator, the committee shall consult with the chairs of the education committees of the house of representatives and the senate. An evaluator shall be selected no later than November 1, 1988."

Laws 1987, Ch. 363, § 22, as amended by Laws 1988, Ch. 237, § 12 provides:

"**Sec. 22. State board of education committee to study the improvement of special education services**

"**A.** The state board of education shall establish a committee to study the improvement of special education services consisting of at least the following:

"1. Two members of the senate, appointed by the president of the senate.

"2. Two members of the house of representatives, appointed by the speaker of the house of representatives.

"3. Five parents of handicapped children, including one parent of a sensory impaired child, one parent of a physically handicapped child, one parent of an educable or trainable mentally handicapped child, one parent of a severely or profoundly mentally handicapped child and one parent of a multiple handicapped child.

"4. One representative from the Arizona state school for the deaf and the blind, appointed by the board of directors of the Arizona state school for the deaf and the blind.

"5. One representative from the department of education who is knowledgeable in the area of special education.

"6. Three representatives from school districts who are experienced in the area of special education.

"7. One county school superintendent or another representative of a county school superintendent's office.

"8. One representative from a university which is under the jurisdiction of the Arizona board of regents, who is knowledgeable in the area of special education, appointed by the Arizona board of regents.

"9. One representative from the sensory impairment advisory committee, established pursuant to § 20 of this act, elected by a majority of the sensory impairment advisory committee.

"**B.** Members of the committee are not eligible to receive compensation, but members appointed pursuant to subsection A, paragraphs 3, 6, 7, 8 and 9 are eligible for reimbursement of expenses by the state board of education pursuant to title 38, chapter 4, article 2, Arizona Revised Statutes.

"**C.** The committee shall:

"1. Review the delivery system of special education services to pupils in, at a minimum, the following handicap categories:

"(a) Visually handicapped.

"(b) Hearing handicapped.

"(c) Physically handicapped.

"(d) Educable mentally handicapped.

"(e) Trainable mentally handicapped.

"(f) Severely or profoundly mentally handicapped.

"(g) Multiple handicapped.

"2. Make recommendations to the state board of education by October 1 of each year beginning in 1988 until 1990 regarding:

"(a) Improvements to the statewide system of delivery of special education services.

"(b) Modifications to existing rules to provide consistent standards for special education programs for pupils in the handicap categories specified in paragraph 1 of this subsection.

"(c) Modifications to existing rules governing the special education voucher process for the Arizona state school for the deaf and the blind, including the criteria on which vouchers are approved or disapproved and the time factors involved in the process.

"3. In developing recommendations, define a role for the Arizona state school for the deaf and the blind with respect to sensory impaired pupils.

"4. Review and make recommendations concerning the role of parents or guardians in the initial referral of and the placement process for special education pupils."

Laws 1987, Ch. 363, § 23, which required the Arizona board of regents to establish loan forgiveness programs for special education teachers, was repealed by Laws 1990, Ch. 340, § 2.

Laws 1987, Ch. 363, § 24, as amended by Laws 1988, Ch. 237, § 13, and Laws 1991, Ch. 292, § 26, effective June 28, 1991, providing for a joint legislative committee to study the Arizona state school for the deaf and the blind was repealed by Laws 1992, Ch. 70, § 2, subsec. I, as amended by Laws 1993, Ch. 174, § 4, on October 10, 1993.

Laws 1987, Ch. 363, § 25, as amended by Laws 1988, Ch. 237, § 14 and Laws 1990, Ch. 348, § 30, effective June 26, 1990, provides:

"**Sec. 25. Appropriations requirements**

"**A.** Notwithstanding section 19 and section 21, subsection F of this act, a program of regional service cooperatives is established and the sensory impairment advisory committee shall serve as the advisory committee for the pilot program of regional service cooperatives only if legislation is enacted by the thirty-eighth legislature, first regular session, appropriating monies for the purpose of planning and establishing the pilot program of regional service cooperatives.

"**B.** Notwithstanding § 23 of this act the Arizona board of regents shall establish a loan forgiveness program for special education teachers only if legislation is enacted by the thirty-eighth legislature, second regular session, appropriating monies for the loan forgiveness program."

Laws 1987, Ch. 363, § 26, as amended by Laws 1988, Ch. 237, § 15, and by Laws 1991, Ch. 298, § 43, provides:

"**Sec. 26. Expiration date**

"Sections 19, 20 and 21 of this act are repealed from and after June 30, 1994."

Laws 1990, Ch. 283, § 3 relating to delayed repeal provisions, was itself repealed by Laws 1991, Ch. 298, § 44.

Laws 1990, Ch. 283, § 4, effective June 12, 1990, provides:

"**Sec. 4. Transition to voucher funding**

"**A.** School districts which have included in their fiscal year 1991–1992 student count, pupils receiving educational programs and related services from a regional services cooperative and for whom a voucher is paid for fiscal year 1991–1992 as providing in § 2 of this act, must reduce their revenue control limit and district support level, capital outlay revenue limit and capital levy revenue limit for fiscal year 1991–1992 by the amounts attributable to these pupils for the days for which the pupil was counted and notify the department of education by July 31, 1991 of the amounts. The department of education shall prescribe the method for determining the amount of the reductions. The department of education shall decrease that school district's apportionment of equalization assistance for the fiscal year 1991–1992 by the corresponding amount.

"**B.** It is the intent of the legislature that monies appropriated from the state general fund to the state board of education and the superintendent of public instruction for basic state aid for fiscal year 1991–1992, in an amount equal to the equalization assistance reduction in subsection A shall be used by the state board of education for the state permanent special education institutional voucher fund pursuant to Title 15, chapter 10, article 7, Arizona Revised Statutes."

Laws 1991, Ch. 298, § 1, par. 22, provides:

"**Section 1. Purpose**"

"22. Laws 1990, chapter 283, § 3 amended Laws 1987, chapter 363, § 26 but failed to include the amendments to that section that were made by Laws 1988, chapter 237, § 15. In order to correct this potentially defective enactment, the Laws 1987, chapter 363, § 26 enactment, as amended by Laws 1988, chapter 237, § 15, is amended to incorporate the Laws 1990, chapter 283, § 3 version and the Laws 1990, chapter 283 version is repealed."

Laws 2003, Ch. 8, § 3, effective Sept. 18, 2003, retroactively effective to July 1, 2003, provides:

"**Sec. 3. Purpose**

"The purpose of the Arizona state schools for the deaf and the blind is to promote and maintain an educational opportunity of adequate scope and quality for sensory impaired children in this state which will lead to an adult life of independence and self-sufficiency, a meaningful personal, family and community life and a useful and productive occupational life."

§ 15-1303. School for the deaf and the blind as public corporation; tax exemption

A. The school shall be a body corporate under the name of "the Arizona state school for the deaf and the blind".

B. The corporation shall:

1. Have perpetual succession.

2. Have a corporate seal.

3. Be deemed a public corporation and its property shall be exempt from all taxes and assessments.

C. The corporation may, in the corporate name:

1. Sue and be sued.

2. Contract and be contracted with.

3. Take and hold by purchase, gift or devise real and personal property required for its use.

4. Convert property received by gift, purchase or devise which is not suitable for its use into money or property which is suitable for its use.

Added by Laws 1981, Ch. 1, § 2, eff. Jan. 23, 1981.

Historical and Statutory Notes

Source:

Laws 1929, Ch. 93, §§ 1, 2.

Code 1939, §§ 54-1501, 54-1502.

A.R.S. former § 15-803.

§ 15-1304. Land reserved for use and benefit of school; schools for the deaf and blind fund

A. The grant of one hundred thousand acres of land for schools for the deaf, dumb and blind made by the enabling act approved June 20, 1910, or the proceeds of such lands as are sold or otherwise disposed of, is forever reserved for the use and benefit of the school for the deaf and the blind.

B. No land exchanges or sales or commercial leases in excess of ten years of land of the grant by the United States for the use and benefit of the school for the deaf and the blind shall be disposed of except by majority approval of the voting members of the board of directors of the school.

C. The superintendent of the school shall annually report to the board on the use of monies which are the proceeds of or income from the proceeds of land of the grant by the United States for the use and benefit of the school.

D. A schools for the deaf and the blind fund is established consisting of monies from expendable earnings of the grant in subsection a of this section, monies from the department of education for special educational vouchers for deaf and blind students pursuant to § 15-1202, except for monies dedicated to regional school cooperatives, which are continuously appropriated, and overage and nonresident student monies collected pursuant to § 15-1345. Monies in the fund are subject to legislative appropriation and are exempt from the provisions of § 35-190 relating to lapsing of appropriations.

Added by Laws 1981, Ch. 1, § 2, eff. Jan. 23, 1981. Amended by Laws 1988, Ch. 237, § 2; Laws 1991, Ch. 80, § 1; Laws 1998, Ch. 242, § 6, eff. July 1, 1999.

Historical and Statutory Notes

Source:

Laws 1929, Ch. 93, §§ 8, 10.

Code 1939, §§ 54-1508, 54-1510.

A.R.S. former § 15-804.

Laws 1991, Ch. 80, § 31 provides:

"**Sec. 31. Validation of prior acts**

"Every transaction involving the disposal of land of the grant of the United States for the use and benefit of the state school for the deaf and blind that was executed after January 23, 1981 and before the effective date of this act without compliance with § 15-1304, Arizona Revised Statutes, is confirmed, ratified, validated and declared legally effective."

§ 15-1305. Arizona state schools for the deaf and the blind; classroom site fund

The Arizona state schools for the deaf and the blind classroom site fund is established consisting of monies received from the department of education pursuant to § 15-977. The Arizona state schools for the deaf and the blind shall administer the fund. Monies in the fund are exempt from the provisions of § 35-190 relating to lapsing of appropriations and are continuously appropriated.

Added by Laws 2001, 2nd S.S., Ch. 6, § 2, eff. Dec. 19, 2001.

§ 15-1306. Arizona state schools for the deaf and the blind telecommunications tax fund

A. The Arizona state schools for the deaf and the blind telecommunications tax fund is established consisting of monies received from the telecommunications tax levied pursuant to § 42-5252, subsection A, paragraph 6. The Arizona state schools for the deaf and the blind shall administer the fund.

B. Monies in the fund shall be used for operating expenses of the Arizona state schools for the deaf and the blind and are subject to legislative appropriation.

C. Monies in the fund are exempt from the provisions of § 35-190 relating to lapsing of appropriations.

Added by Laws 2003, Ch. 263, § 12, eff. Sept. 18, 2003, retroactively effective to July 1, 2003.

Historical and Statutory Notes

Laws 2003, Ch. 263, § 102, provides:

"**Sec. 102. Retroactivity**

"**A.** Sections 5-504, 5-505, 5-522, 28-737, 28-876, 28-2416, 28-8101, 28-8103, 42-5252 and 43-401, Arizona Revised Statutes, as amended by this act, apply retroactively to from and after June 30, 2003 and §§ 4, 87 and 92 of this act and § 15-1306, Arizona Revised Statutes, as added by this act, are effective retroactively to from and after June 30, 2003.

"**B.** Section 100 of this act is effective retroactively to from and after May 31, 2003."

ARTICLE 2. ADMINISTRATION AND EMPLOYMENT OF PERSONNEL

Historical and Statutory Notes

Laws 1988, Ch. 237, § 21, which provided for delayed repeal of Title 15, Ch. 11, effective January 1, 1994, was itself repealed by Laws 1991, Ch. 8, § 1, subsec. F.

§ 15-1321. Board of directors; members; appointment; term; compensation

A. The school for the deaf and the blind shall be governed by a board of directors. The board shall consist of the governor, as an ex officio nonvoting member, the superintendent of public instruction or the superintendent's designee and six appointive members.

B. The governor shall appoint the appointive members of the board to terms of three years. One member shall be an employee of a school district who works with the district's program for sensory impaired pupils. In selecting three of the remaining five appointive members the governor shall give preference to persons who have experience in and knowledge of sensory impaired education. The terms of two members expire on the first Monday of January of each year. Appointment to fill a vacancy resulting other than by expiration of term shall be for the unexpired portion of the term only.

C. Members of the board shall not receive compensation.

Added by Laws 1981, Ch. 1, § 2, eff. Jan. 23, 1981. Amended by Laws 1981, Ch. 314, § 18; Laws 1988, Ch. 237, § 3.

Historical and Statutory Notes

Source:

Laws 1929, Ch. 93, §§ 6, 7.
Code 1939, §§ 54–1506, 54–1507.
A.R.S. former § 15–811.
Laws 1970, Ch. 204, § 32.
Laws 1976, Ch. 113, § 1.

§ 15–1322. Board organization; meetings; quorum

A. The board shall select from its membership a president, a treasurer and a secretary or a president and a secretary-treasurer.

B. A meeting of the board may be called at any time by the governor, the president or the secretary.

C. Four voting members shall constitute a quorum for the transaction of business of the board.

Added by Laws 1981, Ch. 1, § 2, eff. Jan. 23, 1981. Amended by Laws 1988, Ch. 237, § 4.

Historical and Statutory Notes

Source:

Laws 1929, Ch. 93, § 28.
Code 1939, § 54–1528.
A.R.S. former § 15–812.

§ 15–1323. Board of directors; fund; powers and duties

A. The board may bring actions and proceedings necessary to protect the interests of the schools. Such proceedings shall be instituted in the name of the Arizona state schools for the deaf and the blind.

B. The board shall be trustee of all donations of lands, monies or other things of value for the benefit of the schools. Notwithstanding title 35, chapters 1 and 2,[1] the board may invest monies donated to the school through a contract with an investment specialist. The superintendent of the schools shall annually report to the board on the use of monies received as donations or income from donations.

C. The board shall maintain an enterprise fund in which shall be retained fees, rentals and other charges received for the use of school facilities for nonschool events. Monies in the enterprise fund may be used only to pay costs associated with operating facilities for the purpose for which the monies were received.

D. The board shall:

1. Provide from the funds appropriated for the schools all the necessary staff, services, supplies and equipment.

2. Prescribe the system of records and accounts for the schools.

3. Cause to be kept a record of all important papers.

4. Cause to be kept a set of books and accounts which show every transaction made, every appropriation by the legislature for the schools, the purchase, storage and consumption of supplies for subsistence, construction and other purposes, receipts from all sources and all expenditures made.

E. Books and records of the schools shall be open to public inspection, unless otherwise restricted by law.

Added by Laws 1981, Ch. 1, § 2, eff. Jan. 23, 1981. Amended by Laws 1988, Ch. 237, § 5; Laws 1993, Ch. 204, § 3, eff. April 21, 1993.

[1] Sections 35-101 et seq. and 35-301 et seq.

Historical and Statutory Notes

Source:

Laws 1929, Ch. 93, §§ 6, 9, 18.
Code 1939, §§ 54-1506, 54-1509, 54-1518.
A.R.S. former § 15-813.

Laws 1988, Ch. 237, § 17 provides:

"**Sec. 17. Initial term of member of board of directors**

"Notwithstanding § 15-1323, Arizona Revised Statutes, as amended by this act, the initial term of the sixth member of the board of directors of the Arizona state school for the deaf and the blind expires on January 7, 1991."

§ 15-1324. Reports of board of directors

The board shall prepare and file:

1. An annual report to the governor with a detailed statement of the cost of maintaining the school which shows in detail every financial transaction, a complete record of the conditions and work of the school, and including reports by the superintendent and chief medical officer.

2. An estimate for the use of the legislature of appropriations necessary for the support of and for needed improvements to the school, and also a report of the operation of the school for the preceding year.

Added by Laws 1981, Ch. 1, § 2, eff. Jan. 23, 1981.

Historical and Statutory Notes

Source:

Laws 1929, Ch. 93, § 14.
Code 1939, § 54-1514.
A.R.S. former § 15-814.

§ 15-1325. Superintendent and other personnel; appointment; compensation; term of employment; qualifications; nonretention notice

A. There shall be a superintendent of the schools who shall be the executive officer. The superintendent shall be appointed by the board of directors, and the board shall issue one, two or three year contracts for the superintendent. The superintendent is eligible to receive compensation pursuant to § 38-611. The board of directors shall designate the management and supervisory positions. The superintendent, with the approval of and acting on behalf of the board, shall issue one, two or three year contracts for the management and supervisory positions designated by the board pursuant to this section. Compensation for persons issued contracts pursuant to this section shall be paid according to a range of compensation approved by the board of directors.

B. The superintendent and the management and supervisory staff, except for the persons contracted for personnel service and business and finance service shall be persons who are competent educators of the deaf or the blind, or the multiply disabled and sensory impaired, and who are acquainted with school management and class instruction of the deaf or the blind, or the multiply disabled and sensory impaired. A person is eligible to be the superintendent, or hold a position on the management or supervisory staff except for a person contracted for personnel service and business and finance service if the person has had actual experience as a teacher of the deaf or the blind or the multiply disabled and sensory impaired.

C. The board of directors shall establish a system for the evaluation of the performance of the superintendent in consultation with the administration of the schools. The superintendent shall establish a system for the evaluation of the performance of persons contracted pursuant to this section in consultation with the staff of the schools.

D. On or before April 15 preceding the expiration of the superintendent's employment contract, the board shall give written notice to the superintendent of the board's intention to offer or not to offer a new employment contract. On or before April 15 preceding the expiration of the contract of a person contracted by the superintendent, acting on behalf of the board of directors pursuant to this section, the superintendent shall give written notice to the person of the board's intention to offer or not to offer the person a new employment contract. If the board decides to offer the superintendent a new employment contract, the board shall offer the new employment contract on or before May 15 preceding the expiration of the superintendent's current employment contract. If the board decides to offer a new employment contract to a person contracted pursuant to this section, the superintendent, acting on behalf of the board, shall offer the new employment contract on or before May 15 preceding the expiration of the current employment contract. The person offered a contract pursuant to this subsection shall accept the contract by signing and returning it to the board of directors within thirty days or the offer is deemed refused. If the person adds written terms or conditions to the employment contract offered, the person fails to accept the employment contract.

E. Notice of the board of directors' intention not to reemploy the superintendent or a person contracted pursuant to this section shall be delivered to the superintendent or the person contracted by one of the following:

1. The superintendent, in person, acting on behalf of the board.

2. Certified mail, postmarked on or before the deadline prescribed in subsection D of this section and directed to the place of residence as recorded in the agency's records.

Added by Laws 1981, Ch. 1, § 2, eff. Jan. 23, 1981. Amended by Laws 1981, Ch. 32, § 1; Laws 1983, Ch. 1, § 1, eff. Jan. 28, 1983; Laws 1987, Ch. 363, § 11, eff. May 22, 1987; Laws 1991, Ch. 292, § 22, eff. June 28, 1991; Laws 1993, Ch. 204, § 4, eff. April 21, 1993.

Historical and Statutory Notes

Source:

Laws 1929, Ch. 93, §§ 3, 11.
Code 1939, §§ 54–1503, 54–1511.
A.R.S. former § 15–815.
Laws 1962, Ch. 98, § 17.
Laws 1967, Ch. 117, § 1.
Laws 1968, Ch. 173, § 14.
Laws 1970, Ch. 204, § 33.

Laws 1993, Ch. 204, § 17, effective April 21, 1993, provides:

"Sec. 17. **ASDB personnel; initial offer of contract**

"Notwithstanding § 15–1325, Arizona Revised Statutes, as amended by this act:

"1. On or before thirty days after the effective date of this act, the board of directors of the Arizona state schools for the deaf and the blind shall give written notice to the superintendent of the board's intention to offer or not to offer an employment contract. If the board decides to offer the superintendent an employment contract, the board shall offer the employment contract within thirty days after the notice.

"2. On or before thirty days after the effective date of this act, the superintendent of the Arizona state schools for the deaf and the blind, acting on behalf of the board of directors, shall give written notice to a person in a supervisory or management position as designated by the board of the board's intention to offer or not to offer the person an employment contract. If the board decides to offer a contract to a person in a supervisory or management position, the superintendent, acting on behalf of the board, shall offer the employment contract within thirty days after the notice."

§ 15–1326. Employment and discharge of personnel

A. The superintendent, acting on behalf of the board of directors, shall employ all personnel needed for the operation of the schools. The board shall review all personnel appointments on a periodic basis and may require employment justification by the superintendent as it deems necessary.

B. Except as provided in § 15–1325, the superintendent shall place each new employee in a probationary employment status. The board shall determine the term and conditions of probationary employment status. The superintendent may discharge any probationary employee who is unsuited or not qualified for employment at the schools and shall file with the board a written report of the action and the reasons for the discharge. On satisfactory completion of probationary employment, employees shall be granted permanent employment status.

C. The superintendent may discharge, only for cause, any permanent employee at the schools. The superintendent shall file with the board a written report of the action and the reasons for the discharge. Permanent employees discharged from employment at the schools are entitled to due process protections in the manner provided by the board including but not limited to a hearing before the board of directors. The due process procedures will be developed in consultation with the employees.

D. The board shall prescribe policies for employees, including employee conduct and discipline.

Added by Laws 1986, Ch. 193, § 2. Amended by Laws 1993, Ch. 204, § 5, eff. April 21, 1993.

Historical and Statutory Notes

Former § 15–1326, added by Laws 1981, Ch. 1, § 2, derived from Laws 1929, Ch. 93, §§ 11, 15; Code 1939, §§ 54–1511, 54–1515; and A.R.S. former § 15–816, relating to the powers and duties of the superintendent of the state school for the deaf and the blind, was repealed by Laws 1986, Ch. 193, § 1.

§ 15-1326.01. Renumbered as § 15-1327

§ 15-1327. Limitations on reduction of salaries or personnel

A. The board of directors may direct the superintendent to reduce salaries or eliminate permanent employee positions in the Arizona state schools for the deaf and the blind in order to effectuate economies in the operation of the schools or to improve the efficient conduct and administration of the schools. The superintendent, with the approval of the board, may designate the positions to be eliminated within an employee classification, and the reduction of personnel shall occur within and be limited to that specific employee classification. A person whose position is eliminated does not have a preferred right to employment in a different employee classification, except that when a vacancy exists in a teaching position and no teacher who is currently employed at any of the schools applies for the position, a person whose position in a management or supervisory position is eliminated has a preferred right to employment as a teacher, provided that the person is qualified for the teaching position. A person whose position is eliminated and who is transferred to a different position in a lower grade does not have a preferred right to a continued salary based on the former position or to any particular salary level in the lower grade. No reduction in the salary of a certificated teacher or credentialed specialist who has been employed by the schools for more than one year shall be made except in accordance with a general salary reduction in the schools by which the person is employed, and in such case the reduction shall be applied equitably among all permanent employees.

B. Notice of a general salary reduction shall be given to each certificated teacher and credentialed specialist affected not later than May 15 before the fiscal year in which the reduction is to take effect.

C. A permanent employee dismissed for reasons of economy or to improve the efficient conduct and administration of the schools shall have a preferred right of reappointment in the order of original employment by the board of directors in the event of an increase in the number of permanent employees or the reestablishment of services within a period of three years.

Added as § 15-1326.01 by Laws 1993, Ch. 204, § 6, eff. April 21, 1993. Renumbered as § 15-1327. Amended by Laws 2004, Ch. 243, § 2.

Historical and Statutory Notes

Laws 1993, Ch. 204, § 16, effective April 21, 1993, provides:

"**Sec. 16. Legislative intent**

"**A.** The legislature intends to continue the Arizona state school for the deaf and blind to promote and maintain an educational opportunity of adequate scope and quality for sensory impaired children in this state that will lead to an adult life of independence and self-sufficiency, a meaningful personal, family and community life and a useful productive occupational life.

"**B.** This act is intended to allow the Arizona state schools for the deaf and the blind to implement the recommendations made in the auditor general report issued in October, 1992 and the budget recommendation of the staff of the joint legislative budget committee for fiscal year 1993-1994, including a recommended reduction in force limited to management and supervisory personnel and clerical and other staff that support management and supervisory personnel."

The 2004 amendment by Ch. 243, substituted "employee positions" for "employees" in subsec. A; and rewrote subsec. B, which had read:

"**B.** Notice of a general salary reduction shall be given to each certificated teacher and credentialed specialist affected not later than May 1 of the calendar year in which the reduction is to take effect."

Former § 15-1327, added by Laws 1981, Ch. 1, § 2, derived from Laws 1929, Ch. 93, § 25; Code 1939, § 54-1525; A.R.S. former § 15-817; Laws 1970, Ch. 204, § 34, and relating to the powers, duties and compensation of medical officers, was repealed by Laws 1993, Ch. 204, § 7, effective April 21, 1993.

Reviser's Notes:

1993 Note. Pursuant to authority of § 41-1304.02, this section, added by Laws 1993, Ch. 204, sec. 6 as § 15-1326.01, was renumbered as § 15-1327.

§ 15-1328. Repealed by Laws 1993, Ch. 204, § 7, eff. April 21, 1993

Historical and Statutory Notes

The repealed section, added by Laws 1981, Ch. 1, § 2, relating to rules and classifications regarding the board of directors of the state school for the deaf and the blind, was derived from:

Laws 1929, Ch. 93, §§ 11, 13, 16, 17.
Code 1939, §§ 54-1511, 54-1513, 54-1516, 54-1517.
A.R.S. former § 15-818.
Laws 1970, Ch. 190, § 15.
Laws 1971, Ch. 125, § 19.
Laws 1976, Ch. 162, § 15.
Laws 1978, Ch. 201, § 258.

§ 15-1329. Salaries and subsistence of employees; payrolls

A. The board shall determine the salaries and assign an employee classification of persons it employs, except for the superintendent as provided in § 15-1325.

B. All salary schedules for employees of the schools shall become operative on July 1 of each year and shall be included in the estimate of expenses submitted by the superintendent.

C. In addition to the officer's salary, each officer required to live at the school may receive food supplies for the officer's family from the regular supplies furnished to the institution, but such officer's family shall include only such officer's spouse and minor children.

D. The superintendent shall furnish a semimonthly payroll for the school showing the name of each officer and employee, monthly stipend and time of service. The payroll shall be audited by the board and a statement of the amount determined due shall be filed with the department of administration and a warrant issued to each individual name therein contained.

Added by Laws 1981, Ch. 1, § 2, eff. Jan. 23, 1981. Amended by Laws 1983, Ch. 98, § 18; Laws 1983, Ch. 184, § 1; Laws 1993, Ch. 204, § 8, eff. April 21, 1993.

Historical and Statutory Notes

Source:

Laws 1929, Ch. 93, § 12.
Code 1939, § 54-1512.
A.R.S. former § 15-819.
Laws 1968, Ch. 89, § 9.
Laws 1972, Ch. 141, § 8.
Laws 1973, Ch. 172, § 56.

Reviser's Notes:

1983 Note. Prior to the 1993 amendment, this section contained the amendments made by Laws 1983, Ch. 98, § 18 and Ch. 184, § 1 which were blended together pursuant to authority of § 41-1304.03.

§ 15-1330. Fingerprinting personnel; affidavit

A. Certificated personnel employed by the schools shall have valid fingerprint clearance cards issued pursuant to title 41, chapter 12, article 3.1 [1] or shall apply for a fingerprint clearance card within seven working days of employment.

B. In addition to the fingerprint requirement in subsection A of this section, certificated employees shall submit a second set of fingerprints to the school for the purposes of obtaining state and federal criminal records checks. Employment with the schools is conditioned on the results of the fingerprint check required under this subsection and the maintenance of the certificate or license required for employment. Fingerprint checks shall be conducted pursuant to § 41–1750 and Public Law 92–544. The fingerprints shall be submitted on the form prescribed by the school.

C. Noncertificated personnel employed by the schools and nonpaid personnel working in the schools shall be fingerprinted as a condition of employment for the purpose of obtaining state and federal criminal records checks. Noncertificated employees and nonpaid personnel shall submit fingerprints on the form prescribed by the school to the superintendent within twenty days after the date an employee begins work. Employment with the schools is conditioned on the results of the fingerprint check. Fingerprint checks shall be conducted pursuant to § 41–1750 and Public Law 92–544.

D. The department of public safety may exchange the fingerprint data collected pursuant to subsections B and C of this section with the federal bureau of investigation.

E. The schools may charge the employee or nonpaid personnel for the costs of the fingerprint checks.

F. Personnel employed by the schools shall certify on forms that are provided by the schools and notarized that they are not awaiting trial on and have never been convicted of or admitted in open court or pursuant to a plea agreement of committing any criminal offenses in this state or similar offenses in another state or jurisdiction as specified in § 41–1758.03, subsections B and C.

G. Before employment, the schools shall make documented, good faith efforts to contact previous employers of personnel to obtain information and recommendations that may be relevant to a person's fitness for employment. For certificated personnel, the schools may also contact the department of education to obtain information that is contained in the person's certification record and that may be relevant to the person's fitness for employment. For persons in other positions that require licensing, the schools may also contact the agency that issued the license for information relevant to the person's fitness for employment. Agencies and previous employers that provide information pursuant to this subsection are immune from civil liability unless the information provided is false and is acted on to the detriment of the employment applicant by the schools and the previous employer or agency knows the information is false or acts with reckless disregard of the truth or falsity of the information. Employees who rely on information obtained pursuant to this subsection in making employment decisions are immune from civil liability unless the information obtained is false and the employee knows the information is false or acts with reckless disregard of the truth or falsity of the information.

H. The superintendent shall notify the department of public safety if the superintendent receives credible evidence that a person who possesses a valid fingerprint clearance card either:

1. Is arrested for or charged with an offense listed in § 41-1758.03, subsection B.

2. Falsified information on the form required by subsection F of this section.

Added by Laws 1985, Ch. 364, § 39, eff. May 16, 1985. Amended by Laws 1993, Ch. 39, § 3; Laws 1993, Ch. 204, § 9, eff. April 21, 1993; Laws 1997, Ch. 231, § 29; Laws 1998, Ch. 270, § 4, eff. August 17, 1999; Laws 2000, Ch. 251, § 4; Laws 2001, Ch. 241, § 6; Laws 2003, Ch. 214, § 7, eff. Oct. 1, 2003.

[1] Section 41-1758 et seq.

Historical and Statutory Notes

The 1993 blended amendments by Chs. 39 and 204 rewrote the section, which had read:

"**A.** Beginning July 1, 1985, personnel employed by the school shall be fingerprinted as a condition of employment. An employee shall submit fingerprints and the form prescribed in subsection D of this section to the superintendent within twenty days after the date an employee begins work. Employment with the school is conditioned on the results of the fingerprint check.

"**B.** Fingerprint checks shall be conducted pursuant to § 41-1750, subsection G.

"**C.** The school shall assume the costs of fingerprint checks and may charge these costs to its fingerprinted employee.

"**D.** Personnel employed by the school shall certify on forms that are provided by the school and notarized that they are not awaiting trial on and have never been convicted of or admitted committing any of the following criminal offenses in this state or similar offenses in another state or jurisdiction:

"1. Sexual abuse of a minor.

"2. Incest.

"3. First or second degree murder.

"4. Kidnapping.

"5. Arson.

"6. Sexual assault.

"7. Sexual exploitation of a minor.

"8. Contributing to the delinquency of a minor.

"9. Commercial sexual exploitation of a minor.

"10. Felony offenses involving distribution of marijuana or dangerous or narcotic drugs.

"11. Burglary.

"12. Robbery.

"13. A dangerous crime against children as defined in § 13-604.01.

"14. Child abuse.

"15. Sexual conduct with a minor.

"16. Molestation of a child.

"**E.** The school shall make documented, good faith efforts to contact previous employers of personnel to obtain information and recommendations which may be relevant to a person's fitness for employment."

The 1997 amendment by Ch. 231 modified a statutory reference.

The 1998 amendment by Ch. 270 rewrote the section, which had read:

"**A.** Personnel employed by the schools shall be fingerprinted as a condition of employment. For personnel required to be fingerprinted as a condition of certification or licensing for employment, the schools may satisfy the requirements of this subsection by accepting the issuance of the certificate or license. An employee shall submit fingerprints and the form prescribed in subsection D of this section to the superintendent within twenty days after the date an employee begins work. Employment with the schools is conditioned on the results of the fingerprint check and maintenance of the certificate or license required for employment.

"**B.** Fingerprint checks shall be conducted pursuant to § 41-1750, subsection G.

"**C.** The schools shall assume the costs of fingerprint checks and may charge these costs to its fingerprinted employee.

"**D.** Personnel employed by the schools shall certify on forms that are provided by the schools and notarized that they are not awaiting trial on and have never been convicted of or admitted in open court or pursuant to a plea agreement committing any criminal offenses in this state or similar offenses in another state or jurisdiction as specified in § 15-534, subsection E.

"**E.** Before employment, the schools shall make documented, good faith efforts to contact previous employers of personnel to obtain information and recommendations which may be relevant to a person's fitness for employment. For certificated personnel, the schools shall also contact the department of education to obtain information contained in the person's certification record that may be relevant to the person's fitness for employment. For persons in other positions that require licensing, the schools shall also contact the agency that issued the license for information relevant to the person's fitness for employment. Agencies and previous employers that provide information pursuant to this subsection are immune from civil liability unless the information provided is false and is acted on to the detriment of the employment applicant by the schools and the previous employer or agency knows the information is false or acts with reckless disregard of the truth or falsity of the information. Employees who rely on information obtained pursuant to this subsection in making employment decisions are immune from civil liability unless the information obtained is false and the employee knows the information is false or acts with reckless disregard of the truth or falsity of the information."

The 2000 amendment by Ch. 251 added subsec. D, requiring notification by the superintendent of arrests of, or falsifications by, certain fingerprint clearance card possessors.

The 2001 amendment by Ch. 241 rewrote the section, which had read:

"**A.** personnel employed by the schools shall have valid class one or class two fingerprint clearance cards issued pursuant to title 41, chapter 12, article 3.1 or shall apply for a class one or class two fingerprint clearance card within seven working days of employment. For personnel required to be fingerprinted as a condition of certification or licensing for employment, the schools may satisfy the requirements of this subsection by accepting the issuance of the certificate or license. Employment with the schools is conditioned on the results of the fingerprint check and maintenance of the certificate or license required for employment.

"**B.** Personnel employed by the schools shall certify on forms that are provided by the schools and notarized that they are not awaiting trial on and have never been convicted of any criminal offenses in this state or similar offenses in another state or jurisdiction as specified in § 15-534, subsection B.

"**C.** Before employment, the schools shall make documented, good faith efforts to contact previous employers of personnel to obtain information and recommendations which may be relevant to a person's fitness for employment. For certificated personnel, the schools shall also contact the department of education to obtain information contained in the person's certification record that may be relevant to the person's fitness for employment. For persons in other positions that require licensing, the schools shall also contact the agency that issued the license for information relevant to the person's fitness for employment. Agencies and previous employers that provide information pursuant to this subsection are immune from civil liability unless the information provided is false and is acted on to the detriment of the employment applicant by the schools and the previous employer or agency knows the information is false or acts with reckless disregard of the truth or falsity of the information. Employees who rely on information obtained pursuant to this subsection in making employment decisions are immune from civil liability unless the information obtained is false and the employee knows the information is false or acts with reckless disregard of the truth or falsity of the information.

"**D.** The superintendent shall notify the department of public safety if the superintendent receives credible evidence that a person who possesses a valid class one or class two fingerprint clearance card either:

"1. Is arrested for or charged with an offense listed in § 41-1758.03, subsection B or F.

"2. Falsified information on the form required by subsection B of this section."

The 2003 amendment by Ch. 214, deleted "class one or class two" before "fingerprint clearance card(s)" in subsecs. A and H; and modified subsection references to § 41-1758.03 in several place.

Reviser's Notes:

1993 Note. Prior to the 1997 amendment, this section contained the amendments made by Laws 1993, Ch. 39, sec. 3 and Ch. 204, sec. 9 that were blended together pursuant to authority of § 41-1304.03.

§ 15-1331. Equity study for school personnel

A. The department of administration shall:

1. In consultation with the department of education and the board of directors, conduct salary equity studies for teachers, credentialed specialists and other personnel unique to the school. For teachers, compensation for extracurricular activities shall be included. The department of administration shall conduct a full study once every five years by analyzing salary structures

for similar personnel in school districts in this state providing significant programs for sensory impaired children. The average salary increase awarded to similar positions in three school districts included in the full study and selected by the department of administration and department of education in consultation with the board shall be reported for consideration by the joint legislative budget committee.

2. Conduct reclassification studies for all other personnel with follow-up studies as necessary.

B. The board shall use the results of the department of administration's studies in determining salaries pursuant to §15-1329 and in making its budget request. The joint legislative budget committee may consider the results of the studies in making its recommendations for funding of existing personnel services.

Added by Laws 1988, Ch. 237, § 6. Amended by Laws 1995, Ch. 196, § 22.

Historical and Statutory Notes

Laws 1988, Ch. 237, § 19 provides:

"**Sec. 19. Legislative intent**

"The legislature intends to appropriate sufficient monies to the Arizona state school for the deaf and the blind to allow the school to implement the salary recommendations made by the department of administration pursuant to § 15-1331, Arizona Revised Statutes, as added by this act."

Laws 1991, Ch. 288, § 23, effective Sept. 21, 1991, retroactively effective to July 1, 1991, provides:

"**Sec. 23. Use of salary study for fiscal year 1991-1992**

"Notwithstanding the provisions of § 15-1331, subsection B, Arizona Revised Statutes, the joint legislative budget committee shall not use the results of the studies conducted pursuant to § 15-1331, subsection A, Arizona Revised Statutes, in making its recommendations for funding of existing personnel services for fiscal year 1991-1992."

Laws 1995, 1st S.S., Ch. 4, § 5, provides:

"**Sec. 5. School personnel salary equity study; school district average**

"Notwithstanding § 15-1331, subsection A, paragraph 1, Arizona Revised Statutes, the salary equity study shall tie interim increases to the average salary increase awarded to similar positions in five school districts instead of three school districts."

For applicability provisions of Laws 1995, Ch. 196, see the Historical and Statutory Notes following § 1-254.

ARTICLE 3. INSTRUCTION AND STUDENTS

Historical and Statutory Notes

Laws 1988, Ch. 237, § 21, which provided for delayed repeal of Title 15, Ch. 11, effective January 1, 1994, was itself repealed by Laws 1991, Ch. 8, § 1, subsec. F.

§ 15-1341. Instruction of pupils

A. The board of directors shall see that all persons admitted to the school are taught and trained by methods which are to their best interests.

B. The board shall ensure the careful supervision of the care, education and development of pupils to insure that the best care and education known to modern science is given, as nearly as is practicable, and that the best methods of teaching the sensory impaired are used in the school.

C. The board shall give special attention to the methods of care, education and development of the persons admitted, with particular consideration of the humanitarian aspects of their education.

D. The board, if advisable in particular cases, may allow pupils to remain at the school during the entire year.

Added by Laws 1981, Ch. 1, § 2, eff. Jan. 23, 1981. Amended by Laws 1987, Ch. 363, § 12, eff. May 22, 1987.

Historical and Statutory Notes

Source:
Laws 1929, Ch. 93, §§ 19, 22, 26.
Code 1939, §§ 54-1519, 54-1522, 54-1526.
A.R.S. former § 15-831.

§ 15-1342. Admissions

A. Chapter 7, article 4 of this title [1] governs admissions to the school except as provided in this section. The evaluation and consideration of placement in the school shall be made under the direction of the chief administrative official of the school district or accommodation school within the boundaries of which the child resides or a person designated by the official as responsible for special education after consultation with the parent, as defined in § 15-761, of the child. If a parent or legal guardian of a child directly refers a child to the state school for the deaf and the blind, the school shall immediately after notification of referral contact the chief administrative official of the school district or accommodation school within the boundaries of which the child resides. The chief administrative official shall arrange for the establishment of a placement and evaluation team for that child.

B. A placement and evaluation team shall determine the appropriate educational placement for the child based on the development of an individualized education program. Each placement and evaluation team shall document that it has advised the parent or legal guardian of all placement options. The placement and evaluation team shall consist of at least the following persons:

1. The parent or legal guardian of the child.

2. An administrator from the school district in which the child resides.

3. A certified teacher of the sensory impaired who provides or may provide in the future educational services to the child.

4. An evaluator, with preference given to an evaluator who is trained and experienced in evaluating the educational needs of sensory impaired children.

5. A representative of the school.

C. The individualized education program plan of a child continuing in special education placement from the prior school year shall be reviewed annually and revised if necessary. The individualized planning conference shall include a representative of the school district of residence and a representative of the school, the child's teacher, the parent , as defined in § 15-761, of the child and, if appropriate, the child.

D. Except as provided in subsection F of this section, the chief administrative official of the school district or accommodation school within the boundaries of which the child resides or a person designated by the official as responsible for special education shall place the child according to the recommendations of the individualized education program team.

E. A child who is placed in the school but moves from one school district or county to another may remain placed in the school until the next annual review. A representative of the child's new district of residence shall be included on the team conducting the review. The superintendent of the school shall at least quarterly give the chief administrator of the school district or accommodation school notice of any changes in a child's residence.

F. If the chief administrator of the school district or accommodation school or his designee and the superintendent of the school determine that the school cannot provide the appropriate educational programs and services needed by the child, they shall locate or establish a program to meet the child's needs in consultation with the department of education and any other appropriate state agency.

G. A complete record of every person admitted shall be kept from the date of his admission to the date of his discharge or death. The records shall be accessible to the board or a legislative committee or upon order of a judge of a court of record.

H. If there is any question regarding the propriety of the placement or admission of any person received in the school, the governing board of the school district or accommodation school within the boundaries of which the child resides or the board of the school shall make an investigation and take such action as it deems proper.

I. No political or religious belief shall be required as a qualification of any student of the school.

Added by Laws 1981, Ch. 1, § 2, eff. Jan. 23, 1981. Amended by Laws 1988, Ch. 237, § 7; Laws 1992, Ch. 172, § 37.

[1] Section 15-761 et seq.

Historical and Statutory Notes

Source:

Laws 1929, Ch. 93, §§ 11, 19.
Code 1939, §§ 54-1511, 54-1519.
A.R.S. former § 15-832.

§ 15-1343. Persons entitled to education

A. A person is entitled to an education in the schools for the deaf and the blind without charge if the person is a resident of this state, age three through twenty-one years and sensory impaired to an extent that he cannot acquire an appropriate education in the school district of residence.

B. The school district of residence that refers a pupil for admission to the schools shall determine that the pupil is a resident of this state or is otherwise eligible for an education without charge pursuant to §§ 15-823 and 15-824.

Added by Laws 1981, Ch. 1, § 2, eff. Jan. 23, 1981. Amended by Laws 1987, Ch. 363, § 13, eff. May 22, 1987; Laws 1993, Ch. 204, § 10, eff. April 21, 1993.

Historical and Statutory Notes

Source:

Laws 1929, Ch. 93, §§ 4, 5.
Code 1939, §§ 54-1504, 54-1505.
A.R.S. former § 15-833.

§ 15-1344. Authority for enrollment of children under three years of age; definition

A. The board of directors may enroll a child under the age of three years in the schools for the deaf and the blind without charge if the person having legal custody of the child is a resident of this state and the child is sensory impaired to an extent that the person would benefit from a specialized program.

B. For the purposes of this section, the residence of the person having legal custody of the pupil is considered the residence of the pupil.

C. For the purposes of this section, "legal custody" means legal custody pursuant to § 15-824.

Added by Laws 1981, Ch. 1, § 2, eff. Jan. 23, 1981. Amended by Laws 1987, Ch. 363, § 14, eff. May 22, 1987; Laws 1993, Ch. 204, § 11, eff. April 21, 1993.

Historical and Statutory Notes

Source:

Laws 1970, Ch. 144, § 1.
A.R.S. former § 15-833.01.
Laws 1973, Ch. 48, § 1.

Reviser's Notes:

1993 Note. Pursuant to authority of § 41-1304.02, in the section heading "; definition" was added.

§ 15-1345. Overage and nonresident students; deposit

A. Persons older than the age specified in § 15-1343 and persons who are not residents of this state may be admitted to the school if its capacity will permit, but no person shall be received into or retained in the school to the exclusion or detriment of those for whom it is especially founded.

B. persons from other states and countries may have the benefits of the school by complying with the conditions of admission for state citizens and by advance payment to the superintendent of an amount fixed by the board.

C. Monies collected pursuant to subsection B of this section shall be deposited in the schools for the deaf and the blind fund established by § 15-1304.

Added by Laws 1981, Ch. 1, § 2, eff. Jan. 23, 1981. Amended by Laws 1998, Ch. 242, § 7, eff. July 1, 1999.

Historical and Statutory Notes

Source:

Laws 1929, Ch. 93, §§ 22, 24.
Code 1939, §§ 54-1522, 54-1524.
A.R.S. former § 15-834.

§ 15-1346. Payment for personal expenses

A. It is the responsibility of parents or persons having legal custody of a pupil to provide sufficient monies for that pupil enrolled in the school to cover personal care items, including clothing, hearing aids, hearing aid repairs, eyeglasses, eyeglass repairs, medical or dental care and transportation to the school and home at the close of the school term.

B. The superintendent shall periodically make an account of certified expenses for a pupil and shall bill the parent or person having legal custody of the pupil for reimbursement of such expenses. If the superintendent determines that the parent or person having legal custody of the pupil is unable to pay the

account and that the pupil is indigent, the superintendent shall remit the account after one school year to the clerk of the board of supervisors of the county in which the pupil resides for payment from the county general fund.
Added by Laws 1987, Ch. 363, § 16, eff. May 22, 1987.

Historical and Statutory Notes

Former § 15-1346, added by Laws 1981, Ch. 1, § 2, derived from Laws 1929, Ch. 93, § 20; Code 1939, § 54-1520; A.R.S. former § 15-835; and Laws 1978, Ch. 188, § 11, relating to attendance at school for the deaf and the blind, was repealed by Laws 1987, Ch. 363, § 15.

Reviser's Notes:

1987 Note. Pursuant to authority of § 41-1304.02, in subsection B the spelling of "periodically" was corrected as a manifest clerical error.

§§ 15-1347 to 15-1350. Repealed by Laws 1987, Ch. 363, § 15, eff. May 22, 1987

Historical and Statutory Notes

The repealed sections, added by Laws 1981, Ch. 1, § 2, amended by Laws 1984, Ch. 349, § 15, derived from:

Laws 1929, Ch. 93, §§ 21, 23.
Code 1939, §§ 54-1521 to 54-1523.
A.R.S. former §§ 15-836 to 15-839.
Laws 1960, Ch. 127, § 44.
Laws 1972, Ch. 106, § 2.
Laws 1978, Ch. 201, §§ 259, 260.

related to penalties and enforcement of the refusal to send a child to school; payment for students' clothes and transportation; and the establishment of residential facilities for emotionally disturbed children with hearing or visual impairments.

See, now, § 15-802 as to former § 15-1347 and § 15-1346 as to former § 15-1349.

ARTICLE 4. BRANCH SCHOOLS [REPEALED]

Article 4, Branch Schools, consisting of § 15-1361, as added by Laws 1981, Ch. 1, § 2,effective January 23, 1981, was repealed by Laws 1987, Ch. 363, § 17, effective May 22, 1987.

§ 15-1361. Repealed by Laws 1987, Ch. 363, § 17, eff. May 22, 1987

Historical and Statutory Notes

The repealed section, added by Laws 1981, Ch. 1, § 2, derived from Laws 1967, Ch. 117, § 2 and A.R.S. former § 15-851, related to the branch elementary day school for the deaf.

CHAPTER 11.1

STATE EDUCATIONAL SYSTEM FOR COMMITTED YOUTH FUNDING

ARTICLE 1. GENERAL PROVISIONS

Chapter 11.1, State Educational System for Committed Youth Funding,consisting of Article 1, § 15–1371, was added by Laws 1991, Ch. 288, § 9, effective September 21, 1991, retroactively effective to July 1, 1991.

Former Chapter 11.1, State Juvenile Educational System Funding, consisting of Article 1, § 15–1371, as added by Laws 1989, Ch. 266, § 9, effective July 1, 1991, was repealed by Laws 1991, Ch. 288, § 8, Paragraph 1, effective September 21, 1991, retroactively effective to July 1, 1991.

ARTICLE 1. GENERAL PROVISIONS

Historical and Statutory Notes

Laws 1991, Ch. 288, § 12, effective September 21, 1991, retroactively effective to July 1, 1991, was repealed by Laws 1992, Ch. 319, § 56.

Laws 1989, Ch. 266, § 27, subsec. B, as amended by Laws 1990, Ch. 267, § 4 and by Laws 1992, Ch. 319, § 55, provides:

"**Sec. 27. Effective date**"

"**B.** Sections 8, 18 and 20 through 23 and 25 of this act are effective from and after June 30, 1991."

§ 15–1371. Equalization assistance for state educational system for committed youth; state education fund for committed youth

A. The superintendent of the state educational system for committed youth shall calculate a base support level as prescribed in § 15–943 and a capital outlay revenue limit as prescribed in § 15-961 for the educational system established pursuant to § 41-2831, except that:

1. Notwithstanding § 15-901:

(a) The student count shall be determined using the following definitions:

(i) "Daily attendance" means days in which a pupil attends an educational program for a minimum of two hundred forty minutes not including meal and recess periods. Attendance for one hundred twenty or more minutes but fewer than two hundred forty minutes shall be counted as one-half day's attendance.

(ii) "Fractional student" means a pupil enrolled in an educational program of one hundred twenty or more minutes but fewer than two hundred forty minutes a day not including meal and recess periods. A fractional student shall be counted as one-half of a full-time student.

(iii) "Full-time student" means a pupil enrolled in an educational program for a minimum of two hundred forty minutes a day not including meal and recess periods.

(b) "Seriously emotionally disabled pupils enrolled in a school district program as provided in § 15-765" includes seriously emotionally disabled pupils enrolled in the department of juvenile corrections school system.

2. All pupils shall be counted as if they were enrolled in grades nine through twelve.

3. The teacher experience index is 1.

4. The base support level shall be calculated using the base level multiplied by 1.0, except that the state educational system for committed youth is also eligible beginning with fiscal year 1992-1993 for additional teacher compensation monies as specified in § 15-952.

5. Section 15-943, paragraph 1 does not apply.

B. The superintendent may use §§ 15-855, 15-942 and 15-948 in making the calculations prescribed in subsection A of this section, except that for the 1992-1993 fiscal year rapid decline shall not be used. The superintendent of the system and the department of education shall prescribe procedures for determining average daily attendance and average daily membership.

C. Equalization assistance for the state educational system for committed youth for the budget year is determined by adding the amount of the base support level and the capital outlay revenue limit for the budget year calculated as prescribed in subsection A of this section.

D. The state educational system for committed youth shall not receive twenty-five per cent of the equalization assistance unless it is accredited by the north central association of colleges and secondary schools.

E. The state education fund for committed youth is established. Fund monies shall be used for the purposes of the state educational system for committed youth, and notwithstanding § 35-173, monies appropriated to the fund shall not be transferred to or used for any program not within the state educational system for committed youth. State equalization assistance for the state educational system for committed youth as determined in subsection A of this section, other state and federal monies received from the department of education for the state educational system for committed youth and monies appropriated for the state educational system for committed youth, except monies appropriated pursuant to subsection F of this section, shall be deposited in the fund. The state treasurer shall maintain separate accounts for fund monies if the separate accounts are required by statute or federal law.

F. The department of juvenile corrections may seek appropriations for capital needs for land, buildings and improvements, including repairs and maintenance, required to maintain the state educational system for committed youth.

G. The state board of education shall apportion state aid and deposit it, pursuant to §§ 35–146 and 35–147, in the state education fund for committed youth in an amount as determined by subsection A of this section. The apportionments shall be as follows:

1. On July 1, one-third of the total amount to be apportioned during the fiscal year.

2. On October 15, one-twelfth of the total amount to be apportioned during the fiscal year.

3. On December 15, one-twelfth of the total amount to be apportioned during the fiscal year.

4. On January 15, one-twelfth of the total amount to be apportioned during the fiscal year.

5. On February 15, one-twelfth of the total amount to be apportioned during the fiscal year.

6. On March 15, one-twelfth of the total amount to be apportioned during the fiscal year.

7. On April 15, one-twelfth of the total amount to be apportioned during the fiscal year.

8. On May 15, one-twelfth of the total amount to be apportioned during the fiscal year.

9. On June 15, one-twelfth of the total amount to be apportioned during the fiscal year.

H. In conjunction with the department of administration, the superintendent of the state educational system for committed youth shall establish procedures to account for the receipt and expenditure of state education fund for committed youth monies by modifying the current accounting system used for state agencies as necessary.

Added by Laws 1991, Ch. 288, § 9, eff. Sept. 21, 1991, retroactively effective to July 1, 1991. Amended by Laws 1992, Ch. 273, § 5; Laws 1994, Ch. 91, § 8, eff. April 12, 1994; Laws 1995, Ch. 178, § 18; Laws 2000, Ch. 193, § 110; Laws 2000, Ch. 236, § 30, eff. April 12, 2000.

Historical and Statutory Notes

Laws 1989, Ch. 266, § 24, effective July 1, 1991, as amended by Laws 1991, Ch. 288, § 11, effective September 21, 1991, retroactively effective to July 1, 1991, provides:

"**Sec. 24. Equalization assistance for state educational system for committed youth for fiscal years 1991–1992, 1992–1993 and 1993–1994**

"**A.** Notwithstanding § 15–1371, Arizona Revised Statutes:

"1. For fiscal year 1991–1992 the student count is five hundred eighty and the weighted student count is one thousand fifteen for the state educational system for committed youth.

"2. For fiscal years 1992–1993 and 1993–1994, the number of state educational system for committed youth pupils that may be counted as SEH-P as provided in § 15–943, Arizona Revised Statutes, is equal to the larger of twenty-five per cent of the student count or the actual number of pupils determined to be SEH-P.

"**B.** Notwithstanding § 15–1371, Arizona Revised Statutes, the following number of minutes shall be used in determining the definitions of daily attendance and full-time student and one-half of the following number of minutes shall be used in determining the fractional student and one-half day's attendance for the state educational system for committed youth:

"1. For fiscal year 1991–1992, one hundred fifty minutes.

"2. For fiscal year 1992–1993, one hundred ninety-five minutes."

Laws 1991, Ch. 210, § 12, which purportedly amended § 15–1371 as added by Laws 1989, Ch. 266, § 9, effective July 1, 1991, was repealed by Laws 1991, Ch. 288, § 8, par. 2, effective September 21, 1991, retroactively effective to July 1, 1991.

Former § 15–1371, added by Laws 1989, Ch. 266, § 9, relating to juvenile educational system funding, was repealed by Laws 1991, Ch. 288, § 8, par. 1, effective Sept. 21, 1991, retroactively effective to July 1, 1991.

Reviser's Notes:

2000 Note. This section contains the amendments made by Laws 2000, Ch. 193, sec. 110 and Ch. 236, sec. 30 that were blended together as shown above pursuant to authority of § 41–1304.03.

§ 15–1371.01. Renumbered as § 15–1372

§ 15–1372. Equalization assistance for state educational system for persons in the state department of corrections; fund

A. The state department of corrections shall provide educational services for pupils who are under the age of eighteen years and pupils with disabilities who are age twenty-one or younger who are committed to the state department of corrections. The department of education shall provide technical assistance to the state department of corrections on request and shall assist the state department of corrections in establishing program and personnel standards.

B. The state education fund for correctional education is established. Subject to legislative appropriation, fund monies shall be used for the purposes of providing education to pupils as specified in subsection A of this section. Notwithstanding § 35–173, monies appropriated to the fund shall not be transferred to or used for any program not directly related to the educational services required by this section. State equalization assistance, other state and federal monies received from the department of education for which the pupils in correctional education programs qualify and monies appropriated for correctional education except monies appropriated pursuant to subsection C of this section shall be deposited in the fund. The state treasurer shall maintain separate accounts for fund monies if the separate accounts are required by statute or federal law.

C. The state department of corrections may seek appropriations for capital needs for land, buildings and improvements, including repairs and maintenance, required to maintain the educational services required by this section.

D. The state board of education shall apportion state aid and deposit it, pursuant to §§ 35–146 and 35–147, in the state education fund for correctional education in an amount as determined by subsection E of this section. The apportionments are as follows:

1. On July 1, one-third of the total amount to be apportioned during the fiscal year.

2. On October 15, one-twelfth of the total amount to be apportioned during the fiscal year.

3. On December 15, one-twelfth of the total amount to be apportioned during the fiscal year.

4. On January 15, one-twelfth of the total amount to be apportioned during the fiscal year.

5. On February 15, one-twelfth of the total amount to be apportioned during the fiscal year.

6. On March 15, one-twelfth of the total amount to be apportioned during the fiscal year.

7. On April 15, one-twelfth of the total amount to be apportioned during the fiscal year.

8. On May 15, one-twelfth of the total amount to be apportioned during the fiscal year.

9. On June 15, one-twelfth of the total amount to be apportioned during the fiscal year.

E. The director of the state department of corrections shall calculate a base support level as prescribed in § 15–943 and a capital outlay revenue limit as prescribed in § 15–961 for the educational services required by this section, except that:

1. Notwithstanding § 15–901, the student count shall be determined using the following definitions:

(a) "Daily attendance" means days in which a pupil attends an educational program for a minimum of one hundred eighty minutes not including meal and recess periods. Attendance for ninety or more minutes but fewer than one hundred eighty minutes shall be counted as one-half day's attendance.

(b) "Fractional student" means a pupil enrolled in an educational program of ninety or more minutes but fewer than one hundred eighty minutes per day not including meal and recess periods. A fractional student shall be counted as one-half of a full-time student.

(c) "Full-time student" means a pupil enrolled in an educational program for a minimum of one hundred eighty minutes per day not including meal and recess periods.

(d) "Pupil with a disability" has the same meaning as child with a disability prescribed in § 15–761.

2. All pupils shall be counted as if they were enrolled in grades nine through twelve.

3. The teacher experience index is 1.

4. The calculation for additional teacher compensation monies as prescribed in § 15–952 is available.

5. Section 15–943, paragraph 1 does not apply.

6. The base support level and capital outlay amounts calculated pursuant to this section shall be multiplied by 0.67.

7. The school year shall consist of a period of not less than two hundred eight days.

F. The director of the state department of corrections may use §§ 15-855, 15-942 and 15-948 in making the calculations prescribed in subsection E of this section. The director of the state department of corrections and the department of education shall prescribe procedures for calculating average daily attendance and average daily membership.

G. Equalization assistance for correctional education programs provided for those pupils specified in subsection A of this section is determined by adding the amount of the base support level and the capital outlay revenue limit for the budget year calculated as prescribed in subsection E of this section.

H. The director of the state department of corrections shall keep records and provide information as the department of education requires to determine the appropriate amount of equalization assistance. Equalization assistance shall be used to provide educational services in this section.

I. The department of education and the state department of corrections shall enter into an intergovernmental agreement that establishes the necessary accountability between the two departments regarding the administrative and funding requirements contained in subsections A and B of this section. The agreement shall:

1. Provide for appropriate education to all committed youths as required by state and federal law.

2. Provide financial information to meet requirements for equalization assistance.

3. Provide for appropriate pupil intake and assessment procedures.

4. Require pupil performance assessment and the reporting of results.

Added as § 15-1371.01 by Laws 1994, Ch. 195, § 1. Renumbered as § 15-1372. Amended by Laws 1995, Ch. 158, § 2; Laws 1998, Ch. 232, § 3; Laws 1998, Ch. 241, § 8, eff. July 1, 1999; Laws 1999, Ch. 211, § 17; Laws 1999, Ch. 233, § 1; Laws 2000, Ch. 193, § 111.

Historical and Statutory Notes

Laws 1995, Ch. 158, § 8, provides:

"**Sec. 8. Equalization assistance for adult correctional education**

"Notwithstanding § 15-1372, Arizona Revised Statutes:

"1. For fiscal year 1996-1997, the student count is one hundred sixty-four and the weighted student count is 271.051 for the correctional education programs provided by § 15-1372, subsection B, Arizona Revised Statutes, as amended by this act.

"2. For fiscal year 1996-1997, the number of correctional education students that may be counted as ED-P as provided in § 15-943, Arizona Revised Statutes, is equal to twenty-five per cent of the student count or the actual number of pupils determined to be ED-P, whichever is more."

The amendment of this section by Laws 1998, Ch. 241, § 8 was repealed by Laws 1999, Ch. 211, § 18.

Laws 1998, Ch. 241, § 27, provides:

"**Sec. 27. Effective date**

"Sections 1 through 23 and § 26 of this act are effective from and after June 30, 1999."

The amendment of this section by Laws 1998, Ch. 241, § 8 was repealed by Laws 1999, Ch. 233, § 2.

The 1999 amendment of this section by Ch. 211 explicitly amended the amendment of this section by Laws 1998, Ch. 232, § 3.

The 1999 amendment of this section by Ch. 233 explicitly amended the amendment of this section by Laws 1998, Ch. 232, § 3.

Laws 1999, Ch. 211, § 1, par. 9, provides:

"**Section 1. Purpose**"

"9. Section 15-1372, Arizona Revised Statutes, was amended by Laws 1998, chapter 232, § 3 and Laws 1998, chapter 241, § 8. These two versions could not be blended because of the delayed effective date of the chapter 241 version. In order to combine these two versions, this act amends the Laws 1998, chapter 232 version of § 15-1372, Arizona Revised Statutes, to incorporate the amendments made by Laws 1998, chapter 241 and the chapter 241 version is repealed."

Laws 1999, Ch. 211, § 73, subsec. E, provides:

"**Sec. 73. Retroactive application**"

"**E.** Sections 2 through 5, 17, 18, 20, 21, 26, 27, 29 through 36, 39 through 44, 47 through 50 and 63 through 66 of this act apply retroactively to from and after June 30, 1999."

Laws 1999, Ch. 233, §§ 3 and 5, provide:

"**Sec. 3. Equalization assistance for state educational system for persons in the state department of corrections for fiscal year 1998-1999**

"Notwithstanding § 15-1372, Arizona Revised Statutes, as amended by this act, the base support level and capital outlay amounts calculated pursuant to § 15-1372, subsection E, Arizona Revised Statutes, shall be multiplied by 0.50 for fiscal year 1998-1999."

"**Sec. 5. Retroactivity**

"Sections 1 and 2 of this act apply retroactively to from and after June 30, 1999."

Reviser's Notes:

1994 Note. Pursuant to authority of § 41-1304.02, this section, added by Laws 1994, Ch. 195, sec. 1 as § 15-1371.01, was renumbered as § 15-1372 and in the section heading "state" was added after "the".

1995 Note. Pursuant to authority of § 41-1304.02, in subsection E, paragraph 1 the subdivisions were alphabetized with subdivisions (a), (b), (c) and (d) becoming subdivisions (d), (a), (b) and (c), respectively.

1998 Note. The independent and valid amendment of this section by Laws 1998, Ch. 232, sec. 3 and Ch. 241, sec. 8 could not be blended because of the delayed effective date of Ch. 241.

1999 Note. Prior to the 2000 amendment, this section contained the amendments made by Laws 1999, Ch. 211, sec. 17 and Ch. 233, sec. 1 that were blended together pursuant to authority of § 41-1304.03.

§ 15-1373. State education system for committed youth; classroom site fund

The state education system for committed youth classroom site fund is established consisting of monies received from the department of education pursuant to § 15-977. The department of juvenile corrections shall administer the fund. Monies in the fund are exempt from the provisions of § 35-190 relating to lapsing of appropriations and are continuously appropriated.

Added by Laws 2001, 2nd S.S., Ch. 6, § 3, eff. Dec. 19, 2001.

CHAPTER 12

COMMUNITY COLLEGES

ARTICLE 1. GENERAL PROVISIONS FOR AND ESTABLISHMENT OF COMMUNITY COLLEGE DISTRICTS

ARTICLE 2. STATE BOARD OF DIRECTORS FOR COMMUNITY COLLEGES

ARTICLE 3. COMMUNITY COLLEGE DISTRICT BOARDS

ARTICLE 4. COMMUNITY COLLEGE DISTRICT FINANCE

Chapter 12, Community Colleges, consisting of Article 1, §§ 15–1401 to 15–1405, Article 2, §§ 15–1421 to 15–1427, Article 3, §§ 15–1441 to 15–1445, Article 4, §§ 15–1461 to 15–1469, and Article 5, §§ 15–1481 to 15–1491, was added by Laws 1981, Ch. 1, § 2, effective January 23, 1981.

ARTICLE 1. GENERAL PROVISIONS FOR AND ESTABLISHMENT OF COMMUNITY COLLEGE DISTRICTS

Historical and Statutory Notes

Executive Orders:

Executive Order No. 91–13, dated September 17, 1991, terminated and suspended Executive Order No. 88–23, and reestablished the Arizona Commission for Postsecondary Education.

Executive Order No. 93–22, dated Oct. 2, 1993, related to the Arizona Commission for Postsecondary Education and provided for additional responsibilities and a reconstituted membership.

§ 15–1401. Definitions

In this chapter, unless the context otherwise requires:

1. "Accredited" means accredited by a regional accrediting agency recognized by the United States department of education or by the council on postsecondary accreditation.

2. "Additional short-term classes" means those classes which are not in session on the forty-fifth day of the fall or spring semester, which commence at various times during the fiscal year and which are offered over a period of less than sixteen weeks.

3. "Budget year" means the fiscal year for which the community college district is budgeting and which immediately follows the current year.

4. "Community college" means an educational institution that is operated by a district board and that provides a program not exceeding two years' training in the arts, sciences and humanities beyond the twelfth grade of the public or private high school course of study or vocational education, including terminal courses of a technical and vocational nature and basic adult education courses.

5. "Current year" means the fiscal year in which the community college district is operating.

6. "District" means a community college district that is established pursuant to §§ 15–1402 and 15–1403 and that is a political subdivision of this state and, unless otherwise specified, includes provisional community college districts established pursuant to § 15–1409.

7. "District board" means the community college district governing board.

8. "Full–time equivalent student" means student enrollment for fifteen community college semester credit units per semester.

9. "Open entry, open exit classes" means those classes in which students enter or exit based on mastery of specified competencies and which commence at various times during the fiscal year.

10. "Operational expense budget" means the budget as adopted by the district board pursuant to § 15–1461.

11. "Operational expenses" means the administration, instruction, operation of community college plant, maintenance of community college plant, fixed charges and contingencies incurred in the operation of a district exclusive of all capital outlay items, special levies, auxiliary enterprise funds, restricted funds and bond service items.

12. "Provisional community college district" means a community college district organized pursuant to § 15-1409.

Added by Laws 1981, Ch. 1, § 2, eff. Jan. 23, 1981. Amended by Laws 1981, Ch. 287, § 1; Laws 1985, Ch. 210, § 1; Laws 1986, Ch. 203, § 1; Laws 1988, Ch. 234, § 1, eff. Sept. 30, 1988, retroactively effective to July 1, 1986; Laws 1988, Ch. 234, § 2, eff. Oct. 1, 1988; Laws 1989, Ch. 283, § 8, eff. Sept. 15, 1989, retroactively effective to Oct. 1, 1988; Laws 1993, Ch. 167, § 1; Laws 1997, Ch. 300, § 10; Laws 1998, Ch. 113, § 5; Laws 1999, Ch. 340, § 1; Laws 2002, Ch. 330, § 5; Laws 2004, Ch. 336, § 3.

Historical and Statutory Notes

Source:

Laws 1960, Ch. 119, § 1.
A.R.S. former § 15-651.
Laws 1971, Ch. 146, § 1.
Laws 1980, 2nd S.S., Ch. 9, § 27.

Laws 1988, Ch. 234, §§ 5 and 6 provide:

"**Sec. 5. Retroactivity**

"Section 1 of this act is effective retroactively to July 1, 1986.

"**Sec. 6. Effective date**

"Section 15-1401, Arizona Revised Statutes, as amended by § 2 of this act, is effective from and after September 30, 1988."

The 1989 amendment of this section by Ch. 283 explicitly amended the 1988 amendment of this section by Ch. 234, § 1.

Laws 1989, Ch. 283, § 1, par. 2, provides:

"Section 15-1401, Arizona Revised Statutes, was amended by Laws 1988, chapter 234, § 1 and by Laws 1988, chapter 234, § 2. The amendment of this section by Laws 1988, chapter 234, § 2 did not set forth in full the text of the section as amended by Laws 1988, chapter 234, § 1 as required by Constitution of Arizona article IV, part 2, § 14. In order to correct a potentially defective enactment, in this enactment the chapter 234, § 1 version is amended to incorporate the amendments made by chapter 234, § 2 and the chapter 234, § 2 version is repealed."

Amendment of this section by Laws 1988, Ch. 234, § 2 was repealed by Laws 1989, Ch. 283, § 9.

Laws 1989, Ch. 283, § 25, subsec. A, provides:

"**Sec. 25. Retroactivity**

"**A.** Section 15-1401, Arizona Revised Statutes, as amended by this act, is effective retroactively to from and after September 30, 1988."

Laws 1993, Ch. 167, § 4 provides;

"**Sec. 4. Community college; definition; scope**

"An institution that does not meet the definition of community college in § 15-1401, Arizona Revised Statutes, as amended by this act, shall not be considered a community college for the purposes of title 15, chapter 12, Arizona Revised Statutes."

The amendment of this section by Laws 1997, Ch. 300, § 10 was repealed by Laws 1998, Ch. 113, § 6.

Laws 1998, Ch. 113, § 1, par. 4, provides:

"**Section 1. Purpose**"

"4. Section 15-1401, Arizona Revised Statutes, was amended by Laws 1997, chapter 300, § 10. However, the amendment of this section was erroneously included in the title of the act in violation of article IV, part 2, § 13, Constitution of Arizona. In order to correct a potentially defective enactment, this act amends the previous valid version of § 15-1401, Arizona Revised Statutes, to incorporate the amendments made by Laws 1997, chapter 300 and the chapter 300 version is repealed."

The 1998 amendment of this section by Ch. 113 explicitly amended the amendment of this section by Laws 1993, Ch. 167, § 1.

Laws 1998, Ch. 113, § 69, subsec. D, provides:

"**Sec. 69. Retroactive application**"

"**D.** Sections 2, 5, 6, 12 through 15, 32, 33, 42, 52, 53, 61, 62, 64 and 65 of this act apply retroactively to July 21, 1997."

Laws 2002, Ch. 330, became law without the Governor's signature as provided in Arizona Constitution, Article 5, § 7.

Reviser's Notes:

1988 Note. The amendment of this section by Laws 1988, Ch. 234, § 2 failed to set forth in full the text of the section as amended by Laws 1988, Ch. 234, § 1, as required by Constitution of Arizona Art. IV, part 2, § 14.

1997 Note. The amendment of this section by Laws 1997, Ch. 300, § 10 was erroneously included in the title of the act in violation of Constitution of Arizona art. IV, pt. 2, § 13.

§ 15-1402. Community college districts; requirements

A. Community college districts may be organized under the provisions of this chapter for a single county, two or more contiguous counties or an existing community college district and contiguous counties not part of any community college district if the proposed district has a primary assessed valuation, based on the valuation for the preceding year, of at least four hundred forty-eight million, seventeen thousand, two hundred dollars and a minimum population of forty thousand persons who are fifteen or more years of age, as determined by the most recent federal census.

B. Beginning with fiscal year 1993-1994, the minimum primary assessed valuation required to organize a community college district as provided in subsection A increases each year by the percentage change in total primary assessed valuation for all of the districts with a population of less than five hundred thousand persons according to the most recent United States decennial census using actual primary assessed valuation numbers from the prior two years.

Added by Laws 1981, Ch. 1, § 2, eff. Jan. 23, 1981. Amended by Laws 1983, Ch. 141, § 1, eff. April 19, 1983; Laws 1988, Ch. 349, § 1; Laws 1992, Ch. 288, § 16, eff. Sept. 30, 1992, retroactively effective to July 1, 1992; Laws 1992, Ch. 345, § 1.

Historical and Statutory Notes

Source:

Laws 1927, Ch. 84, §§ 1 to 4.
Rev.Code 1928, §§ 1086, 1087, 1087a.
Laws 1931, Ch. 81, § 1.
Code 1939, §§ 54-701, 54-919, 54-920.
A.R.S. former §§ 15-601, 15-611, 15-666.
Laws 1960, Ch. 119, § 1.
Laws 1961, Ch. 68, § 1.
Laws 1977, Ch. 162, § 2.
Laws 1982, Ch. 289, §§ 1 and 2, relating to a moratorium on the formation of a community college district, expired June 30, 1984 by terms of § 1, subsec. B of that act.

Reviser's Notes:

1992 Note. This section contains the amendments made by Laws 1992, Ch. 288, sec. 16 and Ch. 345, sec. 1 that were blended together as shown above pursuant to authority of § 41-1304.03.

§ 15-1403. Procedure to form a district

A. For the purpose of forming a district, not less than ten per cent of the qualified electors in the territory included in the proposed district, or where a district consists of more than one county not less than ten per cent of the qualified electors in each county, shall petition the county school superintendent for the establishment of the district. Where a district consists of more than one county, the signatures of the qualified electors on the petition shall be submitted to the county school superintendent of the county of which the qualified electors are residents, provided that the county school superintendent of the county with the larger population, as determined by the most recent federal census, shall be the custodian of the completed petition. The petition shall set forth the name of the proposed district and its boundaries. The county school superintendent shall verify the signatures thereon, provided that whenever a proposed district consists of more than one county the county school superintendent of the county with the least population shall verify the signatures on the petition from his county prior to submitting the petition to the county school superintendent of the county with the larger population.

B. The county school superintendent who is the custodian of the completed petition shall transmit the petition to the county board of supervisors, or if the district consists of more than one county, to the county board of supervisors of the county with the largest population, which shall determine whether the proposed district meets the minimum standards of assessed valuation and population as provided in § 15–1402.

C. If the county board of supervisors determines that the proposed district meets the minimum standards of assessed valuation and population prescribed in subsection B of this section, the county, or counties, shall call and conduct an election, as prescribed in this article. If the majority of the votes cast in the proposed district, consisting of one county, favors the formation of the district, such a district is deemed to be formed, as provided in § 15–1404. Where the proposed district consists of more than one county there shall be a majority of the votes cast in each county favoring the formation of the district before the district is deemed to be formed, as provided in § 15–1404.

Added by Laws 1981, Ch. 1, § 2, eff. Jan. 23, 1981. Amended by Laws 1983, Ch. 141, § 2, eff. April 19, 1983; Laws 2002, Ch. 330, § 6.

Historical and Statutory Notes

Source:
Rev.Code 1928, §§ 1087b, 1087c.
Laws 1931, Ch. 81, § 1.
Code 1939, §§ 54–702, 54–703.
A.R.S. former §§ 15–612, 15–613, 15–667.
Laws 1960, Ch. 119, § 1.

Laws 2002, Ch. 330, became law without the Governor's signature as provided in Arizona Constitution, Article 5, § 7.

§ 15–1404. Election to determine formation of district; notice; canvass

A. Upon approval of the proposed district, the county board of supervisors shall return the petition with its approval to the county school superintendent, or if the proposed district consists of more than one county, to the county school superintendent of the county with the larger population, as determined by the most recent federal census. The county school superintendent shall transmit notification of approval for formation of the proposed district to the board of supervisors which shall submit the question to the qualified electors of the county at the next general election or at a special election called for that purpose. If a special election is called, notice thereof shall be given by publication for at least two weeks in a newspaper of general circulation published in the county or counties of the proposed district. The election shall be conducted and returns shall be made in the manner provided by law for special elections.

B. A special election conducted pursuant to this section shall be held on a date prescribed by § 16–204.

Added by Laws 1981, Ch. 1, § 2, eff. Jan. 23, 1981. Amended by Laws 1996, Ch. 271, § 15, eff. April 23, 1996; Laws 2002, Ch. 330, § 7.

Historical and Statutory Notes

Source:
Rev.Code 1928, §§ 1087c, 1087d.
Laws 1931, Ch. 81, § 1.
Code 1939, §§ 54–703, 54–704.
A.R.S. former §§ 15–613, 15–614, 15–668.
Laws 1960, Ch. 119, § 1.

For provisions of Laws 1983, Ch. 282 relating to terms of governing board members of organized community college districts, see Historical and Statutory Notes following § 15-1441.

Laws 2002, Ch. 330, became law without the Governor's signature as provided in Arizona Constitution, Article 5, § 7.

§ 15-1405. Presentation of plan to legislature by county board of supervisors

The county board of supervisors shall present a plan to the legislature for formation and establishment of a community college district no later than January 15 subsequent to the election held as provided in § 15-1404.

Added by Laws 1981, Ch. 1, § 2, eff. Jan. 23, 1981. Amended by Laws 2004, Ch. 336, § 4.

Historical and Statutory Notes

Source:

Rev.Code 1928, §§ 1087c, 1087d.
Laws 1931, Ch. 81, § 1.
Code 1939, §§ 54-703, 54-704.
A.R.S. former §§ 15-613, 15-614, 15-669.
Laws 1960, Ch. 119, § 1.

§ 15-1406. District board members and employees; compensation; payment of expenses for employment candidates

A. Sections 38-608, 38-609, 38-610 and 38-613 relating to all public officers and employees apply to district board members and district officers and employees. Except as otherwise provided in subsection B, the other provisions of title 38, chapter 4 [1] relating to public officers and employees of this state do not apply to district board members or district officers or employees.

B. The district board may permit a member, member-elect , officer or employee to travel within or without the state for a community college district purpose and receive reimbursement for lodging and subsistence and transportation expenses according to the procedures and amounts established by the district board as long as the reimbursement rates do not exceed the maximum amounts established pursuant to § 38-623 and § 38-624, subsection C.

C. The district board may pay for the traveling, lodging and other travel related expenses of candidates for employment with the district according to the policies and procedures established by the district board.

Added by Laws 1985, Ch. 344, § 1, eff. May 14, 1985, retroactively effective to April 3, 1985. Amended by Laws 1991, Ch. 274, § 2, eff. June 21, 1991, retroactively effective to April 3, 1985; Laws 1992, Ch. 100, § 1.

[1] Section 38-601 et seq.

Historical and Statutory Notes

Laws 1985, Ch. 344, § 4, effective May 14, 1985, provides:

"**Sec. 4. Retroactivity**

"This act is effective retroactively to April 3, 1985."

Laws 1991, Ch. 274, §§ 5 and 6, effective June 21, 1991, provide:

"**Sec. 5. Prohibition against travel reimbursement for members-elect**

"Notwithstanding § 15-1406, subsection B, Arizona Revised Statutes, as amended by this act, no member-elect may be paid reimbursement for lodging and subsistence and transportation expenses incurred prior to the effective date of this act.

"**Sec. 6. Retroactivity**

"Section 2 of this act is effective retroactively to April 3, 1985."

§ 15–1407. Formation of new district by subdivision of existing district; division of assets

A. If two or more contiguous counties have formed a community college district, a new district may be formed in one or more of the counties by dissolution of the existing district if each county in which a new district is formed meets the requirements prescribed in § 15–1402. Except as provided in this section, the procedures for dissolution of the district shall be as prescribed in § 15–1403 for the formation of a district in more than one county.

B. The election shall be held as provided in § 15–1404, except that a majority of the qualified electors in each of the counties in the existing district must approve the dissolution of the existing district and the formation of the new district.

C. If a county is within a community college district which is dissolved pursuant to this section and the county does not meet the requirements of § 15–1402, the county is no longer part of an established community college district.

D. The district board of the existing district shall prepare a projected list of assets for the existing district before the end of the fiscal year in which the election is held. The district boards of the existing and new district shall prepare a final statement of assets for the existing district as of the end of the fiscal year in which the election was held. The district boards of the existing district and the new district shall set aside sufficient assets or provide other means to satisfy the liabilities of the existing district and approve the final division of all assets by September 15 of the year in which the new district becomes operative.

Added by Laws 1988, Ch. 349, § 2.

§ 15–1408. Use of community college district resources or employees to influence elections; prohibition

A. A community college district shall not use its personnel, equipment, materials, buildings or other resources for the purpose of influencing the outcomes of elections. Notwithstanding this section, a community college district may distribute informational pamphlets on a proposed bond election as provided in § 35–454. Nothing in this section precludes a community college district from reporting on official actions of the governing board.

B. Employees of a community college district may not use the authority of their positions to influence the vote or political activities of any subordinate employee.

C. This section does not prohibit community college districts from permitting student political organizations of political parties, including those that are recognized pursuant to §§ 16–801, 16–802 and 16–803, to conduct lawful meetings in community college buildings or on community college grounds, except as prescribed in subsection A of this section. Each student political organization that is allowed to conduct lawful meetings on community college property shall have equal access as any other student political organization that is allowed to conduct lawful meetings on community college property.

D. Nothing contained in this section shall be construed as denying the civil and political liberties of any employee as guaranteed by the United States and Arizona Constitutions.

Added by Laws 1996, Ch. 286, § 6. Amended by Laws 2003, Ch. 253, § 5, eff. Sept. 18, 2003, retroactively effective to July 1, 2003.

§ 15–1409. Provisional community college districts; formation; provisional community college district governing board; powers and duties; program termination

A. A provisional community college district shall contract with an existing community college district to provide instructional and student services within the provisional community college district.

B. The minimum assessed valuation and population requirements prescribed in § 15–1402 do not apply to provisional community college districts.

C. A provisional community college district shall be formed and a provisional community college district board shall be elected in the same manner prescribed in §§ 15–1403, 15–1404 and 15–1441, except that the county board of supervisors by majority vote may adopt a resolution to submit the question of the formation of a provisional community college district and the approval of a proposed tax rate to fund the provisional community college district directly to the qualified electors of the county at a special or general election called for that purpose as prescribed in § 16–204 and title 35, chapter 3, article 3. [1] The resolution adopted by the county board of supervisors shall include a statement that the primary property tax levy limit for the provisional community college district shall be no less than the levy limit of the most recently formed community college district in this state.

D. Except as provided in this section, a provisional community college district governing board has the same powers and duties specified in § 15–1444 for community college districts.

E. A provisional community college district shall not award degrees, certificates or diplomas.

F. A provisional community college district is not eligible to receive equalization aid pursuant to § 15–1468 or state contribution for capital outlay for initial or additional campuses pursuant to § 15–1463.

G. The state aid eligibility requirements prescribed in § 15–1466, subsection G, paragraphs 1 and 2 do not apply to provisional community college districts.

H. Notwithstanding any other law, the same student shall not be counted twice as a full-time equivalent student in both a provisional community college district and a community college district. Notwithstanding any other law, beginning with the fiscal year after the year in which the provisional community college district is formed and has established its primary tax rate, a district that provides services in a provisional district pursuant to § 15–1470 shall no longer count these students in the district's full-time equivalent student count.

I. If a provisional community college district is converted into a community college district by the formation of a community college district pursuant to § 15–1402, the provisional community college district is dissolved and any equipment, property, personnel, liabilities and assets are transferred to the community college district.

J. If a provisional community college district is formed in a county that provides reimbursement for the attendance of nonresident state students pursuant to § 15-1469, that county shall continue to provide reimbursement payments to community college districts for the remainder of the fiscal year in which the provisional community college district is formed, provided that the county board of supervisors adopts a levy that is at least equal to the sum of the reimbursement payments and the amount of the community college services provided in the fiscal year immediately before the formation of the provisional community college district.

K. The board of supervisors of a county that has formed a provisional community college district may by majority vote enter into an intergovernmental agreement to loan monies to the governing board of the provisional community college district in an amount that does not exceed two hundred thousand dollars. Any loan pursuant to this subsection shall be repaid from the next scheduled collection of property taxes to fund the provisional community college district. The annual interest charges on any loan pursuant to this subsection shall not exceed five per cent.

L. The provisional community college district program established by this section ends on July 1, 2009 pursuant to § 41-3102.

Added by Laws 1999, Ch. 340, § 2. Amended by Laws 2001, Ch. 258, § 1, eff. April 26, 2001; Laws 2002, Ch. 330, § 8.

[1] Section 35-451 et seq.

Historical and Statutory Notes

Laws 2002, Ch. 330, became law without the Governor's signature as provided in Arizona Constitution, Article 5, § 7.

Reviser's Notes:

1999 Note. Pursuant to authority of § 41-1304.02, in the section heading "; program termination" was added after "duties".

§ 15-1410. Credit and noncredit courses

A. Courses offered for credit shall satisfy at least one of the following purposes and requirements:

1. Credit courses shall satisfy one or more of the following purposes:

(a) Qualify students for a community college certificate or degree.

(b) Be acceptable for transfer to a regionally accredited public or private college or university.

(c) Prepare students with skills to seek entry level jobs in the field of specialization.

(d) Improve the student's job skills or prepare the student for promotion in fields of employment.

(e) Provide skills necessary for success in other college courses.

(f) Provide continuing education and lifelong learning.

2. A credit course shall satisfy all of the following requirements:

(a) A formal course outline that defines the objectives and content of the course shall be on file and available for audit.

(b) Students shall be evaluated and given a grade based on their mastery of the objectives and content of the course.

(c) Faculty teaching the course shall meet the standards set by the district to teach in the subject area of the course.

(d) The credits awarded for completion of the course shall be based on the effort required of, and the competencies gained by, the students in accordance with policies adopted by the district governing board.

(e) Before enrollment in the course, students shall have achieved prerequisite competencies as defined in the syllabus or approved course guidelines.

(f) The course shall have been developed using the district's formal curriculum review procedure.

(g) The course shall have an evaluation component. The results of this evaluation shall be used for the purposes of formative and summative evaluation by the institution.

(h) A district board may adopt policies that allow students to receive credit through a variety of other means, including national standardized examinations and credit by evaluation or examination.

B. Noncredit courses are courses that do not meet the criteria established in subsection A. Noncredit courses shall be the financial responsibility of the district.

Added by Laws 2003, Ch. 253, § 6, eff. Sept. 18, 2003, retroactively effective to July 1, 2003.

ARTICLE 2. STATE BOARD OF DIRECTORS FOR COMMUNITY COLLEGES

Termination under Sunset Law

The state board of directors for community colleges shall terminate on July 1, 2008, unless continued. See §§ 41-3008.04 and 41-2955.

Title 15, Chapter 12, Article 2, relating to the state board of directors for community colleges, is repealed on January 1, 2009, by § 41-3008.04.

Historical and Statutory Notes

Laws 1988, Ch. 45, § 1 provides:

"**Section 1. Purpose**

"The purpose of the state board of directors for community colleges is to provide for the government, oversight, planning and coordination of the community college system in areas of statewide concern."

Laws 1988, Ch. 45, § 7, which provided for delayed repeal of title 15, Ch. 12, art. 2, effective January 1, 1999, was itself repealed by Laws 1991, Ch. 8, § 1, subsec. F.

§ 15-1421. Repealed by Laws 2003, Ch. 264, § 6

Historical and Statutory Notes

The repealed section related to the state board of directors for community colleges, and it was added by Laws 1981, Ch. 1, § 2, eff. Jan. 23, 1981, amended by Laws 1981, Ch. 314, § 19; Laws 1985, Ch. 247, § 1, eff. April 29, 1985; Laws 1988, Ch. 45, § 2; Laws 1993, Ch. 167, § 2. It was derived from Laws 1960, Ch. 119, § 1; A.R.S. former §§ 15-656, 15-676; and Laws 1972, Ch. 163, § 12.

§ 15-1422. Repealed by Laws 2003, Ch. 264, § 6

Historical and Statutory Notes

The repealed section, added by Laws 1981, Ch. 1, § 2, related to officers, organization, and meetings of the state board of community colleges. It was derived from Laws 1960, Ch. 119, § 1; A.R.S. former § 15-657; Laws 1972, Ch. 109, § 3; Laws 1974, Ch. 64, § 1; and Laws 1975, Ch. 47, § 1.

§ 15-1423. Repealed by Laws 2002, Ch. 330, § 9

Historical and Statutory Notes

The repealed section, added by Laws 1981, Ch. 1, § 2, amended by Laws 1988, Ch. 234, § 3; Laws 1993, Ch. 167, § 3, derived from Laws 1960, Ch. 119, § 1; A.R.S. former § 15-658; Laws 1970, Ch. 204, § 30; Laws 1971, Ch. 146, § 3; Laws 1975, Ch. 47, § 2; Laws 1978, Ch. 168, § 2, related to compensation of the executive director and board members of the community college state board.

Laws 2002, Ch. 330, became law without the Governor's signature as provided in Arizona Constitution, Article 5, § 7.

§ 15-1424. Repealed by Laws 2004, Ch. 336, § 5

Historical and Statutory Notes

The repealed section, providing general powers of state board, was added by Laws 1981, Ch. 1, § 2, eff. Jan. 23, 1981, was amended by Laws 1981, Ch. 187, § 1; Laws 1981, Ch. 314, § 20; Laws 1982, Ch. 332, § 16; Laws 1984, Ch. 232, § 1; Laws 1984, Ch. 349, § 16; Laws 1986, Ch. 297, § 1; Laws 1988, Ch. 218, § 1; Laws 1989, Ch. 117, § 1; Laws 1990, Ch. 348, § 20, eff. June 26, 1990; Laws 1992, Ch. 172, § 38; Laws 1993, Ch. 189, § 16; Laws 1995, Ch. 191, § 19, eff. April 19, 1995; Laws 1995, Ch. 196, § 23; Laws 1997, Ch. 158, § 1; Laws 1999, Ch. 76, § 4; Laws 2000, Ch. 193, § 112; Laws 2002, Ch. 330, § 10; Laws 2003, Ch. 253, § 7, eff. Sept. 18, 2003, retroactively effective to July 1, 2003. The section was derived from:

Laws 1960, Ch. 119, § 1.
A.R.S. former § 15-659.
Laws 1971, Ch. 146, § 4.
Laws 1973, Ch. 70, § 1.
Laws 1978, Ch. 168, § 3.
Laws 1980, 2nd S.S., Ch. 9, § 28.

The amendment of this section by Laws 1995, Ch. 196, § 23, was repealed by Laws 1996, Ch. 248, § 12.

Laws 2002, Ch. 330, became law without the Governor's signature as provided in Arizona Constitution, Article 5, § 7.

§ 15-1425. Repealed by Laws 2003, Ch. 253, § 8, eff. Sept. 18, 2003, retroactively effective to July 1, 2003

Historical and Statutory Notes

The repealed section, added by Laws 1981, Ch. 1, § 2, eff. Jan. 23, 1981, amended by Laws 1981, Ch. 287, § 2; Laws 1981, Ch. 300, § 1; Laws 1982, Ch. 172, § 1; Laws 1982, Ch. 196, § 1; Laws 1982, Ch. 332, § 17; Laws 1983, Ch. 154, § 3; Laws 1983, Ch. 325, § 12; Laws 1984, Ch. 166, § 1; Laws 1984, Ch. 277, § 4; Laws 1984, Ch. 379, § 16; Laws 1985, Ch. 133, § 1; Laws 1985, Ch. 210, § 2; Laws 1985, Ch. 254, § 5, eff. April 29, 1985; Laws 1989, Ch. 117, § 2; Laws 1990, Ch. 330, § 10; Laws 1991, Ch. 218, § 13, eff. June 10, 1991; Laws 1992, Ch. 345, § 2; Laws 1993, Ch. 202, § 14, eff. April 21, 1993; Laws 1997, Ch. 137, § 3; Laws 1999, Ch. 340, § 3; Laws 2000, Ch. 193, § 113; Laws 2001, Ch. 75, § 1; Laws 2001, Ch.

372, § 1; Laws 2001, Ch. 372, § 2, eff. July 2, 2002; Laws 2001, 2nd S.S., Ch. 6, § 4, eff. July 1, 2002; Laws 2002, Ch. 241, § 2; Laws 2002, Ch. 330, § 11, derived from Laws 1960, Ch. 119, § 1; A.R.S. former § 15-660; Laws 1963, Ch. 13, § 1; Laws 1972, Ch. 52, § 1, Laws 1980, 2nd S.S., Ch. 9, § 29, related to general administrative powers of district boards.

§ 15-1426. Repealed by Laws 2002, Ch. 330, § 13

Historical and Statutory Notes

The repealed section, added by Laws 1981, Ch. 1, § 2, derived from Law 1960, Ch. 119, § 1; A.R.S. former § 15-663, related to employment of legal counsel by community college state board to procure federal loans.

Laws 2002, Ch. 330, became law without the Governor's signature as provided in Arizona Constitution, Article 5, § 7.

§ 15-1427. Annual report

By November 1 of each year, each community college district shall make a report for the preceding fiscal year to the governor and the joint legislative budget committee and shall provide a copy of this report to the secretary of state and the director of the Arizona state library, archives and public records. The report shall set forth the state of progress of the community colleges operated under this chapter, the courses of study included in the curriculums, the number of professors and other instructional staff members employed, the number of students registered and attending classes, the number of full-time equivalent students enrolled during the year, the total number of students not residing in the district, the amount of receipts and expenditures and such other information as the governor and the joint legislative budget committee deem proper.

Added by Laws 1981, Ch. 1, § 2, eff. Jan. 23, 1981. Amended by Laws 1982, Ch. 166, § 1; Laws 2002, Ch. 330, § 14; Laws 2004, Ch. 336, § 6.

Historical and Statutory Notes

Source:

Laws 1960, Ch. 119, § 1.
A.R.S. former § 15-664.

Laws 1982, Ch. 166, § 2 provides:

"**Sec. 2. Intent regarding termination**

"Notwithstanding the provisions of this act, the legislature intends that, if the provisions of title 41, chapter 20 [§ 41-2351 et seq.], Arizona Revised Statutes, operate to terminate the state board of directors for community colleges, any provisions regarding powers, duties, functions or personnel added or amended by this act terminate on the date of termination of the state board of directors for community colleges."

Laws 2002, Ch. 330, became law without the Governor's signature as provided in Arizona Constitution, Article 5, § 7.

§ 15-1428. Repealed by Laws 2004, Ch. 336, § 7

Historical and Statutory Notes

The repealed section, relating to a uniform system of accounting for community college districts and duties of auditor general, was added by Laws 1982, Ch. 196, § 2, and was amended by Laws 2002, Ch. 330, § 15.

Laws 2002, Ch. 330, became law without the Governor's signature as provided in Arizona Constitution, Article 5, § 7.

§ 15-1429. Repealed by Laws 2003, Ch. 253, § 8, eff. Sept. 18, 2003, retroactively effective to July 1, 2003

Historical and Statutory Notes

The repealed section, added by Laws 1999, Ch. 340, § 4, amended by laws 2002, Ch. 330, § 16, related to services outside district boundaries.

ARTICLE 3. COMMUNITY COLLEGE DISTRICT BOARDS

§ 15-1441. Selection of precincts; district board members; terms; qualifications; vacancies

A. The board of supervisors shall establish in the same manner as provided in § 16-411 five precincts in a community college district for the election of a district board member from each precinct. A precinct in a community college district shall be composed of the number of election precincts as determined by the board of supervisors and shall have the same boundaries as are defined for the election precincts under § 16-411. If the board of supervisors redefines the boundaries of election precincts under § 16-411 which are included within a precinct in a community college district, the board of supervisors shall redefine the boundaries of the precinct in the community college district to conform with the election precinct changes. The precincts shall be established in a newly organized district subsequent to the organizational vote and the county school superintendent shall appoint five members, one from each precinct, who are qualified electors.

B. Where two or more counties constitute a district, as many precincts shall be set up by the board of supervisors in each county as the county is entitled to membership. In no case shall a county which is part of a district have more than four precincts, and where a district consists of two or more counties at least one member shall reside in each county.

C. At the first general election held for a district, the candidate having the most votes in each precinct shall be declared elected, provided the candidate meets the requirements provided in subsection A of this section. The two elected members having the highest number of votes receive six year terms, the two elected members receiving the next highest number of votes receive four year terms and the one elected member receiving the lowest number of votes receives a two year term. Thereafter each member's term is six years.

D. The next general election of district board members following the first general election shall be for the precinct where the elected candidate received the lowest number of votes and the second general election for the two precincts where the elected candidates received the next highest number of votes and the third general election for the two precincts where the elected candidates received the highest number of votes. The order of elections as established through this procedure shall thereafter be the order of precinct elections.

E. Vacancies shall be filled by appointment by the county school superintendent for the unexpired term for the precinct where the vacancy occurs, except that if the unexpired term is two years or longer, the county school superintendent may do one of the following:

1. Make an appointment for a term which shall be until the next regular election for district board members, at which time a successor shall be elected to serve the unexpired portion of the term.

2. With the approval of the district board, leave the vacancy until the next regular election for governing board members, at which time a successor shall be elected to serve the unexpired portion of the term.

F. When a vacancy occurs in a district with more than one county, the county school superintendent of the county where the previous incumbent resided shall fill the appointment for the unexpired term.

G. A county officer as provided in § 11-401 is not eligible to serve as a member of a community college district governing board during his term of office.

H. Employees of a community college district or their spouses are not eligible to hold membership on the community college district governing board in the district in which the employee is employed.

Added by Laws 1981, Ch. 1, § 2, eff. Jan. 23, 1981. Amended by Laws 1981, Ch. 85, § 1; Laws 1983, Ch. 282, § 1, eff. April 27, 1983; Laws 1988, Ch. 349, § 3.

Historical and Statutory Notes

Source:

Laws 1927, Ch. 84, §§ 1, 2.
Rev.Code 1928, §§ 1086, 1087e.
Laws 1931, Ch. 81, § 1.
Code 1939, §§ 54-705, 54-919.
A.R.S. former §§ 15-602, 15-621, 15-676, 15-676.01.
Laws 1960, Ch. 119, § 1.
Laws 1963, Ch. 67, § 1.
Laws 1977, Ch. 164, § 9.
Laws 1980, Ch. 157, § 1.

Laws 1977, Ch. 164, § 18, subsec. B provides:

"**Sec. 18. Applicability of prohibition of employees or spouses on school district and community college district boards**

"**B.** Notwithstanding § 15-676.01, community college board members who on the effective date of this act are employees or spouses of employees of a community college district shall be permitted to serve out their elected terms which they are serving as of the effective date of this act [eff. Aug. 27, 1977]."

Laws 1980, Ch. 157, § 4 provides:

"**Sec. 4. Terms of board members**

"**A.** Notwithstanding the provisions of §§ 15-676.01 and 15-677, Arizona Revised Statutes, a person serving as a member of a community college district board on the effective date of this act [July 31, 1980] is eligible to continue to serve until expiration of the current term of office, except that members whose terms of office expire in January of an even-numbered year are eligible to continue to serve until the first Monday in January of the next odd-numbered year.

"**B.** At the general election in 1980 one office on a community college district board shall be filled by election for a term beginning on the first Monday in January, 1981 and ending on the first Monday in January, 1985.

"**C.** At the general election in 1982 two offices on a community college district board shall be filled by election for a term beginning on the first Monday in January, 1983 and ending on the first Monday in January, 1987.

"**D.** At the general election in 1984 three offices on a community college district board shall be filled by election for a term beginning on the first Monday in January, 1985 and ending on the first Monday in January, 1989. Thereafter the term of office of members of a community college district board is four years beginning on the first Monday of January after the general election."

Laws 1983, Ch. 282, § 2, effective April 27, 1983, provides:

"**Sec. 2. Terms of governing board members of organized community college districts**

"**A.** Notwithstanding § 15-1441, Arizona Revised Statutes, as amended by this act, a person serving as a member of a community college district governing board on the effective date of this act is eligible to continue to serve until expiration of the current term of office.

"**B.** For community college districts organized as provided in §§ 15-1404 and 15-1441, Arizona Revised Statutes, on expiration of the terms in January, 1985 of members of a community college district governing board, the two elected members receiving the highest number of votes are eligible to serve one term each ending on the first Monday in January, 1991 and the one elected member receiving the lowest number of votes is eligible to serve one term ending on the first Monday in January, 1989. On expiration of the terms in January, 1987 of members of a community college district governing board, the one elected member receiving the highest number of votes is eligible to serve one term ending on the first Monday in January, 1993 and the one elected member receiving the lowest number of votes is eligible to serve one term ending on the first Monday in January, 1989. Thereafter the terms of office of members of community college district governing boards are six years beginning on the first Monday in January next after the general election."

§ 15-1442. Nominating petitions; election; returns; results; certificate of election; statement of contributions and expenditures

A. Candidates for the district board must file nominating petitions, conforming to the provisions set forth in § 16-314, with the appropriate county officer.

B. Members of the district board shall be elected at the time and place, and in the manner, of general elections as provided in title 16.[1]

C. The county school superintendent and the chairman of the board of supervisors shall meet on the seventh day following the election to canvass the returns in accordance with procedures for the canvass of returns in a general election. The county school superintendent shall declare the results of the election, declare elected the person receiving the highest number of votes for each office to be filled and issue to him a certificate of election.

D. All candidates for the office of community college district governing board member shall file with the clerk of the board of supervisors a statement of contributions and expenditures as provided in § 16-913.

Added by Laws 1981, Ch. 1, § 2, eff. Jan. 23, 1981. Amended by Laws 1984, Ch. 59, § 2; Laws 1993, Ch. 98, § 6, eff. Jan. 1, 1994.

[1] Section 16-101 et seq.

Historical and Statutory Notes

Source:

Rev.Code 1928, § 1087f.
Laws 1931, Ch. 81, § 1.
Code 1939, § 54-706.
A.R.S. former §§ 15-622, 15-677.
Laws 1980, Ch. 157, § 2.

Reviser's Notes:

1993 Note. Pursuant to authority of § 41-1304.02, in the section heading "Nominating petitions;" was added before "Election".

§ 15-1443. Meetings; officers; immunity

A. Within twenty days after appointment of the first district board, the county school superintendent, or county school superintendents by joint action where the district consists of more than one county, shall call a meeting of the district board by giving at least ten days' notice by registered or certified mail to each board member. At the meeting the district board shall organize by electing a president and a secretary from among its members and may transact any other business relating to the affairs of the district.

B. Following the first election of members, the district board shall meet and organize in January each year and shall hold regular meetings at such time and place as the policies of the board provide. Special meetings may be held at the call of the president or upon a call issued in writing signed by a majority of the members of the district board.

C. Members of the district board are immune from personal liability with respect to all acts done and actions taken in good faith within the scope of their authority during duly constituted regular and special meetings.

Added by Laws 1981, Ch. 1, § 2, eff. Jan. 23, 1981. Amended by Laws 1996, Ch. 116, § 1; Laws 2003, Ch. 253, § 9, eff. Sept. 18, 2003, retroactively effective to July 1, 2003.

Historical and Statutory Notes

Source:

Rev.Code 1928, § 1087g.
Laws 1931, Ch. 81, § 1.
Code 1939, § 54-707.
A.R.S. former §§ 15-623, 15-678.
Laws 1960, Ch. 119, § 1.
Laws 1972, Ch. 109, § 4.
Laws 1975, Ch. 47, § 3.

The 1996 amendment by Ch. 116, in subsec. B, first sentence, deleted "on the first Monday" following "organize" and "monthly" preceding "meetings".

The 2003 amendment by Ch. 253, in subsec. B, substituted "policies" for "rules" in the first sentence and inserted "district" before "board" in the second sentence.

§ 15-1444. General powers of district governing boards

A. Except as otherwise provided, the district board shall:

1. Maintain each community college for a period of not less than eight months in each year and, if the funds of the district are sufficient, maintain each community college for a longer period.

2. Adopt policies in a public forum to offer programs that meet the educational needs of the population served by the community college.

3. Enforce the courses of study prescribed by the district board.

4. Visit each community college under its jurisdiction and examine carefully into its management, conditions and needs.

5. Exclude from each community college all books, publications or papers of a sectarian, partisan or denominational character intended for use as textbooks.

6. Appoint and employ a chancellor or chancellors, vice-chancellors, a president or presidents, vice-presidents, deans, professors, instructors, lecturers, fellows and such other officers and employees it deems necessary. The district board may enter into employment contracts with chancellors, vice-chancellors and presidents for a duration of more than one year but not more than five years.

7. Determine the salaries of persons it appoints and employs.

8. Remove any officer or employee if in its judgment the interests of education in this state require the removal.

9. Award degrees, certificates and diplomas upon the completion of courses and curriculum as it deems appropriate.

10. Appoint or employ, if it deems necessary, police officers who shall have the authority and power of peace officers. The police officers who have received a certificate from the Arizona peace officer standards and training board are eligible for membership in and benefits under either title 38, chapter 5, article 2[1] or the public safety personnel retirement system under title 38, chapter 5, article 4.[2]

11. Determine the location within the district of a community college and purchase, receive, hold, make and take leases of, sell and convey real or personal property for the benefit of the community colleges under its jurisdiction.

12. Obtain insurance or be self-insured, or a combination of insurance and self-insurance, against loss, to the extent it is determined necessary on community college buildings of the district. The local district shall have an insurable interest in the buildings.

B. The district board may:

1. Administer trusts declared or created for the district and receive by gift or devise and hold in trust or otherwise property wheresoever located, and if not otherwise provided, dispose of the property for the benefit of the district.

2. Lease real property, as lessor or as lessee. If a district is the lessee, the lease may contain an option to purchase the property. The district board may adopt policies as are deemed necessary and may delegate in writing to the chancellor or president of the district, or their designees, all or any part of its authority to lease property under this paragraph. A district board shall not delegate the authority to execute a lease that exceeds one hundred thousand dollars per year. Any delegation by the district board pursuant to this paragraph may be rescinded in whole or in part at any time by the district board.

3. Sue and be sued.

4. Contract. The district board may adopt such policies as are deemed necessary and may delegate in writing to the chancellor or president of the district, or their designees, all or any part of its authority to contract under this paragraph. Any delegation of authority under this paragraph may be rescinded by the district board at any time in whole or in part.

5. Construct, remodel and repair buildings.

6. In conjunction with other districts, establish policies for procurement of goods and services.

7. Provide a plan or plans for employee benefits which may include optional retirement programs pursuant to § 15–1451, subsection A, which allow for participation in a cafeteria plan that meets the requirements of the United States internal revenue code of 1986. [3]

8. Accept grants or donations of monies from the United States, or from any of its agencies, departments or officers, or from persons, corporations, foundations or associations. A district board shall deposit the monies into a specific fund or account and a district board shall administer the monies in accordance with the purpose of the grant or donation with specific policies or restrictions as described or stipulated in the grant or donation. In the case of personal property granted or donated to or for the benefit of a community college district, a district board shall immediately transfer possession and ownership of the property to the designated district.

9. Enter into intergovernmental agreements or contracts pursuant to § 11–952.01 for participation in programs offered by public agency pools or separately contract with a trustee or board of trustees that provides a common self-insurance program with pooled funds and risks pursuant to § 15–382, subsec-

tion B, paragraph 2. The district board is not required to engage in competitive procurement in order to make the decision to participate in these programs.

C. If a district acquires real or personal property, whether by purchase, exchange, condemnation, gift or otherwise, the district shall pay to the county treasurer any taxes on the property that were unpaid as of the date of acquisition, including penalties and interest. The lien for unpaid delinquent taxes, penalties and interest on property acquired by the district:

1. Is not abated, extinguished, discharged or merged in the title to the property.

2. Is enforceable in the same manner as other delinquent tax liens.

D. From and after December 31, 1988, in a district whose boundaries encompass a vehicle emissions control area as defined in § 49–541 the district board shall require all out of county and out of state students to sign an affidavit at the time of course registration that the student's vehicle meets the requirements of § 49–542. From and after December 31, 1988, the district board on property under its jurisdiction within a vehicle emissions control area shall prohibit the parking of those vehicles which fail to comply with § 49–542.

E. A community college district and a joint technological education district governing board may enter into agreements for the provision of administrative, operational and educational services and facilities.

F. Each district may establish a program for the exchange of students between the community colleges under its jurisdiction and colleges and universities located in Sonora, Mexico. The program may provide for in-state tuition for Sonora students at the community colleges under its jurisdiction in exchange for similar tuition provisions for Arizona students enrolled or seeking enrollment in Sonora colleges and universities. The community colleges may work in conjunction with the Arizona-Mexico commission in the governor's office to coordinate recruitment and admissions activities to provide for in-state tuition for up to fifty Sonora students at the community colleges under its jurisdiction in exchange for similar tuition provisions for up to fifty total Arizona students enrolled or seeking enrollment in Sonora colleges and universities.

G. Each district shall facilitate transfer articulation coordination pursuant to § 15–1824.

Added by Laws 1981, Ch. 1, § 2, eff. Jan. 23, 1981. Amended by Laws 1981, Ch. 187, § 2; Laws 1984, Ch. 232, § 2; Laws 1985, Ch. 280, § 2; Laws 1986, Ch. 297, § 2; Laws 1987, Ch. 154, § 2, eff. April 21, 1987; Laws 1987, Ch. 360, § 1; Laws 1987, Ch. 365, § 6; Laws 1988, Ch. 218, § 2; Laws 1990, Ch. 411, § 1; Laws 1992, Ch. 40, § 1; Laws 1995, Ch. 32, § 7, eff. March 30, 1995; Laws 1998, Ch. 236, § 1; Laws 1999, Ch. 228, § 1; Laws 2000, Ch. 144, § 1; Laws 2001, Ch. 251, § 5; Laws 2002, Ch. 330, § 17; Laws 2003, Ch. 253, § 10, eff. Sept. 18, 2003, retroactively effective to July 1, 2003; Laws 2004, Ch. 230, § 5; Laws 2004, Ch. 336, § 8.

[1] Section 38–711 et seq.

[2] Section 38–841 et seq.

[3] 26 U.S.C.A. § 1 et seq.

Historical and Statutory Notes

Source:

Laws 1927, Ch. 84, §§ 1, 2.
Rev.Code 1928, §§ 1086, 1087h.
Laws 1931, Ch. 81, § 1.
Code 1939, §§ 54–708, 54–919.
A.R.S. former §§ 15–602, 15–624, 15–679.
Laws 1960, Ch. 119, § 1.
Laws 1965, 3rd S.S., Ch. 4, § 1.
Laws 1970, Ch. 199, § 1.
Laws 1973, Ch. 70, § 2.
Laws 1976, Ch. 136, § 1.

Laws 2001, Ch. 251, became law without the Governor's signature as provided in Arizona Constitution, Article 5, § 7.

Laws 2002, Ch. 330, became law without the Governor's signature as provided in Arizona Constitution, Article 5, § 7.

Reviser's Notes:

1987 Note. Prior to the 1988 amendment, this section contained the amendments made by Laws 1987, Ch. 360, § 1 and Ch. 365, § 6 which were blended together pursuant to authority of § 41–1304.03.

2000 Note. In the chapter version in subsection B, paragraph 3, second sentence "~~its~~" should have appeared instead of "~~it's~~". Pursuant to authority of § 41–1304.02, "~~its~~" is substituted in the chapter version to correct a manifest clerical error.

2004 Note. This section contains the amendments made by Laws 2004, Ch. 230, sec. 5 and Ch. 336, sec. 8 that were blended together as shown pursuant to authority of § 41–1304.03.

§ 15–1445. Administrative powers of district governing boards

A district board shall:

1. Adopt policies for the government of the community colleges under its jurisdiction.

2. In conjunction with other district boards, set standards for the establishment, development, administration, operation and accreditation of community colleges in the district.

3. Fix tuitions and graduate the tuitions and fees between institutions and between residents, nonresidents and students from foreign countries. The district board may waive tuitions and fees and graduate tuitions and waivers for an employee or the spouse or dependent child of an employee of the district, or for a nonresident student enrolled in the district if the district board determines the waiver is in the best interest of this state and the student.

4. In conjunction with other district boards, submit to the economic estimates commission before January 10 of each year the estimated number of full-time equivalent students for the district as prescribed in section 15–1466.01.

5. Establish curriculums and designate courses that in its judgment will best serve the interests of this state.

6. Determine academic classes that qualify as open entry, open exit classes and prescribe policies for the operation of open entry, open exit classes.

7. In conjunction with other district boards and the state board for vocational and technological education, review and adopt, within the scope of the statutory definitions of vocational and technological education, program and staff standards with modifications as necessary for courses taught in community colleges. The district board shall base the standards on vocational and technological competence.

8. In conjunction with other district boards, establish qualifications of the instructional staff that, at a minimum, shall be equal to those required to meet accreditation guidelines and establish standards of vocational and technological competence required to instruct in occupational as well as academic subjects.

9. In conjunction with other district boards, prescribe guidelines providing for the transferability between community college district vocational and technological education programs and in conjunction with the state board for vocational and technological education prescribe guidelines for the interrelationship of secondary programs and postsecondary programs.

10. In conjunction with other district boards, prescribe the manner in which the self-evaluation of vocational and technological education programs is conducted as provided in § 15-1452.

11. If requested by the state board for vocational and technological education, assist in the preparation, publication and distribution of an annual state plan and a comprehensive five year state plan.

12. In conjunction with other district boards and the state board for vocational and technological education, develop a process to determine program funding priorities for state aid purposes. Each district board shall submit state aid recommendations to the legislature. The recommendations shall be based on the process and on existing cost studies of vocational and technological education in this state.

13. In conjunction with other district boards, prescribe qualifications for admission to community colleges for honorably discharged veterans who served on active duty in the armed forces for a minimum of one year and who were previously enrolled at a community college or university in this state. For the purpose of determining the qualifications, the district board may not consider prior failing grades received by the veteran at a community college or university in this state.

14. Require the publisher of each literary and nonliterary textbook used in the community colleges of the district to furnish computer software in a standardized format, when software becomes available for nonliterary textbooks, to the district board from which braille versions of the textbook may be produced.

15. Identify students simultaneously enrolled in a course for both high school and college credit by using the same student level data element required by § 15-1042, subsection A. The auditor general shall have access to this information when certifying the full-time equivalent student enrollment pursuant to § 15-1466.01, paragraph 4.

Added by Laws 2003, Ch. 253, § 12, eff. Sept. 18, 2003, retroactively effective to July 1, 2003.

Historical and Statutory Notes

Former § 15-1445, added by Laws 1981, Ch. 1, § 2, amended by Laws 1981, Ch. 134, § 1, relating to reports by president or chancellor, was repealed by Laws 2003, Ch. 253, § 11, eff. Sept. 18, 2003, retroactively effective to July 1, 2003. It was derived from:

Rev.Code 1928, § 1087i.
Laws 1931, Ch. 81, § 1.
Code 1939, § 54-709.
A.R.S. former §§ 15-631, 15-687.
Laws 1960, Ch. 119, § 1.

§ 15-1446. Lease-purchase agreements

A. A district board may enter into lease or lease-purchase agreements for real property, including buildings and improvements to the property.

B. Lease or lease-purchase agreements authorized by subsection A of this section or § 15–1444, subsection A, paragraph 11 shall not create an obligation of payment by the district under the terms of the lease or lease-purchase agreement for periods longer than fifteen years.

C. Notwithstanding subsection B of this section, a district board may enter into lease agreements for real property, including buildings and improvements to the property, that obligate the district for more than fifteen years if such agreements are with an Indian tribe, involve land owned or controlled by the federal government or by a joint powers airport authority organized under title 28, chapter 25, article 8 or involve real property that is owned by a nongovernmental nonprofit corporation and that is offered for lease in an amount not to exceed one thousand dollars per year to a community college district for purposes of expanding health care education programs.

D. The amount of outstanding indebtedness due to acquisition of real property by lease-purchase for each district shall not exceed two million five hundred thousand dollars in any one year and fifteen million dollars in the aggregate. A district board may pledge tuitions, fees, rentals and other charges to any payments due under lease-purchase agreements.

E. Notwithstanding subsection D of this section, periodic payments and any option payments for acquisition of real property by lease-purchase are restricted to payment from capital outlay funds.

F. Districts that acquire real property by lease-purchase are not entitled to receive monies pursuant to § 15–1463 pertaining to the specific real property acquired by lease-purchase.

G. Notwithstanding any other law, payments on lease or lease-purchase agreements entered into pursuant to subsection A of this section or § 15–1444, subsection A, paragraph 11 are obligations of the district within the meaning of the constitutional limit against indebtedness set out in article IX, § 8, Constitution of Arizona.

Added by Laws 2003, Ch. 253, § 13, eff. Sept. 18, 2003, retroactively effective to July 1, 2003. Amended by Laws 2004, Ch. 336, § 9.

Historical and Statutory Notes

The 2004 amendment by Ch. 336 inserted new subsec. C, redesignating existing subsecs. C to F as D to G, and modifying internal references to the subsections, accordingly.

Former § 15–1446, added by Laws 1982, Ch. 332, § 18, amended by Laws 1983, Ch. 325, § 13; Laws 1984, Ch. 379, § 17; Laws 1985, Ch. 254, § 6, relating to county plans for vocational and technical education, was repealed by Laws 1990, Ch. 330, § 11.

§ 15–1447. Reports by president or chancellor

The president or chancellor of every district, at the close of each fiscal year, before and as a prerequisite to receiving the president or chancellor's last month's salary, shall make and subscribe under oath a complete report of the district and each college or campus within the district for the entire school year and shall deliver a copy of the report to the district board. The report shall show the total number of full-time equivalent students enrolled during the year, the actual total number of students, the number of teachers regularly employed and the total number of students not residing within the district.

Added by Laws 2003, Ch. 253, § 15, eff. Sept. 18, 2003, retroactively effective to July 1, 2003.

Historical and Statutory Notes

Former § 15-1447, added by Laws 1982, Ch. 332, § 18, and amended by Laws 2002, Ch. 330, § 18, related to evaluation of vocational and technical education programs, was repealed by Laws 2003, Ch. 253, § 14, effective September 18, 2003, retroactively effective to July 1, 2003.

§ 15-1448. Employment of legal counsel; opinions of counsel

A. If a district lies in two or more counties, the county attorney of the largest county in which the district lies as determined by the last federal decennial census is the attorney for the district.

B. A district board may employ an attorney to represent the district if the county attorney consents. The district board shall state in writing the purpose for which it employs an attorney.

C. A district board may employ an attorney without the consent of the county attorney if it deems it advisable.

D. Compensation for an attorney whom the district board employs as provided in subsections B and C of this section is payable from district monies.

E. If a district board employs an attorney without the consent of the county attorney, the county attorney has no duty to represent the district with regard to any matter for which the attorney was employed and is not responsible to the district for any exercise of, or failure to exercise, professional judgment by the attorney in his representation of the district.

F. The county attorney is not required to assume the duty to represent the district on a matter for which the district board employs an attorney without the consent of the county attorney.

G. An attorney employed pursuant to subsection B or C of this section shall represent the district with the powers of and the duties otherwise performed by the county attorney pursuant to § 11-532, subsection A, paragraph 11.

H. Any county attorney who issues a legal opinion to a community college district shall promptly transmit a copy of the opinion to the attorney general who shall concur, revise or decline to review the opinion of the county attorney. If the attorney general does not concur, revise, or decline to review the county attorney's opinion within sixty days from its receipt, the opinion shall be deemed affirmed. If the attorney general revises the opinion, the opinion of the attorney general shall prevail.

Added by Laws 1985, Ch. 145, § 2. Amended by Laws 2003, Ch. 253, § 16, eff. Sept. 18, 2003, retroactively effective to July 1, 2003.

§ 15-1449. Control of vehicles and nonpedestrian devices on community college property by district board; sanctions; compliance with emissions inspection; definition

A. The district board may adopt policies for the control of vehicles and nonpedestrian devices on property of the institutions under the district board's jurisdiction with respect to the following only:

1. Maximum speed of vehicles and nonpedestrian devices.
2. Direction of travel.
3. Authorized hours of travel.

4. Required stops in traffic.

5. Place, method and time of parking.

6. Nonparking areas and restricted areas.

7. Prohibition of parking in vehicle emissions control areas as defined in § 49-541 of those vehicles which fail to comply with § 49-542.

8. Designation of special parking areas for students, faculty, staff and the general public.

B. The district board may prescribe and collect reasonable fees for specially designated parking areas. The district board shall cause signs and notices to be posted on the property for the regulation of vehicles and nonpedestrian devices.

C. The policies adopted by the district board pursuant to subsection A of this section shall be enforced administratively under procedures approved by the district board for each institution under its jurisdiction. As to students, faculty and staff, these procedures may involve both student and faculty adjudicating bodies if all procedures give the individual notice and an opportunity to be heard concerning the alleged infractions and any sanction to be imposed on the individual. Administrative and disciplinary sanctions may be imposed on students, faculty and staff for a violation of the policies including a reasonable monetary penalty, impoundment, regular institutional discipline, withdrawal or suspension of campus parking privileges, encumbrances of records or grades, or both, and oral or written reprimand. Habitual or flagrant disregard of policies is a ground for suspension or expulsion from the institution for a student and may be taken into consideration as to faculty and staff in regard to amount of salary and continuation of employment.

D. Members of the general public who park their vehicles in an unauthorized manner on the property of an institution under the jurisdiction of the district board shall be warned concerning their unauthorized parking, and if they continue to or habitually park in an unauthorized manner, the vehicles parked in an unauthorized manner may be impounded by the institution and a reasonable fee may be exacted for the cost of impoundment and storage.

E. Members of the general public who violate a policy adopted by the district board pursuant to subsection A of this section regarding the use of nonpedestrian devices on the property of an institution under the jurisdiction of the district board shall be warned of a violation. A nonpedestrian device may be impounded by the institution, and a reasonable fee may be exacted for the cost of impoundment and storage.

F. Except as provided in § 41-1092.08, subsection H, a person who has received a final administrative ruling concerning a sanction imposed on the person as a result of a violation of a policy adopted pursuant to subsection A of this section has the right to have that ruling reviewed by the superior court in the county in which the institution involved is situated pursuant to title 12, chapter 7, article 6. [1]

G. An institution that is under the jurisdiction of the district board and that is located in a vehicle emissions control area as defined in § 49-541 shall prohibit the issuance of annual permits to park on property under its jurisdiction until the applicant submits an affidavit or shows proof that the applicant's vehicle meets the requirements of § 49-542.

H. In this section, "nonpedestrian devices" includes bicycles, tricycles, unicycles, skateboards, roller skates and equines.

Added by Laws 1989, Ch. 274, § 1. Amended by Laws 1997, Ch. 221, § 66; Laws 2000, Ch. 113, § 40; Laws 2002, Ch. 330, § 19; Laws 2003, Ch. 253, § 17, eff. Sept. 18, 2003, retroactively effective to July 1, 2003.

[1] Section 12-901 et seq.

Historical and Statutory Notes

Laws 2002, Ch. 330, became law without the Governor's signature as provided in Arizona Constitution, Article 5, § 7.

§ 15-1450. District board members; participation in employee benefit plan

A. A community college district board may allow its members and spouses and dependents of members to participate in the plan providing health, accident, life and disability benefits for employees of the district and their dependents. A district board member is eligible to participate in the plan provided as an employee benefit if the member pays the full premium and the participation of the member does not result in an expenditure of district monies.

B. If the community college district board allows its members to participate in the plan, as provided in subsection A of this section, a district board may also adopt a policy allowing participation in the plan provided as an employee benefit for board members after they leave the board and for surviving spouses and dependents of board members or former board members under the following conditions:

1. The community college district board may allow a board member and spouses and dependents of members to continue to participate after the board member leaves the board if all of the following apply:

(a) The board member served at least six consecutive years on the board.

(b) The board member was covered under the plan while serving on the board.

(c) The board member pays the full premium.

(d) The board member's participation does not result in an expenditure of district monies.

2. The district board may allow the surviving spouse and dependents of a deceased board member to continue to participate in the plan if all of the following apply:

(a) The surviving spouse or dependents were covered under the board member's or former board member's participation in the plan.

(b) The surviving spouse or dependents pay the full premium.

(c) The participation of the surviving spouse and dependents does not result in the expenditure of district monies.

Added by Laws 1990, Ch. 151, § 1.

§ 15-1451. Optional retirement plans

A. Pursuant to § 15-1444, subsection B, paragraph 5, a community college district board may establish an optional retirement program under which contracts providing retirement and death benefits may be purchased for employees of the institutions under its jurisdiction as designated by the community college district board.

B. An optional retirement program established pursuant to this section shall:

1. Be designed to be a qualified governmental plan under § 401(a) of the internal revenue code.[1]

2. Comply with all requirements of the internal revenue code applicable to governmental plans.

3. Be a qualified plan under § 401(a) of the internal revenue code.

4. Apply for and maintain a current letter of determination issued by the United States internal revenue service.

5. Be a qualified pick-up plan as defined by § 414(h)(2) of the internal revenue code as confirmed by a private letter ruling issued by the United States internal revenue service.

6. Provide benefits through annuity contracts that are fixed or variable in nature or that are a combination of fixed and variable.

C. Eligible employees may elect to participate in an optional retirement plan established by the community college district board. The eligible employee shall make the election in writing and file the election with the Arizona state retirement system and the disbursing officer of the employing institution. The eligible employee shall make the election either:

1. Within thirty days of the employee's effective date of employment.

2. If the employee is a member of the Arizona state retirement system on the date the optional retirement program becomes effective, within ninety days of the effective date of the optional retirement program.

3. Beginning on october 1, 2001 through december 31, 2001.

D. If an employee who is a member of the Arizona state retirement system elects to participate in an optional retirement program pursuant to subsection C of this section, the Arizona state retirement system shall transfer the employee's contributions to the Arizona state retirement system and interest as determined by the board of the Arizona state retirement system to the optional retirement program within the later of ninety days after the election or ninety days after receipt by the optional retirement program of a favorable letter of determination issued by the United States internal revenue service. If an eligible employee fails to make an election as provided in subsection C of this section, the employee is deemed to have elected to participate in the Arizona state retirement system. The election to participate in an optional retirement program is irrevocable and constitutes a waiver of all benefits provided by the Arizona state retirement system. All eligible employees who elect to participate in an optional retirement program shall remain participants in the optional retirement program during the continuance of employment with the community college district.

E. The community college district board shall make contributions from public monies appropriated or any other monies available for this purpose on behalf of each participant in the optional retirement program in an amount that is at least equal to the employer contribution prescribed in title 38, chapter 5, article 2 [2] but that is not more than the amount prescribed in § 15-1628, subsection C.

F. Subject to subsection H of this section, each community college district board that establishes an optional retirement program shall establish program provisions including:

1. Categories of employees that are eligible to elect to participate in the optional retirement program.

2. The employee contribution rate. This rate may be greater than the employee contribution rate prescribed in title 38, chapter 5, article 2.

3. A vesting period for employer contributions, if any. All employee contributions that are picked up by the employer are fully vested at all times.

4. Restrictions on benefits, except that the optional retirement program shall not allow a participant to withdraw employer contributions except as retirement income payable for life or to provide for loans on retirement income.

G. A community college district board may elect to provide health or long-term disability coverage to optional retirement program participants under separate benefit plans. The community college district board may allocate a portion of its employer contribution that would otherwise be made to the optional retirement program under subsection E of this section to the separate benefit plans to provide health or long-term disability coverage.

H. Community college district boards that establish an optional retirement program under this section may enter into intergovernmental agreements appointing a single administrator or designating a single community college district board to administer the optional retirement program. A community college district board may satisfy the requirements of this section by entering into an intergovernmental agreement with another community college district board to participate in that community college district's optional retirement program. The administration shall include, without limitation, the design and implementation of the plan document establishing the optional retirement program, compliance with the qualification requirements prescribed in subsection B of this section and such other duties that are not inconsistent with this section as may be delegated to the administrator pursuant to the intergovernmental agreements entered into among the community college district boards.

I. Although designated as employee contributions, all employee contributions made to an optional retirement program shall be picked up and paid by the community college district in lieu of contributions by the employee. The contributions picked up by a community college district may be made through a reduction in the employees' salary or an offset against future salary increases, or a combination of both. The employees participating in the optional retirement program do not have the option of choosing to receive the contributed amounts directly instead of the community college district paying the amounts to the optional retirement program. It is intended that all employee contributions that are picked up by the community college district as provided in this subsection shall be treated as employer contributions under § 414(h) of the internal revenue code and shall be excluded from the employees' gross income for federal and state income tax purposes and are includable in the gross income of the employees or their beneficiaries only in the taxable year in which they are distributed.

J. A community college district board shall not be liable to any employee, retiree or other person for any reason relating to the community college district board's provision of or failure to provide for an optional retirement program or health or long-term disability coverage.

Added by Laws 1995, Ch. 284, § 1. Amended by Laws 1996, Ch. 185, § 1; Laws 1998, Ch. 236, § 2; Laws 1999, Ch. 327, § 1; Laws 2001, Ch. 136, § 1; Laws 2001, Ch. 138, § 1; Laws 2001, Ch. 280, § 1; Laws 2001, Ch. 380, § 1.

[1] Internal Revenue Code sections may be found in Title 26 of U.S.C.A.

[2] Section 38–711 et seq.

Historical and Statutory Notes

The 1996 amendment by Ch. 185, in subsec. A, substituted "subsection I" for "subsection H"; and in the last sentence of subsec. C, inserted "who elect to participate in an optional retirement program" following "All eligible employees".

The 1998 amendment by Ch. 236, in subsec. A, inserted "and pursuant to § 15–1444, subsection B, paragraph 5,"; deleted subsec. B, par. 7, which had read:

"7. Have at all times at least fifty active participants.";

and, in subsec. G, the 1998 amendment also substituted "may" for "shall" in the first sentence, and inserted the second sentence relating to entering into intergovernmental agreements.

The 1999 amendment by Ch. 327, in subsec. C, substituted "thirty" for "ninety" in the third and fourth sentences, and inserted "within ninety days of" in the fourth sentence.

The 2001 amendment by Ch. 136 deleted "Notwithstanding § 38–729, subsection I, and" from the beginning of the section.

The 2001 amendment by Ch. 138 amended and reorganized subsecs. C and D as C to E, redesignating existing subsecs. D to I, as E to J, accordingly; and made conforming changes. Subsections C and D had read:

"**C.** Eligible employees may elect to participate in an optional retirement plan established by the community college district board. The eligible employee shall make the election in writing and file the election with the Arizona state retirement system and the disbursing officer of the employing institution. The eligible employee shall make the election within thirty days of the employee's effective date of employment or, if the employee is a member of the Arizona state retirement system on the date the optional retirement program becomes effective, within ninety days of the effective date of the optional retirement program. If an employee who is a member of the Arizona state retirement system elects to participate in an optional retirement program within thirty days of the employee's effective date of employment or within ninety days of the effective date of the optional retirement program, the Arizona state retirement system shall transfer the employee's contributions to the Arizona state retirement system and interest as determined by the board of the Arizona state retirement system to the optional retirement program within the later of ninety days after the election or ninety days after receipt by the optional retirement program of a favorable letter of determination issued by the United States internal revenue service. If an eligible employee fails to make an election as provided in this subsection, the employee is deemed to have elected to participate in the Arizona state retirement system. The election to participate in an optional retirement program is irrevocable and constitutes a waiver of all benefits provided by the Arizona state retirement system. All eligible employees who elect to participate in an optional retirement program shall remain participants in the optional retirement program during the continuance of employment with the community college district.

"**D.** The community college district board shall make contributions from public monies appropriated or any other monies available for this purpose on behalf of each participant in the optional retirement program in an amount equal to the employer contribution prescribed in title 38, chapter 5, article 2."

The 2001 amendment by Ch. 280 deleted "Notwithstanding § 38-729, subsection I, and" from the beginning of subsec. A.

The 2001 amendment by Ch. 380 deleted "Notwithstanding § 38-729, subsection I, and" from the beginning of subsec. A.

Reviser's Notes:

2001 Note. This section contains the amendments made by Laws 2001, Ch. 136, sec. 1, Ch. 138, sec. 1, Ch. 280, sec. 1 and Ch. 380, sec. 1 that were blended together as shown pursuant to authority of § 41-1304.03.

§ 15-1452. Evaluation of vocational and technological education programs

A district board shall provide for the evaluation of vocational and technological education programs once every five years. The assessment shall be conducted in cooperation with and with assistance from business, industry and labor representatives. The district board may conduct a self-evaluation.

Added by Laws 2003, Ch. 253, § 18, eff. Sept. 18, 2003, retroactively effective to July 1, 2003.

ARTICLE 4. COMMUNITY COLLEGE DISTRICT FINANCE

§ 15-1461. District budget; annual estimate; computation; notice; hearing; adoption

A. Not later than June 5, each district established pursuant to this chapter, and any other community college established prior to the enactment of this chapter, shall prepare a proposed budget for the budget year on a form which the auditor general prescribes to be transmitted to the district board. The proposed budget shall be accompanied by an estimate of the amount of funds needed for the ensuing year as determined by the district based on the proposed budget prepared by it.

B. The district shall establish and set forth in the proposed budget the per capita expenditure per full-time equivalent student, which shall be the total operational expenses.

C. The district shall establish and set forth in the proposed budget the per capita expenditure per full-time equivalent student, which shall be the total capital outlay expenses.

D. The number of basic full-time equivalent students shall be computed by dividing the total community college credit units by fifteen per semester and shall be based on regular day enrollment. The number of additional short-term full-time equivalent students shall be computed by dividing the total community college credit units from additional short-term classes by thirty. The number of skill center full-time equivalent students shall be computed by dividing the total number of clock hours in approved vocational training programs by six hundred forty.

E. The governing board of each district shall prepare a notice fixing a time not later than June 20 and designating a public place within each district at which a public hearing and special board meeting shall be held. The governing board shall present the proposed budget for consideration of the residents and the taxpayers of the district at such meeting.

F. The governing board of each district shall publish a copy of the proposed budget prior to the meeting and, in addition, a notice of the public hearing and special board meeting not later than fifteen days prior to the meeting. The proposed budget shall contain but need not be limited to the following information:

1. The estimated cost of all operational, capital outlay and debt service expenses.

2. The percentage of increase or decrease in each budget category as compared to each category of the budget for the current year.

3. The total amount of revenues by source that was necessary to meet the district's budget for the current year.

4. The total amount of revenues by source that will be necessary to meet the proposed district budget.

5. The total property tax levy of the district for the current year.

6. The levy for primary property taxes and the levy for secondary property taxes for the current year.

7. The primary property tax rate and secondary property tax rate for the current year.

8. The estimated amount of total property tax levies for the district and the primary property tax and secondary property tax components thereof necessary for the budget year.

9. The maximum amount of primary property tax dollars which the district is permitted to levy pursuant to title 42, chapter 17, article 2 [1] for the budget year.

10. The amount of secondary property tax dollars which the district will levy for the budget year.

11. The amount of monies received from primary property taxation in the previous fiscal year in excess of the maximum allowable amount as calculated pursuant to title 42, chapter 17, article 2.

G. The governing board shall publish the proposed budget and the notice of the public hearing and special board meeting a second time not later than five days prior to the meeting. Publication shall be made in a newspaper of general circulation within the district. The cost of publication shall be a charge against the district. If a truth in taxation notice and hearing is required under § 15-1461.01, the district may combine the notice and hearing under this section with the truth in taxation notice and hearing.

H. If the district fails to publish the proposed budget, notice and statements required by subsection F of this section, the board of supervisors shall levy on the property in the district the lesser of the amount of primary property taxes which were levied for the district in the current year or the amount which would be produced by the primary property tax rate which was levied for the district in the current year.

I. At the time and place fixed in the notice, the members of the governing board shall hold the public hearing and present the proposed budget to the persons attending the hearing. Upon request of any person, the governing board shall explain the budget and any resident or taxpayer of the district may protest the inclusion of any item in the proposed budget.

J. Immediately following the public hearing the chairman shall call to order the special board meeting for the purpose of adopting the budget. The governing board shall adopt the budget making deductions from the budget as it sees fit but making no additions to the budget and shall enter the budget as adopted in its minutes. The governing board shall not adopt the budget if the property tax requirements of the budget, excluding amounts budgeted and levied for secondary property taxes, exceed the amounts authorized pursuant to title 42, chapter 17, article 2.[1]

Added by Laws 1981, Ch. 1, § 2, eff. Jan. 23, 1981. Amended by Laws 1982, Ch. 196, § 3; Laws 1982, Ch. 263, § 2; Laws 1985, Ch. 365, § 1; Laws 1996, 7th S.S., Ch. 3, § 1; Laws 1998, Ch. 1, § 56, eff. Jan. 1, 1999; Laws 2003, Ch. 253, § 19, eff. Sept. 18, 2003, retroactively effective to July 1, 2003.

[1] Section 42-17051 et seq.

Historical and Statutory Notes

Source:

Laws 1960, Ch. 119, § 1.
A.R.S. former § 15-688.
Laws 1977, Ch. 152, § 1.
Laws 1980, 2nd S.S., Ch. 9, § 31.

Laws 1977, Ch. 152, § 25, subsec. A provides:

"**Sec. 25. Effective dates**

"**A.** The provisions of §§ 1 through 7 and 13 through 15 of this act shall become effective January 1, 1978."

Laws 1993, 2nd S.S., Ch. 8, § 11, provides:

"**Sec. 11. Fiscal year 1993-1994 community college maintenance and operating state aid, capital outlay aid and equalization aid; general appropriations amount**

"Notwithstanding the provisions of title 15, chapter 12, article 4, Arizona Revised Statutes, or any other law, the operating state aid, capital outlay and equalization aid for community college districts for the 1993-1994 fiscal year shall be the amounts appropriated in the general appropriations act for the 1993-1994 fiscal year."

Laws 1996, 7th S.S., Ch. 3, § 7, provides:

"**Sec. 7. Applicability**

"This act applies to tax years beginning from and after December 31, 1996."

Reviser's Notes:

1982 Note: Prior to the 1985 amendment, this section contained the amendments made by Laws 1982, Ch. 196, § 3 and Ch. 263, § 2 which were blended together pursuant to authority of § 41-1304.03.

§ 15-1461.01. Truth in taxation notice and hearing; roll call vote on tax increase; definition

A. On or before February 10 of the tax year, the county assessor shall transmit and certify to the property tax oversight commission and to the district governing board the total net primary assessed values that are required to compute the levy limit prescribed by § 42-17051. If the proposed primary property tax levy, excluding amounts that are attributable to new construction, is greater than the amount levied in the preceding tax year by the district:

1. The district governing board shall publish a notice that meets the following requirements:

(a) The notice shall be published twice in a newspaper of general circulation in the district. The first publication shall be at least fourteen but not more than twenty days before the date of the hearing. The second publication shall be at least seven but not more than ten days before the date of the hearing.

(b) The notice shall be published in a location other than the classified or legal advertising section of the newspaper in which it is published.

(c) The notice shall be at least one-fourth page in size and shall be surrounded by a solid black border at least one-eighth inch in width.

(d) The notice shall be in the following form, with the "truth in taxation hearing—notice of tax increase" headline in at least eighteen point type:

Truth in Taxation Hearing

Notice of Tax Increase

In compliance with § 15–1461.01, Arizona Revised Statutes, ________ community college district is notifying its property taxpayers of ________ community college district's intention to raise its primary property taxes over last year's level. The ________ community college district is proposing an increase in primary property taxes of $________ or %________.

For example, the proposed tax increase will cause ________ community college district's primary property taxes on a $100,000 home to increase from $________ (total taxes that would be owed without the proposed tax increase) to $________ (total proposed taxes including the tax increase).

This proposed increase is exclusive of increased primary property taxes received from new construction. The increase is also exclusive of any changes that may occur from property tax levies for voter approved bonded indebtedness or budget and tax overrides.

All interested citizens are invited to attend the public hearing on the tax increase that is scheduled to be held ________ (date and time) at ________ (location).

2. In lieu of publishing the truth in taxation notice, the district board may mail the truth in taxation notice prescribed by paragraph 1, subdivision (d) to all registered voters in the district at least ten but not more than twenty days before the date of the hearing.

3. In addition to publishing the truth in taxation notice under paragraph 1 or mailing the notice under paragraph 2, the district governing board shall issue a press release containing the truth in taxation notice to all newspapers of general circulation in the district.

4. The district board shall consider a motion to levy the increased property taxes by roll call vote.

5. Within three days after the hearing, the district board shall mail a copy of the truth in taxation notice, a statement of its publication or mailing and the result of the district board's vote under paragraph 4 to the property tax oversight commission established by § 42–17002.

6. The district board shall hold the truth in taxation hearing on or before the adoption of the county, city or town budget under § 42–17105.

B. If the governing board fails to comply with the requirements of this section, the governing board shall not fix, levy or assess an amount of primary property taxes that exceeds the preceding year's amount, except for amounts attributable to new construction.

C. For purposes of this section, "amount attributable to new construction" means the net assessed valuation of property added to the tax roll since the previous year multiplied by a property tax rate computed by dividing the district's primary property tax levy in the preceding year by the estimate of the district's total net assessed valuation for the current year, excluding the net assessed valuation attributable to new construction.

Added by Laws 1996, 7th S.S., Ch. 3, § 2. Amended by Laws 1997, Ch. 274, § 6; Laws 1998, Ch. 1, § 57, eff. Jan. 1, 1999; Laws 1999, Ch. 108, § 4; Laws 2000, Ch. 390, § 2; Laws 2001, Ch. 267, § 1; Laws 2003, Ch. 240, § 1.

Historical and Statutory Notes

Laws 1996, 7th S.S., Ch. 3, § 7, provides:

"**Sec. 7. Applicability**

"This act applies to tax years beginning from and after December 31, 1996."

The 1997 amendment by Ch. 274 deleted "When levying taxes" from the beginning of subsec. A, par. 4; and deleted subsec. A, par. 5, which had read:

"5. The governing board shall hold the truth in taxation hearing on or before the adoption of the county, city or town budget under § 42-303."

The 1998 amendment by Ch. 1 substituted "§ 42-17002" for "§ 42-306" at the end of subsec. A, par. 4; and substituted "district board" for "governing board", and "§ 42-17105" for "§ 42-303" in subsec. A, par. 5.

The 1999 amendment by Ch. 108 substituted "the following form" for "substantially the following form" in subsec. A, par. 1(d); and inserted subsec. A, par. 3, relating to press releases, and redesignated existing pars. 3 to 5, as 4 to 6, accordingly.

The 2000 amendment by Ch. 390 substituted "the district governing board" for "the district board" in subsec. A, par. 1; and rewrote subsec. A, par. 3, which had read:

"3. In addition to publishing the truth in taxation notice under paragraph 1, subdivision (d) of this subsection or paragraph 2 of this subsection, the community college district shall issue a press release containing the truth in taxation notice to all newspapers of general circulation in the district."

The 2001 amendment by Ch. 267 rewrote the introductory paragraph of subsec. A, which had read:

"**A.** On or before July 1, the county assessor shall transmit to the district an estimate of the total net assessed valuation of the district, including an estimate of new property that has been added to the tax roll since the previous levy of property taxes in the district. If the proposed primary property tax levy, excluding amounts that are attributable to new construction, is greater than the amount levied in the preceding tax year by the district:"

The 2003 amendment by Ch. 240, inserted a new subsec. B, and redesignated existing subsec. B as C, accordingly.

Reviser's Notes:

1996 Note. Pursuant to authority of § 41-1304.02, in the section heading "roll call" was added after "hearing;" and in subsection A, second sentence "by" was transposed to follow "year" and "in" was transposed to follow "levied".

1998 Note. Pursuant to authority of § 41-1304.02, in subsection A, paragraph 1, subdivision (d) the main words of the notice heading were capitalized to correct an electronic data base error.

§ 15-1462. Special tax levy for maintenance or capital outlay of district; proration of monies

A. The board of supervisors in each district may supply funds from other designated sources or, in lieu thereof, shall annually, at the time of levying other taxes, levy a special community college tax on property to be determined by each county comprising the district for the purpose of maintaining the district or for capital outlay. For purposes of this subsection "capital outlay" means the expenditures which result in the acquisition of fixed properties such as land, temporary, permanent or portable buildings and development or permanent improvements to land or construction of buildings. The tax shall be at a rate sufficient to provide the amount proposed in the annual estimate of funds as needed to maintain the district for the current fiscal year, after deducting from the total estimate the amount of funds appropriated for the district by the legislature, but shall not be in excess of the levy limitation prescribed in title 42, chapter 17, article 2.[1] The tax shall be added to and collected in the same manner as other county taxes on property. The amount of the special community college tax shall be paid into the community college fund of the county.

B. For the first year of operation monies shall be prorated to each county within a district in the ratio that the number of high school graduates of each county within the district bears to the total number of high school graduates in all counties within the district. Thereafter, proration of monies shall be to each county within a district in the ratio that the number of full-time equivalent students of each county within the district bears to the total number of full-time equivalent students in all counties within the district.

Added by Laws 1981, Ch. 1, § 2, eff. Jan. 23, 1981. Amended by Laws 1995, Ch. 173, § 1; Laws 1998, Ch. 1, § 58, eff. Jan. 1, 1999.

[1] Section 42–17051 et seq.

Historical and Statutory Notes

Source:

Laws 1927, Ch. 84, §§ 3, 4.
Rev.Code 1928, §§ 1087, 1087j.
Laws 1931, Ch. 81, § 1.
Code 1939, §§ 54–710, 54–920.
A.R.S. former §§ 15–603, 15–615, 15–689.
Laws 1960, Ch. 119, § 1.
Laws 1969, Ch. 86, § 1.
Laws 1977, Ch. 152, § 2.
Laws 1980, 2nd S.S., Ch. 9, § 32.

Reviser's Notes:

1995 Note. Pursuant to authority of § 41–1304.02, in the section heading "or capital outlay" was added after "maintenance".

§ 15–1463. State contribution for capital outlay for initial or additional campus

A. This state, by legislative appropriation, shall pay to the district a sum equal to fifty per cent of the total cost for capital outlay for an initial campus in a newly formed district or in a county entering into an intergovernmental agreement for providing courses pursuant to § 15–1470, not to exceed one million dollars.

B. If a district board in an existing district determines the need for an additional campus or campuses, it shall submit a request to the joint legislative budget committee for review. This state, by legislative appropriation, shall pay a sum equal to fifty per cent of the total cost for capital outlay for each approved campus within the district, but not to exceed one million dollars at any one campus, including the purchase, erection, remodeling or completion of buildings and the purchase of equipment and facilities for educational or auxiliary purposes of the community college, excluding the cost of any land granted to the district and dormitories erected for the use of students or faculty members.

Added by Laws 1981, Ch. 1, § 2, eff. Jan. 23, 1981. Amended by Laws 1987, Ch. 360, § 2; Laws 1988, Ch. 209, § 1; Laws 1991, Ch. 274, § 3, eff. June 21, 1991; Laws 2002, Ch. 330, § 20; Laws 2003, Ch. 253, § 20, eff. Sept. 18, 2003, retroactively effective to July 1, 2003.

Historical and Statutory Notes

Source:

Laws 1927, Ch. 84, §§ 3, 4.

Rev.Code 1928, §§ 1087, 1087j.
Laws 1931, Ch. 81, § 1.
Code 1939, §§ 54–710, 54–920.
A.R.S. former §§ 15–603, 15–615, 15–686.
Laws 1960, Ch. 119, § 1.
Laws 1965, 3rd S.S., Ch. 4, § 2.
Laws 1970, Ch. 192, § 12.
Laws 1972, Ch. 122, § 1.
Laws 1976, Ch. 163, § 6.
Laws 1978, Ch. 168, § 4.
Laws 1980, 2nd S.S., Ch. 9, § 30.
Laws 1980, Ch. 167, § 3.

Laws 2002, Ch. 330, became law without the Governor's signature as provided in Arizona Constitution, Article 5, § 7.

§ 15–1464. State aid per capita distribution for capital outlay; capital outlay fund; appropriation

A. In addition to the appropriation prescribed in § 15–1463, subsection A, this state shall pay to each community college district state aid for capital outlay in the following manner:

1. For fiscal year 1992–1993 for a community college district which had less than five thousand actual full-time equivalent students according to the most recent fiscal year actual full-time equivalent student count, the amount determined by multiplying the number of actual full-time equivalent students according to the most recent fiscal year actual full-time equivalent student count by two hundred seven dollars.

2. For fiscal year 1992–1993 for a community college district which had five thousand or more actual full-time equivalent students according to the most recent fiscal year actual full-time equivalent student count, the amount determined by multiplying the number of actual full-time equivalent students according to the most recent fiscal year actual full-time equivalent student count by one hundred fifty-eight dollars.

3. Beginning with fiscal year 1993–1994 the legislature shall adjust by the growth rate for common and high school districts as provided by law, subject to appropriation, the amount of state aid to community college districts as provided in paragraphs 1 and 2.

B. The basis for computing full-time equivalent students for the capital outlay per capita distribution shall be on the same basis as the computation prescribed in § 15–1466.01.

C. In addition to the formula to determine the appropriations prescribed in § 15–1463, subsection A and subsection A of this section, this state may pay additional amounts for capital outlay to a community college district based on requests from the district.

D. Appropriations for capital outlay made pursuant to subsections A and C of this section and § 15–1463 shall be made to an account designated as the capital outlay fund.

E. At the beginning of each fiscal year, the district board shall present to the department of administration a claim for the annual amount appropriated by the legislature and assigned to the district for capital outlay purposes. The department of administration shall draw a warrant in payment of the claim and shall transmit the warrant to the state treasurer who shall disburse the funds to the district for capital outlay purposes, to be expended as provided by law. If no community college exists, the department shall establish a fund for new future community college districts to be disbursed as needed.

F. Notwithstanding subsection E of this section, a community college district may request the state treasurer to disburse the monies to the local government investment pool for deposit into the district's account as established in § 35–326.

G. Each district has the option of using up to twenty per cent of its total capital outlay aid appropriation for operating aid purposes or taking this same amount out of the district's total operating state aid appropriation and using it for capital outlay purposes.

Added by Laws 1981, Ch. 1, § 2, eff. Jan. 23, 1981. Amended by Laws 1984, Ch. 61, § 7, eff. April 6, 1984; Laws 1985, Ch. 305, § 1, eff. May 7, 1985; Laws 1987, Ch. 360, § 3; Laws 1990, Ch. 397, § 1, eff. July 1, 1991; Laws 1991, Ch. 288, § 10, eff. Sept. 21, 1991, retroactively effective to July 1, 1991; Laws 1992, Ch. 172, § 39; Laws 1992, Ch. 345, § 3; Laws 1993, Ch. 189, § 17; Laws 1995, Ch. 191, § 20, eff. April 19, 1995; Laws 1999, Ch. 96, § 4; Laws 1999, Ch. 228, § 2; Laws 2002, Ch. 330, § 21.

Historical and Statutory Notes

Source:

Laws 1927, Ch. 84, §§ 3, 4.
Rev.Code 1928, §§ 1087, 1087j.
Laws 1931, Ch. 81, § 1.
Code 1939, §§ 54–710, 54–920.
A.R.S. former §§ 15–603, 15–615, 15–686.
Laws 1960, Ch. 119, § 1.
Laws 1965, 3rd S.S., Ch. 4, § 2.
Laws 1970, Ch. 192, § 12.
Laws 1972, Ch. 122, § 1.
Laws 1976, Ch. 163, § 6.
Laws 1978, Ch. 168, § 4.
Laws 1980, 2nd S.S., Ch. 9, § 30.
Laws 1980, Ch. 167, § 3.

Laws 1990, Ch. 397, § 2, provides:

"**Sec. 2. Effective date**

"The provisions of this act shall be effective from and after June 30, 1991."

The 1991 amendment of this section by Ch. 288 explicitly amended the 1990 amendment of this section by Ch. 397.

Laws 1990, Ch. 397, § 2, establishing a July 1, 1991 effective date for Ch. 397, was repealed by Laws 1991, Ch. 288, § 14, effective September 21, 1991, retroactively effective to July 1, 1991.

Laws 1991, Ch. 288, § 21, effective Sept. 21, 1991, retroactively effective to July 1, 1991, provides:

"**Sec. 21. 1991–1992 fiscal year per capita distribution formula for community college districts**

"Notwithstanding any other provision of law, for the 1991–1992 fiscal year, the increase for the per capita distribution for community college districts shall be determined by using the provisions of § 15–1464, Arizona Revised Statutes, as amended by Laws 1987, chapter 360, § 3, and the provisions of § 15–1464, Arizona Revised Statutes, as amended by Laws 1990, chapter 397, § 1, and by § 11 of this act, and the distribution shall be one-half of such increase."

Laws 1992, Ch. 288, § 20, eff. Sept. 30, 1992, retroactively effective to July 1, 1992, provides:

"Sec. 20. **1992–1993 fiscal year per capita distribution for community college districts**

"Notwithstanding the provisions of § 15–1464, Arizona Revised Statutes, or any other provision of law, for the 1992–1993 fiscal year, the per capita distribution for community college districts shall be the same amounts as appropriated for the 1991–1992 fiscal year."

Laws 1996, 5th S.S., Ch. 4, § 1, provides:

"**Section 1. Community college districts; capital outlay aid; operating aid**

"In fiscal year 1997–1998, for a community college district with declining full-time equivalent student enrollment for each of the fiscal years 1994–1995 and 1995–1996:

"1. Notwithstanding § 15–1464, Arizona Revised Statutes, the state aid per capita distribution for capital outlay shall be the result of multiplying the district's fiscal year 1994–1995 audited full-time equivalent student count by two hundred ten dollars for districts with less than five thousand and by one hundred sixty dollars for districts with five thousand or more.

"2. Notwithstanding § 15–1466, Arizona Revised Statutes, the operating state aid shall be the district's fiscal year 1996–1997 operating state aid appropriation, minus the difference in the fiscal years 1993–1994 and 1994–1995 audited full-time equivalent student count, multiplied by the average dollar amount per full-time equivalent student of operating state aid appropriated for fiscal year 1996–1997 for all districts."

Laws 1999, Ch. 96, § 7, provides:

"**Sec. 7. Retroactivity**

"This act applies retroactively to from and after June 30, 1999."

Laws 2002, Ch. 330, became law without the Governor's signature as provided in Arizona Constitution, Article 5, § 7.

Reviser's Notes:

1992 Note. Prior to the 1993 amendment, this section contained the amendments made by Laws 1992, Ch. 172, sec. 39 and Ch. 345, sec. 3 that were blended together pursuant to authority of § 41-1304.03.

1999 Note. Prior to the 2002 amendment, this section contained the amendments made by Laws 1999, Ch. 96, sec. 4 and Ch. 228, sec. 2 that were blended together pursuant to authority of § 41-1304.03.

§ 15-1465. Election; issuance and sale of bonds for capital outlay; disposition of proceeds; proration of expenditures by counties

A. A district may conduct an election to determine whether or not bonds shall be issued and sold for the purpose of paying its share of the expenditures incurred for capital outlay. The election shall be originated and conducted, the bonds issued, sold and redeemed and a tax levy imposed for payment of interest on such bonds and redemption of bonds in accordance with the provisions of title 35, chapter 3, article 3 [1] and the limitations imposed on school districts by article IX, § 8, Constitution of Arizona, insofar as those provisions are applicable. Bond counsel fees, financial advisory fees, printing costs and paying agent and registrar fees shall be paid from either the amount authorized by the qualified electors of the community college district or current operating funds. Bond election expenses shall be paid from current operating funds only.

B. The proceeds of all bonds sold as provided in subsection A shall be used only for capital outlay, including the purchase of land, the purchase, erection, remodeling or completion of buildings and the purchase of equipment and facilities for educational or auxiliary purposes of the community college district.

C. Where a district contains more than one county, subsections A and B shall be applicable separately to each of the counties as to its portion of the expenditures to be paid for capital outlay in setting up the physical plant of the district even though the proposed plant is to be established, wholly or partly, in one county of the district.

D. The portion of the expenditures for capital outlay to be prorated by each county of a district shall be determined in the ratio that the assessed valuation of each county within the district bears to the total assessed valuation of all counties within the district.

E. If a majority of the qualified electors voting at an election held as provided in this chapter disapproves the issuance of bonds for any purpose, the governing board of the community college district shall not authorize the expenditure of funds from any source for such purpose without subsequent approval of a majority of the qualified electors voting at an election held as provided in this chapter, except that a subsequent vote of the district electors shall not be necessary to:

1. Construct buildings and site improvements on existing campuses.
2. Repair and remodel existing facilities and to purchase equipment.
3. Purchase land adjacent to an existing campus.

Added by Laws 1981, Ch. 1, § 2, eff. Jan. 23, 1981. Amended by Laws 1991, Ch. 135, § 1; Laws 1996, Ch. 286, § 7; Laws 2002, Ch. 330, § 22.

[1] Section 35-451 et seq.

Historical and Statutory Notes

Source:

Laws 1927, Ch. 84, §§ 3, 4.
Rev.Code 1928, §§ 1087, 1087j.
Laws 1931, Ch. 81, § 1.
Code 1939, §§ 54-710, 54-920.
A.R.S. former §§ 15-603, 15-615, 15-686.
Laws 1960, Ch. 119, § 1.
Laws 1965, 3rd S.S., Ch. 4, § 2.
Laws 1970, Ch. 192, § 12.
Laws 1972, Ch. 122, § 1.
Laws 1976, Ch. 163, § 6.
Laws 1978, Ch. 168, § 4.
Laws 1980, 2nd S.S., Ch. 9, § 30.
Laws 1980, Ch. 167, § 3.

Laws 2002, Ch. 330, became law without the Governor's signature as provided in Arizona Constitution, Article 5, § 7.

§ 15-1466. State aid; eligibility; limitations

A. Subject to legislative appropriation, the legislature shall determine and appropriate the amount of state aid each fiscal year for any district possessing the qualifications as prescribed in this chapter.

B. The state shall determine the amount of state aid, as prescribed in subsection F of this section, appropriated to each district for the fiscal year prior to the fiscal year for which the state aid is being calculated.

C. The state shall adjust the amount of state aid appropriated to each district as determined in subsection B of this section by the growth rate referenced by § 15-901, subsection B, paragraph 2. This amount shall be appropriated to the district except as provided in subsection D of this section.

D. In addition to the state aid appropriated in subsection C of this section, each district qualified under this chapter shall have its state aid adjusted in an amount that reflects the growth in the full-time equivalent student count of the district calculated as follows:

1. Calculate the growth in the actual, audited full-time equivalent student count between the second and third most recent fiscal years prior to the fiscal year for which the state aid is being calculated for each district.

2. Calculate the average appropriation per full-time equivalent student for all districts by dividing the amount determined in subsection B of this section by the actual, audited full-time equivalent student count for all districts in the most recent fiscal year.

3. Multiply the amount calculated in paragraph 1 of this subsection by the average appropriation calculated in paragraph 2 of this subsection. This amount shall be appropriated to the district for growth.

E. State aid appropriated to each district shall be allocated and paid in accordance with subsection C of this section before any funding is allocated and paid in accordance with subsection D of this section.

F. The total amount appropriated to each district each fiscal year in accordance with subsections C and D of this section shall serve as the amount of state aid to be adjusted in the next fiscal year.

G. To be eligible for state aid, a district shall:

1. Be equipped with suitable buildings, equipment and campus.

2. Have three hundred twenty full-time equivalent students attending in the district.

3. Have complied with all of the requirements of the district board including budgets and curriculum.

H. Notwithstanding subsection E of this section, the legislature may allocate funding for growth in the full-time equivalent student count prior to or in combination with funding of the growth rate.

I. The total amount of state monies that may be spent in any fiscal year by a district for operating state aid shall not exceed the amount appropriated or authorized by § 35-173 for that purpose. Notwithstanding § 15-1444, this section shall not be construed to impose a duty on an officer, agent or employee of this state to discharge a responsibility or to create any right in a person or group if the discharge or right would require an expenditure of state monies in excess of the expenditure authorized by legislative appropriation for that specific purpose, including any duties prescribed in an employment contract entered into pursuant to § 15-1444, subsection A, paragraph 6.

J. In addition to the formula to determine the state aid appropriations prescribed in this section, the state may pay additional amounts for state aid to a district based on requests included in the district's budget request.

K. This section does not entitle a community college operated by a qualified Indian tribe to state aid for community colleges pursuant to this chapter.
Added by Laws 1992, Ch. 345, § 5. Amended by Laws 1993, 2nd S.S., Ch. 8, § 4; Laws 1993, Ch. 112, § 1; Laws 1993, Ch. 189, § 18; Laws 1995, Ch. 191, § 21, eff. April 19, 1995; Laws 1995, Ch. 196, § 24; Laws 1999, Ch. 228, § 3; Laws 1999, 1st S.S., Ch. 4, § 11; Laws 2002, Ch. 330, § 23; Laws 2003, Ch. 253, § 21, eff. Sept. 18, 2003, retroactively effective to July 1, 2003.

Historical and Statutory Notes

Source:

Rev.Code 1928, § 1087k.
Laws 1935, Ch. 38, § 1.
Laws 1947, Ch. 111, § 1.
Laws 1949, Ch. 57, § 1.
Laws 1953, Ch. 93, § 1.
Code 1939, Supp.1953, § 54-711.
A.R.S. former §§ 15-632, 15-690.
Laws 1957, Ch. 11, § 1.
Laws 1960, Ch. 119, § 1.
Laws 1961, Ch. 127, § 1.
Laws 1965, 3rd S.S., Ch. 4, § 3.
Laws 1972, Ch. 122, § 2.
Laws 1976, Ch. 60, § 1.
Laws 1980, 2nd S.S., Ch. 9, § 33.
A.R.S. former § 15-1466.
Laws 1981, Ch. 1, § 2.
Laws 1981, Ch. 287, § 3.
Laws 1981, Ch. 300, § 2.
Laws 1982, Ch. 196, § 4.
Laws 1982, Ch. 332, § 19.
Laws 1985, Ch. 305, § 2.
Laws 1985, Ch. 365, § 2.
Laws 1987, Ch. 360, § 4.
Laws 1988, Ch. 234, § 4.
Laws 1992, Ch. 172, § 40.

Laws 1992, Ch. 345, § 12, provides:

"**Sec. 12. Yavapai and Coconino county community college districts; full-time student equivalent adjustment for fiscal year 1990-1991**"

"For fiscal year 1993-1994 when determining the amount to be paid for growth in full-time student equivalent under § 15-1466, subsection C, Arizona Revised Statutes, as added by this act, the full-time student equivalent count for the Yavapai county community college district shall be adjusted to reflect a loss of three hundred sixty-one for fiscal year 1990-1991, which will result in a fiscal year 1990-1991 full-time student equivalent count of two thousand two hundred ninety-one. The Coconino county community college district full-time student equivalent count for fiscal year 1990-1991 shall be three hundred sixty-one."

The 1993 amendment of this section by Ch. 112 explicitly amended the 1993 amendment of this section by 2nd S.S., Ch. 8.

The 1993 amendment by Ch. 189 explicitly amended the 1993 amendment of this section by 2nd S.S., Ch. 8.

Laws 1995, 1st S.S., Ch. 4, § 3, provides:

"**Sec. 3. Fiscal year 1995–1996 community college district growth rate**

"Notwithstanding § 15–1466, subsections A through F, Arizona Revised Statutes, and in accordance with § 15–1466, subsection H, Arizona Revised Statutes, the community college district growth rate for fiscal year 1995–1996 is 0.0 per cent."

For applicability provisions of Laws 1995, Ch. 196, see the Historical and Statutory Notes following § 1–254.

The amendment of this section by Laws 1995, Ch. 191, § 21, was repealed by Laws 1996, Ch. 248, § 13.

Laws 1996, 5th S.S., Ch. 4, § 1, provides:

"**Section 1. Community college districts; capital outlay aid; operating aid**

"In fiscal year 1997–1998, for a community college district with declining full-time equivalent student enrollment for each of the fiscal years 1994–1995 and 1995–1996:

"1. Notwithstanding § 15–1464, Arizona Revised Statutes, the state aid per capita distribution for capital outlay shall be the result of multiplying the district's fiscal year 1994–1995 audited full-time equivalent student count by two hundred ten dollars for districts with less than five thousand and by one hundred sixty dollars for districts with five thousand or more.

"2. Notwithstanding § 15–1466, Arizona Revised Statutes, the operating state aid shall be the district's fiscal year 1996–1997 operating state aid appropriation, minus the difference in the fiscal years 1993–1994 and 1994–1995 audited full-time equivalent student count, multiplied by the average dollar amount per full-time equivalent student of operating state aid appropriated for fiscal year 1996–1997 for all districts."

For purpose of Laws 1996, Ch. 248, see Historical and Statutory Notes following § 15–365.

Laws 2002, Ch. 330, became law without the Governor's signature as provided in Arizona Constitution, Article 5, § 7.

Former § 15–1466, added by Laws 1981, Ch. 1, relating to state aid eligibility and calculation of full-time equivalent student enrollment (see Source, ante), was repealed by Laws 1992, Ch. 345, § 4. See, now, this section and § 15–1466.01.

Prior to the repeal of the former section, it was amended by Laws 1992, Ch. 172, § 40.

1993 Note. Prior to the 1995 amendments, this section contained the amendments made by Laws 1993, Ch. 112, sec. 1 and Ch. 189, sec. 18 that were blended together pursuant to authority of § 41–1304.03.

1995 Note. The amendment made by Laws 1995, Ch. 196, sec. 24 was inconsistent and incompatible with Laws 1995, Ch. 191, sec. 21 and therefore could not be blended.

1999 Note. Prior to the 2002 amendment, this section contained the amendments made by Laws 1999, First Regular Session, Ch. 228, sec. 3 and First Special Session, Ch. 4, sec. 11 that were blended together pursuant to authority of § 41–1304.03.

§ 15–1466.01. Calculation of full-time equivalent student enrollment

In determining state aid under §§ 15–1464 and 15–1466 the number of full-time equivalent students shall be calculated in the following manner:

1. For the basic actual full-time equivalent student enrollment, add the number of full-time equivalent students enrolled as of forty-five days after classes begin in the fall semester to the number of full-time equivalent students enrolled as of forty-five days after classes begin in the spring semester, not including additional short-term classes, and divide the sum by two.

2. For the additional short-term and open entry, open exit full-time equivalent student enrollments:

(a) Determine the total number of credit units for students enrolled in additional short-term and open entry, open exit classes for the fiscal year.

(b) Determine the total number of credit units for students who have completed the additional short-term and open entry, open exit classes for the fiscal year. Any student who has not completed the class by June 30 of each fiscal year shall not be eligible to be counted for state aid purposes until the following year.

(c) Add the amounts in subdivisions (a) and (b).

(d) Divide the amount determined in subdivision (c) by two.

(e) Divide the quotient obtained in subdivision (d) by thirty.

(f) The result in subdivision (e) is the additional short-term and open entry, open exit full-time equivalent student enrollments for the fiscal year.

3. For the skill center and adult basic education courses full-time equivalent student enrollment, divide by six hundred forty the total class attended clock hours of persons who complete vocational training. Any student who does not complete vocational training programs by June 30 of each fiscal year shall not be eligible to be counted for state aid purposes until the following year.

4. The total of basic actual, additional short-term and open entry, open exit and skill center full-time equivalent student enrollment shall be the basis of providing state aid. Beginning with the audit for the year ending June 30, 2003, the auditor general shall audit separately any full-time equivalent student enrollment where a student is enrolled in a course for both high school and college credit simultaneously, except for credit received at a private college or a college owned, operated or chartered by an Indian tribe, taking into consideration any relevant law, regulation or rule. The full-time equivalent student enrollment reported by each district for all basic actual, additional short-term and open entry, open exit classes and skill center and adult basic education courses shall be audited annually by the auditor general. The auditor general shall report the results of the audit to the staffs of the joint legislative budget committee and the governor's office of strategic planning and budgeting by October 15 of each year.

Added by Laws 1992, Ch. 345, § 5. Amended by Laws 1997, Ch. 300, § 11; Laws 2001, Ch. 372, § 3, eff. July 2, 2002; Laws 2003, Ch. 253, § 22, eff. Sept. 18, 2003, retroactively effective to July 1, 2003; Laws 2004, Ch. 336, § 10.

Historical and Statutory Notes

Source:

Rev.Code 1928, § 1087k.
Laws 1935, Ch. 38, § 1.
Laws 1947, Ch. 111, § 1.
Laws 1949, Ch. 57, § 1.
Laws 1953, Ch. 93, § 1.
Code 1939, Supp.1953, § 54-711.
A.R.S. former §§ 15-632, 15-690.
Laws 1957, Ch. 11, § 1.
Laws 1960, Ch. 119, § 1.
Laws 1961, Ch. 127, § 1.
Laws 1965, 3rd S.S., Ch. 4, § 3.
Laws 1972, Ch. 122, § 2.
Laws 1976, Ch. 60, § 1.
Laws 1980, 2nd S.S., Ch. 9, § 33.
A.R.S. former § 15-1466.
Laws 1981, Ch. 1, § 2.
Laws 1981, Ch. 287, § 3.
Laws 1981, Ch. 300, § 2.
Laws 1982, Ch. 196, § 4.
Laws 1982, Ch. 332, § 19.
Laws 1985, Ch. 305, § 2.
Laws 1985, Ch. 365, § 2.
Laws 1987, Ch. 360, § 4.
Laws 1988, Ch. 234, § 4.

§ 15-1466.02. Record keeping requirements for full-time equivalent student enrollment

A. On or before July 21 each year, each community college district shall:

1. Provide a certified report to the auditor general of the number of full-time equivalent students calculated by the district pursuant to § 15-1466.01.

2. Separately calculate and report to the auditor general any full-time equivalent student enrollment where a student is enrolled in a course for both high school and college credit simultaneously.

B. Each community college district shall submit to the auditor general a summary of its full-time equivalent student enrollment accounting policies and procedures, compilation procedures and source records used for calculating full-time equivalent student enrollment.

C. Basic actual full-time equivalent student enrollment shall be counted on the forty-fifth day after the basic actual full-time equivalent student enrollment classes begin for the fall and spring semesters, as published in the college catalogs. Class rosters that reflect enrollment as of the forty-fifth day shall be provided by the registrar's office to each professor or instructor for every class section. The class roster shall indicate the course number, course title, time, instructor name and students enrolled. Each professor or instructor is required to review the class roster and make additions or deletions as necessary. On the forty-fifth day class rosters, each professor or instructor shall indicate as withdrawn each student who has not been attending class, even if the student has not formally withdrawn from the course, and that student shall not be counted for state aid purposes. The official forty-fifth day rosters shall include a manual signature and date or an electronic authorization and date by the professor or instructor and shall include the following certification:

I hereby certify that the information contained in this class roster accurately reflects those students who are enrolled and participating.

Students who have withdrawn or who have been withdrawn from classes as of the forty-fifth day shall not be counted for state aid purposes. A record shall be maintained that identifies student withdrawals by date of withdrawal, as of the forty-fifth day and after the forty-fifth day for the entire semester.

D. Additional short-term and open entry, open exit full-time equivalent student enrollment must be counted as of June 30 of each year. Registration records shall be maintained to support the number of credit hours for additional short-term and open entry, open exit classes in which students are enrolled during the fiscal year. Final grade rosters shall be prepared that present initial enrollees, those students who withdrew from the class and those students who completed the class. The final grade rosters shall include a manual signature or electronic authorization by the professor or instructor and shall be used to support the number of credit hours claimed for full-time equivalent student enrollment. For both additional short-term and open entry, open exit classes, only students who have received a grade by June 30 may be counted as completed for state aid purposes and students with a grade of incomplete shall not be counted.

E. Skill center and adult basic education full-time equivalent student enrollment records shall be maintained to support the actual clock hours attended by students in skill center and adult basic education courses.

F. Those students who are simultaneously enrolled in a course for both high school and college credit and the courses, including section numbers, that the students attend shall be specifically identified in the district's full-time equivalent student enrollment records.

G. The community college district's records used to calculate full-time equivalent student enrollment counts shall be provided to the auditor general in an electronic format prescribed by the auditor general.

Added by Laws 2003, Ch. 253, § 23, eff. Sept. 18, 2003, retroactively effective to July 1, 2003.

§ 15–1467. State aid appropriations; disbursement procedure; district fund

A. Appropriations for state aid to districts shall be distributed to each community college district in accordance with § 15–1466.

B. On July 15, October 15, January 15 and April 15, each district shall present to the department of administration a claim for one-fourth of the annual amount appropriated to the district. The department of administration shall draw a warrant in payment of the claim and transmit the warrant to the state treasurer who shall disburse the funds to each district for the support and maintenance of the district, to be expended as provided by law. If no community college exists, the department shall establish a fund for new future districts to be disbursed as needed.

C. Notwithstanding subsection B of this section, a district may request the state treasurer to disburse the monies to the local government investment pool for deposit into the district's account as established in § 35–326.

Added by Laws 1981, Ch. 1, § 2, eff. Jan. 23, 1981. Amended by Laws 1992, Ch. 345, § 6; Laws 1999, Ch. 96, § 5; Laws 2002, Ch. 330, § 24; Laws 2003, Ch. 253, § 24, eff. Sept. 18, 2003, retroactively effective to July 1, 2003.

Historical and Statutory Notes

Source:

Laws 1943, Ch. 20, § 1.
Code 1939, Supp.1952, § 54–712.
A.R.S. former §§ 15–633, 15–691.
Laws 1960, Ch. 119, § 1.
Laws 1970, Ch. 190, §§ 11, 13.
Laws 1972, Ch. 122, § 3.
Laws 1974, Ch. 123, § 1.
Laws 1976, Ch. 60, § 2.

Laws 1999, Ch. 96, § 7, provides:

"**Sec. 7. Retroactivity**

"This act applies retroactively to from and after June 30, 1999."

Laws 2002, Ch. 330, became law without the Governor's signature as provided in Arizona Constitution, Article 5, § 7.

§ 15–1468. Equalization aid for community college districts

A. Subject to legislative appropriation, any district that has less than the amount of primary assessed valuation prescribed in § 15–1402 shall be paid by this state an amount equal to the following:

1. The difference between the prior year's actual primary assessed valuation of the district and the amount of primary assessed valuation prescribed in § 15–1402.

2. The actual prior year's primary property tax rate for the district.

3. The difference determined in paragraph 1 multiplied by the lesser of the tax rate determined in paragraph 2 or one dollar and thirty-seven cents.

B. The equalization aid provided for in subsection A of this section shall be used for the same purposes specified in § 15–1462 and shall be apportioned to any qualifying district pursuant to § 15–1467.

C. This section does not apply to provisional community college districts as prescribed in § 15–1409.

Added by Laws 1992, Ch. 288, § 18, eff. Sept. 30, 1992, retroactively effective to July 1, 1992. Amended by Laws 1992, Ch. 345, § 8; Laws 1995, Ch. 196, § 25; Laws 2003, Ch. 253, § 25, eff. Sept. 18, 2003, retroactively effective to July 1, 2003.

Historical and Statutory Notes

Source:

Rev.Code 1928, § 1087k.
Laws 1935, Ch. 38, § 1.
Laws 1947, Ch. 111, § 1.
Laws 1949, Ch. 57, § 1.
Laws 1953, Ch. 93, § 1.
Code 1939, Supp.1953, § 54–711.
A.R.S. former §§ 15–632, 15–690.01.
Laws 1957, Ch. 11, § 1.
Laws 1961, Ch. 127, § 1.
Laws 1971, Ch. 106, § 2.
Laws 1977, Ch. 116, § 1.
A.R.S. former § 15–1468.
Laws 1981, Ch. 1, § 2.
Laws 1981, Ch. 306, § 1.
Laws 1985, Ch. 305, § 3.

For applicability provisions of Laws 1995, Ch. 196, see the Historical and Statutory Notes following § 1–254.

Former § 15–1468, added by Laws 1981, Ch. 1, relating to similar subject matter (see Source, ante), was repealed by Laws 1992, Ch. 288, § 17, eff. Sept. 30, 1992, retroactively effective to July 1, 1992, and by Laws 1992, Ch. 345, § 7. See, now, this section.

Laws 1981, Ch. 314, § 21, which as amended by Laws 1982, Ch. 217, § 1 also provided for the repeal of the former section on July 1, 1985, was repealed by Laws 1985, Ch. 305, § 5, effective May 7, 1985.

Reviser's Notes:

1992 Note. Prior to the 1995 amendment, this section contained amendments made by Laws 1992, Ch. 288, sec. 18 and Ch. 345, sec. 8 that were blended together pursuant to authority § 41–1304.03. In Laws 1992, Ch. 345 version in subsection A, paragraph 3 the spelling of "lesser" was corrected, pursuant to authority of § 41–1304.02

§ 15–1469. Attendance of nonresident state students; payment of cost by county of residence

A. The district may admit students from any part of this state which is not a part of an established community college district on the same conditions as residents.

B. It shall be the obligation of the county of the student's residence to reimburse the district as provided in this subsection. The amount of reimbursement to each community college district from each county which is not a part of an organized community college district shall be determined as follows:

1. For students attending classes within the established community college district:

(a) Determine the number of full-time equivalent students attending classes within the district from the county for the year preceding the current year.

(b) Determine the operational expenses of the district for the current year excluding direct and indirect costs of noncredit courses.

(c) Determine the amount of state aid the district received for the current year as provided in § 15–1466.

(d) Subtract the amount of state aid received for the current year determined in subdivision (c) from the amount of operational expenses for the current year determined in subdivision (b).

(e) Determine the number of full-time equivalent students enrolled in the district for the current year.

(f) Divide the amount determined in subdivision (d) by the number of full-time equivalent students determined in subdivision (e).

(g) Multiply the amount determined in subdivision (f) by the average number of full-time equivalent students for the county determined as provided in subdivision (a).

The resulting amount is the amount of reimbursement to the district from the county for the budget year for students attending classes within the established community college district.

2. For students attending classes offered by the district within the county pursuant to § 15-1470, the amount specified in the intergovernmental agreement is the amount of reimbursement to the district from the county for the budget year for students attending classes within the county.

C. The county school superintendent of the county of the student's residence shall certify to the community college district board and the board of supervisors that the student is a resident of the county.

D. On or before May 15, the staff of the joint legislative budget committee shall:

1. Determine the amount of reimbursement to each district from each county pursuant to subsection B, paragraph 1 of this section.

2. Notify the board of supervisors of each county of the amount it shall reimburse to each district pursuant to subsection B, paragraph 1 of this section for the budget year.

3. Notify each community college district eligible to receive reimbursement of the amount of reimbursement from each county pursuant to subsection B, paragraph 1 of this section for the budget year.

E. On or before November 15 and May 15, the board of supervisors shall draw warrants on the county treasurer in favor of the community college district for half of the amount due pursuant to subsection B of this section. The board of supervisors shall:

1. Pay monies from the county general fund or levy a community college reimbursement levy pursuant to § 42-17203 for the amount of reimbursement pursuant to an intergovernmental agreement for extension courses as provided in § 15-1470.

2. Pay monies from the county general fund or levy a community college reimbursement levy pursuant to § 42-17203 for the amount of reimbursement pursuant to subsection B, paragraph 1 of this section.

F. Notwithstanding subsection E of this section, a county and a community college district may specify by intergovernmental agreement that the amount of reimbursement due from the county be reduced by the value of in-kind contributions made by the county to the district.

G. For the purposes of subsection B, paragraph 1 of this section full-time equivalent students are determined in the same manner prescribed by § 15-1466.01.

Added by Laws 1981, Ch. 1, § 2, eff. Jan. 23, 1981. Amended by Laws 1983, Ch. 141, § 3, eff. April 19, 1983; Laws 1985, Ch. 305, § 4, eff. May 7, 1985; Laws 1985, Ch. 365, § 3; Laws 1986, Ch. 322, § 1; Laws 1992, Ch. 345, § 9; Laws 1998, Ch. 1, § 59, eff. Jan. 1, 1999; Laws 2002, Ch. 330, § 25; Laws 2003, Ch. 264, § 7; Laws 2004, Ch. 336, § 11.

Historical and Statutory Notes

Source:

Laws 1960, Ch. 119, § 1.
A.R.S. former § 15–693.
Laws 1962, Ch. 128, § 1.
Laws 1980, 2nd S.S., Ch. 9, § 34.

Laws 2002, Ch. 330, became law without the Governor's signature as provided in Arizona Constitution, Article 5, § 7.

Reviser's Notes:

1985 Note. Prior to the 1986 amendment, this section contained the amendments made by Laws 1985, Ch. 305, § 4 and Ch. 365, § 3 which were blended together pursuant to authority of § 41–1304.03.

§ 15–1469.01. Payment of community college nonresident state student cost

A. Any county which is not a part of an established community college district and whose share of transaction privilege taxes, apportioned pursuant to § 42–5029, subsection D, totals less than one per cent of the total distribution base apportioned to all counties shall have any reimbursement to a community college district prescribed by § 15–1469 paid by the state.

B. The state treasurer shall reduce the apportionment pursuant to § 42–5029 to any county whose community college reimbursement as prescribed in § 15–1469 is eligible to be paid by the state pursuant to subsection A of this section by the amount of the reimbursement paid by the state. The state treasurer shall deposit the amount of the reduction in the state general fund.

C. Community college reimbursement payments made by the state on behalf of a county pursuant to this section shall be included under the state appropriation limitation established pursuant to article IX, § 17, Constitution of Arizona, and shall not be included under county expenditure limitations established pursuant to article IX, § 20, Constitution of Arizona.

Added by Laws 1987, 3rd S.S., Ch. 1, § 1, eff. July 22, 1987. Amended by Laws 1998, Ch. 1, § 60, eff. Jan. 1, 1999; Laws 1999, Ch. 183, § 2.

§ 15–1470. Community college courses; intergovernmental agreement

A. A district may offer credit and noncredit courses and services outside of the district in other districts within this state.

B. A district may offer credit and noncredit courses and services outside of the district in counties within this state without an organized district.

C. A district may offer credit and noncredit courses and services outside of this state. A district is not entitled to state aid payments for students who are provided courses and services outside of this state.

D. Before a district may offer courses pursuant to subsection A, the district shall enter into an intergovernmental agreement with the district of the county in which the courses will be held.

E. Before a district may offer courses pursuant to subsection B, the district shall enter into an intergovernmental agreement with the board of supervisors of the county in which the courses will be held. The district and the county shall negotiate the amount of reimbursement payable by the county to the district for courses conducted within the county no later than July 1.

F. The intergovernmental agreement entered into as provided in subsection E may not require or permit the county to reimburse the district for noncredit classes.

G. The intergovernmental agreement entered into as provided in this section shall include provisions for an alternative dispute resolution.

Added by Laws 1983, Ch. 141, § 4, eff. April 19, 1983. Amended by Laws 2002, Ch. 330, § 26; Laws 2003, Ch. 253, § 26, eff. Sept. 18, 2003, retroactively effective to July 1, 2003.

Historical and Statutory Notes

Laws 2002, Ch. 330, became law without the Governor's signature as provided in Arizona Constitution, Article 5, § 7.

Reviser's Notes:

1983 Note. Pursuant to authority of § 41–1304.02, "; intergovernmental agreement" was added to the heading of this section.

§ 15–1471. Expenditure limitations; overrides

A. A district board, on the approval of a majority of the qualified electors in the district voting at a regularly scheduled election on the first Tuesday after the first Monday in November, may authorize expenditures in excess of the district expenditure limitation prescribed pursuant to article IX, § 21, Constitution of Arizona. The excess expenditures authorized shall be a specified percentage of the expenditure limitation. The impact of the authorization shall appear on the ballot and in publicity pamphlets in the same manner as prescribed in § 41–563.03.

B. In the resolution requesting the voters to approve expenditures in excess of the district expenditure limitation prescribed pursuant to article IX, § 21, Constitution of Arizona, the district board shall state the number of years in which the authority to expend in excess of the limitation otherwise prescribed is to be in effect. The district board shall not request authority from the voters for a period of less than two years nor more than seven years.

C. Any authorization of expenditures made pursuant to this section shall be used in determining a modified expenditure limitation which is equal to the expenditure limitation prescribed pursuant to article IX, § 21, Constitution of Arizona, increased by the specified percentage, beginning with the fiscal year immediately following the approval of the qualified electors of the district. The district board shall not authorize expenditures in excess of the modified expenditure limitation in subsequent fiscal years unless subsequent approval for additional excess expenditures is received as provided in subsection A of this section.

Added by Laws 1986, Ch. 322, § 2. Amended by Laws 1992, Ch. 40, § 2; Laws 2003, Ch. 4, § 1.

Historical and Statutory Notes

Reviser's Notes:

1986 Note. Pursuant to authority of § 41–1304.02, in the heading of this section "; definition" was deleted.

§ 15–1472. Community college district workforce development accounts; reports

A. Each community college district shall establish a separate workforce development account to receive only tax revenues authorized pursuant to § 42–5029, subsection E, paragraph 3. Each community college district board shall approve the expenditure of these monies in accordance with § 15–1461 and consistent with subsection B of this section.

B. Monies received pursuant to subsection A of this section shall be expended for workforce development and job training purposes. These expenditures may include:

1. Partnerships with businesses and educational institutions.

2. Additional faculty for improved and expanded classroom instruction and course offerings.

3. Technology, equipment and technology infrastructure for advanced teaching and learning in classrooms or laboratories.

4. Student services such as assessment, advisement and counseling for new and expanded job opportunities.

5. The purchase, lease or lease-purchase of real property, for new construction, remodeling or repair of buildings or facilities on real property.

C. The state treasurer shall transfer monies under this section into each district's workforce development account by the fifteenth day of each month. The state treasurer shall also allocate and distribute any pooled interest earnings earned from revenues authorized in § 42–5029, subsection E, paragraph 3 to each district in accordance with the method prescribed in subsection D, paragraph 2 of this section.

D. Revenues authorized for community college districts in § 42–5029, subsection E, paragraph 3 shall be distributed by the state in the following manner:

1. For thirteen fiscal years beginning in fiscal year 2001–2002 the state treasurer shall allocate one million dollars per fiscal year for the purpose of bringing this state into compliance with the matching capital requirements prescribed in § 15–1463. The state treasurer shall distribute the monies authorized in this subsection to each district in the order in which each campus qualified for funding pursuant to § 15–1463.

2. After the monies have been paid each year to the eligible district pursuant to paragraph 1 of this subsection, the state treasurer shall distribute monies from the workforce development fund to each community college district in the following manner:

(a) Each district shall receive the sum of two hundred thousand dollars.

(b) After each district has received the payments prescribed in subdivision (a), the remainder of monies in the fund shall be distributed to each district according to each district's full-time equivalent student enrollment percentage of the total state wide audited full-time equivalent student enrollment in the preceding fiscal year prescribed in § 15–1466.01. The percentage distribution under this subdivision shall be adjusted annually on October 1 of each year.

E. Revenues received by community college districts shall not be used by the legislature to supplant or reduce any state aid authorized in this chapter or supplant any proceeds from the sale of bonds authorized in this article and article 5 of this chapter. [1]

F. Monies received under this section shall not be considered to be local revenues for purposes of article IX, § 21, Constitution of Arizona.

G. Each community college district shall submit a workforce development plan by April 1 of each year to the department of commerce. The plan shall outline the purpose and goals for which workforce development monies are to be expended by the district.

H. Each community college district or community college that is owned, operated or chartered by a qualifying Indian tribe on its own Indian reservation shall submit a report once every two years of its workforce development plan activities and the expenditures authorized in this section to the governor, president of the senate, speaker of the house of representatives, joint legislative budget committee and department of commerce by December 1 of every even-numbered year. The report shall include the purpose and goals for which the workforce development monies were expended by each district or community college together with a general accounting of the expenditures authorized in subsection B of this section. A copy of the final report shall also be provided to the secretary of state and the director of the Arizona state library, archives and public records. For the purposes of this subsection, "qualifying Indian tribe" has the same meaning prescribed in § 42-5031.01.

Added by Laws 2000, 5th S.S., Ch. 1, § 18. Amended by Laws 2002, Ch. 330, § 27; Laws 2004, Ch. 88, § 1; Laws 2004, Ch. 336, § 12.

[1] Section 15-1481 et seq.

Historical and Statutory Notes

Proposition 301, approved by the electors at the Nov. 7, 2000 general election, effective Nov. 27, 2000, included a provision increasing the state transaction privilege tax rate six-tenths of one per cent. Therefore, the conditions of the 5th S.S. Ch. 1 were met, and the act became effective.

Laws 2002, Ch. 330, became law without the Governor's signature as provided in Arizona Constitution, Article 5, § 7.

Reviser's Notes:

2004 Note. This section contains the amendments made by Laws 2004, Ch. 88, sec. 1 and Ch. 336, sec. 12 that were blended together as shown pursuant to authority of § 41-1304.03. In the Ch. 88 version in subsection H the first "of" was shown as new, or upstyle, language, but is existing language. Pursuant to authority of § 41-1304.02, "of" is shown as existing, or downstyle, language in the chapter version to correct a manifest clerical error.

§ 15-1473. Uniform system of accounting for community college districts; duties of auditor general

A. The auditor general shall determine the accounting systems, accounting methods and accounting procedures for use by the community college districts.

B. The auditor general, in conjunction with the community college districts, shall prescribe a uniform system of accounting as provided in § 41-1279.21 for use by all community college districts.

Added by Laws 2004, Ch. 336, § 13.

ARTICLE 5. ISSUANCE OF BONDS FOR REVENUE PRODUCING BUILDINGS

§ 15-1481. Definitions

In this article, unless the context otherwise requires:

1. "Acquire" includes purchase, erect, build, construct, reconstruct, repair, replace, extend, better, furnish, equip, develop, improve and embellish.

2. "Board" means the governing board of a community college district or its successors, but does not include provisional community college districts as prescribed in § 15-1409.

3. "Bonds" means any bonds issued pursuant to this article.

4. "Federal agency" means the housing and home finance agency, the United States of America or any of its officers or agencies designated or created to make grants or loans of monies for public construction work.

5. "Institution" means any community college district that is organized in this state pursuant to § 15-1402, but does not include provisional community college districts as prescribed in § 15-1409.

6. "Project" means one or more classrooms, student or faculty residence halls, dormitories, dining halls, student union buildings, field houses, stadia and other revenue producing buildings located at the institution, together with sites for the buildings, and including equipment, furnishings, heating, lighting and other service facilities in connection with the buildings.

Added by Laws 1981, Ch. 1, § 2, eff. Jan. 23, 1981. Amended by Laws 1988, Ch. 206, § 1; Laws 2002, Ch. 330, § 28; Laws 2003, Ch. 253, § 27, eff. Sept. 18, 2003, retroactively effective to July 1, 2003.

Historical and Statutory Notes

Source:

Laws 1961, Ch. 117, § 1.
A.R.S. former § 15-696.
Laws 1963, Ch. 14, § 1.

Laws 2002, Ch. 330, became law without the Governor's signature as provided in Arizona Constitution, Article 5, § 7.

§ 15-1482. Powers

The board shall have power, for and in behalf of the institution, to:

1. Acquire any project or projects and own, operate and maintain the same.

2. Accept grants or loans of monies from a federal agency.

3. Borrow monies and issue bonds and provide for the payment of the same and for the rights of the holders thereof.

4. Perform all acts and do all things necessary or convenient to carry out the powers granted by this article.

Added by Laws 1981, Ch. 1, § 2, eff. Jan. 23, 1981.

Historical and Statutory Notes

Source:

Laws 1961, Ch. 117, § 1.
A.R.S. former § 15-696.01.
Laws 1963, Ch. 14, § 2.

§ 15-1483. Issuance of bonds

A. The board for and on behalf of an institution is authorized from time to time to issue negotiable bonds for the purpose of acquiring a project or projects. The bonds shall be authorized by resolution of the board. The bonds may be issued in one or more series, bear such date or dates, be in such denomination or denominations, mature at such time or times, not exceeding forty years from the respective dates thereof, mature in such amount or amounts, bear interest at such rate or rates, as determined by the board, payable semiannually, be in such form either coupon or registered, carry such registration privileges, be executed in such manner, be payable in such medium of payment, at such place or places, and be subject to such term of redemption, with or without premium, as such resolution or other resolutions may provide. The bonds may be sold at not less than par at either public or private sale. The bonds shall be fully negotiable within the meaning and for all the purposes of title 47, chapter 3.[1]

B. Before the issuance of bonds, a district shall submit information regarding the planned projects that will be funded with the bond proceeds to the joint committee on capital review for review. If a bond issuance requires voter approval, the district shall submit the information to the joint committee on capital review before seeking voter approval.

Added by Laws 1981, Ch. 1, § 2, eff. Jan. 23, 1981. Amended by Laws 1982, Ch. 106, § 1, eff. April 14, 1982; Laws 1984, Ch. 77, § 21; Laws 2002, Ch. 330, § 29; Laws 2003, Ch. 264, § 8.

[1] Section 47-3101 et seq.

Historical and Statutory Notes

Source:

Laws 1961, Ch. 117, § 1.
A.R.S. former § 15-696.02.
Laws 1963, Ch. 14, § 3.
Laws 1969, Ch. 75, § 1.
Laws 1970, Ch. 89, § 10.
Laws 1976, Ch. 162, § 14.

Laws 2002, Ch. 330, became law without the Governor's signature as provided in Arizona Constitution, Article 5, § 7.

§ 15-1484. Powers to secure bonds

A. In connection with the issuance of the bonds authorized by § 15-1483, or in order to secure the payment of such bonds and interest thereon, the board shall have power by resolution to:

1. Fix and maintain tuitions, fees, rentals and other charges from students, faculty members and others using or being served by, or having the right to use or the right to be served by, any project.

2. Provide that bonds issued under this article may be secured by a first, exclusive and closed lien on all or any certain part of the income and revenue derived from, and shall be payable from tuitions, fees, rentals and other charges from students, faculty members and others using or being served by, or having the right to use or the right to be served by, any project.

3. Pledge and assign to, or in trust for the benefit of, the holder or holders of the bonds issued hereunder an amount of the income and revenue derived from tuitions, fees, rentals and other charges from students, faculty members

and others using or being served by, or having the right to use or the right to be served by, any project.

4. Covenant with or for the benefit of the holder or holders of bonds issued under this article to acquire any project, that as long as any such bonds remain outstanding and unpaid the board will fix, maintain and collect in such installments as may be agreed upon an amount of the tuitions, fees, rentals and other charges from students, faculty members and others using or being served by, or having the right to use or the right to be served by, any project, which shall be sufficient to pay when due the bonds issued hereunder to acquire such project, and interest thereon, and to create and maintain reasonable reserves therefor and to pay the costs of operation and maintenance of such project including, but not limited to, reserves for extraordinary repairs, insurance and maintenance, which costs of operation and maintenance shall be determined by the board in its absolute discretion.

5. Make and enforce and agree to make and enforce parietal rules that shall insure the use of any project by all students in attendance at the institution to the maximum extent to which such project is capable of serving such students, or if any part of the project is designed for occupancy as living quarters for the faculty members, by as many faculty members as may be served thereby.

6. Covenant that as long as any of the bonds issued under this article remain outstanding and unpaid it will not, except upon such terms and conditions as may be determined:

(a) Voluntarily create or cause to be created any debt, lien, pledge, assignment, encumbrance or other charge having priority to or being on a parity with the lien of the bonds issued under this article upon any of the income and revenues derived from tuitions, fees, rentals and other charges from students, faculty members and others using or being served by, or having the right to use or the right to be served by, any project.

(b) Convey or otherwise alienate the project to acquire which such bonds shall have been issued or the real estate upon which such project shall be located, except at a price sufficient to pay all the bonds then outstanding issued under this article to acquire such project and interest accrued thereon, and then only in accordance with any agreements with the holder or holders of such bonds.

(c) Mortgage or otherwise voluntarily create or cause to be created any encumbrance on the project to acquire which such bonds shall have been issued or the real estate upon which it shall be located.

7. Covenant as to the procedure by which the terms of any contract with a holder or holders of such bonds may be amended or abrogated, the amount or percentage of bonds the holder or holders of which must consent to an amendment or abrogation and the manner in which such consent may be given.

8. Vest in a trustee or trustees the right to receive all or any part of the income and revenue pledged and assigned to, or for the benefit of, the holder or holders of bonds issued hereunder, and to hold, apply and dispose of the same and the right to enforce any covenant made to secure or pay or in relation to the bonds; execute and deliver a trust agreement or trust agreements which may set forth the powers and duties and the remedies available to such trustee

or trustees and limiting the liabilities thereof and describing what occurrences shall constitute events of default and prescribing the terms and conditions upon which such trustee or trustees or the holder or holders of bonds of any specified amount or percentage of such bonds may exercise such rights and enforce any and all such covenants and resort to such remedies as may be appropriate.

9. Vest in a trustee or trustees or the holder or holders of any specified amount or percentage of bonds the right to apply to any court of competent jurisdiction for, and have granted, the appointment of a receiver or receivers of the income and revenue pledged and assigned to or for the benefit of the holder or holders of such bonds, which receiver or receivers may have and be granted such powers and duties as such court may order or decree for the protection of the bondholders.

10. Make covenants with any federal agency, private agency, corporation or individual to perform any and all acts and to do any and all such things as may be necessary or convenient or desirable in order to secure such bonds or as may in the judgment of the board tend to make the bonds more marketable, notwithstanding that such acts or things may not be enumerated herein, and to lease any project for the best interests of the institution, and to perform all acts and to do all things not inconsistent with the constitution of this state as may be necessary or convenient or desirable for the issuance of such bonds and for their security.

11. Enter into any and all contracts and agreements necessary to accomplish the acquisition of the project or projects including agreements for construction, engineering and architectural services and agreements covering disposition and application of the proceeds received from the sale of the bonds.

B. No bond shall be issued for any institution which causes the total aggregate face amount of all bonds issued for classrooms to exceed the greater of twenty-five per cent of all bonds then issued for such institution or one million dollars. For purposes of this subsection, classroom does not include any building which would have been included within the definition of project prior to September 30, 1988.

Added by Laws 1981, Ch. 1, § 2, eff. Jan. 23, 1981. Amended by Laws 1984, Ch. 349, § 17; Laws 1988, Ch. 206, § 2; Laws 1990, Ch. 348, § 21, eff. June 26, 1990; Laws 2002, Ch. 330, § 30.

Historical and Statutory Notes

Source:

Laws 1961, Ch. 117, § 1.
A.R.S. former § 15-696.03.
Laws 1963, Ch. 14, § 4.

Laws 2002, Ch. 330, § 60, provides:

"**Sec. 60. Covenants on existing general obligation or revenue bonds**

"Any and all obligations or covenants of the state board of directors for community colleges with respect to any general obligation bonds, revenue bonds, leases, lease-purchase agreements or any related documents or obligations, including any pledges of revenue therefore, shall hereby be and become the obligations and covenants of the community college district board of the institution for which such financing was undertaken. Such community college district board shall have all rights to take any and all actions under such financing arrangements as the state board of directors for community colleges could have taken and shall discharge all obligations and duties of the state board thereunder."

Laws 2002, Ch. 330, became law without the Governor's signature as provided in Arizona Constitution, Article 5, § 7.

§ 15-1485. Monies of institution

No monies derived from the sale of bonds under the provisions of this article shall be required to be paid into the state treasury but shall be deposited by the treasurer of the board in a separate bank account or accounts in such bank or banks or trust company or trust companies as may be designated by the board, and all deposits of such monies shall, if required by the board, be secured by obligations of the United States of America of a market value equal at all times to the amount of the deposit, and all banks and trust companies are authorized to give such security. Such monies shall be considered as held for and on behalf of the institution for which the bonds have been issued. Such monies shall be disbursed as may be directed by the board and in accordance with the terms of any agreements with the holder or holders of any bonds. This section shall not be construed as limiting the power of the board to agree in connection with the issuance of the bonds as to the custody and disposition of the monies received from the sale of such bonds or the income and revenue pledged and assigned to or in trust for the benefit of the holder or holders thereof.
Added by Laws 1981, Ch. 1, § 2, eff. Jan. 23, 1981.

Historical and Statutory Notes

Source:
Laws 1961, Ch. 117, § 1.
A.R.S. former § 15-696.04.
Laws 1963, Ch. 14, § 5.

§ 15-1486. Validity of bonds

The bonds bearing the signatures of officers in office on the date of the signing thereof shall be valid and binding obligations, notwithstanding that before the delivery thereof and payment therefor any or all of the persons whose signatures appear thereon shall have ceased to be officers of the board. The validity of the bonds shall not be dependent on nor affected by the validity or regularity of any proceedings to acquire the project financed by the bonds or taken in connection therewith.
Added by Laws 1981, Ch. 1, § 2, eff. Jan. 23, 1981.

Historical and Statutory Notes

Source:
Laws 1961, Ch. 117, § 1.
A.R.S. former § 15-696.05.
Laws 1963, Ch. 14, § 6.

§ 15-1487. Prohibitions against obligating the state of Arizona

Nothing in this article shall be construed to authorize the board to contract a debt on behalf of, or in any way to obligate, the state of Arizona, or to pledge, assign or encumber in any way or to permit the pledging, assigning or encumbering in any way of appropriations made by the legislature or revenue derived from the investment of the proceeds of the sale and from the rental of such lands as have been set aside by the Enabling Act approved June 20, 1910, or other legislative enactments of the United States, for the use and benefit of the institution.

Added by Laws 1981, Ch. 1, § 2, eff. Jan. 23, 1981.

Historical and Statutory Notes

Source:
Laws 1961, Ch. 117, § 1.
A.R.S. former § 15-696.06.
Laws 1963, Ch. 14, § 7.

§ 15-1488. Bonds obligations issued for and on behalf of institutions

All bonds issued pursuant to this article shall be obligations issued by the board for and on behalf of the institution payable only in accordance with the terms thereof, and shall not be obligations general, special or otherwise of the state of Arizona. Such bonds shall not constitute a debt, legal or moral, of the state of Arizona, and shall not be enforceable against this state, nor shall payment thereof be enforceable out of any funds of the institution issuing said bonds other than the income and revenue pledged and assigned to, or in trust for the benefit of, the holder or holders of such bonds. No institution shall be dissolved until all of the bonds issued by the board for and on behalf of the institution have been paid in full.

Added by Laws 1981, Ch. 1, § 2, eff. Jan. 23, 1981.

Historical and Statutory Notes

Source:
Laws 1961, Ch. 117, § 1.
A.R.S. former § 15-696.07.
Laws 1963, Ch. 14, § 8.

§ 15-1489. Certification of bonds by attorney general

The board may submit to the attorney general of the state of Arizona any bonds to be issued under this article after all proceedings for the issuance of such bonds have been taken. Upon the submission of such proceedings to the attorney general, it shall be his duty to examine into and pass upon the validity of the bonds and the regularity of all proceedings in connection therewith. If such proceedings conform to the provisions of this article, and if the bonds when delivered and paid for will constitute binding and legal obligations authorized by the board for and on behalf of the institution, enforceable according to the terms thereof, the attorney general shall certify in substance upon the back of each of said bonds that it is issued in accordance with the constitution and laws of the state of Arizona.

Added by Laws 1981, Ch. 1, § 2, eff. Jan. 23, 1981.

Historical and Statutory Notes

Source:
Laws 1961, Ch. 117, § 1.
A.R.S. former § 15-696.08.
Laws 1963, Ch. 14, § 9.

§ 15-1490. Excision of unconstitutional or ineffective parts of article

It is declared that the sections, clauses, sentences and parts of this article are severable, are not matters of mutual essential inducement and any of them may be excised by any court of competent jurisdiction if this article would otherwise be unconstitutional or ineffective. It is the intention of this article to confer upon the board, for and on behalf of the institution, all or any part of the powers in this article provided for, and if any one or more sections, clauses, sentences or parts of this article shall for any reason be questioned in any court of competent jurisdiction and shall be adjudged unconstitutional or invalid, such judgment shall not affect, impair or invalidate the remaining provisions thereof, but shall be confined in its operation to the specific provision or provisions so held unconstitutional or invalid, and the inapplicability or invalidity of any section, clause, sentence or part of this article in any one or more instances shall not be taken to affect or prejudice its applicability or validity in any other instance.

Added by Laws 1981, Ch. 1, § 2, eff. Jan. 23, 1981.

Historical and Statutory Notes

Source:

Laws 1961, Ch. 117, § 1.
A.R.S. former § 15–696.09.
Laws 1963, Ch. 14, § 10.

§ 15–1491. Supplemental nature of article; construction and purpose

The powers conferred by this article shall be in addition to and supplemental to the powers conferred by any other law, general or special, and bonds may be issued under the provisions of this article notwithstanding the provisions of and without regard to the procedure required by any other such law. Insofar as the provisions of this article are inconsistent with the provisions of any other law, general or special, the provisions of this article shall be controlling.

Added by Laws 1981, Ch. 1, § 2, eff. Jan. 23, 1981.

Historical and Statutory Notes

Source:

Laws 1961, Ch. 117, § 1.
A.R.S. former § 15–696.10.

CHAPTER 13

UNIVERSITIES AND RELATED INSTITUTIONS

ARTICLE 1. UNIVERSITIES

ARTICLE 2. ARIZONA BOARD OF REGENTS

Chapter 13, consisting of Article 1, §§ 15–1601 to 15–1606, Article 2, §§ 15–1621 to 15–1632, Article 3, §§ 15–1651 to 15–1653, Article 4, §§ 15–1661 to 15–1669, Article 5, §§ 15–1681 to 15–1695, Article 6, §§ 15–1701 to 15–1711, Article 7, §§ 15–1721 to 15–1726, and Article 8, §§ 15–1741 to 15–1746, was added by Laws 1981, Ch. 1, § 2, effective January 23, 1981.

Laws 1982, Ch. 229, § 25, subsec. A substituted "Universities and Related Institutions" for "Universities and Colleges and Related Institutions" as the heading for this chapter.

ARTICLE 1. UNIVERSITIES

Historical and Statutory Notes

Executive Orders:

Executive Order No. 91-13, dated September 17, 1991, terminated and suspended Executive Order No. 88-23, and reestablished the Arizona Commission for Postsecondary Education.

Laws 1982, Ch. 229, § 25, subsec. B substituted "Universities" for "Universities and Colleges" as the heading for this article.

§ 15-1601. State universities; location; faculty powers

A. The Arizona board of regents shall maintain state universities at Flagstaff in Coconino county, at Tempe in Maricopa county and at Tucson in Pima county, and the universities are respectively designated northern Arizona university, Arizona state university and the university of Arizona. The board shall maintain an Arizona state university campus in western Maricopa county designated as Arizona state university west campus. The board shall maintain an Arizona state university campus in eastern Maricopa county designated as Arizona state university east campus. The board may establish and maintain other colleges and universities subject to legislative authority.

B. The universities shall have colleges, schools and departments and give courses of study and academic degrees as the board approves. Subject to the responsibilities and powers of the board and the university presidents, the faculty members of the universities, through their elected faculty representatives, shall share responsibility for academic and educational activities and matters related to faculty personnel. The faculty members of each university, through their elected faculty representatives, shall participate in the governance of their respective universities and shall actively participate in the development of university policy.

Added by Laws 1982, Ch. 229, § 3. Amended by Laws 1984, Ch. 173, § 1; Laws 1992, Ch. 259, § 1; Laws 1994, Ch. 218, § 2.

Historical and Statutory Notes

Source:

Civ.Code 1901, §§ 3625, 3626, 3634, 3668, 3706.
Laws 1913, 3rd S.S., Ch. 46, §§ 1, 2.
Civ.Code 1913, §§ 4470, 4471, 4479, 4506, 4507.
Laws 1925, Ch. 23, § 1.
Laws 1925, Ch. 55, § 4.
Rev.Code 1928, §§ 1100, 1130, 1136.
Code 1939, §§ 54-1601, 54-1607.
Laws 1944, 2nd S.S., Ch. 6, § 1.
Laws 1945, Ch. 80, § 4.
Code 1939, Supp.1952, §§ 54-1301, 54-1602c.
A.R.S. former §§ 15-701, 15-702, 15-702.01, 15-702.02, 15-703, 15-1602 to 15-1605.
Laws 1959, Initiative and Referendum Measures, Page 403.
Laws 1965, Ch. 37, § 1.
A.R.S. former § 15-1601.
Laws 1981, Ch. 1, § 2.

Laws 1994, ch. 218, § 1, provides:

"**Section 1. Legislative intent**

"It is the intent of the legislature that the Arizona state university east campus be located at the site of the closed Williams air force base upon conveyance from the federal government for that purpose."

Laws 1995, Ch. 298, § 1, provides:

"**Section 1. Legislative intent**

"It is the intent of the legislature to encourage the redevelopment efforts at the former Williams air force base in order to replace the jobs lost with the closure of Williams air force base as soon as possible. The redevelopment efforts emphasize both an airport and an educational reuse component at the former Williams air force base. The operation of a civilian airport requires funds to be matched with federal funds for the construction of infrastructure necessary to attract tenants and users to the airport. The education, research, and training consortium requires funds to renovate buildings, equipment and other facilities to establish an educational campus at the former base. It is the intent of the legislature to provide the funds necessary for the first phase of the redevelopment process."

Former § 15-1601, added by Laws 1981, Ch. 1, § 2 (see Source, ante), and relating to the location and purpose of the university of Arizona, was repealed by Laws 1982, Ch. 229, § 2.

§§ 15-1602 to 15-1605. Repealed by Laws 1982, Ch. 229, § 2

Historical and Statutory Notes

The repealed sections, added by Laws 1981, Ch. 1, § 2, provided for the colleges at the university of Arizona, stated the locations and purposes of the state colleges, designated the Arizona state college at Tempe as Arizona state university, and related to the colleges, departments, and courses of Arizona state university and northern Arizona university. See, now, § 15-1601.

§ 15-1606. Correspondence and extension courses

The universities may offer extension courses at places within the state other than the city where the institution is located, and correspondence courses may be given.

Added by Laws 1981, Ch. 1, § 2, eff. Jan. 23, 1981. Amended by Laws 1982, Ch. 229, § 4.

Historical and Statutory Notes

Source:

Laws 1945, Ch. 80, § 4.

Code 1939, Supp.1952, § 54-1602c.

A.R.S. former § 15-704.

ARTICLE 2. ARIZONA BOARD OF REGENTS

Termination under Sunset Law

The Arizona board of regents shall, if the voters approve amendment repealing authority for the board pursuant to Const. Art. 11, § 5, terminate on July 1, 2012, unless continued. See §§ 41-3012.12 and 41-2955.

Title 15, Chapter 13, Article 2, relating to the Arizona board of regents, is repealed on January 1, 2013, by § 41-3012.12.

Historical and Statutory Notes

Laws 1992, Ch. 307, § 6, provides:

"Sec. 6. **Purpose**

"The purpose of the Arizona board of regents is to adopt, prescribe and regulate administrative and financial policy applicable to universities of this state, to adopt regulations, rules and measures for universities of this state and to supervise the operation of universities of this state."

§ 15-1621. Members; appointment; terms; oath; immunity

A. The Arizona board of regents consists of ten appointive members, including two student members, and the governor and the superintendent of public instruction as ex officio members.

B. Appointive members, except the student members, shall be appointed by the governor pursuant to § 38-211. The term of each appointive member, except the student members, is eight years, to begin and end on the third Monday in January.

C. The governor shall appoint two student members to serve staggered terms. Each year the governor shall designate on a rotation basis a university under the jurisdiction of the Arizona board of regents to submit a list of nominees for the position of student member. The associated students' organization of the designated university, by majority vote of its governing body, shall select three nominees for student member. The governor shall consider the three nominees when making the appointment of the student member but may appoint any qualified student. Before adjournment of the regular session of the legislature, the governor shall submit to the senate for consent of the senate the name of the nominee for student member whose term is to begin on July 1. A student nominated for a full term may not serve until confirmed by the senate. A student member must be a person who is legally domiciled in this state and attends a university under the jurisdiction of the Arizona board of regents on a full- time basis. In the first year of the term the student member may exercise all rights and privileges of a board member, except the right to vote. In the second year of the term the student member may exercise all rights and privileges of a board member, including the right to vote. The term of each student member is two years, beginning on July 1. The governor may remove the student members for cause. A student member who graduates with no more than seven months remaining in the second year of the term may serve the remainder of the term. A vacancy in the office of student member shall be filled as follows:

1. If a vacancy occurs during the first year of a student member's term, the office shall be filled for the unexpired term. A student member nominated by the governor to fill a vacancy pursuant to this paragraph may serve the balance of the term without being confirmed by the senate.

2. If a vacancy occurs during the second year of a student member's term, the remaining student member shall assume all rights and privileges of a board member, including the right to vote. A new student member shall be nominated to a two year term to begin on July 1 as provided in this subsection.

D. Each appointive member of the board shall take the oath of office before entering upon the duties of the member's office.

E. Members of the board are immune from personal liability with respect to all acts done and actions taken in good faith within the scope of their authority during duly constituted regular and special meetings with approval of a majority of the board.

Added by Laws 1981, Ch. 1, § 2, eff. Jan. 23, 1981. Amended by Laws 1987, Ch. 76, § 1, eff. April 16, 1987; Laws 1989, Ch. 7, § 1; Laws 2000, Ch. 128, § 1.

Historical and Statutory Notes

Source:

Civ.Code 1901, §§ 3627-3629.
Laws 1912, Ch. 40, § 1.
Civ.Code 1913, §§ 4472-4474.
Laws 1919, Ch. 36, §§ 1, 2.
Rev.Code 1928, § 1131.
Laws 1945, Ch. 80, § 1.
Code 1939, Supp.1952, § 54-1602.
A.R.S. former § 15-721.
Laws 1971, Ch. 125, § 18.
Laws 1972, Ch. 109, § 5.
Laws 1972, Ch. 163, § 13.

Laws 1981, Ch. 155, § 1, as amended by Laws 1984, Ch. 319, § 1, and Laws 1985, Ch. 97, § 1, which provided for the appointment of a student member to the Arizona board of regents, expired July 1, 1987 by provisions of § 2 of that act.

Laws 2000, Ch. 128, § 3, provides:

"**Sec. 3. Student members; initial transition to two-year terms**"

"This act does not extend the term of the current student member. The governor shall not appoint a second student member for the 2000–2001 term. Notwithstanding § 15–1621, Arizona Revised Statutes, as amended by this act, for the 2001–2002 term, two student members shall be appointed. One student member shall be appointed to a one-year term and one student member shall be appointed to a two-year term. The student member appointed for one year shall immediately assume all the rights and privileges of a member of the Arizona board of regents, including the right to vote. Every year thereafter, one student member shall be appointed to a two-year term."

Laws 2002, Ch. 170, § 3, provides:

"**Sec. 3. Purpose**

"Pursuant to § 41–2955, subsection B, Arizona Revised Statutes, the legislature continues the Arizona board of regents to adopt, prescribe and regulate administrative and financial policies applicable to universities of this state, to adopt regulations, rules and measures for universities of this state and to supervise the operation of universities of this state."

Reviser's Notes:

2000 Note. Pursuant to authority of § 41–1304.02, in subsection C, paragraph 2, last sentence the spelling of "two year" was corrected.

§ 15–1622. Officers; organization; quorum

A. The board shall select from its membership a president, secretary, treasurer and such other officers it deems necessary. The same person shall not hold the offices of secretary and treasurer. The board may require the treasurer to give additional bond.

B. A majority of the membership of the board shall constitute a quorum for transaction of business at any meeting regularly called, but a number less than a quorum may adjourn from time to time.

Added by Laws 1981, Ch. 1, § 2, eff. Jan. 23, 1981.

Historical and Statutory Notes

Source:

Laws 1945, Ch. 80, § 3.
Code 1939, Supp.1952, § 54–1602b.
A.R.S. former § 15–722.

§ 15–1623. Compensation of members

A. The Secretary of the Arizona board of regents shall receive compensation as determined pursuant to § 38–611.

B. Appointed members shall receive compensation as determined pursuant to § 38–611 for each day of attendance at board meetings, except the compensation of no member of the board shall exceed five hundred dollars in any year.

Added by Laws 1981, Ch. 1, § 2, eff. Jan. 23, 1981.

Historical and Statutory Notes

Source:

Laws 1945, Ch. 80, § 3.
Code 1939, Supp.1952, § 54–1602b.
A.R.S. former § 15–723.
Laws 1970, Ch. 204, § 31.

§ 15–1624. Meetings of board advisory committees; student records; executive session

Notwithstanding the provisions of § 38–431.01, subsection A, meetings of advisory committees to the board involving student records may be held in executive session. A student whose records are to be considered may request that the meeting be held as a public meeting in which case the meeting pertaining to such student's records shall not be in executive session.

Added by Laws 1981, Ch. 1, § 2, eff. Jan. 23, 1981.

Historical and Statutory Notes

Source:

Laws 1945, Ch. 80, § 5.
Laws 1947, Ch. 70, § 1.
Code 1939, Supp.1952, § 54–1602d.
A.R.S. former § 15–725.
Laws 1966, Ch. 110, § 2.
Laws 1972, Ch. 52, § 2.
Laws 1974, Ch. 125, § 1.
Laws 1976, Ch. 60, § 3.
Laws 1977, Ch. 31, § 2.
Laws 1978, Ch. 169, § 1.
Laws 1979, Ch. 168, § 1.

§ 15–1625. General powers of board as body corporate

A. The Arizona board of regents is a body corporate with perpetual succession. The board has jurisdiction and control over the universities.

B. The board may:

1. Adopt a corporate seal.

2. Contract.

3. Sue and be sued.

4. Purchase, receive, hold, make and take leases and long-term leases of and sell real and personal property for the benefit of this state and for the use of the institutions under its jurisdiction.

Added by Laws 1981, Ch. 1, § 2, eff. Jan. 23, 1981. Amended by Laws 1982, Ch. 229, § 5; Laws 1984, Ch. 349, § 18.

Historical and Statutory Notes

Source:

Laws 1945, Ch. 80, § 2.
Code 1939, Supp.1952, § 54–1602a.
A.R.S. former § 15–724.

§ 15–1626. General administrative powers of board

A. The board shall:

1. Have and exercise the powers necessary for the effective governance and administration of the institutions under its control. To that end, the board may adopt, and authorize each university to adopt, such regulations, policies, rules or measures as are deemed necessary and may delegate in writing to its committees, to its university presidents, or their designees, or to other entities under its control, any part of its authority for the administration and governance of such institutions, including those powers enumerated in § 15–1625, subsection B, paragraphs 2 and 4, paragraphs 3, 4, 7, 8, 10 and 11 of this subsection, and subsection B of this section. Any delegation of authority may be rescinded by the board at any time in whole or in part.

2. Appoint and employ and determine the compensation of presidents with such power and authority and for such purposes in connection with the operation of the institutions as the board deems necessary.

3. Appoint and employ and determine the compensation of vice-presidents, deans, professors, instructors, lecturers, fellows and such other officers and employees with such power and authority and for such purposes in connection with the operation of the institutions as the board deems necessary, or delegate its authority pursuant to paragraph 1 of this subsection.

4. Remove any officer or employee when the interests of education in this state so require in accordance with its personnel rules and policies.

5. Fix tuitions and fees to be charged and graduate the tuitions and fees between institutions and between residents, nonresidents and students from foreign countries. The amount of tuition, registration fees and other revenues included in the operating budget for the university adopted by the board as prescribed in paragraph 12 of this subsection shall be deposited, pursuant to §§ 35-146 and 35-147. All other tuition and fee revenue shall be retained by each university for expenditure as approved by the board. Except as provided in subsection H of this section, the Arizona board of regents shall adopt rules to govern its tuition and fee setting process which shall provide for the following:

(a) At least one public hearing at each university as an opportunity for students and members of the public to comment upon any proposed increase in tuition or fees.

(b) Publication of the notice of public hearing at least ten days prior to the hearing in a newspaper of general circulation in Maricopa county, Coconino county and Pima county. The notice shall include the date, time and location of the public hearing.

(c) Public disclosure by each university of any proposed increases in tuition or fees at least ten days prior to the public hearing.

(d) Final board action on changes in tuition or fees shall be taken by roll call vote.

The procedural requirements of subdivisions (a), (b), (c) and (d) apply only to those changes in tuition or fees that require board approval.

6. Pursuant to § 35-115, submit a budget request for each institution under its jurisdiction that includes the estimated tuition and fee revenue available to support the programs of the institution as described in the budget request. The estimated available tuition and fee revenue shall be based on the tuition and registration fee rates in effect at the time the budget request is submitted with adjustments for projected changes in enrollment as provided by the board.

7. Establish curriculums and designate courses at the several institutions which in its judgment will best serve the interests of this state.

8. Award such degrees and diplomas upon the completion of such courses and curriculum requirements as it deems appropriate.

9. Prescribe qualifications for admission of all students to the universities. The board shall establish policies for guaranteed admission that assure fair and equitable access to students in this state from public, private, charter and home schools. For the purpose of determining the qualifications of honorably discharged veterans, veterans are those who served in the armed forces for a minimum of two years and who were previously enrolled at a university or community college in this state. No prior failing grades received by the veteran at the university or community college in this state may be considered.

10. Adopt any energy conservation standards promulgated by the department of administration for the construction of new buildings.

11. Employ for such time and purposes as the board requires attorneys whose compensation shall be fixed and paid by the board. Litigation to which the board is a party and for which self-insurance is not provided may be compromised or settled at the direction of the board.

12. Adopt annually an operating budget for each university equal to the sum of appropriated general fund monies and the amount of tuition, registration fees and other revenues approved by the board and allocated to each university operating budget.

13. In consultation with the state board of education and other education groups, develop and implement a program to award honors endorsements to be affixed to the high school diplomas of qualifying high school pupils and to be included in the transcripts of pupils who are awarded endorsements. The board shall develop application procedures and testing criteria and adopt testing instruments and procedures to administer the program. In order to receive an honors endorsement, a pupil must demonstrate an extraordinary level of knowledge, skill and competency as measured by the testing instruments adopted by the board in mathematics, English, science and social studies. Additional subjects may be added at the determination of the board. The program is voluntary for pupils.

14. Require the publisher of each literary and nonliterary textbook used in the universities of this state to furnish computer software in a standardized format when software becomes available for nonliterary textbooks, to the Arizona board of regents from which braille versions of the textbooks may be produced.

15. Require universities that provide a degree in education to require courses that are necessary to obtain a provisional structured English immersion endorsement as prescribed by the state board of education.

B. The board shall adopt personnel rules. All nonacademic employees of the universities are subject to these rules except for university presidents, university vice-presidents, university deans, legal counsel and administrative officers. The personnel rules shall be similar to the personnel rules under § 41–783. The rules shall include provisions for listing available positions with the department of economic security, competitive employment processes for applicants, probationary status for new nonacademic employees, nonprobationary status on successful completion of probation and due process protections of nonprobationary employees after discharge. The board shall provide notice of proposed rule adoption and an opportunity for public comment on all personnel rules proposed for adoption.

C. The Arizona board of regents may employ legal assistance in procuring loans for the institutions from the United States government. Fees or compensation paid for such legal assistance shall not be a claim upon the general fund of this state but shall be paid from funds of the institutions.

D. The board shall approve or disapprove any contract or agreement entered into by the university of Arizona hospital with the Arizona health facilities authority.

E. The board may adopt policies which authorize the institutions under its jurisdiction to enter into employment contracts with nontenured employees for periods of more than one year but not more than five years. The policies shall prescribe limitations on the authority of the institutions to enter into employment contracts for periods of more than one year but not more than five years, including the requirement that the board approve the contracts.

F. The board may adopt a plan or plans for employee benefits which allow for participation in a cafeteria plan that meets the requirements of the United States internal revenue code of 1986.[1]

G. The board may establish a program for the exchange of students between the universities under the jurisdiction of the board and colleges and universities located in the state of Sonora, Mexico. Notwithstanding subsection A, paragraph 5 of this section, the program may provide for in-state tuition at the universities under the jurisdiction of the board for fifty Sonoran students in exchange for similar tuition provisions for up to fifty Arizona students enrolled or seeking enrollment in Sonoran colleges or universities. The board may direct the universities to work in conjunction with the Arizona-Mexico commission to coordinate recruitment and admissions activities.

H. Subsection A, paragraph 5, subdivisions (a), (b), (c) and (d) of this section do not apply to fee increases that are set by individual universities and that do not require approval by the Arizona board of regents before the fee increase becomes effective.

Added by Laws 1981, Ch. 1, § 2, eff. Jan. 23, 1981. Amended by Laws 1981, Ch. 262, § 1; Laws 1983, Ch. 190, § 2; Laws 1983, Ch. 289, § 1; Laws 1986, Ch. 321, § 1; Laws 1987, Ch. 154, § 3, April 21, 1987; Laws 1988, Ch. 299, § 1; Laws 1992, Ch. 213, § 1; Laws 1992, Ch. 307, § 2; Laws 1993, 2nd S.S., Ch. 8, § 5; Laws 1994, Ch. 59, § 1; Laws 1997, Ch. 137, § 4; Laws 1997, Ch. 230, § 1; Laws 1999, Ch. 259, § 1; Laws 2000, Ch. 128, § 2; Laws 2000, Ch. 193, § 114; Laws 2001, 2nd S.S., Ch. 9, § 5; Laws 2004, Ch. 322, § 1.

[1] 26 U.S.C.A. § 125.

Historical and Statutory Notes

Source:

Laws 1935, Ch. 18, § 1.
Code 1939, § 54-1201.
Laws 1945, Ch. 80, § 5.
Laws 1947, Ch. 70, § 1.
Code 1939, Supp.1952, § 54-1602d.
A.R.S. former §§ 15-725, 15-726.
Laws 1966, Ch. 110, § 2.
Laws 1972, Ch. 52, § 2.
Laws 1974, Ch. 125, § 1.
Laws 1976, Ch. 60, § 3.
Laws 1977, Ch. 31, § 2.
Laws 1978, Ch. 169, § 1.
Laws 1979, Ch. 168, § 1.

For provision of Laws 1979, Ch. 46, relating to education of Arizona students as osteopathic physicians in schools located in other states, see Historical and Statutory Notes following § 15-1742.

Laws 1992, Ch. 307, § 1, provides:

"**Section 1. Legislative intent**

"It is the intent of the legislature by this act to authorize the Arizona board of regents to make such delegation of its powers as the board deems necessary for the following purposes:

"1. To enable the board to properly exercise its policymaking and oversight responsibilities; and

"2. To enable the institutions under its control to function in an efficient manner."

Laws 1997, Ch. 230, § 2, provides:

"**Sec. 2. Implementation progress report**

"The board of regents shall submit to the governor, the speaker of the house of representatives and the president of the senate an implementation progress report on the honors endorsement program established in § 15-1626, subsection A, paragraph 13, Arizona Revised Statutes, as amended by this act, by December 15, 1997."

Reviser's Notes:

1983 Note. Prior to the 1986 amendment, this section contained the amendments made by Laws 1983, Ch. 190, § 2 and Ch. 289, § 1 which were blended together pursuant to authority of § 41-1304.03. Additionally, pursuant to authority of § 41-1304.02, subsection D, as added by Laws 1983, Ch. 190, was relettered as subsection C and subsection C, as added by Laws 1983, Ch. 289, was published as temporary law with the section heading "Arizona board of regents; comprehensive merit pay plan".

1992 Note. Prior to the 1993 amendment this section contained the amendments made by Laws 1992, Ch. 213, sec. 1 and Ch. 307, sec. 2

that were blended together pursuant to authority of § 41-1304.03.

1997 Note. Prior to the 1999 amendment, this section contained the amendments made by Laws 1997,Ch. 137, § 4 and Ch. 230, § 1 that were blended together pursuant to authority of § 41-1304.03.

2000 Note. Prior to the 2001 2nd S.S. amendment, this section contained the amendments made by Laws 2000, Ch. 128, sec. 2 and Ch. 193, sec. 114 that were blended together pursuant to authority of § 41-1304.03.

2004 Note. Pursuant to authority of § 41-1304.02, in subsection A, paragraph 5, subdivision (d) the second sentence was moved to start at the left margin to correct a manifest clerical error.

§ 15-1627. Control of vehicles and nonpedestrian devices on university property; sanctions; compliance with emissions inspection; definition

A. Each university may adopt rules for the control of vehicles and nonpedestrian devices on its property with respect to the following only: maximum speed of vehicles and nonpedestrian devices, direction of travel, authorized hours of travel, required stops in traffic, place of parking, method of parking, time of parking, nonparking areas, restricted areas, prohibition of parking in vehicle emissions control areas as defined in § 49-541 of those vehicles which fail to comply with § 49-542 and designation of special parking areas for students, faculty, staff and the general public. Each university may prescribe and collect reasonable fees for specially designated parking areas. Each university shall cause signs and notices to be posted upon the property for the regulation of vehicles and nonpedestrian devices.

B. The rules adopted by each university pursuant to subsection A of this section shall be enforced administratively by each university. As to students, faculty and staff, these procedures may, but need not, involve both student and faculty adjudicating bodies, as long as all procedures give the individual notice and an opportunity to be heard concerning the alleged infractions and any sanction to be imposed upon him. Administrative and disciplinary sanctions may be imposed upon students, faculty and staff for a violation of the rules including, but not limited to: a reasonable monetary penalty, impoundment, regular institutional discipline, withdrawal or suspension of campus parking privileges, encumbrances of records or grades, or both, and oral or written reprimand. Habitual or flagrant disregard of rules shall be a ground for suspension or expulsion from the university for a student and may be taken into consideration as to faculty and staff in regard to amount of salary and continuation of employment.

C. Members of the general public who park their vehicles in an unauthorized manner upon the property of a university shall be warned concerning their unauthorized parking and, if they continue, or if such persons habitually park in such an unauthorized manner, the vehicles so parked may be impounded by the institution and a reasonable fee exacted for the cost of impoundment and storage.

D. Members of the general public who violate a rule adopted by the university pursuant to subsection A of this section regarding the use of nonpedestrian devices shall be warned of a violation and any nonpedestrian devices may be impounded by the university and a reasonable fee may be exacted for the cost of impoundment and storage.

E. Any person who has received a final administrative ruling concerning a sanction imposed upon him as a result of a violation of a rule pursuant to subsection A of this section shall have the right to have that ruling reviewed by the superior court in the county in which the institution involved is situated, in accordance with the provisions of the administrative review act, title 12, chapter 7, article 6.[1]

F. This section shall be considered supplemental in nature to the general common law and statutory powers of institutions under control of the board as to the internal control and activities of their students, faculty and staff.

G. An institution under the jurisdiction of the board of regents and which is located in a vehicle emissions control area as defined in § 49-541 shall prohibit the issuance of annual permits to park on property under its jurisdiction until the applicant submits an affidavit or shows proof that his vehicle meets the requirements of § 49-542.

H. For the purposes of this section, "nonpedestrian devices" includes bicycles, tricycles, unicycles, skateboards, roller skates and equines.

Added by Laws 1981, Ch. 1, § 2, eff. Jan. 23, 1981. Amended by Laws 1985, Ch. 280, § 3; Laws 1987, Ch. 246, § 1; Laws 1987, Ch. 365, § 7; Laws 1988, Ch. 252, § 2; Laws 1992, Ch. 307, § 3; Laws 1994, Ch. 59, § 2.

[1] Section 12-901 et seq.

Historical and Statutory Notes

Source:

Laws 1967, Ch. 101, § 1.
A.R.S. former § 15-725.01.
Laws 1968, Ch. 86, § 1.

Reviser's Notes:

1987 Note. Prior to the 1988 amendment, this section contained the amendments made by Laws 1987, Ch. 246, § 1 and Ch. 365, § 7 which were blended together pursuant to authority of § 41-1304.03. Pursuant to authority of § 41-1304.02, in the section heading "violation; classification;" was removed.

§ 15-1628. Powers and procedures pertaining to optional retirement programs

A. The Arizona board of regents may establish optional retirement programs under which contracts providing retirement and death benefits may be purchased for members of the faculty and administrative officers of the institutions under its jurisdiction. The benefits to be provided for or on behalf of participants in the optional retirement program shall be provided through annuity contracts, fixed or variable in nature, or a combination thereof, or other retirement plans approved by the Arizona board of regents.

B. Elections to participate in the optional retirement programs shall be made as follows:

1. Eligible employees initially appointed on or after August 9, 1974 shall elect to become members of the Arizona state retirement system or to participate in an optional retirement program established by the Arizona board of regents. The election shall be made in writing and filed with the Arizona state retirement system and the disbursing officer of the employing institution and shall be effective as of the effective date of appointment. If an eligible employee fails to make an election as provided in this paragraph, the eligible

employee shall be deemed to have elected membership in the Arizona state retirement system.

2. Eligible employees initially appointed before August 9, 1974 may elect to participate in the optional retirement programs. The election shall be made in writing and filed with the Arizona state retirement system and the disbursing officer of the employing institution on or before December 14, 1974, shall become effective as of January 1, 1975 and shall constitute a waiver of all benefits provided by the Arizona state retirement system, except all such benefits as are expressly provided by law.

3. Any employee who becomes eligible may elect an optional retirement program. The election shall be made in writing and filed with the Arizona state retirement system and the disbursing officer of the employing institution within thirty days after notice in writing to the employee of the employee's eligibility, and shall become effective on the first day of the pay period following such election, and shall constitute a waiver of all benefits provided by the Arizona state retirement system, except all such benefits as are expressly provided by law.

4. Any eligible employee who is a member of the Arizona state retirement system at the time the employee elects to participate in the optional retirement program shall leave the funds in the employee's retirement account on deposit with the Arizona state retirement system during the continuance of employment. Additional contributions to the employee's retirement account shall not be required and continued service with the Arizona board of regents or an institution under the jurisdiction of the Arizona board of regents while under an optional retirement program shall be deemed to be member service in the Arizona state retirement system for the purpose of determining eligibility for any benefits under such system. The amount of any such benefits under such system shall be computed only on the basis of service otherwise creditable to a member of the system and the employee's compensation during such service. For purposes of subsection D of this section, years of member service in the Arizona state retirement system shall count as years of service under the optional retirement programs.

C. The Arizona board of regents shall contribute public funds appropriated or any other funds available for such purpose on behalf of each participant in the optional retirement programs in an amount equal to seven per cent of the participant's compensation. Each participant shall also contribute an amount equal to seven per cent of the participant's compensation. The appropriation to each university for purposes of enabling the Arizona board of regents to make the contribution provided in this subsection shall not exceed the employer contribution required under the Arizona state retirement system as prescribed by title 38, chapter 5, article 2.[1] Funds utilized by the board of regents or by a university to pay that portion of the contribution that represents the difference between the employer contribution as prescribed by title 38, chapter 5, article 2 and the contribution rate provided in this subsection for an optional retirement program do not constitute a use of appropriated monies for supplemental retirement.

D. In the case of an electing employee initially appointed on or after August 9, 1974, contributions pursuant to subsection C of this section shall not be made by the Arizona board of regents until the employee's completion of five years of service. Employee contributions required during this initial five year period and during continued service with an institution under the jurisdiction of the Arizona board of regents shall be promptly remitted to the optional retirement programs approved by the Arizona board of regents. At the end of an electing employee's completion of five years of service, a single contribution in an amount determined pursuant to subsection C of this section, with interest, shall be made by the chief financial officer of the employing institution to the approved company or companies on behalf of such employee. In the case of an electing employee who does not continue in service with an institution under the jurisdiction of the Arizona board of regents for at least five years, the amount of employer contributions, with interest, shall be refunded to this state.

E. If an employee's service is terminated by death prior to the completion of five years of service, a death benefit equal to the sums appropriated for such employee, plus interest, shall be paid to the beneficiary designated by the participant under the participant's optional retirement program.

F. The provisions of subsection D of this section shall not apply to any electing employee who, at the time of initial appointment, owns a contract determined by the Arizona board of regents to be acceptable for use in the optional retirement program.

G. The Arizona board of regents may provide for the administration of such optional retirement programs and perform or authorize the performance of such functions as may be necessary for such purposes. The Arizona board of regents shall approve the company or companies from which benefits may be purchased under the optional retirement programs. Such optional retirement programs shall not permit loans. In giving its approval, the board shall consider:

1. The nature and extent of the rights and benefits to be provided for participants and their beneficiaries.

2. The relation of such rights and benefits to the amount of contributions to be made.

3. The suitability of such rights and benefits to the needs of the participants and the interests of the institutions under its jurisdiction in the recruitment and retention of faculty and administrative officers.

4. The ability of the approved company or companies to provide such suitable rights and benefits.

H. Any eligible employee initially appointed after August 9, 1974, electing to participate in the optional retirement programs, shall be ineligible for membership in the Arizona state retirement system as long as the employee remains continuously employed in any position by the Arizona board of regents or by an institution under its jurisdiction, except as expressly provided by law.

I. The benefits, annuities and employee and employer contributions provided for in this section, and all interest, earnings and other credits pertaining to such benefits, annuities and contributions, shall not be subject to execution or attachment and shall be nonassignable. The employee and employer contributions provided for in this section and all interest, earnings and other credits pertaining to such contributions are exempt from state, county and municipal taxes. The benefits and annuities received by an employee under this section after December 31, 1988 are subject to tax pursuant to title 43.[2]

J. Subject to amendment of the federal-state agreement provided for in § 38-702, every eligible employee electing to participate in the optional retirement programs shall have old age, survivors and disability insurance coverage provided by the federal social security act in accordance with the provisions of title 38, chapter 5, article 1.[3]

Added by Laws 1981, Ch. 1, § 2, eff. Jan. 23, 1981. Amended by Laws 1984, Ch. 398, § 1, eff. May 16, 1984; Laws 1989, Ch. 312, § 4; Laws 1995, Ch. 32, § 8, eff. March 30, 1995; Laws 2001, Ch. 380, § 2.

[1] Section 38-711 et seq.

[2] Section 43-101 et seq.

[3] Section 38-701 et seq.

Historical and Statutory Notes

Source:

Laws 1974, Ch. 125, § 4.
A.R.S. former § 15-725.02.

Laws 1987, Ch. 319, § 1, subsec. B, provides:

"**Section 1. Retirement contribution rate; reduction of appropriations; state aid to schools; reversion; adjustment for appropriations report**"

"**B.** Notwithstanding § 15-1628, Arizona Revised Statutes, the amount appropriated for fiscal year 1987-1988 to each university for contribution to optional retirement programs under the jurisdiction of the Arizona board of regents shall be reduced by subtracting an amount equivalent to one and sixteen hundredths per cent of the compensation of employees participating in optional retirement programs from the amount appropriated for contribution to optional retirement programs, all of which shall be reflected in the general fund appropriation."

Laws 1989, Ch. 312, § 25, subsec. A provides:

"**Sec. 25. Retroactivity**

"**A.** Sections 4, 6, 7, 8, 9, 10, 12, 13, 14, 15 and 16 of this act apply retroactively to taxable years beginning from and after December 31, 1988."

Laws 1990, Ch. 235, § 6, effective September 1, 1990, provides:

"**Sec. 6. Eligibility**

"**A.** Any member of the Arizona state retirement system and their covered dependents who are receiving long-term liability benefits from a program established prior to July 1, 1988, by a participating employer member of the plan are eligible for coverage pursuant to § 2 of this act.

"**B.** Any member of the public safety personnel retirement system, the elected officials' retirement plan, the corrections officer retirement plan or the optional retirement programs authorized pursuant to § 15-1628 who is receiving group health and accident insurance provided by the department of administration for active state employees on the effective date of this act is eligible to continue with such coverage."

§ 15-1629. Annual report

Within ninety days after the close of each fiscal year the Arizona board of regents shall make a report for the fiscal year to the governor. The report shall set forth the state of progress of the universities in their several colleges, schools and departments, the courses of study included in their curricula, the number of professors, other instructional faculty and staff members employed, the number of students registered and attending classes, the amount of receipts and expenditures and such other information as the board deems proper.

Added by Laws 1981, Ch. 1, § 2, eff. Jan. 23, 1981. Amended by Laws 1982, Ch. 229, § 6.

Historical and Statutory Notes

Source:

Civ.Code 1901, §§ 3638, 3690.
Laws 1913, 3rd S.S., Ch. 46, § 18.
Civ.Code 1913, §§ 4483, 4523.
Laws 1915, Ch. 17, § 3.
Laws 1925, Ch. 55, § 7.
Rev.Code 1928, §§ 1114, 1138.
Laws 1945, Ch. 80, § 7.
Code 1939, § 54–1609.
Code 1939, Supp.1952, § 54–1315.
A.R.S. former § 15–727.

§ 15–1630. Abortion at educational facility prohibited; exception

No abortion shall be performed at any facility under the jurisdiction of the Arizona board of regents unless such abortion is necessary to save the life of the woman having the abortion.

Added by Laws 1981, Ch. 1, § 2, eff. Jan. 23, 1981.

Historical and Statutory Notes

Source:

Laws 1974, Ch. 171, § 15.
A.R.S. former § 15–730.

§ 15–1631. State museum

A. There shall be a state museum for the collection and preservation of the archaeological resources, specimens of the mineral wealth and the flora and fauna of this state.

B. The Arizona board of regents shall direct and manage the museum and shall set apart sufficient space to accommodate it.

Added by Laws 1981, Ch. 1, § 2, eff. Jan. 23, 1981.

Historical and Statutory Notes

Source:

Civ.Code 1901, §§ 3642 to 3644.
Civ.Code 1913, §§ 4487 to 4489.
Rev.Code 1928, § 1145.
Code 1939, § 54–1616.
A.R.S. former § 15–705.

§ 15–1632. University property of expelled students; classification

A. A student who is expelled by a university shall surrender all university property. The university shall refund the deposit for any property to the student.

B. An expelled student who fails or refuses to return university property is guilty of a petty offense.

Added by Laws 1981, Ch. 1, § 2, eff. Jan. 23, 1981. Amended by Laws 1982, Ch. 229, § 7.

Historical and Statutory Notes

Source:

Civ.Code 1901, §§ 3649 to 3651.
Civ.Code 1913, §§ 4498 to 4500.
Rev.Code 1928, § 1153.
Code 1939, § 54–1618.
A.R.S. former § 15–728.
Laws 1978, Ch. 201, § 257.

The 1982 amendment rewrote this section, which had read:

"A. A student of the university who is expelled by the faculty or the Arizona board of regents shall surrender his cadet uniform. The board shall pay from the university of Arizona fund not otherwise appropriated the cost price of the uniform to the parent or guardian of the student.

"B. An expelled student who wears a cadet uniform in a public place is guilty of a petty offense."

§ 15-1633. Repealed by Laws 1984, Ch. 251, § 8, eff. Jan. 1, 1985

Historical and Statutory Notes

The repealed section, added by Laws 1982, Ch. 128, § 1, related to bidding, contracting and purchasing procedures for institutions under the jurisdiction of the Board of Regents. See, now, § 41-2533.

§ 15-1634. Intergovernmental agreements; special assessments

A. Pursuant to § 48-582 or 48-920 or in conjunction with any street improvement made pursuant to any other statute, the board on behalf of this state or any university may enter into and shall be bound by intergovernmental agreements with one or more cities, counties or improvement districts for the purpose of improving streets adjacent to or running through university property by the construction of any or all of the improvements authorized in either title 48, chapter 4, articles 1 and 2 or title 48, chapter 6, article 1.[1]

B. The agreement may provide that assessments may be levied against university property to secure repayment of the cost of the improvements. So long as this state or the board owns the land so assessed the assessment liens may not be enforced by sale or foreclosure. The agreement may also provide that the university's share of any incidental cost may be paid by the board from any available fund of that university. The board shall pay or cause to be paid the installments of principal and interest coming due on the assessments and may pledge for the payment thereof any monies of the respective university which do not cause the agreement or assessment to become a debt of this state under, or contrary to, any constitutional provision and which do not violate any contract rights of any other person to be paid from the same source. The agreement shall provide that the payments due under the agreement include any penalties and additional interest that the owner of property subject to assessment would be required to pay on the delinquency of an installment of principal or interest.

C. In the agreement the board may waive any formal requirement, notice or prerequisite to levying an assessment.

D. If the board leases, long-term leases or sells any parcel subject to an assessment, the board shall require that the lessee's or purchaser's initial payment be in an amount at least sufficient to reimburse the board for the parcel's allocative share of the monies previously expended to pay the assessment. The board shall return such amount to be reimbursed to the source of the monies under subsection B of this section.

E. Upon the sale of any parcel subject to an assessment, the lien of the assessment may be enforced by foreclosure and sale in the manner set forth in the respective statute authorizing the levying of the assessment.

Added by Laws 1983, Ch. 284, § 6, eff. April 27, 1983. Amended by Laws 1984, Ch. 349, § 19; Laws 1985, Ch. 190, § 33.

[1] Sections 48-501 et seq., 48-571 et seq., and 48-901 et seq.

§ 15-1635. University research development purposes; product development; corporations

Text of section pending conditional enactment

A. In order to stimulate the flow of capital into the development of specific products which have advanced beyond the theoretical stage and are capable of being reduced to practice on a commercial scale, the board may by resolution organize one or more corporations under the provisions of title 10.[1] At least one-half of any voting shares of each such corporation shall be held by the board, or a majority of the directors, trustees or members of the corporation shall be designated or appointed by the board. No member or employee of the board may receive any direct or indirect compensation, other than reimbursement for actual expenses incurred in the performance of his duties, by reason of serving as a member, director or trustee of a corporation organized under this section.

B. No such corporation may be organized unless the board finds in its organizational resolution that its formation will stimulate and encourage the development of new products within this state in situations in which financial aid would not otherwise be reasonably available from conventional lending sources. In addition to the powers each corporation may have, each corporation may:

1. Enter into product development agreements with persons doing business in this state, on such terms and conditions as are consistent with the research development purposes of the board, to advance financial aid to such persons for the development of specific products, procedures and techniques to be developed and produced in this state and to condition such agreements on contractual assurances that the benefits of increasing or maintaining employment and tax revenues shall remain in this state and accrue to it.

2. Acquire, lease, purchase, manage, hold and dispose of real and personal property in this state and lease, convey or deal in or enter into contracts with respect to such property on any terms necessary or incidental to carrying out these research and development purposes.

3. Hold patents, copyrights, trademarks or any other evidences of protection or exclusivity as to any products issued under the laws of the United States or any state or nation.

C. Before organizing such a corporation, the board shall develop a procedure for applications for financial aid to be forwarded, together with an application fee prescribed by the board, to the board. The board shall investigate and prepare a report concerning the advisability of approving the proposed financial aid for such person and concerning any other factors deemed relevant. The investigation and report shall include such facts about the person under consideration as his history, wage standards, job opportunities, stability of employment, past and present financial condition and structure, pro forma income statements, present and future markets and prospects and integrity of management as well as the feasibility of the proposed project to be granted financial aid, including the state of development of the product as well as the likelihood of its commercial feasibility. After receipt and consideration of the report and after other action as is deemed appropriate, the board shall approve or deny the application. The board shall promptly notify the applicant of such action. Approval shall be conditioned on payment to the board, within such reasonable time after notification of approval as the board may specify, of a commitment fee prescribed by the board.

D. The board may receive and accept aid or contributions of monies from any source, including gifts or grants from private sources or from any department or agency of the United States or this state, for the purposes of carrying out the provisions of this section.

E. The board may also enter into research and development agreements, royalty agreements, development agreements, licensing agreements and profit sharing agreements concerning the research, development, production, storing or marketing of new products developed or to be developed through university research.

Added by Laws 1983, Ch. 284, § 6, eff. April 27, 1983. Amended by Laws 1984, Ch. 349, § 20; Laws 1990, Ch. 348, § 22, eff. June 26, 1990.

[1] Section 10–002 et seq.

For text of conditional enactment, see § 15–1635, post

Conditional Repeal

This section is conditionally repealed by Laws 2003, Ch. 257, § 2, if the Constitution of Arizona is amended by a vote of the people at the next general election. See note, post.

Historical and Statutory Notes

Laws 2003, Ch. 257, § 4, provides:

"**Sec. 4. Conditional enactment**

"**A.** This act is not effective unless the Constitution of Arizona is amended by vote of the people at the next general election to authorize the Arizona board of regents and state universities to acquire, hold, pledge and dispose of securities.

"**B.** The enactment of any provision of this act, conditioned on the results of an election, does not constitute a submission of those provisions to the voters under the power of the referendum."

§ 15–1635. Ownership of business interest in exchange for technology or intellectual property; annual report; definitions

Text of conditional enactment

A. In its capacity as a corporate body, the board by resolution may acquire an ownership interest, in the form of securities, in a business enterprise as all or part of the consideration for the license or other disposition of any interest in technology or intellectual property created or acquired, in whole or in part, or managed by the board. The board may also enter into research and development agreements, royalty agreements, development agreements, licensing agreements, joint venture agreements and profit sharing agreements concerning the research, development, production, storing or marketing of new products or services developed or to be developed based in whole or in part on university research, technology or intellectual property.

B. The board shall not contribute money or other property to the issuer of the securities under subsection A, except for the assigned or licensed technology or intellectual property. A member of the board shall not receive any direct or indirect compensation for serving as a member, director or trustee of any such issuer of securities, other than reimbursement for actual expenses incurred in performing the member's duties. This state, the board and institutions under the board's jurisdiction are not liable for any debt or other obligation of any company, corporation or individual due to ownership of securities pursuant to this section, whether in tort, contract or otherwise.

C. The board may acquire, hold, pledge and dispose of securities described in subsection A for the benefit of one or more of the state universities. Securities the board acquires under this section shall be treated as endowment assets subject to title 10, chapter 41. [1]

D. The board may designate one or more technology development companies to acquire, hold, pledge and dispose of the securities on behalf of the board or universities. The board may assign or license, in whole or in part, its interest in technology or intellectual property, or the board may assign, in whole or in part, its interest in securities acquired pursuant to this section, to any technology development company, in consideration of the assignee's or licensee's undertaking to develop or to cause to be developed the technology or intellectual property for the benefit of the board or university. The technology development company may hold the technology, intellectual property or securities directly or through subsidiary entities that are directly or indirectly wholly owned by the technology development company. Any technology development company or wholly owned subsidiary entity is not considered to be an agency or instrumentality of this state.

E. An issuer of securities acquired by the board pursuant to subsection A, whether held by the board or by another entity pursuant to subsection D, shall provide the board with all information that a corporation is required to furnish to shareholders pursuant to title 10, chapter 16, article 2. The board may inspect the records of the issuer of securities as provided by title 10, chapter 16, article 1. [2]

F. This section does not cause an issuer of securities described in subsection A or a technology development company or other entity described in subsection D to be:

1. Considered an agency or instrumentality of this state.

2. Subject to the public records, public meetings or public finance laws of this state, except for information received by the board pursuant to subsection E.

G. For the purposes of carrying out this section, the board may receive and accept aid or contributions of monies from any source, including gifts or grants from private sources or from any department or agency of the United States or this state.

H. On or before March 1 of each year, the board shall issue a public report of its activities under this section during the preceding calendar year. The board shall submit a copy of the report to the governor, the president of the senate and the speaker of the house of representatives and shall provide a copy of this report to the secretary of state, the director of the Arizona state library, archives and public records and any other person who requests a copy. The report shall include information, by university, relating to:

1. The business enterprises in which the board receives an ownership interest.

2. Technology, intellectual property and other products transferred to the business enterprises.

3. Agreements relating to the research, development, production, storing or marketing of new products or services developed based on university research, technology or intellectual property.

4. Revenues produced from activities under this section.

I. For the purposes of this section:

1. "Securities" means corporate stock or other equity securities, debentures, warrants, options or other contractual rights that may be converted into options, debt securities, limited partnership interests, membership interests in a limited liability company, beneficial interests in trusts, joint venture interests and any other interests, however denominated, in any form of firm or company if holding the security does not cause this state or the board to be personally liable for the obligations of the issuer of the security.

2. "Technology development company" means a nonprofit corporation, a foundation, a trust, a fund, a for-profit corporation or a limited liability company whose sole and direct or indirect beneficiary, stockholder or member, as applicable, is the board or one or more of the state universities.

Added by Laws 2003, Ch. 257, § 3.

[1] Section 10–11801 et seq.

[2] Section 10–1601 et seq.

For text of section pending conditional enactment, see § 15–1635, ante

Historical and Statutory Notes

Laws 2003, Ch. 257, § 1, provides:

"**Section 1. Intent**

"The legislature intends to facilitate technology transfer by the Arizona board of regents and the state universities and that it be carried out according to policies established by the board for the following purposes:

"1. To transfer university technology to the private sector to enable the public to benefit from its use.

"2. To obtain an appropriate return on university technology.

"3. To induce closer ties with the private sector.

"4. To contribute to economic development.

"5. To recruit, retain and reward faculty, other researchers and other inventors.

"6. To provide students with opportunities to participate in the process of using university technology to benefit the public.

"7. To accomplish other purposes that the board determines to be appropriate."

Laws 2003, Ch. 257, § 4, provides:

"**Sec. 4. Conditional enactment**

"**A.** This act is not effective unless the Constitution of Arizona is amended by vote of the people at the next general election to authorize the Arizona board of regents and state universities to acquire, hold, pledge and dispose of securities.

"**B.** The enactment of any provision of this act, conditioned on the results of an election, does not constitute a submission of those provisions to the voters under the power of the referendum."

Reviser's Notes:

2003 Note. Pursuant to authority of § 41–1304.02, in subsection I, paragraph 2 the spelling of "universities" was corrected.

§ 15-1635.01. Transfer of technology developed by universities; patent policies; officer or employee interest in private entity

A. To encourage sponsored research at institutions under the jurisdiction of the Arizona board of regents and to encourage transfer of such technology to the private sector, the Arizona board of regents shall consider the establishment of patent policies which permit, on a case by case negotiated basis, either the giving of title or the granting of licenses to the sponsor of the research.

B. Notwithstanding title 38, chapter 3, article 8,[1] an officer or employee of an institution under the jurisdiction of the Arizona board of regents may, subject to subsection C, apply to the board for permission to establish and maintain a substantial interest in a private entity which supplies equipment, material, supplies or services to the institution in order to facilitate the transfer of technology developed by the officer or employee of an institution under the jurisdiction of the board from the institution to commercial and industrial enterprises for the economic development of this state.

C. Before an officer or employee makes an application to the board pursuant to subsection B, the officer or employee must receive the approval of the president of the institution at which he is employed. The president of the institution may grant approval and the officer or employee may submit the application to the board only if all of the following conditions are met:

1. The officer or employee provides a detailed description of his interest in the private entity to the president.

2. The nature of the private entity's proposed undertaking is fully described to the president.

3. The officer or employee demonstrates to the satisfaction of the president that the proposed undertaking will benefit the economy of this state by contributing to the development of private enterprise.

4. The proposed undertaking does not violate any existing contracts.

5. The officer or employee demonstrates to the satisfaction of the president that the proposed undertaking will not adversely affect research, public service or instructional activities at the institution.

6. The officer's or employee's interest in the private entity or benefit from the interest will not adversely affect any state interest.

D. The board may authorize an officer or employee of one of the institutions under its jurisdiction to establish and maintain a substantial interest in a private entity if all of the following conditions are met:

1. The application is approved by the president of the institution at which the officer or employee is employed.

2. The application contains a detailed description of the officer's or employee's interest in the private entity.

3. The application contains a detailed description of the private entity's proposed undertaking.

4. The application demonstrates to the satisfaction of the board that the proposed undertaking will benefit the economy of this state by contributing to the development of private enterprise.

5. The proposed undertaking does not violate any existing contracts.

6. The application demonstrates to the satisfaction of the board that the proposed undertaking will not adversely affect research, public service or instructional activities at the institutions under the jurisdiction of the board.

7. The officer's or employee's interest in the private entity or benefit from the interest will not adversely affect any state interest.

E. On recommendation of the board, the president of the institution at which the officer or employee is employed may require that the institution have a share in any royalties or other proceeds from the proposed undertaking of the private entity.

F. If the technology was developed solely using monies from a private sector sponsor, the board shall not authorize an officer or employee of an institution under its jurisdiction to establish and maintain a substantial interest in a private entity which would exploit that technology unless the board determines that patent, licensing and royalty rights are in accordance with the provisions of the agreement under which the technology was developed.

G. The board may establish policies for the implementation of this section.

Added as § 41-1509 by Laws 1986, Ch. 240, § 2. Renumbered as § 15-1635.01.

[1] Section 38-501 et seq.

Historical and Statutory Notes

Laws 1986, Ch. 240, § 1 provides:

"**Section 1. Legislative intent**

"It is the intent of the legislature to foster a partnership between the public and private sectors in this state by further encouraging the exchange of technological expertise and other valuable information between private enterprise and this state's university system. Such a strengthened partnership is an extension of one of the founding intentions for the university system and remains essential due to the external challenges posed by rapid technological advancements and economic growth. The legislature recognizes that the greatest public good will result from the hand in hand cooperation of the public and private sectors as the economic and social benefits to be derived from such an effort are virtually unlimited for the further economic development of this state. Therefore, the legislature further recognizes that private enterprise should share with and act as a partner with the universities in studies, research and development, and it is the purpose of this act to promote such a partnership for the greater well-being of the residents of this state and the nation."

Reviser's Notes:

1986 Note. Pursuant to authority of § 41-1304.02, this section, added by Laws 1986, Ch. 240, § 2 as § 41-1509, was renumbered as § 15-1635.01.

§ 15-1636. Lease of real property and improvements in research park; prohibited and permitted uses

A. The board shall not lease real property located in an area designated as a research park pursuant to § 35-701, paragraph 10 unless the lease contains a covenant that prohibits unlimited manufacturing on the site and allows the board to enforce the covenant by appropriate means, which may include termination of the lease.

B. The board may take title to and lease improvements constructed on land located in an area defined as a research park pursuant to § 35-701, paragraph

10, if the lease contains a covenant that restricts the use of the subject property to the uses permitted under this section. The lease shall allow the board to enforce the covenant by appropriate means, including termination of the lease. The board may lease unimproved lots or parcels located in an area designated as a research park pursuant to § 35-701, paragraph 10, for any use by a lessee.

C. The requirements of subsection B of this section do not apply to improvements constructed before the effective date of subsection B of this section or to a lease entered into between the board and a lessee, subsidiary, successor, sublessee or assignee of a lessee, who originally entered into any lease with the board before July 31, 1996.

D. The subject property may be used only for the following purposes:

1. Laboratories, offices and other facilities for testing, consulting and information processing, related to research and development.

2. Production, assembly or sale of products pursuant to research and development activities.

3. Pilot plants in which processes planned for use in production elsewhere can be tested and assembled.

4. Regional or national headquarters of the lessee or its subsidiaries that are engaged in research and development or education activities.

5. Education and training facilities.

6. Operations required to maintain or support any permitted use, including maintenance shops, power plants, wastewater treatment facilities, the keeping of animals, machine shops, common area improvements and facilities and professional and commercial services supporting permitted uses, such as child development centers, food services and post office and mailing centers.

Added by Laws 1983, Ch. 284, § 6, eff. April 27, 1983. Amended by Laws 1984, Ch. 236, § 3; Laws 1986, Ch. 281, § 4, eff. May 2, 1986; Laws 1996, Ch. 349, § 3.

Historical and Statutory Notes

Reviser's Notes:

1996 Note. Pursuant to authority of § 41-1304.02, in subsection D, paragraph 6 "waste water" was combined as one word.

§ 15-1637. Lease of property for health care institution; requirements; conditions; reports; directors, members and officers of nonprofit corporation; definition

A. The Arizona board of regents may lease real property, improvements or personal property owned by the board to a nonprofit corporation as lessee for purposes of operating a health care institution as defined in § 36-401. If the board leases such property for such purposes, whether title to improvements on the property rests in the board or in the lessee, the lease agreement and any amendments, renewals or extensions of the agreement shall be deemed binding and effective according to its terms. If, under the provisions of the lease, improvements or personal property related to the operation of a health care institution are conveyed to the nonprofit corporation, they shall be presumed to have been conveyed for their then fair market value.

B. Any lease agreement entered into pursuant to subsection A of this section may, at the discretion of the Arizona board of regents, contain provisions requiring the nonprofit corporation to acquire the approval of the Arizona board of regents prior to entering into any business transactions that may adversely affect the interests of this state or that are contained in subsection G, paragraph 2 of this section. The Arizona board of regents shall specify in the lease agreement the type and nature of such transactions which require prior approval of the board.

C. To satisfy the requirements of § 103 of the internal revenue code,[1] as defined in § 43-105, any nonprofit corporation which is a lessee as described in subsection A of this section is declared to be:

1. A validly organized and existing body politic and corporate exercising its powers for the benefit of the people, to improve their health and welfare and to increase their prosperity.

2. Engaged in a purpose essential to public health care.

3. Performing an essential governmental function.

D. Any nonprofit corporation which is a lessee as described in subsection A of this section is exempt from property taxation by this state or any agency or subdivision of this state and possesses and may exercise only those powers of the Arizona board of regents which are delegated to the nonprofit corporation by the Arizona board of regents and which are necessary to satisfy the requirements of § 103 of the internal revenue code, as defined in § 43-105, as specified in the terms, conditions, restrictions and agreements of the lease agreement. These powers are in addition to all those powers granted to a nonprofit corporation by title 10, chapters 24 through 40.[2]

E. Any nonprofit corporation which is a lessee as described in subsection A of this section may issue bonds and incur obligations and pledge its revenues as security for the payment of the bonds or other obligations for health care institutional purposes to the extent provided by the lease agreement or amendments, renewals or extensions of the agreement. Nothing in this section shall be construed to authorize the incurrence of a debt by the state within the meaning of any constitutional restriction on debt.

F. Except as provided in subsection G of this section, any nonprofit corporation which is a lessee as described in subsection A of this section may acquire by purchase, lease or otherwise, and may operate, other health care institutions and real and personal property for purposes of providing products and services related to the operation of health care institutions owned, leased or operated by it. Such acquisition or operation does not affect the powers, rights, privileges or immunities conferred on such nonprofit corporation by this section.

G. No nonprofit corporation which is a lessee as described in subsection A of this section shall:

1. Until September 1, 1986 enter into any agreement with a county or a nonprofit corporation to which property is conveyed pursuant to § 11-256.03, subsection A if the agreement provides for the conveyance of any ownership interest whatever in the nonprofit corporation to which property is conveyed pursuant to § 11-256.03, subsection A or in the property described in § 11-

256.03, subsection A. After August 31, 1986 any such agreement must be approved by the Arizona board of regents and the legislature. This subsection does not prevent the grant of an option to purchase such property, provided that the option may not be exercised before September 1, 1986 and the exercise of the option must be approved by the Arizona board of regents and the legislature. Under no circumstances shall any state general fund monies be used to acquire any interest in such property.

2. Own, lease, manage or operate any other health care institution or other real or personal property unless such acquisition, management or operation either:

(a) Relates to and furthers the educational or research purposes and goals of the university of Arizona hospital.

(b) Promotes the efficient and economical operation of the university of Arizona hospital or any other health care institution acquired pursuant to paragraph 1 of this subsection.

H. A nonprofit corporation which is a lessee as described in subsection A of this section may manage and operate property described in § 11–256.03, subsection A subject to the restrictions of subsection G of this section. Any management or operation agreement shall provide that the nonprofit corporation which is a lessee as described in subsection A of this section shall not be liable for any bonds or other obligation of any kind relating to the ownership or operation of the property described in § 11–256.03, subsection A incurred before the property is conveyed to such nonprofit corporation in accordance with subsection G of this section.

I. A health care institution which is the subject of a lease agreement as described in subsection A of this section is subject to § 15–1630.

J. A nonprofit corporation which is a lessee as described in subsection A of this section shall make semiannual progress reports as to its financial status and deliver them on January 1 and July 1 of each year to the Arizona board of regents, the president of the senate, the speaker of the house of representatives and the governor. The nonprofit corporation shall present an independently audited financial statement to the auditor general within ninety days of the close of the previous fiscal year. The auditor general shall review such statements and transmit them together with a report to officers entitled to receive progress reports by this subsection.

K. Any nonprofit corporation which is a lessee as described in subsection A of this section shall:

1. Be organized as a nonprofit corporation pursuant to title 10, chapters 24 through 40 only upon the approval of the Arizona board of regents.

2. Be governed by a board of directors, the members of which are appointed by the Arizona board of regents, provided that no more than forty-nine per cent of the members of such board of directors of the nonprofit corporation shall be officers or employees of this state and of such forty-nine per cent only two members of such board of directors may be members of the Arizona board of regents. Members of the Arizona board of regents who are appointed to the board of directors of such nonprofit corporation shall be residents of different

counties unless all members of the board of regents are residents of the same county.

3. Be organized under articles of incorporation or bylaws approved by the Arizona board of regents which shall provide among other things that:

(a) No earnings of the nonprofit corporation shall inure to the benefit of or be distributable to its members, directors, officers or other individuals, except that the nonprofit corporation shall be authorized to pay reasonable compensation for services rendered to it by individuals other than members of the board of directors of the nonprofit corporation acting solely in such capacity, to reimburse expenses in connection with services rendered to or expenses incurred on behalf of the nonprofit corporation and to make payments and distributions in furtherance of the purposes of the nonprofit corporation.

(b) Upon the dissolution or liquidation of the nonprofit corporation, the board of directors of the nonprofit corporation shall, after paying or making provision for the payment of all of the liabilities of the nonprofit corporation, distribute all of the assets of the nonprofit corporation to the Arizona board of regents or its successor.

(c) Neither the articles of incorporation nor the bylaws of the nonprofit corporation shall be amended without the approval of the Arizona board of regents.

(d) The board of directors of the nonprofit corporation may adopt nondiscriminatory rules and regulations providing for the use of the university of Arizona hospital by, and staff privileges for, any persons licensed under title 32, chapter 7, 13 or 17[3] whether or not such persons have a faculty teaching appointment with the school of medicine, providing, however, that such rules and regulations shall contain requirements sufficient to protect the educational and research purposes and goals of the university of Arizona hospital.

L. No member of the Arizona board of regents who is also a member or director of a nonprofit corporation which is a lessee as described in subsection A of this section shall as a regent vote upon any matter pertaining to such a corporation as may come before the Arizona board of regents.

M. For the purposes of this section "nonprofit corporation" means a corporation as defined in § 10–3140.

Added by Laws 1984, Ch. 316, § 2. Amended by Laws 1985, Ch. 269, § 1; Laws 1987, Ch. 243, § 1; Laws 1990, Ch. 57, § 4; Laws 1994, Ch. 41, § 4; Laws 1995, Ch. 241, § 7, eff. Jan. 1, 1996; Laws 1999, Ch. 297, § 26, eff. May 18, 1999.

[1] Internal Revenue Code sections may be found in Title 26 of U.S.C.A.

[2] Sections 10–3101 et seq. through 10–11701 et seq.

[3] Sections 32–801 et seq., 32–1401 et seq., 32–1800 et seq.

Historical and Statutory Notes

The 1995 amendment of this section by Ch. 241, § 7, explicitly amended the 1994 amendment of this section by Ch. 41, § 4.

The amendment of this section by Laws 1994, Ch. 223, § 85, eff. Jan. 1, 1996, was repealed by Laws 1995, Ch. 241, § 8, eff. Jan. 1, 1996.

Laws 1995, Ch. 241, § 1, par. 4, provides:

"**Section 1. Purpose**"

"4. Section 15–1637, Arizona Revised Statutes, was amended by Laws 1994, chapter 41, § 4 and Laws 1994, chapter 223, § 85. These two versions could not be blended because of the delayed effective date of the chapter 223 version. In order to combine these versions, this act amends the Laws 1994, chapter 41 version of § 15-1637, Arizona Revised Statutes, to incorporate the amendments made by Laws 1994, chapter 223 and the chapter 223 version is repealed."

Laws 1995, Ch. 241, § 61, subsec. B, provides:

"**Sec. 61. Delayed effective date**"

"B. Sections 2, 7, 10, 14, 16 and 47 of this act are effective on January 1, 1996."

Reviser's Notes:

1984 Note. Pursuant to authority of § 41-1304.02, "Lease of property for health care institution to nonprofit corporation; powers and duties of board and lessee; reports" was substituted for the previous section heading [section heading was subsequently amended in 1985]. In subsection G, paragraph 1, in two places the word "Arizona" before "state legislature" was transposed before "board of regents".

1994 Note. The independent and valid amendment of this section by Laws 1994, Ch. 41, sec. 4 and Ch. 223, sec. 85 could not be blended because of the delayed effective date of Ch. 223.

§ 15-1638. Disclosure of records and other matters; exception; definition

A. A nonprofit corporation that is a lessee pursuant to § 15-1637, subsection A shall disclose and make available records and other matters in the same manner as is required of a public body pursuant to title 39, chapter 1,[1] except that the nonprofit corporation is not required to disclose or make available any records or other matters that:

1. Identify the care or treatment of an individual patient who receives services provided by the nonprofit corporation, including billings, unless the patient or patient's representative consents in writing to the disclosure.

2. Reveal proprietary information provided to the nonprofit corporation by a nongovernmental source.

3. Would cause demonstrable and material harm to the nonprofit corporation and that would place it at a competitive disadvantage in the marketplace.

4. Would violate an exception, privilege or confidentiality granted or imposed by statute or common law.

B. The provisions of this section do not apply to reports of statistical and demographic data required by § 36-125.05.

C. In this section, "nongovernmental" means an entity other than the federal government, an agency or instrumentality of the federal government or a public body as defined in § 39-121.01.

Added by Laws 1988, Ch. 224, § 1.

[1] Section 39-101 et seq.

Historical and Statutory Notes

Reviser's Notes:

1988 Note. Laws 1988, Ch. 305, sec. 1 and Ch. 343, sec. 1 added another new § 15-1638 which were renumbered as §§ 15-1639 and 15-1641, respectively, pursuant to authority of § 41-1304.02. Additionally, subsection B was relettered as subsection C and the following subsection was relettered accordingly and in the section heading; "definition" was transposed to follow "exception".

§ 15-1639. University recruitment and retention program for economically disadvantaged, minority and underrepresented student populations

A. The three universities under the jurisdiction of the board of regents shall each establish a comprehensive plan to initiate new programs and expand existing student recruitment and retention programs directed at economically disadvantaged, minority and underrepresented student populations. The plan shall incorporate at least the following:

1. Programs which are directed at Arizona resident students and which include outreach programs established to work with potential students at the high school level.

2. A program overview which illustrates the coordination between existing and new recruitment and retention programs.

3. Methods for the evaluation of program impact and the establishment of target goals for success. The results of these evaluations shall be reported to the board of regents utilizing a standard format distributed by the board.

B. Monies appropriated for this program shall not be used to support remedial course work.

C. Students admitted to the universities must meet the admission criteria established by the board of regents.

Added as § 15-1638 by Laws 1988, Ch. 305, § 1. Renumbered as § 15-1639.

Historical and Statutory Notes

Reviser's Notes:

1988 Note. Pursuant to authority of § 41-1304.02, this section, added by Laws 1988, Ch. 305, sec. 1 as § 15-1638, was renumbered as § 15-1639. Additionally, subsection B was placed into temporary law under the heading "University comprehensive plans; submission" and subsections C and D were relettered as B and C. In relettered subsection B a space was added between the words "course" and "work" as a correction of a manifest clerical error.

§ 15-1640. Public records exemption; intellectual property; historical records; donor records

A. The following records of a university under the jurisdiction of the Arizona board of regents are exempt from the provisions of title 39, chapter 1, article 2: [1]

1. Intellectual property that is a trade secret as defined in § 44-401 and that is contained in any of the following:

(a) Unfunded grant applications or proposals.

(b) Proprietary data or research material provided to a university by a third party who has an expectation that the data or material will remain confidential. In order to qualify for the exemption prescribed in this subdivision, the intellectual property must be provided to the university pursuant to a contract executed between the third party and the university that meets all of the following requirements:

(i) The contract specifies that the intellectual property is being provided to the university and that there is a need for confidentiality.

(ii) The contract is approved before the contract becomes effective by an official of the university who is authorized to sign research contracts.

(iii) The contract includes the name or names of the third party, a general description of the research or other work that is the subject of the contract in a manner sufficient to provide the public with the information necessary to understand the nature of that research or other work and a statement that the intellectual property that is the subject of the contract will be conveyed by the third party to the university pursuant to the terms of the contract.

(iv) The contract will become a public document that is subject to title 39, chapter 1, article 2 when the contract is executed.

(c) Proprietary data or research material that is developed by persons employed by a university, if the disclosure of this data or material would be contrary to the best interests of this state.

2. Historical records and materials donated to a university by a private person or a private entity, if restricted access is a condition of the donation. The exemption provided by this paragraph shall expire no later than twenty years after the original donation.

3. All records concerning donors or potential donors to a university, other than the names of the donors and the description, date, amount and conditions of these donations.

B. Any exemption provided by this section shall no longer be applicable if the subject matter of the records becomes available to the general public.

Added by Laws 2001, Ch. 216, § 1.

[1] Section 39-121 et seq.

Historical and Statutory Notes

Former § 15-1640, added as § 15-1639 by Laws 1988, Ch. 305, § 2, renumbered as § 15-1640, amended by Laws 1996, Ch. 284, § 70, which provided for a teacher loan forgiveness program, was repealed by Laws 1988, Ch. §305, § 6, eff. July 1, 2000.

§ 15-1641. Collegiate special plate funds; purpose

A. The Arizona board of regents shall establish a separate collegiate special plate fund for each university, as described in section 15-1601, consisting of monies received by the board from collegiate plate annual donations pursuant to § 28-2412.

B. The board of regents shall require each university, as described in § 15-1601, to submit a plan for approval of the expenditure of monies in the appropriate fund. All monies in the fund shall only be used for academic scholarships. Each university shall annually report to the board of regents the percentage of monies that was expended on behalf of minority applicants.

C. The board of regents may delegate to a state university foundation approved by each university, as described in § 15-1601, the right to market and promote the purchase of collegiate special plates. No dues, fees or charges except those specified in § 28-2412 may be levied or collected by a state university foundation in connection with collegiate special plates.

D. The fund established in this section is exempt from section 35-190, relating to lapsing of appropriations. At the direction of the board the state treasurer may invest and divest inactive monies in the fund as provided by § 35-313. The state treasurer shall credit all interest earned on the fund monies to the fund.

Added as § 15-1638 by Laws 1988, Ch. 343, § 1, eff. Jan. 1, 1989. Renumbered as § 15-1641. Amended by Laws 1992, Ch. 208, § 2, eff. Jan. 1, 1993; Laws 1992, Ch. 349, § 2, eff. Jan. 1, 1993; Laws 1997, Ch. 1, § 35, eff. Oct. 1, 1997.

Historical and Statutory Notes

Laws 1988, Ch. 343, § 8 provides:

"Sections 1 through 4 of this act are effective from and after December 31, 1988."

The 1992 amendment of this section by Ch. 349, specifically amended the 1992 amendment of this section by Ch. 208.

Reviser's Notes:

1988 Note. Pursuant to authority of § 41-1304.02, this section, added by Laws 1988, Ch. 343, § 2 as § 15-1638, was renumbered as § 15-1641.

§ 15-1641.01. Renumbered as § 15-1646

§ 15-1642. Financial aid trust fund; aid to students with verifiable financial need; endowment

A. The Arizona board of regents may establish a financial aid trust fund for the purposes of providing immediate aid to students with verifiable financial need, including students who are underrepresented in the population of university students or who by virtue of their special circumstances present unique needs for financial aid, and creating an endowment for future financial aid. Subject to the limitations provided in subsection B, paragraph 3, the board may assess a surcharge upon registration fees paid by students for deposit in the fund.

B. The board shall adopt rules to govern the financial aid trust fund, including the following:

1. Fifty per cent of the monies received each year shall be placed in the trust fund as a permanent endowment. The remaining monies received shall be used for immediate aid for students with verifiable financial need. At least fifty per cent of the immediate aid monies shall be used for grant aid.

2. The immediate aid monies shall be distributed to the universities on a pro rata basis based on relative student contributions to the fund.

3. The surcharge on student registration shall not exceed one per cent of the registration fee for students taking more than six credit surcharge hours. The surcharge hours for students taking fewer than seven credit hours shall equal one-half the surcharge assessed students taking more than six credit hours.

C. Monies raised pursuant to the surcharge on student registration shall be matched by monies appropriated by the legislature.

D. The board shall report every three years to the legislature on the status of the financial aid trust fund. The report shall include the use to which the monies have been put and the impact of such use.

E. Fund monies shall only be used in university assistance programs approved by the board and such monies shall be in addition to, and not in replacement of, existing state or institutional financial aid monies. Assistance may be provided to full-time or part-time students. Monies appropriated by this state shall not be used to provide assistance to students who are not residents of this state.

Added by Laws 1989, Ch. 123, § 1. Amended by Laws 1994, Ch. 298, § 1.

§ 15-1643. Arizona area health education system; centers; governing boards; duties

A. The Arizona board of regents shall establish the Arizona area health education system in the college of medicine of the university of Arizona. The board shall appoint a system director.

B. The system shall consist of five area health education centers administered by the director of the Arizona area health education system. Each center shall represent a geographic area with specified populations that the system determines currently lack services by the health care professions.

C. The Arizona board of regents shall appoint a governing board for each center consisting of not fewer than ten people and not more than twenty people. Board membership shall consist of health care providers and consumers and shall reflect the ethnic representation of the center's geographic area. Each governing board shall make recommendations to the director regarding health professionals' educational needs, local program priorities and the allocation of system monies. Board members are not eligible to receive compensation or reimbursement of expenses.

D. Each center shall conduct:

1. Physician and other health professional education programs that consist of any of the following:

(a) An undergraduate clinical training program.

(b) A graduate program.

(c) Postgraduate continuing education.

2. Programs to recruit and retain minority students in health professions.

3. Continuing education programs for health professionals.

E. The director shall submit a written report on or before November 15 of each year to the governor, the president of the senate and the speaker of the house of representatives. The report shall contain the following:

1. The fiscal status of each center.

2. Information regarding center education, outreach and training programs.

3. Information regarding placement of health care personnel in areas the director determines are underserved by these professionals.

4. An assessment of system accomplishments.

5. Recommendations for possible legislative action.

F. The system shall provide expertise and administrative services to each center.

Added by Laws 1990, Ch. 342, § 1.

Historical and Statutory Notes

Reviser's Notes:

1990 Note. Laws 1990, Ch. 266, § 5 added another § 15-1643 that was renumbered as § 15-1646 pursuant to authority of § 41-1304.02.

§ 15–1644. Statewide commission; membership; qualifications; duties; compensation; staffing

A. The Arizona board of regents shall appoint a statewide area health education centers commission consisting of not fewer than ten members and not more than twenty members who are knowledgeable about the delivery of health care in this state. Members of the commission shall advise the director on a regular basis on the management of the system and on the expenditure of monies appropriated for the system.

B. Commission members serve at the pleasure of the Arizona board of regents and are not eligible to receive compensation or reimbursement of expenses.

C. The Arizona area health education system shall provide staffing for the commission.

Added by Laws 1990, Ch. 342, § 1.

§ 15–1645. Health professions field scholarships; purpose; amount; repayment; definition

A. Each area health education center located in this state may grant and administer a scholarship in an amount of not more than eight thousand dollars for each student for each school year to at least two students who are residents of the center's geographic area and who are enrolled in a health professions program at an Arizona university. The scholarship shall be used to defray educational expenses including room and board.

B. A scholarship shall be granted on the condition that the student contractually agree to practice in the center's geographic area for two years or one year of service for each year of scholarship support, whichever is longer, after completing post-graduation training. If the recipient withdraws from school, the recipient shall repay all scholarship monies within one year of the withdrawal. If the student is dismissed, an appropriate mechanism shall be negotiated to arrange repayment of the remaining unforgiven balance with eight per cent interest.

C. For good cause a center may extend the time period for training prior to scholarship repayment.

D. The Arizona board of regents shall waive all tuition and fees for students granted a scholarship under this section if the legislature appropriates funds for this purpose.

E. For the purposes of this section "health professions program" means enrollment in a school of medicine, nursing, pharmacy or physical therapy.

Added by Laws 1990, Ch. 342, § 1.

§ 15–1646. Board of regents and university scholarships

The state public universities under the jurisdiction of the Arizona board of regents shall establish policies which assure fair and equitable access by Arizona students from public, private, charter and home schools to scholarships, including tuition waivers, which are issued solely on the basis of academic merit and for which the universities establish and administer fair and equitable selection criteria. The universities under the jurisdiction of the Arizona board of regents shall report annually to the board information including the number of such scholarships issued on the basis of academic merit to students from public, private, charter and home schools.

Added as § 15-1641.01 by Laws 1999, Ch. 63, § 1. Renumbered as § 15-1646.

Historical and Statutory Notes

Former § 15-1646, added as § 15-1643 by Laws 1990, Ch. 266, § 5, renumbered as § 15-1646 by the reviser, which related to environmental education training programs, was repealed by Laws 1995, Ch. 268, § 52.

Reviser's Notes:

1999 Note. Pursuant to authority of § 41-1304.02, this section, added by Laws 1999, Ch. 63, sec. 1 as § 15-1641.01, was renumbered as § 15-1646.

§ 15-1647. Distribution of licensing and patent income; Arizona state university; report

A. Notwithstanding any other law, Arizona state university shall distribute the gross or net income derived from the licensing and other revenues derived from patents including anticancer, antiviral, antifungal or antimicrobial drug discoveries or inventions, including up-front payments, royalties and any other subsequent or eventual revenue attributable to commercialization.

B. The distribution of income received pursuant to subsection A shall be detailed by Arizona state university in an audited annual report. Arizona state university shall specify the expenditures and actual expenses in the audited annual report. The report shall be distributed annually to the president of the Arizona board of regents, the governor, the president of the senate, the speaker of the house of representatives, the secretary of state and the department of library, archives and public records.

Added by Laws 2000, Ch. 332, § 1.

§ 15-1648. Technology and research initiative fund; purpose

A. The technology and research initiative fund is established consisting of revenues transferred to the fund pursuant to § 42-5029, subsection E, paragraph 2. The Arizona board of regents shall administer the fund. The monies in the fund are continuously appropriated to the Arizona board of regents for distribution pursuant to this section and are exempt from the provisions of § 35-190 relating to lapsing of appropriations.

B. The board shall adopt rules to administer the technology and research initiative fund in accordance with this section. The board may allocate up to twenty per cent of the monies in the fund to be used for capital projects relating to new economy initiatives, including debt service, for the universities under its jurisdiction, pursuant to chapter 13, article 5 of this title. [1]

C. The Arizona board of regents shall receive requests from the individual universities and shall determine the amount and duration of each award. The criteria for the evaluation of each request shall be as follows:

1. The award must be related to one of the following:

(a) A specific academic or research field.

(b) Designed to expand access to baccalaureate or post-baccalaureate education for time-bound and place-bound students.

(c) To implement recommendations of the Arizona partnership for the new economy or the governor's task force on higher education.

2. The award may be used to develop new and existing programs that will prepare students to contribute in high technology industries located in this state.

3. The award may be used in conjunction with matching financial assistance from private industry.

4. The Arizona board of regents shall give preference to requests that are developed in conjunction with private industry, private entities or federal agencies.

D. The Arizona board of regents shall submit a report to the governor, the president of the senate and the speaker of the house of representatives on September 1 of each year on the technology and research award program and shall transmit a copy to the secretary of state and the director of the Arizona state library, archives and public records. The report shall include a description of the amount and duration of each new award distributed and a description of the purpose and goals for each award. For existing awards, the Arizona board of regents shall use a detailed set of performance measures to determine the overall effectiveness of each award.

Added by Laws 2000, 5th S.S., Ch. 1, § 19.

[1] Section 15-1681 et seq.

Historical and Statutory Notes

Laws 2000, 5th S.S., Ch. 1, §§ 66 and 67, provide:

"**Sec. 66. Delayed implementation**

"This act shall not be implemented until from and after May 31, 2001.

"**Sec. 67. Conditional enactment**

"This act does not become effective unless the qualified electors of this state in the general election that will be held in November, 2000 approve an increase in state transaction privilege tax rates of six-tenths of one per cent in order to fund the provisions of this act." See note, post.

Proposition 301, approved by the electors at the Nov. 7, 2000 general election, effective Nov. 27, 2000, included a provision increasing the state transaction privilege tax rate six-tenths of one per cent. Therefore, the conditions of the 5th S.S. Ch. 1 were met, and the act became effective.

ARTICLE 3. TEACHER TRAINING SCHOOLS

§ 15-1651. Teacher training schools

A. Every teacher training school established in connection with the state universities shall be a part of the school system and a branch of the school district within which the training school is located.

B. Training schools shall be governed by the laws and regulations relating to schools except as otherwise provided in this article.

C. Students in the state universities may, under rules prescribed by the Arizona board of regents, teach in the training schools and other schools without being certificated teachers.

Added by Laws 1981, Ch. 1, § 2, eff. Jan. 23, 1981. Amended by Laws 1982, Ch. 229, § 8.

Historical and Statutory Notes

Source:

Laws 1909, Ch. 87, §§ 1, 2.
Laws 1913, 3rd S.S., Ch. 46, §§ 10, 11.
Civ.Code 1913, §§ 4515, 4516.
Rev.Code 1928, § 1109.
Code 1939, § 54-1310.
A.R.S. former § 15-901.
Laws 1960, Ch. 127, § 45.

§ 15-1652. Management and expenses

A. Every teacher training school shall be under the supervision and management of the Arizona board of regents. All teachers in the school, except the principal, shall be employed by the Arizona board of regents and the governing board of the school district in which the training school is located, acting jointly.

B. The school district shall pay towards the expense of a teacher training school an amount equal to one-half of the school monies which it is entitled to have apportioned to it based on the student count at the training school during the preceding school year, but pupils attending from another school district shall not be credited with enrollment in the school district in which the university is located.

Added by Laws 1981, Ch. 1, § 2, eff. Jan. 23, 1981. Amended by Laws 1982, Ch. 229, § 9.

Historical and Statutory Notes

Source:

Laws 1909, Ch. 87, § 3.
Laws 1913, 3rd S.S., Ch. 46, § 12.
Civ.Code 1913, § 4517.
Rev.Code 1928, § 1110.
Code 1939, § 54-1311.
A.R.S. former § 15-902.
Laws 1974, 1st S.S., Ch. 3, § 14.
Laws 1980, 2nd S.S., Ch. 9, § 35.

§ 15-1653. Authority to prescribe rules governing admission and attendance

The Arizona board of regents and the governing board of the school district in which a teacher training school is located shall jointly prescribe rules and regulations governing admission and attendance at the training school of children of school age who reside within the school district and governing all pupils in changing their attendance from the training school to another school in the school district. The Arizona board of regents may admit all children of school age residing within the school district who are not then registered during that year for attendance at another school of the school district for attendance at the training school up to such number as necessary for the conduct of the training school.

Added by Laws 1981, Ch. 1, § 2, eff. Jan. 23, 1981.

Historical and Statutory Notes

Source:

Laws 1909, Ch. 87, § 4.
Laws 1913, 3rd S.S., Ch. 46, § 13.
Civ.Code 1913, § 4518.
Rev.Code 1928, § 1111.
Code 1939, § 54-1312.
A.R.S. former § 15-903.

§ 15-1654. Qualifications for admission to teacher training program

On or before January 1, 1993, each university under the jurisdiction of the Arizona board of regents shall establish qualifications for entrance into the teacher training program of its respective colleges of education.

Added by Laws 1992, Ch. 305, § 18.

ARTICLE 4. FINANCIAL PROVISIONS

§ 15-1661. Annual appropriation; expenditure; balance; salaries

A. There shall be appropriated in the general appropriation bill for each fiscal year a sum of monies not less than eighty-five one-hundredths of one mill on the dollar of the assessed valuation of all taxable property in the state for the improvement, support and maintenance of the institutions under the Arizona board of regents' jurisdiction, including payment of salaries, current expenses, purchase of equipment, making necessary repairs, construction of new buildings, purchase of lands and in general for payment of all such expenses connected with the management of the institutions under the Arizona board of regents' jurisdiction. The department of revenue shall, upon compiling the aggregate assessed valuation of all taxable property within this state, compute the amount of monies so determined and certify such amount over its seal to the department of administration and the state treasurer.

B. Amounts appropriated as provided by subsection A shall be paid as other claims against this state are paid.

C. The balance of appropriations as provided by subsection A at the end of the fiscal year, if any, shall not revert to the general fund but shall be carried forward for the continued use for which appropriated.

D. Monies appropriated to a university under the jurisdiction of the Arizona board of regents for cost of living salary increases for university employees shall be used to provide cost of living salary increases to all university employees including graduate student assistants. If monies are appropriated to a university for salary increases based on merit, the monies shall be used to provide merit increases according to the merit pay plan adopted by the Arizona board of regents.

Added by Laws 1981, Ch. 1, § 2, eff. Jan. 23, 1981. Amended by Laws 1990, Ch. 138, § 1; Laws 1994, Ch. 323, § 2, eff. Jan. 1, 1996.

Historical and Statutory Notes

Source:

Laws 1921, Ch. 81, § 1.
Laws 1922, Ch. 35, § 128.
Laws 1925, Ch. 34, § 8.
Rev.Code 1928, § 1155.
Laws 1933, Ch. 7, § 2.
Code 1939, § 54-1620.
A.R.S. former § 15-741.
Laws 1970, Ch. 190, § 14.
Laws 1976, Ch. 163, § 7.

Laws 1994, Ch. 323, § 54, subsec. A, as amended by Laws 1995, Ch. 249, § 42, Laws 1996, Ch. 351, § 53, provides:

"**Sec. 54. Delayed effective date**

"**A.** Sections 1 through 7, 9, 11, 16, 25, 26, 29, 30, 32, 33, 34, 36, 37, 38, 40 through 43 and 45 through 48 of this act are effective from and after December 31, 1995."

Laws 1996, Ch. 351, § 58, subsec. C, provides:

"**Sec. 58. Retroactive application**"

"**C.** Sections 29 through 32, 53 and 54 of this act apply retroactively to from and after July 31, 1995."

§ 15-1662. Universities; funds and accounts

A. The state treasurer shall maintain the following separate permanent funds and accounts:

1. Universities land fund. Distributions from the fund pursuant to article X, § 7, Constitution of Arizona and all monies derived from the lease, sale or other

disposition of lands granted by the United States for the use and benefit of the universities shall be deposited in the universities land fund as provided in this section and § 37-522. Monies accruing to the universities under the laws of the United States pertaining to timber lands shall be deposited in the universities timber land account established by § 37-482, subsection B and may be used for the payment of expenditures which the state land department incurs for the conservation, sale and other administration of timber or timber products as provided in this section and §§ 37-482 and 37-522.

2. Normal schools land fund. Distributions from the fund pursuant to article X, § 7, Constitution of Arizona and all monies derived from the lease, sale or other disposition of lands granted by the United States for the use and benefit of normal schools shall be deposited in the normal schools land fund as provided in this section and § 37-523.

3. Agricultural and mechanical colleges land fund. Distributions from the fund pursuant to article X, § 7, Constitution of Arizona and all monies derived from the lease, sale or other disposition of lands granted by the United States for the use and benefit of agricultural and mechanical colleges shall be deposited in the agricultural and mechanical colleges land fund as provided in this section and § 37-524.

4. School of mines land fund. Distributions from the fund pursuant to article X, § 7, Constitution of Arizona and all monies derived from the lease, sale or other disposition of lands granted by the United States for the use and benefit of schools of mines shall be deposited in the school of mines land fund as provided in this section and § 37-524.

5. Military institutes land fund. Distributions from the fund pursuant to article X, § 7, Constitution of Arizona and all monies derived from the lease, sale or other disposition of lands granted by the United States for the use and benefit of military institutes shall be deposited in the military institutes land fund as provided in this section and § 37-525 .

B. The Arizona board of regents shall maintain a separate permanent fund to be known as the universities fund. All monies other than those specified in subsection A which are derived from the lease, sale or other disposition of lands or property which are given by any person or by law as a trust fund to be administered by the board in conformity with the terms of the gift shall be deposited in the universities fund. Such monies shall be invested and administered as designated for the use of the universities except such monies as are appropriated for specific purposes from the general fund of this state for the use of the universities.

C. The state treasurer shall keep the monies of the land funds invested in safe interest bearing securities and prudent equity pursuant to article X, § 7, Constitution of Arizona and as provided by §§ 35-313 and 35-314.01, and monies earned from investment shall be credited to the funds.

D. Monies shall not be taken from one fund or deposited in any other fund nor shall any fund or the income from the fund be taken or expended for any object other than that of the original gift or appropriation.

Added by Laws 1981, Ch. 1, § 2, eff. Jan. 23, 1981. Amended by Laws 1982, Ch. 229, § 10, eff. July 2, 1983; Laws 1998, Ch. 173, § 1; Laws 1999, Ch. 74, § 1; Laws 2000, Ch. 193, § 115.

Historical and Statutory Notes

Source:

Civ.Code 1901, § 3640.
Civ.Code 1913, § 4485.
Laws 1925, Ch. 55, § 8.
Rev.Code 1928, § 1140.
Code 1939, § 54–1611.
A.R.S. former § 15–742.

Laws 1982, Ch. 229, § 27 provides:

"**Sec. 27. Effective date**

"Sections 10, 11, 19, 20, 21 and 22 of this act are effective from and after July 1, 1983."

§ 15–1663. Expenditure of land funds; eminent scholars matching grant fund

A. Except as provided in subsection B of this section, the Arizona board of regents may expend, as it deems expedient and as is not inconsistent with the provisions of any appropriation, the income of the land funds established pursuant to the enabling act in accordance with the purposes specified in the enabling act for each land fund specified in § 15–1662.

B. Beginning with the 1998–1999 fiscal year, the universities land fund shall be known as the eminent scholars matching grant fund and shall consist of the annual income from the universities land fund. The eminent scholars matching grant fund shall be used to provide to the universities matching monies for the interest earned on nonpublic endowment monies donated to attract and retain eminent faculty. Appropriations to the Arizona board of regents for the eminent scholars matching grant fund shall commence in the 1998–1999 fiscal year. The eminent scholars matching grant fund shall be allocated as follows:

1. Monies in the eminent scholars matching grant fund shall be used to supplement and not supplant any other sources of monies for the universities. Monies shall be allocated to each university on a dollar-for-dollar match basis. The amount allocated shall be equal to the amount of interest earned in the previous calendar year by each university on the nonpublic endowment monies donated from and after December 31, 1997 which are designated by the universities as being solely for the purpose of attracting and retaining eminent faculty.

2. If the monies appropriated by the legislature for the eminent scholars matching grant fund are greater than the amount of interest earned on the nonpublic endowment monies designated by the universities for expenditure as provided in this subsection, the board may allocate the excess monies as provided in subsection A of this section.

3. If the monies appropriated by the legislature for the eminent scholars matching grant fund are less than the amount of interest earned on the nonpublic endowment monies designated by the universities for expenditure as provided in this subsection, the board shall allocate the monies to each university in a manner deemed appropriate.

Added by Laws 1981, Ch. 1, § 2, eff. Jan. 23, 1981. Amended by Laws 1982, Ch. 229, § 11, eff. July 2, 1983; Laws 1983, Ch. 232, § 1; Laws 1991, Ch. 45, § 1; Laws 1998, Ch. 173, § 2.

Historical and Statutory Notes

Source:

Civ.Code 1901, § 3637.
Civ.Code 1913, § 4482.
Laws 1925, Ch. 55, § 6.
Rev.Code 1928, § 1137.

Code 1939, § 54–1608.
A.R.S. former § 15–743.

Reviser's Notes:

1998 Note. Pursuant to authority of § 41–1304.02, in the section heading "; eminent scholars matching grant fund" was added and in subsection B, first sentence after "year", the second "the" was removed to correct a manifest clerical error.

§ 15–1664. Expenditure of monies

All monies for the use and benefit of an institution under its jurisdiction shall be expended under the direction and control of the Arizona board of regents for the support and maintenance of such institution, buildings and grounds, and for any other purpose the board deems expedient if not inconsistent with provisions of any appropriations.
Added by Laws 1981, Ch. 1, § 2, eff. Jan. 23, 1981.

Historical and Statutory Notes

Source:
Civ.Code 1901, §§ 3682, 3697.
Laws 1913, 3rd S.S., Ch. 46, § 16.
Civ.Code 1913, § 4521.
Laws 1922, Ch. 35, § 135.
Rev.Code 1928, § 1113.
Laws 1945, Ch. 80, § 6.
Code 1939, Supp.1952, § 54–1314.
A.R.S. former § 15–744.
Laws 1965, Ch. 37, § 3.

§ 15–1665. Acceptance of federal and other monies

The Arizona board of regents may accept grants of monies from the United States or any of its officers or agencies designated or created to make grants for public construction work, or from any individual, group of individuals, corporation or association.
Added by Laws 1981, Ch. 1, § 2, eff. Jan. 23, 1981.

Historical and Statutory Notes

Source:
Laws 1945, Ch. 64, § 1.
Laws 1945, Ch. 82, § 1.
Laws 1947, Ch. 26, § 1.
Laws 1947, Ch. 39, § 1.
Laws 1949, Ch. 81, § 1.
Laws 1949, Ch. 105, § 1.
Code 1939, Supp.1952, §§ 54–1320, 54–1365, 54–1622, 54–1623.
A.R.S. former § 15–745.

§ 15–1666. Federal monies; deposit and expenditure

Monies obtained by the universities from the United States under special acts of congress for specific purposes shall be deposited in a special fund by the board, and it shall be administered in accordance with the purpose of the act of congress.
Added by Laws 1981, Ch. 1, § 2, eff. Jan. 23, 1981. Amended by Laws 1982, Ch. 229, § 12.

Historical and Statutory Notes

Source:
Civ.Code 1901, § 3637.
Civ.Code 1913, § 4482.
Laws 1925, Ch. 55, § 6.
Rev.Code 1928, § 1137.
Code 1939, § 54–1608.
A.R.S. former § 15–746.

§ 15–1667. Federal aid to experiment stations

The state assents to the provisions and accepts the benefits of the act of congress entitled "An Act to authorize the more complete endowment of agricultural experiment stations and for other purposes, approved February 24, 1925." The Arizona board of regents is designated as a state board for the purposes of this section and is empowered to cooperate with agencies of the federal government in administering the federal law.

Added by Laws 1981, Ch. 1, § 2, eff. Jan. 23, 1981.

Historical and Statutory Notes

Source:

Laws 1927, Ch. 105, §§ 1, 2.
Rev.Code 1928, § 1154.
Code 1939, § 54-1619.
A.R.S. former § 15-747.

§ 15-1668. Deposits of universities monies to be secured; exception

A. Monies deposited by the universities shall be secured by regularly issued and interest-bearing bonds of the United States government or state, county, municipal or school district improvement bonds of this state of a market value equal at all times to the amount of the deposits, and all public depositories are directed to give such security.

B. The public depository may, in lieu of depositing bonds described in this section, deposit the safekeeping receipt of a federal reserve bank or any bank located in a central reserve city whose combined capital and surplus on the date of the safekeeping receipt is ten million dollars or more, evidencing the deposit therein of such securities. The safekeeping receipt shall be endorsed or assigned to the comptroller of the respective institution making the deposit.

C. The condition of the deposit of securities, or a safekeeping receipt in lieu thereof, shall be that the public depository will upon lawful demand therefor promptly pay the monies in its custody to the institution making the deposit.

D. Notwithstanding the requirements of this section, any public depository under the provisions of title 35, chapter 2 [1] may accept deposits of public monies to the total authorized insurance on accounts insured by the federal deposit insurance corporation or the federal savings and loan insurance corporation without depositing a surety bond or securities in lieu of such security bond.

Added by Laws 1981, Ch. 1, § 2, eff. Jan. 23, 1981.

[1] Section 35-301 et seq.

Historical and Statutory Notes

Source:

Laws 1961, Ch. 47, § 1.
A.R.S. former § 15-748.
Laws 1975, Ch. 126, § 1.

§ 15-1669. Payment of salaries; sick leave

A. The Arizona board of regents may provide for payment of annual salaries of any person appointed or employed as provided in § 15-1626, subsection A, paragraph 2, over a twelve month pay period pursuant to agreement between such person and the board.

B. The Arizona board of regents shall require institutions under its jurisdiction as part of payroll reporting procedures to identify and report hours of sick leave earned by any person appointed or employed as provided in § 15-1626, subsection A, paragraph 2, and absences on account of sickness. Compensation paid to employees on account of sickness shall be so identified in the accounting records of the institution.

Added by Laws 1981, Ch. 1, § 2, eff. Jan. 23, 1981. Amended by Laws 1981, Ch. 285, § 1.

Historical and Statutory Notes

Source:

A.R.S. former § 15-749.
Laws 1972, Ch. 178, § 1.

§ 15-1670. Appropriation for university research infrastructure facilities; definition

A. In fiscal years 2007-2008 through 2030-2031, the following sums are appropriated each year from the state general fund to the respective universities for lease-purchase capital financing for research infrastructure projects:

1. $14,472,000 to Arizona state university.
2. $14,253,000 to the university of Arizona.
3. $5,900,000 to northern Arizona university.

B. Lease-purchase financing agreements under subsection A of this section:

1. Must be entered into before July 1, 2006.
2. Are subject to the requirements of § 15-1682.01.

C. The appropriations under subsection A of this section constitute continuing year-to-year appropriations but do not constitute an obligation of the legislature or this state to continue the appropriation in any fiscal year. The annual appropriation is a current expense of this state in the fiscal year in which it occurs and is not a general obligation indebtedness of this state or of any university. If the appropriation is discontinued in any fiscal year, this state and the university are relieved of any subsequent obligation pursuant to this section.

D. Beginning in fiscal year 2007-2008 and in each subsequent fiscal year for which an appropriation is made pursuant to subsection A of this section, each university shall deposit no later than October 1 with the state treasurer in the state general fund an amount equal to:

1. Twenty per cent of the income from licensure and royalty payments received by the university during the preceding fiscal year.

2. Twenty-five per cent of the income received by the university during the preceding fiscal year from the sale or transfer of intellectual property developed by the university.

3. If a constitutional amendment authorizing ownerships and securities by the Arizona board of regents is approved by the qualified electors voting at a statewide general election, thirty per cent of the income received in the preceding fiscal year resulting from the conveyance of ownership interests in business enterprises acquired to develop technology or intellectual property

based in whole or in part on the university's research, technology or intellectual property.

E. The aggregate amount transferred in each fiscal year for deposit in the state general fund by all universities from all sources listed under subsection D of this section shall not exceed the aggregate amounts appropriated in that fiscal year under subsection A of this section. If amounts under subsection D of this section would otherwise exceed the limit prescribed by this subsection, the deposited amounts shall be proportionately reduced for each university.

F. On or before October 1 of each year, each university shall report to the joint legislative budget committee the total amount of income the university received in the preceding fiscal year from each category of income that is subject to deposit pursuant to subsection D of this section.

G. For the purposes of this section, "research infrastructure" means installations and facilities for continuance and growth of scientific and technological research activities at the university.
Added by Laws 2003, Ch. 267, § 1.

ARTICLE 5. ISSUANCE OF BONDS

Historical and Statutory Notes

Laws 1984, Ch. 395, § 1, as amended by Laws 1986, Ch. 187, § 1, provides:

"**Section 1. Authorization for acquisition and completion of cancer center and the issuance of bonds**

"**A.** The legislature approves and authorizes the Arizona board of regents, or its successor, to acquire and complete the cancer center for the university of Arizona and authorizes the issuance of revenue bonds for such purpose pursuant to title 15, chapter 13, article 5, Arizona Revised Statutes, [§ 15-1681 et seq.] in one or more series and in various denominations but not exceeding in the aggregate three million dollars.

"**B.** The Arizona board of regents shall designate the cancer center to be included in the system of building facilities at the university of Arizona, and the bonds authorized by this section shall be secured and are payable as provided in title 15, chapter 13, article 5, Arizona Revised Statutes."

Laws 1986, Ch. 260, § 1, effective April 30, 1986, provides:

"**Section 1. Authorization for acquisition of projects and issuance of bonds**

"**A.** The legislature approves and authorizes the Arizona board of regents, or its successor, to acquire for and on behalf of the institutions under its jurisdiction the following projects, and authorizes the issuance of revenue bonds for such purposes pursuant to title 15, chapter 13, article 5, Arizona Revised Statutes, in one or more series but not exceeding in the aggregate the amount specified for each project as follows:

"1. For and on behalf of Arizona state university:

"(a) An addition to Sun Devil Stadium, eight million dollars.

"(b) Student recreational facilities, twenty million dollars.

"(c) Student housing facilities, ten million dollars.

"2. For and on behalf of the university of Arizona:

"(a) Student recreational facilities, fifteen million one hundred sixty-three thousand dollars.

"(b) Parking facilities, twelve million three hundred eighty thousand dollars.

"(c) Student housing facilities, five million dollars.

"3. For and on behalf of northern Arizona university, six million dollars for a student recreation facility.

"**B.** The Arizona board of regents shall designate the projects authorized by this act to be included in the system of facilities of Arizona state university or the university of Arizona, as appropriate, and the bonds authorized by this act shall be secured and made payable as provided in title 15, chapter 13, article 5, Arizona Revised Statutes."

§ 15–1681. Definitions

In this article, unless the context otherwise requires:

1. "Acquire" includes to purchase, lease, lease-purchase, erect, build, construct, reconstruct, raze, remodel, repair, replace, alter, extend, expand, better, equip, furnish, develop, improve and embellish a project, and the acquisition, preparation and development of a site or sites therefor.

2. "Board" means the Arizona board of regents or its successor.

3. "Bonds" means any bonds issued pursuant to this article.

4. "Federal agency" means the United States of America, the president of the United States of America, the department of housing and urban development or such other agency or agencies of the United States of America as may be designated or created to make loans or grants, or both.

5. "Institution" means the university of Arizona, Arizona state university and northern Arizona university or any other college or university under the jurisdiction and control of the board or its successor.

6. "Project" means and includes buildings, structures, areas and facilities which, as determined by the board, are required by or necessary for the use or benefit of each of such institutions, including, without limiting the generality of the foregoing, student, faculty or staff housing facilities, residence halls, dormitories and apartments; student union and recreational buildings and stadiums; other facilities for student, faculty or staff services; any facility or building leased to the United States of America; parking garages and areas; offices, classrooms, laboratories, dining halls and food service facilities, libraries, auditoriums, or parts thereof, or additions or extensions thereto; heating, lighting and other utility service facilities in connection therewith, or parts thereof, or additions or extensions thereto; whether heretofore acquired and now or hereafter used for any or all of the purposes aforesaid, or as may be hereafter acquired under this article, with all equipment and appurtenant facilities; or any one, or more than one, or all of the foregoing, or any combination thereof, for any institution, including sites therefor.

7. "System of building facilities" means such project or projects as the board by resolution shall collectively designate to be included in a system of building facilities at each institution, either:

(a) Hereafter acquired for each of such institutions under the terms of this article.

(b) Heretofore acquired for each of such institutions prior to May 17, 1974 under the terms of any other law and now located on the campus of each of such institutions, whether unencumbered by or encumbered by a pledge of and lien on the income and revenues derived from the operation thereof for the payment of any bonds theretofore issued by the board for the acquisition thereof.

(c) As provided in both subdivisions (a) and (b).

(d) Any combination of as provided in subdivisions (a), (b) and (c).

Added by Laws 1981, Ch. 1, § 2, eff. Jan. 23, 1981. Amended by Laws 1984, Ch. 349, § 21; Laws 1990, Ch. 348, § 23, eff. June 26, 1990; Laws 2001, 2nd S.S., Ch. 2, § 3, eff. Jan. 1, 2002.

Historical and Statutory Notes

Source:

Laws 1974, Ch. 182, § 2.
A.R.S. former § 15-782.

Laws 1980, Ch. 51, § 1, effective April 17, 1980, as amended by Laws 1981, Ch. 20, § 1, effective March 16, 1981, provides:

"**Section 1. Authorization and approval of bonds**

"**A.** The legislature approves and authorizes the Arizona board of regents, or its successor, to acquire any dormitory project or projects for northern Arizona university as provided in title 15, chapter 13, article 5, Arizona Revised Statutes, as added by Laws 1981, chapter 1, § 2, by the issuance of revenue bonds in various denominations but not exceeding in the aggregate nine million dollars.

"**B.** The Arizona board of regents, or its successor, may establish a separate new fee, tuition or other charge in addition to all fees, tuitions and other charges currently imposed. The bonds authorized by this act may be made payable from such new fee, tuition or charge in addition to and in the same manner as the sources of payment provided in title 15, chapter 13, article 5 [§ 15-1681 et seq.], Arizona Revised Statutes, as added by Laws 1981, chapter 1, § 2."

Laws 1980, Ch. 67, § 1 provides:

"**Section 1. Authorization and approval of bonds**

"**A.** The legislature approves and authorizes the Arizona board of regents, or its successor, to acquire any memorial union annex and high-rise parking project or projects for Arizona state university as provided in title 15, chapter 7, article 6, Arizona Revised Statutes, by the issuance of revenue bonds in various denominations but not exceeding in the aggregate fifteen million dollars.

"**B.** The Arizona board of regents, or its successor, may establish a separate new fee, tuition or other charge in addition to all fees, tuitions and other charges currently imposed. The bonds authorized by this act may be made payable from such new fee, tuition or charge in addition to and in the same manner as the sources of payment provided in title 15, chapter 7, article 6."

Laws 1980, Ch. 241, § 1, effective April 24, 1980, provides:

"**Section 1. Authorization for issuance of bonds**

"**A.** The legislature approves and authorizes the Arizona board of regents, or its successor, to acquire for and on behalf of the university of Arizona any one or more of the projects defined in § 15-782, Arizona Revised Statutes, and authorizes the issuance of revenue bonds for such purpose pursuant to title 15, chapter 7, article 6, [§ 15-782 et seq.] Arizona Revised Statutes, in one or more series but not exceeding in the aggregate twenty-five million dollars.

"**B.** The legislature approves and authorizes the Arizona board of regents, or its successor, to acquire for and on behalf of Arizona state university any one or more of the projects defined in § 15-782, Arizona Revised Statutes, and authorizes the issuance of revenue bonds for such purpose pursuant to title 15, chapter 7, article 6, Arizona Revised Statutes, in one or more series but not exceeding in the aggregate twenty-five million dollars.

"**C.** The legislature approves and authorizes the Arizona board of regents, or its successor, to acquire for and on behalf of northern Arizona university any one or more of the projects defined in § 15-782, Arizona Revised Statutes, and authorizes the issuance of revenue bonds for such purpose pursuant to title 15, chapter 7, article 6, Arizona Revised Statutes, in one or more series but not exceeding in the aggregate twelve million five hundred thousand dollars.

"**D.** The board shall increase tuitions and fees as may be necessary to secure the payment of any bonds and interests thereon issued under the provisions of title 15, chapter 7, article 6 and this act.

"**E.** The Arizona board of regents or its successor shall not issue bonds authorized by this act for any project unless the project has first been approved by the joint legislative budget committee."

Laws 1982, Ch. 265, § 1 effective April 27, 1982, provides:

"**Section 1. Authorization for acquisition of projects and the issuance of bonds**

"**A.** The legislature approves and authorizes the Arizona board of regents or its successor, to acquire laboratory and research facilities for the university of Arizona, and authorizes the issuance of revenue bonds for such purpose pursuant to title 15, chapter 13, article 5, Arizona Revised Statutes, in one or more series and in various denominations but not exceeding in the aggregate thirty-five million dollars.

"**B.** The Arizona board of regents shall designate the project or projects authorized by subsection A of this section to be included in the system of building facilities at the university of Arizona, and the bonds authorized by this act shall be secured and are payable as provided in title 15, chapter 13, article 5, Arizona Revised Statutes.

"**C.** The legislature approves and authorizes the Arizona board of regents, or its successor, to acquire for and on behalf of the university of Arizona any one or more of the projects defined in § 15-1681, Arizona Revised Statutes, and authorizes the issuance of revenue bonds for such purpose pursuant to title 15, chapter 13, article 5, Arizona Revised Statutes, in one or more series but not exceeding in the aggregate ten million dollars.

"**D.** The legislature approves and authorizes the Arizona board of regents, or its successor, to acquire for and on behalf of Arizona state university any one or more of the projects defined in § 15-1681, Arizona Revised Statutes, and authorizes the issuance of revenue bonds for such purpose pursuant to title 15, chapter 13, article 5, Arizona Revised Statutes, in one or more series but not exceeding in the aggregate ten million dollars.

"**E.** The Arizona board of regents may increase tuitions, fees and other charges as is necessary to secure the payment of any bonds and interest on the bonds issued under the provisions of title 15, chapter 13, article 5, Arizona Revised Statutes, and this act. The board may establish a separate new fee, tuition or other charge in addition to all fees, tuitions and other charges it currently imposes. The bonds authorized by this act are payable from the new fee, tuition or charge in addition to and in the same manner as provided for payments in title 15, chapter 13, article 5, Arizona Revised Statutes.

"**F.** The Arizona board of regents, or its successor, shall not issue bonds authorized by this act for any project unless the project is first approved by the joint legislative budget committee."

Laws 1990, Ch. 195, § 1, provides:

"**Section 1. Authorization for acquisition of a project and issuance of bonds**

"**A.** Subject to subsection B, the legislature approves and authorizes the Arizona board of regents, or its successor, to acquire for and on behalf of northern Arizona university its portion of the project known as the Southwest forest science complex, a joint project with the federal government, and, subject to subsection B, authorizes the issuance of revenue bonds for such purposes pursuant to title 15, chapter 13, article 5, Arizona Revised Statutes, in one or more series but not exceeding in the aggregate five million dollars.

"**B.** The Arizona board of regents, or its successor, shall not issue revenue bonds as authorized by this act for the project unless the project is first reviewed by the joint committee on capital review and the federal portion of funding for the northern Arizona university facility is assured."

Laws 1996, Ch. 334, § 1, provides:

"**Section 1. Authorization for acquisition of projects and issuance of bonds**

"**A.** The Arizona board of regents may acquire for and on behalf of the universities under its jurisdiction one or more of the projects defined in § 15-1681, Arizona Revised Statutes, and may issue revenue bonds for this purpose subject to the provisions of subsections C and D of this section in one or more series but not exceeding in the aggregate two hundred forty-five million four hundred thousand dollars.

"**B.** The Arizona board of regents, on the basis of the system of building facilities priorities, shall determine the amount and timing of the bond authorization for the universities under its jurisdiction. The board shall base its determination on the priorities of the system of building facilities, the need and ability of the university for which the bonds are issued to meet the necessary debt service on the bonds from revenues available for the payment of the bonds and any interest on the bonds.

"**C.** The Arizona board of regents shall provide a comprehensive, multi-year bonding plan to the joint committee on capital review and the governor, prior to the issuance of revenue bonds pursuant to this section. The joint committee on capital review shall review the bonding plan and any revisions thereto that are submitted by the Arizona board of regents, and shall invite comment on the bonding plan from the governor or his representative. No revenue bonds shall be issued for a project which does not appear in the plan. The bonding plan shall include:

"1. A description of the specific projects to be financed by the revenue bonds authorized by this section.

"2. An identification of the source of funds for repayment of the bonds for each specific project.

"3. An estimate of the cost of debt service for each project.

"**D.** The Arizona board of regents shall not issue revenue bonds pursuant to this section for any project unless the project is first included in the bonding plan required by subsection C of this section and the project is subsequently approved by the joint committee on capital review. The governor or his representative shall be invited to comment prior to the joint committee on capital review taking action on a project."

Laws 2001, Ch. 233, § 6, provides:

"**Sec. 6. Board of regents; authorization for acquisition of projects and issuance of bonds**

"**A.** The Arizona board of regents may acquire for and on behalf of northern Arizona university one or more of the projects defined in § 15-1681, Arizona Revised Statutes, and may issue revenue bonds for this purpose subject to subsections B and C of this section, in one or more series but not exceeding in the aggregate $39,100,000 more than any remaining bonding authority of northern Arizona university.

"**B.** Before the issuance of revenue bonds pursuant to this section, the Arizona board of regents shall provide a comprehensive multi-year bonding plan to the joint committee on capital review and to the governor. The joint committee on capital review shall review the multiyear bonding plan and any revisions that are submitted by the board of regents and shall solicit comment on the bonding plan from the governor's office. Revenue bonds shall not be issued for a project that does not appear in the multiyear bonding plan. The multiyear bonding plan shall include the following:

"1. A description of the specific projects that will be financed with the revenue bonds.

"2. An identification of the source of monies that will be used to repay the bonds for each project.

"3. An estimate of the cost to service the debt for each project.

"**C.** The Arizona board of regents shall not issue revenue bonds pursuant to this section for any project unless the project is included in the multiyear bonding plan required by subsection B of this section and the project is subsequently approved by the joint committee on capital review."

§ 15-1682. Powers

The board shall have power for each institution, as defined in this article, to:

1. Acquire, if authorized by the legislature, any project or projects, or any combination thereof, and to own, operate and maintain the same and establish, own, operate and maintain a system of building facilities.

2. Acquire by purchase, contract, lease-purchase, lease or gift, and hold or dispose of, real or personal property or rights or interest therein.

3. Accept grants, subsidies or loans of monies from a federal agency, or others, upon such terms and conditions as may be imposed, and to pledge the proceeds of grants, subsidies or loans of monies received or to be received from the United States of America or any agency or instrumentality thereof, or others, pursuant to agreements entered into between such board and the United States of America, or any agency or instrumentality thereof, or others.

4. Borrow monies and issue bonds to acquire any one project, or more than one, or any combination thereof, if authorized by the legislature, and to refund bonds heretofore or hereafter issued to acquire any project or projects, or to refund any such refunding bonds, or for any one, or more than one, or all of such purposes, or any combination thereof, and to provide for the security and payment of such bonds and for the rights of the holders thereof.

5. Make contracts and leases and execute all instruments and perform all acts and do all things necessary or convenient to carry out the powers granted in this article.

6. Retain in its treasury:

(a) All monies received from the sale of all bonds issued under this article.

(b) All fees, tuitions, rentals and other charges from students, faculty, staff members and others using or being served by, or having the right to use or the right to be served by, or to operate, any project.

(c) All fees for student activities, student services and all other fees, tuitions and charges collected from students matriculated, registered or otherwise enrolled at and attending each institution pledged under the terms of any resolution authorizing bonds pursuant to this article.

(d) All rentals from any facility or building leased to the United States of America.

Added by Laws 1981, Ch. 1, § 2, eff. Jan. 23, 1981. Amended by Laws 1984, Ch. 349, § 22; Laws 1990, Ch. 348, § 24, eff. June 26, 1990; Laws 2001, 2nd S.S., Ch. 2, § 4, eff. Jan. 1, 2002.

Historical and Statutory Notes

Source:

Laws 1974, Ch. 182, § 2.
A.R.S. former § 15-782.01.

§ 15-1682.01. Lease-purchase agreements

A. Any lease-purchase agreement executed by the board relating to land acquisition, capital projects, energy systems or energy management systems shall provide that:

1. The obligation of this state to make any payment under the agreement is a current expense of the board and is not a general obligation indebtedness of this state or the board.

2. If the legislature fails to appropriate monies or the board fails to allocate monies for any periodic payment or renewal term of the agreement, the agreement terminates at the end of the current term and this state and the board are relieved of any subsequent obligation under the agreement.

3. The joint committee on capital review shall review the project before the lease-purchase agreement takes effect.

B. A lease-purchase agreement under this section shall comply with the constitution and other laws of this state.

Added by Laws 2001, 2nd S.S., Ch. 2, § 5, eff. Jan. 1, 2002.

§ 15-1683. Issuance of bonds

The board shall have power, and is hereby authorized from time to time, to issue bonds:

1. To acquire any one project, or more than one, or any combination thereof, for such institution, provided that both of the following conditions are met:

(a) As of the date of issuance of bonds or certificates of participation for any institution, projected debt service on bonds and certificates of participation then outstanding and proposed to be issued for such institution, as shown in the most recent capital improvement plan reported to the board may not exceed, in any fiscal year shown in such capital improvement plan, more than eight per cent of such institution's total projected expenditures and mandatory transfers. The calculation of compliance with this condition shall be as set forth in and approved by the board in its adopted capital improvement plan for such institution.

(b) The project to be acquired with the proceeds of the bonds is reviewed by the joint committee on capital review.

2. To refund bonds heretofore and hereafter issued to acquire any project or projects for such institution as hereinafter provided for.

3. To refund any such refunding bonds.

4. For any one, or more than one, or all of such purposes, or any combination thereof.

All bonds shall be authorized by resolution of the board and may be issued in one or more series, may bear such date or dates, may be in such denomination or denominations, may mature at such time or times not exceeding forty years from the respective dates thereof, may mature in such amount or amounts, may bear interest at such rate or rates as shall be determined by the board, payable at such time or times, may be in such form, either coupon or registered as to principal only or as to both principal and interest, may carry such registration privileges, including the conversion of a fully registered bond to a coupon bond or bonds and the conversion of a coupon bond to a fully registered bond, may be executed in such manner, may be made payable in such medium of payment, at such place or places within or without the state, and may be subject to such terms of redemption prior to their expressed maturity, with or without premium, as such resolution or other resolutions may provide. All bonds issued under this article shall be sold as the board shall determine. Such resolution may provide that one of the officers of the board shall sign such bonds manually and that the other signatures may be printed, lithographed, engraved or otherwise reproduced thereon. The coupon bonds shall be fully negotiable within the meaning of the uniform commercial code, title 47. [1]

Added by Laws 1981, Ch. 1, § 2, eff. Jan. 23, 1981. Amended by Laws 1981, Ch. 20, § 2, eff. March 16, 1981; Laws 1984, Ch. 77, § 22; Laws 2002, Ch. 202, § 1.

[1] Section 47-1101 et seq.

Historical and Statutory Notes

Source:

Laws 1974, Ch. 182, § 2.
A.R.S. former § 15-782.02.

§ 15-1684. Refunding bonds

The board shall have power, and is hereby authorized from time to time, to issue refunding bonds:

1. To refund unpaid matured bonds.

2. To refund unpaid mature coupons evidencing interest upon its unpaid matured bonds.

3. To refund interest at the coupon rate upon its unpaid matured bonds that has accrued since the maturity of those bonds, provided that such refunding bonds may be exchanged for the bonds to be refunded on a par for par basis of the bonds, interest coupons and interest not represented by coupons, if any, or may be sold at not less than par, or may be exchanged in part and sold in part, and the proceeds received at any such sale shall be used to pay the bonds, interest coupons and interest not represented by coupons, if any, and all bonds

and interest coupons which have been received in exchange or paid shall be cancelled and the obligation for interest not represented by coupons which has been discharged shall be evidenced by a written acknowledgment of the exchange or payment thereof.

4. To refund bonds at or prior to their maturity or which by their terms are subject to redemption before maturity, or both, in an amount necessary to refund the principal amount of the bonds to be refunded, the interest to accrue up to and including the maturity date or dates or to the next succeeding redemption date thereof, and the applicable redemption premiums, if any, and may be exchanged for not less than an equal principal amount of bonds to be refunded or may be sold as the board shall determine, or may be exchanged in part and sold in part, and all proceeds received at the sale thereof, excepting the accrued interest received, shall be used:

(a) If the bonds to be refunded are then due, for the payment thereof.

(b) If the bonds to be refunded are voluntarily surrendered with the consent of the holder or holders thereof, for the payment thereof.

(c) If the bonds to be refunded are then subject to prior redemption at the option of the board and if such option has been exercised, for the redemption thereof.

(d) If the bonds to be refunded are not then subject to payment or redemption, or if the bonds are subject to prior redemption and the board chooses to defer exercising the option to a later date or chooses to exercise the option at any prior redemption date and sets the date for such redemption or chooses not to exercise such option, to invest the proceeds received at the sale in obligations issued by or guaranteed by the United States of America or any department, agency or instrumentality thereof, that will mature at such time or times, with interest thereon or the proceeds received therefrom, to provide funds adequate to pay when due or called for redemption prior to maturity the bonds to be refunded, or the bonds issued to refund the bonds to be refunded, together with the interest accrued thereon and any redemption premium due thereon, and such proceeds or obligations of the United States of America shall, with all other funds legally available for such purpose, be deposited in escrow with a banking corporation or national banking association with power to accept and execute trusts, or any successor thereto, which is also a member of the federal deposit insurance corporation and of the federal reserve system, to be held in an irrevocable trust solely for and until the payment and redemption of the bonds so to be refunded, and any balance remaining in such escrow after the payment and retirement of the bonds to be refunded shall be used and held for use by such board as revenues pledged for the payment of such refunding bonds.

(e) For any combination thereof as provided in subdivisions (a) through (d).

Added by Laws 1981, Ch. 1, § 2, eff. Jan. 23, 1981.

Historical and Statutory Notes

Source:
Laws 1974, Ch. 182, § 2.
A.R.S. former § 15–782.03.
Laws 1975, Ch. 32, § 1.

§ 15-1685. Security of bonds

In connection with the issuance of any bonds under this article, and in order to secure the payment of any such bonds and the interest thereon, the board shall have power for each institution:

1. To fix, maintain and collect:

(a) Fees, tuitions, rentals and other charges from students, faculty, staff members and others using or being served by, or having the right to use or the right to be served by, or to operate, any project or system of institution building facilities.

(b) Fees for student activities, student services and all other fees and charges from students matriculated, registered or otherwise enrolled at and attending each such institution.

(c) Rentals from any facility or building leased to the United States of America, the aggregate of which shall be sufficient at all times to pay the bonds at maturity and accruing interest thereon in accordance with their terms, and to create and maintain all reserves therefor as provided by the resolution authorizing such bonds, and to pay all necessary expenses of the operation and maintenance of any project and system of building facilities.

2. To provide that bonds issued under this article shall be payable from and secured by a pledge of and lien on all or any part of the income and revenues derived from, and to pledge and assign to, or in trust for the benefit of, the holder or holders of bonds issued under this article all or any part of the income and revenues derived from:

(a) Fees, tuitions, rentals and other charges from students, faculty, staff members and others using or being served by, or having the right to use or the right to be served by, or to operate, any project or system of building facilities.

(b) Fees for student activities, student services, and all other fees and charges collected from students matriculated, registered or otherwise enrolled at and attending each such institution.

(c) Rentals from any facility or building leased to the United States of America, except that, if such board provides that any bonds issued under this article shall also be payable from the income and revenues of any project heretofore acquired for each such institution, any such provision for the payment of such bonds from the income and revenues of any such project heretofore acquired for each such institution shall be subject to, and in all respects in full conformity and compliance with, the rights of the holders of any bonds or obligations payable from the income and revenues of any such project heretofore issued for each institution and then outstanding.

(d) Interest and earnings on investments.

3. To covenant with or for the benefit of the holder or holders of the bonds issued under this article that so long as any such bonds shall remain outstanding and unpaid the board will fix, maintain and collect in such installments as may be agreed upon:

(a) Fees, rentals and other charges from students, faculty, staff members and others using or being served by, or having the right to use or the right to be served by, or to operate any project or system of building facilities.

(b) Fees for student activities, student services and all other fees from students matriculated, registered or otherwise enrolled at and attending each institution pledged under the terms of any resolution authorizing bonds pursuant to this article.

(c) Rentals from any facility or building leased to the United States of America, the aggregate of which shall be sufficient at all times to pay the proportionate share of the bonds at maturity and accruing interest thereon in accordance with their terms and to create and maintain all reserves therefor as provided by the resolution authorizing such bonds until such bonds and accruing interest have been paid in accordance with their terms and to pay all necessary expenses of the operation and maintenance of any project or system of building facilities.

4. To covenant with or for the benefit of the holder or holders of bonds issued under this article as to all matters deemed advisable by the board, including:

(a) The purposes, terms and conditions for the issuance of additional parity or junior lien bonds that may thereafter be issued, and for the payment of the principal, redemption premiums and interest on such bonds.

(b) The kind and amount of all insurance to be carried, the cost of which shall be charged as an operation and maintenance expense of any project or system of building facilities.

(c) The operation, maintenance and management of any project or system of building facilities to assure the maximum use and occupancy thereof; the accounting for, and the keeping of records, reports and audits of, all income and revenue from, and all expenses of, any project or system of building facilities; and the employment of engineers and consultants.

(d) The obligation of the board to maintain any project or system of building facilities in good condition and to operate the same at all times in an economical and efficient manner.

(e) The terms and conditions for creating and maintaining sinking funds, reserve funds and such other special funds as may be created in the resolution authorizing such bonds, separate and apart from all other funds and accounts of such board and each institution.

(f) The procedure by which the terms of any contract with the holders of the bonds may be amended, the amount of the bonds the holders of which must consent thereto and the manner in which consent may be given.

(g) Providing the procedure for refunding such bonds.

(h) Such other covenants as may be deemed necessary or desirable to assure a successful operation of any project or system of building facilities and the prompt payment of the principal of and interest upon the bonds so authorized.

5. To make and enforce and agree to make and enforce parietal rules that shall insure the use of any project or system of building facilities to the

maximum extent to which the same is capable of serving students, faculty, staff members and others using or being served by, or having the right to use or the right to be served by, or to operate, any project or system of building facilities.

6. To covenant that so long as any of the bonds issued under this article shall remain outstanding and unpaid it will not, except upon such terms and conditions as may be determined:

(a) Voluntarily create or cause to be created any debt, lien, mortgage, pledge, assignment, encumbrance or other charge having priority to the lien of the bonds issued under this article upon any of the income and revenue derived from:

(i) All fees, rentals and other charges from students, faculty, staff members and others using or being served by, or having the right to use or the right to be served by, or to operate, any project or system of building facilities.

(ii) Fees for student activities, student services and all other fees collected from students matriculated, registered or otherwise enrolled at and attending each institution.

(iii) All rentals from any facility or building leased to the United States of America.

(b) Convey or otherwise alienate any project or the real estate upon which such project shall be located, except at a price sufficient to pay all the bonds issued for such project then outstanding and interest accrued thereon, and then only in accordance with any agreements with the holder or holders of such bonds.

7. To vest in a trustee or trustees the right to receive all or any part of the income and revenue pledged and assigned to or for the benefit of the holder or holders of bonds issued under this article, and to hold, apply and dispose of the same and the right to enforce any covenant made to secure or pay or in relation to the bonds; execute and deliver a trust agreement or trust agreements which may set forth the powers and duties and remedies available to such trustee or trustees and limiting the liabilities thereof and describing what occurrences shall constitute events of default and prescribing the terms and conditions upon which such trustee or trustees or the holder or holders of any specified amount or percentage of such bonds may exercise such rights and enforce any and all such covenants and resort to such remedies as may be appropriate.

8. To covenant to perform any and all acts and to do any and all such things as may be necessary or convenient or desirable in order to secure its bonds, or as may in the judgment of the board tend to make the bonds more marketable, notwithstanding that such acts or things may not be enumerated herein, it being the intention hereof to give the board issuing bonds pursuant to this article power to make all covenants, to perform all acts and to do all things not inconsistent with the constitution of Arizona.

Added by Laws 1981, Ch. 1, § 2, eff. Jan. 23, 1981.

Historical and Statutory Notes

Source:

Laws 1974, Ch. 182, § 2.
A.R.S. former § 15-782.04.

§ 15-1686. Effect on bonds authorized but unissued

All acts granting authority to the board to construct or acquire any buildings, projects or facilities and to issue bonds therefor shall be kept in full force and effect but shall be supplemented by this enactment if both of the following occur:

1. Bonds remain authorized but not sold and the land, project, buildings or facilities have not been fully acquired or constructed.

2. Due to the issuance of bonds authorized by this article, any revenues which otherwise would have been used to secure the unissued bonds, in whole or in part, have been applied to payment of bonds authorized by this article, then the board may issue the remaining bonds so authorized solely for the purposes of acquiring or constructing or completing the acquisition and construction of the projects heretofore authorized as parity bonds, notwithstanding the fact that the acts authorizing such additional bonds may limit the revenues available to be pledged for their repayment to specified revenues of the board.

Added by Laws 1981, Ch. 1, § 2, eff. Jan. 23, 1981.

Historical and Statutory Notes

Source:

Laws 1974, Ch. 182, § 2.
A.R.S. former § 15-782.05.

§ 15-1687. Enforcement of contract

The provisions of this article and of any resolution or other proceeding authorizing the issuance of bonds shall constitute a contract with the holders of such bonds and the provisions thereof shall be enforceable either in law or in equity, by suit, action, mandamus or other proceeding in any court of competent jurisdiction to enforce and compel the performance of all duties required by this article, and by any resolution authorizing the issuance of bonds adopted responsive hereto.

Added by Laws 1981, Ch. 1, § 2, eff. Jan. 23, 1981.

Historical and Statutory Notes

Source:

Laws 1974, Ch. 182, § 2.
A.R.S. former § 15-782.06.

§ 15-1688. Monies of the board

No monies derived from the sale of bonds issued under the provisions of this article or pledged or assigned to or in trust for the benefit of the holder or holders of the bonds shall be required to be paid into the state treasury but shall be invested in obligations issued by or guaranteed by the United States or any of the senior debt of its agencies, sponsored agencies, corporations, sponsored corporations or instrumentalities, or shall be deposited by the treasurer or other fiscal officer of the board in such bank or banks or trust company or trust companies as may be designated by the board, and all deposits of such monies shall, if required by the board, be secured by obligations of the United States of a market value equal at all times to the amount of such monies on deposit. Such monies shall be disbursed as may be directed by the board and in accordance with the terms of any agreements with the holder or holders of any bonds. This section shall not be construed as limiting the power of the board to agree in connection with the issuance of any of its bonds as to the custody and disposition of the monies received from the sale of such bonds or from the income and revenues pledged or assigned to or in trust for the benefit of the holder or holders of the bonds.

Added by Laws 1981, Ch. 1, § 2, eff. Jan. 23, 1981. Amended by Laws 2001, Ch. 117, § 6.

Historical and Statutory Notes

Source:

Laws 1974, Ch. 182, § 2.
A.R.S. former § 15-782.07.

§ 15-1689. Validity of bonds

The bonds bearing the signatures of officers of the board in office on the date of the signing thereof shall be valid and binding obligations, notwithstanding that before the delivery thereof and payment therefor any or all persons whose signatures appear thereon shall have ceased to be such officers. The validity of the bonds shall not be dependent on nor affected by the validity or regularity of any proceedings to acquire any project financed by the bonds, or to refund outstanding bonds, or taken in connection therewith.

Added by Laws 1981, Ch. 1, § 2, eff. Jan. 23, 1981.

Historical and Statutory Notes

Source:

Laws 1974, Ch. 182, § 2.
A.R.S. former § 15-782.08.

§ 15-1690. Prohibitions against obligating state of Arizona

Nothing in this article shall be construed to authorize the board to contract a debt on behalf of, or in any way to obligate, the state of Arizona, or to pledge, assign or encumber in any way, or to permit the pledging, assigning or encumbering in any way, of appropriations made by the legislature or revenue derived from the investment of the proceeds of the sale and from the rental of such lands as have been set aside by the Enabling Act approved June 20, 1910, or other legislative enactments of the United States, for the use and benefit of the board or the institution.

Added by Laws 1981, Ch. 1, § 2, eff. Jan. 23, 1981.

Historical and Statutory Notes

Source:

Laws 1974, Ch. 182, § 2.
A.R.S. former § 15-782.09.

§ 15-1691. Bonds; obligations of board

All bonds issued pursuant to this article shall be obligations of the board issuing such bonds, payable only in accordance with the terms thereof, and shall not be obligations general, special or otherwise of the state of Arizona. Such bonds shall not constitute a debt, legal or moral, of the state of Arizona, and shall not be enforceable against the state, nor shall payment thereof be enforceable out of any funds of the board or the institution issuing such bonds other than the income and revenue pledged and assigned to, or in trust for the benefit of, the holder or holders of such bonds.

Added by Laws 1981, Ch. 1, § 2, eff. Jan. 23, 1981.

Historical and Statutory Notes

Source:

Laws 1974, Ch. 182, § 2.
A.R.S. former § 15-782.10.

§ 15-1692. Certification of bonds by attorney general

The board may submit to the attorney general of the state of Arizona any bonds to be issued hereunder after all proceedings for the issuance of such bonds have been taken. Upon the submission of such proceedings to the attorney general, it shall be the duty of the attorney general to examine into and pass upon the validity of such bonds and the regularity of all proceedings in connection therewith. If such proceedings conform to the provisions of this article and such bonds when delivered and paid for will constitute binding and legal obligations of the board enforceable according to the terms thereof, the attorney general shall certify in substance upon the back of each of such bonds that it is issued in accordance with the constitution and laws of the state of Arizona.

Added by Laws 1981, Ch. 1, § 2, eff. Jan. 23, 1981.

Historical and Statutory Notes

Source:

Laws 1974, Ch. 182, § 2.
A.R.S. former § 15-782.11.

§ 15-1693. Bonds as legal investments

The state and all counties, cities, towns and other municipal corporations, political subdivisions and public bodies, and public officers of any thereof, all banks, bankers, trust companies, savings banks and institutions, building and loan associations, investment companies and other persons carrying on a banking business, all insurance companies, insurance associations and other persons carrying on an insurance business and all executors, administrators, guardians, trustees and other fiduciaries may legally invest any debt service funds, monies or other funds belonging to them or within their control in any bonds issued pursuant to this article, it being the purpose of this section to authorize the investment in such bonds of all debt service, insurance, retirement compensation, pension and trust funds, whether owned or controlled by private or public persons or officers, except that nothing contained in this section may be construed as relieving any person, firm or corporation from any duty of exercising reasonable care in selecting securities for purchase or investment.

Added by Laws 1981, Ch. 1, § 2, eff. Jan. 23, 1981.

Historical and Statutory Notes

Source:

Laws 1974, Ch. 182, § 2.
A.R.S. former § 15–782.12.

§ 15–1694. Excision of unconstitutional and ineffective parts of article

It is hereby declared that the sections, clauses, sentences and parts of this article are severable, are not matters of mutual essential inducement and any of them may be excised by any court of competent jurisdiction if this article would otherwise be unconstitutional or ineffective. It is the intention of this article to confer upon the board the whole or any part of the powers in this article provided for, and if any one or more sections, clauses, sentences or parts of this article shall for any reason be questioned in any court of competent jurisdiction and shall be adjudged unconstitutional or invalid, such judgment shall not affect, impair or invalidate the remaining provisions thereof but shall be confined in its operation to the specific provision or provisions so held unconstitutional or invalid, and the inapplicability or invalidity of any section, clause, sentence or part of this article in any one or more instances shall not be taken to affect or prejudice its applicability or validity in any other instance.
Added by Laws 1981, Ch. 1, § 2, eff. Jan. 23, 1981.

Historical and Statutory Notes

Source:

Laws 1974, Ch. 182, § 2.
A.R.S. former § 15–782.13.

§ 15–1695. Supplemental nature of article; construction and purpose

The powers conferred by this article shall be in addition to and supplemental to the powers conferred by any other law, general or special, and bonds may be issued under this article notwithstanding the provisions of any other such law and without regard to the procedure required by any other such laws. Insofar as the provisions of this article are inconsistent with the provisions of any other law, general or special, the provisions of this article shall be controlling.
Added by Laws 1981, Ch. 1, § 2, eff. Jan. 23, 1981.

Historical and Statutory Notes

Source:

Laws 1974, Ch. 182, § 2.
A.R.S. former § 15–782.14.

ARTICLE 6. ISSUANCE OF BONDS BY TWENTY–SEVENTH LEGISLATURE [REPEALED]

Article 6, Issuance of Bonds by Twenty-Seventh Legislature, consisting of §§ 15–1701 to 15–1711, as added by Laws 1981, Ch. 1, § 2, effective January 23, 1981, was repealed by Laws 1981, Ch. 314, § 22, effective July 25, 1981.

§§ 15-1701 to 15-1711. Repealed by Laws 1981, Ch. 314, § 22

Historical and Statutory Notes

The repealed sections, added by Laws 1981, Ch. 1, § 2, and derived from Laws 1966, Ch. 110, § 1; A.R.S. former §§ 15-771 to 15-781; and Laws 1970, Ch. 89, § 11, related to the issuance of bonds by the twenty-seventh legislature.

ARTICLE 7. MEDICAL STUDENT LOANS

Termination under Sunset Law

The board of medical student loans shall terminate on July 1, 2011, unless continued. See §§ 41-3011.03 and 41-2955.

Title 15, Chapter 13, Article 7, relating to the board of medical student loans, is repealed on January 1, 2012, by § 41-3011.03.

§ 15-1721. Definitions

In this article, unless the context otherwise requires:

1. "Board" means the board of medical student loans.

2. "Medically underserved area" means an area of this state designated by the department of health services pursuant to title 36, chapter 24, article 1 [1] or by federal law.

3. "Medically underserved population" means an area designated by the United States department of health and human services.

4. "Rural" means either of the following:

(a) A county with a population of less than four hundred thousand persons.

(b) A census county division with less than fifty thousand persons in a county with a population of at least four hundred thousand persons.

Added by Laws 1981, Ch. 1, § 2, eff. Jan. 23, 1981. Amended by Laws 2001, Ch. 27, § 1.

[1] Section 36-2351 et seq.

Historical and Statutory Notes

Source:

Laws 1977, Ch. 171, § 1.
A.R.S. former § 15-768.

Laws 1996, Ch. 154, § 5, provides:

"**Sec. 5. Purpose**

"The purpose of the board of medical student loans is to administer the medical student loan fund."

Laws 2001, Ch. 27, § 7, provides:

"**Sec. 7. Purpose**

"Pursuant to § 41-2955, subsection B, Arizona Revised Statutes, the legislature continues the board of medical student loans to administer the medical student loan program."

§ 15-1722. Board of medical student loans; members; terms; officers; compensation

A. The board of medical student loans is established and consists of the following eight members:

1. Two members who are appointed by the chairman of the Arizona medical board.

2. Three who are members appointed by the governor and who are knowledgeable in the problems of health care in Arizona.

3. One member who is appointed from the staff of the college of medicine of the university of Arizona and who is appointed by the president of the university of Arizona.

4. One member who is licensed pursuant to title 32, chapter 17 and who is appointed by the board of osteopathic examiners in medicine and surgery.

5. The director of the department of health services or the director's designee who is the ex officio nonvoting eighth member of the board.

B. The terms of members are four years beginning on the third Monday in January.

C. The board shall select a chairman and vice-chairman and such other officers as it deems necessary.

D. Board members shall be compensated as determined pursuant to § 38–611.

Added by Laws 1981, Ch. 1, § 2, eff. Jan. 23, 1981. Amended by Laws 1981, Ch. 314, § 23; Laws 1999, Ch. 79, § 1; Laws 2002, Ch. 254, § 4.

Historical and Statutory Notes

Source:

Laws 1977, Ch. 171, § 1.
A.R.S. former § 15–768.01.

§ 15–1723. Medical student loans; amount; qualifications; requirements

A. The board may grant loans from the medical student loan fund established by § 15–1725 to defray the expenses of the medical education of those students at a public or private school of medicine in this state who intend to enter and complete a residency program approved by the accreditation council for graduate medical education or by the american osteopathic association to become board certified in family practice, general pediatrics, obstetrics and gynecology, general internal medicine, or combined medicine and pediatrics and who are deemed qualified by the board to receive such loans. Loans shall be granted upon such terms and conditions as may be imposed by the board. One of the qualifications shall be Arizona residency, which shall be determined according to the same criteria prescribed for in-state student status in § 15–1802. The board may grant forty loans each year.

B. The loans granted by the board shall provide for tuition plus no more than ten thousand dollars for each student in 1992–1993. Beginning in 1993–1994 and continuing each year thereafter until June 30, 2002, each loan shall provide for tuition plus no more than ten thousand dollars per year adjusted by the percentage change in the GDP price deflator from the second preceding calendar year to the calendar year immediately preceding the current year. The amount provided for tuition shall not exceed the cost of registration for a full-time student at a college of medicine at a university under the jurisdiction of the Arizona Board of regents. For 2002–2003, each loan shall provide for tuition plus no more than sixteen thousand dollars for each student. Beginning in 2003–2004 and continuing each year thereafter, each loan shall provide for tuition plus no more than sixteen thousand dollars for each student per year adjusted by the percentage change in the GDP price deflator from the second preceding calendar year to the calendar year immediately preceding the current year. For purposes of this subsection, "GDP price deflator" means the average of the four implicit price deflators for the gross domestic product reported by the United States department of commerce for the four quarters of the calendar year.

C. The board shall make a full and careful investigation of the ability, character and qualification of each applicant through a written application and interview process and determine the applicant's fitness to become a loan recipient. The investigation of each applicant shall include an examination of the ability of the applicant to pay the expenses of a medical education. The board shall give preference to qualified applicants who are unable to pay the expenses of obtaining a medical education and to qualified applicants who demonstrate a commitment to serve in an area listed in subsection E of this section.

D. The services to be performed are service to the state by practicing general practice, family practice, general pediatrics, combined medicine and pediatrics, obstetrics and gynecology, or general internal medicine in An area listed in subsection E of this section. The service location is subject to approval by the board.

E. The board may approve service in any of the following locations:

1. A rural and medically underserved area of this state.

2. A medically underserved area of this state.

3. A medically underserved population of this state.

4. Any Indian reservation that is located in this state.

F. The board may specify an area listed in subsection E of this section in the student's contract to permit the student to seek employment in that area as a physician. After the area is specified by the board, that area shall be designated in the student's subsequent contracts as an approved area and as an approved service location.

G. The board shall collect and maintain data on the retention of doctors who practice in an area listed in subsection E of this section. The board shall collect this data for at least ten years after each loan recipient completes the recipient's service commitment.

H. Private schools of medicine shall reimburse the university of Arizona for any administrative costs related to the processing of loans for students at private schools of medicine pursuant to subsection A of this section.

Added by Laws 1981, Ch. 1, § 2, eff. Jan. 23, 1981. Amended by Laws 1981, Ch. 314, § 24; Laws 1992, Ch. 338, § 1; Laws 1993, Ch. 112, § 2; Laws 1996, Ch. 154, § 1; Laws 1999, Ch. 79, § 2; Laws 2001, Ch. 27, § 2.

Historical and Statutory Notes

Source:

Laws 1977, Ch. 171, § 1.
A.R.S. former § 15-768.02.

Laws 2001, Ch. 27, § 6, provides:

"**Sec. 6. Retroactive application**

"**A.** Section 15-1723, Arizona Revised Statutes, subsection E, as amended by this act, applies retroactively to from and after June 30, 1978.

"**B.** Section 15-1724, Arizona Revised Statutes, subsections E and G, as amended by this act, apply retroactively to from and after June 30, 1978.

"**C.** Service locations approved by the board of medical student loans before July 1, 2000 are deemed to be approved service locations until the program participants fulfill the conditions of their contracts."

Reviser's Notes:

2001 Note. In the chapter version in subsection G, first sentence a stricken comma appears after "~~rural~~". Pursuant to authority of § 41-1304.02, in the chapter version the stricken comma is removed to correct a manifest clerical error.

§ 15-1724. Medical student loans; interest; obligations; penalty; authority of attorney general

A. Each applicant who is approved for a loan by the board may be granted a loan for a period of up to five years.

B. The loans shall bear interest at the rate of seven per cent per year.

C. Each loan shall be evidenced by a contract between the student and the board, acting on behalf of this state. The contract shall provide for the payment by the state of a stated sum or sums defraying the costs of a medical education at a public or private school of medicine in this state and shall be conditioned upon the contractual agreement by the recipient of such loan to complete the service required by § 15-1723. The contract shall provide that the recipient serving as a physician in an area listed in § 15-1723, subsection E may receive compensation from the board for such service and other services designated in the contract which compensation shall be credited against amounts due under the loan and shall not exceed the amount of the loan and any interest accrued on the loan. Such service shall be full time as determined by the board and shall be for two years or one year of service for each year of loan support, whichever is longer. A loan and the interest accrued thereon may be fully paid with compensation received for services as required by the contract or at the option of the recipient by payment of all monies, interest and penalties for failure to fulfill the contract.

D. A loan recipient shall begin the service for which the recipient contracted as a condition of the loan within three years of completion of the recipient's undergraduate medical education unless extended to four years by the board. A recipient who is ordered into military service or for other cause beyond the recipient's control deemed sufficient by the board is unable to commence the required service within three years of such graduation shall begin service within one year after completing military service or the termination of such other cause.

E. If a recipient decides not to fulfill the conditions of the contract by serving in an area listed in § 15-1723, subsection E, the contract shall provide that the recipient shall be required to repay the full amount borrowed, including tuition, at the seven per cent interest rate plus a penalty for liquidated damages in an amount equivalent to the full amount borrowed, including tuition, less the amount credited for time actually served in a site approved by the board, to be calculated on a prorated monthly basis. The board for good reason may provide for extensions of the period of repayment specified in the loan recipient's contract. The board may waive the payment of principal, interest and liquidated damages if it determines that death or permanent physical disability accounts for the recipient's failure to fulfill the contract. For recipients entering into a contract prior to January 1, 1992, the board may, for the purpose of retaining the recipient's service in a federally designated medically underserved area of this state, release the recipient from obligations to the program if the recipient enters into a legally binding service contract with the United States public health service. The contracted term of service for the United States public health service must be for the same or longer term than the recipient's service commitment to this state under the medical student loan program.

F. If a recipient withdraws or is dismissed from medical school, the recipient shall be required to repay the loan to the board with interest with no penalty within one year of withdrawal. The board may for good reason provide for extensions on the period of repayment.

G. On receipt of supporting documentation, the board for good cause shown may defer the loan recipient's service or payment obligation or may enter into repayment arrangements with the loan recipient or allow service that is equivalent to full-time service if the board determines that this action is justified after a review of the individual's circumstances.

H. The attorney general may commence whatever actions are necessary to enforce the contract and achieve repayment of loans provided by the board pursuant to this article.

Added by Laws 1981, Ch. 1, § 2, eff. Jan. 23, 1981. Amended by Laws 1992, Ch. 338, § 2; Laws 1994, Ch. 272, § 1, eff. July 17, 1994, retroactively effective to July 1, 1994; Laws 1999, Ch. 79, § 3; Laws 2001, Ch. 27, § 3.

Historical and Statutory Notes

Source:

Laws 1977, Ch. 171, § 1.
A.R.S. former § 15-768.03.

Laws 1994, Ch. 272, § 6, provides:

"**Sec. 6. Retroactivity**

"This act is effective retroactively to July 1, 1994."

Laws 2001, Ch. 27, § 6, provides:

"**Sec. 6. Retroactive application**

"**A.** Section 15-1723, Arizona Revised Statutes, subsection E, as amended by this act, applies retroactively to from and after June 30, 1978.

"**B.** Section 15-1724, Arizona Revised Statutes, subsections E and G, as amended by this act, apply retroactively to from and after June 30, 1978.

"**C.** Service locations approved by the board of medical student loans before July 1, 2000 are deemed to be approved service locations until the program participants fulfill the conditions of their contracts."

§ 15-1725. Medical student loan fund

A. The medical student loan fund is established. All monies appropriated to carry out the provisions of this article shall be deposited in the fund, and all payments of principal and interest received by the board shall be deposited, pursuant to §§ 35-146 and 35-147, in the fund. Monies in the fund are subject to legislative appropriation.

B. Monies in the medical student loan fund are exempt from the provisions of § 35-190 relating to lapsing of appropriations.

Added by Laws 1981, Ch. 1, § 2, eff. Jan. 23, 1981. Amended by Laws 1996, Ch. 335, § 11, eff. July 1, 1997; Laws 2000, Ch. 193, § 116.

Historical and Statutory Notes

Source:

Laws 1977, Ch. 171, § 1.
A.R.S. former § 15-768.04.

§ 15-1726. Repealed by Laws 2003, Ch. 104, § 10

Historical and Statutory Notes

The repealed section, which provided a requirement for reports, was added by Laws 1981, Ch. 1, § 2. The section was derived from Laws 1977, Ch. 171, § 1; and A.R.S. former § 15-768.05.

ARTICLE 8. COMPACT FOR WESTERN REGIONAL COOPERATION IN HIGHER EDUCATION

Termination under Sunset Law

The western interstate commission for higher education shall terminate on July 1, 2008, unless continued. See §§ 41-3008 and 41-2955.

Title 15, Chapter 13, Article 8, relating to the compact for western regional cooperation in higher education, is repealed on January 1, 2009, by § 41-3008.

Historical and Statutory Notes

Laws 1988, Ch. 43, § 1 provides:

"**Section 1. Purpose**

"The western interstate commission for higher education was established to enter into agreements with institutions in the region offering graduate or professional education or with compacting states or territories to provide adequate services and facilities of graduate and professional education for the citizens of this state."

Laws 1988, Ch. 43, § 9, which provided for delayed repeal of Title 15, Ch. 13, Art. 8, effective January 1, 1999, was itself repealed by Laws 1991, Ch. 8, § 1, subsec. F.

§ 15-1741. Definitions

In this article, unless the context otherwise requires:

1. "Board" means the Arizona board of regents or its successor.

2. "Commission" means the Western Interstate Commission for Higher Education.

3. "Compact" means the Compact for Western Regional Cooperation in Higher Education.

Added by Laws 1981, Ch. 1, § 2, eff. Jan. 23, 1981.

Historical and Statutory Notes

Source:

Laws 1953, Ch. 59, § 2.
Code 1939, Supp.1953, § 54-1903.
A.R.S. former § 15-762.

§ 15-1742. Authority of governor to enter compact; terms of compact

The governor, for and in behalf of the state, may enter into compacts for western regional cooperation in higher education with the states of Alaska, California, Colorado, Hawaii, Idaho, Montana, Nevada, New Mexico, Oregon,

Utah, Washington and Wyoming, or any one or more of such states or territories. Under such compacts, the following covenants may be agreed to:

ARTICLE I

WHEREAS, the future of this nation and of the western states is dependent upon the quality of the education of its youth; and

WHEREAS, many of the western states individually do not have sufficient numbers of potential students to warrant the establishment and maintenance within their borders of adequate facilities in all of the essential fields of technical, professional and graduate training, nor do all of the states have the financial ability to furnish within their borders institutions capable of providing acceptable standards of training in all of the fields mentioned above; and

WHEREAS, it is believed that the western states, or groups of such states within the region, cooperatively can provide acceptable and efficient educational facilities to meet the needs of the region and of the students thereof:

Now, therefore, the states of Alaska, Arizona, California, Colorado, Hawaii, Idaho, Montana, Nevada, New Mexico, Oregon, Utah, Washington and Wyoming do hereby covenant and agree as follows:

ARTICLE II

Each of the compacting states and territories pledges to each of the other compacting states and territories faithful cooperation in carrying out all the purposes of this compact.

ARTICLE III

The compacting states and territories hereby create the western interstate commission for higher education, hereinafter called the commission. Said commission shall be a body corporate of each compacting state and territory and an agency thereof. The commission shall have all the powers and duties set forth herein, including the power to sue and be sued, and such additional powers as may be conferred upon it by subsequent action of the respective legislatures of the compacting states and territories.

ARTICLE IV

The commission shall consist of three resident members from each compacting state or territory. At all times one commissioner from each compacting state or territory shall be an educator engaged in the field of higher education in the state or territory from which he is appointed.

The commissioners from each state and territory shall be appointed by the governor thereof as provided by law in such state or territory. Any commissioner may be removed or suspended from office as provided by the law of the state or territory from which he shall have been appointed.

The terms of each commissioner shall be four years; provided however that the first three commissioners shall be appointed as follows: one for two years, one for three years and one for four years. Each commissioner shall hold office until his successor shall be appointed and qualified. If any office becomes vacant for any reason, the governor shall appoint a commissioner to fill the office for the remainder of the unexpired term.

ARTICLE V

Any business transacted at any meeting of the commission must be by affirmative vote of a majority of the whole number of compacting states and territories.

One or more commissioners from a majority of the compacting states and territories shall constitute a quorum for the transaction of business.

Each compacting state and territory represented at any meeting of the commission is entitled to one vote.

ARTICLE VI

The commission shall elect from its number a chairman and a vice-chairman, and may appoint, and at its pleasure dismiss or remove, such officers, agents and employees as may be required to carry out the purpose of this compact; and shall fix and determine their duties, qualifications and compensation, having due regard for the importance of the responsibilities involved.

The commissioners shall serve without compensation but shall be reimbursed for their actual and necessary expenses from the funds of the commission.

ARTICLE VII

The commission shall adopt a seal and bylaws and shall adopt and promulgate rules and regulations for its management and control.

The commission may elect such committees as it deems necessary for the carrying out of its functions.

The commission shall establish and maintain an office within one of the compacting states for the transaction of its business and may meet at any time, but in any event must meet at least once a year. The chairman may call such additional meetings and upon the request of a majority of the commissioners of three or more compacting states or territories shall call additional meetings.

The commission shall submit a budget to the governor of each compacting state and territory at such time and for such period as may be required.

The commission shall, after negotiations with interested institutions, determine the cost of providing the facilities for graduate and professional education for use in its contractual agreements throughout the region.

On or before the fifteenth day of January of each year, the commission shall submit to the governors and legislatures of the compacting states and territories a report of its activities for the preceding calendar year.

The commission shall keep accurate books of account, showing in full its receipts and disbursements, and said books of account shall be open at any reasonable time for inspection by the governor of any compacting state or territory or his designated representative. The commission shall not be subject to the audit and accounting procedure of any of the compacting states or territories. The commission shall provide for an independent annual audit.

ARTICLE VIII

It shall be the duty of the commission to enter into such contractual agreements with any institutions in the region offering graduate or professional education and with any of the compacting states or territories as may be required in the judgment of the commission to provide adequate services and facilities of graduate and professional education for the citizens of the respective compacting states or territories. The commission shall first endeavor to provide adequate services and facilities in the fields of dentistry, medicine, public health and veterinary medicine and may undertake similar activities in other professional and graduate fields.

For this purpose the commission may enter into contractual agreements:

(a) With the governing authority of any educational institution in the region or with any compacting state or territory to provide such graduate or professional educational services upon terms and conditions to be agreed upon between contracting parties, and

(b) With the governing authority of any educational institution in the region or with any compacting state or territory to assist in the placement of graduate or professional students in educational institutions in the region providing the desired services and facilities, upon such terms and conditions as the commission may prescribe.

It shall be the duty of the commission to undertake studies of needs for professional and graduate educational facilities in the region, the resources for meeting such needs and the long-range effects of the compact on higher education; and from time to time to prepare comprehensive reports on such research for presentation to the western governors' conference and to the legislatures of the compacting states and territories. In conducting such studies, the commission may confer with any national or regional planning body which may be established. The commission shall draft and recommend to the governors of the various compacting states and territories uniform legislation dealing with problems of higher education in the region.

For the purposes of this compact the word "region" shall be construed to mean the geographical limits of the several compacting states and territories.

ARTICLE IX

The operating costs of the commission shall be apportioned equally among the compacting states and territories.

ARTICLE X

This compact shall become operative and binding immediately as to those states and territories adopting it whenever five or more of the states of Alaska, Arizona, California, Colorado, Hawaii, Idaho, Montana, Nevada, New Mexico, Oregon, Utah, Washington and Wyoming have duly adopted it prior to July 1, 1953. This compact shall become effective as to any additional states or territories adopting thereafter at the time of such adoption.

ARTICLE XI

This compact may be terminated at any time by consent of a majority of the compacting states or territories. Consent shall be manifested by passage and signature in the usual manner of legislation expressing such consent by the legislature and governor of such terminating state. Any state or territory may at any time withdraw from this compact by means of appropriate legislation to that end. Such withdrawal shall not become effective until two years after written notice thereof by the governor of the withdrawing state or territory, accompanied by a certified copy of the requisite legislative action, is received by the commission. Such withdrawal shall not relieve the withdrawing state or territory from its obligations hereunder accruing prior to the effective date of withdrawal. The withdrawing state or territory may rescind its action of withdrawal at any time within the two year period. Thereafter, the withdrawing state or territory may be reinstated by application to and the approval by a majority vote of the commission.

ARTICLE XII

If any compacting state or territory shall at any time default in the performance of any of its obligations assumed or imposed in accordance with the provisions of this compact, all rights, privileges and benefits conferred by this compact or agreements hereunder shall be suspended from the effective date of such default as fixed by the commission.

Unless such default shall be remedied within a period of two years following the effective date of such default, this compact may be terminated with respect to such defaulting state or territory by affirmative vote of three-fourths of the other member states or territories.

Any such defaulting state may be reinstated by performing all acts and obligations upon which it has heretofore defaulted and by application to and the approval by a majority vote of the commission.

Added by Laws 1981, Ch. 1, § 2, eff. Jan. 23, 1981.

Historical and Statutory Notes

Source:

Laws 1952, Ch. 104, § 1.
Code 1939, Supp.1952, § 54–1901.
A.R.S. former § 15–761.

Laws 1979, Ch. 46, § 7 provides:

"**Sec. 7. Education of Arizona students as osteopathic physicians in schools located in other states**

"**A.** The legislature finds that it is in the public interest that opportunity be provided for Arizona students to become osteopathic physicians.

"**B.** The Arizona board of regents shall seek to contract through the western interstate commission for higher education with schools of osteopathic medicine located in other states, who have a nondiscriminatory policy as to race or religion, for placement of Arizona residents. The number of placements in colleges of osteopathic medicine shall not exceed twenty.

"**C.** Selection of students for spaces obtained through contract by the Arizona board of regents through the western interstate commission for higher education and the out-of-state schools shall be the responsibility of the individual school, provided that any student for whom space is contracted shall be required to enter into an agreement with the Arizona board of regents to practice osteopathic medicine in this state under the terms and conditions prescribed by § 15–764, Arizona Revised Statutes.

"**D.** The board of regents through the western interstate commission for higher education is authorized to establish terms and conditions of contracts with schools of osteopathic medicine including the amount of payment to be made to each school."

Laws 1998, Ch. 40, § 3, provides:

"Sec. 3. Purpose

"The western interstate commission for higher education was established to enter into agreements with institutions in the region offering graduate or professional education or with compacting states or territories to provide adequate services and facilities of graduate and professional education for the citizens of this state."

Complementary Legislation:

Alaska—AS 14.44.010 to 14.44.035.
Cal.—West's Ann.Cal.Educ.Code, §§ 99000 to 99005.

Complementary Legislation:

Colo.—West's C.R.S.A. § 24-60-601.
Hawaii—HRS §§ 310-1 to 310-8.
Idaho—I.C. §§ 33-3601 to 33-3604.
Mont.—MCA 20-25-801 to 20-25-806.
Nev.—N.R.S. 397.010 to 397.080.
N.M.—NMSA 1978, §§ 11-10-1 to 11-10-3.
Ore.—ORS 351.770 to 351.840.
U.S.—Aug. 8, 1953, c. 380, 67 Stat. 490.
Utah—U.C.A.1953, §§ 53B-4-101 to 53B-4-103.
Wash.—West's RCWA 28B.70.010 to 28B.70.050.
Wyo.—Wyo.Stat.Ann. §§ 21-16-201, 21-16-202.

§ 15-1743. Authorizing agreements for education of Arizona students outside compact area; limitations

A. The western interstate commission for higher education is authorized to act on behalf of this state in making arrangements for the placement of students in institutions and programs of higher learning outside the states which are parties to the compact for establishing the commission. For that purpose, the commission may negotiate and enter into arrangements and contracts with the Arizona board of regents, with public and private educational institutions and agencies and with other states. These arrangements and contracts may provide for the obtaining of one or more places for students on either a special or continuing basis; the payment of partial or full tuition and other charges not to exceed the cost of agreements within the compact area; and the furnishing of reciprocal, compensating or other advantages and benefits in support of the educational program involved.

B. The authority conferred by subsection A shall be exercised only pursuant to written agreement between the commission and the Arizona board of regents. Any such agreements shall include provisions for the payment of tuition and any other costs, and no such agreement shall be made which commits this state or any agency or officer of it to any obligation for which funds have not been appropriated or otherwise made available in accordance with law.

C. Nothing in this section alters any of the obligations or restricts or impairs any rights which this state may have under the compact establishing the commission.

Added by Laws 1981, Ch. 1, § 2, eff. Jan. 23, 1981.

Historical and Statutory Notes

Source:

Laws 1976, Ch. 9, § 1.
A.R.S. former § 15-761.01.

§ 15-1744. Processing and certification of students

A. The board shall, within the limitations and on the terms fixed by the commission and by this article, determine the number of students desiring to take advantage of the educational facilities afforded by the compact and, from those indicating such a desire, select a group in each allowable professional field. In making the selections the board shall only include students who:

1. Have at least an average scholastic attainment record.

2. Are citizens of the United States.

3. Have been actual bona fide residents of Arizona for at least the last five years.

4. Have completed such preliminary education as will qualify them for admission to the professional or graduate school provided by the commission.

B. The names of the students selected shall be certified by the board to the commission through the Arizona members of the commission, along with such data as the commission may require.

Added by Laws 1981, Ch. 1, § 2, eff. Jan. 23, 1981.

Historical and Statutory Notes

Source:
Laws 1953, Ch. 59, § 3.
Code 1939, Supp.1953, § 54–1904.
A.R.S. former § 15–763.
Laws 1958, Ch. 92, § 1.
Laws 1980, Ch. 140, § 1.

§ 15–1745. Contract with student certified by board

A. Before certifying a student to the commission the board shall, on behalf of this state, enter into a written contract with the student. The contract shall set forth the methods and terms of repayment by the student to this state and shall be on terms and conditions and in a form provided by the board. The contract shall provide:

1. That the student shall within one year after completing his professional education and internship begin the practice of his profession within Arizona. If the student engages in postgraduate studies and does so without a lapse of more than one year following the completion of his professional course, then he shall begin practice within this state within one year after completing the graduate studies. If the student is involuntarily inducted into military service, or for other cause beyond his control deemed sufficient by the board is unable to begin the practice of his profession within one year after completing his professional education, internship and any graduate studies, then he shall begin practice within this state within one year after completing his required military service or the termination of such other cause.

2. That if the student engages in the practice of his profession within this state or while completing military service resulting from involuntary induction, his indebtedness to this state may be discharged in one of the following ways:

(a) By payment to this state of one-half of all sums expended by this state for and in behalf of the student with interest at the rate prescribed in subsection B.

(b) For each year of practice or internship within this state or in military service there shall be discharged his obligation for one academic year of study for which a portion of the cost was paid by this state, except that each six months of practice shall discharge his obligation for one academic year of study if such practice is confined to a locality within the state where there is an exceptional need for his professional services as determined and certified by the medical board of examiners or licensing board of his profession.

3. That if the student fails to complete the required course of professional study, or if the course of study is interrupted by one school year or more for a cause or causes not resulting from involuntary induction into military service or other cause beyond his control deemed sufficient by the board, or if the student fails to practice his profession within the state for such continuous time as completely discharges his obligation, except for delays resulting from an excusable cause as prescribed in this section, one-half of the entire sum paid for or on behalf of the student by this state and not repaid or discharged as herein provided shall be due and payable forthwith with interest at the rate prescribed in subsection B. The board may extend the time of payment over a period not exceeding fifteen years and shall not require payment of interest during the existence of any excusable cause as prescribed in this section.

4. That if the student does not begin practice in this state within the time prescribed in this section but shall have repaid an agreed part of the sum expended by this state in his behalf, the board may permit him to discharge the balance of his obligation by subsequent practice within this state.

5. That in the event of the death of the student during the period of his education, internship or practice, his obligation to this state under this article shall cease except as to any portion which is then due.

B. The interest rate for a student's contract is the rate in effect for the fiscal year during which the student begins the approved course of professional study. The board shall establish the interest rate by November 1 of the current year for the following fiscal year. The board shall establish a rate equal to the average interest rate of auctioned ninety-one day United States treasury bills over the twenty-four month period ending September 30 of the current year, except that the board may round the rate to the nearest one-half per cent. Accrual of interest charges provided by the contract begins on the first day of the first complete month following graduation of the student or, for students who fail to complete their required course of study, the first day of the first complete month following the date when the student was no longer enrolled.

Added by Laws 1981, Ch. 1, § 2, eff. Jan. 23, 1981. Amended by Laws 1987, Ch. 15, § 1.

Historical and Statutory Notes

Source:

Laws 1953, Ch. 59, § 4.
Code 1939, Supp.1953, § 54-1905.
A.R.S. former § 15-764.
Laws 1958, Ch. 92, § 2.
Laws 1976, Ch. 9, § 2.
Laws 1980, Ch. 140, § 2.

Laws 1987, Ch. 15, § 2, provides:

"**Sec. 2. Interest rates for fiscal year 1987-1988; applicability to existing contracts**

"**A.** Notwithstanding § 15-1745, Arizona Revised Statutes, as amended by this act, the Arizona board of regents may establish the interest rate prescribed in § 15-1745, Arizona Revised Statutes, for fiscal year 1987-1988 by September 1, 1987.

"**B.** For contracts entered into pursuant to § 15-1745, Arizona Revised Statutes, which are in effect on the effective date of this act and which specify an interest rate of twelve per cent, the Arizona board of regents may reduce the interest rate on the outstanding principal balance to the rate established as provided in subsection A of this section. The obligation of a person to pay any interest which has accrued prior to the effective date of this act remains."

§ 15–1746. Collections revolving fund; expenditures; employment of legal counsel; exemption from lapsing

A. A collections revolving fund is established which consists of:

1. Monies repaid to the board as provided in § 15–1745.
2. Monies which the legislature appropriates.

B. The board shall use monies in the collections revolving fund for payment of expenses incurred in enforcing contracts entered into with students as provided in § 15–1745, including expenditures for filing fees, court costs, travel, depositions, transcripts, reproduction costs, expert witness fees, investigations and similar costs and expenses. Except for payment of attorney fees due on the initial recovery of monies as provided in subsection C of this section, the board may not use monies in the fund to compensate or employ attorneys.

C. The board may, in legal actions taken outside of this state to enforce the contracts entered into with students as provided in § 15–1745, employ legal counsel on a contingent fee basis plus court costs. The employment and payment of legal counsel under this subsection is not subject to the bidding and contracting requirements under title 41, chapter 23.[1]

D. At no time shall the amount of monies in the collections revolving fund retained to pay expenses incurred in enforcing contracts entered into with students exceed ten thousand dollars.

E. The board shall not retain more than ten thousand dollars in the collections revolving fund. Monies collected in excess of ten thousand dollars shall be deposited in the state general fund.

F. Monies in the collections revolving fund, up to an amount of ten thousand dollars, are exempt from § 35–190, relating to lapsing of appropriations.

Added by Laws 1983, Ch. 188, § 1. Amended by Laws 1984, Ch. 251, § 9, eff. Jan. 1, 1985; Laws 1988, Ch. 43, § 2; Laws 1988, Ch. 43, § 3, eff. July 1, 1993.

[1] Section 41–2501 et seq.

Historical and Statutory Notes

Laws 1988, Ch. 43, § 8 provides:

"**Sec. 8. Effective date**

"Section 15–1746, Arizona Revised Statutes, as amended by § 3 of this act, is effective from and after June 30, 1993."

Former § 15–1746, added by Laws 1981, Ch. 1, § 2, derived from Laws 1953, Ch. 59, § 6 (A.R.S. former § 15–765), and making this article exempt from § 35–190 relating to lapsing appropriations, was repealed by Laws 1981, Ch. 314, § 25.

ARTICLE 9. MEDICAL PROGRAMS

Article 9, Medical Programs, consisting of §§ 15-1750 to 15–1753, was added by Laws 1994, Ch. 257, § 1, effective July 17, 1994.

Historical and Statutory Notes

Laws 1994, Ch. 257, § 2, provides:

"**Sec. 2. Primary care disciplines; plan; reports**

"**A.** The Arizona board of regents shall:

"1. Report to the president of the senate and the speaker of the house of representatives by November 15, 1994 on the status of these efforts to strengthen primary health care in this state.

"2. Set goals for the university of Arizona school of medicine for increasing the percentage of graduates who enter residencies and careers in primary care.

"3. Initiate changes necessary within university of Arizona admissions, advising, curriculum and other areas to ensure that the requirements established in §§ 15–1751, 15–1752 and 15–1753, Arizona Revised Statutes, are met.

"4. Work with the area health education centers and other entities and adopt policies necessary to ensure that the university of Arizona school of medicine has sufficient medical residency positions for medical school graduates in these primary care disciplines.

"B. The university of Arizona school of medicine shall submit a plan to the Arizona board of regents by October 15, 1994 with strategies to reach these goals of increasing the number of graduates entering primary care disciplines."

§ 15–1751. Positions at the university of Arizona

The university of Arizona school of medicine shall give priority consideration to applicants who demonstrate a willingness to practice in medically underserved areas of this state.

Added by Laws 1994, Ch. 257, § 1.

§ 15–1752. Repealed by Laws 1996, Ch. 237, § 1

Historical and Statutory Notes

The repealed section, added by Laws 1994, Ch. 257, § 1, related to rural rotation programs for medical students, residents, nurse practitioners and certified nurse midwives. See, now, § 15–1754.

§ 15–1753. Primary care disciplines; definition

A. The university of Arizona school of medicine shall prepare a plan with the goal of encouraging students to enter the primary care disciplines. At least sixty per cent of the residency positions available at the university of Arizona school of medicine shall be reserved for medical school graduates entering programs defined as primary care disciplines of which at least twelve per cent of the residency positions available at the university of Arizona school of medicine shall be reserved for medical school graduates entering the family medicine program.

B. Beginning October 1, 1995 and each year thereafter, the university of Arizona shall submit a report to the president of the senate and the speaker of the house of representatives. The report shall include the number of residents who graduated from the university of Arizona in a primary care discipline and who are practicing in primary care and the number who have elected to enter into specialty practices.

C. The information provided in subsection B of this section shall be made available to the chairmen of the appropriations committees in the house of representatives and the senate for their use in future funding decisions for the university of Arizona medical school.

D. For purposes of this section, "primary care disciplines" includes family medicine, general internal medicine, general pediatrics, obstetrics and gynecology.

Added by Laws 1994, Ch. 257, § 1. Amended by Laws 1995, Ch. 207, § 2; Laws 1996, Ch. 237, § 2.

Historical and Statutory Notes

A purported amendment of this section by Laws 1995, Ch. 207, § 3, which was to become effective July 1, 1998 according to § 4 of that act, was repealed by Laws 1996, Ch. 237, § 3.

The 1996 amendment of this section by Ch. 237 explicitly amended the 1995 amendment of this section by Ch. 207, § 2.

Reviser's Notes:

1994 Note. Pursuant to authority of § 41-1304.02, in the section heading "; definition" was added.

§ 15-1754. Rural health professions program; definition

A. The three universities under the jurisdiction of the Arizona board of regents shall select ten nurse practitioner students, fifteen medical students and four pharmacy students each year to participate in a rural health professions program. The three universities shall develop application procedures for students to apply for voluntary participation in the program. The three universities shall attempt to ensure that each individual participating student be able to fulfill the program requirements in a single rural practice setting.

B. The university of Arizona shall choose the fifteen medical students, four pharmacy students and four nurse practitioner students, Arizona state university shall choose four nurse practitioner students, and Northern Arizona university shall choose two nurse practitioner students who will participate at the respective universities.

C. Pharmacy students and medical students selected to participate in the program shall be placed in a rural practice or rural location in this state. Each placement shall be for a duration of at least one month and shall occur during the summer months between academic years, as part of the required curriculum during a clinical clerkship and in the final year of training.

D. Nurse practitioner students selected to participate in the program shall be placed in a rural practice or rural location in this state during the summer months between the first and second year of their academic instruction. A participating nurse practitioner student's internship shall also be conducted in a clinical setting located in a rural area of this state.

E. Students who participate in the program shall be teamed with two mentors throughout their period of academic instruction. The mentors shall provide guidance and counseling to students who participate in the program concerning the fulfillment of rural health professions program requirements, the selection of elective curricula and the selection of residency programs or internships. One of the faculty mentors shall be a physician, pharmacist or nurse who works closely with the participating student during the student's rural placement, and one of the mentors shall be a faculty member of the university where the program participant is enrolled. At least one of the mentors shall be available at all times to support the student's interest in rural health care.

F. For purposes of this section, "rural" means either:

1. A county with a population of less than four hundred thousand persons according to the most recent United States decennial census.

2. A census county division with less than fifty thousand persons in a county with a population of four hundred thousand or more persons according to the most recent United States decennial census.
Added by Laws 1996, Ch. 237, § 4.

Historical and Statutory Notes

Source:
A.R.S. former § 15-1752.
Laws 1994, Ch. 257, § 1.
Laws 1995, Ch. 207, § 1.

ARTICLE 10. UNIFORM ATHLETE AGENTS ACT

Article 10, Uniform Athlete Agents Act, consisting of §§ 15-1761 to 15-1776, was added by Laws 2001, Ch. 175, § 2, effective April 21, 2001.

Former Article 10, Athlete Agents, consisting of §§ 15-1761 to 15-1765, added by Laws 1999, Ch. 39, § 1, was repealed by Laws 2001, Ch. 175, § 1, effective April 21, 2001.

ATHLETE AGENTS ACT (2000)

Table of Jurisdictions Wherein 2000 Act Has Been Adopted

For text of Uniform Acts, and variation notes and annotation materials for adopting jurisdictions, see Uniform Laws Annotated, Master Edition, Volume 7B.

Jurisdiction	Laws	Effective Date	Statutory Citation
Alabama	2001, Act 701	10-1-2001	Code, 1975, §§ 8-26A-1 to 8-26A-31.
Arizona	2001, c. 175	4-21-2001	A.R.S. §§ 15-1761 to 15-1776.
Arkansas	2001, Act 1622	4-16-2001*	A.C.A. §§ 17-16-101 to 17-16-122.
Delaware	2001, c. 144	1-1-2002	24 Del.C. §§ 5401 to 5420.
Idaho	2001, c. 202	7-1-2001	I.C. §§ 54-4801 to 54-4820.
Indiana	2001, P.L. 54-2001	7-1-2001	West's A.I.C. 25-5.2-1-1 to 25-5.2-2-16.
Mississippi	2001, c. 536	7-1-2001	Code 1972, §§ 73-42-1 to 73-42-35.
Nevada	2001, c. 284	10-1-2001	NRS 398.400 to 398.496.
Tennessee	2001, c. 342	7-1-2001	T.C.A. §§ 49-7-2122 to 49-7-2141.
Utah	2001, c. 237	4-30-2001	U.C.A.1953, 15-9-101 to 15-9-119.
West Virginia	2001, c. 238	7-1-2001	Code, 30-39-1 to 30-39-21.

* Date of approval.

§ 15-1761. Short title

This article may be cited as the Uniform Athlete Agents Act.
Added by Laws 2001, Ch. 175, § 2, eff. April 21, 2001.

Historical and Statutory Notes

Former § 15-1761, added by Laws 1999, Ch. 39, § 1, containing definitions, was repealed by Laws 2001, Ch. 175, § 1, effective April 21, 2001. See, now, § 15-1762.

§ 15-1762. Definitions

In this article, unless the context otherwise requires:

1. "Agency contract" means an agreement in which a student athlete authorizes a person to negotiate or solicit a professional sports services contract or an endorsement contract on behalf of the student athlete.

2. "Athlete agent" means an individual who enters into an agency contract with a student athlete or, directly or indirectly, recruits or solicits a student athlete to enter into an agency contract. Athlete agent includes an individual who represents to the public that the individual is an athlete agent. Athlete agent does not include a spouse, parent, sibling, grandparent or guardian of the student athlete or an individual acting solely on behalf of a professional sports team or a professional sports organization.

3. "Athletic director" means an individual responsible for administering the overall athletic program of an educational institution or, if an educational institution has separately administered athletic programs for male students and female students, the athletic program for males or the athletic program for females.

4. "Contact" means a direct or indirect communication between an athlete agent and a student athlete to recruit or solicit the student athlete to enter into an agency contract.

5. "Endorsement contract" means an agreement under which a student athlete is employed or receives consideration to use on behalf of the other party any value that the student athlete may generate because of publicity, reputation, following or fame that was obtained because of athletic ability or performance.

6. "Intercollegiate sport" means a sport that is played at the collegiate level and for which eligibility requirements for participation by a student athlete are established by a national association for the promotion or regulation of collegiate athletics.

7. "Person" means an individual, a corporation, a business trust, an estate, a trust, a partnership, a limited liability company, an association, a joint venture, a government, a governmental subdivision, a government agency, a government instrumentality, a public corporation or any other legal or commercial entity.

8. "Professional sports services contract" means an agreement under which an individual is employed, or agrees to render services, as a player on a professional sports team, with a professional sports organization or as a professional athlete.

9. "Record" means information that is inscribed on a tangible medium or that is stored in an electronic format or any other medium and that is retrievable in perceivable form.

10. "Registration" means registration as an athlete agent pursuant to this article.

11. "State" means a State of the United States, the District of Columbia, Puerto Rico, the United States Virgin Islands or any territory or insular possession subject to the jurisdiction of the United States.

12. "Student athlete" means an individual who engages in, is eligible to engage in or may be eligible in the future to engage in any intercollegiate sport. If an individual is permanently ineligible to participate in a particular intercollegiate sport, the individual is not a student athlete for purposes of that sport.

Added by Laws 2001, Ch. 175, § 2, eff. April 21, 2001.

Historical and Statutory Notes

Source:

Laws 1999, Ch. 39, § 1.
A.R.S. former § 15-1761.

Former § 15-1762, added by Laws 1999, Ch. 39, § 1, relating to violations of the article, was repealed by Laws 2001, Ch. 175, § 1, effective April 21, 2001. See, now, § 15-1774.

§ 15-1763. Service of process; subpoenas

A. By acting as an athlete agent in this State, a nonresident individual constructively appoints the Secretary of State as the individual's agent for service of process in any civil action in this State related to the individual's athlete agent activities in this State.

B. The Secretary of State may issue subpoenas for any material that is relevant to the administration of this article.

Added by Laws 2001, Ch. 175, § 2, eff. April 21, 2001.

Historical and Statutory Notes

Former § 15-1763, added by Laws 1999, Ch. 39, § 1, relating to agreements between an athlete and athlete agent entered into before the athlete's eligibility to participate in intercollegiate sports at an institution of higher education has terminated, was repealed by Laws 2001, Ch. 175, § 1, effective April 21, 2001.

§ 15-1764. Athlete agents; registration; void contracts

A. Except as otherwise provided in subsection b of this section, an individual may not act as an athlete agent in this State without holding a certificate of registration under Section 15-1766 or 15-1768.

B. Before being issued a certificate of registration, an individual may act as an athlete agent in this state for all purposes other than signing an agency contract, if both:

1. A student athlete or another person acting on behalf of the student athlete initiates communication with the individual.

2. Within seven days after an initial act as an athlete agent, the individual submits an application for registration as an athlete agent in this State.

C. An agency contract resulting from conduct in violation of this section is void, and the athlete agent shall return any consideration received under the contract.

Added by Laws 2001, Ch. 175, § 2, eff. April 21, 2001.

Historical and Statutory Notes

Former § 15-1764, added by Laws 1999, Ch. 39, § 1, relating to applicability of the article, was repealed by Laws 2001, Ch. 175, § 1, effective April 21, 2001.

§ 15-1765. Registration as athlete agent; form; requirements

A. An applicant for registration as an athlete agent shall submit an application for registration to the Secretary of State in a form prescribed by the Secretary of State. An application filed under this section is a public record under title 39. [1] The application shall be in the name of an individual and, except as otherwise provided in subsection b of this section, shall be signed or otherwise authenticated by the applicant under penalty of perjury. The application shall state or contain the following:

1. The name of the applicant and the address of the applicant's principal place of business.

2. The name of the applicant's business or employer, if applicable.

3. Any business or occupation engaged in by the applicant for the five years immediately preceding the date of the submission of the application.

4. A description of the applicant's:

(a) Formal training as an athlete agent.

(b) Practical experience as an athlete agent.

(c) Educational background relating to the applicant's activities as an athlete agent.

5. The names and addresses of three individuals who are not related to the applicant and who are willing to serve as references for the applicant.

6. The name, sport and last known team of each individual for whom the applicant acted as an athlete agent during the five years immediately preceding the date of the submission of the application.

7. The names and addresses of all persons who are:

(a) With respect to the athlete agent's business if it is not a corporation, the partners, members, officers, managers, associates or profit sharers of the business.

(b) With respect to a corporation employing the athlete agent, the officers, the directors and any shareholder of the corporation that has an ownership interest of five per cent or more in the corporation.

8. Whether the applicant or any person named pursuant to paragraph 7 of this subsection has been convicted of a crime that, if committed in this State, would be a crime involving moral turpitude or a felony. If the applicant gives an affirmative response to the information requested pursuant to this paragraph, the applicant shall list each specific criminal conviction.

9. Whether there has been any administrative or judicial determination that the applicant or any person named pursuant to paragraph 7 of this subsection has made a false, misleading, deceptive or fraudulent representation.

10. Any instance in which the conduct of the applicant or any person named pursuant to paragraph 7 of this subsection resulted in the imposition on a student athlete or an educational institution of a sanction, suspension or declaration of ineligibility to participate in an interscholastic or intercollegiate athletic event.

11. Any sanction, suspension or disciplinary action that was taken against the applicant or any person named pursuant to paragraph 7 of this subsection and that arose out of occupational or professional misconduct.

12. Whether there has been any denial of an application for, suspension or revocation of or refusal to renew the registration or licensure of the applicant or any person named pursuant to paragraph 7 of this subsection as an athlete agent in any State.

B. An individual who has submitted an application for and holds a certificate of registration or licensure as an athlete agent in another State may submit a copy of the application and certificate in lieu of submitting an application in the form prescribed pursuant to subsection a. The Secretary of State shall accept the application and the certificate from the other State as an application for registration in this State if the application to the other State meets all of the following requirements:

1. Was submitted in the other State within the six months immediately preceding the submission of the application in this State and the applicant certifies that the information contained in the application is current and correct.

2. Contains information that is substantially similar to or more comprehensive than that required in an application submitted in this State.

3. Was signed by the applicant under penalty of perjury.

Added by Laws 2001, Ch. 175, § 2, eff. April 21, 2001.

[1] Section 39-4101 et seq.

Historical and Statutory Notes

Former § 15-1765, added by Laws 1999, Ch. 39, § 1, relating to civil liability for failure to comply with the article, was repealed by Laws 2001, Ch. 175, § 1, effective April 21, 2001. See, now, § 15-1775.

Reviser's Notes:

2001 Note. Pursuant to authority of § 41-1304.02, in subsection A, paragraph 10 the words "on a student athlete or an educational institution" were transposed to follow "imposition".

§ 15-1766. Certificate of registration; issuance or denial; renewal

A. Except as otherwise provided in subsection B of this section, the Secretary of State shall issue a certificate of registration to an individual who complies with Section 15-1765, subsection a or whose application has been accepted under Section 15-1765, subsection B.

B. The Secretary of State may refuse to issue a certificate of registration if the Secretary of State determines that the applicant has engaged in conduct that has a significant adverse effect on the applicant's fitness to act as an athlete agent. In making the determination, the Secretary of State may consider whether the applicant has:

1. Been convicted of a crime that, if committed in this State, would be a crime involving moral turpitude or would be a felony.

2. Made a materially false, misleading, deceptive or fraudulent representation in the application or as an athlete agent.

3. Engaged in conduct that would disqualify the applicant from serving in a fiduciary capacity.

4. Engaged in conduct that is prohibited by Section 15-1774.

5. Has had a registration or licensure as an athlete agent suspended, revoked or denied or has been refused renewal of registration or licensure as an athlete agent in any State.

6. Engaged in conduct that resulted in a sanction, suspension or declaration of ineligibility to participate being imposed on a student athlete or an educational institution in an interscholastic or an intercollegiate athletic event.

7. Engaged in conduct that significantly adversely reflects on the applicant's credibility, honesty or integrity.

C. In making a determination under subsection B of this section, the Secretary of State shall consider all of the following:

1. The time between the conduct that occurred and the date of the application.

2. The nature of the conduct and the context in which the conduct occurred.

3. Any other relevant conduct of the applicant.

D. An athlete agent may apply to renew a registration by submitting an application for renewal in a form prescribed by the Secretary of State. An application for renewal that is filed pursuant to this subsection is a public record under title 39. [1] The application for renewal shall be signed by the applicant under penalty of perjury and must contain current information concerning all matters required in an original registration.

E. An individual who has submitted an application for renewal of registration or licensure in another State, in lieu of submitting an application for renewal in the form prescribed pursuant to subsection d of this section, may file a copy of the application for renewal and a valid certificate of registration or licensure from the other State. The Secretary of State shall accept the application for renewal from the other State as an application for renewal in this State if the application to the other State meets all of the following requirements:

1. Was submitted in the other State within the six months immediately preceding the filing in this State and the applicant certifies the information contained in the application for renewal is current and correct.

2. Contains information that is substantially similar to or more comprehensive than that required in an application for renewal submitted in this State.

3. Was signed by the applicant under penalty of perjury.

F. A certificate of registration or a renewal of a registration is valid for two years from the date of issuance.

Added by Laws 2001, Ch. 175, § 2, eff. April 21, 2001.

[1] Section 39-4101 et seq.

§ 15-1767. Suspension, revocation or refusal to renew registration

A. The Secretary of State may suspend, revoke or refuse to renew a registration for conduct that would have justified denial of registration under Section 15-1766, subsection B.

B. The Secretary of State may deny, suspend, revoke or refuse to renew a certificate of registration only after proper notice and an opportunity for a hearing pursuant to title 41, chapter 6. [1]

Added by Laws 2001, Ch. 175, § 2, eff. April 21, 2001.

[1] Section 41-1001 et seq.

§ 15-1768. Temporary registration

The Secretary of State may issue a temporary certificate of registration while an application for registration or renewal of registration pursuant to this article is pending.

Added by Laws 2001, Ch. 175, § 2, eff. April 21, 2001.

§ 15-1769. Registration and renewal fees

An application for registration or renewal of registration shall be accompanied by the payment to the secretary of state of a fee in the following amounts:

1. For an initial application for registration, twenty dollars.

2. For an application for registration based on a certificate of registration or licensure issued by another State, twenty dollars.

3. For an application for renewal of registration, twenty dollars.

4. For an application for renewal of registration based on an application for renewal of registration or licensure submitted in another State, twenty dollars.

Added by Laws 2001, Ch. 175, § 2, eff. April 21, 2001.

§ 15-1770. Required form of contract

A. An agency contract shall be a record that is signed or otherwise authenticated by the parties.

B. An agency contract shall state or contain the following:

1. The amount and method of calculating the consideration to be paid by the student athlete for services to be provided by the athlete agent under the contract and any other consideration the athlete agent has received or will receive from any other source for entering into the contract or for providing the services.

2. The name of any person who is not listed in the application for registration or renewal of registration and who will be compensated because the student athlete signed the agency contract.

3. A description of any expenses that the student athlete agrees to reimburse the athlete agent.

4. A description of the services to be provided to the student athlete.

5. The duration of the contract.

6. The date of the execution of the contract.

C. An agency contract shall contain, in close proximity to the signature of the student athlete, a conspicuous notice in bold-faced type in capital letters that states the following:

WARNING TO STUDENT ATHLETE

IF YOU SIGN THIS CONTRACT:

1. YOU MAY LOSE YOUR ELIGIBILITY TO COMPETE AS A STUDENT ATHLETE IN YOUR SPORT.

2. IF YOU HAVE AN ATHLETIC DIRECTOR, WITHIN 72 HOURS AFTER ENTERING INTO THIS CONTRACT OR BEFORE THE NEXT ATHLETIC EVENT IN WHICH THE STUDENT ATHLETE MAY PARTICIPATE, WHICHEVER COMES FIRST, BOTH YOU AND YOUR ATHLETE AGENT MUST NOTIFY YOUR ATHLETIC DIRECTOR.

3. YOU MAY CANCEL THIS CONTRACT WITHIN 14 DAYS AFTER SIGNING IT. CANCELLATION OF THIS CONTRACT MAY NOT REINSTATE YOUR ELIGIBILITY.

D. An agency contract that does not conform to this section is voidable by the student athlete. If a student athlete voids an agency contract, the student athlete is not required to pay any consideration under the contract or to return any consideration that was received from the athlete agent and that was given to induce the student athlete to enter into the contract.

E. The athlete agent shall give a copy of the signed or otherwise authenticated agency contract to the student athlete at the time of execution.

Added by Laws 2001, Ch. 175, § 2, eff. April 21, 2001.

§ 15–1771. Notice to educational institution

A. Within seventy-two hours after entering into an agency contract or before the next scheduled athletic event in which the student athlete may participate, whichever occurs first, the athlete agent shall give notice in a record of the existence of the contract to the athletic director of the educational institution at which the student athlete is enrolled or the educational institution at which the athlete agent has reasonable grounds to believe the student athlete intends to enroll.

B. Within seventy-two hours after entering into an agency contract or before the next athletic event in which the student athlete may participate, whichever occurs first, the student athlete shall inform the athletic director of the educational institution at which the student athlete is enrolled that he or she has entered into an agency contract.

Added by Laws 2001, Ch. 175, § 2, eff. April 21, 2001.

§ 15–1772. Student athlete's right to cancel contract

A. A student athlete may cancel an agency contract by giving notice of the cancellation to the athlete agent in a record within fourteen days after the contract is signed.

B. A student athlete may not waive the right to cancel an agency contract.

C. If a student athlete cancels an agency contract, the student athlete is not required to pay any consideration under the contract or to return any consideration received from the athlete agent to induce the student athlete to enter into the contract.

Added by Laws 2001, Ch. 175, § 2, eff. April 21, 2001.

§ 15–1773. Required records

A. An athlete agent shall retain all of the following records for a period of five years:

1. The name and address of each individual represented by the athlete agent.

2. Any agency contract entered into by the athlete agent.

3. Documentation of any direct costs incurred by the athlete agent in the recruitment or solicitation of a student athlete to enter into an agency contract.

B. The Records required to be retained pursuant to subsection a shall be open to inspection by the Secretary of State during normal business hours.
Added by Laws 2001, Ch. 175, § 2, eff. April 21, 2001.

§ 15-1774. Prohibited conduct; violation; classification

A. It is unlawful for An athlete agent, with the intent to induce a student athlete to enter into an agency contract, to engage in any of the following conduct:

1. Give any materially false or misleading information or make a materially false promise or representation.

2. Furnish anything of value to a student athlete before the student athlete enters into the agency contract.

3. Furnish anything of value to any individual other than the student athlete or another registered athlete agent.

B. It is unlawful for An athlete agent to intentionally commit any of the following conduct:

1. Initiate contact with a student athlete unless the athlete agent is registered with the secretary of state pursuant to this article.

2. Refuse or fail to retain or permit inspection of the records required to be retained by Section 15-1773.

3. Fail to register if required by Section 15-1764.

4. Provide materially false or misleading information in an application for registration or renewal of registration.

5. Predate or postdate an agency contract.

6. Fail to notify a student athlete before the student athlete signs or otherwise authenticates an agency contract for a particular sport that the signing or authentication may make the student athlete ineligible to participate as a student athlete in that sport.

C. A person who violates this section is guilty of a class 1 misdemeanor.
Added by Laws 2001, Ch. 175, § 2, eff. April 21, 2001.

Historical and Statutory Notes

Source:

Laws 1999, Ch. 39, § 1.
A.R.S. former § 15-1762.

§ 15-1775. Civil remedies

A. An educational institution may bring a cause of action against an athlete agent or a former student athlete for damages caused by a violation of this article. The court may award to the prevailing party costs and reasonable attorney fees in any action brought pursuant to this section.

B. An educational institution may recover damages pursuant to subsection a including losses and expenses incurred as a result of the conduct of an athlete agent or a former student athlete if the educational institution was injured by a violation of this article or was penalized, disqualified or suspended from participation in athletics by a national association for the promotion and regulation of athletics, by an athletic conference or by reasonable self-imposed disciplinary action taken to mitigate sanctions likely to be imposed by such an organization.

C. A right of action under this section does not accrue until the educational institution discovers or by the exercise of reasonable diligence should have discovered the violation by the athlete agent or the former student athlete.

D. Any liability of the athlete agent or the former student athlete under this section is several and not joint.

E. This article does not restrict other legal or equitable rights, remedies or defenses of any person.

Added by Laws 2001, Ch. 175, § 2, eff. April 21, 2001.

Historical and Statutory Notes

Source:

Laws 1999, Ch. 39, § 1.
A.R.S. former § 15–1765.

§ 15–1776. Administrative penalties

The Secretary of State may assess a civil penalty against an athlete agent in an amount of not to exceed twenty-five thousand dollars for each violation of this article.

Added by Laws 2001, Ch. 175, § 2, eff. April 21, 2001.

CHAPTER 14

PROVISIONS RELATING TO BOTH COMMUNITY COLLEGES AND UNIVERSITIES

ARTICLE 1. CLASSIFICATION OF STUDENTS FOR TUITION PURPOSES

ARTICLE 2. ADMISSION OF STUDENTS

ARTICLE 3. VOCATIONAL PROGRAMS

ARTICLE 4. SELECTIVE SERVICE REGISTRATION AND STUDENT LOAN REPAYMENT

ARTICLE 5. COMMISSION FOR POSTSECONDARY EDUCATION

ARTICLE 6. GUARANTEED TUITION PROGRAMS [REPEALED]

ARTICLE 7. COLLEGE SAVINGS PLAN

Chapter 14, consisting of Article 1, §§ 15–1801 to 15–1807, was added by Laws 1981, Ch. 1, § 2, effective January 23, 1981.

Laws 1982, Ch. 229, § 25, subsec. C substituted "Provisions Relating to Both Community Colleges and Universities" for "Provisions Relating to Both Community Colleges and Universities and Colleges" as the heading for this chapter.

ARTICLE 1. CLASSIFICATION OF STUDENTS FOR TUITION PURPOSES

§ 15–1801. Definitions

In this article, unless the context otherwise requires:

1. "Armed forces of the United States" means the army, the navy, the air force, the marine corps, the coast guard, the commissioned corps of the United States public health services, the national oceanographic and atmospheric administration, the national guard and any military reserve unit of any branch of the armed forces of the united states.

2. "Continuous attendance" means enrollment at an educational institution in this state as a full-time student, as such term is defined by the governing body of the educational institution, for a normal academic year since the beginning of the period for which continuous attendance is claimed. Such person need not attend summer sessions or any other intersession beyond the normal academic year in order to maintain continuous attendance.

3. "Domicile" means a person's true, fixed and permanent home and place of habitation. It is the place where he intends to remain and to which he

expects to return when he leaves without intending to establish a new domicile elsewhere.

4. "Emancipated person" means a person who is neither under a legal duty of service to his parent nor entitled to the support of such parent under the laws of this state.

5. "Parent" means a person's father or mother, or if one parent has custody, that parent, or if there is no surviving parent or the whereabouts of the parents are unknown, then a guardian of an unemancipated person if there are not circumstances indicating that such guardianship was created primarily for the purpose of conferring the status of an in-state student on such unemancipated person.

Added by Laws 1981, Ch. 1, § 2, eff. Jan. 23, 1981. Amended by Laws 1982, Ch. 229, § 13; Laws 1984, Ch. 86, § 1, eff. April 12, 1984; Laws 1998, Ch. 201, § 1.

Historical and Statutory Notes

Source:

Laws 1972, Ch. 101, § 2.
A.R.S. former § 15-791.

§ 15-1802. In-state student status

A. Except as otherwise provided in this article no person having a domicile elsewhere than in this state is eligible for classification as an in-state student for tuition purposes.

B. A person is not entitled to classification as an in-state student until the person is domiciled in this state for one year, except that a person whose domicile is in this state is entitled to classification as an in-state student if the person meets one of the following requirements:

1. The person's parent's domicile is in this state and the parent is entitled to claim the person as an exemption for state and federal tax purposes.

2. The person is an employee of an employer which transferred the person to this state for employment purposes or the person is the spouse of such employee.

3. The person is an employee of a school district in this state and is under contract to teach on a full-time basis, or is employed as a full-time noncertified classroom aide, at a school within that school district. For purposes of this paragraph, the person is eligible for classification as an in-state student only for courses necessary to complete the requirements for certification by the state board of education to teach in a school district in this state. No member of the person's family is eligible for classification as an in-state student if the person is eligible for classification as an in-state student pursuant to this paragraph.

C. The domicile of an unemancipated person is that of such person's parent.

D. Any unemancipated person who remains in this state when such person's parent, who had been domiciled in this state, removes from this state is entitled to classification as an in-state student until attainment of the degree for which currently enrolled, as long as such person maintains continuous attendance.

E. A person who is a member of the armed forces of the United States and who is stationed in this state pursuant to military orders or who is the spouse or a dependent child as defined in § 43–1001 of a person who is a member of the armed forces of the United States and who is stationed in this state pursuant to military orders is entitled to classification as an in-state student. The student, while in continuous attendance toward the degree for which currently enrolled, does not lose in-state student classification.

F. A person who is a member of the armed forces of the United States or the spouse or a dependent as defined in § 43–1001 of a member of the armed forces of the United States is entitled to classification as an in-state student if the member of the armed forces has claimed this state as the person's state of legal residence for at least twelve consecutive months before the member of the armed forces, spouse or dependent enrolls in a university under the jurisdiction of the Arizona board of regents or a community college under the jurisdiction of a community college district governing board. For purposes of this subsection, the requirement that a person be domiciled in this state for one year before enrollment to qualify for in-state student classification does not apply.

G. A person who is honorably discharged from the armed forces of the United States shall be granted immediate classification as an in-state student on honorable discharge from the armed forces and, while in continuous attendance toward the degree for which currently enrolled, does not lose in-state student classification if the person has met all of the following requirements:

1. Declared Arizona as the person's legal residence with the person's branch of service at least one year prior to discharge from the armed forces.

2. Demonstrated objective evidence of intent to be a resident of Arizona which, for the purposes of this section, includes at least one of the following:

(a) An Arizona driver license.

(b) Arizona motor vehicle registration.

(c) Employment history in Arizona.

(d) Arizona voter registration.

(e) Transfer of major banking services to Arizona.

(f) Change of permanent address on all pertinent records.

(g) Other materials of whatever kind or source relevant to domicile or residency status.

3. Filed an Arizona income tax return with the department of revenue during the previous tax year.

H. A person who is a member of an Indian tribe recognized by the United States department of the interior whose reservation land lies in this state and extends into another state and who is a resident of the reservation is entitled to classification as an in-state student.

Added by Laws 1981, Ch. 1, § 2, eff. Jan. 23, 1981. Amended by Laws 1982, Ch. 229, § 14; Laws 1985, Ch. 133, § 2; Laws 1998, Ch. 202, § 1; Laws 1999, Ch. 5, § 3; Laws 1999, Ch. 124, § 1; Laws 2000, Ch. 322, § 1; Laws 2002, Ch. 330, § 31.

Historical and Statutory Notes

Source:

Laws 1972, Ch. 101, § 2.
A.R.S. former § 15–792.
Laws 1978, Ch. 167, § 1.
Laws 1979, Ch. 168, § 2.

Laws 2002, Ch. 330, became law without the Governor's signature as provided in Arizona Constitution, Article 5, § 7.

Reviser's Notes:

1999 Note. Prior to the 2000 amendments, this section contained the amendments made by Laws 1999, Ch. 5, sec. 3 and Ch. 124, sec. 1 that were blended together pursuant to authority of § 41–1304.03.

§ 15–1802.01. County residency status; community college districts

A. Each community college district shall adopt policies regarding domicile requirements that include, at a minimum, the following:

1. Each student shall have the question of domicile determined before the time of registration and payment of fees. It is the responsibility of the student to register under the correct domicile determination.

2. Enforcement of domicile requirements shall be the responsibility of the chief executive officer of each community college district.

3. The chief executive officer of each community college district shall designate a representative at each college or campus who is responsible for documents and who is qualified to administer oaths as defined in § 41–311 in connection with statements and testimony relative to student domicile status for tuition purposes.

4. In addition to the requirements prescribed in § 15–1802, subsection G, any of the following may be used in determining a student's domicile:

(a) An income tax return.

(b) The place of graduation from high school.

(c) The source of financial support.

(d) Dependency as indicated on a federal income tax return.

(e) Ownership of real property.

(f) A notarized statement of a landlord or employer.

(g) Bank accounts.

B. Each community college district shall adopt policies regarding classification procedures for a student for nonresident or resident tuition purposes that include, at a minimum, the following:

1. In determining a student's classification, the college may consider all evidence, written or oral, presented by the student and any other information received from any source that is relevant to determining classification. The college may request written sworn statements or sworn testimony of the student.

2. The decision as to classification shall be made by the representative designated pursuant to subsection A, paragraph 3 of this section. In making the decision the representative may consult with other college officials. Decisions by the representative shall be made as soon as possible after all relevant information is acquired.

3. If the representative classifies the student as a nonresident for tuition purposes, the decision shall be communicated to the student by mail to the most recent address furnished to the college. If the student is classified as a nonresident for tuition purposes, the student must make satisfactory provision for payment of nonresident tuition and other charges.

C. Each community college district shall adopt a review and appeals process for students contesting a domicile decision by the college.

D. An individual domiciled in this state, but not in a community college district, shall be required to sign a notarized statement as to county residency stating that the individual has resided in the county for at least fifty days before the first day of classes.

Added by Laws 2003, Ch. 253, § 28, eff. Sept. 18, 2003, retroactively effective to July 1, 2003. Amended by Laws 2004, Ch. 336, § 14.

§ 15-1803. Alien in-state student status

An alien is entitled to classification as an in-state refugee student if such person has been granted refugee status in accordance with all applicable laws of the United States and has met all other requirements for domicile.

Added by Laws 1982, Ch. 229, § 15.

Historical and Statutory Notes

Source:

Laws 1977, Ch. 73, § 3.
A.R.S. former §§ 15-792.01, 15-1803.
Laws 1981, Ch. 1, § 2.

Former § 15-1803, added by Laws 1981, Ch. 1, § 2, and relating to alien instate student status, was repealed by Laws 1981, Ch. 314, § 25.

§ 15-1804. Presumptions relating to student status; definition

A. Unless the contrary appears to the satisfaction of the registering authority of the community college or university at which a student is registering, it shall be presumed that:

1. No emancipated person has established a domicile in this state while attending any educational institution in this state as a full-time student, as such status is defined by subsection B for community college students or as defined by the Arizona board of regents for university students, in the absence of a clear demonstration to the contrary.

2. Once established, a domicile is not lost by mere absence unaccompanied by intention to establish a new domicile.

3. A person who has been domiciled in this state immediately prior to becoming a member of the armed forces of the United States shall not lose in-state status by reason of such person's presence in any other state or country while a member of the armed forces of the United States.

B. For the purposes of this section, "full-time student" means a community college student who registers for at least twelve semester hours per semester at a community college in this state.

Added by Laws 1981, Ch. 1, § 2, eff. Jan. 23, 1981. Amended by Laws 1982, Ch. 229, § 16; Laws 2004, Ch. 336, § 15.

Historical and Statutory Notes

Source:
Laws 1972, Ch. 101, § 2.
A.R.S. former § 15-793.
Laws 1978, Ch. 167, § 2.

§ 15-1805. Student status guidelines

A. The Arizona board of regents shall adopt guidelines applicable to all institutions under their jurisdiction that will ensure uniform criteria to aid the institutions in determining the tuition status of any student and that will establish uniform procedures for review of that status.

B. Community college districts shall adopt policies applicable to all institutions under their jurisdiction that will ensure uniform criteria to aid the institutions in determining the tuition status of any student and that will establish uniform procedures for review of that status.

Added by Laws 1981, Ch. 1, § 2, eff. Jan. 23, 1981. Amended by Laws 2003, Ch. 253, § 29, eff. Sept. 18, 2003, retroactively effective to July 1, 2003.

Historical and Statutory Notes

Source:
Laws 1972, Ch. 101, § 2.
A.R.S. former § 15-794.

Reviser's Notes:

2003 Note. Pursuant to authority of § 41-1304.02, in the section heading "guidelines" was substituted for "regulations".

§ 15-1805.01. Admissions; enrollments; community colleges

A. Admissions to the community colleges in this state may be granted to any person who meets any one of the following criteria:

1. Is a graduate of a high school that is accredited by a regional accrediting association as defined by the United States office of education or approved by a state board of education or other appropriate state educational agency.

2. Has a high school certificate of equivalency.

3. Is eighteen years of age or older and demonstrates evidence of potential success in the community college.

4. Is a transfer student in good standing from another college or university.

B. Each community college district shall adopt policies regarding the admission of students under eighteen years of age that include, at a minimum, the following requirements:

1. Admission to the community colleges in this state shall be granted to any student who is under eighteen years of age and who achieves a composite score of 930 or more on the scholastic aptitude test or a composite score of twenty-two or more on the American college test.

2. A community college may limit the number of semester hours in which the student may enroll to not more than six credit hours.

C. Students may be admitted on an individual basis with the approval of college officials if the student meets the established requirements of the courses for which the student enrolls and the college officials determine that the student's admission is in the best interest of the student.

Added by Laws 2003, Ch. 253, § 30, eff. Sept. 18, 2003, retroactively effective to July 1, 2003.

§ 15-1806. Testimony concerning student status; designation of persons to administer oaths

The Arizona board of regents and each community college district shall designate a person employed at each institution under their respective jurisdictions to administer oaths or affirmations in connection with the taking of testimony relative to student status for tuition purposes.

Added by Laws 1981, Ch. 1, § 2, eff. Jan. 23, 1981. Amended by Laws 2003, Ch. 253, § 31, eff. Sept. 18, 2003, retroactively effective to July 1, 2003.

Historical and Statutory Notes

Source:

Laws 1972, Ch. 101, § 2.
A.R.S. former § 15-795.

§ 15-1807. Concurrent enrollment; nonresident tuition

A. It is unlawful for any nonresident student to register concurrently in two or more public institutions of higher education in this state including any university or community college for a combined student credit hour enrollment of more than six semester hours without payment of nonresident tuition at one of such institutions.

B. Any nonresident student desiring to enroll concurrently in two or more public institutions of higher education in this state including any university or community college for a combined total of more than six semester hours who is not subject to nonresident tuition at any of such institutions shall pay the nonresident tuition at the institution of his choice in an amount equivalent to nonresident tuition at such institution for the combined total of semester hours for which the nonresident student is concurrently enrolled.

Added by Laws 1981, Ch. 1, § 2, eff. Jan. 23, 1981. Amended by Laws 1982, Ch. 229, § 17.

Historical and Statutory Notes

Source:

Laws 1980, Ch. 164, § 1.
A.R.S. former § 15-798.

§ 15-1808. Tuition waiver of child or spouse of peace officer, correctional officer, fire fighter, emergency paramedic or national guard member killed in the line of duty; disabled national guard member; definitions

A. The board of regents, after verification by the Arizona peace officers memorial board, by the Arizona fire fighters and emergency paramedics memorial board or by the adjutant general of the national guard that a person is a child or a spouse of a peace officer, correctional officer, fire fighter, emergency paramedic or national guard member who was a resident of the state of Arizona and who was killed in the line of duty or who died from injuries suffered in the line of duty while traveling to or from duty, shall provide the person who qualifies under subsection B of this section and who otherwise meets the qualifications for admission with a tuition waiver scholarship at any university under the jurisdiction of the board. A district as defined in § 15-1401, after verification by the Arizona peace officers memorial board, by the Arizona fire fighters and emergency paramedics memorial board or by the adjutant general of the national guard that a person is the child or the spouse of a peace officer, correctional officer, fire fighter, emergency paramedic or national guard member who was a resident of Arizona and who was killed in the line of duty or who died from injuries suffered in the line of duty while traveling to or from duty, shall provide the person who qualifies under subsection B of this section and who otherwise meets the qualifications for admission with a tuition waiver scholarship at any community college under the jurisdiction of the board.

B. The tuition waiver scholarships shall be limited to children who are thirty years of age or younger or a spouse who has not remarried and shall be limited for a spouse or for any one child to no more than sixty-four credit hours at Arizona community colleges and a total number of credits including any transfer credits from an Arizona community college equal to the number of credits required for a baccalaureate degree at Arizona universities for that student's initially declared course of study.

C. A member of the Arizona national guard who received a purple heart citation on or after September 11, 2001 or a former member of the Arizona national guard who was medically discharged from the Arizona national guard due to an injury or disability suffered during status under title 10, United States code, in weekend training status, in annual training status or in response to a state of emergency declared by the governor is eligible for a tuition waiver scholarship provided for in this section.

D. For the purposes of this section:

1. "Correctional officer" means a person, other than an elected official, who is employed by this state or a county, city or town and who is responsible for the supervision, protection, care, custody or control of inmates in a state, county or municipal correctional institution, including counselors but excluding secretarial, clerical and professionally trained personnel.

2. "Emergency paramedic" means a person who has been trained in an emergency paramedic training program certified by the director of the department of health services or in an equivalent training program and who is certified by the director of the department of health services to render services pursuant to § 36-2205.

3. "Fire fighter" means a professional fire fighter who is a member of a state, federal, tribal, city, county, district or private fire department.

4. "Peace officers" means sheriffs of counties, constables, marshals, police officers of cities and towns, commissioned personnel of the department of public safety and police officers appointed by community college district governing boards or the Arizona board of regents, who have received a certificate from the Arizona peace officer standards and training board, and other state, federal, tribal, city or county officers vested by law with a duty to maintain public order and make arrests.

Added by Laws 1989, Ch. 117, § 3. Amended by Laws 1990, Ch. 206, § 1; Laws 1998, Ch. 60, § 1, eff. May 7, 1998, retroactively effective to January 4, 1997; Laws 2003, Ch. 253, § 32, eff. Sept. 18, 2003, retroactively effective to July 1, 2003; Laws 2004, Ch. 224, § 1.

Historical and Statutory Notes

Reviser's Notes:

1989 Note. Pursuant to authority of § 41–1304.02, in the section heading "child of" was substituted for "killed" and "killed in the line of duty" was added after "officer".

1990 Note. Pursuant to authority of § 41–1304.02, in the section heading "or spouse" was added after "child".

2004 Note. Pursuant to authority of § 41–1304.02, in subsection D the definitions were alphabetized with paragraph 4 renumbered as paragraph 1 and paragraphs 1, 2 and 3 renumbered as paragraphs 2, 3 and 4, respectively.

ARTICLE 2. ADMISSION OF STUDENTS

Article 2, Admission of Students, consisting of § 15–1821, was added by Laws 1984, Ch. 311, § 3, effective August 3, 1984.

§ 15–1821. Special admission of students under age eighteen; enrollment information; reports

A. Each community college district board shall adopt policies which require community colleges under its jurisdiction to admit students under age eighteen who have not yet attained a high school diploma or high school certificate of equivalency and who meet the established requirements of the courses for which they enroll. The Arizona board of regents shall adopt rules which require the universities under its jurisdiction to admit students under age eighteen who have not yet attained a high school diploma or high school certificate of equivalency and who meet the established requirements of the courses for which they enroll.

B. The policies and rules as provided in subsection A shall include the following provisions:

1. No student under age eighteen shall be denied admission because of age, lack of a high school diploma or high school certificate of equivalency, grade in school, lack of permission of school officials or lack of concurrent enrollment in a public or private school, if the student has achieved at least a specified score on a college entrance examination.

2. A community college or university which admits a student pursuant to paragraph 1 of this subsection may limit the number of semester credit hours in which the student may enroll to no less than six semester credit hours.

3. A student admitted to a community college or university pursuant to paragraph 1 of this subsection is not guaranteed admission to a specific degree program or to all courses offered by the community college or university.

C. Each community college district and the Arizona board of regents shall provide all high schools in this state with information which describes the policies and rules, as appropriate, the types of courses available and other information related to the enrollment of students under the age of eighteen. Each unified or high school district school shall make this information available to all students in at least grades nine through twelve.

D. On or before November 15, each community college district and the Arizona board of regents shall submit a report to the president of the senate, the speaker of the house of representatives and the state board of education and shall provide a copy of this report to the secretary of state and the director of the Arizona state library, archives and public records, on students under eighteen years of age who had not yet attained a high school diploma or high school certificate of equivalency and who were enrolled in a university or community college course or a program for community college or university credit during the time period of September of the previous fiscal year through August of the current fiscal year. The annual report shall include at least the following:

1. The number of students who were enrolled.

2. A general narrative of the types of courses or programs in which the students were enrolled.

3. The rules adopted pursuant to subsection A.

E. On or before September 30, each institution under the jurisdiction of the Arizona board of regents shall submit to the Arizona board of regents in the form specified by the Arizona board of regents the information that the Arizona board of regents needs to compile the report required in subsection D.

Added by Laws 1984, Ch. 311, § 3. Amended by Laws 1989, Ch. 158, § 1; Laws 2003, Ch. 253, § 33, eff. Sept. 18, 2003, retroactively effective to July 1, 2003; Laws 2004, Ch. 336, § 16.

Historical and Statutory Notes

Reviser's Notes:

1989 Note. Pursuant to authority of § 41-1304.02, in the section heading "; enrollment information; reports" was added.

§ 15-1821.01. Dual enrollment information

On a determination by a community college district governing board that it is in the best interest of the citizens of a district, the district governing board may authorize district community colleges to offer college courses that may be counted toward both high school and college graduation requirements at the high school during the school day subject to the following:

1. The community college district governing board and the governing board of the school district or organization of which the high school is a part shall enter into an agreement or contract that, at a minimum, shall address the responsibility of the community college and of the high school for payment for facilities, personnel and other costs, and the manner in which the college tuition is to be paid by or on behalf of each student shall be clearly stated.

2. Students shall be admitted to the community college under the policies adopted by each district, subject to the following:

(a) All students enrolled for college credit shall be high school juniors or seniors. All students in the course, including those not electing to enroll for college credit, shall satisfy the prerequisites for the course as published in the college catalog and shall comply with college policies regarding student placement in courses.

(b) A community college may waive the class status requirements specified in subdivision (a) of this paragraph for up to twenty-five per cent of the students enrolled by a college in courses provided that the community college has an established written criteria for waiving the requirements for each course. These criteria shall include a demonstration, by an examination of the specific purposes and requirements of the course, that freshman and sophomore students who meet course prerequisites are prepared to benefit from the college level course. All exceptions and the justification for the exceptions shall be reported as provided in paragraph 6 of this section.

3. The courses shall be previously evaluated and approved through the curriculum approval process of the district, shall be at a higher level than taught by the high school and shall be transferable to a university under the jurisdiction of the Arizona board of regents or be applicable to an established community college occupational degree or certificate program. Physical education courses shall not be available for dual enrollment purposes.

4. College approved textbooks, syllabuses, course outlines and grading standards that are applicable to the courses if taught at the community college shall apply to these courses and to all students in the courses offered pursuant to this section. The chief executive officer of each community college shall establish an advisory committee of full-time faculty who teach in the disciplines offered at the community college to assist in course selection and implementation in the high schools and to review and report at least annually to the chief executive officer whether the course goals and standards are understood, the course guidelines are followed and the same standards of expectation and assessment are applied to these courses as though they were being offered at the community college.

5. Each faculty member shall meet the requirements established by the governing board pursuant to § 15-1444. The chief executive officer of each community college district shall establish an advisory committee of full-time faculty who teach in the disciplines offered at the community college district to assist in the selection, orientation, ongoing professional development and evaluation of faculty teaching college courses in conjunction with the high schools.

6. Each community college district shall annually, on or before September 1, provide a report to the joint legislative budget committee on the courses offered in conjunction with high schools during the previous fiscal year. In the case of a multicollege district, the multicollege district shall provide a separate report for each college. This report shall include the following:

(a) Documentation of compliance with the requirements identified in paragraphs 3, 4 and 5 of this section.

(b) The number of students in each course who did not meet the criteria prescribed in paragraph 2 of this section.

(c) The total enrollments listed by location, by high school grade level, by course and by whether the program was academic or occupational.

(d) Summary data on the performance of students enrolled for college credit in courses offered in conjunction with high schools, including completion rates and grade distribution.

7. Each community college district shall conduct tracking studies of subsequent academic or occupational achievement of students enrolled in courses

offered pursuant to this section. The report of the results of the first tracking study shall be submitted to the joint legislative budget committee on or before September 1, 2003 and subsequent reports shall be submitted to the joint legislative budget committee on or before September 1 of each odd-numbered year thereafter, subject to the following:

(a) The tracking studies prescribed in this paragraph may involve statistically valid sampling techniques and shall include, at a minimum, the high school graduation rate, the number of students continuing their studies after graduation at a community college in this state or a university under the jurisdiction of the Arizona board of regents, the performance of the students in subsequent college courses in the same discipline or occupational field and the student's grade point average after one year at an Arizona community college or university as compared to the student's college grade point average for courses completed while still in high school.

(b) On receipt of the report of the tracking studies prescribed in this paragraph, the joint legislative budget committee shall convene an ad hoc committee that includes community college academic officers, faculty and other experts in the field to review the manner in which these courses are provided. This committee may make recommendations to the joint legislative budget committee regarding desirable changes in this section or in the manner in which this section is being implemented. A copy of this report shall be provided to each district governing board.

8. A school district shall ensure that a pupil is a full-time student as defined in § 15-901 and is enrolled in and attending a full-time instructional program at a school in the school district before that pupil is allowed to enroll in a college course pursuant to this section, except that high school seniors who satisfy high school graduation requirements with less than a full-time instructional program shall be exempt from this subdivision. [1]

Added by Laws 2003, Ch. 253, § 34, eff. Sept. 18, 2003, retroactively effective to July 1, 2003.

[1] So in original. Should read "paragraph".

Historical and Statutory Notes

Reviser's Notes:

2003 Note. Pursuant to authority of § 41-1304.02, in paragraph 1 the second "shall" was transposed to follow "minimum,".

§ 15-1822. Report; academic performance of high school graduates

A. On or before October 31, each community college district and the Arizona board of regents shall submit a report to the president of the senate, the speaker of the house of representatives, the superintendent of public instruction and the state board of education and shall provide a copy of this report to the secretary of state and the director of the Arizona state library, archives and public records, on the academic performance of the preceding year's graduates from high schools in this state enrolled in institutions under their jurisdiction during the year ending on June 30 of the current calendar year. The report shall include for each school at least the following:

1. The number of graduates of the school who were enrolled in the institution during the reporting period.

2. Information about the academic performance of graduates of the school in mathematics and English courses.

B. On or before September 1, each institution under the jurisdiction of the Arizona board of regents shall submit to the Arizona board of regents in the form specified by the Arizona board of regents the information that the Arizona board of regents needs to compile the report required under this section.

C. The superintendent of public instruction shall provide each high school in this state with a copy of the portion of the report that is applicable to its graduates.

Added by Laws 1986, Ch. 304, § 1, eff. Jan. 1, 1987. Amended by Laws 2003, Ch. 253, § 35, eff. Sept. 18, 2003, retroactively effective to July 1, 2003; Laws 2004, Ch. 336, § 17.

Historical and Statutory Notes

Laws 1986, Ch. 304, § 2 provides:

"**Sec. 2. Effective date**

"This act is effective from and after December 31, 1986."

§ 15-1823. Identification numbers; social security numbers

A. From and after June 30, 2002, if a university under the jurisdiction of the Arizona board of regents assigns an individual identification number to faculty, staff or students at a university, the identification number shall not be identical to the individual's social security number. The university shall not allow the display of the individual's social security number, or any four or more consecutive numbers contained in the individual's social security number, on any internet site maintained by the university or other publicly accessible document for any purpose.

B. On request of an individual, a university under the jurisdiction of the Arizona board of regents shall assign faculty, staff or students an individual identification number that is identical to an individual's social security number. A university shall notify faculty, staff or students of the option to obtain an identification number for no additional fee that is identical to the individual's social security number on a form distributed at the time that the individual identification number is assigned.

C. If a community college or community college district assigns an individual identification number to faculty, staff or students at a community college that is identical to an individual's social security number, the community college or community college district shall not allow the display of an individual's social security number, or any four or more consecutive numbers contained in the individual's social security number, on any internet site maintained by the community college or community college district or other publicly accessible document for any purpose.

D. On the request of a student, a community college or community college district shall assign the student an identification number that is not identical to the student's social security number. Beginning January 1, 2004, if a high school student is enrolled in a college course offered by a community college district pursuant to § 15-1821.01, the identification number assigned to that student pursuant to this subsection shall correspond to the identification number assigned to that student in connection with the student accountability information system established by § 15-1041. A community college or community college district shall notify students of the option to obtain an individual identification number for no additional fee that is not identical to an individual's social security number in applications for admission, through telecommunications registration procedures, and in college catalogs. Notification in catalogs shall occur no later than June 30, 2000, or in the next printed edition of the catalog after the current one in print, whichever is sooner.

E. On the request of a faculty or staff member, a community college or community college district shall assign the faculty or staff member an identification number that is not identical to the faculty or staff member's social security number. A community college or community college district shall provide notification to faculty and staff members of the option to obtain an individual identification number that is not identical to a faculty or staff member's social security number.

F. This section does not exempt any regulated institution from any duty of compliance it may have with any federal law that may:

1. Regulate that institution's collection or use of social security numbers.
2. Protect the privacy rights of faculty, staff or students.

G. This section does not prohibit the electronic transfer of student transcripts between educational institutions.

Added by Laws 1999, Ch. 239, § 1. Amended by Laws 2000, Ch. 264, § 1; Laws 2003, Ch. 253, § 36, eff. Sept. 18, 2003, retroactively effective to July 1, 2003.

Retroactive Application

Section 15-1823, as amended by Laws 2000, Ch. 264, applies retroactively to August 6, 1999.

Historical and Statutory Notes

Reviser's Notes:

1999 Note. Pursuant to authority of § 41-1304.02, in § 1 [of Chapter 239] the article heading "Article 8. Student Identification Numbers" was removed to correct a manifest clerical error.

1999 Note. Pursuant to authority of § 41-1304.02, in the section heading "prohibited" was removed.

2000 Note. Pursuant to authority of § 41-1304.02, in the section heading "Student" was removed.

§ 15-1824. Transfer articulation; annual report

A. The community college districts and universities shall cooperate in operating a statewide articulation and transfer system, including the process for transfer of lower division general education credits, general elective credits and curriculum requirements for approved majors, to facilitate the transfer of community college students to Arizona public universities without a loss of credit toward a baccalaureate degree and to ensure that the postsecondary education needs of students statewide are met without unnecessary duplication of programs.

B. The Arizona board of regents and the community college districts shall submit an annual report of their progress on both articulation and meeting statewide postsecondary education needs to the joint legislative budget committee on or before December 15 and shall provide a copy of this report to the secretary of state and the director of the Arizona state library, archives and public records.

Added by Laws 2002, Ch. 330, § 32. Amended by Laws 2003, Ch. 253, § 37, eff. Sept. 18, 2003, retroactively effective to July 1, 2003; Laws 2004, Ch. 336, § 18.

Historical and Statutory Notes

Laws 2002, Ch. 330, became law without the Governor's signature as provided in Arizona Constitution, Article 5, § 7.

Reviser's Notes:

2002 Note. Pursuant to authority of § 41–1304.02, in subsection A "post secondary" was combined as one word.

ARTICLE 3. VOCATIONAL PROGRAMS

Article 3, Vocational Programs, consisting of § 15–1831, was added by Laws 1985, Ch. 338, § 1, effective August 7, 1985.

§ 15–1831. Information on persons who have completed vocational programs; definitions

A. The center for vocational education shall:

1. By the end of each calendar year publish and distribute a report of the placement rates and average salaries earned by persons completing vocational programs in this state during the prior fiscal year. This report may include information on a program which would be a vocational program except that it was not completed by at least twenty-five persons during the fiscal year.

2. Establish an advisory committee consisting of representatives of both public and private institutions which offer vocational programs. The advisory committee shall advise the center in the implementation of this section.

3. Prescribe the format in which institutions which offer vocational programs shall provide the information necessary to produce the report prescribed in paragraph 1 of this subsection.

B. The governing board of each community college district shall:

1. Transmit to the center for vocational education the following information within thirty days of the end of the fiscal year:

(a) The social security number of each person who completed a vocational program during the previous fiscal year.

(b) Such information as the center may require in order to conduct a follow-up survey of a sample of persons who have completed vocational programs.

2. Make available to students prior to or at the time of registration the report distributed by the center for vocational education as prescribed in this section.

C. In this section, unless the context otherwise requires:

1. "Center for vocational education" means the center for vocational education at a university under the jurisdiction of the Arizona board of regents designated by the board.

2. "Vocational program" means a program completed by at least twenty-five persons during the fiscal year and which is one of the following:

(a) Operated by a community college district organized pursuant to chapter 12 of this title[1] and designated as a vocational program, including vocational programs operated by a skill center.

(b) A private vocational program licensed pursuant to § 32-3021 which does not provide a baccalaureate degree.

Added by Laws 1985, Ch. 338, § 1. Amended by Laws 2003, Ch. 253, § 38, eff. Sept. 18, 2003, retroactively effective to July 1, 2003.

[1] Section 15-401 et seq.

ARTICLE 4. SELECTIVE SERVICE REGISTRATION AND STUDENT LOAN REPAYMENT

Article 4, Selective Service Registration and Student Loan Repayment, consisting of § 15-1841, was added by Laws 1988, Ch. 147, § 1, effective September 30, 1988.

§ 15-1841. Selective service registration; applicability

A. Except as provided in subsection B, a person is not eligible for any financial aid by the state from the expenditure of public funds for grants, loans or scholarships at a university or community college in this state unless the person has registered with the selective service system if required by the Federal Military Selective Service Act (62 Stat. 604; 50 United States Code App. § 453[1]).

B. A person may not be denied a right, privilege or benefit by reason of subsection A if either of the following applies:

1. The requirement for the person to so register has terminated or become inapplicable to the person.

2. The person shows by a preponderance of the evidence that the failure of the person to register with the selective service system was not a knowing and willful failure to register.

Added by Laws 1988, Ch. 147, § 1.

[1] 50 U.S.C.A. App. § 453.

Historical and Statutory Notes

Reviser's Notes:

1988 Note. Pursuant to authority of § 41-1304.02, in the section heading the words "and students loan repayment" were deleted.

ARTICLE 5. COMMISSION FOR POSTSECONDARY EDUCATION

Article 5, Commission For Postsecondary Education, consisting of §§ 15-1851 to 15-1853, was added by Laws 1994, Ch. 298, § 2, effective July 17, 1994.

Termination under Sunset Law

The commission for postsecondary education shall terminate on July 1, 2008, unless continued. See §§ 41–3008.14 and 41–2955.

Title 15, Chapter 14, Article 5, relating to the commission for postsecondary education, is repealed on January 1, 2009, by § 41–3008.14.

§ 15–1851. Commission for postsecondary education; purpose; report; members; terms; powers and duties; compensation; quorum; personal liability; definition

A. The commission for postsecondary education is established as the postsecondary review entity for this state for the conduct, supervision and coordination of the review of postsecondary education institutions in order to determine the eligibility of those institutions for student financial aid monies pursuant to the provisions of part H, subpart one of the higher education amendments of 1992 (P.L. 102–325; 106 Stat. 638; 20 United States Code § 1099a). The commission shall accomplish the purpose of this subsection through the accumulation of information, the performance of studies and the determination of compliance by the postsecondary education institutions with the provisions of part H, subpart one of the higher education amendments of 1992. The review authority of the commission shall be limited to circumstances where the United States department of education has referred an institution to the commission for review or where the United States department of education has approved the review of an institution in accordance with criteria established by the United States department of education. The commission shall keep records of its activities, and the commission shall provide information when requested to the United States secretary of education for financial and compliance audits and for institution evaluation. The scope of authority of the commission acting as a postsecondary review entity to review any educational institution is limited specifically to compliance by the institution with title IV, part H, subpart one of the higher education amendments of 1992. Any review of any institution conducted by the commission shall be performed in the context of the institution's individual mission and purposes. The commission shall not exercise planning, policy, coordinating, supervisory, budgeting or administrative powers over any postsecondary institution in this state.

B. The commission shall also administer the applicable programs identified under § 1203 of the higher education act amendments of 1998 (P.L. 105–244), including the leveraging educational assistance partnership program, the federal family education loan program and the Paul Douglas teacher scholarships program, and shall supervise the state guarantee agency under the higher education act amendments of 1998.

C. In addition to the responsibilities prescribed in subsections A and B of this section, the commission shall:

1. Provide a forum to public and private postsecondary education institutions for discussion of issues of mutual interest, including the following:

(a) The postsecondary needs of unserved and underserved individuals in this state.

(b) The resources of public and private institutions, organizations and agencies that are located in this state and that are capable of providing postsecondary education opportunities.

(c) Enrollment demand and public policy options to meet statewide needs for postsecondary education services.

(d) Cooperative comprehensive instructional and capital planning.

2. Provide reports pursuant to this subsection on discussions of issues of mutual interest.

3. Coordinate and promote collaborative studies on issues of mutual interest to public and private postsecondary education institutions.

4. Compile and disseminate information to the public regarding postsecondary education opportunities in this state.

5. Prepare an annual report that summarizes the results of the commission's activities prescribed in this section and § 15–1852. The annual report shall be submitted to the speaker of the house of representatives, the president of the senate, the governor and the Arizona state library, archives and public records by December 28.

D. The commission consists of the executive director of the Arizona board of regents, the executive director of the state board for private postsecondary education and the following additional members who shall be appointed by the governor pursuant to § 38–211:

1. Two members who hold senior executive or managerial positions in a university under the jurisdiction of the Arizona board of regents.

2. Two members who hold senior executive or managerial positions in a community college district, one representing a community college district in a county with a population of five hundred thousand persons or more and one representing a community college district in a county with a population of less than five hundred thousand persons.

3. Two members who hold senior executive or managerial positions in private postsecondary institutions of higher education that are licensed under title 32, chapter 30, [1] that are located in this state, that offer bachelor or higher degrees and that are accredited by a regional accreditation agency approved by the United States department of education.

4. Two members who hold senior executive or managerial positions in private postsecondary institutions of higher education that are licensed under title 32, chapter 30, that are located in this state, that offer vocational education programs and that are accredited by a national accreditation agency approved by the United States department of education.

5. One member who holds a senior executive or managerial position in a private cosmetology school that is licensed under title 32, chapter 5, [2] that is located in this state, that offers cosmetology programs approved by the board of cosmetology and that is accredited by a national accreditation agency approved by the United States department of education.

6. One member who holds a senior executive or managerial position in an institution that is licensed under title 32, chapter 23 [3] or under the provisions of

14 Code of Federal Regulations part 147, that offers vocational education programs at the postsecondary level, that is located in this state and that is not an institution that is qualified under any other category.

7. One member who has held a senior executive or managerial level position in commerce or industry in this state for at least three years before the member's appointment and who is not qualified to serve under any other category.

8. Two members who hold senior executive or managerial positions in the high school education system in this state.

9. One member who is an owner, operator or administrator of a charter school in this state.

E. Members of the commission appointed pursuant to subsection D, paragraphs 1 through 9 of this section shall serve four year terms. Appointed members of the commission shall be residents of this state. Appointed members of the commission at all times during their terms shall continue to be eligible for appointment under the category that they were appointed to represent. Terms of appointed members of the commission begin on the third Monday in January. No appointed member of the commission may serve more than two consecutive terms.

F. The executive director of the Arizona board of regents and the executive director of the state board for private postsecondary education serve as members of the commission during their respective terms of office and are not eligible to vote with respect to the commission's review of any postsecondary institution.

G. Members appointed pursuant to subsection D, paragraphs 1 through 9 of this section are eligible to receive compensation pursuant to § 38-611 for each day spent in the performance of commission duties and may be reimbursed for expenses properly incurred in connection with the attendance at meetings or hearings of the commission.

H. The governor shall appoint a chairman from among the members of the commission who shall serve a one year term that begins on the third Monday in January.

I. Except as provided in subsection J of this section, a majority of the members of the commission constitutes a quorum for the transaction of commission business. The vote of a majority of the quorum constitutes authority for the commission to act.

J. For all purposes relating to title IV, part H, subpart one of the higher education amendments of 1992 the commission membership shall consist only of the members appointed pursuant to subsection D, paragraphs 1 through 7 of this section, and all commission actions taken pursuant to title IV, part H, subpart one of the higher education act of 1992 require the affirmative vote of at least six members.

K. Members of the commission are immune from personal liability with respect to all actions that are taken in good faith and within the scope of the commission's authority.

L. For the purposes of this section, "community college district" means a community college district that is established pursuant to §§ 15-1402 and 15-1403 and that is a political subdivision of this state.

Added by Laws 1994, Ch. 298, § 2. Amended by Laws 1996, Ch. 354, § 1; Laws 1998, Ch. 235, § 1, eff. May 29, 1998; Laws 1999, Ch. 21, § 1, eff. April 19, 1999; Laws 2000, Ch. 88, § 19; Laws 2003, Ch. 187, § 1; Laws 2003, Ch. 253, § 39, eff. Sept. 18, 2003, retroactively effective to July 1, 2003; Laws 2004, Ch. 336, § 19.

[1] Section 32-3001.

[2] Section 32-501.

[3] Section 32-2351.

Historical and Statutory Notes

Laws 1994, Ch. 289, § 7, as amended by Laws 1995, Ch. 241, § 56, provides:

"**Sec. 7. Initial terms of members of commission for postsecondary education**

"**A.** Notwithstanding § 15-1851, Arizona Revised Statutes, as added by this act, the initial terms of the members of the commission for postsecondary education are, for each appointment made pursuant to section 15-1851, subsection D, paragraphs 1, 2, 3, 4 and 8, Arizona Revised Statutes, as added by this act, one member shall serve a term ending on the third Monday in January, 1996 and one member shall serve a term ending on the third Monday in January, 1997.

"**B.** The governor shall make all other and subsequent appointments as prescribed by statute."

Laws 1995, Ch. 241, § 1, par. 31, provides:

"**Section 1. Purpose**"

"31. Laws 1994, chapter 298, § 7 prescribed the initial terms of the members of the commission for postsecondary education. However, one set of terms begins and ends in the same year. To correct this problem this act amends Laws 1994, chapter 298, § 7 to change '1995' to '1996'."

Laws 1995, Ch. 241, § 60, subsec. A, provides:

"**Sec. 60. Retroactive application**

"**A.** Sections 5, 6, 12, 13, 34, 35, 56, 57 and 58 of this act apply retroactively to July 17, 1994."

Laws 1996, Ch. 354, § 4, provides:

"**Sec. 4. Purpose**

"The purpose of this act is to improve the efficiency and cost effectiveness of public and private higher education programs in this state."

Laws 1998, Ch. 235, § 8, provides:

"**Sec. 8. Purpose**

"The purpose of the commission for postsecondary education is to:

"1. Conduct, supervise and coordinate the review of public and private postsecondary education institutions in this state to determine their eligibility for student financial aid monies.

"2. Administer specifically identified federal and state financial aid programs.

"3. Provide a forum to public and private postsecondary education institutions for discussion of issues of mutual interest.

"4. Coordinate and promote studies of interest to postsecondary institutions.

"5. Provide information to the public on postsecondary education opportunities in this state."

Executive Orders:

Executive Order No. 98-11, dated November 3, 1998, established the Arizona Task Force for the Western Governors' University.

Reviser's Notes:

1994 Note. Pursuant to authority of § 41-1304.02, in subsection A, first sentence "1099a" was substituted for "1099A" as a correction of a manifest clerical error. In the chapter version in subsection D, paragraph 4 before "accreditation" "regional" appears instead of "national" contrary to amendment instructions. Pursuant to authority of § 41-1304.02, "national" is substituted.

2003 Note. Prior to the 2004 amendment, this section contained the amendments made by Laws 2003, Ch. 187, sec. 1 and Ch. 253, sec. 39 that were blended together pursuant to authority of § 41-1304.03.

§ 15-1852. Additional powers and duties

A. In addition to the powers and duties prescribed in § 15-1851, the commission for postsecondary education shall:

1. Meet at least four times each year.

2. Adopt rules to carry out the purposes of this article.

3. Administer and enforce the provisions of this article and rules adopted pursuant to this article.

4. Keep a record of its proceedings.

5. Contract, on behalf of this state, with the United States secretary of education for the purpose of complying with the provisions of part H of the higher education amendments of 1992.

6. Enter into agreements and contracts with state regulatory agencies or entities, accrediting bodies and other peer review systems for the purpose of complying with the provisions of title IV program eligibility reviews as set forth in part H of the higher education amendments of 1992. Agreements and contracts executed pursuant to this subsection shall be for the purpose of conducting fact-finding activities, eligibility reviews, compliance assessments and recommendations, program reviews and consumer complaint studies. The review authority of the commission shall be limited to those circumstances specified in § 15-1851, subsection A. The commission shall provide sufficient monies to the agency or contractor to perform review functions.

7. Establish procedures for the performance of the title IV eligibility reviews as prescribed in part H, subpart one of the higher education amendments of 1992, the evaluation and assessment of the reviews performed, the evaluation and assessment of the postsecondary institution's initial and continuing title IV eligibility, the notification of the results of the reviews and the enforcement of an appeals process that provides for due process for postsecondary education institutions. The review authority of the commission shall be limited to those circumstances specified in § 15-1851, subsection A.

8. Establish procedures by which agencies of this state that are responsible for oversight of postsecondary institutions receive notification of eligibility reviews, eligibility determinations and actions and other actions taken or planned against postsecondary institutions.

9. Comply with the provisions of title 38, chapter 3, article 3.1 [1] and title 39. [2]

B. The commission may:

1. Adopt an official seal.

2. Contract.

3. Sue and be sued.

4. Receive, hold, make and take leases of and sell personal property for the benefit of the commission.

5. Employ permanent or temporary personnel as the commission deems necessary to carry out this article. The commission may designate the duties of these personnel. The commission employees are subject to title 41, chapter 4, articles 5 and 6. [3]

6. Conduct investigations, hold hearings and determine methods of enforcement of the provisions of this article.

7. Issue subpoenas to compel the attendance of witnesses and the production of documents, administer oaths, take testimony, hear proof and receive exhibits into evidence.

8. Establish policy centers under its control to conduct studies.

9. Coordinate and promote studies of interest to postsecondary institutions in this state.

C. The commission is exempt from title 41, chapter 6 but shall adopt rules in a manner substantially similar to title 41, chapter 6.[4]

Added by Laws 1994, Ch. 298, § 2. Amended by Laws 1996, Ch. 354, § 2; Laws 1996, Ch. 354, § 3, eff. July 1, 1997; Laws 1998, Ch. 235, § 2, eff. May 29, 1998.

[1] Section 38–431 et seq.

[2] Section 39–101 et seq.

[3] Sections 41–761 et seq., 41–781 et seq.

[4] Section 41–1001 et seq.

Historical and Statutory Notes

The 1996 amendment of this section by Ch. 354, § 3, explicitly amended the amendment of this section by Ch. 354, § 2.

Laws 1996, Ch. 354, § 5, provides:

"**Sec. 5. Delayed effective date**

"Section 3 of this act is effective on July 1, 1997."

Reviser's Notes:

1994 Note. Pursuant to authority of § 41–1304.02, in subsection A, paragraph 6, second sentence the spelling of "fact-finding" was corrected.

§ 15–1853. Funding; federal monies; postsecondary education fund; report

A. The postsecondary education fund is established consisting of:

1. Monies appropriated by the legislature.

2. Monies received from state agencies and political subdivisions of this state.

3. Monies received from the United States government, including monies received from the United States department of education pursuant to subsection B of this section.

4. Gifts, grants and donations received from any private source to carry out the duties and responsibilities of the commission.

B. The commission may receive monies distributed by the United States department of education for the reimbursement of the costs of performing review requirements. The costs may include expenses for the instruction of personnel needed to serve the purpose of § 15–1851, subsection A, the supplementation of existing review functions, work performed by subcontractors or consultants in connection with the review functions of the commission and any other administrative expenses necessary for compliance with part H, subpart one of the higher education amendments of 1992. No more than thirteen per cent of amounts received by the commission from the United States department of education may be utilized for administrative purposes by the commission.

C. The commission shall administer the fund in compliance with the requirements of this article. The commission shall separately account for monies received from each source listed in subsection a of this section and may establish accounts and subaccounts of the fund as necessary to carry out the requirements of this subsection.

D. Monies obtained pursuant to subsection A, paragraphs 1 through 3 of this section are subject to legislative appropriation. The commission shall not use these monies for purposes other than those designated by special line items for which the monies are received.

E. Monies obtained pursuant to subsection A, paragraph 4 of this section are continuously appropriated. These monies shall be used in accordance with the requests of the donor. If no request is specified, the monies may be used for additional responsibilities of the board prescribed in § 15-1851, subsection C and § 15-1852, subsection B, paragraphs 8 and 9.

F. The commission shall report quarterly to the joint legislative budget committee on fund deposits and expenditures.

Added by Laws 1994, Ch. 298, § 2. Amended by Laws 1998, Ch. 235, § 3, eff. May 29, 1998.

§ 15-1854. Private postsecondary education student financial assistance program; private postsecondary education student financial assistance fund; definition

A. A private postsecondary education student financial assistance program is established. The commission shall develop, implement and administer the program. A student who obtains an associate degree from a community college district or from a community college under the jurisdiction of an Indian tribe in this state that meets the same accreditation standards as a community college district and who registers for enrollment as a full-time student in a baccalaureate program at a private, nationally or regionally accredited four year degree granting college or university chartered in this state is eligible to submit an application to the commission for participation in the program. The commission shall establish eligibility criteria for the program including financial need and academic merit, shall develop application forms, procedures and deadlines and shall select qualifying students each year for participation in the program. Participating students shall receive an award in an amount of up to one thousand five hundred dollars annually for not to exceed two years and three thousand dollars to be used to pay all or a portion of the tuition and fees charged at the private, accredited four year college or university.

B. A private postsecondary education student financial assistance fund is established consisting of legislative appropriations. The commission shall administer the fund. Monies in the fund are exempt from the provisions of § 35-190, relating to lapsing of appropriations. The commission shall make awards for payment of tuition at eligible colleges or universities to students who are selected to participate in the private postsecondary education student financial assistance program pursuant to subsection A.

C. The commission shall develop a program evaluation procedure in order to determine the effectiveness of the private postsecondary education student financial assistance program in shifting students who would have otherwise attended a public four year college or university to private four year degree granting colleges or universities.

D. A student who fails to receive a baccalaureate degree within a three year period of receipt of the program award shall reimburse the private postsecondary education student financial assistance fund for all awards received pursuant to subsection A.

E. For the purposes of this section, "community college district" means a community college district established pursuant to §§ 15–1402 and 15–1403 that is a political subdivision of this state.

Added by Laws 1996, Ch. 341, § 1. Amended by Laws 1997, Ch. 265, § 1; Laws 1998, Ch. 235, § 4, eff. May 29, 1998; Laws 2003, Ch. 253, § 40, eff. Sept. 18, 2003, retroactively effective to July 1, 2003.

Historical and Statutory Notes

Reviser's Notes:

1996 Note. Pursuant to authority of § 41–1304.02, in the section heading "pilot" was added after the first "voucher" and in subsection A, third and last sentences and subsection C, in two places the spelling of "four year" was corrected.

ARTICLE 6. GUARANTEED TUITION PROGRAMS [REPEALED]

Article 6, Guaranteed Tuition Programs, consisting of §§ 15–1861 to 15–1864, was added by Laws 1994, Ch. 298, § 3, effective July 17, 1994, and was repealed by Laws 2004, Ch. 126, § 1.

Termination Under Sunset Law

The Arizona student program investing resources in education selection committee was to have terminated on July 1, 2004, and Title 15, Chapter 14, Article 6, relating to the Arizona student program investing resources in education selection committee was to have been repealed on January 1, 2005 by §41–3004.10. However, § 41–3004.10 and Title 15, Ch. 14, Art. 6 were repealed by Laws 2004, Ch. 126, § 2.

Historical and Statutory Notes

Laws 1994, Ch. 298, § 6, provides:

"**Sec. 6. Legislative intent**

"**A.** The legislative intent of the Arizona student program investing resources for education is to:

"1. Demonstrate the efficacy of such a model for the entire state through a pilot program system.

"2. Make students the primary beneficiaries of this program by providing the students with the means to afford a college education and with additional support by the schools through the consolidation and enhancement of support programs.

"3. Allow students to remain in the program if they move away from a school chosen to participate in the program unless they leave the state. It is expected that the schools they later attend will provide the additional support components to the students that were provided in the original school.

"4. Be a 'last dollar' assistance program providing financial aid up to a student's unmet financial need as calculated using the federal financial need model.

"**B.** The purpose of the commission for postsecondary education is to supervise, coordinate and review postsecondary education institutions to determine eligibility of those programs for student financial aid monies."

§§ 15–1861 to 15–1864. Repealed by Laws 2004, Ch. 126, § 1

Historical and Statutory Notes

Section 15–1861, providing definitions, was added by Laws 1994, Ch. 298, § 3.

Section 15–1861 was purportedly amended by Laws 2004, Ch. 336, § 20.

Section 15–1862, relating to the Arizona student program investing resources for education, was added by Laws 1994, Ch. 298, § 3.

Section 15–1863, relating to the Arizona student program investing resources for education selection committee, its membership and duties, was added by Laws 1994, Ch. 298, § 3.

Section 15–1863 was purportedly amended by Laws 2004, Ch. 336, § 21.

Section 15–1864, relating to the Arizona student program investing resources in education scholarship fund, was added by Laws 1994, Ch. 298, § 3, and was amended by Laws 2000, Ch. 193, § 117.

Historical and Statutory Notes

Section 15–1861, providing definitions, was added by Laws 1994, Ch. 298, § 3.

Section 15–1862, relating to the Arizona student program investing resources for education, was added by Laws 1994, Ch. 298, § 3.

Section 15–1863, relating to the Arizona student program investing resources for education selection committee, its membership and duties, was added by Laws 1994, Ch. 298, § 3.

Section 15–1864, relating to the Arizona student program investing resources in education scholarship fund, was added by Laws 1994, Ch. 298, § 3, and was amended by Laws 2000, Ch. 193, § 117.

ARTICLE 7. COLLEGE SAVINGS PLAN

Article 7, College Savings Plan, consisting of §§ 15–1871 to 15–1879, was added by Laws 1997, Ch. 171, § 1, effective April 24, 1997.

§ 15–1871. Definitions

In this article, unless the context otherwise requires:

1. "Account" means an individual trust account in the fund established as prescribed in this article.

2. "Account owner" means the person who enters into a tuition savings agreement pursuant to this article, who is an account owner within the meaning of § 529 of the internal revenue code[1] and who is designated at the time an account is opened as having the right to withdraw monies from the account before the account is disbursed to or for the benefit of the designated beneficiary.

3. "Commission" means the commission for postsecondary education established by § 15–1851.

4. "Committee" means the family college savings program oversight committee.

5. "Designated beneficiary" means a person who qualifies as a designated beneficiary under § 529 of the internal revenue code and, except as provided in § 15–1875, subsections R and S, with respect to an account, who is designated at the time the account is opened as the person whose higher education expenses are expected to be paid from the account or, if this designated beneficiary is replaced in accordance with § 15–1875, subsections E, F and G, the replacement beneficiary.

6. "Eligible educational institution" means an institution of higher education that qualifies under § 529 of the internal revenue code as an eligible educational institution.

7. "Financial institution" means any bank, commercial bank, national bank, savings bank, savings and loan association, credit union, insurance company, brokerage firm or other similar entity that is authorized to do business in this state.

8. "Fund" means the family college savings program trust fund that constitutes a public instrumentality of this state established by § 15–1873.

9. "Member of the family" means any of the following:

(a) A son or daughter of a person or a descendant of the son or daughter of the person.

(b) A stepson or stepdaughter of a person.

(c) A brother, sister, stepbrother or stepsister of a person. For the purposes of this subdivision, "brother" and "sister" includes a brother or sister by the half-blood.

(d) The father or mother of a person or the ancestor of the father or mother of a person.

(e) A stepfather or stepmother of a person.

(f) A son or daughter of a person's brother or sister. For the purposes of this subdivision, "brother" and "sister" includes a brother or sister by the half-blood.

(g) A brother or sister of the person's father or mother. For the purposes of this subdivision, "brother" and "sister" includes a brother or sister by the half-blood.

(h) A son-in-law, daughter-in-law, father-in-law, mother-in-law, brother-in-law or sister-in-law of a person.

(i) The spouse of a person or the spouse of any individual described in this paragraph.

(j) A first cousin of a person.

(k) Any individual who meets the criteria for family membership described in this paragraph as a result of legal adoption.

10. "Nonqualified withdrawal" means a withdrawal from an account other than one of the following:

(a) A qualified withdrawal.

(b) A withdrawal made as the result of the death or disability of the designated beneficiary of an account.

(c) A withdrawal that is made on the account of a scholarship, or the allowance or payment described in § 135(d)(1)(B) or (C) of the internal revenue code, and that is received by the designated beneficiary, but only to the extent of the amount of this scholarship, allowance or payment.

(d) A rollover or change of designated beneficiary.

11. "Person" means an individual, an individual's legal representative or any other legal entity authorized to establish a savings account under § 529 of the internal revenue code and the corresponding regulations.

12. "Program" means the family college savings program established under this article that constitutes a qualified tuition program as defined in § 529 of the internal revenue code.

13. "Qualified higher education expenses" means tuition, fees, books, supplies, room and board and equipment required for enrollment or attendance of a designated beneficiary at an eligible educational institution and expenses for special needs services in the case of a special needs beneficiary that are incurred in connection with enrollment or attendance, if these expenses meet the definition of qualified higher education expenses in § 529 of the internal revenue code.

14. "Qualified withdrawal" means a withdrawal from an account to pay the qualified higher education expenses of the designated beneficiary of the account, but only if the withdrawal is made in accordance with this article.

15. "Section 529 of the internal revenue code" means § 529 of the internal revenue code of 1986, as amended, and the final regulations issued pursuant to that section.

16. "Trust interest" means an account owner's interest in the fund created by a tuition savings agreement for the benefit of a designated beneficiary.

17. "Tuition savings agreement" means an agreement between the commission, as trustee of the fund, and an account owner that creates an interest in the fund and that provides for participation in the program.

Added by Laws 1997, Ch. 171, § 1, eff. April 24, 1997. Amended by Laws 1999, Ch. 98, § 1, eff. April 28, 1999; Laws 2002, Ch. 122, § 1; Laws 2004, Ch. 327, § 1.

[1] Internal Revenue Code sections may be found in Title 26 of U.S.C.A.

Retroactive Application

This section, as amended by Laws 2002 Ch. 122, applies retroactively to January 1, 2002.

Historical and Statutory Notes

Laws 1997, Ch. 171, § 3, effective April 24, 1997, provides:

"**Sec. 3. Legislative intent**

"The legislature intends to establish the family college savings program in recognition that the general welfare and well-being of the state of Arizona are directly related to the educational levels and skills of its citizens. Therefore, a vital and valid public purpose of the state of Arizona is served by the establishment and implementation of the program that will encourage and make possible the attainment of an accessible, affordable postsecondary education by the greatest number of citizens through a savings program. The legislature further intends that the Arizona commission for postsecondary education may achieve this purpose most effectively through a public-private partnership using selected financial institutions to serve as depositories for individual family college savings accounts."

Laws 2002, Ch. 122, § 5, provides:

"**Sec. 5. Retroactivity**

"This act applies retroactively to from and after December 31, 2001."

Reviser's Notes:

1997 Note. Pursuant to authority of § 41-1304.02, in paragraph 9, subdivisions (a) and (b) a period was substituted for a comma at the end of the sentence to correct manifest clerical errors.

§ 15–1872. Family college savings program oversight committee; membership; powers and duties

A. The family college savings program oversight committee is established in the commission for postsecondary education. The committee consists of the following members:

1. The state treasurer or the state treasurer's designee.

2. The director of the securities division of the Arizona corporation commission or the director's designee.

3. A president or chancellor of a community college district who is appointed by the governor.

4. The chairperson of the state board for private postsecondary education or the chairperson's designee.

5. Three members of the general public, each of whom possesses knowledge, skill and experience in accounting, risk management or investment management or as an actuary. The governor shall appoint these members to serve staggered four year terms pursuant to § 38–211. The initial members appointed pursuant to this paragraph shall assign themselves by lot to serve two, three and four year terms. The chairperson shall notify the governor's office on appointments of these terms. All subsequent members appointed pursuant to this paragraph serve four year terms.

6. A certified financial planner who is appointed by the governor.

7. A certified public accountant who is appointed by the governor.

8. An attorney with a state bar of Arizona certification in estates and trusts who is appointed by the governor.

B. The commission shall select a chairperson and a vice-chairperson from among the committee's membership. A majority of the membership constitutes a quorum for the transaction of business. The committee shall meet at least once each calendar quarter. The chairperson may call additional meetings.

C. Members of the family college savings program oversight committee appointed pursuant to subsection A, paragraph 8 [1] of this section are eligible to receive compensation as determined pursuant to § 38–611 for each day of attendance at committee meetings, except that the compensation of any member shall not exceed five hundred dollars in any year. The commission shall pay compensation pursuant to this subsection from monies of the commission.

D. The committee shall recommend financial institutions for approval by the commission to act as the depositories and managers of family college savings accounts pursuant to § 15–1874.

E. The committee may submit proposed rules to the commission to assist in the implementation and administration of this article.

F. Members of the committee are immune from personal liability with respect to all actions that are taken in good faith and within the scope of the committee's authority.

Added by Laws 1997, Ch. 171, § 1, eff. April 24, 1997. Amended by Laws 2004, Ch. 327, § 2; Laws 2004, Ch. 336, § 22.

[1] So in original. Probably should read "paragraphs 5 through 8".

Historical and Statutory Notes

Reviser's Notes:

1997 Note. Pursuant to authority of § 41-1304.02, in subsection A, paragraph 8 the last sentence was transposed to follow the third sentence.

2004 Note. This section contains the amendments made by Laws 2004, Ch. 327, sec. 2 and Ch. 336, sec. 22 that were blended together as shown pursuant to authority of § 41-1304.03.

§ 15-1873. Commission for postsecondary education; powers and duties; family college savings program trust fund

A. The commission shall:

1. Develop and implement the program in a manner consistent with this article through the adoption of rules, guidelines and procedures.

2. Retain professional services, if necessary, including accountants, auditors, consultants and other experts.

3. Seek rulings and other guidance from the United States department of the treasury and the internal revenue service relating to the program.

4. Make changes to the program required for the participants in the program to obtain the federal income tax benefits or treatment provided by § 529 of the internal revenue code. [1]

5. Interpret, in rules, policies, guidelines and procedures, the provisions of this article broadly in light of its purpose and objectives.

6. Charge, impose and collect administrative fees and service charges in connection with any agreement, contract or transaction relating to the program.

7. Negotiate and select the financial institution or institutions to act as the depository and manager of the program in accordance with this article.

8. As an agency of this state, act as trustee of the fund.

9. Maintain the program on behalf of this state as required by § 529 of the internal revenue code.

10. Enter into tuition savings agreements with account owners pursuant to this article.

B. The family college savings program trust fund is established consisting of the assets of the family college savings program. The commission shall administer the fund and shall act as the sole trustee of the fund. Monies in the fund are continuously appropriated. The fund is designated a public instrumentality of this state that is created for an essential public purpose. Trust interests in the fund shall be designated by the commission for each account owner. The fund shall be separated into a trust account and an operating account. The trust account shall include amounts received by the family college savings program from account owners pursuant to tuition savings agreements and interest and investment income earned by the fund. The commission shall make transfers from the trust account to the operating account as necessary for the immediate payment of obligations under tuition savings agreements, operating expenses and administrative costs of the family college savings program. The commission shall deposit and invest monies or other amounts in the fund with financial institutions in accordance with § 15–1874.

Added by Laws 1997, Ch. 171, § 1, eff. April 24, 1997. Amended by Laws 2004, Ch. 327, § 3.

[1] Internal Revenue Code sections may be found in Title 26 of U.S.C.A.

Historical and Statutory Notes

Reviser's Notes:

2004 Note. Pursuant to authority of § 41–1304.02, in the section heading "family college savings program;" was removed.

§ 15–1874. Use of contractor as account depository and manager

A. The commission shall implement the operation of the program through the use of one or more financial institutions to act as the depositories of the fund and managers of the program. Under the program, persons may submit applications for enrollment in the program and establish accounts in the fund at the financial institution. Monies paid by account owners to the fund for deposit in accounts maintained by the fund at a financial institution shall be paid to the financial institution as an agent of the fund and the tuition savings agreements shall provide that all monies paid by account owners to fund accounts held at financial institutions are being paid to the fund.

B. The committee shall solicit proposals from financial institutions to act as the depositories of fund monies and managers of the program. Financial institutions that submit proposals must describe the financial instruments that will be held in accounts. The commission shall select proposals from financial institutions to act as depositories and managers and that the solicitation and selection process is exempt from the procurement code requirements of title 41, chapter 23. [1]

C. On the recommendation of the committee, the commission shall select the financial institution or institutions to implement the operation of the program from among bidding financial institutions that demonstrate the most advantageous combination, both to potential program participants and this state, of the following factors:

1. Financial stability and integrity.

2. The safety of the investment instruments being offered, taking into account any insurance provided with respect to these instruments.

3. The ability of the investment instruments to track estimated costs of higher education as calculated by the commission and provided by the financial institution to the account holder.

4. The ability of the financial institutions, directly or through a subcontract, to satisfy record keeping and reporting requirements.

5. The financial institution's plan for promoting the program and the investment it is willing to make to promote the program.

6. The fees, if any, proposed to be charged to persons for maintaining accounts.

7. The minimum initial deposit and minimum contributions that the financial institution will require for the investment of fund monies and the willingness of the financial institution to accept contributions through payroll deduction plans and other deposit plans.

8. Any other benefits to this state or its residents included in the proposal, including an account opening fee payable to the commission by the account owner and an additional fee from the financial institution for statewide program marketing by the commission.

D. The commission shall enter into a contract with a financial institution, or except as provided in subsection E of this section, contracts with financial institutions, to serve as program managers and depositories. Program management contracts shall provide the terms and conditions by which financial institutions shall sell interests in the fund to account owners, invest monies in the fund and manage the program.

E. The commission may select more than one financial institution and investment for the program if both of the following conditions exist:

1. The United States internal revenue service has provided guidance that giving a contributor a choice of two investment instruments under a state plan will not cause the plan to fail to qualify for favorable tax treatment under § 529 of the internal revenue code. [2]

2. The commission concludes that the choice of instrument vehicles is in the best interest of college savers and will not interfere with the promotion of the program.

F. A program manager shall:

1. Take all action required to keep the program in compliance with the requirements of this article and all action not contrary to this article or its contract to manage the program so that it is treated as a qualified tuition plan under § 529 of the internal revenue code.

2. Keep adequate records of each of the fund's accounts, keep each account segregated from each other account and provide the commission with the information necessary to prepare statements required by § 15–1875, subsections O, P and Q or file these statements on behalf of the commission.

3. Compile and total information contained in statements required to be prepared under § 15–1875, subsections O, P and Q and provide these compilations to the commission.

4. If there is more than one program manager, provide the commission with this information to assist the commission to determine compliance with § 15–1875, subsection N.

5. Provide representatives of the commission, including other contractors or other state agencies, access to the books and records of the program manager to the extent needed to determine compliance with the contract.

6. Hold all accounts in the name of and for the benefit of the fund and this state.

G. Any contract executed between the commission and a financial institution pursuant to this section shall be for a term of at least three years and not more than seven years.

H. The commission may terminate a contract with a financial institution at any time for good cause on the recommendation of the committee. If a contract is terminated pursuant to this subsection, the commission shall take custody of accounts held at that financial institution and shall seek to promptly transfer the accounts to another financial institution that is selected as a program manager and into investment instruments as similar to the original investments as possible.

I. If the commission determines not to renew the appointment of a financial institution as a program manager, the commission may take action consistent with the interests of the program and the accounts and in accordance with its duties as the trustee of the fund, including termination of all services or continuation of certain management and administrative services of that financial institution for accounts of the program managed by that financial institution during its term as a program manager, if any continuation of services is only permitted under the following conditions:

1. The commission and the financial institution enters into a written agreement specifying the rights of the program and the commission and the responsibilities of the financial institution, including the standards that continue to be applicable to the accounts as accounts of the program.

2. Any services provided by the financial institution to accounts continue to be subject to the control of the commission as the trustee of the fund with responsibility of all accounts of the program.

Added by Laws 1997, Ch. 171, § 1, eff. April 24, 1997. Amended by Laws 2002, Ch. 122, § 2; Laws 2004, Ch. 327, § 4.

[1] Section 41–2501 et seq.

[2] Internal Revenue Code sections may be found in Title 26 of U.S.C.A.

Historical and Statutory Notes

Laws 2002, Ch. 122, § 5, provides:

"**Sec. 5. Retroactivity**

"This act applies retroactively to from and after December 31, 2001."

§ 15–1875. Program requirements

A. The program shall be operated through the use of accounts in the fund established by account owners. Payments to the fund for participation in the program shall be made by account owners pursuant to tuition savings agreements. An account may be opened by any person who desires to invest in the fund and to save to pay qualified higher education expenses by satisfying each of the following requirements:

1. Completing an application in the form prescribed by the commission. The application shall include the following information:

(a) The name, address and social security number or employer identification number of the contributor.

(b) The name, address and social security number of the account owner if the account owner is not the contributor.

(c) The name, address and social security number of the designated beneficiary.

(d) The certification relating to no excess contributions required by subsection N.

(e) Any other information that the commission may require.

2. Paying the one-time application fee established by the commission.

3. Making the minimum contribution required by the commission or by opening an account.

4. Designating the type of account to be opened if more than one type of account is offered.

B. Any person may make contributions to an account after the account is opened.

C. Contributions to accounts may be made only in cash.

D. Account owners may withdraw all or part of the balance from an account on sixty days' notice, or a shorter period as may be authorized by the commission, under rules prescribed by the commission. These rules shall include provisions that will generally enable the commission or program manager to determine if a withdrawal is a nonqualified withdrawal or a qualified withdrawal. The rules may, but need not, require one or more of the following:

1. Account owners seeking to make a qualified withdrawal or other withdrawal that is not a nonqualified withdrawal shall provide certifications, copies of bills for qualified higher education expenses or other supporting material.

2. Qualified withdrawals from an account shall be made only by a check payable as designated by the account owner.

3. Withdrawals not meeting certain requirements shall be treated as nonqualified withdrawals by the program manager, and if these withdrawals are not nonqualified withdrawals, the account owner must seek refunds of penalties, if any, directly from the commission.

E. An account owner may change the designated beneficiary of an account to an individual who is a member of the family of the former designated beneficiary in accordance with procedures established by the commission.

F. On the direction of an account owner, all or a portion of an account may be transferred to another account of which the designated beneficiary is a member of the family of the designated beneficiary of the transferee account.

G. Changes in designated beneficiaries and rollovers under this section are not permitted if the changes or rollovers would violate either of the following:

1. Subsection N, relating to excess contributions.

2. Subsection K, relating to investment choice.

H. In the case of any nonqualified withdrawal from an account, a penalty may be imposed if the penalty is required for purposes of qualifying the program as a qualified tuition program under § 529 of the internal revenue code. [1] The commission may adopt rules to establish the parameters for the assessment of penalties. Any penalties assessed shall be paid to the commission for use in operating and marketing the program and for student financial aid.

I. Each account shall be maintained separately from each other account under the program.

J. Separate records and accounting shall be maintained for each account for each designated beneficiary.

K. No contributor to, account owner of or designated beneficiary of any account may direct the investment, within the meaning of § 529 of the internal revenue code, of any contributions to an account or the earnings from the account.

L. If the commission terminates the authority of a financial institution to hold accounts and accounts must be moved from that financial institution to another financial institution, the commission shall select the financial institution and type of investment to which the balance of the account is moved unless the internal revenue service provides guidance stating that allowing the account owner to select among several financial institutions that are then contractors would not cause a plan to cease to be a qualified tuition plan.

M. Neither an account owner nor a designated beneficiary may use an interest in an account as security for a loan. Any pledge of an interest in an account is of no force and effect.

N. On the recommendation of the committee, the commission shall adopt rules to prevent contributions on behalf of a designated beneficiary in excess of those necessary to pay the qualified higher education expenses of the designated beneficiaries. The rules shall address the following:

1. Procedures for aggregating the total balances of multiple accounts established for a designated beneficiary.

2. The establishment of a maximum total balance for the purpose of prohibiting contributions to accounts established for a designated beneficiary if the contributions would cause the maximum total balance to be exceeded.

3. The commission shall review the quarterly reports received from participating financial institutions and certify that the balance in all qualified tuition programs, as defined in § 529 of the internal revenue code, of which that person is the designated beneficiary does not exceed the lesser of:

(a) A maximum college savings amount established by the commission from time to time.

(b) The cost in current dollars of qualified higher education expenses that the contributor reasonably anticipates the designated beneficiary will incur.

4. Requirements that any excess contributions with respect to a designated beneficiary be promptly withdrawn in a nonqualified withdrawal or rolled over to another account in accordance with this section.

O. If there is any distribution from an account to any person or for the benefit of any person during a calendar year, the distribution shall be reported to the internal revenue service and the account owner or the designated beneficiary to the extent required by federal law.

P. The financial institution shall provide statements to each account owner at least once each year within thirty-one days after the twelve month period to which they relate. The statement shall identify the contributions made during a preceding twelve month period, the total contributions made through the end of the period, the value of the account as of the end of this period, distributions made during this period and any other matters that the commission requires be reported to the account owner.

Q. Statements and information returns relating to accounts shall be prepared and filed to the extent required by federal or state tax law.

R. A state or local government or organizations described in § 501(c)(3) of the internal revenue code may open and become the account owner of an account to fund scholarships for persons whose identity will be determined after an account is opened.

S. In the case of any account described in subsection R, the requirement that a designated beneficiary be designated when an account is opened does not apply and each person who receives an interest in the account as a scholarship shall be treated as a designated beneficiary with respect to the interest.

T. Any social security numbers, addresses or telephone numbers of individual account holders and designated beneficiaries that come into the possession of the commission are confidential, are not public records and shall not be released by the commission.

U. An account owner may transfer ownership rights to another eligible account owner.

V. An account owner may designate successor account owners.

Added by Laws 1997, Ch. 171, § 1, eff. April 24, 1997. Amended by Laws 1999, Ch. 98, § 2, eff. April 28, 1999; Laws 2002, Ch. 122, § 3; Laws 2004, Ch. 327, § 5.

[1] Internal Revenue Code sections may be found in Title 26 of U.S.C.A.

Historical and Statutory Notes

Laws 2002, Ch. 122, § 5, provides:

"**Sec. 5. Retroactivity**

"This act applies retroactively to from and after December 31, 2001."

§ 15–1876. Higher education expenses; exemption from taxation

Notwithstanding any other law, the amount of any distribution to a designated beneficiary, as defined in § 529(e)(1) of the internal revenue code,[1] from an individual trust account or savings account established under this article is exempt from taxation under title 43 [2] but only to the extent that this income is used to pay qualified higher education expenses of the designated beneficiary.

Added by Laws 1997, Ch. 171, § 1, eff. April 24, 1997.

[1] 26 U.S.C.A. § 529.

[2] Section 41–101 et seq.

Historical and Statutory Notes

Reviser's Notes:

1997 Note. Pursuant to authority of § 41–1304.02, in the section heading "taxation" was substituted for "income".

§ 15–1877. Scholarships and financial aid provisions

A. Any student loan program, student grant program or other financial assistance program established or administered by this state shall treat the balance in an account of which the student is a designated beneficiary as neither an asset of the parent of the designated beneficiary nor as a scholarship, a grant or an asset of the student for determining a student's or parent's income, assets or financial need.

B. Subsection A applies to any state appropriated financial assistance program administered by a college or university in this state including the financial aid trust fund, established by § 15–1642, the leveraging educational assistance program established by § 1203 of the Higher Education Act amendments of 1998 (P.L. 105–244; 112 stat. 1581; 20 United States Code § 1001) and the private postsecondary education student financial assistance program established by § 15–1854.

C. Subsections A and B do not apply if any of the following conditions exist:

1. Federal law requires all or a portion of the amount in an account to be taken into consideration in a different manner.

2. Federal benefits could be lost if all or a portion of the amount in an account is not taken into consideration in a different manner.

3. A specific grant establishing a financial assistance program requires that all or a portion of the amount in an account be taken into consideration.
Added by Laws 1997, Ch. 171, § 1, eff. April 24, 1997. Amended by Laws 2001, Ch. 172, § 1.

§ 15–1878. Limitations of article

A. Nothing in this article shall be construed to:

1. Give any designated beneficiary any rights or legal interest with respect to an account unless the designated beneficiary is the account owner.

2. Guarantee that a designated beneficiary will be admitted to an eligible educational institution or be allowed to continue enrollment at or graduate from an eligible educational institution located in this state after admission.

3. Establish state residency for a person merely because the person is a designated beneficiary.

4. Guarantee that amounts saved pursuant to the program will be sufficient to cover the qualified higher education expenses of a designated beneficiary.

B. Nothing in this article establishes any obligation of this state or any agency or instrumentality of this state to guarantee for the benefit of any account owner, contributor to an account or designated beneficiary any of the following:

1. The return of any amounts contributed to an account.

2. The rate of interest or other return on any account.

3. The payment of interest or other return on any account.

4. Tuition rates or the cost of related higher education expenditures.

C. Under rules adopted by the commission, every contract, application, deposit slip or other similar document that may be used in connection with a contribution to an account shall clearly indicate that the account is not insured by this state and neither the principal deposited nor the investment return is guaranteed by this state.

Added by Laws 1997, Ch. 171, § 1, eff. April 24, 1997. Amended by Laws 2002, Ch. 122, § 4.

Historical and Statutory Notes

Laws 2002, Ch. 122, § 5, provides:

"Sec. 5. Retroactivity

"This act applies retroactively to from and after December 31, 2001."

§ 15–1879. Annual report

The commission shall submit an annual report to the speaker of the house of representatives, the president of the senate and the governor by February 1 that summarizes the commission's findings and recommendations concerning the program established by this article.

Added by Laws 1997, Ch. 171, § 1, eff. April 24, 1997.

CHAPTER 15

INTERSTATE COMPACTS

ARTICLE 1. COMPACT FOR EDUCATION

Chapter 15, Interstate Compacts, consisting of Article 1, § 15–1901, was added as Article 2, § 15–121 of Chapter 1 of this title by Laws 1981, Ch. 1, § 2, effective January 23, 1981, but was renumbered as Chapter 15, Article 1, § 15–1901, and the chapter heading was added.

ARTICLE 1. COMPACT FOR EDUCATION

§ 15–1901. Authority of governor to enter compact; terms of compact for education

The governor is authorized in the name of this state to join with other states legally joining in the compact for education, which compact shall be in the following form:

COMPACT FOR EDUCATION

ARTICLE I—PURPOSE AND POLICY

SECTION A. It is the purpose of this compact to:

1. Establish and maintain close cooperation and understanding among executive, legislative, professional educational and lay leadership on a nationwide basis at the state and local levels.

2. Provide a forum for the discussion, development, crystallization and recommendation of public policy alternatives in the field of education.

3. Provide a clearinghouse of information on matters relating to educational problems and how they are being met in different places throughout the nation, so that the executive and legislative branches of state government and of local communities may have ready access to the experience and record of the entire country and so that both lay and professional groups in the field of education

may have additional avenues for the sharing of experience and the interchange of ideas in the formation of public policy in education.

4. Facilitate the improvement of state and local educational systems so that they will be able to meet adequate and desirable goals in a society which requires continuous qualitative and quantitative advance in educational opportunities, methods and facilities.

SECTION B. It is the policy of this compact to encourage and promote local and state initiative in the development, maintenance, improvement and administration of educational systems and institutions in a manner which will accord with the needs and advantages of diversity among localities and states.

SECTION C. The party states recognize that each has an interest in the quality and quantity of education furnished in each of the other states, as well as in the excellence of its own educational systems and institutions, because of the highly mobile character of individuals within the nation and because the products and services contributing to the health, welfare and economic advancement of each state are supplied in significant part by persons educated in other states.

ARTICLE II—STATE DEFINED

As used in this compact, "state" means a state, territory or possession of the United States, the District of Columbia or the Commonwealth of Puerto Rico.

ARTICLE III—THE COMMISSION

SECTION A. The education commission of the states, hereinafter called "the commission", is hereby established. The commission shall consist of seven members representing each party state. Four shall be members of the state legislature, two selected by the president of the senate and two selected by the speaker of the house of representatives and serving in such manner as the legislature may determine and three shall be appointed by and serve at the pleasure of the governor, unless the laws of the state otherwise provide. In addition to any other principles or requirements which a state may establish for the appointment and service of its members of the commission, the guiding principle for the composition of the membership on the commission from each party state shall be that the members representing the state shall, by virtue of their training, experience, knowledge or affiliations, be in a position collectively to reflect broadly the interests of the state government, higher education, the state education system, local education and lay and professional public and nonpublic educational leadership. Of the gubernatorial appointees, one shall be the head of a state agency or institution, designated by the governor, having responsibility for one or more programs of public education. In addition to the members of the commission representing the party states, there may be, not to exceed ten, nonvoting commissioners selected by the steering committee for terms of one year. The nonvoting commissioners shall represent leading national organizations of professional educators or persons concerned with educational administration.

SECTION B. The members of the commission shall be entitled to one vote each on the commission. No action of the commission shall be binding unless taken at a meeting at which a majority of the total number of votes on the commission are cast in favor thereof. Action of the commission shall be only at a meeting at which a majority of the commissioners are present. The commission shall meet at least once a year. In its bylaws, and subject to such directions and limitations as may be contained therein, the commission may delegate the exercise of any of its powers to the steering committee or the executive director, except for the power to approve budgets or requests for appropriations, the power to make policy recommendations pursuant to article IV and adoption of the annual report pursuant to section J of this article.

SECTION C. The commission shall have a seal.

SECTION D. The commission shall elect annually, from among its members, a chairman, who shall be a governor, a vice-chairman and a treasurer. The commission shall provide for the appointment of an executive director. The executive director shall serve at the pleasure of the commission and, together with the treasurer and such other personnel as the commission may deem appropriate, shall be bonded in such amount as the commission shall determine. The executive director shall be the secretary.

SECTION E. Irrespective of the civil service, personnel or other merit system laws of any of the party states, the executive director, subject to the approval of the steering committee, shall appoint, remove or discharge such personnel as may be necessary for the performance of the functions of the commission and shall fix the duties and compensation of such personnel. The commission in its bylaws shall provide for the personnel policies and programs of the commission.

SECTION F. The commission may borrow, accept or contract for the services of personnel from any party jurisdiction, the United States or any subdivision or agency of such governments, or from any agency of two or more of the party jurisdictions or their subdivisions.

SECTION G. The commission may accept for any of its purposes and functions under this compact any and all donations and grants of money, equipment, supplies, materials and services, conditional or otherwise, from any state, the United States or any other governmental agency or from any person, firm, association, foundation or corporation and may receive, utilize and dispose of the same. Any donation or grant accepted by the commission pursuant to this section or services borrowed pursuant to section F of this article shall be reported in the annual report of the commission. The report shall include the nature, amount and conditions of the donation, grant or services borrowed and the identity of the donor or lender.

SECTION H. The commission may establish and maintain such facilities as may be necessary for the transacting of its business. The commission may acquire, hold and convey real and personal property and any interest therein.

SECTION I. The commission shall adopt bylaws for the conduct of its business and shall have the power to amend and rescind such bylaws. The commission shall publish its bylaws in convenient form and shall file a copy of the bylaws and a copy of any amendment to the bylaws with the appropriate agency or officer in each of the party states.

SECTION J. The commission annually shall make to the governor and legislature of each party state a report covering the activities of the commission for the preceding year. The commission may make such additional reports as it may deem desirable.

ARTICLE IV—POWERS

In addition to authority conferred on the commission by other provisions of the compact, the commission shall have authority to:

1. Collect, correlate, analyze and interpret information and data concerning educational needs and resources.

2. Encourage and foster research in all aspects of education, but with special reference to the desirable scope of instruction, organization, administration and instructional methods and standards employed or suitable for employment in public educational systems.

3. Develop proposals for adequate financing of education as a whole and at each of its many levels.

4. Conduct or participate in research of the types referred to in this article in any instance where the commission finds that such research is necessary for the advancement of the purposes and policies of this compact, utilizing fully the resources of national associations, regional compact organizations for higher education and other agencies and institutions, both public and private.

5. Formulate suggested policies and plans for the improvement of public education as a whole, or for any segment of public education, and make recommendations with respect thereto available to the appropriate governmental units, agencies and public officials.

6. Do such other things as may be necessary or incidental to the administration of any of its authority or functions pursuant to this compact.

ARTICLE V—COOPERATION WITH FEDERAL GOVERNMENT

SECTION A. If the laws of the United States specifically so provide, or if administrative provision is made therefor within the federal government, the United States may be represented on the commission by not to exceed ten representatives. Any representative or representatives of the United States shall be appointed and serve in such manner as may be provided by or pursuant to federal law and may be drawn from any one or more branches of the federal government, but no such representative shall have a vote on the commission.

SECTION B. The commission may provide information and make recommendations to any executive or legislative agency or officer of the federal government concerning the common educational policies of the states and may advise with any such agencies or officers concerning any matter of mutual interest.

ARTICLE VI—COMMITTEES

SECTION A. To assist in the expeditious conduct of its business when the full commission is not meeting, the commission shall elect a steering committee of thirty-two members which, subject to the provisions of this compact and consistent with the policies of the commission, shall be constituted and function as provided in the bylaws of the commission. One-fourth of the voting membership of the steering committee shall consist of governors, one-fourth shall consist of legislators and the remainder shall consist of other members of the commission. A federal representative on the commission may serve with the steering committee, but without vote. The voting members of the steering committee shall serve for terms of two years, except that members elected to the first steering committee of the commission shall be elected as follows: sixteen for one year and sixteen for two years. The chairman, vice-chairman and treasurer of the commission shall be members of the steering committee and, anything in this section to the contrary notwithstanding, shall serve during their continuance in these offices. Vacancies in the steering committee shall not affect its authority to act, but the commission at its next regularly ensuing meeting following the occurrence of any vacancy shall fill it for the unexpired term. No person shall serve more than two terms as a member of the steering committee, provided that service for a partial term of one year or less shall not be counted toward the two term limitation.

SECTION B. The commission may establish advisory and technical committees composed of state, local and federal officials and private persons to advise it with respect to any one or more of its functions. Any advisory or technical committee may, on request of the states concerned, be established to consider any matter of special concern to two or more of the party states.

SECTION C. The commission may establish such additional committees as its bylaws may provide.

ARTICLE VII—FINANCE

SECTION A. The commission shall advise the governor or designated officer or officers of each party state of its budget and estimated expenditures for such period as may be required by the laws of that party state. Each of the commissioner's budgets of estimated expenditures shall contain specific recommendations of the amount or amounts to be appropriated by each of the party states.

SECTION B. The total amount of appropriation requests under any budget shall be apportioned among the party states. In making the apportionment, the commission shall devise and employ a formula which takes equitable account of the populations and per capita income levels of the party states.

SECTION C. The commission shall not pledge the credit of any party state. The commission may meet any of its obligations in whole or in part with funds available to it pursuant to article III, section G of this compact, provided that the commission takes specific action setting aside such funds prior to incurring an obligation to be met in whole or in part in such manner. Except where the commission makes use of funds available to it pursuant to article III, section G, the commission shall not incur any obligation prior to the allotment of funds by the party states adequate to meet the same.

SECTION D. The commission shall keep accurate accounts of all receipts and disbursements. The receipts and disbursements of the commission shall be subject to the audit and accounting procedures established by its bylaws. All receipts and disbursements of funds handled by the commission shall be audited yearly by a qualified public accountant, and the report of the audit shall be included in and become part of the annual reports of the commission.

SECTION E. The accounts of the commission shall be open at any reasonable time for inspection by duly constituted officers of the party states and by any persons authorized by the commission.

SECTION F. Nothing contained herein shall be construed to prevent commission compliance with laws relating to audit or inspection of accounts by or on behalf of any government contributing to the support of the commission.

ARTICLE VIII—ELIGIBLE PARTIES; ENTRY INTO AND WITHDRAWAL

SECTION A. This compact shall have as eligible parties all states, territories and possessions of the United States, the District of Columbia and the Commonwealth of Puerto Rico. In respect of any such jurisdiction not having a governor, the term "governor", as used in this compact, shall mean the closest equivalent official of such jurisdiction.

SECTION B. Any state or other eligible jurisdiction may enter into this compact, and it shall become binding when it has adopted the compact.

SECTION C. Any party state may withdraw from this compact by enacting a statute repealing the compact. No withdrawal shall affect any liability already incurred by or chargeable to a party state prior to the time of such withdrawal.

ARTICLE IX—CONSTRUCTION AND SEVERABILITY

The provisions of this compact shall be severable and if any phrase, clause, sentence or provision of this compact is declared to be contrary to the constitution of any state or of the United States, or if the application thereof to any government, agency, person or circumstance is held invalid, the validity of the remainder of this compact and the applicability of the compact to any government, agency, person or circumstance shall not be affected thereby. If this compact shall be held contrary to the constitution of any state participating therein, the compact shall remain in full force and effect as to the state affected as to all severable matters.

Added as § 15–121 by Laws 1981, Ch. 1, § 2, eff. Jan. 23, 1981. Renumbered as § 15–1901.

Historical and Statutory Notes

Reviser's Notes:

1981 Note. The above article and section which comprises it were added by Laws 1981, Ch. 1, § 2 as Chapter 1, article 2 and § 15–121, and were renumbered as Chapter 15, article 1 and § 15–1901 pursuant to authority of § 41–1304.02. Additionally, pursuant to authority of § 41–1304.02, in the heading of Chapter 15 the words "Interstate Compacts" were added.

Complementary Legislation:

Ala.—Code 1975, §§ 16–44–1 to 16–44–3.
Alaska—AS 14.44.050 to 14.44.060.
Ark.—A.C.A. §§ 6–4–201 to 6–4–203.
Cal.—West's Ann.Cal.Educ.Code §§ 12510 to 12515.5.
Colo.—West's C.R.S.A. 24–60–1201 to 24–60–1204.
Conn.—C.G.S.A. §§ 10–374 to 10–376.
Del.—14 Del.C. §§ 8201, 8211.
D.C.—D.C. Official Code, 2001 Ed. §§ 38–3001 to 38–3004.
Fla.—West's F.S.A. §§ 244.06 to 244.08.
Ga.—O.C.G.A. §§ 20–6–20 to 20–6–24.
Hawaii—HRS §§ 311–1 to 311–6.
Idaho—I.C. §§ 33–4101 to 33–4103.
Ill.—S.H.A. 45 ILCS 90/0.01 to 90/4.
Ind.—West's A.I.C. 20–11–1–1 to 20–11–1–6.
Iowa—I.C.A. §§ 272B.1 to 272B.3.

Kan.—K.S.A. 72-6011 to 72-6014.
Ky.—KRS 156.710, 156.720.
La.—LSA-R.S. 17:1911 to 17:1913.
Me.—20-A M.R.S.A. §§ 601 to 609.
Md.—Code, Education, §§ 25-101 to 25-104.
Mass.—M.G.L.A. c. 69 App., §§ 1-1 to 1-3.
Mich.—M.C.L.A. §§ 388.1301 to 388.1304.
Minn.—M.S.A. §§ 127A.80, 127A.81.
Miss.—Code 1972, §§ 37-135-11 to 37-135-15.
Mo.—V.A.M.S. §§ 173.300 to 173.330, 173.715 to 173.721.
Nev.—N.R.S. 399.015
N.H.—RSA 200-G:1 to 200-G:3.
N.J.—N.J.S.A. 18A:75-1 to 18A:75-12.
N.M.—NMSA 1978, §§ 11-8-1 to 11-8-11.
N.Y.—McKinney's Education Law, § 107.
N.C.—G.S. § 115C-104.
Ohio—R.C. §§ 3301.48, 3301.49.
Okl.—70 Okl.St.Ann. §§ 506.1 to 506.3.
Ore.—L.1967, c. 606.
Pa.—24 P.S. §§ 5401 to 5403.
Puerto Rico—18 L.P.R.A. §§ 1221 to 1226.
R.I.—Gen.Laws 1956, § 16-47-1.
S.C.—Code 1976, §§ 59-11-10 to 59-11-30.
Tenn.—T.C.A. §§ 49-12-201 to 49-12-203.
Tex.—V.T.C.A., Education Code §§ 161.01 to 161.04.
Utah—U.C.A.1953, 53A-27-101 to 53A-27-103.
V.I.—17 V.I.C. §§ 551 to 559.
Va.—Code 1950, §§ 22.1-336 to 22.1-338.
W.Va.—Code, 18-10D-1 to 18-10D-7.
Wis.—W.S.A. 39.75, 39.76.
Wyo.—Wyo.Stat.Ann. §§ 21-16-301, 21-16-302.

Source:

Laws 1980, Ch. 161, § 1.
A.R.S. former §§ 15-1139, 15-1199.

CHAPTER 16

SCHOOL CAPITAL FINANCE

ARTICLE 1. SCHOOL FACILITIES BOARD

ARTICLE 2. BUILDING ADEQUACY STANDARDS

ARTICLE 3. DEFICIENCIES CORRECTION

ARTICLE 4. BUILDING RENEWAL

ARTICLE 5. NEW SCHOOL FACILITIES

ARTICLE 6. STATE SCHOOL FACILITIES REVENUE BONDS

ARTICLE 7. STATE SCHOOL IMPROVEMENT REVENUE BONDS

Chapter 16, School Capital Finance, consisting of Article 1, §§ 15–2001 to 15–2003, Article 2, § 15–2011, Article 3, § 15–2021, Article 4, § 15–2031, Article 5, § 15–2041, Article 6, §§ 15–2051 to 15–2066, was added by Laws 1998, 5th S.S., Ch. 1, effective July 9, 1998.

Termination under Sunset Law

The school facilities board shall terminate on July 1, 2008, unless continued. See §§ 41–3008.19 and 41–2955.

Title 15, Chapter 16, relating to school capital finance, is repealed on January 1, 2009, by § 41–3008.19.

Historical and Statutory Notes

The purported addition of this chapter by Laws 1998, 3rd S.S., Ch. 1, failed to became effective because Ch. 1 was repealed in its entirety by Laws 1998, 5th S.S., Ch. 1, § 2, effective July 1, 1998.

ARTICLE 1. SCHOOL FACILITIES BOARD

§ 15–2001. School facilities board; conflict of interest

A. The school facilities board is established consisting of the following members who shall be appointed by the governor pursuant to § 38–211 in such a manner as to provide for approximate geographic balance and approximate balance between public and private members:

1. One member who is an elected member of a school district governing board with knowledge and experience in the area of finance.

2. One private citizen who represents an organization of taxpayers.

3. One member with knowledge and experience in school construction.

4. One member who is a registered professional architect and who has current knowledge and experience in school architecture.

5. One member with knowledge and experience in school facilities management in a public school system.

6. One member with knowledge and experience in demographics.

7. One member who is a teacher and who currently provides classroom instruction.

8. One member who is a registered professional engineer and who has current knowledge and experience in school engineering.

9. One member who is an owner or officer of a private business.

B. In addition to the members appointed pursuant to subsection A of this section, the superintendent of public instruction or the superintendent's designee shall serve as an advisory nonvoting member of the school facilities board.

C. The governor shall appoint a chairperson from members appointed pursuant to subsection A of this section.

D. Members of the school facilities board serve four year terms. The school facilities board shall meet as often as the members deem necessary. A majority of the members constitutes a quorum for the transaction of business.

E. The unexcused absence of a member for more than three consecutive meetings is justification for removal by a majority vote of the board. If the member is removed, notice shall be given of the removal pursuant to § 38–292.

F. The governor shall fill a vacancy by appointment of a qualified person as provided in subsection A of this section.

G. Members of the board who are employed by government entities are not eligible to receive compensation. Members of the board who are not employed by government entities are entitled to payment of one hundred fifty dollars for each meeting attended, prorated for partial days spent for each meeting, up to two thousand five hundred dollars each year. All members are eligible for reimbursement of expenses pursuant to title 38, chapter 4, article 2.[1] These expenses and the payment of compensation are payable to a member from monies appropriated to the board from the new school facilities fund.

H. Members of the school facilities board are subject to title 38, chapter 3, article 8.[2]

Added by Laws 1998, 5th S.S., Ch. 1, § 39, eff. July 9, 1998. Amended by Laws 1999, Ch. 3, § 1, eff. March 1, 1999.

[1] Section 38–621 et seq.

[2] Section 38–501 et seq.

Historical and Statutory Notes

Laws 1998, 5th S.S., Ch. 1, §§ 47, 48 and 51, provide:

"**Sec. 47. Purpose**

"The purpose of the school facilities board is to evaluate the school capital needs of school districts and to distribute monies to school districts in order to cure existing deficiencies, for building renewal and for the construction of new facilities.

"**Sec. 48. School facilities board; initial members; transition**

"**A.** Notwithstanding § 15-2001, Arizona Revised Statutes, as added by this act, of the initial members appointed by the governor to the school facilities board, the governor shall appoint three members of the board to two-year terms in office, three members to three-year terms in office and three members to four-year terms in office. The governor shall appoint all subsequent members as prescribed by § 15-2001, Arizona Revised Statutes.

"**B.** Notwithstanding Laws 1997, chapter 4, § 16, as amended by Laws 1997, first special session, chapter 9, § 1, the school facilities board succeeds to the functions of the state board for school capital facilities established pursuant to Laws 1996, fifth special session, chapter 8. All administrative and financial matters, contracts, proceedings and authorizations, whether completed, pending or in process, of the state board for school capital facilities are transferred to and retain the same status with the school facilities board. This act does not alter the effect of any actions that were taken or impair the valid obligations of the state board for school capital facilities that were in existence on the effective date of this act.

"**C.** The school facilities board shall assume responsibility for the operation of the school capital equity fund."

"**Sec. 51. Initial report of building renewal fund distribution amount**

"Notwithstanding § 15-2031, Arizona Revised Statutes, as added by this act, the school facilities board shall submit its initial report on the proposed distribution of building renewal monies to the president of the senate, the speaker of the house of representatives, the department of library, archives and public records and the governor as soon as practical but no later than May 1, 1999."

Laws 1998, 5th S.S., Ch. 1, § 55, as amended by Laws 1999, Ch. 299, § 39; Laws 2000, Ch. 163, § 2; Laws 2001, Ch. 11, § 9, effective March 15, 2001, retroactively effective to January 1, 2001, provides:

"**Sec. 55. Exemption from rule making requirements; delayed effective date of rules**

"Notwithstanding any other law, the school facilities board is exempt from the provisions of title 41, chapter 6, Arizona Revised Statutes, until December 31, 2001. By March 31, 1999, the school facilities board shall provide a final draft of proposed minimum school facility adequacy guidelines to the governor, the speaker of the house of representatives and the president of the senate and the school facilities board shall make copies of the final draft available to the public. The school facilities board shall provide the public with an opportunity to comment on the proposed rules and shall hold at least one public hearing on the proposed rules. The rules adopted pursuant to this section do not become effective until April 30, 1999."

Laws 1998, 5th S.S., Ch. 1, § 60, as amended by Laws 2000, Ch. 163, § 3; Laws 2001, Ch. 11, § 10, effective March 15, 2001, retroactively effective to January 1, 2001, provides:

"**Sec. 60. School facilities board; procurement**

"Notwithstanding any other provision of law, the school facilities board is exempt from the provisions of title 41, chapter 23, Arizona Revised Statutes, until from and after December 31, 2001."

The 1999 amendment by Ch. 3, deleted "pursuant to § 38-211" following "chairperson" in subsec. C; and deleted the last two sentences of subsec. H, which read:

"A member or employee of the school facilities board shall not have a direct or indirect financial interest in any property purchased, facility constructed or contract financed with monies made available by the board or any other public monies. A violation of this subsection is a class 1 misdemeanor."

Laws 1999, 1st S.S., Ch. 4, §§ 18 and 19, provide:

"**Sec. 18. New school facilities funding**

"Notwithstanding title 15, chapter 16, Arizona Revised Statutes, the school facilities board established pursuant to § 15-2001, Arizona Revised Statutes, may disburse monies from the new school facilities fund established pursuant to § 15-2041, Arizona Revised Statutes, before publishing minimum school facility adequacy guidelines pursuant to § 15-2011, subsection F, Arizona Revised Statutes and Laws 1998, fifth special session, chapter 1, § 55.

"**Sec. 19. Retroactivity**

"Section 18 of this act, relating to new school facilities funding, applies retroactively to from and after January 1, 1999."

Laws 1999, Ch. 299, § 42, provides:

"**Sec. 42. Exemption from local match requirement**

"**A.** Notwithstanding Laws 1998, fifth special session, chapter 1, § 48, a school district that received funding for a capital project from the former state board for school capital facilities established by Laws 1996, fifth special session, chapter 8, § 13 shall not be required to provide an additional matching share if all of the following conditions are met:

"1. At the time the former state board for school capital facilities approved the capital project, Laws 1997, chapter 4, § 16 as amended by Laws 1997, first special session, chapter 9, § 1 had been enacted by the legislature and the school district was entitled to a significant amount of funding that could have been used to meet part of its required local match.

"2. The repeal of Laws 1997, chapter 4, § 16 as amended by Laws 1997, first special session, chapter 9, § 1 necessitated that the school district pass a bond in order to provide the local match.

"3. The school district would have qualified for new facilities without any local match under Laws 1998, fifth special session, chapter 1.

"4. The school district has paid at least one million dollars in local match for a capital project.

"5. The 1998 combined tax rate for the majority of the district is at least fifty per cent higher than the average statewide property tax rate as published by the department of revenue.

"B. The school facilities board may use monies from the deficiencies correction fund established by § 15–2021, Arizona Revised Statutes, as amended by this act, or the new school facilities fund established by § 15–2041, Arizona Revised Statutes, as amended by this act, to complete any projects previously approved by the former state board for school capital facilities."

Laws 1999, Ch. 299, § 43, provides:

"**Sec. 43. Retroactivity**

"Section 39 of this act is effective retroactively to from and after April 30, 1999."

Laws 2001, Ch. 11, § 13, provides:

"**Sec. 13. Retroactivity**

"Sections 9 and 10 of this act are effective retroactively to from and after December 31, 2000."

§ 15–2002. Powers and duties; executive director; staffing; report

A. The school facilities board shall:

1. Make assessments of school facilities and equipment deficiencies pursuant to § 15–2021 and approve the distribution of grants as appropriate.

2. Develop a database for administering the building renewal formula prescribed in § 15–2031 and administer the distribution of monies to school districts for building renewal.

3. Inspect school buildings at least once every five years to ensure compliance with the building adequacy standards prescribed in § 15–2011 and routine preventative maintenance guidelines as prescribed in this section with respect to construction of new buildings and maintenance of existing buildings. The school facilities board shall randomly select twenty school districts every thirty months and inspect them pursuant to this paragraph.

4. Review and approve student population projections submitted by school districts to determine to what extent school districts are entitled to monies to construct new facilities pursuant to § 15–2041. The board shall make a final determination within six months of the receipt of an application by a school district for monies from the new school facilities fund.

5. Certify that plans for new school facilities meet the building adequacy standards prescribed in § 15–2011.

6. Develop prototypical elementary and high school designs. The board shall review the design differences between the schools with the highest academic productivity scores and the schools with the lowest academic productivity scores. The board shall also review the results of a valid and reliable survey of parent quality rating in the highest performing schools and the lowest performing schools in this state. The survey of parent quality rating shall be administered by the department of education. The board shall consider the design elements of the schools with the highest academic productivity scores and parent quality ratings in the development of elementary and high school

designs. The board shall develop separate school designs for elementary, middle and high schools with varying pupil capacities.

7. Develop application forms, reporting forms and procedures to carry out the requirements of this article.

8. Review and approve or reject requests submitted by school districts to take actions pursuant to § 15–341, subsection F.

9. Submit an annual report by December 15 to the speaker of the house of representatives, the president of the senate, the superintendent of public instruction, the director of the Arizona state library, archives and public records and the governor that includes the following information:

(a) A detailed description of the amount of monies distributed by the school facilities board in the previous fiscal year.

(b) A list of each capital project that received monies from the school facilities board during the previous fiscal year, a brief description of each project that was funded and a summary of the board's reasons for the distribution of monies for the project.

(c) A summary of the findings and conclusions of the building maintenance inspections conducted pursuant to this article during the previous fiscal year.

(d) A summary of the findings of common design elements and characteristics of the highest performing schools and the lowest performing schools based on academic productivity including the results of the parent quality rating survey.

For the purposes of this paragraph, "academic productivity" means academic year advancement per calendar year as measured with student-level data using the statewide nationally standardized norm-referenced achievement test.

10. By December 1 of each year, report to the joint committee on capital review the amounts necessary to fulfill the requirements of §§ 15–2021, 15–2022, 15–2031 and 15–2041 for the following fiscal year and the estimated amounts necessary to fulfill the requirements of §§ 15–2021, 15–2022, 15–2031 and 15–2041 for the fiscal year following the next fiscal year. No later than January 1 of each year, the board shall instruct the state treasurer as to the amounts under the transaction privilege tax to be credited in equal quarterly installments for the following state fiscal year. The board shall provide copies of both reports to the president of the senate, the speaker of the house of representatives and the governor.

11. Adopt minimum school facility adequacy guidelines to provide the minimum quality and quantity of school buildings and the facilities and equipment necessary and appropriate to enable pupils to achieve the educational goals of the Arizona state schools for the deaf and the blind. The school facilities board shall establish minimum school facility adequacy guidelines applicable to the Arizona state schools for the deaf and the blind by December 31, 2000.

12. Beginning August 15, 2004, and each even-numbered year thereafter, report to the joint committee on capital review the amounts necessary to fulfill the requirements of §§ 15–2031 and 15–2041 for the Arizona state schools for the deaf and the blind for the following two fiscal years. Notwithstanding

paragraph 10 of this subsection or any other law, the school facilities board shall not include these amounts in the building renewal or new school facilities transfer instructions to the state treasurer. The Arizona state schools for the deaf and the blind shall incorporate the findings of the report in any request for building renewal monies and new school facilities monies. Any monies provided to the Arizona state schools for the deaf and the blind for building renewal and for new school facilities are subject to legislative appropriation.

13. By October 15 of each year, the school facilities board shall submit information regarding demographic assumptions, a proposed construction schedule and new school construction cost estimates for the following fiscal year to the joint committee on capital review for its review.

B. The school facilities board may contract for private services in compliance with the procurement practices prescribed in title 41, chapter 23.[1]

C. The governor shall appoint an executive director of the school facilities board pursuant to § 38-211. The executive director is eligible to receive compensation as determined pursuant to § 38-611 and may hire and fire necessary staff as approved by the legislature in the budget. The executive director shall have demonstrated competency in school finance, facilities design or facilities management, either in private business or government service. The executive director serves at the pleasure of the governor. The staff of the school facilities board is exempt from title 41, chapter 4, articles 5 and 6.[2] The executive director:

1. Shall analyze applications for monies submitted to the board by school districts.

2. Shall assist the board in developing forms and procedures for the distribution and review of applications and the distribution of monies to school districts.

3. May review or audit, or both, the expenditure of monies by a school district for deficiencies corrections, building renewal and new school facilities.

4. Shall assist the board in the preparation of the board's annual report.

5. Shall research and provide reports on issues of general interest to the board.

6. May aid school districts in the development of reasonable and cost-effective school designs in order to avoid statewide duplicated efforts and unwarranted expenditures in the area of school design.

7. May assist school districts in facilitating the development of multijurisdictional facilities.

8. Shall assist the board in any other appropriate matter or method as directed by the members of the board.

9. Shall establish procedures to ensure compliance with the notice and hearing requirements prescribed in § 15-905. The notice and hearing procedures adopted by the board shall include the requirement, with respect to the board's consideration of any application filed after July 1, 2001 or after December 31 of the year in which the property becomes territory in the vicinity of a military airport or ancillary military facility as defined in § 28-8461 for

monies to fund the construction of new school facilities proposed to be located in territory in the vicinity of a military airport or ancillary military facility, that the military airport receive notification of the application by first class mail at least thirty days before any hearing concerning the application.

10. May expedite any request for funds in which the local match was not obtained for a project that received preliminary approval by the state board for school capital facilities.

11. Shall expedite any request for funds in which the school district governing board submits an application that shows an immediate need for a new school facility.

12. Shall make a determination as to administrative completion within one month after the receipt of an application by a school district for monies from the new school facilities fund.

13. Shall provide technical support to school districts as requested by school districts in connection with the construction of new school facilities and the maintenance of existing school facilities.

D. When appropriate, the school facilities board shall review and use the statewide school facilities inventory and needs assessment conducted by the joint committee on capital review and issued in July, 1995.

E. The school facilities board shall contract with one or more private building inspectors to complete an initial assessment of school facilities and equipment provided in § 15–2021 and shall inspect each school building in this state at least once every five years to ensure compliance with § 15–2011. A copy of the inspection report, together with any recommendations for building maintenance, shall be provided to the school facilities board and the governing board of the school district.

F. The school facilities board may consider appropriate combinations of facilities or uses in making assessments of and curing deficiencies pursuant to subsection A, paragraph 1 of this section and in certifying plans for new school facilities pursuant to subsection A, paragraph 5 of this section.

G. The board shall not award any monies to fund new facilities that are financed by class A bonds that are issued by the school district.

H. The board shall not distribute monies to a school district for replacement or repair of facilities if the costs associated with the replacement or repair are covered by insurance or a performance or payment bond.

I. The board may contract for construction services and materials that are necessary to correct existing deficiencies in school district facilities as determined pursuant to § 15–2021. The board may procure the construction services necessary pursuant to this subsection by any method including construction-manager-at-risk, design-build, design-bid-build or job-order-contracting as provided by title 41, chapter 23. The construction planning and services performed pursuant to this subsection are exempt from § 41–791.01.

J. The school facilities board may enter into agreements with school districts to allow school facilities board staff and contractors access to school property for the purposes of performing the construction services necessary pursuant to subsection I of this section.

K. By October 1, 2002, each school district shall develop routine preventative maintenance guidelines for its facilities. The guidelines shall be submitted to the school facilities board for review and approval by February 1, 2003. If upon inspection by the school facilities board it is determined that a school district facility was inadequately maintained pursuant to the school district's routine preventative maintenance guidelines, the school district shall use building renewal monies pursuant to § 15-2031, subsection J to return the building to compliance with the school district's routine preventative maintenance guidelines. Once the district is in compliance, it no longer is required to use building renewal monies for preventative maintenance.

L. The school facilities board may temporarily transfer monies between the capital reserve fund established by § 15-2003, the deficiencies correction fund established by § 15-2021, the emergency deficiencies correction fund established by § 15-2022, the building renewal fund established by § 15-2031 and the new school facilities fund established by § 15-2041 if all of the following conditions are met:

1. The transfer is necessary to avoid a temporary shortfall in the fund into which the monies are transferred.

2. The transferred monies are restored to the fund where the monies originated as soon as practicable after the temporary shortfall in the other fund has been addressed.

3. The school facilities board reports to the joint committee on capital review the amount of and the reason for any monies transferred.

Added by Laws 1998, 5th S.S., Ch. 1, § 39, eff. July 9, 1998. Amended by Laws 1999, Ch. 76, § 5; Laws 1999, Ch. 299, § 33; Laws 2000, Ch. 88, § 20; Laws 2000, Ch. 163, § 1; Laws 2001, Ch. 11, § 3, eff. March 15, 2001; Laws 2001, Ch. 23, § 6; Laws 2001, Ch. 297, § 2; Laws 2002, Ch. 241, § 4; Laws 2002, Ch. 330, § 33; Laws 2003, Ch. 215, § 3, eff. May 14, 2003, retroactively effective to Aug. 22, 2002; Laws 2003, Ch. 264, § 9; Laws 2004, Ch. 111, § 6; Laws 2004, Ch. 314, § 2.

[1] Section 41-2501 et seq.

[2] Section 41-761 et seq. and 41-781 et seq.

Retroactive Application

This section, as amended by Laws 2001, Ch. 23, applies retroactively to July 2, 2001.

This section, as amended by Laws 2002, Ch. 241, applies retroactively to August 9, 2001.

Historical and Statutory Notes

The purported amendment of this section by Laws 1998, Ch. 164 failed to become effective because Chapter 164 was repealed in its entirety by Laws 1998, 5th S.S., Ch. 1, § 2, effective July 1, 1998.

Laws 1999, 1st S.S., Ch. 4, § 17, provides:

"**Sec. 17. State treasurer; school facilities transfer**

"Notwithstanding § 15-2002, subsection A, paragraph 11, Arizona Revised Statutes, or any other law, the state treasurer shall disregard the instructions of the school facilities board relating to the new school facilities fund transfer for fiscal year 1999-2000 and instead transfer the sum of $200,000,000 from transaction privilege revenues to the new school facilities fund established by § 15-2041, Arizona Revised Statutes."

This section was purportedly amended by Laws 2000, 4th S.S., Ch. 1, § 21. Section 27 of Laws 2000, 4th S.S., Ch. 1 provides:

"**Sec. 27. Conditional enactment**

"Sections 21 through 25 of this act are not effective unless the Constitution of Arizona is amended by the voters at the next general election and the enabling act of June 20, 1910 is amended by Congress to allow the designation of state trust lands for the Arizona conservation reserve and the donation of state trust lands for school sites."

However, Proposition 100, based on Laws 2000, S.C.R. 1001, proposing amendment to the Constitution of Arizona by amendment of Article 10, §§ 1 to 4, 7 and 10 and addition of Article 10, §§ 12 to 14, relating to state lands, was rejected by the electors at the November 7, 2000 general election as proclaimed by the governor on November 27, 2000. Therefore, the condition of the amendment of this section by Laws 2000, 4th S.S., Ch. 1, was not met, and the amendment did not become effective.

Laws 2001, Ch. 23, § 18, subsec. C, provides:

"**Sec. 18. Retroactivity**

"**C.** Sections 15–2002 and 15–2041, Arizona Revised Statutes, as amended by this act, apply retroactively to from and after July 1, 2001."

The amendment of this section by Laws 2001, Ch. 297, § 2 was repealed by Laws 2002, Ch. 241, § 5; Laws 2002, Ch. 330, § 34.

The 2002 amendments of this section by Chs. 241 and 330, explicitly amended the amendment of this section by Laws 2001, Ch. 11, § 3, and by Laws 2001, Ch. 23, § 6.

Laws 2002, Ch. 241, § 1, par. 2, provides:

"**Section 1. Purpose**

"2. Section 15–2002, Arizona Revised Statutes, was amended by Laws 2001, chapter 11, § 3, Laws 2001, chapter 23, § 6 and Laws 2001, chapter 297, § 2. The chapter 297 version could not be blended because it failed to amend the chapter 11 version, which was an emergency enactment, and therefore did not comply with article IV, part 2, § 14, Constitution of Arizona. To accomplish the intent of these enactments, this act amends the 2001 blended version of § 15–2002, Arizona Revised Statutes, to incorporate the amendments made by Laws 2001, chapter 297 and the chapter 297 version is repealed."

Laws 2002, Ch. 241, § 36, subsec. B, provides:

"**Sec. 36. Retroactive application**

"**B.** Sections 4, 5, 9, 10, 11, 12, 15, 16, 17, 18, 29 and 30 of this act apply retroactively to August 9, 2001."

Laws 2002, Ch. 330, became law without the Governor's signature as provided in Arizona Constitution, Article 5, § 7.

Laws 2003, Ch. 215, § 5, eff. May 14, 2003, provides:

"**Sec. 5. Retroactivity**

"This act is effective retroactively to August 22, 2002."

The amendment of this section by Laws 2003, Ch. 264, § 9 was repealed by Laws 2004, Ch. 111, § 7.

The amendment of this section by Laws 2003, Ch. 264, § 9 was repealed by Laws 2004, Ch. 314, § 3.

Laws 2003, Ch. 264, § 35, as amended by Laws 2004, Ch. 274, § 4, provides:

"**Sec. 35. Project bids; joint committee on capital review approval**

"**A.** Before the issuance in fiscal year 2003–2004 of any state school trust revenue bonds pursuant to laws 2003, chapter 264, as amended by this act, the school facilities board shall:

"1. Receive bids for the cost of all deficiencies correction projects that will be financed with the revenue bond proceeds.

"2. Submit a list of the projects, the project bids and the estimated annual principal and interest payments related to the bond agreement to the joint committee on capital review for approval.

"**B.** Before the issuance in fiscal year 2004–2005 of any state school trust revenue bonds pursuant to laws 2003, chapter 264, as amended by this act, the school facilities board shall submit the bond proposal to the joint committee on capital review for review.

"**C.** The school facilities board shall report to the joint committee on capital review the cost of the remaining projects in the Tucson Unified School District, the Mesa Unified School District and the Glendale Union High School District after receiving bids for projects in those districts."

Laws 2003, Ch. 264, § 45, provides:

"**Sec. 45. Retroactivity**

"**A.** Section 15–2031, Arizona Revised Statutes, as amended by this act, Laws 2003, first special session, chapter 3, § 1, as amended by this act, and §§ 17, 18 and 38 of this act apply retroactively to from and after June 30, 2003.

"**B.** Section 15–121, Arizona Revised Statutes, as amended by this act, applies retroactively to from and after April 30, 2003."

The 2004 amendment of this section by Ch. 111, § 6 explicitly amended the amendment of this section by Laws 2003, Ch. 215, § 3.

Laws 2004, Ch. 274, § 9, provides:

"**Sec. 9. Retroactivity**

"Sections 2 through 7 of this act are effective retroactively to from and after June 30, 2004."

Laws 2004, Ch. 314, § 1, par. 1, provides:

"**Section 1. Purpose**

"1. Section 15-2002, Arizona Revised Statutes, was amended by Laws 2003, chapter 215, § 3 and Laws 2003, chapter 264, § 9. The chapter 264 version could not be blended because it failed to amend the chapter 215 version, which was an emergency enactment, and therefore did not comply with article IV, part 2, § 14, Constitution of Arizona. To accomplish the intent of these enactments, this act amends the Laws 2003, chapter 215 version of § 15-2002, Arizona Revised Statutes, to incorporate the amendments made by Laws 2003, chapter 264 and the chapter 264 version is repealed."

The 2004 amendment of this section by Ch. 314, § 2 explicitly amended the amendment of this section by Laws 2003, Ch. 215, § 3.

Laws 2004, Ch. 314, § 16, subsec. A, provides:

"**Sec. 16. Retroactive application**

"**A.** Sections 2, 3, 4, 5, 8, 9, 14 and 15 of this act apply retroactively to September 18, 2003."

Reviser's Notes:

1998 Note.. Pursuant to authority of § 41-1304.02, in subsection A, paragraph 10 the subdivision (e) designation was removed and the text was moved to start at the left margin.

1999 Note. Prior to the 2000 amendments, this section contained the amendments made by Laws 1999, Ch. 76, sec. 5 and Ch. 299, sec. 33 that were blended together pursuant to authority of § 41-1304.03.

2000 Note. Prior to the 2001 amendments, this section contained the amendments made by Laws 2000, Ch. 88, sec. 20 and Ch. 163, sec. 1 that were blended together pursuant to authority of § 41-1304.03.

2001 Note. The amendment of this section by Laws 2001, Ch. 297, sec. 2 failed to set forth in full the text of the section as amended by Laws 2001, Ch. 11, sec. 3, an emergency act, as required by Constitution of Arizona art. IV, pt. 2, sec. 14.

2001 Note. Prior to the 2002 amendment, this section contained the amendments made by Laws 2001, Ch. 11, sec. 3 and Ch. 23, sec. 6 that were blended together pursuant to authority of § 41-1304.03.

2002 Note. Prior to the 2003 amendment, this section contained the amendments made by Laws 2002, Ch. 241, sec. 4 and Ch. 330, sec. 33 that were blended together pursuant to authority of § 41-1304.03.

2003 Note. The amendment of this section by Laws 2003, Ch. 264, sec. 9 failed to set forth in full the text of the section as amended by Laws 2003, Ch. 215, sec. 3, an emergency act, as required by Constitution of Arizona art. IV, pt. 2, sec. 14.

2004 Note. This section contains the amendments made by Laws 2004, Ch. 111, sec. 6 and Ch. 314, sec. 2 that were blended together as shown pursuant to authority of § 41-1304.03.

§ 15-2003. Capital reserve fund

A. A capital reserve fund is established consisting of monies that are credited to the fund from the new school facilities fund established by § 15-2041, subsection A.

B. The school facilities board shall administer the fund. On notice from the school facilities board, the state treasurer shall invest and reinvest monies in the fund as provided by § 35-313, and monies earned on investments shall be credited to the capital reserve fund.

C. Monies in the capital reserve fund are subject to legislative appropriation only to the deficiencies correction fund established by § 15-2021 or the new school facilities fund established by § 15-2041.

Added by Laws 1998, 5th S.S., Ch. 1, § 39, eff. July 9, 1998.

Historical and Statutory Notes

The purported amendment of this section by Laws 1998, Ch. 164 failed to become effective because Chapter 164 was repealed in its entirety by Laws 1998, 5th S.S., Ch. 1, § 2, effective July 1, 1998.

§ 15-2004. School facilities board lease-to-own; fund

A. In order to fulfill the requirements of § 15-2041, the school facilities board may acquire school facilities for the use of one or more school districts by entering into one or more lease-to-own transactions in accordance with this section. For purposes of this section, providing school facilities includes land acquisition, related infrastructure, fixtures, furnishings, equipment and costs of the lease-to-own transaction. The school facilities board may provide monies to provide school facilities in part pursuant to § 15–2041 and in part through a lease-to-own transaction.

B. A lease-to-own transaction may provide for:

1. The ground lease of the land for the facilities to a private entity for the term of the lease-to-own transaction or for a term of up to one and one-half times the term of the lease-to-own transaction, subject to earlier termination on completion of performance of the lease-to-own agreement. The ground lessor may either be the school district or the school facilities board, whichever holds title to the land.

2. The lease of the completed school facilities by a private entity to the school facilities board for an extended term of years pursuant to a lease-to-own agreement.

3. The sublease of the completed school facilities by the school facilities board to the school district during the term of the lease-to-own agreement. The sublease shall provide for the use, maintenance and operation of the school facilities by the school district and for the transfer of ownership of the school facilities to the school district on completion of performance of the lease-to-own agreement.

4. The option for the school facilities board's purchase of the school facilities and transfer of ownership of the school facilities to the school district before the expiration of the lease-to-own agreement.

5. The services of trustees, financial advisors, paying agents, transfer agents, underwriters, lawyers and other professional service providers, credit enhancements or liquidity facilities and all other services considered necessary by the school facilities board in connection with the lease-to-own transaction, and related agreements and arrangements including arrangements for the creation and sale of certificates of participation evidencing proportionate interests in the lease payments to be made by the school facilities board pursuant to the lease-to-own agreement.

C. The sublease of the school facilities to the school district is subject to this section and to the provisions of the lease-to-own agreement. Neither a ground lease by the school district as lessor nor a sublease of the school facilities to the school district is required to be authorized by a vote of the school district electors. A ground lease is not subject to any limitations or requirements applicable to leases or lease-purchase agreements pursuant to § 15–342 or any other section of this title.

D. Any school facility that is constructed through a lease-to-own agreement shall meet the minimum building adequacy standards set forth in § 15–2011.

E. School districts may use local monies to exceed the minimum adequacy standards and to build athletic fields and any other capital project for leased-to-own facilities.

F. The school facilities board shall include any square footage of new school facilities constructed through lease-to-own agreements in the computations prescribed in § 15-2011.

G. Pursuant to § 15-2031, a school district is eligible to receive building renewal monies for any facility constructed through a lease-to-own agreement. If a facility's building maintenance renewal is included in the lease-to-own agreement, then the facility shall not be included in the district's building renewal calculation.

H. A lease-to-own fund is established consisting of monies appropriated by the legislature. The school facilities board shall administer the fund and distribute monies in the fund to make payments pursuant to lease-to-own agreements entered into by the school facilities board pursuant to this section, to make payments to or for the benefit of school districts pursuant to local lease-to-own agreements entered into by school districts pursuant to § 15-2005 and to pay costs considered necessary by the school facilities board in connection with lease-to-own transactions and local lease-to-own transactions. Payments by the school facilities board pursuant to a lease-to-own agreement or local lease-to-own agreement shall be made only from the lease-to-own fund. On notice from the school facilities board, the state treasurer shall invest and divest monies in the fund as provided by § 35-313, and monies earned from investment shall be credited to the lease-to-own fund.

I. A lease-to-own agreement entered into by the school facilities board pursuant to this section shall provide that:

1. At the completion of the lease-to-own agreement, ownership of the school facilities and land associated with the lease-to-own agreement shall be transferred to the school district as specified in the agreement.

2. The obligation of the school facilities board to make any payment under the lease-to-own agreement is a current expense, payable exclusively from appropriated monies, and is not a general obligation indebtedness of this state or the school facilities board. The obligation of a school district to make expenditures under a sublease pursuant to subsection B, paragraph 3 of this section is a current expense, payable exclusively from budgeted monies, and is not a general obligation indebtedness of the school district.

3. If the legislature fails to appropriate monies or the school facilities board fails to allocate such monies for any periodic payment or renewal term of the lease-to-own agreement, the lease-to-own agreement terminates at the end of the current term and this state and the school facilities board are relieved of any subsequent obligation under the agreement and the school district is relieved of any subsequent obligation under the sublease.

4. The lease-to-own agreement shall be reviewed and approved by the attorney general before the agreement may take effect.

5. Before the agreement takes effect and after review by the attorney general, the project or projects related to the agreement shall be submitted for review by the joint committee on capital review.

J. The school facilities board may covenant to use its best efforts to budget, obtain, allocate and maintain sufficient appropriated monies to make payments under a lease-to-own agreement, but the lease-to-own agreement shall acknowledge that appropriating state monies is a legislative act and is beyond the control of the school facilities board or of any other party to the lease-to-own agreement.

K. The land and the school facilities on the land are exempt from taxation during the term of the lease-to-own agreement and during construction and subsequent occupancy by the school district pursuant to the sublease.

L. The powers prescribed in this section are in addition to the powers conferred by any other law. Without reference to any other provision of this title or to any other law, this section is authority for the completion of the purposes prescribed in this section for the school facilities board to provide school facilities for use by school districts through lease-to-own transactions pursuant to this section without regard to the procedure required by any other law. Except as otherwise provided in this section, the provisions of this title that relate to the matters contained in this section are superseded because this section is the exclusive law on these matters.

Added by Laws 2002, Ch. 330, § 35. Amended by Laws 2003, Ch. 264, § 19.

Historical and Statutory Notes

Laws 2002, Ch. 330, § 55, provides:

"**Sec. 55. New school facilities; lease–to–own**

"**A.** The school facilities board shall enter into lease-to-own transactions pursuant to §§ 15–2004, 15–2005 and 15–2006, Arizona Revised Statutes, as added by this act, to pay for the costs of new school facilities in fiscal year 2002–2003.

"**B.** Notwithstanding § 15–2006, Arizona Revised Statutes, as added by this act, the school facilities board shall enter into lease-to-own transactions in an amount not to exceed $400,000,000 in fiscal year 2002–2003 in order to fulfill the requirements of § 15–2041, Arizona Revised Statutes.

"**C.** Notwithstanding § 15–2041, Arizona Revised Statutes, as amended by this act, the school facilities board may transfer monies from the new school facilities fund to the lease-to-own fund established by § 15–2004, Arizona Revised Statutes, as added by this act, in fiscal year 2002–2003 for the purposes of that section."

Laws 2002, Ch. 330, became law without the Governor's signature as provided in Arizona Constitution, Article 5, § 7.

Laws 2003, Ch. 264, § 19, provides:

"**Sec. 19. New school facilities; lease–to–own**

"**A.** The school facilities board shall enter into lease-to-own transactions pursuant to §§ 15–2004, 15–2005 and 15–2006, Arizona Revised Statutes, to pay for the costs of new school facilities in fiscal year 2003–2004.

"**B.** Notwithstanding § 15–2006, Arizona Revised Statutes, the school facilities board shall enter into lease-to-own transactions in an amount not to exceed $250,000,000 in fiscal year 2003–2004 in order to fulfill the requirements of § 15–2041, Arizona Revised Statutes.

"**C.** Notwithstanding § 15–2041, Arizona Revised Statutes, the school facilities board may transfer monies from the new school facilities fund to the lease-to-own fund established by § 15–2004, Arizona Revised Statutes, in fiscal year 2003–2004 for the purposes of that section."

Laws 2004, Ch. 274, § 6, provides:

"**Sec. 6. New school facilities; lease–to–own**

"**A.** The school facilities board shall enter into lease-to-own transactions pursuant to §§ 15–2004, 15–2005 and 15–2006, Arizona Revised Statutes, to pay for the costs of new school facilities in fiscal year 2004–2005.

"**B.** Notwithstanding § 15–2006, Arizona Revised Statutes, the school facilities board shall enter into lease-to-own transactions in an amount not to exceed $250,000,000 in fiscal year 2004–2005 in order to fulfill the requirements of § 15–2041, Arizona Revised Statutes.

"**C.** Notwithstanding § 15–2041, Arizona Revised Statutes, the school facilities board may transfer monies from the new school facilities fund to the lease-to-own fund established by § 15–2004, Arizona Revised Statutes, in fiscal year 2004–2005 for the purposes of that section.

"**D.** Notwithstanding § 35–190, Arizona Revised Statutes, monies remaining in the lease-to-own fund established by § 15–2004, Arizona

Revised Statutes, at the end of fiscal year 2003-2004 shall not revert to the state general fund."

Laws 2004, Ch. 274, § 9, provides:

"Sec. 9. Retroactivity

"Sections 2 through 7 of this act are effective retroactively to from and after June 30, 2004."

§ 15-2005. Local lease-to-own by school districts

A. In order to fulfill the requirements of § 15-2041, with the approval of the school facilities board, a school district may acquire school facilities by entering into a local lease-to-own transaction in accordance with this section. For purposes of this section, providing school facilities includes land acquisition, related infrastructure, fixtures, furnishings, equipment and costs of the local lease-to-own transaction. The school facilities board may provide monies to provide school facilities in part pursuant to § 15-2041 and in part through payments to or for the benefit of a school district for a local lease-to-own transaction.

B. A local lease-to-own transaction may provide for:

1. The ground lease of the land for the facilities to a private entity for the term of the local lease-to-own transaction or for a term of up to one and one-half times the term of the local lease-to-own transaction, subject to earlier termination on completion of performance of the local lease-to-own agreement. The ground lessor may either be the school district or the school facilities board, whichever holds title to the land.

2. The lease of the completed school facilities by a private entity to the school district for an extended term of years pursuant to a local lease-to-own agreement. The local lease-to-own agreement shall provide for the use, maintenance and operation of the school facilities by the school district and for the transfer of ownership of the school facilities to the school district on completion of performance of the local lease-to-own agreement.

3. The option for the school district's purchase of the school facilities and transfer of ownership of the school facilities to the school district before the expiration of the local lease-to-own agreement.

4. The services of trustees, financial advisors, paying agents, transfer agents, underwriters, lawyers and other professional service providers, credit enhancements or liquidity facilities and all other services considered necessary by the school district or the school facilities board in connection with the local lease-to-own transaction, and related agreements and arrangements including arrangements for the creation and sale of certificates of participation evidencing proportionate interests in the lease payments to be made by the school district pursuant to the local lease-to-own agreement.

C. Neither a ground lease by the school district as lessor nor a local lease-to-own agreement is required to be authorized by a vote of the school district electors. A ground lease is not subject to any limitations or requirements applicable to leases or lease-purchase agreements pursuant to § 15-342 or any other section of this title.

D. The school facilities board may make payments to or for the benefit of the school district from the lease-to-own fund established by § 15-2004 for the payment of amounts payable under the local lease-to-own agreement.

E. Any school facility that is constructed through a lease-to-own agreement shall meet the minimum building adequacy standards set forth in § 15–2011.

F. School districts may use local monies to exceed the minimum adequacy standards and to build athletic fields and any other capital project for leased-to-own facilities.

G. The school facilities board shall include any square footage of new school facilities constructed through lease-to-own agreements in the computations prescribed in § 15–2011.

H. Pursuant to § 15–2031, a school district is eligible to receive building renewal monies for any facility constructed through a lease-to-own agreement. If a facility's building maintenance renewal is included in the lease-to-own agreement, then the facility shall not be included in the district's building renewal calculation.

I. A local lease-to-own agreement entered into by a school district pursuant to this section shall provide that:

1. At the completion of the lease-to-own agreement, ownership of the school facilities and land associated with the lease-to-own agreement shall be transferred to the school district as specified in the agreement.

2. The obligation of the school district to make any payment or expenditure under the local lease-to-own agreement is a current expense, payable exclusively from properly budgeted monies, and is not a general obligation indebtedness of this state, the school facilities board or the school district, and that any payment by the school facilities board to or for the benefit of the school district from the lease-to-own fund established by § 15–2004 for payments of amounts payable under the local lease-to-own agreement is a current expense, payable exclusively from appropriated monies, and is not a general obligation indebtedness of this state or the school facilities board.

3. If the school district fails to properly budget for payments under the local lease-to-own agreement or if the legislature fails to appropriate monies or the school facilities board fails to allocate monies for periodic payment to or for the benefit of the school district for payments under the local lease-to-own agreement, the local lease-to-own agreement terminates at the end of the current term and the school district, the school facilities board and this state are relieved of any subsequent obligation under the local lease-to-own agreement.

4. The local lease-to-own agreement shall be reviewed and approved by the attorney general before the agreement may take effect.

5. Before the agreement takes effect and after review by the attorney general, the project or projects related to the agreement shall be submitted for review by the joint committee on capital review.

J. The school district may covenant to use its best efforts to budget, obtain, allocate and maintain sufficient monies to make payments under a local lease-to-own agreement, but the local lease-to-own agreement shall acknowledge that budgeting school district monies is a governmental act of the school district governing board that may not be contracted away. The school facilities board is not required to covenant to budget, obtain, allocate or maintain sufficient monies in the lease-to-own fund to make payments to or for the benefit of a school district for payments under a local lease-to-own agreement.

K. The land and the school facilities on the land are exempt from taxation during the term of the local lease-to-own agreement and during construction and subsequent occupancy by the school district pursuant to the local lease-to-own agreement.

L. The powers prescribed in this section are in addition to the powers conferred by any other law. Without reference to any other provision of this title or to any other law, this section is authority for the completion of the purposes prescribed in this section for school districts to provide school facilities through local lease-to-own transactions pursuant to this section without regard to the procedure required by any other law. Except as otherwise provided in this section, the provisions of this title that relate to the matters contained in this section are superseded because this section is the exclusive law on these matters.

Added by Laws 2002, Ch. 330, § 35. Amended by Laws 2003, Ch. 264, § 19.

Historical and Statutory Notes

Laws 2002, Ch. 330, § 55, provides:

"**Sec. 55. New school facilities; lease-to-own**

"**A.** The school facilities board shall enter into lease-to-own transactions pursuant to §§ 15–2004, 15–2005 and 15–2006, Arizona Revised Statutes, as added by this act, to pay for the costs of new school facilities in fiscal year 2002–2003.

"**B.** Notwithstanding § 15–2006, Arizona Revised Statutes, as added by this act, the school facilities board shall enter into lease-to-own transactions in an amount not to exceed $400,000,000 in fiscal year 2002–2003 in order to fulfill the requirements of § 15–2041, Arizona Revised Statutes.

"**C.** Notwithstanding § 15–2041, Arizona Revised Statutes, as amended by this act, the school facilities board may transfer monies from the new school facilities fund to the lease-to-own fund established by § 15–2004, Arizona Revised Statutes, as added by this act, in fiscal year 2002–2003 for the purposes of that section."

Laws 2002, Ch. 330, became law without the Governor's signature as provided in Arizona Constitution, Article 5, § 7.

Laws 2003, Ch. 264, § 19, provides:

"**Sec. 19. New school facilities; lease-to-own**

"**A.** The school facilities board shall enter into lease-to-own transactions pursuant to §§ 15–2004, 15–2005 and 15–2006, Arizona Revised Statutes, to pay for the costs of new school facilities in fiscal year 2003–2004.

"**B.** Notwithstanding § 15–2006, Arizona Revised Statutes, the school facilities board shall enter into lease-to-own transactions in an amount not to exceed $250,000,000 in fiscal year 2003–2004 in order to fulfill the requirements of § 15–2041, Arizona Revised Statutes.

"**C.** Notwithstanding § 15–2041, Arizona Revised Statutes, the school facilities board may transfer monies from the new school facilities fund to the lease-to-own fund established by § 15–2004, Arizona Revised Statutes, in fiscal year 2003–2004 for the purposes of that section."

Laws 2004, Ch. 274, § 6, provides:

"**Sec. 6. New school facilities; lease-to-own**

"**A.** The school facilities board shall enter into lease-to-own transactions pursuant to §§ 15–2004, 15–2005 and 15–2006, Arizona Revised Statutes, to pay for the costs of new school facilities in fiscal year 2004–2005.

"**B.** Notwithstanding § 15–2006, Arizona Revised Statutes, the school facilities board shall enter into lease-to-own transactions in an amount not to exceed $250,000,000 in fiscal year 2004–2005 in order to fulfill the requirements of § 15–2041, Arizona Revised Statutes.

"**C.** Notwithstanding § 15–2041, Arizona Revised Statutes, the school facilities board may transfer monies from the new school facilities fund to the lease-to-own fund established by § 15–2004, Arizona Revised Statutes, in fiscal year 2004–2005 for the purposes of that section.

"**D.** Notwithstanding § 35–190, Arizona Revised Statutes, monies remaining in the lease-to-own fund established by § 15–2004, Arizona Revised Statutes, at the end of fiscal year 2003–2004 shall not revert to the state general fund."

Laws 2004, Ch. 274, § 9, provides:

"**Sec. 9. Retroactivity**

"Sections 2 through 7 of this act are effective retroactively to from and after June 30, 2004."

§ 15-2006. Lease-to-own amount

In order to fulfill the requirements of § 15-2041, the school facilities board may enter into lease-to-own transactions for up to a maximum of two hundred million dollars in any fiscal year.

Added by Laws 2002, Ch. 330, § 35. Amended by Laws 2003, Ch. 264, § 19.

Historical and Statutory Notes

Laws 2002, Ch. 330, § 55, provides:

"**Sec. 55. New school facilities; lease-to-own**

"**A.** The school facilities board shall enter into lease-to-own transactions pursuant to §§ 15-2004, 15-2005 and 15-2006, Arizona Revised Statutes, as added by this act, to pay for the costs of new school facilities in fiscal year 2002-2003.

"**B.** Notwithstanding § 15-2006, Arizona Revised Statutes, as added by this act, the school facilities board shall enter into lease-to-own transactions in an amount not to exceed $400,000,000 in fiscal year 2002-2003 in order to fulfill the requirements of § 15-2041, Arizona Revised Statutes.

"**C.** Notwithstanding § 15-2041, Arizona Revised Statutes, as amended by this act, the school facilities board may transfer monies from the new school facilities fund to the lease-to-own fund established by § 15-2004, Arizona Revised Statutes, as added by this act, in fiscal year 2002-2003 for the purposes of that section."

Laws 2002, Ch. 330, became law without the Governor's signature as provided in Arizona Constitution, Article 5, § 7.

Laws 2003, Ch. 264, § 19, provides:

"**Sec. 19. New school facilities; lease-to-own**

"**A.** The school facilities board shall enter into lease-to-own transactions pursuant to §§ 15-2004, 15-2005 and 15-2006, Arizona Revised Statutes, to pay for the costs of new school facilities in fiscal year 2003-2004.

"**B.** Notwithstanding § 15-2006, Arizona Revised Statutes, the school facilities board shall enter into lease-to-own transactions in an amount not to exceed $250,000,000 in fiscal year 2003-2004 in order to fulfill the requirements of § 15-2041, Arizona Revised Statutes.

"**C.** Notwithstanding § 15-2041, Arizona Revised Statutes, the school facilities board may transfer monies from the new school facilities fund to the lease-to-own fund established by § 15-2004, Arizona Revised Statutes, in fiscal year 2003-2004 for the purposes of that section."

Laws 2004, Ch. 274, § 6, provides:

"**Sec. 6. New school facilities; lease-to-own**

"**A.** The school facilities board shall enter into lease-to-own transactions pursuant to §§ 15-2004, 15-2005 and 15-2006, Arizona Revised Statutes, to pay for the costs of new school facilities in fiscal year 2004-2005.

"**B.** Notwithstanding § 15-2006, Arizona Revised Statutes, the school facilities board shall enter into lease-to-own transactions in an amount not to exceed $250,000,000 in fiscal year 2004-2005 in order to fulfill the requirements of § 15-2041, Arizona Revised Statutes.

"**C.** Notwithstanding § 15-2041, Arizona Revised Statutes, the school facilities board may transfer monies from the new school facilities fund to the lease-to-own fund established by § 15-2004, Arizona Revised Statutes, in fiscal year 2004-2005 for the purposes of that section.

"**D.** Notwithstanding § 35-190, Arizona Revised Statutes, monies remaining in the lease-to-own fund established by § 15-2004, Arizona Revised Statutes, at the end of fiscal year 2003-2004 shall not revert to the state general fund."

Laws 2004, Ch. 274, § 9, provides:

"**Sec. 9. Retroactivity**

"Sections 2 through 7 of this act are effective retroactively to from and after June 30, 2004."

ARTICLE 2. BUILDING ADEQUACY STANDARDS

§ 15-2011. Minimum school facility adequacy requirements; definition

A. The school facilities board shall, as determined and prescribed in this chapter, provide funding to school districts for new construction as the projected number of pupils in the district will fill the existing school facilities and require more pupil space.

B. School buildings in a school district are adequate if all of the following requirements are met:

1. The buildings contain sufficient and appropriate space and equipment that comply with the minimum school facility adequacy guidelines established pursuant to subsection F of this section. The state shall not fund facilities for elective courses that require the school district facilities to exceed minimum school facility adequacy requirements. The school facilities board shall determine whether a school building meets the requirements of this paragraph by analyzing the total square footage that is available for each pupil in conjunction with the need for specialized spaces and equipment.

2. The buildings are in compliance with federal, state and local building and fire codes and laws that are applicable to the particular building. An existing school building is not required to comply with current requirements for new buildings unless this compliance is specifically mandated by law or by the building or fire code of the jurisdiction where the building is located.

3. The building systems, including roofs, plumbing, telephone systems, electrical systems, heating systems and cooling systems, are in working order and are capable of being properly maintained.

4. The buildings are structurally sound.

C. The standards that shall be used by the school facilities board to determine whether a school building meets the minimum adequate gross square footage requirements are as follows:

1. For a school district that provides instruction to pupils in programs for preschool children with disabilities, kindergarten programs and grades one through six, eighty square feet per pupil in programs for preschool children with disabilities, kindergarten programs and grades one through six.

2. For a school district that provides instruction to up to eight hundred pupils in grades seven and eight, eighty-four square feet per pupil in grades seven and eight.

3. For a school district that provides instruction to more than eight hundred pupils in grades seven and eight, eighty square feet per pupil in grades seven and eight or sixty-seven thousand two hundred square feet, whichever is more.

4. For a school district that provides instruction to up to four hundred pupils in grades nine through twelve, one hundred twenty-five square feet per pupil in grades nine through twelve.

5. For a school district that provides instruction to more than four hundred and up to one thousand pupils in grades nine through twelve, one hundred twenty square feet per pupil in grades nine through twelve or fifty thousand square feet, whichever is more.

6. For a school district that provides instruction to more than one thousand and up to one thousand eight hundred pupils in grades nine through twelve, one hundred twelve square feet per pupil in grades nine through twelve or one hundred twenty thousand square feet, whichever is more.

7. For a school district that provides instruction to more than one thousand eight hundred pupils in grades nine through twelve, ninety-four square feet per

pupil in grades nine through twelve or two hundred one thousand six hundred square feet, whichever is more.

D. The school facilities board may modify the square footage requirements prescribed in subsection C of this section or modify the amount of monies awarded to cure the square footage deficiency pursuant to this section for particular school districts based on extraordinary circumstances for any of the following considerations:

1. The number of pupils served by the school district.

2. Geographic factors.

3. Grade configurations other than those prescribed in subsection C of this section.

E. In measuring the square footage per pupil requirements of subsection C of this section, the school facilities board shall:

1. Use the most recent one hundredth day average daily membership.

2. For each school, use the lesser of either:

(a) Total gross square footage.

(b) Student capacity multiplied by the appropriate square footage per pupil prescribed by subsection C of this section.

3. Consider the total space available in all schools in use in the school district, except that the school facilities board shall allow an exclusion of the square footage for certain schools and the pupils within the schools' boundaries if the school district demonstrates to the board's satisfaction unusual or excessive busing of pupils or unusual attendance boundary changes between schools.

4. Compute the gross square footage of all buildings by measuring from exterior wall to exterior wall. Square footage used solely for district administration, storage of vehicles and other nonacademic purposes shall be excluded from the gross square footage.

5. Include all portable and modular buildings.

6. Include in the gross square footage new construction funded wholly or partially by the school facilities board based on the square footage funded by the school facilities board. If the new construction is to exceed the square footage funded by the school facilities board, then the excess square footage shall not be included in the gross square footage if any of the following apply:

(a) The excess square footage was constructed before July 1, 2002 or funded by a class B bond, impact aid revenue bond or capital outlay override approved by the voters after August 1, 1998 and before June 30, 2002 or funded from unrestricted capital outlay expended before June 30, 2002.

(b) The excess square footage of new school facilities does not exceed twenty-five per cent of the minimum square footage requirements pursuant to subsection C of this section.

(c) The excess square footage of expansions to school facilities does not exceed twenty-five per cent of the minimum square footage requirements pursuant to subsection C of this section.

7. Require that excess square footage that is constructed after July 1, 2002 and that is not excluded pursuant to paragraph 6 of this subsection meets the minimum school facility adequacy guidelines in order to be eligible for building renewal monies as computed in § 15-2031.

F. The school facilities board shall adopt rules establishing minimum school facility adequacy guidelines. The executive director of the school facilities board shall report monthly to the joint committee on capital review on the progress of the development of the proposed rules establishing the guidelines. The joint committee on capital review shall review the proposed guidelines before the school facilities board adopts the rules to establish the minimum school facility adequacy guidelines. The guidelines shall provide the minimum quality and quantity of school buildings and facilities and equipment necessary and appropriate to enable pupils to achieve the academic standards pursuant to § 15-203, subsection A, paragraphs 12 and 13 and §§ 15-701 and 15-701.01. At a minimum, the school facilities board shall address all of the following in developing these guidelines:

1. School sites.
2. Classrooms.
3. Libraries and media centers, or both.
4. Cafeterias.
5. Auditoriums, multipurpose rooms or other multiuse space.
6. Technology.
7. Transportation.
8. Facilities for science, arts and physical education.
9. Other facilities and equipment that are necessary and appropriate to achieve the academic standards prescribed pursuant to § 15-203, subsection A, paragraphs 12 and 13 and §§ 15-701 and 15-701.01.
10. Appropriate combinations of facilities or uses listed in this section.

G. The board shall consider the facilities and equipment of the schools with the highest academic productivity scores, as prescribed in § 15-2002, subsection A, paragraph 9, subdivision (d), and the highest parent quality ratings in the establishment of the guidelines.

H. The school facilities board may consider appropriate combinations of facilities or uses in making assessments of and curing existing deficiencies pursuant to § 15-2002, subsection A, paragraph 1 and in certifying plans for new school facilities pursuant to § 15-2002, subsection A, paragraph 5.

I. For the purposes of this section, "student capacity" means the capacity adjusted to include any additions to or deletions of space, including modular or portable buildings at the school. The school facilities board shall determine the student capacity for each school in conjunction with each school district, recognizing each school's allocation of space as of July 1, 1998, to achieve the academic standards prescribed pursuant to § 15-203, subsection A, paragraphs 12 and 13 and §§ 15-701 and 15-701.01.

Added by Laws 1998, 5th S.S., Ch. 1, § 39, eff. July 9, 1998. Amended by Laws 1999, Ch. 299, § 34; Laws 2002, Ch. 330, § 36.

Historical and Statutory Notes

The purported amendment of this section by Laws 1998, Ch. 164 failed to become effective because Chapter 164 was repealed in its entirety by Laws 1998, 5th S.S., Ch. 1, § 2, effective July 1, 1998.

Laws 1999, 1st S.S., Ch. 4, §§ 18 and 19, provide:

"**Sec. 18. New school facilities funding**

"Notwithstanding title 15, chapter 16, Arizona Revised Statutes, the school facilities board established pursuant to § 15-2001, Arizona Revised Statutes, may disburse monies from the new school facilities fund established pursuant to § 15-2041, Arizona Revised Statutes, before publishing minimum school facility adequacy guidelines pursuant to § 15-2011, subsection F, Arizona Revised Statutes and Laws 1998, fifth special session, chapter 1, § 55.

"**Sec. 19. Retroactivity**

"Section 18 of this act, relating to new school facilities funding, applies retroactively to from and after January 1, 1999."

Laws 2001, 2nd S.S., Ch. 6, § 9, eff. Dec. 19, 2001, providing for school facilities board rules, was itself repealed by Laws 2002, Ch. 330, § 41.

Laws 2002, Ch. 330, § 57, provides:

"**Sec. 57. Minimum school facility adequacy guidelines; temporary limitation on changes**

"Notwithstanding § 15-2011, Arizona Revised Statutes, as amended by this act, or any other law, through fiscal year 2003-2004 the school facilities board shall not adopt rules that change minimum school facility adequacy guidelines unless those changes are necessary in order to comply with building, health, fire or safety codes or would reduce state costs."

Laws 2002, Ch. 330, became law without the Governor's signature as provided in Arizona Constitution, Article 5, § 7.

Reviser's Notes:

1998 Note. Pursuant to authority of § 41-1304.02, in subsection E, paragraph 3 the words "to the board's satisfaction" were transposed to follow "demonstrates".

ARTICLE 3. DEFICIENCIES CORRECTION

Historical and Statutory Notes

Laws 1998, 5th S.S., Ch. 1, § 61, providing for delayed repeal of Title 15, Chapter 16, Article 3, July 1, 2003, was itself repealed by Laws 2002, Ch. 330, § 42.

§ 15-2021. Deficiencies correction fund

A. A deficiencies correction fund is established consisting of monies appropriated by the legislature and monies credited to the fund pursuant to § 42-5030.01. The school facilities board shall administer the fund and distribute monies to school districts and pay contractors for the purpose of correcting existing deficiencies. Monies in the fund are continuously appropriated and are exempt from the provisions of § 35-190 relating to lapsing of appropriations.

B. School districts are eligible for monies from the deficiencies correction fund for either of the following purposes:

1. To correct any square footage deficiency pursuant to section 15-2011. School districts shall submit a summary notice on a form prescribed by the school facilities board that the school district believes it has a square footage deficiency pursuant to § 15-2011, subsection C to the school facilities board by December 1, 1998. If the school district exceeds the standard by ten per cent or more, the school district may be required to pay for the cost of an on-site space assessment by the school facilities board. By June 30, 1999, the school facilities board shall assess all alleged square footage deficiencies from the school district notices.

2. To correct quality deficiencies based on the district's inability to comply with the minimum school facility adequacy requirements established in and

pursuant to § 15-2011. This state shall not correct quality deficiencies pursuant to this paragraph for elective courses that require the school district facilities to exceed building adequacy standards. School districts shall submit a summary notice on a form prescribed by the school facilities board that the school district has a quality deficiency need to the school facilities board by August 1, 1999.

C. The school facilities board shall calculate the amount of distribution for square footage deficiencies based on the square footage prescribed in § 15-2011, subsection C and the cost per square foot based on the amounts prescribed in § 15-2041, subsection D, paragraph 3, subdivision (c), adjusted as needed to bring the school district into compliance with the minimum school facility adequacy requirements established in and pursuant to § 15-2011.

D. The school facilities board may distribute monies for new construction to a school district if the board determines after its assessment that the new construction is more cost-effective than correcting the deficiencies in the existing school building or buildings.

E. The school facilities board shall distribute monies from the deficiencies correction fund to school districts and pay contractors for the purpose of correcting existing deficiencies in an amount approved by the board. The school facilities board shall review and award monies to correct deficiencies pursuant to this section by June 30, 2001 and shall ensure that school districts correct deficiencies pursuant to this section by June 30, 2004. The school facilities board shall not distribute monies to school districts from the deficiencies correction fund for projects that are commenced after June 30, 2003 or that were approved by the school facilities board after May 10, 2002.

F. School districts that receive monies from the deficiencies correction fund shall establish a school district deficiencies correction fund and shall use the monies in the school district deficiencies correction fund only for the purposes prescribed in this section. Ending cash balances in a school district's deficiencies correction fund may be used in following fiscal years only for the purposes prescribed in this section. Each school district that receives monies from the deficiencies correction fund shall annually report the expenditures in the previous fiscal year to the school facilities board by October 15 and provide an accounting of the monies remaining in the deficiencies correction fund at the end of the previous fiscal year. This state shall annually provide sufficient monies to the deficiencies correction fund established in this section in order to correct existing deficiencies of all schools in this state by June 30, 2004.

G. A deficiency correction project awarded pursuant to this section may be combined with the deficiency correction projects of one or more additional school districts for purposes of procuring construction services and materials that are necessary to correct deficiencies if the school facilities board determines that combining the projects maximizes the purchasing value of the public monies of this state.

Added by Laws 1998, 5th S.S., Ch. 1, § 39, eff. July 9, 1998. Amended by Laws 1999, Ch. 5, § 4; Laws 1999, Ch. 299, § 35; Laws 2000, Ch. 88, § 21; Laws 2001, Ch. 11, § 4, eff. Mar. 15, 2001; Laws 2001, Ch. 117, § 7; Laws 2002, Ch. 330, § 37; Laws 2003, 1st S.S., Ch. 2, § 2, eff. March 28, 2003.

Repeal

The repeal of this section by Laws 1998, 5th S.S., Ch. 1, § 61, effective July 1, 2003, was itself repealed by Laws 2002, Ch. 330, § 42.

This section is repealed effective July 1, 2005 by Laws 2002, Ch. 330, § 43, as amended by Laws 2003, 1st S.S., Ch. 2, § 9, effective March 28, 2003.

Historical and Statutory Notes

The purported amendment of this section by Laws 1998, Ch. 164 failed to become effective because Chapter 164 was repealed in its entirety by Laws 1998, 5th S.S., Ch. 1, § 2, effective July 1, 1998.

Laws 1999, Ch. 299, § 42, provides:

"**Sec. 42. Exemption from local match requirement**

"**A.** Notwithstanding Laws 1998, fifth special session, chapter 1, § 48, a school district that received funding for a capital project from the former state board for school capital facilities established by Laws 1996, fifth special session, chapter 8, § 13 shall not be required to provide an additional matching share if all of the following conditions are met:

"1. At the time the former state board for school capital facilities approved the capital project, Laws 1997, chapter 4, § 16 as amended by Laws 1997, first special session, chapter 9, § 1 had been enacted by the legislature and the school district was entitled to a significant amount of funding that could have been used to meet part of its required local match.

"2. The repeal of Laws 1997, chapter 4, § 16 as amended by Laws 1997, first special session, chapter 9, § 1 necessitated that the school district pass a bond in order to provide the local match.

"3. The school district would have qualified for new facilities without any local match under Laws 1998, fifth special session, chapter 1.

"4. The school district has paid at least one million dollars in local match for a capital project.

"5. The 1998 combined tax rate for the majority of the district is at least fifty per cent higher than the average statewide property tax rate as published by the department of revenue.

"**B.** The school facilities board may use monies from the deficiencies correction fund established by § 15–2021, Arizona Revised Statutes, as amended by this act, or the new school facilities fund established by § 15–2041, Arizona Revised Statutes, as amended by this act, to complete any projects previously approved by the former state board for school capital facilities."

Laws 2000, Ch. 375, § 9, provides:

"**Sec. 9. Retention of tax revenues pending funding of students FIRST deficiencies corrections fund**

"Notwithstanding § 42–6108.01, Arizona Revised Statutes, as added by this act the state treasurer shall retain revenues from the tax on hotels that are payable to the tourism fund until the school facilities board, in consultation with the governor's office of strategic planning and budgeting, and after review by the joint legislative budget committee, certifies that sufficient monies are dedicated to the deficiencies correction fund to make the school improvements required pursuant to § 15–2021, Arizona Revised Statutes."

The 2001 amendment of this section by Ch. 117 explicitly amended the amendment of this section by Laws 2001, Ch. 11, § 4.

Laws 2001, Ch. 11, § 12, provides:

"**Sec. 12. Transfer of new school facilities fund monies**

"On the effective date of this act, the school facilities board may transfer monies in the new school facilities fund established pursuant to § 15–2041, Arizona Revised Statutes, to the deficiencies correction fund established pursuant to § 15–2021, Arizona Revised Statutes, until June 30, 2001. The school facilities board shall transfer monies in the deficiencies correction fund to the new school facilities fund at any time during fiscal year 2001–2002 in an amount not to exceed the amount of any monies transferred from the new school facilities fund to the deficiencies correction fund during fiscal year 2000–2001."

Laws 2001, Ch. 233, § 5, as amended by Laws 2001, 2nd S.S., Ch. 6, § 8, eff. Dec. 19, 2001, provides:

"**Sec. 5. State treasurer; school facilities transfer**

"Notwithstanding § 15–2002, subsection A, paragraph 10, Arizona Revised Statutes, or any other law, the state treasurer shall disregard any instructions of the school facilities board relating to the deficiencies correction fund transfers for fiscal year 2001–2002 and fiscal year 2002–2003 and instead shall not make any transfer in fiscal year 2001–2002 and fiscal year 2002–2003 from transaction privilege revenues to the deficiencies correction fund established by § 15-2021, Arizona Revised Statutes."

Laws 2002, Ch. 330, § 43, as amended by Laws 2003, 1st S.S., Ch. 2, § 9, effective March 28, 2003, provides:

"**Sec. 43. Delayed repeal**

"Section 15-2021, Arizona Revised Statutes, as amended by Laws 2002, chapter 330, section 37 and this act, is repealed from and after June 30, 2005."

Laws 2002, Ch. 330, § 52, provides:

"**Sec. 52. Deficiencies correction deadlines**

"**A.** Notwithstanding the delayed repeal of § 15-2021, Arizona Revised Statutes, pursuant to this act, the dates by which various actions must be completed to correct deficiencies do not apply to the Arizona state schools for the deaf and the blind. The school facilities board shall ensure that deficiencies in the facilities of the Arizona state schools for the deaf and the blind are assessed by December 31, 2002.

"**B.** Notwithstanding § 15-2021, Arizona Revised Statutes, monies to correct deficiencies identified in the assessment pursuant to subsection A of this section shall be subject to legislative appropriation."

Laws 2002, Ch. 330, § 63, provides:

"**Sec. 63. Retroactivity**

"**A.** Section 15-2021, Arizona Revised Statutes, as amended by this act, applies retroactively to from and after May 10, 2002.

"**B.** Section 61 of this act, relating to the building renewal formula and legislative intent, applies retroactively to from and after June 30, 2002."

Laws 2002, Ch. 330, became law without the Governor's signature as provided in Arizona Constitution, Article 5, § 7.

Laws 2003, Ch. 264, § 22, as amended by Laws 2004, Ch. 274, § 2, provides:

"**Sec. 22. Authorization of state school trust revenue bonds for fiscal years 2003-2004 and 2004-2005**

"**A.** The school facilities board shall issue in fiscal year 2003-2004 and fiscal year 2004-2005 negotiable state school trust revenue bonds pursuant to laws 2003, chapter 264, as amended by this act, in a principal amount not exceeding $247,135,000 in fiscal year 2003-2004 and $25,000,000 in fiscal year 2004-2005 to:

"1. Provide monies to pay the cost of:

"(a) Correcting existing deficiencies as prescribed by section 15-2021, Arizona Revised Statutes.

"(b) Bond related expenses including any expenses incurred by the school facilities board to issue and administer its bonds including underwriting fees and costs, trustee fees, financial consultant fees, printing and advertising costs, paying agent fees, transfer agent fees, legal, accounting, feasibility consultant and other professional fees and expenses, bond insurance or other credit enhancements or liquidity facilities, attorney and accounting fees and expenses related to credit enhancement, bond insurance or liquidity enhancement, remarketing fees, rating agency fees and costs, travel and telecommunications expenses and all other fees considered necessary by the school facilities board in order to market and administer the bonds.

"2. Fully or partially fund any reserves or sinking accounts for debt service on the bonds established by the bond resolution.

"**B.** The school facilities board shall authorize the bonds by resolution. The resolution shall prescribe:

"1. The fixed or variable rate or rates of interest, the date or dates on which interest is payable and the denominations of the bonds.

"2. The date or dates of the bonds and maturity, within twenty years after the date of issuance.

"3. The form of the bonds.

"4. The manner of executing the bonds.

"5. The medium and place of payment.

"6. The terms of redemption, which may provide for a premium for early redemption.

"**C.** The bonds issued pursuant to laws 2003, chapter 264, as amended by this act, shall be known as state school trust revenue bonds.

"**D.** Notwithstanding subsection A of this section, state school trust revenue bonds shall not be issued in a principal amount or with terms such that the total annual debt service on all outstanding state school trust revenue bonds issued pursuant to laws 2003, chapter 264, as amended by this act, all outstanding state school facilities revenue bonds issued pursuant to title 15, chapter 16, article 6, Arizona Revised Statutes, all outstanding qualified zone academy bonds issued pursuant to title 15, chapter 16, article 7, Arizona Revised Statutes, and all other bonds or other obligations issued pursuant to law and payable from amounts available for debt service pursuant to § 37-521, Arizona Revised Statutes, would exceed the amount available for debt service under § 37-521, Arizona Revised Statutes."

Laws 2003, Ch. 264, § 23, as amended by Laws 2004, Ch. 274, § 3, provides:

"**Sec. 23. Issuance and sale of revenue bonds; use of bond proceeds**

"**A.** For fiscal year 2003-2004 and fiscal year 2004-2005, the school facilities board shall issue state school trust revenue bonds authorized by laws 2003, chapter 264, § 22, as amended by this act in the number and amount provided in the resolution.

"B. The bonds shall be sold at public or private sale at the price and on the terms prescribed in the resolution at, above or below par.

"C. If the school facilities board issues state school trust revenue bonds pursuant to laws 2003, chapter 264, as amended by this act, the board shall establish a state school trust revenue bond proceeds fund consisting of the net proceeds received from the sale of the bonds.

"D. The school facilities board may use monies in the school trust revenue bond proceeds fund only for the purposes provided in laws 2003, chapter 264, § 22, subsection A, as amended by this act. Monies in the state school trust revenue bond proceeds fund are exempt from lapsing under § 35-190, Arizona Revised Statutes.

"E. The state treasurer or bond trustee shall administer and account for the state school trust revenue bond proceeds fund."

Laws 2003, Ch. 264, § 29, provides:

"Sec. 29. Investment of monies in state school trust revenue bond proceeds fund and state school trust revenue bond debt service fund

"A. The school facilities board may authorize the state treasurer or bond trustee to invest monies in the state school trust revenue bond proceeds fund and the state school trust revenue bond debt service fund.

"B. The order directing an investment may state a specified time when the monies invested will be used. The state treasurer or bond trustee shall make the investment in such a way as to mature at the specified date.

"C. All monies earned as interest or otherwise derived from the investment of the monies in the state school trust revenue bond proceeds fund and the state school trust revenue bond debt service fund shall be credited to the deficiencies correction fund established by § 15-2021, Arizona Revised Statutes, while the deficiencies correction fund exists and thereafter to the state school trust revenue bond debt service fund established pursuant to this act.

"D. At the direction of the school facilities board, the state treasurer or bond trustee may invest or reinvest monies in the state school trust revenue bond proceeds fund and the state school trust revenue debt service fund in any investments authorized by § 35-313, Arizona Revised Statutes. The purchase of the securities shall be made by the state treasurer or bond trustee on authority of a resolution of the board. The treasurer or bond trustee shall act as custodian of all securities purchased. The securities may be sold on an order of the board."

Laws 2003, Ch. 264, § 35, as amended by Laws 2004, Ch. 274, § 4, provides:

"Sec. 35. Project bids; joint committee on capital review approval

"A. Before the issuance in fiscal year 2003-2004 of any state school trust revenue bonds pursuant to laws 2003, chapter 264, as amended by this act, the school facilities board shall:

"1. Receive bids for the cost of all deficiencies correction projects that will be financed with the revenue bond proceeds.

"2. Submit a list of the projects, the project bids and the estimated annual principal and interest payments related to the bond agreement to the joint committee on capital review for approval.

"B. Before the issuance in fiscal year 2004-2005 of any state school trust revenue bonds pursuant to laws 2003, chapter 264, as amended by this act, the school facilities board shall submit the bond proposal to the joint committee on capital review for review.

" C. The school facilities board shall report to the joint committee on capital review the cost of the remaining projects in the Tucson Unified School District, the Mesa Unified School District and the Glendale Union High School District after receiving bids for projects in those districts."

Laws 2003, Ch. 264, § 45, provides:

"Sec. 45. Retroactivity

"A. Section 15-2031, Arizona Revised Statutes, as amended by this act, Laws 2003, first special session, chapter 3, § 1, as amended by this act, and §§ 17, 18 and 38 of this act apply retroactively to from and after June 30, 2003.

"B. Section 15-121, Arizona Revised Statutes, as amended by this act, applies retroactively to from and after April 30, 2003."

Laws 2003, 1st S.S., Ch. 2, §§ 22 to 24, provide:

"Sec. 22. School deficiencies correction; completion exemption

"Notwithstanding § 15-2021, Arizona Revised Statutes, as amended by this act, the Mesa unified school district, Glendale union school district and Tucson unified school district shall have until June 30, 2005 to correct existing deficiencies.

"Sec. 23. School deficiencies correction; reimbursement; conditions

"A. Notwithstanding § 15-2021, Arizona Revised Statutes, as amended by this act, a school district may transfer monies distributed to the school district deficiencies correction fund to another school district fund to reimburse that fund for monies used for projects to correct identified deficiencies as described in § 15-2011, Arizona Revised Statutes, if, prior to the school district expending any of its own monies to correct deficiencies, the school facilities board:

"1. Approved the identified deficiency correction projects pursuant to § 15–2021, Arizona Revised Statutes.

"2. Certified that the identified deficiency correction projects would be delayed until after June 30, 2004.

"3. Is provided by the school district, prior to the district spending any of its own monies, an accounting of the monies to be spent from each school district fund.

"**B.** If monies are transferred into the unrestricted capital outlay fund pursuant to subsection A of this section, the unrestricted capital budget limit is increased by the amount of the monies transferred.

"**Sec. 24. Delayed repeal**

"Section 23 of this act, relating to school deficiencies correction reimbursement and conditions, is repealed from and after June 30, 2005."

Laws 2004, Ch. 274, § 9, provides:

"**Sec. 9. Retroactivity**

"Sections 2 through 7 of this act are effective retroactively to from and after June 30, 2004."

Reviser's Notes:

1999 Note. Prior to the 2000 amendment, this section contained the amendments made by Laws 1999, Ch. 5, sec. 4 and Ch. 299, sec. 35 that were blended together pursuant to authority of § 41–1304.03.

2001 Note. Pursuant to authority of § 41–1304.02, in [Laws 2001, Ch. 11, § 12] the first sentence the spelling of the second "established" was corrected.

§ 15–2022. Emergency deficiencies correction fund; definition

A. An emergency deficiencies correction fund is established consisting of monies transferred from the deficiencies correction fund established by § 15–2021 or the new school facilities fund established by § 15–2041. The school facilities board shall administer the fund and distribute monies in accordance with the rules of the school facilities board to school districts for emergency purposes. The school facilities board shall not transfer monies from the deficiencies correction fund and the new school facilities fund if the transfer will affect, interfere with, disrupt or reduce any capital projects that the school facilities board has approved pursuant to §§ 15–2021 and 15–2041. The School facilities board shall transfer to the emergency deficiencies correction fund the amount necessary each fiscal year to fulfill the requirements of this section. Monies in the fund are continuously appropriated and are exempt from the provisions of § 35–190 relating to lapsing of appropriations.

B. If the school facilities board determines that there are insufficient monies in the emergency deficiencies correction fund to correct an emergency, the school district may correct the emergency pursuant to § 15–907.

C. If a school district has an emergency, the school district shall apply to the school facilities board for funding for the emergency. The school district's application shall disclose any insurance or building renewal monies available to the school district to pay for the emergency.

D. The school facilities board staff shall notify the school district of the staff's recommendation within five business days of receiving the application. The school facilities board shall decide on the staff's recommendation for funding at the next scheduled school facilities board meeting.

E. For the purposes of this section, "emergency" means a serious need for materials, services or construction or expenses in excess of the district's adopted budget for the current fiscal year and that seriously threaten the functioning of the school district, the preservation or protection of property or public health, welfare or safety.

Added by Laws 2001, Ch. 297, § 3.

Historical and Statutory Notes

The repeal of Chapter 16, Article 3 by Laws 1998, 5th S.S., Ch. 1, § 61, effective July 1, 2003, was itself repealed by Laws 2002, Ch. 330, § 42.

ARTICLE 4. BUILDING RENEWAL

§ 15-2031. Building renewal fund; definitions

A. A building renewal fund is established consisting of monies appropriated by the legislature and monies credited to the fund pursuant to § 42-5030.01. The school facilities board shall administer the fund and distribute monies to school districts for the purpose of maintaining the adequacy of existing school facilities. Monies in the fund are continuously appropriated and are exempt from the provisions of § 35-190 relating to lapsing of appropriations.

B. The school facilities board shall inventory and inspect all school buildings in this state in order to develop a database to administer the building renewal formula. The database shall include the student capacity of the building as determined by the school facilities board. The board shall distribute monies from the building renewal fund to school districts in an amount computed pursuant to subsection G of this section. A school district that receives monies from the building renewal fund shall use the monies primarily for any buildings in the database developed or created under subsection D of this section and secondly for any other buildings owned by the school district for any of the following:

1. Major renovations and repairs of a building.

2. Upgrading systems and areas that will maintain or extend the useful life of the building.

3. Infrastructure costs.

4. Relocation and placement of portable and modular buildings.

C. Monies received from the building renewal fund shall not be used for any of the following purposes:

1. New construction.

2. Remodeling interior space for aesthetic or preferential reasons.

3. Exterior beautification.

4. Demolition.

5. The purchase of soft capital items pursuant to § 15-962, subsection D.

6. Routine maintenance except as provided in § 15-2002, subsection K and subsection J of this section.

D. The school facilities board shall maintain the building renewal database and use the database for the computation of the building renewal formula distributions. The board shall ensure that the database is updated on at least an annual basis to reflect changes in the ages and value of school buildings. The facilities listed in the database shall include only those buildings that are owned by school districts that are required to meet academic standards. Each school district shall report to the school facilities board no later than September 1 of each year the number and type of school buildings owned by the district, the square footage of each building, the age of each building, the nature of any renovations completed and the cost of any renovations completed. The school facilities board may review or audit, or both, to confirm the information submitted by a school district. The board shall adjust the age of each school facility in the database whenever a building is significantly upgraded or remodeled. The age of a building that has been significantly upgraded or remodeled shall be recomputed as follows:

1. Divide the cost of the renovation by the building capacity value of the building determined in subsection G, paragraph 3 of this section.

2. Multiply the quotient determined in paragraph 1 of this subsection by the currently listed age of the building in the database.

3. Subtract the product determined in paragraph 2 of this subsection from the currently listed age of the building in the database, rounded to the nearest whole number. If the result is negative, use zero.

E. The school facilities board shall submit an annual report to the president of the senate, the speaker of the house of representatives, the Arizona state library, archives and public records and the governor by October 1 that includes the computation of the amount of monies to be distributed from the building renewal fund for the current fiscal year. The joint committee on capital review shall review the school facilities board's calculation of the building renewal fund distributions. After the joint committee on capital review reviews the distributions computed by the school facilities board, the school facilities board shall distribute the monies from the building renewal fund to school districts in two equal installments in November and May of each year.

F. School districts that receive monies from the building renewal fund shall establish a district building renewal fund and shall use the monies in the district building renewal fund only for the purposes prescribed in subsection B of this section. Ending cash balances in a school district's building renewal fund may be used in following fiscal years for building renewal pursuant to subsection B of this section. By October 15 of each year, each school district shall report to the school facilities board the projects funded at each school in the previous fiscal year with monies from the district building renewal fund, an accounting of the monies remaining in the district building renewal fund at the end of the previous fiscal year and a comprehensive five-year plan that details the proposed use of building renewal monies. If a school district fails to submit the report by October 15, the school facilities board shall withhold building renewal monies from the school district until the school facilities board determines that the school district has complied with the reporting requirement. When the school facilities board determines that the school district has complied with the reporting requirement, the school facilities board shall restore the full amount of withheld building renewal monies to the school district.

G. Notwithstanding any other provision of this chapter, if a school district converts space that is listed in the database maintained pursuant to this section to space that will be used for administrative purposes, the school district is responsible for any costs associated with the conversion, maintenance and replacement of that space. The building renewal amount for each school building shall be computed as follows:

1. Divide the age of the building as computed pursuant to subsection D of this section by one thousand two hundred seventy-five or, in the case of modular or portable buildings, by two hundred ten.

2. Multiply the quotient determined in paragraph 1 of this subsection by 0.67.

3. Determine the building capacity value as follows:

(a) Multiply the student capacity of the building by the per student square foot capacity established by § 15-2041.

(b) Multiply the product determined in subdivision (a) of this paragraph by the cost per square foot established by § 15-2041.

4. Multiply the product determined in paragraph 2 of this subsection by the product determined in paragraph 3, subdivision (b) of this subsection.

H. If the school facilities board determines that a school district has spent monies from the building renewal fund for purposes other than those prescribed in subsection B of this section, the school facilities board shall notify the superintendent of public instruction. Notwithstanding any other law, the superintendent of public instruction shall withhold a corresponding amount from the monies that would otherwise be due the school district under the capital outlay revenue limit until these monies are repaid.

I. Beginning on July 1, 2002, a school district is not entitled to receive monies from the building renewal fund for any buildings that are to be replaced with new buildings that are funded with deficiencies corrections monies pursuant to § 15-2021. The replacement buildings are not eligible to receive building renewal funding until the fiscal year following the completion of the building.

J. Notwithstanding subsections B and C of this section, a school district may use eight per cent of the building renewal amount computed pursuant to subsection G of this section for routine preventative maintenance. The board, after consultation with maintenance specialists in school districts, shall provide examples of recommended services that are routine preventative maintenance.

K. A school district that uses building renewal monies for routine preventative maintenance shall use the building renewal monies to supplement and not supplant expenditures from other funds for the maintenance of school buildings. The auditor general shall prescribe a method for determining compliance with the requirements of this subsection. A school district, in connection with any audit conducted by a certified public accountant, shall also contract for an independent audit to determine whether the school district used building renewal monies to reduce the school district's existing level of routine preventative maintenance funding. The auditor general may conduct discretionary reviews of a school district that is not required to contract for an independent audit.

L. For the purposes of this section:

1. "Routine preventative maintenance" means services that are performed on a regular schedule at intervals ranging from four times a year to once every three years and that are intended to extend the useful life of a building system and reduce the need for major repairs.

2. "Student capacity" has the same meaning prescribed in § 15-2011.

Added by Laws 1998, 5th S.S., Ch. 1, § 39, eff. July 9, 1998. Amended by Laws 1999, Ch. 5, § 5; Laws 1999, Ch. 299, § 36; Laws 2000, Ch. 88, § 22; Laws 2000, Ch. 158, § 1; Laws 2001, Ch. 117, § 8. Amended by Laws 2002, Ch. 330, § 38; Laws 2003, Ch. 102, § 1.

Historical and Statutory Notes

The purported amendment of this section by Laws 1998, Ch. 164 failed to become effective because Chapter 164 was repealed in its entirety by Laws 1998, 5th S.S., Ch. 1, § 2, effective July 1, 1998.

Laws 2002, Ch. 330, § 61, provides:

"**Sec. 61. Building renewal formula; legislative intent**

"**A.** Notwithstanding § 15-2031, Arizona Revised Statutes, as amended by this act, or any other law, the building renewal formula is suspended for fiscal year 2002-2003 and fiscal year 2003-2004. For fiscal year 2002-2003, the amount for building renewal shall be as provided in this act.

"**B.** It is the intent of the legislature to suspend the building renewal formula through fiscal year 2003-2004 as monies necessary for school facilities required to meet academic standards will be provided from the deficiencies corrections fund established by § 15-2021, Arizona Revised Statutes, which is repealed by this act from and after June 30, 2004.

"**C.** It is also the intent of the legislature that the facilities and equipment necessary and appropriate to enable students to achieve the academic standards pursuant to § 15-203, subsection A, paragraphs 12 and 13, Arizona Revised Statutes, and §§ 15-701 and 15-702, Arizona Revised Statutes, are exclusively the facilities and equipment addressed by the school facilities board in the minimum school facility adequacy guidelines adopted pursuant to § 15-2011, Arizona Revised Statutes."

Laws 2002, Ch. 330, became law without the Governor's signature as provided in Arizona Constitution, Article 5, § 7.

Laws 2003, Ch. 102, became law without the Governor's signature as provided in Arizona Constitution, Article 5, § 7.

The amendment of this section by Laws 2003, Ch. 264, was line item vetoed by the Governor. See Governor's veto message dated June 17, 2003. The vetoed amendment read:

"**A.** A building renewal fund is established consisting of monies appropriated by the legislature and monies credited to the fund pursuant to § 42-5030.01. The school facilities board shall administer the fund and distribute monies to school districts for the purpose of maintaining the adequacy of existing school facilities. Monies in the fund are continuously appropriated and are exempt from the provisions of section 35-190 relating to lapsing of appropriations.

"**B.** The school facilities board shall inventory and inspect all school buildings in this state in order to develop a database to administer the building renewal formula. The database shall include the student capacity of the building as determined by the school facilities board. The board shall distribute monies from the building renewal fund to school districts in an amount computed pursuant to subsection G of this section. A school district that receives monies from the building renewal fund shall use the monies primarily for any buildings in the database developed or created under subsection D of this section and secondly for any other buildings owned by the school district for any of the following:

"1. Major renovations and repairs of a building.

"2. Upgrading systems and areas that will maintain or extend the useful life of the building.

"3. Infrastructure costs.

"4. Relocation and placement of portable and modular buildings.

"**C.** Monies received from the building renewal fund shall not be used for any of the following purposes:

"1. New construction.

"2. Remodeling interior space for aesthetic or preferential reasons.

"3. Exterior beautification.

"4. Demolition.

"5. The purchase of soft capital items pursuant to § 15-962, subsection D.

"6. Routine maintenance except as provided in § 15-2002, subsection K and subsection J of this section.

"**D.** The school facilities board shall maintain the building renewal database and use the database for the computation of the building renewal formula distributions. The board shall ensure that the database is updated on at least an annual basis to reflect changes in the ages and value of school buildings. The facilities listed in the database shall include only those buildings that are owned by school districts that are required to meet academic standards. Each school district shall report to the school facilities board no later than September 1 of each year the number and type of school buildings owned by the district, the square footage of each building, the age of each building, the nature of any renovations completed and the cost of any renovations completed. The school facilities board may review or audit, or both, to confirm the information submitted by a school district. The board shall adjust the age of each school facility in the database whenever a building is significantly upgraded or remodeled. The age of a building that has been significantly upgraded or remodeled shall be recomputed as follows:

"1. Divide the cost of the renovation by the building capacity value of the building determined in subsection G, paragraph 3 of this section.

"2. Multiply the quotient determined in paragraph 1 of this subsection by the currently listed age of the building in the database.

"3. Subtract the product determined in paragraph 2 of this subsection from the currently listed age of the building in the database, rounded to the nearest whole number. If the result is negative, use zero. If the result is greater than thirty, use thirty.

"**E.** The school facilities board shall submit an annual report to the president of the senate, the speaker of the house of representatives, the Arizona state library, archives and public records and the governor by October 1 that includes the computation of the amount of monies to be distributed from the building renewal fund for the current fiscal year. The joint committee on capital review shall review the school facilities board's calculation of the building renewal fund distributions. After the joint committee on capital review reviews the distributions computed by the school facilities board, the school facilities board shall distribute the monies from the building renewal fund to school districts in two equal installments in November and May of each year.

"**F.** School districts that receive monies from the building renewal fund shall establish a district building renewal fund and shall use the monies in the district building renewal fund only for the purposes prescribed in subsection B of this section. Ending cash balances in a school district's building renewal fund may be used in following fiscal years for building renewal pursuant to subsection B of this section. By October 15 of each year, each school district shall report to the school facilities board the projects funded at each school in the previous fiscal year with monies from the district building renewal fund, an accounting of the monies remaining in the district building renewal fund at the end of the previous fiscal year and a comprehensive five-year plan that details the proposed use of building renewal monies.

"**G.** Notwithstanding any other provision of this chapter, if a school district converts space that is listed in the database maintained pursuant to this section to space that will be used for administrative purposes, the school district is responsible for any costs associated with the conversion, maintenance and replacement of that space. The building renewal amount for each school building shall be computed as follows:

"1. Divide the age of the building as computed pursuant to subsection D of this section by one thousand two hundred seventy-five.

"2. Multiply the quotient determined in paragraph 1 of this subsection by 0.67.

"3. Determine the building capacity value as follows:

"(a) Multiply the student capacity of the building by the square footage per pupil requirements established by § 15-2011.

"(b) Multiply the product determined in subdivision (a) by the replacement cost per square foot. For the purposes of this subdivision, "replacement cost" means eighty-five per cent of the cost per square foot for new school construction for the specific grade configuration prescribed in § 15-2041.

"4. Multiply the product determined in paragraph 2 of this subsection by the product determined in paragraph 3, subdivision (b) of this subsection.

"**H.** If the school facilities board determines that a school district has spent monies from the building renewal fund for purposes other than those prescribed in subsection B of this section, the school facilities board shall notify the superintendent of public instruction. Notwithstanding any other law, the superintendent of public instruction shall withhold a corresponding amount from the monies that would otherwise be due the school district under the capital outlay revenue limit until these monies are repaid.

"**I.** Beginning on July 1, 2002, a school district is not entitled to receive monies from the building renewal fund for any buildings that are to be replaced with new buildings that are funded with deficiencies corrections monies pursuant to § 15-2021. The replacement buildings are not eligible to receive building renewal funding until the fiscal year following the completion of the building.

"J. Notwithstanding subsections B and C of this section, a school district may use eight per cent of the building renewal amount computed pursuant to subsection G of this section for routine preventative maintenance. The board, after consultation with maintenance specialists in school districts, shall provide examples of recommended services that are routine preventative maintenance.

"K. A school district that uses building renewal monies for routine preventative maintenance shall use the building renewal monies to supplement and not supplant expenditures from other funds for the maintenance of school buildings. The auditor general shall prescribe a method for determining compliance with the requirements of this subsection. A school district, in connection with any audit conducted by a certified public accountant, shall also contract for an independent audit to determine whether the school district used building renewal monies to reduce the school district's existing level of routine preventative maintenance funding. The auditor general may conduct discretionary reviews of a school district that is not required to contract for an independent audit.

"L. For the purposes of this section:

"1. "Routine preventative maintenance" means services that are performed on a regular schedule at intervals ranging from four times a year to once every three years and that are intended to extend the useful life of a building system and reduce the need for major repairs.

"2. "Student capacity" has the same meaning prescribed in section 15–2011.

Laws 2003, Ch. 264, § 45, provides:

"**Sec. 45. Retroactivity**

"A. Section 15–2031, Arizona Revised Statutes, as amended by this act, Laws 2003, first special session, chapter 3, § 1, as amended by this act, and §§ 17, 18 and 38 of this act apply retroactively to from and after June 30, 2003.

"B. Section 15–121, Arizona Revised Statutes, as amended by this act, applies retroactively to from and after April 30, 2003."

The purported amendment of this section by Laws 2004, Ch. 274, § 1, was line item vetoed by the Governor in the Act approved May 28, 2004.

Reviser's Notes:

1999 Note. Prior to the 2000 amendments, this section contained the amendments made by Laws 1999, Ch. 5, sec. 5 and Ch. 299, sec. 36 that were blended together pursuant to authority of § 41–1304.03.

2000 Note. Prior to the 2001 amendment, this section contained the amendments made by Laws 2000, Ch. 88, sec. 22 and Ch. 158, sec. 1 that were blended together pursuant to authority of § 41–1304.03.

2002 Note. Pursuant to authority of § 41–1304.02, in the section heading "definitions" was substituted for "definition".

ARTICLE 5. NEW SCHOOL FACILITIES

§ 15–2041. New school facilities fund; capital plan

A. A new school facilities fund is established consisting of monies appropriated by the legislature and monies credited to the fund pursuant to § 37–221 or 42–5030.01. The school facilities board shall administer the fund and distribute monies, as a continuing appropriation, to school districts for the purpose of constructing new school facilities. On June 30 of each fiscal year, any unobligated contract monies in the new school facilities fund shall be transferred to the capital reserve fund established by § 15–2003.

B. The school facilities board shall prescribe a uniform format for use by the school district governing board in developing and annually updating a capital plan that consists of each of the following:

1. Enrollment projections for the next five years for elementary schools and eight years for middle and high schools, including a description of the methods used to make the projections.

2. A description of new schools or additions to existing schools needed to meet the building adequacy standards prescribed in § 15–2011. The description shall include:

(a) The grade levels and the total number of pupils that the school or addition is intended to serve.

(b) The year in which it is necessary for the school or addition to begin operations.

(c) A timeline that shows the planning and construction process for the school or addition.

3. Long–term projections of the need for land for new schools.

4. Any other necessary information required by the school facilities board to evaluate a school district's capital plan.

5. If a school district pays tuition for all or a portion of the school district's high school pupils to another school district, the capital plan shall indicate the number of pupils for which the district pays tuition to another district. If a school district accepts pupils from another school district pursuant to § 15–824, subsection A, the school district shall indicate the projections for this population separately. This paragraph does not apply to a small isolated school district as defined in § 15–901.

C. If the capital plan indicates a need for a new school or an addition to an existing school within the next four years or a need for land within the next ten years, the school district shall submit its plan to the school facilities board by September 1 and shall request monies from the new school facilities fund for the new construction or land. Monies provided for land shall be in addition to any monies provided pursuant to subsection D of this section.

D. The school facilities board shall distribute monies from the new school facilities fund as follows:

1. The school facilities board shall review and evaluate the enrollment projections and either approve the projections as submitted or revise the projections. In determining new construction requirements, the school facilities board shall determine the net new growth of pupils that will require additional square footage that exceeds the building adequacy standards prescribed in § 15–2011. If the projected growth and the existing number of pupils exceeds three hundred fifty pupils who are served in a school district other than the pupil's resident school district, the school facilities board, the receiving school district and the resident school district shall develop a capital facilities plan on how to best serve those pupils. A small isolated school district as defined in § 15–901 is not required to develop a capital facilities plan pursuant to this paragraph.

2. If the approved projections indicate that additional space will not be needed within the next two years for elementary schools or three years for middle or high schools in order to meet the building adequacy standards prescribed in § 15–2011, the request shall be held for consideration by the school facilities board for possible future funding and the school district shall annually submit an updated plan until the additional space is needed.

3. If the approved projections indicate that additional space will be needed within the next two years for elementary schools or three years for middle or high schools in order to meet the building adequacy standards prescribed in § 15–2011, the school facilities board shall provide an amount as follows:

(a) Determine the number of pupils requiring additional square footage to meet building adequacy standards. This amount for elementary schools shall not be less than the number of new pupils for whom space will be needed in the next year and shall not exceed the number of new pupils for whom space will be needed in the next five years. This amount for middle and high schools shall not be less than the number of new pupils for whom space will be needed in the next four years and shall not exceed the number of new pupils for whom space will be needed in the next eight years.

(b) Multiply the number of pupils determined in subdivision (a) of this paragraph by the square footage per pupil. The square footage per pupil is ninety square feet per pupil for preschool children with disabilities, kindergarten programs and grades one through six, one hundred square feet for grades seven and eight, one hundred thirty-four square feet for a school district that provides instruction in grades nine through twelve for fewer than one thousand eight hundred pupils and one hundred twenty-five square feet for a school district that provides instruction in grades nine through twelve for at least one thousand eight hundred pupils. The total number of pupils in grades nine through twelve in the district shall determine the square footage factor to use for net new pupils. The school facilities board may modify the square footage requirements prescribed in this subdivision for particular schools based on any of the following factors:

(i) The number of pupils served or projected to be served by the school district.

(ii) Geographic factors.

(iii) Grade configurations other than those prescribed in this subdivision.

(iv) Compliance with minimum school facility adequacy requirements established pursuant to § 15-2011.

(c) Multiply the product obtained in subdivision (b) of this paragraph by the cost per square foot. The cost per square foot is ninety dollars for preschool children with disabilities, kindergarten programs and grades one through six, ninety-five dollars for grades seven and eight and one hundred ten dollars for grades nine through twelve. The cost per square foot shall be adjusted annually for construction market considerations based on an index identified or developed by the joint legislative budget committee as necessary but not less than once each year. The school facilities board shall multiply the cost per square foot by 1.05 for any school district located in a rural area. The school facilities board may modify the base cost per square foot prescribed in this subdivision for particular schools based on geographic conditions or site conditions. For the purposes of this subdivision, "rural area" means an area outside a thirty-five mile radius of a boundary of a municipality with a population of more than fifty thousand persons according to the most recent United States decennial census.

(d) Once the school district governing board obtains approval from the school facilities board for new facility construction funds, additional portable or modular square footage created for the express purpose of providing temporary space for pupils until the completion of the new facility shall not be included by the school facilities board for the purpose of new construction funding calculations. On completion of the new facility construction project, if the portable or modular facilities continue in use, then the portable or modular facilities shall be included as prescribed by this chapter, unless the school facilities board approves their continued use for the purpose of providing temporary space for pupils until the completion of the next new facility that has been approved for funding from the new school facilities fund.

4. For projects approved after December 31, 2001, and notwithstanding paragraph 3 of this subsection, a unified school district that does not have a high school is not eligible to receive high school space as prescribed by § 15-2011 and this section unless the unified district qualifies for geographic factors prescribed by paragraph 3, subdivision (b), item (ii) of this subsection.

E. Monies for architectural and engineering fees shall be distributed on the completion of the analysis by the school facilities board of the school district's request. After receiving monies pursuant to this subsection, the school district shall submit a design development plan for the school or addition to the school facilities board before any monies for construction are distributed. If the school district's request meets the building adequacy standards, the school facilities board may review and comment on the district's plan with respect to the efficiency and effectiveness of the plan in meeting state square footage and facility standards before distributing the remainder of the monies. The school facilities board may decline to fund the project if the square footage is no longer required due to revised enrollment projections.

F. The school facilities board shall distribute the monies needed for land for new schools so that land may be purchased at a price that is less than or equal to fair market value and in advance of the construction of the new school. If necessary, the school facilities board may distribute monies for land to be leased for new schools if the duration of the lease exceeds the life expectancy of the school facility by at least fifty per cent. The proceeds derived through the sale of any land purchased or partially purchased with monies provided by the school facilities board shall be returned to the state fund from which it was appropriated and to any other participating entity on a proportional basis. If a school district acquires real property by donation at an appropriate school site approved by the school facilities board, the school facilities board shall distribute an amount equal to twenty per cent of the fair market value of the donated real property that can be used for academic purposes. The school district shall place the monies in the unrestricted capital outlay fund and increase the unrestricted capital outlay limit by the amount of monies placed in the fund. Monies distributed under this subsection shall be distributed from the new school facilities fund. A school district shall not pay a consultant a percentage of the value of any of the following:

1. Donations of real property, services or cash from any of the following:

(a) Entities that have offered to provide construction services to the school district.

(b) Entities that have been contracted to provide construction services to the school district.

(c) Entities that build residential units in that school district.

(d) Entities that develop land for residential use in that school district.

2. Monies received from the school facilities board on behalf of the school district.

3. Monies paid by the school facilities board on behalf of the school district.

G. In addition to distributions to school districts based on pupil growth projections, a school district may submit an application to the school facilities board for monies from the new school facilities fund if one or more school buildings have outlived their useful life. If the school facilities board determines that the school district needs to build a new school building for these reasons, the school facilities board shall remove the square footage computations that represent the building from the computation of the school district's total square footage for purposes of this section. If the square footage recomputation reflects that the school district no longer meets building adequacy standards, the school district qualifies for a distribution of monies from the new school construction formula in an amount determined pursuant to subsection D of this section. Buildings removed from a school district's total square footage pursuant to this subsection shall not be included in the computation of monies from the building renewal fund established by § 15–2031. The school facilities board may modify the base cost per square foot prescribed in this subsection under extraordinary circumstances for geographic factors or site conditions.

H. School districts that receive monies from the new school facilities fund shall establish a district new school facilities fund and shall use the monies in the district new school facilities fund only for the purposes prescribed in this section. By October 15 of each year, each school district shall report to the school facilities board the projects funded at each school in the previous fiscal year with monies from the district new school facilities fund and shall provide an accounting of the monies remaining in the new school facilities fund at the end of the previous fiscal year.

I. If a school district has surplus monies received from the new school facilities fund, the school district may use the surplus monies only for capital purposes for the project for up to one year after completion of the project. If the school district possesses surplus monies from the new school construction project that have not been expended within one year of the completion of the project, the school district shall return the surplus monies to the school facilities board for deposit in the new school facilities fund.

J. The board's consideration of any application filed after July 1, 2001 or after December 31 of the year in which the property becomes territory in the vicinity of a military airport or ancillary military facility as defined in § 28–8461 for monies to fund the construction of new school facilities proposed to be located in territory in the vicinity of a military airport or ancillary military facility shall include, if after notice is transmitted to the military airport pursuant to § 15–2002 and before the public hearing the military airport provides comments and analysis concerning compatibility of the proposed school facilities with the high noise or accident potential generated by military airport or ancillary military facility operations that may have an adverse effect on public health and safety, consideration and analysis of the comments and analysis provided by the military airport before making a final determination.

K. If a school district uses its own project manager for new school construction, the members of the school district governing board and the project manager shall sign an affidavit stating that the members and the project manager understand and will follow the minimum adequacy requirements prescribed in § 15–2011.

L. The school facilities board shall establish a separate account in the new school facilities fund designated as the litigation account to pay attorney fees, expert witness fees and other costs associated with litigation in which the school facilities board pursues the recovery of damages for deficiencies correction that resulted from alleged construction defects or design defects that the school facilities board believes caused or contributed to a failure of the school building to conform to the building adequacy requirements prescribed in § 15–2011. Attorney fees paid pursuant to this subsection shall not exceed the market rate for similar types of litigation. Monies recovered as damages pursuant to this subsection shall be used to offset debt service on the correction of existing deficiencies as prescribed by § 15–2021. The joint committee on capital review shall conduct an annual review of the litigation account, including the costs associated with current and potential litigation.

M. Until the state board of education and the auditor general adopt rules pursuant to § 15–213, subsection J, the school facilities board may allow school districts to contract for construction services and materials through the qualified select bidders list method of project delivery for new school facilities pursuant to this section.

Added by Laws 1998, 5th S.S., Ch. 1, § 39, eff. July 9, 1998. Amended by Laws 1999, Ch. 5, § 6; Laws 1999, Ch. 179, § 1, eff. May 6, 1999; Laws 1999, Ch. 299, § 37; Laws 2001, Ch. 23, § 7; Laws 2001, Ch. 117, § 9; Laws 2002, Ch. 286, § 2, eff. Aug. 22, 2002, retroactively effective to March 2, 2002; Laws 2002, Ch. 321, § 1, eff. May 30, 2002; Laws 2002, Ch. 330, § 39; Laws 2003, Ch. 215, § 4, eff. May 14, 2003, retroactively effective to Aug. 22, 2002; Laws 2004, Ch. 111, § 8.

Retroactive Application

This section, as amended by Laws 2001, Ch. 23, applies retroactively to July 2, 2001.

Historical and Statutory Notes

The purported amendment of this section by Laws 1998, Ch. 164 failed to become effective because Chapter 164 was repealed in its entirety by Laws 1998, 5th S.S., Ch. 1, § 2, effective July 1, 1998.

Laws 1999, Ch. 299, § 42, provides:

"**Sec. 42. Exemption from local match requirement**

"**A.** Notwithstanding Laws 1998, fifth special session, chapter 1, § 48, a school district that received funding for a capital project from the former state board for school capital facilities established by Laws 1996, fifth special session, chapter 8, § 13 shall not be required to provide an additional matching share if all of the following conditions are met:

"1. At the time the former state board for school capital facilities approved the capital project, Laws 1997, chapter 4, § 16 as amended by Laws 1997, first special session, chapter 9, § 1 had been enacted by the legislature and the school district was entitled to a significant amount of funding that could have been used to meet part of its required local match.

"2. The repeal of Laws 1997, chapter 4, § 16 as amended by Laws 1997, first special session, chapter 9, § 1 necessitated that the school district pass a bond in order to provide the local match.

"3. The school district would have qualified for new facilities without any local match under Laws 1998, fifth special session, chapter 1.

"4. The school district has paid at least one million dollars in local match for a capital project.

"5. The 1998 combined tax rate for the majority of the district is at least fifty per cent higher than the average statewide property tax rate as published by the department of revenue.

"**B.** The school facilities board may use monies from the deficiencies correction fund established by § 15-2021, Arizona Revised Statutes, as amended by this act, or the new school facilities fund established by § 15-2041, Arizona Revised Statutes, as amended by this act, to complete any projects previously approved by the former state board for school capital facilities."

Laws 1999, 1st S.S., Ch. 4, § 17, provides:

"**Sec. 17. State treasurer; school facilities transfer**

"Notwithstanding § 15-2002, subsection A, paragraph 11, Arizona Revised Statutes, or any other law, the state treasurer shall disregard the instructions of the school facilities board relating to the new school facilities fund transfer for fiscal year 1999-2000 and instead transfer the sum of $200,000,000 from transaction privilege revenues to the new school facilities fund established by § 15-2041, Arizona Revised Statutes."

Laws 1999, 1st S.S., Ch. 4, §§ 18 and 19, provide:

"**Sec. 18. New school facilities funding**

"Notwithstanding title 15, chapter 16, Arizona Revised Statutes, the school facilities board established pursuant to § 15-2001, Arizona Revised Statutes, may disburse monies from the new school facilities fund established pursuant to § 15-2041, Arizona Revised Statutes, before publishing minimum school facility adequacy guidelines pursuant to § 15-2011, subsection F, Arizona Revised Statutes and Laws 1998, fifth special session, chapter 1, § 55.

"**Sec. 19. Retroactivity**

"Section 18 of this act, relating to new school facilities funding, applies retroactively to from and after January 1, 1999."

Laws 2001, Ch. 23, § 18, subsec. C, provides:

"**Sec. 18. Retroactivity**

"**C.** Sections 15-2002 and 15-2041, Arizona Revised Statutes, as amended by this act, apply retroactively to from and after July 1, 2001."

Laws 2002, Ch. 286, § 3, provides:

"**Sec. 3. Retroactivity**

"This act is effective retroactively to from and after March 1, 2002."

Laws 2002, Ch. 330, became law without the Governor's signature as provided in Arizona Constitution, Article 5, § 7.

Laws 2003, Ch. 215, § 5, eff. May 14, 2003, provides:

"**Sec. 5. Retroactivity**

"This act is effective retroactively to August 22, 2002."

Laws 2004, Ch. 274, § 6, provides:

"**Sec. 6. New school facilities; lease-to-own**

"**A.** The school facilities board shall enter into lease-to-own transactions pursuant to §§ 15-2004, 15-2005 and 15-2006, Arizona Revised Statutes, to pay for the costs of new school facilities in fiscal year 2004-2005.

"**B.** Notwithstanding § 15-2006, Arizona Revised Statutes, the school facilities board shall enter into lease-to-own transactions in an amount not to exceed $250,000,000 in fiscal year 2004-2005 in order to fulfill the requirements of § 15-2041, Arizona Revised Statutes.

"**C.** Notwithstanding § 15-2041, Arizona Revised Statutes, the school facilities board may transfer monies from the new school facilities fund to the lease-to-own fund established by § 15-2004, Arizona Revised Statutes, in fiscal year 2004-2005 for the purposes of that section.

"**D.** Notwithstanding § 35-190, Arizona Revised Statutes, monies remaining in the lease-to-own fund established by § 15-2004, Arizona Revised Statutes, at the end of fiscal year 2003-2004 shall not revert to the state general fund."

Laws 2004, Ch. 274, § 9, provides:

"**Sec. 9. Retroactivity**

"Sections 2 through 7 of this act are effective retroactively to from and after June 30, 2004."

Reviser's Notes:

1999 Note. Prior to the 2001 amendment, this section contained the amendments made by Laws 1999, Ch. 5, sec. 6, Ch. 179, sec. 1 and Ch. 299, sec. 37 that were blended together pursuant to authority of § 41-1304.03. Pursuant to authority of § 41-1304.02, in subsection A, first sentence the reference to "§ 37-221" was substituted for the reference to "§ 37-225" to conform to the reviser's renumbering of that section.

2001 Note. Prior to the 2002 amendment, this section contained the amendments made by Laws 2001, Ch. 23, sec. 7 and Ch. 117, sec. 9 that were blended together pursuant to authority of § 41-1304.03.

2002 Note. Prior to the 2003 amendment, this section contained the amendments made by Laws 2002, Ch. 286, sec. 2, Ch. 321, sec. 1 and Ch. 330, sec. 39 that were blended together pursuant to authority of § 41-1304.03.

ARTICLE 6. STATE SCHOOL FACILITIES REVENUE BONDS

§ 15–2051. Authorization of state school facilities revenue bonds

A. The school facilities board may issue negotiable revenue bonds pursuant to this article. If authorized by the legislature, bonds may be issued under this article in a principal amount not exceeding two hundred million dollars in a fiscal year to:

1. Provide monies to pay the cost of:

(a) Acquiring real property and constructing new school facilities as provided by § 15–2041.

(b) Bond related expenses including any expenses incurred by the school facilities board to issue and administer its bonds including underwriting fees and costs, trustee fees, financial consultant fees, printing and advertising costs, paying agent fees, transfer agent fees, legal, accounting, feasibility consultant and other professional fees and expenses, bond insurance or other credit enhancements or liquidity facilities, attorney and accounting fees and expenses related to credit enhancement, bond insurance or liquidity enhancement, remarketing fees, rating agency fees and costs, travel and telephone expenses and all other fees considered necessary by the school facilities board in order to market and administer the bonds.

2. Fully or partially fund any reserves or sinking accounts established by the bond resolution.

B. The school facilities board shall authorize the bonds by resolution. The resolution shall prescribe:

1. The fixed or variable rate or rates of interest, the date or dates on which interest is payable and the denominations of the bonds.

2. The date or dates of the bonds and maturity, within ten years after the date of issuance.

3. The form of the bonds.

4. The manner of executing the bonds.

5. The medium and place of payment.

6. The terms of redemption, which may provide for a premium for early redemption.

C. The bonds issued pursuant to this article shall be known as state school facilities revenue bonds.

Added by Laws 1998, 5th S.S., Ch. 1, § 39, eff. July 9, 1998. Amended by Laws 2000, 5th S.S., Ch. 1, § 20

Historical and Statutory Notes

Proposition 301, approved by the electors at the Nov. 7, 2000 general election, effective Nov. 27, 2000, included a provision increasing the state transaction privilege tax rate six-tenths of one per cent. Therefore, the conditions of the 5th S.S. Ch. 1 were met, and the act became effective.

Laws 2003, Ch. 264, § 22, as amended by Laws 2004, Ch. 274, § 2, provides:

"**Sec. 22. Authorization of state school trust revenue bonds for fiscal years 2003–2004 and 2004–2005**

"**A.** The school facilities board shall issue in fiscal year 2003–2004 and fiscal year 2004–2005 negotiable state school trust revenue bonds pursuant to laws 2003, chapter 264, as amended by this act, in a principal amount not exceeding $247,135,000 in fiscal year 2003–2004 and $25,000,000 in fiscal year 2004–2005 to:

"1. Provide monies to pay the cost of:

"(a) Correcting existing deficiencies as prescribed by section 15–2021, Arizona Revised Statutes.

"(b) Bond related expenses including any expenses incurred by the school facilities board to issue and administer its bonds including underwriting fees and costs, trustee fees, financial consultant fees, printing and advertising costs, paying agent fees, transfer agent fees, legal, accounting, feasibility consultant and other professional fees and expenses, bond insurance or other credit enhancements or liquidity facilities, attorney and accounting fees and expenses related to credit enhancement, bond insurance or liquidity enhancement, remarketing fees, rating agency fees and costs, travel and telecommunications expenses and all other fees considered necessary by the school facilities board in order to market and administer the bonds.

"2. Fully or partially fund any reserves or sinking accounts for debt service on the bonds established by the bond resolution.

"**B.** The school facilities board shall authorize the bonds by resolution. The resolution shall prescribe:

"1. The fixed or variable rate or rates of interest, the date or dates on which interest is payable and the denominations of the bonds.

"2. The date or dates of the bonds and maturity, within twenty years after the date of issuance.

"3. The form of the bonds.

"4. The manner of executing the bonds.

"5. The medium and place of payment.

"6. The terms of redemption, which may provide for a premium for early redemption.

"**C.** The bonds issued pursuant to laws 2003, chapter 264, as amended by this act, shall be known as state school trust revenue bonds.

"**D.** Notwithstanding subsection A of this section, state school trust revenue bonds shall not be issued in a principal amount or with terms such that the total annual debt service on all outstanding state school trust revenue bonds issued pursuant to laws 2003, chapter 264, as amended by this act, all outstanding state school facilities revenue bonds issued pursuant to title 15, chapter 16, article 6, Arizona Revised Statutes, all outstanding qualified zone academy bonds issued pursuant to title 15, chapter 16, article 7, Arizona Revised Statutes, and all other bonds or other obligations issued pursuant to law and payable from amounts available for debt service pursuant to § 37–521, Arizona Revised Statutes, would exceed the amount available for debt service under § 37–521, Arizona Revised Statutes."

Laws 2003, Ch. 264, § 23, as amended by Laws 2004, Ch. 274, § 3, provides:

"**Sec. 23. Issuance and sale of revenue bonds; use of bond proceeds**

"**A.** For fiscal year 2003–2004 and fiscal year 2004–2005, the school facilities board shall issue state school trust revenue bonds authorized by laws 2003, chapter 264, § 22, as amended by this act in the number and amount provided in the resolution.

"**B.** The bonds shall be sold at public or private sale at the price and on the terms prescribed in the resolution at, above or below par.

"**C.** If the school facilities board issues state school trust revenue bonds pursuant to laws 2003, chapter 264, as amended by this act, the board shall establish a state school trust revenue bond proceeds fund consisting of the net proceeds received from the sale of the bonds.

"**D.** The school facilities board may use monies in the school trust revenue bond proceeds fund only for the purposes provided in laws 2003, chapter 264, § 22, subsection A, as amended by this act. Monies in the state school trust revenue bond proceeds fund are exempt from lapsing under § 35–190, Arizona Revised Statutes.

"**E.** The state treasurer or bond trustee shall administer and account for the state school trust revenue bond proceeds fund."

Laws 2004, Ch. 274, § 9, provides:

"**Sec. 9. Retroactivity**

"Sections 2 through 7 of this act are effective retroactively to from and after June 30, 2004."

§ 15–2052. Issuance and sale of revenue bonds

A. The school facilities board shall issue the bonds in the number and amount provided in the resolution.

B. The bonds shall be sold at public or private sale at the price and on the terms prescribed in the resolution at, above or below par.

C. The net proceeds of the sale of the bonds shall be deposited in the revenue bond proceeds fund established pursuant to § 15–2053.

Added by Laws 1998, 5th S.S., Ch. 1, § 39, eff. July 9, 1998. Amended by Laws 1999, Ch. 299, § 38; Laws 2000, 5th S.S., Ch. 1, § 21.

Historical and Statutory Notes

Proposition 301, approved by the electors at the Nov. 7, 2000 general election, effective Nov. 27, 2000, included a provision increasing the state transaction privilege tax rate six-tenths of one per cent. Therefore, the conditions of the 5th S.S. Ch. 1 were met, and the act became effective.

§ 15-2053. School facilities revenue bond proceeds fund; use for new school facilities

A. If the school facilities board issues revenue bonds under this article, the board shall establish a school facilities revenue bond proceeds fund consisting of the net proceeds received from the sale of the bonds.

B. The school facilities board may use monies in the school facilities revenue bond proceeds fund only for the purposes provided in § 15-2051, subsection A. Monies in the revenue bond proceeds fund are exempt from lapsing under § 35-190.

C. The state treasurer or bond trustee shall administer and account for the school facilities revenue bond proceeds fund.

Added by Laws 1998, 5th S.S., Ch. 1, § 39, eff. July 9, 1998. Amended by Laws 2000, 5th S.S., Ch. 1, § 22.

Historical and Statutory Notes

Proposition 301, approved by the electors at the Nov. 7, 2000 general election, effective Nov. 27, 2000, included a provision increasing the state transaction privilege tax rate six-tenths of one per cent. Therefore, the conditions of the 5th S.S. Ch. 1 were met, and the act became effective.

§ 15-2054. School facilities revenue bond debt service fund

A. The school facilities board shall establish a school facilities revenue bond debt service fund consisting of monies transferred to the fund pursuant to §§ 37-521 and 42-5030.01.

B. Monies in the school facilities revenue bond debt service fund may be used only for the purposes authorized by this article.

C. The state treasurer or bond trustee shall administer and account for the school facilities revenue bond debt service fund.

Added by Laws 1998, 5th S.S., Ch. 1, § 39, eff. July 9, 1998. Amended by Laws 2000, 5th S.S., Ch. 1, § 23.

Historical and Statutory Notes

Proposition 301, approved by the electors at the Nov. 7, 2000 general election, effective Nov. 27, 2000, included a provision increasing the state transaction privilege tax rate six-tenths of one per cent. Therefore, the conditions of the 5th S.S. Ch. 1 were met, and the act became effective.

Laws 2003, Ch. 264, § 24, provides:

"**Sec. 24. State school trust revenue bond debt service fund**

"**A.** If it issues state school trust revenue bonds, the school facilities board shall establish a state school trust revenue bond debt service fund consisting of monies transferred to the fund pursuant to § 37-521, subsection B, Arizona Revised Statutes, as amended by this act.

"**B.** Monies in the state school trust revenue bond debt service fund may be used only for the purposes authorized by this act.

"**C.** The state treasurer or bond trustee shall administer and account for the state school trust revenue bond debt service fund."

Laws 2003, Ch. 264, § 25, provides:

"**Sec. 25. Securing principal and interest; refunding bonds**

"**A.** In connection with issuing state school trust revenue bonds authorized by this act and to secure the principal and interest on the bonds, the school facilities board by resolution may:

"1. Segregate the state school trust revenue bond debt service fund into one or more accounts and subaccounts and provide that bonds issued under this act may be secured by a lien on all or part of the monies paid into the state school trust revenue bond debt service fund or into any account or subaccount in the fund.

"2. Provide that the bonds issued under this act are secured by a first lien on the monies paid into the state school trust revenue bond debt service fund as provided in this act and pledge and assign to or in trust for the benefit of the holder or holders of the bonds all or part of the monies in the state school trust revenue bond debt service fund, in any account or subaccount in the state school trust revenue bond debt service fund or in the state school trust revenue bond proceeds fund as is necessary to secure and pay the principal, the interest and any premium on the bonds as they come due.

"3. Establish priorities among bondholders based on criteria adopted by the board.

"4. Set aside, regulate and dispose of reserves and sinking accounts.

"5. Prescribe the procedure, if any, by which the terms of any contract with bondholders may be amended or abrogated, the amount of bonds the holders of which must consent to and the manner in which the consent may be given.

"6. Provide for payment of bond related expenses from the proceeds of the sale of the bonds or other revenues authorized by this act and available to the board.

"7. Provide for the services of trustees, cotrustees, agents and consultants and other specialized services with respect to the bonds.

"8. Take any other action that in any way may affect the security and protection of the bonds or interest on the bonds.

"9. Refund any bonds issued by the board by issuing new bonds, if these bonds are secured from the same source of revenues as the bonds authorized by this act.

"10. Issue bonds partly to refund outstanding bonds and partly for any other purpose consistent with this act.

"**B.** If bonds are issued pursuant to this act, the executive director of the school facilities board shall provide to the state treasurer and the state land department a schedule of the amount needed to pay each fiscal year's debt service on outstanding state school trust revenue bonds including sinking fund deposits pursuant to the terms of the bonds, and the state treasurer and the state land department shall follow the schedule in making transfers to the state school trust revenue bond debt service fund pursuant to this act.

"**C.** Bonds issued to refund any bonds issued by the board as provided by subsection A, paragraphs 9 and 10 of this section are not subject to the limit on principal amount prescribed by § 22, subsection A of this act but are subject to the limitation on total annual debt service prescribed by § 22, subsection D of this act."

Laws 2003, Ch. 264, § 26, provides:

"**Sec. 26. Lien of pledge**

"**A.** Any pledge made under this act in connection with state school trust revenue bonds is valid and binding from the time when the pledge is made.

"**B.** The monies pledged and received by the school facilities board to be placed in the state school trust revenue bond debt service fund are immediately subject to the lien of the pledge without any future physical delivery or further act. Any lien of any pledge is valid and binding against all parties that have claims of any kind against the board, regardless of whether the parties have notice of the lien. The official resolution or trust indenture or any instrument by which this pledge is created, when adopted by the school facilities board, is notice to all concerned of the creation of the pledge, and those instruments need not be recorded in any other place to perfect the pledge."

Laws 2003, Ch. 264, § 28, provides:

"**Sec. 28. Payment of revenue bonds**

"**A.** The state school trust revenue bonds shall be paid solely from monies from the state school trust revenue bond debt service fund established pursuant to this act.

"**B.** The state treasurer or the paying agent for the revenue bonds shall cancel all revenue bonds when paid."

§ 15–2055. Securing principal and interest

A. In connection with issuing bonds authorized by this article and to secure the principal and interest on the bonds, the school facilities board by resolution may:

1. Segregate the school facilities revenue bond debt service fund into one or more accounts and subaccounts and provide that bonds issued under this

article may be secured by a lien on all or part of the monies paid into the school facilities revenue bond debt service fund or into any account or subaccount in the fund.

2. Provide that the bonds issued under this article are secured by a first lien on the monies paid into the school facilities revenue bond debt service fund as provided by § 37–521, subsection B, paragraph 1 and § 42–5030.01, subsection A, and pledge and assign to or in trust for the benefit of the holder or holders of the bonds all or part of the monies in the school facilities revenue bond debt service fund, any account or subaccount in the fund or in the school facilities revenue bond proceeds fund as is necessary to secure and pay the principal, the interest and any premium on the bonds as they come due.

3. Establish priorities among bondholders based on criteria adopted by the board.

4. Set aside, regulate and dispose of reserves and sinking accounts.

5. Prescribe the procedure, if any, by which the terms of any contract with bondholders may be amended or abrogated, the amount of bonds the holders of which must consent to and the manner in which the consent may be given.

6. Provide for payment of bond related expenses from the proceeds of the sale of the bonds or other revenues authorized by this article and available to the board.

7. Provide for the services of trustees, cotrustees, agents and consultants and other specialized services with respect to the bonds.

8. Take any other action that in any way may affect the security and protection of the bonds or interest on the bonds.

9. Refund any bonds issued by the board, if these bonds are secured from the same source of revenues as the bonds authorized by this article, by issuing new bonds.

10. Issue bonds partly to refund outstanding bonds and partly for any other purpose consistent with this article.

B. Bonds issued to refund any bonds issued by the board as provided by subsection A, paragraphs 9 and 10 of this section are not subject to legislative authorization or the two hundred million dollar limitation prescribed by § 15–2051, subsection A.

Added by Laws 1998, 5th S.S., Ch. 1, § 39, eff. July 9, 1998. Amended by Laws 2000, 5th S.S., Ch. 1, § 24.

Historical and Statutory Notes

Proposition 301, approved by the electors at the Nov. 7, 2000 general election, effective Nov. 27, 2000, included a provision increasing the state transaction privilege tax rate six-tenths of one per cent. Therefore, the conditions of the 5th S.S. Ch. 1 were met, and the act became effective.

§ 15–2056. Lien of pledge

A. Any pledge made under this article is valid and binding from the time when the pledge is made.

B. The monies so pledged and received by the board to be placed in the school facilities revenue bond debt service fund are immediately subject to the lien of the pledge without any future physical delivery or further act. Any lien of any pledge is valid and binding against all parties that have claims of any kind against the board, regardless of whether the parties have notice of the lien. The official resolution or trust indenture or any instrument by which this pledge is created, when adopted by the board, is notice to all concerned of the creation of the pledge, and those instruments need not be recorded in any other place to perfect the pledge.

Added by Laws 1998, 5th S.S., Ch. 1, § 39, eff. July 9, 1998. Amended by Laws 2000, 5th S.S., Ch. 1, § 25.

Historical and Statutory Notes

Proposition 301, approved by the electors at the Nov. 7, 2000 general election, effective Nov. 27, 2000, included a provision increasing the state transaction privilege tax rate six-tenths of one per cent. Therefore, the conditions of the 5th S.S. Ch. 1 were met, and the act became effective.

§ 15-2057. Bond purchase; cancellation

The school facilities board may purchase bonds for cancellation out of any monies available for the purchase, at a price of not more than either of the following:

1. If the bonds are redeemable at the time of the purchase, the applicable redemption price plus accrued interest to the next interest payment date on the bonds.

2. If the bonds are not redeemable at the time of the purchase, the applicable redemption price on the first date after the purchase on which the bonds become subject to redemption plus accrued interest to that date.

Added by Laws 1998, 5th S.S., Ch. 1, § 39, eff. July 9, 1998.

Historical and Statutory Notes

Laws 2003, Ch. 264, § 27, provides:

"**Sec. 27. Bond purchase; cancellation**

"The school facilities board may purchase bonds for cancellation out of any monies available for the purchase, at a price of not more than either of the following:

"1. If the bonds are redeemable at the time of the purchase, the applicable redemption price plus accrued interest to the next interest payment date on the bonds.

"2. If the bonds are not redeemable at the time of the purchase, the applicable redemption price on the first date after the purchase on which the bonds become subject to redemption plus accrued interest to that date."

§ 15-2058. Repealed by Laws 2000, 5th S.S., Ch. 1, § 25

Historical and Statutory Notes

Laws 2000, 5th S.S., Ch. 1, § 26, provides:

"**Sec. 26. Repeal**

"Section 15-2058, Arizona Revised Statutes, is repealed."

Proposition 301, approved by the electors at the Nov. 7, 2000 general election, effective Nov. 27, 2000, included a provision increasing the state transaction privilege tax rate six-tenths of one per cent. Therefore, the conditions of the 5th S.S. Ch. 1 were met, and the act became effective. [Therefore, the repeal of this section is effective.]

The repealed section, which related to cancellation of unsold revenue bonds and hearing related thereto, was added by Laws 1998, 5th S.S., Ch. 1, § 39, eff. July 9, 1998.

§ 15-2059. Payment of revenue bonds

A. The revenue bonds shall be paid solely from monies from the school facilities revenue bond debt service fund established by § 15-2054 and other monies that are credited to the school facilities revenue bond debt service fund.

B. The state treasurer or the paying agent for the revenue bonds shall cancel all revenue bonds when paid.

Added by Laws 1998, 5th S.S., Ch. 1, § 39, eff. July 9, 1998. Amended by Laws 2000, 5th S.S., Ch. 1, § 27.

Historical and Statutory Notes

Proposition 301, approved by the electors at the Nov. 7, 2000 general election, effective Nov. 27, 2000, included a provision increasing the state transaction privilege tax rate six-tenths of one per cent. Therefore, the conditions of the 5th S.S. Ch. 1 were met, and the act became effective.

§ 15-2060. Investment of monies in school facilities revenue bond proceeds fund

A. As provided by § 15-2062, the school facilities board may authorize the state treasurer or bond trustee to invest monies in the school facilities revenue bond proceeds fund established by § 15-2053.

B. The order directing an investment shall state a specified time when the proceeds from the sale of the bonds will be used. The state treasurer or bond trustee shall make the investment in such a way as to mature at the specified date.

C. All monies earned as interest or otherwise derived from the investment of the monies in the school facilities revenue bond proceeds fund shall be credited to the school facilities revenue bond debt service fund established by § 15-2054.

Added by Laws 1998, 5th S.S., Ch. 1, § 39, eff. July 9, 1998. Amended by Laws 2000, 5th S.S., Ch. 1, § 28.

Historical and Statutory Notes

Proposition 301, approved by the electors at the Nov. 7, 2000 general election, effective Nov. 27, 2000, included a provision increasing the state transaction privilege tax rate six-tenths of one per cent. Therefore, the conditions of the 5th S.S. Ch. 1 were met, and the act became effective.

Laws 2003, Ch. 264, § 29, provides:

"**Sec. 29. Investment of monies in state school trust revenue bond proceeds fund and state school trust revenue bond debt service fund**

"**A.** The school facilities board may authorize the state treasurer or bond trustee to invest monies in the state school trust revenue bond proceeds fund and the state school trust revenue bond debt service fund.

"**B.** The order directing an investment may state a specified time when the monies invested will be used. The state treasurer or bond trustee shall make the investment in such a way as to mature at the specified date.

"**C.** All monies earned as interest or otherwise derived from the investment of the monies in the state school trust revenue bond proceeds fund and the state school trust revenue bond debt service fund shall be credited to the deficiencies correction fund established by § 15-2021, Arizona Revised Statutes, while the deficiencies correction fund exists and thereafter to the state school trust revenue bond debt service fund established pursuant to this act.

"**D.** At the direction of the school facilities board, the state treasurer or bond trustee may invest or reinvest monies in the state school trust revenue bond proceeds fund and the state school trust revenue debt service fund in any investments authorized by § 35-313, Arizona Revised Statutes. The purchase of the securities shall be made by the state treasurer or bond trustee on authority of a resolution of the board.

The treasurer or bond trustee shall act as custodian of all securities purchased. The securities may be sold on an order of the board."

Laws 2003, Ch. 264, § 34, provides:

"**Sec. 34. State treasurer and state board of investment to comply with agreements**

"Notwithstanding any other law, the state treasurer and the state board of investment shall comply with all agreements made by the school facilities board with or for the benefit of the owners of its state school trust revenue bonds regarding the investment of the assets of the permanent state school fund."

§ 15–2061. Investment of monies in the school facilities revenue bond debt service fund

A. The school facilities board may authorize the state treasurer or bond trustee to invest and reinvest any monies in the school facilities revenue bond debt service fund as provided by § 15–2062.

B. All monies earned as interest or otherwise derived from the investment of the monies in the school facilities revenue bond debt service fund shall be credited to that fund.

Added by Laws 1998, 5th S.S., Ch. 1, § 39, eff. July 9, 1998. Amended by Laws 2000, 5th S.S., Ch. 1, § 29.

Historical and Statutory Notes

Proposition 301, approved by the electors at the Nov. 7, 2000 general election, effective Nov. 27, 2000, included a provision increasing the state transaction privilege tax rate six-tenths of one per cent. Therefore, the conditions of the 5th S.S. Ch. 1 were met, and the act became effective.

Laws 2003, Ch. 264, § 29, provides:

"**Sec. 29. Investment of monies in state school trust revenue bond proceeds fund and state school trust revenue bond debt service fund**

"**A.** The school facilities board may authorize the state treasurer or bond trustee to invest monies in the state school trust revenue bond proceeds fund and the state school trust revenue bond debt service fund.

"**B.** The order directing an investment may state a specified time when the monies invested will be used. The state treasurer or bond trustee shall make the investment in such a way as to mature at the specified date.

"**C.** All monies earned as interest or otherwise derived from the investment of the monies in the state school trust revenue bond proceeds fund and the state school trust revenue bond debt service fund shall be credited to the deficiencies correction fund established by § 15–2021, Arizona Revised Statutes, while the deficiencies correction fund exists and thereafter to the state school trust revenue bond debt service fund established pursuant to this act.

"**D.** At the direction of the school facilities board, the state treasurer or bond trustee may invest or reinvest monies in the state school trust revenue bond proceeds fund and the state school trust revenue debt service fund in any investments authorized by § 35–313, Arizona Revised Statutes. The purchase of the securities shall be made by the state treasurer or bond trustee on authority of a resolution of the board. The treasurer or bond trustee shall act as custodian of all securities purchased. The securities may be sold on an order of the board."

§ 15–2062. Authorized investments of fund monies

A. On notice from the school facilities board, the state treasurer or bond trustee shall invest and divest monies in either the school facilities revenue bond proceeds fund or the school facilities revenue debt service fund in any of the following:

1. Obligations issued or guaranteed by the united states or any of the senior debt of its agencies, sponsored agencies, corporations, sponsored corporations or instrumentalities.

2. State, county or municipal bonds issued in this state on which the payments of interest have not been deferred.

3. Investment agreements and repurchase agreements collateralized by investments described in paragraph 1.

B. The purchase of the securities shall be made by the state treasurer or bond trustee on authority of a resolution of the board. The treasurer or bond trustee shall act as custodian of all securities purchased. The securities may be sold on an order of the board.

Added by Laws 1998, 5th S.S., Ch. 1, § 39, eff. July 9, 1998. Amended by Laws 2000, Ch. 193, § 118; Laws 2000, 5th S.S., Ch. 1, § 30; Laws 2002, Ch. 49, § 1, eff. April 20, 2002.

Historical and Statutory Notes

Proposition 301, approved by the electors at the Nov. 7, 2000 general election, effective Nov. 27, 2000, included a provision increasing the state transaction privilege tax rate six-tenths of one per cent. Therefore, the conditions of the 5th S.S. Ch. 1 were met, and the act became effective.

§ 15-2063. Audit

A. The school facilities board shall cause an annual audit to be made of the school facilities revenue bond proceeds fund established in § 15-2053 and the school facilities revenue bond debt service fund established in § 15-2054, including all accounts and subaccounts in the funds. A certified public accountant shall conduct the audit within ninety days after the end of the fiscal year.

B. The school facilities board shall immediately file a certified copy of the audit with the auditor general. The auditor general may make any further audits and examinations that are necessary and take appropriate action relating to the audit or examination pursuant to title 41, chapter 7, article 10.1. [1] If the auditor general takes no official action within thirty days after the audit is filed, the audit is considered to be sufficient.

C. The school facilities board shall pay negotiated and approved fees and costs of the certified public accountant and auditor general under this section from the school facilities revenue bond debt service fund established by § 15-2054.

Added by Laws 1998, 5th S.S., Ch. 1, § 39, eff. July 9, 1998. Amended by Laws 2000, 5th S.S., Ch. 1, § 31.

[1] Section 41-1278 et seq.

Historical and Statutory Notes

Proposition 301, approved by the electors at the Nov. 7, 2000 general election, effective Nov. 27, 2000, included a provision increasing the state transaction privilege tax rate six-tenths of one per cent. Therefore, the conditions of the 5th S.S. Ch. 1 were met, and the act became effective.

Laws 2003, Ch. 264, § 30, provides:

"**Sec. 30. Audit**

"**A.** The school facilities board shall cause an annual audit to be made of the state school trust revenue bond proceeds fund established pursuant to this act and the state school trust revenue bond debt service fund established pursuant to this act, including all accounts and subaccounts in the funds. A certified public accountant shall conduct the audit within ninety days after the end of each fiscal year.

"**B.** The school facilities board shall immediately file a certified copy of the audit with the auditor general. The auditor general may make any further audits and examinations that are necessary and may take appropriate action relating to the audit or examination pursuant to title 41, chapter 7, article 10.1, Arizona Revised Statutes. If the auditor general takes no official action within thirty days after the audit is filed, the audit is considered to be sufficient.

"C. The school facilities board shall pay negotiated and approved fees and costs of the certified public accountant and auditor general under this section from the state school trust revenue bond debt service fund established pursuant to this act."

§ 15–2064. Characteristics of bonds; negotiable; exemption from taxation; obligation; legal investments

A. Bonds issued under this article are fully negotiable within the meaning and for all purposes of the uniform commercial code, subject only to any provisions for registration, regardless of whether the bonds actually constitute negotiable instruments under the uniform commercial code.

B. The bonds, their transfer and the income from the bonds are at all times free from taxation in this state.

C. Bonds issued under this article:

1. Are obligations of the board. The members of the board and persons executing the bonds are not personally liable for payment of the bonds.

2. Are payable only according to their terms.

3. Are not general, special or other obligations of this state.

4. Do not constitute a debt of this state.

5. Are not enforceable against this state nor is payment of the bonds enforceable out of any monies other than the revenue pledged and assigned to, or in trust for the benefit of, the holder or holders of the bonds.

6. Are securities in which public officers and bodies of this state and of municipalities and political subdivisions of this state, all companies, associations and other persons carrying on an insurance business, all financial institutions, investment companies and other persons carrying on a banking business, all fiduciaries and all other persons who are authorized to invest in government obligations may properly and legally invest.

7. Are securities that may be deposited with public officers or bodies of this state and municipalities and political subdivisions of this state for purposes that require the deposit of government bonds or obligations.

Added by Laws 1998, 5th S.S., Ch. 1, § 39, eff. July 9, 1998.

Historical and Statutory Notes

Laws 2003, Ch. 264, § 31, provides:

"**Sec. 31. Characteristics of bonds; negotiable; exemption from taxation; obligation; legal investments**

"**A.** State school trust revenue bonds issued under this act are fully negotiable within the meaning and for all purposes of the uniform commercial code, subject only to any provisions for registration, regardless of whether the bonds actually constitute negotiable instruments under the uniform commercial code.

"**B.** The bonds, their transfer and the income from the bonds are at all times free from taxation in this state.

"**C.** Bonds issued under this act:

"1. Are obligations of the school facilities board. The members of the board and persons executing the bonds are not personally liable for payment of the bonds.

"2. Are payable only according to their terms.

"3. Are not general, special or other obligations of this state.

"4. Do not constitute a debt of this state.

"5. Are not enforceable against this state nor is the payment of the bonds enforceable out of any monies other than the revenue pledged and assigned to, or in trust for the benefit of, the holder or holders of the bonds.

"6. Are securities in which public officers and bodies of this state and of municipalities and political subdivisions of this state, all companies, associations and other persons carrying on an insurance business, all financial institutions, investment companies and other persons carrying on a banking business, all fiduciaries and all other persons who are authorized to invest in government obligations may properly and legally invest.

"7. Are securities that may be deposited with public officers or bodies of this state and municipalities and political subdivisions of this state for purposes that require the deposit of government bonds or obligations."

§ 15-2065. Effect of changing circumstances on bonds; agreement of state

A. Bonds issued under this article remain valid and binding obligations of the board notwithstanding that before the delivery of the bonds any of the persons whose signatures appear on the bonds cease to be members of the school facilities board.

B. An amendment of any provision of this article does not diminish or impair the validity of bonds issued under this article or the remedies and rights of bondholders.

C. This state pledges to and agrees with the holders of the bonds authorized by this article that this state will not limit, alter or impair the rights and remedies of the bondholders, until all bonds issued under this article, together with interest on the bonds, interest on any unpaid installments of principal or interest and all costs and expenses in connection with any action or proceedings by or on behalf of the bondholders, are fully met and discharged. The board, as agent for this state, may include this pledge and undertaking in its resolutions and indentures authorizing and securing the bonds.

Added by Laws 1998, 5th S.S., Ch. 1, § 39, eff. July 9, 1998.

Historical and Statutory Notes

Laws 2003, Ch. 264, § 32, provides:

"**Sec. 32. Effect of changing circumstances on bonds; agreement of state**

"**A.** State school trust revenue bonds issued under this act remain valid and binding obligations of the school facilities board notwithstanding that before the delivery of the bonds any of the persons whose signatures appear on the bonds cease to be members of the school facilities board.

"**B.** An amendment of any provision of this act does not diminish or impair the validity of bonds issued under this act or the remedies and rights of bondholders.

"**C.** This state pledges to and agrees with the holders of the bonds authorized by this act that this state will not limit, alter or impair the rights and remedies of the bondholders, until all bonds issued under this act, together with interest on the bonds, interest on any unpaid installments of principal or interest and all costs and expenses in connection with any action or proceedings by or on behalf of the bondholders, are fully met and discharged. The school facilities board, as agent for this state, may include this pledge and undertaking in its resolutions and indentures authorizing and securing the bonds."

§ 15-2066. Validity of bonds; certification by attorney general

A. This article constitutes full authority for authorizing and issuing bonds without reference to any other law of this state. No other law with regard to authorizing or issuing obligations or that in any way impedes or restricts performing the acts authorized by this article may be construed to apply to any proceedings taken or acts done pursuant to this article.

B. The validity of bonds issued under this article does not depend on and is not affected by the legality of any proceeding relating to any action by the school facilities board in granting or lending monies or the acquisition, construction or improvement of any facility paid with monies provided by the board.

C. The school facilities board may submit to the attorney general revenue bonds to be issued under this article after all proceedings for authorizing the bonds have been completed. Within fifteen days after submission, the attorney general shall examine the bonds and pass on the validity of the bonds and the regularity of the proceedings. If the bonds and proceedings comply with the constitution of Arizona and this article, and if the bonds when delivered and paid for will constitute binding and legal obligations of the board, the attorney general shall certify in substance that the bonds are issued according to the constitution and laws of this state. The certificate shall also state that the bonds are also validly secured by the obligation to transfer monies from designated sources of revenue, including income on the permanent state school fund established by § 37–521, to cover any insufficiencies.

D. The bonds shall recite that they are regularly issued pursuant to this article. That recital, together with the certification by the attorney general under subsection C of this section, constitutes prima facie evidence of the legality and validity of the bonds. From and after the sale and delivery of the bonds, they are incontestable by the school facilities board or this state.
Added by Laws 1998, 5th S.S., Ch. 1, § 39, eff. July 9, 1998.

Historical and Statutory Notes

Laws 2003, Ch. 264, § 33, provides:

"**Sec. 33. Validity of bonds; certification by attorney general**

"**A.** This act constitutes full authority for authorizing and issuing state school trust revenue bonds without reference to any other law of this state. No other law with regard to authorizing or issuing obligations or that in any way impedes or restricts performing the acts authorized by this act may be construed to apply to any proceedings taken or acts done pursuant to this act.

"**B.** The validity of bonds issued under this act does not depend on and is not affected by the legality of any proceeding relating to any action by the school facilities board in granting or lending monies or the acquisition, construction or improvement of any facility paid with monies provided by the school facilities board.

"**C.** The school facilities board may submit to the attorney general revenue bonds to be issued under this act after all proceedings for authorizing the bonds have been completed. Within fifteen days after submission, the attorney general shall examine the bonds and pass on the validity of the bonds and the regularity of the proceedings. If the bonds and proceedings comply with the Constitution of Arizona and this act, and if the bonds when delivered and paid for will constitute binding and legal obligations of the board, the attorney general shall certify in substance that the bonds are issued according to the constitution and laws of this state. The certificate shall also state that the bonds are also validly secured by the obligation to transfer monies from designated sources of revenue, including income on the permanent state school fund as provided by this act, to cover any insufficiencies.

"**D.** The bonds shall recite that they are regularly issued pursuant to this act. That recital, together with the certification by the attorney general under subsection C of this section, constitutes prima facie evidence of the legality and validity of the bonds. From and after the sale and delivery of the bonds, they are incontestable by the school facilities board or this state."

ARTICLE 7. STATE SCHOOL IMPROVEMENT REVENUE BONDS

Article 7, State School Improvement Revenue Bonds, consisting of §§ 15–2081 to 15–2095, was added by Laws 2000, 5th S.S., Ch. 1, § 33.

Historical and Statutory Notes

Laws 2000, 5th S.S., Ch. 1, § 59, which purportedly repealed this article effective July 1, 2005, was itself repealed by Laws 2001, Ch. 11, § 11, effective March 15, 2001.

Laws 2000, 5th S.S., Ch. 1, §§ 66 and 67, provide:

"**Sec. 66. Delayed implementation**

"This act shall not be implemented until from and after May 31, 2001.

"**Sec. 67. Conditional enactment**

"This act does not become effective unless the qualified electors of this state in the general election that will be held in November, 2000 approve an increase in state transaction privilege tax rates of six-tenths of one per cent in order to fund the provisions of this act."

Proposition 301, approved by the electors at the Nov. 7, 2000 general election, effective Nov. 27, 2000, included a provision increasing the state transaction privilege tax rate six-tenths of one per cent. Therefore, the conditions of the 5th S.S. Ch. 1 were met, and the act became effective.

§ 15-2081. Authorization of state school improvement revenue bonds; expiration

A. The school facilities board may issue revenue bonds in a principal amount not to exceed eight hundred million dollars pursuant to this article. The school facilities board may also issue qualified zone academy bonds within the meaning of § 1397e of the United States internal revenue code of 1986 [1] or successor provisions pursuant to this article in a principal amount not to exceed twenty million dollars. The qualified zone academy bonds shall be separately accounted for within the school improvement revenue bond proceeds fund established by § 15-2083. All bonds authorized by this section may be issued for the following purposes:

1. To provide monies to pay the cost of:

(a) Correcting existing deficiencies as prescribed by § 15-2021.

(b) Bond related expenses including any expenses incurred by the school facilities board to issue and administer its bonds including underwriting fees and costs, trustee fees, financial consultant fees, printing and advertising costs, paying agent fees, transfer agent fees, legal, accounting, feasibility consultant and other professional fees and expenses, bond insurance or other credit enhancements or liquidity facilities, attorney and accounting fees and expenses related to credit enhancement, bond insurance or liquidity enhancement, remarketing fees, rating agency fees and costs, travel and telephone expenses and all other fees considered necessary by the school facilities board in order to market and administer the bonds.

2. To fully or partially fund any reserves or sinking accounts established by the bond resolution.

B. The school facilities board shall authorize the bonds by resolution. The resolution shall prescribe:

1. The fixed or variable rate or rates of interest, the date or dates on which interest is payable and the denominations of the bonds.

2. The date or dates of the bonds and maturity, within twenty years after the date of issuance.

3. The form of the bonds.

4. The manner of executing the bonds.

5. The medium and place of payment.

6. The terms of redemption, which may provide for a premium for early redemption.

C. The bonds issued pursuant to this article shall be known as state school improvement revenue bonds.

D. The authority of the school facilities board to issue school improvement revenue bonds pursuant to this article expires from and after June 30, 2003, except for bonds issued to refund any bonds issued by the board.

Added by Laws 2000, 5th S.S., Ch. 1, § 32. Amended by Laws 2001, Ch. 11, § 5, eff. Mar. 15, 2001; Laws 2001, 2nd S.S., Ch. 6, § 5, eff. Dec. 19, 2001.

[1] Internal Revenue Code sections may be found in Title 26 of U.S.C.A.

Repeal

Laws 2000, 5th S.S., Ch. 1, § 59, which purportedly repealed this article effective July 1, 2005, was itself repealed by Laws 2001, Ch. 11, § 11, effective March 15, 2001.

Historical and Statutory Notes

Proposition 301, approved by the electors at the Nov. 7, 2000 general election, effective Nov. 27, 2000, included a provision increasing the state transaction privilege tax rate six-tenths of one per cent. Therefore, the conditions of the 5th S.S. Ch. 1 were met, and the act became effective.

Reviser's Notes:

2001 Note. Pursuant to authority of § 41–1304.02, in the section heading "; expiration" was added.

§ 15–2082. Issuance and sale of school improvement revenue bonds

A. The school facilities board shall issue the school improvement revenue bonds in the number and amount provided in the resolution.

B. The bonds shall be sold at public or private sale at the price and on the terms prescribed in the resolution at, above or below par.

C. The net proceeds of the sale of the bonds shall be deposited in the school improvement revenue bond proceeds fund established pursuant to § 15–2083.

Added by Laws 2000, 5th S.S., Ch. 1, § 32.

Repeal

Laws 2000, 5th S.S., Ch. 1, § 59, which purportedly repealed this article effective July 1, 2005, was itself repealed by Laws 2001, Ch. 11, § 11, effective March 15, 2001.

Historical and Statutory Notes

Proposition 301, approved by the electors at the Nov. 7, 2000 general election, effective Nov. 27, 2000, included a provision increasing the state transaction privilege tax rate six-tenths of one per cent. Therefore, the conditions of the 5th S.S. Ch. 1 were met, and the act became effective.

§ 15–2083. School improvement revenue bond proceeds fund; use for school improvements

A. If the school facilities board issues revenue bonds under this article, the board shall establish a school improvement revenue bond proceeds fund consisting of the net proceeds received from the sale of the bonds.

B. The school facilities board may use monies in the school improvement revenue bond proceeds fund only for the purposes provided in § 15–2081, subsection A. Monies in the school improvement revenue bond proceeds fund are exempt from lapsing under § 35–190.

C. The state treasurer or bond trustee shall administer and account for the school improvement revenue bond proceeds fund.

Added by Laws 2000, 5th S.S., Ch. 1, § 32.

Repeal

Laws 2000, 5th S.S., Ch. 1, § 59, which purportedly repealed this article effective July 1, 2005, was itself repealed by Laws 2001, Ch. 11, § 11, effective March 15, 2001.

Historical and Statutory Notes

Proposition 301, approved by the electors at the Nov. 7, 2000 general election, effective Nov. 27, 2000, included a provision increasing the state transaction privilege tax rate six-tenths of one per cent. Therefore, the conditions of the 5th S.S. Ch. 1 were met, and the act became effective.

§ 15–2084. School improvement revenue bond debt service fund

A. The school facilities board shall establish a school improvement revenue bond debt service fund consisting of monies received by the school facilities board pursuant to § 42–5029, subsection E and section 37–521, subsection B, paragraph 1. All monies received pursuant to section 42–5029, subsection e shall be accounted for separately and shall be used only for debt service of school improvement revenue bonds. All monies received pursuant to § 37–521, subsection B, paragraph 1 shall be accounted for separately and shall be used only for debt service of qualified zone academy bonds.

B. Monies in the school improvement revenue bond debt service fund may be used only for the purposes authorized by this article.

C. The state treasurer or bond trustee shall administer and account for the school improvement revenue bond debt service fund.

Added by Laws 2000, 5th S.S., Ch. 1, § 32. Amended by Laws 2001, 2nd S.S., Ch. 6, § 6, eff. Dec. 19, 2001.

Repeal

Laws 2000, 5th S.S., Ch. 1, § 59, which purportedly repealed this article effective July 1, 2005, was itself repealed by Laws 2001, Ch. 11, § 11, effective March 15, 2001.

Historical and Statutory Notes

Proposition 301, approved by the electors at the Nov. 7, 2000 general election, effective Nov. 27, 2000, included a provision increasing the state transaction privilege tax rate six-tenths of one per cent. Therefore, the conditions of the 5th S.S. Ch. 1 were met, and the act became effective.

§ 15–2085. Securing principal and interest

A. In connection with issuing bonds authorized by this article and to secure the principal and interest on the bonds, the school facilities board by resolution may:

1. Segregate the school improvement revenue bond debt service fund into one or more accounts and subaccounts and provide that bonds issued under this article may be secured by a lien on all or part of the monies paid into the revenue bond debt service fund or into any account or subaccount in the fund.

2. Provide that the bonds issued under this article are secured by a first lien on the monies paid into the school improvement revenue bond debt service fund as provided by § 42-5029, subsection E, paragraph 1 and pledge and assign to or in trust for the benefit of the holder or holders of the bonds all or part of the monies in the school improvement revenue bond debt service fund, in any account or subaccount in the fund or in the school improvement revenue bond proceeds fund as is necessary to secure and pay the principal, the interest and any premium on the bonds as they come due.

3. Establish priorities among bondholders based on criteria adopted by the board.

4. Set aside, regulate and dispose of reserves and sinking accounts.

5. Prescribe the procedure, if any, by which the terms of any contract with bondholders may be amended or abrogated, the amount of bonds the holders of which must consent to and the manner in which the consent may be given.

6. Provide for payment of bond related expenses from the proceeds of the sale of the bonds or other revenues authorized by this article and available to the board.

7. Provide for the services of trustees, cotrustees, agents and consultants and other specialized services with respect to the bonds.

8. Take any other action that in any way may affect the security and protection of the bonds or interest on the bonds.

9. Refund any bonds issued by the board, if these bonds are secured from the same source of revenues as the bonds authorized by this article, by issuing new bonds, whether at or before maturity of the bonds being refunded.

10. Issue bonds partly to refund outstanding bonds and partly for any other purpose consistent with this article.

B. Bonds issued to refund any bonds issued by the board as provided by subsection A, paragraphs 9 and 10 of this section are not subject to legislative authorization or subject to the eight hundred million dollar limitation prescribed by § 15-2081, subsection A.

Added by Laws 2000, 5th S.S., Ch. 1, § 32. Amended by Laws 2001, Ch. 11, § 6, eff. Mar. 15, 2001.

Repeal

Laws 2000, 5th S.S., Ch. 1, § 59, which purportedly repealed this article effective July 1, 2005, was itself repealed by Laws 2001, Ch. 11, § 11, effective March 15, 2001.

Historical and Statutory Notes

Proposition 301, approved by the electors at the Nov. 7, 2000 general election, effective Nov. 27, 2000, included a provision increasing the state transaction privilege tax rate six-tenths of one per cent. Therefore, the conditions of the

5th S.S. Ch. 1 were met, and the act became effective.

§ 15-2086. Lien of pledge

A. Any pledge made under this article is valid and binding from the time when the pledge is made.

B. The monies so pledged and received by the board to be placed in the school improvement revenue bond debt service fund are immediately subject to the lien of the pledge without any future physical delivery or further act. Any lien of any pledge is valid and binding against all parties that have claims of any kind against the board, regardless of whether the parties have notice of the lien. The official resolution or trust indenture or any instrument by which this pledge is created, when adopted by the board, is notice to all concerned of the creation of the pledge, and those instruments need not be recorded in any other place to perfect the pledge.

Added by Laws 2000, 5th S.S., Ch. 1, § 32.

Repeal

Laws 2000, 5th S.S., Ch. 1, § 59, which purportedly repealed this article effective July 1, 2005, was itself repealed by Laws 2001, Ch. 11, § 11, effective March 15, 2001.

Historical and Statutory Notes

Proposition 301, approved by the electors at the Nov. 7, 2000 general election, effective Nov. 27, 2000, included a provision increasing the state transaction privilege tax rate six-tenths of one per cent. Therefore, the conditions of the 5th S.S. Ch. 1 were met, and the act became effective.

§ 15-2087. Bond purchase; cancellation

The school facilities board may purchase bonds for cancellation out of any monies available for the purchase at a price of not more than either of the following:

1. If the bonds are redeemable at the time of the purchase, the applicable redemption price plus accrued interest to the next interest payment date on the bonds.

2. If the bonds are not redeemable at the time of the purchase, the applicable redemption price on the first date after the purchase on which the bonds become subject to redemption plus accrued interest to that date.

Added by Laws 2000, 5th S.S., Ch. 1, § 32.

Repeal

Laws 2000, 5th S.S., Ch. 1, § 59, which purportedly repealed this article effective July 1, 2005, was itself repealed by Laws 2001, Ch. 11, § 11, effective March 15, 2001.

Historical and Statutory Notes

Proposition 301, approved by the electors at the Nov. 7, 2000 general election, effective Nov. 27, 2000, included a provision increasing the state transaction privilege tax rate six-tenths of one per cent. Therefore, the conditions of the

5th S.S. Ch. 1 were met, and the act became effective.

§ 15-2088. Payment of revenue bonds

A. The revenue bonds shall be paid solely from monies from the school improvement revenue bond debt service fund established pursuant to § 15-2084 and other monies that are credited to the school improvement revenue bond debt service fund.

B. The state treasurer or the paying agent for the revenue bonds shall cancel all revenue bonds when paid.

Added by Laws 2000, 5th S.S., Ch. 1, § 32.

Repeal

Laws 2000, 5th S.S., Ch. 1, § 59, which purportedly repealed this article effective July 1, 2005, was itself repealed by Laws 2001, Ch. 11, § 11, effective March 15, 2001.

Historical and Statutory Notes

Proposition 301, approved by the electors at the Nov. 7, 2000 general election, effective Nov. 27, 2000, included a provision increasing the state transaction privilege tax rate six-tenths of one per cent. Therefore, the conditions of the 5th S.S. Ch. 1 were met, and the act became effective.

§ 15-2089. Investment of monies in school improvement revenue bond proceeds fund

A. As provided by § 15-2091, the school facilities board may authorize the state treasurer or bond trustee to invest monies in the school improvement revenue bond proceeds fund established pursuant to § 15-2083.

B. The order directing an investment shall state a specified time when the proceeds from the sale of the bonds will be used. The state treasurer or bond trustee shall make the investment in such a way as to mature at the specified date.

C. All monies earned as interest or otherwise derived from the investment of the monies in the school improvement revenue bond proceeds fund shall be credited to the school improvement revenue bond debt service fund established by § 15-2084.

Added by Laws 2000, 5th S.S., Ch. 1, § 32.

Repeal

Laws 2000, 5th S.S., Ch. 1, § 59, which purportedly repealed this article effective July 1, 2005, was itself repealed by Laws 2001, Ch. 11, § 11, effective March 15, 2001.

Historical and Statutory Notes

Proposition 301, approved by the electors at the Nov. 7, 2000 general election, effective Nov. 27, 2000, included a provision increasing the state transaction privilege tax rate six-tenths of one per cent. Therefore, the conditions of the 5th S.S. Ch. 1 were met, and the act became effective.

§ 15–2090. Investment of monies in the school improvement revenue bond debt service fund

A. The school facilities board may authorize the state treasurer or bond trustee to invest and reinvest any monies in the school improvement revenue bond debt service fund as provided by section 15–2091.

B. All monies earned as interest or otherwise derived from the investment of the monies in the school improvement revenue bond debt service fund shall be credited to that fund.

Added by Laws 2000, 5th S.S., Ch. 1, § 32. Amended by Laws 2002, Ch. 49, § 2, eff. April 20, 2002.

Repeal

Laws 2000, 5th S.S., Ch. 1, § 59, which purportedly repealed this article effective July 1, 2005, was itself repealed by Laws 2001, Ch. 11, § 11, effective March 15, 2001.

Historical and Statutory Notes

Proposition 301, approved by the electors at the Nov. 7, 2000 general election, effective Nov. 27, 2000, included a provision increasing the state transaction privilege tax rate six-tenths of one per cent. Therefore, the conditions of the 5th S.S. Ch. 1 were met, and the act became effective.

§ 15–2091. Authorized investments of fund monies

A. On notice from the school facilities board, the state treasurer or bond trustee shall invest and divest monies in either the school improvement revenue bond proceeds fund or the school improvement revenue debt service fund in any of the following:

1. Obligations issued or guaranteed by the United States or any of the senior debt of its agencies, sponsored agencies, corporations, sponsored corporations or instrumentalities.

2. State, county or municipal bonds that are issued in this state and on which the payments of interest have not been deferred.

3. Investment agreements and repurchase agreements collateralized by investments described in paragraph 1 of this subsection.

B. The purchase of the securities shall be made by the state treasurer or bond trustee on authority of a resolution of the board. The treasurer or bond trustee shall act as custodian of all securities purchased. The securities may be sold on an order of the board.

Added by Laws 2000, 5th S.S., Ch. 1, § 32. Amended by Laws 2002, Ch. 49, § 3, eff. April 20, 2002.

Repeal

Laws 2000, 5th S.S., Ch. 1, § 59, which purportedly repealed this article effective July 1, 2005, was itself repealed by Laws 2001, Ch. 11, § 11, effective March 15, 2001.

Historical and Statutory Notes

Proposition 301, approved by the electors at the Nov. 7, 2000 general election, effective Nov. 27, 2000, included a provision increasing the state transaction privilege tax rate six-tenths of one per cent. Therefore, the conditions of the 5th S.S. Ch. 1 were met, and the act became effective.

§ 15-2092. Audit

A. The school facilities board shall cause an annual audit to be made of the school improvement revenue bond proceeds fund established by § 15-2083 and the school improvement revenue bond debt service fund established by § 15-2084, including all accounts and subaccounts in the funds. A certified public accountant shall conduct the audit within ninety days after the end of the fiscal year.

B. The school facilities board shall immediately file a certified copy of the audit with the auditor general. The auditor general may make any further audits and examinations that are necessary and may take appropriate action relating to the audit or examination pursuant to title 41, chapter 7, article 10.1.[1] If the auditor general takes no official action within thirty days after the audit is filed, the audit is considered to be sufficient.

C. The school facilities board shall pay negotiated and approved fees and costs of the certified public accountant and auditor general under this section from the revenue bond debt service fund established by § 15-2084.

Added by Laws 2000, 5th S.S., Ch. 1, § 32.

[1] Section 41-1278 et seq.

Repeal

Laws 2000, 5th S.S., Ch. 1, § 59, which purportedly repealed this article effective July 1, 2005, was itself repealed by Laws 2001, Ch. 11, § 11, effective March 15, 2001.

Historical and Statutory Notes

Proposition 301, approved by the electors at the Nov. 7, 2000 general election, effective Nov. 27, 2000, included a provision increasing the state transaction privilege tax rate six-tenths of one per cent. Therefore, the conditions of the 5th S.S. Ch. 1 were met, and the act became effective.

§ 15-2093. Characteristics of bonds; negotiable; exemption from taxation: obligation; legal investments

A. Bonds issued under this article are fully negotiable within the meaning and for all purposes of the uniform commercial code, subject only to any provisions for registration, regardless of whether the bonds actually constitute negotiable instruments under the uniform commercial code.

B. The bonds, their transfer and the income from the bonds are at all times free from taxation in this state.

C. Bonds issued under this article:

1. Are obligations of the board. The members of the board and persons executing the bonds are not personally liable for payment of the bonds.

2. Are payable only according to their terms.

3. Do not constitute a debt of this state.

4. Are not enforceable against this state nor is payment of the bonds enforceable out of any monies other than the revenue pledged and assigned to, or in trust for the benefit of, the holder or holders of the bonds.

5. Are securities in which public officers and bodies of this state and of municipalities and political subdivisions of this state, all companies, associations and other persons carrying on an insurance business, all financial institutions, investment companies and other persons carrying on a banking business, all fiduciaries and all other persons who are authorized to invest in government obligations may properly and legally invest.

6. Are securities that may be deposited with public officers or bodies of this state and municipalities and political subdivisions of this state for purposes that require the deposit of government bonds or obligations.

Added by Laws 2000, 5th S.S., Ch. 1, § 32.

Repeal

Laws 2000, 5th S.S., Ch. 1, § 59, which purportedly repealed this article effective July 1, 2005, was itself repealed by Laws 2001, Ch. 11, § 11, effective March 15, 2001.

Historical and Statutory Notes

Proposition 301, approved by the electors at the Nov. 7, 2000 general election, effective Nov. 27, 2000, included a provision increasing the state transaction privilege tax rate six-tenths of one per cent. Therefore, the conditions of the 5th S.S. Ch. 1 were met, and the act became effective.

§ 15–2094. Effect of changing circumstances on bonds; agreement of state

A. Bonds issued under this article remain valid and binding obligations of the board notwithstanding that before the delivery of the bonds any of the persons whose signatures appear on the bonds cease to be members of the school facilities board.

B. An amendment of any provision of this article does not diminish or impair the validity of bonds issued under this article or the remedies and rights of bondholders.

C. This state pledges to and agrees with the holders of the bonds authorized by this article that this state will not limit, alter or impair the rights and remedies of the bondholders until all bonds issued under this article, together with interest on the bonds, interest on any unpaid installments of principal or interest and all costs and expenses in connection with any action or proceedings by or on behalf of the bondholders, are fully met and discharged. The board, as agent for this state, may include this pledge and undertaking in its resolutions and indentures authorizing and securing the bonds.

Added by Laws 2000, 5th S.S., Ch. 1, § 32.

Repeal

Laws 2000, 5th S.S., Ch. 1, § 59, which purportedly repealed this article effective July 1, 2005, was itself repealed by Laws 2001, Ch. 11, § 11, effective March 15, 2001.

Historical and Statutory Notes

Proposition 301, approved by the electors at the Nov. 7, 2000 general election, effective Nov. 27, 2000, included a provision increasing the state transaction privilege tax rate six-tenths of one per cent. Therefore, the conditions of the 5th S.S. Ch. 1 were met, and the act became effective.

§ 15-2095. Validity of bonds; certification by attorney general

A. This article constitutes full authority for authorizing and issuing bonds without reference to any other law of this state. No other law with regard to authorizing or issuing obligations or that in any way impedes or restricts performing the acts authorized by this article may be construed to apply to any proceedings taken or acts done pursuant to this article.

B. The validity of bonds issued under this article does not depend on and is not affected by the legality of any proceeding relating to any action by the school facilities board in granting or lending monies or the acquisition, construction or improvement of any facility paid with monies provided by the board.

C. The school facilities board may submit to the attorney general revenue bonds to be issued under this article after all proceedings for authorizing the bonds have been completed. Within fifteen days after submission, the attorney general shall examine the bonds and pass on the validity of the bonds and the regularity of the proceedings. If the bonds and proceedings comply with the Constitution of Arizona and this article, and if the bonds when delivered and paid for will constitute binding and legal obligations of the board, the attorney general shall certify in substance that the bonds are issued according to the constitution and laws of this state.

D. The bonds shall recite that they are regularly issued pursuant to this article. That recital, together with the certification by the attorney general under subsection C of this section, constitutes prima facie evidence of the legality and validity of the bonds. From and after the sale and delivery of the bonds, they are incontestable by the school facilities board or this state.
Added by Laws 2000, 5th S.S., Ch. 1, § 32.

Repeal

Laws 2000, 5th S.S., Ch. 1, § 59, which purportedly repealed this article effective July 1, 2005, was itself repealed by Laws 2001, Ch. 11, § 11, effective March 15, 2001.

Historical and Statutory Notes

Proposition 301, approved by the electors at the Nov. 7, 2000 general election, effective Nov. 27, 2000, included a provision increasing the state transaction privilege tax rate six-tenths of one per cent. Therefore, the conditions of the 5th S.S. Ch. 1 were met, and the act became effective.

ARTICLE 8. IMPACT AID REVENUE BONDS

Article 8, Impact Aid Revenue Bonds, consisting of §§ 15-2101 to 15-2115, was added by Laws 2001, Ch. 228, § 4, effective August 9, 2001.

§ 15–2101. Definition

For the purposes of this article, "impact and revenues" [1] means the revenues received by the school district pursuant to 20 United States Code §§ 7701 through 7714.

Added by Laws 2001, Ch. 228, § 4.

[1] So in original. Should read "impact aid revenues".

§ 15–2102. Authorization of school district impact aid revenue bonds

A. On voter approval pursuant to § 15–491, a school district governing board may issue negotiable impact aid revenue bonds pursuant to this article. Bonds may be issued under this article in a total aggregate amount not to exceed three times the average of the school district's annual impact aid revenues for the five years immediately preceding the issuance of the bonds. The bond proceeds may be used to:

1. Provide monies to pay the cost of:

(a) Capital projects authorized under chapter 4, article 5 of this title. [1]

(b) Bond related expenses including any expenses incurred by the school district to issue and administer its bonds including underwriting fees and costs, trustee fees, financial consultant fees, printing and advertising costs, paying agent fees, transfer agent fees, legal, accounting, feasibility consultant and other professional fees and expenses, bond insurance or other credit enhancements or liquidity facilities, attorney and accounting fees and expenses related to credit enhancement, bond insurance or liquidity enhancement, remarketing fees, rating agency fees and costs, travel and telephone expenses and all other fees considered necessary by the governing board in order to market and administer the bonds.

2. Fully or partially fund any reserves or sinking accounts established by the bond resolution.

B. The governing board shall authorize the bonds by resolution. The resolution shall prescribe:

1. The fixed or variable rate or rates of interest, payable semiannually, and the denominations of the bonds.

2. The date or dates of the bonds and maturity, within twenty years after the date of issuance.

3. The form of the bonds.

4. The manner of executing the bonds.

5. The medium and place of payment.

6. The terms of redemption, which may provide for a premium for early redemption.

C. The bonds issued pursuant to this article shall be known as impact aid revenue bonds.

D. An accommodation school may issue impact aid revenue bonds only if the accommodation school is located on a military base.

Added by Laws 2001, Ch. 228, § 4. Amended by Laws 2004, Ch. 313, § 1.

[1] Section 15–491 et seq.

Historical and Statutory Notes

Laws 2004, Ch. 313, §§ 2 and 3, provide:

"**Sec. 2. Guidebook on impact aid monies**

"By July 1, 2005, the Arizona department of education shall assemble a guidebook for distribution to school districts that receive federal impact aid that compiles the approved uses of impact aid monies as determined by the federal government and pursuant to state law. The Arizona department of education shall not make any determination concerning the use of impact aid monies unless the use listed in the guidebook is indisputably supported by a previous determination by the federal government or indisputably supported by state law.

"**Sec. 3. Federal base relocation and closure commission affirmation**

"An accommodation school located on a military base may not issue impact aid revenue bonds until after the Federal Base Relocation and Closure Commission has affirmed that the base on which the accommodation school is located will remain open, except that it may proceed with the election for voter approval under § 15–491, Arizona Revised Statutes as required by § 15–2102, subsection A, Arizona Revised Statutes."

Reviser's Notes:

2001 Note. Pursuant to authority of § 41–1304.02, in the section heading "; definition" was removed.

§ 15–2103. Issuance and sale of impact aid revenue bonds

A. The governing board shall issue the bonds in the number and amount provided in the resolution.

B. The bonds shall be sold at public or private sale at the price and on the terms prescribed in the resolution for at, above or below par.

C. The proceeds of the sale of the bonds shall be deposited in the county treasury to the credit of the school district's Impact Aid revenue bond building fund. These deposits may be drawn out for the purposes authorized by this article as other school monies are drawn.

D. Revenue Bond proceeds shall not be expended for items whose useful life is less than the average life of the bonds issued, except that bond proceeds shall not be expended for items whose useful life is less than five years.

Added by Laws 2001, Ch. 228, § 4.

§ 15–2104. Impact aid revenue bond building and debt service funds

A. If a school district issues Impact Aid revenue bonds under this article, the governing board shall establish:

1. An impact aid revenue bond building fund consisting of the net proceeds received from the sale of the bonds. The fund shall be a continuing fund that is not subject to reversion.

2. An impact aid revenue bond debt service fund consisting of monies received by the school district from impact aid revenues.

B. Monies in the impact aid revenue bond building fund and the impact aid revenue bond debt service fund may be used only for the purposes authorized by this article.

C. The school district shall provide the county treasurer with an impact aid revenue bond debt service schedule. The county treasurer shall keep an account of all school district debt service funds that shows the school district to which each fund belongs. The county treasurer shall credit to the impact aid revenue bond debt service fund an amount from impact aid revenues equal to the principal and interest that will become due on the impact aid revenue bonds during the current year. The treasurer shall receive and credit any interest or income earned by the debt service fund.

D. Notwithstanding any other provision in this article, the annual payment of principal and interest on impact aid revenue bonds each year shall not exceed seventy-five per cent of the net impact aid revenues of the school district for the current year. For the purposes of this subsection, "net impact aid revenues" mean impact aid revenues for the year after deducting the sum of the following amounts:

1. The amount of any increase in the school district's general budget limit pursuant to § 15–905, subsections K, O and P.

2. The amount necessary to fund any budget override adopted pursuant to § 15–481, subsection F, J or M.

3. The amount that would be produced by levying the applicable qualifying tax rate as provided in § 15–971, subsection B, minus the amount levied for primary school district taxes for the year pursuant to § 15–992, except that if the result is a negative number, use zero.

Added by Laws 2001, Ch. 228, § 4.

Historical and Statutory Notes

Reviser's Notes:

2001 Note. Pursuant to authority of § 41–1304.02, in subsection D, second sentence the quotation marks were added to enclose "net impact aid revenues" to correct a manifest clerical error.

§ 15–2105. Securing principal and interest

To secure the principal and interest on the impact aid revenue bonds, the governing board by resolution may:

1. Segregate the impact aid revenue bond debt service fund into one or more accounts and subaccounts and provide that bonds issued under this article may be secured by a lien on all or part of the monies paid into the impact Aid revenue bond debt service fund or into any account or subaccount in the fund.

2. Provide that the bonds issued under this article are secured by a first lien on the monies paid in the impact aid revenue bond debt service fund as provided by § 15–2104 and Pledge and assign to or in trust for the benefit of the holder or holders of the bonds all or part of the monies in the impact aid revenue bond debt service fund or an account or subaccount as is necessary to secure and pay the principal, the interest and any premium on the bonds as they come due.

3. Establish priorities among bondholders based on criteria adopted by the governing board.

4. Set aside, regulate and dispose of reserves and sinking accounts.

5. Prescribe the procedure, if any, by which the terms of any contract with bondholders may be amended or abrogated, the amount of bonds the holders of which must consent to and the manner in which the consent may be given.

6. Provide for payment of bond related expenses from the proceeds of the sale of the bonds or other revenues authorized by this article available to the school district.

7. Provide for the services of trustees, cotrustees, agents and consultants and other specialized services with respect to the bonds.

8. Take any other action that in any way may affect the security and protection of the bonds or interest on the bonds.

9. Refund any bonds issued by the school district, if these bonds are secured from the same source of revenues as the bonds authorized by this article, by issuing new bonds.

10. Issue bonds partly to refund outstanding bonds and partly for any other purpose consistent with this article.

Added by Laws 2001, Ch. 228, § 4.

§ 15–2106. Cancellation of unsold impact aid revenue bonds

A. If an impact aid revenue bond issue remains unsold for six months after being offered for sale, the governing board of the school district or any school district comprised wholly or partly of territory that was part of the school district at the time of issuing the bonds may cancel the unsold bonds.

B. The governing board shall fix a time for a hearing on the proposed cancellation of the unsold bonds. The governing board shall give notice of the time, place and subject of the hearing. The notice shall be published for ten days before the hearing in a newspaper of general circulation in the district.

C. At the time and place designated in the notice, the governing board shall hear reasons for or against the proposed cancellation of the unsold bonds, and if the board considers it to be in the school district's best interests, it shall order the unsold bonds to be cancelled and the bonds and the vote by which they were authorized to be issued are void.

Added by Laws 2001, Ch. 228, § 4.

§ 15–2107. Payment of impact aid revenue bonds; use of surplus monies

A. The impact aid revenue bonds shall be paid solely from monies distributed to the school district from impact aid revenues and other monies that are authorized by this article and that are credited to the school district's impact aid revenue bond debt service fund.

B. The county treasurer or the paying agent for the impact aid revenue bonds shall cancel all impact aid revenue bonds when paid. Any surplus monies remaining in the impact aid revenue bond debt service fund shall be transferred back to the school district's capital outlay fund.

C. If a balance remains in the school district's impact aid revenue bond building fund after the acquisition or construction of facilities for which the bonds were issued is completed and the payment of other related costs, the balance remaining in the impact aid revenue bond building fund shall be transferred to the school district's capital outlay fund.

Added by Laws 2001, Ch. 228, § 4.

§ 15-2108. Investment of monies in impact aid revenue bond building fund

A. If monies in the Impact aid revenue bond building fund are not required to be used for a period of ten days or more, the governing board may authorize their investment.

B. The order directing an investment shall state a specified time when the proceeds from the sale of the bonds will be used. The governing board shall make the investment in such a way as to mature at the specified date.

C. All monies earned as interest or otherwise derived from the investment of the monies in the impact aid revenue bond building fund shall be credited to the impact aid revenue bond debt service fund.

Added by Laws 2001, Ch. 228, § 4.

§ 15-2109. Investment of monies in impact aid revenue bond debt service fund

A. The governing board may authorize the investment and reinvestment of any monies in the school district's impact aid revenue bond debt service fund.

B. All monies earned as interest or otherwise derived from the investment of the monies in the impact aid revenue bond debt service fund shall be credited to that fund.

C. The impact aid revenue bond debt service fund is a continuing fund and is not subject to reversion.

Added by Laws 2001, Ch. 228, § 4.

§ 15-2110. Authorized investments of fund monies

A. The monies in either the impact aid revenue bond building fund or debt service fund may be invested and reinvested at the direction of the governing board in any of the investments authorized by § 15-2062.

B. The purchase of the securities shall be made by the county treasurer or the treasurer's designated agent on authority of a resolution of the governing board. The county treasurer shall act as custodian of all securities purchased. The securities may be sold on an order of the governing board.

Added by Laws 2001, Ch. 228, § 4.

§ 15-2111. Audit

A. The governing board shall cause an annual audit to be made of the impact aid revenue bond building fund and the impact aid revenue bond debt service fund, including all accounts and subaccounts in the funds. A certified public accountant shall conduct the audit within ninety days after the end of the fiscal year.

B. The governing board shall immediately file a certified copy of the audit with the auditor general. The auditor general may make any further audits and examinations that are considered to be necessary and take appropriate action relating to the audit or examination pursuant to title 41, chapter 7, article 10.1.[1] If the auditor general takes no official action within thirty days after the audit is filed, the audit is considered to be sufficient.

C. The governing board shall pay negotiated and approved fees and costs of the certified public accountant and auditor general under this section from the impact aid revenue bond debt service fund.

Added by Laws 2001, Ch. 228, § 4.

[1] Section 41–1278 et seq.

§ 15–2112. Lien of pledge

A. Any pledge made under this article is valid and binding from the time when the pledge is made.

B. The monies so pledged and received by the school district to be placed in the impact aid revenue bond debt service fund are immediately subject to the lien of the pledge without any future physical delivery or further act. Any lien of any pledge is valid and binding against all parties that have claims of any kind against the school district, regardless of whether the parties have notice of the lien. The official resolution or trust indenture or any instrument by which this pledge is created, when adopted by the governing board, is notice to all concerned of the creation of the pledge, and those instruments need not be recorded in any other place to perfect the pledge.

Added by Laws 2001, Ch. 228, § 4.

§ 15–2113. Characteristics of bonds; negotiable; exemption from taxation; obligation; legal investments

A. Bonds issued under this article are fully negotiable within the meaning and for all purposes of the uniform commercial code, subject only to any provisions for registration, regardless of whether the bonds actually constitute negotiable instruments under the uniform commercial code.

B. The bonds, their transfer and the income from the bonds are at all times free from taxation in this state.

C. Bonds issued under this article:

1. Are obligations of the school district. The members of the governing board and persons executing the bonds are not personally liable for payment of the bonds.

2. Are payable only according to their terms.

3. Are not general, special or other obligations of the county or of this state.

4. Do not constitute a debt of the county or of this state.

5. Are not enforceable against the county or this state nor is payment of the bonds enforceable out of any monies other than the revenue pledged and assigned to, or in trust for the benefit of, the holder or holders of the bonds.

6. Are securities in which public officers and bodies of this state and of municipalities and political subdivisions of this state, all companies, associations and other persons carrying on an insurance business, all financial institutions, investment companies and other persons carrying on a banking business, all fiduciaries and all other persons who are authorized to invest in government obligations may properly and legally invest.

7. Are securities that may be deposited with public officers or bodies of this state and municipalities and political subdivisions of this state for purposes that require the deposit of government bonds or obligations.
Added by Laws 2001, Ch. 228, § 4.

§ 15-2114. Effect of changing circumstances on bonds; agreement of state

A. Bonds issued under this article remain valid and binding obligations of the school district notwithstanding that before the delivery of the bonds any of the persons whose signatures appear on the bonds cease to be officers of the school district.

B. An amendment of any provision of this article does not diminish or impair the validity of bonds issued under this article or the remedies and rights of bondholders.

C. This state pledges to and agrees with the holders of the bonds authorized by this article that this state will not limit, alter or impair the ability of a school district to qualify for impact aid revenues, or in any way impair the rights and remedies of the bondholders, until all bonds issued under this article, together with interest on the bonds, interest on any unpaid installments of principal or interest and all costs and expenses in connection with any action or proceedings by or on behalf of the bondholders, are fully met and discharged. The governing board, as agent for this state, may include this pledge and undertaking in its resolutions and indentures authorizing and securing the bonds.
Added by Laws 2001, Ch. 228, § 4.

§ 15-2115. Validity of bonds; certification by attorney general

A. This article constitutes full authority for authorizing and issuing bonds without reference to any other law of this state. No other law with regard to authorizing or issuing obligations or that in any way impedes or restricts performing the acts authorized by this article may be construed to apply to any proceedings taken or acts done pursuant to this article.

B. The validity of bonds issued under this article is not dependent on or affected by the legality of any proceeding relating to the acquisition, construction or improvement of any school district capital project for which the bonds are issued.

C. The governing board may submit to the attorney general revenue bonds to be issued under this article after all proceedings for authorizing the bonds have been completed. Within fifteen days after submission, the attorney general shall examine the bonds and pass on the validity of the bonds and the regularity of the proceedings. If the bonds and proceedings comply with the Arizona constitution and this article, and if the bonds when delivered and paid for will constitute binding and legal obligations of the school district, the attorney general shall certify in substance that the bonds are issued according to the constitution and laws of this state. The certificate shall also state that the bonds are also validly secured by the obligation to transfer impact aid revenues to cover any insufficiencies.

D. The bonds shall recite that they are regularly issued pursuant to this article. From and after the sale and delivery of the bonds, they are incontestable by this state or the school district.
Added by Laws 2001, Ch. 228, § 4.

CHAPTER 17

LOCAL EDUCATION ACCOUNTABILITY PROGRAM

ARTICLE 1. GENERAL PROVISIONS

Chapter 17, Local Education Accountability Program, containing Article 1, consisting of §§ 15–2201 to 15–2203, was added by Laws 2000, 5th S.S., Ch. 1, § 32.

Laws 2000, 5th S.S., Ch. 1, §§ 66 and 67, provide:

"**Sec. 66. Delayed implementation**

"This act shall not be implemented until from and after May 31, 2001.

"**Sec. 67. Conditional enactment**

"This act does not become effective unless the qualified electors of this state in the general election that will be held in November, 2000 approve an increase in state transaction privilege tax rates of six-tenths of one per cent in order to fund the provisions of this act."

Proposition 301, approved by the electors at the Nov. 7, 2000 general election, effective Nov. 27, 2000, included a provision increasing the state transaction privilege tax rate six-tenths of one per cent. Therefore, the conditions of the 5th S.S. Ch. 1 were met, and the act became effective.

ARTICLE 1. GENERAL PROVISIONS

§ 15–2201. Local education accountability program; phase-in

A. The local education accountability program is established to provide direct funding associated with teacher salaries, average daily membership, and transportation of pupils to local individual schools.

B. By January 1 of each year, principals of schools not participating in the local education accountability program may provide written notice to the district superintendent of schools and the department of education of intent to apply for participation in the program.

C. Each school district shall, from the applications made and by March 1 of each year, select at least one school to participate in the program and shall select additional schools as necessary to reach ten per cent of the number of schools in the district. If applications are received from more than ten per cent of the schools, the district may, at its sole option, determine the schools making up ten per cent of the schools in the district which shall participate in the program. Nothing in this section shall be construed as a limitation of the number of schools which the district may admit to the program in any one year.

D. The principal of each school selected to participate in the program may:

1. Adopt a corporate seal.

2. Contract, except that the principal shall not enter into any contract for goods or services in which the total cost of the transaction exceeds five thousand dollars without written approval from the school district governing

board. The school district governing board shall approve any proposed contract submitted by the principal pursuant to this paragraph if the contract is in proper form and if the contract is for a lawful purpose. The principal shall honor any existing contractual obligations between the school district and any provider of goods or services to the school.

3. Sue and be sued.

E. The principal of each financially and operationally independent school shall negotiate employment contracts with teachers who provide instruction at the school, except that the principal shall honor any existing employment agreements between those teachers and the school district. The salary paid to a teacher who provides instruction at a financially and operationally independent school shall not be less than the salary earned by that teacher before the school became financially and operationally independent and shall not be less than the salary offered by that school district to teachers with comparable work experience and a comparable level of education.

F. Each financially and operationally independent school shall procure liability insurance, property damage insurance, workers' compensation insurance and any other forms of insurance deemed necessary or desirable by the principal of the school.

G. Taxpayers are eligible to receive a tax credit pursuant to § 43–1089.01 for contributions to financially and operationally independent schools.

H. A school district governing board shall not take any personnel action against a principal applying to participate in the local education accountability program.

I. A school district governing board shall not take any personnel action against a principal of a financially and operationally independent school that is directly or indirectly contingent on the amount of services that the school will contract to purchase from the school district. As used in this subsection "personnel action" means any of the following:

1. A disciplinary or corrective action.
2. A transfer or reassignment.
3. A suspension, demotion or dismissal.
4. An unfavorable performance evaluation.
5. A reduction in pay, benefits or awards.
6. Other significant changes in duties or responsibilities that are inconsistent with the principal's salary or employment classification.

Added by Laws 2000, 5th S.S., Ch. 1, § 33.

Historical and Statutory Notes

Proposition 301, approved by the electors at the Nov. 7, 2000 general election, effective Nov. 27, 2000, included a provision increasing the state transaction privilege tax rate six-tenths of one per cent. Therefore, the conditions of the 5th S.S. Ch. 1 were met, and the act became effective.

§ 15–2202. Responsibilities of principals

A. The principal of each financially and operationally independent school shall follow existing school district policies unless the principal provides written notification to the school district governing board of any modifications to existing district policies that will be in effect at the school.

B. The principal of each financially and operationally independent school may:

1. Renew or decline to renew teacher employment contracts. The dismissal of teachers employed at the school shall conform to chapter 5 of this title [1] and rules adopted by the state board of education for the evaluation and dismissal of teachers.

2. Approve, adopt and purchase academic curricula, publications and supporting materials, notwithstanding any curriculum adopted by the school district to the contrary. Any curricula adopted by the principal shall be in accordance with the academic standards adopted by the state board of education.

Added by Laws 2000, 5th S.S., Ch. 1, § 33.

[1] Section 15-2202 et seq.

Historical and Statutory Notes

Proposition 301, approved by the electors at the Nov. 7, 2000 general election, effective Nov. 27, 2000, included a provision increasing the state transaction privilege tax rate six-tenths of one per cent. Therefore, the conditions of the 5th S.S. Ch. 1 were met, and the act became effective.

§ 15-2203. Distribution of monies from school districts to schools

A. By April 1 the governing board of each school district shall provide a detailed written menu of services that the district will offer to provide to financially and operationally independent schools. The cost charged to the financially and operationally independent schools for services provided by the school district shall not exceed the costs charged to other schools in the school district.

B. After deducting necessary expenses that are directly related to the administration of the school district, each school district shall distribute all monies that are associated with teacher salaries, average daily membership and transportation of pupils directly to the principal of each school in the school district in the same manner as prescribed for school districts pursuant to § 15-973, subsection B, except that special education weighted funding prescribed pursuant to § 15-943 shall be distributed to and administered by the school district. The school district shall enter into a good faith agreement with the principal for the distribution of special education monies. The distribution of special education monies to the financially and operationally independent school need not necessarily conform to the amount of the group B weights prescribed in § 15-943.

C. By June 1 the principal of each individual school shall notify the governing board of the school district which, if any, services that the school will contract to purchase from the school district.

D. On July 1 of the first year of each school's financial and operation independence from the school district, the department of education shall apportion to the school one-third of the total amount of the monies to be apportioned during the fiscal year that are associated with average daily membership and transportation of pupils.

E. If the qualified electors of the school district approve a school district budget override pursuant to § 15–481, a financially and operationally independent school is entitled to the same amount of proceeds from the override election that the school would be entitled to receive if the school were not financially and operationally independent from the school district.

F. The school district is responsible for providing interscholastic athletic services for financially and operationally independent schools. The school district may charge the costs of providing interscholastic athletic services to financially and operationally independent schools that participate in interscholastic athletic activities.

Added by Laws 2000, 5th S.S., Ch. 1, § 33.

Historical and Statutory Notes

Proposition 301, approved by the electors at the Nov. 7, 2000 general election, effective Nov. 27, 2000, included a provision increasing the state transaction privilege tax rate six-tenths of one per cent. Therefore, the conditions of the 5th S.S. Ch. 1 were met, and the act became effective.

CHAPTER 18

HAZING PREVENTION POLICIES

ARTICLE 1. GENERAL PROVISIONS

Chapter 18, Hazing Prevention Policies, consisting of Article 1, § 15–2301, was added by Laws 2001, Ch. 230, § 1, effective August 9, 2001.

ARTICLE 1. GENERAL PROVISIONS

§ 15–2301. Hazing prevention policies; definitions

A. Every public educational institution in this state shall adopt, Post and enforce a hazing prevention policy. The hazing prevention policy shall be printed in every student handbook for distribution to parents and students. Each hazing prevention policy shall include:

1. A definition of hazing pursuant to subsection C, paragraph 2 of this section.

2. A statement that hazing is prohibited.

3. A statement that any solicitation to engage in hazing is prohibited.

4. A Statement that aiding and abetting another person who is engaged in hazing is prohibited.

5. A statement that it is not a defense to a violation of the hazing prevention policy if the hazing victim consented to or acquiesced in the hazing activity.

6. A statement that all students, teachers and staff shall take reasonable measures within the scope of their individual authority to prevent violations of the hazing prevention policy.

7. A description of the procedures for students, teachers and staff to report violations of the hazing prevention policy and the procedures to file a complaint for a violation of the hazing prevention policy.

8. Procedures to investigate reports of violations of the hazing prevention policy and to investigate complaints for a violation of the hazing prevention policy.

9. A description of the circumstances under which a violation of the hazing prevention policy shall be reported to the appropriate law enforcement agency.

10. A Description of appropriate penalties, sanctions and appeals mechanisms for persons and organizations that violate the hazing prevention policy. The sanctions shall include the revocation or suspension of an organization's permission to conduct operations at the educational institution if the organization knowingly permitted, authorized or condoned the hazing activity. Any teacher or staff who knowingly permitted, authorized or condoned the hazing activity is subject to disciplinary action by the educational institution.

B. Violations of hazing prevention policies adopted pursuant to this section do not include either of the following:

1. Customary athletic events, contests or competitions that are sponsored by an educational institution.

2. Any activity or conduct that furthers the goals of a legitimate educational curriculum, a legitimate extracurricular program or a legitimate military training program.

C. For purposes of this section:

1. "Educational institution" means any of the following:

(a) A public school that provides instruction to pupils in any combination of kindergarten programs and grades one through twelve.

(b) A public community college or a vocational education program that provides academic instruction or training not exceeding two years' duration in the arts, sciences and humanities beyond the twelfth grade of the public or private high school course of study.

(c) Any public college or university that provides academic instruction beyond the twelfth grade of the public or private high school course of study and that offers any combination of baccalaureate, master's or doctoral degrees to students that complete specified academic requirements.

2. "Hazing" means any intentional, knowing or reckless act committed by a student, whether individually or in concert with other persons, against another student, and in which both of the following apply:

(a) The act was committed in connection with an initiation into, an affiliation with or the maintenance of membership in any organization that is affiliated with an educational institution.

(b) The act contributes to a substantial risk of potential physical injury, mental harm or degradation or causes physical injury, mental harm or personal degradation.

3. "Organization" means an athletic team, association, order, society, corps, cooperative, club or other similar group that is affiliated with an educational institution and whose membership consists primarily of students enrolled at that educational institution.

4. "Student" means any person who is enrolled at an educational institution, any person who has been promoted or accepted for enrollment at an educational institution or any person who intends to enroll at or be promoted to an educational institution within the next twelve calendar months. The hazing prevention policy of the educational institution where a person has been accepted for or promoted to enrollment, or where a person intends to enroll or be promoted to within the next twelve calendar months, shall be the effective policy. A person who meets the definition of a student for purposes of this paragraph shall continue to be defined as a student for purposes of this section until the person graduates, transfers, is promoted or withdraws from the educational institution.

Added by Laws 2001, Ch. 230, § 1.

Historical and Statutory Notes

Laws 2001, Ch. 230, § 2, provides:

"**Sec. 2. Intent**

"It is the intent of the legislature and the policy of this state that all educational institutions in this state provide students with safe, orderly, civil and positive learning environments. The legislature believes that no student in this state shall feel threatened while enrolled in a school in this state. The legislature hereby declares that hazing activities are not permissible and will not be tolerated in the schools of this state."

Reviser's Notes:

2001 Note. Pursuant to authority of § 41-1304.02, in subsection A, paragraph 1 was renumbered as paragraph 2 and paragraph 2 was renumbered as paragraph 1.

Section

Title 13, the revised Criminal Code, consisting of Chapters 1 to 38, [illegible]

§ 13-914. Intensive probation; evaluation; sentence; criteria; limits; conditions

A. An adult probation officer shall prepare a presentence report for every offender who has either:

1. Been convicted of a felony and for whom the granting of probation is not prohibited by law.

2. Violated probation by the commission of a technical violation that was not chargeable or indictable as a criminal offense.

B. The adult probation officer shall evaluate the needs of the offender and the offender's risk to the community, including the nature of the offense and criminal history of the offender. If the nature of the offense and the prior criminal history of the offender indicate that the offender should be included in an intensive probation program pursuant to supreme court guidelines for intensive probation, the adult probation officer may recommend to the court that the offender be granted intensive probation.

TITLE 13

CRIMINAL CODE

Selected Provisions From Title 13, Criminal Code

TITLE 13

Title 13, the revised Criminal Code, consisting of Chapters 1 to 33, 35, 35.1, and 36 to 38, was adopted by Laws 1977, Ch. 142, §§ 1 to 178, effective October 1, 1978, Laws 1978, Ch. 200, § 3, effective October 1, 1978, and Laws 1978, Ch. 215, § 3, effective October 1, 1978.

§ 13–914. Intensive probation; evaluation; sentence; criteria; limit; conditions

A. An adult probation officer shall prepare a presentence report for every offender who has either:

1. Been convicted of a felony and for whom the granting of probation is not prohibited by law.

2. Violated probation by commission of a technical violation that was not chargeable or indictable as a criminal offense.

B. The adult probation officer shall evaluate the needs of the offender and the offender's risk to the community, including the nature of the offense and criminal history of the offender. If the nature of the offense and the prior criminal history of the offender indicate that the offender should be included in an intensive probation program pursuant to supreme court guidelines for intensive probation, the adult probation officer may recommend to the court that the offender be granted intensive probation.

C. The court may suspend the imposition or execution of the sentence and grant the offender a period of intensive probation in accordance with this chapter. Except for sentences that are imposed pursuant to § 13-3601, the sentence is tentative to the extent that it may be altered or revoked pursuant to this chapter, but for all other purposes it is a final judgment of conviction. This subsection does not preclude the court from imposing a term of intensive probation pursuant to § 13-3601.

D. When granting intensive probation the court shall set forth on the record the factual and legal reasons in support of the sentence.

E. Intensive probation shall be conditioned on the offender:

1. Maintaining employment or maintaining full-time student status at a school subject to the provisions of title 15 [1] or title 32, chapter 30 [2] and making progress deemed satisfactory to the probation officer, or both, or being involved in supervised job searches and community service work at least six days a week throughout the offender's term of intensive probation.

2. Paying restitution and probation fees of not less than fifty dollars unless, after determining the inability of the offender to pay the fee, the court assesses a lesser fee. Probation fees shall be deposited in the adult probation services fund established by § 12-267. Any amount greater than forty dollars of the fee assessed pursuant to this subsection shall only be used to supplement monies currently used for the salaries of adult probation and surveillance officers and for support of programs and services of the superior court adult probation departments.

3. Establishing a residence at a place approved by the intensive probation team and not changing the offender's residence without the team's prior approval.

4. Remaining at the offender's place of residence at all times except to go to work, to attend school, to perform community service and as specifically allowed in each instance by the adult probation officer.

5. Allowing administration of drug and alcohol tests if requested by a member of the intensive probation team.

6. Performing not less than forty hours of community service each month. Full-time students may be exempted or required to perform fewer hours of community service. For good cause, the court may reduce the number of community service hours performed to not less than twenty hours each month.

7. Meeting any other conditions imposed by the court to meet the needs of the offender and limit the risks to the community, including participation in a program of community punishment authorized in title 12, chapter 2, article 11. [3]

Added as § 12-292 by Laws 1984, 1st S.S., Ch. 11, § 1, eff. July 1, 1985. Amended by Laws 1986, Ch. 208, § 1; Laws 1988, Ch. 324, § 1. Renumbered as § 13-914 and amended by Laws 1989, Ch. 18, §§ 1, 4, eff. April 12, 1989. Amended by Laws 1995, Ch. 192, § 6, eff. Oct. 1, 1995; Laws 1998, Ch. 111, § 1; Laws 1998, Ch. 294, § 4; Laws 2002, Ch. 291, § 9.

[1] Section 15-101 et seq.

[2] Section 32-3001 et seq.

[3] Section 12-299 et seq.

Historical and Statutory Notes

The 1988 amendment, in subsec. A(1), preceding "felony", deleted reference to class 4, 5, or 6; in subsec. (C), in the first sentence, substituted "The court" for "If the court accepts the recommendation of the adult probation officer to grant an offender intensive probation it"; rewrote subsec. E which had read:

"A person who was granted parole and is subject to § 31-415 may be placed on intensive probation supervision pursuant to § 31-417 in the county in which he resides if the board of pardons and paroles finds that he has committed a technical violation of parole that is not chargeable or indictable as a criminal offense."

and in subsec. F(7) [now subsec. E], following court, deleted reference to board of pardons and paroles and inserted requirement of participation in a program of community punishment.

The 1989 amendment, in subsec. C, substituted "this chapter" for the references to the specific article or title and chapter, and deleted the provision which required minimum incarceration as a condition of intensive probation; deleted subsec. E which limited the court's power to grant intensive probation to an offender convicted of a class 2 or 3 felony; redesignated former subsec. F as subsec. E; and substituted "title 12, chapter 2, article 11" for "article 11 of this chapter" in subsec. E, par. 7.

The 1995 amendment by Ch. 192 substituted "adult probation services fund established by § 12-267" for "probation services fund" in subsec. E, par. 2.

The 1998 amendment by Ch. 111, in subsec. C, inserted the exception proviso in the second sentence, and added the last sentence relating to intensive probation; and inserted the last sentence of subsec. E, par. 6, relating to reduction of community service hours.

The 1998 amendment by Ch. 294 inserted the exception clause at the beginning of the second sentence of subsec. C and further inserted in such subsection the third sentence, relating to § 13-3601; and made nonsubstantive, gender-neutral changes in subsec. E.

The 2002 amendment by Ch. 291, rewrote subsec. E, par. 2, which had read:

[E.] "2. Paying restitution and probation fees of not less than forty dollars unless, after determining the inability of the offender to pay the fee, the court assesses a lesser fee. Probation fees shall be deposited in the adult probation services fund established by § 12-267."

Former § 13-914, relating to the disposal of weapons, was repealed by Laws 1977, Ch. 142, § 29, effective October 1, 1978.

Reviser's Notes:

1998 Note. Prior to the 2002 amendment, this section contained the amendments made by Laws 1998, Ch. 111, sec. 1 and Ch. 294, sec. 4 that were blended together pursuant to authority of § 41-1304.03.

§ 13-1204. Aggravated assault; classification; definition

A. A person commits aggravated assault if the person commits assault as defined in § 13-1203 under any of the following circumstances:

1. If the person causes serious physical injury to another.

2. If the person uses a deadly weapon or dangerous instrument.

3. If the person commits the assault after entering the private home of another with the intent to commit the assault.

4. If the person is eighteen years of age or older and commits the assault upon a child the age of fifteen years or under.

5. If the person commits the assault knowing or having reason to know that the victim is a peace officer, or a person summoned and directed by the officer while engaged in the execution of any official duties.

6. If the person commits the assault knowing or having reason to know the victim is a teacher or other person employed by any school and the teacher or other employee is upon the grounds of a school or grounds adjacent to the school or is in any part of a building or vehicle used for school purposes, or any teacher or school nurse visiting a private home in the course of the teacher's or nurse's professional duties, or any teacher engaged in any authorized and organized classroom activity held on other than school grounds.

7. If the person meets both of the following conditions:

(a) Is imprisoned or otherwise subject to the custody of any of the following:

(i) The state department of corrections.

(ii) The department of juvenile corrections.

(iii) A law enforcement agency.

(iv) A county or city jail or an adult or juvenile detention facility of a city or county.

(v) Any other entity that is contracting with the state department of corrections, the department of juvenile corrections, a law enforcement agency, another state, any private correctional facility, a county, a city or the federal bureau of prisons or other federal agency that has responsibility for sentenced or unsentenced prisoners.

(b) Commits an assault knowing or having reason to know that the victim is acting in an official capacity as an employee of any of the entities prescribed by subdivision (a) of this paragraph.

8. If the person commits the assault while the victim is bound or otherwise physically restrained or while the victim's capacity to resist is substantially impaired.

9. If the person commits the assault knowing or having reason to know that the victim is a fire fighter, fire investigator, fire inspector, emergency medical technician or paramedic engaged in the execution of any official duties, or a person summoned and directed by such individual while engaged in the execution of any official duties.

10. If the person commits the assault knowing or having reason to know that the victim is a licensed health care practitioner who is certified or licensed pursuant to title 32, chapter 13, 15, 17 or 25,[1] or a person summoned and directed by the licensed health care practitioner while engaged in the person's professional duties. The provisions of this paragraph do not apply if the person who commits the assault is seriously mentally ill, as defined in § 36-550, or is afflicted with Alzheimer's disease or related dementia.

11. If the person commits assault by any means of force which causes temporary but substantial disfigurement, temporary but substantial loss or impairment of any body organ or part, or a fracture of any body part.

12. If the person commits assault as prescribed by § 13-1203, subsection A, paragraph 1 or 3 and the person is in violation of an order of protection issued against the person pursuant to § 13-3602 or 13-3624.

13. If the person commits the assault knowing or having reason to know that the victim is a prosecutor.

B. Except pursuant to subsections C and D of this section, aggravated assault pursuant to subsection A, paragraph 1 or 2 of this section is a class 3 felony except if the victim is under fifteen years of age in which case it is a class 2 felony punishable pursuant to § 13-604.01. Aggravated assault pursuant to subsection A, paragraph 11 of this section is a class 4 felony. Aggravated assault pursuant to subsection A, paragraph 7 of this section is a class 5 felony.

Aggravated assault pursuant to subsection A, paragraph 3, 4, 5, 6, 8, 9, 10, 12 or 13 of this section is a class 6 felony.

C. Aggravated assault pursuant to subsection A, paragraph 1 or 2 of this section committed on a peace officer while the officer is engaged in the execution of any official duties is a class 2 felony. Aggravated assault pursuant to subsection A, paragraph 11 of this section committed on a peace officer while the officer is engaged in the execution of any official duties is a class 3 felony. Aggravated assault pursuant to subsection A, paragraph 5 of this section resulting in any physical injury to a peace officer while the officer is engaged in the execution of any official duties is a class 5 felony.

D. Aggravated assault pursuant to:

1. Subsection A, paragraph 1 or 2 of this section is a class 2 felony if committed on a prosecutor.

2. Subsection A, paragraph 11 of this section is a class 3 felony if committed on a prosecutor.

3. Subsection A, paragraph 13 of this section is a class 5 felony if the assault results in a physical injury to a prosecutor.

E. For the purposes of this section, "prosecutor" means county attorney, municipal prosecutor or attorney general and an assistant or deputy county attorney, municipal prosecutor or attorney general.

Added by Laws 1977, Ch. 142, § 61, eff. Oct. 1, 1978. Amended by Laws 1980, Ch. 229, § 15, eff. April 23, 1980; Laws 1984, Ch. 325, § 2; Laws 1985, Ch. 364, § 14, eff. May 16, 1985; Laws 1990, Ch. 152, § 1; Laws 1991, Ch. 225, § 2; Laws 1994, Ch. 121, § 1; Laws 1994, Ch. 200, § 12, eff. April 19, 1994; Laws 1995, Ch. 127, § 1; Laws 1996, Ch. 32, § 1, eff. March 25, 1996; Laws 1999, Ch. 261, § 16. Amended by Laws 2001, Ch. 124, § 3.

[1] Sections 32-1401 et seq., 32-1601 et seq., 32-1800 et seq., 32-2501 et seq.

Historical and Statutory Notes

Source:

Pen.Code 1901, §§ 184, 185, 193, 215 to 219, 381, 392, 427.
Pen.Code 1913, §§ 183, 184, 193, 215 to 220, 425, 432, 467, 610.
Rev.Code 1928, §§ 4592, 4593, 4613 to 4616, 4723, 4726, 4832.
Code 1939, §§ 43-603 to 43-606, 43-1802, 43-2201, 43-2204, 43-2207, 43-3801.
Laws 1955, Ch. 103, § 1.
A.R.S. former §§ 13-245, 13-248 to 13-251, 13-521, 13-915 to 13-917, 13-920, 13-922, 13-1022.
Laws 1962, Ch. 88, § 1.
Laws 1962, Ch. 104, § 1.
Laws 1967, Ch. 62, §§ 1 to 3, 7.
Laws 1968, Ch. 67, § 1.
Laws 1969, Ch. 133, §§ 7, 8.
Laws 1970, Ch. 58, § 1.
Laws 1970, Ch. 166, § 5.
Laws 1971, Ch. 38, § 2.
Laws 1972, Ch. 179, § 1.
Laws 1973, Ch. 138, §§ 3, 8.
Laws 1973, Ch. 172, § 33.
Laws 1975, Ch. 68, § 1.
Laws 1976, Ch. 111, §§ 1, 2, 7.

The 1980 amendment rewrote pars. 6 and 7 of subsec. A, which had read:

"6. If such person commits the assault knowing or having reason to know the victim is a teacher or other person employed by any school and such teacher or other employee is upon the grounds of a school or grounds adjacent to such school or is in any part of a building or vehicle used for school purposes, or any teacher or school nurse visiting a private home in the course of his professional duties.

"7. If such person is imprisoned in the custody of the department of corrections or subject to the custody of personnel from such department and commits the assault knowing or having reason to know the victim is an employee of such department acting in an official capacity."

The 1984 amendment inserted the second sentence of subsec. B; and deleted a reference to par. 7 in the last sentence of subsec. B.

The 1985 amendment inserted the exception in the first sentence of subsec. B.

The 1990 amendment, in subsec. A, inserted par. 9.

The 1991 amendment added par. 10 to subsec. A, and inserted the second sentence in subsec. B.

The 1994 amendment by Ch. 121 provided for emergency medical technicians in par. 9, inserted par. 10, and renumbered former par. 10 as par. 11 in subsec. A; and in subsec. B, added the reference to paragraph 10 of subsection A.

The 1994 amendment by Ch. 200 inserted at the beginning of subsec. B "Except pursuant to subsection C of this section"; and added subsec. C.

The 1995 amendment by Ch. 127, in paragraph 7 of subsec. A, inserted "or any other entity contracting with the state department of corrections, a law enforcement agency, a county, a city or the federal bureau of prisons, or other federal agency that has responsibility for sentenced or unsentenced prisoners," and inserted ", entity" following "jail" twice; made nonsubstantive changes in par. 10 of subsec. A; and, in subsec. C, substituted "subsection A, paragraph 11" for "subsection A, paragraph 10", and substituted "while the officer is engaged" for "while engaged" twice.

The 1996 amendment by Ch. 32 rewrote subsec. A, par. 7, which had read:

"7. If such person is imprisoned in the custody of the state department of corrections, a law enforcement agency, county or city jail, or adult or juvenile detention facility of a city or county or any other entity contracting with the state department of corrections, a law enforcement agency, a county, a city or the federal bureau of prisons, or other federal agency that has responsibility for sentenced or unsentenced prisoners, or subject to the custody of personnel from such department, agency, jail, entity or detention facility and commits the assault knowing or having reason to know the victim is an employee of such department, agency, jail, entity or detention facility acting in an official capacity."

The 1999 amendment by Ch. 261 modified a statutory reference.

The 2001 amendment by Ch. 124 inserted subsec. A, par. 13; and added subsecs. D and E.

Former § 13-1204, was renumbered as § 13-3804.

Reviser's Notes:

1990 Note. Pursuant to authority of § 41-1304.02, in subsection B, last sentence a comma was added after "6" to correct a manifest clerical error.

1994 Note. Prior to the 1995 amendment, this section contained amendments made by Laws 1994, Ch. 121, sec. 1 and Ch. 200, sec. 12 that were blended together pursuant to authority of § 41-1304.03.

§ 13-1604. Aggravated criminal damage; classification

A. A person commits aggravated criminal damage by intentionally or recklessly without the express permission of the owner:

1. Defacing, damaging or in any way changing the appearance of any building, structure, personal property or place used for worship or any religious purpose.

2. Defacing or damaging any building, structure or place used as a school or as an educational facility.

3. Defacing, damaging or tampering with any cemetery, mortuary or personal property of the cemetery or mortuary or other facility used for the purpose of burial or memorializing the dead.

B. Aggravated criminal damage is punishable as follows:

1. Aggravated criminal damage is a class 4 felony if the person intentionally or recklessly does any act described in subsection A which causes damage to the property of another in an amount of ten thousand dollars or more.

2. Aggravated criminal damage is a class 5 felony if the person intentionally or recklessly damages property of another in an amount of one thousand five hundred dollars or more but less than ten thousand dollars.

3. In all other cases aggravated criminal damage is a class 6 felony.

C. In determining the amount of damage to property, damages include the cost of repair or replacement of the property that was damaged.

Added by Laws 1981, Ch. 191, § 5. Amended by Laws 1994, Ch. 17, § 1.

Historical and Statutory Notes

The 1994 amendment made nonsubstantive changes for the sake of clarity in par. 3 of subsec. A; and in subsec. B, rewrote par. 3 and deleted par. 4. Paragraphs 3 and 4 of subsec. B had read:

"3. Aggravated criminal damage is a class 6 felony if the person intentionally or recklessly damages property of another in an amount of one hundred dollars or more but less than one thousand five hundred dollars.

"4. In all other cases aggravated criminal damage is a class 1 misdemeanor."

§ 13–1818. Misappropriation of charter school monies; violation; classification

A. A person commits misappropriation of charter school monies if without lawful authority and with an intent to defraud the person converts monies provided by this state under a charter school contract in a manner that does not further the purposes of the charter and is not reasonably related to the business of the charter school.

B. A violation of subsection A is a class 4 felony, except that if the amount of monies converted is twenty-five thousand dollars or more a violation of subsection A is a class 2 felony.

Added as § 13–1816 by Laws 2000, Ch. 90, § 1. Renumbered as § 13–1818.

Historical and Statutory Notes

Reviser's Notes:

2000 Note. Pursuant to authority of § 41–1304.02, this section, added by Laws 2000, Ch. 90, sec. 1 as § 13–1816, was renumbered as § 13–1818.

§ 13–2905. Loitering; classification

A. A person commits loitering if such person intentionally:

1. Is present in a public place and in an offensive manner or in a manner likely to disturb the public peace solicits another person to engage in any sexual offense; or

2. Is present in a transportation facility and after a reasonable request to cease or unless specifically authorized to do so solicits or engages in any business, trade or commercial transactions involving the sale of merchandise or services; or

3. Is present in a public place to beg, unless specifically authorized by law; or

4. Is present in a public place, unless specifically authorized by law, to gamble with any cards, dice or other similar gambling devices; or

5. Is present in or about a school, college or university building or grounds after a reasonable request to leave and either does not have any reason or relationship involving custody of or responsibility for a pupil or student or any other specific legitimate reason for being there or does not have written permission to be there from anyone authorized to grant permission.

B. Loitering under subsection A, paragraph 5 is a class 1 misdemeanor. Loitering under subsection A, paragraphs 1, 2, 3 and 4 is a class 3 misdemeanor.

Added by Laws 1977, Ch. 142, § 91, eff. Oct. 1, 1978. Amended by Laws 1978, Ch. 201, § 171, eff. Oct. 1, 1978; Laws 1981, Ch. 264, § 7, eff. Sept. 1, 1981; Laws 1987, Ch. 307, § 12; Laws 1988, Ch. 194, § 1.

Historical and Statutory Notes

Source:

Pen.Code 1901, § 599.
Pen.Code 1913, § 693.
Rev.Code 1928, § 4868.
Code 1939, § 43-5901.
Laws 1939, Ch. 13, § 1.
Laws 1951, Ch. 111, § 1.
Code 1939, Supp.1952, § 43-5902.
A.R.S. former §§ 13-991 to 13-993.
Laws 1965, Ch. 20, § 4.
Laws 1972, Ch. 162, § 2.

Adopted from California, see West's Ann.Pen. Code § 647.

Laws 1978, Ch. 201, § 171 added the phrase "after a reasonable request to leave" to par. 6 of subsec. A.

The 1981 amendment substituted "marijuana" for "cannabis or" in par. 3 of subsec. A.

For conditional enactment provision of Laws 1981, Ch. 264 and information as to occurrence of the condition, see Historical and Statutory Notes preceding § 13-3401.

The 1987 amendment inserted at the beginning of par. 3 of subsec. A the exception pertaining to § 13-3411.

The 1988 amendment, in subsec. A, deleted former par. 3, which read:

"Except as provided in § 13-3411, is present in a public place with one or more persons to unlawfully possess, use or sell marijuana, dangerous drugs or narcotic drugs; or";

redesignated former subds. (4) to (6) as subds. (3) to (5); and, in subsec. B, deleted a sentence, which read: "Loitering under subsection A, paragraph 3 is a class 6 felony."

Reviser's Notes:

1988 Note. The substance of the amendments made by Laws 1988, Ch. 194, sec. 1 was not reflected in the title to this act as required by Constitution of Arizona Art. IV, part 2, § 13.

§ 13-2911. Interference with or disruption of an educational institution; violation; classification; definitions

A. A person commits interference with or disruption of an educational institution by doing any of the following:

1. Intentionally, knowingly or recklessly interfering with or disrupting the normal operations of an educational institution by either:

(a) Threatening to cause physical injury to any employee or student of an educational institution or any person on the property of an educational institution.

(b) Threatening to cause damage to any educational institution, the property of any educational institution or the property of any employee or student of an educational institution.

2. Intentionally or knowingly entering or remaining on the property of any educational institution for the purpose of interfering with the lawful use of the property or in any manner as to deny or interfere with the lawful use of the property by others.

3. Intentionally or knowingly refusing to obey a lawful order given pursuant to subsection C of this section.

B. To constitute a violation of this section, the acts that are prohibited by subsection A, paragraph 1 of this section are not required to be directed at a specific individual, a specific educational institution or any specific property of an educational institution.

C. The chief administrative officer of an educational institution or an officer or employee designated by the chief administrative officer to maintain order may order a person to leave the property of the educational institution if the officer or employee has reasonable grounds to believe either that:

1. Any person or persons are committing any act that interferes with or disrupts the lawful use of the property by others at the educational institution.

2. Any person has entered on the property of an educational institution for the purpose of committing any act that interferes with or disrupts the lawful use of the property by others at the educational institution.

D. The appropriate governing board of every educational institution shall adopt rules pursuant to title 41, chapter 6 [1] for the maintenance of public order on all property of any educational institution under its jurisdiction that is used for educational purposes and shall provide a program for the enforcement of its rules. The rules shall govern the conduct of students, faculty and other staff and all members of the public while on the property of the educational institution. Penalties for violations of the rules shall be clearly set forth and enforced. Penalties shall include provisions for the ejection of a violator from the property and, in the case of a student, faculty member or other staff violator, the violator's suspension or expulsion or any other appropriate disciplinary action. A governing board shall amend its rules as necessary to ensure the maintenance of public order. Any deadly weapon, dangerous instrument or explosive that is used, displayed or possessed by a person in violation of a rule adopted pursuant to this subsection shall be forfeited and sold, destroyed or otherwise disposed of pursuant to chapter 39 of this title.[2] This subsection does not do either of the following:

1. Preclude school districts from conducting approved gun safety programs on school campuses.

2. Apply to private universities, colleges, high schools or common schools or other private educational institutions.

E. An educational institution is not eligible to receive any state aid or assistance unless rules are adopted in accordance with this section.

F. This section does not prevent or limit the authority of the governing board of any educational institution to discharge any employee or expel, suspend or otherwise punish any student for any violation of its rules, even though the violation is unlawful under this chapter or is otherwise an offense.

G. This section may be enforced by any peace officer in this state wherever and whenever a violation occurs.

H. Restitution under §§ 8-341, 8-345 and 13-603 applies to any financial loss that is suffered by a person or educational institution as a result of a violation of this section.

I. Interference with or disruption of an educational institution pursuant to subsection A, paragraph 1 of this section is a class 6 felony. Interference with or disruption of an educational institution pursuant to subsection A, paragraph 2 or 3 of this section is a class 1 misdemeanor.

J. For the purposes of this section:

1. "Educational institution" means, except as otherwise provided, any university, college, community college, high school or common school in this state.

2. "Governing board" means the body, whether appointed or elected, that has responsibility for the maintenance and government of an educational institution.

3. "Interference with or disruption of" includes any act that might reasonably lead to the evacuation or closure of any property of the educational institution or the postponement, cancellation or suspension of any class or other school activity. For the purposes of this paragraph, an actual evacuation, closure, postponement, cancellation or suspension is not required for the act to be considered an interference or disruption.

4. "Property of an educational institution" means all land, buildings and other facilities that are owned, operated or controlled by the governing board of an educational institution and that are devoted to educational purposes.

Added by Laws 1977, Ch. 142, § 91, eff. Oct. 1, 1978. Amended by Laws 1986, Ch. 232, § 25, eff. Jan. 1, 1987; Laws 1989, Ch. 196, § 1; Laws 2000, Ch. 226, § 1, eff. April 10, 2000; Laws 2002, Ch. 181, § 3.

[1] Section 41-1001 et seq.

[2] Section 13-4301 et seq.

Historical and Statutory Notes

Source:

Pen.Code 1901, § 607.
Pen.Code 1913, § 697.
Rev.Code 1928, § 4870.
Code 1939, § 43-1309.
A.R.S. former §§ 13-374, 13-1091 to 13-1094.
Laws 1970, Ch. 222, § 2.

Laws 1977, Ch. 142, § 185 provides:

"**Sec. 185. Exemption**

"Governing boards of educational institutions which have rules and regulations for the maintenance of public order upon property under such governing board's jurisdiction in effect on the date of this act shall be exempt from the provisions of § 13-2911, subsections C and D."

The 2000 amendment by Ch. 226 rewrote the section, which prior thereto read:

"**A.** A person commits interference with the peaceful conduct of educational institutions by knowingly:

"1. Going upon or remaining upon the property of any educational institution in violation of any rule of such institution or for the purpose of interfering with the lawful use of such property by others or in such manner as to deny or interfere with the lawful use of such property by others; or

"2. Refusing to obey a lawful order given pursuant to subsection B of this section.

"**B.** When the chief administrative officer of an educational institution or an officer or employee designated by him to maintain order has reasonable grounds to believe that any person or persons are committing any act which interferes with or disrupts the lawful use of such property by others at the educational institution or has reasonable grounds to believe any person has entered upon the property for the purpose of committing such an act, such officer or employee may order such person to leave the property of the educational institution.

"**C.** The appropriate governing board of every educational institution shall adopt rules for the maintenance of public order upon all property under its jurisdiction which is used for educational purposes and shall provide a program for the enforcement of such rules. Such rules shall govern the conduct of students, faculty and other staff and all members of the public while on the property. Penalties for violations of such rules shall be clearly set forth and enforced. Penalties shall include provisions for the ejection of a violator from the property and, in the case of a student, faculty member or other staff violator, his suspension, expulsion or other appropriate disciplinary action. Adoption of all rules required by this section shall be governed by title 41, chapter 6, and such rules shall be amended as necessary to ensure the maintenance of public order. Any deadly weapon, dangerous instrument or explosive used, displayed or possessed by a person in violation of a rule adopted pursuant to this subsection shall be forfeited and sold, destroyed, or otherwise disposed of according to chapter

39 of this title. Nothing in this subsection shall preclude school districts from conducting approved gun safety programs on school campuses. This subsection shall not apply to private universities, colleges, high schools or common schools or other private educational institutions.

"**D.** No educational institution shall be eligible to receive any state aid or assistance unless rules are adopted in accordance with this section.

"**E.** No provision in this section shall prevent or limit the authority of the governing board of any educational institution to discharge any employee or expel, suspend or otherwise punish any student for violation of its rules, even though such violation is unlawful under this chapter or is otherwise an offense.

"**F.** The provisions of this section may be enforced by any peace officer in the state wherever and whenever a violation occurs.

"**G.** For the purposes of this section:

"1. "Educational institution" means, except as otherwise provided, any university, college, community college, high school or common school in this state.

"2. "Governing board" means the body, whether appointed or elected, which has responsibility for the maintenance and government of an educational institution.

"3. "Property" means all land, buildings and other facilities owned, operated or controlled by the governing board of an educational institution and devoted to educational purposes.

"**H.** Interference with the peaceful conduct of educational institutions is a class 1 misdemeanor."

The 2002 amendment by Ch. 181 rewrote the section, which had read:

"**A.** A person commits interference with or disruption of an educational institution by doing any of the following:

"1. For the purpose of causing, or in reckless disregard of causing, interference with or disruption of an educational institution, threatening to cause physical injury to any employee of an educational institution or any person attending an educational institution.

"2. For the purpose of causing, or in reckless disregard of causing, interference with or disruption of an educational institution, threatening to cause damage to any educational institution, the property of any educational institution, the property of any employee of an educational institution or the property of any person attending an educational institution.

"3. Knowingly going on or remaining on the property of any educational institution for the purpose of interfering with or disrupting the lawful use of the property or in any manner as to deny or interfere with the lawful use of the property by others.

"4. Knowingly refusing to obey a lawful order given pursuant to subsection C of this section.

"**B.** To constitute a violation of this section, the acts that are prohibited by subsection A, paragraph 1 or 2 of this section are not required to be directed at a specific individual, a specific educational institution or any specific property of an educational institution.

"**C.** When The chief administrative officer of an educational institution or an officer or employee designated by him to maintain order has reasonable grounds to believe that any person or persons are committing any act that interferes with or disrupts the lawful use of the property by others at the educational institution or has reasonable grounds to believe any person has entered on the property of an educational institution for the purpose of committing such an act, the officer or employee may order the person to leave the property of the educational institution.

"**D.** The appropriate governing board of every educational institution shall adopt rules for the maintenance of public order on all property of any educational institution under its jurisdiction that is used for educational purposes and shall provide a program for the enforcement of its rules. The rules shall govern the conduct of students, faculty and other staff and all members of the public while on the property of the educational institution. Penalties for violations of the rules shall be clearly set forth and enforced. Penalties shall include provisions for the ejection of a violator from the property and, in the case of a student, faculty member or other staff violator, the violator's suspension, expulsion or other appropriate disciplinary action. Adoption of all rules required by this section shall be governed by title 41, chapter 6, and the rules shall be amended as necessary to ensure the maintenance of public order. Any deadly weapon, dangerous instrument or explosive that is used, displayed or possessed by a person in violation of a rule adopted pursuant to this subsection shall be forfeited and sold, destroyed or otherwise disposed of pursuant to chapter 39 of this title. This subsection does not preclude school districts from conducting approved gun safety programs on school campuses. This subsection does not apply to private universities, colleges, high schools or common schools or other private educational institutions.

"**E.** An educational institution is not eligible to receive any state aid or assistance unless rules are adopted in accordance with this section.

"**F.** This section does not prevent or limit the authority of the governing board of any educational institution to discharge any employee or expel, suspend or otherwise punish any student for any violation of its rules, even though the violation is unlawful under this chapter or is otherwise an offense.

"**G.** This section may be enforced by any peace officer in this state wherever and whenever a violation occurs.

"**H.** Restitution under §§ 8-341, 8-345 and 13-603 applies to any financial loss that is suffered by a person or educational institution as a result of a violation of this section.

"**I.** Interference with or disruption of an educational institution pursuant to subsection A, paragraph 1 or 2 of this section is a class 6 felony. Interference with or disruption of an educational institution pursuant to subsection A, paragraph 3 or 4 of this section is a class 1 misdemeanor.

"**J.** For the purposes of this section:

"1. 'Educational institution' means, except as otherwise provided, any university, college, community college, high school or common school in this state.

"2. 'Governing board' means the body, whether appointed or elected, that has responsibility for the maintenance and government of an educational institution.

"3. 'Interference with or disruption of' includes causing an employee of an educational institution to take any action to protect the educational institution, or the employees, students or property of an educational institution.

"4. 'Property of an educational institution' means all land, buildings and other facilities that are owned, operated or controlled by the governing board of an educational institution and that are devoted to educational purposes."

§ 13-2917. Public nuisance; abatement; classification

A. It is a public nuisance, and is no less a nuisance because the extent of the annoyance or damage inflicted is unequal, for anything:

1. To be injurious to health, indecent, offensive to the senses or an obstruction to the free use of property that interferes with the comfortable enjoyment of life or property by an entire community or neighborhood or by a considerable number of persons.

2. To unlawfully obstruct the free passage or use, in the customary manner, of any navigable lake, river, bay, stream, canal or basin, or any public park, square, street or highway.

B. It is a public nuisance for any person to sell, offer to sell, transfer, trade or disseminate any item which is obscene as defined in § 13-3501, within two thousand feet, measured in a straight line, of the nearest boundary line of any of the following:

1. Any building used as a private or public elementary or high school.

2. Any public park.

3. Any residence district as defined in § 28-101.

C. The county attorney, the attorney general or the city attorney may bring an action in superior court to abate, enjoin and prevent the activity described in subsections A and B of this section.

D. Any person who knowingly maintains or commits a public nuisance or who knowingly fails or refuses to perform any legal duty relating to the removal of a public nuisance is guilty of a class 2 misdemeanor.

Formerly § 13-601. Amended by Laws 1976, Ch. 159, § 5, eff. June 27, 1976. Renumbered as § 13-2917 and amended by Laws 1978, Ch. 201, §§ 173, 179, eff. Oct. 1, 1978. Amended by Laws 1999, Ch. 261, § 22.

Historical and Statutory Notes

The 1976 amendment added par. B.

The 1978 amendment substituted "§ 13–3501" for "§ 13–531.01" in par. B and added par. C.

The 1999 amendment by Ch. 261 rewrote the section, which had read:

"**A.** Anything which is injurious to health, or is indecent, or offensive to the senses, or an obstruction to the free use of property, so as to interfere with the comfortable enjoyment of life or property by an entire community or neighborhood, or by a considerable number of persons, or which unlawfully obstructs the free passage or use, in the customary manner, of any navigable lake, river, bay, stream, canal or basin, or any public park, square, street or highway, is a public nuisance, and is no less a nuisance because the extent of the annoyance or damage inflicted is unequal.

"**B.** It is a public nuisance for any person to sell, offer to sell, transfer, trade or disseminate any item which is obscene as defined by § 13–3501, within two thousand feet, measured in a straight line, of the nearest boundary line of any building used as a private or public elementary or high school, of any public park, or of any residence district as defined by § 28–101.

"**C.** Any person who knowingly maintains or commits a public nuisance or who knowingly fails or refuses to perform any legal duty relating to the removal of a public nuisance is guilty of a class 2 misdemeanor."

Reviser's Notes:

1978 Note. Pursuant to authority of § 41–1304.02, "; classification" was added to the heading of this section.

§ 13–3102. Misconduct involving weapons; defenses; classification; definitions

A. A person commits misconduct involving weapons by knowingly:

1. Carrying a deadly weapon without a permit pursuant to § 13–3112 except a pocket knife concealed on his person; or

2. Carrying a deadly weapon without a permit pursuant to § 13–3112 concealed within immediate control of any person in or on a means of transportation; or

3. Manufacturing, possessing, transporting, selling or transferring a prohibited weapon; or

4. Possessing a deadly weapon or prohibited weapon if such person is a prohibited possessor; or

5. Selling or transferring a deadly weapon to a prohibited possessor; or

6. Defacing a deadly weapon; or

7. Possessing a defaced deadly weapon knowing the deadly weapon was defaced; or

8. Using or possessing a deadly weapon during the commission of any felony offense included in chapter 34 of this title; [1] or

9. Discharging a firearm at an occupied structure in order to assist, promote or further the interests of a criminal street gang, a criminal syndicate or a racketeering enterprise; or

10. Unless specifically authorized by law, entering any public establishment or attending any public event and carrying a deadly weapon on his person after a reasonable request by the operator of the establishment or the sponsor of the event or the sponsor's agent to remove his weapon and place it in the custody of the operator of the establishment or the sponsor of the event; or

11. Unless specifically authorized by law, entering an election polling place on the day of any election carrying a deadly weapon; or

12. Possessing a deadly weapon on school grounds; or

13. Unless specifically authorized by law, entering a nuclear or hydroelectric generating station carrying a deadly weapon on his person or within the immediate control of any person; or

14. Supplying, selling or giving possession or control of a firearm to another person if the person knows or has reason to know that the other person would use the firearm in the commission of any felony; or

15. Using, possessing or exercising control over a deadly weapon in furtherance of any act of terrorism as defined in § 13-2301 or possessing or exercising control over a deadly weapon knowing or having reason to know that it will be used to facilitate any act of terrorism as defined in § 13-2301.

B. Subsection A, paragraph 1 of this section shall not apply to a person in his dwelling, on his business premises or on real property owned or leased by that person.

C. Subsection A, paragraphs 1, 2, 3, 7, 10, 11, 12 and 13 of this section shall not apply to:

1. A peace officer or any person summoned by any peace officer to assist and while actually assisting in the performance of official duties; or

2. A member of the military forces of the United States or of any state of the United States in the performance of official duties; or

3. A warden, deputy warden or correctional officer of the state department of corrections; or

4. A person specifically licensed, authorized or permitted pursuant to a statute of this state or of the United States.

D. Subsection A, paragraphs 3 and 7 of this section shall not apply to:

1. The possessing, transporting, selling or transferring of weapons by a museum as a part of its collection or an educational institution for educational purposes or by an authorized employee of such museum or institution, if:

(a) Such museum or institution is operated by the United States or this state or a political subdivision of this state, or by an organization described in § 170(c) of title 26 of the United States Code as a recipient of a charitable contribution; and

(b) Reasonable precautions are taken with respect to theft or misuse of such material.

2. The regular and lawful transporting as merchandise; or

3. Acquisition by a person by operation of law such as by gift, devise or descent or in a fiduciary capacity as a recipient of the property or former property of an insolvent, incapacitated or deceased person.

E. Subsection A, paragraph 3 of this section shall not apply to the merchandise of an authorized manufacturer of or dealer in prohibited weapons, when such material is intended to be manufactured, possessed, transported, sold or transferred solely for or to a dealer, a regularly constituted or appointed state, county or municipal police department or police officer, a detention facility, the military service of this or another state or the United States, a museum or educational institution or a person specifically licensed or permitted pursuant to federal or state law.

F. Subsection A, paragraph 1 of this section shall not apply to a weapon or weapons carried in a belt holster which holster is wholly or partially visible, or carried in a scabbard or case designed for carrying weapons which scabbard or case is wholly or partially visible or carried in luggage. Subsection A, paragraph 2 of this section shall not apply to a weapon or weapons carried in a case, holster, scabbard, pack or luggage that is carried within a means of transportation or within a storage compartment, trunk or glove compartment of a means of transportation.

G. Subsection A, paragraph 10 of this section shall not apply to shooting ranges or shooting events, hunting areas or similar locations or activities.

H. Subsection A, paragraph 3 of this section shall not apply to a weapon described in § 13-3101, subsection A, paragraph 7, subdivision (e), if such weapon is possessed for the purposes of preparing for, conducting or participating in lawful exhibitions, demonstrations, contests or athletic events involving the use of such weapon. Subsection A, paragraph 12 of this section shall not apply to a weapon if such weapon is possessed for the purposes of preparing for, conducting or participating in hunter or firearm safety courses.

I. Subsection A, paragraph 12 of this section shall not apply to the possession of a:

1. Firearm that is not loaded and that is carried within a means of transportation under the control of an adult provided that if the adult leaves the means of transportation the firearm shall not be visible from the outside of the means of transportation and the means of transportation shall be locked.

2. Firearm for use on the school grounds in a program approved by a school.

J. Misconduct involving weapons under subsection A, paragraph 9, 14 or 15 of this section is a class 3 felony. Misconduct involving weapons under subsection A, paragraph 3, 4, 8 or 13 of this section is a class 4 felony. Misconduct involving weapons under subsection A, paragraph 12 of this section is a class 1 misdemeanor unless the violation occurs in connection with conduct which violates the provisions of § 13-2308, subsection A, paragraph 5, § 13-2312, subsection C, § 13-3409 or § 13-3411, in which case the offense is a class 6 felony. Misconduct involving weapons under subsection A, paragraph 5, 6 or 7 of this section is a class 6 felony. Misconduct involving weapons under subsection A, paragraph 1, 2, 10 or 11 of this section is a class 1 misdemeanor.

K. For the purposes of this section:

1. "Public establishment" means a structure, vehicle or craft that is owned, leased or operated by this state or a political subdivision of this state.

2. "Public event" means a specifically named or sponsored event of limited duration either conducted by a public entity or conducted by a private entity with a permit or license granted by a public entity. Public event does not include an unsponsored gathering of people in a public place.

3. "School" means a public or nonpublic kindergarten program, common school or high school.

4. "School grounds" means in, or on the grounds of, a school.

Added by Laws 1977, Ch. 142, § 94, eff. Oct. 1, 1978. Amended by Laws 1978, Ch. 201, § 195, eff. Oct. 1, 1978; Laws 1980, Ch. 229, § 30, eff. April 23, 1980; Laws 1982, Ch. 238, § 5; Laws 1984, Ch. 261, § 2; Laws 1990, Ch. 366, § 5; Laws 1991, Ch. 237, § 1; Laws 1991, Ch. 316, § 3, eff. July 3, 1991; Laws 1992, Ch. 319, § 2; Laws 1993, Ch. 228, § 1; Laws 1994, Ch. 109, § 1; Laws 1994, Ch. 200, § 19, eff. April 19, 1994; Laws 1997, Ch. 136, § 17; Laws 2000, Ch. 376, § 1; Laws 2002, Ch. 219, § 18; Laws 2004, Ch. 134, § 2.

[1] Section 13-3401 et seq.

Historical and Statutory Notes

Source:

Pen.Code 1901, §§ 382 to 384, 387, 427.
Pen.Code 1913, §§ 426 to 429, 467.
Rev.Code 1928, §§ 4616, 4724, 4725.
Code 1939, §§ 43-2201, 43-2205, 43-2206.
Laws 1953, Ch. 116, §§ 1 to 3.
Code 1939, Supp.1953, §§ 43-2210, 43-2211, 43-2212.
A.R.S. former §§ 13-911 to 13-913, 13-915, 13-919.
Laws 1970, Ch. 166, § 2.
Laws 1976, Ch. 157, § 2.

The 1978 amendment renumbered former subsec. H as subsec. I, added a new subsec. H, and made certain clerical changes.

The 1980 amendment inserted "of this section" throughout the section.

The 1982 amendment made a conforming change in the statutory citation in subsec. H.

The 1984 amendment rewrote subsec. I, which had read:

"Misconduct involving weapons under paragraphs 3 through 7 of subsection A of this section is a class 6 felony. Misconduct involving weapons under paragraphs 1, 2, 8 and 9 of subsection A of this section is a class 1 misdemeanor."

The 1990 amendment, in subsec. A, inserted par. 8, and renumbered former pars. 8 and 9 as pars. 9 and 10; in subsec. B, inserted "on his" following "dwelling,"; in subsec. C, substituted "9 and 10" for "8 and 9" following "7," in the introduction; in subsec. G, substituted "9" for "8" following "paragraph"; and in subsec. I, inserted "or 8" following "3" in the first sentence, and "9 and 10" for "8 and 9" following "2," in the second sentence.

The 1991 amendment by Ch. 237 inserted par. 11 in subsec. A; substituted "paragraphs 1, 2, 3, 7, 9, 10 and 11" for "paragraphs 1, 2, 3, 7, 9 and 10" in the introductory paragraph of subsec. C; substituted "case, holster, scabbard, pack or luggage which are carried within a means of transportation or within a storage compartment, trunk or glove compartment" for "case, holster or scabbard in a means of transportation or a storage compartment, trunk, pack, luggage, or glove compartment" in subsec. F; inserted the second sentence in subsec. H; inserted a new subsec. I; redesignated existing subsec. I as subsec. J; and added subsec. K.

The 1991 amendment by Ch. 316 inserted par. 9 of subsec. A and redesignated former pars. 9 and 10 as pars. 10 and 11 accordingly; inserted the first sentence of subsec. I classifying misconduct involving weapons as a class 3 felony; and made nonsubstantive changes.

The amendment of this section made by Laws 1991, Ch. 316, § 3 was repealed by Laws 1992, Ch. 319, § 3.

The 1992 amendment, by Ch. 319, a corrections bill, made changes identical to those made by Laws 1991, Ch. 316 amendment.

The 1992 amendment of this section by Ch. 319 explicitly amended the 1991 amendment of this section by Ch. 237.

Laws 1992, Ch. 319, § 1, par. 1, provides:

"Section 1. Purpose

"1. Section 13-3102, Arizona Revised Statutes, was amended by Laws 1991, chapter 237, § 1 and Laws 1991, chapter 316, § 3. These two versions could not be blended because the chapter 316 version failed to conform an internal reference in subsection C. To accomplish the intent of these enactments, in this act the Laws 1991, chapter 237 version of § 13-3102, Arizona Revised Statutes, is amended to conform the internal reference in subsection C and to incorporate the amendments made by Laws 1991, chapter 316 and the chapter 316 version is repealed."

The 1993 amendment, in subsec. F, substituted "is" for "are" following "luggage which" in the second sentence; in subsec. H, substituted "paragraph 7" for "paragraph 6" following "§ 13-3101"; in subsec. I, rewrote par. 1 and deleted par. 3; and in subsec. J, inserted the second sentence and substituted "paragraphs 1, 2, 10 and 11" for " paragraphs 1, 2, 10, 11 and

12" following "weapons under subsection A" in the last sentence.

Prior to the 1993 amendment, pars. 1 and 3 of subsec. I read, respectively:

"1. Firearm which is not loaded and which is carried in a locked container within a means of transportation which is not under the control of a pupil."

"3. Weapon or weapons carried within a means of transportation when a pupil is being transported to or from school grounds by a parent, guardian, or person, other than the pupil, who is authorized to transport the pupil to or from school grounds."

The 1994 amendment by Ch. 109 inserted in pars. 1 and 2 "without a permit pursuant to § 13–3112" and added par. 13 in subsec. A, added reference to new par. 13 in subsecs. C and J, and inserted "and which is" preceding "carried" in par. 1 of subsec. I.

The 1994 amendment by Ch. 200 deleted at the end of subsec. A par. 9 "when such conduct does not result in the death or physical injury of another person", inserted a new subsec. B and redesignated subsequent subsections accordingly, and in subsec. K substituted "paragraphs 5, 6 and 7" for "paragraphs 4 through 7".

The 1997 amendment by Ch. 136 redesignated former subsec. B as subsec. A, par. 14; redesignated former subsecs. C to L as B to K, accordingly; in newly designated subsec. C inserted new par. 3 and redesignated former par. 3 as par. 4; and made other nonsubstantive changes.

The 2000 amendment by Ch. 376 inserted, in subsec. K, pars. 1 and 2 defining "public establishment" and "public event"; and redesignated former pars. 1 and 2 of subsec. K as pars. 2 and 3.

The 2002 amendment by Ch. 219, substituted "nuclear or hydroelectric generating station" for "commercial nuclear generating station" in subsec. A, par. 13; inserted subsec. A, par. 15; and modified internal references in subsec. J.

The 2004 amendment by Ch. 134, made nonsubstantive changes to subsecs. E and K.

Reviser's Notes:

1991 Note. Pursuant to authority of § 41–1304.02, in the section heading "; definitions" was added after "classification".

1991 Note. The amendment made by Laws 1991, Ch. 316, sec. 3 was inconsistent and incompatible with Laws 1991, Ch. 237, sec. 1 and therefore could not be blended.

1993 Note. In the chapter version in subsection I, paragraph 3, "(a)" was shown as stricken instead of removed pursuant to amendment instructions.

1994 Note. Prior to the 1997 amendment, this section contained the amendments made by Laws 1994, Ch. 109, sec. 1 and Ch. 200, sec. 19 that were blended together pursuant to authority of § 41–1304.03.

2000 Note. Pursuant to authority of § 41–1304.02, quotation marks were removed at the end of subsection K, paragraph 4 to correct a manifest clerical error.

§ 13–3107. Unlawful discharge of firearms; exceptions; classification; definitions

A. A person who with criminal negligence discharges a firearm within or into the limits of any municipality is guilty of a class 6 felony.

B. Notwithstanding the fact that the offense involves the discharge of a deadly weapon, unless the dangerous nature of the felony is charged and proven pursuant to § 13–604, subsection P, the provisions of § 13–702, subsection G apply to this offense.

C. This section does not apply if the firearm is discharged:

1. As allowed pursuant to the provisions of chapter 4 of this title. [1]

2. On a properly supervised range.

3. In an area recommended as a hunting area by the Arizona game and fish department, approved and posted as required by the chief of police, but any such area may be closed when deemed unsafe by the chief of police or the director of the game and fish department.

4. For the control of nuisance wildlife by permit from the Arizona game and fish department or the United States fish and wildlife service.

5. By special permit of the chief of police of the municipality.

6. As required by an animal control officer in the performance of duties as specified in § 9-499.04.

7. Using blanks.

8. More than one mile from any occupied structure as defined in § 13-3101.

9. In self-defense or defense of another person against an animal attack if a reasonable person would believe that deadly physical force against the animal is immediately necessary and reasonable under the circumstances to protect oneself or the other person.

D. For the purposes of this section:

1. "Municipality" means any city or town and includes any property that is fully enclosed within the city or town.

2. "Properly supervised range" means a range that is operated:

(a) By a club affiliated with the national rifle association of America, the amateur trapshooting association, the national skeet association or any other nationally recognized shooting organization, or by any public or private school, or

(b) Approved by any agency of the federal government, this state, a county or city within which the range is located or

(c) With adult supervision for shooting air or carbon dioxide gas operated guns, or for shooting in underground ranges on private or public property. Added as § 13-917.01 by Laws 1962, Ch. 104, § 2. Renumbered as § 13-3107 by Laws 1977, Ch. 142, § 95, eff. Oct. 1, 1978. Amended by Laws 1978, Ch. 201, § 196, eff. Oct. 1, 1978; Laws 1980, Ch. 13, § 2, eff. March 17, 1980; Laws 2000, Ch. 119, § 1.

[1] Section 13-401 et seq.

Historical and Statutory Notes

The 1978 amendment deleted 2 exceptions (self defense and defense of property) to the prohibition of the discharge of firearms in municipalities, added the exception set out in par. 1 of subsec. A, made violation a class 2 misdemeanor, and deleted former subsec. C which defined "firearm".

The 1980 amendment inserted par. 6 in subsec. A.

The 2000 amendment by Ch. 119 rewrote the section, which had read:

"**A.** Discharge of a firearm within the limits of any municipality is a class 2 misdemeanor except:

"1. As allowed pursuant to the provisions of chapter 4 of this title.

"2. On a properly supervised range.

"3. In an area recommended as a hunting area by the Arizona game and fish department, approved and posted as required by the chief of police, but any such area may be closed when deemed unsafe by the chief of police or the director of the game and fish department.

"4. For the control of nuisance wildlife by permit from the Arizona game and fish department or the United States fish and wildlife service.

"5. By special permit of the chief of police of the municipality.

"6. As required by an animal control officer in the performance of duties as specified in § 9-499.04.

"**B.** A properly supervised range for the purposes of this section means a range operated by a club affiliated with the national rifle association of America, the amateur trapshooting association, the national skeet association, or any other nationally recognized shooting organization, any agency of the federal government, state of Arizona, county or city within which the range is located, or any public or private school, and, in the case of air or carbon dioxide gas operated guns, or underground ranges on private or public property, such ranges may be operated with adult supervision."

Laws 2000, Ch. 119, § 2, provides:

"**Sec. 2. Short title**

"This act shall be known and may be cited as 'Shannon's Law' ".

Reviser's Notes:

1980 Note. In the section heading, the comma after "hunting" was deleted, pursuant to authority of § 41–1304.02.

2000 Note. In subsection A an existing colon is shown after "~~except~~" even though the sentence ends with a period. Pursuant to authority of § 41–1304.02, in the chapter version the colon is shown as stricken to correct a manifest clerical error and in subsection C, paragraph 9 the spelling of "self-defense" was corrected.

§ 13–3111. Minors prohibited from carrying or possessing firearms; exceptions; seizure and forfeiture; penalties; classification

A. Except as provided in subsection B, an unemancipated person who is under eighteen years of age and who is unaccompanied by a parent, grandparent or guardian, or a certified hunter safety instructor or certified firearms safety instructor acting with the consent of the unemancipated person's parent or guardian, shall not knowingly carry or possess on his person, within his immediate control, or in or on a means of transportation a firearm in any place that is open to the public or on any street or highway or on any private property except private property owned or leased by the minor or the minor's parent, grandparent or guardian.

B. This section does not apply to a person who is fourteen, fifteen, sixteen or seventeen years of age and who is any of the following:

1. Engaged in lawful hunting or shooting events or marksmanship practice at established ranges or other areas where the discharge of a firearm is not prohibited.

2. Engaged in lawful transportation of an unloaded firearm for the purpose of lawful hunting.

3. Engaged in lawful transportation of an unloaded firearm between the hours of 5:00 a.m. and 10:00 p.m. for the purpose of shooting events or marksmanship practice at established ranges or other areas where the discharge of a firearm is not prohibited.

4. Engaged in activities requiring the use of a firearm that are related to the production of crops, livestock, poultry, livestock products, poultry products or ratites or in the production or storage of agricultural commodities.

C. If the minor is not exempt under subsection B and is in possession of a firearm, a peace officer shall seize the firearm at the time the violation occurs.

D. In addition to any other penalty provided by law a person who violates subsection A shall be subject to the following penalties:

1. If adjudicated a delinquent juvenile for an offense involving an unloaded firearm, a fine of not more than two hundred fifty dollars, and the court may order the suspension or revocation of the person's driver license until the person reaches eighteen years of age. If the person does not have a driver license at the time of the adjudication, the court may direct that the department of transportation not issue a driver license to the person until the person reaches eighteen years of age.

2. If adjudicated a delinquent juvenile for an offense involving a loaded firearm, a fine of not more than five hundred dollars, and the court may order the suspension or revocation of the person's driver license until the person reaches eighteen years of age. If the person does not have a driver license at

the time of the adjudication, the court may direct that the department of transportation not issue a driver license to the person until the person reaches eighteen years of age.

3. If adjudicated a delinquent juvenile for an offense involving a loaded or unloaded firearm, if the person possessed the firearm while the person was the driver or an occupant of a motor vehicle, a fine of not more than five hundred dollars and the court shall order the suspension or revocation of the person's driver license until the person reaches eighteen years of age. If the person does not have a driver license at the time of adjudication, the court shall direct that the department of transportation not issue a driver license to the person until the person reaches eighteen years of age. If the court finds that no other means of transportation is available, the driving privileges of the child may be restricted to travel between the child's home, school and place of employment during specified periods of time according to the child's school and employment schedule.

E. Firearms seized pursuant to subsection C shall be held by the law enforcement agency responsible for the seizure until the charges have been adjudicated or disposed of otherwise or the person is convicted. Upon adjudication or conviction of a person for a violation of this section, the court shall order the firearm forfeited. However, the law enforcement agency shall return the firearm to the lawful owner if the identity of that person is known.

F. If the court finds that the parent or guardian of a minor found responsible for violating this section knew or reasonably should have known of the minor's unlawful conduct and made no effort to prohibit it, the parent or guardian is jointly and severally responsible for any fine imposed pursuant to this section or for any civil actual damages resulting from the unlawful use of the firearm by the minor.

G. This section is supplemental to any other law imposing a criminal penalty for the use or exhibition of a deadly weapon. A minor who violates this section may be prosecuted and convicted for any other criminal conduct involving the use or exhibition of the deadly weapon.

H. This section applies only in counties with populations of more than five hundred thousand persons according to the most recent decennial census. Counties with populations of five hundred thousand persons or less according to the most recent decennial census, or cities or towns within those counties, may adopt an ordinance identical to this section.

I. A person who violates subsection A is guilty of a class 6 felony.

Added by Laws 1993, Ch. 259, § 1. Amended by Laws 1994, Ch. 109, § 3; Laws 1994, Ch. 201, § 17; Laws 1997, Ch. 136, § 18; Laws 1997, Ch. 222, § 63, eff. July 1, 1998.

Historical and Statutory Notes

Laws 1993, Ch. 259, § 2, provides:

"**Sec. 2. Findings and intent**

"**A.** The legislature finds that:

"1. The overwhelming majority of minors in this state who keep and bear arms do so responsibly and in a law-abiding manner under the supervision of parents or guardians.

"2. A minute number of juvenile offenders disproportionately threaten the public peace through their unlawful use or threatening exhibition of deadly weapons or dangerous instruments.

"3. A minority of parents or guardians have not exercised appropriate authority over or responsibility for their minor's possession of firearms.

"4. The subject of minors carrying, possessing or transporting firearms is a matter of statewide concern and that state law must continue to preempt local ordinances on the subject of minors who carry, possess or transport firearms. Under § 13-3108, Arizona Revised Statutes, the state reaffirms that laws on this subject must continue to be uniform so that minors have a fair opportunity to know the rules, the act of crossing a city boundary will not inadvertently subject a minor to criminal penalties and all citizens in this state can have full confidence that they are fully protected by the same law.

"**B.** The legislature expressly intends that the provisions of § 13-3111, Arizona Revised Statutes, as added by this act:

"1. Protect the constitutional rights of law-abiding parents and minors who do not criminally misuse firearms.

"2. Regulate the possession of firearms by minors.

"3. Preempt the regulation of the carrying, possessing or transporting of firearms by minors."

The 1994 amendment by Ch. 109 rewrote subsecs. C and D, added new subsec. E, and rewrote provisions formerly contained in subsecs. E and F (now subsecs. F and G). Prior to amendment, subsecs. C to F provided:

"**C.** If the minor is not exempt under subsection B of this section and is in possession of a firearm, a peace officer may seize the firearm and hold it until the agency returns the firearm to the parent or guardian or initiates forfeiture proceedings pursuant to chapter 39 of this title.

"**D.** A person who violates subsection A of this section is an incorrigible child and shall be subject to the following penalties:

"1. For an offense involving an unloaded firearm, a fine of not more than two hundred fifty dollars and the court may order the suspension or revocation of the person's driver's license.

"2. For an offense involving a loaded firearm, a fine of not more than five hundred dollars and the court may order the suspension or revocation of the person's driver's license.

"**E.** If the firearm is not returned to the parent or guardian pursuant to subsection C of this section it shall be held by the law enforcement agency responsible for the seizure until the charges have been adjudicated or otherwise disposed of and until the conclusion of any forfeiture proceedings. Upon adjudication of a person for a violation of this section, the court in accordance with chapter 39 of this title shall order the firearm forfeited and sold, destroyed or disposed of otherwise.

"**F.** If the court finds that the parent or guardian of a minor found responsible for violating this section knew of the minor's unlawful conduct and made no effort to prohibit it, the parent or guardian is jointly and severally responsible for any fine imposed pursuant to this section.

"**G.** This section is supplemental to any other law imposing a criminal penalty for the use or exhibition of a deadly weapon. A minor who violates this section may be prosecuted and convicted for any other criminal conduct involving the use or exhibition of the deadly weapon.

"**H.** This section applies only in counties with populations of more than five hundred thousand persons according to the most recent decennial census. Counties with populations of less than five hundred thousand persons according to the most recent decennial census, or cities or towns within those counties, may adopt an ordinance identical to this section."

The 1994 amendment by Ch. 201, in subsec. D, substituted "a delinquent" for "an incorrigible" in the introductory paragraph, and inserted par. 3; inserted the last sentence in subsec. E; and substituted "five hundred thousand persons or less" for "less than five hundred thousand persons" in subsec. H.

For severability provisions of Laws 1994, Ch. 201, see Historical and Statutory Notes under § 4-244.01.

The 1997 amendment by Ch. 136 inserted subsec. B, par. 4; inserted "In addition to any other penalty provided by law" and deleted "of this section is a delinquent child" following "violates subsection A" in subsec. D; inserted "If adjudicated a delinquent juvenile" at the beginning of subsec. D, pars. 1, 2 and 3; deleted former subsec. E; redesignated former subsecs. F to I as E to H; and added new subsec. I. Former subsec. E had read, "A violation of this section shall be charged, heard and disposed of pursuant to § 8-232."

The 1997 amendment by Ch. 222 made a change in a statutory reference to conform to renumbering of sections.

The amendment of this section by Laws 1997, Ch. 222, § 63 was repealed by Laws 1998, Ch. 113, § 4, and by Laws 1998, Ch. 289, § 12.

Laws 1998, Ch. 113, § 1, par. 3, provides:

"**Section 1. Purpose**"

"3. Section 13-3111, Arizona Revised Statutes, was amended by Laws 1997, chapter 136, § 18 and Laws 1997, chapter 222, § 63. The only change made by chapter 222 was to conform an internal reference in subsection E. In the chapter 136 version, subsection E was stricken. In order to eliminate the double amendment activity, this act repeals § 13-3111, Arizona Revised Statutes, as amended by Laws 1997, chapter 222, § 63."

Reviser's Notes:

1994 Note. Prior to the 1997 amendment, this section contained the amendments made by Laws 1994, Ch. 109, sec. 3 and Ch. 201, sec. 17 that were blended together pursuant to authority of § 41-1304.03.

1997 Note. The independent and valid amendment of this section by Laws 1997, Ch. 136, sec. 18 and Ch. 222, sec. 63 could not be blended because of the delayed effective date of Ch. 222.

1997 Note. Pursuant to authority of § 41-1304.02, in the section heading "violation;" was removed and in subsection B, paragraph 4 the comma before "ratites" was transposed to follow "livestock products" and the "or" before "poultry products" was transposed to follow "poultry products".

§ 13-3411. Possession, use, sale or transfer of marijuana, peyote, prescription drugs, dangerous drugs or narcotic drugs or manufacture of dangerous drugs in a drug free school zone; violation; classification; definitions

A. It is unlawful for a person to do any of the following:

1. Intentionally be present in a drug free school zone to sell or transfer marijuana, peyote, prescription-only drugs, dangerous drugs or narcotic drugs.

2. Possess or use marijuana, peyote, dangerous drugs or narcotic drugs in a drug free school zone.

3. Manufacture dangerous drugs in a drug free school zone.

B. A person who violates subsection A of this section is guilty of the same class of felony that the person would otherwise be guilty of had the violation not occurred within a drug free school zone, but the minimum, maximum and presumptive sentence for that violation shall be increased by one year. A person convicted of violating subsection A of this section is not eligible for suspension of sentence, probation, pardon or release from confinement on any basis except pursuant to § 31-233, subsection A or B until the sentence imposed by the court has been served or commuted. The additional sentence imposed under this subsection is in addition to any enhanced punishment that may be applicable under § 13-604 or other provisions of this chapter.

C. In addition to any other penalty prescribed by this title, the court shall order a person convicted of a violation of this section to pay a fine of not less than two thousand dollars or three times the value as determined by the court of the drugs involved in or giving rise to the charge, whichever is greater, and not more than the maximum authorized by chapter 8 of this title.[1] A judge shall not suspend any part or all of the imposition of any fine required by this subsection.

D. Each school district's governing board or its designee, or the chief administrative officer in the case of a nonpublic school, shall place and maintain permanently affixed signs located in a visible manner at the main entrance of each school that identifies the school and its accompanying grounds as a drug free school zone.

E. The drug free school zone map prepared pursuant to title 15 [2] shall constitute an official record as to the location and boundaries of each drug free school zone. The school district's governing board or its designee, or the chief administrative officer in the case of any nonpublic school, shall promptly notify the county attorney of any changes in the location and boundaries of any school property and shall file with the county recorder the original map prepared pursuant to title 15.

F. All school personnel who observe a violation of this section shall immediately report the violation to a school administrator. The administrator shall immediately report the violation to a peace officer. It is unlawful for any school personnel or school administrator to fail to report a violation as prescribed in this section.

G. School personnel having custody or control of school records of a student involved in an alleged violation of this section shall make the records available to a peace officer upon written request signed by a magistrate. Records disclosed pursuant to this subsection are confidential and may be used only in a judicial or administrative proceeding. A person furnishing records required under this subsection or a person participating in a judicial or administrative proceeding or investigation resulting from the furnishing of records required under this subsection is immune from civil or criminal liability by reason of such action unless the person acted with malice.

H. A person who violates subsection F of this section is guilty of a class 3 misdemeanor.

I. For purposes of this section:

1. "Drug free school zone" means the area within three hundred feet of a school or its accompanying grounds, any public property within one thousand feet of a school or its accompanying grounds, a school bus stop or on any school bus or bus contracted to transport pupils to any school.

2. "School" means any public or nonpublic kindergarten program, common school or high school.

Added by Laws 1987, Ch. 307, § 24. Amended by Laws 1988, Ch. 194, § 6; Laws 1990, Ch. 366, § 15; Laws 1992, Ch. 196, § 1; Laws 1993, Ch. 255, § 47, eff. Jan. 1, 1994; Laws 1997, Ch. 209, § 3; Laws 1999, Ch. 261, § 25.

[1] Section 13–801 et seq.

[2] Section 15–101 et seq.

Application

Laws 1993, Ch. 255, § 99, as amended by Laws 1994, Ch. 236, § 17, effective July 17, 1994, retroactively effective to January 1, 1994, provides:

*"Sec. 99. **Applicability***

"The provisions of §§ 1 through 86 and §§ 89 through 95 of this act apply only to persons who commit a felony offense after the effective date of this act."

Historical and Statutory Notes

The 1988 amendment added subsec. D defining "school".

The 1990 amendment, in subsec. A, substituted "Any" for "Both" in the introduction, deleted "with one or more persons" following "present", and inserted ", or to be present on any public property within one thousand feet of a school or its accompanying grounds or a school bus stop," following "grounds" in pars. 1 and 2, and added pars. 3 and 4; and in subsec. B, inserted "or 3" following "paragraph 1" in par. 1, and inserted "or 4" following "paragraph 2" in par. 2.

Unlawful use of narcotic drug is lesser included offense of loitering offense involving use of drugs, notwithstanding the disparity in punishment. State v. Bowling (App.1989) 163 Ariz. 22, 785 P.2d 591, redesignated as opinion.

The 1992 amendment rewrote the section. Pars. 3 and 4, of subsec. A, had read:

"3. For a person to intentionally be present on a school bus to possess, use or sell marijuana.

"4. For a person to intentionally be present on a school bus to possess, use or sell a dangerous drug or a narcotic drug."

The 1993 amendment, in subsec. B, deleted "or commutation" following "not eligible for suspension", deleted ", parole, work furlough" preceding "or release from confinement", deleted "other" following "released from confinement on any", deleted "entire" preceding "sentence imposed by the court", and inserted "or commuted" following "imposed by the court has been served".

Laws 1993, Ch. 255, § 101, provides:

"**Sec. 101. Legislative intent**

"It is the intent of the legislature that the provisions of this act relating to parole, work furlough, home arrest, earned release credits and other early release programs have only prospective effect. For any person convicted for an offense committed before the effective date of this act the provisions of this act shall have no effect and such person shall be eligible for and may participate in such programs as though this act has not passed."

The 1997 amendment by Ch. 209 inserted subsec. A, par. 3; substituted "violation of this section" for "violation of this subsection" in subsec. G; and substituted "bus contracted to transport pupils" for "bus which transports pupils" in subsec. I, par. 1.

The 1999 amendment by Ch. 261 inserted "or transfer" before "marijuana" in subsec. A, par. 1; substituted "is not eligible" for "shall not be eligible" in subsec. B; and substituted "is immune from civil or criminal liability" for "shall be immune from any civil or criminal liability" in subsec. G.

Another § 13-3411 was renumbered as § 13-3415.

Reviser's Notes:

1987 Note. Pursuant to authority of § 41-1304.02, in the section heading "school grounds" was added after "on".

1992 Note. Pursuant to authority of § 41-1304.02, in the section heading "in a drug free school zone" was substituted for "on school grounds or near schools" and "definitions" was substituted for "definition" and in subsection D and subsection E, second sentence the spelling of "nonpublic" was corrected.

1999 Note. Pursuant to authority of § 41-1304.02, in the section heading a comma was substituted for the first "or" and "or transfer" was added after "sale".

§ 13-3620. Duty to report abuse, physical injury, neglect and denial or deprivation of medical or surgical care or nourishment of minors; medical records; exception; violation; classification; definitions

A. Any person who reasonably believes that a minor is or has been the victim of physical injury, abuse, Child abuse, a reportable offense or neglect that appears to have been inflicted on the minor by other than accidental means or that is not explained by the available medical history as being accidental in nature or who reasonably believes there has been a denial or deprivation of necessary medical treatment or surgical care or nourishment with the intent to cause or allow the death of an infant who is protected under § 36-2281 shall immediately report or cause reports to be made of this information to a peace officer or to child protective services in the department of economic security, except if the report concerns a person who does not have care, custody or control of the minor, the report shall be made to a peace officer only. A member of the clergy, christian science practitioner or priest who has received a confidential communication or a confession in that person's role as a member of the clergy, christian science practitioner or a priest in the course of the discipline enjoined by the church to which the member of the clergy, christian science practitioner or priest belongs may withhold reporting of the communication or confession if the member of the clergy, christian science practitioner or priest determines that it is reasonable and necessary within the concepts of the religion. This exemption applies only to the communication or confession and not to personal observations the member of the clergy, christian science practitioner or priest may otherwise make of the minor. For the purposes of this subsection, "person" means:

1. Any physician, physician's assistant, optometrist, dentist, osteopath, chiropractor, podiatrist, behavioral health professional, nurse, psychologist, counselor or social worker who develops the reasonable belief in the course of treating a patient.

2. Any peace officer, member of the clergy, priest or christian science practitioner.

3. The parent, stepparent or guardian of the minor.

4. School personnel or domestic violence victim advocate who develop the reasonable belief in the course of their employment.

5. Any other person who has responsibility for the care or treatment of the minor.

B. A report is not required under this section for conduct prescribed by §§ 13-1404 and 13-1405 if the conduct involves only minors who are fourteen, fifteen, sixteen or seventeen years of age and there is nothing to indicate that the conduct is other than consensual.

C. If a physician, psychologist or behavioral health professional receives a statement from a person other than a parent, stepparent, guardian or custodian of the minor during the course of providing sex offender treatment that is not court ordered or that does not occur while the offender is incarcerated in the state department of corrections or the department of juvenile corrections, the physician, psychologist or behavioral health professional may withhold the reporting of that statement if the physician, psychologist or behavioral health professional determines it is reasonable and necessary to accomplish the purposes of the treatment.

D. Reports shall be made immediately by telephone or in person and shall be followed by a written report within seventy-two hours. The reports shall contain:

1. The names and addresses of the minor and the minor's parents or the person or persons having custody of the minor, if known.

2. The minor's age and the nature and extent of the minor's abuse, child abuse, physical injury or neglect, including any evidence of previous abuse, child abuse, physical injury or neglect.

3. Any other information that the person believes might be helpful in establishing the cause of the abuse, child abuse, physical injury or neglect.

E. A health care professional who is regulated pursuant to title 32 and who, after a routine newborn physical assessment of a newborn infant's health status or following notification of positive toxicology screens of a newborn infant, reasonably believes that the newborn infant may be affected by the presence of alcohol or a drug listed in § 13-3401 shall immediately report this information, or cause a report to be made, to child protective services in the department of economic security. For the purposes of this subsection, "newborn infant" means a newborn infant who is under thirty days of age.

F. Any person other than one required to report or cause reports to be made under subsection A of this section who reasonably believes that a minor is or has been a victim of abuse, child abuse, physical injury, a reportable offense or neglect may report the information to a peace officer or to child protective services in the department of economic security, except if the report concerns a person who does not have care, custody or control of the minor, the report shall be made to a peace officer only.

G. A person who has custody or control of medical records of a minor for whom a report is required or authorized under this section shall make the records, or a copy of the records, available to a peace officer or child protective services worker investigating the minor's neglect, child abuse, physical injury or abuse on written request for the records signed by the peace officer or child protective services worker. Records disclosed pursuant to this subsection are confidential and may be used only in a judicial or administrative proceeding or investigation resulting from a report required or authorized under this section.

H. When telephone or in-person reports are received by a peace officer, the officer shall immediately notify child protective services in the department of economic security and make the information available to them. Notwithstanding any other statute, when child protective services receives these reports by telephone or in person, it shall immediately notify a peace officer in the appropriate jurisdiction.

I. Any person who is required to receive reports pursuant to subsection A of this section may take or cause to be taken photographs of the minor and the vicinity involved. Medical examinations of the involved minor may be performed.

J. A person who furnishes a report, information or records required or authorized under this section, or a person who participates in a judicial or administrative proceeding or investigation resulting from a report, information or records required or authorized under this section, is immune from any civil or criminal liability by reason of that action unless the person acted with malice or unless the person has been charged with or is suspected of abusing or neglecting the child or children in question.

K. Except for the attorney client privilege or the privilege under subsection L of this section, no privilege applies to any:

1. Civil or criminal litigation or administrative proceeding in which a minor's neglect, dependency, abuse, child abuse, physical injury or abandonment is an issue.

2. Judicial or administrative proceeding resulting from a report, information or records submitted pursuant to this section.

3. Investigation of a minor's child abuse, physical injury, neglect or abuse conducted by a peace officer or child protective services in the department of economic security.

L. In any civil or criminal litigation in which a child's neglect, dependency, physical injury, abuse, child abuse or abandonment is an issue, a member of the clergy, a christian science practitioner or a priest shall not, without his consent, be examined as a witness concerning any confession made to him in his role as a member of the clergy, a christian science practitioner or a priest in the course of the discipline enjoined by the church to which he belongs. Nothing in this subsection discharges a member of the clergy, a christian science practitioner or a priest from the duty to report pursuant to subsection A of this section.

M. If psychiatric records are requested pursuant to subsection G of this section, the custodian of the records shall notify the attending psychiatrist, who may excise from the records, before they are made available:

1. Personal information about individuals other than the patient.

2. Information regarding specific diagnosis or treatment of a psychiatric condition, if the attending psychiatrist certifies in writing that release of the information would be detrimental to the patient's health or treatment.

N. If any portion of a psychiatric record is excised pursuant to subsection M of this section, a court, upon application of a peace officer or child protective services worker, may order that the entire record or any portion of the record that contains information relevant to the reported abuse, child abuse, physical injury or neglect be made available to the peace officer or child protective services worker investigating the abuse, child abuse, physical injury or neglect.

O. A person who violates this section is guilty of a class 1 misdemeanor, except if the failure to report involves a reportable offense, the person is guilty of a class 6 felony.

P. For the purposes of this section:

1. "Abuse" has the same meaning prescribed in § 8–201.

2. "Child abuse" means child abuse pursuant to § 13–3623.

3. "Neglect" has the same meaning prescribed in § 8–201.

4. "Reportable offense" means any of the following:

(a) Any offense listed in chapters 14 and 35.1 of this title [1] or § 13–3506.01.

(b) Surreptitious photographing, videotaping, filming or digitally recording of a minor pursuant to § 13–3019.

(c) Child prostitution pursuant to § 13–3212.

(d) Incest pursuant to § 13–3608.

Added as § 13–842.01 by Laws 1964, Ch. 76, § 2. Amended by Laws 1976, Ch. 171, § 3, eff. June 27, 1976. Renumbered as § 13–3620 by Laws 1977, Ch. 142, § 99, eff. Oct. 1, 1978. Amended by Laws 1978, Ch. 201, § 235, eff. Oct. 1, 1978; Laws 1982, Ch. 272, § 2; Laws 1983, Ch. 296, § 1, eff. July 2, 1984; Laws 1984, Ch. 114, § 1; Laws 1984, Ch. 355, § 1; Laws 1985, Ch. 364, § 30, eff. May 16, 1985; Laws 1986, Ch. 347, § 1, eff. May 9, 1986; Laws 1989, Ch. 270, § 5; Laws 1990, Ch. 237, § 12; Laws 1990, Ch. 384, § 5; Laws 1998, Ch. 276, § 37; Laws 1998, Ch. 289, § 14; Laws 2003, Ch. 222, § 2.

[1] Section 13–3401 et seq.

Historical and Statutory Notes

The 1976 amendment rewrote subsec. A, which had read:

"**A.** Any physician, including a hospital intern or resident physician, whose examination of any minor discloses evidence of injury or physical neglect not explained by the available medical history as being accidental in nature, shall immediately report or cause reports to be made of such information to a municipal or county peace officer. Such reports shall be made forthwith by telephone or in person forthwith, and shall be followed by a written report. Such reports shall contain:

"1. The names and addresses of the minor and his parents or person or persons having custody of such minor, if known.

"2. The minor's age and the nature and extent of his injuries or physical neglect, including any evidence of previous injuries or physical neglect.

"3. Any other information that the physician believes might be helpful in establishing the cause of the injury or physical neglect.";

deleted former subsec. B, which read:

"When the attendance of the physician is pursuant to the performance of services as a member of the staff of a hospital or similar institution, he shall notify the person in charge of the institution or his designated delegate who shall make the necessary reports.";

added subsecs. B and C; relettered the former subsec. C as subsec. D and rewrote the subsection, which had read:

"Anyone participating in the making of reports required under the provisions of this section, or anyone participating in a judicial proceeding resulting from such reports, shall be immune from any civil or criminal liability that might otherwise be incurred or imposed as a result of such actions. Notwithstanding the provisions of § 13–1802, paragraph 4, the physician-patient privilege shall not be a ground for excluding evidence regarding a minor's injuries or physical neglect, or the cause thereof in any judicial proceeding resulting from a report submitted pursuant to this section.";

relettered former subsec. D as subsec. E and rewrote the subsection, which had read:

"A person who violates any provision of this section is guilty of a misdemeanor punishable by a fine of not more than one hundred dollars, by imprisonment for not more than ten days, or both.";

and relettered former subsec. E as subsec. F, and substituted "eighteen" for "sixteen" in the subsection, which had read:

"For the purpose of this section, "minor" means a person under the age of sixteen years.".

The 1978 amendment inserted "class 2" preceding "misdemeanor" in subsec. E; and deleted subsec. F.

The 1982 amendment inserted the exception to subsec. E in subsec. D; inserted a new subsec. E; and designated former subsec. E as subsec. F.

The 1983 amendment inserted the provision pertaining to denial or deprivation of necessary medical treatment or surgical care or nourishment with the intent to cause or allow the death of a child protected under § 36–2281 in subsec. A; and made a nonsubstantive change in subsec. C.

The 1984 blended amendment of Chs. 114 and 355, in subsec. A, inserted "parent or counselor", inserted "or treatment", substituted "reasonable grounds to believe that a minor is or has been the victim" for "evidence", substituted "who has reasonable grounds to believe there has been a" for "evidence of", and substituted "an infant" for "a child".

The 1985 amendment required that reports to a municipal or county peace officer or to the protective services be followed up in writing within seventy-two hours of the telephone or in person report by those required to report, and added the provision requiring the child protective services to immediately notify a municipal or county peace officer upon receiving a report of a violation by telephone or in person from those required to report.

The 1986 amendment rewrote the section.

The 1989 amendment rewrote the first sentence of subsec. A which had read:

"Any physician, hospital intern or resident, surgeon, dentist, osteopath, chiropractor, podiatrist, county medical examiner, nurse, psychologist, school personnel, social worker, peace officer, parent or counselor or any other person having responsibility for the care or treatment of children whose observation or examination of any minor discloses reasonable grounds to believe that a minor is or has been the victim of injury, sexual molestation, death, abuse or physical neglect which appears to have been inflicted upon such minor by other than accidental means or which is not explained by the available medical history as being accidental in nature or who has reasonable grounds to believe there has been a denial or deprivation of necessary medical treatment or surgical care or nourishment with the intent to cause or allow the death of an infant protected under § 36–2281 shall immediately report or cause reports to be made of such information to a peace officer or to the protective services of the department of economic security."

The 1990 amendment by Ch. 237 inserted the reference to § 8–201 in subsec. A.

The 1990 amendment by Ch. 384, in subsec. A, deleted "or" preceding "counselor" and inserted ", clergyman or priest" following "counselor" in the first sentence, and inserted the second through fourth sentences.

The 1998 amendment by Ch. 276 inserted new subsec. B, and redesignated former subsecs. B to J as new subsecs. C to K.

The 1998 amendment by Ch. 289 inserted new subsec. B, relating to reporting of newborn affected by alcohol or other substance; redesignated existing subsecs. B to J as C to K; and made other nonsubstantive changes.

The 2003 amendment by Ch. 222, rewrote the section, which had read:

"**A.** Any physician, hospital intern or resident, surgeon, dentist, osteopath, chiropractor, podiatrist, county medical examiner, nurse, psychologist, school personnel, social worker, peace officer, parent, counselor, clergyman or priest or any other person having responsibility for the care or treatment of children whose observation or examination of any minor discloses reasonable grounds to believe that a minor is or has been the victim of injury, sexual abuse pursuant to § 13–1404, sexual conduct with a minor pursuant to § 13–1405, sexual assault pursuant to § 13–1406, molestation of a child pursuant to § 13–1410, commercial sexual exploitation of a minor pursuant to § 13–3552, sexual exploitation of a minor pursuant to § 13–3553, incest pursuant to § 13–3608 or child prostitution pursuant to § 13–3212, death, abuse pursuant to § 8–201, or physical neglect which appears to have been inflicted on that minor by other than accidental means or which is not explained by the available medical history as being accidental in nature or who has reasonable grounds to believe there has been a denial or deprivation of necessary medical treatment or surgical care or nourishment with the intent to cause or allow the death of an infant less than one year of age protected under § 36–2281 shall immediately report or cause reports to be made of this information to a peace officer or to child protective services in the department of economic security. A clergyman or priest who has received a confidential communication or a confession in that person's role as a clergyman or a priest in the course of the discipline enjoined by the church to which the clergyman or priest belongs may withhold reporting of the communication or confession if the clergyman or priest determines that it is reasonable and necessary within the concepts of the religion. This exemption applies only to the communication or confession and not to personal observations the clergyman or priest may otherwise make of the minor. A report is not required under this section for conduct prescribed by §§ 13–1404 and 13–1405 if the conduct involves only minors age fourteen, fifteen, sixteen or seventeen and there is nothing to indicate that the conduct is other than consensual. Reports shall be made forthwith by telephone or in person forthwith and shall be followed by a written report within seventy-two hours. The reports shall contain:

"1. The names and addresses of the minor and the minor's parents or the person or persons having custody of the minor, if known.

"2. The minor's age and the nature and extent of the minor's injuries or physical neglect, including any evidence of previous injuries or physical neglect.

"3. Any other information that the person believes might be helpful in establishing the cause of the injury or physical neglect.

"**B.** A health care professional who is regulated pursuant to title 32 and whose routine newborn physical assessment of a newborn infant's health status or whose notification of positive toxicology screens of a newborn infant gives the professional reasonable grounds to believe that the newborn infant may be affected by the presence of alcohol or a substance prohibited by chapter 34 of this title shall immediately report this information, or cause a report to be made, to child protective services in the department of economic security. For the purposes of this subsection 'newborn infant' means a newborn infant who is under thirty days of age.

"**C.** Any person other than one required to report or cause reports to be made in subsection A of this section who has reasonable grounds to believe that a minor is or has been a victim of abuse or neglect may report the information to a peace officer or to child protective services in the department of economic security.

"**D.** A person having custody or control of medical records of a minor for whom a report is required or authorized under this section shall make the records, or a copy of the records, available to a peace officer or child protective services worker investigating the minor's neglect or abuse on written request for the records signed by the peace officer or child protective services worker. Records disclosed pursuant to this subsection are confidential and may be used only in a judicial or administrative proceeding or investigation resulting from a report required or authorized under this section.

"**E.** When such telephone or in-person reports are received by the peace officer, they shall immediately notify child protective services in the department of economic security and make the information available to them. Notwithstanding any other statute, when child protective services receives these reports by telephone or in person, it shall immediately notify a peace officer in the appropriate jurisdiction.

"**F.** Any person required to receive reports pursuant to subsection A of this section may take or cause to be taken photographs of the child and the vicinity involved. Medical examinations including, but not limited to, radiological examinations of the involved child may be performed.

"**G.** A person furnishing a report, information or records required or authorized under this section, or a person participating in a judicial or administrative proceeding or investigation resulting from a report, information or records required or authorized under this section, shall be immune from any civil or criminal liability by reason of such action unless the person acted with malice or unless the person has been charged with or is suspected of abusing or neglecting the child or children in question. Except as provided in subsection H of this section, the physician-patient privilege, the husband-wife privilege or any privilege except the attorney-client privilege, provided for by professions such as the practice of social work or nursing covered by law or a code of ethics regarding practitioner-client confidences, both as they relate to the competency of the witness and to the exclusion of confidential communications, shall not pertain in any civil or criminal litigation or administrative proceeding in which a child's neglect, dependency, abuse or abandonment is an issue nor in any judicial or administrative proceeding resulting from a report, information or records submitted pursuant to this section nor in any investigation of a child's neglect or abuse conducted by a peace officer or child protective services in the department of economic security.

"**H.** In any civil or criminal litigation in which a child's neglect, dependency, abuse or abandonment is an issue, a clergyman or priest shall not, without his consent, be examined as a witness concerning any confession made to him in his role as a clergyman or a priest in the course of the discipline enjoined by the church to which he belongs. Nothing in this subsection discharges a clergyman or priest from the duty to report pursuant to subsection A of this section.

"**I.** If psychiatric records are requested pursuant to subsection D of this section, the custodian of the records shall notify the attending psychiatrist, who may excise from the records, before they are made available:

"1. Personal information about individuals other than the patient.

"2. Information regarding specific diagnosis or treatment of a psychiatric condition, if the attending psychiatrist certifies in writing that release of the information would be detrimental to the patient's health or treatment.

"**J.** If any portion of a psychiatric record is excised pursuant to subsection I of this section, a court, upon application of a peace officer or child protective services worker, may order that the entire record or any portion of the record containing information relevant to the reported abuse or neglect be made available to the peace officer or child protective services worker investigating the abuse or neglect.

"**K.** A person who violates this section is guilty of a class 1 misdemeanor."

Reviser's Notes:

1984 Note. Prior to the 1986 amendment, this section contained the amendments made by Laws 1984, Ch. 114, § 1 and Ch. 355, § 1 which were blended together pursuant to authority of § 41-1304.03.

1990 Note. Prior to the 1998 amendments, this section contained the amendments made by Laws 1990, Ch. 237, § 12 and Ch. 384, § 5 which were blended together pursuant to authority of § 41-1304.03.

1998 Note. Prior to the 2003 amendment, this section contained the amendments made by Laws 1998, Ch. 276, sec. 37 and Ch. 289, sec. 14 that were blended together pursuant to authority of § 41-1304.03.

§ 13-3716. Notice of conviction of dangerous crime against children or child abuse; violation; classification

A. It is unlawful for a person who has been convicted of a dangerous crime against children as defined in § 13-604.01 or child abuse pursuant to § 13-3623, subsection A or subsection B, paragraph 1 to fail to give notice of the fact of the conviction to a business institution or organization when applying for employment or volunteering for service with any business institution or organization that sponsors any activity in which adults supervise children. For the purposes of this section, business institutions or organizations include schools, preschools, child care providers and youth organizations.

B. A person who violates this section is guilty of a class 5 felony.

Added by Laws 1987, Ch. 194, § 1. Amended by Laws 1996, Ch. 108, § 1; Laws 2000, Ch. 50, § 5.

Historical and Statutory Notes

The 1996 amendment by Ch. 108 inserted "or child abuse pursuant to § 13-3623, subsection B or subsection C, paragraph 1" in the first sentence of subsec. A.

The 2000 amendment by Ch. 50, in the first sentence of subsec. A, changed the references from "§ 13-3623, subsection B or subsection C" to "§ 13-3623, subsection A or subsection B"; and made nonsubstantive wording changes.

Reviser's Notes:

1987 Note. Pursuant to authority of § 41-1304.02, "Notice of conviction of dangerous crime against children; violation; classification" was substituted for the previous section heading.

§ 13-3990. Notice of conviction of teachers

On the conviction of a person of an offense in this title or of any felony, if the person is certified to teach by the state board of education or is teaching in a community college district or charter school, a copy of the judgment and sentence, and of the opinion of the court or magistrate, if any opinion is filed, shall be sent by the clerk of the court, or by the magistrate, to the state board of education, to the community college district or to the charter school.

Added by Laws 1986, Ch. 40, § 1. Amended by Laws 2002, 5th S.S., Ch. 4, § 1, eff. Aug. 5, 2002; Laws 2004, Ch. 336, § 1.

Historical and Statutory Notes

The 2002 amendment by 5th S.S., Ch. 4, inserted "or is teaching in a charter school," and "or to the charter school".

The 2004 amendment by Ch. 336 rewrote the section, which had read:

"On the conviction of a person of an offense in this title or of any felony, if the person is certified to teach by the state board of education or state board of directors for community colleges, or is teaching in a charter school, a copy of the judgment and sentence, and of the opinion of the court or magistrate, if any opinion is filed, shall be sent by the clerk of the court, or by the magistrate, to the certifying board or to the charter school."

Historical and Statutory Notes

TITLE 34

PUBLIC BUILDINGS AND IMPROVEMENTS

COMPUTER ACCESS

§ 13-3990. Notice of conviction of teachers

ARTICLE 1. ACCESS BY MINORS

On the conviction of a person of an offense in this title or of any felony, if the person is certified to teach by the state board of education or is teaching in a community college district or charter school, a copy of the judgment and sentence, and of the opinion of the court or magistrate if any opinion is filed, shall be sent by the clerk of the court to the state board of education or to the community college district or to the charter school.

Added by Laws 1996, Ch. 40, § 1. Amended by Laws 2002, 5th S.S., Ch. 3, § 1, eff. Aug. 5, 2002; Laws 2009, Ch. 3, § 1.

Historical and Statutory Notes

§ 34-501. Definitions

(b) Is frequently or regularly used directly by a minor.

(c) Is connected to any computer communication system.

Added by Laws 1999, Ch. 26.

§ 34-502. Computer access; harmful to minors

A. A public school that provides a public access computer shall equip the computer with software that seeks to prevent minors from gaining access to material that is harmful to minors or purchase internet connectivity from an internet service provider that provides filter services to limit access to material that is harmful to minors. Standards and rules for the enforcement of this subsection shall be prescribed by the governing board of each school district.

B. A public library that provides a public access computer shall do one or both of the following:

1. Equip the computer with software that will limit minors' ability to gain access to material that is harmful to minors or purchase internet connectivity from an internet service provider that provides filter services to limit access to material that is harmful to minors.

2. Develop and implement by January 1, 2000 a policy that establishes measures to restrict minors from gaining computer access to material that is harmful to minors.

TITLE 34

PUBLIC BUILDINGS AND IMPROVEMENTS

CHAPTER 5

COMPUTER ACCESS

ARTICLE 1. ACCESS BY MINORS

Chapter 5, Computer Access, consisting of §§ 34–501, 34–502, was added by Laws 1999, Ch. 73, § 1, effective August 6, 1999.

ARTICLE 1. ACCESS BY MINORS

§ 34–501. Definitions

In this article, unless the context otherwise requires:

1. "Harmful to minors" has the same meaning as prescribed in § 13–3501, paragraph 1.

2. "Public access computer" means a computer that:

(a) Is located in a public school or public library.

(b) Is frequently or regularly used directly by a minor.

(c) Is connected to any computer communication system.

Added by Laws 1999, Ch. 73, § 1.

§ 34–502. Computer access; harmful to minors

A. A public school that provides a public access computer shall equip the computer with software that seeks to prevent minors from gaining access to material that is harmful to minors or purchase internet connectivity from an internet service provider that provides filter services to limit access to material that is harmful to minors. Standards and rules for the enforcement of this subsection shall be prescribed by the governing board of every school district.

B. A public library that provides a public access computer shall do one or both of the following:

1. Equip the computer with software that will limit minors' ability to gain access to material that is harmful to minors or purchase internet connectivity from an internet service provider that provides filter services to limit access to material that is harmful to minors.

2. Develop and implement by January 1, 2000, a policy that establishes measures to restrict minors from gaining computer access to material that is harmful to minors.

C. Rules for the enforcement of subsection B shall be adopted by the director of the Arizona state library, archives and public records.

D. A public school that complies with subsection A or a public library that complies with subsection B shall not be criminally liable or liable for any damages that might arise from a minor gaining access to material that is harmful to minors through the use of a public access computer that is owned or controlled by the public school or public library.

Added by Laws 1999, Ch. 73, § 1. Amended by Laws 2000, Ch. 88, § 39.

Historical and Statutory Notes

The 2000 amendment by Ch. 88 rewrote subsec. C which had read:

"**C.** Rules and regulations for the enforcement of subsection B shall be established by the director of the department of library, archives and public records."

TITLE 38

PUBLIC OFFICERS AND EMPLOYEES

CHAPTER 3

CONDUCT OF OFFICE

ARTICLE 3.1. PUBLIC MEETINGS AND PROCEEDINGS

ARTICLE 8. CONFLICT OF INTEREST OF OFFICERS AND EMPLOYEES

ARTICLE 9. DISCLOSURE OF INFORMATION BY PUBLIC EMPLOYEES

ARTICLE 3.1. PUBLIC MEETINGS AND PROCEEDINGS

Article 3.1, consisting of §§ 38–431 to 38–431.06, was added by Laws 1962, Ch. 138, § 2, effective June 21, 1962.

§ 38–431. Definitions

In this article, unless the context otherwise requires:

1. "Advisory committee" means a committee that is officially established, upon motion and order of a public body or by the presiding officer of the public body, and whose members have been appointed for the specific purpose of making a recommendation concerning a decision to be made or considered or a course of conduct to be taken or considered by the public body.

2. "Executive session" means a gathering of a quorum of members of a public body from which the public is excluded for one or more of the reasons prescribed in § 38–431.03. In addition to the members of the public body, officers, appointees and employees as provided in § 38–431.03 and the auditor general as provided in § 41–1279.04, only individuals whose presence is reasonably necessary in order for the public body to carry out its executive session responsibilities may attend the executive session.

3. "Legal action" means a collective decision, commitment or promise made by a public body pursuant to the constitution, the public body's charter, bylaws or specified scope of appointment and the laws of this state.

4. "Meeting" means the gathering, in person or through technological devices, of a quorum of members of a public body at which they discuss, propose or take legal action, including any deliberations by a quorum with respect to such action.

5. "Political subdivision" means all political subdivisions of this state, including without limitation all counties, cities and towns, school districts and special districts.

6. "Public body" means the legislature, all boards and commissions of this state or political subdivisions, all multimember governing bodies of departments, agencies, institutions and instrumentalities of the state or political subdivisions, including without limitation all corporations and other instrumentalities whose boards of directors are appointed or elected by the state or political subdivision. Public body includes all quasi-judicial bodies and all standing, special or advisory committees or subcommittees of, or appointed by, such public body.

7. "Quasi-judicial body" means a public body, other than a court of law, possessing the power to hold hearings on disputed matters between a private person and a public agency and to make decisions in the general manner of a court regarding such disputed claims.

Added by Laws 1962, Ch. 138, § 2. Amended by Laws 1974, Ch. 196, § 1, eff. May 22, 1974; Laws 1978, Ch. 86, § 1; Laws 1982, Ch. 278, § 1; Laws 1985, Ch. 203, § 1; Laws 2000, Ch. 358, § 1.

Historical and Statutory Notes

Laws 1962, Ch. 138, § 1, provided:

"It is the public policy of this state that proceedings in meetings of governing bodies of the state and political subdivisions thereof exist to aid in the conduct of the people's business. It is the intent of this act that their official deliberations and proceedings be conducted openly."

Senate Bill 1059 (Laws 1974, Ch. 196) having remained with the governor ten days, Sundays excluded, after final adjournment of the legislature, became law without the governor's approval, as provided by Const. Art. 5, § 7, effective May 22, 1974, the date the bill was filed in the office of the secretary of state.

Reviser's Notes:

1978 Note. Pursuant to authority of § 41–1304.02, the quotation marks which enclosed the words "public body" were omitted in the second sentence of paragraph 4 [now 5].

§ 38–431.01. Meetings shall be open to the public

A. All meetings of any public body shall be public meetings and all persons so desiring shall be permitted to attend and listen to the deliberations and proceedings. All legal action of public bodies shall occur during a public meeting.

B. All public bodies, except for subcommittees and advisory committees, shall provide for the taking of written minutes or a recording of all their meetings, including executive sessions. For meetings other than executive sessions, such minutes or recording shall include, but not be limited to:

1. The date, time and place of the meeting.
2. The members of the public body recorded as either present or absent.
3. A general description of the matters considered.
4. An accurate description of all legal actions proposed, discussed or taken, and the names of members who propose each motion. The minutes shall also include the names of the persons, as given, making statements or presenting material to the public body and a reference to the legal action about which they made statements or presented material.

C. Minutes of executive sessions shall include items set forth in subsection B, paragraphs 1, 2 and 3 of this section, an accurate description of all instructions given pursuant to § 38–431.03, subsection A, paragraphs 4, 5 and 7 and such other matters as may be deemed appropriate by the public body.

D. The minutes or a recording shall be open to public inspection three working days after the meeting except as otherwise specifically provided by this article.

E. All or any part of a public meeting of a public body may be recorded by any person in attendance by means of a tape recorder, camera or other means of sonic reproduction, provided that there is no active interference with the conduct of the meeting.

F. The secretary of state for state public bodies, the city or town clerk for municipal public bodies and the county clerk for all other local public bodies shall distribute open meeting law materials prepared and approved by the attorney general to a person elected or appointed to a public body prior to the day that person takes office.

G. A public body may make an open call to the public during a public meeting, subject to reasonable time, place and manner restrictions, to allow individuals to address the public body on any issue within the jurisdiction of the public body. At the conclusion of an open call to the public, individual members of the public body may respond to criticism made by those who have addressed the public body, may ask staff to review a matter or may ask that a matter be put on a future agenda. However, members of the public body shall not discuss or take legal action on matters raised during an open call to the public unless the matters are properly noticed for discussion and legal action.

H. A member of a public body shall not knowingly direct any staff member to communicate in violation of this article.

Added by Laws 1962, Ch. 138, § 2. Amended by Laws 1974, Ch. 196, § 2, eff. May 22, 1974; Laws 1975, Ch. 48, § 1; Laws 1978, Ch. 86, § 2; Laws 1982, Ch. 278, § 2; Laws 2000, Ch. 358, § 2.

Historical and Statutory Notes

The 1974 amendment inserted the subsection numbering; deleted, from subsec. A, the former second sentence, which read: "All minutes of such meetings as are required by law shall be properly and accurately recorded and open to public inspection except as otherwise specifically provided by statute"; and added subsec. B.

The 1975 amendment substituted "All governing bodies" for "Governing bodies" and "official meetings" for "meetings" in the first sentence, rewrote the second sentence, which had read: "Such minutes shall be properly and accurately recorded as to all legal action taken and open to public inspection except as otherwise specifically provided by statute.", and added pars. 1 to 3 [now pars. 1, 2, and 4] in subsec. B; and added subsecs. C and D [now subsecs. D and E].

Laws 1975, Ch. 48, § 6 provides:

"**Sec. 6. Retroactivity**

"The provisions of this act shall be retroactive to, from and after December 31, 1974."

The 1978 amendment substituted "public body" for "governing body" in par. 2 of subsec. B and in subsec. D [now subsec. E], substituted "All meetings of any public body" for "All official meetings at which any legal action is taken by governing bodies" in subsec. A; rewrote the first sentence, which had read: "All governing bodies, except for subcommittees, shall provide for the taking of written minutes of all their official meetings.", and inserted "or recording" in the second sentence of the introductory paragraph of subsec. B; and rewrote the first sentence, which had read: "An accurate description of all matters proposed, discussed or decided and the names of members who propose and second each motion.", and added the second sentence in par. 3 of subsec. B.

The 1982 amendment added ", including executive sessions" in the first sentence and substituted "For meetings other than executive session, such" for "Such" in the second sentence of the introductory paragraph of subsec. B; inserted par. 3 and renumbered former par. 3 as par. 4 in subsec. B; and inserted subsec. C, redesignated former subsecs. C and D as subsecs. D and E, and added subsec. F.

§ 38-431.02. Notice of meetings

A. Public notice of all meetings of public bodies shall be given as follows:

1. The public bodies of the state shall file a statement with the secretary of state stating where all public notices of their meetings will be posted and shall give such additional public notice as is reasonable and practicable as to all meetings.

2. The public bodies of the counties, school districts and other special districts shall file a statement with the clerk of the board of supervisors stating where all public notices of their meetings will be posted and shall give such additional public notice as is reasonable and practicable as to all meetings.

3. The public bodies of the cities and towns shall file a statement with the city clerk or mayor's office stating where all public notices of their meetings will be posted and shall give such additional public notice as is reasonable and practicable as to all meetings.

C) on paper

B. If an executive session will be held, the notice shall be given to the members of the public body, and to the general public, stating the specific provision of law authorizing the executive session.

C. Except as provided in subsections D and E, meetings shall not be held without at least twenty-four hours' notice to the members of the public body and to the general public.

D. In case of an actual emergency, a meeting, including an executive session, may be held upon such notice as is appropriate to the circumstances. If this subsection is utilized for conduct of an emergency session or the consideration of an emergency measure at a previously scheduled meeting the public body must post a public notice within twenty-four hours declaring that an emergency session has been held and setting forth the information required in subsections H and I.

E. A meeting may be recessed and resumed with less than twenty-four hours' notice if public notice of the initial session of the meeting is given as required in subsection A, and if, prior to recessing, notice is publicly given as to the time and place of the resumption of the meeting or the method by which notice shall be publicly given.

F. A public body which intends to meet for a specified calendar period, on a regular day, date or event during such calendar period, and at a regular place and time, may post public notice of such meetings at the beginning of such period. Such notice shall specify the period for which notice is applicable.

G. Notice required under this section shall include an agenda of the matters to be discussed or decided at the meeting or information on how the public may obtain a copy of such an agenda. The agenda must be available to the public at least twenty-four hours prior to the meeting, except in the case of an actual emergency under subsection D.

H. Agendas required under this section shall list the specific matters to be discussed, considered or decided at the meeting. The public body may discuss, consider or make decisions only on matters listed on the agenda and other matters related thereto.

I. Notwithstanding the other provisions of this section, notice of executive sessions shall be required to include only a general description of the matters to be considered. Such agenda shall provide more than just a recital of the statutory provisions authorizing the executive session, but need not contain information that would defeat the purpose of the executive session, compromise the legitimate privacy interests of a public officer, appointee or employee, or compromise the attorney-client privilege.

J. Notwithstanding subsections H and I, in the case of an actual emergency a matter may be discussed and considered and, at public meetings, decided, where the matter was not listed on the agenda provided that a statement setting forth the reasons necessitating such discussion, consideration or decision is placed in the minutes of the meeting and is publicly announced at the public meeting. In the case of an executive session, the reason for consideration of the emergency measure shall be announced publicly immediately prior to the executive session.

K. Notwithstanding subsection H, the chief administrator, presiding officer or a member of a public body may present a brief summary of current events without listing in the agenda the specific matters to be summarized, provided that:

1. The summary is listed on the agenda.

2. The public body does not propose, discuss, deliberate or take legal action at that meeting on any matter in the summary unless the specific matter is properly noticed for legal action.

Added by Laws 1974, Ch. 196, § 4, eff. May 22, 1974. Amended by Laws 1978, Ch. 86, § 3; Laws 1982, Ch. 278, § 3; Laws 2000, Ch. 358, § 3; Laws 2002, Ch. 247, § 1.

Historical and Statutory Notes

Former § 38–431.02, added by Laws 1962, Ch. 138, § 2, and relating to nonapplicability of article to executive sessions, was repealed by Laws 1974, Ch. 196, § 3.

Reviser's Notes:

In subsection D (now E) "subsection" was substituted for "paragraph" pursuant to authority of § 41–1304.02.

§ 38–431.03. Executive sessions

A. Upon a public majority vote of the members constituting a quorum, a public body may hold an executive session but only for the following purposes:

1. Discussion or consideration of employment, assignment, appointment, promotion, demotion, dismissal, salaries, disciplining or resignation of a public officer, appointee or employee of any public body, except that, with the exception of salary discussions, an officer, appointee or employee may demand that the discussion or consideration occur at a public meeting. The public body shall provide the officer, appointee or employee with written notice of the executive session as is appropriate but not less than twenty-four hours for the officer, appointee or employee to determine whether the discussion or consideration should occur at a public meeting.

2. Discussion or consideration of records exempt by law from public inspection, including the receipt and discussion of information or testimony that is specifically required to be maintained as confidential by state or federal law.

3. Discussion or consultation for legal advice with the attorney or attorneys of the public body.

4. Discussion or consultation with the attorneys of the public body in order to consider its position and instruct its attorneys regarding the public body's position regarding contracts that are the subject of negotiations, in pending or contemplated litigation or in settlement discussions conducted in order to avoid or resolve litigation.

5. Discussions or consultations with designated representatives of the public body in order to consider its position and instruct its representatives regarding negotiations with employee organizations regarding the salaries, salary schedules or compensation paid in the form of fringe benefits of employees of the public body.

6. Discussion, consultation or consideration for international and interstate negotiations or for negotiations by a city or town, or its designated representa-

tives, with members of a tribal council, or its designated representatives, of an Indian reservation located within or adjacent to the city or town.

7. Discussions or consultations with designated representatives of the public body in order to consider its position and instruct its representatives regarding negotiations for the purchase, sale or lease of real property.

B. Minutes of and discussions made at executive sessions shall be kept confidential except from:

1. Members of the public body which met in executive session.

2. Officers, appointees or employees who were the subject of discussion or consideration pursuant to subsection A, paragraph 1 of this section.

3. The auditor general on a request made in connection with an audit authorized as provided by law.

4. A county attorney or the attorney general when investigating alleged violations of this article.

C. The public body shall instruct persons who are present at the executive session regarding the confidentiality requirements of this article.

D. Legal action involving a final vote or decision shall not be taken at an executive session, except that the public body may instruct its attorneys or representatives as provided in subsection A, paragraphs 4, 5 and 7 of this section. A public vote shall be taken before any legal action binds the public body.

E. Except as provided in § 38–431.02, subsections I and J, a public body shall not discuss any matter in an executive session which is not described in the notice of the executive session.

F. Disclosure of executive session information pursuant to this section or § 38–431.06 does not constitute a waiver of any privilege, including the attorney-client privilege. Any person receiving executive session information pursuant to this section or § 38–431.06 shall not disclose that information except to the attorney general or county attorney, by agreement with the public body or to a court in camera for purposes of enforcing this article. Any court that reviews executive session information shall take appropriate action to protect privileged information.

Added by Laws 1974, Ch. 196, § 6, eff. May 22, 1974. Amended by Laws 1978, Ch. 86, § 4; Laws 1982, Ch. 278, § 4; Laws 1983, Ch. 274, § 2, eff. April 27, 1983; Laws 1990, Ch. 56, § 1, eff. April 12, 1990; Laws 2000, Ch. 358, § 4.

Historical and Statutory Notes

Former § 38–431.03, as added by Laws 1962, Ch. 138, § 2, was renumbered as § 38–431.04 by Laws 1974, Ch. 196, § 6, effective May 22, 1974.

Reviser's Notes:

1982 Note. Pursuant to authority of § 41–1304.02, "Nonapplicability to" was deleted from the section heading.

2000 Note. Pursuant to authority of § 41–1304.02, in subsection B, in the lead-in language a colon was substituted for the semicolon to correct a manifest clerical error.

§ 38-431.04. Writ of mandamus

Where the provisions of this article are not complied with, a court of competent jurisdiction may issue a writ of mandamus requiring that a meeting be open to the public.

Added as § 38-431.03 by Laws 1962, Ch. 138, § 2. Renumbered as § 38-431.04 by Laws 1974, Ch. 196, § 6, eff. May 22, 1974.

Historical and Statutory Notes

Former § 38-431.04, added by Laws 1962, Ch. 138, § 2, was renumbered as § 38-431.05 by Laws 1974, Ch. 196, § 6, effective May 22, 1974.

§ 38-431.05. Meeting held in violation of article; business transacted null and void; ratification

A. All legal action transacted by any public body during a meeting held in violation of any provision of this article is null and void except as provided in subsection B.

B. A public body may ratify legal action taken in violation of this article in accordance with the following requirements:

1. Ratification shall take place at a public meeting within thirty days after discovery of the violation or after such discovery should have been made by the exercise of reasonable diligence.

2. The notice for the meeting shall include a description of the action to be ratified, a clear statement that the public body proposes to ratify a prior action and information on how the public may obtain a detailed written description of the action to be ratified.

3. The public body shall make available to the public a detailed written description of the action to be ratified and all deliberations, consultations and decisions by members of the public body that preceded and related to such action. The written description shall also be included as part of the minutes of the meeting at which ratification is taken.

4. The public body shall make available to the public the notice and detailed written description required by this section at least seventy-two hours in advance of the public meeting at which the ratification is taken.

Added as § 38-431.04 by Laws 1962, Ch. 138, § 2. Renumbered as § 38-431.05 by Laws 1974, Ch. 196, § 6, eff. May 22, 1974. Amended by Laws 1978, Ch. 86, § 5; Laws 1982, Ch. 278, § 5.

Historical and Statutory Notes

Former § 38-431.05, added by Laws 1962, Ch. 138, § 2, relating to noneffectiveness on right to appeal, was repealed by Laws 1974, Ch. 196, § 5.

§ 38-431.06. Investigations; written investigative demands

A. On receipt of a written complaint signed by a complainant alleging a violation of this article or on their own initiative, the attorney general or the county attorney for the county in which the alleged violation occurred may begin an investigation.

B. In addition to other powers conferred by this article, in order To carry out the duties prescribed in this article, the attorney general or the county attorney for the county in which the alleged violation occurred, or their designees, may:

1. Issue written investigative demands to any person.

2. Administer an oath or affirmation to any person for testimony.

3. Examine under oath any person in connection with the investigation of the alleged violation of this article.

4. Examine by means of inspecting, studying or copying any account, book, computer, document, minutes, paper, recording or record.

5. Require any person to file on prescribed forms a statement or report in writing and under oath of all the facts and circumstances requested by the attorney general or county attorney.

C. The written investigative demand shall:

1. Be served on the person in the manner required for service of process in this state or by certified mail, return receipt requested.

2. Describe the class or classes of documents or objects with sufficient definiteness to permit them to be fairly identified.

3. Prescribe a reasonable time at which the person shall appear to testify and within which the document or object shall be produced and advise the person that objections to or reasons for not complying with the demand may be filed with the attorney general or county attorney on or before that time.

4. Specify a place for the taking of testimony or for production of a document or object and designate a person who shall be the custodian of the document or object.

D. If a person objects to or otherwise fails to comply with the written investigation demand served on the person pursuant to subsection C, the attorney general or county attorney may file an action in the superior court for an order to enforce the demand. Venue for the action to enforce the demand shall be in Maricopa county or in the county in which the alleged violation occurred. Notice of hearing the action to enforce the demand and a copy of the action shall be served on the person in the same manner as that prescribed in the Arizona rules of civil procedure. If a court finds that the demand is proper, including that the compliance will not violate a privilege and that there is not a conflict of interest on the part of the attorney general or county attorney, that there is reasonable cause to believe there may have been a violation of this article and that the information sought or document or object demanded is relevant to the violation, the court shall order the person to comply with the demand, subject to modifications the court may prescribe. If the person fails to comply with the court's order, the court may issue any of the following orders until the person complies with the order:

1. Adjudging the person in contempt of court.

2. Granting injunctive relief against the person to whom the demand is issued to restrain the conduct that is the subject of the investigation.

3. Granting other relief the court deems proper.

Added by Laws 2000, Ch. 358, § 5.

Historical and Statutory Notes

Former § 38–431.06, added by Laws 1962, Ch. 138, § 2, and amended by Laws 1978, Ch. 201, § 677, which provided penalties for violations, was repealed by Laws 1982, Ch. 278, § 6. See, now, § 38–431.07

§ 38–431.07. Violations; enforcement; removal from office; in camera review

A. Any person affected by an alleged violation of this article, the attorney general or the county attorney for the county in which an alleged violation of this article occurred may commence a suit in the superior court in the county in which the public body ordinarily meets, for the purpose of requiring compliance with, or the prevention of violations of, this article, by members of the public body, or to determine the applicability of this article to matters or legal actions of the public body. For each violation the court may impose a civil penalty not to exceed five hundred dollars against a person who violates this article or who knowingly aids, agrees to aid or attempts to aid another person in violating this article and order such equitable relief as it deems appropriate in the circumstances. The civil penalties awarded pursuant to this section shall be deposited into the general fund of the public body concerned. The court may also order payment to a successful plaintiff in a suit brought under this section of the plaintiff's reasonable attorney fees, by the defendant state, the political subdivision of the state or the incorporated city or town of which the public body is a part or to which it reports. If the court determines that a public officer with intent to deprive the public of information violated any provision of this article the court may remove the public officer from office and shall assess the public officer or a person who knowingly aided, agreed to aid or attempted to aid the public officer in violating this article, or both, with all of the costs and attorney fees awarded to the plaintiff pursuant to this section.

B. A public body shall not expend public monies to employ or retain legal counsel to provide legal services or representation to the public body or any of its officers in any legal action commenced pursuant to any provisions of this article, unless the public body has authority to make such expenditure pursuant to other provisions of law and takes a legal action at a properly noticed open meeting approving such expenditure prior to incurring any such obligation or indebtedness.

C. In any action brought pursuant to this section challenging the validity of an executive session, the court may review in camera the minutes of the executive session, and if the court in its discretion determines that the minutes are relevant and that justice so demands, the court may disclose to the parties or admit in evidence part or all of the minutes.

Added by Laws 1974, Ch. 196, § 7, eff. May 22, 1974. Amended by Laws 1978, Ch. 86, § 6; Laws 1982, Ch. 278, § 7; Laws 2000, Ch. 358, § 6.

Historical and Statutory Notes

Source:

A.R.S. former § 38–431.06.
Laws 1962, Ch. 138, § 2.
Laws 1978, Ch. 201, § 677.

The 1978 amendment substituted "public body" for "governing body" four times and substituted references to legal actions for references to decisions twice in the first sentence, and inserted "also" following "The court may" and substituted "the defendant state, political subdivision of the state or the incorporated city or town of which the public body" for "the governing body of which it" in the third sentence.

The 1982 amendment inserted the subsection lettering and added subsecs. B and C; and substituted "Any person affected by an alleged violation of this article, the attorney general or the county attorney for the county in which an alleged violation of this article occurred may commence a suit in the superior court in the county" for "Any person affected by a legal action of a public body may commence a suit in the superior court for the county" in the first sentence, inserted "impose a civil penalty not to exceed five hundred dollars against a person who violates this article and" in the second sentence, inserted the third sentence, substituted "attorney fees" for "attorney's fees" in the fourth sentence, and added the fifth sentence in subsec. A.

The 2000 amendment by Ch. 358 substituted, in the second sentence of subsec. A, "five hundred dollars for each violation against a person who violates this article or who knowingly aids, agrees to aid or attempts to aid another person in violating this article" for "five hundred dollars against a person who violates this article"; deleted, from the fifth sentence of subsec. A, "or of the opportunity to be heard" following "deprive the public of information"; substituted, in the same sentence, "shall assess the public officer or a person who knowingly aided, agreed to aid or attempted to aid the public officer in violating this article, or both" for "shall assess him"; and made nonsubstantive wording changes.

Reviser's Notes:

2000 Note. Pursuant to authority of § 41–1304.02, in subsection A, second sentence the words "For each violation" were transposed to the beginning of the sentence.

§ 38–431.08. Exceptions; limitation

A. This article does not apply to:

1. Any judicial proceeding of any court or any political caucus of the legislature.

2. Any conference committee of the legislature, except that all such meetings shall be open to the public.

3. The commissions on appellate and trial court appointments and the commission on judicial qualifications.

4. Good cause exception determinations and hearings conducted by the board of fingerprinting pursuant to § 41–619.55.

B. A hearing held within a prison facility by the board of executive clemency is subject to this article, except that the director of the state department of corrections may:

1. Prohibit, on written findings that are made public within five days of so finding, any person from attending a hearing whose attendance would constitute a serious threat to the life or physical safety of any person or to the safe, secure and orderly operation of the prison.

2. Require a person who attends a hearing to sign an attendance log. If the person is over sixteen years of age, the person shall produce photographic identification which verifies the person's signature.

3. Prevent and prohibit any articles from being taken into a hearing except recording devices, and if the person who attends a hearing is a member of the media, cameras.

4. Require that a person who attends a hearing submit to a reasonable search on entering the facility.

C. The exclusive remedies available to any person who is denied attendance at or removed from a hearing by the director of the state department of corrections in violation of this section shall be those remedies available in § 38-431.07, as against the director only.

D. Either house of the legislature may adopt a rule or procedure pursuant to article IV, part 2, § 8, Constitution of Arizona, to provide an exemption to the notice and agenda requirements of this article or to allow standing or conference committees to meet through technological devices rather than only in person.

Added by Laws 1974, Ch. 196, § 7, eff. May 22, 1974. Amended by Laws 1975, Ch. 71, § 1, eff. May 20, 1975; Laws 1977, Ch. 128, § 1; Laws 1982, Ch. 278, § 8; Laws 1990, Ch. 298, § 1, eff. June 16, 1990; Laws 1998, Ch. 232, § 8; Laws 1998, Ch. 270, § 12, eff. August 17, 1999; Laws 1999, Ch. 211, § 33; Laws 2000, Ch. 251, § 14; Laws 2000, Ch. 358, § 7.

Historical and Statutory Notes

The amendment of this section by Laws 1998, Ch. 20, § 12 was repealed by Laws 1999, Ch. 211, § 34.

The 1999 amendment of this section by Ch. 211 explicitly amended the amendment of this section by Laws 1998, Ch. 232, § 8.

Laws 1999, Ch. 211, § 1, par. 19, provides:

"**Section 1. Purpose**"

"19. Section 38-431.08, Arizona Revised Statutes, was amended by Laws 1998, chapter 232, § 8 and Laws 1998, chapter 270, § 12. These two versions could not be blended because of the delayed effective date of the chapter 270 version. In order to combine these two versions, this act amends the Laws 1998, chapter 232 version of § 38-431.08, Arizona Revised Statutes, to incorporate the amendments made by Laws 1998, chapter 270 and the chapter 270 version is repealed."

Laws 1999, Ch. 211, § 73, subsec. E, provides:

"**Sec. 73. Retroactive application**"

"**E.** Sections 2 through 5, 17, 18, 20, 21, 26, 27, 29 through 36, 39 through 44, 47 through 50 and 63 through 66 of this act apply retroactively to from and after June 30, 1999."

Reviser's Notes:

1998 Note. The independent and valid amendment of this section by Laws 1998, Ch. 232, sec. 8 and Ch. 270, sec. 12 could not be blended because of the delayed effective date of Ch. 270.

2000 Note. This section contains the amendments made by Laws 2000, Ch. 251, sec. 14 and Ch. 358, sec. 7 that were blended together as shown above pursuant to authority of § 41-1304.03.

§ 38-431.09. Declaration of public policy

It is the public policy of this state that meetings of public bodies be conducted openly and that notices and agendas be provided for such meetings which contain such information as is reasonably necessary to inform the public of the matters to be discussed or decided. Toward this end, any person or entity charged with the interpretations of this article shall construe any provision of this article in favor of open and public meetings.

Added by Laws 1978, Ch. 86, § 7. Amended by Laws 1982, Ch. 278, § 9; Laws 2000, Ch. 358, § 8.

ARTICLE 8. CONFLICT OF INTEREST OF OFFICERS AND EMPLOYEES

Article 8, consisting of §§ 38-501 to 38-504, was added by Laws 1968, Ch. 88, § 1, effective June 20, 1968.

§ 38-501. Application of article

A. This article shall apply to all public officers and employees of incorporated cities or towns, of political subdivisions and of the state and any of its departments, commissions, agencies, bodies or boards.

B. Notwithstanding the provisions of any other law, or the provisions of any charter or ordinance of any incorporated city or town to the contrary, the provisions of this article shall be exclusively applicable to all officers and employees of every incorporated city or town or political subdivision or the state and any of its departments, commissions, agencies, bodies or boards and shall supersede the provisions of any other such law, charter provision or ordinance.

C. Other prohibitions in the state statutes against any specific conflict of interests shall be in addition to this article if consistent with the intent and provisions of this article.

Added by Laws 1968, Ch. 88, § 1. Amended by Laws 1978, Ch. 208, § 1, eff. Oct. 1, 1978; Laws 1992, Ch. 140, § 1.

Historical and Statutory Notes

Source:

Laws 1919, Ch. 173, § 28.
Code 1939, § 75–1028.
A.R.S. former § 30–365.

Laws 1978, Ch. 208, § 7 provides:

"**Sec. 7. Effective date**

"The provisions of this act shall become effective on October 1, 1978."

§ 38–502. Definitions

In this article, unless the context otherwise requires:

1. "Compensation" means money, a tangible thing of value or a financial benefit.

2. "Employee" means all persons who are not public officers and who are employed on a full-time, part-time or contract basis by an incorporated city or town, a political subdivision or the state or any of its departments, commissions, agencies, bodies or boards for remuneration.

3. "Make known" means the filing of a paper which is signed by a public officer or employee and which fully discloses a substantial interest or the filing of a copy of the official minutes of a public agency which fully discloses a substantial interest. The filing shall be in the special file established pursuant to § 38–509.

4. "Official records" means the minutes or papers, records and documents maintained by a public agency for the specific purpose of receiving disclosures of substantial interests required to be made known by this article.

5. "Political subdivision" means all political subdivisions of the state and county, including all school districts.

6. "Public agency" means:

(a) All courts.

(b) Any department, agency, board, commission, institution, instrumentality or legislative or administrative body of the state, a county, an incorporated town or city and any other political subdivision.

(c) The state, county and incorporated cities or towns and any other political subdivisions.

7. "Public competitive bidding" means the method of purchasing defined in title 41, chapter 4, article 3,[1] or procedures substantially equivalent to such method of purchasing, or as provided by local charter or ordinance.

8. "Public officer" means all elected and appointed officers of a public agency established by charter, ordinance, resolution, state constitution or statute.

9. "Relative" means the spouse, child, child's child, parent, grandparent, brother or sister of the whole or half blood and their spouses and the parent, brother, sister or child of a spouse.

10. "Remote interest" means:

(a) That of a nonsalaried officer of a nonprofit corporation.

(b) That of a landlord or tenant of the contracting party.

(c) That of an attorney of a contracting party.

(d) That of a member of a nonprofit cooperative marketing association.

(e) The ownership of less than three per cent of the shares of a corporation for profit, provided the total annual income from dividends, including the value of stock dividends, from the corporation does not exceed five per cent of the total annual income of such officer or employee and any other payments made to him by the corporation do not exceed five per cent of his total annual income.

(f) That of a public officer or employee in being reimbursed for his actual and necessary expenses incurred in the performance of official duty.

(g) That of a recipient of public services generally provided by the incorporated city or town, political subdivision or state department, commission, agency, body or board of which he is a public officer or employee, on the same terms and conditions as if he were not an officer or employee.

(h) That of a public school board member when the relative involved is not a dependent, as defined in § 43–1001, or a spouse.

(i) That of a public officer or employee, or that of a relative of a public officer or employee, unless the contract or decision involved would confer a direct economic benefit or detriment upon the officer, employee or his relative, of any of the following:

(i) Another political subdivision.

(ii) A public agency of another political subdivision.

(iii) A public agency except if it is the same governmental entity.

(j) That of a member of a trade, business, occupation, profession or class of persons consisting of at least ten members which is no greater than the interest of the other members of that trade, business, occupation, profession or class of persons.

11. "Substantial interest" means any pecuniary or proprietary interest, either direct or indirect, other than a remote interest.

Added by Laws 1968, Ch. 88, § 1. Amended by Laws 1973, Ch. 116, § 6; Laws 1974, Ch. 199, § 1; Laws 1977, Ch. 164, § 17; Laws 1978, Ch. 151, § 7; Laws 1978, Ch. 208, § 2, eff. Oct. 1, 1978; Laws 1979, Ch. 145, § 36; Laws 1992, Ch. 140, § 2.

[1] Section 41-722 et seq.

Historical and Statutory Notes

Senate Bill 1121 (Laws 1974, Ch. 199) having remained with the governor ten days, Sundays excluded, after final adjournment of the legislature, became law without the governor's approval, as provided by Const. Art. 5, § 7.

For purpose, effective date, and retroactivity provisions of Laws 1979, Ch. 145, §§ 1 and 40, see Historical and Statutory Notes following § 43-104.

Reviser's Notes:

1978 Note. Prior to the 1979 amendment, this section contained the amendments made by Laws 1978, chapter 151, section 7 and chapter 208, section 2 which were blended together pursuant to authority of § 41-1304.03.

§ 38-503. Conflict of interest; exemptions; employment prohibition

A. Any public officer or employee of a public agency who has, or whose relative has, a substantial interest in any contract, sale, purchase or service to such public agency shall make known that interest in the official records of such public agency and shall refrain from voting upon or otherwise participating in any manner as an officer or employee in such contract, sale or purchase.

B. Any public officer or employee who has, or whose relative has, a substantial interest in any decision of a public agency shall make known such interest in the official records of such public agency and shall refrain from participating in any manner as an officer or employee in such decision.

C. Notwithstanding the provisions of subsections A and B of this section, no public officer or employee of a public agency shall supply to such public agency any equipment, material, supplies or services, unless pursuant to an award or contract let after public competitive bidding, except that:

1. A school district governing board may purchase, as provided in §§ 15-213 and 15-323, supplies, materials and equipment from a school board member.

2. Political subdivisions other than school districts may purchase through their governing bodies, without using public competitive bidding procedures, supplies, materials and equipment not exceeding three hundred dollars in cost in any single transaction, not to exceed a total of one thousand dollars annually, from a member of the governing body if the policy for such purchases is approved annually.

D. Notwithstanding subsections A and B of this section and as provided in §§ 15-421 and 15-1441, the governing board of a school district or a community college district may not employ a person who is a member of the governing board or who is the spouse of a member of the governing board.

Added by Laws 1968, Ch. 88, § 1. Amended by Laws 1978, Ch. 208, § 3, eff. Oct. 1, 1978; Laws 1980, Ch. 170, § 3; Laws 1986, Ch. 17, § 3; Laws 1986, Ch. 246, § 1; Laws 1987, Ch. 138, § 2.

Historical and Statutory Notes

Source:

Civ.Code 1901, §§ 217 to 219, 999.
Civ.Code 1913, §§ 173 to 175, 2446.
Rev.Code 1928, § 91.
Code 1939, § 12-401.
A.R.S. former § 38-446.

§ 38–504. Prohibited acts

A. A public officer or employee shall not represent another person for compensation before a public agency by which the officer or employee is or was employed within the preceding twelve months or on which the officer or employee serves or served within the preceding twelve months concerning any matter with which the officer or employee was directly concerned and in which the officer or employee personally participated during the officer's or employee's employment or service by a substantial and material exercise of administrative discretion.

B. During the period of a public officer's or employee's employment or service and for two years thereafter, a public officer or employee shall not disclose or use for the officer's or employee's personal profit, without appropriate authorization, any information acquired by the officer or employee in the course of the officer's or employee's official duties which has been clearly designated to the officer or employee as confidential when such confidential designation is warranted because of the status of the proceedings or the circumstances under which the information was received and preserving its confidentiality is necessary for the proper conduct of government business. A public officer or employee shall not disclose or use, without appropriate authorization, any information that is acquired by the officer or employee in the course of the officer's or employee's official duties and that is declared confidential by law.

C. A public officer or employee shall not use or attempt to use the officer's or employee's official position to secure any valuable thing or valuable benefit for the officer or employee that would not ordinarily accrue to the officer or employee in the performance of the officer's or employee's official duties if the thing or benefit is of such character as to manifest a substantial and improper influence on the officer or employee with respect to the officer's or employee's duties.

Added by Laws 1974, Ch. 199, § 3. Amended by Laws 1995, Ch. 76, § 5; Laws 1999, Ch. 40, § 1.

Historical and Statutory Notes

For effective date of Laws 1974, Ch. 199, see Historical and Statutory Notes following § 38–502.

The 1995 amendment added subsec. D.

The 1999 amendment by Ch. 40 rewrote the section which had read:

"**A.** No public officer or employee may represent another person for compensation before a public agency by which he is or was employed within the preceding twelve months or on which he serves or served within the preceding twelve months concerning any matter with which such officer or employee was directly concerned and in which he personally participated during his employment or service by a substantial and material exercise of administrative discretion.

"**B.** During the period of his employment or service and for two years thereafter, no public officer or employee may disclose or use for his personal profit, without appropriate authorization, any information acquired by him in the course of his official duties which has been clearly designated to him as confidential when such confidential designation is warranted because of the status of the proceedings or the circumstances under which the information was received and preserving its confidentiality is necessary to the proper conduct of government business. No public officer or employee shall disclose or use, without appropriate authorization, any information acquired by him in the course of his official duties which is declared confidential by law.

"**C.** No public officer or employee may use or attempt to use his official position to secure any valuable thing or valuable benefit for himself that would not ordinarily accrue to him in the performance of his official duties, which thing or benefit is of such character as to manifest a substantial and improper influence upon him with respect to his duties.

"**D.** Notwithstanding subsection A, neither the director of the department of gaming nor any other employee of the department of gaming may be employed within the gaming industry or represent another person for compensation before the department of gaming for a period of two years from the last day of the person's employment with the department of gaming."

Former § 38-504, added by Laws 1968, Ch. 88, § 1, relating to penalties, was repealed by Laws 1974, Ch. 199, § 2.

§ 38-505. Additional income prohibited for services

A. No public officer or employee may receive or agree to receive directly or indirectly compensation other than as provided by law for any service rendered or to be rendered by him personally in any case, proceeding, application, or other matter which is pending before the public agency of which he is a public officer or employee.

B. This section shall not be construed to prohibit the performance of ministerial functions including, but not limited to, the filing, or amendment of tax returns, applications for permits and licenses, incorporation papers, and other documents.

Added by Laws 1974, Ch. 199, § 3.

§ 38-506. Remedies

A. In addition to any other remedies provided by law, any contract entered into by a public agency in violation of this article is voidable at the instance of the public agency.

B. Any person affected by a decision of a public agency may commence a civil suit in the superior court for the purpose of enforcing the civil provisions of this article. The court may order such equitable relief as it deems appropriate in the circumstances including the remedies provided in this section.

C. The court may in its discretion order payment of costs, including reasonable attorney's fees, to the prevailing party in an action brought under subsection B.

Added by Laws 1978, Ch. 208, § 5, eff. Oct. 1, 1978.

Historical and Statutory Notes

Laws 1979, Ch. 195, § 1, par. 14 provides:

"**Section 1. Purpose**"

"14. Section 38-506, Arizona Revised Statutes, was amended by Laws 1978, chapter 201, § 687 with a delayed effective date. Laws 1978, chapter 208, with the same delayed effective date, in § 4 repealed § 38-506 and in section 5 added new §§ 38-506 through 38-510. Section 38-510 as added by chapter 208, a penalty section, relates to the same subject matter as that of § 38-506 which was repealed by chapter 208. In order to accomplish the intent of Laws 1978, chapter 208, §§ 4 and 5, in this enactment the chapter 201 version of § 38-506 is repealed."

Former § 38-506, added by Laws 1974, Ch. 199, § 3, relating to the subject matter of § 38-510, was repealed by Laws 1978, Ch. 208, § 4, effective October 1, 1978.

Former § 38-506, added by Laws 1974, Ch. 199, § 3, and amended by Laws 1978, Ch. 201, § 687 (see Reviser's Note, post), was repealed by Laws 1979, Ch. 195, § 24. See, now, § 38-510.

Reviser's Notes:

1978 Note. Section 38-506, the penalty section of title 38, chapter 3, article 8 added by Laws 1974, Ch. 199, § 3, was repealed by Laws 1978, Ch. 208, § 4. Its subject matter, with classifications of violations, was included in § 38-510 added by Laws 1978, Ch. 208, § 5, effective October 1, 1978. Section 38-506 added by Laws 1974, Ch. 199, § 3 was amended by Laws 1978, Ch. 201, § 687, effective October 1, 1978, to read:

"**38-506. Violation; classification**

Any public officer or employee who knowingly conceals or fails to disclose any substantial interest or who violates any provision of this article shall be guilty of a class 5 felony, and upon conviction shall forfeit his office."

The two measures which became Chapter 208 and Chapter 201 were sent to the governor on May 31 and June 1, respectively, and were signed by the governor on June 14 and June 9, respectively. Chapter 208 related only to conflicts of interest and Chapter 201 amended sections throughout Arizona Revised Statutes to conform to the structure of the Revised Criminal Code, effective October 1, 1978.

Pursuant to authority of § 41-1304.02, in the heading of this section "; action by resident" was omitted.

§ 38-507. Opinions of the attorney general, county attorneys, city or town attorneys and house and senate ethics committee

Requests for opinions from either the attorney general, a county attorney, a city or town attorney, the senate ethics committee or the house of representatives ethics committee concerning violations of this article shall be confidential, but the final opinions shall be a matter of public record. The county attorneys shall file opinions with the county recorder, the city or town attorneys shall file opinions with the city or town clerk, the senate ethics committee shall file opinions with the senate secretary and the house of representatives ethics committee shall file opinions with the chief clerk of the house of representatives.

Added by Laws 1978, Ch. 208, § 5, eff. Oct. 1, 1978. Amended by Laws 1992, Ch. 140, § 3.

Historical and Statutory Notes

Another § 38-507, added by Laws 1978, Ch. 189, was renumbered as § 38-511.

§ 38-508. Authority of public officers and employees to act

A. If the provisions of § 38-503 prevent an appointed public officer or a public employee from acting as required by law in his official capacity, such public officer or employee shall notify his superior authority of the conflicting interest. The superior authority may empower another to act or such authority may act in the capacity of the public officer or employee on the conflicting matter.

B. If the provisions of § 38-503 prevent a public agency from acting as required by law in its official capacity, such action shall not be prevented if members of the agency who have apparent conflicts make known their substantial interests in the official records of their public agency.

Added by Laws 1978, Ch. 208, § 5, eff. Oct. 1, 1978.

§ 38-509. Filing of disclosures

Every political subdivision and public agency subject to this article shall maintain for public inspection in a special file all documents necessary to memorialize all disclosures of substantial interest made known pursuant to this article.

Added by Laws 1978, Ch. 208, § 5, eff. Oct. 1, 1978.

§ 38–510. Penalties

A. A person who:

1. Intentionally or knowingly violates any provision of §§ 38–503 through 38–505 is guilty of a class 6 felony.

2. Recklessly or negligently violates any provision of §§ 38–503 through 38–505 is guilty of a class 1 misdemeanor.

B. A person found guilty of an offense described in subsection A of this section shall forfeit his public office or employment if any.

C. It is no defense to a prosecution for a violation of §§ 38–503 through 38–505 that the public officer or employee to whom a benefit is offered, conferred or agreed to be conferred was not qualified or authorized to act in the desired way.

D. It is a defense to a prosecution for a violation of §§ 38–503 through 38–505 that the interest charged to be substantial was a remote interest.

Added by Laws 1978, Ch. 208, § 5, eff. Oct. 1, 1978.

Historical and Statutory Notes

Source:

Laws 1974, Ch. 199, § 3.

Laws 1978, Ch. 201, § 687.

A.R.S. former § 38–506.

§ 38–511. Cancellation of political subdivision and state contracts; definition

A. The state, its political subdivisions or any department or agency of either may, within three years after its execution, cancel any contract, without penalty or further obligation, made by the state, its political subdivisions, or any of the departments or agencies of either if any person significantly involved in initiating, negotiating, securing, drafting or creating the contract on behalf of the state, its political subdivisions or any of the departments or agencies of either is, at any time while the contract or any extension of the contract is in effect, an employee or agent of any other party to the contract in any capacity or a consultant to any other party of the contract with respect to the subject matter of the contract.

B. Leases of state trust land for terms longer than ten years cancelled under this section shall respect those rights given to mortgagees of the lessee by § 37–289 and other lawful provisions of the lease.

C. The cancellation under this section by the state or its political subdivisions shall be effective when written notice from the governor or the chief executive officer or governing body of the political subdivision is received by all other parties to the contract unless the notice specifies a later time.

D. The cancellation under this section by any department or agency of the state or its political subdivisions shall be effective when written notice from such party is received by all other parties to the contract unless the notice specifies a later time.

E. In addition to the right to cancel a contract as provided in subsection A of this section, the state, its political subdivisions or any department or agency of either may recoup any fee or commission paid or due to any person significantly involved in initiating, negotiating, securing, drafting or creating the contract on behalf of the state, its political subdivisions or any department or agency of either from any other party to the contract arising as the result of the contract.

F. Notice of this section shall be included in every contract to which the state, its political subdivisions, or any of the departments or agencies of either is a party.

G. For purposes of this section, "political subdivisions" do not include entities formed or operating under title 48, chapter 11, 12, 13, 17, 18, 19 or 22.[1]

Added as § 38–507 by Laws 1978, Ch. 189, § 1. Renumbered as § 38–511. Amended by Laws 1985, Ch. 155, § 1; Laws 1988, Ch. 169, § 1; Laws 1992, Ch. 45, § 1.

[1] Sections 48–1501 et seq., 48–1701 et seq., 48–1901 et seq., 48–2301 et seq., 48–2601 et seq., 48–2901 et seq., 48–3701 et seq.

Historical and Statutory Notes

Laws 1988, ch. 169, § 2, provides:

"**Sec. 2. Applicability**

"The provisions of this act, with respect to contracts of political subdivisions or any of the departments or agencies of a political subdivision, shall apply to contracts made by a political subdivision or any department or agency of a political subdivision after the effective date of this act."

Reviser's Notes:

1978 Note. The above section was added by Laws 1978, Ch. 189, sec. 1 as § 38–507 and was renumbered as § 38–511 pursuant to authority of § 41–1304.02.

1988 Note. Pursuant to authority of § 41–1304.02, in the section heading "political subdivision and" was added after "of" and "; definition" was added after "contracts" and subsection F was relettered as subsection G and subsection G was relettered as subsection F.

ARTICLE 9. DISCLOSURE OF INFORMATION BY PUBLIC EMPLOYEES

Article 9, consisting of §§ 38–531 and 38–532, was added by Laws 1985, Ch. 189, § 1, effective April 26, 1985.

§ 38–531. Definitions

In this article, unless the context otherwise requires:

1. "Employee" means an officer or employee of this state or any of its departments, commissions, agencies or boards. Employee includes employees and officers of community college districts, school districts and counties of this state but does not include officers or employees of a municipal corporation established for the purpose of reclamation and distribution of water and the generation of electricity.

2. "Former employee" means an employee who was dismissed.

3. "Personnel action" means:

(a) Appointment.

(b) Promotion.

(c) Disciplinary or corrective action.

(d) Detail, transfer or reassignment.

(e) Suspension, demotion or dismissal.

(f) Reinstatement.

(g) Restoration.

(h) Reemployment.

(i) Performance evaluation.

(j) Decision concerning pay, benefits or awards.

(k) Elimination of the employee's position without a reduction in force by reason of lack of monies or work.

(*l*) Other significant change in duties or responsibilities which is inconsistent with the employee's salary or grade level.

4. "Public body" means the attorney general, the legislature, the governor, a federal, state or local law enforcement agency, the county attorney, the governing board of a community college district or school district, the board of supervisors of a county or an agency director.

5. "Reprisal" means to take a personnel action the result of which is adverse to an employee.

Added by Laws 1985, Ch. 189, § 1, eff. April 26, 1985. Amended by Laws 1989, Ch. 285, § 1; Laws 1990, Ch. 373, § 1.

§ 38-532. Prohibited personnel practice; violation; reinstatement; exceptions; civil penalty

A. It is a prohibited personnel practice for an employee who has control over personnel actions to take reprisal against an employee for a disclosure of information of a matter of public concern by the employee to a public body which the employee reasonably believes evidences:

1. A violation of any law.

2. Mismanagement, a gross waste of monies or an abuse of authority.

B. The disclosure by an employee to a public body alleging a violation of law, mismanagement, gross waste of monies or abuse of authority shall be in writing and shall contain the following information:

1. The date of the disclosure.

2. The name of the employee making the disclosure.

3. The nature of the alleged violation of law, mismanagement, gross waste of monies or abuse of authority.

4. If possible, the date or range of dates on which the alleged violation of law, mismanagement, gross waste of monies or abuse of authority occurred.

C. An employee who knowingly commits a prohibited personnel practice shall be ordered by the state personnel board, a community college district governing board, a school district governing board or other appropriate independent personnel board established or authorized pursuant to § 38-534 to pay a civil penalty of up to five thousand dollars to the state general fund, a county general fund, a community college district unrestricted general fund or a school district maintenance and operation fund, whichever is appropriate. The employee who committed the prohibited personnel practice, not the governmental entity, shall pay the civil penalty. Upon a finding that an employee committed a prohibited personnel practice, the employer shall take appropriate disciplinary action including dismissal.

D. An employee or former employee against whom a prohibited personnel practice is committed may recover attorney fees, costs, back pay, general and special damages and full reinstatement for any reprisal resulting from the prohibited personnel practice as determined by the court.

E. An employee does not commit a prohibited personnel practice if he takes reprisal against an employee if that employee discloses information in a manner prohibited by law or the materials or information are prescribed as confidential by law.

F. This section may not be used as a defense in a disciplinary action where the employee is being disciplined for cause pursuant to § 41-770, except in a hearing on a complaint brought pursuant to this section by an employee or former employee who believes he has been the subject of a prohibited personnel practice as prescribed in this section as the result of a disclosure of information.

G. On request or at any time an employee alleges reprisal, an employer shall provide an employee who is subject to disciplinary or corrective action, suspension, demotion or dismissal with a copy of this section.

H. If an employee or former employee believes that a personnel action taken against him is the result of his disclosure of information under this section, he may make a complaint to an appropriate independent personnel board, if one is established or authorized pursuant to § 38-534 or to a community college district governing board or school district governing board. If an independent personnel board has not been established or authorized, or if a school district governing board or a community college district governing board does not hear and decide personnel matters brought pursuant to this section, the employee or former employee may make a complaint to the state personnel board. A complaint made pursuant to this subsection shall be made within ten days of the effective date of the action taken against him. The state personnel board, a school district governing board, a community college governing board or other appropriate independent personnel board, shall, pursuant to the rules governing appeals under § 41-785, make a determination concerning:

1. The validity of the complaint.

2. Whether a prohibited personnel practice was committed against the employee or former employee as a result of disclosure of information by the employee or former employee.

I. If the state personnel board, a community college district governing board, a school district governing board or other appropriate independent personnel board established or authorized pursuant to § 38-534 determines that a prohibited personnel practice was committed as a result of disclosure of information by the employee or former employee, it shall rescind the personnel action and order that all lost pay and benefits be returned to the employee or former employee. The employee, former employee, employee alleged to have committed a prohibited personnel practice pursuant to subsection A of this section or employer may appeal the decision of the state personnel board, a community college district governing board, a school district governing board or other appropriate independent personnel board established or authorized pursuant to § 38–534 to the superior court as provided in title 12, chapter 7, article 6.[1] Notwithstanding § 12–910, an appeal to the superior court under this subsection shall be tried de novo.

J. For purposes of a hearing by the state personnel board, a school district governing board, a community college district governing board or other appropriate independent personnel board conducted under this section, the employee, former employee, employee alleged to have committed the prohibited personnel practice pursuant to subsection A of this section and employer may be represented by counsel. In addition, representation by counsel in such hearings shall meet any other requirements stipulated by the state personnel board, a school district governing board, a community college district governing board or other appropriate independent personnel board or as required by law.

K. An employee or former employee may also seek injunctive relief as is otherwise available in civil actions.

L. This section shall not be construed to limit or extend the civil or criminal liability of an employee or former employee for any disclosure of information or to limit an employee's right to a separate pretermination hearing with the employee's employer, as provided by law.

M. An employee who knowingly makes a false accusation that a public officer or employee who has control over personnel actions has engaged in a violation of any law, mismanagement, a gross waste of monies or an abuse of authority is personally subject to a civil penalty of up to twenty-five thousand dollars and dismissal from employment by the employer.

Added by Laws 1985, Ch. 189, § 1, eff. April 26, 1985. Amended by Laws 1989, Ch. 285, § 2; Laws 1990, Ch. 373, § 2.

[1] Section 12–901 et seq.

Historical and Statutory Notes

The 1989 amendment rewrote the section which had read:

"**A.** It is a prohibited personnel practice for an employee who has control over personnel actions to take reprisal against an employee for a disclosure of information by the employee to a public body which the employee reasonably believes evidences:

"1. A violation of any law.

"2. Mismanagement, a gross waste of monies or an abuse of authority.

"**B.** An employee who commits a prohibited personnel practice shall be suspended without pay for up to thirty days or dismissed.

"**C.** An employee does not commit a prohibited personnel practice if he takes reprisal against a person if that person discloses information in a manner prohibited by law or the materials or information are prescribed as confidential by law.

"**D.** This subsection may not be used as a defense in a disciplinary action where the person is being disciplined for cause pursuant to § 41–770.

"**E.** This section shall not be construed to limit or extend civil or criminal liability of a person for any disclosure of information or the consequences of disclosing information."

The 1990 amendment rewrote the section, which had read:

"**A.** It is a prohibited personnel practice for an employee who has control over personnel actions to take reprisal against an employee for a disclosure of information by the employee to a public body which the employee reasonably believes evidences:

"1. A violation of any law.

"2. Mismanagement, a gross waste of monies or an abuse of authority.

"**B.** An employee who knowingly commits a prohibited personnel practice is personally subject to a civil penalty of up to twenty-five thousand dollars and shall be dismissed.

"**C.** An employee or former employee against whom a prohibited personnel practice is committed may recover attorney fees, costs, back pay, general and special damages and full reinstatement for any reprisal resulting from the prohibited personnel practice as determined by the court.

"**D.** An employee does not commit a prohibited personnel practice if he takes reprisal against an employee if that employee discloses information in a manner prohibited by law or the materials or information are prescribed as confidential by law.

"**E.** This section may not be used as a defense in a disciplinary action where the employee is being disciplined for cause pursuant to § 41–770, except in an appeal before the state personnel board by an employee or former employee who believes he has been the subject of a prohibited personnel practice as defined in this section as the result of a disclosure of information.

"**F.** An employer shall provide an employee who is subject to disciplinary or corrective action, suspension, demotion or dismissal with a copy of this section at the time the action is taken.

"**G.** If an employee or former employee believes that a personnel action taken against him is the result of his disclosure of information under this section, he may make an appeal to the state personnel board within ten days of the effective date of the action taken against him. The state personnel board shall, pursuant to the rules governing appeals under § 41–785, make a determination concerning:

"1. The validity of the complaint.

"2. Whether a prohibited personnel practice was committed against the employee or former employee as a result of disclosure of information by the employee or former employee.

"**H.** If the state personnel board determines that a prohibited personnel practice was committed as a result of disclosure of information by the employee or former employee, it shall order the employee or former employee to be reinstated with back pay. The employee, former employee or the employer may appeal the decision of the board to the superior court as provided in title 12, chapter 7, article 6. Notwithstanding § 12–910, an appeal to the superior court under this subsection shall be tried de novo.

"**I.** For purposes of an appeal to the state personnel board conducted under this section either party may be represented by counsel. In addition, representation by counsel in such hearings must meet any other requirements stipulated by the state personnel board or required by law.

"**J.** An employee or former employee may also seek injunctive relief as is otherwise available in civil actions.

"**K.** This section shall not be construed to limit or extend the civil or criminal liability of an employee or former employee for any disclosure of information. Neither shall any provision of this section be construed to limit an employee's right to a separate pretermination hearing with the employee's employer, as provided by law.

"**L.** An employee who knowingly makes a false accusation that a public officer or employee who has control over personnel actions has engaged in a violation of any law, mismanagement, a gross waste of monies or an abuse of authority is personally subject to a civil penalty of up to twenty-five thousand dollars and dismissal from employment."

Reviser's Notes:

1989 Note. Pursuant to authority of § 41–1304.02, in the section heading "classification;" was deleted and "; civil penalty" was added after "exceptions" and in the second sentence of subsection K the spelling of "pretermination" was corrected.

1990 Note. Pursuant to authority of § 41–1304.02, in subsection J, first sentence, the comma after the fourth "board" was transposed to follow the first "section".

§ 38–533. Exemptions

This article does not apply to an employee or former employee of a state university or the board of regents which has in effect at the time a personnel action is taken against the employee a rule or provision for the protection of its employees from reprisal for the disclosure of information to a public body, except that the employee or former employee may appeal the final administrative decision to the superior court as provided in title 12, chapter 7, article 6.[1]

Notwithstanding § 12-910, an employee or former employee who has been dismissed is entitled to a trial de novo in superior court.
Added by Laws 1989, Ch. 285, § 3. Amended by Laws 1990, Ch. 373, § 3.

[1] Section 12-901 et seq.

§ 38-534. Appropriate independent personnel boards

A. A community college district, county and school district may either:

1. Establish an appropriate independent personnel board to hear and decide personnel matters brought pursuant to § 38-532.

2. Authorize an existing independent board to hear and decide personnel matters brought pursuant to § 38-532.

B. Notwithstanding subsection A of this section, a school district governing board or a community college district governing board may hear and decide personnel matters brought pursuant to § 38-532.

C. If a community college district, county or school district does not establish an appropriate independent personnel board to hear and decide personnel matters brought pursuant to § 38-532, or does not authorize an existing independent board to hear and decide personnel matters brought pursuant to § 38-532, or if a school district governing board or a community college district governing board does not hear and decide personnel matters brought pursuant to § 38-532, complaints filed pursuant to this article shall be heard by the state personnel board.
Added by Laws 1990, Ch. 373, § 4.

CHAPTER 5

SOCIAL SECURITY AND RETIREMENT

ARTICLE 1. SOCIAL SECURITY FOR PUBLIC OFFICERS AND EMPLOYEES

ARTICLE 2. ARIZONA STATE RETIREMENT SYSTEM

ARTICLE 1. SOCIAL SECURITY FOR PUBLIC OFFICERS AND EMPLOYEES

Article 1, consisting of §§ 38–701 to 38–705, was added by Laws 1995, Ch. 32, § 14, effective March 30, 1995.

Former Article 1, consisting of §§ 38–701 to 38–707, enacted as part of the revision effective January 9, 1956, was repealed by Laws 1995, Ch. 32, § 13, effective March 30, 1995.

Historical and Statutory Notes

Laws 1986, Ch. 287, §§ 1 and 2 provide:

"**Section 1. Permanent retirement benefit increases**

"**A.** Effective July 1, 1986, each person who was receiving retirement benefits including survivors' benefits on or before June 30, 1985 pursuant to title 38, chapter 5, article 2 or 2.1, Arizona Revised Statutes, shall receive a permanent increase in their monthly benefit equal to sixty cents for each year of credited future service, credited past service and prior service plus sixty cents for each year the person has been retired as of June 30, 1986. The sum of the years of credited future service, credited past service and prior service and years retired shall be rounded to the nearest whole number.

"**B.** Notwithstanding the provisions of subsection A of this section, the maximum monthly benefit increase shall not exceed eight per cent of the current monthly benefit.

"**Sec. 2. Funding**

"The cost of the benefit increases is payable from the current assets of the retirement plan. The cost of the benefit increases shall be added to the unfunded liability of the retirement plan."

Laws 1989, Ch. 310, § 19 provides:

"**Sec. 19. Permanent tax equity benefit allowance for retirees; funding**

"**A.** Retroactive to January 1, 1989, each person receiving retirement benefits on or before January 1, 1989 pursuant to title 38, chapter 5, article 2 or 2.1, Arizona Revised Statutes, is entitled to receive a tax equity benefit allowance consisting of a permanent increase of three per cent in his base benefit being received on January 1, 1989. The cost of the benefit increase provided by this subsection is payable from the assets of the applicable retirement system or plan. The cost of the benefit increase shall be added to the unfunded liability of the applicable retirement system or plan.

"**B.** Retroactive to January 1, 1989, each person receiving retirement benefits on or before January 1, 1989 pursuant to title 38, chapter 5, article 3, Arizona Revised Statutes, and former title 38, chapter 5, article 3.1, Arizona Revised Statutes, is entitled to receive a tax equity benefit allowance consisting of a permanent increase of three per cent in his base benefit being received on January 1, 1989. The cost of the benefit increase provided by this subsection is payable from the current assets of the elected officials' retirement plan.

"C. Retroactive to January 1, 1989, each person receiving retirement benefits on or before January 1, 1989 pursuant to title 38, chapter 5, article 4, Arizona Revised Statutes, is entitled to receive a tax equity benefit allowance consisting of a permanent increase of three per cent in his base benefit received on January 1, 1989. The cost of the benefit increase provided by this subsection is payable from the applicable employer cost of the public safety personnel retirement system.

"D. Retroactive to January 1, 1989, each person who was receiving retirement benefits on or before January 1, 1989 pursuant to title 38, chapter 5, article 6, Arizona Revised Statutes, is entitled to receive a tax equity benefit allowance consisting of a permanent increase of 1.5 per cent of his base benefit being received on January 1, 1989. The cost of the benefit increase provided by this subsection is payable from the current assets of the corrections officer retirement plan [for authority of Legislative Council to add last seven words of subsec. D, see Attorney General Opinion, Arizona, R89-108].

"E. Each person that retires after January 1, 1989 and before the effective date of this act and who receives retirement benefits pursuant to title 38, chapter 5, article 2 or 2.1, Arizona Revised Statutes, is entitled to receive a tax equity benefit allowance retroactive to the date of retirement consisting of a permanent increase of three per cent of his base benefit. The cost of the benefit increase provided by this subsection is payable from the assets of the applicable retirement system or plan. The cost of the benefit increase shall be added to the unfunded liability of the applicable retirement system or plan.

"F. Each person that retires after January 1, 1989 and before the effective date of this act and who receives retirement benefits pursuant to title 38, chapter 5, article 3, Arizona Revised Statutes, and former title 38, chapter 5, article 3.1, Arizona Revised Statutes, is entitled to receive a tax equity benefit allowance retroactive to the date of retirement consisting of a permanent increase of three per cent of his base benefit. The cost of the benefit increase provided by this subsection is payable from the current assets of the elected officials' retirement plan.

"G. Each person that retires after January 1, 1989 and before the effective date of this act and who receives retirement benefits pursuant to title 38, chapter 5, article 4, Arizona Revised Statutes, is entitled to receive a tax equity benefit allowance retroactive to the date of retirement consisting of a permanent increase of three per cent of his base benefit. The cost of the benefit increase provided by this subsection is payable from the applicable employer cost of the public safety personnel retirement system.

"H. Each person that retires after January 1, 1989 and before the effective date of this act and who receives retirement benefits pursuant to title 38, chapter 5, article 6, Arizona Revised Statutes, is entitled to receive a tax equity benefit allowance retroactive to the date of retirement consisting of a permanent increase of 1.5 per cent of his base benefit. The cost of the benefit increase provided by this subsection is payable from the current assets of the corrections officer retirement plan [for authority of legislative council to add subsec. H, see Attorney General Opinion, Arizona, R89-108]."

Laws 1989, Ch. 310, § 27, subsec. F, as amended by Laws 1990, Ch. 68, § 1, provides:

"**Sec. 27. Retroactivity and applicability**

"Section 19 of this act is effective retroactively to January 1, 1989."

Laws 1996, Ch. 18, § 3, provides:

"**Sec. 3. Purpose**

"The purpose of the public retirement plans is to manage and invest retirement monies and distribute retirement benefits to retired members of the plans."

§ 38-701. Definitions

In this article, unless the context otherwise requires:

1. "Commissioner of social security" includes any individual to whom the commissioner of social security has delegated any of the commissioner's functions under the social security act with respect to coverage under the act of employees of states and their political subdivisions.

2. "Employee" means any person in the employ of this state or a political subdivision of this state and includes an elective or appointive officer of this state or an eligible political subdivision of this state.

3. "Employment" means any service performed by an employee in the employ of this state or a political subdivision of this state, for the employer,

except service that in the absence of an agreement entered into under this article would constitute "employment" as defined in the social security act, or service that under the social security act may not be included in an agreement between this state and the commissioner of social security entered into under this article.

4. "Political subdivision" includes counties, incorporated cities or towns and school districts in this state, and any other political subdivision as defined in article XIII, § 7, Constitution of Arizona.

5. "Social security act" means the federal social security act (42 United States Code chapter 7),[1] including regulations and requirements issued pursuant to that act.

6. "State agency" means the Arizona state retirement system board established pursuant to § 38–713.

Added by Laws 1995, Ch. 32, § 14, eff. March 30, 1995.

[1] 42 U.S.C.A. § 301 et seq.

Historical and Statutory Notes

Source:

Laws 1951, Ch. 126, § 2.
Code 1939, Supp.1952, § 12–830.
A.R.S. former § 38–701.
Laws 1959, Ch. 31, § 1.

Former § 38–701, enacted as part of the revision effective January 9, 1956, (see Source, ante), relating to similar subject matter, was repealed by Laws 1995, Ch. 32, § 13, eff. March 30, 1995.

§ 38–702. Federal-state agreement

A. On behalf of this state the governor may enter into an agreement with the commissioner of social security, consistent with this article, for the purpose of extending the benefits of the federal old age and survivors insurance system to employees of this state or any political subdivision of this state with respect to services that are specified in the agreement and that constitute employment.

B. The agreement may contain provisions relating to coverage, benefits, contributions, effective date, modification of the agreement, notification of dissolution of entities, administration and other appropriate provisions to which the state agency and commissioner of social security agree, except that the agreement shall provide in effect the following, unless otherwise required under the social security act:

1. Benefits shall be provided for employees whose services are covered by the agreement, and their dependents and survivors, on the same basis as though the services constituted employment within the meaning of title II of the social security act.[1]

2. The agreement is effective with respect to services in employment covered by the agreement performed after a date specified in the agreement, but in no event may it be effective with respect to services performed before the first day of the calendar year in which the agreement is entered into or in which the modification of the agreement making it applicable to the services is entered into, but an agreement or modification of an agreement entered into within the period permitted for retroactive coverage of employees under the agreement by title II of the social security act may provide in the agreement or modification of the agreement that the agreement or modification of the agreement is

effective with respect to services performed after January 1, 1951, or any date after that date.

3. All services that constitute employment and that are performed in the employ of this state by employees of this state are covered by the agreement.

4. All services that constitute employment performed in the employ of an eligible political subdivision of this state and that are covered by a plan that is in conformity with the terms of the agreement and that has been approved by the state agency under § 38–703 are covered by the agreement.

5. All services described in either paragraph 3 or 4 and performed by individuals in positions covered by a retirement system with respect to which the governor has issued a certificate to the commissioner of social security pursuant to § 38–706.

Added by Laws 1995, Ch. 32, § 14, eff. March 30, 1995. Amended by Laws 2001, Ch. 136, § 2.

[1] 42 U.S.C.A. § 401 et seq.

Historical and Statutory Notes

Source:

Laws 1951, Ch. 126, 3.
Laws 1952, Ch. 46, § 1.
Laws 1953, Ch. 90, § 1.
Code 1939, Supp.1953, § 12–831.
A.R.S. former § 38–702.

The 2001 amendment by Ch. 136 added par. 5 of subsec. B.

Former § 38–702, enacted as part of the revision effective January 9, 1956, (see Source, ante), relating to similar subject matter, was repealed by Laws 1995, Ch. 32, § 13, eff. March 30, 1995.

Reviser's Notes:

1995 Note. Pursuant to authority of § 41–1304.02, in subsection A the spelling of "survivors" was corrected.

§ 38–703. Plans for coverage of employees of eligible political subdivisions; payroll audits

A. Each eligible political subdivision of this state may submit for approval by the state agency a plan for extending the benefits of title II of the social security act, in conformity with applicable provisions of the social security act, to employees of the eligible political subdivisions. The state agency shall approve each plan and any amendment of the plan if it finds that the plan or amendment of the plan is in conformity with requirements provided in rules of the state agency, except that a plan shall not be approved unless:

1. It is in conformity with the requirements of the social security act and with the agreement entered into under § 38–702.

2. It provides that all services that constitute employment and that are performed in the employ of the eligible political subdivision by employees of the political subdivision are covered by the plan.

3. It provides for such methods of administration of the plan by the eligible political subdivisions that the state agency finds to be necessary for the proper and efficient administration of the plan.

4. It provides that the eligible political subdivision make reports, in the form and containing the information, the state agency from time to time requires, and comply with provisions the state agency or the commissioner of social

security from time to time finds necessary to assure the correctness and verification of the reports.

B. The state agency shall not finally refuse to approve a plan submitted by an eligible political subdivision under subsection A of this section without reasonable notice and the opportunity for a hearing to the political subdivision affected by the refusal.

Added by Laws 1995, Ch. 32, § 14, eff. March 30, 1995.

Historical and Statutory Notes

Source:

Laws 1951, Ch. 126, § 5.
Code 1939, Supp.1952, § 12-833.
Code 1939, Supp.1954, § 12-833a.
Laws 1955, Ch. 71, §§ 1, 2.
A.R.S. former § 38-704.
Laws 1961, Ch. 93, § 1.
Laws 1970, Ch. 190, § 58.
Laws 1972, Ch. 51, § 3.
Laws 1976, Ch. 163, § 31.
Laws 1982, Ch. 141, § 1.
Laws 1983, Ch. 98, § 111.

Former § 38-703, enacted as part of the revision effective January 9, 1956, amended by Laws 1972, Ch. 51, § 2, derived from Laws 1951, Ch. 126, § 4, and Code 1939, Supp.1952, § 12-832, relating to contributions by state employees, was repealed by Laws 1992, Ch. 320, § 1.

§ 38-704. Rule making powers of state agency

The state agency shall adopt rules that are not inconsistent with this article and that it finds necessary or appropriate for the efficient administration of the functions with which it is charged under this article.

Added by Laws 1995, Ch. 32, § 14, eff. March 30, 1995.

Historical and Statutory Notes

Source:

Laws 1951, Ch. 126, § 7.
Code 1939, Supp.1952, § 12-835.
A.R.S. former § 38-706.

Former § 38-704, enacted as part of the revision effective January 9, 1956, derived from:

Laws 1951, Ch. 126, § 5.
Code 1939, Supp.1952, § 12-833.
Code 1939, Supp.1954, § 12-833a.
Laws 1955, Ch. 71, §§ 1, 2.
Laws 1961, Ch. 93, § 1.
Laws 1970, Ch. 190, § 58.
Laws 1972, Ch. 51, § 3.
Laws 1976, Ch. 163, § 31.
Laws 1982, Ch. 141, § 1.
Laws 1983, Ch. 98, § 111.

relating to coverage plans for employees of eligible political subdivisions and payroll audits, was repealed by Laws 1995, Ch. 32, § 13, eff. March 30, 1995. See, now, § 38-703.

§ 38-705. Studies and reports by state agency

The state agency may:

1. Conduct studies concerning the problem of old age and survivors insurance protection for employees and concerning the operation of agreements made and plans approved under this article.

2. Submit a report to the legislature at the beginning of each regular session covering the administration and operation of this article during the preceding calendar year, including recommendations for amendments to this article it considers proper.

Added by Laws 1995, Ch. 32, § 14, eff. March 30, 1995. Amended by Laws 1996, Ch. 185, § 2.

Historical and Statutory Notes

Source:

Laws 1951, Ch. 126, § 8.
Code 1939, Supp.1952, § 12-836.
A.R.S. former § 38-707.

Former § 38-705, enacted as part of the revision effective January 9, 1956, amended by Laws 1972, Ch. 51, § 4, derived from:

Laws 1951, Ch. 126, § 6.
Laws 1952, Ch. 103, § 1.
Laws 1953, Ch. 90, § 2.
Code 1939, Supp.1953, § 12-834.

relating to an old age survivors disability insurance account, was repealed by Laws 1995, Ch. 32, § 13, eff. March 30, 1995.

§ 38-706. Referenda and certification

A. On request of the board of trustees of a retirement system established by this state, the governor may authorize a referendum. On request of the governing body of any political subdivision that has established a retirement system, the governor shall authorize a referendum.

B. The referendum shall be conducted and the governor shall designate an agency or individual to supervise its conduct, in accordance with the requirements of § 218(d)(3) of the social security act, on the question of whether service in positions covered by the retirement system should be excluded from or included under an agreement under this article. The notice of referendum required by § 218(d)(3)(c) of the social security act to be given to employees shall contain or shall be accompanied by a statement, in the form and detail deemed necessary and sufficient by the agency or individual designated to supervise the referendum, to inform the employees of the rights that will accrue to them and their dependents and survivors, and the liabilities to which they will be subject, if their services are included under an agreement under this article.

C. On receipt of evidence satisfactory to the governor that with respect to any referendum the conditions specified in § 218(d)(3) of the social security act have been met, the governor shall so certify to the commissioner of social security.

Added by Laws 2001, Ch. 136, § 3.

Historical and Statutory Notes

Former § 38-706, enacted as part of the revision effective January 9, 1956, derived from Laws 1951, Ch. 126, § 7, and Code 1939, Supp. 1952, § 12-835, which related to state agency rulemaking powers, was repealed by Laws 1995, Ch. 32, § 13, effective March 30, 1995.

See, now, § 38-704.

§ 38-707. Repealed by Laws 1995, Ch. 32, § 13, eff. March 30, 1995

Historical and Statutory Notes

The repealed section, enacted as part of the revision effective January 9, 1956, derived from Laws 1951, Ch. 126, § 8, and Code 1939, Supp. 1952, § 12-836, related to state agency studies and reports.

See, now, § 38-705.

ARTICLE 2. ARIZONA STATE RETIREMENT SYSTEM

Article 2, consisting of §§ 38–711 to 38–721, 38–727 to 38–730, 38–735 to 38–746, 38–755 to 38–772, 38–781 to 38–783, and 38–791 to 38–794, was added by Laws 1995, Ch. 32, § 14, effective March 30, 1995.

Former Article 2, State Employees Retirement System, consisting of §§ 38–741 to 38–754, 38–756, 38–758 to 38–764, enacted as part of the revision effective January 9, 1956, § 38–743.01, added by Laws 1975, Ch. 53, § 4, § 38–743.05, added by Laws 1970, Ch. 136, § 5, § 38–743.06, added by Laws 1992, Ch. 188, § 1, § 38–746.01, added by Laws 1975, Ch. 52, § 1, § 38–752.01, added by Laws 1970, Ch. 136, § 11, § 38–757, added by Laws 1985, Ch. 257, § 3, § 38–759.01, added by Laws 1975, Ch. 57, § 2, §§ 38–765 to 38–775, added by Laws 1959, Ch. 145, § 2, § 38–777, added by Laws 1960, Ch. 42, § 3, and § 38–778, added by Laws 1968, Ch. 84, § 6, was repealed by Laws 1995, Ch. 32, § 13, effective March 30, 1995.

Termination under Sunset Law

The Arizona state retirement system shall terminate on July 1, 2006, unless continued. See §§ 41–3006.08 and 41–2955.

Title 38, Chapter 5, Article 2, relating to the Arizona state retirement system, is repealed on January 1, 2007 by § 41–3006.08.

DERIVATION TABLE

Showing where the subject matter of certain sections of Title 38 was incorporated in the Reorganization of Title 38 following the repeal of those sections by Laws 1995, Ch. 32, effective March 30, 1995.

New Sections	Former Sections
38–711	38–781.01
38–712	38–781
38–713	38–742
38–714	38–743
38–715	38–743.01
38–716	38–743.05, 38–781.17
38–717	38–743.06
38–718	38–752.01
38–719	38–757, 38–781.23
38–720	38–753, 38–781.21
38–721	38–756
38–727	38–745, 38–781.03
38–728	38–781.37
38–729	38–752, 38–781.20
38–730	38–781.24
38–735	38–781.14
38–736	38–748, 38–781.04
38–737	38–781.05
38–738	38–750, 38–781.19
38–739	None
38–740	38–758
38–741	38–758
38–742	38–781.40
38–743	38–781.39
38–744	38–746.01, 38–781.29
38–745	38–746, 38–781.42
38–746	38–781.38
38–747	None
38–755	38–744, 38–781.18
38–756	38–781.18
38–757	38–759, 38–781.07
38–758	38–781.08
38–759	38–781.09
38–760	38–781.10
38–761	None
38–762	None
38–763	None
38–764	38–781.13
38–765	38–781.15
38–766	38–781.16
38–767	38–781.27
38–768	38–781.26
38–769	38–781.38
38–770	38–781.45
38–771	38–781.44
38–772	38–781.05
38–773	None
38–781	38–781.31
38–782	38–781.25
38–783	38–781.41

New Sections	Former Sections
38–791	38–781.16
38–792	38–762, 38–781.22
38–793	38–763, 38–781.32
38–794	38–764, 38–781.33

Historical and Statutory Notes

Laws 1984, Ch. 397, § 1, effective May 16, 1984, provides:

"**Section 1. Permanent retirement benefit increases**

"Effective July 1, 1984, each person who was receiving retirement benefits on or before June 30, 1983, pursuant to Title 38, chapter 5, article 2 or 2.1, [Sections 38–741 et seq. or 38–781.01 et seq.] Arizona Revised Statutes, shall receive a permanent increase of forty dollars monthly in the base benefit being received on June 30, 1983."

Laws 1984, Ch. 397, § 2, as amended by Laws 1986, Ch. 13, § 1, effective April 14, 1986, provides:

"**Sec. 2. Funding**

"The cost of the benefit increases are payable from the current assets of the retirement plan. The cost of the benefit increases shall be added to the unfunded liability of the retirement plan."

Laws 1985, Ch. 270, § 1, effective May 1, 1985, provides:

"**Section 1. Permanent retirement benefit increases**

"Effective July 1, 1985, each person who was receiving retirement benefits on or before June 30, 1984 pursuant to title 38, chapter 5, article 2 or 2.1, Arizona Revised Statutes, shall receive a permanent increase of forty dollars per month in the base benefit received on June 30, 1985."

Laws 1985, Ch. 270, § 2, as amended by Laws 1986, Ch. 13, § 2, effective April 14, 1986, provides:

"**Sec. 2. Funding**

"The cost of the benefit increases is payable from the current assets of the retirement plan. The cost of the benefit increases shall be added to the unfunded liability of the retirement plan."

Laws 1986, Ch. 13, § 3 provides:

"**Sec. 3. Reimbursement by the state retirement plan to the state retirement system**

"The state retirement plan shall reimburse the state retirement system from the current assets of the retirement plan for any amounts paid by the system pursuant to Laws 1984, chapter 397, § 2 and Laws 1985, chapter 270, § 2."

Laws 1987, Ch. 281, §§ 1 and 2, effective May 12, 1987, provide:

"**Section 1. Permanent retirement benefit increases**

"**A.** Effective July 1, 1987, each person who was receiving retirement benefits on or before June 30, 1986 pursuant to title 38, chapter 5, article 2 or 2.1, Arizona Revised Statutes, shall receive a permanent increase in their monthly benefit equal to sixty cents for each year of credited future service, credited past service and prior service plus sixty cents for each year the person has been retired as of June 30, 1987. The sum of the years of credited future service, credited past service and prior service and years retired shall be rounded to the nearest whole number.

"**B.** Notwithstanding the provisions of subsection A of this section, the monthly benefit increase for any retired member shall not exceed ten per cent of the current monthly benefit nor shall it be less than two per cent.

"**Sec. 2. Funding**

"The cost of the benefit increases shall be added to the applicable employer cost of the retirement plan as determined pursuant to § 38–781.05, Arizona Revised Statutes."

For provision of Laws 1987, Ch. 133 relating to transfer of assets for nonjoinder members, see Historical and Statutory Notes following § 38–884.

Laws 1989, Ch. 310, § 18 provides:

"**Sec. 18. Permanent retirement benefit increases; funding**

"**A.** Effective July 1, 1989, each person who was receiving retirement benefits on or before June 30, 1988 pursuant to title 38, chapter 5, article 2 or 2.1, Arizona Revised Statutes, is entitled to receive a permanent increase of two per cent of his base benefit being received on December 31, 1988.

"**B.** Effective July 1, 1990, each person who was receiving retirement benefits on or before June 30, 1989 pursuant to title 38, chapter 5, article 2 or 2.1, Arizona Revised Statutes, is entitled to receive a permanent increase of two per cent of his base benefit being received on June 30, 1990.

"**C.** The cost of the benefit increase in subsections A and B of this section is payable from the current assets of the retirement plan. The cost of the benefit increase shall be added to the unfunded liability of the retirement plan."

Laws 1989, Ch. 310, § 27, subsec. G, as amended by Laws 1990, Ch. 68, § 1, provides:

"**Sec. 27. Retroactivity and applicability**"

"**G.** Section 18 of this act is effective retroactively to July 1, 1989."

Laws 1990, Ch. 217, § 1, provides:

"**Section 1. Permanent tax equity benefit allowance for retirees of the Arizona state retirement system; funding**

"Each person who retires after September 14, 1989 but before September 15, 1990 and who receives retirement benefits pursuant to title 38, chapter 5, article 2 or 2.1, Arizona Revised Statutes, is entitled to receive a tax equity benefit allowance retroactive to the date of retirement consisting of a permanent increase of three per cent of his base benefit. The cost of the benefit increase provided by this section is payable from the assets of the applicable retirement system or plan. The cost of the benefit increase shall be added to the unfunded liability of the applicable retirement system or plan."

Laws 1990, Ch. 235, § 7, effective September 1, 1990, provides:

"**Sec. 7. Transfer**

"The contracts, records and personnel relating to the retiree health insurance program shall be transferred from the department of administration to the Arizona state retirement system on the effective date of this act."

Laws 1995, Ch. 134, § 17, provides:

"**Sec. 17. Employer and member contributions**

"**A.** Notwithstanding §§ 38-736 and 38-737, Arizona Revised Statutes, for fiscal year 1995-1996, the contribution rate for the Arizona state retirement system established pursuant to title 38, chapter 5, article 2, Arizona Revised Statutes, is 3.36 per cent of payroll for both employers and members of the Arizona state retirement system.

"**B.** For fiscal year 1995-1996, the contribution rate for employers and members covered by the long-term disability program established by title 38, chapter 5, article 2.1, Arizona Revised Statutes, as added by this act, is .49 per cent of payroll for both employers and members."

Section 41-2996.02, which was to have repealed Title 38, Chapter 5, Article 2, effective January 1, 1997, was repealed by Laws 1996, Ch. 18, § 1, effective July 20, 1996, retroactively effective to July 1, 1996.

Laws 1997, Ch. 280, § 21, provides:

"**Sec. 21. Recalculation of costs of redeemed service; refund**

"**A.** The Arizona state retirement system shall recalculate the cost of redeemed service as provided in this section effective retroactively to the date of redemption of service by a retired member or a deceased retired member whose beneficiary is receiving benefits on account of a deceased retired member of the Arizona state retirement system if the retired member redeemed previously forfeited service pursuant to Laws 1986, chapter 77, § 1 or Laws 1992, chapter 137, § 1.

"**B.** The Arizona state retirement system shall recalculate the cost of redeemed service as provided in this section effective retroactively to the date of redemption of the service by an active member of the Arizona state retirement system if the active member redeemed previously forfeited service pursuant to Laws 1986, chapter 77, § 1 or Laws 1992, chapter 137, § 1.

"**C.** The Arizona state retirement system shall determine the amount a member described in subsection A or B of this section would have paid for the purchase of the member's previously forfeited service if § 38-742, Arizona Revised Statutes, as amended by Laws 1996, chapter 185, § 8, had been in effect at the time of purchase pursuant to Laws 1986, chapter 77, § 1 or Laws 1992, chapter 137, § 1.

"**D.** The Arizona state retirement system shall subtract the amount determined pursuant to subsection C of this section from the amount the member actually paid pursuant to Laws 1986, chapter 77, § 1 or Laws 1992, chapter 137, § 1. If the remainder is greater than zero and notwithstanding any other law, the Arizona state retirement system shall refund the remainder to the active member, the retired member or the retired member's beneficiary. The Arizona state retirement system shall pay a refund pursuant to this subsection to an active member at the time it makes retirement benefit payments.

"**E.** The Arizona state retirement system shall pay interest on any amounts refunded pursuant to this section. The interest shall be compounded annually at the interest rate assumption approved by the board from time to time for actuarial equivalency.

"**F.** Before retirement, an active member who is entitled to a payment pursuant to subsections D and E of this section may apply the amount of the payment to a purchase of additional service pursuant to § 38-742, 38-743 or 38-745, Arizona Revised Statutes, if the active member is eligible to purchase such service."

§ 38-711. Definitions

In this article, unless the context otherwise requires:

1. "Active member" means a member as defined in paragraph 23, subdivision (b) of this section who satisfies the eligibility criteria prescribed in § 38-

727 and who is currently making member contributions as prescribed in § 38–736.

2. "Actuarial equivalent" means equality in value of the aggregate amounts expected to be received under two different forms of payment, based on mortality and interest rate assumptions approved from time to time by the board.

3. "ASRS" means the Arizona state retirement system established by this article.

4. "Assets" means the resources of ASRS including all cash, investments or securities.

5. "Average monthly compensation" means:

(a) For a member whose membership in ASRS commenced before January 1, 1984 and who left the member's contributions on deposit or reinstated forfeited credited service pursuant to § 38–742 for a period of employment that commenced before January 1, 1984, the monthly average of compensation on which contributions were remitted during a period of sixty consecutive months during which the member receives the highest compensation within the last one hundred twenty months of credited service. Any month for which no contributions are reported to ASRS or that falls within a period of nonpaid or partially paid leave of absence or sabbatical leave shall be excluded from the computation. The sixty consecutive months may entirely precede, may be both before and after or may be completely after any excluded months. If the member was employed for less than sixty consecutive months, the average monthly compensation is based on the total consecutive months worked.

(b) Effective July 1, 1985, the monthly average of compensation on which contributions were remitted during a period of thirty-six consecutive months during which a member receives the highest compensation within the last one hundred twenty months of credited service. Any month for which no contributions are reported to ASRS or that falls within a period of nonpaid or partially paid leave of absence or sabbatical leave shall be excluded from the computation. The thirty-six consecutive months may entirely precede, may be both before and after or may be completely after any excluded months. If the member was employed for less than thirty-six consecutive months, the average monthly compensation shall be based on the total consecutive months worked. This subdivision applies only to members whose membership in ASRS was effective after December 31, 1983 or who agree in writing as a binding condition of eligibility for being granted the benefit advantages available under this subdivision to have their benefit computed on the basis of the definition of compensation.

6. "Board" means the ASRS board established in § 38–713.

7. "Compensation" means the gross amount paid to a member by an employer as salary or wages, including amounts that are subject to deferred compensation or tax shelter agreements, for services rendered to or for an employer, or that would have been paid to the member except for the member's election or a legal requirement that all or part of the gross amount be used for other purposes, but does not include amounts paid in excess of compensation limits established in § 38–746. Compensation includes amounts paid as salary

or wages to a member by a second employer. Compensation, as provided in paragraph 5, subdivision (b) of this section, does not include:

(a) Lump sum payments, on termination of employment, for accumulated vacation or annual leave, sick leave, compensatory time or any other form of termination pay whether the payments are made in one payment or by installments over a period of time.

(b) Damages, costs, attorney fees, interest or other penalties paid pursuant to a court order or a compromise settlement or agreement to satisfy a grievance or claim even though the amount of the payment is based in whole or in part on previous salary or wage levels, except that, if the court order or compromise settlement or agreement directs salary or wages to be paid for a specific period of time, the payment is compensation for that specific period of time. If the amount directed to be paid is less than the actual salary or wages that would have been paid for the period if service had been performed, the contributions for the period shall be based on the amount of compensation that would have been paid if the service had been performed.

(c) Payment, at the member's option, in lieu of fringe benefits that are normally paid for or provided by the employer.

(d) Merit awards pursuant to § 38–613 and performance bonuses paid to assistant attorneys general pursuant to § 41–192.

8. "Contingent annuitant" means the person named by a member to receive retirement income payable following a member's death after retirement as provided in § 38–760.

9. "Credited service" means, subject to § 38–739, the number of years standing to the member's credit on the books of ASRS during which the member made the required contributions.

10. "Current annual compensation" means the greater of:

(a) Annualized compensation of the full pay period immediately before the date of a request to ASRS to purchase credited service pursuant to § 38–743 or 38–745.

(b) Annualized compensation of the partial year if the member has less than twelve months total credited service on the date of a request to purchase credited service pursuant to § 38–743 or 38–745.

(c) The sum of the twelve months of compensation immediately before the date of a request to ASRS to purchase credited service pursuant to § 38–743 or 38–745.

(d) The sum of the thirty-six months of compensation immediately before the date of a request to ASRS to purchase credited service pursuant to § 38–743 or 38–745 divided by three.

(e) If the member has retired one or more times from ASRS, the average monthly compensation that was used for calculating the member's last pension benefit times twelve.

11. "Early retirement" means retirement before a member's normal retirement date after five years of total credited service and attainment of age fifty.

12. "Effective date" means July 1, 1970, except with respect to employers and members whose contributions to ASRS commence thereafter, the effective date of their membership in ASRS is as specified in the applicable joinder agreement.

13. "Employer" means:

(a) This state.

(b) Participating political subdivisions.

(c) Participating political subdivision entities.

14. "Employer contributions" means all amounts paid into ASRS by an employer on behalf of a member.

15. "Fiscal year" means the period from July 1 of any year to June 30 of the following year.

16. "Inactive member" means a member who previously made contributions to ASRS and who satisfies each of the following:

(a) Has not retired.

(b) Is not eligible for active membership in ASRS.

(c) Is not currently making contributions to ASRS.

(d) Has not withdrawn contributions from ASRS.

17. "Interest" means the assumed actuarial investment earnings rate approved by the board.

18. "Internal revenue code" means the United States internal revenue code of 1986, as amended. [1]

19. "Investment management" means the persons, companies, banks, insurance company investment funds, mutual fund companies, management or any combinations of those entities that are appointed by ASRS and that have responsibility and authority for investment of the monies of ASRS.

20. "Late retirement" means retirement after normal retirement.

21. "Leave of absence" means any unpaid leave authorized by the employer, including leaves authorized for sickness or disability or to pursue education or training.

22. "Life annuity" means equal monthly installments payable during the member's lifetime after retirement.

23. "Member":

(a) Means any employee of an employer on the effective date.

(b) Means all employees of an employer who are eligible for membership pursuant to § 38-727 and who are engaged to work at least twenty weeks in each fiscal year and at least twenty hours each week.

(c) Means any person receiving a benefit under ASRS.

(d) Means any person who is a former active member of ASRS and who has not withdrawn contributions from ASRS pursuant to § 38-740.

(e) Does not include any employee of an employer who is otherwise eligible pursuant to this article and who begins service in a limited appointment for not more than eighteen months on or after July 1, 1979. If the employment exceeds eighteen months, the employee shall be covered by ASRS as of the beginning of the nineteenth month of employment. In order to be excluded under this subdivision, classifications of employees designated by employers as limited appointments must be approved by the director.

(f) Does not include any leased employee. For the purposes of § 414(n) of the internal revenue code, "leased employee" means an individual who:

(i) Is not otherwise an employee of an employer.

(ii) Pursuant to a leasing agreement between the employer and another person, performs services for the employer on a substantially full-time basis for at least one year.

(iii) Performs services under the primary direction or control of the employer.

24. "Member contributions" means all amounts paid to ASRS by a member.

25. "Normal costs" means the sum of the individual normal costs for all active members for each fiscal year. The normal cost for an individual active member is the cost that is assigned to the fiscal year using the projected unit credit method.

26. "Normal retirement age" means the age at which a member reaches the member's normal retirement date.

27. "Normal retirement date" means the earliest of the following:

(a) A member's sixty-fifth birthday.

(b) A member's sixty-second birthday and completion of at least ten years of credited service.

(c) The first day that the sum of a member's age and years of total credited service equals eighty.

28. "Political subdivision" means any political subdivision of this state and includes a political subdivision entity.

29. "Political subdivision entity" means an entity:

(a) That is located in this state.

(b) That is created in whole or in part by political subdivisions, including instrumentalities of political subdivisions.

(c) Where a majority of the membership of the entity is composed of political subdivisions.

(d) Whose primary purpose is the performance of a government related service.

30. "Retired member" means a member who is receiving retirement benefits pursuant to this article.

31. "Service year" means fiscal year, except that:

(a) If the normal work year required of a member is less than the full fiscal year but is for a period of at least nine months, the service year is the normal work year.

(b) For a salaried member employed on a contract basis under one contract, or two or more consecutive contracts, for a total period of at least nine months, the service year is the total period of the contract or consecutive contracts.

(c) In determining average monthly compensation pursuant to paragraph 5 of this section, the service year is considered to be twelve months of compensation.

32. "State" means this state, including any department, office, board, commission, agency, institution or other instrumentality of this state.

33. "Vested" means that a member is eligible to receive a future retirement benefit.

Added by Laws 1995, Ch. 32, § 14, eff. March 30, 1995. Amended by Laws 1996, Ch. 185, § 3; Laws 1997, Ch. 280, § 1; Laws 1998, Ch. 1, § 110, eff. Jan. 1, 1999; Laws 1998, Ch. 155, § 1; Laws 1999, Ch. 327, § 2; Laws 2000, Ch. 132, § 1; Laws 2001, Ch. 136, § 4; Laws 2003, Ch. 164, § 1, eff. May 7, 2003; Laws 2004, Ch. 246, § 1.

[1] Internal Revenue Code sections may be found in Title 26 of U.S.C.A.

Historical and Statutory Notes

Source:

Laws 1953, Ch. 128, § 3.
Code 1939, Supp.1953, § 12-839.
Laws 1954, Ch. 116, § 1.
A.R.S. former § 38-741.
Laws 1957, Ch. 96, § 1.
Laws 1965, Ch. 87, § 1.
A.R.S. former § 38-781.01.
Laws 1970, Ch. 134, § 2.
Laws 1970, Ch. 136, § 2.
Laws 1972, Ch. 51, § 14.
Laws 1974, Ch. 120, §§ 1 and 6.
Laws 1975, Ch. 53, §§ 1 and 2.
Laws 1978, Ch. 54, § 1.
Laws 1979, Ch. 221, § 2.
Laws 1981, Ch. 284, § 2.
Laws 1983, Ch. 293, § 1.
Laws 1985, Ch. 196, § 1.
Laws 1985, Ch. 294, §§ 1 and 3.
Laws 1986, Ch. 285, § 1.
Laws 1987, Ch. 274, § 1.
Laws 1989, Ch. 310, § 2.
Laws 1990, Ch. 145, § 1.
Laws 1990, Ch. 396, § 1.
Laws 1991, Ch. 170, § 1.
Laws 1991, Ch. 270, § 4.
Laws 1992, Ch. 319, § 32.
Laws 1992, Ch. 320, § 5.
Laws 1994, Ch. 356, § 8.

Laws 1995, Ch. 134, § 17, provides:

"**Sec. 17. Employer and member contributions**

"**A.** Notwithstanding §§ 38-736 and 38-737, Arizona Revised Statutes, for fiscal year 1995-1996, the contribution rate for the Arizona state retirement system established pursuant to title 38, chapter 5, article 2, Arizona Revised Statutes, is 3.36 per cent of payroll for both employers and members of the Arizona state retirement system.

"**B.** For fiscal year 1995-1996, the contribution rate for employers and members covered by the long-term disability program established by title 38, chapter 5, article 2.1, Arizona Revised Statutes, as added by this act, is .49 per cent of payroll for both employers and members."

The 1998 amendments by Ch. 1 and 155 made changes in statutory references to conform to the reorganization of Title 42.

The 1999 amendment by Ch. 327 deleted "or (c)" following "subdivision (b)" in par. 1; inserted in par. 7 the sentence reading "Compensation includes amounts paid as salary or wages to a member by a second employer."; and deleted, in par. 22, former subd. (c), redesignating former subds. (d) and (e) as subds. (c) and (d). Former subd. (c) had read:

"(c) Means all employees of an employer who are eligible pursuant to this article and whose work for more than one employer totals at least twenty weeks in a fiscal year and at least twenty hours each week and includes work provided on a part-time basis to an employer who is not the full-time employer of the employee."

Laws 1999, Ch. 327, § 27, providing for withdrawal of contributions from the Arizona state retirement system, was repealed by sec. 31 of the act, eff. Jan. 1, 2001.

Laws 1999, Ch. 327, § 28, effective July 1, 2000, provides:

"**Sec. 28. Arizona state retirement system defined benefit retirees; benefit increase**

"A member or a member's beneficiary who is receiving a benefit under the Arizona state retirement system defined benefit program established by title 38, chapter 5, article 2, Arizona Revised Statutes, on July 1, 2000 is entitled to receive a one-time permanent increase of five per cent of the member's or beneficiary's monthly benefit amount."

Laws 1999, Ch. 327, § 30, provides:

"**Sec. 30. Retroactivity**

"**A.** Section 38-797.07, Arizona Revised Statutes, as amended by this act, applies retroactively to from and after June 30, 1996.

"**B.** Section 27 of this act, relating to withdrawal of contributions from the Arizona state retirement system, is effective retroactively to from and after December 31, 1998."

Laws 1999, Ch. 327, § 32, provides:

"**Sec. 32. Delayed effective date**

"Section 38-757, Arizona Revised Statutes, as amended by this act, and § 28 of this act, relating to benefit increases for Arizona state retirement system defined benefits retirees, are effective from and after June 30, 2000."

The 2000 amendment by Ch. 132 added new par. 25, "normal retirement age", redesignating subsequent paragraphs accordingly.

The 2001 amendment by Ch. 136 rewrote pars. 1 and 22, which had read:

"1. "Active member" means a member as defined in paragraph 22, subdivision (b) of this section who satisfies the eligibility criteria prescribed in § 38-727 and who either is currently making member contributions as prescribed in § 38-736 or is receiving credited service under article 2.1 of this chapter.

"22. "Member":

"(a) Means any employee of an employer on the effective date.

"(b) Means all employees of an employer who are eligible for membership pursuant to § 38-727 and who are engaged to work at least twenty weeks in each fiscal year and at least twenty hours each week.

"(c) Means any person receiving a benefit under ASRS.

"(d) Does not include any employee of an employer who is otherwise eligible pursuant to this article and who begins service in a limited appointment for not more than eighteen months on or after July 1, 1979. If the employment exceeds eighteen months, the employee shall be covered by ASRS as of the beginning of the nineteenth month of employment. In order to be excluded under this subdivision, classifications of employees designated by employers as limited appointments must be approved by the director."

Laws 2001, Ch. 380, § 16, provides:

"**Sec. 16. Termination of the tax deferred annuity and deferred compensation pilot program**

"This act terminates the pilot program option for legislative employees and state elected officials to elect to participate in a tax deferred annuity and deferred compensation program pursuant to title 38, chapter 5, article 5, Arizona Revised Statutes, in lieu of participation in the Arizona state retirement system pursuant to title 38, chapter 5, article 2, Arizona Revised Statutes. All legislative employees and state elected officials who elected on or before the effective date of this act to participate in a deferred tax annuity and deferred compensation program in lieu of participation in the Arizona state retirement system shall continue to participate in that option pursuant to the irrevocable election made by the employee or state elected official and the employer shall continue to pay an amount equal to five per cent of the employee's or state elected official's base salary directly to the program in lieu of employer contributions to a public retirement system."

The 2003 amendment by Ch. 164, inserted new par. 10, defining "Current annual compensation"; redesignated existing pars. 10 to 31, as 11 to 32, accordingly; and modified internal references to paragraphs to accommodate the redesignations of the paragraph numbers.

The 2004 amendment by Ch. 246 inserted new subd. (c) in par. 13; inserted "and includes a political subdivision entity" in par. 28; inserted new par. 29, and redesignated existing pars. 29 through 32 as 30 through 33 accordingly; and rewrote par. 25, which had read:

"25. 'Normal costs' means costs of ASRS as computed under the projected unit credit method of actuarial computation that would have arisen if the benefits in effect at the time of the computation had always been in effect from the time of earliest eligibility of the current members."

Laws 2004, Ch. 246, § 2, provides:

"**Sec. 2. Current participating political subdivision entities; retroactive effective date**

"The effective date of any current participating political subdivision entity that meets the definition of political subdivision entity as added by this act is retroactively effective to the political subdivision entity's effective date as specified in the applicable joinder agreement."

Reviser's Notes:

1998 Note. Prior to the 1999 amendment, this section contained the amendments made by Laws 1998, Ch. 1, sec. 110 and Ch. 155, sec. 1 that were blended together pursuant to authority of § 41-1304.03.

§ 38-712. ASRS purpose; trust fund

A. The primary intent of ASRS is to:

1. Provide an incentive in the recruitment and retention of employees of the highest possible quality.

2. Contribute toward providing a total compensation package that is generally equivalent to comparable employment in other public and private organizations in this state.

3. Provide a retirement system that encourages employees to remain in service for periods of time that will provide public employers with the full benefit of the training and experience gained by the employees.

4. Provide an orderly method of promoting and maintaining a high level of service to the public through an equitable separation procedure that is available to employees at retirement or on becoming disabled.

5. Provide a base retirement benefit that is less than one hundred per cent of a member's post-retirement income requirements, recognizing that personal savings and social security also contribute toward total post-retirement income requirements.

B. ASRS is a defined benefit plan as described in § 414(j) of the internal revenue code.[1] As provided in § 38-771, some eligible members of ASRS are entitled to benefits under the defined contribution program administered by ASRS. With respect to the portion of ASRS that provides benefits to members entitled to benefits under the defined contribution program that are derived from employer contributions and that are based partly on the balance of the separate account of a member, ASRS is a plan described in § 414(k) of the internal revenue code and shall comply with all applicable provisions of § 414(k) of the internal revenue code.

C. A public employee's retirement trust fund is established to afford an optimum degree of security to the members of ASRS. All monies and other assets of ASRS are a part of the trust fund. All accounts, depositories and funds of ASRS are included within the trust fund.

D. Except as provided in § 38-738, an employer does not have a beneficial interest in any asset of the trust fund, and no part of the trust fund may ever revert to or be paid, directly or indirectly, to an employer. All liabilities with respect to members and their beneficiaries shall be satisfied before any part of the corpus or income of the trust fund is used for or diverted to purposes other than for the exclusive benefit of members or their beneficiaries.

Added by Laws 1995, Ch. 32, § 14, eff. March 30, 1995. Amended by Laws 1997, Ch. 280, § 2.

[1] 26 U.S.C.A. § 414.

Historical and Statutory Notes

Source:

A.R.S. former § 38-781.
Laws 1991, Ch. 270, § 3.

The 1997 amendment by Ch. 280 inserted a new subsec. B describing ASRS; redesignated former subsec. B as subsec. C and deleted the second sentence which prohibited the use or appropriation of trust fund assets for any purpose inconsistent with protecting the assets of ASRS for the benefit of members; and added subsec. D relating to beneficial interest in and use of trust fund assets.

§ 38-713. ASRS board; qualifications; term; compensation

A. The ASRS board is established consisting of the following nine members appointed by the governor pursuant to § 38-211:

1. Five members from among the members of ASRS to represent the members of ASRS as follows:

(a) An educator.

(b) An employee of a political subdivision.

(c) A retired member.

(d) An employee of this state.

(e) An at large member who may represent any ASRS member group. 2. Four members who are not members of ASRS to represent the public.

B. Four of the members shall have at least ten years' substantial experience as any one or a combination of the following:

1. A portfolio manager acting in a fiduciary capacity.

2. A securities analyst.

3. An employee or principal of a trust institution, investment organization or endowment fund acting either in a management or an investment related capacity.

4. A chartered financial analyst in good standing as determined by the association for investment management and research.

5. A professor at the university level teaching economics or investment related subjects.

6. An economist.

7. Any other professional engaged in the field of public or private finances.

C. Each member who represents an ASRS member group shall have not less than five years of administrative management experience.

D. The following persons are not eligible for membership on the board:

1. A person who is a stockbroker or bond broker and who is actively engaged in the profession of a stockbroker or bond broker.

2. A person who holds a real estate license pursuant to title 32, chapter 20.[1]

E. A member may be reappointed. Vacancies occurring other than by expiration of a term shall be filled for the balance of the term in the same manner as for initial appointment. On the expiration of any term, the governor shall appoint a successor for a full term of three years that expires on the third Monday in January of the appropriate year.

F. Board members are eligible to receive compensation for performing their duties in an amount of fifty dollars a day, but not more than one thousand dollars in any one fiscal year, and are eligible for reimbursement of expenses pursuant to chapter 4, article 2 of this title.[2]

Added by Laws 1995, Ch. 32, § 14, eff. March 30, 1995. Amended by Laws 1995, Ch. 134, § 2, eff. April 17, 1995; Laws 1997, Ch. 143, § 1, eff. Jan. 1, 1998; Laws 2003, Ch. 63, § 1.

[1] Section 32–2101 et seq.

[2] Section 38–621 et seq.

Historical and Statutory Notes

Source:

Laws 1953, Ch. 128, § 15.
Code 1939, Supp.1953, § 12-851.
Laws 1954, Ch. 116, § 8.
Laws 1955, Ch. 104, § 2.
A.R.S. former § 38-742.
Laws 1970, Ch. 136, § 3.
Laws 1970, Ch. 204, § 145.
Laws 1971, Ch. 90, § 2.
Laws 1972, Ch. 163, § 39.
Laws 1974, Ch. 180, § 1.
Laws 1975, Ch. 158, § 1.
Laws 1987, Ch. 75, § 1.
Laws 1994, Ch. 101, § 1.

The 1995 amendment by Ch. 134, in subsec. E, inserted "for performing their duties" following "compensation", and substituted "a day" for "for each day the board meets" following "fifty dollars".

The 1997 amendment by Ch. 143 rewrote the section which had read:

"**A.** The ASRS board is established consisting of the following seven members appointed by the governor pursuant to § 38-211:

"1. Four members from among the members of ASRS to represent the members of ASRS as follows:

"(a) An educator.

"(b) An employee of a political subdivision.

"(c) A retired member.

"(d) An employee of this state.

"2. Three members who are not members of ASRS to represent the public.

"**B.** Each member shall have not less than five years of administrative management experience.

"**C.** Two of the seven members shall also serve as members of the investment advisory council established pursuant to § 38-716. A member of the board who is also a member of the investment advisory council shall not serve as the presiding officer of the meetings of the board and the council during the same time period.

"**D.** A member may be reappointed. Vacancies occurring other than by expiration of a term shall be filled for the balance of the term in the same manner as for initial appointment. On the expiration of any term, the governor shall appoint a successor for a full term of three years that expires on the third Monday in January of the appropriate year.

"**E.** Board members are eligible to receive compensation for performing their duties in an amount of fifty dollars a day, but not more than one thousand dollars in any one fiscal year, and are eligible for reimbursement of expenses pursuant to chapter 4, article 2 of this title."

Laws 1997, Ch. 143, §§ 9 and 10, provide:

"**Sec. 9. Investment advisory council members; retention on ASRS board; initial terms of new ASRS board members**

"**A.** Any member of the investment advisory council who is not a member of the Arizona state retirement system board on the effective date of this act becomes a member of the Arizona state retirement system board on the effective date of this act. The term of a person who becomes a member of the Arizona state retirement system board pursuant to this subsection expires on the same day that the person's term on the investment advisory council would have expired.

"**B.** Notwithstanding § 38-713, Arizona Revised Statutes, as amended by this act:

"1. A person who does not meet the membership requirements prescribed by this act may continue to serve until the expiration of the member's normal term.

"2. The initial terms of new members of the Arizona state retirement system board are as follows:

"(a) The initial term of the new public member expires on the third Monday in January, 1998.

"(b) The initial term of the at large member expires on the third Monday in January, 2000.

"**Sec. 10. Delayed effective date**

"This act is effective from and after December 31, 1997."

The 2003 amendment by Ch. 63, inserted "as determined by the association for investment management and research", in subsec. A, par. 4.

§ 38-714. Powers and duties of ASRS and board

A. ASRS shall have the powers and privileges of a corporation, shall have an official seal and shall transact all business in the name "Arizona state retirement system", and in that name may sue and be sued.

B. The board is responsible for supervising the administration of this article by the director of ASRS, except the investment powers and duties of investment management.

C. The board is responsible for the performance of fiduciary duties and other responsibilities required to preserve and protect the retirement trust fund established by § 38–712.

D. The board shall:

1. Prescribe investment goals, objectives and policies that are consistent with the purposes of this article and the limitations and standard of care prescribed in § 38–719, subsection B.

2. Allocate assets to meet the investment goals, objectives and policies it prescribes.

3. Adopt specific policy directives for the guidance of investment management.

4. Meet with each investment manager at least annually or at the request of a board member to review the investment manager's performance and the investment manager's attainment of and adherence to the board's investment goals, objectives and policies.

E. The board shall not advocate for or against legislation providing for benefit modifications, except that the board shall provide technical and administrative information regarding the impact of benefit modification legislation.

F. The board may:

1. Determine the rights, benefits or obligations of any person under this article and afford any person dissatisfied with a determination a hearing on the determination.

2. Determine the amount, manner and time of payment of any benefits under this article.

3. Assign, transfer and deliver all stocks, bonds and other investments owned by ASRS if it is not inconsistent with or does not in any way contravene the authority of investment management for investing, reinvesting, purchasing and selling stocks, bonds and other investments.

4. Recommend amendments to this article and articles 2.1 and 7 of this chapter [1] that are required for efficient and effective administration.

5. Adopt, amend or repeal rules for the administration of this article.

6. Prescribe investment diversification programs and assign investment management responsibilities regarding those programs as it deems appropriate to achieve its investment goals, objectives and policies.

G. The board shall submit to the governor and legislature for each fiscal year no later than eight months after the close of the fiscal year a report of its operations and the operations of ASRS. The report shall follow generally accepted accounting principles and generally accepted financial reporting standards and shall include:

1. A report on an actuarial valuation of ASRS assets and liabilities.

2. Any other statistical and financial data that may be necessary for the proper understanding of the financial condition of ASRS and the results of board operations.

H. The board shall:

1. Prepare and publish a synopsis of the annual report for the information of ASRS members.

2. Contract for a study of the mortality, disability, service and other experiences of the members and employers participating in ASRS. The study shall be conducted for fiscal year 1990–1991 and for at least every fifth fiscal year thereafter. A report of the study shall be completed within eight months of the close of the applicable fiscal year and shall be submitted to the governor and the legislature.

3. Conduct an annual actuarial valuation of ASRS assets and liabilities.

I. The auditor general may make an annual audit of ASRS and transmit the results to the governor and the legislature.

Added by Laws 1995, Ch. 32, § 14, eff. March 30, 1995. Amended by Laws 1997, Ch. 143, § 2, eff. Jan. 1, 1998; Laws 1997, Ch. 221, § 179; Laws 1997, Ch. 280, § 3; Laws 1999, Ch. 327, § 3.

[1] Sections 38–781 et seq., 38–921 et seq.

Historical and Statutory Notes

Source:

Laws 1953, Ch. 128, § 15.
Code 1939, Supp.1953, § 12–851.
Laws 1954, Ch. 116, § 8.
Laws 1955, Ch. 104, § 2
A.R.S. former § 38–743.
Laws 1975, Ch. 53, § 4.
Laws 1979, Ch. 220, § 1.
Laws 1982, Ch. 141, § 2.
Laws 1991, Ch. 270, § 1.
Laws 1992, Ch. 53, § 1.
Laws 1994, Ch. 101, § 2.
Laws 1994, Ch. 356, § 4.

The 1997 amendment by Ch. 143 deleted "and the investment advisory council" following "investment management" in subsec. B; inserted a new subsec. D relating to the board's responsibilities pertaining to investment goals and management; redesignated former subsecs. D through H as subsecs. E through I; and added subsec. F, par. 7, relating to the board's power to prescribe investment diversification programs and assign investment management responsibilities.

The 1997 amendment by Ch. 221, in subsec. E, deleted former par. 6, which had read:

"6. Designate a hearing officer to conduct hearings requested by persons who are dissatisfied with determinations made by the board pursuant to paragraph 1 of this subsection."

The 1997 amendment by Ch. 280 added the reference to article 2.1 in subsec. E, par. 4; and rewrote subsec. F which had read:

"**F.** The board shall submit to the governor and legislature for each fiscal year no later than eight months after the close of the fiscal year a report of its operations and the operations of ASRS. The report shall include:

"1. Investment information including:

"(a) A statement of the realized and unrealized capital gain and loss experience of each investment manager.

"(b) A statement of the net amount of investment income produced by each investment manager.

"(c) A summary statement of changes in the investment portfolio of each investment manager, and the net cost of all purchases and sales.

"(d) A list of all investments owned.

"(e) A balance sheet for ASRS funds.

"(f) A statement of income and expenditures for the year for ASRS funds.

"(g) The total rate of return, yield on cost and per cent of cost to market value of ASRS funds.

"2. A report on an actuarial valuation of ASRS assets and liabilities.

"3. Any other statistical and financial data that may be necessary for the proper understanding of the financial condition of ASRS and the results of board operations."

The 1999 amendment by Ch. 327, inserted in subsec. D, par. 4.

Reviser's Notes:

1995 Note. Pursuant to authority of § 41-1304.02, the material contained in subsection I was moved to § 38–715 and relettered as subsection F.

1997 Note. Prior to the effective date of the 1997 blend of Ch. 143, § 2, Ch. 221, § 179, and Ch. 280, § 3, this section contained the amendments made by Laws 1997, Ch. 221, sec. 179 and Ch. 280, sec. 3 that were blended together pursuant to authority of § 41–1304.03.

Prior to the 1999 amendment, this section contained the amendments made by Laws 1997, Ch. 143, sec. 2, Ch. 221, sec. 179 and Ch. 280, sec. 3 that were blended together pursuant to authority of § 41-1304.03.

§ 38-715. Director; powers and duties

A. The board shall appoint a director. The term of the director is one year and expires on June 30. On expiration of a director's term, the board may reappoint the director for another term. The board may remove the director at any time for cause.

B. The director shall appoint a deputy director and assistant directors with the approval of the board.

C. The director, under the supervision of the board, shall:

1. Administer this article, except the investment powers and duties of investment management.

2. Hire employees and services the director deems necessary and prescribe their duties.

3. Prescribe procedures to be followed by members and their beneficiaries in filing applications for benefits.

4. Be responsible for:

(a) Income and the collection of income and the accuracy of all expenditures.

(b) Maintaining books and maintaining and processing records of ASRS.

(c) The investment of temporary surplus monies only in obligations of the United States government or agencies whose obligations are guaranteed by the United States government, commercial paper or banker's acceptances for a term of not more than fifteen days.

(d) Providing continuing education programs for the board to keep the board members informed of current issues and information needed to carry out their duties.

5. Perform additional powers and duties as may be prescribed by the board and delegated to the director.

D. The director, under the supervision and approval of the board, may:

1. Delegate duties and responsibilities to such state departments as the director deems feasible and desirable to administer this article.

2. Appoint a custodian for the safekeeping of all investments owned by ASRS and register stocks, bonds and other investments in the name of a nominee.

3. Invest marketable securities owned by ASRS by entering into security loan agreements with one or more security lending entities. For the purpose of this paragraph:

(a) "Marketable securities" means securities that are freely and regularly traded on recognized exchanges or marketplaces.

(b) "Security loan agreement" means a written contract under which ASRS, as lender, agrees to lend specific marketable securities for a period of not more than one year. ASRS, under a security loan agreement, shall retain the right to collect from the borrower all dividends, interest, premiums and rights and any other distributions to which ASRS otherwise would have been entitled. During the term of a security loan agreement ASRS shall waive the right to vote the securities that are the subject of the agreement. A security loan agreement shall provide for termination by either party on terms mutually acceptable to the parties. The borrower shall deliver collateral to ASRS or its designated representative. At all times during the term of any security loan agreement the collateral shall be in an amount equal to at least one hundred per cent of the market value of the loaned securities. A security loan agreement shall provide for payment of additional collateral on a daily basis, or at such other less frequent intervals as the value of the loaned securities increases. A security loan agreement with a security lending entity shall contain the terms and conditions of the fees to be paid to a security lending entity for servicing the security loan agreement. ASRS shall pay the fees approved by the board to the security lending entity for servicing a security loan agreement from the revenues of the security lending program.

4. Establish one or more reserve holding accounts, into which the board shall close periodically the account balances of inactive accounts. If any person files a claim and furnishes proof of ownership of any amounts in any inactive account the claim shall be paid from the reserve holding account on the same basis as if no action had been taken under this paragraph. Interest and supplemental credits shall be allocated to each reserve holding account on June 30 of each year, as determined by the board. For the purposes of this paragraph, "inactive account" means an account to which contributions have not been paid for six months or more.

5. Make retirement under this article effective retroactively to on or after the day following the date employment is terminated if the member was unable to apply before the retroactive effective date through no fault of the member.

E. The director, under supervision of the governing committee for tax deferred annuity and deferred compensation plans, may hire and supervise employees and obtain services the director deems necessary to administer article 5 of this chapter.[1] The tax deferred annuity and deferred compensation programs established pursuant to article 5 of this chapter shall bear the costs for these employees and services.

F. The director and all persons employed by the director shall be compensated as determined pursuant to § 38-611.

Added by Laws 1995, Ch. 32, § 14, eff. March 30, 1995. Amended by Laws 1995, Ch. 134, § 3, eff. April 17, 1995; Laws 1996, Ch. 185, § 4; Laws 1996, Ch. 351, § 20; Laws 1997, Ch. 143, § 3, eff. Jan. 1, 1998; Laws 1997, Ch. 280, § 4.

[1] Section 38-871 et seq.

Historical and Statutory Notes

Source:

A.R.S. former § 38-743.01.
Laws 1975, Ch. 53, § 4.
Laws 1977, Ch. 140, § 4.
Laws 1985, Ch. 48, § 1.
Laws 1985, Ch. 294, § 2.
Laws 1994, Ch. 101, § 3.
Laws 1994, Ch. 356, § 5.

The 1995 amendment by Ch. 134, in subsec. A, deleted "to serve at the pleasure of the board" at the end of the first sentence, and added the second through fourth sentences, relating to the term, reappointment, and removal of the director, respectively; and in subsec. D, deleted "either:", and added former subd. (a) to the end of the introduction, and deleted former subds. (b) and (c) of par. 4, which had read:

"(b) An account with less than five years of credited service.

"(c) An account with a balance of less than one thousand dollars and on which the member has failed to contact ASRS for three years or more."

Amendment of this section by Laws 1995, Ch. 134, § 3, was repealed by Laws 1996, Ch. 185, § 5, and by Laws 1996, Ch. 351, § 21.

The 1996 amendment by Ch. 185 rewrote subsec. A, which had read:

"**A.** The board shall appoint a director to serve at the pleasure of the board."

The 1996 amendment also rewrote the last sentence of subsec. D, par. 4, which had read:

"For the purposes of this paragraph, 'inactive account' means either:"

"(a) An account to which contributions have not been paid for six months or more.

"(b) An account with less than five years of credited service.

"(c) An account with a balance of less than one thousand dollars and on which the member has failed to contact ASRS for three years or more."

Finally, the 1996 amendment substituted "ninety days" for "sixty days" in subsec. D, par. 5 (b).

The 1996 amendment of this section by Ch. 185 explicitly amended the addition of this section by Laws 1995, Ch. 32, § 14.

The 1996 amendment by Ch. 351 rewrote subsec. A; in subsec. D, par. 4, included the material in subd. (a) in the first paragraph and deleted subds. (b) and (c) relating to accounts with less than five years of credited service and to certain accounts with a balance of less than one thousand dollars. Prior to the 1996 amendment, subsec. A had read:

"**A.** The board shall appoint a director to serve at the pleasure of the board."

The 1996 amendment of this section by Ch. 351 explicitly amended the 1995 amendment of this section by Ch. 32, § 14.

Laws 1996, Ch. 351, § 1, par. 9, provides:

"**Section 1. Purpose**"

"9. Section 38-715, Arizona Revised Statutes, was amended by Laws 1995, chapter 134, § 3. However, due to an error four words of existing text in subsection B were omitted from the act. In order to comply with article IV, part 2, § 14, Constitution of Arizona, in this act the previous valid version of § 38-715, Arizona Revised Statutes, is amended to incorporate the amendments made by Laws 1995, chapter 134, § 3 and the chapter 134 version is repealed."

Laws 1996, Ch. 351, § 58, subsec. A, provides:

"**Sec. 58. Retroactive application**

"**A.** Sections 18 through 21 of this act apply retroactively to April 17, 1995."

The 1997 amendment by Ch. 143 substituted "for the board to keep the board members informed" for "for the board and the investment advisory council to keep them informed" in subsec. C, par. 4(d); and deleted subsec. C, par. 5, relating to the provision or procurement of materials and services for the investment advisory council.

The 1997 amendment by Ch. 280 rewrote subsec. D, pars. 3 and 5 which had read:

"3. Invest marketable securities owned by ASRS by entering into security loan agreements. For the purpose of this paragraph:

"(a) 'Marketable securities' means securities that are freely and regularly traded on recognized exchanges or marketplaces.

"(b) 'Security loan agreement' means a written contract under which ASRS, as lender, agrees to lend specific marketable securities for a period of not more than one year. ASRS, under a security loan agreement, shall retain the right to collect from the borrower all dividends, interest, premiums and rights and any other distributions to which ASRS otherwise would have been entitled. During the term of a security loan agreement ASRS shall waive the right to vote the securities that are the subject of the agreement. A security loan agreement shall provide for termination by either party on terms mutually acceptable to the parties. The borrower shall deliver collateral to ASRS or its designated representative in the form of cash. At all times during the term of any security loan agreement the collateral shall be in an amount equal to at least one hundred per cent of the market value of the loaned securities. A security loan agreement shall provide for payment of additional collateral on a daily basis, or at such other less frequent intervals as the value of the loaned securities increases. Each security loan agreement shall be subject to a custodial agreement between ASRS and the custodian appointed pursuant to paragraph 2 of this subsection. The custodial agreement shall contain the terms and conditions of the fees to be paid to the custodian for servicing the security loan agreement. ASRS shall pay the fees approved by the board to the custodian for servicing the security loan agreements from the income of the investment of marketable securities pursuant to this paragraph."

"5. Make retirement under this article effective retroactively to on or after the day following the date employment is terminated if both of the following conditions are met:

"(a) The member was unable to apply before the retroactive effective date through no fault of the member.

"(b) The retroactive effective date is not more than ninety days before the date the director receives the retirement application."

Reviser's Notes:

1995 Note. Pursuant to authority of § 41–1304.02, subsection F consists of material that was added as § 38–714, subsection I and that was moved to this section.

1995 Note. The amendment of this section by Laws 1995, Ch. 134, sec. 3 failed to set forth in full the text of the section as amended [added] by Laws 1995, Ch. 32, sec. 14, an emergency act, as required by Constitution of Arizona art. IV, pt. 2, sec. 14.

1996 Note. Prior to the 1997 amendments, this section contained the amendments made by Laws 1996, Ch. 185, sec. 4 and Ch. 351, sec. 20 that were blended together pursuant to authority of § 41–1304.03.

1997 Note. This section contains the amendments made by Laws 1997, Ch. 143, sec. 3 and Ch. 280, sec. 4 that were blended together as shown above pursuant to authority of § 41–1304.03.

§ 38–716. Repealed by Laws 1997, Ch. 143, § 4, eff. Jan. 1, 1998

Historical and Statutory Notes

The repealed section, added by Laws 1995, Ch. 32, § 14, relating to the investment advisory council, was derived from:

A.R.S. former §§ 38–743.05, 38–781.17.

Laws 1970, Ch. 134, § 2.

Laws 1970, Ch. 136, § 5.

Laws 1973, Ch. 21, § 1.

Laws 1979, Ch. 104, first § 2.

Laws 1987, Ch. 75, § 2.

Laws 1992, Ch. 321, § 1.

Laws 1994, Ch. 101, § 4.

§ 38–717. Liability insurance and immunity for the board

A. The department of administration shall provide coverage pursuant to title 41, chapter 3.1, article 1 [1] against all liability for acts or omissions of any nature by members of the board while acting in an authorized governmental or proprietary capacity and within the course and scope of their employment or authority.

B. Notwithstanding any other law, a member of the board is immune from civil liability and is not subject to suit directly or by way of contribution for any act or omission resulting in any damage or injury if the member was acting in good faith and within the scope of the member's official capacity, unless the damage or injury was caused by wilful and wanton or grossly negligent conduct of the member. For the purposes of this subsection, "official capacity" means any decision or act taken by a member of the board to further the purpose for which the board is established.

Added by Laws 1995, Ch. 32, § 14, eff. March 30, 1995. Amended by Laws 1997, Ch. 143, § 5, eff. Jan. 1, 1998.

[1] Section 41–621 et seq.

Historical and Statutory Notes

Source:

A.R.S. former § 38–743.06.
Laws 1992, Ch. 188, § 1.

The 1997 amendment by Ch. 143 deleted references to the investment advisory council throughout.

§ 38–718. Investment management; qualifications; term; removal; general powers and duties

A. The board shall appoint investment management. Investment management shall have:

1. The highest professional and fiduciary recommendations.

2. Not less than three years' experience at handling institutional investments of at least two hundred fifty million dollars and not less than two hundred fifty million dollars currently under management.

3. Had responsibility for investment decision making as an insurance company investment fund, an investment division of a bank, a mutual fund, an investment organization, a pension fund or an investment adviser who is designated as a chartered financial analyst by the association for investment management and research.

B. A bank serving as investment management does not have a conflict of interest because it is also a depository in which ASRS monies are deposited.

C. The board shall appoint the investment management for a term of one year and may appoint the investment management to succeeding terms. The board may remove investment management for not complying with this article or for failure to comply with or adhere to the board's investment goals, objectives or policies.

D. Investment management:

1. Has the sole authority to invest and reinvest in the name of ASRS all ASRS monies assigned to investment management and shall purchase and sell in the name of ASRS any of the securities and investments held by ASRS under this article.

2. Is responsible for making and executing all investment decisions.

3. Shall be multiple.

E. Investment management shall not directly or indirectly:

1. Have an interest in making an investment or purchasing annuities from a private insurer or in the gains or profits accruing from an investment or annuities.

2. As investment management or as agent or partner of others borrow monies, funds or deposits of ASRS or use monies, funds or deposits in any manner except as directed under this article.

3. Be an endorser, surety or obligor on investments made under this article.

F. Subject to the limitations in § 38-719, the board may authorize the director to make investments that are designated by the board and that do not exceed fifty per cent of the assets of the investment account measured at cost.

G. For the purpose of exercising the investment responsibilities prescribed in this section, the board may enter into contracts to receive market data and other market information from securities, commodities, options and monetary exchanges. These contracts may be interpreted and enforced under the laws of a jurisdiction other than this state and are not subject to § 35-214 or 38-511 or title 41, chapter 23. [1]

Added by Laws 1995, Ch. 32, § 14, eff. March 30, 1995. Amended by Laws 1997, Ch. 143, § 6, eff. Jan. 1, 1998; Laws 1997, Ch. 280, § 5; Laws 1999, Ch. 327, § 4; Laws 2003, Ch. 63, § 2; Laws 2004, Ch. 76, § 1.

[1] Section 41-2501 et seq.

Historical and Statutory Notes

Source:

A.R.S. former § 38–752.01.
Laws 1970, Ch. 136, § 11.
Laws 1971, Ch. 90, § 4.
Laws 1975, Ch. 53, § 5.
Laws 1982, Ch. 141, § 3.
Laws 1994, Ch. 101, § 5.

The 1997 amendment by Ch. 143 substituted references to the board for references to the investment advisory council throughout; and deleted provisions requiring the board to approve the appointment and removal of management by the council.

The 1997 amendment by Ch. 280 rewrote subsec. G which had read:

"**G.** Subject to the limitations in § 38–719, the investment advisory council may authorize the director to make investments that are designated by the investment advisory council and that do not exceed twenty per cent of the assets of the investment account measured at cost."

The 1999 amendment by Ch. 327 deleted former subsec. F, which had read, "The board does not have authority over investment management except in the performance of it administrative powers and duties."; redesignated former subsec. G as subsec. F and, in redesignated subsec. F, substituted "fifty" for "the following" and deleted three paragraphs which had allowed investments of assets of the investment account not to exceed percentages of 30% from July 1, 1997 to June 30, 1998, 40% from July 1, 1998 to June 30, 1999, and 50% from July 1, 1999 onward; and added new subsec. G.

The 2003 amendment by Ch. 63, inserted "who is" following "investment adviser", and substituted "association for investment management and research" for "institute of chartered financial analysts", in subsec. A, par. 3.

The 2004 amendment by Ch. 76 rewrote par. 2 of subsec. A, which had read:

"2. Not less than five years' experience at handling investments of not less than ten per cent of the total assets of ASRS per year."

Reviser's Notes:

1997 Note. Prior to the 1999 amendment, this section contained the amendments made by Laws 1997, Ch. 143, sec. 6 and Ch. 280, sec. 5 that were blended together pursuant to authority of § 41–1304.03.

§ 38–719. Investment of monies; limitations

A. Investment management may invest and reinvest the monies in its accounts and may hold, purchase, sell, assign, transfer and dispose of any of the securities and investments in which any of its account monies are invested. Investment management shall redeposit the proceeds of sales, maturities and calls in the ASRS depository.

B. Investment management shall discharge the duties of the position with the care, skill, prudence and diligence under the circumstances then prevailing that a prudent person acting in a like capacity and familiar with the same matters would use in the conduct of an enterprise of a like character and with like aims as that of ASRS, except that:

1. No more than eighty per cent of ASRS assets may be invested at any given time in corporate stocks or equity equivalents, based on cost value of the stocks or equity equivalents irrespective of capital appreciation.

2. No more than five per cent of ASRS assets may be invested in securities issued by any one institution, agency or corporation, other than securities issued as direct obligations of or fully guaranteed by the United States government or mortgage backed securities and agency debentures issued by federal agencies.

3. No more than five per cent of the voting stock of any one corporation may be owned.

4. No more than twenty per cent of ASRS assets may be invested in foreign equity securities, and those investments shall be made only by investment managers with demonstrated expertise in those investments.

5. No more than ten per cent of ASRS assets may be invested in bonds or other evidences of indebtedness of those multinational development banks in which the United States is a member nation, including the international bank for reconstruction and development, the African development bank, the Asian development bank and the Inter-American development bank.

6. No more than one per cent of ASRS assets may be invested in economic development projects authorized as eligible for investment by the department of commerce.

C. Notwithstanding any other law, investment management shall not be required to invest in any type of investment that is dictated or required by any entity of the federal government and that is intended to fund economic development projects, public works or social programs but may consider such economically targeted investments pursuant to its fiduciary responsibility.

Added by Laws 1995, Ch. 32, § 14, eff. March 30, 1995. Amended by Laws 1995, Ch. 80, § 1; Laws 1995, Ch. 223, § 1; Laws 1997, Ch. 280, § 6; Laws 2001, Ch. 136, § 5.

Historical and Statutory Notes

Source:

Laws 1953, Ch. 128, § 16.
Code 1939, Supp.1953, § 12-852.
Laws 1954, Ch. 116, § 9.
Laws 1955, Ch. 104, § 3.
A.R.S. former §§ 38-757, 38-781.23.
Laws 1957, Ch. 96, § 3.
Laws 1961, Ch. 92, § 1.
Laws 1962, Ch. 44, § 1.
Laws 1968, Ch. 155, § 1.
Laws 1970, Ch. 134, § 2.
Laws 1970, Ch. 136, § 16.
Laws 1972, Ch. 118, § 8.
Laws 1974, Ch. 170, § 1.
Laws 1975, Ch. 37, § 8.
Laws 1975, Ch. 158, § 5.
Laws 1976, Ch. 178, § 1.
Laws 1979, Ch. 104, second § 2, § 4.
Laws 1980, Ch. 42, § 1.
A.R.S. former § 38-757.
Laws 1985, Ch. 257, § 3.
Laws 1986, Ch. 341, § 1.
Laws 1989, Ch. 203, § 10.
Laws 1992, Ch. 325, § 1.
Laws 1994, Ch. 101, § 6.

The 1995 amendment by Ch. 80, in subsec. B, substituted "eighty per cent" for "sixty per cent" in par. 1, and substituted "twenty per cent" for "fifteen per cent" and inserted "equity" in the phrase "foreign equity securities" in par. 4.

The 1995 amendment by Ch. 223 added subsec. C relating to investments required by any entity of the federal government that are intended to fund economic development projects, public works or social programs.

Laws 1995, Ch. 223, § 5, provides:

"**Sec. 5. Conditional enactment**

"Section 1 of this act does not become effective unless senate bill 1109, forty-second legislature, first regular session, relating to the Arizona state retirement system, is enacted into law." [S.B. 1109 was enacted as Ch. 32]

The 1997 amendment by Ch. 280 rewrote subsec. B, par. 4, which had read:

"4. No more than twenty per cent of ASRS assets may be invested in foreign equity securities or the sale of options, and those investments shall be made only by investment managers with demonstrated expertise in those investments. This paragraph does not authorize any investment in precious metals, venture capital or the purchase of options except closing purchases of options that have been previously sold."

The 2001 amendment by Ch. 136 inserted "or mortgage backed securities and agency debentures issued by federal agencies" at the end of subsec. B, par. 2.

Reviser's Notes:

1995 Note. Prior to the 1997 amendment, this section contained the amendments made by Laws 1995, Ch. 80, sec. 1 and Ch. 223, sec. 1 that were blended together pursuant to authority of § 41-1304.03.

§ 38-720. ASRS depository

A. Exclusively for the purposes of this article, the board shall establish an ASRS depository that is separate and apart from all other public monies or funds of this state. The ASRS depository shall be a bank in which ASRS monies are deposited and collateralized as provided by law. The ASRS depository consists of subsidiary accounts for administration, retirement and investment. ASRS shall place all monies that come into its custody from any source in the ASRS depository.

B. Any monies not currently needed in the administration account or the retirement account may be invested to provide the maximum income.

Added by Laws 1995, Ch. 32, § 14, eff. March 30, 1995.

Historical and Statutory Notes

Source:

Laws 1953, Ch. 128, § 18.
Code 1939, Supp.1953, § 12–854.
Laws 1954, Ch. 116, § 10.
A.R.S. former §§ 38–753, 38–781.21.
Laws 1960, Ch. 90, § 1.
Laws 1965, Ch. 87, § 2.
Laws 1966, Ch. 74, § 1.
Laws 1968, Ch. 192, § 2.
Laws 1970, Ch. 134, § 2.
Laws 1970, Ch. 136, § 12.
Laws 1972, Ch. 51, § 9.

§ 38–721. Administration account

A. ASRS shall maintain an administration account consisting of all monies for administrative purposes. The following monies shall be deposited in the administration account:

1. All monies appropriated by the legislature to pay administrative expenses of ASRS.

2. All monies received for proportionate shares of administrative expenses from departments that pay the salaries of their officers and employees wholly or in part from monies received from sources other than appropriations from the state general fund.

3. All monies received for proportionate shares of administrative expenses from political subdivisions paying employer contributions.

4. Monies that the director transfers from the investment account and that are necessary for the payment of expenditures made pursuant to subsections C and D of this section.

B. Except as provided in subsection C of this section, expenditures from the administration account shall be made in accordance with board directives, subject to legislative appropriation.

C. Expenditures for the following are continuously appropriated and shall be paid from the administration account in the amount deemed necessary by the board:

1. Investment management fees and related consulting fees necessary to meet the board's investment objectives.

2. Rent.

3. Actuarial consulting fees.

4. Retiree payroll.

D. With the approval of the board, the director:

1. May expend monies from the administration account for staff, expenses and related consulting fees necessary to implement § 38–714, subsection F,

paragraphs 1 and 6 and subsection H, paragraphs 2 and 3 and §§ 38-755 and 38-756.

2. Shall pay from the administration account the costs for administering the health insurance program for retired members pursuant to § 38-782, the cost of continuing education programs for the board and the cost of legal counsel.

Added by Laws 1995, Ch. 32, § 14, eff. March 30, 1995. Amended by Laws 1995, Ch. 134, § 4, eff. April 17, 1995; Laws 1996, Ch. 335, § 21, eff. July 1, 1997; Laws 1997, Ch. 143, § 7, eff. Jan. 1, 1998; Laws 2001, Ch. 136, § 6.

Historical and Statutory Notes

Source:

Laws 1953, Ch. 128, § 21.
Code 1939, Supp.1953, § 12-857.
A.R.S. former § 38-756.
Laws 1970, Ch. 136, § 15.
Laws 1987, Ch. 321, § 1.
Laws 1988, Ch. 277, § 2.
Laws 1990, Ch. 235, § 2.
Laws 1990, Ch. 271, § 1.
Laws 1991, Ch. 270, § 2.
Laws 1992, Ch. 53, § 2.
Laws 1992, Ch. 320, § 4.
Laws 1994, Ch. 356, § 6.

The 1995 amendment by Ch. 134, in subsec. D, made a nonsubstantive punctuation change in the introduction, and deleted "the contract fees of the administrator of the long term disability program established pursuant to § 38-781," following "§ 38-782," in par. 2.

The 1996 amendment by Ch. 335, in subsec. B, substituted "Except as provided in subsection C of this section," for "All" at the beginning, and provided that expenditures were subject to legislative appropriation; and in subsec. C, inserted "are continuously appropriated and" following "objectives".

The 1997 amendment by Ch. 143, in subsec. C, substituted "the board's" for "the investment advisory council's", and deleted "investment advisory council with approval of the" following "necessary by the"; and, in subsec. D, substituted "subsection F" for "subsection E" and "subsection H" for "subsection G" in par. 1, and deleted "and the investment advisory council" following "the board" in par. 2.

The 1997 amendment of this section by Ch. 143 explicitly amended the amendment of this section by Laws 1996, Ch. 335, § 21.

The 2001 amendment by Ch. 136 rewrote subsec. C, which had read:

"**C.** Expenditures for investment management fees and related consulting fees necessary to meet the board's investment objectives are continuously appropriated and shall be paid from the administration account in the amount deemed necessary by the board."

§ 38-727. Eligibility; options

The following provisions apply to all employees hired on or after the effective date:

1. All employees and officers of this state and all officers and employees of political subdivisions establishing a retirement plan administered by the board pursuant to this article who as a result of state service or service for the political subdivision are included in agreements providing for their coverage under the federal old age and survivors insurance system are subject to this article, except that membership is not mandatory:

(a) On the part of any employee who is eligible and who elects to participate in the optional retirement programs established by the Arizona board of regents pursuant to the authority conferred by § 15-1628 or by a community college district board pursuant to authority conferred by § 15-1451.

(b) For a state elected official who is subject to term limits, who is eligible for participation in ASRS because the state elected official elected not to participate in the elected officials' retirement plan as provided in § 38-804, subsection A and who elects not to participate in ASRS as provided in paragraph 7 of this section.

(c) On the part of any employee or officer who is eligible to participate and who participates in the elected officials' retirement plan pursuant to article 3 of this chapter,[1] the public safety personnel retirement system pursuant to article 4 of this chapter[2] or the corrections officer retirement plan pursuant to article 6 of this chapter.[3]

2. All employees and officers of political subdivisions whose compensation is provided wholly or in part from state monies and who are declared to be state employees and officers by the legislature for retirement purposes are subject, on legislative enactment, to this article and are members of ASRS.

3. Any member whose service terminates other than by death or withdrawal from membership is deemed to be a member of ASRS until the member's death benefit is paid.

4. Employees and officers shall not become members of ASRS and, if they are members immediately before becoming employed as provided by this section, shall have their membership status suspended while they are employed by state departments paying the salaries of their officers and employees wholly or in part from monies received from sources other than appropriations from the state general fund for the period or periods payment of the employer contributions is not made by or on behalf of the departments.

5. Notwithstanding other provisions of this section, a temporary employee of the legislature whose projected term of employment is for not more than six months is ineligible for membership in ASRS. If the employment continues beyond six successive months, the employee may elect to either:

(a) Receive credit for service for the first six months of employment and establish membership in ASRS as of the beginning of the current term of employment if, within forty-five days after the first six months of employment, both the employer and the employee contribute to ASRS the amount that would have been required to be contributed to ASRS during the first six months of employment as if the employee had been a member of ASRS during those six months.

(b) Establish membership in ASRS as of the day following the completion of six months of employment.

6. A person who is employed in postgraduate training in an approved medical residency training program of an employer is ineligible for membership in ASRS.

7. A state elected official who is subject to term limits and who is eligible for participation in ASRS because the state elected official elected not to participate in the elected officials' retirement plan as provided in § 38-804, subsection A may elect not to participate in ASRS. The election not to participate is specific for that term of office. The state elected official who is subject to term limits shall make the election in writing and file the election with ASRS within thirty days after the elected official's retirement plan mails the notice to the state elected official of the state elected official's eligibility to participate in ASRS. The election is effective on the first day of the state elected official's eligibility. If a state elected official who is subject to term limits fails to make an election as provided in this paragraph, the state elected official is deemed to have elected to participate in ASRS. The election not to participate in ASRS is

irrevocable and constitutes a waiver of all benefits provided by ASRS for the state elected official's entire term, except for any benefits accrued by the state elected official in ASRS for periods of participation prior to being elected to an office subject to term limits or any benefits expressly provided by law.

Added by Laws 1995, Ch. 32, § 14, eff. March 30, 1995. Amended by Laws 1995, Ch. 85, § 1; Laws 1995, Ch. 284, § 2; Laws 1996, Ch. 185, § 6; Laws 1997, Ch. 127, § 1; Laws 1999, Ch. 329, § 1; Laws 2001, Ch. 136, § 7; Laws 2001, Ch. 280, § 2; Laws 2001, Ch. 380, § 3.

[1] Section 38-801 et seq.

[2] Section 38-841 et seq.

[3] Section 38-881 et seq.

Historical and Statutory Notes

Source:

Laws 1953, Ch. 128, § 4.
Code 1939, Supp.1953, § 12-840.
Laws 1954, Ch. 116, § 2.
A.R.S. former §§ 38-745, 38-781.03.
Laws 1964, Ch. 142, § 1.
Laws 1970, Ch. 134, § 2.
Laws 1974, Ch. 125, §§ 2, 3.
Laws 1975, Ch. 44, §§ 3, 4.
Laws 1981, Ch. 1, §§ 13, 17.
Laws 1982, Ch. 292, § 15.
Laws 1986, Ch. 108, § 1.
Laws 1990, Ch. 145, § 2.
Laws 1992, Ch. 320, § 7.

The 1995 amendment by Ch. 85, in par. 5, added ", the employee may elect to either" at the end of the introductory paragraph, and rewrote subds. (a) and (b), which formerly read:

"(a) The employee shall participate in ASRS and the employee's membership is established as of the beginning of the current term of employment.

"(b) The employee's employer shall pay into ASRS the amount that both the employer and the employee would have been required to contribute to ASRS during only the first six months of employment as if the employee had been a member of ASRS during those six months.";

and deleted former subd. (c), which had read:

"(c) The employee is eligible to receive credit for service for the first six months of the employee's employment."

Laws 1995, Ch. 85, § 2, provides:

"**Sec. 2. Conditional enactment**

"This act does not become effective unless Senate Bill 1109, forty-second legislature, first regular session, relating to the Arizona state retirement system, is enacted into law. [Senate Bill 1109 was enacted as Ch. 32.]"

The 1995 amendment by Ch. 284 added "or by a community college district board pursuant to authority conferred by § 15-1451" at the end of par. 1.

The 1995 amendment of this section by Ch. 284 explicitly amended the addition of this section by Ch. 32, § 14.

The 1996 amendment by Ch. 185 deleted "and shall participate in ASRS" following "this article" in the first sentence of par. 1.

The 1997 amendment by Ch. 127 allowed the exception for elected officials in par. 1; and added par. 7 relating to elected official participation.

Laws 1997, Ch. 127, § 4, provides:

"**Sec. 4. County elected officials; election to join elected officials' retirement plan; payment of contributions**

"**A.** Any current county elected official of a county that is not presently participating in the elected officials' retirement plan may file a written election with the fund manager electing to become a contributing member of the plan. The fund manager must receive the written election within thirty days after the effective date of this section. In order for the election to become effective, the county elected official shall contribute to the plan or cause to be contributed to the plan:

"1. The amount of member contributions that the elected official would have contributed to the plan had the elected official been a member of the plan.

"2. The amount of employer contributions required of the county had the elected official been a member of the plan.

"3. Interest on the amount required in paragraphs 1 and 2 of this subsection at the rate of the net effective yield of the plan for the applicable year as published by the fund manager in the annual report.

"**B.** Credited service shall not apply to the elected official until the amounts required under subsection A of this section are paid to the fund manager. The elected official shall pay or cause to be paid the amounts required under subsection A of this section by October 31, 1997.

"**C.** Effective October 31, 1997, all eligible elected officials of a county that is not participating in the plan shall participate in the plan unless an eligible elected official has not filed an election pursuant to subsection A of this section. However, all elected county officials who failed to make the election allowed under subsection A of this section shall become members of the plan if they subsequently, either through reelection or election, become an eligible elected official.

"**D.** Notwithstanding § 38–815, Arizona Revised Statutes, an elected official acting pursuant to subsection A of this section may transfer assets from a private existing retirement program if they agree to forfeit all benefits under that retirement program other than a lump sum return of the amounts contributed from that retirement program.

"**E.** The terms used in this section have the same meaning as the terms in title 38, chapter 5, article 3, Arizona Revised Statutes."

The 1999 amendment by Ch. 329, in par. 1, inserted the item designations; in par. 1, item (a), deleted "or" from the end; in par. 1, item (b), substituted "For a state elected official" for "For an elected official" and "the state elected official" for "the elected official"; added items (c) and (d) of par. 1; in par. 7, inserted "state" where appearing; and added par. 8.

The 2001 amendment by Ch. 136 inserted par. 1(e).

The 2001 amendment by Ch. 280 par. 1(c) and (d) and par. 8, which had read:

[1]"(c) For an employee of the legislature who elects as provided in paragraph 8 of this section to participate in a tax deferred annuity and deferred compensation program established pursuant to article 5 of this chapter in lieu of participation in ASRS.

[1]"(d) For exempt state officers or employees as defined in § 38–951 who elect to participate in the defined contribution retirement plan option pursuant to article 8 of this chapter."

"8. In lieu of participation in ASRS or the defined contribution retirement plan option pursuant to article 8 of this chapter, an employee of the legislature may elect pursuant to this paragraph to participate in a tax deferred annuity and deferred compensation program established pursuant to article 5 of this chapter. An employee of the legislature shall make the election in writing and file the written election with ASRS. If an employee of the legislature elects to participate in a tax deferred annuity and deferred compensation program pursuant to this paragraph, the election is irrevocable and constitutes a waiver of all benefits provided by ASRS, except for any benefits accrued by the employee before election pursuant to this paragraph. If an employee of the legislature elects to participate in a tax deferred annuity and deferred compensation program pursuant to this paragraph, the employee's employer shall pay an amount equal to five per cent of the employee's base salary directly to the program in lieu of employer contributions to ASRS."

The 2001 amendment by Ch. 380 deleted par. 1(c) and (d), and par. 8, which had read:

[1.] "(c) For an employee of the legislature who elects as provided in paragraph 8 of this section to participate in a tax deferred annuity and deferred compensation program established pursuant to article 5 of this chapter in lieu of participation in ASRS.

"(d) For exempt state officers or employees as defined in § 38–951 who elect to participate in the defined contribution retirement plan option pursuant to article 8 of this chapter."

"8. In lieu of participation in ASRS or the defined contribution retirement plan option pursuant to article 8 of this chapter, an employee of the legislature may elect pursuant to this paragraph to participate in a tax deferred annuity and deferred compensation program established pursuant to article 5 of this chapter. An employee of the legislature shall make the election in writing and file the written election with ASRS. If an employee of the legislature elects to participate in a tax deferred annuity and deferred compensation program pursuant to this paragraph, the election is irrevocable and constitutes a waiver of all benefits provided by ASRS, except for any benefits accrued by the employee before election pursuant to this paragraph. If an employee of the legislature elects to participate in a tax deferred annuity and deferred compensation program pursuant to this paragraph, the employee's employer shall pay an amount equal to five per cent of the employee's base salary directly to the program in lieu of employer contributions to ASRS."

Reviser's Notes:

1995 Note. Prior to the 1996 amendment, this section contained the amendments made by Laws 1995, Ch. 85, sec. 1 and Ch. 284, sec. 2 that were blended together pursuant to authority of § 41–1304.03. Pursuant to authority of § 41–1304.02, in paragraph 5, subdivision (a) the words ", within forty-five days after the first six months of employment," were transposed to follow the first "if".

1997 Note. Pursuant to authority of § 41–1304.02, in paragraph 7, third sentence "official's" was substituted for "officials".

1999 Note. Pursuant to authority of § 41–1304.02, "Eligibility; options" was substituted for the previous section heading.

2001 Note. This section contains the amendments made by Laws 2001, Ch. 136, sec. 7, Ch. 280, sec. 2 and Ch. 380, sec. 3 that were blended together as shown pursuant to authority of § 41–1304.03.

§ 38-728. Elected officers of incorporated cities and towns; plan membership

Notwithstanding any other law, each elected officer of an incorporated city or town may elect membership under this article.

Added by Laws 1995, Ch. 32, § 14, eff. March 30, 1995.

Historical and Statutory Notes

Source:

A.R.S. former § 38-781.37.
Laws 1974, Ch. 120, § 11.

§ 38-729. Political subdivision plans

A. The governing body of any political subdivision may adopt, by appropriate legislation, a supplemental retirement plan for employees and officers of the political subdivision who are included within agreements entered into between the governing body and the state agency providing for the extension of federal old age and survivors insurance benefits to the officers and employees. The supplemental retirement plan shall provide the same retirement benefits and require the same obligations for entitlement as are provided for other members under this article, except that:

1. The supplemental retirement plan shall specify the date of commencement of the supplemental retirement plan as the first day of the month following board approval of the supplemental plan of the political subdivision as provided in this section.

2. Employer and employee obligations shall be paid to ASRS in accordance with that date.

B. The governing body of the political subdivision shall submit the supplemental retirement plan to the board in the form of an agreement. The agreement shall state the terms of the supplemental retirement plan as provided in this section. The board shall either approve or disapprove the supplemental retirement plan submitted by the governing body of the political subdivision.

C. On approval, the board shall administer the supplemental plan of the political subdivision.

D. The employer's share of contributions and payments in excess of those required of the employer under § 38-737 shall be paid from monies of the political subdivision.

E. On establishment of the supplemental retirement plan the governing body of the political subdivision shall deduct member contributions in the same amounts and in the same manner as provided in this article for state employees and shall pay those contributions, together with the employer contributions for the political subdivision, to ASRS for deposit in the ASRS depository. The governing body of the political subdivision shall reimburse ASRS in a similar manner for its pro rata share of administrative costs attributable to coverage of employees of the political subdivision.

F. In addition to the employer contributions required under § 38-737, on establishment of the supplemental retirement plan the governing body of the political subdivision shall pay to ASRS the amounts, as determined by the board, required to fund additional costs of benefits attributable to service for the political subdivision before the effective date of the supplemental retirement plan. The board may authorize payments to be made at such times as the board requires and in amounts that are less than the amount required for fully funding the additional costs.

G. If the supplemental retirement plan is authorized by a political subdivision, then on or after the effective date of the supplemental retirement plan the governing body of the political subdivision and the board may sign an agreement to waive the provisions of subsection F of this section and to authorize benefits under the supplemental retirement plan only for service with the political subdivision after the effective date of the supplemental retirement plan. In lieu of waiving benefits for all service before the effective date of the supplemental retirement plan, the governing body of the political subdivision may elect to waive benefits for a portion of that service. Amendments to the agreement may increase but shall not reduce the service for which a member is entitled to benefits. The governing body of the political subdivision shall certify for each member the years of service before the effective date of the supplemental retirement plan for which the member is entitled to benefits. In addition to the employer contributions required in § 38–737, the governing body of the political subdivision shall pay to ASRS the amount, as determined by the board, required to fund the cost of the benefits attributable to service before the effective date of the supplemental retirement plan for which members are entitled to benefits.

H. The new political subdivision shall designate the classification of employees that is eligible for membership in ASRS and shall make contributions each year as provided in this section.

I. The liability of the political subdivision providing a supplemental retirement plan within ASRS arises in consideration of the officer's or employee's retention in or entrance into service for the political subdivision.

Added by Laws 1995, Ch. 32, § 14, eff. March 30, 1995. Amended by Laws 1996, Ch. 185, § 7; Laws 2001, Ch. 136, § 8; Laws 2001, Ch. 280, § 3; Laws 2001, Ch. 380, § 4.

Historical and Statutory Notes

Source:

Laws 1953, Ch. 128, § 25.
Code 1939, Supp.1953, § 12–861.
Laws 1954, Ch. 116, § 11.
A.R.S. former §§ 38–752, 38–781.20.
Laws 1960, Ch. 123, § 1.
Laws 1967, Ch. 84, § 4.
Laws 1968, Ch. 192, § 1.
Laws 1970, Ch. 134, § 2.
Laws 1970, Ch. 136, § 10.
Laws 1972, Ch. 51, §§ 8, 22.
Laws 1978, Ch. 209, § 4.
Laws 1979, Ch. 91, §§ 1, 2.
Laws 1982, Ch. 141, § 4.

The 1996 amendment by Ch. 185 rewrote subsec. A, par. 1; inserted subsec. B; and redesignated former subsecs. B to J as C to K, accordingly. Former subsec. A had read:

"**A.** The governing body of any political subdivision may adopt, by appropriate legislation, a supplemental retirement plan for employees and officers of the political subdivision who are included within agreements entered into between the governing body and the state agency providing for the extension of federal old age and survivors insurance benefits to the officers and employees. The supplemental retirement plan shall provide the same retirement benefits and require the same obligations for entitlement as are provided for other members under this article, except that the supplemental retirement plan shall specify the date of commencement of the supplemental retirement plan as the first day of any fiscal year including July 1, 1971, and fiscal years thereafter, and that employer and employee obligations shall be paid to ASRS in accordance with that date."

The 2001 amendment by Ch. 136 deleted subsecs. I and J, and redesignated existing subsec. K as I, accordingly. Subsecs. I and J had read:

"I. Before the effective date of membership and as a condition of an employer's membership in ASRS, the employer shall formally terminate any existing retirement program administered by the board on behalf of the designated eligible employee group included in ASRS and shall formally agree that no retirement program, exclusive of ASRS and the federal social security system, may thereafter be established on behalf of that group.

"J. The board shall transfer all assets under any existing retirement program administered by the board, to the extent attributable to the employer's designated employee group, from that program to ASRS no later than sixty days after the effective date of the supplemental retirement plan. The transferred assets shall be considered in determining any additional payments prescribed in subsections F and G of this section."

The 2001 amendment by Ch. 280 deleted subsec. I, and redesignated existing subsecs. J and K as I and J, accordingly. Former subsec. I had read:

"I. Before the effective date of membership and as a condition of an employer's membership in ASRS, the employer shall formally terminate any existing retirement program administered by the board on behalf of the designated eligible employee group included in ASRS and shall formally agree that no retirement program, exclusive of ASRS and the federal social security system, may thereafter be established on behalf of that group."

The 2001 amendment by Ch. 380 deleted subsec. I, and redesignated existing subsecs J and K as I and J, accordingly. Subsection I had read:

"I. Before the effective date of membership and as a condition of an employer's membership in ASRS, the employer shall formally terminate any existing retirement program administered by the board on behalf of the designated eligible employee group included in ASRS and shall formally agree that no retirement program, exclusive of ASRS and the federal social security system, may thereafter be established on behalf of that group."

Reviser's Notes:

2001 Note. This section contains the amendments made by Laws 2001, Ch. 136, sec. 8, Ch. 280, sec. 3 and Ch. 380, sec. 4 that were blended together as shown pursuant to authority of § 41-1304.03.

§ 38-730. Charter city retirement systems; transfers

A. On application the retirement service credits of an employee of a charter city that is not an employer under ASRS or an employee of an employer that is an employer under ASRS whose job functions are shifted by law from one employer jurisdiction to another shall be transferred to the retirement system of the new employer.

B. An employee of a charter city that is not an employer under ASRS or an employee of an employer that is an employer under ASRS who becomes employed by the other employer jurisdiction may apply to have the employee's retirement service credits transferred to the retirement system of the new employer. The retirement service credits of an employee of a charter city that is not an employer under ASRS shall not be transferred unless the governing body of that city approves the transfer. The retirement service credits of an employee of an employer that is an employer under ASRS shall not be transferred unless the board approves the transfer.

C. The retirement system that transfers the retirement service credits shall pay to the retirement system of the new employer an amount equal to the present value, as of the date of the transfer, of all benefits generated by the transferred service credits in the retirement system of the new employer as determined by the governing board of the retirement system of the new employer. The amount of any payment under this subsection shall include the accumulated retirement contributions of the employee whose retirement service credits are transferred.

D. The accumulated retirement contributions of an employee whose retirement service credits are transferred that are paid to the retirement system of the new employer shall not be withdrawn by the employee unless the employee's employment terminates.

Added by Laws 1995, Ch. 32, § 14, eff. March 30, 1995.

Historical and Statutory Notes

Source:

A.R.S. former § 38-781.24.
Laws 1984, Ch. 136, § 2.
Laws 1992, Ch. 320, § 15.

§ 38-735. Payment of contributions

A. All amounts deducted from a member's compensation as provided in § 38-736 and employer contributions required pursuant to § 38-737 shall be paid to ASRS for deposit in the ASRS depository.

B. Each employer shall certify on each payroll the amount to be contributed and shall remit that amount to ASRS.

C. Payments made pursuant to this article by employers become delinquent after the due date prescribed in the board's rules and thereafter shall be increased by interest from and after that date until payment is received by ASRS. ASRS shall charge interest on the delinquent payments at an annual rate equal to the interest rate assumption approved by the board from time to time for actuarial equivalency. Delinquent payments due under this subsection, together with interest charges as provided in this subsection, may be recovered by action in a court of competent jurisdiction against a political subdivision liable for payments or, at the request of the director, may be deducted from any other monies, including excise revenue taxes, payable to the political subdivision by any department or agency of this state.

Added by Laws 1995, Ch. 32, § 14, eff. March 30, 1995. Amended by Laws 1997, Ch. 280, § 7.

Historical and Statutory Notes

Source:

A.R.S. former § 38-781.14.
Laws 1970, Ch. 134, § 2.
Laws 1978, Ch. 209, § 9.

The 1997 amendment by Ch. 280 substituted "equal to the interest rate assumption approved by the board from time to time for actuarial equivalency" for "determined monthly as the weighted average annual rate of return on all repurchase agreement or other short term investment transactions in the ASRS investment account during the preceding month" in subsec. C.

§ 38-736. Member contributions

A. Member contributions are required as a condition of employment and shall be made by payroll deductions. Member contributions shall begin simultaneously with membership in ASRS. Beginning July 1, 1985, member contributions are a percentage of a member's compensation equal to the employer contribution required pursuant to § 38-737. Amounts so deducted by employers shall be deposited in the ASRS depository.

B. The employer shall pay the member contributions required of members on account of compensation earned. The paid contributions shall be treated as employer contributions for the purpose of determining tax treatment under the internal revenue code.[1] The effective date of the employer payment shall not be before the date ASRS has received notification from the United States internal revenue service that pursuant to § 414(h) of the internal revenue code[2] the member contributions paid will not be included in gross income for income tax purposes until the paid contributions are distributed by refund or retirement benefit payments. The employer shall pay the member contributions from monies that are established and available in the retirement deduction account and that would otherwise have been designated as member contributions and paid to ASRS. Member contributions paid pursuant to this subsection shall be treated for all other purposes, in the same manner and to the same extent, as member contributions made before the approval of the United States internal revenue service pursuant to this section.

Added by Laws 1995, Ch. 32, § 14, eff. March 30, 1995.

[1] 26 U.S.C.A. § 1 et seq.

[2] 26 U.S.C.A. § 414(h).

Historical and Statutory Notes

Source:

Laws 1953, Ch. 128, § 11.
Code 1939, Supp.1953, § 12-847.
Laws 1954, Ch. 116, § 7.
A.R.S. former §§ 38-748, 38-781.04.
Laws 1967, Ch. 84, § 2.
Laws 1970, Ch. 134, § 2.
Laws 1970, Ch. 136, § 7.
Laws 1974, Ch. 167, § 2.
Laws 1975, Ch. 158, § 3.
Laws 1978, Ch. 209, § 3.
Laws 1984, 1st S.S., Ch. 12, § 1.
Laws 1985, Ch. 294, § 4.
Laws 1992, Ch. 320, § 8.

Laws 1995, Ch. 134, § 17, provides:

"**Sec. 17. Employer and member contributions**

"**A.** Notwithstanding §§ 38-736 and 38-737, Arizona Revised Statutes, for fiscal year 1995-1996, the contribution rate for the Arizona state retirement system established pursuant to title 38, chapter 5, article 2, Arizona Revised Statutes, is 3.36 per cent of payroll for both employers and members of the Arizona state retirement system.

"**B.** For fiscal year 1995-1996, the contribution rate for employers and members covered by the long-term disability program established by title 38, chapter 5, article 2.1, Arizona Revised Statutes, as added by this act, is .49 per cent of payroll for both employers and members."

§ 38-737. Employer contributions; definition

A. Employer contributions for the biennial period shall be a percentage of compensation of all employees of the employers, excluding the compensation of those employees who are members of the defined contribution program administered by ASRS, as determined by the ASRS actuary pursuant to this section for June 30 of the even-numbered year immediately preceding the biennial period, except that beginning with fiscal year 2001-2002 the contribution rate shall not be less than two per cent of compensation of all employees of the employers. The total employer contribution shall be determined on the projected unit credit method. Except as provided in subsection D of this section, the total employer contributions shall be equal to the employer normal cost plus the amount required to amortize the past service funding requirement over a rolling thirty-year period.

B. All contributions made by the employer and allocated to the fund established by § 38-712 are irrevocable and shall be used as benefits under this article or to pay expenses of ASRS.

C. The required employer contributions shall be determined every other year by an actuary who is selected by the board and who is a fellow of the society of actuaries. ASRS shall provide a preliminary report by November 1 and a final report by December 15 of each even-numbered year to the governor, the speaker of the house of representatives and the president of the senate on the contribution rate for the two ensuing fiscal years.

D. For the fiscal years ending June 30, 1995 through June 30, 1997 and commencing with fiscal year ending June 30, 1998 through June 30, 2013 the funding period used to determine the valuation of ASRS and employer contributions payable beginning July 1 of the following year or biennial period shall be determined by the ASRS actuary using the following schedule:

Valuation for the Fiscal year ending	Biennial period	Funding period ends
June 30, 1995		June 30, 2005
June 30, 1996		June 30, 2007
June 30, 1997		June 30, 2009
June 30, 1998	July 1, 1999 to June 30, 2001	June 30, 2011
June 30, 2000	July 1, 2001 to June 30, 2003	June 30, 2015
June 30, 2002	July 1, 2003 to June 30, 2005	June 30, 2019
June 30, 2004	July 1, 2005 to June 30, 2007	June 30, 2023
June 30, 2006	July 1, 2007 to June 30, 2009	June 30, 2027
June 30, 2008	July 1, 2009 to June 30, 2011	June 30, 2031
June 30, 2010	July 1, 2011 to June 30, 2013	June 30, 2035
June 30, 2012	July 1, 2013 to June 30, 2015	June 30, 2039

E. If at any time between June 30, 1995 and June 30, 2013 ASRS becomes underfunded, the funding period immediately and permanently reverts to the period provided in subsection A of this section.

F. For the purposes of this section "biennial period" means the two year period beginning on July 1 of an odd-numbered year and ending on June 30 of the next odd-numbered year.

Added by Laws 1995, Ch. 32, § 14, eff. March 30, 1995. Amended by Laws 1997, Ch. 210, § 23, eff. March 1, 1998; Laws 1999, Ch. 327, § 5.

Historical and Statutory Notes

Source:

A.R.S. former § 38–781.05.
Laws 1970, Ch. 134, § 2.
Laws 1972, Ch. 51, § 15.
Laws 1974, Ch. 167, § 3.
Laws 1978, Ch. 54, § 2.
Laws 1984, 1st S.S., Ch. 12, § 2.
Laws 1989, Ch. 310, § 3.
Laws 1992, Ch. 320, § 9.
Laws 1993, 2nd S.S., Ch. 3, § 4.
Laws 1994, Ch. 356, § 9.

Laws 1995, Ch. 134, § 17, provides:

"**Sec. 17. Employer and member contributions**

"**A.** Notwithstanding §§ 38–736 and 38–737, Arizona Revised Statutes, for fiscal year 1995–1996, the contribution rate for the Arizona state retirement system established pursuant to title 38, chapter 5, article 2, Arizona Revised Statutes, is 3.36 per cent of payroll for both employers and members of the Arizona state retirement system.

"**B.** For fiscal year 1995-1996, the contribution rate for employers and members covered by the long-term disability program established by title 38, chapter 5, article 2.1, Arizona Revised Statutes, as added by this act, is .49 per cent of payroll for both employers and members."

The 1997 amendment by Ch. 210 rewrote the section which had read:

A. Employer contributions shall be a percentage of compensation of all employees of the employers, excluding the compensation of those employees who are members of the defined contribution program administered by ASRS, as determined by the ASRS actuary pursuant to this section for June 30 of the fiscal year preceding the preceding fiscal year. The total employer contribution shall be determined on the projected unit credit method. Except as provided in subsection D of this section, the total employer contributions shall be equal to the employer normal cost plus the amount required to amortize the past service funding requirement over a rolling thirty-year period.

B. All contributions made by the employer and allocated to the fund established by § 38-712 are irrevocable and shall be used as benefits under this article or to pay expenses of ASRS.

C. The required employer contributions shall be determined on an annual basis by an actuary who is selected by the board and who is a fellow of the society of actuaries.

D. For the fiscal years ending June 30, 1995 through June 30, 2013 the funding period used to determine the valuation of ASRS and employer contributions payable beginning July 1 of the following year shall be determined by the ASRS actuary using the following schedule:

Fiscal year ending	Funding period ends
June 30, 1995	June 30, 2005
June 30, 1996	June 30, 2007
June 30, 1997	June 30, 2009
June 30, 1998	June 30, 2011
June 30, 1999	June 30, 2013
June 30, 2000	June 30, 2015
June 30, 2001	June 30, 2017
June 30, 2002	June 30, 2019
June 30, 2003	June 30, 2021
June 30, 2004	June 30, 2023
June 30, 2005	June 30, 2025
June 30, 2006	June 30, 2027
June 30, 2007	June 30, 2029
June 30, 2008	June 30, 2031
June 30, 2009	June 30, 2033
June 30, 2010	June 30, 2035
June 30, 2011	June 30, 2037
June 30, 2012	June 30, 2039
June 30, 2013	June 30, 2041

E. If at any time between June 30, 1995 and June 30, 2013 ASRS becomes underfunded, the funding period immediately and permanently reverts to the period provided in subsection A of this section.

Laws 1997, Ch. 210, § 40, subsec. A, provides:

"**Sec. 40. Delayed effective dates**

"**A.** Sections 3, 6 through 12, 14, 23 through 27, 29 through 31 of this act are effective from and after February 28, 1998."

The 1999 amendment by Ch. 327, in subsec. A, inserted the exception clause at the end of the first sentence.

§ 38-738. Adjustment and refund

A. If more than the correct amount of employer or member contributions is paid into ASRS by an employer through a mistake of fact, ASRS shall return those contributions to the employer if the employer requests return of the contributions within one year after the date of overpayment. ASRS shall not pay an employer earnings attributable to excess contributions but shall reduce the amount returned to an employer pursuant to this section by the amount of losses attributable to the excess contributions.

B. If less than the correct amount of employer or member contributions is paid into ASRS by an employer, the following apply:

1. The member shall pay an amount that is equal to the amount that would have been paid in member contributions for the period in question. The member's payments shall be made as provided in § 38-747. If the member does not make the payment within ninety days of being notified by ASRS that the employer has paid all amounts due from the employer, the unpaid amount accrues interest until the amount is paid in full. The member is responsible for

payment of the unpaid amount and interest. The interest rate is the interest rate assumption that is approved by the board for actuarial equivalency for the period in question to the date payment is received.

2. If the member contributions to ASRS made pursuant to this subsection exceed the limits prescribed in § 38–747, subsection E when taking into account other annual additions of the member for the limitation year, the amount to be paid by the member shall be adjusted as provided in § 38–747. For the purposes of this subsection, "limitation year" has the same meaning prescribed in § 38–769.

3. The employer shall pay to ASRS an amount equal to the amount that would have been paid in employer contributions for the period in question together with accumulated interest that would have accrued on both the employer and member contributions due. If the employer does not remit full payment of all employer contributions and all interest due within ninety days of being notified by ASRS of the amount due, the unpaid amount accrues interest until the amount is paid in full. The interest rate is the interest rate assumption that is approved by the board for actuarial equivalency for the period in question to the date payment is received.

4. On satisfaction of the requirements of this subsection, the member's salary history on the records of ASRS shall be adjusted and any additional service credits acquired by the member shall be reinstated.

5. If the member retires before all contributions are made pursuant to this subsection, the member's benefits shall be calculated only based on the contributions actually made.

6. Annual additions shall be determined as provided in § 38–747, subsection O.

7. The initiator of the request for correction of salary history and service credits on records of ASRS is responsible for providing credible evidence of past employment and compensation to ASRS in a form or forms that would lead a reasonable person to conclude that a period of employment occurred under circumstances that made the employee eligible for membership in ASRS during that period. A determination of eligibility by ASRS may be appealed to the ASRS board in a manner prescribed by the board.

C. Subsection B of this section applies to eligible verified service that occurred less than or equal to fifteen years before the date the initiator of the request for correction of salary history and service credits on the records of ASRS provides ASRS with credible evidence in writing that less than the correct amount of contributions were paid into ASRS or ASRS otherwise determines that less than the correct amount of contributions were made.

D. Eligible verified service that is more than fifteen years before the date the initiator of the request for correction of salary history and service credits on the records of ASRS provides ASRS with credible evidence in writing that less than the correct amount of contributions were paid into ASRS or ASRS otherwise determines that less than the correct amount of contributions were made is considered public service credit. The member may purchase this service pursuant to § 38–743.

Added by Laws 1995, Ch. 32, § 14, eff. March 30, 1995. Amended by Laws 1997, Ch. 280, § 8; Laws 1999, Ch. 327, § 6; Laws 2001, Ch. 136, § 9; Laws 2002, Ch. 213, § 1, eff. May 15, 2002; Laws 2003, Ch. 132, § 1; Laws 2003, Ch. 132, § 2, eff. July 1, 2004.

Historical and Statutory Notes

Source:

Laws 1953, Ch. 128, § 14.
Code 1939, Supp.1953, § 12–850.
A.R.S. former §§ 38–750, 38–781.19.
Laws 1970, Ch. 134, § 2.
Laws 1970, Ch. 136, § 9.
Laws 1994, Ch. 356, § 14.

The 1997 amendment by Ch. 280 rewrote subsec. B, pars. 1 and 6, which had read:

"1. The member shall pay an amount that is equal to the amount that would have been paid in member contributions for the period in question. The member's payments shall be made in a lump sum to the employer who shall remit the amount to ASRS. In any one fiscal year, contributions made by the member shall not exceed the lesser of either:

"(a) Thirty thousand dollars or one-fourth of the dollar limitation prescribed in § 38–769, subsection A, paragraph 1, as adjusted by the board, whichever is more.

"(b) Twenty-five per cent of the member's compensation for the fiscal year.

"6. 'Compensation' has the same meaning prescribed in § 38–769."

The 1999 amendment by Ch. 327, in subsec. B, rewrote pars 1 and 2, which had read:

"1. The member shall pay an amount that is equal to the amount that would have been paid in member contributions for the period in question. The member's payments shall be made in a lump sum to the employer who shall remit the amount to ASRS. In any one fiscal year, contributions made by the member under this section shall be treated as an annual addition, shall be added to all other annual additions of the member during the limitation year and are subject to the limits prescribed in § 38–747, subsection E.

"2. If the member contributions to ASRS made pursuant to this subsection exceed the limits prescribed in paragraph 1 of this subsection when taking into account other member contributions made to ASRS for the fiscal year, the amount to be paid by the member shall be reduced to not exceed the limits prescribed in paragraph 1 of this subsection, and the reduced amount shall be carried forward to the next fiscal year, unless the limits would be exceeded. If the limits are exceeded in the next fiscal year, the procedure prescribed by this paragraph shall be repeated until all contributions have been made."

The 2001 amendment by Ch. 136 substituted subsec. B, pars. 6 and 7 for former 6, which had read:

"6. 'Annual additions' and 'limitation year' have the same meaning prescribed in § 38–769."

The 2002 amendment by Ch. 213, substituted "subsection O" for "subsection M", at the end of subsec. B, par. 6.

The 2003 amendment by Ch. 132, § 1, rewrote the section, which had read:

"**A.** If more than the correct amount of employer or member contributions is paid into ASRS by an employer through a mistake of fact, ASRS shall return those contributions to the employer if the employer requests return of the contributions within one year after the date of overpayment. ASRS shall not pay an employer earnings attributable to excess contributions but shall reduce the amount returned to an employer pursuant to this section by the amount of losses attributable to the excess contributions.

"**B.** If less than the correct amount of employer or member contributions is paid into ASRS by an employer, the following apply:

"1. The member shall pay an amount that is equal to the amount that would have been paid in member contributions for the period in question. The member's payments shall be made as provided in § 38–747.

"2. If the member contributions to ASRS made pursuant to this subsection exceed the limits prescribed in § 38–747, subsection E when taking into account other annual additions of the member for the limitation year, the amount to be paid by the member shall be adjusted as provided in § 38–747.

"3. The employer shall pay to ASRS an amount equal to the amount that would have been paid in employer contributions for the period in question together with accumulated interest that would have accrued on both the employer and member contributions due at the interest rate assumption approved by the board for actuarial equivalency for the period in question to the date payment is received.

"4. On satisfaction of the requirements of this subsection, the member's salary history on the records of ASRS shall be adjusted and any additional service credits acquired by the member shall be reinstated.

"5. If the member retires before all contributions are made pursuant to this subsection, the member's benefits shall be calculated only based on the contributions actually made.

"6. Annual additions shall be determined as provided in § 38–747, subsection O.

"7. 'Limitation year' has the same meaning prescribed in § 38–769."

The 2003 amendment by Ch. 132, added subsecs. C and D.

Laws 2003, Ch. 132, § 3, provides:

"**Sec. 3. Effective date**

"Section 2 of this act is effective from and after June 30, 2004."

§ 38–739. Credited service

A. A member shall not earn more than one year of credited service in any fiscal year.

B. A member shall earn proportionate credited service for each month for which the member performs service and is compensated equal to the ratio that the month bears to the number of months in the member's service year.

C. If a member is compensated for less than a full service year, the member shall earn credited service equal to the ratio that the number of months actually compensated bears to the number of months in the full service year.

D. If a member holds two or more concurrent contracts in any fiscal year, credited service shall be determined on the basis of the terms of the contract with the longest term.

E. Members on sabbatical leave for which they are paid on a full or partial basis shall make appropriate contributions while on sabbatical leave and are considered to be employed full time.

F. The following years of service are excluded from credited service under this article:

1. Years of prior service. For the purposes of this paragraph, "prior service" has the same meaning prescribed in § 38–772.

2. Years in which the member made contributions to the defined contribution program administered by ASRS or the Arizona teachers' retirement system before membership in the defined contribution program administered by ASRS and for which those contributions were subsequently withdrawn and paid to the member.

Added by Laws 1995, Ch. 32, § 14, eff. March 30, 1995. Amended by Laws 1999, Ch. 327, § 7.

Historical and Statutory Notes

The 1999 amendment by Ch. 327 substituted "month" or "months" for "pay period" or "pay periods" in subsecs. B and C.

§ 38–740. Return of contributions

A. Any member who leaves employment other than by retirement or death may elect to receive a return of the contributions as follows:

1. If the member has less than five years of credited service, the member shall receive the member's contributions.

2. If a member has five or more years of credited service, the member shall receive the member's contributions and an amount equal to a percentage of the employer contributions paid on behalf of the member. The percentage of employer contributions paid on behalf of the member shall be as follows:

(a) 5.0 to 5.9 years of credited service, twenty-five per cent.

(b) 6.0 to 6.9 years of credited service, forty per cent.

(c) 7.0 to 7.9 years of credited service, fifty-five per cent.

(d) 8.0 to 8.9 years of credited service, seventy per cent.

(e) 9.0 to 9.9 years of credited service, eighty-five per cent.

(f) 10.0 or more years of credited service, one hundred per cent.

3. Interest on the returned contributions as determined by the board.

B. Withdrawal of contributions with interest constitutes a withdrawal from membership in ASRS and results in a forfeiture of all other benefits under ASRS.

C. Notwithstanding any other provision of this article, a member who has not received a return of contributions pursuant to this section may combine any two or more periods of service for purposes of determining the member's benefits.

D. If a member receives more than the amount due to a member pursuant to this section, the member shall repay the amount of the overpayment together with interest at the interest rate earned on ASRS investments as reported on a quarterly basis, but not less than the valuation rate established by the board, from the time of overpayment to the settlement of the debt.

Added by Laws 1995, Ch. 32, § 14, eff. March 30, 1995. Amended by Laws 1999, Ch. 327, § 8.

Historical and Statutory Notes

Source:

Laws 1953, Ch. 128, § 5.
Code 1939, Supp.1953, § 12–841.
Laws 1954, Ch. 116, § 3.
A.R.S. former § 38–758.
Laws 1957, Ch. 96, § 4.
Laws 1958, Ch. 44, § 1.
Laws 1959, Ch. 99, § 1.
Laws 1965, Ch. 87, § 3.
Laws 1970, Ch. 136, § 17.
Laws 1974, Ch. 120, § 2.

The 1999 amendment by Ch. 327 rewrote the section, which had read:

"**A.** Any member who leaves employment other than by retirement or death may elect a return of the member's contributions with interest as determined by the board.

"**B.** Notwithstanding any other provisions of this article, a member, within thirty days of retirement, may elect the return of the member's contributions with interest as determined by the board in lieu of all other benefits under ASRS. Withdrawal of contributions with interest constitutes a withdrawal from membership in ASRS and results in a forfeiture of all other benefits under ASRS.

"**C.** Notwithstanding any other provision of this article, a member who has not received a return of contributions pursuant to subsection A or B may combine any two or more periods of service for purposes of determining the member's vested benefits."

§ 38–741. Reemployment of inactive member

A. ASRS shall return to active status an inactive member who terminates employment with an employer without terminating membership in ASRS and who later is reemployed by the same or another employer.

B. On retirement, the member shall receive benefits derived from service for all employers that employed the member.

C. Retirement benefits attributable to service before membership in ASRS, if any, shall be paid only by the employer from which the retiring member obtained entitlement to the benefits as provided in § 38-729.

Added by Laws 1995, Ch. 32, § 14, eff. March 30, 1995.

Historical and Statutory Notes

Source:

Laws 1953, Ch. 128, § 5.
Code 1939, Supp.1953, § 12-841.
Laws 1954, Ch. 116, § 3.
A.R.S. former § 38-758.
Laws 1957, Ch. 96, § 4.
Laws 1958, Ch. 44, § 1.
Laws 1959, Ch. 99, § 1.
Laws 1965, Ch. 87, § 3.
Laws 1970, Ch. 136, § 17.
Laws 1974, Ch. 120, § 2.

Former § 38-741, enacted as part of the revision effective January 9, 1959, amended by: Laws 1957, Ch. 96, § 1. Laws 1965, Ch. 87, § 1. Laws 1970, Ch. 136, § 2. Laws 1974, Ch. 120, § 1. Laws 1975, Ch. 53, §§ 1, 2. Laws 1985, Ch. 294, § 1. Laws 1992, Ch. 320, § 3.

which was derived from Laws 1953, Ch. 128, § 3, Code 1939, Supp.1953, § 12-839, and Laws 1954, Ch. 116, § 1, defining terms, was repealed by Laws 1995, Ch. 32, § 13. See, now, § 38-711.

§ 38-742. Reinstatement

A. If an active member who received a return of contributions on termination of employment and by receipt of those contributions forfeited credited service earned on that employment, as provided in § 38-740, subsection A, is subsequently reemployed by an employer, the member's service shall be credited only from the date the member's most recent reemployment period commenced.

B. Notwithstanding subsection A of this section, the member may redeposit the amount of the contributions the member received at the time of the member's separation from service, with interest on that amount to the date of redeposit at the interest rate assumption approved by the board for actuarial equivalency. On satisfaction of this obligation, the member's service credits acquired by the previous employment shall be reinstated. If a member redeposits less than the amount required under this subsection, ASRS shall proportionately reduce the member's reinstated service credits.

C. A member who is receiving benefits pursuant to § 38-797.07 and who received a return of contributions on termination of employment and by receipt of those contributions forfeited credited service earned on that employment, as provided in § 38-740, subsection A, may redeposit the amount of the contributions the member received at the time of the member's previous separation from service, with interest on that amount to the date of redeposit at the interest rate assumption approved by the board for actuarial equivalency. On redeposit of the contributions and interest, the member's service credit acquired by the previous employment shall be reinstated. If a member redeposits less than the amount required under this subsection, ASRS shall proportionately reduce the member's reinstated service credits.

Added by Laws 1995, Ch. 32, § 14, eff. March 30, 1995. Amended by Laws 1996, Ch. 185, § 8; Laws 1997, Ch. 280, § 9; Laws 1999, Ch. 327, § 9; Laws 2001, Ch. 136, § 10.

Historical and Statutory Notes

Source:

A.R.S. former § 38–781.40.
Laws 1987, Ch. 208, § 1.

The 1996 amendment by Ch. 185 rewrote the section, which had read:

"**A.** All active members of ASRS who had previous service in ASRS and who forfeited accumulated retirement benefits at or after termination of employment may elect at the time of retirement to redeem any part of the credited service by paying into ASRS the amounts required under subsection B of this section.

"**B.** A person who elects to redeem any part of the person's credited service under subsection A of this section shall pay into ASRS a lump sum equal to the increase in the actuarial present value of benefits computed at the time of retirement that results from adding the number of years or partial years of credited service received under subsection A of this section.

"**C.** If a member who received a return of contributions on termination of employment and by receipt of those contributions forfeited credited service earned on that employment, as provided in § 38–740, subsection A, is subsequently reemployed by an employer, the member's service shall be credited only from the date the member's most recent reemployment period commenced.

"**D.** Notwithstanding subsection C of this section, if a member's reemployment occurred within two years after the member's termination date and, within one hundred eighty days after reemployment, the member signs a written election consenting to a timely reimbursement to ASRS, the member shall redeposit the amount of the member's accumulated contributions at the time of the member's separation from service, with interest on that amount to the date of redeposit at the interest rate assumption approved by the board for actuarial equivalency. On satisfaction of this obligation, the member's service credits acquired by the previous employment shall be reinstated."

The 1997 amendment by Ch. 280, in subsec. B, added the last sentence relating to situations where a member redeposits less than the amount required under the subsection.

Laws 1999, Ch. 260, § 1, provides:

"**Section 1. Arizona game and fish department employees; purchase of forfeited credited service with the Arizona state retirement system**

"**A.** Notwithstanding § 38–742, Arizona Revised Statutes, the Arizona state retirement system shall allow employees of the Arizona game and fish department who became eligible to participate in the public safety personnel retirement system before September 15, 1989, who transferred to the public safety personnel retirement system and who received a return of member contributions from the Arizona state retirement system to purchase their forfeited credited service by paying the amount withdrawn plus interest on the amount withdrawn at the rate of three per cent for each year compounded each year from the date of withdrawal to the date of repayment.

"**B.** Upon the reinstatement of the forfeited credited service, the Arizona state retirement system shall, at the request of the employee, transfer service credits of the employees to the public safety personnel retirement system as provided in title 38, chapter 5, article 7, Arizona Revised Statutes."

The 1999 amendment by Ch. 327, in subsec. B, deleted "member's accumulated" preceding, and inserted "the member received" following, the word "contributions" in the first sentence.

The 2001 amendment by Ch. 136 added subsec. C.

Former § 38–742, enacted as part of the revision effective January 9, 1956 (see Source, following § 38–713), relating to the state retirement board, was repealed by Laws 1995, Ch. 32, § 13.

§ 38–743. Public service credit

A. If an active member of ASRS or a member who is receiving benefits pursuant to § 38–797.07 was previously employed by the United States government, a state of the United States or a political subdivision of a state of the United States, excluding any time worked for a prison while the member was incarcerated, the member may receive credited service for this prior employment if the member pays into ASRS the amount prescribed in subsection B of this section.

B. A member who elects to receive credit for service with the United States government, a state of the United States or a political subdivision of a state of the United States shall pay to ASRS an amount equal to the present value of the additional benefit that is derived from the purchased credited service using the actuarial assumptions that are approved by the board.

C. A member who previously was a member of another public employee retirement system and who receives or is eligible to receive retirement benefits from that system for any period of employment is ineligible to receive retirement benefits from ASRS for the same period.

Added by Laws 1995, Ch. 32, § 14, eff. March 30, 1995. Amended by Laws 1995, Ch. 134, § 5, eff. April 17, 1995; Laws 1996, Ch. 185, § 9; Laws 1999, Ch. 327, § 10; Laws 2001, Ch. 136, § 11; Laws 2004, Ch. 252, § 1.

Historical and Statutory Notes

Source:

A.R.S. former § 38-781.39.
Laws 1987, Ch. 182, § 1.
Laws 1994, Ch. 356, § 18.

The 1995 amendment by Ch. 134, in subsec. A, deleted "At the time of retirement" at the beginning, and deleted "and who is not receiving retirement benefits as a result of that employment" following the second reference to "university"; in subsec. B, substituted "projected benefits resulting" for "benefits computed at the time of retirement that results" following "value of"; and added subsec. C, relating to ineligibility of certain employees.

The 1996 amendment by Ch. 185 rewrote the section, which had read:

"**A.** A teacher, professor, instructor or administrator of a school district, community college or university who is an active member of ASRS, who previously was a member of a public employee retirement system in another state while employed as a teacher, professor, instructor or school administrator of a school district, community college or university may receive up to five years of credited service for this prior employment if the teacher, professor, instructor or administrator pays into ASRS the amount prescribed in subsection B.

"**B.** A teacher, professor, instructor or administrator who elects to receive credit for service outside this state shall pay to ASRS the amount equal to the increase in the actuarial present value of projected benefits resulting from adding the number of years or partial years of credited service received under subsection A.

"**C.** A teacher, professor, instructor or administrator of a school district, community college or university who is a member of ASRS, who previously was a member of a public employee retirement system in another state while employed as a teacher, professor, instructor or school administrator of a school district, community college or university and who receives or is eligible to receive retirement benefits from that system for any period of employment is ineligible to receive retirement benefits from ASRS for the same period."

The 1999 amendment by Ch. 327, in subsec. A, substituted "employed by the United States government, a state of the United States or a political subdivision of a state of the United States" for "a member of another public employee retirement system"; and, in subsec. B, substituted "the United States government, a state of the United States or a political subdivision of a state of the United States" for "another public employee retirement system".

The 2001 amendment by Ch. 136 rewrote the section, which had read:

"**A.** An active member of ASRS who previously was a member of another public employee retirement system may receive credited service for this prior employment if the member pays into ASRS the amount prescribed in subsection B.

"**B.** A member who elects to receive credit for service with another public employee retirement system shall pay to ASRS the amount equal to the Product of the member's current annual compensation times the normal cost rate for ASRS for the fiscal year during which the purchase of credited service is being made times the years or partial years of credited service being purchased.

"**C.** A member of ASRS, who previously was a member of another public employee retirement system and who receives or is eligible to receive retirement benefits from that system for any period of employment is ineligible to receive retirement benefits from ASRS for the same period."

Laws 2004, Ch. 246, § 3, provides:

"**Sec. 3. Active members; purchase of public service credits**

"**A.** An active member of ASRS may purchase credited service pursuant to § 38-743, Arizona Revised Statutes, for employment that occurred before or after the effective date of this act from a political subdivision entity that is eligible for participation in ASRS pursuant to this act even if the eligible political subdivision entity is not participating in ASRS.

"**B.** Any employee of a political subdivision entity that becomes a member of ASRS after

December 31, 2003 but before January 1, 2005 may purchase credited service pursuant to this section and § 38-743, Arizona Revised Statutes, under the statute that was in effect before January 1, 2004 if the employee applies for the credited service purchase on or before December 31, 2004."

The 2004 amendment by Ch. 252 inserted "excluding any time worked for a prison while the member was incarcerated," in subsec. A; and rewrote subsec. B, which had read:

"**B.** A member who elects to receive credit for service with the United States government, a state of the United States or a political subdivision of a state of the United States shall pay to ASRS the amount equal to the product of the member's current annual compensation times the normal cost rate for ASRS for the fiscal year during which the purchase of credited service is being made times the years or partial years of credited service being purchased."

Former § 38-743, added by Laws 1975, Ch. 53, § 4, (see Source, following § 38-714), relating to powers and duties of the state retirement system and board, was repealed by Laws 1995, Ch. 32, § 13.

Another former § 38-743, enacted as part of the revision effective January 9, 1956, derived from Laws 1953, Ch. 128, § 15, Code 1939, Supp.1953, § 12-851, Laws 1954, Ch. 116, § 8, and Laws 1955, Ch. 104, § 2, amended by Laws 1970, Ch. 136, § 4, Laws 1970, Ch. 204, § 146, Laws 1971, Ch. 90, § 3, and Laws 1972, Ch. 51, § 5, and relating to the powers and duties of the state retirement system and board, was repealed by Laws 1975, Ch. 53, § 3, effective May 19, 1975.

Reviser's Notes:

1995 Note. In the chapter version, in subsection A "the" was shown before the first "ASRS", but it is not existing law. Pursuant to authority of § 41-1304.02, "the" is deleted to correct a manifest clerical error.

§ 38-743.01. Repealed by Laws 1995, Ch. 32, § 13, eff. March 30, 1995

Historical and Statutory Notes

The repealed section, added by Laws 1975, Ch. 53, § 4, amended by Laws 1977, Ch. 140, § 4; Laws 1985, Ch. 48, § 1; Laws 1985, Ch. 294, § 2; Laws 1994, Ch. 101, § 3, and Laws 1994, Ch. 356, § 5, related to powers and duties of the director.

See, now, § 38-715.

§ 38-743.02. Repealed by Laws 1972, Ch. 51, § 29, eff. August 13, 1972

Historical and Statutory Notes

The repealed section added by Laws 1970, Ch. 136, § 5, related to the powers and duties of subsidiary boards.

§§ 38-743.03, 38-743.04. Repealed by Laws 1975, Ch. 53, § 3, eff. May 19, 1975

Historical and Statutory Notes

The repealed sections, added by Laws 1970, Ch. 136, § 5, related to the powers and duties of the finance manager and the administrator.

§§ 38-743.05, 38-743.06. Repealed by Laws 1995, Ch. 32, § 13, eff. March 30, 1995

Historical and Statutory Notes

Section 38-743.05, added by Laws 1970, Ch. 136, § 5, amended by Laws 1973, Ch. 21, § 1; Laws 1979, Ch. 104, first § 2; Laws 1987, Ch. 75, § 2; Laws 1992, Ch. 321, § 1, and Laws 1994, Ch. 101, § 4, related to the investment advisory council.

See, now, § 38-716.

Section 38-743.06, added by Laws 1992, Ch. 188, § 1, related to liability insurance and immunity for the state retirement system board and the investment advisory council.

See, now, § 38-717.

§ 38–744. Leave of absence; credit for leave without pay

A. If an active member of ASRS or a member who is receiving benefits pursuant to § 38–797.07 is officially granted a leave of absence from employment without pay and returns to employment with the same employer, unless employment could not be resumed because of disability or nonavailability of a position, the member may elect to be credited with service for retirement purposes for not more than one year of the leave by paying to ASRS the amounts as provided in subsection B of this section, if the member has not withdrawn contributions from ASRS and the member's employer has certified that the leave of absence benefits or is in the best interests of the employer.

B. A member who elects to be credited with a leave period as provided in subsection A of this section shall pay to ASRS an amount equal to the present value of the additional benefit that is derived from the purchased credited service using the actuarial assumptions that are approved by the board.

C. For the purposes of subsection A of this section, each employer shall adopt rules establishing guidelines for a leave of absence that benefits or is in the best interests of the employer.

Added by Laws 1995, Ch. 32, § 14, eff. March 30, 1995. Amended by Laws 1995, Ch. 134, § 6, eff. April 17, 1995; Laws 1996, Ch. 185, § 10; Laws 2001, Ch. 136, § 12; Laws 2004, Ch. 252, § 2.

Historical and Statutory Notes

Source:

A.R.S. former §§ 38–746.01, 38–781.29.
Laws 1970, Ch. 134, § 2.
Laws 1975, Ch. 52, §§ 1, 2.
Laws 1985, Ch. 294, § 7.
Laws 1992, Ch. 320, § 17.

Laws 1995, Ch. 32, § 24, as amended by Laws 1999, Ch. 66, § 1, provides:

"**Sec. 24. Savings clause; beneficiary longevity reserve account; definitions**

"**A.** The repeal of §§ 38–744, 38–745, 38–746, 38–746.01, 38–747 through 38–752, 38–752.01, 38–753, 38–754, 38–758, 38–759, 38–760, 38–762 through 38–775, 38–777 and 38–778, Arizona Revised Statutes, does not affect the rights and duties of members of the state highway patrol retirement system and the Arizona state retirement system that matured or proceedings that were begun before March 30, 1995.

"**B.** ASRS shall maintain the beneficiary longevity reserve account as a part of its accounts for the purpose of maintaining benefits payable to retired system members as follows:

"1. The following amounts shall be credited to the beneficiary longevity reserve account:

"(a) Interest attributable to the system that is earned by ASRS in excess of the annual rate of interest adopted by the board.

"(b) Actuarial gains experienced in the operation of the system as determined by the actuary employed by the board.

"(c) Other available system funds.

"2. ASRS shall charge the following amounts to the beneficiary longevity reserve account:

"(a) Actuarial losses experienced in the operation of the system as determined by the actuary employed by the board.

"(b) Any surplus amounts in the beneficiary longevity reserve account that may be allocated by the board to increase retirement benefits for members pursuant to paragraph 3 of this subsection.

"3. The board, after giving due consideration to the recommendation of its actuary, shall determine the amount required in the beneficiary longevity reserve account to maintain benefits payable to retired system members. Any surplus in the beneficiary longevity reserve account in excess of the amount determined by the actuary may be allocated by the board to increase retirement benefits for system members. The portion of the surplus to be allocated with respect to retired system members shall bear the same ratio to the total of the surplus as the retirement account reserves applicable to those retired system members bear to the retirement account reserves applicable to all system members, and the balance of the surplus shall be allocated with respect to system members who retire after the allocation. The portion of the surplus to be allocated with respect to retired system members shall be allocated in the ratio that each retired system member's retirement account reserve bears to the total retirement account reserves of all retired system members and shall be used to provide a life income to cease at the retired system member's death in an amount determined by the interest and life expectancy tables applicable on the date of allocation and based on the attained age of the retired system member on that date. The portion of the surplus to be allocated with respect to system members retiring after the allocation shall be allocated in the ratio that the balance in each such system member's retirement account arising from employer contributions bears at the time of allocation to the total of those balances of all those system members and shall be credited as an employer contribution to each such system member's retirement account. The life income or increased amount of retirement benefits may be reduced or eliminated if subsequent experience determines that the account is inadequate to maintain necessary reserves and to pay the life incomes or benefits.

"4. Notwithstanding paragraph 3 of this subsection, with respect to retired system members and their beneficiaries receiving retirement benefits, the board may allocate any surplus to those retired system members and their beneficiaries that may arise due to a change in the interest and life expectancy tables that reduced liabilities, other than liabilities for prior service, to maintain benefits payable to those retired system members and their beneficiaries on the date of the change. The surplus shall:

"(a) Be applied for each retired system member and retired system member's beneficiary, in the ratio that the retired system member's or retired system member's beneficiary's reserve held in the retirement account bears to the total reserves for all retired system members and their beneficiaries.

"(b) Provide income in an amount determined by the interest and life expectancy tables applicable on the date of allocation and based on the attained age of the retired system member or retired system member's beneficiary on that date.

"(c) Be payable in a manner that is suitable to the retired system member's or retired system member's beneficiary's method of payment. The income may be reduced or eliminated if subsequent experience determines that the account is inadequate to maintain necessary reserves and to pay the income.

"5. A retired system member who has elected an optional form of retirement benefit may elect to receive the retirement benefits provided in paragraph 3 of this subsection in the same optional form of retirement benefits as the member elected at retirement. If a retired system member elects to receive the benefits provided in paragraph 3 of this subsection in an optional form pursuant to this paragraph, all existing retirement benefits payable to the member pursuant to paragraph 3 of this subsection shall be reannuitized, all future retirement benefits payable to the member pursuant to paragraph 3 of this subsection shall be annuitized and benefits shall be paid to the member or the member's surviving beneficiary based on the optional retirement benefit that the member has elected. The amount of the optional benefits payable pursuant to this paragraph shall be equal to the current actuarial lump sum value of the life income benefits payable to the retired system member under paragraph 3 of this subsection, adjusted actuarially to reflect the benefit payment option and the ages of the retired system member and the member's contingent annuitant, in the case of a joint and survivor annuity option, and the number of years remaining in the original period, in the case of a period certain and life annuity option. The beneficiary of a deceased retired system member who had elected to receive an optional form of retirement benefit pursuant to this paragraph is not eligible for additional benefit increases under paragraph 3 of this section after the death of the retired system member.

"**C.** For the purposes of this section:

"1. 'ASRS' means the Arizona state retirement system established by title 38, chapter 5, article 2, Arizona Revised Statutes.

"2. 'Board' means the ASRS board established in § 38-713, Arizona Revised Statutes.

"3. 'Prior service' means service for this state or a political subdivision of this state before membership in the system.

"4. 'Retirement account' means the combined member and employer contributions with interest or earnings on the contributions including allocations credited as employer contributions pursuant to this section.

"5. 'System' means the defined contribution program administered by ASRS."

The 1995 amendment by Ch. 134, in subsec. B, lengthened the payment period from 180 days to five years.

The 1996 amendment by Ch. 185 rewrote subsecs. A and B, which had read:

"**A.** Any active member of ASRS who is officially granted a leave of absence from employment without pay may elect to be credited with service for retirement purposes for not more than one year of the leave by paying to ASRS the amounts as provided in subsection B, if the member has not withdrawn contributions from ASRS and the member's employer has certified that the leave of absence benefits or is in the best interests of the employer.

"**B.** An active member of ASRS who elects to be credited with a leave period as provided in subsection A shall pay to ASRS, within five years after terminating the leave and resuming employment, unless employment could not be resumed because of disability or nonavailability of a position with the same employer, the amount equal to the employer and member contributions for the leave period together with interest at the interest rate assumption approved by the board for actuarial equivalency, based on the salary received by the member before the leave of absence began."

The 2001 amendment by Ch. 136 rewrote the section, which had read:

"**A.** Any active member of ASRS who is officially granted a leave of absence from employment without pay and who returns to employment with the same employer, unless employment could not be resumed because of disability or nonavailability of a position, may elect to be credited with service for retirement purposes for not more than one year of the leave by paying to ASRS the amounts as provided in subsection B, if the member has not withdrawn contributions from ASRS and the member's employer has certified that the leave of absence benefits or is in the best interests of the employer.

"**B.** An active member of ASRS who elects to be credited with a leave period as provided in subsection A shall pay to ASRS, unless an amount equal to the employer and member contributions for the leave period together with interest at the interest rate assumption approved by the board for actuarial equivalency, based on the salary received by the member before the leave of absence began.

"**C.** For the purposes of subsection A, each employer shall adopt rules establishing guidelines for a leave of absence that benefits or is in the best interests of the employer."

The 2004 amendment by Ch. 252 rewrote subsec. B, which had read:

"**B.** A member who elects to be credited with a leave period as provided in subsection A of this section shall pay to ASRS an amount equal to the employer and member contributions for the leave period together with interest at the interest rate assumption approved by the board for actuarial equivalency, based on the salary received by the member before the leave of absence began."

Former § 38–744, enacted as part of the revision effective January 9, 1956 (see Source, following § 38–755), relating to information regarding members' accounts, was repealed by Laws 1995, Ch. 32, § 13. See, now, § 38–755.

§ 38–745. Credit for military service

A. An active member of ASRS or a member who is receiving benefits pursuant to § 38–797.07 may purchase credited service in ASRS for active military service if both of the following apply:

1. The member was honorably separated from the military service.

2. The member submits a copy of the member's military service record (DD–214) or its equivalent with the member's application for military service credit.

B. The cost to purchase military service credit is an amount equal to the present value of the additional benefit that is derived from the purchased credited service using the actuarial assumptions that are approved by the board.

C. An active member of ASRS who is called to active military service may receive credited service for not more than sixty months of active military service, except as provided by the uniformed services employment and reemployment rights act (38 United States code § 4312(c)). The member's employer shall make employer contributions and member contributions for the member if the member meets the following requirements:

1. Was an active member of ASRS on the day before the member began active military service.

2. Is a member of the Arizona national guard or is a member of the reserves of any military establishment of the United States.

3. Volunteers or is ordered into active military service of the United States as part of a presidential call-up.

4. Is honorably separated from active military service and returns to employment for the same employer from which the member left for active military service within ninety days after the date active military service is terminated, is hospitalized as a result of military service and returns to employment for the same employer from which the member left for active military service within ninety days after release from service related hospitalization or dies as a result of the military service.

D. Contributions made pursuant to subsection C of this section shall be for the period of time beginning on the date the member began active military service and ending on one of the following dates:

1. The date the member is separated from active military service.

2. The date the member is released from service related hospitalization or one year after initiation of service related hospitalization, whichever date is earlier.

3. The date the member dies as a result of active military service.

E. Notwithstanding any other law, on payment of the contributions made pursuant to subsection C of this section, the member shall be credited with service for retirement purposes for the period of time of active military service of not more than sixty months.

F. The employer shall make contributions pursuant to subsection C of this section based on the salary being received by the member immediately before the member volunteered or was ordered into active military service in a lump sum and without penalty when the member returns to employment or on receipt of the member's death certificate. If a member suffers a service related death, the employer shall make the employer and member contributions up to and including the date of the member's death. Death benefits shall be calculated as prescribed by law.

G. In computing the length of total credited service of a member for the purpose of determining retirement benefits or eligibility, the period of military service, as prescribed by this section, shall be included.

H. Notwithstanding any other law, the member is not required to reimburse the member's employer or ASRS for any contribution made pursuant to subsection C of this section.

I. In addition to, but not in duplication of, the provisions of subsection C, contributions, benefits and credited service provided pursuant to this section shall be provided in accordance with § 414(u) of the internal revenue code. [1]

Added by Laws 1995, Ch. 32, § 14, eff. March 30, 1995. Amended by Laws 1996, Ch. 185, § 11; Laws 1997, Ch. 280, § 10; Laws 1999, Ch. 327, § 11; Laws 2001, Ch. 136, § 13; Laws 2004, Ch. 252, § 3.

[1] Internal Revenue Code sections may be found in Title 26 of U.S.C.A.

Historical and Statutory Notes

Source:

Laws 1953, Ch. 128, § 6.

Code 1939, Supp.1953, § 12–842.

A.R.S. former §§ 38–746, 38–781.42.
Laws 1989, Ch. 310, § 5.
Laws 1992, Ch. 320, § 19.
Laws 1994, Ch. 207, § 1.

For state highway patrol retirement system and Arizona state retirement system savings clause and beneficiary longevity reserve account provisions of Laws 1995, Ch. 32, see Historical and Statutory Notes following § 38–744.

The 1996 amendment by Ch. 185 rewrote subsecs. A, B and H, which had read:

"**A.** An active member of ASRS may receive credited service for active military service if:

"1. The member was honorably separated from the military service.

"2. The period of military service for which the member receives credited service does not exceed forty-eight months.

"3. The period of military service for which the participant receives credited service is not on account with any other retirement system.

"**B.** Except as provided in subsection C, the cost to purchase military service credit is based on the amount necessary to equal the increase in the actuarial present value of projected benefits resulting from the credit."

"**H.** An applicant shall submit a copy of the military discharge certificate (DD-256A) and a copy of the military service record (DD-214) or its equivalent with the application when applying for military service credit, except that members of the Arizona national guard and military reserves ordered into active military service as part of a presidential call-up are only required to submit a copy of the military service record (DD-214) or its equivalent."

The 1997 amendment by Ch. 280 rewrote subsecs. A to C; deleted subsec. H; and added a new subsec. H relating to reimbursement of a member's employer or ASRS for certain contributions. Prior to amendment, subsecs. A to C, and H had read:

"**A.** An active member of ASRS may receive credited service for active military service if:

"1. The member was honorably separated from the military service.

"2. The period of military service for which the participant receives credited service is not on account with any other retirement system.

"**B.** Except as provided in subsection C, the cost to purchase military service credit is an amount equal to the product of the member's current annual compensation times the normal cost rate for ASRS for the fiscal year during which the purchase of credited service is being made times the years or partial years of credited service being purchased.

"**C.** For a period of time of active military service but for not more than forty-eight months, an employer shall make employer contributions and member contributions for a person who was an active member of ASRS on the day before the member began active military service, who satisfies the requirements of subsection A, paragraph 2 and who meets the following requirements:

"1. Is a member of the Arizona national guard or is a member of the reserves of any military establishment of the United States.

"2. Volunteers or is ordered into active military service of the United States as part of a presidential call-up.

"3. Is honorably separated from active military service and returns to employment for the same employer from which the member left for active military service within ninety days after the date active military service is terminated, is hospitalized as a result of military service and returns to employment for the same employer from which the member left for active military service within ninety days after release from service related hospitalization or dies as a result of the military service."

"**H.** An applicant shall submit a copy of the military service record (DD-214) or its equivalent with the application when applying for military service credit."

The 1999 amendment by Ch. 327 added subsec. I.

The 2001 amendment by Ch. 136 rewrote subsec. A; and made other nonsubstantive changes. Subsection A had read:

"**A.** An active member of ASRS may purchase credited service in ASRS for active military service if:

"1. The member was honorably separated from the military service.

"2. The member submits a copy of the member's military service record (DD-214) or its equivalent with the member's application for military service credit.

"3. The period of military service for which the participant receives credited service is not on account with any other retirement system.

The 2004 amendment by Ch. 252 inserted "both of the following apply" at the end of the introductory clause of subsec. A; rewrote subsec. B and the first sentence of subsec. C; and substituted "active military service of not more than sixty months" for "active military service of not more than forty-eight months" in subsec. E. Subsection B and the first sentence of subsec. C had read:

"**B.** The cost to purchase military service credit is an amount equal to the product of the member's current annual compensation times the normal cost rate for ASRS for the fiscal year during which the purchase of credited service is being made times the years or partial years of credited service being purchased.

"C. An active member of ASRS who is called to active military service may receive credited service for not more than forty-eight months of active military service."

Former § 38–745, enacted as part of the revision effective January 9, 1956 (see Source, following § 38–727), relating to retirement system membership, was repealed by Laws 1995, Ch. 32, § 13, eff. March. 30, 1995. See, now, § 38–727.

§ 38–746. Compensation limitation; adjustments

A. Except as provided in subsection E, beginning on July 1, 2002, the annual compensation of each employee taken into account under ASRS for any fiscal year or for any other specified twelve consecutive month period shall not exceed two hundred thousand dollars. In determining benefit accruals under ASRS for fiscal years beginning after December 31, 2001 and except as provided for in subsection E, the annual compensation limit under this subsection for fiscal years beginning before January 1, 2002 is two hundred thousand dollars.

B. If compensation under ASRS is determined on a period of time that contains fewer than twelve calendar months, the compensation limit for that period of time is equal to the dollar limit for the calendar year during which the period of time begins, multiplied by the fraction in which the numerator is the number of full months in that period of time and the denominator is twelve.

C. For fiscal years beginning before July 1, 1997, the annual compensation limit prescribed in this section also applies to the combined compensation of a member who is a member of the group of ten highly compensated employees, as defined in § 414(q) of the internal revenue code,[1] and who is paid the highest compensation during the fiscal year and any family member of the member who is either the member's spouse or the member's lineal descendant and who has not attained the age of nineteen before the close of the fiscal year. If the maximum compensation is adjusted pursuant to subsection D, the adjusted limitation shall be prorated among the affected members' compensation determined pursuant to this section before application of the adjusted limitation to the other provisions of this article.

D. The board shall adjust the maximum compensation under subsection A at the same time and in the same manner as adjusted by the United States secretary of the treasury under § 401(a)(17)(B) of the internal revenue code.[2] The adjustment under this subsection for a calendar year applies to annual compensation for the fiscal year of ASRS that begins with or within the calendar year.

E. The dollar limitation prescribed in subsection A does not apply to an eligible member to the extent that the annual compensation of an eligible member taken into account by ASRS for any fiscal year or for any other specified twelve consecutive month period would be reduced below two hundred thirty-five thousand eight hundred forty dollars. This was the amount of compensation taken into account by ASRS as of July 1, 1993. The board shall adjust this amount as of the effective date of the increase prescribed by the United States secretary of the treasury. For the purposes of this subsection, "eligible member" means a person who first became a member of ASRS before July 1, 1996.

Added by Laws 1995, Ch. 32, § 14, eff. March 30, 1995. Amended by Laws 1996, Ch. 185, § 12; Laws 1997, Ch. 280, § 11; Laws 2002, Ch. 213, § 2, eff. July 1, 2002.

[1] 26 U.S.C.A. § 414(q).

[2] 26 U.S.C.A. § 401(a)(17)(B).

Historical and Statutory Notes

Source:

A.R.S. former § 38–781.38.
Laws 1985, Ch. 294, § 8.
Laws 1986, Ch. 168, § 7.
Laws 1991, Ch. 170, § 8.
Laws 1994, Ch. 356, § 17.

For state highway patrol retirement system and Arizona state retirement system savings clause and beneficiary longevity reserve account provisions of Laws 1995, Ch. 32, see Historical and Statutory Notes following § 38–744.

The 1996 amendment by Ch. 185 rewrote the section, which had read:

"**A.** Effective July 1, 1989, the annual compensation of each employee taken into account under ASRS for any fiscal year or for any other specified twelve consecutive month period shall not exceed two hundred thousand dollars.

"**B.** If compensation under ASRS is determined on a period of time that contains fewer than twelve calendar months, the compensation limit for that period of time is equal to the dollar limit for the calendar year during which the period of time begins, multiplied by the fraction in which the numerator is the number of full months in that period of time and the denominator is twelve.

"**C.** The annual compensation limit prescribed in this section also applies to the combined compensation of a member who is a member of the group of ten highly compensated employees, as defined in § 414(q) of the internal revenue code, and who is paid the highest compensation during the fiscal year and any family member of the member who is either the member's spouse or the member's lineal descendant and who has not attained the age of nineteen before the close of the fiscal year.

"**D.** The board shall adjust the maximum compensation under subsection A at the same time and in the same manner as adjusted by the United States secretary of the treasury under § 415(d) of the internal revenue code. If, pursuant to this subsection, the maximum compensation is adjusted, the adjusted limitation shall be prorated among the affected member's compensation determined pursuant to this section before application of the adjusted limitation to the other provisions of this article."

The 1997 amendment by Ch. 280 inserted "For fiscal years beginning before July 1, 1997," at the beginning of subsec. C.

The 2002 amendment by Ch. 213, rewrote subsec. A; inserted the last sentence of subsec. D; and substituted "amount of compensation taken" for "amount allowed to be taken" in the second sentence of subsec. E. Subsection A had read:

"**A.** Except as provided in subsection E, beginning on July 1, 1996, the annual compensation of each employee taken into account under ASRS for any fiscal year or for any other specified twelve consecutive month period shall not exceed one hundred fifty thousand dollars."

Former § 38–746, enacted as part of the revision effective January 9, 1956 (see Source, following § 38–745), relating to creditable service, was repealed by Laws 1995, Ch. 32, § 13, eff. March 30, 1995.

§ 38–746.01. Repealed by Laws 1995, Ch. 32, § 13, eff. March 30, 1995

Historical and Statutory Notes

The repealed section, added by Laws 1975, Ch. 52, § 1, related to credit as service for limited leave of absence without pay. See, now, § 38–744.

§ 38–747. Purchase of credited service; payment; limitations; definitions

A. A member who purchases credited service pursuant to § 38–738, 38–742, 38–743, 38–744, 38–745 or 38–922 shall either:

1. Make payments directly to ASRS as provided in subsection H of this section.

2. Elect to have the member's employer make payments as provided in subsection B of this section.

B. A member may elect to have the member's employer make payments for all or any portion of the amounts payable for the member's purchase of credited service pursuant to the sections prescribed in subsection A of this section through a salary reduction program in accordance with the following:

1. The amounts paid pursuant to a salary reduction program are in lieu of contributions by the electing member. The electing member's salary or other compensation shall be reduced by the amount paid by the employer pursuant to this subsection. For the purposes of this paragraph, "other compensation" includes a member's termination pay.

2. The member shall make an election pursuant to this subsection at any time on or after the date the member elects to purchase credited service pursuant to the sections prescribed in subsection A of this section and before the member's termination of employment. The election shall specify the number of payroll periods that deductions will be made from the member's compensation and the dollar amount of deductions for each payroll period during the specified number of payroll periods. In the case of an election to utilize all or any part of the member's termination pay to purchase credited service, the member's election shall be made at least three full calendar months before the date of the member's termination of employment and entitlement to receive the termination pay. After an election is made pursuant to this subsection, the election is binding on and irrevocable for the member and the member's employer during the member's remaining period of current employment. After a member makes an irrevocable election pursuant to this subsection, the member does not have the option of choosing to receive the contributed amounts directly. For the purposes of this paragraph, "termination pay" means any lump sum that is paid at the member's termination of employment for accrued vacation, sick leave or overtime pay.

3. A member who makes an irrevocable election pursuant to this subsection to have the member's employer make payments for less than all of the amounts payable for the member's purchase of credited service may irrevocably elect to have the member's employer make payments for all or any portion of the remaining amounts payable for the member's purchase of credited service. A member who makes one or more irrevocable elections pursuant to this subsection may also make other contributions to ASRS pursuant to subsection H of this section to the extent of any remaining amounts payable for which the member has not made an election pursuant to this subsection. An additional election or contribution with respect to a portion of the amounts payable for the member's purchase of credited service does not alter, amend or revoke an irrevocable election already made pursuant to this subsection for any other portion of the amounts payable for the member's purchase of credited service.

4. If on termination of the member's current employment all amounts have not been paid to ASRS pursuant to the member's irrevocable election pursuant to this subsection, the member may pay ASRS, within thirty days after the member's termination of employment and subject to other limitations prescribed in this section, all or any portion of the unpaid amounts as provided in subsection H of this section. These payments do not alter, amend or revoke any irrevocable election already made pursuant to this subsection with respect

to any amount to be paid by the member's employer while the member is employed by the member's employer.

5. Amounts paid by an employer pursuant to this subsection shall be treated as employer contributions for the purpose of determining tax treatment under the internal revenue code. [1] The effective date of employer payments pursuant to this subsection shall not be before the date ASRS receives notification from the United States internal revenue service that pursuant to § 414(h)(2) of the internal revenue code the amounts paid by an employer pursuant to this subsection will not be included in the member's gross income for income tax purposes until those amounts are distributed by refund or retirement benefit payments.

6. Unless otherwise provided, member contributions paid by an employer pursuant to this subsection are treated for all other purposes under ASRS in the same manner and to the same extent as member contributions that are not paid by an employer pursuant to this subsection. ASRS shall not grant credited service for contributions made pursuant to this subsection until those contributions are received by ASRS. ASRS may assess interest or administrative charges attributable to any salary reduction election made pursuant to this subsection. The interest or administrative charges shall be added to the amount of contributions that is made to ASRS by the member each payroll period and that is paid by the member's employer. The interest or administrative charges shall not be treated as member contributions for any purposes under this article and a member or a member's beneficiary does not have a right to the return of the interest or administrative charges pursuant to any other provision of this article. Interest assessed pursuant to this subsection shall be at the rate specified by the board pursuant to § 38–711, paragraph 2.

C. A member who elects before July 1, 1999 to receive retirement benefits based on § 38–771, subsection C, paragraph 2 or a member who elects to make contributions to ASRS pursuant to § 38–771.01, subsection F, paragraph 4 shall either make the member's additional contributions required pursuant to § 38–771, subsection E or allowed pursuant to § 38–771.01, subsection F, paragraph 4 directly to ASRS as provided in subsection H of this section or shall elect to have the member's employer make payments for those additional contributions as provided in subsection D of this section. A member who elected to be covered or who was deemed to be covered by § 38–771 on or before December 31, 1995 or who elects to make member contributions pursuant to § 38–771.01, subsection F, paragraph 3 is deemed to have made an irrevocable election pursuant to subsection D of this section to make the member's contributions to ASRS that are required by § 38–771, subsection D or allowed by § 38–771.01, subsection F, paragraph 3.

D. Any member contributions that are required by § 38–771, subsection D or that are allowed pursuant to § 38–771.01, subsection F, paragraph 3 are deemed to be made by the member to ASRS through a salary reduction program in accordance with the following:

1. A member may make member contributions pursuant to § 38–771, subsection E or § 38–771.01, subsection F, paragraph 4 through a salary reduction program elected pursuant to this subsection. If a member makes an irrevocable election pursuant to this subsection before July 1, 1999 to have the

member's employer make payments for additional contributions pursuant to § 38-771, subsection E, the election continues in effect from and after June 30, 1999 and shall not be revoked, amended or altered by any election made pursuant to § 38-771.01 or otherwise. The amounts paid pursuant to a salary reduction program are in lieu of contributions by the electing member. The member's salary or other compensation shall be reduced by the amount paid by the employer pursuant to this subsection.

2. Before a member's termination of employment, the member may make an election pursuant to this subsection at any time after the date the member elects to receive retirement benefits based on § 38-771, subsection C, paragraph 2 but before July 1, 1999 or at any time after the member elects to make member contributions pursuant to § 38-771.01, subsection F, paragraph 4. The election shall specify the number of payroll periods that deductions will be made from the member's compensation and the dollar amount of deductions for each payroll period during the specified number of payroll periods. After an election is made pursuant to this subsection, the election is binding on and irrevocable for the member and the member's employer during the member's remaining period of current employment.

3. After a member makes or is deemed to have made an irrevocable election pursuant to this subsection, the member does not have the option of choosing to receive the contributed amounts directly. A member who makes an irrevocable election pursuant to this subsection to have the member's employer make payments for less than all of the amounts payable for the member's additional contributions allowed by § 38-771.01, subsection F, paragraph 4 may irrevocably elect to have the member's employer make payments for all or any portion of the remaining amounts payable for the member's additional contributions. A member who makes one or more irrevocable elections pursuant to this subsection may also make other contributions to ASRS pursuant to § 38-771.01, subsection F, paragraph 4 or pursuant to subsection H of this section to the extent of any remaining amounts payable for which the member has not made an election pursuant to this subsection. An additional election or contribution with respect to a portion of the amounts payable for the member's additional contributions pursuant to § 38-771.01, subsection F, paragraph 4 does not alter, amend or revoke an irrevocable election already made pursuant to this subsection for any other portion of the amounts payable for the member's additional contributions allowed by § 38-771.01, subsection F, paragraph 4.

4. If on termination of the member's current employment all amounts have not been paid to ASRS pursuant to the member's irrevocable election pursuant to this subsection, the member may pay ASRS, within thirty days after the member's termination of employment and subject to other limitations prescribed in this section, all or any portion of the unpaid amounts as provided in subsection H of this section. These payments do not alter, amend or revoke any irrevocable election already made pursuant to this subsection with respect to any amount to be paid by the member's employer while the member is employed by the member's employer.

5. Amounts paid by an employer pursuant to this subsection shall be treated as employer contributions for the purpose of determining tax treatment under

the internal revenue code. The effective date of employer payments pursuant to this subsection shall not be before the date ASRS receives notification from the United States internal revenue service that pursuant to § 414(h)(2) of the internal revenue code the amounts paid by an employer pursuant to this subsection will not be included in the member's gross income for income tax purposes until those amounts are distributed by refund or retirement benefit payments.

6. Unless otherwise provided, member contributions paid by an employer pursuant to this subsection are treated for all other purposes under ASRS in the same manner and to the same extent as member contributions that are not paid by an employer pursuant to this subsection.

E. The following limits apply to contributions to ASRS:

1. Except to the extent paragraphs 2 and 3 of this subsection apply to certain contributions made by a member to ASRS and to the extent permitted under § 414(v) of the internal revenue code, if applicable, in any one limitation year, the annual additions contributed or allocated to ASRS for or on behalf of a member shall not exceed the lesser of either:

(a) Forty thousand dollars or a larger amount that is prescribed by the board and that is due to any cost of living adjustment announced by the United States secretary of the treasury pursuant to § 415(d) of the internal revenue code. The board shall increase the amount prescribed by this subdivision as of the effective date of the increase announced by the United States secretary of the treasury.

(b) One hundred per cent of the member's compensation for the limitation year. The compensation limit prescribed in this subdivision does not apply to any contribution to ASRS for medical benefits after a member's separation from service, within the meaning prescribed in § 401(h) or 419A(f)(2) of the internal revenue code, that is otherwise treated as an annual addition.

2. Unless paragraph 4 of this subsection applies, for plan years beginning on or after July 1, 1998, in any one limitation year, the annual additions credited to ASRS for or on behalf of a member who makes contributions to ASRS to purchase credited service pursuant to § 38–743, 38–744, 38–745 or 38–922 and with respect to which an irrevocable election has not been made pursuant to subsection B of this section shall not exceed the greater of either:

(a) The requirements of § 38–769. For the purposes of applying the limits prescribed in § 38–769 under this subdivision, the accrued benefit derived from the contributions shall be treated as an annual benefit and the reduced limit for certain early retirement in § 38–769, subsection C, paragraph 2 does not apply.

(b) Except as provided in paragraph 3 of this subsection, the requirements of paragraph 1 of this subsection. The contributions shall be treated as annual additions and any of the member's other annual additions for the limitation year shall be taken into account. For the purposes of applying the requirements of paragraph 1 of this subsection under this subdivision, the percentage of compensation limit in paragraph 1, subdivision (b) of this paragraph does not apply.

3. For plan years beginning on or after July 1, 1998, the requirements of paragraph 1 of this subsection shall not be applied to reduce the amount of credited service that may be purchased by an eligible member pursuant to § 38–743, 38–744, 38–745 or 38–922 to an amount that is less than the amount of credited service allowed to be purchased pursuant to those sections on August 5, 1997 without the application of any of the limits prescribed in this section or § 415 of the internal revenue code. For the purposes of this paragraph, "eligible member" means a person who first becomes a member of ASRS before July 1, 1999.

4. Member contributions to ASRS to purchase credited service pursuant to § 38–743, 38–744 or 38–922 shall not be made by a member if recognition of that service would cause a member to receive a retirement benefit for the same service from ASRS and one or more other retirement plans. This paragraph does not apply to either of the following:

(a) Contributions made by an eligible member as defined in paragraph 3 of this subsection, except that any service purchase by an eligible member is subject to any other limitations, including limitations on duplicative service purchase, otherwise provided in this article.

(b) Any member contributions with respect to which an irrevocable election has been made by a member pursuant to subsection B of this section, except that the service purchase is subject to any other limitations, including limitations on duplicative service purchase, otherwise provided in this article.

F. If a member's contributions are subject to the limitations of subsection E of this section, the contributions shall be treated as being made to a separate defined contribution plan. If the member's contributions exceed the limits prescribed in subsection E of this section when taking into account other member and employer contributions to ASRS on behalf of the member for the limitation year, the amount to be paid by the member shall be reduced to not exceed the limits prescribed in subsection E of this section and the remaining amount shall be carried forward to the next limitation year, unless the limits are exceeded in the next limitation year. If the limits are exceeded in the next limitation year, the procedure prescribed by this subsection shall be repeated until all payments have been made.

G. If, after the application of subsection F of this section, the annual additions on behalf of a member exceed the limitations prescribed in subsection E of this section, ASRS shall dispose of excess amounts by either of the following:

1. Returning to the member any contributions that are made by the member and that are nondeductible under the internal revenue code.

2. Holding the amounts in a suspense account established pursuant to subsection L of this section and allocating the amounts as either member or employer contributions for the benefit of the member in the next limitation year and before any further member or employer contributions are made that would constitute annual additions made to a defined contribution plan pursuant to § 415 of the internal revenue code. ASRS shall allocate contributions as prescribed in this section, and the amount allocated shall reduce the amount of

the member or employer contributions for the limitation year in which the allocation is made.

H. To the extent that a payment under this subsection does not alter, amend or revoke any one or more currently effective irrevocable elections made by the member pursuant to subsection B or D of this section, the board may accept contributions made pursuant to § 38–771 or member contributions for the payment for credited service purchases pursuant to § 38–738, 38–742, 38–743, 38–744, 38–745 or 38–922 or contributions made pursuant to § 38–771.01, subsection F, paragraph 4, in whole or in part, by any one or a combination of the following methods:

1. In lump sum payments.

2. Subject to the limitations prescribed in §§ 401(a)(31) and 402(c) of the internal revenue code and subsection J of this section, accepting a direct rollover of or a contribution by a member of an eligible rollover distribution from one or more:

(a) Retirement programs that are qualified under § 401(a) or 403(a) of the internal revenue code.

(b) Annuity contracts described in § 403(b) of the internal revenue code.

(c) Eligible deferred compensation plans described in § 457(b) of the internal revenue code that are maintained by a state, a political subdivision of a state or any agency or instrumentality of a state or a political subdivision of a state.

3. Subject to the limitations prescribed in § 408(d)(3)(A)(ii) of the internal revenue code, accepting from a member a rollover contribution of that portion of a distribution from an individual retirement account or individual retirement annuity described in § 408(a) or 408(b) of the internal revenue code that is eligible to be rolled over and would otherwise be includable as gross income.

4. Providing by rule that the contributions may be made in installment payments over a period of time.

I. To the extent that a payment under this subsection does not alter, amend or revoke any one or more currently effective irrevocable elections made by a member pursuant to subsection B or D of this section, the board may accept a direct trustee-to-trustee transfer from retirement programs that are qualified under § 401(a) or 403(a) of the internal revenue code, an annuity contract described in § 403(b) of the internal revenue code or an eligible deferred compensation plan described in § 457(b) of the internal revenue code for the payment for credited service purchases pursuant to § 38–742, 38–743, 38–744, 38–745 or 38–922. If a direct trustee-to-trustee transfer is from a retirement program qualified under § 401(a) of the internal revenue code, which includes a cash or deferred arrangement described in § 401(k) of the internal revenue code, the member on whose behalf the transfer was made is not eligible to retire under § 38–764, subsection J, before the date the member attains age fifty and one-half.

J. ASRS shall separately account for all amounts rolled over or directly transferred to ASRS.

K. ASRS shall not grant credited service under § 38–738, 38–742, 38–743, 38–744 or 38–922 for contributions made pursuant to subsection H of this section until the contributions are received by ASRS. ASRS may assess interest or administrative charges attributable to any installment payment made pursuant to subsection H, paragraph 4 of this section to purchase credited service pursuant to § 38-738, 38-742, 38-743, 38-744 or 38-922. The interest or administrative charges shall be added to the amount of contributions made to ASRS by the member. The interest or administrative charges shall not be treated as member contributions for any purposes under this article, and a member or a member's beneficiary does not have a right to the return of the interest or administrative charges pursuant to any other provision of this article. Interest assessed pursuant to this subsection shall be at the rate specified by the board pursuant to § 38-711, paragraph 2.

L. ASRS shall establish a suspense account that conforms with 26 Code of Federal Regulations § 1.415-6(b)(6) regarding excess annual additions.

M. If the member retires before all payments are made pursuant to this section, ASRS shall calculate the member's benefits based only on the payments actually made.

N. On satisfaction of the requirements of this section, ASRS shall adjust the member's credited service history and add any additional service credits acquired.

O. Annual additions on behalf of a member in any limitation year shall be the sum of:

1. The amount of the member contributions made to ASRS to purchase credited service pursuant to § 38-738, 38-743, 38-744, 38-745 or 38-922 and with respect to which an irrevocable election made pursuant to subsection B of this section is not in effect.

2. The amount of member and employer contributions made to ASRS on behalf of a member who elected or was deemed to have elected to receive retirement benefits pursuant to § 38-771 or who is entitled to benefits pursuant to § 38-771.01, except that, other than as provided in subsection P of this section, corrective contributions shall be considered annual additions for the limitation years to which the contributions relate and interest and gains shall not be considered as annual additions for the purpose of any limitation prescribed in this article or in § 415 of the internal revenue code. If the corrective contributions exceed the limit on annual additions for a limitation year prior to the limitation year in which the corrective contributions are contributed by the employer to ASRS, the retirement benefit attributable to the excess corrective contributions shall be treated as an excess benefit and shall be payable to the member as any other excess benefit is payable pursuant to § 38-774, and the employer shall pay the excess corrective contributions to the separate unfunded governmental excess benefit arrangement administered by the board pursuant to § 38-774.

3. Any member or employer contributions made to ASRS or any other plan that are treated as being made to a defined contribution plan maintained by an employer of the member.

4. Any forfeitures, including any income attributable to forfeitures, allocated for or on behalf of a member of ASRS or any other plan that are treated as

being allocated under a defined contribution plan maintained by an employer of the member.

P. To the extent any portion of the subject benefits, if treated as subject to the benefit limitations of § 415(b) of the internal revenue code, exceed the applicable limitation on benefits pursuant to § 38–769 for the form of distribution, a percentage of corrective contributions and interest and gains shall be treated as annual additions for the limitation year in which contributed by the employer to ASRS. This percentage of corrective contributions and interest and gains shall be equal to the percentage determined by dividing the subject benefits that exceed the limitation on benefits pursuant to § 38–769 by the subject benefits. If the corrective contributions and interest and gains that are treated as annual additions for the limitation year in which the corrective contributions and interest and gains are contributed by the employer to ASRS exceed the limit on annual additions for the limitation year, the retirement benefit attributable to the excess shall be treated as an excess benefit and shall be payable to the member as any other excess benefit is payable pursuant to § 38–774, and the employer shall pay the excess to the separate unfunded governmental excess benefit arrangement administered by the board pursuant to § 38–774.

Q. Subsection O of this section shall be construed and interpreted in accordance with 26 Code of Federal Regulations § 1.415–6 to the extent that section is applicable.

R. For the purposes of this section:

1. "Compensation" has the same meaning prescribed in § 38–769.

2. "Corrective contributions" means any contributions that are paid by an employer pursuant to § 38–771.01, subsection C, paragraph 3 and that are attributable to employer contributions that should have been made for prior limitation years.

3. "Defined contribution plan" has the same meaning prescribed in § 38–769.

4. "Interest and gains" means employer contributions to ASRS pursuant to § 38–771.01, subsection C, paragraphs 3, 5 and 6 that are attributable to earnings and supplemental credits that would have been earned or added to a member's annuity payment.

5. "Limitation year" has the same meaning prescribed in § 38–769.

6. "Subject benefits" means the retirement benefit received by a member pursuant to § 38–771.01 minus the sum of the portion of such retirement benefit attributable to contributions that were made by or on behalf of the member to the defined contribution program administered by ASRS for periods before July 1, 1981 and contributions that were made by the member after June 30, 1981 and that were not picked up as provided in § 414(h)(2) of the internal revenue code.

Added by Laws 1995, Ch. 134, § 7, eff. April 17, 1995. Amended by Laws 1996, Ch. 185, § 13; Laws 1997, Ch. 280, § 12; Laws 1998, Ch. 155, § 2; Laws 1999, Ch. 266, § 1, eff. July 1, 1999; Laws 1999, Ch. 327, § 12; Laws 2000, Ch. 315, § 1; Laws 2001, Ch. 136, § 14; Laws 2002, Ch. 213, § 3, eff. May 15, 2002; Laws 2002, Ch. 213, § 4, eff. July 1, 2002; Laws 2004, Ch. 252, § 4.

[1] Internal Revenue Code sections may be found in Title 26 of U.S.C.A.

Historical and Statutory Notes

The 1996 amendment by Ch. 185 rewrote the section, which had read:

"**A.** A member who purchases credited service pursuant to §§ 38–742, 38–743, 38–744, 38–745 or 38–771 shall make payments in a lump sum to ASRS.

"**B.** In any one limitation year, payments shall not exceed the lesser of either:

"1. Thirty thousand dollars or one-fourth of the dollar limitation prescribed in § 38–769, subsection A, paragraph 1, as adjusted by the board as provided in § 38–769, whichever is more.

"2. Twenty-five per cent of the member's compensation for the limitation year.

"**C.** If the member's payments due to ASRS under this section exceed the limits prescribed in subsection B of this section when taking into account other member and employer contributions to ASRS on behalf of the member for the limitation year, the amount to be paid by the member shall be reduced to not exceed the limits prescribed in subsection B of this section and the reduced amount shall be carried forward to the next limitation year, unless the limits are exceeded in the next limitation year. If the limits are exceeded in the next limitation year, the procedure prescribed by this subsection shall be repeated until all payments have been made.

"**D.** If the member retires before all payments are made pursuant to this section, ASRS shall calculate the member's benefits based only on the payments actually made.

"**E.** On satisfaction of the requirements of this section, ASRS shall adjust the member's credited service history and add any additional service credits acquired.

"**F.** For the purposes of this section, the terms 'limitation year' and 'compensation' have the same meaning prescribed in § 38–769."

The 1997 amendment by Ch. 280 rewrote the section which had read:

"**A.** A member who purchases credited service pursuant to § 38–742, 38–743, 38–744, 38–745 or 38–922 shall make payments to ASRS.

"**B.** In any one limitation year, the annual additions credited to ASRS for or on behalf of a member who purchases credited service under the sections prescribed in subsection A of this section shall not exceed the lesser of either:

"1. Thirty thousand dollars or a larger amount that is prescribed by the board and that is due to any cost of living adjustment announced by the United States Secretary of the Treasury pursuant to § 415(d) of the Internal Revenue Code. The board shall increase the amount prescribed by this paragraph as of the effective date of the increase announced by the United States Secretary of the Treasury.

"2. Twenty-five per cent of the member's compensation for the limitation year.

"**C.** A member's contributions under this section are treated as being made to a separate defined contribution plan. If the member's payments under this section exceed the limits prescribed in subsection B of this section when taking into account other member and employer contributions to ASRS on behalf of the member for the limitation year, the amount to be paid by the member shall be reduced to not exceed the limits prescribed in subsection B of this section and the remaining amount shall be carried forward to the next limitation year, unless the limits are exceeded in the next limitation year. If the limits are exceeded in the next limitation year, the procedure prescribed by this subsection shall be repeated until all payments have been made.

"**D.** If, after the application of subsection C of this section, the annual additions on behalf of a member exceed the limitations prescribed in subsection B of this section, ASRS shall dispose of excess amounts by either of the following:

"1. Returning to the member any contributions that are made by the member and that are nondeductible under the Internal Revenue Code.

"2. Holding the amounts in a suspense account established pursuant to subsection F of this section and allocating the amounts as either member or employer contributions for the benefit of the member in the next limitation year and before any further member or employer contributions are made that would constitute annual additions made to a defined contribution plan pursuant to § 415 of the Internal Revenue Code. ASRS shall allocate contributions as prescribed in this section, and the amount allocated shall reduce the amount of the member or employer contributions for the limitation year in which the allocation is made.

"**E.** The board may accept member contributions for the payment for credited service purchases pursuant to §§ 38–742, 38–743, 38–744, 38–745 or 38–922, in whole or in part, by either or both of the following methods:

"1. Accepting eligible rollover distributions from one or more qualified retirement programs, subject to the limitations prescribed in § 402(c) of the Internal Revenue Code.

"2. Providing by rule that the contributions may be made in installment payments over a period of time, except that ASRS shall not grant credited service for contributions that have not been received by ASRS.

"F. ASRS shall establish a suspense account that conforms with 26 Code of Federal Regulations § 1.415-6(b)(6) regarding excess annual additions.

"G. If the member retires before all payments are made pursuant to this section, ASRS shall calculate the member's benefits based only on the payments actually made.

"H. On satisfaction of the requirements of this section, ASRS shall adjust the member's credited service history and add any additional service credits acquired.

"I. Annual additions on behalf of a member in any limitation year shall be the sum of:

"1. The amount of the member contributions made to ASRS to purchase credited service pursuant to § 38-742, 38-743, 38-744, 38-745 or 38-922.

"2. Any member or employer contributions made to ASRS or any other plan that are treated as being made to a defined contribution plan maintained by an employer of the member.

"3. Any forfeitures, including any income attributable to forfeitures, allocated for or on behalf of a member of ASRS or any other plan that are treated as being allocated under a defined contribution plan maintained by an employer of the member.

"J. Subsection I of this section shall be construed and interpreted in accordance with 26 Code of Federal Regulations § 1.415-6 to the extent that section is applicable.

"K. For the purposes of this section:

"1. 'Limitation year', 'defined contribution plan' and 'compensation' have the same meaning prescribed in § 38-769.

"2. In determining the annual additions credited to a member of ASRS, 'annual additions' has the same meaning prescribed in 26 Code of Federal Regulations § 1.415-6(b)."

The 1998 amendment by Ch. 155 inserted "the date" following "anytime on or after" in subsecs. B and D; and rewrote subsecs. E, F and H, which had read:

"E. In any one limitation year, the annual additions credited to ASRS for or on behalf of a member who purchases credited service pursuant to § 38-743, 38-744, 38-745 or 38-922 and with respect to which an irrevocable election has not been made pursuant to subsection B of this section or who has elected to receive retirement benefits pursuant to § 38-771 shall not exceed the lesser of either:

"1. Thirty thousand dollars or a larger amount that is prescribed by the board and that is due to any cost of living adjustment announced by the United States secretary of the treasury pursuant to § 415(d) of the internal revenue code. The board shall increase the amount prescribed by this paragraph as of the effective date of the increase announced by the United States secretary of the treasury.

"2. Twenty-five per cent of the member's compensation for the limitation year.

"F. Subject to the limitations prescribed in subsection E of this section, a member's contributions under this section are treated as being made to a separate defined contribution plan. If the member's contributions under this section exceed the limits prescribed in subsection E of this section when taking into account other member and employer contributions to ASRS on behalf of the member for the limitation year, the amount to be paid by the member shall be reduced to not exceed the limits prescribed in subsection E of this section and the remaining amount shall be carried forward to the next limitation year, unless the limits are exceeded in the next limitation year. If the limits are exceeded in the next limitation year, the procedure prescribed by this subsection shall be repeated until all payments have been made."

"H. To the extent that a payment under this subsection does not alter, amend or revoke any one or more currently effective irrevocable elections made by the member pursuant to subsection B or D of this section, the board may accept member contributions for the payment for credited service purchases pursuant to §§ 38-742, 38-743, 38-744, 38-745 or 38-922, in whole or in part, by any one or a combination of the following methods:

"1. In lump sum payments.

"2. Accepting eligible rollover distributions from one or more qualified retirement programs, subject to the limitations prescribed in § 402(c) of the internal revenue code.

"3. Subject to the limitations prescribed in § 408(d)(3)(A)(ii) of the internal revenue code, accepting conduit rollover contributions from one or more individual retirement accounts.

"4. Providing by rule that the contributions may be made in installment payments over a period of time."

The 1999 amendment by Ch. 266 substituted "In accordance with the following:" for "Employers shall implement this subsection no later than July 1, 1999." in subsec. B; rewrote subsecs. C, D and E; modified statutory references in subsec. H; and rewrote subsec. M, par. 2.

Laws 1999, Ch. 266, § 6, provides:

"**Sec. 6. Conditional enactment; retroactivity**

"**A.** The effective date of this act shall be the later of the date the Arizona state retirement system receives notification from the United States internal revenue service that the employer contributions required by this act do not exceed the limitations of § 415 of the internal revenue code or the date the judgment entered by the court in the class action titled James J. Burke v. ASRS, et al., Pima County Cause No. 316479 pursuant to the settlement of the parties becomes final. If, for any reason prior to January 1, 2000, the Arizona state retirement system does not receive notification from the United States internal revenue service or the final judgment is not entered by the court, then this act does not become effective. The Arizona state retirement system shall notify the director of the Arizona legislative council of the date on which the condition is met.

"**B.** Notwithstanding the date on which the conditions prescribed in subsection A are met, the provisions of this act that are designated to be effective on July 1, 1999 apply retroactively to July 1, 1999."

EDITOR'S NOTE: [Letter dated December 29, 1999 from Arizona State Retirement System to Arizona Legislative Council indicated conditional enactment provisions have been met and that Laws 1999, Ch. 266 is retroactively effective to July 1, 1999.]

The 1999 amendment by Ch. 327 inserted "Unless paragraph 4 of this subsection applies," at the beginning of par. 2, subsec. E; added par. 4, subsec. E; substituted "the contributors" for "and" in the first sentence of subsec. F; and inserted "contributions made pursuant to § 38-771 or" in subsec. H.

The 2000 amendment by Ch. 315 modified a statutory reference in subsec. E, par. 4; rewrote subsec. M, par. 2; inserted a new subsec. N and redesignated existing subsecs. N and O as O and P, accordingly; and rewrote former subsec.O (now P). Subsec. M, par. 2, and subsec. O had read:

"2. The amount of member and employer contributions made to ASRS on behalf of a member who elects to receive retirement benefits pursuant to § 38-771."

"**O.** For the purposes of this section:

"1. 'Compensation' has the same meaning prescribed in § 38-769, except that in determining a member's compensation for purposes of calculating the limits prescribed in subsection E of this section and effective for limitation years beginning on or after July 1, 1998, compensation includes any elective deferrals as defined in § 402(g)(3) of the internal revenue code and any amount that is contributed or deferred by an employer at the election of a member and that is not includable in the gross income of the member pursuant to § 125 or 457 of the internal revenue code.

"2. 'Limitation year' and 'defined contribution plan' have the same meaning prescribed in § 38-769.

"3. In determining the annual additions credited to a member of ASRS, 'annual additions' has the same meaning prescribed in 26 Code of Federal Regulations § 1.415-6(b)."

Laws 2000, Ch. 315, § 4, provides:

"**Sec. 4. Retroactivity**

"Sections 38-747 and 38-771.01, Arizona Revised Statutes, as amended by this act, apply retroactively to July 1, 1999."

The 2001 amendment by Ch. 136 rewrote the section, which had read:

"**A.** A member who purchases credited service pursuant to §§ 38-738, 38-742, 38-743, 38-744, 38-745 or 38-922 shall either:

"1. Make payments directly to ASRS as provided in subsection H of this section.

"2. Elect to have the member's employer make payments as provided in subsection B of this section.

"**B.** A member may elect to have the member's employer make payments for all or any portion of the amounts payable for the member's purchase of credited service pursuant to the sections prescribed in subsection A of this section through a salary reduction program in accordance with the following:

"1. The amounts paid pursuant to a salary reduction program are in lieu of contributions by the electing member. The electing member's salary or other compensation shall be reduced by the amount paid by the employer pursuant to this subsection.

"2. The member shall make an election pursuant to this subsection at any time on or after the date the member elects to purchase credited service pursuant to the sections prescribed in subsection A of this section and before the member's termination of employment. The election shall specify the number of payroll periods that deductions will be made from the member's compensation and the dollar amount of deductions for each payroll period during the specified number of payroll periods. After an election is made pursuant to this subsection, the election is binding on and irrevocable for the member and the member's employer during the member's remaining period of current employment. After a member makes an irrevocable election pursuant to this subsection, the member does not have the option of choosing to receive the contributed amounts directly.

"3. A member who makes an irrevocable election pursuant to this subsection to have the member's employer make payments for less than all of the amounts payable for the member's purchase of credited service may irrevocably elect to have the member's employer make payments for all or any portion of the remaining amounts payable for the member's purchase of credited service. A member who makes one or more irrevocable elections pursuant to this subsection may also make other contributions to ASRS pursuant to subsection H of this section to the extent of any remaining amounts payable for which the member has not made an election pursuant to this subsection. An additional election or contribution with respect to a portion of the amounts payable for the member's purchase of credited service does not alter, amend or revoke an irrevocable election already made pursuant to this subsection for any other portion of the amounts payable for the member's purchase of credited service.

"4. If on termination of the member's current employment all amounts have not been paid to ASRS pursuant to the member's irrevocable election pursuant to this subsection, the member may pay ASRS, within thirty days after the member's termination of employment and subject to other limitations prescribed in this section, all or any portion of the unpaid amounts as provided in subsection H of this section. These payments do not alter, amend or revoke any irrevocable election already made pursuant to this subsection with respect to any amount to be paid by the member's employer while the member is employed by the member's employer.

"5. Amounts paid by an employer pursuant to this subsection shall be treated as employer contributions for the purpose of determining tax treatment under the internal revenue code. The effective date of employer payments pursuant to this subsection shall not be before the date ASRS receives notification from the United States internal revenue service that pursuant to § 414(h)(2) of the internal revenue code the amounts paid by an employer pursuant to this subsection will not be included in the member's gross income for income tax purposes until those amounts are distributed by refund or retirement benefit payments.

"6. Unless otherwise provided, member contributions paid by an employer pursuant to this subsection are treated for all other purposes under ASRS in the same manner and to the same extent as member contributions that are not paid by an employer pursuant to this subsection. ASRS shall not grant credited service for contributions made pursuant to this subsection until those contributions are received by ASRS. ASRS may assess interest or administrative charges attributable to any salary reduction election made pursuant to this subsection. The interest or administrative charges shall be added to the amount of contributions that is made to ASRS by the member each payroll period and that is paid by the member's employer. The interest or administrative charges shall not be treated as member contributions for any purposes under this article and a member or a member's beneficiary does not have a right to the return of the interest or administrative charges pursuant to any other provision of this article. Interest assessed pursuant to this subsection shall be at the rate specified by the board pursuant to § 38–711, paragraph 2.

"**C.** A member who elects before July 1, 1999 to receive retirement benefits based on § 38–771, subsection C, paragraph 2 or a member who elects to make contributions to ASRS pursuant to § 38–771.01, subsection F, paragraph 4 shall either make the member's additional contributions required pursuant to § 38–771, subsection E or allowed pursuant to § 38–771.01, subsection F, paragraph 4 directly to ASRS as provided in subsection H of this section or shall elect to have the member's employer make payments for those additional contributions as provided in subsection D of this section. A member who elected to be covered or who was deemed to be covered by § 38–771 on or before December 31, 1995 or who elects to make member contributions pursuant to § 38–771.01, subsection F, paragraph 3 is deemed to have made an irrevocable election pursuant to subsection D of this section to make the member's contributions to ASRS that are required by § 38–771, subsection D or allowed by § 38–771.01, subsection F, paragraph 3.

"**D.** Any member contributions that are required by § 38–771, subsection D or that are allowed pursuant to § 38–771.01, subsection F, paragraph 3 are deemed to be made by the member to ASRS through a salary reduction program in accordance with the following:

"1. A member may make member contributions pursuant to § 38–771, subsection E or § 38–771.01, subsection F, paragraph 4 through a salary reduction program elected pursuant to this subsection. If a member makes an irrevocable election pursuant to this subsection before July 1, 1999 to have the member's employer make payments for additional contributions pursuant to § 38–771, subsection E, the election continues in effect from and after June 30, 1999 and shall not be revoked, amended or altered by any election made pursuant to § 38–771.01 or otherwise. The amounts paid pursuant to a salary reduction program are in lieu of contributions by the electing member. The member's salary or other compensation shall be reduced by the amount paid by the employer pursuant to this subsection.

"2. Before a member's termination of employment, the member may make an election pursuant to this subsection at any time after the date the member elects to receive retirement benefits based on § 38–771, subsection C, paragraph 2 but before July 1, 1999 or at any time after the member elects to make member contributions pursuant to § 38–771.01, subsection F, paragraph 4. The election shall specify the number of payroll periods that deductions will be made from the member's compensation and the dollar amount of deductions for each payroll period during the specified number of payroll periods. After an election is made pursuant to this subsection, the election is binding on and irrevocable for the member and the member's employer during the member's remaining period of current employment.

"3. After a member makes or is deemed to have made an irrevocable election pursuant to this subsection, the member does not have the option of choosing to receive the contributed amounts directly. A member who makes an irrevocable election pursuant to this subsection to have the member's employer make payments for less than all of the amounts payable for the member's additional contributions allowed by § 38–771.01, subsection F, paragraph 4 may irrevocably elect to have the member's employer make payments for all or any portion of the remaining amounts payable for the member's additional contributions. A member who makes one or more irrevocable elections pursuant to this subsection may also make other contributions to ASRS pursuant to § 38–771.01, subsection F, paragraph 4 or pursuant to subsection H of this section to the extent of any remaining amounts payable for which the member has not made an election pursuant to this subsection. An additional election or contribution with respect to a portion of the amounts payable for the member's additional contributions pursuant to § 38–771.01, subsection F, paragraph 4 does not alter, amend or revoke an irrevocable election already made pursuant to this subsection for any other portion of the amounts payable for the member's additional contributions allowed by § 38–771.01, subsection F, paragraph 4.

"4. If on termination of the member's current employment all amounts have not been paid to ASRS pursuant to the member's irrevocable election pursuant to this subsection, the member may pay ASRS, within thirty days after the member's termination of employment and subject to other limitations prescribed in this section, all or any portion of the unpaid amounts as provided in subsection H of this section. These payments do not alter, amend or revoke any irrevocable election already made pursuant to this subsection with respect to any amount to be paid by the member's employer while the member is employed by the member's employer.

"5. Amounts paid by an employer pursuant to this subsection shall be treated as employer contributions for the purpose of determining tax treatment under the internal revenue code. The effective date of employer payments pursuant to this subsection shall not be before the date ASRS receives notification from the United States internal revenue service that pursuant to § 414(h)(2) of the internal revenue code the amounts paid by an employer pursuant to this subsection will not be included in the member's gross income for income tax purposes until those amounts are distributed by refund or retirement benefit payments.

"6. Unless otherwise provided, member contributions paid by an employer pursuant to this subsection are treated for all other purposes under ASRS in the same manner and to the same extent as member contributions that are not paid by an employer pursuant to this subsection.

"**E.** The following limits apply to contributions to ASRS:

"1. Except as provided in paragraphs 2 and 3 of this subsection, in any one limitation year, the annual additions credited to ASRS for or on behalf of a member shall not exceed the lesser of either:

"(a) Thirty thousand dollars or a larger amount that is prescribed by the board and that is due to any cost of living adjustment announced by the United States secretary of the treasury pursuant to § 415(d) of the internal revenue code. The board shall increase the amount prescribed by this subdivision as of the effective date of the increase announced by the United States secretary of the treasury.

"(b) Twenty-five per cent of the member's compensation for the limitation year.

"2. Unless paragraph 4 of this subsection applies, for plan years beginning on or after July 1, 1998, in any one limitation year, the annual additions credited to ASRS for or on behalf of a member who makes contributions to ASRS to purchase credited service pursuant to § 38–738, 38–743, 38–744, 38–745 or 38–922 and with respect to which an irrevocable election has not been made pursuant to subsection B of this section shall not exceed the greater of either:

"(a) The requirements of § 38–769. For the purposes of applying the limits prescribed in § 38–769 under this subdivision, the accrued benefit derived from the contributions shall be treated as an annual benefit and the reduced limit for certain early retirement in § 38–769, subsection C, paragraph 2 does not apply.

"(b) Except as provided in paragraph 3 of this subsection, the requirements of paragraph 1 of this subsection. The contributions shall be treated as annual additions and any of the member's other annual additions for the limitation year shall be taken into account. For the purposes of applying the requirements of paragraph 1 of this subsection under this subdivision, the percentage of compensation limit in paragraph 1, subdivision (b) of this paragraph does not apply.

"3. For plan years beginning on or after July 1, 1998, the requirements of paragraph 1 of this subsection shall not be applied to reduce the amount of credited service that may be purchased by an eligible member pursuant to § 38–738, 38–743, 38–744, 38–745 or 38–922 to an amount that is less than the amount of credited service allowed to be purchased pursuant to those sections on August 5, 1997 without the application of any of the limits prescribed in this section or § 415 of the internal revenue code. For the purposes of this paragraph, "eligible member" means a person who first becomes a member of ASRS before July 1, 1999.

"4. Contributions to ASRS to purchase credited service pursuant to § 38-743, 38-744, 38-745 or 38-922 do not qualify for treatment under paragraph 2 of this subsection if recognition of that service would cause a member to receive a retirement benefit for the same service from ASRS and one or more other retirement plans.

"**F.** If a member's contributions are subject to the limitations of subsection E of this section, the contributions shall be treated as being made to a separate defined contribution plan. If the member's contributions exceed the limits prescribed in subsection E of this section when taking into account other member and employer contributions to ASRS on behalf of the member for the limitation year, the amount to be paid by the member shall be reduced to not exceed the limits prescribed in subsection E of this section and the remaining amount shall be carried forward to the next limitation year, unless the limits are exceeded in the next limitation year. If the limits are exceeded in the next limitation year, the procedure prescribed by this subsection shall be repeated until all payments have been made.

"**G.** If, after the application of subsection F of this section, the annual additions on behalf of a member exceed the limitations prescribed in subsection E of this section, ASRS shall dispose of excess amounts by either of the following:

"1. Returning to the member any contributions that are made by the member and that are nondeductible under the internal revenue code.

"2. Holding the amounts in a suspense account established pursuant to subsection J of this section and allocating the amounts as either member or employer contributions for the benefit of the member in the next limitation year and before any further member or employer contributions are made that would constitute annual additions made to a defined contribution plan pursuant to § 415 of the internal revenue code. ASRS shall allocate contributions as prescribed in this section, and the amount allocated shall reduce the amount of the member or employer contributions for the limitation year in which the allocation is made.

"**H.** To the extent that a payment under this subsection does not alter, amend or revoke any one or more currently effective irrevocable elections made by the member pursuant to subsection B or D of this section, the board may accept contributions made pursuant to § 38-771 or member contributions for the payment for credited service purchases pursuant to § 38-738, 38-742, 38-743, 38-744, 38-745 or 38-922 or contributions made pursuant to § 38-771.01, subsection F, paragraph 4, in whole or in part, by any one or a combination of the following methods:

"1. In lump sum payments.

"2. Subject to the limitations prescribed in §§ 401(a)(31) and 402(c) of the internal revenue code, accepting eligible rollover distributions directly from one or more retirement programs that are qualified under § 401(a) of the internal revenue code or accepting rollovers directly from a member.

"3. Subject to the limitations prescribed in § 408(d)(3)(A)(ii) of the internal revenue code, accepting from a member conduit rollover contributions that are received by the member from one or more conduit rollover individual retirement accounts previously established by the member.

"4. Providing by rule that the contributions may be made in installment payments over a period of time.

"**I.** ASRS shall not grant credited service under § 38-738, 38-742, 38-743, 38-744 or 38-922 for contributions made pursuant to subsection H of this section until the contributions are received by ASRS. ASRS may assess interest or administrative charges attributable to any installment payment made pursuant to subsection H, paragraph 4 of this section to purchase credited service pursuant to § 38-738, 38-742, 38-743, 38-744 or 38-922. The interest or administrative charges shall be added to the amount of contributions made to ASRS by the member. The interest or administrative charges shall not be treated as member contributions for any purposes under this article, and a member or a member's beneficiary does not have a right to the return of the interest or administrative charges pursuant to any other provision of this article. Interest assessed pursuant to this subsection shall be at the rate specified by the board pursuant to § 38-711, paragraph 2.

"**J.** ASRS shall establish a suspense account that conforms with 26 Code of Federal Regulations § 1.415-6(b)(6) regarding excess annual additions.

"**K.** If the member retires before all payments are made pursuant to this section, ASRS shall calculate the member's benefits based only on the payments actually made.

"**L.** On satisfaction of the requirements of this section, ASRS shall adjust the member's credited service history and add any additional service credits acquired.

"**M.** Annual additions on behalf of a member in any limitation year shall be the sum of:

"1. The amount of the member contributions made to ASRS to purchase credited service pursuant to § 38-738, 38-743, 38-744, 38-745 or 38-922 and with respect to which an irrevocable election made pursuant to subsection B of this section is not in effect.

"2. The amount of member and employer contributions made to ASRS on behalf of a member who elected or was deemed to have elected to receive retirement benefits pursuant to § 38–771 or who is entitled to benefits pursuant to § 38–771.01, except that, other than as provided in subsection N of this section, corrective contributions shall be considered annual additions for the limitation years to which the contributions relate and interest and gains shall not be considered as annual additions for the purpose of any limitation prescribed in this article or in § 415 of the internal revenue code. If the corrective contributions exceed the limit on annual additions for a limitation year prior to the limitation year in which the corrective contributions are contributed by the employer to ASRS, the retirement benefit attributable to the excess corrective contributions shall be treated as an excess benefit and shall be payable to the member as any other excess benefit is payable pursuant to § 38–774, and the employer shall pay the excess corrective contributions to the separate unfunded governmental excess benefit arrangement administered by the board pursuant to § 38–774.

"3. Any member or employer contributions made to ASRS or any other plan that are treated as being made to a defined contribution plan maintained by an employer of the member.

"4. Any forfeitures, including any income attributable to forfeitures, allocated for or on behalf of a member of ASRS or any other plan that are treated as being allocated under a defined contribution plan maintained by an employer of the member.

"**N.** To the extent any portion of the subject benefits, if treated as subject to the benefit limitations of § 415(b) of the internal revenue code, exceed the applicable limitation on benefits pursuant to § 38–769 for the form of distribution, a percentage of corrective contributions and interest and gains shall be treated as annual additions for the limitation year in which contributed by the employer to ASRS. This percentage of corrective contributions and interest and gains shall be equal to the percentage determined by dividing the subject benefits that exceed the limitation on benefits pursuant to § 38–769 by the subject benefits. If the corrective contributions and interest and gains that are treated as annual additions for the limitation year in which the corrective contributions and interest and gains are contributed by the employer to ASRS exceed the limit on annual additions for the limitation year, the retirement benefit attributable to the excess shall be treated as an excess benefit and shall be payable to the member as any other excess benefit is payable pursuant to § 38–774, and the employer shall pay the excess to the separate unfunded governmental excess benefit arrangement administered by the board pursuant to § 38–774.

"O. Subsection M of this section shall be construed and interpreted in accordance with 26 Code of Federal Regulations § 1.415–6 to the extent that section is applicable.

"P. For the purposes of this section:

"1. In determining the annual additions credited to a member of ASRS, "annual additions" has the same meaning prescribed in 26 Code of Federal Regulations § 1.415–6(b).

"2. "Compensation" has the same meaning prescribed in § 38–769, except that in determining a member's compensation for purposes of calculating the limits prescribed in subsection E of this section and effective for limitation years beginning on or after July 1, 1998, compensation includes any elective deferrals as defined in § 402(g)(3) of the internal revenue code and any amount that is contributed or deferred by an employer at the election of a member and that is not includable in the gross income of the member pursuant to § 125 or 457 of the internal revenue code.

"3. "Corrective contributions" means any contributions that are paid by an employer pursuant to § 38–771.01, subsection C, paragraph 3 and that are attributable to employer contributions that should have been made for prior limitation years.

"4. "Defined contribution plan" has the same meaning prescribed in § 38–769.

"5. "Interest and gains" means employer contributions to ASRS pursuant to § 38–771.01, subsection C, paragraphs 3, 5 and 6 that are attributable to earnings and supplemental credits that would have been earned or added to a member's annuity payment.

"6. "Limitation year" has the same meaning prescribed in § 38–769.

"7. "Subject benefits" means the retirement benefit received by a member pursuant to § 38–771.01 minus the sum of the portion of such retirement benefit attributable to Contributions made by or on behalf of the member to the defined contribution program administered by ASRS for periods before July 1, 1981 and Contributions made by the member after June 30, 1981 that were not picked up as provided in § 414(h)(2)of the internal revenue code."

The 2002 amendment by Ch. 213, § 3, substituted "annual additions contributed or allocated to ASRS" for "annual additions credited to ASRS", in subsec. E, par. 1; rewrote subsec. H; inserted new subsecs. I and J, redesignating existing subsecs. I to P, as K to R, accordingly; and made nonsubstantive, conforming changes to internal references. Subsection H had read:

"**H.** To the extent that a payment under this subsection does not alter, amend or revoke any one or more currently effective irrevocable elections made by the member pursuant to subsection B or D of this section, the board may accept contributions made pursuant to § 38–771 or member contributions for the payment for credited service purchases pursuant to § 38–738, 38–742, 38–743, 38–744, 38–745 or 38–922 or contributions made pursuant to § 38–771.01, subsection F, paragraph 4, in whole or in part, by any one or a combination of the following methods:

"1. In lump sum payments.

"2. Subject to the limitations prescribed in §§ 401(a)(31) and 402(c) of the internal revenue code, accepting eligible rollover distributions directly from one or more

"(a) Retirement programs that are qualified under § 401(a) of the internal revenue code or accepting rollovers directly from a member.

"3. Subject to the limitations prescribed in § 408(d)(3)(A)(ii) of the internal revenue code, accepting from a member conduit rollover contributions that are received by the member from one or more conduit rollover individual retirement accounts previously established by the member.

"4. Providing by rule that the contributions may be made in installment payments over a period of time."

The 2002 amendment by Ch. 213, § 4, inserted "and to the extent permitted under § 414(v) of the internal revenue code, if applicable" in subsec. E, par. 1; substituted "Forty thousand dollars" for "Thirty thousand dollars" in subsec. E, par. 1(a); and rewrote subsec. E, par. 1(b) and subsec. R, par. 1, which had read:

[E.] "(b) Twenty-five per cent of the member's compensation for the limitation year."

[R.] "1. 'Compensation' has the same meaning prescribed in § 38–769, except that in determining a member's compensation for purposes of calculating the limits prescribed in subsection E of this section and effective for limitation years beginning on or after July 1, 1998, compensation includes any elective deferrals as defined in § 402(g)(3) of the internal revenue code and any amount that is contributed or deferred by an employer at the election of a member and that is not includable in the gross income of the member pursuant to § 125 or 457 of the internal revenue code."

The 2002 amendment of this section by Ch. 213, § 4 explicitly amended the amendment of this section by Laws 2002, Ch. 213, § 3.

Laws 2002, Ch. 213, § 9, subsec. B, provides:

"**Sec. 9. Retroactivity**"

"**B.** Section 38–747, Arizona Revised Statutes, as amended by § 3 of this act, and § 38–770, Arizona Revised Statutes, as amended by this act, apply retroactively to January 1, 2002."

The 2004 amendment by Ch. 252 inserted the last sentence of subsec B, par. 1; and rewrote subsec. B, par. 2 and subsec. I, which had read:

"**[B.]** 2. The member shall make an election pursuant to this subsection at any time on or after the date the member elects to purchase credited service pursuant to the sections prescribed in subsection A of this section and before the member's termination of employment. The election shall specify the number of payroll periods that deductions will be made from the member's compensation and the dollar amount of deductions for each payroll period during the specified number of payroll periods. After an election is made pursuant to this subsection, the election is binding on and irrevocable for the member and the member's employer during the member's remaining period of current employment. After a member makes an irrevocable election pursuant to this subsection, the member does not have the option of choosing to receive the contributed amounts directly."

"**I.** To the extent that a payment under this subsection does not alter, amend or revoke any one or more currently effective irrevocable elections made by a member pursuant to subsection B or D of this section, the board may accept a direct trustee-to-trustee transfer from an annuity contract described in § 403(b) of the internal revenue code or an eligible deferred compensation plan described in § 457(b) of the internal revenue code for the payment for credited service purchases pursuant to § 38–742, 38–743, 38–744, 38–745 or 38–922. "

Former § 38–747 enacted as part of the revision effective January 9, 1956, amended by Laws 1957, Ch. 96, § 2; Laws 1962, Ch. 20, § 1, eff. July 1, 1962; Laws 1964, Ch. 142, § 2; Laws 1967, Ch. 84, § 1; Laws 1970, Ch. 134, § 3; Laws 1972, Ch. 51, § 7; Laws 1981, Ch. 1, § 14, eff. Jan. 23, 1981; Laws 1981, Ch. 314, § 26, derived from Laws 1953, Ch. 128, § 7; Code 1939, Supp.1953, § 12–843; Laws 1954, Ch. 116, § 4, which related to prior service credit, was repealed by Laws 1995, Ch. 32, § 13, eff. March 30, 1995.

Reviser's Notes:

1996 Note. Pursuant to authority of § 41–1304.02, in the section heading "definitions" was substituted for "definition".

1998 Note. Pursuant to authority of § 41–1304.02, in subsection E, paragraph 1 the spelling of "subsection" was corrected.

1999 Note. Prior to the 2000 amendment, this section contained the amendments made by Laws 1999, Ch. 266, sec. 1 and Ch. 327, sec. 12 that were blended together pursuant to authority of § 41–1304.03.

§ 38-748. Employers; termination option

A. To encourage active members to continue to work beyond normal retirement age, an employer may elect to offer to eligible employees who are active members of ASRS a termination option as provided in subsection B of this section.

B. An employer may enter into a written agreement with an eligible active member who has attained at least a normal retirement age and who has at least five years of credited service that provides that if the member agrees to and performs work for at least six but not more than thirty-six months after the effective date of the agreement the member is eligible to receive:

1. At least six but not more than thirty-six months of credited service in ASRS for the work performed under the agreement if the member purchases an equal amount of credited service pursuant to paragraph 2. The agreement shall provide that the employer and the member shall not make retirement contributions to ASRS for the period of credited service but shall make contributions for the long-term disability program pursuant to § 38-797.05.

2. Eligibility to purchase credited service equal to the period that the member has agreed to work. This purchase shall be made without regard to previous public service, but the cost of the credited service shall be an amount equal to the product of the member's current annual compensation at the time of entering into the agreement times the greater of the contribution rate or the normal cost rate for ASRS for the fiscal year during which the purchase of credited service is being made times the years or partial years of credited service being purchased. A member may purchase no more than an aggregate of five years of credited service pursuant to this paragraph under all agreements the member may have with any one or more employers.

C. The member and employer shall make contributions as agreed between the member and employer to be paid during the term of the agreement. These contributions shall be paid into a supplemental defined contribution plan established pursuant to § 38-952 for the purpose of purchasing the additional credited service authorized by subsection B, paragraph 2 of this section.

D. The written agreement entered into pursuant to subsection B of this section shall include conditions that constitute a breach of the agreement between the employer and the member.

E. A member who does not complete the terms of the agreement forfeits any credited service provided under the agreement, except that any employer or member contributions to a supplemental defined contribution plan are the property of the member or the member's estate. If a member is unable to complete the terms of the agreement due to a termination of employment because the member is considered totally disabled pursuant to § 38-797. 07 or because of death, the member is considered to have completed the agreement for the period through the date of the member's termination of employment. Notwithstanding the six month minimum service requirement of subsection B of this section, the member or the member's beneficiary is eligible to purchase and receive credited service, as provided by subsection B of this section, for the period of the agreement that was completed.

F. An employer who fails to complete the terms of the agreement shall make all contributions required by the agreement to the supplemental defined contribution plan.

G. A member who enters into an agreement under this section is not eligible to purchase other credited service for other public service as provided in § 38-742, 38-743, 38-744 or 38-745.

H. If a member transfers employment between state agencies or from one participating employer to another participating employer, the member and the member's successor agency or employer may complete the terms of the agreement if the successor agency or employer agrees to assume all remaining obligations of the prior agency or employer under the terms of the agreement between the member and the prior agency or employer. A member may have only one agreement in effect at any one time with a single agency or employer.

Added by Laws 2001, Ch. 380, § 5. Amended by Laws 2003, Ch. 196, § 1; Laws 2004, Ch. 252, § 5.

Historical and Statutory Notes

Former § 38-748, enacted as part of the revision effective January 9, 1956 (see Source following § 38-736), which related to contributions by employee members, was repealed by Laws 1995, Ch. 32, § 13, effective March 30, 1995.

§ 38-749. Employer retirement incentive option; employer payment of actuarial cost; definition

Effective July 1, 2005

A. If a retirement incentive program that is offered by an employer results in an actuarial unfunded liability to ASRS, the employer shall pay to ASRS the amount of the unfunded liability. ASRS shall determine the amount of the unfunded liability in consultation with its actuary.

B. An employer shall notify ASRS if the employer plans to implement a retirement incentive program that may affect ASRS funding.

C. If ASRS determines that an employer has implemented a retirement incentive program that results in an actuarial unfunded liability to ASRS, ASRS shall assess the cost of the unfunded liability to that employer. If the employer does not remit full payment of all monies due within ninety days after being notified by ASRS of the amount due, the unpaid amount accrues interest until the amount is paid in full. The interest rate is the interest rate assumption that is approved by the board for actuarial equivalency for the period in question to the date payment is received.

D. For the purposes of this section, "retirement incentive program":

1. Means a total increase in compensation of thirty per cent or more that is given to a member in any one or more years of the last three years before retirement if that increase in compensation is used to calculate the member's retirement benefit and that increase in compensation is not attributed to a:

(a) Promotion.

(b) Reclassification of the position.

(c) Merit or a cost of living increase.

2. Means any monies, credited service or points that the employer provides to a member in exchange for a member's written agreement to retire on a date certain.

3. Does not include payments to an employee for:

(a) Compensation for accrued vacation.

(b) Compensation for accrued sick leave.

(c) Compensatory time.

Added by Laws 2004, Ch. 106, § 1, eff. July 1, 2005.

Historical and Statutory Notes

Former § 38-749, enacted as part of the revision effective January 9, 1956, amended by Laws 1967, Ch. 84, § 3; Laws 1970, Ch. 136, § 8; Laws 1975, Ch. 158, § 4, derived from Laws 1953, Ch. 128, § 12; Code 1939, Supp. 1953, § 12-848, which related to contributions by the state and by political subdivisions, was repealed by Laws 1995, Ch. 32, § 13, eff. March 30, 1995

§§ 38-750 to 38-752. Repealed by Laws 1995, Ch. 32, § 13, eff. March 30, 1995

Historical and Statutory Notes

Section 38-750, enacted as part of the revision effective January 9, 1956 (see Source following § 38-738), provided for contribution adjustment and refund. See now, § 38-738.

Section 38-751, enacted as part of the revision effective January 9, 1956, amended by Laws 1981, Ch. 1, § 15; Laws 1981, Ch. 314, § 27; Laws 1982, Ch. 229, § 24, derived from Laws 1953, Ch. 128, § 13; Code 1939, Supp. 1953, § 12-849, provided for transfer of teachers' retirement credits.

Section 38-752, enacted as part of the revision effective January 9, 1956 (see Source following § 38-729), related to political subdivision retirement systems. See now, § 38-729.

§ 38-752.01. Repealed by Laws 1995, Ch. 32, § 13, eff. March 30, 1995

Historical and Statutory Notes

Section 38-752.01, enacted as part of the revision effective January 9, 1956 (see Source following § 38-718) related to investment management. See now, § 38-718.

§§ 38-753, 38-754. Repealed by Laws 1995, Ch. 32, § 13, eff. March 30, 1995

Historical and Statutory Notes

Section 38-753, enacted as part of the revision effective January 9, 1956 (see Source following § 38-720), provided for a retirement system depository. See now, § 38-720.

Section 38-754, enacted as part of the revision effective January 9, 1956, amended by Laws 1970, Ch. 136, § 13, derived from Laws 1953, Ch. 128, § 19; Code 1939, Supp.1953, § 12-855, provided for a prior service credits account.

For state highway patrol retirement system and Arizona state retirement system savings clause and beneficiary longevity reserve account provisions of Laws 1995, Ch. 32, see Historical and Statutory Notes following § 38-744.

§ 38-755. Information as to member's status

Subject to rules prescribed by the board, on application of a member, the board shall furnish information concerning the member's status. In addition, the board shall annually furnish to each member an account statement showing the status of the member's account including the name of the member's beneficiary as last listed with the board. The member may change the member's beneficiary at any time pursuant to rules adopted by the board and on forms furnished by the board.

Added by Laws 1995, Ch. 32, § 14, eff. March 30, 1995.

Historical and Statutory Notes

Source:

Laws 1953, Ch. 128, § 17.
Code 1939, Supp.1953, § 12-853.
Laws 1955, Ch. 104, § 4.
Code 1939, Supp.1955, § 12-853a.
A.R.S. former §§ 38-744, 38-781.18.
Laws 1970, Ch. 134, § 2.
Laws 1970, Ch. 136, § 6.
Laws 1972, Ch. 51, §§ 6, 21.
Laws 1990, Ch. 271, § 2.
Laws 1992, Ch. 320, § 14.

Former § 38-755, added by Laws 1972, Ch. 51, § 11, relating to transfer of a lieu pension account, was repealed by Laws 1992, Ch. 320, § 1.

Another former § 38-755, derived from Code 1939, Supp.1953, § 12-856, Laws 1953, Ch. 128, § 20, enacted as part of the revision effective January 9, 1956, and amended by Laws 1970, Ch. 136, § 14, which related to lieu pension fund, was repealed by Laws 1972, Ch. 51, § 10, effective August 13, 1972.

§ 38-756. Outreach education program

A. The director shall develop, implement and maintain an outreach education program for members of ASRS that is designed to provide basic information on retirement planning.

B. The outreach education program prescribed in subsection A shall include at least the following:

1. Information on the benefits available to members before retirement.
2. Information on the financial benefits available at retirement including a detailed explanation of the benefits and benefit options under ASRS.
3. Information on how ASRS is organized.
4. Information on how the benefits of the members are funded.
5. Information on the social issues related to retirement.
6. The use of audiovisual, electronic and other educational aids that are designed to provide information on retirement education and planning.
7. The development of a creative promotional program using available media outlets.

C. ASRS shall present the outreach education program prescribed in subsection A at least once each year in each county of this state. Attendance of active members at outreach education program presentations is voluntary.

Added by Laws 1995, Ch. 32, § 14, eff. March 30, 1995. Amended by Laws 1995, Ch. 134, § 8, eff. April 17, 1995.

Historical and Statutory Notes

Source:

A.R.S. former § 38-781.18.
Laws 1970, Ch. 134, § 2.
Laws 1972, Ch. 51, § 21.
Laws 1990, Ch. 271, § 2.
Laws 1992, Ch. 320, § 14.

The 1995 amendment by Ch. 134, in subsec. A, deleted "Until October 1, 1995" at the beginning.

Former § 38-756, enacted as part of the revision effective January 9, 1956 (see Source, following § 38-721), relating to an administration account, was repealed by Laws 1995, Ch. 32, § 13, eff. March 30, 1995.

§ 38–757. Normal retirement

A. After application on a form prescribed by the director, a member may retire on reaching the member's normal retirement date.

B. Except as provided in § 38–768 and subsection C of this section, a member who meets the requirements for retirement benefits at normal retirement shall receive a monthly life annuity that equals the result of paragraph 1 multiplied by paragraph 2 when those paragraphs are defined as follows:

1. The number of whole and fractional years of credited service times the following:

(a) 2.10 per cent if the member does not have more than 19.99 years of credited service.

(b) 2.15 per cent if the member has at least 20.00 years of credited service but not more than 24.99 years of credited service.

(c) 2.20 per cent if the member has at least 25.00 years of credited service but not more than 29.99 years of credited service.

(d) 2.30 per cent if the member has at least 30.00 years of credited service.

2. The member's average monthly compensation.

C. For a person who becomes a member on or after the effective date of this amendment to this section, The amount of a member's monthly life annuity computed pursuant to subsection B of this section shall not be more than eighty per cent of the member's average monthly compensation. This limitation does not preclude benefit increases pursuant to § 38–767.

D. Employers shall provide evidence of, and certify to, in a manner provided by the board, the member's average monthly compensation if that information is not already available from the records of ASRS.

Added by Laws 1995, Ch. 32, § 14, eff. March 30, 1995. Amended by Laws 1999, Ch. 327, § 13, eff. July 1, 2000; Laws 2001, Ch. 380, § 6.

Historical and Statutory Notes

Source:

Laws 1953, Ch. 128, § 8.
Code 1939, Supp.1953, § 12–844.
Laws 1954, Ch. 116, § 5.
Laws 1955, Ch. 104, § 1.
A.R.S. former §§ 38–759, 38–781.07.
Laws 1957, Ch. 96, § 5.
Laws 1958, Ch. 95, § 1.
Laws 1970, Ch. 134, § 2.
Laws 1970, Ch. 136, § 18.
Laws 1972, Ch. 51, § 16.
Laws 1974, Ch. 120, §§ 3, 7.
Laws 1974, Ch. 167, § 4.
Laws 1975, Ch. 54, § 2.
Laws 1978, Ch. 54, § 4.
Laws 1978, Ch. 209, §§ 5, 8.
Laws 1981, Ch. 284, §§ 1, 3.
Laws 1983, Ch, 293, § 2.
Laws 1985, Ch. 294, § 5.
Laws 1985, Ch. 309, §§ 1, 2.
Laws 1986, Ch. 168, § 2.
Laws 1987, Ch. 274, § 2.
Laws 1988, Ch. 256, § 1.
Laws 1991, Ch. 170, § 2.
Laws 1992, Ch. 320, § 10.
Laws 1994, Ch. 356, § 7.
Laws 1994, Ch. 357, § 1.

The 1999 amendment by Ch. 327 inserted "and one-tenth" in par. 1 of subsec. B.

Laws 1999, Ch. 327, § 32, provides:

"**Sec. 32. Delayed effective date**

"Section 38–757, Arizona Revised Statutes, as amended by this act, and § 28 of this act, relating to benefit increases for Arizona state retirement system defined benefits retirees, are effective from and after June 30, 2000."

The 2001 amendment by Ch. 380 rewrote the section, which had read:

"A. After application on a form prescribed by the director, a member may retire on reaching the member's normal retirement date.

"B. Except as provided in § 38–768, a member who meets the requirements for retirement benefits at normal retirement shall receive a monthly life annuity that equals the result of paragraph 1 multiplied by paragraph 2 when those paragraphs are defined as follows:

"1. The number of whole and fractional years of credited service times two and one-tenth per cent.

"2. The member's average monthly compensation.

"C. Employers shall provide evidence of, and certify to, in a manner provided by the board, the member's average monthly compensation if that information is not already available from the records of ASRS."

Former § 38–757, added by Laws 1985, Ch. 257, § 3 (see Source, following § 38–719), relating to investment of monies, was repealed by Laws 1995, Ch. 32, § 13 eff. March 30, 1995.

§ 38–758. Early retirement

A. A member who has attained age fifty and who has five years of total credited service is eligible to elect, in a form and manner prescribed by the board, to receive a reduced retirement income.

B. The benefit payable to a member electing early retirement shall be determined by reducing the normal retirement benefit computed in accordance with § 38–757 either:

1. At the rate of three per cent per year from age sixty to age sixty-five and five per cent per year from age fifty to age sixty. The reduction in normal retirement benefits pursuant to this paragraph for an eligible member electing early retirement shall be based on the period from the date of commencement of early retirement benefits to the member's sixtieth birthday if the member has at least twenty years of total credited service, sixty-second birthday if the member has at least ten but less than twenty years of total credited service or sixty-fifth birthday if the member has at least five but less than ten years of total credited service.

2. If the sum of a member's age and years of total credited service equals seventy-seven or more, but is less than eighty, at the rate of three per cent for each unit of one or fraction of one by which the sum is less than eighty.

Added by Laws 1995, Ch. 32, § 14, eff. March 30, 1995.

Historical and Statutory Notes

Source:

A.R.S. former § 38–781.08.
Laws 1981, Ch. 284, § 5.
Laws 1983, Ch. 293, § 3.
Laws 1988, Ch. 272, § 1.
Laws 1990, Ch. 396, § 2.
Laws 1991, Ch. 170, § 3.
Laws 1991, Ch. 270, § 5.
Laws 1992, Ch. 319, § 34.
Laws 1994, Ch. 356, § 10.

For state highway patrol retirement system and Arizona state retirement system savings clause and beneficiary longevity reserve account provisions of Laws 1995, Ch. 32, see Historical and Statutory Notes following § 38–744.

Former § 38–758, enacted as part of the revision effective January 9, 1956 (see Source, following § 38–740), relating to termination of membership before retirement, was repealed by Laws 1995, Ch. 32, § 13, eff. March 30, 1995.

§ 38–759. Late retirement

A. A member who is eligible for normal retirement benefits on the member's normal retirement date may elect to defer receiving retirement benefits.

B. Notwithstanding this section, payment of a member's deferred benefits shall not commence later than the April 1 following the calendar year in which the member attains seventy and one-half years of age or the calendar year in which the member terminates employment, whichever occurs later.

Added by Laws 1995, Ch. 32, § 14, eff. March 30, 1995.

Historical and Statutory Notes

Source:

A.R.S. former § 38-781.09.
Laws 1970, Ch. 134, § 2.
Laws 1972, Ch. 51, § 17.
Laws 1974, Ch. 120, § 9.
Laws 1983, Ch. 293, § 4.
Laws 1986, Ch. 168, § 3.

For state highway patrol retirement system and Arizona state retirement system savings clause and beneficiary longevity reserve account provisions of Laws 1995, Ch. 32, see Historical and Statutory Notes following § 38-744.

Former § 38-759, enacted as part of the revision effective January 9, 1956 (see Source, following § 38-757), relating to retirement from service and reemployment, was repealed by Laws 1995, Ch. 32, § 13, eff. March 30, 1995.

§ 38-759.01. Repealed by Laws 1988, Ch. 256, § 2, eff. June 29, 1988

Historical and Statutory Notes

Section 38-759.01, added by Laws 1975, Ch. 57, § 2, amended by Laws 1978, Ch. 209, § 7; Laws 1981, Ch. 1, § 16; Laws 1983, Ch. 98, § 112, related to retirement contributions and benefits for employment beyond age seventy.

Former section 38-759.01, added by Laws 1974, Ch. 120, § 4, effective July 1, 1975, and relating to employment beyond the normal retirement date, was repealed by Laws 1975, Ch. 57, § 1, effective May 16, 1975.

§ 38-760. Optional forms of retirement benefits

A. On retirement, members may elect an optional form of retirement benefit as provided in this section.

B. The optional retirement benefits available under this section include the following:

1. Joint and survivor annuity in a reduced amount payable to the retiring member during life, with the provisions that after the member's death all, two-thirds or one-half of the retirement income, as the member elects, shall be continued during the lifetime of the contingent annuitant designated by the retiring member subject to the restrictions prescribed in § 38-764. The amount of retirement income shall be the actuarial equivalent of the retirement income to which the member would be entitled under normal or early retirement. The election in a manner prescribed by the board shall name the contingent annuitant. The election may be revoked at any time before the member's effective date of retirement. At any time after benefits have commenced, the member may name a different contingent annuitant or rescind the election by written notice to the board as follows:

(a) If a different contingent annuitant is named, the annuity of the member under the same joint and survivor annuity option previously elected shall be adjusted to the actuarial equivalent of the original annuity, based on the age of the new contingent annuitant. The adjustment shall include all post-retirement increases in retirement income that are authorized by law after the member's date of retirement. Payment of this adjusted annuity shall continue under the provisions of the option previously elected by the member.

(b) If the member rescinds the election, the member shall thereafter receive a straight life annuity equal to what the member would otherwise be entitled to receive if the member had not elected the joint and survivor annuity option, including all post-retirement increases in retirement income that are authorized by law after the date of retirement. The increased payment shall continue during the remainder of the member's lifetime.

(c) If the member reverts to a straight life annuity pursuant to subdivision (b), the member may name a new contingent annuitant subject to the same restrictions prescribed in subdivision (a).

2. A period certain and life annuity actuarially reduced with payments for five, ten or fifteen years that are not dependent on the continued lifetime of the member but whose payments continue for the member's lifetime beyond the five, ten or fifteen year period. At any time, a member who retires after the effective date of this amendment to this section may rescind the election of a period certain and life annuity. If the member rescinds the election of a period certain and life annuity, the member shall thereafter receive a straight life annuity equal to what the member would otherwise be entitled to receive if the member had not elected the period certain and life annuity option, including all postretirement increases in retirement income that are authorized by law after the date of retirement. The increased payment shall continue during the remainder of the member's lifetime. If the member reverts to a straight life annuity pursuant to this paragraph, the member may again elect a period certain and life annuity subject to the same provisions of the period certain and life annuity previously elected by the member.

3. Beginning on july 1, 2002, a lump sum payment equal to not more than thirty–six months of the member's retirement benefits under the benefit option elected by the member. The member's benefit shall be actuarially reduced to provide for the lump sum payment. The lump sum payment shall be made at the time of retirement. Any benefit increase granted to a member who elects a lump sum payment pursuant to this paragraph is subject to the following conditions:

(a) If the benefit increase is a percentage increase of the member's retirement benefit, the increase shall be based on the actuarially reduced retirement benefit of the member.

(b) If the benefit increase is pursuant to § 38–767, the amount of the member's benefit increase shall be calculated without regard to the lump sum payment pursuant to this paragraph.

4. Other forms of actuarially reduced optional benefits prescribed by the board.

Added by Laws 1995, Ch. 32, § 14, eff. March 30, 1995. Amended by Laws 1999, Ch. 121, § 1; Laws 2001, Ch. 136, § 15; Laws 2001, Ch. 380, § 7.

Historical and Statutory Notes

Source:

A.R.S. former § 38–781.10.
Laws 1970, Ch. 134, § 2.
Laws 1972, Ch. 51, § 18.
Laws 1985, Ch. 294, § 6.
Laws 1986, Ch. 83, § 1.
Laws 1986, Ch. 168, § 4.
Laws 1990, Ch. 396, § 3.
Laws 1991, Ch. 170, § 4.
Laws 1991, Ch. 217, § 1.
Laws 1991, Ch. 270, § 6.
Laws 1992, Ch. 252, § 1.
Laws 1994, Ch. 356, § 11.

For state highway patrol retirement system and Arizona state retirement system savings clause and beneficiary longevity reserve account provisions of Laws 1995, Ch. 32, see Historical and Statutory Notes following § 38-744.

The 1999 amendment by Ch. 121, in subsec. B, par. 1, inserted "subject to the restrictions prescribed in § 38-764" in the first sentence of the first paragraph, and added subpar. (c) relating to the situation where a member reverts to a straight life annuity.

The 2001 amendment by Ch. 136 inserted the second, third and fourth sentences of subsec. B, par. 2.

The 2001 amendment by Ch. 380 inserted new subsec. B, par. 3, and redesignated existing par. 3 as par. 4, accordingly.

Former § 38-760, enacted as part of the revision effective January 9, 1956, amended by Laws 1957, Ch. 96, § 6, Laws 1965, Ch. 87, § 4, and Laws 1970, Ch. 134, § 4, derived from Laws 1953, Ch. 128, § 9, Code 1939, Supp. 1953, § 12-845, and Laws 1954, Ch. 116, § 6, relating to disability retirement, was repealed by Laws 1995, Ch. 32, § 13, eff. March 30, 1995.

Reviser's Notes:

2001 Note. This section contains the amendments made by Laws 2001, Ch. 136, sec. 15 and Ch. 380, sec. 7 that were blended together as shown pursuant to authority of § 41-1304.03.

§ 38-761. Level income alternative

A. Any member who retires before age sixty-two may elect, at any time before the date the first payment on account of the member's retirement benefit normally becomes due, to convert the retirement benefit otherwise payable to the member after retirement into a reduced retirement benefit that is its actuarial equivalent and is of an amount that, with the member's primary insurance amount under title II of the social security act,[1] the member will receive, as far as possible, the same amount each year before and after the primary insurance amount begins.

B. A member may rescind the member's election of the reduced retirement benefit provided by subsection A within six months after the member's date of retirement if the member reimburses ASRS with a lump sum payment for any additional benefits paid to the member pursuant to this section.

Added by Laws 1995, Ch. 32, § 14, eff. March 30, 1995.

[1] 42 U.S.C.A. § 401 et seq.

Historical and Statutory Notes

Former § 38-761, enacted as part of the revision effective January 9, 1956, amended by Laws 1974, Ch. 120, § 5, derived from Laws 1953, Ch. 128, § 10, and Code 1939, Supp. 1953, § 12-846, relating to lieu pensions, was repealed by Laws 1992, Ch. 320, § 1.

§ 38-762. Survivor benefits before retirement; definition

A. On the termination of employment by death of any active or inactive member before retirement, the designated beneficiary of the member shall be paid a survivor benefit equal to the sum of both of the following:

1. Two times the member's contribution and interest to the defined benefit plan established by this article for credited service that a member earned by working for an employer, plus all contributions and interest made for the purchase of military service, leave without pay or other public service credit.

2. The amount of the member's employee account and the member's employer account together with supplemental credits, if any, transferred from the defined contribution program administered by ASRS to the defined benefit program established by this article.

B. Subsection A, paragraphs 1 and 2 shall be accumulated at compound interest at the valuation rate established by the board through the day of the payment of the benefit.

C. In lieu of a single payment, a designated beneficiary who is eligible for a survivor benefit pursuant to subsection A of more than five thousand dollars may elect to receive the actuarial equivalent of the survivor benefit pursuant to one of the following options:

1. A monthly income for five, ten or fifteen years certain and for life thereafter.

2. Another form of optional benefits approved by the board.

D. On the death of an active or inactive member who has reached an early retirement date applicable to the member or who has a minimum of fifteen years of credited service and whose designated beneficiary is a spouse, child under the age of twenty-one or handicapped child age twenty-one or older, including a legally adopted child or a stepchild, ASRS shall pay the designated beneficiary a survivor benefit equal to the present value, on the date following the date of the member's death, of the life annuity that would have been payable to the designated beneficiary if the member had retired on the date of the member's death and elected to receive an annuity in the form of a joint and survivor annuity providing the same amount of annuity to the surviving beneficiary as the reduced amount that would have been payable during the lifetime of the member. If there is more than one designated beneficiary under this subsection, ASRS shall determine the amount of the annuity and its present value as if the oldest of the beneficiaries was the sole beneficiary. Payment under this subsection shall be in lieu of, but not less than, any payment under subsection A. Payment under this subsection, at the election of the designated beneficiary, may be made in a single sum or may be made in accordance with subsection C. A beneficiary may not elect this option unless a benefit of twenty-five dollars or more per month is payable to the designated beneficiary or the designated beneficiary's estate.

E. If a member dies before distribution of the member's benefits commences, the member's entire benefits shall be distributed no later than five years after the member's death, except to the extent that, if any portion of the member's interest is payable to a designated beneficiary, distributions may be made in substantially equal installments over the life expectancy of the designated beneficiary or over a period not extending beyond the life expectancy of the beneficiary commencing no later than one year after the member's death.

F. If a deceased member did not designate a beneficiary or the beneficiary named by a member predeceases the member, ASRS shall pay the member's survivor benefit to the following persons in the following order of priority:

1. The member's surviving spouse.

2. The member's surviving children, including adopted children, in equal shares.

3. The member's surviving parents in equal shares.

4. The member's estate.

G. Any payment pursuant to this section is payment for the account of the member or the member's beneficiary and all persons entitled to payment and, to the extent of the payment, is a full and complete discharge of all liability of the board or ASRS, or both, under or in connection with ASRS.

H. For purposes of this section, "designated beneficiary" means any individual designated by the member as the member's beneficiary.

Added by Laws 1995, Ch. 32, § 14, eff. March 30, 1995. Amended by Laws 1996, Ch. 185, § 14; Laws 1999, Ch. 327, § 14; Laws 2001, Ch. 136, § 16; Laws 2004, Ch. 252, § 6.

Historical and Statutory Notes

For state highway patrol retirement system and Arizona state retirement system savings clause and beneficiary longevity reserve account provisions of Laws 1995, Ch. 32, see Historical and Statutory Notes following § 38-744.

The 1996 amendment by Ch. 185 substituted "the defined benefit plan established by this article" for "ASRS" in subsec. A, par. 1; designated existing text as subsec. B, and amended that text to conform to redesignation of subsections of this section; and redesignated former subsecs. B to G as C to H, accordingly.

The 1999 amendment by Ch. 327, in subsec. B, substituted "through" for "to", deleted "first" preceding "day", and substituted "payment of the benefit" for "month next preceding the date of death".

The 2001 amendment by Ch. 136 rewrote subsec. F, which had read:

"F. If a deceased member did not designate a beneficiary, the board, in its sole discretion, may direct payment to the member's estate or to another person or persons the board determines to be lawfully entitled to receive payment."

The 2004 amendment by Ch. 252 rewrote subsec. A, par. 1, which had read:

"1. Two times the member's contribution to the defined benefit plan established by this article."

Former § 38-762, enacted as part of the revision effective January 9, 1956 (see Source, following § 38-792), relating to exemption of benefits and contributions from taxation and execution, was repealed by Laws 1995, Ch. 32, § 13, eff. March 30, 1995.

§ 38-763. Survivor benefits after retirement

A. Except as provided in subsection B, if a member dies after distribution of retirement benefits commences, ASRS shall continue to distribute the remaining portion of retirement benefits at least as rapidly as under the method of distribution used before the retired member's death.

B. On the death of a retired member who is receiving benefits , the estate or beneficiary of the member is entitled to receive at least the amount of the member's contribution to ASRS plus interest, as determined by the director, less the benefits received by the member. This amount is payable either as a lump sum or at the same periodic rate in effect at the time of the member's death, as determined by the estate or beneficiary.

Added by Laws 1995, Ch. 32, § 14, eff. March 30, 1995. Amended by Laws 1997, Ch. 280, § 13.

Historical and Statutory Notes

For state highway patrol retirement system and Arizona state retirement system savings clause and beneficiary longevity reserve account provisions of Laws 1995, Ch. 32, see Historical and Statutory Notes following § 38-744.

The 1997 amendment by Ch. 280 deleted "based on a period certain and life annuity or a straight life annuity retirement option" following "is receiving benefits" in subsec. B.

Former § 38-763, enacted as part of the revision effective January 9, 1956 (see Source, following § 38-793), relating to violations, was repealed by Laws 1995, Ch. 32, § 13, eff. March 30, 1995.

§ 38–764. Commencement of retirement; payment of retirement benefits; lump sum payments

A. Retirement is deemed to commence on a date elected by the member. That date shall not be earlier than the day following the date of termination of employment, the date ASRS receives the member's completed retirement application or the date specified by the member pursuant to subsection J of this section.

B. Except as provided in subsection C of this section, all retirement benefits:

1. Are normally payable in monthly installments beginning on the commencement of retirement as prescribed in subsection A of this section.

2. Continue to and include the first day of the month in which death occurs or continue until the date of their cessation in accordance with any optional method of payment that may have been elected.

C. In the case of incapacity of a retired member or contingent annuitant, or in the case of any other emergency, as determined by the board, the board may make the payment to or on behalf of the retired member or contingent annuitant or to another person or persons the board determines to be lawfully entitled to receive payment. The payment is payment for the account of the retired member or contingent annuitant and all persons entitled to payment and, to the extent of the payment, is a full and complete discharge of all liability of the board or ASRS, or both, under or in connection with ASRS.

D. Except as provided in subsection E of this section, at the request of a retired member, a retired member's guardian or a court appointed conservator, the board may pay any increase in retirement benefits or the entire retirement benefit in a lump sum payment based on the actuarial present value of the benefit or the increase in the benefit if the payment of the benefits would result in ineligibility, reduction or elimination of social service programs provided to the member by this state, its political subdivisions or the federal government.

E. The board may pay the entire retirement benefit in a lump sum pursuant to subsection D of this section only if continued membership in ASRS will result in additional requests for lump sum payments based on cost of living adjustments or the establishment of minimum benefit awards.

F. If any benefit that is payable as a series of periodic payments amounts to less than twenty dollars per month, the board, in its sole discretion and based on uniform rules it establishes, may order the amount to be paid quarterly, semiannually, annually or in a lump sum. A member who receives a lump sum payment pursuant to this subsection remains a member of ASRS.

G. All distributions of retirement benefits to a member shall be distributed either:

1. Over a period not exceeding the life of the member or over the lives of the member and the member's contingent annuitant.

2. Over a period not extending beyond the life expectancy of the member or the life expectancy of the member and the member's contingent annuitant.

H. A member may elect to cancel the effective date of retirement within thirty days of retirement or before the member's receipt of retirement benefits, whichever is later.

I. Notwithstanding any other provision of this article, all distributions under this article shall be made in accordance with the distribution requirements of § 401(a)(9) of the internal revenue code.[1]

J. A member who attains a normal retirement date may retire at any time without terminating employment if the member is employed for less than the hours required for active membership pursuant to § 38-711, paragraph 23, subdivision (b).

Added by Laws 1995, Ch. 32, § 14, eff. March 30, 1995. Amended by Laws 1996, Ch. 185, § 15; Laws 1999, Ch. 327, § 15; Laws 2003, Ch. 164, § 2, eff. May 7, 2003.

[1] 26 U.S.C.A. § 401(a)(9).

Historical and Statutory Notes

Source:

A.R.S. former § 38-781.13.
Laws 1970, Ch. 134, § 2.
Laws 1983, Ch. 293, § 5.
Laws 1987, Ch. 274, § 3.
Laws 1990, Ch. 90, § 1.
Laws 1992, Ch. 320, § 12.
Laws 1994, Ch. 356, § 13.

For state highway patrol retirement system and Arizona state retirement system savings clause and beneficiary longevity reserve account provisions of Laws 1995, Ch. 32, see Historical and Statutory Notes following § 38-744.

The 1996 amendment by Ch. 185, inserted subsec. A; redesignated former subsec. A as subsec. B and rewrote the subsection; and redesignated former subsecs. B to G as C to H, accordingly. Former subsec. A had read:

"**A.** Except as provided in subsection B, all retirement benefits:

"1. Are normally payable in monthly installments commencing on the latest of the following:

"(a) The date of termination of employment.

"(b) The date ASRS receives the member's completed retirement application.

"(c) Another date the member elects on the application form prescribed by the board.

"2. Continue to and include the first day of the month in which death occurs or continue until the date of their cessation in accordance with any optional method of payment that may have been elected."

The 1999 amendment by Ch. 327, in the second sentence of subsec. A, deleted "or" following "employment" and inserted "or the date specified by the member pursuant to subsection I"; added the last sentence in subsec. F, relating to lump sum payment; added a new subsec. H and redesignated former subsec. H as subsec. I; and added subsec. J.

The 2003 amendment by Ch. 164, substituted "subsection J of this section" for "subsection I of this section", in subsec. A; and substituted "paragraph 23, subdivision (b)" for "paragraph 22, subdivision (b)", in subsec. J.

Laws 2003, Ch. 164, §§ 3 and 4, provide:

"**Sec. 3. Recalculation of costs of redeemed active military service; refund**

"**A.** If a retired member or a deceased retired member whose beneficiary is receiving benefits on account of a deceased retired member of the Arizona state retirement system received credited service for active military service from the Arizona state retirement system before July 20, 1996, the Arizona state retirement system shall recalculate the cost of that credited service as provided in this section effective retroactively to the date of receipt of the credited service.

"**B.** If an active member of the Arizona state retirement system received credited service for active military service from the Arizona state retirement system before July 20, 1996, the Arizona state retirement system shall recalculate the cost of that credited service as provided in this section effective retroactively to the date of receipt of the credited service.

"**C.** The Arizona state retirement system shall determine the amount a member described in subsection A or B of this section would have paid for credited service for active military service on or after July 20, 1996.

"**D.** The Arizona state retirement system shall subtract the amount determined pursuant to subsection C of this section from the amount the member actually paid for credited service for active military service. If the difference is greater than zero and notwithstanding any other law, the Arizona state retirement system shall refund the difference to the active member, the retired member or the retired member's beneficiary. The Arizona state retirement system shall pay a refund pursuant to this subsection to an active member at the time it makes retirement benefit payments.

"**E.** The Arizona state retirement system shall pay interest on any amounts refunded pursuant to this section. The interest shall be compounded annually at the interest rate assumption approved by the board from time to time for actuarial equivalency.

"**F.** Before retirement, an active member who is entitled to a payment pursuant to subsections D and E of this section may apply the amount of the payment to a purchase of additional active military service pursuant to § 38-745, Arizona Revised Statutes, if the member is eligible to purchase that service.

"**Sec. 4. Member notification; publication**

"The Arizona state retirement system shall notify members who might be eligible for a refund pursuant to § 3 of this act by publishing a summary of the provisions of § 3 of this act in the following publications according to the following schedule:

"1. In four successive Arizona state retirement system quarterly newsletters immediately following the effective date of this act.

"2. In two successive annual statements for individual members immediately following the effective date of this act."

Former § 38-764, enacted as part of the revision effective January 9, 1956 (see Source, following § 38-794), relating to reservation of the right to amend or repeal the former article, was repealed by Laws 1995, Ch. 32, § 13, eff. March 30, 1995.

§ 38-765. Errors; benefit recomputation

If any change or error in the records results in any member or beneficiary receiving from ASRS more or less than the member or beneficiary would have been entitled to receive if the records had been correct, the board shall correct the error and as far as practicable shall adjust the payments in a manner so that the actuarial equivalent of the benefit to which the member or beneficiary was correctly entitled is paid. The board shall correct any change or error and shall pay the appropriate monies to a member or beneficiary or shall recover monies from the member or beneficiary if the member or beneficiary is overpaid.

Added by Laws 1995, Ch. 32, § 14, eff. March 30, 1995.

Historical and Statutory Notes

Source:

A.R.S. former § 38-781.15.
Laws 1970, Ch. 134, § 2.
Laws 1972, Ch. 51, § 19.
Laws 1975, Ch. 54, § 3.
Laws 1987, Ch. 274, § 4.
Laws 1988, Ch. 19, § 2.
Laws 1990, Ch. 145, § 3.
Laws 1992, Ch. 320, § 13.

For state highway patrol retirement system and Arizona state retirement system savings clause and beneficiary longevity reserve account provisions of Laws 1995, Ch. 32, see Historical and Statutory Notes following § 38-744.

Former § 38-765, added by Laws 1959, Ch. 145, § 2, relating to state highway patrol retirement system administration and membership, was repealed by Laws 1995, Ch. 32, § 13, eff. March 30, 1995.

§ 38-766. Retired members; return to work; maximum benefit

A. A retired member who is engaged to work by an employer for at least twenty weeks in each fiscal year and at least twenty hours per week resumes active membership in ASRS. ASRS shall suspend payment of the member's retirement benefits until the member either:

1. Terminates employment.

2. Attains a normal retirement date and no longer meets the requirements for active membership pursuant to this subsection.

B. A member who satisfies subsection A, paragraph 1 or 2 of this section is entitled to receive an annuity recomputed to include the additional compensation and credited service. However, the recomputed annuity shall be in the original optional form chosen pursuant to § 38-760, with the same beneficiary, if applicable, as when the member first retired. A member who retired under a provision of law allowing increased benefits if the retirement occurred during a specific period of time and who subsequently becomes an employee under ASRS shall not retain the increased benefits under the prior law when benefits are computed for the member's most recent retirement.

C. Section 38-769, subsection L applies when determining the maximum benefit that may be paid to a retired member who resumes active membership and subsequently retires.

Added by Laws 1995, Ch. 32, § 14, eff. March 30, 1995. Amended by Laws 1997, Ch. 280, § 14; Laws 1999, Ch. 327, § 16; Laws 2002, Ch. 213, § 5, eff. May 15, 2002.

Historical and Statutory Notes

Source:

A.R.S. former § 38-781.15.
Laws 1970, Ch. 134, § 2.
Laws 1972, Ch. 51, § 19.
Laws 1975, Ch. 54, § 3.
Laws 1987, Ch. 274, § 4.
Laws 1988, Ch. 19, § 2.
Laws 1990, Ch. 145, § 3.
Laws 1992, Ch. 320, § 13.

For state highway patrol retirement system and Arizona state retirement system savings clause and beneficiary longevity reserve account provisions of Laws 1995, Ch. 32, see Historical and Statutory Notes following § 38-744.

The 1997 amendment by Ch. 280 added subsec. C relating to the application of § 38-769, subsec. M.

The 1999 amendment by Ch. 327 rewrote subsec. A, which had read:

"**A.** If a retired member is engaged to work by an employer for at least twenty weeks in each fiscal year and at least twenty hours per week, the retired member resumes active membership in ASRS. ASRS shall suspend payment of the member's retirement benefits until the member terminates employment and the benefit is recomputed pursuant to subsection B of this section."

The amendment by Ch. 327 also substituted "On the termination of employment of a previously retired member, the member" for "A member who satisfies subsection A, paragraph 1 or 2 of this section" in the first sentence of subsec. B; and substituted "N" for "M" in subsec. C.

The 2002 amendment by Ch. 213, modified an internal reference.

Laws 2002, Ch. 213, § 9, subsec. A, provides:

"**Sec. 9. Retroactivity**

"**A.** Sections 38-766 and 38-769, Arizona Revised Statutes, as amended by this act, apply retroactively to July 1, 2001."

Former § 38-766, added by Laws 1959, Ch. 145, § 2, and amended by Laws 1968, Ch. 192, § 3, relating to a state highway patrol retirement fund, was repealed by Laws 1995, Ch. 32, § 13, eff. March 30, 1995.

§ 38-766.01. Retired members; return to work

A. Notwithstanding § 38-766, a retired member may return to work and still be eligible to receive retirement benefits if all of the following requirements are satisfied:

1. The retired member has attained the member's normal retirement age.

2. The retired member terminated employment at least twelve months before returning to work.

3. If the retired member returns to work as a teacher, the retired member is working as a certificated teacher.

4. If the retired member returns to work as a teacher, the retired member's employment is not subject to the requirements prescribed in §§ 15-538, 15-538.01 and 15-539 through 15-543.

5. The retired member acknowledges in writing the provisions of this section.

B. An employer of a retired member who returns to work pursuant to this section shall not pay contributions on behalf of the retired member pursuant to § 38–736, 38–737 or 38–797.05. A retired member who returns to work pursuant to this section does not accrue credited service, retirement benefits or long-term disability program benefits pursuant to article 2.1 of this chapter for the period the retired member returns to work.

Added by Laws 2000, Ch. 132, § 2. Amended by Laws 2001, Ch. 68, § 1.

Historical and Statutory Notes

Laws 2000, Ch. 132, § 4, which provided for delayed repeal of this section on July 1, 2003, was itself repealed by Laws 2002, Ch. 213, § 8, eff. May 15, 2002.

The 2001 amendment by Ch. 68 inserted "If the retired member returns to work as a teacher," in subsec. A, pars. 3 and 4.

Reviser's Notes:

2000 Note. Pursuant to authority of § 41–1304.02, in subsection B, last sentence the spelling of "long-term" was corrected.

§ 38–767. Benefit increases

A. Effective July 1 of each year, each retired member or beneficiary of a retired member is entitled to receive a permanent benefit increase in the base benefit equal to the amount determined in subsection D of this section if the retired member or beneficiary of a retired member was receiving benefits on or before July 31 of the previous calendar year. The annual permanent benefit increases shall be paid on a monthly basis. The benefit increase shall commence on July 1.

B. The total amount of the percentage increase provided in subsection A of this section shall not exceed four per cent in aggregate for all persons eligible for an increase. The percentage payable from excess investment earnings shall be determined as follows:

1. Determine any excess investment earnings account balance available.

2. Determine the total excess investment earnings as provided in subsection C of this section.

3. Add the amount determined in paragraph 1 of this subsection to the amount determined in paragraph 2 of this subsection.

4. Determine one per cent of the actuarial present value of benefits for retired members and beneficiaries as of June 30 of the year prior to the year for which an increase is being granted.

5. Divide the amount determined in paragraph 3 of this subsection by the amount determined in paragraph 4 of this subsection. If the quotient is equal to or more than four, the percentage increase payable from excess investment earnings on accounts associated with those persons eligible for an annual benefit increase pursuant to subsection A of this section is four per cent. If the quotient is one or more but less than four, the percentage increase payable from excess investment earnings on accounts associated with those persons eligible for an annual benefit increase pursuant to subsection A of this section is

that per cent rounded to the nearest tenth of a per cent. If the quotient is less than one, no benefit increases shall be granted.

C. The excess investment earnings on accounts associated with those persons eligible for an annual benefit increase pursuant to subsection A of this section are equal to the actuarial present value of benefits for all retired members and beneficiaries as of June 30 of the year prior to the year for which an increase is being granted multiplied by the positive difference, if any, between the yield rate on the actuarial value of ASRS assets for the fiscal year that ended June 30 of the year prior to the year for which an increase is being granted and eight per cent. The excess investment earnings on accounts associated with those persons eligible for an annual benefit increase pursuant to subsection A of this section are zero if the yield rate on ASRS assets is less than or equal to eight per cent.

D. The permanent benefit increase for each person entitled to receive an increase pursuant to subsection A of this section shall be determined based on years of credited service as follows:

1. Multiply the percentage determined in subsection B, paragraph 5 of this section by the actuarial present value of benefits for retired members and beneficiaries as of June 30 of the year prior to the year for which an increase is being granted.

2. Determine the actuarial present value of a one dollar per year of credited service annual increase in the base benefit amounts as of June 30 of the year prior to the year for which an increase is being granted, received by all persons entitled to receive an increase pursuant to subsection A of this section.

3. Divide the amount determined in paragraph 1 of this subsection by the amount determined in paragraph 2 of this subsection.

4. Multiply the amount determined in paragraph 3 of this subsection by the number of years of credited service for each retired member and the number of years of credited service earned by a retired member for each beneficiary entitled to receive an increase pursuant to subsection A of this section.

E. Any excess investment earnings on accounts associated with those persons eligible for an annual benefit increase pursuant to subsection A of this section from any year that are not used for benefit adjustments for that year are available for future benefit increases in the following years.

F. Monies available for future benefit increases shall earn interest at a rate of eight per cent per year. This interest shall be used to pay the additional benefit increases provided for in subsection G of this section.

G. In addition to a benefit increase pursuant to subsection A of this section, if a retired member had more than ten years of credited service, the retired member or beneficiary of the retired member is entitled to receive a benefit increase based on the number of years following retirement as follows:

1. At least five years but less than ten years, a monthly benefit increase equal to the amount determined in subsection H of this section.

2. At least ten years but less than fifteen years, a monthly benefit increase equal to two times the amount determined in subsection H of this section.

3. At least fifteen years but less than twenty years, a monthly benefit increase equal to three times the amount determined in subsection H of this section.

4. At least twenty years but less than twenty-five years, a monthly benefit increase equal to four times the amount determined in subsection H of this section.

5. At least twenty-five years but less than thirty years, a monthly benefit increase equal to five times the amount determined in subsection H of this section.

6. At least thirty years, a monthly benefit increase equal to six times the amount determined in subsection H of this section.

H. The amount of the monthly benefit increase under subsection G of this section for a retired member or beneficiary of a retired member who is entitled to the increase when at least five years but less than ten years have elapsed since the retired member's retirement date is equal to the amount obtained by dividing the amount of interest credited pursuant to subsection F of this section by the amount that equals the sum of:

1. The actuarial present value, as of June 30 of the year prior to the year for which the increase is granted, of a benefit increase of one dollar per month for the retired members and beneficiaries of retired members who are eligible for an increase under subsection G of this section and for whom at least five years but less than ten years have elapsed since the retired members' retirement dates.

2. The actuarial present value, as of June 30 of the year prior to the year for which the increase is granted, of a benefit increase of two dollars per month for the retired members and beneficiaries of retired members who are eligible for an increase under subsection G of this section and for whom at least ten years but less than fifteen years have elapsed since the retired members' retirement dates.

3. The actuarial present value, as of June 30 of the year prior to the year for which the increase is granted, of a benefit increase of three dollars per month for the retired members and beneficiaries of retired members who are eligible for an increase under subsection G of this section and for whom at least fifteen years but less than twenty years have elapsed since the retired members' retirement dates.

4. The actuarial present value, as of June 30 of the year prior to the year for which the increase is granted, of a benefit increase of four dollars per month for the retired members and beneficiaries of retired members who are eligible for an increase under subsection G of this section and for whom at least twenty years but less than twenty-five years have elapsed since the retired members' retirement dates.

5. The actuarial present value, as of June 30 of the year prior to the year for which the increase is granted, of a benefit increase of five dollars per month for the retired members and beneficiaries of retired members who are eligible for an increase under subsection G of this section and for whom at least twenty-five

years but less than thirty years have elapsed since the retired members' retirement dates.

6. The actuarial present value, as of June 30 of the year prior to the year for which the increase is granted, of a benefit increase of six dollars per month for the retired members and beneficiaries of retired members who are eligible for an increase under subsection G of this section and for whom at least thirty years have elapsed since the retired members' retirement dates.

I. A member of the defined contribution program administered by ASRS is only eligible for the benefit increases pursuant to this section if the member elects to transfer irrevocably from the defined contribution program administered by ASRS to the defined benefit program established by this article.

J. The cost of the benefit increases granted pursuant to this section shall be added to the existing liabilities of ASRS.

K. As used in this section, the actuarial present value of benefits for retired members and beneficiaries does not include the value of benefits provided pursuant to § 38-783.

Added by Laws 1995, Ch. 32, § 14, eff. March 30, 1995. Amended by Laws 1995, Ch. 134, § 9, eff. April 17, 1995; Laws 1995, Ch. 205, § 1; Laws 1997, Ch. 280, § 15; Laws 1999, Ch. 174, § 1; Laws 2000, Ch. 66, § 1; Laws 2001, Ch. 380, § 8.

Historical and Statutory Notes

Source:

A.R.S. former § 38-781.27.
Laws 1994, Ch. 357, § 2.

The purported repeal of this section by Laws 1995, Ch. 32, § 26, which was to be effective July 1, 2000, was itself repealed by Laws 1998, Ch. 264, § 6.

For state highway patrol retirement system and Arizona state retirement system savings clause and beneficiary longevity reserve account provisions of Laws 1995, Ch. 32, see Historical and Statutory Notes following § 38-744.

The 1995 amendment by Ch. 134, in subsec. A, deleted "and members receiving long-term disability benefits pursuant to § 38-781 on or before June 30, 1995" following "calendar year" in the first sentence.

Laws 1995, Ch. 134, § 16, provides:

"**Sec. 16. Benefit increases**

"**A.** Members of the Arizona state retirement system who were eligible to receive long-term disability benefits pursuant to § 38-781, Arizona Revised Statutes, as repealed by this act, on or before June 30, 1995 are eligible to receive an increased benefit equal to the benefit increase provided to retired members pursuant to § 38-767, Arizona Revised Statutes, as amended by this act.

"**B.** The benefit increases provided by subsection A of this section shall be added to the liabilities of the long-term disability program established by title 38, chapter 5, article 2.1, Arizona Revised Statutes, as added by this act."

The 1995 amendment by Ch. 205 substituted "The percentage" for "One-half of the percentage" in subsec. B, par. 1.

The 1997 amendment by Ch. 280 substituted "on July 1" for "the following January 1 with retroactive payments from July 1 through December 31" in subsec. A; rewrote subsec. B, par. 2, subsec. C, and subsec. D, par. 1; deleted "or member receiving long-term disability benefits" following "each retired member" in subsec. D, par. 4; added subsec. H limiting the value of benefits included actuarial present value of benefits. Prior to amendment subsec. B, par. 2, subsec. C, and subsec. D, par. 1, had read:

"2. The percentage payable from excess investment earnings determined as follows:

"(a) Determine the excess investment earnings account balance on the accounts associated with those persons eligible for an annual benefit increase pursuant to subsection A of this section.

"(b) Determine the total excess investment earnings on accounts associated with those persons eligible for an annual benefit increase pursuant to subsection A of this section as provided in subsection C of this section.

"(c) Add the amount determined in subdivision (a) of this paragraph to the amount determined in subdivision (b) of this paragraph.

"(d) Determine the actuarial present value of a one per cent benefit increase for each person entitled to receive an increase pursuant to subsection A of this section.

"(e) Divide the amount determined in subdivision (c) of this paragraph by the amount determined in subdivision (d) of this paragraph. If the quotient is equal to or more than three, the percentage increase payable from excess investment earnings on accounts associated with those persons eligible for an annual benefit increase pursuant to subsection A of this section is three per cent. If the quotient is one or more but less than three, the percentage increase payable from excess investment earnings on accounts associated with those persons eligible for an annual benefit increase pursuant to subsection A of this section is that per cent rounded to the nearest tenth of a per cent. If the quotient is less than one, no benefit increases shall be granted.

"**C.** The excess investment earnings on accounts associated with those persons eligible for an annual benefit increase pursuant to subsection A of this section are equal to the average of the actuarial present value of accounts associated with those persons eligible for an annual benefit increase pursuant to subsection A of this section during the fiscal year that ended June 30 of the year prior to the year for which an increase is being granted multiplied by the positive difference, if any, between the yield rate on the actuarial value of ASRS assets for the fiscal year that ended June 30 of the year prior to the year for which an increase is being granted and nine per cent. The excess investment earnings on accounts associated with those persons eligible for an annual benefit increase pursuant to subsection A of this section are zero if the yield rate on ASRS assets is less than or equal to nine per cent.

"**D.** The permanent benefit increase for each person entitled to receive an increase pursuant to subsection A of this section shall be determined based on years of credited service as follows:

"1. Multiply the percentage determined in subsection B, paragraph 2, subdivision (e) of this section by the actuarial present value of the base benefits being received, as of June 30 of the year prior to the year for which an increase is being granted, by all persons entitled to receive an increase pursuant to subsection A of this section."

Laws 1997, Ch. 280, § 23, provides:

"**Sec. 23. Retroactivity**

"Section 38–767, Arizona Revised Statutes, as amended by this act, applies retroactively to July 1, 1997."

The 1999 amendment by Ch. 174 rewrote subsec. B; substituted "eight per cent" for "nine per cent" twice in subsec. C; and substituted "paragraph five" for "paragraph 2, subdivision (e)" in subsec. D, par. 1. Prior to amendment, subsec. B had read:

"**B.** The total amount of the percentage increase provided in subsection A of this section, not to exceed three per cent in aggregate for all persons eligible for an increase, is equal to the lesser of:

"1. The percentage change in the all items component of the consumer price index for all urban consumers as published by the United States department of labor, bureau of labor statistics, for the calendar year preceding the year for which the increase is being calculated.

"2. The percentage payable from excess investment earnings determined as follows:

"(a) Determine any excess investment earnings account balance available.

"(b) Determine the total excess investment earnings as provided in subsection C of this section.

"(c) Add the amount determined in subdivision (a) of this paragraph to the amount determined in subdivision (b) of this paragraph.

"(d) Determine one per cent of the actuarial present value of benefits for retired members and beneficiaries as of June 30 of the year prior to the year for which an increase is being granted.

"(e) Divide the amount determined in subdivision (c) of this paragraph by the amount determined in subdivision (d) of this paragraph. If the quotient is equal to or more than three, the percentage increase payable from excess investment earnings on accounts associated with those persons eligible for an annual benefit increase pursuant to subsection A of this section is three per cent. If the quotient is one or more but less than three, the percentage increase payable from excess investment earnings on accounts associated with those persons eligible for an annual benefit increase pursuant to subsection A of this section is that per cent rounded to the nearest tenth of a per cent. If the quotient is less than one, no benefit increases shall be granted."

The 2000 amendment by Ch. 66 rewrote subsec. A, which formerly read:

"**A.** Effective July 1 of each year, all retired members or beneficiaries of retired members who were fifty-five years of age or older on the respective applicable date and who were receiving benefits on or before June 30 of the previous calendar year are entitled to receive a permanent benefit increase in their base benefit equal to the amount determined in subsection D of this section. Beneficiaries of retired members are entitled to receive annual permanent benefit increases in their base benefit as provided in this subsection regardless of the beneficiary's age if the retired member attained at least age fifty-five before the retired member's death and if the beneficiary was receiving benefits on or before June 30 of the previous year. The annual permanent benefit increases shall be paid on a monthly basis. The benefit increase shall commence on July 1."

The 2001 amendment by Ch. 380 inserted new subsecs. F, G and H, and redesignated existing subsecs. F, G and H as subsecs. I, J and k, accordingly.

Former § 38–767, added by Laws 1959, Ch. 145, § 2, relating to state highway patrol retirement system contributions, was repealed by Laws 1995, Ch. 32, § 13, eff. March 30, 1995.

Reviser's Notes:

1995 Note. Prior to the 1997 amendment, this section contained the amendments made by Laws 1995, Ch. 134, sec. 9 and Ch. 205, sec. 1 that were blended together pursuant to authority of § 41–1304.03.

§ 38–768. Minimum retirement benefit

A. Notwithstanding any other provision of this article, a retired member or beneficiary who is entitled to a benefit under this article shall receive at least a minimum monthly benefit that is computed pursuant to subsection B of this section if the retired member or beneficiary is at least seventy-five years of age and if the retired member or beneficiary is any of the following:

1. Retired from ASRS with at least twenty years of credited service.

2. A beneficiary of ASRS who is receiving benefits derived from a retired member who had at least twenty years of credited service.

3. A member with at least twenty years of service who irrevocably revokes the receipt of benefits determined on the basis of membership in the defined contribution program administered by ASRS and who elects to receive benefits under this article.

4. A beneficiary who is receiving benefits derived from a retired member who had at least twenty years of service, who irrevocably revoked the receipt of benefits determined on the basis of membership in the defined contribution program administered by ASRS and who elected to receive benefits under this article.

B. The minimum monthly benefit provided by subsection A of this section:

1. For retired members is six hundred dollars.

2. For beneficiaries is the amount determined by paragraph 1 of this subsection and reduced in accordance with the option chosen by multiplying the amount determined by paragraph 1 of this subsection by the actuarial figure for the option chosen and by the percentage of the option chosen.

C. If the minimum monthly benefit pursuant to subsections A and B of this section is more than the retired member's or beneficiary's current monthly benefit, the retired member or beneficiary is eligible to receive a monthly benefit equal to the minimum benefit. If the retired member's or beneficiary's current monthly benefit is more than the minimum benefit, the retired member's or beneficiary's benefit remains the same.

D. A member who receives a lump sum payment pursuant to § 38–764, subsection D is not eligible for a minimum benefit as provided by this section.

Added by Laws 1995, Ch. 32, § 14, eff. March 30, 1995. Amended by Laws 1996, Ch. 185, § 16.

Historical and Statutory Notes

Source:

A.R.S. former § 38-781.26.
Laws 1994, Ch. 357, § 2.

For state highway patrol retirement system and Arizona state retirement system savings clause and beneficiary longevity reserve account provisions of Laws 1995, Ch. 32, see Historical and Statutory Notes following § 38-744.

The 1996 amendment by Ch. 185 made a conforming change to the reference to § 38-764 in subsec. D.

Former § 38-768, added by Laws 1959, Ch. 145, § 2, relating to state highway patrol retirement system service determination, was repealed by Laws 1995, Ch. 32, § 13, eff. March 30, 1995.

§ 38-769. Maximum retirement benefits; termination; definitions

A. Notwithstanding any other provision of this article, except as provided in subsection C of this section, the employer provided portion of a member's annual benefit payable in the form of a straight life annuity, at any time within a limitation year, shall not exceed one hundred sixty thousand dollars or a larger amount that is effective as of January 1 of each calendar year, is prescribed by the board and is due to any cost of living adjustment announced by the United States secretary of the treasury pursuant to § 415(d) of the internal revenue code.[1] The board shall increase the amount pursuant to this subsection as of the effective date of the increase as prescribed by the United States secretary of the treasury. Benefit increases provided in this section resulting from the increase in the limitations of § 415(b) of the internal revenue code as amended by the economic growth and tax relief reconciliation act of 2001 shall be provided to all current and former members who have benefits that are limited by § 415(b) of the internal revenue code and who have an accrued benefit under ASRS immediately before July 1, 2001, other than an accrued benefit resulting from a benefit increase solely as a result of the increases provided by this section resulting from the increase in the limitations of § 415(b) of the internal revenue code as amended by the economic growth and tax relief reconciliation act of 2001.

B. Notwithstanding the limitations of subsection A of this section, the benefits payable to a member are deemed not to exceed the limitations determined under subsection A of this section if the retirement benefits payable to the member under this article do not exceed ten thousand dollars for the limitation year and if an employer has not at any time maintained a defined contribution plan in which the member has participated.

C. The limitations determined under subsection A of this section are subject to the following adjustments:

1. If a member has less than ten years of membership in ASRS, the maximum dollar limitation determined under subsection A of this section shall be multiplied by a fraction, the numerator of which is the number of years, or partial years, of membership in ASRS and the denominator of which is ten. The reduction provided in this paragraph also applies to the ten thousand dollar floor limitation provided in subsection B of this section, except that the reduction applies to years of service with an employer rather than to years of membership in ASRS. The reduction in this paragraph does not reduce the limitations determined under subsection A of this section to an amount less than one-tenth of the limitations as determined without regard to this paragraph.

2. If a member's annual benefit commences before the member attains sixty-two years of age, the

defined benefit dollar limitation applicable to the member at the earlier age is an annual benefit payable in the form of a straight life annuity beginning at the earlier age that is the actuarial equivalent of the defined benefit dollar limitation applicable to the member at age sixty-two and that is adjusted under paragraph 1 of this subsection, if required. The defined benefit dollar limitation applicable at an age before age sixty-two is determined as the lesser of:

(a) The actuarial equivalent at that age of the defined benefit dollar limitation computed using the interest rate specified by the board in § 38–711, paragraph 2 and the mortality table or other tabular factors prescribed in paragraph 5 of this subsection.

(b) The actuarial equivalent at that age of the defined benefit dollar limitation computed using a five per cent interest rate and the applicable mortality table prescribed in paragraph 5 of this subsection. Any decrease in the defined benefit dollar limitation determined in accordance with this paragraph shall not reflect a mortality decrement if benefits are not forfeited on the death of the member. If any benefits are forfeited on death, the full mortality decrement is taken into account.

3. If a member's annual benefit commences after sixty-five years of age, the limitation determined under subsection A of this section applicable to the member at the later age is the annual benefit payable in the form of a straight life annuity beginning at the later age that is actuarially equivalent to the defined benefit dollar limitation applicable to the participant at age sixty-five and that is adjusted under paragraph 1 of this subsection, if required. The actuarial equivalent of the defined benefit dollar limitation applicable at an age after age sixty-five is determined as the lesser of:

(a) The actuarial equivalent at that age of the defined benefit dollar limitation computed using the interest rate specified by the board as provided in § 38–711, paragraph 2 and the mortality table or other tabular factors prescribed in paragraph 5 of this subsection.

(b) The actuarial equivalent at that age of the defined benefit dollar limitation computed using a five per cent interest rate assumption and the applicable mortality table prescribed in paragraph 5 of this subsection. For the purposes of this subdivision, mortality between age sixty-five and the age at which benefits commence shall be ignored.

4. If the member's benefit is paid in a form other than a straight life annuity, the benefit paid may not exceed the actuarial equivalent of the maximum annual benefit payable as a straight life annuity disregarding the portion of any joint and survivor annuity that constitutes a qualified joint and survivor annuity as defined in § 417 of the internal revenue code. Actuarial equivalency under this paragraph shall be determined by the use of an interest rate assumption equal to the greater of five per cent a year or the rate specified by the board as provided in § 38–711, paragraph 2.

5. For the purposes of adjusting any benefit or limitation under paragraph 2, 3 or 4 of this subsection, the board shall use the mortality table prescribed by

the United States secretary of the treasury as required by § 415(b)(2)(E)(v) of the internal revenue code.

D. Subsection C, paragraphs 1 and 2 of this section do not apply to income received from ASRS as a pension, annuity or similar allowance as a result of the recipient becoming disabled by personal injury or sickness or to amounts received from ASRS by beneficiaries, survivors or the estate of a member as a result of the death of the member.

E. Notwithstanding any other provision of this section, the annual benefit payable under this article may be reduced to the extent necessary, as determined by the board, to prevent disqualification of ASRS under § 415 of the internal revenue code that imposes additional limitations on the annual benefits payable to members who also may be participating in another tax qualified pension or savings plan of this state. An employer shall not provide employee retirement or deferred benefits if the benefits authorized by this section and as required by federal law result in the failure of ASRS to meet federal qualification standards as applied to public pension plans. The board shall advise affected members of any additional information concerning their annual benefits required by this subsection.

F. If the maximum amount of benefit allowed under § 415 of the internal revenue code is increased after the commencement date of a member's benefit due to any cost of living adjustment announced by the United States secretary of the treasury pursuant to the provisions of § 415(d) of the internal revenue code, the amount of the monthly benefit payable under ASRS to a member whose benefit is restricted due to the provisions of § 415(d) of the internal revenue code shall be increased by the board as of the date prescribed by the United States secretary of the treasury on which the increase shall become effective. The increase shall reflect the increase in the amount of retirement income that may be payable under this article as a result of the cost of living adjustment.

G. In determining the adjustments to the defined benefit dollar limitation authorized by subsection A of this section, the board shall prescribe a larger defined benefit dollar limitation if prescribed by the United States secretary of the treasury pursuant to § 415(d) of the internal revenue code. An adjustment to the defined benefit dollar limitation prescribed in subsection A of this section is not effective before the first calendar year for which the United States secretary of the treasury publishes the adjustment. After it is prescribed by the board, the new defined benefit dollar limitation applies to the limitation year ending with or within the calendar year for which the secretary of the treasury makes the adjustment.

H. For the purposes of the limitations prescribed by this section, all member and employer contributions made to ASRS to provide a member benefits pursuant to § 38–771 or 38–771.01 and all member contributions that are not treated as picked up by the employer under § 414(h)(2) of the internal revenue code shall be treated as made to a separate defined contribution plan.

I. On termination of ASRS the accrued benefit of each member is, as of the date of termination, fully vested and nonforfeitable.

J. If ASRS terminates, the benefit of any highly compensated employee as defined in § 414(q) of the internal revenue code and any highly compensated former employee is limited to a benefit that is nondiscriminatory under § 401(a)(4) of the internal revenue code and as follows:

1. Benefits distributed to any of the twenty-five active and former highly compensated employees with the greatest compensation in the current or any prior fiscal year are restricted so that the annual payments are no greater than an amount equal to the payment that would be made on behalf of the member under a straight life annuity that is the actuarial equivalent of the sum of the member's accrued benefit, the member's other benefits under ASRS, excluding a social security supplement as defined in 26 Code of Federal Regulations § 1.411(a)–7(C)(4)(ii), and the amount the member is entitled to receive under a social security supplement.

2. Paragraph 1 of this subsection does not apply if either:

(a) After payment of the benefit to a member described in paragraph 1 of this subsection, the value of ASRS assets equals or exceeds one hundred ten per cent of the value of the current liabilities, as defined in § 412(*l*)(7) of the internal revenue code, of ASRS.

(b) The value of the benefits for a member described in paragraph 1 of this subsection is less than one per cent of the value of the current liabilities, as defined in § 412(*l*)(7) of the internal revenue code, of ASRS before distribution.

(c) The value of the benefits payable by ASRS to a member described in paragraph 1 of this subsection does not exceed three thousand five hundred dollars.

K. For the purposes of subsection J of this section, "benefit" includes loans in excess of the amount prescribed in § 72(p)(2)(A) of the internal revenue code, any periodic income, any withdrawal values payable to a living member and any death benefits not provided for by insurance on the member's life.

L. On retirement of a member who was a retired member, who resumed active membership and who subsequently retires, the limitations of this section in effect on the member's subsequent retirement apply to the member's retirement benefit payable as recomputed pursuant to § 38–766. In addition, the sum of the present value of the member's recomputed retirement benefits plus the present value of the benefits the member received during the member's prior retirement shall not exceed the present value of the limitations in effect on the member's subsequent retirement. The limitations prescribed in this subsection shall not reduce a member's retirement benefit below the retirement benefit the member was receiving before the member resumed active membership. For the purposes of determining present value under this subsection, the board shall use the actuarial equivalent assumptions provided in § 38–711, paragraph 2.

M. For the purposes of this section:

1. Annual additions shall be determined as provided in § 38–747, subsection O.

2. "Annual benefit" means a benefit, including any portion of a member's retirement benefit payable to an alternate payee under a qualified domestic

relations order that satisfies the requirements prescribed in § 414(p)(1)(A)(i) of the internal revenue code and § 38–773, payable annually in the form of a straight life annuity, disregarding the portion of a joint and survivor annuity that constitutes a qualified joint and survivor annuity as defined in § 417 of the internal revenue code, with no ancillary or incidental benefits or rollover contributions and excluding any portion of the benefit derived from member contributions or other contributions that are treated as a separate defined contribution plan under § 415 of the internal revenue code but including any of those contributions that are picked up by the employer under § 414(h) of the internal revenue code, or that otherwise are not treated as a separate defined contribution plan. If the benefit is payable in another form, the determination as to whether the limitation described in subsection A of this section has been satisfied shall be made by the board by adjusting the benefit so that it is actuarially equivalent to the annual benefit described in this paragraph in accordance with the regulations promulgated by the United States secretary of the treasury. In addition, for determining the annual benefit attributable to member contributions, the factors described in § 411(c)(2)(B) of the internal revenue code and the regulations promulgated under the internal revenue code shall be used by the board regardless of whether § 411 of the internal revenue code applies to ASRS. The factors described in § 411(c)(2)(B) of the internal revenue code shall be those factors described under § 417(e)(3) of the internal revenue code and determined on the basis of the 417(e) mortality table and an interest rate equal to the annual yield for thirty-year treasury constant maturities, as reported in federal reserve statistical release G–13 and H–15, for the third full calendar month preceding the plan year for which the determination is made. For the purposes of this paragraph, "the 417(e) mortality table" means the mortality table that is published by the United States treasury department as the table to be used for the purposes of § 417(e) of the internal revenue code to determine the single sum value of an accrued benefit.

3. "Compensation" means the member's earned income, wages, salaries, fees for professional service and other amounts received for personal services actually rendered in the course of employment with the employer and includes amounts described in §§ 104(a)(3) and 105(a) of the internal revenue code, but only to the extent that these amounts are includable in the gross income of the member. Compensation also includes any elective deferral as defined in § 402(g)(3) of the internal revenue code and any amount that is contributed or deferred by an employer at the election of a member and that is not includable in the gross income of the member by reason of § 125, 132(f)(4) or 457 of the internal revenue code. Compensation does not mean:

(a) Employer contributions to a plan of deferred compensation to the extent the contributions are not included in the gross income of the employee for the taxable year in which contributed and any distributions from a plan of deferred compensation, regardless of whether the amounts are includable in gross income of the employee when distributed, except that any amount received by a member pursuant to an unfunded nonqualified plan may be considered as compensation for the purposes of this section in the year the amounts are includable in the gross income of the member under the internal revenue code.

(b) Other amounts that receive special tax benefits, such as premiums for group term life insurance, but only to the extent that the premiums are not includable in the gross income of the employee.

4. "Defined benefit dollar limitation" means the dollar limitation determined under subsection A of this section.

5. "Defined benefit plan" has the same meaning prescribed in § 414(j) of the internal revenue code.

6. "Defined contribution plan" has the same meaning prescribed in § 414(i) of the internal revenue code.

7. "Limitation year" and "years of service" means the fiscal year.

Added by Laws 1995, Ch. 32, § 14, eff. March 30, 1995. Amended by Laws 1996, Ch. 185, § 17; Laws 1997, Ch. 280, § 16; Laws 1998, Ch. 155, § 3; Laws 2001, Ch. 136, § 17; Laws 2002, Ch. 213, § 6, eff. May 15, 2002.

[1] Internal Revenue Code sections may be found in Title 26 of U.S.C.A.

Historical and Statutory Notes

Source:

A.R.S. former § 38–781.38.
Laws 1986, Ch. 168, § 7.
Laws 1991, Ch. 170, § 8.
Laws 1994, Ch. 356, § 17.

For state highway patrol retirement system and Arizona state retirement system savings clause and beneficiary longevity reserve account provisions of Laws 1995, Ch. 32, see Historical and Statutory Notes following § 38–744.

The 1996 amendment by Ch. 185 rewrote the section, which had read:

"**A.** Notwithstanding any other provision of this article, except as provided in subsection C of this section, the employer provided portion of a member's annual benefit, at any time within a limitation year, shall not exceed the lesser of:

"1. Ninety thousand dollars or a larger amount that is prescribed by the board and that is due to any cost of living adjustment announced by the United States internal revenue service pursuant to § 415(d) of the internal revenue code. The board shall increase the amount pursuant to this paragraph as of the effective date of the increase as prescribed by the United States secretary of the treasury or the secretary's designee.

"2. One hundred per cent of the member's average compensation for the member's high three consecutive years of service as provided in § 415 of the internal revenue code. For purposes of this paragraph, a member's high three consecutive years of service is the period of three consecutive years or the actual number of consecutive years of employment for a member who is employed less than three consecutive years with the employer during which the member had the greatest aggregate compensation from the employer.

"**B.** Notwithstanding the limitations of subsection A of this section, the benefits payable to a member are deemed not to exceed the limitations determined under subsection A of this section if the retirement benefits payable to the member under this article do not exceed ten thousand dollars for the limitation year and if an employer has not at any time maintained a defined contribution plan in which the member has participated.

"**C.** The limitations determined under subsection A of this section are subject to the following adjustments:

"1. Effective retroactively to July 1, 1987, if a member has less than ten years of membership in ASRS, the limitation determined under subsection A of this section shall be multiplied by a fraction, the numerator of which is the number of years, or part of the number of years, of membership in ASRS and the denominator of which is ten. The reduction provided in this paragraph also applies to the one hundred per cent of compensation limitation and the ten thousand dollar floor limitation provided in subsection B of this section, except that the reductions apply to years of service with an employer rather than to years of membership in ASRS. The reduction in this paragraph does not reduce the limitations determined under subsection A of this section to an amount less than one-tenth of the limitations as determined without regard to this paragraph.

"2. If a member's annual benefit commences before the member attains sixty-two years of age, the limitation determined under subsection A of this section shall be adjusted to the actuarial equivalent of an annual benefit equal to the dollar limitation commencing at sixty-two years of age. The actuarial equivalent under this paragraph shall not be less than seventy-five thousand dollars if a member's annual benefit commences at or after fifty-five years of age. If a member's annual benefit commences before fifty-five years of age, the actuarial equivalent shall equal the greater of:

"(a) The actuarial equivalent of a seventy-five thousand dollar annual benefit for fifty-five years of age.

"(b) The actuarial equivalent of a ninety thousand dollar annual benefit for sixty-two years of age.

"Actuarial equivalency under this paragraph shall be determined by the use of an interest rate assumption equal to the greater of five per cent a year or the rate specified by the board as provided in § 38–711, paragraph 2.

"3. If a member's annual benefit commences after sixty-five years of age, the limitation determined under subsection A of this section shall be adjusted to the actuarial equivalent of an annual benefit equal to the dollar limitation commencing at sixty-five years of age. Actuarial equivalency under this paragraph shall be determined by the use of an interest rate assumption equal to the lesser of five per cent a year or the rate specified by the board as provided in § 38–711, paragraph 2.

"4. If the member's benefit is paid in a form other than an annual benefit, the benefit paid may not exceed the actuarial equivalent of the maximum annual benefit payable as a straight life annuity disregarding the portion of any joint and survivor annuity that constitutes a qualified joint and survivor annuity as defined in § 417 of the internal revenue code. Actuarial equivalency under this paragraph shall be determined by the use of an interest rate assumption equal to the greater of five per cent a year or the rate specified by the board as provided in § 38–711, paragraph 2.

"**D.** Notwithstanding subsections A, B, C and F of this section, the annual benefit payable under this article may be reduced to the extent necessary, as determined by the board, to prevent disqualification of ASRS under § 415 of the internal revenue code that imposes additional limitations on the annual benefits payable to members who also may be participating in another tax qualified pension or savings plan of this state, provided that for purposes of maximum benefits under this section, the benefit of ASRS is considered primary. An employer shall not provide employee retirement or deferred benefits if the benefits authorized by this section and as required by federal law result in the failure of ASRS to meet federal qualification standards as applied to public pension plans. The board shall advise affected members of any additional information concerning their annual benefits required by this subsection.

"**E.** If the maximum amount of benefit allowed under § 415 of the internal revenue code is increased after the commencement date of a member's benefit due to any cost of living adjustment announced by the United States internal revenue service pursuant to the provisions of § 415(d) of the internal revenue code, the amount of the monthly benefit payable under ASRS to a member whose benefit is restricted due to the provisions of § 415(d) of the internal revenue code shall be increased by the board as of the date prescribed by the United States secretary of the treasury or the secretary's designee on which the increase shall become effective. The increase shall reflect the increase in the amount of retirement income that may be payable under this article as a result of the cost of living adjustment.

"**F.** On termination of ASRS the accrued benefit of each member is, as of the date of termination, fully vested and nonforfeitable.

"**G.** In determining the adjustments authorized by subsections A and B of this section, the board shall prescribe a larger amount if prescribed by the United States secretary of the treasury pursuant to § 415(d) of the internal revenue code. To the extent provided in regulations promulgated by the United States secretary of the treasury, the adjustments to the limitation made by the board pursuant to subsection C, paragraph 1 of this section shall be applied separately to each change in the benefit structure of ASRS.

"**H.** For purposes of this section:

"1. 'Annual benefit' means a benefit payable annually in the form of a straight life annuity, disregarding the portion of a joint and survivor annuity that constitutes a qualified joint and survivor annuity as defined in § 417 of the internal revenue code, with no ancillary or incidental benefits or rollover contributions and excluding any portion of the benefit derived from member contributions or other contributions that are treated as a separate defined contribution plan under § 415 of the internal revenue code but including any of those contributions that are picked up by the employer under § 414(h) of the internal revenue code, or that otherwise are not treated as a separate defined contribution plan. If the benefit is payable in another form, the determination as to whether the limitation described in subsection C, paragraph 1 of this section has been satisfied shall be made by the board by adjusting the benefit so that it is actuarially equivalent to the annual benefit described in this section in accordance with the regulations promulgated by the United States secretary of the treasury for determining the annual benefit attributable to member contributions. The factors described in § 411(c)(2)(B) of the internal revenue code and the regulations promulgated under the internal revenue code shall be used by the board regardless of whether § 411 of the internal revenue code applies to ASRS.

"2. 'Compensation' means the member's earned income, wages, salaries, fees for professional service and other amounts received for personal services actually rendered in the course of employment with the employer. Compensation does not mean:

"(a) Employer contributions to a plan of deferred compensation to the extent the contributions are not included in the gross income of the employee for the taxable year in which contributed, on behalf of an employee to a simplified employee pension plan described in § 408(k) of the internal revenue code and any distributions from a plan of deferred compensation, regardless of whether the amounts are includable in gross income of the employee when distributed.

"(b) Other amounts that receive special tax benefits, such as premiums for group term life insurance, but only to the extent that the premiums are not includable in the gross income of the employee, or contributions made by the employer, whether or not under a salary reduction agreement, towards the purchase of an annuity contract described in § 403(b) of the internal revenue code, whether or not the contributions are excludable from the gross income of the employee.

"3. 'Defined benefit plan' has the same meaning prescribed in § 414(j) of the internal revenue code.

"4. 'Defined contribution plan' has the same meaning prescribed in § 414(i) of the internal revenue code.

"5. 'Limitation year' and 'years of service' means the fiscal year."

The 1997 amendment by Ch. 280 rewrote subsec. A; in subsec. C, par. 1, deleted ", paragraph 1" following "under subsection A", deleted "one hundred per cent of compensation limitation prescribed in subsection A, paragraph 2 of this section and the" following "also applies to the", and substituted "reduction applies" for "reductions apply"; substituted "the dollar limitation determined under subsection A of this section" for "a ninety thousand dollar annual benefit" in subsec. C, par. 2(b); inserted a new subsec. D relating to application of certain portions of subsec. C; redesignated former subsecs. D through L as subsecs. E through M and made changes in corresponding internal references; in subsec. E (former D), inserted "For limitation years beginning before July 1, 2000" in the introductory paragraph, and rewrote par. 1; in subsec. F (former E), inserted "beginning before July 1, 2000" in the introductory paragraph; deleted ", paragraph 1" following "in subsection A" in subsec. I (former H); deleted "Retroactive to July 1, 1996," from the beginning of subsec. J (former I); inserted a new subsec. N relating to retirement of members who were retired, who resumed active membership and who subsequently retire; redesignated former subsec. M as subsec. O, and in par. 3 of that subsection inserted the provision including amounts described in §§ 104(a)(3) and 105(a) of the Internal Revenue Code in the definition of compensation. Prior to amendment subsec. A and subsec. E (former D), par. 1, had read:

"**A.** Notwithstanding any other provision of this article, except as provided in subsection C of this section, the employer provided portion of a member's annual benefit, at any time within a limitation year, shall not exceed the lesser of:

"1. Ninety thousand dollars or a larger amount that is prescribed by the board and that is due to any cost of living adjustment announced by the United States secretary of the treasury pursuant to § 415(d) of the internal revenue code. The board shall increase the amount pursuant to this paragraph as of the effective date of the increase as prescribed by the United States secretary of the treasury .

"2. One hundred per cent of the member's average compensation for the member's high three consecutive years of service as provided in § 415 of the internal revenue code. For purposes of this paragraph, a member's high three consecutive years of service is the period of three consecutive years or the actual number of consecutive years of employment for a member who is employed less than three consecutive years with the employer during which the member had the greatest aggregate compensation from the employer."

"**D.** The board shall limit benefits payable to a member who is a member of ASRS and any other defined benefit plan maintained by the member's employer and a defined contribution plan maintained by the member's employer in a manner it determines to be necessary to prevent the sum of the following fractions from exceeding 1.0:

"1. The projected annual benefit of the member under ASRS and any other defined benefit plan maintained by the member's employer in which the member participated as of the date of determination divided by the lesser of:

"(a) The product of 1.25 multiplied by the dollar limitation in effect under subsection A, paragraph 1 of this section for the limitation year.

"(b) One hundred forty per cent of the member's average compensation for the member's high three consecutive years of service, as described in subsection A, paragraph 2 of this section."

The 1998 amendment by Ch. 155 added subsec. C, par. 5, relating to use of the mortality table; inserted "subdivision (a)" in subsec. E, par. 2(a); and rewrote subsec. O, par. 2, which had read:

"2. 'Annual benefit' means a benefit, including any portion of a member's retirement benefit payable to an alternate payee under a qualified domestic relations order that satisfies the requirements prescribed in § 414(p)(1)(A)(i) of the internal revenue code and § 38–773, payable annually in the form of a straight life annuity, disregarding the portion of a joint and survivor annuity that constitutes a qualified joint and survivor annuity as defined in § 417 of the internal revenue code, with no ancillary or incidental benefits or rollover contributions and excluding any portion of the benefit derived from member contributions or other contributions that are treated as a separate defined contribution plan under § 415 of the internal revenue code but including any of those contributions that are picked up by the employer under § 414(h) of the internal revenue code, or that otherwise are not treated as a separate defined contribution plan. If the benefit is payable in another form, the determination as to whether the limitation described in subsection C, paragraph 1 of this section has been satisfied shall be made by the board by adjusting the benefit so that it is actuarially equivalent to the annual benefit described in this section in accordance with the regulations promulgated by the United States secretary of the treasury for determining the annual benefit attributable to member contributions. The factors described in § 411(c)(2)(B) of the internal revenue code and the regulations promulgated under the internal revenue code shall be used by the board regardless of whether § 411 of the internal revenue code applies to ASRS."

The 2001 amendment by Ch. 136 deleted "Except for the limitations prescribed in subsection B of this section," and inserted "or 38–771.01" in subsec. J; and rewrote subsec. O, par. 1, which had read:

"**O.** For purposes of this section:

"1. "Annual additions" has the same meaning prescribed in 26 Code of Federal Regulations § 1.415–6(b)."

The 2002 amendment by Ch. 213, rewrote the section, which had read:

"**A.** Notwithstanding any other provision of this article, except as provided in subsection C of this section, the employer provided portion of a member's annual benefit, at any time within a limitation year, shall not exceed ninety thousand dollars or a larger amount that is prescribed by the board and that is due to any cost of living adjustment announced by the United States secretary of the treasury pursuant to § 415(d) of the internal revenue code. The board shall increase the amount pursuant to this paragraph as of the effective date of the increase as prescribed by the United States secretary of the treasury.

"**B.** Notwithstanding the limitations of subsection A of this section, the benefits payable to a member are deemed not to exceed the limitations determined under subsection A of this section if the retirement benefits payable to the member under this article do not exceed ten thousand dollars for the limitation year and if an employer has not at any time maintained a defined contribution plan in which the member has participated.

"**C.** The limitations determined under subsection A of this section are subject to the following adjustments:

"1. If a member has less than ten years of membership in ASRS, the maximum dollar limitation determined under subsection A of this section shall be multiplied by a fraction, the numerator of which is the number of years, or partial years, of membership in ASRS and the denominator of which is ten. The reduction provided in this paragraph also applies to the ten thousand dollar floor limitation provided in subsection B of this section, except that the reduction applies to years of service with an employer rather than to years of membership in ASRS. The reduction in this paragraph does not reduce the limitations determined under subsection A of this section to an amount less than one-tenth of the limitations as determined without regard to this paragraph.

"2. If a member's annual benefit commences before the member attains sixty-two years of age, the limitation determined under subsection A of this section shall be adjusted to the actuarial equivalent of an annual benefit equal to the dollar limitation commencing at sixty-two years of age. The actuarial equivalent under this paragraph shall not be less than seventy-five thousand dollars if a member's annual benefit commences at or after fifty-five years of age. If a member's annual benefit commences before fifty-five years of age, the actuarial equivalent shall equal the greater of:

"(a) The actuarial equivalent of a seventy-five thousand dollar annual benefit for fifty-five years of age.

"(b) The actuarial equivalent of the dollar limitation determined under subsection A of this section for sixty-two years of age.

"Actuarial equivalency under this paragraph shall be determined by the use of an interest rate assumption equal to the greater of five per cent a year or the rate specified by the board as provided in § 38–711, paragraph 2.

"3. If a member's annual benefit commences after sixty-five years of age, the limitation determined under subsection A of this section shall be adjusted to the actuarial equivalent of an annual benefit equal to the dollar limitation commencing at sixty-five years of age. Actuarial equivalency under this paragraph shall be determined by the use of an interest rate assumption equal to the lesser of five per cent a year or the rate specified by the board as provided in § 38–711, paragraph 2.

"4. If the member's benefit is paid in a form other than an annual benefit, the benefit paid may not exceed the actuarial equivalent of the maximum annual benefit payable as a straight life annuity disregarding the portion of any joint and survivor annuity that constitutes a qualified joint and survivor annuity as defined in § 417 of the internal revenue code. Actuarial equivalency under this paragraph shall be determined by the use of an interest rate assumption equal to the greater of five per cent a year or the rate specified by the board as provided in § 38–711, paragraph 2.

"5. For the purposes of adjusting any benefit or limitation under paragraph 2, 3 or 4 of this subsection, the board shall use the mortality table prescribed by the United States secretary of the treasury as required by § 415(b)(2)(E)(v) of the internal revenue code.

"**D.** Subsection C, paragraphs 1 and 2 of this section do not apply to income received from ASRS as a pension, annuity or similar allowance as a result of the recipient becoming disabled by personal injury or sickness or to amounts received from ASRS by beneficiaries, survivors or the estate of a member as a result of the death of the member.

"**E.** For limitation years beginning before July 1, 2000, the board shall limit benefits payable to a member who is a member of ASRS and any other defined benefit plan maintained by the member's employer and a defined contribution plan maintained by the member's employer in a manner it determines to be necessary to prevent the sum of the following fractions from exceeding 1.0:

"1. The projected annual benefit of the member under ASRS and any other defined benefit plan maintained by the member's employer in which the member participated as of the date of determination divided by the lesser of:

"(a) The product of 1.25 multiplied by the dollar limitation in effect under subsection A of this section for the limitation year.

"(b) One hundred forty per cent of the member's average compensation for the member's high three consecutive years of service. For the purposes of this subdivision, a member's high three consecutive years of service is the period of three consecutive years or the actual number of consecutive years of employment for a member who is employed less than three consecutive years with the employer during which the member had the greatest aggregate compensation from the employer.

"2. The sum of the annual additions on behalf of the member as of the limitation year in which the determination is made under ASRS and any defined contribution plan maintained by the member's employer divided by the lesser of the following amounts determined for the limitation year and for each prior year of service with the employer:

"(a) The product of 1.25 multiplied by the dollar limitation in effect under § 38–747, subsection E, paragraph 1, subdivision (a) for the limitation year.

"(b) Thirty–five per cent of the member's compensation in the limitation year.

"**F.** ASRS shall compute the fractions prescribed in subsection E of this section as of the close of any limitation year beginning before July 1, 2000. For the purposes of determining a member's projected annual benefit adjusted to an actuarially equivalent straight life annuity if the benefit is expressed in a form other than a straight life annuity or a qualified joint and survivor annuity as defined in § 417 of the internal revenue code under any defined benefit plan maintained by an employer and subject to the limitation prescribed by subsection E of this section, the benefit shall be based on the following assumptions:

"1. The member will continue covered employment until reaching the member's normal retirement date determined under the defined benefit plan or the current date, whichever is later.

"2. The member's compensation for the limitation year under consideration will remain constant until the member's normal retirement date or actual retirement.

"3. All other relevant factors used to determine benefits under the defined benefit plan will remain constant for all future limitation years.

"**G.** Notwithstanding any other provision of this section, the annual benefit payable under this article may be reduced to the extent necessary, as determined by the board, to prevent disqualification of ASRS under § 415 of the internal revenue code that imposes additional limitations on the annual benefits payable to members who also may be participating in another tax qualified pension or savings plan of this state. An employer shall not provide employee retirement or deferred benefits if the benefits authorized by this section and as required by federal law result in the failure of ASRS to meet federal qualification standards as applied to public pension plans. The board shall advise affected members of any additional information concerning their annual benefits required by this subsection.

"**H.** If the maximum amount of benefit allowed under § 415 of the internal revenue code is increased after the commencement date of a member's benefit due to any cost of living adjustment announced by the United States secretary of the treasury pursuant to the provisions of § 415(d) of the internal revenue code, the amount of the monthly benefit payable under ASRS to a member whose benefit is restricted due to the provisions of § 415(d) of the internal revenue code shall be increased by the board as of the date prescribed by the United States secretary of the treasury on which the increase shall become effective. The increase shall reflect the increase in the amount of retirement income that may be payable under this article as a result of the cost of living adjustment.

"**I.** In determining the adjustments authorized by subsections A and B of this section, the board shall prescribe a larger amount if prescribed by the United States secretary of the treasury pursuant to § 415(d) of the internal revenue code. An adjustment to the dollar limitation prescribed in subsection A of this section is not effective before the first calendar year for which the United States secretary of the treasury publishes the adjustment. After it is prescribed by the board, the new dollar limitation applies to the limitation year ending with or within the calendar year for which the secretary of the treasury makes the adjustment. To the extent provided in regulations promulgated by the United States secretary of the treasury, the adjustments to the limitation made by the board pursuant to subsection C, paragraph 1 of this section shall be applied separately to each change in the benefit structure of ASRS.

"**J.** For the purposes of the limitations prescribed by this section, all member and employer contributions made to ASRS to provide a member benefits pursuant to § 38–771 or 38–771.01 and all member contributions that are not treated as picked up by the employer under § 414(h)(2) of the internal revenue code shall be treated as made to a separate defined contribution plan.

"**K.** On termination of ASRS the accrued benefit of each member is, as of the date of termination, fully vested and nonforfeitable.

"**L.** If ASRS terminates, the benefit of any highly compensated employee as defined in § 414(q) of the internal revenue code and any highly compensated former employee is limited to a benefit that is nondiscriminatory under § 401(a)(4) of the internal revenue code and as follows:

"1. Benefits distributed to any of the twenty-five active and former highly compensated employees with the greatest compensation in the current or any prior fiscal year are restricted so that the annual payments are no greater than an amount equal to the payment that would be made on behalf of the member under a straight life annuity that is the actuarial equivalent of the sum of the member's accrued benefit, the member's other benefits under ASRS, excluding a social security supplement as defined in 26 Code of Federal Regulations § 1.411(a)–7(C)(4)(ii), and the amount the member is entitled to receive under a social security supplement.

"2. Paragraph 1 of this subsection does not apply if either:

"(a) After payment of the benefit to a member described in paragraph 1 of this subsection, the value of ASRS assets equals or exceeds one hundred ten per cent of the value of the current liabilities, as defined in § 412(*l*)(7) of the internal revenue code, of ASRS.

"(b) The value of the benefits for a member described in paragraph 1 of this subsection is less than one per cent of the value of the current liabilities, as defined in § 412(*l*)(7) of the internal revenue code, of ASRS before distribution.

"(c) The value of the benefits payable by ASRS to a member described in paragraph 1 of this subsection does not exceed three thousand five hundred dollars.

"**M.** For the purposes of subsection L of this section, 'benefit' includes loans in excess of the amount prescribed in § 72(p)(2)(A) of the internal revenue code, any periodic income, any withdrawal values payable to a living member and any death benefits not provided for by insurance on the member's life.

"**N.** On retirement of a member who was a retired member, who resumed active membership and who subsequently retires, the limitations of this section in effect on the member's subsequent retirement apply to the member's retirement benefit payable as recomputed pursuant to § 38–766. In addition, the sum of the present value of the member's recomputed retirement benefits plus the present value of the benefits the member received during the member's prior retirement shall not exceed the present value of the limitations in effect on the member's subsequent retirement. The limitations prescribed in this subsection shall not reduce a member's retirement benefit below the retirement benefit the member was receiving before the member resumed active membership. For the purposes of determining present value under this subsection, the board shall use the actuarial equivalent assumptions provided in § 38–711, paragraph 2.

"**O.** For purposes of this section:

"1. Annual additions shall be determined as provided in § 38–747, subsection M.

"2. 'Annual benefit' means a benefit, including any portion of a member's retirement benefit payable to an alternate payee under a qualified domestic relations order that satisfies the requirements prescribed in § 414(p)(1)(A)(i) of the internal revenue code and § 38–773, payable annually in the form of a straight life annuity, disregarding the portion of a joint and survivor annuity that constitutes a qualified joint and survivor annuity as defined in § 417 of the internal revenue code, with no ancillary or incidental benefits or rollover contributions and excluding any portion of the benefit derived from member contributions or other contributions that are treated as a separate defined contribution plan under § 415 of the internal revenue code but including any of those contributions that are picked up by the employer under § 414(h) of the internal revenue code, or that otherwise are not treated as a separate defined contribution plan. If the benefit is payable in another form, the determination as to whether the limitation described in subsection A of this section has been satisfied shall be made by the board by adjusting the benefit so that it is actuarially equivalent to the annual benefit described in this paragraph in accordance with the regulations promulgated by the United States secretary of the treasury. In addition, for determining the annual benefit attributable to member contributions, the factors described in § 411(c)(2)(B) of the internal revenue code and the regulations promulgated under the internal revenue code shall be used by the board regardless of whether § 411 of the internal revenue code applies to ASRS. The factors described in § 411(c)(2)(B) of the internal revenue code shall be those factors described under § 417(e)(3) of the internal revenue code and determined on the basis of the 417(e) mortality table and an interest rate equal to the annual yield for thirty-year treasury constant maturities, as reported in federal reserve statistical release G-13 and H-15, for the third full calendar month preceding the plan year for which the determination is made. For the purposes of this paragraph, 'the 417(e) mortality table' means the mortality table that is published by the United States treasury department as the table to be used for the purposes of § 417(e) of the internal revenue code to determine the single sum value of an accrued benefit.

"3. 'Compensation' means the member's earned income, wages, salaries, fees for professional service and other amounts received for personal services actually rendered in the course of employment with the employer and includes amounts described in §§ 104(a)(3) and 105(a) of the internal revenue code, but only to the extent that these amounts are includable in the gross income of the member. Compensation does not mean:

"(a) Employer contributions to a plan of deferred compensation to the extent the contributions are not included in the gross income of the employee for the taxable year in which contributed, on behalf of an employee to a simplified employee pension plan described in § 408(k) of the internal revenue code and any distributions from a plan of deferred compensation, regardless of whether the amounts are includable in gross income of the employee when distributed, except that any amount received by a member pursuant to an unfunded nonqualified plan may be considered as compensation for the purposes of this section in the year the amounts are includible in the gross income of the member under the internal revenue code.

"(b) Other amounts that receive special tax benefits, such as premiums for group term life insurance, but only to the extent that the premiums are not includable in the gross income of the employee, or contributions made by the employer, whether or not under a salary reduction agreement, towards the purchase of an annuity contract described in § 403(b) of the internal revenue code, whether or not the contributions are excludable from the gross income of the employee.

"4. 'Defined benefit plan' has the same meaning prescribed in § 414(j) of the internal revenue code.

"5. 'Defined contribution plan' has the same meaning prescribed in § 414(i) of the internal revenue code.

"6. 'Limitation year' and 'years of service' means the fiscal year."

Laws 2002, Ch. 213, § 9, subsec. A, provides:

"**Sec. 9. Retroactivity**

"**A.** Sections 38-766 and 38-769, Arizona Revised Statutes, as amended by this act, apply retroactively to July 1, 2001."

Former § 38-769, added by Laws 1959, Ch. 145, § 2, relating to state highway patrol retirement system retirement, was repealed by Laws 1995, Ch. 32, § 13, eff. March 30, 1995.

Reviser's Notes:

1997 Note. Pursuant to authority of § 41-1304.02, in subsection O, paragraph 2, first sentence, in the citation to section 414 of the internal revenue code "(i)" was substituted for "(I)" to correct a manifest clerical error.

§ 38-770. Eligible rollover distribution; definitions

A. Notwithstanding any other provision of this article that would limit a distributee's election under this section, a distributee may elect, at any time and in the manner prescribed by the board, to have any portion of an eligible rollover distribution paid directly to an eligible retirement plan specified by the distributee in a direct rollover.

B. An eligible rollover distribution may commence less than thirty days after the notice required under § 402(f) of the internal revenue code [1] is given to the distributee, provided that both:

1. ASRS clearly informs the distributee that the distributee has a right to a period of at least thirty days after receiving the notice to consider the decision of whether or not to elect a direct rollover.

2. The distributee, after receiving the notice, affirmatively elects a distribution.

C. For the purposes of this section:

1. "Direct rollover" means a payment by ASRS to the eligible retirement plan specified by the distributee.

2. "Distributee" means a member, a member's surviving spouse or a member's spouse or former spouse who is the alternate payee under an acceptable domestic relations order as defined in § 38–773.

3. "Eligible retirement plan" means any of the following that accepts a distributee's eligible rollover distribution:

(a) An individual retirement account described in § 408(a) of the internal revenue code.

(b) An individual retirement annuity described in § 408(b) of the internal revenue code.

(c) An annuity plan described in § 403(a) of the internal revenue code.

(d) A qualified trust described in § 401(a) of the internal revenue code.

(e) An annuity contract described in § 403(b) of the internal revenue code.

(f) An eligible deferred compensation plan described in § 457(b) of the internal revenue code that is maintained by a state, a political subdivision of a state or any agency or instrumentality of a state or a political subdivision of a state and that agrees to separately account for amounts transferred into the eligible deferred compensation plan from ASRS.

4. "Eligible rollover distribution" means distribution of all or any portion of the balance to the credit of the distributee but does not include any of the following:

(a) Any distribution that is one of a series of substantially equal periodic payments made not less frequently than annually for the life or life expectancy of the member or the joint lives or joint life expectancies of the member and the member's designated beneficiary or for a specified period of ten years or more.

(b) Any distribution to the extent the distribution is required under § 401(a)(9) of the internal revenue code.

(c) Except as provided in this paragraph, the portion of any distribution that is not includable in gross income. A distribution does not fail to be an eligible rollover distribution merely because the portion consists of after-tax employee contributions that are not includable in gross income if the portion is paid only to an individual retirement account or annuity described in § 408(a) or 408(b) of the internal revenue code or to a qualified defined contribution plan described in § 401 (a) or 403(a) of the internal revenue code that agrees to separately account for amounts so transferred, including separately accounting for the portion of the distribution that is includable in gross income and the portion of the distribution that is not includable in gross income.

(d) Any distribution that is made due to hardship of the member.

Added by Laws 1995, Ch. 32, § 14, eff. March 30, 1995. Amended by Laws 2002, Ch. 213, § 7, eff. May 15, 2002.

[1] Internal Revenue Code sections may be found in Title 26 of U.S.C.A.

Historical and Statutory Notes

Source:

A.R.S. former § 38-781.45.
Laws 1994, Ch. 356, § 20.

For state highway patrol retirement system and Arizona state retirement system savings clause and beneficiary longevity reserve account provisions of Laws 1995, Ch. 32, see Historical and Statutory Notes following § 38-744.

The 2002 amendment by Ch. 213, rewrote subsec. C, which had read:

"**C.** For the purposes of this section:

"1. 'Direct rollover' means a payment by ASRS to the eligible retirement plan specified by the distributee.

"2. 'Distributee' means a member, a member's surviving spouse or a member's former spouse.

"3. 'Eligible retirement plan' means:

"(a) For a member any of the following that accepts the distributee's eligible rollover distribution:

"(i) An individual retirement account described in § 408(a) of the internal revenue code.

"(ii) (b) An individual retirement annuity described in § 408(b) of the internal revenue code.

"(iii) An annuity plan described in § 403(a) of the internal revenue code.

"(iv) A qualified trust described in § 401(a) of the internal revenue code.

"(b) For a surviving or former spouse any of the following that accepts the distributee's eligible rollover distribution:

"(i) An individual retirement account described in § 408(a) of the internal revenue code.

"(ii) An individual retirement annuity described in § 408(b) of the internal revenue code.

"4. 'Eligible rollover distribution' means distribution of all or any portion of the balance to the credit of the distributee but does not include any of the following:

"(a) Any distribution that is one of a series of substantially equal periodic payments made not less frequently than annually for the life or life expectancy of the member or the joint lives or joint life expectancies of the member and the member's designated beneficiary or for a specified period of ten years or more.

"(b) Any distribution to the extent the distribution is required under § 401(a)(9) of the internal revenue code.

"(c) the portion of any distribution that is not includable in gross income.

"(c) the portion of any distribution that is not includable in gross income."

Laws 2002, Ch. 213, § 9, subsec. B, provides:

"**Sec. 9. Retroactivity**"

"**B.** Section 38-747, Arizona Revised Statutes, as amended by § 3 of this act, and § 38-770, Arizona Revised Statutes, as amended by this act, apply retroactively to January 1, 2002."

Former § 38-770, added by Laws 1959, Ch. 145, § 2, amended by Laws 1960, Ch. 42, § 1, relating to state highway patrol retirement system benefits, was repealed by Laws 1995, Ch. 32, § 13, eff. March 30, 1995.

§ 38-771. Benefit options for transferred defined contribution program members; definitions

A. On or before December 31, 1995 a nonretired ASRS member who was a member of the defined contribution program administered by ASRS and who was transferred to the defined benefit program established by this article on July 1, 1981 shall elect to receive either retirement benefits provided under this section or retirement benefits as otherwise provided by this article. An election under this subsection is irrevocable. A member who fails to make an election under this subsection is deemed to have elected to receive retirement benefits provided under this section.

B. A member who elects to receive retirement benefits provided under this section is eligible only for those benefits.

C. If a member elects to receive retirement benefits provided under this section, the member shall elect to receive retirement benefits based on either of the following:

1. The contributions paid by the member and member's employer, plus all earnings attributed to the member's retirement account, through the member's retirement date.

2. Except as provided in subsections E and F of this section, contributions paid by the member and member's employer at the contribution rate in effect before July 1, 1975 and an employee and employer contribution rate of seven per cent calculated from July 1, 1975, plus all earnings attributed to the member's retirement account, through the member's retirement date.

D. Notwithstanding §§ 38–736 and 38–737, members who elect to receive retirement benefits provided under this section and their employers shall each make contributions at a rate of seven per cent of the member's compensation and, beginning on July 1, 1998, employers shall make contributions to ASRS on behalf of their respective members who have elected to receive retirement benefits provided under this section to pay the actuarially determined amount necessary to provide the group health and accident insurance benefits for those retired members and their dependents as provided under § 38–783. Member contributions pursuant to this subsection shall be salary reduction contributions pursuant to § 38–747, subsections C and D.

E. Subject to subsection F of this section, if a member desires to receive retirement benefits based on subsection C, paragraph 2 of this section, the member shall make the election on or before June 30, 1999 and during the member's active employment. The election shall be made in accordance with § 38–747, subsections C, D and H. If a member elects to receive retirement benefits based on subsection C, paragraph 2 of this section, both the member and the member's employer shall pay to ASRS the difference between the contributions made and seven per cent of the member's gross compensation from July 1, 1984 through December 31, 1995. If a member elects to have the member's employer make payments for all or a portion of the contributions pursuant to § 38–747, subsection D, the member's employer shall make the contributions as required by § 38–747, subsection D. If a member elects to make contributions pursuant to § 38–747, subsection H, both the member and the member's employer shall pay to ASRS the portion of the difference between the total required contributions and that portion of the required contributions that the member has elected to have the member's employer pay pursuant to § 38–747, subsection D. The member's employer shall make the employer's contributions attributable to a member's period of employment before July 1, 1999 in a single lump sum payment at the time and computed in the manner prescribed in § 38–771.01, subsections G and H. If a member elects pursuant to subsection C, paragraph 2 of this section to have contributions made or to make contributions pursuant to § 38–747, subsection D or H for less than the full amount permitted by this subsection the member's benefits shall be computed only with reference to the contributions actually made. A member shall make an election pursuant to this section with respect to contributions to be made by the member before July 1, 1999. This election shall remain in full force and effect on and after July 1, 1999 and may be modified or revoked by the member only if the modification or revocation is specifically authorized in § 38–747. Section 38–771.01 governs any elections made by a member with respect to contributions to be made by the member to ASRS on or after July 1, 1999.

F. Contributions made to ASRS by a member and the member's employer pursuant to subsections D and E of this section shall not exceed, in any one limitation year, the limits of § 38–747, subsection E. If for any reason, the member and employer contributions to ASRS made pursuant to subsections D and E of this section would, at the time such contributions are due, taking into account other employer and member contributions due to ASRS for the limitation year, exceed the limits of § 38–747, the amount to be paid by the member and the member's employer under subsection E of this section shall be proportionately reduced and such reduction shall be carried into the succeeding limitation year and paid by the member and the member's employer within thirty days of the beginning of such limitation year, unless the limits of § 38–747 would again be exceeded, in which event this procedure will be repeated until all such contributions have been made. If more than one employer is contributing on behalf of a member, the reduction and contributions in succeeding years shall be proportionately allocated among the employers. If a member retires prior to making all contributions under subsections D and E of this section because of the limitations of § 38–747, the member's benefits under this section shall be calculated only with reference to the contributions actually made. For purposes of this subsection, "limitation year" has the same meaning prescribed in § 38–769.

G. A member who elects to receive retirement benefits provided under this section is subject to the provisions of § 38–771.01, subsection K that are equivalent to those imposed before the member's transfer from the defined contribution program administered by ASRS to the defined benefit program established by this article.

H. ASRS shall handle all retirement accounts of members who elect retirement benefits provided under this section and all member and employer contributions attributable to those members in the same manner as retirement accounts and contributions that are part of the defined contribution program administered by ASRS. Retirement accounts of members who elect to receive retirement benefits provided under this section are eligible for interest and supplemental credits on the same basis as members who retired under the defined contribution program administered by ASRS.

I. The election of retirement benefits by a member pursuant to this section is a waiver of all claims and demands by the member that the retirement benefits are less than the amount of retirement benefits payable to the member under the defined contribution program administered by ASRS if the member had remained a member of the defined contribution program administered by ASRS.

J. For purposes of this section:

1. "Member's employer" means an employer who compensated the member during a period when the member's contributions were less than seven per cent.

2. "Retirement account" means the combined member and employer contributions with interest or earnings on the contributions including any allocations credited as employer contributions.

Added by Laws 1995, Ch. 32, § 14, eff. March 30, 1995. Amended by Laws 1995, Ch. 134, § 10, eff. April 17, 1995; Laws 1996, Ch. 135, § 1; Laws 1997, Ch. 280, § 17; Laws 1999, Ch. 266, § 2, eff. July 1, 1999; Laws 1999, Ch. 327, § 17.

Historical and Statutory Notes

Source:

A.R.S. former § 38–781.44.
Laws 1991, Ch. 144, § 1.

For state highway patrol retirement system and Arizona state retirement system savings clause and beneficiary longevity reserve account provisions of Laws 1995, Ch. 32, see Historical and Statutory Notes following § 38–744.

The 1995 amendment by Ch. 134 rewrote the section, which formerly read:

"**A.** An ASRS member who was a member of the defined contribution program administered by ASRS and who was transferred to the defined benefit program established by this article on July 1, 1981 may elect one of the following benefit options at the time of retirement or termination:

"1. Retirement benefits provided under this article.

"2. Retirement benefits provided by the defined contribution program administered by ASRS.

"**B.** If a member elects benefits pursuant to subsection A, paragraph 2, the member shall elect to receive benefits based on either of the following:

"1. The contributions paid by the member and member's employer.

"2. Contributions paid by the member and member's employer before July 1, 1975 and an employee and employer contribution rate of seven per cent calculated from July 1, 1975 to the date of retirement or termination as provided in subsection C.

"**C.** If a member chooses benefits pursuant to subsection B, paragraph 2, both the member and the member's employer shall pay to ASRS the difference between the contribution made and seven per cent of the member's gross salary from July 1, 1984 to the date the member retires or terminates. Interest and supplemental credits shall be charged to the assets of ASRS.

"**D.** The election of benefits by a member pursuant to this section is a waiver of all claims and demands by the member that the benefits are less than the amount of benefits payable to the member under the defined contribution program administered by ASRS if the member had remained a member of the defined contribution program administered by ASRS.

"**E.** For purposes of this section, 'member's employer' means the employer who compensated the member during a period when the member's contributions were less than seven per cent."

Laws 1995, Ch. 134, § 19, provides:

"**Sec. 19. Legislative intent; election; definitions**

"**A.** The purpose of § 38–771, Arizona Revised Statutes, as amended by this act, is to preserve the benefit rights of nonretired members of the system who were transferred from the system to the plan pursuant to Laws 1980, chapter 238. Laws 1980, chapter 238 guaranteed that benefits payable under the plan to a member of the system who was transferred to membership in the plan under that act would not be less than the retirement benefits payable to the member under the system if the member had remained a member of the system.

"**B.** The legislature does not intend that the benefit rights of members of the plan who were transferred from the system to the plan be affected by this act.

"**C.** In order to comply with article II, § 25, Constitution of Arizona, the Arizona state retirement system shall hold an election pursuant to § 38–771, Arizona Revised Statutes, as amended by this act, for members of the plan with benefit rights established by Laws 1980, chapter 238.

"**D.** For the purpose of this section:

"1. 'Plan' means the defined benefit program established pursuant to title 38, chapter 5, article 2, Arizona Revised Statutes.

"2. 'System' means the defined contribution program administered by the Arizona state retirement system."

The 1996 amendment by Ch. 135 inserted the exception provision at the beginning of subsec. C, par. 2; in subsec. E, substituted "June 30, 1999" for "December 31, 1995" and added the last sentence, including pars. 1 and 2; and made nonsubstantive changes.

Laws 1996, Ch. 135, § 2, provides:

"**Sec. 2. Retroactivity**

"This act applies retroactively to April 17, 1995."

Laws 1997, Ch. 203, § 1, providing for benefit options for transferred defined contribution program members, and Laws 1997, Ch. 203, § 3, as amended by Laws 1999, Ch. 266, § 4, eff. July 1, 1999, providing for the definition of eligible member, and Laws 1997, Ch. 203, § 2, were repealed by Laws 1997, Ch. 203, § 4, effective January 1, 2003 and January 1, 2001, respectively.

The 1997 amendment by Ch. 280 rewrote subsecs. D and E which had read:

"**D.** Beginning January 1, 1996 and notwithstanding §§ 38–736 and 38–737, members who elect to receive retirement benefits provided under this section and their employers shall each make contributions at a rate of seven per cent of the member's compensation.

"**E.** Subject to subsection F of this section, if a member elects to receive retirement benefits based on subsection C, paragraph 2 of this section, both the member and the member's employer shall pay to ASRS on or before June 30, 1999 or the member's retirement date, whichever is earlier, the difference between the contributions made and seven per cent of the member's gross compensation from July 1, 1984 through December 31, 1995 or the member's retirement date, whichever is earlier. Interest and supplemental credits for the additional contributions shall be credited to the member's retirement account and charged to the assets of ASRS at the time the additional contributions are paid. If a member makes additional contributions for less than the full amount required by this subsection:

"1. The member's employer shall pay only the reduced amount.

"2. The member's benefits shall be calculated only with reference to the contributions actually made."

The 1999 amendment by Ch. 266 rewrote the section.

Laws 1999, Ch. 266, § 6, provides:

"**Sec. 6. Conditional enactment; retroactivity**

"**A.** The effective date of this act shall be the later of the date the Arizona state retirement system receives notification from the United States internal revenue service that the employer contributions required by this act do not exceed the limitations of § 415 of the internal revenue code or the date the judgment entered by the court in the class action titled James J. Burke v. ASRS, et al., Pima County Cause No. 316479 pursuant to the settlement of the parties becomes final. If, for any reason prior to January 1, 2000, the Arizona state retirement system does not receive notification from the United States internal revenue service or the final judgment is not entered by the court, then this act does not become effective. The Arizona state retirement system shall notify the director of the Arizona legislative council of the date on which the condition is met.

"**B.** Notwithstanding the date on which the conditions prescribed in subsection A are met, the provisions of this act that are designated to be effective on July 1, 1999 apply retroactively to July 1, 1999."

EDITOR'S NOTE: [Letter dated December 29, 1999 from Arizona State Retirement System to Arizona Legislative Council indicated conditional enactment provisions have been met and that Laws 1999, Ch. 266 is retroactively effective to July 1, 1999.]

The 1999 amendment by Ch. 327, in subsec. F, rewrote pars. 5 and 6, which had read:

"5. If a retired member who is receiving retirement benefits provided under this section is engaged to work by an employer for twenty or more weeks in a fiscal year and twenty hours or more per week and is required or elects to be covered by the defined benefit program established by this article, the retired member commences active membership in the defined benefit program and the member's retirement benefit payments under this section are suspended until the member terminates employment.

"6. On termination of employment of a retired member previously receiving retirement benefits provided under this section, ASRS shall reinstate the member's retirement benefits provided under this section and the member is entitled to receive retirement benefits as provided in § 38–760 for the credited service earned by the member after the member's active membership in the defined benefit program established pursuant to this article commenced."

The amendment of this section by Laws 1999, Ch. 327, § 17 was repealed by Laws 2000, Ch. 315, § 2.

Former § 38–771, added by Laws 1959, Ch. 145, § 2, relating to state highway patrol retirement system disability benefits, was repealed by Laws 1995, Ch. 32, § 13, eff. March 30, 1995.

§ 38–771.01. Alternative benefits for transferred defined contribution program members; definitions

A. A retired or nonretired ASRS member who was a member of the defined contribution program administered by ASRS, who was transferred to the defined benefit program established by this article on July 1, 1981, who is determined by ASRS to qualify under paragraph 1 of this subsection and who is not excluded under paragraph 2 of this subsection shall receive defined contribution benefits pursuant to this section, or, if greater, defined benefit retirement benefits pursuant to this article. A retired or nonretired ASRS member qualifies or is excluded under this section based on the following criteria:

1. A member is entitled to receive benefits under this section only if the member satisfies at least one of the following requirements:

(a) Is not retired as of July 1, 1999 even though the member may have previously elected to receive benefits under the defined benefit program established by this article, may have transferred employment between or among employers on or after July 1, 1981 or may have terminated employment on or after July 1, 1981 and after that termination date returned to employment with an employer.

(b) Retired on or after July 1, 1984 and elected to receive benefits under the defined benefit program established by this article.

(c) Retired on or after July 1, 1984 and is receiving benefits under the defined contribution program administered by ASRS.

2. Even if the member otherwise qualifies under paragraph 1 of this subsection, a member is not entitled to receive benefits under this section if any of the following applies to the member:

(a) The member retired before July 1, 1984.

(b) The member is entitled to receive benefits pursuant to § 38–771 and has paid to ASRS pursuant to § 38–771 before July 1, 1999 the entire amount that is attributable to service performed on or after July 1, 1984 and that is equal to the contribution rate of seven per cent of compensation, the contribution has been matched by an equal contribution to ASRS by the member's employers and all applicable earnings and supplemental credits have been credited for the member's account.

(c) The member withdrew the member's contributions from the defined contribution program administered by ASRS and, as of July 1, 1999, is not entitled to any benefit under the defined contribution program administered by ASRS.

(d) The member transferred the member's benefits under either the defined benefit program established by this article or the defined contribution program administered by ASRS to any other retirement system.

B. A beneficiary is entitled to receive benefits pursuant to this section only if the beneficiary satisfies the requirements of paragraph 1 of this subsection and is not excluded under paragraph 2 of this subsection based on the following criteria:

1. The beneficiary is a beneficiary of a retired or nonretired member who qualifies for benefits under subsection A, paragraph 1 of this section, is not excluded under subsection A, paragraph 2 of this section and as of July 1, 1999 either:

(a) Is receiving a monthly benefit from the defined benefit program established by this article or the defined contribution program administered by ASRS.

(b) Is living, is a survivor of a deceased retired or nonretired member and elected to receive a lump sum distribution of the survivor benefit that was payable on the death of the member.

2. Even if the beneficiary satisfies the requirements of paragraph 1 of this subsection, a beneficiary is not entitled to receive benefits under this section if the beneficiary is a beneficiary of a deceased retired member who elected a form of benefit under either the defined benefit program established by this article or the defined contribution program administered by ASRS that did not provide for survivor benefits after the death of the retired member.

C. A member or a deceased member's beneficiary who receives benefits pursuant to this section shall receive benefits based on the sum of the following:

1. Contributions paid by the member and the member's employer at the contribution rates in effect before July 1, 1984, together with all applicable earnings and supplemental credits on those contributions.

2. Contributions paid by the member's employer at the contribution rates in effect beginning on July 1, 1984 through the earlier of June 30, 1999 or the member's retirement or death, together with all applicable earnings and supplemental credits on those contributions computed through the earlier of June 30, 1999 or the member's retirement or death.

3. The excess of employer contributions computed at the rate of seven per cent of compensation beginning on July 1, 1984 through June 30, 1999 over the actual contributions paid by the member's employer as described in paragraph 2 of this subsection, together with all earnings and supplemental credits that would have been earned on those excess contributions computed from the date the contributions would have been paid to ASRS.

4. Contributions paid by the member at the contribution rate in effect on and after July 1, 1984, together with all earnings on those contributions.

5. With respect to member contributions that were not paid to ASRS before July 1, 1999 pursuant to § 38–771, subsection C, paragraph 2, forty per cent of the earnings that would have been credited on those contributions through the earlier of June 30, 1999 or the member's retirement or death as if those member contributions had been paid.

6. Contributions paid by the member to ASRS before July 1, 1999 pursuant to an election under § 38–771, subsection C, paragraph 2 and subsection E, together with all earnings on those contributions.

7. Contributions paid by the member to ASRS on or after July 1, 1999 pursuant to an election under § 38–771, subsection C, paragraph 2 and subsection E, together with earnings on those contributions.

8. Contributions paid by the member to ASRS on or after July 1, 1999 pursuant to this section, together with earnings on those contributions.

9. Contributions paid by the member's employer to ASRS on or after July 1, 1999 pursuant to this section, together with all applicable earnings and supplemental credits on those contributions.

D. Effective on July 1, 1999, ASRS shall adjust the retirement account reserves under the defined contribution program administered by ASRS for retired members and the beneficiaries of deceased retired members entitled to benefits pursuant to this section to give effect to additional contributions, earnings and supplemental credits for those retired members prescribed in subsection C, paragraphs 1 through 6 of this section for the periods of the members' employment before July 1, 1999 and to give effect to the recomputation, adjustment and payment of benefits pursuant to subsection G of this section. After this recomputation, adjustment and payment, ASRS shall credit and charge these retirement account reserves with the amounts prescribed under the defined contribution program administered by ASRS based on the adjustments prescribed in this section.

E. Effective on July 1, 1999, ASRS shall adjust each nonretired member's accounts under the defined contribution program administered by ASRS to equal the sum of the contribution amounts prescribed in subsection C, paragraphs 1 through 6 of this section with respect to periods of a member's employment before July 1, 1999. After the adjustment, these accounts shall accrue applicable interest and supplemental credits based on the entire amounts credited to the accounts.

F. For periods of a nonretired member's employment on or after July 1, 1999, a nonretired member who is entitled to receive benefits pursuant to this section and the nonretired member's employer shall each make contributions to ASRS at the rates established pursuant to §§ 38–736 and 38–737, except as follows:

1. If a nonretired member made an election pursuant to § 38–771, subsection C, paragraph 2 and § 38–747, subsections C and D before July 1, 1999, the member's employer shall continue to make pickup contributions to ASRS on behalf of the member pursuant to the member's election, except that with respect to employer contributions that are required pursuant to § 38–771, subsection E for periods of a member's employment before July 1, 1999, the employer shall make a lump sum payment to ASRS as computed pursuant to subsection G of this section and required to be paid to ASRS pursuant to subsection H of this section.

2. If a nonretired member elected or was deemed to have elected benefits pursuant to § 38–771 before December 31, 1995, for periods of a member's employment from and after the election or deemed election the nonretired member's employer and the member shall each continue to pay to ASRS an amount equal to seven per cent of the member's compensation in lieu of the rates established pursuant to §§ 38–736 and 38–737.

3. A nonretired member who is entitled to receive benefits pursuant to this section and who never elected to receive benefits pursuant to § 38–771 may elect pursuant to § 38–747, subsections C and D to make contributions at the rate of seven per cent of the member's compensation for periods of a member's employment on or after July 1, 1999. If a member makes an election pursuant

to this paragraph, the election is irrevocable as provided in § 38-747, subsection D and the member and the member's employer shall each make contributions at a rate of seven per cent of the member's compensation beginning on the effective date of the election.

4. A nonretired member who is entitled to receive benefits pursuant to this section may elect pursuant to § 38-747, subsections C, D and H to make contributions with respect to member contributions that were not made to ASRS but that could have been made pursuant to § 38-771, subsection C, paragraph 2 for periods of employment before July 1, 1999 other than member contributions for which an irrevocable election pursuant to § 38-747, subsections C and D was in effect before July 1, 1999.

5. In addition to any other employer contributions required pursuant to this section, a nonretired member's employer shall make contributions to ASRS on behalf of the nonretired member who will receive retirement benefits pursuant to this section to pay the actuarially determined amount necessary to provide the group health and accident insurance benefits for the nonretired member and the nonretired member's dependents as provided under § 38-783.

6. Notwithstanding any other provision of this article, an election permitted pursuant to this section shall not revoke, amend or alter any irrevocable election made by a member before July 1, 1999 pursuant to §§ 38-747 and 38-771.

G. Effective on July 1, 1999, ASRS shall recompute the monthly and annual benefits for retired members entitled to receive benefits pursuant to this section and the monthly or lump sum survivor's benefits payable to beneficiaries entitled to receive benefits pursuant to this section. The recomputation of benefits shall be as if the member's retirement account or retirement reserve account on the date of retirement or death had been computed based on the amounts that would have been credited to the account as of that date based on the contribution amounts prescribed in subsection C, paragraphs 1 through 6 of this section. In addition and after recomputing benefits described in this subsection, with respect to members who retired on or after July 1, 1984, ASRS shall recompute the annual payments that would have been made to the member or beneficiary of a deceased member entitled to receive benefits under this section in excess of the annual payments actually made. The recomputation shall be calculated and paid as follows:

1. The recomputation shall be calculated and paid based on the member's and, if applicable, the member's beneficiary's age, the benefit option selected at the date of the initial benefit payments and the actuarial assumptions used by ASRS at the time the initial benefit payments were computed.

2. Before July 1, 2000, ASRS shall pay to the retired member or beneficiary in a lump sum the difference between the recomputed amount and the actual distributions paid to the member or beneficiary through July 1, 1999, together with interest at the rate of eight per cent a year, compounded monthly, computed from the date each excess payment should have been paid through the date of payment to the retired member or beneficiary.

3. If the retired member is living, ASRS shall pay the lump sum payment to the member. If the member is deceased and is survived by a beneficiary who is

then living and receiving a monthly benefit on account of the deceased member, ASRS shall pay the lump sum payment to the beneficiary. The payment to the beneficiary shall include the recomputed amount that is payable pursuant to this section and that would have been paid to the member through the date of the member's death plus the recomputed amount that is payable pursuant to this section and that would have been payable to the beneficiary from the member's date of death. Section 38-770 applies to a payment to a member or the member's beneficiary who is the surviving spouse of the member, if the payment is substantially larger or smaller than the monthly benefit payable by ASRS to the member.

4. With respect to a beneficiary who is a survivor of a deceased nonretired member who would have been entitled to benefits under this section and who elected a lump sum distribution of the survivor benefit that was payable on the death of the nonretired member, ASRS shall pay the recomputed amount in a lump sum to the beneficiary. If the beneficiary is the surviving spouse of the member, § 38-770 applies to the payment.

5. Effective on July 1, 1999, ASRS shall increase the member's or beneficiary's monthly and annual benefit to the recomputed amount. After that adjustment, ASRS shall adjust the member's or beneficiary's annual benefit as otherwise provided under the defined contribution program administered by ASRS.

H. Before July 1, 2002, the employer of each nonretired or retired member or deceased member who has a beneficiary entitled to adjustments and payments pursuant to subsections E and G of this section for periods of a member's employment before July 1, 1999 shall pay to ASRS in one or more installments those amounts required by ASRS to make the recomputations and adjustments pursuant to this section. ASRS shall determine the amount to be paid by the employer to ASRS as of July 1, 1999, plus interest at the rate of eight per cent a year, compounded monthly, from July 1, 1999 through the date the payment is made by the employer to ASRS. Any payments by the employer shall first be applied to accrued and unpaid interest and then to the amount to be paid by the employer to ASRS. ASRS shall allocate the payment to the assets maintained under the defined contribution program administered by ASRS. When determining the amounts required to be paid by employers for the recomputations and adjustments pursuant to this section, ASRS first shall transfer on July 1, 1999 from the assets maintained by ASRS under the defined benefit program established by this article to the assets maintained by ASRS under the defined contribution program administered by ASRS an amount equal to the sum of the defined benefit program equity balances of the retired and nonretired members or their beneficiaries whose benefits are transferred from the defined benefit program to the defined contribution program pursuant to this section, except that the amount transferred for any member or beneficiary shall not be more than the amount required to fund the recomputations and adjustments required by this section for the member or beneficiary. The defined benefit program equity balance for a member or beneficiary of a deceased member shall equal the sum of the member's employee and employer account balances on the earlier of June 30, 1999 or the member's retirement or death, less the monthly annuity payments to a retired member or beneficiary, plus the earnings on the average balance of that amount for a plan year.

I. If a member retired before July 1, 1999, elected to receive benefits pursuant to § 38–771, subsection C, paragraph 2 and did not make all contributions pursuant to § 38–771, subsection E because of the limitations prescribed in § 38–747, subsection E, the member has the option of receiving the employer contributions prescribed in subsection C, paragraphs 3 and 5 of this section in a lump sum payment. If the retired member elects to receive a lump sum payment, ASRS shall pay the amount on or before July 1, 2000 and the amount shall be deducted from the member's account when computing the annuity benefits to which the member is otherwise entitled pursuant to this section. In no case shall the payment under this subsection duplicate the payment under subsection G of this section. Section 38–770 applies to a payment to a member under this subsection if the payment is substantially larger or smaller than the monthly benefit payable by ASRS to the member.

J. Contributions made to ASRS by a member and the member's employer pursuant to subsection F of this section, other than employer contributions required pursuant to subsections G and H of this section, shall not exceed, in any one limitation year, the limits prescribed in § 38–747, subsection E. If for any reason the member and applicable employer contributions made pursuant to subsection F of this section would at the time the contributions are due, taking into account other annual additions due to ASRS for the limitation year, exceed the limits prescribed in § 38–747, subsection E, the amount to be paid by the member and the member's employer pursuant to subsection F of this section, other than employer contributions required pursuant to subsections G and H of this section, shall be proportionately reduced and the reduction shall be carried into the succeeding limitation year and paid by the member and the member's employer within thirty days after the beginning of that limitation year, unless the limits prescribed in § 38–747, subsection E would again be exceeded. If the limits are exceeded again, the procedure prescribed in this subsection shall be repeated until all of the contributions are made. If more than one employer is contributing on behalf of a member, the reduction and contributions in succeeding years shall be proportionately allocated among the employers. If a member retires before making all contributions pursuant to this section because of the limitations prescribed in § 38–747, subsection E, the member's benefits pursuant to this section shall be computed only with reference to the contributions actually made. For the purposes of this subsection, "limitation year" has the same meaning prescribed in § 38–769.

K. Unless otherwise provided in this section, a member who receives retirement benefits pursuant to this section and § 38–771 is subject to conditions that are equivalent to those imposed before the member's transfer from the defined contribution program administered by ASRS to the defined benefit program established by this article. Those conditions include the following:

1. A member who attains sixty-five years of age may retire and, on application, shall receive a life annuity derived from the member's prior service credit, if any, together with a life annuity derived from the member's retirement account. The annuity is payable in equal monthly installments. The amount of the installments is based on the age of the member at the date of commence-

ment of retirement and is determined by the interest and life expectancy tables applicable at the date of the commencement of retirement.

2. If a retired member who is receiving retirement benefits pursuant to this section dies before receipt of annuity payments in an amount equal to the member's retirement account balance immediately before retirement, ASRS shall pay the member's designated beneficiary or estate in a lump sum the difference between the retirement account balance and the total amount of annuity payments received.

3. A member who attains sixty-five years of age with at least five years of creditable service may retire and, on application, may elect to receive in lieu of the annuity payments from the member's prior service, if any, together with a life annuity derived from the member's retirement account as provided in paragraph 1 of this subsection, the actuarial equivalent of those retirement benefits under one of the options established by the board.

4. A member who attains sixty years of age with at least five years of creditable service may retire and, on application, may receive a life annuity derived from the actuarial equivalent of the member's prior service credit, if any, together with a life annuity derived from the member's retirement account. The annuity shall be determined and paid in the manner set forth in paragraph 1 of this subsection.

5. In lieu of the retirement benefits pursuant to paragraph 4 of this subsection, on application, a member may elect to receive the actuarial equivalent of those retirement benefits under one of the options established by the board.

6. If a retired member who is receiving retirement benefits pursuant to this section is engaged to work by an employer for twenty or more weeks in a fiscal year and twenty hours or more a week, the member's retirement benefit payments pursuant to this section are suspended until the member terminates employment. On return to employment, the member shall accrue benefits pursuant to this section, unless the member elects to be covered by the defined benefit program established by this article. If a formerly retired member elects to be covered by the defined benefit program established by this article, the formerly retired member shall be an active member in the defined benefit program with respect to all service performed after the member's return to work and shall not accrue additional benefits pursuant to this section. Notwithstanding the other provisions of this paragraph, if a retired member begins or returns to employment as an elected official or to any other type of service or employment that does not require the retired member to begin active membership in the defined contribution program administered by ASRS or the defined benefit program established by this article, the payment of retirement benefits pursuant to this section shall not be terminated, withheld or interrupted because of beginning or returning to the service or employment or holding the elected office, unless the formerly retired member actually elects to recommence active participation in the defined benefit program established by this article or pursuant to this section.

7. On termination of employment of a retired member previously receiving retirement benefits pursuant to this section, ASRS shall reinstate the member's retirement benefits pursuant to this section and, on reinstatement of retirement

benefits, the benefit shall be recomputed on the basis of the member's attained age and shall be adjusted for retirement benefits previously received and additional contributions, interest and supplemental credits accrued during the period of employment. On this reinstatement of retirement benefits, if the member elected to be covered by the defined benefit program established by this article on the member's return to employment, the member is also entitled to receive retirement benefits pursuant to the defined benefit program established by this article for the credited service earned by the member after the member's active membership in the defined benefit program established by this article began.

L. ASRS shall handle all retirement accounts of members who elect retirement benefits provided pursuant to this section and all member and employer contributions attributable to those members in the same manner as retirement accounts and contributions that are part of the defined contribution program administered by ASRS. Retirement accounts of members who elect to receive retirement benefits pursuant to this section are eligible for interest and supplemental credits on the same basis as members who retired under the defined contribution program administered by ASRS.

M. The receipt of retirement benefits by a member pursuant to this section is a waiver of all claims and demands by the member that the retirement benefits are less than the amount of retirement benefits payable to the member under the defined contribution program administered by ASRS if the member had remained a member of the defined contribution program administered by ASRS.

N. The board may administer and interpret this section in order to prevent any duplication of benefits provided by ASRS and the defined contribution program administered by ASRS and to provide all eligible members and beneficiaries with the benefits they are entitled to under the laws of this state.

O. For purposes of this section:

1. "Beneficiary" means the individual designated by the member in writing on forms approved by ASRS to receive benefits pursuant to this article after the death of the member.

2. "Creditable service" means service after April 8, 1953 in a position not subject to the defined contribution program administered by ASRS, prior service and membership service.

3. "Member's employer" means an employer who compensated the member during a period when the member's contributions were less than seven per cent.

4. "Pension" means equal monthly installments that are derived from a member's prior service credits and that are payable during the member's lifetime after retirement.

5. "Prior service" means service for this state or a political subdivision before membership in the defined contribution program administered by ASRS.

6. "Prior service credits" means the amount that is allowed for services before membership in the defined contribution program administered by ASRS and that is payable as a pension on retirement.

7. "Retirement account" means the combined member and employer contributions with applicable interest and supplemental credits on the contributions as computed pursuant to subsection C of this section.

8. "Service" means any compensated employment by the state or a political subdivision and includes periods of nonpaid leave, including military leave, provided employment has not been terminated at the commencement of the leave period and employment is state service for retirement purposes or service for any political subdivision establishing a defined contribution program administered by ASRS.38-771.

Added by Laws 1999, Ch. 266, § 3, eff. July 1, 1999. Amended by Laws 2000, Ch. 315, § 3.

Historical and Statutory Notes

Laws 1999, Ch. 266, §§ 5 and 6, provide:

"**Sec. 5. Applicability; prior election void; attorney fees and costs**

"**A.** Section 38-771.01, Arizona Revised Statutes, as added by this act, only provides benefits for members of ASRS or their beneficiaries who are described in § 38-771.01, Arizona Revised Statutes, as added by this act, and who do not elect to opt out of coverage within the class action suit titled James J. Burke v. ASRS, et al., Pima County Cause No. 316479. If a member or beneficiary elects to opt out of coverage under that class action suit, the member or beneficiary is not entitled to any benefits provided pursuant to § 38-771.01, Arizona Revised Statutes, as added by this act, but is entitled to benefits only as provided in § 38-771, Arizona Revised Statutes, and Laws 1997, chapter 203 or as otherwise provided by title 38, chapter 5, article 2, Arizona Revised Statutes.

"**B.** If an eligible member as defined in Laws 1997, chapter 203, § 3, as amended by this act, previously received or elected to receive payment from the member's employer as provided in Laws 1997, chapter 203 and that member is entitled to benefits under § 38-771.01, Arizona Revised Statutes, as added by this act, the member's election to receive the payment is void and of no further force and effect.

"**C.** If a member described in subsection B of this section previously received a payment from the member's employer pursuant to Laws 1997, chapter 203, the member shall return to the employer the gross amount of the payment, undiminished by any federal and state income taxes withheld by the employer from the payment and without interest, on or before December 31, 1999, unless the court in the class action titled James J. Burke v. ASRS, et al., Pima County Cause No. 316479 orders the member not to return all or any portion of the payment based on objective criteria not specific to any one member submitted to the court demonstrating that the member is not financially capable of returning all or a portion of the payment.

"**D.** If the member obtains an order not to return all or any portion of the payment to the employer, the gross amount of the payment, undiminished by any federal and state income and employment taxes withheld by the employer from the payment, that was previously paid to the member and that is not returned to the employer shall be subtracted by ASRS in computing the amount that ASRS will credit to the member's account pursuant to § 38-771.01, subsection C, Arizona Revised Statutes, as added by this act. Notwithstanding any provision to the contrary in § 38-771.01, Arizona Revised Statutes, as added by this act, if a member described in subsection C of this section does not return the entire payment to the employer on or before July 1, 1999, ASRS shall not recompute the member's account pursuant to § 38-771.01, subsection C, Arizona, Revised Statutes, as added by this act, until the earlier of the date the member repays the payment, the date the member obtains a court order that the amount will not be required to be returned to the employer or December 31, 1999. If the total repayment has not been made by December 31, 1999 and the member has not previously obtained a court order that the repayment is not required, in recomputing the member's account pursuant to § 38-771.01, Arizona Revised Statutes, as added by this act, ASRS shall subtract the unpaid amount from the recomputation until the member repays the payment to the employer. Any amount repaid after December 31, 1999 shall bear interest at eight per cent a year, compounded monthly.

"**E.** The employers whose former or present employees are entitled to benefits under § 38-771.01, Arizona Revised Statutes, as added by this act, shall pay the reasonable attorney fees and costs incurred by the plaintiffs in the class action suit titled James J. Burke v. ASRS, et al., Pima County Cause No. 316479, as may be awarded by the court. The attorney fees and costs shall be prorated among the employers based on the amount each employer is required to contribute to ASRS pursuant to § 38-771.01, Arizona Revised Statutes, as added by this act, as compared to the total amount all such employers are required to contribute to ASRS. ASRS shall compute the amount each employer is required to contribute to ASRS for the attorney fees and costs and inform each employer of the amount of the payment no later than December 31, 1999. Each employer shall pay its portion of the attorney fees and costs to ASRS on or before June 30, 2000. ASRS shall deposit the amounts paid in accounts that are separate from the assets of the defined contribution program administered by ASRS and the defined benefit program established by title 38, chapter 5, article 2, Arizona Revised Statutes. ASRS shall pay the attorney fees and costs from the monies maintained by ASRS in the separate accounts.

"**F.** The terms used in this section have the same meaning prescribed in § 38–711, Arizona Revised Statutes, and § 38–771.01, Arizona Revised Statutes, as added by this act.

"**Sec. 6. Conditional enactment; retroactivity**

"**A.** The effective date of this act shall be the later of the date the Arizona state retirement system receives notification from the United States internal revenue service that the employer contributions required by this act do not exceed the limitations of § 415 of the internal revenue code or the date the judgment entered by the court in the class action titled James J. Burke v. ASRS, et al., Pima County Cause No. 316479 pursuant to the settlement of the parties becomes final. If, for any reason prior to January 1, 2000, the Arizona state retirement system does not receive notification from the United States internal revenue service or the final judgment is not entered by the court, then this act does not become effective. The Arizona state retirement system shall notify the director of the Arizona legislative council of the date on which the condition is met.

"**B.** Notwithstanding the date on which the conditions prescribed in subsection A are met, the provisions of this act that are designated to be effective on July 1, 1999 apply retroactively to July 1, 1999."

EDITOR'S NOTE: [Letter dated December 29, 1999 from Arizona State Retirement System to Arizona Legislative Council indicated conditional enactment provisions have been met and that Laws 1999, Ch. 266 is retroactively effective to July 1, 1999.]

The 2000 amendment by Ch. 315 rewrote subsec. G, par. 3, and the last sentence of subsec. I, which had read:

[G.] "3. If the retired member is living, ASRS shall pay the lump sum payment to the member. If the member is deceased and is survived by a beneficiary who is then living and receiving a monthly benefit on account of the deceased member, ASRS shall pay the lump sum payment to the beneficiary. The payment to the beneficiary shall include the recomputed amount payable pursuant to this section that would have been paid to the member through the date of the member's death plus the recomputed amount payable pursuant to this section that would have been payable to the beneficiary from the member's date of death. Section 38–770 does not apply to these payments."

[I.] . . . "Section 38–770 applies to payments."

Laws 2000, Ch. 315, § 4, provides:

"**Sec. 4. Retroactivity**

"Sections 38–747 and 38–771.01, Arizona Revised Statutes, as amended by this act, apply retroactively to July 1, 1999."

Reviser's Notes:

2000 Note. Pursuant to authority of § 41–1304.02, in subsection H, third sentence "ASRS" was substituted for "aSRS" and in subsection K, paragraph 7, first sentence "recomputed" was substituted for "recomputeD" to correct electronic database errors.

§ 38–772. Prior service under defined contribution program administered by ASRS; definitions

A. Amounts required of employers as provided in § 38–737, subsections A and B are in addition to any payments required of employers on behalf of prior service credits under the defined contribution program administered by ASRS arising from members of ASRS. Payments made to ASRS on behalf of members with those prior service credits shall reduce by that amount the payments required to be paid to the defined contribution program administered by ASRS for those prior service credits.

B. Notwithstanding § 38–757, subsection B, any prior service credits to which the member was entitled under the defined contribution program administered by ASRS shall be added to the product of § 38–757, subsection B, paragraphs 1 and 2.

C. For the purposes of this section:

1. "Prior service" means service for this state or a political subdivision of this state before membership in the defined contribution program administered by ASRS.

2. "Prior service credits" means the amount that is allowed for services before membership in the defined contribution program administered by ASRS and that is payable as a retirement benefit.

Added by Laws 1995, Ch. 32, § 14, eff. March 30, 1995.

Historical and Statutory Notes

Source:

A.R.S. former § 38-781.05.
Laws 1970, Ch. 134, § 2.
Laws 1972, Ch. 51, § 15.
Laws 1974, Ch. 167, § 3.
Laws 1978, Ch. 54, § 2.
Laws 1984, 1st S.S., Ch. 12, § 2.
Laws 1989, Ch. 310, § 3.
Laws 1992, Ch. 320, § 9.
Laws 1993, 2nd S.S., Ch. 3, § 4.
Laws 1994, Ch. 356, § 9.

For state highway patrol retirement system and Arizona state retirement system savings clause and beneficiary longevity reserve account provisions of Laws 1995, Ch. 32, see Historical and Statutory Notes following § 38-744.

Former § 38-772, added by Laws 1959, Ch. 145, § 2, amended by Laws 1973, ch. 172, § 96, relating to state highway patrol retirement system survivor benefits, was repealed by Laws 1995, Ch. 32, § 13, eff. March 30, 1995.

§ 38-773. Benefit payments to alternate payee under acceptable domestic relations order; termination of marriage; revocation of beneficiary designation; definitions

A. The board shall review any domestic relations order to which a member is a party and that is submitted to the board to determine if the domestic relations order is acceptable under this section. After a determination that a domestic relations order is acceptable under this section, the board shall notify the member and the named alternate payee of its acceptance of the domestic relations order and ASRS shall pay benefits in accordance with the applicable requirements of the order.

B. An acceptable domestic relations order shall not require the board to provide any type, form or time of payment of severance, survivor or retirement benefits or any severance, survivor or retirement benefit option that is not provided under this article.

C. An acceptable domestic relations order shall specify all of the following:

1. The name and last known mailing address of the member.

2. The name and last known mailing address of each alternate payee covered by the order.

3. The method of determining the amount of the member's severance, survivor or retirement benefits to be paid by ASRS to each alternate payee covered by the order.

4. The number of payments or period to which the order applies.

D. Except as provided by the express terms of a domestic relations order, the divorce or annulment of a member's marriage revokes any revocable:

1. Disposition or appointment of benefits made by a divorced member to that member's former spouse or to a relative of the divorced member's former

spouse in an instrument executed by the member before the divorce or annulment of the member's marriage to the former spouse.

2. Provision in an instrument executed by the member before the divorce or annulment of the member's marriage to the former spouse conferring any power or right on the divorced member's former spouse or on a relative of the divorced member's former spouse.

E. ASRS shall give effect to provisions of an instrument executed by a member before the divorce or annulment of the member's marriage to a former spouse as follows:

1. In the case of disposition or appointment of benefits, as if the former spouse and relatives of the former spouse disclaimed all provisions revoked by this section.

2. In the case of a revoked power or right, as if the former spouse and relatives of the former spouse died immediately before the divorce or annulment.

F. Provisions of an instrument revoked solely as provided by this section are revived by the divorced member's remarriage to the former spouse or by a nullification of the member's divorce or annulment.

G. For the purposes of this section:

1. "Domestic relations order" means any judgment, decree, order or approval of a property settlement agreement entered in a court of competent jurisdiction that:

(a) Relates to marital property rights of a spouse or former spouse.

(b) Creates or recognizes in the spouse or former spouse the existence of an alternate payee's right to severance, survivor or retirement benefits.

(c) Assigns the spouse or former spouse as alternate payee the right to receive all or part of the severance, survivor or retirement benefits payable to the member.

2. "Relative of the divorced member's former spouse" means a person who is related to the divorced member's former spouse by blood, adoption or affinity and who, after the divorce or annulment, is not related to the divorced member by blood, adoption or affinity.

Added by Laws 1995, Ch. 134, § 11, eff. March 30, 1995.

Historical and Statutory Notes

For state highway patrol retirement system and Arizona state retirement system savings clause and beneficiary longevity reserve account provisions of Laws 1995, Ch. 32, see Historical and Statutory Notes following § 38-744.

Former § 38-773, added by Laws 1959, Ch. 145, § 2, amended by Laws 1960, Ch. 42, § 2; Laws 1971, Ch. 74, § 1; Laws 1984, Ch. 188, § 48, which provided for the applicability of the workers' compensation law, was repealed by Laws 1995, Ch. 32, § 13, eff. March 30, 1995.

Reviser's Notes:

1995 Note. Pursuant to authority of § 41-1304.02, in the section heading "definitions" was substituted for "definition".

§ 38-774. Excess benefit arrangement

A. A separate unfunded governmental excess benefit arrangement is established outside of and apart from the trust fund established by § 38-712 to pay members benefits that are otherwise payable by ASRS and that exceed the limitations on benefits imposed by § 415 of the internal revenue code.[1] The board shall administer this excess benefit arrangement as a qualified governmental excess benefit arrangement pursuant to section 415(m) of the internal revenue code.

B. The board may adopt rules to implement this section subject to the following:

1. Benefits under this section are subject to § 38–773 and § 38–791, subsections D and F and are exempt from execution to the same extent as provided in § 38–792.

2. Contributions to this arrangement are not held in trust and shall not be commingled with other monies of ASRS.

C. A member is entitled to a monthly benefit under this section in an amount equal to the amount that the member's benefit that is payable by ASRS has been reduced by the limitation on benefits imposed by § 38–769 and § 415 of the internal revenue code. The benefit that is payable by this arrangement shall be paid at such time or times and in such form as the benefit under ASRS would be paid.

D. The benefit that is payable under this section shall be paid with employer contributions that would otherwise be made to ASRS under § 38–737. In lieu of the employer contributions being paid to the trust fund established by § 38–712, an amount determined by ASRS as necessary to pay benefits under this section shall be paid on a monthly basis to a separate account established by the board for this arrangement and may include amounts needed to pay reasonable and necessary expenses of this arrangement. The director may invest the monies in this account in suitable short-term investments between receipt of the monies and disbursement of the monies. The amount shall be paid to the account at least fifteen days before a disbursement is to be made under this section.

E. A member shall not directly or indirectly elect to defer compensation to purchase benefits provided under this section.

F. This section shall not be construed as requiring an employer or ASRS to purchase any investment or any contract to secure any obligations under this section. If an employer or ASRS purchases an investment or contract that the employer or ASRS earmarks to pay benefits under this section, title to and beneficial ownership of the investment or contract remain at all times in the employer or ASRS, and the member and the member's beneficiaries, if any, do not have any proprietary interest in any specific assets of the employer or ASRS. Any rights of the member and the member's beneficiaries, if any, to payment of any amounts under this section shall be those of general unsecured creditors of the employer or ASRS. This section and any action taken pursuant to this section by the employer or ASRS do not create and shall not be construed to create an irrevocable trust of any kind.

Added by Laws 1998, Ch. 155, § 4, eff. Aug. 21, 1998, retroactively effective to January 1, 1996.

[1] Internal Revenue Code sections may be found in Title 26 of U.S.C.A.

Historical and Statutory Notes

Laws 1998, Ch. 155, § 5, provides:

"**Sec. 5. Retroactivity**

"Section 38-774, Arizona Revised Statutes, as added by this act, is effective retroactively to from and after December 31, 1995."

Former § 38-774, added by Laws 1959, Ch. 145, § 2, relating to the effect of authorized leave of absence, including military service leaves, was repealed by Laws 1995, Ch. 32, § 13, eff. March 30, 1995.

§ 38-775. Repealed by Laws 1995, Ch. 32, § 13, eff. March 30, 1995

Historical and Statutory Notes

The repealed section, added by Laws 1959, Ch. 145, § 2, related to the effective dates of benefits.

§ 38-776. Repealed by Laws 1973, Ch. 97, § 1

Historical and Statutory Notes

The repealed section, which placed limitations upon employment by members of the state highway patrol retirement system qualifying for benefits under provisions of the article, was added by Laws 1959, Ch. 145, § 2.

§§ 38-777, 38-778. Repealed by Laws 1995, Ch. 32, § 13, eff. March 30, 1995

Historical and Statutory Notes

Section 38-777, added by Laws 1960, Ch. 42, § 3, amended by Laws 1973, Ch. 172, § 97, provided for termination of highway patrol retirement system membership.

Section 38-778, added by Laws 1968, Ch. 84, § 6, amended by Laws 1970, Ch. 211, § 4; Laws 1973, Ch. 97, § 2, related to the inapplicability of certain sections.

§ 38-781. Repealed by Laws 1995, Ch. 134, § 12, eff. October 2, 1995

Historical and Statutory Notes

The repealed section, added by Laws 1995, Ch. 32, § 1, eff. March 30, 1995, derived from:

A.R.S. former § 38-781.31.
Laws 1987, Ch. 112, § 1.
Laws 1988, Ch. 183, § 1.
Laws 1992, Ch. 145, § 1.
Laws 1994, Ch. 356, § 16.

related to a long-term disability program.

See, now, § 38-797 et seq.

Laws 1995, Ch. 134, §§ 16 and 18, provide:

"**Sec. 16. Benefit increases**

"**A.** Members of the Arizona state retirement system who were eligible to receive long-term disability benefits pursuant to § 38-781, Arizona Revised Statutes, as repealed by this act, on or before June 30, 1995 are eligible to receive an increased benefit equal to the benefit increase provided to retired members pursuant to § 38-767, Arizona Revised Statutes, as amended by this act.

"**B.** The benefit increases provided by subsection A of this section shall be added to the liabilities of the long-term disability program established by title 38, chapter 5, article 2.1, Arizona Revised Statutes, as added by this act."

"**Sec. 18. Transfer of members**

"On October 1, 1995 all members of the Arizona state retirement system who participated in the long-term disability program established by section 38-781, Arizona Revised Statutes, as repealed by this act, shall be transferred to the long-term disability program established by title 38, chapter 5, article 2.1, Arizona Revised Statutes, as added by this act."

Former § 38-781, added by Laws 1991, Ch. 270, § 3, relating to the purpose of the state retirement system and a public employee's retirement trust fund, was repealed by Laws 1995, Ch. 32, § 13, eff. March 30 1995.

§§ 38-781.01 to 38-781.27. Repealed by Laws 1995, Ch. 32, § 13, eff. March 30, 1995

Historical and Statutory Notes

Section 38-781.01, added by Laws 1970, Ch. 134, § 2 (see Source following § 38-711, provided definitions for former Article 2.1, Retirement Plan.

Section 38-781.02, added by Laws 1970, Ch. 134, § 2, amended by Laws 1975, Ch. 53, § 6, related to administration of former Article 2.1, Retirement Plan.

Section 38-781.03, added by Laws 1970, Ch. 134, § 2 (see Source following § 38-727), related to eligibility for retirement plan.

Section 38-781.04, added by Laws 1970, Ch. 134, § 2 (see Source following § 38-736), related to employee contributions.

Section 38-781.05, added by Laws 1970, Ch. 134, § 2 (see Source following § 38-727), related to employer contributions.

Section 38-781.06, added by Laws 1970, Ch. 134, § 2, related to transfer of accounts of participants with credited service in the retirement system.

Section 38-781.07, added by Laws 1970, Ch. 134, § 2 (see Source following § 38-757), related to normal retirement age and pension.

Section 38-781.08, added by Laws 1981, Ch. 284, § 5 (see Source following § 38-758), provided for early retirement.

Former § 38-781.08 added by Laws 1970, ch. 134, § 2, and amended by Laws 1974, ch. 120, § 8, Laws 1974, ch. 167, § 5, and Laws 1978, ch. 54, § 6 was repealed by Laws 1978, ch. 54, § 5, and Laws 1981, ch. 284, § 4. The repeal by Laws 1978, ch. 54, § 5 was of former § 38-781.08 as amended by Laws 1974, ch. 167, § 5.

Section 38-781.09, added by Laws 1970, Ch. 134, § 2 (see Source following § 38-759), related to late retirement.

Section 38-781.10, added by Laws 1970, Ch. 134, § 2 (see Source following § 38-760) related to optional retirement benefits.

Section 38-781.11, added by Laws 1970, Ch. 134, § 2, amended by Laws 1976, Ch. 178, § 2; Laws 1982, Ch. 269, § 1; Laws 1986, Ch. 168, § 5; Laws 1986, Ch. 415, § 15; Laws 1988, Ch. 249, § 1; Laws 1990, Ch. 170, § 5, related to death benefits.

Section 38-781.12, added by Laws 1970, Ch. 134, § 2, amended by Laws 1982, Ch. 231, § 1; Laws 1992, Ch. 320, § 11, and Laws 1994, Ch. 356, § 12, related to severance benefits.

Section 38-781.13, added by Laws 1970, Ch. 134, § 2 (see Source following § 38-764), related to facility of payment of retirement benefits.

Section 38-781.14, added by Laws 1970, Ch. 134, § 2, amended by Laws 1978, Ch. 209, § 9, related to contributions by members.

Section 38-781.15, added by Laws 1970, Ch. 134, § 2 (see Source following § 38-765), related to limitations on pension payments, contributions and credited service.

Section 38-781.16, added by Laws 1970, Ch. 134, § 2, amended by Laws 1972, Ch. 51, § 20; Laws 1989, Ch. 267, § 13, related to assurances and liabilities.

Section 38-781.17, added by Laws 1970, Ch. 134, § 2 (see Source following § 38-716), related to the investment advisory council.

Section 38-781.18, added by Laws 1970, Ch. 134, § 2 (see Source following § 38-755), related to information as to a participant's status.

Section 38-781.19, added by Laws 1970, Ch. 134, § 2 (see Source following § 38-738), provided for adjustment and refund of contributions.

Section 38-781.20, added by Laws 1970, Ch. 134, § 2 (see Source following § 38-729), related to political subdivision plans for retirement of employees and officers.

Section 38-781.21, added by Laws 1970, Ch. 134, § 2 (see Source following § 38-720), provided for a retirement plan depository.

Section 38-781.22, added by Laws 1970, Ch. 134, § 2 (see Source following § 38-792), provided for exemptions of benefits and contributions to employee retirement benefit plans from taxation and execution.

Section 38-781.23, added by Laws 1970, Ch. 134, § 2 (see Source following § 38-719), related to investment and management of retirement plan monies.

Section 38-781.24, added by Laws 1984, Ch. 136, § 2 (see Source following § 38-730), related to charter city retirement systems.

Former § 38-781.24, added by Laws 1970, Ch. 134, § 2, amended by Laws 1972, Ch. 51, § 24, and requiring mandatory security valuation reserve, was repealed by Laws 1976, Ch. 161, § 16, effective June 27, 1976.

Another former § 38-781.24, added by Laws 1983, Ch. 293, § 6, and relating to charter city and other political subdivision retirement systems and the transfers of credited service from one system to another, was repealed by Laws 1984, Ch. 136, § 1.

Section 38-781.25, added by Laws 1990, Ch. 235, § 3, amended by Laws 1991, Ch. 170, § 6, Laws 1992, Ch. 320, § 16, and Laws 1994, Ch.

356, § 15, related to group health and accident coverage for retired public employees and elected officials and their dependents.

Former § 38-781.25, providing for guarantees and actuarial reserves to provide for increases in benefits, was added by Laws 1970, Ch. 134, § 2, and amended by Laws 1972, Ch. 51 § 25, and was repealed by Laws 1976, Ch. 161, § 16, eff. June 27, 1976.

Section 38-781.26, added by Laws 1994, Ch. 357, § 2, related to minimum retirement benefits.

Former § 38-781.26, pertaining to the application of assets and surplus thereof, was added by Laws 1970, Ch. 134, § 2, and was repealed by Laws 1976, Ch. 161, § 16, eff. June 27, 1976.

Section 38-781.27, added by Laws 1994, Ch. 357, § 2, related to benefit increases.

Laws 1994, chapter 357, § 3, which was to repeal § 38-781.27 effective July 1, 2000, was itself repealed by Laws 1995, Ch. 32, § 25, eff. March 30, 1995.

Former 38-781.27, pertaining to surplus amounts, was added by Laws 1970, Ch. 134, § 2, and was repealed by Laws 1976, Ch. 161, § 16, eff. June 27, 1976.

§ 38-781.28. Repealed by Laws 1991, Ch. 170, § 7

Historical and Statutory Notes

The repealed section, added by Laws 1970, Ch. 134, § 2, amended by Laws 1972, Ch. 51, § 26; Laws 1973, Ch. 113, § 2; Laws 1974, Ch. 67, § 3, related to retired members benefits.

§ 38-781.29. Repealed by Laws 1995, Ch. 32, § 13, eff. March 30, 1995

Historical and Statutory Notes

Section 38-781.29, added by Laws 1970, Ch. 134, § 2, amended by Laws 1975, Ch. 52, § 2; Laws 1985, Ch. 294, § 7; Laws 1992, Ch. 320, § 17, related to participation in retirement plan during leave of absence.

See, now, § 38-744.

§ 38-781.30. Repealed by Laws 1991, Ch. 170, § 7

Historical and Statutory Notes

Section 38-781.30, added by Laws 1970, Ch. 134, § 2, amended by Laws 1974, Ch. 120, § 10; Laws 1976, Ch. 178, § 3, allowed for retirement pension upon disability.

§§ 38-781.31 to 38-781.33. Repealed by Laws 1995, Ch. 32, § 13, eff. March 30, 1995

Historical and Statutory Notes

Section § 38-781.31, added by Laws 1987, Ch. 112, § 1, amended by Laws 1988, Ch. 183, § 1, Laws 1992, Ch. 145, § 1, and Laws 1994, Ch. 356, § 16, related to a long term disability benefit program.

Former § 38-781.31, repealed by Laws 1981, Ch. 284, § 6, providing for retirement benefits for elected state officers and providing exceptions was added by Laws 1970, Ch. 134, § 2, and amended by Laws 1974, Ch. 167, § 6.

Section 38-781.32, added by Laws 1970, Ch. 134, § 2, amended by Laws 1978, Ch. 201, § 692, related to violations and criminal classification of crimes concerning retirement plans.

Section 38-781.33, added by Laws 1970, Ch. 134, § 2, provided the right to modify, amend or repeal the article or its provisions was reserved to the legislature.

See, now, §§ 38-793 and 38-794.

§ 38-781.34. Repealed by Laws 1981, Ch. 284, § 6

Historical and Statutory Notes

The repealed section, providing for retirement benefits for elected officers of counties was added by Laws 1972, Ch. 88, § 1.

See, now, § 38-801 et seq.

§ 38-781.35. Repealed by Laws 1991, Ch. 170, § 7

Historical and Statutory Notes

The repealed section, added by Laws 1973, Ch. 113, § 3, provided for a continuing appropriation to the Arizona state retirement system board.

§ 38-781.36. Repealed by Laws 1987, Ch. 274, § 5, eff. Aug. 18, 1987, retroactively effective to June 30, 1987

Historical and Statutory Notes

The repealed section, added by Laws 1975, Ch. 57, § 4, amended by Laws 1978, Ch. 54, § 7; Laws 1978, Ch. 209, § 10; Laws 1981, Ch. 1, § 18, related to retirement contributions and benefits for continuation of employment of state employees beyond age seventy.

Former section 38-781.36, added by Laws 1974, Ch. 120, § 11, effective July 1, 1975, and relating to employment beyond normal retirement date, was repealed by Laws 1975, Ch. 57, § 3, effective May 16, 1975.

§§ 38-781.37 to 38-781.42. Repealed by Laws 1995, Ch. 32, § 13, eff. March 30, 1995

Historical and Statutory Notes

Section 38-781.37, added by Laws 1974, Ch. 120, § 11, related to retirement benefits for elected officers of incorporated cities and towns.

Section 38-781.38, added by Laws 1986, Ch. 168, § 7, amended by Laws 1990, Ch. 170, § 8, and by Laws 1994, Ch. 356, § 17, related to maximum benefits.

Former § 38-781.38, added by Laws 1985, Ch. 294, § 8, relating to compliance with the internal revenue code, was repealed by Laws 1986, Ch. 168, § 6, effective April 23, 1986.

Section 38-781.39, added by Laws 1987, Ch. 182, § 1, amended by Laws 1994, Ch. 356, § 18, related to out of state service credit for teachers, professors, instructors, and administrators

Section 38-781.40, added by Laws 1987, Ch. 208, § 1, related to redemption of contributions and credited service.

Section 38-781.41, added by Laws 1988, Ch. 277, § 3, and by Laws 1988, Ch. 307, § 1, amended by Laws 1989, Ch. 310, § 4; Laws 1990, Ch. 235, § 4; Laws 1991, Ch. 170, § 9; Laws 1992, Ch. 320, § 18; Laws 1994, Ch. 356, § 19, related to health and accident insurance for retired and disabled state retirement system members.

Section 38-781.42, added by Laws 1989, Ch. 310, § 5, amended by Laws 1992, Ch. 320, § 19, and Laws 1994, Ch. 207, § 1, related to military service credit.

§ 38-781.43. Repealed by Laws 1991, Ch. 175, § 6, eff. Dec. 31, 1992

Historical and Statutory Notes

The repealed section, added by Laws 1991, Ch.175, § 1, related to contributions paid during military service.

Another § 38-781.43 was renumbered as § 38-781.44.

Reviser's Notes:

1991 Note. Laws 1991, Ch. 144, sec. 1 added another new § 38-781.43 that was renumbered as § 38-781.44, pursuant to authority of § 41-1304.02.

§§ 38-781.44, 38-781.45. Repealed by Laws 1995, Ch. 32, § 13, eff. March 30, 1995

Historical and Statutory Notes

Section 38-781.44, added as § 38-781.43 by Laws 1991, Ch. 144, § 1, and renumbered as § 38-781.44, related to benefit options for transferred system members.

See, now, § 38-771.

Repealed

Section 38-781.45, added by Laws 1994, Ch. 356, § 20, related to eligible rollover distribution.

See, now, § 38-770.

§ 38-782. Group health and accident coverage for retired public employees and elected officials and their dependents

A. The board shall establish group health and accident coverage for eligible retired and disabled members and their dependents. Eligible retired and disabled members are those members who are receiving retirement benefits from ASRS or long-term disability benefits pursuant to § 38-651.03 or article 2.1 of this chapter [1] and who elect not to obtain health and accident insurance through their former employer. If an insured retired or disabled member dies before the insured member's dependent beneficiary or an insured surviving dependent, the dependent beneficiary or insured surviving dependent is entitled to coverage at group rates if the dependent beneficiary or surviving dependent elects to continue in the coverage within six months of the insured member's death and the dependent beneficiary or surviving dependent agrees to pay the cost of the premium for group health and accident insurance. On notification of the insured member's death, the board shall immediately notify a dependent beneficiary or an insured surviving dependent of the provisions of this section.

B. Retired members of the public safety personnel retirement system, the elected officials' retirement plan, the corrections officer retirement plan or the optional retirement programs authorized pursuant to §§ 15-1451 and 15-1628 and their dependents who are receiving benefits from the public safety personnel retirement system, the elected officials' retirement plan, the corrections officer retirement plan or the optional retirement programs authorized pursuant to §§ 15-1451 and 15-1628 and who are not covered by § 38-651.01 may participate in group health and accident coverage provided pursuant to this section. On the death of an insured member of the public safety personnel retirement system, the elected officials' retirement plan, the corrections officer retirement plan or the optional retirement programs authorized pursuant to §§ 15-1451 and 15-1628, the insured surviving dependent is entitled to coverage at group rates. Except as provided in subsection H of this section, the surviving dependent shall be charged amounts that are sufficient to pay for the premium and administrative expense of providing the coverage.

C. The board may enter into agreements with retired and disabled members of ASRS who elect to obtain the coverage provided pursuant to subsection A of this section. Those agreements may include provision for the deduction from the retirement benefits of the members who elect to obtain the coverage of amounts sufficient to pay for the premium not covered under retirement benefits and the administrative expense of providing the coverage.

D. The fund manager of the public safety personnel retirement system may enter into agreements with retired members of the public safety personnel retirement system, the elected officials' retirement plan, the corrections officer retirement plan and their dependents who elect to obtain the coverage provided pursuant to this section. Those agreements may include provisions for the deduction from the retirement benefits of the members who elect to obtain the coverage of amounts sufficient to pay for the premium not covered under their retirement benefits and the administrative expense of providing the coverage.

E. The board may enter into agreements with retired members of the optional retirement programs authorized pursuant to §§ 15–1451 and 15–1628 and their dependents who elect to obtain the coverage provided pursuant to this section. Those agreements may include provisions for the payment of amounts sufficient to pay for the premium and administrative expense of providing the coverage.

F. If an insured member receiving long-term disability benefits pursuant to article 2.1 of this chapter becomes ineligible for the long-term disability benefits, the member and the covered dependents of the member may continue to participate in the group health and accident coverage provided pursuant to this section subject to the following conditions:

1. Participation in the coverage is limited to twelve months from the date the member ceases eligibility for benefits under article 2.1 of this chapter or the member commences employment, whichever occurs first.

2. The member shall pay the full premium cost of the coverage selected, and the member is not eligible for benefits pursuant to § 38–783.

3. If a member who participates in the coverage dies during the twelve month period provided by this subsection, covered dependents of the member may continue coverage after the death of the member through the end of the twelve month period. Covered dependents of the member who continue coverage pursuant to this paragraph shall pay the full premium cost of the coverage selected and are not eligible for benefits pursuant to § 38–783.

G. Retired or disabled members who are not eligible for medicare, who live in this state, who enroll in a qualifying health maintenance organization under this section and who reside outside the area of a qualifying health maintenance organization shall be offered the option of enrolling with a qualified health maintenance organization offered through their provider under the same premiums as if they lived within the area boundaries of the qualified health maintenance organization provided that:

1. All medical services are rendered and received at an office designated by the qualifying health maintenance organization or at a facility referred by the health maintenance organization.

2. All nonemergency or nonurgent travel, ambulatory and other expenses from the residence area of the member to the designated office of the qualifying health maintenance organization or the facility referred by the health maintenance organization are the responsibility of and at the expense of the member.

3. All emergency or urgent travel, ambulatory and other expenses from the residence area of the member to the designated office of the qualifying health maintenance organization or the facility referred by the health maintenance organization shall be paid pursuant to any agreement between the health maintenance organization and the member living outside the area of the qualifying health maintenance organization.

H. Public monies shall not be spent to pay all or any part of the insurance premium pursuant to this section except for monies authorized to be paid for any insured from the retirement plan from which the insured is receiving benefits.

Added by Laws 1995, Ch. 32, § 14, eff. March 30, 1995. Amended by Laws 1995, Ch. 134, § 13, eff. April 17, 1995; Laws 1997, Ch. 291, § 4, eff. July 1, 1998; Laws 1998, Ch. 236, § 3; Laws 1999, Ch. 300, § 15; Laws 2001, Ch. 136, § 18.

[1] Section 38-797 et seq.

Historical and Statutory Notes

Source:

A.R.S. former § 38-781.25.
Laws 1990, Ch. 235, § 3.
Laws 1991, Ch. 170, § 6.
Laws 1992, Ch. 320, § 16.
Laws 1994, Ch. 356, § 15.

The 1995 amendment by Ch. 134 substituted references to article 2.1 of this chapter for references to § 38-781 throughout; and, in subsec. A, substituted "retirement benefits" for "income" following "receiving" in the second sentence.

The 1997 amendment by Ch. 291 inserted "or as provided in § 38-615" at the end of subsec. H.

The 1998 amendment by Ch. 236 altered statutory references.

The amendment of this section by Laws 1998, Ch. 236, § 3 explicitly amended the amendment of this section by Laws 1997, Ch. 291, § 4.

The 1999 amendment by Ch. 300 deleted "or as provided in § 38-615" from the end of subsec. H.

The 2001 amendment by Ch. 136 substituted "who elect not to obtain health and accident insurance" for "who are not eligible to obtain health and accident insurance" in the second sentence of subsec. A; and rewrote subsec. F, par. 3, which had read:

"3. If a member who participates in the coverage dies during the twelve month period provided by this subsection, covered dependents of the member are not eligible to continue coverage after the death of the member."

Laws 2003, Ch. 247, § 5, provides:

"**Sec. 5. Arizona state retirement system report on health insurance coverage for government retirees**

"**A.** In preparing the request for proposals for the contract for the group health and accident insurance coverage for eligible retired and disabled members and their dependents as prescribed by § 38-782, Arizona Revised Statutes, the Arizona state retirement system shall seek to provide coverage that:

"1. Is affordable to all members who retire under a public retirement system or plan of this state and who are eligible to receive the coverage.

"2. Is meaningful, timely and appropriate to all members who retire under a public retirement system or plan of this state and who are eligible to receive the coverage.

"3. Is accessible and available.

"**B.** On or before December 15, 2004, the Arizona state retirement system shall report to the speaker of the house of representatives and the president of the senate as to the progress and success of the system in obtaining a group health and accident insurance contract for eligible retired and disabled members that achieves the goals of subsection A of this section."

§ 38-783. Retired members; dependents; health insurance; premium payment; separate account; definitions

A. Subject to subsections J, K and L of this section, the board shall pay from ASRS assets part of the single coverage premium of any health and accident insurance for each retired, contingent annuitant or disabled member of ASRS if the member elects to participate in the coverage provided by ASRS or § 38-651.01 or elects to participate in a health and accident insurance program provided or administered by an employer or paid for, in whole or in part, by an employer to an insurer. A contingent annuitant must be receiving a monthly retirement benefit from ASRS in order to obtain any premium payment provided by this section. The board shall pay:

1. Up to one hundred fifty dollars per month for a member of ASRS who is not eligible for medicare if the retired or disabled member has ten or more years of credited service.

2. Up to one hundred dollars per month for each member of ASRS who is eligible for medicare if the retired or disabled member has ten or more years of credited service.

B. Subject to subsections J, K and L of this section, the board shall pay from ASRS assets part of the family coverage premium of any health and accident insurance for a retired, contingent annuitant or disabled member of ASRS who elects family coverage and who otherwise qualifies for payment pursuant to subsection A of this section. If a member of ASRS and the member's spouse are both either retired or disabled under ASRS and apply for family coverage, the member who elects family coverage is entitled to receive the payments under this section as if they were both applying under a single coverage premium unless the payment under this section for family coverage is greater. Payment under this subsection is in the following amounts:

1. Up to two hundred sixty dollars per month if the member of ASRS and one or more dependents are not eligible for medicare.

2. Up to one hundred seventy dollars per month if the member of ASRS and one or more dependents are eligible for medicare.

3. Up to two hundred fifteen dollars per month if either:

(a) The member of ASRS is not eligible for medicare and one or more dependents are eligible for medicare.

(b) The member of ASRS is eligible for medicare and one or more dependents are not eligible for medicare.

C. In addition each retired, contingent annuitant or disabled member of ASRS with less than ten years of credited service and a dependent of such a retired, contingent annuitant or disabled member who elects to participate in the coverage provided by ASRS or § 38–651.01 or who elects to participate in a health and accident insurance program provided or administered by an employer or paid for, in whole or in part, by an employer to an insurer is entitled to receive a proportion of the full benefit prescribed by subsection A, B, E or F of this section according to the following schedule:

1. 9.0 to 9.9 years of credited service, ninety per cent.

2. 8.0 to 8.9 years of credited service, eighty per cent.

3. 7.0 to 7.9 years of credited service, seventy per cent.

4. 6.0 to 6.9 years of credited service, sixty per cent.

5. 5.0 to 5.9 years of credited service, fifty per cent.

6. Those with less than five years of credited service do not qualify for the benefit.

D. The board shall not pay more than the amount prescribed in this section for a member of ASRS.

E. In addition to the payments provided by subsection A of this section, through June 30, 2005, the board shall pay an insurance premium benefit for medical coverage, not including limited benefit coverage as defined in § 20–1137, for each retired, contingent annuitant or disabled member of ASRS who is eligible for a premium benefit payment pursuant to subsection A of this section and who lives in a nonservice area as follows:

1. Up to three hundred dollars per month for a member of ASRS who is not eligible for medicare if the retired or disabled member has ten or more years of credited service. From and after June 30, 2003, to qualify for this additional benefit, a retired or disabled member of ASRS shall pay out-of-pocket medical insurance premiums of at least one hundred twenty-five dollars per month.

2. Up to one hundred seventy dollars per month for a member of ASRS who is eligible for medicare if the retired or disabled member has ten or more years of credited service. From and after June 30, 2003, to qualify for this additional benefit, a retired or disabled member of ASRS shall pay out-of-pocket medical insurance premiums of at least one hundred dollars per month.

F. In addition to the payments provided by subsection B of this section, through June 30, 2005, the board shall pay from ASRS assets part of the family coverage premium for medical coverage, not including limited benefit coverage as defined in § 20–1137, for a retired, contingent annuitant or disabled member of ASRS who is eligible for a premium benefit payment pursuant to subsection B of this section, who is enrolled in a family medical plan and who lives in a nonservice area as follows:

1. Up to six hundred dollars per month if the member of ASRS and one or more dependents are not eligible for medicare and the retired or disabled member of ASRS has ten or more years of credited service. From and after June 30, 2003, to qualify for this additional benefit, a retired or disabled member shall pay out-of-pocket medical insurance premiums of at least four hundred twenty-five dollars per month.

2. Up to three hundred fifty dollars per month if the member of ASRS and one or more dependents are eligible for medicare and the retired or disabled member of ASRS has ten or more years of credited service. From and after June 30, 2003, to qualify for this additional benefit, a retired or disabled member shall pay out-of-pocket medical insurance premiums of at least two hundred dollars per month.

3. If the retired or disabled member of ASRS has ten or more years of credited service, up to four hundred seventy dollars per month if either:

(a) The member of ASRS is not eligible for medicare and one or more dependents are eligible for medicare.

(b) The member of ASRS is eligible for medicare and one or more dependents are not eligible for medicare.

From and after June 30, 2003, to qualify for this additional benefit, a retired or disabled member shall pay out-of-pocket medical insurance premiums of at least four hundred dollars per month.

G. A retired, contingent annuitant or disabled member of ASRS who is enrolled in a managed care program in a nonservice area is not eligible for the payment prescribed in subsection E or F of this section if the member terminates coverage under the managed care program.

H. A retired, contingent annuitant or disabled member of ASRS may elect to purchase individual health care coverage and receive a payment pursuant to this section through the retired or disabled member's employer if that employer assumes the administrative functions associated with the payment, including verification that the payment is used to pay for health insurance coverage if the payment is made to the retired or disabled member.

I. The board shall establish a separate account that consists of the benefits provided by this section. The board shall not use or divert any part of the corpus or income of the account for any purpose other than the provision of benefits under this section unless the liabilities of ASRS to provide the benefits are satisfied. If the liabilities of ASRS to provide the benefits described in this section are satisfied, the board shall return any amount remaining in the account to the employer.

J. Payment of the benefits provided by this section is subject to the following conditions:

1. The payment of the benefits is subordinate to the payment of retirement benefits payable by ASRS.

2. The total of contributions for the benefits and actual contributions for life insurance protection, if any, shall not exceed twenty-five per cent of the total actual employer and employee contributions to ASRS, less contributions to fund past service credits, after the day the account is established.

3. The board shall deposit the benefits provided by this section in the account.

4. The contributions by the employer to the account shall be reasonable and ascertainable.

K. A member who elects to receive a retirement benefit pursuant to § 38–760, subsection B, paragraph 1 may elect at the time of retirement an optional form of health and accident insurance premium benefit payment pursuant to this subsection as follows:

1. The optional premium benefit payment shall be an amount prescribed by subsection A, B, C, E or F of this section that is actuarially reduced to the retiring member for life. The amount of the optional premium benefit payment shall be the actuarial equivalent of the premium benefit payment to which the retired member would otherwise be entitled. The election in a manner prescribed by the board shall name the contingent annuitant and may be revoked at any time before the retiring member's effective date of retirement. At any time after benefits have commenced, the member may name a different contingent annuitant or rescind the election by written notice to the board as follows:

(a) If the retired member names a different contingent annuitant, the optional premium benefit payment shall be adjusted to the actuarial equivalent of the original premium benefit payment based on the age of the new contingent annuitant. The adjustment shall include all postretirement increases or decreases in amounts prescribed by subsection A, B, C, E or F of this section that are authorized by law after the retired member's date of retirement. Payment of this adjusted premium benefit payment shall continue under the provisions of the optional premium benefit payment previously elected by the retired member. A retired member cannot name a different contingent annuitant if the retired member has at any time rescinded the optional form of health and accident insurance premium benefit payment.

(b) If the retired member rescinds the election, the retired member shall thereafter receive the premium benefit payment that the retired member would otherwise be entitled to receive if the retired member had not elected the optional premium benefit payment, including all postretirement increases or decreases in amounts prescribed by subsection A, B, C, E or F of this section that are authorized by law after the member's date of retirement. The increased benefit payment shall continue during the remainder of the retired member's lifetime. The decision to rescind shall be irrevocable.

2. If, at the time of the retired member's death:

(a) The retired member was receiving a reduced premium benefit payment based on an amount prescribed in subsection B, C or F of this section and the contingent annuitant is eligible for family health and accident insurance coverage, the contingent annuitant is entitled to receive a premium benefit payment based on an amount prescribed in subsection B, C or F of this section times the reduction factor applied to the retired member's premium benefit payment times the joint and survivor option reduction factor elected by the retired member at the time of retirement pursuant to § 38–760, subsection B, paragraph 1.

(b) The retired member was receiving a reduced premium benefit payment based on an amount prescribed in subsection A, C or E of this section and the contingent annuitant is eligible for single health and accident insurance coverage, the contingent annuitant is entitled to receive a premium benefit payment based on an amount prescribed in subsection A, C or E of this section times the reduction factor applied to the retired member's premium benefit payment times the joint and survivor option reduction factor elected by the retired member at the time of retirement pursuant to § 38–760, subsection B, paragraph 1.

(c) The retired member was receiving a reduced premium benefit payment based on an amount prescribed in subsection B, C or F of this section and the contingent annuitant is not eligible for family health and accident insurance coverage, the contingent annuitant is entitled to receive a premium benefit payment based on an amount prescribed in subsection A, C or E of this section times the reduction factor applied to the retired member's premium benefit payment times the joint and survivor option reduction factor elected by the retired member at the time of retirement pursuant to § 38–760, subsection B, paragraph 1.

L. A member who elects to receive a retirement benefit pursuant to § 38–760, subsection B, paragraph 2 may elect at the time of retirement an optional form of health and accident insurance premium benefit payment pursuant to this subsection as follows:

1. The optional premium benefit payment shall be an amount prescribed by subsection A, B, C, E or F of this section that is actuarially reduced with payments for five, ten or fifteen years that are not dependent on the continued lifetime of the retired member but whose payments continue for the retired member's lifetime beyond the five, ten or fifteen year period. The election in a

manner prescribed by the board shall name the contingent annuitant and may be revoked at any time before the retiring member's effective date of retirement. At any time after benefits have commenced, the member may name a different contingent annuitant or rescind the election by written notice to the board. If the retired member rescinds the election, the retired member shall thereafter receive the premium benefit payment that the retired member would otherwise be entitled to receive if the retired member had not elected the optional premium benefit payment, including all postretirement increases or decreases in amounts prescribed by subsection A, B, C, E or F of this section that are authorized by law after the member's date of retirement. The increased benefit payment shall continue during the remainder of the retired member's lifetime. The decision to rescind shall be irrevocable.

2. If, at the time of the retired member's death:

(a) The retired member was receiving a reduced premium benefit payment based on an amount prescribed in subsection B, C or F of this section and the contingent annuitant is eligible for family health and accident insurance coverage, the contingent annuitant is entitled to receive a premium benefit payment based on an amount prescribed in subsection B, C or F of this section times the period certain and life option reduction factor elected by the retired member at the time of retirement pursuant to § 38–760, subsection B, paragraph 2.

(b) The retired member was receiving a reduced premium benefit payment based on an amount prescribed in subsection A, C or E of this section and the contingent annuitant is eligible for single health and accident insurance coverage, the contingent annuitant is entitled to receive a premium benefit payment based on an amount prescribed in subsection A, C or E of this section times the period certain and life option reduction factor elected by the retired member at the time of retirement pursuant to § 38–760, subsection B, paragraph 2.

(c) The retired member was receiving a reduced premium benefit payment based on an amount prescribed in subsection B, C or F of this section and the contingent annuitant is not eligible for family health and accident insurance coverage, the contingent annuitant is entitled to receive a premium benefit payment based on an amount prescribed in subsection A, C or E of this section times the period certain and life option reduction factor elected by the retired member at the time of retirement pursuant to § 38–760, subsection B, paragraph 2.

M. If, at the time of retirement, a retiring member does not elect to receive a reduced premium benefit payment pursuant to subsection K or L of this section, the retired member's contingent annuitant is not eligible at any time for the optional premium benefit payment.

N. A contingent annuitant is not eligible for any premium benefit payment if the contingent annuitant was not enrolled in an eligible health and accident insurance plan at the time of the retired member's death or if the contingent annuitant is not the dependent beneficiary or insured surviving dependent as provided in § 38–782.

O. For the purposes of this section:

1. "Account" means the separate account established pursuant to subsection I of this section.

2. "Credited service" includes prior service.

3. "Nonservice area" means an area in this state in which ASRS pursuant to § 38–782, the department of administration pursuant to § 38–651.01 or any employer does not provide or administer a health care services organization program, excluding any preferred provider organization program or individual health indemnity policy, for which the retired, contingent annuitant or disabled member of ASRS is eligible.

4. "Prior service" means service for this state or a political subdivision of this state before membership in the defined contribution program administered by ASRS.

Added by Laws 1995, Ch. 32, § 14, eff. March 30, 1995. Amended by Laws 1997, Ch. 280, § 18; Laws 2001, Ch. 136, § 19; Laws 2001, Ch. 376, § 1; Laws 2001, Ch. 383, § 1; Laws 2003, Ch. 171, § 1; Laws 2003, Ch. 247, § 1; Laws 2004, Ch. 87, § 1, eff. April 16, 2004.

Historical and Statutory Notes

Source:

A.R.S. former § 38–781.41.
Laws 1988, Ch. 277, § 3.
Laws 1988, Ch. 307, § 1.
Laws 1989, Ch. 310, § 4.
Laws 1990, Ch. 235, § 4.
Laws 1991, Ch. 170, § 9.
Laws 1992, Ch. 320, § 18.
Laws 1994, Ch. 356, § 19.

The 1997 amendment by Ch. 280 rewrote subsec. B; inserted a new subsec. D providing that the board shall not pay more than the amount prescribed in subsecs. A or B; redesignated former subsecs. D through F as subsecs. E through G and made changes in corresponding internal references; and added subsec. F, par. 3, defining prior service. Prior to amendment subsec. B had read:

"**B.** Subject to subsection E of this section, in addition to the benefits provided by subsection A of this section the board shall pay from ASRS assets part of the premium for dependent coverage for each retired or disabled member of ASRS who elects to participate in the health insurance premium payments provided pursuant to subsection A of this section. The payment may be up to eighty dollars per month for one or more dependents who are not eligible for medicare and up to fifty dollars per month for one or more dependents who are eligible for medicare."

The 2001 amendment by Ch. 136 rewrote the first sentences of subsecs. A and C, which had read, respectively:

"**A.** Subject to subsection F of this section, the board shall pay from ASRS assets part of the single coverage premium of any group health and accident insurance for each retired or disabled member of ASRS if the member elects to participate in the coverage provided by ASRS or § 38–651.01 or elects to participate in any other health and accident insurance coverage provided or administered by an employer."

"**C.** In addition each retired or disabled member of ASRS with less than ten years of credited service and a dependent of such a retired or disabled member who elects to participate in the coverage provided by ASRS or § 38–651.01 or who elects to participate in any other health and accident coverage program provided or administered by an employer is entitled to receive a proportion of the full benefit prescribed by subsection A or B of this section according to the following schedule:"

The 2001 amendment by Ch. 376 modified internal references to conform to reorganization of the section; rewrote subsec. D; inserted new subsecs. E to H, redesignating existing subsecs. E to G as I to K, accordingly; and inserted subsec. K, par. 3. Subsection D had read:

"**D.** The board shall not pay more than the amount prescribed in subsection A or B of this section or the applicable proportion prescribed in subsection C of this section for a retired or disabled member of ASRS."

Laws 2001, Ch. 376, § 5, provides:

"**Sec. 5. Retroactivity**

"This act applies retroactively to from and after June 30, 2001."

The 2001 amendment by Ch. 383 increased the dollar amounts in subsec. A, pars. 1 and 2, and in subsec. B, pars. 1, 2 and 3; and deleted "subsection A or B of this section or the applicable proportion prescribed in subsection C of" following "prescribed in" in subsec. D.

Laws 2001, Ch. 383, § 6, provides:

"**Sec. 6. Retroactivity**

"This act applies retroactively to from and after June 30, 2001."

The 2003 amendment by Ch. 171, rewrote subsec. A; substituted "subsections J, K, and L" for "subsection" in subsec. B; inserted "contingent annuitant" before "or disabled member" throughout; deleted "retired or disabled" before "member" throughout; inserted "insurance" before program in subsec. C; substituted "if the retired or disabled member" for "and who" in subsec. E, pars. 1 and 2; inserted subsecs. K, L, M, and N; and redesignated existing subsec. K as O. Subsec. A had read:

"**A.** Subject to subsection J of this section, the board shall pay from ASRS assets part of the single coverage premium of any health and accident insurance for each retired or disabled member of ASRS if the member elects to participate in the coverage provided by ASRS or § 38–651.01 or elects to participate in a health and accident insurance program provided or administered by an employer or paid for, in whole or in part, by an employer to an insurer. The board shall pay:

"1. Up to one hundred fifty dollars per month for a retired or disabled member of ASRS who is not eligible for medicare and who has ten or more years of credited service.

"2. Up to one hundred dollars per month for each retired or disabled member of ASRS who is eligible for medicare and who has ten or more years of credited service."

Laws 2003, Ch.171, § 3, provides:

"**Sec. 3. Applicability**

"The optional premium benefit payment provided by this act applies to members who retire from and after December 31, 2003."

The 2003 amendment by Ch. 247, rewrote the section, which had read:

"**A.** Subject to subsection J of this section, the board shall pay from ASRS assets part of the single coverage premium of any health and accident insurance for each retired or disabled member of ASRS if the member elects to participate in the coverage provided by ASRS or § 38–651.01 or elects to participate in a health and accident insurance program provided or administered by an employer or paid for, in whole or in part, by an employer to an insurer. The board shall pay:

"1. Up to one hundred fifty dollars per month for a retired or disabled member of ASRS who is not eligible for medicare and who has ten or more years of credited service.

"2. Up to one hundred dollars per month for each retired or disabled member of ASRS who is eligible for medicare and who has ten or more years of credited service.

"**B.** Subject to subsection J of this section, the board shall pay from ASRS assets part of the family coverage premium of any health and accident insurance for a retired or disabled member of ASRS who elects family coverage and who otherwise qualifies for payment pursuant to subsection A of this section. Payment under this subsection is in the following amounts:

"1. Up to two hundred sixty dollars per month if the retired or disabled member of ASRS and one or more dependents are not eligible for medicare.

"2. Up to one hundred seventy dollars per month if the retired or disabled member of ASRS and one or more dependents are eligible for medicare.

"3. Up to two hundred fifteen dollars per month if either:

"(a) The retired or disabled member of ASRS is not eligible for medicare and one or more dependents are eligible for medicare.

"(b) The retired or disabled member of ASRS is eligible for medicare and one or more dependents are not eligible for medicare.

"**C.** In addition each retired or disabled member of ASRS with less than ten years of credited service and a dependent of such a retired or disabled member who elects to participate in the coverage provided by ASRS or § 38–651.01 or who elects to participate in a health and accident program provided or administered by an employer or paid for, in whole or in part, by an employer to an insurer is entitled to receive a proportion of the full benefit prescribed by subsection A or B of this section according to the following schedule:

"1. 9.0 to 9.9 years of credited service, ninety per cent.

"2. 8.0 to 8.9 years of credited service, eighty per cent.

"3. 7.0 to 7.9 years of credited service, seventy per cent.

"4. 6.0 to 6.9 years of credited service, sixty per cent.

"5. 5.0 to 5.9 years of credited service, fifty per cent.

"6. Those with less than five years of credited service do not qualify for the benefit.

"**D.** The board shall not pay more than the amount prescribed in this section for a retired or disabled member of ASRS.

"**E.** Through June 30, 2003, the board shall pay an insurance premium benefit for each retired or disabled member of ASRS who is eligible for a premium benefit payment pursuant to subsection A of this section and who lives in a nonservice area as follows:

"1. Up to three hundred dollars per month for a retired or disabled member of ASRS who is not eligible for medicare and who has ten or more years of credited service.

"2. Up to one hundred seventy dollars per month for a retired or disabled member of ASRS who is eligible for medicare and who has ten or more years of credited service.

"**F.** Through June 30, 2003, the board shall pay from asrs assets part of the family coverage premium of any group health and accident insurance coverage for a retired or disabled member of ASRS who is eligible for a premium benefit payment pursuant to subsection B of this section and who lives in a nonservice area as follows:

"1. Up to six hundred dollars per month if the retired or disabled member of ASRS and one or more dependents are not eligible for medicare.

"2. Up to three hundred fifty dollars per month if the retired or disabled member of ASRS and one or more dependents are eligible for medicare.

"3. Up to four hundred seventy dollars per month if either:

"(a) The retired or disabled member of ASRS is not eligible for medicare and one or more dependents are eligible for medicare.

"(b) The retired or disabled member of ASRS is eligible for medicare and one or more dependents are not eligible for medicare.

"**G.** A retired or disabled member of ASRS who is enrolled in a managed care program in a nonservice area is not eligible for the payment prescribed in subsection E or F of this section if the member terminates coverage under the managed care program.

"**H.** Through June 30, 2003, a retired or disabled member of ASRS may elect to purchase individual health care coverage and receive a payment pursuant to this section through the retired or disabled member's employer if that employer assumes the administrative functions associated with the payment, including verification that the payment is used to pay for health insurance coverage if the payment is made to the retired or disabled member.

"**I.** The board shall establish a separate account that consists of the benefits provided by this section. The board shall not use or divert any part of the corpus or income of the account for any purpose other than the provision of benefits under this section unless the liabilities of ASRS to provide the benefits are satisfied. If the liabilities of ASRS to provide the benefits described in this section are satisfied, the board shall return any amount remaining in the account to the employer.

"**J.** Payment of the benefits provided by this section is subject to the following conditions:

"1. The payment of the benefits is subordinate to the payment of retirement benefits payable by ASRS.

"2. The total of contributions for the benefits and actual contributions for life insurance protection, if any, shall not exceed twenty-five per cent of the total actual employer and employee contributions to ASRS, less contributions to fund past service credits, after the day the account is established.

"3. The board shall deposit the benefits provided by this section in the account.

"4. The contributions by the employer to the account shall be reasonable and ascertainable.

"**K.** For the purposes of this section:

"1. "Account" means the separate account established pursuant to subsection I of this section.

"2. "Credited service" includes prior service.

"3. "Nonservice area" means an area in this state in which ASRS pursuant to § 38-782, the department of administration pursuant to § 38-651.01 or any employer does not provide or administer a health care services organization program, excluding any preferred provider organization program or individual health indemnity policy, for which the retired or disabled member of ASRS is eligible.

"4. "Prior service" means service for this state or a political subdivision of this state before membership in the defined contribution program administered by ASRS."

Laws 2003, Ch. 247, § 7, provides:

"**Sec. 7. Retroactivity**

"Sections 38-783, 38-817, 38-857 and 38-906, Arizona Revised Statutes, as amended by this act, apply retroactively to from and after June 30, 2003."

The 2004 amendment by Ch. 87, in subsec. B, inserted the second sentence.

Laws 2004, Ch. 87, § 2 provides:

"**Sec. 2. Retroactivity**

"Section 38-783, Arizona Revised Statutes, as amended by this act applies retroactively to from and after March 31, 2004."

Reviser's Notes:

1997 Note. Pursuant to authority of § 41-1304.02, in subsection G, paragraph 3 the quotation marks following "ASRS." were deleted to correct a manifest clerical error.

2001 Note. Prior to the 2003 amendment, this section contained the amendments made by Laws 2001, Ch. 136, sec. 19, Ch. 376, sec. 1 and Ch. 383, sec. 1 that were blended together pursuant to authority of § 41-1304.03.

2003 Note. Prior to the 2004 amendment, this section contained the amendments made by Laws 2003, Ch. 171, sec. 1 and Ch. 247, sec. 1

that were blended together pursuant to authority of § 41–1304.03.

§ 38–791. Assurances and liabilities

A. Nothing contained in this article shall be construed as:

1. A contract of employment between an employer and any employee.

2. A right of any employee to continue in the employment of an employer.

3. A limitation of the rights of an employer to discharge any of its employees, with or without cause.

B. A member does not have any right to, or interest in, any ASRS assets on termination of the member's employment or otherwise, except as provided from time to time by ASRS, and then only to the extent of the benefits payable to the member out of ASRS assets. All payments of benefits shall be made solely out of ASRS assets and neither the employers, the board nor any member of the board is liable for payment of benefits in any manner.

C. Payment of compensation less contributions as provided in this article fully discharges any claim or demand for the service rendered by a member during the period covered by the payment, except with respect to benefits provided under this article.

D. Benefits, employee contributions or employer contributions, including interest, earnings and all other credits, payable under this article are not subject in any manner to anticipation, alienation, sale, transfer, assignment, pledge, encumbrance, charge, garnishment, execution or levy of any kind, either voluntary or involuntary, before actually being received by a person entitled to the benefit, contribution, earning or credit, and any attempt to anticipate, alienate, sell, transfer, assign, pledge, encumber, charge, garnish, execute or levy or otherwise dispose of any benefit, contribution, earning or credit under this article is void. ASRS is not in any manner liable for, or subject to, the debts, contracts, liabilities, engagements or torts of any person entitled to any benefit, contribution, earning or credit under this article.

E. Neither the employers, the board nor any member of the board guarantees the fund established by § 38–712 in any manner against loss or depreciation, and they are not liable for any act or failure to act that is made in good faith pursuant to this article. The employers are not responsible for any act or failure to act of the board or any member of the board. Neither the board nor any member of the board is responsible for any act or failure to act of any employer.

F. This section does not exempt employee benefits of any kind from a writ of attachment, a writ of execution, a writ of garnishment and orders of assignment issued by a court of record as the result of a judgment for arrearages of child support or for child support debt.

Added by Laws 1995, Ch. 32, § 14, eff. March 30, 1995.

Historical and Statutory Notes

Source:

A.R.S. former § 38–781.16.

Laws 1970, Ch. 134, § 2.

Laws 1972, Ch. 51, § 20.

Laws 1989, Ch. 267, § 13.

§ 38-792. Exemptions from execution, attachment and taxation; exception

A. The benefits and annuities, the member and employer contributions and the securities in ASRS accounts provided for in this article are not subject to execution or attachment and are nonassignable except as specifically provided in this article. The member and employer contributions and the securities in ASRS accounts are exempt from state, county and municipal income taxes. Contributions that are withdrawn after December 31, 1974 by a public officer or employee from the accounts of ASRS and that are not received as benefits from ASRS and benefits and annuities received by a public officer or employee from ASRS after December 31, 1988 are subject to tax pursuant to title 43.

B. Interest, earnings and all other credits pertaining to benefits and annuities are not subject to execution or attachment and are nonassignable.

Added by Laws 1995, Ch. 32, § 14, eff. March 30, 1995.

Historical and Statutory Notes

Source:

Laws 1953, Ch. 128, § 22.
Code 1939, Supp.1953, § 12-858.
A.R.S. former §§ 38-762, 38-781.22.
Laws 1970, Ch. 134, § 2.
Laws 1970, Ch. 136, § 19.
Laws 1972, Ch. 51, §§ 13, 23.
Laws 1975, Ch. 48, §§ 2, 3.
Laws 1989, Ch. 312, §§ 6, 7.

§ 38-793. Violation; classification

A person who knowingly makes any false statement or who falsifies or permits to be falsified any record of ASRS with an intent to defraud ASRS is guilty of a class 6 felony.

Added by Laws 1995, Ch. 32, § 14, eff. March 30, 1995.

Historical and Statutory Notes

Source:

Laws 1953, Ch. 128, § 23.
Code 1939, Supp.1953, § 12-859.
A.R.S. former §§ 38-763, 38-781.32.
Laws 1970, Ch. 134, § 2.
Laws 1978, Ch. 201, §§ 691, 692.

§ 38-794. Reservation to legislature

The right to modify, amend or repeal this article, or any provisions of this article, is reserved to the legislature.

Added by Laws 1995, Ch. 32, § 14, eff. March 30, 1995.

Historical and Statutory Notes

Source:

Laws 1953, Ch. 128, § 24.
Code 1939, Supp.1953, § 12-860.
A.R.S. former §§ 38-764, 38-781.33.
Laws 1970, Ch. 134, § 2.

ARTICLE 2.1. LONG-TERM DISABILITY PROGRAM

Article 2.1, consisting of §§ 38-797 to 38-797.13, was added by Laws 1995, Ch. 134, § 14, effective April 17, 1994.

Former Article 2.1, Retirement Plan, consisting of § 38-781, added by Laws 1991, Ch. 270, § 3, §§ 38-781.01 to 38-781.24, added by Laws 1970, Ch. 134, § 2, § 38-781.25, added by Laws 1990, Ch. 235, § 3,

§§ 38-781.26 and 38-781.27, added by Laws 1994, Ch. 357, § 2, §§ 38-781.29 and 38-781.30, added by Laws 1970, Ch. 134, § 2, § 38-781.31, added by Laws 1987, Ch. 112, § 1, § 38-781.32 and 38-781.33, added by laws 1970, Ch. 134, § 2, § 38-781.35, added by Laws 1973, Ch. 113, § 3, § 38-781.36, added by Laws 1975, Ch. 57, § 4, § 38-781.37, added by Laws 1974, Ch. 120, § 11, § 38-781.38, added by Laws 1986, Ch. 168. § 7, § 38-781.39, added by Laws 1987, Ch. 182, § 1, § 38-781.40, added by Laws 1987, Ch. 208, § 1, § 38-781.41, added by Laws 1988, Ch. 277, § 3, § 38-781.42, added by Laws 1989, Ch. 310, § 5, § 38-781.44, added by Laws 1991, Ch. 144, § 1, and § 38-781.45, added by Laws 1994, Ch. 356, § 20, was repealed by Laws 1995, Ch. 32, § 13, eff. March 30, 1995.

Termination under Sunset Law

The long-term disability program shall terminate on July 1, 2006, unless continued. See §§ 41-3006.08 and 41-2955.

Title 38, Chapter 5, Article 2.1, relating to the long-term disability program, is repealed on January 1, 2007 by § 41-3006.08.

Section 41-2996.02, which was to have repealed Title 38, Chapter 5, Article 2.1, effective January 1, 1997, was repealed by Laws 1996, Ch. 18, § 1, effective July 20, 1996, retroactively effective to July 1, 1996.

Historical and Statutory Notes

Laws 1995, Ch. 134, §§ 16 and 18, provide:

"**Sec. 16. Benefit increases**

"**A.** Members of the Arizona state retirement system who were eligible to receive long-term disability benefits pursuant to § 38-781, Arizona Revised Statutes, as repealed by this act, on or before June 30, 1995 are eligible to receive an increased benefit equal to the benefit increase provided to retired members pursuant to § 38-767, Arizona Revised Statutes, as amended by this act.

"**B.** The benefit increases provided by subsection A of this section shall be added to the liabilities of the long-term disability program established by title 38, chapter 5, article 2.1, Arizona Revised Statutes, as added by this act."

"**Sec. 18. Transfer of members**

"On October 1, 1995 all members of the Arizona state retirement system who participated in the long-term disability program established by section 38-781, Arizona Revised Statutes, as repealed by this act, shall be transferred to the long-term disability program established by title 38, chapter 5, article 2.1, Arizona Revised Statutes, as added by this act."

§ 38-797. Definitions

In this article, unless the context otherwise requires:

1. "ASRS" means the Arizona state retirement system established by article 2 of this chapter.[1]

2. "Assets" means the accumulated resources of the LTD program.

3. "Board" means the ASRS board established pursuant to § 38-713.

4. "Compensation" means the gross amount paid to a member by an employer as salary or wages, including amounts that are subject to deferred compensation or tax shelter agreements, for services rendered to or for an employer, or that would have been paid to the member except for the member's election or a legal requirement that all or part of the gross amount be used for other purposes. Compensation does not include:

(a) Lump sum payments on termination of employment for accumulated vacation or annual leave, sick leave, compensatory time or any other form of termination pay whether the payments are made in one payment or by installments over a period of time.

(b) Damages, costs, attorney fees, interest or other penalties paid pursuant to a court order or a compromise settlement or agreement to satisfy a grievance or claim even though the amount of the payment is based in whole or in part on previous salary or wage levels, except that, if the court order or compromise settlement or agreement directs salary or wages to be paid for a specific period of time, the payment is compensation for that specific period of time.

(c) Payment, at the member's option, in lieu of fringe benefits that are normally paid for or provided by the employer.

(d) Merit awards pursuant to § 38–613 and performance bonuses paid to assistant attorneys general pursuant to § 41–192.

5. "Depository" means a bank in which the monies of the LTD program are deposited and collateralized as provided by law.

6. "Employer" means:

(a) This state.

(b) Participating political subdivisions.

7. "Employer contributions" means all amounts paid into the LTD program by an employer.

8. "Fiscal year" means the period from July 1 of any year to June 30 of the following year.

9. "LTD program" means the long-term disability program established by this article.

10. "Member" has the same meaning prescribed in § 38–711.

11. "Monthly compensation" means one-twelfth of a member's annual compensation paid and payable in the fiscal year during which a member becomes disabled.

12. "Normal retirement date" means the earliest of the following:

(a) A member's sixty-fifth birthday.

(b) A member's sixty-second birthday and completion of at least ten years of credited service.

(c) The first day that the sum of a member's age and years of total credited service equals eighty.

13. "Political subdivision" means any political subdivision of this state.

14. "State" means this state, including any department, office, board, commission, agency, institution or other instrumentality of this state.

Added by Laws 1995, Ch. 134, § 14, eff. April 17, 1995. Amended by Laws 1997, Ch. 280, § 19.

[1] Section 38–711 et seq.

Historical and Statutory Notes

The 1997 amendment by Ch. 280 deleted "immediately following the day" following "The first day" in par. 12(c).

§ 38-797.01. LTD program

A. A long-term disability program is established.

B. The program is known as the LTD program.

Added by Laws 1995, Ch. 134, § 14, eff. April 17, 1995.

§ 38-797.02. LTD trust fund

A. A LTD trust fund is established for the purpose of paying benefits under and costs of administering the LTD program.

B. The LTD fund consists of all monies paid into it in accordance with this article, whether in the form of cash, securities or other assets, and all monies received from any other source.

C. Custody, management and investment of the LTD fund are as prescribed by this article and article 2 of this chapter.[1]

Added by Laws 1995, Ch. 134, § 14, eff. April 17, 1995.

[1] Section 38-711 et seq.

§ 38-797.03. ASRS board; personnel; duties

A. The board shall administer the LTD program. ASRS officers, contractors and personnel shall perform the duties prescribed by this article.

B. The board may enter into a contract with an insurance company or another entity to administer all or part of the LTD program and to determine eligibility for benefits under the LTD program.

C. The board shall pay from the LTD trust fund the amounts necessary to pay benefits under and costs of administering the LTD program.

Added by Laws 1995, Ch. 134, § 14, eff. April 17, 1995.

§ 38-797.04. Eligibility

All members are subject to this article and shall participate in the LTD program.

Added by Laws 1995, Ch. 134, § 14, eff. April 17, 1995.

§ 38-797.05. Employer and member contributions

A. Beginning July 1, 1996, employers shall contribute the percentage of the compensation of all of the members under their employment so that the total employer contributions equals the amount that the board determines is necessary to pay one-half of all benefits under and costs of administering the LTD program.

B. Beginning July 1, 1996, a member shall contribute a percentage of the member's compensation equal to the employer contribution for the member required pursuant to subsection A of this section.

C. The employer shall pay the member contributions required of members on account of compensation earned. All employer and member contributions shall be paid to the board. The board shall allocate the contributions to the LTD trust fund and shall place the contributions in the LTD program's depository.

D. Each employer shall certify on each payroll the amount to be contributed to the LTD program and shall remit that amount to the board. The contributions are irrevocable.

E. Payments due pursuant to this article by employers become delinquent after the due date prescribed in the board's rules and thereafter shall be increased by interest from and after that date until payment is received by the board. The board shall charge interest on the delinquent payments at an annual rate equal to the interest rate assumption approved by the board for actuarial equivalency pursuant to article 2 of this chapter. [1] Delinquent payments due under this subsection, together with interest charges as provided in this subsection, may be recovered by an action in a court of competent jurisdiction against an employer liable for payments or, at the request of the director, may be deducted from any monies, including excise revenue taxes, payable to the employer by any department or agency of this state.

F. If more than the correct amount of contributions required is paid by an employer, proper adjustment shall be made in connection with subsequent payments. The board shall return excess contributions to the employer if the employer requests return of the contributions within one year after the date of overpayment.

G. Member contributions are not refundable and are not included in the calculation of survivor benefits pursuant to § 38-762.

Added by Laws 1995, Ch. 134, § 14, eff. April 17, 1995. Amended by Laws 2001, Ch. 136, § 20.

[1] Section 38-711 et seq.

Historical and Statutory Notes

The 2001 amendment by Ch. 136 rewrote subsec. E, which had read:

E. Payments due pursuant to this article by employers become delinquent after the due date prescribed in the board's rules and thereafter shall be increased by interest from and after that date until payment is received by the board. The board shall charge interest on the delinquent payments at an annual rate determined monthly as the weighted average annual rate of return on all repurchase agreements or other short-term investment transactions in the ASRS investment account established in article 2 of this chapter during the preceding month. Delinquent payments due under this subsection, together with interest charges as provided in this subsection, may be recovered by an action in a court of competent jurisdiction against an employer liable for payments or, at the request of the director, may be deducted from any monies, including excise revenue taxes, payable to the employer by any department or agency of this state."

§ 38-797.06. Contribution rate; annual report; definition

A. The board shall:

1. After consulting with its actuary, determine a biennial period contribution rate based on the LTD program experience of the employers and the costs of administering the LTD program.

2. Annually report the current contribution rate to the governor, the president of the senate, the speaker of the house of representatives and each participating political subdivision.

B. For the purposes of this section, "biennial period" means the two year period beginning on July 1 of an odd-numbered year and ending on June 30 of the next odd-numbered year.

Added by Laws 1995, Ch. 134, § 14, eff. April 17, 1995. Amended by Laws 2000, Ch. 132, § 3.

Historical and Statutory Notes

The 2000 amendment by Ch. 132 added subsec. B.

Laws 2000, Ch. 132, § 5 provides:

"**Sec. 5. Retroactivity**

"Section 38-797.06, Arizona Revised Statutes, as amended by this act, applies retroactively to from and after June 30, 1999."

§ 38-797.07. LTD program benefits; limitations; definitions

A. The LTD program is subject to the following limitations:

1. Except as provided in paragraph 7 of this subsection, monthly benefits shall not exceed two-thirds of a member's monthly compensation at the time disability commences, reduced by:

(a) Sixty-four per cent of social security disability benefits that the member or the member's dependents are eligible to receive.

(b) Eighty-three per cent of social security retirement benefits that the member is eligible to receive.

(c) All of any workers' compensation benefits.

(d) All of any payments for a veteran's disability if both of the following apply:

(i) The veteran's disability payment is for the same condition or a condition related to the condition currently causing the member's total disability.

(ii) The veteran's disability is due to, or a result of, service in the armed forces of the United States.

(e) All of any other benefits by reason of employment that are financed partly or wholly by an employer, including payments for sick leave.

(f) Fifty per cent of any salary, wages, commissions or other employment related pay that the member receives or is entitled to receive from any gainful employment in which the member actually engages.

2. Monthly benefits are not payable until a member has been totally disabled for a period of six consecutive months.

3. Monthly benefits are not payable to a member who is receiving retirement benefits from ASRS.

4. Monthly benefits are not payable to a member whose disability is due to, or a result of, any of the following:

(a) An intentionally self-inflicted injury.

(b) War, whether declared or not.

(c) An injury incurred while engaged in a felonious criminal act or enterprise.

(d) An injury or sickness for which the member received medical treatment within three months before the date of the member's coverage under the LTD program. This subdivision does not apply to a member who either:

(i) Has been an active member of an employer for twelve continuous months.

(ii) Is employed by an employer as of June 30, 1988.

5. Monthly benefits cease to be payable to a member at the earliest of the following:

(a) The date the member ceases to be totally disabled.

(b) The date the member:

(i) Ceases to be under the direct care of a doctor.

(ii) Refuses to undergo any medical examination or refuses to participate in any work rehabilitation program for which the member is reasonably qualified by education, training or experience and that is requested by the insurance company or claims administrator that is selected by the board to administer the LTD program.

(c) The date the member withdraws employee contributions with interest and ceases to be a member.

(d) The later of the following:

(i) The member's normal retirement date.

(ii) The month following sixty months of payments if disability occurs before sixty-five years of age.

(iii) The month following attainment of seventy years of age if disability occurs at sixty-five years of age or after but before sixty-nine years of age.

(iv) The month following twelve months of payments if disability occurs at or after sixty-nine years of age.

(e) If the member is convicted of a criminal offense and sentenced to more than six months in a jail, prison or other penal institution, the first day of the month following the first thirty continuous days of the member's confinement for the remainder of the confinement.

6. Monthly benefits are payable under the LTD program only for disabilities that commence on or after July 1, 1988.

7. The minimum benefit for a member who is entitled to receive benefits under the LTD program is fifty dollars per month.

8. Members are eligible to receive the benefits and payments described in paragraph 1 of this subsection, and the reductions provided by paragraph 1 of this subsection apply even though the benefits are not actually paid as follows:

(a) For primary and dependent social security benefits, the members are eligible for the benefits until the benefits are actually awarded, or if the benefits are denied, until the member pursues the social security appeal process through a hearing before a social security administrative law judge or until the insurance company or claims administrator determines that the member is not eligible for social security disability benefits.

(b) For benefits and payments from any other source provided in paragraph 1 of this subsection, the members are eligible for the benefits if it is reasonable to believe that the benefits will be paid on proper completion of the claim or would have been paid except for the failure of the member to pursue the claim in time.

9. A member shall be considered totally disabled if:

(a) During the first thirty months of a period of disability, the member is unable to perform all duties of the position held by the member when the member became totally disabled.

(b) For a member who has received monthly benefits for twenty-four months within a five-year period, the member is unable to perform any work for compensation or gain for which the member is reasonably qualified by education, training or experience in an amount at least equal to the scheduled benefits prescribed in paragraph 1 of this subsection.

B. A member who receives monthly benefits from the LTD program is entitled to receive service credit pursuant to article 2 of this chapter[1] from the time disability commences until benefits cease to be payable, except that for a member who receives monthly benefits from the LTD program on or after June 30, 1999 the number of years of service credited to the member's retirement account during the period the member receives LTD benefit payments shall not cause the member's total credited service for retirement benefits to exceed the greater of thirty years or the total years of service credited to the member's retirement account on the commencement of disability.

C. This section does not prohibit a member whose disability has been established to the satisfaction of the board from relying on treatment by prayer through spiritual means in accordance with the tenets and practice of a recognized church, religious denomination or native american traditional medicine by a duly accredited practitioner of the church, denomination or native american traditional medicine without suffering reduction or suspension of the member's monthly benefits.

D. For the purposes of this section:

1. "Received medical treatment" means that the member consulted with or received the advice of a licensed medical or dental practitioner, including advice given during a routine examination, and it includes situations in which the member received medical or dental care, treatment or services, including the taking of drugs, medication, insulin or similar substances.

2. "Social security" and "social security disability" includes the railroad retirement act of 1974 (P.L. 93-445; 88 Stat. 1305; 45 United States Code §§ 231 through 231u).

Added by Laws 1995, Ch. 134, § 14, eff. April 17, 1995. Amended by Laws 1996, Ch. 185, § 18; Laws 1999, Ch. 146, § 1; Laws 1999, Ch. 327, § 18; Laws 2001, Ch. 136, § 21; Laws 2004, Ch. 107, § 1.

[1] Section 38-711 et seq.

Historical and Statutory Notes

Source: A.R.S. former § 38-781.31.

Laws 1987, Ch. 112, § 1.
Laws 1988, Ch. 183, § 1.
Laws 1992, Ch. 145, § 1.
Laws 1994, Ch. 356, § 16.

The 1996 amendment by Ch. 185 added subsec. C.

The 1999 amendment by Ch. 146 inserted "for a member who receives monthly benefits from the LTD program on or after June 30, 1999", and substituted "thirty years" for "twenty-five years", in subsec. B.

Laws 1999, Ch. 146, § 2, provides:

"**Sec. 2. Retroactivity**

"Section 38–797.07, Arizona Revised Statutes, as amended by this act, applies retroactively to June 30, 1999."

The 1999 amendment by Ch. 327, in par. 4, subsec. A, rewrote subd. (d), which had read:

"(d) An injury or sickness for which the member received medical treatment within three months before the date of the member's coverage under the LTD program. This subdivision does not apply to a member who has been a member for twelve continuous months nor to a member who is employed by an employer as of June 30, 1988. For the purposes of this subdivision, 'received medical treatment' means that the member consulted with or received the advice of a licensed medical or dental practitioner, including advice given during a routine examination, and it includes situations in which the member received medical or dental care, treatment or services, including the taking of drugs, medication, insulin or similar substances."

The amendment by Ch. 327 also added a new par. 1 in subsec. C and redesignated the material that formerly constituted the whole of subsec. C as par. 2 thereof.

Laws 1999, Ch. 327, § 30, provides:

"**Sec. 30. Retroactivity**

"**A.** Section 38–797.07, Arizona Revised Statutes, as amended by this act, applies retroactively to from and after June 30, 1996.

"**B.** Section 27 of this act, relating to withdrawal of contributions from the Arizona state retirement system, is effective retroactively to from and after December 31, 1998".

The 2001 amendment by Ch. 136 inserted "in an amount at least equal to the scheduled benefits prescribed in paragraph 1 of this subsection" at the end of subsec. A, par. 9(b).

The 2004 amendment by Ch. 107 rewrote the section, which had read:

"**A.** The LTD program is subject to the following limitations:

"1. Except as provided in paragraph 7, monthly benefits shall not exceed two-thirds of a member's monthly compensation at the time disability commences, reduced by:

"(a) Sixty-four per cent of social security disability benefits that the member or the member's dependents are eligible to receive.

"(b) Eighty-three per cent of social security retirement benefits that the member is eligible to receive.

"(c) All of any workers' compensation benefits.

"(d) All of any payments for a veteran's disability if both of the following apply:

"(i) The veteran's disability payment is for the same condition or a condition related to the condition currently causing the member's total disability.

"(ii) The veteran's disability is due to, or a result of, service in the armed forces of the United States.

"(e) All of any other benefits by reason of employment that are financed partly or wholly by an employer, including payments for sick leave.

"(f) Fifty per cent of any salary, wages, commissions or similar pay that the member receives or is entitled to receive from any gainful employment in which the member actually engages.

"2. Monthly benefits are not payable until a member has been totally disabled for a period of six consecutive months.

"3. Monthly benefits are not payable to a member who is receiving retirement benefits from ASRS.

"4. Monthly benefits are not payable to a member whose disability is due to, or a result of, any of the following:

"(a) An intentionally self-inflicted injury.

"(b) War, whether declared or not.

"(c) An injury incurred while engaged in a felonious criminal act or enterprise.

"(d) An injury or sickness for which the member received medical treatment within three months before the date of the member's coverage under the LTD program. This subdivision does not apply to a member who either:

"(i) Has been an employee of an employer for twelve continuous months.

"(ii) Is employed by an employer as of June 30, 1988.

"5. Monthly benefits cease to be payable to a member at the earliest of the following:

"(a) The date the member ceases to be totally disabled.

"(b) The date the member ceases to be under the direct care of a doctor or refuses to undergo any medical examination requested by the insurance company selected by the board to administer the LTD program.

"(c) The date the member withdraws employee contributions with interest and ceases to be a member.

"(d) The later of the following:

"(i) The member's normal retirement date.

"(ii) The month following sixty months of payments if disability occurs before sixty-five years of age.

"(iii) The month following attainment of seventy years of age if disability occurs at sixty-five years of age or after but before sixty-nine years of age.

"(iv) The month following twelve months of payments if disability occurs at or after sixty-nine years of age.

"6. Monthly benefits are payable under the LTD program only for disabilities that commence on or after July 1, 1988.

"7. The minimum benefit for a member who is entitled to receive benefits under the LTD program is fifty dollars per month.

"8. Members are eligible to receive the benefits and payments described in paragraph 1, and the reductions provided by paragraph 1 apply even though the benefits are not actually paid as follows:

"(a) For primary or dependent social security benefits, the members are eligible for the benefits until the benefits are actually awarded, or if the benefits are denied, until notice of the denial of the appeal of the first denial is received.

"(b) For benefits and payments from any other source provided in paragraph 1, the members are eligible for the benefits if it is reasonable to believe that the benefits will be paid on proper completion of the claim or would have been paid except for the failure of the member to pursue the claim in time.

"9. A member shall be considered totally disabled if:

"(a) During the first thirty months of a period of disability, the member is unable to perform all duties of the position held by the member when the member became totally disabled.

"(b) For a member who has received monthly benefits for twenty-four consecutive months, that a member is unable to perform any work for compensation or gain for which the member is reasonably qualified by education, training or experience in an amount at least equal to the scheduled benefits prescribed in paragraph 1 of this subsection.

"**B.** A member who receives monthly benefits from the LTD program is entitled to receive service credit pursuant to article 2 of this chapter from the time disability commences until benefits cease to be payable, except that for a member who receives monthly benefits from the LTD program on or after June 30, 1999 the number of years of service credited to the member's retirement account during the period the member receives LTD benefit payments shall not cause the member's total credited service for retirement benefits to exceed the greater of thirty years or the total years of service credited to the member's retirement account on the commencement of disability.

"**C.** For the purposes of this section:

"1. 'Received medical treatment' means that the member consulted with or received the advice of a licensed medical or dental practitioner, including advice given during a routine examination, and it includes situations in which the member received medical or dental care, treatment or services, including the taking of drugs, medication, insulin or similar substances.

"2. 'Social security' and 'social security disability' includes the railroad retirement act of 1974 (P.L. 93-445; 88 Stat. 1305; 45 United States Code §§ 231 through 231u)."

Reviser's Notes:

1995 Note. Pursuant to authority of § 41-1304.02, in the section heading "; limitations" was added.

1996 Note. Pursuant to authority of § 41-1304.02, in the section heading "; definitions" was added after "limitations" and in subsection C "Code" was substituted for "Codes" to correct a manifest clerical error.

1999 Note. Prior to the 2001 amendment, this section contained the amendments made by Laws 1999, Ch. 146, sec. 1 and Ch. 327, sec. 18 that were blended together pursuant to authority of § 41-1304.03.

§ 38-797.08. Errors; benefit recomputation

If any change or error in the records results in any member receiving from the LTD program more or less than the member would have been entitled to receive if the records had been correct, the board shall correct the error and shall adjust the payments in a manner so that the equivalent of the benefit to which the member was correctly entitled is paid. The board shall correct any change or error and shall pay the appropriate monies to a member or shall recover monies from the member if the member is overpaid.

Added by Laws 1995, Ch. 134, § 14, eff. April 17, 1995.

§ 38-797.09. Facility of payment

In the case of incapacity of a member receiving LTD program benefits, or in the case of any other emergency as determined by the board, the board may make LTD program benefit payments on behalf of the member to another person or persons the board determines to be lawfully entitled to receive payment. The payment is payment for the account of the member and all persons entitled to payment and, to the extent of the payment, is a full and complete discharge of all liability of the board or the LTD program, or both, under or in connection with the LTD program.

Added by Laws 1995, Ch. 134, § 14, eff. April 17, 1995.

§ 38-797.10. Assurances and liabilities

A. Nothing contained in this article shall be construed as:

1. A contract of employment between an employer and any employee.

2. A right of any member to continue in the employment of an employer.

3. A limitation of the rights of an employer to discharge any of its employees, with or without cause.

B. A member does not have any right to, or interest in, any LTD program assets on termination of the member's employment or otherwise, except as provided from time to time in the LTD program, and then only to the extent of the benefits payable to the member out of LTD program assets. All payments of benefits shall be made solely out of LTD program assets and neither the employers, the board nor any member of the board is liable for payment of benefits in any manner.

C. Benefits, employer and member contributions, earnings and all other credits payable under this article are not subject in any manner to anticipation, alienation, sale, transfer, assignment, pledge, encumbrance, charge, garnishment, execution or levy of any kind, either voluntary or involuntary, before actually being received by a person entitled to the benefit, earning or credit, and any attempt to anticipate, alienate, sell, transfer, assign, pledge, encumber, charge, garnish, execute or levy or otherwise dispose of any benefit, earning or credit under this article is void. The LTD program is not in any manner liable for, or subject to, the debts, contracts, liabilities, engagements or torts of any person entitled to any benefit, earning or credit under this article.

D. Neither the employers, the board nor any member of the board guarantees the LTD trust fund established by § 38-797.02 in any manner against loss or depreciation, and they are not liable for any act or failure to act that is made in good faith pursuant to this article. The employers are not responsible for any act or failure to act of the board or any member of the board. Neither the board nor any member of the board is responsible for any act or failure to act of any employer.

E. This section does not exempt benefits of any kind from a writ of attachment, a writ of execution, a writ of garnishment and orders of assignment issued by a court of record as the result of a judgment for arrearages of child support or for child support debt.

Added by Laws 1995, Ch. 134, § 14, eff. April 17, 1995.

§ 38–797.11. Exemptions from execution, attachment and taxation; exception

A. The benefits, the employer and member contributions and the securities in the LTD trust fund established by § 38–797.02 are not subject to execution or attachment and are nonassignable except as specifically provided in this article. The employer and member contributions and the securities in the LTD trust fund established by § 38–797.02 are exempt from state, county and municipal income taxes. Benefits received by a member from the LTD program are subject to tax pursuant to title 43.

B. Interest, earnings and all other credits pertaining to benefits are not subject to execution or attachment and are nonassignable.

Added by Laws 1995, Ch. 134, § 14, eff. April 17, 1995.

§ 38–797.12. Violation; classification

A person who knowingly makes any false statement or who falsifies or permits to be falsified any record of the LTD program with an intent to defraud the LTD program is guilty of a class 6 felony.

Added by Laws 1995, Ch. 134, § 14, eff. April 17, 1995.

§ 38–797.13. Reservation to legislature

The right to modify, amend or repeal this article, or any provisions of this article, is reserved to the legislature.

Added by Laws 1995, Ch. 134, § 14, eff. April 17, 1995.

§ 38–797.14. Liquidation of LTD program

If the legislature determines that the LTD program is no longer to be operated for the purposes set forth in this article, any monies remaining in the LTD trust after paying all liabilities of the trust or after making adequate provision for paying those liabilities revert to the general funds of the employers that were making contributions to the LTD program at the time the legislature terminates the LTD program. The reverted monies shall be prorated according to the gross amount of contributions made by the employers to the LTD program.

Added by Laws 1997, Ch. 280, § 20.

ARTICLE 5. TAX DEFERRED ANNUITY AND DEFERRED COMPENSATION PROGRAMS

Article 5, consisting of §§ 38–871 to 38–874, was added by Laws 1972, Ch. 133, § 3, effective August 13, 1972.

§ 38–871. Annuity and deferred compensation governing committee; members; powers and duties

Text of section effective until January 1, 2006

A. A governing committee for tax deferred annuity and deferred compensation plans is established that consists of the following seven members:

1. Three employees of the state appointed by the governor.

2. The director of the department of administration or the director's designee.

3. The superintendent of the state banking department or the superintendent's designee.

4. The director of insurance or the director's designee.

5. The director of the Arizona state retirement system or the director's designee.

B. The governing committee may:

1. Investigate and approve tax deferred compensation and annuity programs which give employees of the state income tax benefits authorized by title 26, United States Code Annotated.[1]

2. In carrying out the purposes of this article, enter into agreements with life insurance companies authorized to do business in this state and with bank trustees or custodians and investment counseling firms registered with the securities exchange commission.

C. The governing committee shall:

1. Arrange for consolidated billing and efficient administrative services in order that any such plans approved shall operate without cost or contribution from the state except for the incidental expense of administering the payroll salary deduction or reduction and remittance thereof to the trustee or custodian of the plan or plans.

2. Meet monthly or more frequently as the chairman of the committee deems necessary.

3. Arrange for an annual financial audit of the programs and a performance audit of the programs at least once every three years.

4. Adopt rules governing the solicitation of employees by persons offering tax deferred compensation or annuity plans to such employees.

Added by Laws 1972, Ch. 133, § 3. Amended by Laws 1973, Ch. 91, § 3; Laws 1973, Ch. 157, § 48; Laws 1975, Ch. 104, § 34, eff. May 27, 1975; Laws 1983, Ch. 98, § 114; Laws 1985, Ch. 48, § 2; Laws 2001, Ch. 136, § 22.

[1] 26 U.S.C.A. § 1 et seq.

For text of section effective January 1, 2006, see § 38-871, post

§ 38-871. Annuity and deferred compensation governing committee; members; powers and duties

Text of section effective January 1, 2006

A. A governing committee for tax deferred annuity and deferred compensation plans is established that consists of the following seven members:

1. Three employees of the state appointed by the governor.

2. The director of the department of administration or the director's designee.

3. The superintendent of financial institutions or the superintendent's designee.

4. The director of insurance or the director's designee.

5. The director of the Arizona state retirement system or the director's designee.

B. The governing committee may:

1. Investigate and approve tax deferred compensation and annuity programs which give employees of the state income tax benefits authorized by title 26, United States Code Annotated. [1]

2. In carrying out the purposes of this article, enter into agreements with life insurance companies authorized to do business in this state and with bank trustees or custodians and investment counseling firms registered with the securities exchange commission.

C. The governing committee shall:

1. Arrange for consolidated billing and efficient administrative services in order that any such plans approved shall operate without cost or contribution from the state except for the incidental expense of administering the payroll salary deduction or reduction and remittance thereof to the trustee or custodian of the plan or plans.

2. Meet monthly or more frequently as the chairman of the committee deems necessary.

3. Arrange for an annual financial audit of the programs and a performance audit of the programs at least once every three years.

4. Adopt rules governing the solicitation of employees by persons offering tax deferred compensation or annuity plans to such employees.

Added by Laws 1972, Ch. 133, § 3. Amended by Laws 1973, Ch. 91, § 3; Laws 1973, Ch. 157, § 48; Laws 1975, Ch. 104, § 34, eff. May 27, 1975; Laws 1983, Ch. 98, § 114; Laws 1985, Ch. 48, § 2; Laws 2001, Ch. 136, § 22; Laws 2004, Ch. 188, § 38, eff. Jan. 1, 2006.

[1] 26 U.S.C.A. § 1 et seq.

For text of section effective until January 1, 2006, see § 38–871, ante

Historical and Statutory Notes

Laws 1973, Ch. 91, § 3 deleted "§§ 401, 403 and 404," preceding "United States Code Annotated" in par. 1 of subsec. B.

Laws 1973, Ch. 157, § 48 substituted "The assistant director of the department of administration for the division of finance" for "The commissioner of finance" in par. 4 of subsec. A.

The 1975 amendment rewrote pars. 2 and 4 of subsec. A, which had read:

"2. The director of the state personnel commission."

"4. The commissioner of finance."

The 1983 amendment rewrote pars. 2 and 4 of subsec. A, which had read:

"2. The department of administration assistant director for personnel administration."

"4. The department of administration assistant director for finance."

Laws 1985, Ch. 48, § 2, amended subsec. A by substituting "The director of the department of administration or his appointee." for "An employee of the department of administration knowledgeable in the area of personnel administration appointed by the director of the department of administration." in par. 2, by substituting pars. 4 and 5 for former pars. 4 and 5 which read:

"4. An employee of the department of administration knowledgeable in the area of finance appointed by the director of the department of administration.

"5. The attorney general."; and amended subsec. C by redesignating former par. 2 as par. 4 and by inserting pars. 2 and 3.

The 2001 amendment by Ch. 136 substituted "the director's designee" and "the superintendent's designee" for "his appointee" several places in subsec. A; and substituted "Adopt rules governing" for "Promulgate rules and regulations governing" at the beginning of subsec. C, par. 4.

Laws 2001, Ch. 380, § 16, provides:

"**Sec. 16. Termination of the tax deferred annuity and deferred compensation pilot program**

"This act terminates the pilot program option for legislative employees and state elected officials to elect to participate in a tax deferred annuity and deferred compensation program pursuant to title 38, chapter 5, article 5, Arizona Revised Statutes, in lieu of participation in the Arizona state retirement system pursuant to title 38, chapter 5, article 2, Arizona Revised Statutes. All legislative employees and state elected officials who elected on or before the effective date of this act to participate in a deferred tax annuity and deferred compensation program in lieu of participation in the Arizona state retirement system shall continue to participate in that option pursuant to the irrevocable election made by the employee or state elected official and the employer shall continue to pay an amount equal to five per cent of the employee's or state elected official's base salary directly to the program in lieu of employer contributions to a public retirement system."

The 2004 amendment by Ch. 188, in subsec. A, par. 3, substituted "financial institutions" for "the state banking department".

Reviser's Notes:

1975 Note. Laws 1973, Chs. 91 and 157 amended this section. The Ch. 91 version deletes part of a reference to federal statutes. The Ch. 157 version omitted the previously deleted reference, which had not yet become effective, and made unrelated changes to conform to the establishment of the department of administration. Under a correctional enactment, Laws 1975, Ch. 104, the Ch. 91 version was amended to conform to the text changes of the Ch. 157 enactment and the Ch. 157 version repealed.

1985 Note. Pursuant to authority of § 41–1304.02, "powers and" was added in the section heading before "duties".

§ 38–872. Voluntary participation; authorization

A. State employees may participate in tax deferred annuity and deferred compensation programs established pursuant to the provisions of § 38–871.

B. Participants in such plans shall authorize their employers in writing to make reductions or deductions in their remuneration as provided in an executed deferred compensation agreement.

Added by Laws 1972, Ch. 133, § 3.

§ 38–873. Payroll salary deductions; department of administration

The department of administration shall initiate payroll salary reductions or deductions for the plans adopted pursuant to § 38–871 as directed by each employee participating in such plans.

Added by Laws 1972, Ch. 133, § 3. Amended by Laws 1973, Ch. 157, § 49; Laws 1983, Ch. 98, § 115.

Historical and Statutory Notes

The 1973 amendment substituted "The department of administration division of finance" for "The state department of finance".

The 1983 amendment substituted "The department of administration" for "The department of administration division of finance".

§ 38–874. Effect of participation

A. Any benefits provided pursuant to the provisions of this article shall be in addition to any other benefits provided by law for any employees of this state and shall be supplemental to the provisions of the state retirement system provided pursuant to title 38, chapter 5, article 2.[1]

B. Any income deferred under a plan established pursuant to this article shall be included as regular compensation for the purpose of computing the retirement and pension benefits earned by any employee participating in such plan.

Added by Laws 1972, Ch. 133, § 3. Amended by Laws 1995, Ch. 32, § 18, eff. March 30, 1995.

[1] Section 38-711 et seq.

Historical and Statutory Notes

The 1995 amendment by Ch. 32, in subsec. A, deleted a reference to the state retirement plan, and deleted a reference to article 2.1.

INDEX

COUNTY

SECTION

†